P9-DMX-219

THE MALCONTENTS

The Malcontents

The Best Bitter, Cynical, and Satirical Writing in the World

Edited, with Commentary, by

Joe Queenan

RUNNING PRESS
PHILADELPHIA · LONDON

Printed in the United States

9 8 7 6 5 4 3 2 1
Digit on the right indicates the number of this printing

Library of Congress Cataloging-in-Publication Number 2002100439

ISBN 0-7624-1344-1

Cover design by Whitney Cookman
Interior design by Serrin Bodmer
Edited by Jennifer Worick
Biographies researched by Jeanine Rosen
Fly photograph by Bill Jones
Author photograph by Sigrid Estrada
Typography: Concorde BE and Granjon

This book may be ordered by mail from the publisher.
Please include $2.50 for postage and handling.
But try your bookstore first!

Running Press Book Publishers
125 South Twenty-second Street
Philadelphia, Pennsylvania 19103-4399

Visit us on the web!
www.runningpress.com

For John Mullen

Contents

A Note on the Texts

The texts in this book are based on early printed editions. We have made no attempt to modernize the authors' (or translators') own distinct usage, spelling, or punctuation, or to make the texts consistent with each other in this regard. In some cases, we have relied on texts published a few years after the first editions, but have tried to select texts that remain true to the author's original intention and style.

Introduction

by Joe Queenan

When I was a young man pretending to be a young writer in Paris in 1972, I met a prematurely compulsive man who spent all his time compiling a list of the world's ten greatest composers. Obsessed with bringing order and finality to the world of ideas—a fairly common activity among young people in Paris at that time—this very intense German-American would turn up at the *Alliance Française* bar every lunchtime, and make a concerted—and quite public—effort to determine, once and for all, who were the ten greatest composers in the history of Western music. Presumably, once this list was cast in stone, he could move on to the world's ten greatest impresarios.

In this daily ranking enterprise, the man was happy to enlist anyone who happened to be within easy striking distance. As the rest of us were usually drinking heavily, we were happy to indulge him. Herr Rankem—I forget his real name, but his natty pre-Age of Irony fedora is burned into my memory forever—would always start the list with the indisputable titans—Bach, Beethoven, and Mozart—and then quickly add Verdi and Wagner, whose claims to be included in the Pantheon of the Immortals seemed only slightly less unassailable. He would then grudgingly include Brahms (whom he did not like, but whose stature could not be denied) and Schubert, who died young and penniless and brilliant. But mostly brilliant.

After that, the trouble started. The competition for the remaining five slots included Handel, Haydn, Mendelssohn, Schumann, Chopin, Liszt, Tchaikovsky, Debussy, Bartók, and Stravinsky. (He never even bothered to consider such lightweights as Puccini, Donizetti, Monteverdi, Vivaldi, Gluck, Scarlatti, Bruckner, Dvoràk, Mussorgsky, Strauss, or Ravel, much less such out-and-out barbarians as Webern and Schoenberg.)

Every single day, this decidedly eccentric man would rearrange the list, marshalling cogent arguments as to why one composer should be included and another eliminated. When asked my opinion, I told him to simply chuck out Handel, Lizst, Mendelssohn, Stravinsky, and Schumann, which would bring his list down to a perfect ten. But then I would impishly remind him that he had failed to include Berlioz, which meant that yet another composer had to be deleted. This would have the desired effect of sending him into an emotional tailspin, during which the rest of us tended to drink even more. At this juncture, I would helpfully volunteer that he might consider expanding his list to twelve or fifteen or even thirty-five. "After all, *mon vieux*," I would point out, "There is no law against it."

Herr Rankem insisted that this would not solve the problem, that no matter what number was finally settled upon, sooner or later it would come down to a ridiculously arbitrary choice between Fauré and Rimsky-Korsakov or Saint-Saëns and Shostakovich for the final slot. This seemed like a good time for us to drink ourselves into oblivion. The next day he would reappear at our regular gathering place at the *Alliance Française* bar and start all over again.

After I left Paris in July 1973, I never saw Herr Rankem again. In fact, I did not even think about him again until the editors of Running Press called me in the summer of the year 2001 and asked if I would like to write the introduction to a book about the world's greatest bitter, cynical, and/or satirical writing. I was overjoyed to undertake the project, because it would give me a chance to reread Swift, Wilde, Shaw, Twain, Saki, Pope, Molière, and the rest of my boyhood heroes, and would force me to finally polish off *Don Quixote* (which I had capriciously abandoned after a scant one hundred pages a quarter-century earlier). It would also oblige me to read Rabelais' *Gargantua and Pantagruel*, a summit that I had never even attempted to scale.

This part of the assignment was enormous fun. Indeed, one of the great pleasures in reading books that are hundreds and even thousands of years old is in discovering how little the targets of the satirist have changed over the centuries. Working one's way through Aristophanes and Rabelais and Molière, it is clear that jackasses, pedants, buffoons, and charlatans have always been a clear and present danger to humanity, and that they are not merely a modern health hazard. Thus, when Voltaire, tongue in cheek, writes that without Columbus's landing on the island that introduced syphilis to the Western World none of us would have ever known the joys of chocolate, he sounds exactly like modern-day editorial writers who grudgingly approve of poverty because it is character-building. Proving, once again, that there is nothing new under the sun. Especially if it involves morons. Or editorial writers.

Obviously, there were other treats. For example, it was a pure delight to rediscover the malice in Mark Twain that a generation of hagiographers, toadies, documentary filmmakers, and Mark Twain impersonators had moved heaven and earth to submerge from view. In attempting to defang the profoundly misanthropic Twain and transform him into a toothless, tiresome curmudgeon of the deadly Andy Rooney variety, the Hal Holbrookians among us had very nearly eradicated the memory of Mark Twain, the Ornery Son of a Bitch. But no sooner did I start paging through his *Collected Essays* than I realized what a thoroughly malicious personality he possessed. Great to have you back, Mr. Clemens. The reports of your demise *had* been greatly exaggerated.

Other pleasures lay in store. Wilde's *Picture of Dorian Gray* was as twisted and operatic as I remembered it the last time I read it, and Saki's weird little stories had gotten even stranger. And yes, it still seemed odd that Voltaire, who had written thousands and thousands of pages of serious prose in his life, should be best remembered for a satirical work that could be read in an hour or so. But there you have it. Reading these classics was such a joy that for months on end I refused to watch television, entertain guests, or pay my bills. For two solid weeks I refused to come to the door or answer the phone while I was reading *Don Quixtote*; based on the quality of the visits and phone calls I generally get, I wish the book had been longer.

This blissful interlude came to an abrupt end when the time came to make the final selections. Here, it was not merely a question of who to include, but which of each author's works were most appropriate for the anthology. For example, *Pygmalion* is a wittier, more entertaining play than *Mrs. Warren's Profession*, but, placed in its historical context, *Mrs. Warren's Profession* is far more important, presenting Shaw at his most implacably rigid and cynical. *Pygmalion* was eventually repackaged as a heartwarming, life-affirming musical comedy that lifted the hearts of millions. *Mrs. Warren's Profession* wasn't. (While I was reading his greatest hits, it occurred to me that Shaw, like Leo Tolstoy, Rip Van Winkle, Victor Hugo, Father Christmas, Casey Stengel, and King Lear, is one of those people who does not seem to have ever been young. He is always depicted as a wise old man with a flowing beard and a furrowed brow, and always seems to be around ninety-three. In fact, he wrote *Mrs. Warren's Profession* in 1894 when he was only thirty-eight.)

A similar problem arose with the work of Molière. From the very beginning of the selection process, it was obvious that the greatest French playwright of all time was going to make the final cut, if only because he is buried in the same cemetery as America's *numero uno poète maudit*, Jim Morrison. Also, since Molière began coughing blood on the stage during a performance of *The Imaginary Invalid* the night he died, it was clear that he had an amazing sense of occasion, as well as a keen sense of irony.

The question was which play to include. While *Tartuffe*, in which Molière mercilessly pillories religious shams—the forerunners of our modern tele-evangelists—seemed like the most obvious choice—in part because it is the play that infuriated the most people in his life—it is not Molière's best work. And while *The Miser*, *The Misanthrope*, *The Imaginary Invalid*, *Don Juan*, or *The Doctor in Spite of Himself* might better fit the classification of "bitter" or "cynical," I finally chose *The Bourgeois Gentleman* because it is more relevant to our times and our culture, and because it illustrates how it is possible for a satirist to utterly eviscerate a target while displaying a grudging affection for his victim.

SINCE MOLIÈRE BEGAN COUGHING BLOOD ON THE STAGE DURING A PERFORMANCE OF **THE IMAGINARY INVALID** THE NIGHT HE DIED, IT WAS CLEAR THAT HE HAD AN AMAZING SENSE OF OCCASION, AS WELL AS A KEEN SENSE OF IRONY.

Monsieur Jourdain, the gullible, pretentious protagonist of *The Bourgeois Gentleman*, is the sort of harmless simpleton who, were he alive today, would be designing his own McMansion, learning ethnic haiku at the local Writer's Center, festooning his house with overpriced tribal pottery, and taking a Danish film appreciation course at a nearby community college. Jourdain is the kind of jackass you would hate to have move in next door to you—unless you yourself were a harmless jackass—but not the kind of person whose house deserves to be fire-bombed. With its merciless ridicule of the *nouveau riche*, the most persistently infuriating yet ultimately hapless people on the face of the earth, *The Bourgeois Gentleman* could have been written yesterday. Though that would make Molière pretty old.

One thing I wish to make clear is that, in compiling this anthology, I was determined to array the complete range of styles used by our assorted Malcontents to register their rage, disappointment, or stupefaction over the centuries. Many of the choices were obvious: Machiavelli's *The Prince*, Voltaire's

Candide, Jonathan Swift's "A Modest Proposal," perhaps the most influential, and certainly the most economical, piece of satire ever written. Oscar Wilde's *The Picture of Dorian Gray* was an equally obvious choice; in it Wilde not only taunted an entire society, but at the same time expressed his own fatigue with the spiritually empty art-for-art's sake philosophy that he had helped to popularize.

This is one of the rare instances where a satirist not only loathes his contemporaries, but seems to loathe himself. Unlike *Lady Windemere's Fan*, *The Ideal Husband*, *A Woman of No Importance*, and even *The Importance of Being Earnest*, *The Picture of Dorian Gray* reveals a Wilde who is no longer content with being clever; he is now determined to be in some way profound. This was an herculean task for a writer who had personally elevated insincerity to an art form. And what a curious book it is. Alternately vicious and sentimental—Sybil Vane is one of the most ridiculously one-dimensional characters in the history of literature, and some of the prose is of an almost incandescent purple hue—*Dorian Gray* is one of the strangest novels ever written, a peculiar hybrid with few antecedents and even fewer progeny. It's a bit like *Fidelio*: an amazing one-off.

FIRST, HAD I NOT INCLUDED THE MOST FAMOUS SATIRICAL POEM EVER WRITTEN IN THE COLLECTION, I WOULD LOOK LIKE A NITWIT. SECOND, BY MAKING THIS SELECTION, I COULD HOLD DOWN THE QUANTITY OF POETRY TO A BARE MINIMUM. WE WANT TO SELL A FEW BOOKS HERE.

Another automatic selection was Alexander Pope's *The Rape of the Lock*. There are two reasons for this. First, had I not included the most famous satirical poem ever written in the collection, I would look like a nitwit. Second, by making this selection, I could hold down the quantity of poetry to a bare minimum. We want to sell a few books here. Nor am I a man entirely without compassion for the reader.

In other cases, I selected less-famous works by celebrated Malcontents purely because I believe these works should be more famous. While the genius of "The Man That Corrupted Hadleyburg," the ingenuity of "The $30,000 Bequest," and the profound misanthropy of "The Mysterious Stranger" are not to be denied, these stories have been widely anthologized elsewhere, and at this late date, reading them is getting to be like homework. More to the point, I have long been an aficionado of the lesser-loved works of the dearly beloved. One of the greatest influences on my life was my college French teacher, Thomas Donahue, who believed that Henry Miller would be longer remembered for *The Colossus of Maroussi* than *Tropic of Cancer*, *Tropic of Capricorn*, and all those other semi-tropical works, and also contended that James Baldwin was more artistically formidable in *Giovanni's Room* than in *Go Tell It on the Mountain* or *The Fire Next Time*.

I have enormous sympathy for this point of view; I honestly believe that Twain's "In Defense of Harriet Shelley" is one of the most brilliant pieces of intellectual vivisection ever written; it should be the template for every reviewer condemned to read a book of literary criticism. I also believe that Twain's perverted homilies "The Story of the Good Little Boy" and "Marjorie Fleming, the Wonder Child" are as hilarious as anything in *The Adventures of Huckleberry Finn* or *Pudd'nhead Wilson*, and probably tell us more about the man who wrote them. That is: He was not very nice.

Still, for appearance's sake, I have also included the frightfully well-known essay, "Fenimore Cooper's Literary Offenses," because it is irresponsible, mean-spirited, desecrates a national icon, shoots fish in the barrel, and spits in the eye of the public—all the things great satire is supposed to do. Finally, though it is heresy to say so, I must admit that I prefer Twain's shorter works to his longer works, and prefer his more cerebral, urbane writing to the rustic, homespun tales for which he is most famous. When my fifteen-year-old son recently confessed that he found *The Adventures of Tom Sawyer* hopelessly boring and thoroughly dated, I surprised him by saying that I agreed.

I have similar feelings about the work of Ambrose Bierce. Justly revered for *The Devil's Dictionary*, Bierce should be better known for stories such as "A Revolt of the Gods," which begins with the words: "My father was a deodorizer of dead dogs, my mother kept the only shop for the sale of cats'-meat in my native city. They did not live happily; the difference in social rank was a chasm which could not be bridged by the vows of marriage." Whereas *The Devil's Dictionary* announces its malice beforehand, stories like this surprise the reader with their casual, disingenuous insanity. "My mother's air of surprise when any of us went wrong in any way was very terrible to us," Bierce's narrator divulges at another juncture. "One day, when in a fit of peevish temper, I had taken the liberty to cut off the baby's ear, her simple words, 'John, you surprise me!' appeared to me so sharp a reproof that after a sleepless night I went into tears, and throwing myself at her feet, exclaimed: 'Mother, forgive me for surprising you.'" Bierce and Saki are masters of miniaturized malice, in the way that Satie and Fauré are masters of miniaturized charm. But let's not get into that.

Some of the writers presented here are included because they should be far better known. It has been said that Ben Jonson is the greatest unread writer in the English language, making him a kind of inverted-image Tom Clancy. For the record, Saki can do more in seven pages than P.G. Wodehouse did in his entire career. Actually, he could do it in two. And Flann O'Brien's account of setting up a professional book-reading service for illiterate but affluent nincompoops is the cleverest article to ever appear in a newspaper anywhere. Yes, I have checked.

And what of Rabelais? Since it took me, a satirist of sorts, fifty-one years to get around to reading one of the sacred texts I should have devoured when I was seventeen, isn't that some indication that *Gargantua and Pantagruel* is not exactly indispensable reading material? No, what it proves is this:

1. The best things in life are worth waiting for.
2. I am a complete and utter fool.

True, Rabelais is crude, scatological, pedantic, and unstructured, and sometimes his writing makes enormous demands on the reader. All the same, when he is at the top of his game (inventing absurd card games with names like *Shit-in-His-Beard* or *The Salvo of Farts*, or discussing how a goose makes an excellent substitute for toilet paper), his work is as funny as anything ever written. He certainly raised the bar for other practitioners of the trade with chapter headings like "How the Lords Licksole and Suckfist Did Plead Before Pantagruel Without an Attorney." *Gargantua and Pantagruel* falls into that enviable category of books that rural American schoolboards would insist on having banned—and perhaps even burned—if they only knew of their existence.

Moreover, because of his enormous influence on Laurence Sterne, Tobias Smollett, and Henry Fielding, my decision to include selections from *Gargantua and Pantagruel* gave me a perfect excuse to leave those three out. In the best of all possible worlds, this book would be 3,000 pages long and would include lengthy, cunningly translated excerpts from Martial, Horace, Petronius, Samuel Johnson, Richard Sheridan, and William Congreve, not to mention snippets from Aesop, La Fontaine, Beaumarchais, Marivaux, Edgar Allan Poe, and a score of others. But, as we learn from Voltaire's astonishingly bitter *Candide* (another automatic selection), this is not the best of all possible worlds. And, to be perfectly honest, I'm not sure that a 3,000-page book brimming with excerpts from Petronius's *Satyricon* or Smollet's *Humphrey Clinker* is exactly what the public is looking for.

Some of the authors who appear here were chosen because of their influence on subsequent writers. Without Gogol's "The Nose," there could be no Jarry, no Ionesco, no Borges, no Genet, no Philip Roth, no Ishmael Reed, no Woody Allen. Without Twain there could be no James Thurber, no Garrison Keillor; without

Swift, there could be no H.L. Mencken, no George Orwell, no P.J. O'Rourke. Without Saki there could be no Evelyn Waugh, no Roald Dahl, no J.G. Ballard. Without Aristophanes and Molière, there could be no Tom Wolfe (though I sometimes suspect that the author of *Radical Chic* would have probably figured out a way to get here all on his own). And without Ambrose Bierce, there could be no Ray Bradbury, no Rod Serling, no Stephen King, no Harlan Ellison. I admit this is a mixed blessing.

Other writers were chosen because they were masters of getting up people's noses. Rabelais was always in trouble with the Church. Molière was always in trouble with the Church. Voltaire was always in trouble with the Church. And the Marquis de Sade was always in trouble with everybody. Of all the authors in this collection, de Sade is both the most appropriate and the least welcome. This is because of all the authors, de Sade best fits the profile of the "malcontent," yet at the same time manages to remain a pariah long after his death. With Swift, Pope, Aristophanes, Twain, and even Wilde, we generally feel some sort of kinship with the author; sooner or later, we come to believe that we are fighting on the same side, that the miscreants he torments and the abuses he denounces are miscreants we want to see tormented and abuses we want to see denounced. This is the kind of retroactive sophistication that encourages our belief that, had we been alive at the time, we would have immediately recognized the genius of Vincent Van Gogh, Franz Schubert, and Satchel Paige.

Not so with Comte Donatien-Alphonse-François de Sade. Almost two hundred years after his death, de Sade still remains a supremely unapproachable figure, a shadowy outcast who somehow managed to alienate all the right people while remaining the wrong kind of person himself. Imprisoned by the aristocracy, the Terror, and Napoleon Bonaparte himself, de Sade from a distance seems like an idiosyncratic libertarian who we would all like to include among our intellectual influences. He is, to paraphrase Wilde, the sort of writer who had execrable taste in friends, but impeccable taste in enemies. But then, once we start reading what de Sade actually wrote—which almost no one ever does—well, things get a bit complicated . . .

It's the whips and truncheons and branding irons, of course, that cause all the fuss. As clever and insightful and honest as he could be in analyzing politics, economics, and morality, de Sade always goes and spoils things by getting the entire population of the Loire Valley to gang-rape some impressionable virgin just for the hell of it. Just when it seems like he's winning over the reader with his merciless evisceration of corrupt politicians and pedophile prelates, he goes and wears out his welcomes with a totally extraneous but exquisitely detailed description of an innocent young woman's public disemboweling. Sad to say, you can take de Sade out of the cathouse but you can't take the cathouse out of de Sade.

And yet, it would be unforgivable if de Sade were not included in this anthology. If ever a human being fit the bill as a malcontent, the Marquis de Sade was it. Which is why I implore the reader to approach *Justine* with an open mind. It is true that de Sade feverishly and enthusiastically writes about unspeakable sexual practices that most of us would find deeply repugnant, with the obvious exception of people in certain rather obvious East and West Coast zip codes. It is undeniable that de Sade is in the fullest sense of the word "depraved." Not to mention "perverted." It is indisputable that reading *Justine* will not give the reader as much pleasure as perusing Jane Austen. Especially if you're reading it to the kids.

Yet, there are passages in de Sade that are as hilarious—in a decidedly twisted way—as anything anyone has ever written in the history of mankind. My personal favorite is the scene toward the end of the book where Thérèse (who is really Justine) tells Monsieur de Corville (who is really her long-lost sister Juliette's husband) that she is reluctant to supply any more juicy details about her adventures among the scum of the earth because the material is just too salacious. A complete dunce who never learns a thing from her myriad misfortunes, Thérèse bleats: "I was absorbed in these musings when suddenly I heard the door to my cell open; 'tis Roland: the villain has come to complete his outraging of me by making me serve his hideous eccentricities: you may well imagine, Madame, that they were to be as ferocious as his other proceedings and that such a man's love-makings are necessarily tainted by his abhorrent character. But how can I abuse your patience by relating these new horrors? Have I not already more than soiled your imagination with infamous recitations? Dare I hazard additional ones?"

The response is not long in coming.

"Yes, Thérèse," Monsieur de Corville put in, "yes, we insist upon the details, you veil them with a decency that removes their edge of horror; there remains only what is useful to whoever seeks to perfect his understanding of enigmatic man. You may not fully apprehend how these tableaux help toward the development of the human spirit; our backwardness in this branch of learning may very well be due to the stupid restraint of those who venture to write upon such matters. Inhibited by absurd fears, they only discuss the puerilities with which every fool is familiar, and dare not, by addressing themselves boldly to the investigation of the human heart, offer its gigantic idiosyncrasies to our view."

In other words: *If you've got the slime, I've got the time.*

Not everyone will agree with the selections in this book. Why did I choose Jane Austen's less famous and somewhat atypical *Lady Susan* rather than an excerpt from *Sense and Sensibility*, *Emma*, or *Pride and Prejudice*? Because as much as possible I wanted to use complete works rather than fragments, and because this little jewel is unbelievably vicious. Also, it is a superb example of the novel composed entirely of letters, and one can never have too many of those in a collection. Similarly, some will say that Juvenal's misogynistic Sixth Satire or the ferociously homophobic Second Satire is more representative of this spectacularly unpleasant human being's *oeuvre* than his First, and that in selecting this uncharacteristically restrained work I am protecting Juvenal from himself, disingenuously shielding the public from the great Latin satirist's reputation as a complete son of a bitch.

That is exactly right, but I have a very good reason for doing so. On his deathbed, my father, a huge, huge Juvenal fan despite his working-class background, made me swear on his not-yet-dug grave or the blood of my Celtic forbears—I can never remember which—that I would do everything in my power to increase Juvenal's renown in this country, even if it meant suppressing the truth about his horrible misogyny and repugnant homophobia. To be perfectly honest, I'd be pleased as punch if somebody came along and complained that Juvenal's misogynistic Sixth Satire or the ferociously homophobic Second Satire were more representative of this spectacularly unpleasant human's being's oeuvre than his First, and that in selecting this uncharacteristically restrained work I am protecting Juvenal from himself, disingenuously shielding the public from the great Latin satirist's reputation as a complete son of a bitch. But frankly, I don't think it's going to happen.

> ALTHOUGH HE IS NOT HIMSELF A FUNNY HUMAN BEING — AND WHO WOULD EXPECT A FLORENTINE CHUCKLE KING AFTER TORTURE AT THE HANDS OF THE MEDICI? — MACHIAVELLI HAS HAD AN ENORMOUS INFLUENCE ON EVERYONE WHO HAS TRIED TO BE FUNNY SINCE HIS TIME. WELL, MAYBE NOT MARTIN LAWRENCE. OR MOLLY IVINS.

Some of the selections in this anthology are easy to read and some are not. Prodigiously well-read and a compulsive show-off, Ben Jonson fills *Volpone* with arcane mythological and historical references that will probably be lost on most modern readers, including me. I do not think that this detracts from the overall impact of his work, but it certainly places more demands on the reader. Apparently, Orson Welles once had big plans for a Broadway production of the seventeenth-century masterpiece, with Jackie Gleason in the title role. It is unlikely that Mr. Gleason would have understood many of the playwright's enigmatic allusions either, but the fact that he was even interested in the project demonstrates that Jonson had written a play capable of stirring modern audiences three centuries after his death. True, of all the selections in this book *Volpone* is probably the toughest assignment. But as an indictment of doctors, lawyers, politicians, and sycophants it is virtually without peer. It rewards those who stick with it. So stick with it.

Machiavelli is the only writer included in this anthology who is not overtly funny. In fact, he is quite spectacularly humorless, though not as spectacularly humorless as the pinheads who try to repackage his principles into motivational guides for hapless businessmen: *Machiavelli for Middle-Management*, *The Prince for Paupers* . . . that sort of thing. Yet the ultimate effect he achieves on the reader can be quite hilarious, in part because one is never sure just how serious Machiavelli is when he makes his dry, oracular pronouncements.

"A Prince . . . cannot without injury to himself practise the virtue of liberality," he writes in the chapter "Of Liberality and Miserliness" in *The Prince*. "There is no quality so self-destructive as liberality; for while you practise it you lose the means whereby it can be practised, and become poor and despised, or else, to avoid poverty, you become rapcious and hated." This mood of deadpan amorality is exactly the sort of tone Swift strove for in "A Modest Proposal," and its overall impact is magnified by the maddening self-assurance of the obviously deranged speaker. Thus, although he is not himself a funny human being—and who would expect a Florentine Chuckle King after torture at the hands of the Medici?—Machiavelli has had an enormous influence on everyone who has tried to be funny since his time. Well, maybe not Martin Lawrence. Or Molly Ivins.

This brings me all the way back to the strange man at the Parisian bistro who used to spend all his waking hours compiling a list of the ten greatest composers. At the time I repeatedly warned him that if he left out Brahms, the general public would be up in arms, but that if he included Brahms at the expense of Alban Berg, fans of 12-tone music would go ballistic. (I did not actually use the term "go ballistic" at the time, as that vacuous banality had not yet been invented; I suspect I resorted to something more contemporary like "flip out," as in: "Fans of the diatonic scale will totally flip out if you pick Johannes Brahms and leave out Alban Berg." Moreover, I did not honestly believe that the general public would be up in arms if he left Brahms off his list, as the general public rarely gets up in arms about that sort of thing. To be perfectly honest, I was merely striving for effect.)

Yet my reasoning was irreproachable, and many years later the same logic applies here. In making this or that selection, or this or that omission, one must be prepared to defend one's choices. Attic comedy buffs will undoubtedly wonder why I picked *The Birds* over *Lysistrata* or *The Frogs* or *The Clouds*. The answer: I felt like it. Besides, with Aristophanes and Molière, one is faced with an embarrassment of riches; it's impossible to make a bad choice. Others will wonder why I ignored Congreve and Sheridan. Simple: I hate them. I know that they're great in the same way that George Romney, Sir Joshua Reynolds, Theodore Dreiser, William Thackeray, and Sergei Rachmaninoff are great. But I still hate them. They're just too, too precious.

Others may complain that the relatively good-natured Cervantes does not belong in a book called *The Malcontents*. Oh yes, he does. Though his satire is usually gentle and bittersweet, his work reflects a deep dissatisfaction with the contemporary world and profound disappointment with mankind in general, putting him in the same general class as Molière. Besides, having waited fifty-one years to read *Don Quixote*, which I now believe to be the second-greatest book ever written (right after *The Iliad*), I'd be a complete dunce not to include selections from it here. But in fairness to Cervantes, I decided upon a good-natured excerpt from the novel which reflects Cervantes' true feelings toward his lovable but insane hero, rather than the more cynical, better-known, but atypical "Tale of Inappropriate Curiosity."

Corn-fed, hale and hearty, good-natured people opening these pages may ask how the Malcontents ended up being so miserable, or, at the very least, so cranky. The answer: That's what jail will do to you. Oscar Wilde ended up in jail. Machiavelli ended up in jail. Voltaire served time, as did Jonson, and de Sade couldn't stay out of the calaboose. Cervantes not only ended up in jail, but he ended up in a Turkish jail, the central character in a late medieval *Midnight Express*. And even as refined a figure as Jane Austen spent her entire life living with her family, which is a different kind of penal servitude. No, if you spent as much time busting rocks and plying oars as the titans contained in this collection, you would probably end up with a fairly pessimistic view of the world yourself.

Satire is sometimes referred to as an obscure, inaccessible form of entertainment that closes on Saturday night. Like Fitzgerald's dictum "There are no second acts in American life," this statement has a beguiling surface beauty but is still basically stupid. Satire, cynicism, a jaundiced view of the world, what have you, have flourished since the days of the ancient Greeks and will continue to flourish because it is one of mankind's most effective weapons against arrogance, greed, and ignorance. In my own lifetime, I saw a president driven from office by the power of satire. It wasn't the war in Vietnam that caused Lyndon Baines Johnson to resign. It was the Smothers Brothers. Or at least that's what my generation likes to believe.

> IT WASN'T THE WAR IN VIETNAM THAT CAUSED LYNDON BAINES JOHNSON TO RESIGN. IT WAS THE SMOTHERS BROTHERS. OR AT LEAST THAT'S WHAT MY GENERATION LIKES TO BELIEVE.

This collection ended up with nineteen writers, the number of years Jean Valjean spent in the galleys for stealing a loaf of bread. It could have been ten or fifteen or thirty, but it isn't. If I learned anything from Herr Rankem, it is that one sometimes has to call it a day.

Although this book is aimed at the general reader, I hope that it will also be of use to anyone seriously considering a career in the malcontentedness field. The authors arrayed herein are the immortals; these are the keepers of the flame, the top guns, the A Team. For best results, neophyte wise-acres should study the authors' biographies to see how they fit into their societies, then read through the selections to see which author best suits their style of misanthropy. C.S. Lewis once said that we read in order to know that we are not alone. The Malcontents teach us not only that we are not alone, but that some of the people we are sharing the planet with are scoundrels, lechers, thugs, or simpletons. But the Malcontents also provide future generations of writers with the moral authority to do what they're not supposed to do, to write what they're not supposed to write. Should anyone complain that a satirist is gratuitously cruel, tell him to reread his Oscar Wilde. If anyone complains about beating a dead horse, tell him to consult Rabelais and de Sade. If anyone registers an objection to a writer's using the same material over and over again, tell him to take a gander at Molière. If anyone complains about being completely over the top, or in hopelessly poor taste, tell him to re-read Swift and Voltaire and Machiavelli. One final bit of advice to young writers: After reading these masters, steal everything that isn't nailed down. To paraphrase T.S. Eliot: Bad poets borrow, good poets steal.

Aristophanes

(c. 447–388 B.C.)

For more than two millennia, audiences and critics alike have termed the work of Athens' fifth-century B.C. playwrights the "Old Comedy," a dramatic form that grew out of early Dionysian rites. In Greek, *komoidia* literally means "song of the *komos.*" Like the *komos* (a ritualized drunken revel with all the best features of a Bourbon Street Mardi Gras or an eighteenth-century Parisian salon), the Old Comedy is typified by depictions of carousal, often grotesque costumes, and vicious character assassination. Of all the playwrights of this period—Chionides, Cratinus, Magnes, Ecphantides, and others—only Aristophanes, the foremost exponent of the Old Comedy, is known to the modern world as more than a name. The author of forty-four plays, victor in Athenian playwriting competitions half a dozen times, his great reputation rests today on the eleven plays that survive: *The Acharnians*, *The Knights*, *The Clouds*, *The Wasps*, *The Peace*, *The Birds*, *Lysistrata*, *Women at the Thesmophoria*, *The Frogs*, *Ecclesiazusae*, and *Plutus*. Almost everything that is known or supposed about Aristophanes' life comes directly from the plays. Independent of the works, it can be safely asserted that Aristophanes served as a councillor of the city of Athens and had two sons. He was born circa 447 B.C. in Athens, though it has been argued otherwise in an attempt to portray him as a non-citizen of Athens and thus discredit him. Wherever he was born, he *did* grow up in Athens and was schooled there, during the last peaceful decade before the onset of the war with Sparta.

Aristophanes began his career in the dramatic arts in 427 B.C. with a play entitled *The Banqueteers* (now lost), cutting his teeth on a satire of his peers' moral and educational theories. His plays focused on the social, literary, and philosophical concerns of Athens during the Peloponnesian War (431–404 B.C.) between reactionary Sparta and imperialist Athens. Aristophanes was opposed to the jingoistic rhetoric of statesmen who dominated the Athenian government during this troubled period.

Aristophanes' *The Birds* was first performed at the Dionysian festival in Athens in early 414 B.C. The festival was a welcome diversion for the Athenian adult males (no women or children were allowed to attend) who were not able to fight. The Peloponnesian War had taken a physical and psychic toll on the citizenry, who packed into the 16,000-seat amphitheater for a little respite and also to watch Aristophanes take a swing at the Athenian establishment. At the moment the plays in the festival were being staged, the Athenian army lay in wait under the walls of Syracuse, plotting a bold attack on the formerly neutral site on the island of Sicily. Some say the play itself was a satirical attack on the imperialistic vision that led to this ill-fated Sicilian expedition. Though it is one of the most lyrical of Aristophanes' plays, it won only second prize at the festival.

The Birds tells the story of a regular Athenian citizen, Pisthetairos (Trusty), who journeys out with his friend Euelpides to escape the drudgery of city life. The two old men are feeling beleaguered by civic duties, politics, and the military presence in Athens. They seek out the Hoopee, a bird that has been a king named Thereus until the gods transformed him in punishment for his heinous crimes. The Hoopee tells the two men that there is no refuge in the known world from the grip of the Athenian empire. Despairing, they listen to the Hoopee's tales of the glorious life of birds and decide that they will found a "city of birds," suspended between earth and heaven, and live among them. They amass an exotic array of birds and try to forge a man-bird alliance and diminish the influence of the gods in their new paradise.

Athenians try to infiltrate the bird kingdom (named Nephelokokkygia or Cloudcuckooland) and impose their corrupt ways, but are turned away by Pisthetairos, "the Wise may learn many things from their foes." Pisthetairos fends off the interlopers and is crowned king of his bird empire—an image that would not have sat well with the democratic Athenians. The hero, an everyman, has his triumph because his fantasy world is a success. The gods are bested but not demoralized, the paradise is maintained, corrupt Athenian influence is kept out. The play is an escape for those caught in the grip of what seemed a never-ending war and the powerlessness that had permeated their once-great region.

Plato, in one of his epigrams, says that the Graces chose Aristophanes' soul for their abode. He included Aristophanes as a character in his *Symposium* and sent to Dionysius the Younger a copy of Aristophanes' play *The Clouds* as a primer on the Athenian republic. Aristophanes was thought of not only as an authority on the foibles and flaws of the great city-state of Athens but also as a master of witty dialogue, pointed topical allusions, brilliant parodies, and lyric verse. His writing, which delivers the news of the day in mocking, poetic style, reveals Aristophanes' desire to use his work for the good of his native city as he watched its steady decline.

The Birds

DRAMATIS PERSONÆ

EUELPIDES
PISTHETÆRUS
EPOPS (the Hoopoe)
TROCHILUS, Servant to Epops
PHŒNICOPTERUS
HERALDS
A PRIEST
A POET
A PROPHET
METON, a Geometrician
A COMMISSIONER
A DEALER IN DECREES
IRIS
A PARRICIDE
CINESIAS, a Dithyrambic Bard
AN INFORMER
PROMETHEUS
POSIDON
TRIBALLUS
HERACLES
SERVANT OF PISTHETÆRUS
MESSENGERS
CHORUS OF BIRDS

SCENE: A wild, desolate tract of open country; broken rocks and brushwood occupy the centre of the stage.

EUELPIDES [*to his jay*] Do you think I should walk straight for yon tree?

PISTHETÆRUS [*to his crow*] Cursed beast, what are you croaking to me? . . . to retrace my steps?

EUELPIDES Why, you wretch, we are wandering at random, we are exerting ourselves only to return to the same spot; 'tis labour lost.

PISTHETÆRUS To think that I should trust to this crow, which has made me cover more than a thousand furlongs!

EUELPIDES And I to this jay, who has torn every nail from my fingers!

PISTHETÆRUS If only I knew where we were. . . .

EUELPIDES Could you find your country again from here?

PISTHETÆRUS No, I feel quite sure I could not, any more than could Execestides find his.

EUELPIDES Oh dear! A dear!

PISTHETÆRUS Aye, aye, my friend, 'tis indeed the road of "oh dears" we are following.

EUELPIDES That Philocrates, the bird-seller, played us a scurvy trick, when he pretended these two guides could help us to find Tereus, the Epops, who is a bird, without being born of one. He has indeed sold us this jay, a true son of Tharelides, for an obolus, and this crow for three, but what can they do? Why, nothing whatever but bite and scratch!—What's the matter with you then, that you keep opening your beak? Do you want us to fling ourselves headlong down these rocks? There is no road that way.

PISTHETÆRUS Not even the vestige of a track in any direction.

EUELPIDES And what does the crow say about the road to follow?

PISTHETÆRUS By Zeus, it no longer croaks the same thing it did.

EUELPIDES And which way does it tell us to go now?

PISTHETÆRUS It says that, by dint of gnawing, it will devour my fingers.

EUELPIDES What misfortune is ours! we strain every nerve to get to the birds, do everything we can to that end, and we cannot find our way! Yes, spectators, our madness is quite different from that of Sacas. He is not a citizen, and would fain be one at any cost; we, on the contrary, born of an honourable tribe and family and living in the midst of our fellow-citizens, we have fled from our country as hard as ever we could go. 'Tis not that we hate it; we recognize it to be great and rich, likewise that everyone has the right to ruin himself, but the crickets only chirrup among the fig-trees for a month or two, whereas the Athenians spend their whole lives in chanting forth judgments from their law-courts. That is why we started off with a basket, a stewpot and some myrtle boughs and have come to seek a quiet country in which to settle. We are going to Tereus, the Epops, to learn from him, whether, in his aerial flights, he has noticed some town of this kind.

PISTHETÆRUS Here! look!

EUELPIDES What's the matter?

PISTHETÆRUS Why, the crow has been pointing me to something up there for some time now.

EUELPIDES And the jay is also opening its beak and craning its neck to show me I know not what. Clearly, there are some birds about here. We shall soon know, if we kick up a noise to start them.

PISTHETÆRUS Do you know what to do? Knock your leg against this rock.

EUELPIDES And you your head to double the noise.

PISTHETÆRUS Well then use a stone instead; take one and hammer with it.

EUELPIDES Good idea! Ho there, within! Slave! slave!

PISTHETÆRUS What's that, friend! You say, "slave," to summon Epops! 'Twould be much better to shout, "Epops, Epops!"

EUELPIDES Well then, Epops! Must I knock again? Epops!

TROCHILUS Who's there? Who calls my master?

EUELPIDES Apollo the Deliverer! what an enormous beak!

TROCHILUS Good god! they are bird-catchers.

EUELPIDES The mere sight of him petrifies me with terror. What a horrible monster!

TROCHILUS Woe to you!

EUELPIDES But we are not men.

TROCHILUS What are you, then?

EUELPIDES I am the Fearling, an African bird.

TROCHILUS You talk nonsense.

EUELPIDES Well, then, just ask it of my feet.

TROCHILUS And this other one, what bird is it?

PISTHETÆRUS I? I am a Cackling, from the land of the pheasants.

EUELPIDES But you yourself, in the name of the gods! what animal are you?

TROCHILUS Why, I am a slave-bird.

EUELPIDES Why, have you been conquered by a cock?

TROCHILUS No, but when my master was turned into a peewit, he begged me to become a bird too, to follow and to serve him.

EUELPIDES Does a bird need a servant, then?

TROCHILUS 'Tis no doubt because he was a man. At times he wants to eat a dish of loach from Phalerum; I seize my dish and fly to fetch him some. Again he wants some pea-soup; I seize a ladle and a pot and run to get it.

EUELPIDES This is, then, truly a running-bird. Come, Trochilus, do us the kindness to call your master.

TROCHILUS Why, he has just fallen asleep after a feed of myrtle-berries and a few grubs.

EUELPIDES Never mind; wake him up.

TROCHILUS I am certain he will be angry. However, I will wake him to please you.

PISTHETÆRUS You cursed brute! why, I am almost dead with terror!

EUELPIDES Oh! my god! 'twas sheer fear that made me lose my jay.

PISTHETÆRUS Ah! you great coward! were you so frightened that you let go your jay?

EUELPIDES And did you not lose your crow, when you fell sprawling on the ground? Pray tell me that.

PISTHETÆRUS No, no.

EUELPIDES Where is it, then?

PISTHETÆRUS It has flown away.

EUELPIDES Then you did not let it go! Oh! you brave fellow!

EPOPS Open the forest, that I may go out!

EUELPIDES By Heracles! what a creature! what plumage! What means this triple crest?

EPOPS Who wants me?

EUELPIDES The twelve great gods have used you ill, meseems.

EPOPS Are you chaffing me about my feathers? I have been a man, strangers.

EUELPIDES 'Tis not you we are jeering at.

EPOPS At what, then?

EUELPIDES Why, 'tis your beak that looks so odd to us.

EPOPS This is how Sophocles outrages me in his tragedies. Know, I once was Tereus.

EUELPIDES You were Tereus, and what are you now? a bird or a peacock?

EPOPS I am a bird.

EUELPIDES Then where are your feathers? For I don't see them.

EPOPS They have fallen off.

EUELPIDES Through illness?

EPOPS No. All birds moult their feathers, you know, every winter, and others grow in their place. But tell me, who are you?

EUELPIDES We? We are mortals.

EPOPS From what country?

EUELPIDES From the land of the beautiful galleys.

EPOPS Are you dicasts?

EUELPIDES No, if anything, we are anti-dicasts.

EPOPS Is that kind of seed sown among you?

EUELPIDES You have to look hard to find even a little in our fields.

EPOPS What brings you here?

EUELPIDES We wish to pay you a visit.

EPOPS What for?

EUELPIDES Because you formerly were a man, like we are, formerly you had debts, as we have, formerly you did not want to pay them, like ourselves; furthermore, being turned into a bird, you have when flying seen all lands and seas. Thus you have all human knowledge as well as that of birds. And hence we have come to you to beg you to direct us to some cosy town, in which one can repose as if on thick coverlets.

EPOPS And are you looking for a greater city than Athens?

EUELPIDES No, not a greater, but one more pleasant to dwell in.

EPOPS Then you are looking for an aristocratic country.

EUELPIDES I? Not at all! I hold the son of Scellias in horror.

EPOPS But, after all, what sort of city would please you best?

EUELPIDES A place where the following would be the most important business transacted.—Some friend would come knocking at the door quite early in the morning saying, "By Olympian Zeus, be at my house early, as soon as you have bathed, and bring your children too. I am giving a nuptial feast, so don't fail, or else don't cross my threshold when I am in distress."

EPOPS Ah! that's what may be called being fond of hardships. And what say you?

PISTHETÆRUS My tastes are similar.

EPOPS And they are?

PISTHETÆRUS I want a town where the father of a handsome lad will stop in the street and say to me reproachfully as if I had failed him, "Ah! Is this well done, Stilbonides! You met my son coming from the bath after the gymnasium and you neither spoke to him, nor embraced him, nor took him with you, nor ever once twitched his parts. Would anyone call you an old friend of mine?"

EPOPS Ah! wag, I see you are fond of suffering. But there is a city of delights, such as you want. 'Tis on the Red Sea.

EUELPIDES Oh, no. Not a sea-port, where some fine morning the

Salaminian galley can appear, bringing a writ-server along. Have you no Greek town you can propose to us?

EPOPS Why not choose Lepreum in Elis for your settlement?

EUELPIDES By Zeus! I could not look at Lepreum without disgust, because of Melanthius.

EPOPS Their, again, there is the Opuntian, where you could live.

EUELPIDES I would not be Opuntian for a talent. But come, what is it like to live with the birds? You should know pretty well.

EPOPS Why, 'tis not a disagreeable life. In the first place, one has no purse.

EUELPIDES That does away with much roguery.

EPOPS For food the gardens yield us white sesamé, myrtle-berries, poppies and mint.

EUELPIDES Why, 'tis the life of the newly-wed indeed.

PISTHETÆRUS Ha! I am beginning to see a great plan, which will transfer the supreme power to the birds, if you will but take my advice.

EPOPS Take your advice? In what way?

PISTHETÆRUS In what way? Well, firstly, do not fly in all directions with open beak; it is not dignified. Among us, when we see a thoughtless man, we ask, "What sort of bird is this?" and Teleas answers, "'Tis a man who has no brain, a bird that has lost his head, a creature you cannot catch, for it never remains in any one place."

EPOPS By Zeus himself! your jest hits the mark. What then is to be done?

PISTHETÆRUS Found a city.

EPOPS We birds? But what sort of city should we build?

PISTHETÆRUS Oh, really, really! 'tis spoken like a fool! Look down.

EPOPS I am looking.

PISTHETÆRUS Now look upwards.

EPOPS I am looking.

PISTHETÆRUS Turn your head round.

EPOPS Ah! 'twill be pleasant for me, if I end up twisting my neck!

PISTHETÆRUS What have you seen?

EPOPS The clouds and the sky.

PISTHETÆRUS Very well! is not this the pole of the birds then?

EPOPS How their pole?

PISTHETÆRUS Or, if you like it, the land. And since it turns and passes through the whole universe, it is called, 'pole.' If you build and fortify it, you will turn your pole into a fortified city. In this way you will reign over mankind as you do over the grasshoppers and cause the gods to die of rabid hunger.

EPOPS How so?

PISTHETÆRUS The air is 'twixt earth and heaven. When we want to go to Delphi, we ask the Bœotians for leave of passage; in the same way, when men sacrifice to the gods, unless the latter pay you tribute, you exercise the right of every nation towards strangers and don't allow the smoke of the sacrifices to pass through your city and territory.

EPOPS By earth! by snares! by network! I never heard of anything more cleverly conceived; and, if the other birds approve, I am going to build the city along with you.

PISTHETÆRUS Who will explain the matter to them?

EPOPS You must yourself. Before I came they were quite ignorant, but since I have lived with them I have taught them to speak.

PISTHETÆRUS But how can they be gathered together?

EPOPS Easily. I will hasten down to the coppice to waken my dear Procné! as soon as they hear our voices, they will come to us not willingly.

PISTHETÆRUS My dear bird, lose no time, I beg. Fly at once into the coppice and awaken Procné.

EPOPS Chase off drowsy sleep, dear companion. Let the sacred hymn arise from thy divine throat in melodious strains; roll forth in soft cadence your refreshing melodies to bewail the fate of Itys, which has been the cause of so many tears to us both. Your pure notes rise through the thick leaves of the yew-tree right up to the throne of Zeus, where Phœbus listens to you, Phœbus with his golden hair. And his ivory lyre responds to your plaintive accents; he gathers the choir of the gods and from their immortal lips rushes a sacred chant of blessed voices.

[*The flute is played behind the scene.*]

PISTHETÆRUS Oh! by Zeus! what a throat that little bird possesses. He has filled the whole coppice with honey-sweet melody!

EUELPIDES Hush!

PISTHETÆRUS What's the matter?

EUELPIDES Will you keep silence?

PISTHETÆRUS What for?

EUELPIDES Epops is going to sing again.

EPOPS [*in the coppice*] Epopoi, poi, popoi, epopoi, popoi, here, here, quick, quick, quick, my comrades in the air; all you, who pillage the fertile lands of the husbandmen, the numberless tribes who gather and devour the barley seeds, the swift flying race who sing so sweetly. And you whose gentle twitter resounds through the fields with the little cry of tio, tio, tio, tio, tio, tio, tio, tio; and you who hop about the branches of the ivy in the gardens; the mountain birds, who feed on the wild olive berries or the arbutus, hurry to come at my call, trioto, trioto, totobrix; you also, who snap up the sharp-stinging gnats in the marshy vales, and you who dwell in the fine plain of Marathon, all damp with dew, and you, the francolin with speckled wings; you too, the halcyons, who flit over the swelling waves of the sea, come hither to hear the tidings; let all the tribes of long-necked birds assemble here; know that a clever old man has come to us, bringing an entirely new idea and proposing great reforms. Let all come to the debate here, here, here, here. Torotorotorotorotix, kikkobau, kikkobau, torotorotorotorolililix.

PISTHETÆRUS Can you see any bird?

EUELPIDES By Phœbus, no! and yet I am straining my eyesight to scan the sky.

PISTHETÆRUS 'Twas really not worth Epops' while to go and bury himself in the thicket like a plover when a-hatching.

PHOENICOPTERUS Torotina, torotina.

PISTHETÆRUS Hold, friend, here is another bird.

EUELPIDES I' faith, yes! 'tis a bird, but of what kind? Isn't it a peacock?

PISTHETÆRUS Epops will tell us. What is this bird?

EPOPS 'Tis not one of those you are used to seeing; 'tis a bird from the marshes.

PISTHETÆRUS Oh! oh! but he is very handsome with his wings as crimson as flame.

EPOPS Undoubtedly; indeed he is called flamingo.

EUELPIDES Hi! I say! You!

PISTHETÆRUS What are you shouting for?

EUELPIDES Why, here's another bird.

PISTHETÆRUS Aye, indeed; 'tis a foreign bird too. What is this bird from beyond the mountains with a look as solemn as it is stupid?

EPOPS He is called the Mede.

PISTHETÆRUS The Mede! But, by Heracles! how, if a Mede, has he flown here without a camel?

EUELPIDES Here's another bird with a crest.

PISTHETÆRUS Ah! that's curious. I say, Epops, you are not the only one of your kind then?

EPOPS This bird is the son of Philocles, who is the son of Epops; so that, you see, I am his grandfather; just as one might say, Hipponicus, the son of Callias, who is the son of Hipponicus.

PISTHETÆRUS Then this bird is Callias! Why, what a lot of his feathers he has lost!

EPOPS That's because he is honest; so the informers set upon him and the women too pluck out his feathers.

PISTHETÆRUS By Posidon, do you see that many-coloured bird? What is his name?

EPOPS This one? 'Tis the glutton.

PISTHETÆRUS Is there another glutton besides Cleonymus? But why, if he is Cleonymus, has he not thrown away his crest? But what is the meaning of all these crests? Have these birds come to contend for the double stadium prize?

EPOPS They are like the Carians, who cling to the crests of their mountains for greater safety.

PISTHETÆRUS Oh, Posidon! do you see what swarms of birds are gathering here?

EUELPIDES By Phœbus! what a cloud! The entrance to the stage is no longer visible, so closely do they fly together.

PISTHETÆRUS Here is the partridge.

EUELPIDES Faith! there is the francolin.

PISTHETÆRUS There is the poachard.

EUELPIDES Here is the kingfisher. And over yonder?

EPOPS 'Tis the barber.

EUELPIDES What? a bird a barber?

PISTHETÆRUS Why, Sporgilus is one. Here comes the owl.

EUELPIDES And who is it brings an owl to Athens?

PISTHETÆRUS Here is the magpie, the turtle-dove, the swallow, the horned owl, the buzzard, the pigeon, the falcon, the ring-dove, the cuckoo, the red-foot, the red-cap, the purple-cap, the kestrel, the diver, the ousel, the osprey, the woodpecker.

EUELPIDES Oh! oh! What a lot of birds! what a quantity of blackbirds! how they scold, how they come rushing up! What a noise! what a noise! Can they be bearing us ill-will? Oh! there! there! they are opening their beaks and staring at us.

PISTHETÆRUS Why, so they are.

CHORUS Popopopopopopopoi. Where is he who called me? Where am I to find him?

EPOPS I have been waiting for you this long while! I never fail in my word to my friends.

CHORUS Tititititititi. What good thing have you to tell me?

EPOPS Something that concerns our common safety, and that is just as pleasant as it is to the purpose. Two men, who are subtle reasoners, have come here to seek me.

CHORUS Where? What? What are you saying?

EPOPS I say, two old men have come from the abode of men to propose a vast and splendid scheme to us.

CHORUS Oh! 'tis a horrible, unheard-of crime! What are you saying?

EPOPS Nay! never let my words scare you.

CHORUS What have you done then?

EPOPS I have welcomed two men, who wish to live with us.

CHORUS And you have dared to do that!

EPOPS Aye, and am delighted at having done so.

CHORUS Where are they?

EPOPS In your midst, as I am.

CHORUS Ah! ah! we are betrayed; 'tis sacrilege! Our friend, he who picked up corn-seeds in the same plains as ourselves, has violated our ancient laws; he has broken the oaths that bind all birds; he has laid a snare for me, he has handed us over to the attacks of that impious race which, throughout all time, has never ceased to war against us. As for this traitorous bird, we will decide his case later, but the two old men shall be punished forthwith; we are going to tear them to pieces.

PISTHETÆRUS 'Tis all over with us.

EUELPIDES You are the sole cause of all our trouble. Why did you bring me from down yonder?

PISTHETÆRUS To have you with me.

EUELPIDES Say rather to have me melt into tears.

PISTHETÆRUS Go to! you are talking nonsense.

EUELPIDES How so?

PISTHETÆRUS How will you be able to cry when once your eyes are pecked out?

CHORUS Io! io! forward to the attack, throw yourselves upon the foe, spill his blood; take to your wings and surround them on all sides. Woe to them! let us get to work with our beaks, let us devour them. Nothing can save them from our wrath, neither the mountain forests, nor the clouds that float in the sky, nor the foaming deep. Come, peck, tear to ribbons. Where is the chief of the cohort? Let him engage the right wing.

EUELPIDES This is the fatal moment. Where shall I fly to, unfortunate wretch that I am?

PISTHETÆRUS Stay! stop here!

EUELPIDES That they may tear me to pieces?

PISTHETÆRUS And how do you think to escape them?

EUELPIDES I don't know at all.

PISTHETÆRUS Come, I will tell you. We must stop and fight them. Let us arm ourselves with these stew-pots.

EUELPIDES Why with the stew-pots?

PISTHETÆRUS The owl will not attack us.

EUELPIDES But do you see all those hooked claws?

PISTHETÆRUS Seize the spit and pierce the foe on your side.

EUELPIDES And how about my eyes?

PISTHETÆRUS Protect them with this dish or this vinegar-pot.

EUELPIDES Oh! what cleverness! what inventive genius! You are a great general, even greater than Nicias, where stratagem is concerned.

CHORUS Forward, forward, charge with your beaks! Come, no delay. Tear, pluck, strike, flay them, and first of all smash the stew-pot.

EPOPS Oh, most cruel of all animals, why tear these two men to pieces, why kill them? What have they done to you? They belong to the same tribe, to the same family as my wife.

CHORUS Are wolves to be spared? Are they not our most mortal foes? So let us punish them.

EPOPS If they are your foes by nature, they are your friends in heart, and they come here to give you useful advice.

CHORUS Advice or a useful word from their lips, from them, the enemies of my forebears!

EPOPS The wise can often profit by the lessons of a foe, for caution is the mother of safety. 'Tis just such a thing as one will not learn from a friend and which an enemy compels you to know. To begin with, 'tis the foe and not the friend that taught cities to build high walls, to equip long vessels of war; and 'tis this knowledge that protects our children, our slaves and our wealth.

CHORUS Well then, I agree, let us first hear them, for 'tis best; one can even learn something in an enemy's school.

PISTHETÆRUS Their wrath seems to cool. Draw back a little.

EPOPS 'Tis only justice, and you will thank me later.

CHORUS Never have we opposed your advice up to now.

PISTHETÆRUS They are in a more peaceful mood; put down your stew-pot and your two dishes; spit in hand, doing duty for a spear, let us mount guard inside the camp close to the pot and watch in our arsenal closely; for we must not fly.

EUELPIDES You are right. But where shall we be buried, if we die?

PISTHETÆRUS In the Ceramicus; for, to get a public funeral, we shall tell the Strategi that we fell at Orneæ, fighting the country's foes.

CHORUS Return to your ranks and lay down your courage beside your wrath as the Hoplites do. Then let us ask these men who they are, whence they come, and with what intent. Here, Epops, answer me.

EPOPS Are you calling me? What do you want of me?

CHORUS Who are they? From what country?

EPOPS Strangers, who have come from Greece, the land of the wise.

CHORUS And what fate has led them hither to the land of the birds?

EPOPS Their love for you and their wish to share your kind of life; to dwell and remain with you always.

CHORUS Indeed, and what are their plans?

EPOPS They are wonderful, incredible, unheard of.

CHORUS Why, do they think to see some advantage that determines them to settle here? Are they hoping with our help to triumph over their foes or to be useful to their friends?

EPOPS They speak of benefits so great it is impossible either to describe or conceive them; all shall be yours, all that we see here, there, above and below us; this they vouch for.

CHORUS Are they mad?

EPOPS They are the sanest people in the world.

CHORUS Clever men?

EPOPS The slyest of foxes, cleverness its very self, men of the world, cunning, the cream of knowing folk.

CHORUS Tell them to speak and speak quickly; why, as I listen to you, I am beside myself with delight.

EPOPS Here, you there, take all these weapons and hang them up inside close to the fire, near the figure of the god who presides there and under his protection; as for you, address the birds, tell them why I have gathered them together.

PISTHETÆRUS Not I, by Apollo, unless they agree with me as the little ape of an armourer agreed with his wife, not to bite me, nor pull me by the parts, nor shove things up my . . .

CHORUS You mean the . . . [*Puts finger to bottom.*] Oh! be quite at ease.

PISTHETÆRUS No, I mean my eyes.

CHORUS Agreed.

PISTHETÆRUS Swear it.

CHORUS I swear it and, if I keep my promise, let judges and spectators give me the victory unanimously.

PISTHETÆRUS It is a bargain.

CHORUS And if I break my word, may I succeed by one vote only.

HERALD Hearken, ye people! Hoplites, pick up your weapons and return to your firesides; do not fail to read the decrees of dismissal we have posted.

CHORUS Man is a truly cunning creature, but nevertheless explain. Perhaps you are going to show me some good way to extend my power, some way that I have not had the wit to find out and which you have discovered. Speak! 'tis to your own interest as well as to mine, for if you secure me some advantage, I will surely share it with you. But what object can have induced you to come among us? Speak boldly, for I shall not break the truce, until you have told us all.

PISTHETÆRUS I am bursting with desire to speak; I have already mixed the dough of my address and nothing prevents me from kneading it. . . . Slave! bring the chaplet and water, which you must pour over my hands. Be quick!

EUELPIDES Is it a question of feasting? What does it all mean?

PISTHETÆRUS By Zeus, no! but I am hunting for fine, tasty words to break down the hardness of their hearts.—I grieve so much for you, who at one time were kings . . .

CHORUS We kings! Over whom?

PISTHETÆRUS . . . of all that exists, firstly of me and of this man, even of Zeus himself. Your race is older than Saturn, the Titans and the Earth.

CHORUS What, older than the Earth!

PISTHETÆRUS By Phœbus, yes.

CHORUS By Zeus, but I never knew that before!

PISTHETÆRUS 'Tis because you are ignorant and heedless, and have never read your Æsop. 'Tis he who tells us that the lark was born before all other creatures, indeed before the Earth; his father died of sickness, but the Earth did not exist then; he remained unburied for five days, when the bird in its dilemma decided, for want of a better place, to entomb its father in its own head.

EUELPIDES So that the lark's father is buried at Cephalæ.

EPOPS Hence, if we existed before the Earth, before the gods, the kingship belongs to us by right of priority.

EUELPIDES Undoubtedly, but sharpen your beak well; Zeus won't be in a hurry to hand over his sceptre to the woodpecker.

PISTHETÆRUS It was not the gods, but the birds, who were formerly the masters and kings over men; of this I have a thousand proofs. First of all, I will point you to the cock, who governed the Persians before all other monarchs, before Darius and Megabyzus. 'Tis in memory of his reign that he is called the Persian bird.

EUELPIDES For this reason also, even to-day, he alone of all the birds wears his tiara straight on his head, like the Great King.

PISTHETÆRUS He was so strong, so great, so feared, that even now, on account of his ancient power, everyone jumps out of bed as soon as ever he crows at daybreak. Blacksmiths, potters, tanners, shoemakers, bathmen, corn-dealers, lyre-makers and armourers, all put on their shoes and go to work before it is daylight.

EUELPIDES I can tell you something anent that. 'Twas the cock's fault that I lost a splendid tunic of Phrygian wool. I was at a feast in town, given to celebrate the birth of a child; I had drunk pretty freely and had just fallen asleep, when a cock, I suppose in a greater hurry than the rest, began to crow. I thought it was dawn and set out for Alimos. I had hardly got beyond the walls, when a footpad struck me in the back with his bludgeon; down I went and wanted to shout, but he had already made off with my mantle.

PISTHETÆRUS Formerly also the kite was ruler and king over the Greeks.

EPOPS The Greeks?

PISTHETÆRUS And when he was king, 'twas he who first taught them to fall on their knees before the kites.

EUELPIDES By Zeus! 'tis what I did myself one day on seeing a kite; but at the moment I was on my knees, and leaning backwards with mouth agape, I bolted an obolus and was forced to carry my bag home empty.

PISTHETÆRUS The cuckoo was king of Egypt and of the whole of Phœnicia. When he called out "cuckoo," all the Phœnicians hurried to the fields to reap their wheat and their barley.

EUELPIDES Hence no doubt the proverb, "Cuckoo! cuckoo! go to the fields, ye circumcised."

PISTHETÆRUS So powerful were the birds, that the kings of Grecian cities, Agamemnon, Menelaus, for instance, carried a bird on the lip of their sceptres, who had his share of all presents.

EUELPIDES That I didn't know and was much astonished when I saw Priam come upon the stage in the tragedies with a bird, which kept watching Lysicrates to see if he got any present.

PISTHETÆRUS But the strongest proof of all is, that Zeus, who now reigns, is represented as standing with an eagle on his head as a symbol of his royalty; his daughter has an owl, and Phœbus, as his servant, has a hawk.

EUELPIDES By Demeter, 'tis well spoken. But what are all these birds doing in heaven?

PISTHETÆRUS When anyone sacrifices and, according to the rite, offers the entrails to the gods, these birds take their share before Zeus. Formerly men always swore by the birds and never by the gods; even now Lampon swears by the goose, when he wants to lie. . . . Thus 'tis clear that you were great and sacred, but now you are looked upon as slaves, as fools, as Helots; stones are thrown at you as at raving madmen, even in holy places. A crowd of bird-catchers sets snares, traps, limed-twigs and nets of all sorts for you; you are caught, you are sold in heaps and the buyers finger you over to be certain you are fat. Again, if they would but serve you up simply roasted; but they rasp cheese into a mixture of oil, vinegar and laserwort, to which another sweet and greasy sauce is added, and the whole is poured scalding hot over your back, for all the world as if you were diseased meat.

CHORUS Man, your words have made my heart bleed; I have groaned over the treachery of our fathers, who knew not how to transmit to us the high rank they held from their forefathers. But 'tis a benevolent Genius, a happy Fate, that sends you to us; you shall be our deliverer and I place the destiny of my little ones and my own in your hands with every confidence. But hasten to tell me what must be done; we should not be worthy to live, if we did not seek to regain our royalty by every possible means.

PISTHETÆRUS First I advise that the birds gather together in one city and that they build a wall of great bricks, like that at Babylon, round the plains of the air and the whole region of space that divides earth from heaven.

EPOPS Oh, Cebriones! oh, Porphyrion! what a terribly strong place!

PISTHETÆRUS This, this being well done and completed, you demand back the empire from Zeus; if he will not agree, if he refuses and does not at once confess himself beaten, you declare a sacred war against him and forbid the gods henceforward to pass through your country with lust, as hitherto, for the purpose of fondling their Alcmenas, their Alopés, or their Semelés! If they try to pass through, you infibulate them with rings so that they can work no longer. You send another messenger to mankind, who will proclaim to them that the birds are kings, that for the future they must first of all sacrifice to them, and only afterwards to the gods; that it is fitting to appoint to each deity the bird that has most in common with it. For instance, are they sacrificing to Aphrodité, let them at the same time offer barley to the coot; are they immolating a sheep to Posidon, let them consecrate wheat in honour of the duck; is a steer being offered to Heracles, let honey-cakes be dedicated to the gull; is a goat being slain for King Zeus, there is a King-Bird, the wren, to whom the sacrifice of a male gnat is due before Zeus himself even.

EUELPIDES This notion of an immolated gnat delights me! And now let the great Zeus thunder!

EPOPS But how will mankind recognize us as gods and not as jays? Us, who have wings and fly?

PISTHETÆRUS You talk rubbish! Hermes is a god and has wings and flies, and so do many other gods. First of all, Victory flies with golden wings, Eros is undoubtedly winged too, and Iris is compared by Homer to a timorous dove. If men in their blindness do not recognize you as gods and continue to worship the dwellers in Olympus, then a cloud of sparrows greedy for corn must descend upon their fields and eat up all their seeds; we shall see their if Demeter will mete them out any wheat.

EUELPIDES By Zeus, she'll take good care she does not, and you will see her inventing a thousand excuses.

PISTHETÆRUS The crows too will prove your divinity to them by pecking out the eyes of their flocks and of their draught-oxen; and then let Apollo cure them, since he is a physician and is paid for the purpose.

EUELPIDES Oh! don't do that! Wait first until I have sold my two young bullocks.

PISTHETÆRUS If on the other hand they recognize that you are God, the principle of life, that you are Earth, Saturn, Posidon, they shall be loaded with benefits.

EPOPS Name me one of these then.

PISTHETÆRUS Firstly, the locusts shall not eat up their vine-blossoms; a legion of owls and kestrels will devour them. Moreover, the gnats and the gall-bugs shall no longer ravage the figs; a flock of thrushes shall swallow the whole host down to the very last.

EPOPS And how shall we give wealth to mankind? This is their strongest passion.

PISTHETÆRUS When they consult the omens, you will point them to the richest mines, you will reveal the paying ventures to the diviner, and not another shipwreck will happen or sailor perish.

EPOPS No more shall perish? How is that?

PISTHETÆRUS When the auguries are examined before starting on a voyage, some bird will not fail to say, "Don't start! there will be a storm," or else, "Go! you will make a most profitable venture."

EUELPIDES I shall buy a trading-vessel and go to sea. I will not stay with you.

PISTHETÆRUS You will discover treasures to them, which were buried in former times, for you know them. Do not all men say, "None know where my treasure lies, unless perchance it be some bird."

EUELPIDES I shall sell my boat and buy a spade to unearth the vessels.

EPOPS And how are we to give them health, which belongs to the gods?

PISTHETÆRUS If they are happy, is not that the chief thing towards health? The miserable man is never well.

EPOPS Old Age also dwells in Olympus. How will they get at it? Must they die in early youth?

PISTHETÆRUS Why, the birds, by Zeus, will add three hundred years to their life.

EPOPS From whom will they take them?

PISTHETÆRUS From whom? Why, from themselves. Don't you know the cawing crow lives five times as long as a man?

EUELPIDES Ah! ah! these are far better kings for us than Zeus!

PISTHETÆRUS Far better, are they not? And firstly, we shall not have to build them temples of hewn stone, closed with gates of gold; they will dwell amongst the bushes and in the thickets of green oak; the most venerated of birds will have no other temple than the foliage of the olive tree; we shall not go to Delphi or to Ammon to sacrifice; but standing erect in the midst of arbutus and wild olives and holding forth our hands filled with wheat and barley, we shall pray them to admit us to a share of the blessings they enjoy and shall at once obtain them for a few grains of wheat.

CHORUS Old man, whom I detested, you are now to me the dearest of all; never shall I, if I can help it, fail to follow your advice. Inspirited by your words, I threaten my rivals the gods, and I swear that if you march in alliance with me against the gods and are faithful to our just, loyal and sacred bond, we shall soon have shattered their sceptre. 'Tis our part to undertake the toil, 'tis yours to advise.

EPOPS By Zeus! 'tis no longer the time to delay and loiter like Nicias; let us act as promptly as possible. . . . In the first place, come, enter my nest built of brushwood and blades of straw, and tell me your names.

PISTHETÆRUS That is soon done; my name is Pisthetærus.

EPOPS And his?

PISTHETÆRUS Euelpides, of the deme of Thria.

EPOPS Good! and good luck to you.

PISTHETÆRUS We accept the omen.

EPOPS Come in here.

PISTHETÆRUS Very well, 'tis you who lead us and must introduce us.

EPOPS Come then.

PISTHETÆRUS Oh! my god! do come back here. Hi! tell us how we are to follow you. You can fly, but we cannot.

EPOPS Well, well.

PISTHETÆRUS Remember Æsop's fables. It is told there, that the fox faired very ill, because he had made an alliance with the eagle.

EPOPS Be at ease. You shall eat a certain root and wings will grow on your shoulders.

PISTHETÆRUS Then let us enter. Xanthias and Manes, pick up our baggage.

CHORUS Hi! Epops! do you hear me?

EPOPS What's the matter?

CHORUS Take them off to dine well and call your mate, the melodious Procné, whose songs are worthy of the Muses; she will delight our leisure moments.

PISTHETÆRUS Oh! I conjure you, accede to their wish; for this delightful bird will leave her rushes at the sound of your voice; for the sake of the gods, let her come here, so that we may contemplate the nightingale.

EPOPS Let it be as you desire. Come forth, Procné, show yourself to these strangers.

PISTHETÆRUS Oh! great Zeus! what a beautiful little bird! what a dainty form! what brilliant plumage!

EUELPIDES Do you know how dearly I should like to split her legs for her?

PISTHETÆRUS She is dazzling all over with gold, like a young girl.

EUELPIDES Oh! how I should like to kiss her!

PISTHETÆRUS Why, wretched man, she has two little sharp points on her beak.

EUELPIDES I would treat her like an egg, the shell of which we remove before eating it; I would take off her mask and then kiss her pretty face.

EPOPS Let us go in.

PISTHETÆRUS Lead the way, and may success attend us.

CHORUS Lovable golden bird, whom I cherish above all others, you, whom I associate with all my songs, nightingale, you have come, you have come, to show yourself to me and to charm me with your notes. Come, you, who play spring melodies upon the harmonious flute, lead off our anapœsts.

Weak mortals, chained to the earth, creatures of clay as frail as the foliage of the woods, you unfortunate race, whose life is but darkness, as unreal as a shadow, the illusion of a dream, hearken to us, who are immortal beings, ethereal, ever young and occupied with eternal thoughts, for we shall teach you about all celestial matters; you shall know thoroughly what is the nature of the birds, what the origin of the gods, of the rivers, of Erebus, and Chaos; thanks to us, Prodicus will envy you your knowledge.

At the beginning there was only Chaos, Night, dark Erebus, and deep Tartarus. Earth, the air and heaven had no existence. Firstly, black-winged Night laid a germless egg in the bosom of the infinite deeps of Erebus, and from this, after the revolution of long ages, sprang the graceful Eros with his glittering golden wings, swift as the whirlwinds of the tempest. He mated in deep Tartarus with dark Chaos, winged like himself, and thus hatched forth our race, which was the first to see the light. That of the Immortals did not exist until Eros had brought together all the ingredients of the world, and from their marriage Heaven, Ocean, Earth and the imperishable race of blessed gods sprang into being. Thus our origin is very much older than that of the dwellers in Olympus. We are the offspring of Eros; there are a thousand proofs to show it. We have wings and we lend assistance to lovers. How many handsome youths, who had sworn to remain insensible, have not been vanquished by our power and have yielded themselves to their lovers when almost at the end of their youth, being led away by the gift of a quail, a waterfowl, a goose, or a cock.

And what important services do not the birds render to mortals! First of all, they mark the seasons for them, springtime, winter, and autumn. Does the screaming crane migrate to Libya,—it warns the husbandman to sow, the pilot to take his ease beside his tiller hung up in his dwelling, and Orestes to weave a tunic, so that the rigorous cold may not drive him any more to strip other folk.

When the kite reappears, he tells of the return of spring and of the period when the fleece of the sheep must be clipped. Is the swallow in sight? All hasten to sell their warm tunic and to buy some light clothing. We are your Ammon, Delphi, Dodona, your Phœbus Apollo. Before undertaking anything, whether a business transaction, a marriage, or the purchase of food, you consult the birds by reading the omens, and you give this name of omen to all signs that tell of the future. With you a word is an omen, you call a sneeze an omen, a meeting an omen, an unknown sound an omen, a slave or an ass an omen.

Is it not clear that we are a prophetic Apollo to you? If you recognize us as gods, we shall be your divining Muses, through us you will know the winds and the seasons, summer, winter, and the temperate months. We shall not withdraw ourselves to the highest clouds like Zeus, but shall be among you and shall give to you and to your children and the children of your children, health and wealth, long life, peace, youth, laughter, songs and feasts; in short, you will all be so well off, that you will be weary and satiated with enjoyment.

Oh, rustic Muse of such varied note, tio, tio, tio, tiotinx, I sing with you in the groves and on the mountain tops, tio, tio, tio, tio, tiotinx. I pour forth sacred strains from my golden throat in honour of the god Pan, tio, tio, tio, tiotinx, from the top of the thickly leaved ash, and my voice mingles with the mighty choirs who extol Cybelé on the mountain tops, totototototototototinx. 'Tis to our concerts that Phrynichus comes to pillage like a bee the ambrosia of his songs, the sweetness of which so charms the ear, tio, tio, tio, tio, tinx.

If there be one of you spectators who wishes to spend the rest of his life quietly among the birds, let him come to us. All that is disgraceful and forbidden by law on earth is on the contrary honourable among us, the birds. For instance, among you 'tis a crime to beat your father, but with us 'tis an estimable deed; it's considered fine to run straight at your father and hit him, saying, "Come, lift your spur if you want to fight." The runaway slave, whom you brand, is only a spotted francolin with us. Are you Phrygian like Spintharus? Among us you would be the Phrygian bird, the goldfinch, of the race of Philemon. Are you a slave and a Carian like Execestides? Among us you can create yourself forefathers; you can always find relations. Does the son of Pisias want to betray the gates of the city to the foe? Let him become a partridge, the fitting offspring of his father; among us there is no shame in escaping as cleverly as a partridge.

So the swans on the banks of the Hebrus, tio, tio, tio, tio, tiotinx, mingle their voices to serenade Apollo, tio, tio, tio, tio, tiotinx, flapping their wings the while, tio, tio, tio, tio, tiotinx; their notes reach beyond the clouds of heaven; all the dwellers in the forests stand still with astonishment and delight; a calm rests upon the waters, and the Graces and the choirs in Olympus catch up the strain, tio, tio, tio, tio, tiotinx.

There is nothing more useful nor more pleasant than to have wings. To begin with, just let us suppose a spectator to be dying with hunger and to be weary of the choruses of the tragic poets; if he were winged, he would fly off, go home to dine and come back with his stomach filled. Some Patroclides in urgent need would not have to soil his cloak, but could fly off, satisfy his requirements, and, having recovered his breath, return. If one of you, it matters not who, had adulterous relations and saw the husband of his mistress in the seats of the senators, he might stretch his wings, fly thither, and, having appeased his craving, resume his place. Is it not the most priceless gift of all, to be winged? Look at Diitrephes! His wings were only wickerwork ones, and yet he got himself chosen Phylarch and then Hipparch; from being nobody, he has risen to be famous; 'tis now the finest gilded cock of his tribe.

PISTHETÆRUS Halloa! What's this? By Zeus! I never saw anything so funny in all my life.

EUELPIDES What makes you laugh?

PISTHETÆRUS 'Tis your bits of wings. D'you know what you look like? Like a goose painted by some dauber-fellow.

EUELPIDES And you look like a close-shaven blackbird.

PISTHETÆRUS 'Tis ourselves asked for this transformation, and, as Æschylus has it, "These are no borrowed feathers, but truly our own."

EPOPS Come now, what must be done?

PISTHETÆRUS First give our city a great and famous name, then sacrifice to the gods.

EUELPIDES I think so too.

EPOPS Let's see. What shall our city be called?

PISTHETÆRUS Will you have a high-sounding Laconian name? Shall we call it Sparta?

EUELPIDES What! call my town Sparta? Why, I would not use esparto for my bed, even though I had nothing but bands of rushes.

PISTHETÆRUS Well then, what name can you suggest?

EUELPIDES Some name borrowed from the clouds, from these lofty regions in which we dwell—in short, some well-known name.

PISTHETÆRUS Do you like Nephelococcygia?

EPOPS Oh! capital! truly 'tis a brilliant thought!

EUELPIDES Is it in Nephelococcygia that all the wealth of Theovenes and most of Aeschines' is?

PISTHETÆRUS No, 'tis rather the plain of Phlegra, where the gods withered the pride of the sons of the Earth with their shafts.

EUELPIDES Oh! what a splendid city! But what god shall be its patron? for whom shall we weave the peplus?

PISTHETÆRUS Why not choose Athené Polias?

EUELPIDES Oh! what a well-ordered town 'twould be to have a female deity armed from head to foot, while Clisthenes was spinning!

PISTHETÆRUS Who then shall guard the Pelargicon?

EPOPS One of ourselves, a bird of Persian strain, who is everywhere proclaimed to be the bravest of all, a true chick of Ares.

EUELPIDES Oh! noble chick! what a well-chosen god for a rocky home!

PISTHETÆRUS Come! into the air with you to help the workers who are building the wall; carry up rubble, strip yourself to mix the mortar, take up the hod, tumble down the ladder, an [sic] you like, post sentinels, keep the fire smouldering beneath the ashes, go round the walls, bell in hand, and go to sleep up there yourself, then despatch two heralds, one to the gods above, the other to mankind on earth and come back here.

EUELPIDES As for yourself, remain here, and may the plague take you for a troublesome fellow!

PISTHETÆRUS Go, friend, go where I send you, for without you my orders cannot be obeyed. For myself, I want to sacrifice to the new god, and I am going to summon the priest who must preside at the ceremony. Slaves! slaves! bring forward the basket and the lustral water.

CHORUS I do as you do, and I wish as you wish, and I implore you to address powerful and solemn prayers to the gods, and in addition to immolate a sheep as a token of our gratitude. Let us sing the Pythian chant in honour of the god, and let Chæris accompany our voices.

PISTHETÆRUS [*to the flute-player*] Enough! but, by Heracles! what is this? Great gods! I have seen many prodigious things, but I never saw a muzzled raven.

EPOPS Priest! 'tis high time! Sacrifice to the new gods.

PRIEST I begin, but where is he with the basket? Pray to the Vesta of the birds, to the kite, who presides over the hearth, and to all the god and goddess-birds who dwell in Olympus.

CHORUS Oh! Hawk, the sacred guardian of Sunium, oh, god of the storks!

PRIEST Pray to the swan of Delos, to Latona the mother of the quails, and to Artemis, the goldfinch.

PISTHETÆRUS 'Tis no longer Artemis Colænis, but Artemis the goldfinch.

PRIEST And to Bacchus, the finch and Cybelé, the ostrich and mother of the gods and mankind.

CHORUS Oh! sovereign ostrich, Cybelé, the mother of Cleocritus, grant health and safety to the Nephelococcygians as well as to the dwellers in Chios . . .

PISTHETÆRUS The dwellers in Chios! I am delighted they should be thus mentioned on all occasions.

CHORUS . . . to the heroes, the birds, to the sons of heroes, to the porphyrion, the pelican, the spoon-bill, the redbreast, the grouse, the peacock, the horned-owl, the teal, the bittern, the heron, the stormy petrel, the fig-pecker, the titmouse . . .

PISTHETÆRUS Stop! stop! you drive me crazy with your endless list. Why, wretch, to what sacred feast are you inviting the vultures and the sea-eagles? Don't you see that a single kite could easily carry off the lot at once? Begone, you and your fillets and all; I shall know how to complete the sacrifice by myself.

PRIEST It is imperative that I sing another sacred chant for the rite of the lustral water, and that I invoke the immortals, or at least one of them, provided always that you have some suitable food to offer him; from what I see here, in the shape of gifts, there is naught whatever but horn and hair.

PISTHETÆRUS Let us address our sacrifices and our prayers to the winged gods.

A POET Oh, Muse! celebrate happy Nephelococcygia in your hymns.

PISTHETÆRUS What have we here? Where do you come from, tell me? Who are you?

POET I am he whose language is sweeter than honey, the zealous slave of the Muses, as Homer has it.

PISTHETÆRUS You a slave! and yet you wear your hair long?

POET No, but the fact is all we poets are the assiduous slaves of the Muses, according to Homer.

PISTHETÆRUS In truth your little cloak is quite holy too through zeal! But, poet, what ill wind drove you here?

POET I have composed verses in honour of your Nephelococcygia, a host of splendid dithyrambs and parthenians, worthy of Simonides himself.

PISTHETÆRUS And when did you compose them? How long since?

POET Oh! 'tis long, aye, very long, that I have sung in honour of this city.

PISTHETÆRUS But I am only celebrating its foundation with this sacrifice; I have only just named it, as is done with little babies.

POET "Just as the chargers fly with the speed of the wind, so does the voice of the Muses take its flight. Oh! then noble founder of the town of Ætna, thou, whose name recalls the holy sacrifices, make us such gift as thy generous heart shall suggest."

PISTHETÆRUS He will drive us silly if we do not get rid of him by some present. Here! you, who have a fur as well as your tunic, take it off and give it to this clever poet. Come, take this fur; you look to me to be shivering with cold.

POET My Muse will gladly accept this gift; but engrave these verses of Pindar's on your mind.

PISTHETÆRUS Oh! what a pest! 'Tis impossible then to be rid of him.

POET "Straton wanders among the Scythian nomads, but has no linen garment. He is sad at only wearing an animal's pelt and no tunic." Do you conceive my bent?

PISTHETÆRUS I understand that you want me to offer you a tunic. Hi! you [*to* EUELPIDES], take off yours; we must help the poet. . . . Come, you, take it and begone.

POET I am going, and these are the verses that I address to this city: "Phœbus of the golden throne, celebrate this shivery, freezing city; I have travelled through fruitful and snow-covered plains. Tralala! Tralala!"

PISTHETÆRUS What are you chanting us about frosts? Thanks to the tunic, you no longer fear them. Ah! by Zeus! I could not have believed this cursed fellow could so soon have learnt the way to our city. Come, priest, take the lustral water and circle the altar.

PRIEST Let all keep silence!

A PROPHET Let not the goat be sacrificed.

PISTHETÆRUS Who are you?

PROPHET Who am I? A prophet.

PISTHETÆRUS Get you gone.

PROPHET Wretched man, insult not sacred things. For there is an oracle of Bacis, which exactly applies to Nephelococcygia.

PISTHETÆRUS Why did you not reveal it to me before I founded my city?

PROPHET The divine spirit was against it.

PISTHETÆRUS Well, 'tis best to know the terms of the oracle.

PROPHET "But when the wolves and the white crows shall dwell together between Corinth and Sicyon. . . ."

PISTHETÆRUS But how do the Corinthians concern me?

PROPHET 'Tis the regions of the air that Bacis indicated in this manner. "They must first sacrifice a white-fleeced goat to Pandora, and give the prophet, who first reveals my words, a good cloak and sandals."

PISTHETÆRUS Are the sandals there?

PROPHET Read. "And besides this a goblet of wine and a good share of the entrails of the victim."

PISTHETÆRUS Of the entrails—is it so written?

PROPHET Read. "If you do as I command, divine youth, you shall be an eagle among the clouds; if not, you shall be neither turtle-dove, nor eagle, nor woodpecker."

PISTHETÆRUS Is all that there?

PROPHET Read.

PISTHETÆRUS This oracle in no sort of way resembles the one Apollo dictated to me: "If an impostor comes without invitation to annoy you during the sacrifice and to demand a share of the victim, apply a stout stick to his ribs."

PROPHET You are drivelling.

PISTHETÆRUS "And don't spare him, were he an eagle from out of the clouds, were it Lampon himself or the great Diopithes."

PROPHET Is all that there?

PISTHETÆRUS Here, read it yourself, and go and hang yourself.

CHORUS Oh! unfortunate wretch that I am.

PISTHETÆRUS Away with you, and take your prophecies elsewhere.

METON I have come to you.

PISTHETÆRUS Yet another pest. What have you come to do? What's your plan? What's the purpose of your journey? Why these splendid buskins?

METON I want to Survey the plains of the air for you and to parcel them into lots.

PISTHETÆRUS In the name of the gods, who are you?

METON Who am I? Meton, known throughout Greece and at Colonus.

PISTHETÆRUS What are these things?

METON Tools for measuring the air. In truth, the spaces in the air have precisely the form of a furnace. With this bent ruler I draw a line from top to bottom; from one of its points I describe a circle with the compass. Do you understand?

PISTHETÆRUS Not the very least.

METON With the straight ruler I set to work to inscribe a square within this circle; in its centre will be the market-place, into which all the straight streets will lead, converging to this centre like a star, which, although only orbicular, sends forth its rays in a straight line from all sides.

PISTHETÆRUS Meton, you new Thales . . .

METON What d'you want with me?

PISTHETÆRUS I want to give you a proof of my friendship. Use your legs.

METON Why, what have I to fear?

PISTHETÆRUS 'Tis the same here as in Sparta. Strangers are driven away, and blows rain down as thick as hail.

METON Is there sedition in your city?

PISTHETÆRUS No, certainly not.

METON What's wrong then?

PISTHETÆRUS We are agreed to sweep all quacks and impostors far from our borders.

METON Then I'm off.

PISTHETÆRUS I fear me 'tis too late. The thunder growls already.

[*Beats him.*]

METON Oh, woe! oh, woe!

PISTHETÆRUS I warned you. Now, be off, and do your surveying somewhere else.

[*METON takes to his heels.*]

AN INSPECTOR Where are the Proxeni?

PISTHETÆRUS Who is this Sardanapalus?

INSPECTOR I have been appointed by lot to come to Nephelococcygia as inspector.

PISTHETÆRUS An inspector! and who sends you here, you rascal?

INSPECTOR A decree of Taleas.

PISTHETÆRUS Will you just pocket your salary, do nothing, and be off?

INSPECTOR I' faith! that I will; I am urgently needed to be at Athens to attend the assembly; for I am charged with the interests of Pharnaces.

PISTHETÆRUS Take it then, and be off. See, here is your salary.

[*Beats him.*]

INSPECTOR What does this mean?

PISTHETÆRUS 'Tis the assembly where you have to defend Pharnaces.

INSPECTOR You shall testify that they dare to strike me, the inspector.

PISTHETÆRUS Are you not going to clear out with your urns? 'Tis not to be believed; they send its inspectors before we have so much as paid sacrifice to the gods.

A DEALER IN DECREES "If the Nephelococcygian does wrong to the Athenian . . ."

PISTHETÆRUS Now whatever are these cursed parchments?

DEALER IN DECREES I am a dealer in decrees, and I have come here to sell you the new laws.

PISTHETÆRUS Which?

DEALER IN DECREES "The Nephelococcygians shall adopt the same weights, measures and decrees as the Olophyxians."

PISTHETÆRUS And you shall soon be imitating the Ototyxians.

[*Beats him.*]

DEALER IN DECREES Hullo! what are you doing?

PISTHETÆRUS Now will you be off with your decrees? For I am going to let you see some severe ones.

INSPECTOR [*returning*] I summon Pisthetærus for outrage for the month of Munychion.

PISTHETÆRUS Ha! my friend! are you still there?

DEALER IN DECREES "Should anyone drive away the magistrates and not receive them, according to the decree duly posted . . ."

PISTHETÆRUS What! rascal! you are there too?

INSPECTOR Woe to you! I'll have you condemned to a fine of ten thousand drachmæ.

PISTHETÆRUS And I'll smash your urns.

INSPECTOR Do you recall that evening when you stooled against the column where the decrees are posted?

PISTHETÆRUS Here! here! let him be seized. [THE INSPECTOR *runs off.*] Well! don't you want to stop any longer?

PRIEST Let us get indoors as quick as possible; we will sacrifice the goat inside.

CHORUS Henceforth it is to me that mortals must address their sacrifices and their prayers. Nothing escapes my sight nor my might. My glance embraces the universe, I preserve the fruit in the flower by destroying the thousand kinds of voracious insects the soil produces, which attack the trees and feed on the germ when it has scarcely formed in the calyx; I destroy those who ravage the balmy terrace gardens like a deadly plague; all these gnawing crawling creatures perish beneath the lash of my wing. I hear it proclaimed everywhere: "A talent for him who shall kill Diagoras of Melos, and a talent for him who destroys one of the dead tyrants." We likewise wish to make our proclamation: "A talent to him among you who shall kill Philocrates, the Strouthian; four, if he brings him to us alive. For this Philocrates skewers the finches together and sells them at the rate of an obolus for seven. He tortures the thrushes by blowing them out, so that they may look bigger, sticks their own feathers into the nostrils of black-birds, and collects pigeons, which he shuts up and forces them, fastened in a net, to decoy others." That is what we wish to proclaim. And if anyone is keeping birds shut up in his yard, let him hasten to let them loose; those who disobey shall be seized by the birds and we shall put them in chains, so that in their turn they may decoy other men.

Happy indeed is the race of winged birds who need no cloak in winter! Neither do I fear the relentless rays of the fiery dogdays; when the divine grasshopper, intoxicated with the sunlight, when noon is burning the ground, is breaking out into shrill melody, my home is beneath the foliage in the flowery meadows. I winter in deep caverns, where I frolic with the mountain nymphs, while in spring I despoil the gardens of the Graces and gather the white, virgin berry on the myrtle bushes. I want now to speak to the judges about the prize they are going to award; if they are favourable to us, we will load them with benefits far greater than those Paris received. Firstly, the owls of Laurium, which every judge desires above all things, shall never be wanting to you; you shall see them coming with you, building their nests in your money-bags and laying coins. Besides, you shall be housed like the gods, for we shall erect gables over your dwellings; if you hold some public post and want to do a little pilfering, we will give you the sharp claws of a hawk. Are you dining in town, we will provide you with crops. But, if your award is against us, don't fail to have metal covers fashioned for yourselves, like those they place over statues; else, look out! for the day you wear a white tunic all the birds will soil it with their droppings.

PISTHETÆRUS Birds! the sacrifice is propitious. But I see no messenger coming from the wall to tell us what is happening. Ah! here comes one running himself out of breath as though he were running the Olympic stadium.

MESSENGER Where, where is he? Where, where, where is he? Where, where, where is he? Where is Pisthetærus, our leader?

PISTHETÆRUS Here am I.

MESSENGER The wall is finished.

PISTHETÆRUS That's good news.

MESSENGER 'Tis a most beautiful, a most magnificent work of art. The wall is so broad, that Proxenides, the Braggartian, and Theogenes could pass each other in their chariots, even if they were drawn by steeds as big as the Trojan horse.

PISTHETÆRUS 'Tis wonderful!

MESSENGER Its length is one hundred stadia; I measured it myself.

PISTHETÆRUS A decent length, by Posidon! And who built such a wall?

MESSENGER Birds—birds only; they had neither Egyptian brickmaker, nor stonemason, nor carpenter; the birds did it all themselves; I could hardly believe my eyes. Thirty thousand cranes came from Libya with a supply of stones, intended for the foundations. The water-rails chiselled them with their beaks. Ten thousand storks were busy making bricks; plovers and other water fowl carried water into the air.

PISTHETÆRUS And who carried the mortar?

MESSENGER Herons, in hods.

PISTHETÆRUS But how could they put the mortar into hods?

MESSENGER Oh! 'twas a truly clever invention; the geese used their feet like spades; they buried them in the pile of mortar and then emptied them into the hods.

PISTHETÆRUS Ah! to what use cannot feet be put?

MESSENGER You should have seen how eagerly the ducks carried bricks. To complete the tale, the swallows came flying to the work, their beaks full of mortar and their trowel on their back, just the way little children are carried.

PISTHETÆRUS Who would want paid servants after this? But, tell me, who did the woodwork?

MESSENGER Birds again, and clever carpenters too, the pelicans, for they squared up the gates with their beaks in such a fashion that one would have thought they were using axes; the noise was just like a dockyard. Now the whole wall is tight everywhere, securely bolted and well guarded; it is patrolled, bell in hand; the sentinels stand everywhere and beacons burn on the towers. But I must run off to clean myself; the rest is your business.

CHORUS Well! what do you say to it? Are you not astonished at the wall being completed so quickly?

PISTHETÆRUS By the gods, yes, and with good reason. 'Tis really not to be believed. But here comes another messenger from the wall to bring us some further news! What a fighting look he has!

SECOND MESSENGER Oh! oh! oh! oh! oh! oh!

PISTHETÆRUS What's the matter?

SECOND MESSENGER A horrible outrage has occurred; a god sent by Zeus has passed through our gates and has penetrated the realms of the air without the knowledge of the jays, who are on guard in the daytime.

PISTHETÆRUS 'Tis an unworthy and criminal deed. What god was it?

SECOND MESSENGER We don't know that. All we know is, that he has got wings.

PISTHETÆRUS Why were not guards sent against him at once?

SECOND MESSENGER We have despatched thirty thousand hawks of the legion of mounted archers. All the hook-clawed birds are moving against him, the kestrel, the buzzard, the vulture, the great-horned owl; they cleave the air, so that it resounds with the flapping of their wings; they are looking everywhere for the god, who cannot be far away; indeed, if I mistake not, he is coming from yonder side.

PISTHETÆRUS All arm themselves with slings and bows! This way, all our soldiers; shoot and strike! Some one give me a sling!

CHORUS War, a terrible war is breaking out between us and the gods! Come, let each one guard the Air, the son of Erebus, in which the clouds float. Take care no immortal enters it without your knowledge. Scan all sides with your glance. Hark! methinks I can bear the rustle of the swift wings of a god from heaven.

PISTHETÆRUS Hi! you woman! where are you flying to? Halt, don't stir! keep motionless! not a beat of your wing!—Who are you and from what country? You must say whence you come.

IRIS I come from the abode of the Olympian gods.

PISTHETÆRUS What's your name, ship or cap?

IRIS I am swift Iris.

PISTHETÆRUS Paralus or Salaminia?

IRIS What do you mean?

PISTHETÆRUS Let a buzzard rush at her and seize her.

IRIS Seize me! But what do all these insults betoken?

PISTHETÆRUS Woe to you!

IRIS 'Tis incomprehensible.

PISTHETÆRUS By which gate did you pass through the wall, wretched woman?

IRIS By which gate? Why, great gods, I don't know.

PISTHETÆRUS You hear how she holds us in derision. Did you present yourself to the officers in command of the jays? You don't answer. Have you a permit, bearing the seal of the storks?

IRIS Am I awake?

PISTHETÆRUS Did you get one?

IRIS Are you mad?

PISTHETÆRUS No head-bird gave you a safe-conduct?

IRIS A safe-conduct to me, you poor fool!

PISTHETÆRUS Ah! and so you slipped into this city on the sly and into these realms of air-land that don't belong to you.

IRIS And what other road can the gods travel?

PISTHETÆRUS By Zeus! I know nothing about that, not I. But they won't pass this way. And you still dare to complain! Why, if you were treated according to your deserts, no Iris would ever have more justly suffered death.

IRIS I am immortal.

PISTHETÆRUS You would have died nevertheless.—Oh! 'twould be truly intolerable! What! should the universe obey us and the gods alone continue their insolence and not understand that they must submit to the law of the strongest in their due turn? But tell me, where are you flying to?

IRIS I? The messenger of Zeus to mankind, I am going to tell them to sacrifice sheep and oxen on the altars and to fill their streets with the rich smoke of burning fat.

PISTHETÆRUS Of which gods are you speaking?

IRIS Of which? Why, of ourselves, the gods of heaven.

PISTHETÆRUS You, gods?

IRIS Are there others then?

PISTHETÆRUS Men now adore the birds as gods, and 'tis to them, by Zeus, that they must offer sacrifices, and not to Zeus at all!

IRIS Oh! fool! fool! Rouse not the wrath of the gods, for 'tis terrible indeed. Armed with the brand of Zeus, Justice would annihilate your race; the lightning would strike you as it did Lycimnius and consume both your body and the porticos of your palace.

PISTHETÆRUS Here! that's enough tall talk. Just you listen and keep quiet! Do you take me for a Lydian or a Phrygian and think to frighten me with your big words? Know, that if Zeus worries me again, I shall go at the head of my eagles, who are armed with lightning, and reduce his dwelling and that of Amphion to cinders. I shall send more than six hundred porphyrions clothed in leopards' skins up to heaven against him; and formerly a single Porphyrion gave him enough to do. As for you, his messenger, if you annoy me, I shall begin by stretching your legs asunder and so conduct myself, Iris though you be, that despite my age, you will be astonished. I will show you something that will make you three times over.

IRIS May you perish, you wretch, you and your infamous words!

PISTHETÆRUS Won't you be off quickly? Come, stretch your wings or look out for squalls!

IRIS If my father does not punish you for your insults . . .

PISTHETÆRUS Ha! . . . but just you be off elsewhere to roast younger folk than us with your lightning.

CHORUS We forbid the gods, the sons of Zeus, to pass through our city and the mortals to send them the smoke of their sacrifices by this road.

PISTHETÆRUS 'Tis odd that the messenger we sent to the mortals has never returned.

HERALD Oh! blessed Pisthetærus, very wise, very illustrious, very gracious, thrice happy, very . . . Come, prompt me, somebody, do.

PISTHETÆRUS Get to your story!

HERALD All peoples are filled with admiration for your wisdom, and they award you this golden crown.

PISTHETÆRUS I accept it. But tell me, why do the people admire me?

HERALD Oh you, who have founded so illustrious a city in the air, you know not in what esteem men hold you and how many there are who burn with desire to dwell in it. Before your city was built, all men had a mania for Sparta; long hair and fasting were held in honour, men went dirty like Socrates and carried staves. Now all is changed. Firstly, as soon as 'tis dawn, they all spring out of bed together to go and seek their food, the same as you do; then they fly off towards the notices and finally devour the decrees. The bird-madness is so clear, that they actually bear the names of birds. There is a halting victualler, who styles himself the partridge; Menippus calls himself the swallow; Opontius the one-eyed crow; Philocles the lark; Theogenes the fox-goose; Lycurgus the ibis; Chærephon the bat; Syracosius the magpie; Midias the quail; indeed he looks like a quail that has been hit heavily over the head. Out of love for the birds they repeat all the songs which concern the swallow, the teal, the goose or the pigeon; in each verse you see wings, or at all events a few feathers. This is what is happening down there. Finally, there are more than ten thousand folk who are coming here from earth to ask you for feathers and hooked claws; so, mind you supply yourself with wings for the immigrants.

PISTHETÆRUS Ah! by Zeus, 'tis not the time for idling. Go as quick as possible and fill every hamper, every basket you can find with wings. Manes will bring them to me outside the walls, where I will welcome those who present themselves.

CHORUS This town will soon be inhabited by a crowd of men.

PISTHETÆRUS If fortune favours us.

CHORUS Folk are more and more delighted with it.

PISTHETÆRUS Come, hurry up and bring them along.

CHORUS Will not man find here everything that can please him—wisdom, love, the divine Graces, the sweet face of gentle peace?

PISTHETÆRUS Oh! you lazy servant! won't you hurry yourself?

CHORUS Let a basket of wings be brought speedily. Come, beat him as I do, and put some life into him; he is as lazy as an ass.

PISTHETÆRUS Aye, Manes is a great craven.

CHORUS Begin by putting this heap of wings in order; divide them in three parts according to the birds from whom they came; the singing, the prophetic and the aquatic birds; then you must take care to distribute them to the men according to their character.

PISTHETÆRUS [*to* MANES] Oh! by the kestrels! I can keep my hands off you no longer; you are too slow and lazy altogether.

A PARRICIDE Oh! might I but become an eagle, who soars in the skies! Oh! might I fly above the azure waves of the barren sea!

PISTHETÆRUS Ha! 'twould seem the news was true; I hear someone coming who talks of wings.

PARRICIDE Nothing is more charming than to fly; I burn with desire to live under the same laws as the birds; I am bird-mad and fly towards you, for I want to live with you and to obey your laws.

PISTHETÆRUS Which laws? The birds have many laws.

PARRICIDE All of them; but the one that pleases me most is, that among the birds it is considered a fine thing to peck and strangle one's father.

PISTHETÆRUS Aye, by Zeus! according to us, he who dares to strike his father, while still a chick, is a brave fellow.

PARRICIDE And therefore I want to dwell here, for I want to strangle my father and inherit his wealth.

PISTHETÆRUS But we have also an ancient law written in the code of the storks, which runs thus, "When the stork father has reared his young and has taught them to fly, the young must in their turn support the father."

PARRICIDE 'Tis hardly worthwhile coming all this distance to be compelled to keep my father!

PISTHETÆRUS No, no, young friend, since you have come to us with such willingness, I am going to give you these black wings, as though you were an orphan bird; furthermore, some good advice, that I received myself in infancy. Don't strike your father, but take these wings in one hand and these spurs in the other; imagine you have a cock's crest on your head and go and mount guard and fight; live on your pay and respect your father's life. You're a gallant fellow! Very well, then! Fly to Thrace and fight.

PARRICIDE By Bacchus! 'Tis well spoken; I will follow your counsel.

PISTHETÆRUS 'Tis acting wisely, by Zeus.

CINESIAS "On my light pinions I soar off to Olympus; in its capricious flight my Muse flutters along the thousand paths of poetry in turn . . ."

PISTHETÆRUS This is a fellow will need a whole shipload of wings.

CINESIAS ". . . and being fearless and vigorous, it is seeking fresh outlet."

PISTHETÆRUS Welcome, Cinesias, you lime-wood man! Why have you come here a-twisting your game leg in circles?

CINESIAS "I want to become a bird, a tuneful nightingale."

PISTHETÆRUS Enough of that sort of ditty. Tell me what you want.

CINESIAS Give me wings and I will fly into the topmost airs to gather fresh songs in the clouds, in the midst of the vapours and the fleecy snow.

PISTHETÆRUS Gather songs in the clouds?

CINESIAS 'Tis on them the whole of our latter-day art depends. The most brilliant dithyrambs are those that flap their wings in void space and are clothed in mist and dense obscurity. To appreciate this, just listen.

PISTHETÆRUS Oh! no, no, no!

CINESIAS By Hermes! but indeed you shall. "I shall travel through thine ethereal empire like a winged bird, who cleaveth space with his long neck . . ."

PISTHETÆRUS Stop! easy all, I say!

CINESIAS " . . . as I soar over the seas, carried by the breath of the winds . . ."

PISTHETÆRUS By Zeus! but I'll cut your breath short.

CINESIAS ". . . now rushing along the tracks of Notus, now nearing Boreas across the infinite wastes of the ether." [PISTHETÆRUS *beats him*.] Ah! old man, that's a pretty and clever idea truly!

PISTHETÆRUS What, are you not delighted to be cleaving the air?

CINESIAS To treat a dithyrambic poet, for whom the tribes dispute with each other, in this style!

PISTHETÆRUS Will you stay with us and form a chorus of winged birds as slender as Leotrophides for the Cecropid tribe?

CINESIAS You are making game of me, 'tis clear; but know that I shall never leave you in peace if I do not have wings wherewith to traverse the air.

AN INFORMER What are these birds with downy feathers, who look so pitiable to me? Tell me, oh swallow with the long dappled wings.

PISTHETÆRUS Oh! but 'tis a perfect invasion that threatens us. Here comes another of them, humming along.

INFORMER Swallow with the long dappled wings, once more I summon you.

PISTHETÆRUS It's his cloak I believe he's addressing; 'faith, it stands in great need of the swallows' return.

INFORMER Where is he who gives out wings to all comers?

PISTHETÆRUS 'Tis I, but you must tell me for what purpose you want them.

INFORMER Ask no questions. I want wings, and wings I must have.

PISTHETÆRUS Do you want to fly straight to Pellené?

INFORMER I? Why, I am an accuser of the islands, an informer . . .

PISTHETÆRUS A fine trade, truly!

INFORMER . . . a hatcher of lawsuits. Hence I have great need of wings to prowl round the cities and drag them before justice.

PISTHETÆRUS Would you do this better if you had wings?

INFORMER No, but I should no longer fear the pirates; I should return with the cranes, loaded with a supply of lawsuits by way of ballast.

PISTHETÆRUS So it seems, despite all your youthful vigour, you make it your trade to denounce strangers?

INFORMER Well, and why not? I don't know how to dig.

PISTHETÆRUS But, by Zeus! there are honest ways of gaining a living at your age without all this infamous trickery.

INFORMER My friend, I am asking you for wings, not for words.

PISTHETÆRUS 'Tis just my words that give you wings.

INFORMER And how can you give a man wings with your words?

PISTHETÆRUS 'Tis thus that all first start.

INFORMER All?

PISTHETÆRUS Have you not often heard the father say to young men in the barbers' shops, "It's astonishing how Diitrephes' advice has made my son fly to horse-riding."—"Mine," says another, "has flown towards tragic poetry on the wings of his imagination."

INFORMER So that words give wings?

PISTHETÆRUS Undoubtedly; words give wings to the mind and make a man soar to heaven. Thus I hope that my wise words will give you wings to fly to some less degrading trade.

INFORMER But I do not want to.

PISTHETÆRUS What do you reckon on doing then?

WORDS GIVE WINGS TO THE MIND AND MAKE A MAN SOAR TO HEAVEN.

INFORMER I won't belie my breeding; from generation to generation we have lived by informing. Quick, therefore, give me quickly some light, swift hawk or kestrel wings, so that I may summon the islanders, sustain the accusation here, and haste back there again on flying pinions.

PISTHETÆRUS I see. In this way the stranger will be condemned even before he appears.

INFORMER That's just it.

PISTHETÆRUS And while he is on his way here by sea, you will be flying to the islands to despoil him of his property.

INFORMER You've hit it, precisely; I must whirl hither and thither like a perfect humming-top.

PISTHETÆRUS I catch the idea. Wait, i' faith, I've got some fine Corcyræan wings. How do you like them?

INFORMER Oh! woe is me! Why, 'tis a whip!

PISTHETÆRUS No, no; these are the wings, I tell you, that set the top a-spinning.

INFORMER Oh! oh! oh!

PISTHETÆRUS Take your flight, clear off, you miserable cur, or you will soon see what comes of quibbling and lying. Come, let us gather up our wings and withdraw.

CHORUS In my ethereal flights I have seen many things new and strange and wondrous beyond belief. There is a tree called Cleonymus belonging to an unknown species; it has no heart, is good for nothing and is as tall as it is cowardly. In springtime it shoots forth calumnies instead of birds and in autumn it strews the ground with bucklers in place of leaves.

Far away in the regions of darkness, where no ray of light ever enters, there is a country, where men sit at the table of the heroes and dwell with them always—save always in the evening. Should any mortal meet the hero Orestes at night, he would soon be stripped and covered with blows from head to foot.

PROMETHEUS Ah! by the gods! if only Zeus does not espy me! Where is Pisthetærus?

PISTHETÆRUS Ha! what is this? A masked man!

PROMETHEUS Can you see any god behind me?

PISTHETÆRUS No, none. But who are you, pray?

PROMETHEUS What's the time, please?

PISTHETÆRUS The time? Why, it's past noon. Who are you?

PROMETHEUS Is it the fall of day? Is it no later than that?

PISTHETÆRUS Oh! 'pon my word! but you grow tiresome.

PROMETHEUS What is Zeus doing? Is he dispersing the clouds or gathering them?

PISTHETÆRUS Take care, lest I lose all patience.

PROMETHEUS Come, I will raise my mask.

PISTHETÆRUS Ah! my dear Prometheus!

PROMETHEUS Stop! stop! speak lower!

PISTHETÆRUS Why, what's the matter, Prometheus?

PROMETHEUS H'sh, h'sh! Don't call me by my name; you will be my ruin, if Zeus should see me here. But, if you want me to tell you how things are going in heaven, take this umbrella and shield me, so that the gods don't see me.

PISTHETÆRUS I can recognize Prometheus in this cunning trick. Come, quick then, and fear nothing; speak on.

PROMETHEUS Then listen.

PISTHETÆRUS I am listening, proceed!

PROMETHEUS It's all over with Zeus.

PISTHETÆRUS Ah! and since when, pray?

PROMETHEUS Since you founded this city in the air. There is not a man who now sacrifices to the gods; the smoke of the victims no longer reaches us. Not the smallest offering comes! We fast as though it were the festival of Demeter. The barbarian gods, who are dying of hunger, are bawling like Illyrians and threaten to make an armed descent upon Zeus, if he does not open markets where joints of the victims are sold.

PISTHETÆRUS What! there are other gods besides you, barbarian gods who dwell above Olympus?

PROMETHEUS If there were no barbarian gods, who would be the patron of Execestides?

PISTHETÆRUS And what is the name of these gods?

PROMETHEUS Their name? Why, the Triballi.

PISTHETÆRUS Ah, indeed! 'tis from that no doubt that we derive the word 'tribulation.'

PROMETHEUS Most likely. But one thing I can tell you for certain, namely, that Zeus and the celestial Triballi are going to send deputies here to sue for peace. Now don't you treat, unless Zeus restores the sceptre to the birds and gives you Basileia in marriage.

PISTHETÆRUS Who is this Basileia?

PROMETHEUS A very fine young damsel, who makes the lightning for Zeus; all things come from her, wisdom, good laws, virtue, the fleet, calumnies, the public paymaster and the triobolus.

PISTHETÆRUS Ah! then she is a sort of general manageress to the god.

PROMETHEUS Yes, precisely. If he gives you her for your wife, yours will be the almighty power. That is what I have come to tell you; for you know my constant and habitual goodwill towards men.

PISTHETÆRUS Oh, yes! 'tis thanks to you that we roast our meat.

PROMETHEUS I hate the gods, as you know.

PISTHETÆRUS Aye, by Zeus, you have always detested them.

PROMETHEUS Towards them I am a veritable Timon; but I must return in all haste, so give me the umbrella; if Zeus should see me from up there, he would think I was escorting one of the Canephori.

PISTHETÆRUS Wait, take this stool as well.

CHORUS Near by the land of the Sciapodes there is a marsh, from the borders whereof the odious Socrates evokes the souls of men. Pisander came one day to see his soul, which he had left there when still alive. He offered a little victim, a camel, slit his throat and, following the example of Ulysses, stepped one pace backwards. Then that bat of a Chærephon came up from hell to drink the camel's blood.

POSIDON This is the city of Nephelococcygia, Cloud-cuckoo-town, whither we come as ambassadors. [*To* TRIBALLUS] Hi! what are you up to? you are throwing your cloak over the left shoulder. Come, fling it quick over the right! And why, pray, does it draggle in this fashion? Have you ulcers to hide like Læspodias? Oh! democracy! whither, oh! whither are you leading us? Is it possible that the gods have chosen such an envoy?

TRIBALLUS Leave me alone.

POSIDON Ugh! the cursed savage! you are by far the most barbarous of all the gods.—Tell me, Heracles, what are we going to do?

HERACLES I have already told you that I want to strangle the fellow who has dared to block us in.

POSIDON But, my friend, we are envoys of peace.

HERACLES All the more reason why I wish to strangle him.

PISTHETÆRUS Hand me the cheese-grater; bring me the silphium for sauce; pass me the cheese and watch the coals.

HERACLES Mortal! we who greet you are three gods.

PISTHETÆRUS Wait a bit till I have prepared my silphium pickle.

HERACLES What are these meats?

PISTHETÆRUS These are birds that have been punished with death for attacking the people's friends.

HERACLES And you are seasoning them before answering us?

PISTHETÆRUS Ah! Heracles! welcome, welcome! What's the matter?

HERACLES The gods have sent us here as ambassadors to treat for peace.

A SERVANT There's no more oil in the flask.

PISTHETÆRUS And yet the birds must be thoroughly basted with it.

HERACLES We have no interest to serve in fighting you; as for you, be friends and we promise that you shall always have rain-water in your pools and the warmest of warm weather. So far as these points go we are armed with plenary authority.

PISTHETÆRUS We have never been the aggressors, and even now we are as well disposed for peace as yourselves, provided you agree to one equitable condition, namely, that Zeus yield his sceptre to the birds. If only this is agreed to, I invite the ambassadors to dinner.

HERACLES That's good enough for me. I vote for peace.

POSIDON You wretch! you are nothing but a fool and a glutton. Do you want to dethrone your own father?

PISTHETÆRUS What an error! Why, the gods will be much more powerful if the birds govern the earth. At present the mortals are hidden beneath the clouds, escape your observation, and commit perjury in your name; but if you had the birds for your allies, and a man, after having sworn by the crow and Zeus, should fail to keep his oath, the crows would dive down upon him unawares and pluck out his eye.

POSIDON Well thought of, by Posidon!

HERACLES My notion too.

PISTHETÆRUS [*to the* TRIBALLIAN] And you, what's your opinion?

TRIBALLUS Nabaisatreu.

PISTHETÆRUS D'you see? he also approves. But hear another thing in which we can serve you. If a man vows to offer a sacrifice to some god, and then procrastinates, pretending that the gods can wait, and thus does not keep his word, we shall punish his stinginess.

POSIDON Ah! ah! and how?

PISTHETÆRUS While he is counting his money or is in the bath, a kite will relieve him, before he knows it, either in coin or in clothes, of the value of a couple of sheep, and carry it to the god.

HERACLES I vote for restoring them the sceptre.

POSIDON Ask the Triballian.

HERACLES Hi! Triballian, do you want a thrashing?

TRIBALLUS Saunaka baktarikrousa.

HERACLES He says, "Right willingly."

POSIDON If that be the opinion of both of you, why, I consent too.

HERACLES Very well! we accord the sceptre.

PISTHETÆRUS Ah! I was nearly forgetting another condition. I will leave Heré to Zeus, but only if the young Basileia is given me in marriage.

POSIDON Then you don't want peace. Let us withdraw.

PISTHETÆRUS It matters mighty little to me. Cook, look to the gravy.

HERACLES What an odd fellow this Posidon is! Where are you off to? Are we going to war about a woman?

POSIDON What else is there to do?

HERACLES What else? Why, conclude peace.

POSIDON Oh! the ninny! do you always want to be fooled? Why, you are seeking your own downfall. If Zeus were to die, after having yielded them the sovereignty, you would be ruined, for you are the heir of all the wealth he will leave behind.

PISTHETÆRUS Oh! by the gods! bow he is cajoling you. Step aside, that I may have a word with you. Your uncle is getting the better of you, my poor friend. The law will not allow you an obolus of the paternal property, for you are a bastard and not a legitimate child.

HERACLES I a bastard! What's that you tell me?

PISTHETÆRUS Why, certainly; are you not born of a stranger woman? Besides, is not Athené recognized as Zeus' sole heiress? And no daughter would be that, if she had a legitimate brother.

HERACLES But what if my father wished to give me his property on his death-bed, even though I be a bastard?

PISTHETÆRUS The law forbids it, and this same Posidon would be the first to lay claim to his wealth, in virtue of being his legitimate brother. Listen; thus runs Solon's law: "A bastard shall not inherit, if there are legitimate children;

and if there are no legitimate children, the property shall pass to the nearest kin."

HERACLES And I get nothing whatever of the paternal property?

PISTHETÆRUS Absolutely nothing. But tell me, has your father had you entered on the registers of his phratria?

HERACLES No, and I have long been surprised at the omission.

PISTHETÆRUS What ails you, that you should shake your fist at heaven? Do you want to fight it? Why, be on my side, I will make you a king and will feed you on bird's milk and honey.

HERACLES Your further condition seems fair to me. I cede you the young damsel.

POSIDON But I, I vote against this opinion.

PISTHETÆRUS Then all depends on the Triballian. [*To the* TRIBALLIAN.] What do you say?

POSIDON Big bird give daughter pretty and queen.

PISTHETÆRUS You say that you give her?

POSIDON Why no, he does not say anything of the sort, that he gives her; else I cannot understand any better than the swallows.

PISTHETÆRUS Exactly so. Does he not say she must be given to the swallows?

POSIDON Very well! you two arrange the matter; make peace, since you wish it so; I'll hold my tongue.

HERACLES We are of a mind to grant you all that you ask. But come up there with us to receive Basileia and the celestial bounty.

PISTHETÆRUS Here are birds already cut up, and very suitable for a nuptial feast.

HERACLES You go and, if you like, I will stay here to roast them.

PISTHETÆRUS You to roast them! you are too much the glutton; come along with us.

HERACLES Ah! how well I would have treated myself!

PISTHETÆRUS Let some bring me a beautiful and magnificent tunic for the wedding.

CHORUS At Phanæ, near the Clepsydra, there dwells a people who have neither faith nor law, the Englottogastors, who reap, sow, pluck the vines and the figs with their tongues; they belong to a barbaric race, and among them the Philippi and the Gorgiases are to be found; 'tis these Englottogastorian Philippi who introduced the custom all over Attica of cutting out the tongue separately at sacrifices.

A MESSENGER Oh, you, whose unbounded happiness I cannot express in words, thrice happy race of airy birds, receive your king in your fortunate dwellings. More brilliant than the brightest star that illumes the earth, he is approaching his glittering golden palace; the sun itself does not shine with more dazzling glory. He is entering with his bride at his side, whose beauty no human tongue can express; in his hand he brandishes the lightning, the winged shaft of Zeus; perfumes of unspeakable sweetness pervade the ethereal realms. 'Tis a glorious spectacle to see the clouds of incense wafting in light whirlwinds before the breath of the Zephyr! But here he is himself. Divine Muse! let thy sacred lips begin with songs of happy omen.

CHORUS Fall back! to the right! to the left! advance! Fly around this happy mortal, whom Fortune loads with her blessings. Oh! oh! what grace! what beauty! Oh, marriage so auspicious for our city! All honour to this man! 'tis through him that the birds are called to such glorious destinies. Let your nuptial hymns, your nuptial songs, greet him and his Basileia! 'Twas in the midst of such festivities that the Fates formerly united Olympian Heré to the King who governs the gods from the summit of his inaccessible throne. Oh! Hymen! oh! Hymenæus! Rosy Eros with the golden wings held the reins and guided the chariot; 'twas he, who presided over the union of Zeus and the fortunate Heré. Oh! Hymen! oh! Hymenæus!

PISTHETÆRUS I am delighted with your songs, I applaud your verses. Now celebrate the thunder that shakes the earth, the flaming lightning of Zeus and the terrible flashing thunderbolt.

CHORUS Oh, thou golden flash of the lightning! oh, ye divine shafts of flame, that Zeus has hitherto shot forth! Oh, ye rolling thunders, that bring down the rain! 'Tis by the order of *our* king that ye shall now stagger the earth! Oh, Hymen! 'tis through thee that he commands the universe and that he makes Basileia, whom he has robbed from Zeus, take her seat at his side. Oh! Hymen! oh! Hymenæus!

PISTHETÆRUS Let all the winged tribes of our fellow-citizens follow the bridal couple to the palace of Zeus and to the nuptial couch! Stretch forth your hands, my dear wife! Take hold of me by my wings and let us dance; I am going to lift you up and carry you through the air.

CHORUS Oh, joy! Io Pæan! Tralala! victory is thine, oh, thou greatest of the gods!

Juvenal

(c. 55 to 60–c. 127 A.D.)

In all of Roman literature there is no more personally enigmatic author than Juvenal. Unlike his predecessors Horace and Persius, Juvenal's works are devoid of personal history.

Details regarding his life are few and unreliable. Born around 55 A.D. in Aquinum, Italy, Decimus Junius Juvenalis was thought to have been from a well-to-do family and joined the army as an officer hoping to land a post in the government of the Emperor Domitian (81–96 A.D.). But he was unsuccessful in his quest for promotion, engendering the bitterness and disgust he felt for Roman life and society. This blow was a defining moment for Juvenal, and set the stage for his life's work. He began writing satire, attacking the corruption and stagnation evident during this era of the Roman Empire. In one of his earliest works, Juvenal took on what he saw as a corrupt army system, writing a satire asserting that court favorites had too much influence in the promotion of officers. As a result, Juvenal was stripped of property and banished to Egypt until 96 A.D., when he returned to Rome after Domitian was assassinated.

Poor and without a vocation after his return, Juvenal remained unbowed by his circumstances and continued his searing rhetoric with the support of several patrons. Juvenal's sixteen satirical poems were published in five books (as a collection entitled *The Satires)* and dealt mainly with life in Rome under the rule of Domitian and his successors Nerva (96–98), Trajan (98–117), and Hadrian (117–138). The books are thought to have been issued during the years 100–127 A.D.

The Satires feature a two-pronged attack: the corruption of Roman society and man's barbaric and foolish nature. In the first Satire, Juvenal writes that crime, vice, and the abuse of power and wealth have corrupted Rome so completely that ridicule is inevitable. "Why do I write satire?" Juvenal asks in a famous verse. "Say, rather, how could I help it?" He insulates himself against retaliation by claiming to only criticize dead powerful men, implying that Rome has had a rotten core for many generations. No one group is spared his blistering prose, except perhaps children: "The greatest reverence is due a child! If you are contemplating a wicked act, despise not your child's tender years." He denigrates homosexuals, women, intellectuals, the rich, greedy parents, professional soldiers, hereditary nobility, his own patrons, and the government.

The philosophical points in *The Satires* are often delineated by anecdotes about friends and events he has witnessed, confirming his low opinion of Rome and its inhabitants. His phrasing and descriptive powers are skillfully expressive. The overall structure of the individual Satires is clear and commanding and the text itself is filled with acicular phrases and memorable epigrams, many known to people who have never heard of Juvenal: "Who will guard the guards?," "bread and circuses," "slow rises worth, by poverty oppressed," "the itch for writing." His vocabulary has a street-corner quality, his humor is grim, and his abrasive style pulls no punches.

Book I, containing Satires I–V, was issued around 110 A.D. *Book II*, including only Satire VI—an enormous rant against Roman women and marriage—followed about five years later. *Book III*, with Satires VII, VIII, and IX, was published after the accession of Hadrian. There is no datable allusion in *Book IV*, which holds Satires X–XII. *Book V*—which has the last four pieces, XIII, XIV, XV, and XVI—has two references to the year 127. After Hadrian rose to power, the tone of his material began to change, perhaps because his personal environment was improving; it is said that he obtained a small farm at Tivoli and a house in Rome where he could entertain company. Perhaps Juvenal tempered the attacks on bad literature that so displeased the Emperor and in turn, Hadrian may have bestowed a pension and property upon Juvenal as a patron of arts. Once Juvenal achieved "modest competence," much of the impulse for his biting invective fell away. This does not make the satire any less valid, though it does reveal that his moral resentment was shaped and nurtured by personal motives. Though no actual details of his death exist, Juvenal probably died in or after 127 A.D.

Satire I, the work included in this anthology, introduced the major themes that Juvenal returns to time and again in the rest of his work, namely how can you not write satire when all around you begs its cause?

Don't you want to cram whole notebooks with scribbled invective
When you stand at the corner and see some forger carried past
On the necks of six porters, lounging back like Maecenas
In his open litter?

His favorite targets were the corrupting power of wealth, social or sexual vulgarity, and literature that mines well-trodden themes or subjects. His contention was that writers who used these mythological platitudes were anxious to avoid the real issues that need examination.

The stale themes are bellowed daily
In rich patrons' colonnades, till their marble pillars
Crack with a surfeit of rhetoric.

There is nothing new written under the Roman sun, according to Juvenal. You must take risks in writing, he exclaims:

If you want to be someone one day you must nerve yourself
For deeds that could earn you an island exile or years in gaol.

Yet Juvenal himself attacks those already dead or uses fake names to deride current adversaries. This is to avoid retaliation but also to bring the recent past and present together in one decadent, corrupt circle. He uses long-dead men as examples on which to drape a moral generalization. He claimed that revealing the mistakes of the past was important because he "saw the empire as one long process of degeneration." What once was sacred and morally powerful becomes tainted and suspect.

What's in a senator's purple stripe, if true-blue nobles
Are reduced to herding sheep up-country, while I have more
Stashed away in the bank than any Imperial favourite?

He doesn't approve of diluting social classes, of lower classes rising up through the caste system. Where would he fit into a new world order? Still, he is reluctant to identify any of this contemptuous nouveau riche, calling them "Johnny-come-latelys."

Juvenal ends Satire I with a defense of his oblique approach:

> It's too late for a soldier
> To change his mind about fighting when he's armed in the battle-line
> For myself, I shall try my hand on the famous dead, whose ashes,
> Rest beside the Latin and the Flaminian Ways.

He wants to live to write another day. So he uses the dead as effigies of the unnamed living scoundrels.

Like so many writers who feel that their present world is awry, Juvenal is constantly harking back to the distant past. He never skips an opportunity to compare the simplicity, patriotism, thrift, and decency of the good old days with the excess and moral turpitude he observes around him. He longs for the days when Rome was gaining strength and rues the fact that he has to sit by and watch that strength dwindling. He failed as a bureaucrat and could not effect change from within, so he chose the satirist's role to sit on the outside and rail against Rome's surrender to decay.

Satire I

Must I *always* be stuck in the audience at these poetry-readings, never
Up on the platform myself, taking it out on Cordus
For the times he's bored me to death with ranting speeches
From that *Theseid* of his? Is X to get off scot-free
After inflicting his farces on me, or Y his elegies? Is there
No recompense for whole days wasted on prolix
Versions of *Telephus*? And what about that *Orestes*—
Each margin of the roll crammed solid, top and bottom,
More on the back, and *still* it wasn't finished!
I know all the mythical landscapes like my own back-room:
The grove of Mars, that cave near Aeolus' island
Belonging to Vulcan. The stale themes are bellowed daily
In rich patrons' colonnades, till their marble pillars
Crack with a surfeit of rhetoric. The plane-trees echo
Every old trope—what the winds are up to, whose ghost
Aeacus has on his hellish rack, from what far country
The other fellow is sneaking off with that golden sheepskin,
The monstrous size of those ash-trees the Centaurs used for
  spears:
You get the same stuff from them all, established poet
And raw beginner alike.[1] I too have winced under the cane
And concocted 'Advice to Sulla': *Let the despot retire*
Into private life, take a good long sleep, and so on.[2] When you
  find
Hordes of poets on each street-corner, it's misplaced kindness
To refrain from writing. The paper will still be wasted.
Why then have I chosen to drive my team down the track
Which great Lucilius[3] blazed? If you have the leisure to listen
Calmly and reasonably, I will enlighten you.

When a flabby eunuch marries, when well-born girls go
crazy
For pig-sticking up-country, bare-breasted, spear in fist;
When the barber who rasped away at my youthful beard has
risen
To challenge good society with his millions; when
Crispinus[4]—
That Delta-bred house-slave, silt washed down by the Nile—
Now hitches his shoulders under Tyrian purple, airs
A thin gold ring in summer on his sweaty finger
('My dear, I couldn't *bear* to wear my *heavier* jewels')—
Why then, it is harder *not* to be writing satires; for who
Could endure this monstrous city, however callous at heart,
And swallow his wrath? Look: here comes a brand-new litter,
Crammed with its corpulent owner, some chiselling advocate.
Who's next? An informer. He turned in his noble patron,
And soon he'll have gnawed away that favourite bone of his,
The aristocracy. Lesser informers dread him, grease
His palm with ample bribes, while the wives of trembling actors
Grease him the other way. Today we are elbowed aside
By men who earn legacies in bed, who rise to the top
Via that quickest, most popular route—the satisfied desires
Of some rich old matron. Each lover will get his cut,
A twelfth share in the estate, or eleven-twelfths, depending
On the size of his—services rendered. I suppose he deserves
Some recompense for all that sweat and exertion: he looks
As pale as the man who steps barefoot on a snake—or is waiting
His turn to declaim, at Lyons, in Caligula's competitions.[5]

Need I tell you how anger burns in my heart when I see
The bystanders jostled back by a mob of bravos
Whose master first debauched his ward, and later
Defrauded the boy as well? The courts condemned him,
But the verdict was a farce. Who cares for reputation
If he keeps his cash? A provincial governor, exiled
For extortion, boozes and feasts all day, basks cheerfully
In the wrathful eyes of the Gods; it's still his province,
After winning the case against him, that feels the pinch.

Are not such themes well worthy of Horace's pen? Should I
Not attack them too? Must I stick to the usual round
Of Hercules' labours, what Diomede did, the bellowing
Of that thingummy in the Labyrinth, or the tale of the flying
Carpenter, and how his son went splash in the sea?[6]
Will *these* suffice in an age when each pimp of a husband
Takes these gifts from his own wife's lover—if she is barred in law
From inheriting legacies—and, while they paw each other,
Tactfully stares at the ceiling, or snores, wide awake, in his wine?
Will *these* suffice, when the young blade who has squandered
His family fortune on racing-stables still reckons to get
Command of a cohort? Just watch him lash his horses
Down the Flaminian Way like Achilles' charioteer,
Reins bunched in one hand, showing off to his mistress
Who stands beside him, wrapped in his riding-cloak!
Don't you want to cram whole notebooks scribbled with invective
When you stand at the corner and see some forger carried past
On the necks of six porters, lounging back like Maecenas
In his open litter? A counterfeit seal, a will, a mere scrap
Of paper—these were enough to convert him to wealth and honour.
Do you see that distinguished lady? She has the perfect dose
For a thirsty husband—old wine with a dash of toad's blood.
Locusta's a child to her[7]; she trains her untutored neighbors
To ignore all unkind rumours, to stalk through angry crowds
With their black and bloated husbands before them on the hearse.
If you want to be someone today you must nerve yourself
For deeds that could earn you an island exile, or years in gaol.
Honesty's praised, but honest men freeze. Wealth springs from crime:
Landscape-gardens, palaces, furniture, antique silver—
Those cups embossed with prancing goats—all, all are tainted.
Who can sleep easy today? If your greedy daughter-in-law
Is not being seduced for cash, it'll be your bride: mere schoolboys

Are adulterers now. Though talent be wanting, yet
Indignation will drive me to verse, such as I—or any
scribbler—
May still command. All human endeavours, men's prayers,
Fears, angers, pleasures, joys and pursuits, these make
The mixed mash of my verse.[8]
Since the days of the Flood,
When Deucalion anchored his ship on a mountain peak
To search for a sign, the days when hard stones quivered
To living softness and warmth, and Pyrrha confronted
The first men with their naked mates, has there ever
Been so rich a crop of vices? When has the purse
Of greed yawned wider? When was gambling more frantic
Than it is today? Men face the table's hazards
Not with their purse but their strong-box open beside them.
Here you'll see notable battles, with the croupier for squire,
Holding stakes instead of a shield. Is it not plain lunacy
To lose ten thousand on a turn of the dice, yet grudge
A shirt to your shivering slave? Which of our grandfathers
Would have built himself so many country houses, or dined
Off seven courses, *alone*? Clients were guests in those days.
But now Roman citizens are reduced to scrambling
For a little basket of scraps on their patron's doorstep.[9]
He peers into each face first, scared stiff that some imposter
May give a false name and cheat him: you must be identified
Before you get your ration. The crier has his orders:
Each man to answer to his name, nobility included—
Oh yes, our Upper-Ten are scrounging with the rest.
'The praetor first, then the tribune'—but a freedman blocks
Their way. '*I* got here first,' he says, 'why shouldn't I keep
My place? I don't give *that* for you. Oh, I know I'm foreign:
Look here, at my pierced ears, no use denying it—born
Out East, on the Euphrates. But my five shops bring in
Four hundred thousand, see? So I qualify for the gentry.[10]
What's in a senator's purple stripe, if true-blue nobles
Are reduced to herding sheep up-country, while I have more
Stashed away in the bank than any Imperial favourite?'

So let the Tribunes wait, and money reign supreme;
Let the Johnny-come-lately, whose feet only yesterday were
white
With the chalk of the slave-market, flout this sacrosanct office![11]
Why not? Though as yet, pernicious Cash, you lack
A temple of your own, though we have raised no altars
To Sovereign Gold (as already we worship Honour,
Peace, Victory, Virtue, or Concord—whose roosting storks
Rattle and flap on the roof when you salute their nest),
Still it is Wealth, not God, that compels our deepest reverence.
When the Consul himself tots up, at the end of his year,[12]
What the dole is worth, how much it adds to his income, how
Are we poor dependents to manage? Out of this pittance
We must pay for decent clothes and shoes—not to mention our
food
And the fuel for heating. But plenty who can afford
A litter still queue up for their bob-a-day; some husbands
Go the rounds with a sick or pregnant wife in tow,
Or better (a well-known dodge) pretend she's there when she isn't
And claim for both, displaying a curtained, empty sedan.
'My Galla's in there,' he says. 'Come on, let us through! You
doubt me?
Galla! Put out your head, girl! I'm sorry, she must be asleep—
No don't disturb her, please—!'
And so the day wears on
With its prescribed routine, its fascinating round.
Dole in the pocket, we next attend my lord to the Forum;
Stare, bored, at all those statues—Apollo beside the Law
Courts
(He must be an expert by now) or that jumped-up Egyptian
Pasha[13] who's had the nerve to gate-crash Triumph Row:
His effigy's only fit for pissing on—or worse.
[Experienced clients follow their patron home again],[14]
Hoping against hope for that dinner-invitation
Which never comes: worn out, they drift away to purchase
(Poor souls) their cabbage and kindling. But *he* meanwhile will
loll

Alone at his guestless meal, wolfing the choicest produce
Of sea and woodland. These fellows will gobble up
Whole legacies at one course, off fine big antique tables:
Soon there won't be a parasite left. But who could stomach
Such measures in gourmands? What a grossly ravening maw
That man must have who dines off whole roast boar—a beast
Ordained for convivial feasting! But you'll pay the price
All too soon, my friend, when you undress and waddle
Into the bath, your belly still swollen with undigested
Peacock-meat—a lightning heart-attack, with no time
To make your final will. The story circulates
As a dinner-table joke, the latest thing. But no one
Cares about you. Your corpse is borne out to ironical
Cheers from your cheated friends. Posterity can add
No more, or worse, to our ways; our grandchildren will act
As we do, and share our desires. Today every vice
Has reached its ruinous zenith. So, satirist, hoist your sails,
Cram on every stitch of canvas! But where, you may ask,
Is a talent to match the theme? And where our outspoken
Ancestral bluntness, that wrote what burning passion dictated?
'Show me the man I dare not name,' Lucilius cried,
'What odds if the noble Consul forgive my libel or not?'
But name an Imperial favourite, and you will soon enough
Blaze like those human torches, half-choked, half-grilled to
death,
Those calcined corpses they drag with hooks from the arena,
And leave a broad black trail behind them in the sand.[15]

But what, you may ask, about the man who has poisoned
Three uncles with belladonna—are we to let *him* ride
In his feather-bedded litter, and look down his nose at us?
Yes; and when he approaches, keep mum, clap a hand to your
mouth—
Just to say *That's the man* will brand you as an informer.
It's safe enough to retell how Aeneas fought fierce Turnus;
No one's a penny the worse for Achilles' death, or the frantic
Search for Hylas, that time he tumbled in after his pitcher.
But when fiery Lucilius rages with satire's naked sword

His hearers go red; their conscience is cold with crime,
Their innards sweat at the thought of their secret guilt:
Hence wrath and tears. So ponder these things in your mind
Before the trumpet sounds. It's too late for a soldier
To change his mind about fighting when he's armed in the
    battle-line.
For myself, I shall try my hand on the famous dead, whose
    ashes
Rest beside the Latin and the Flaminian Ways.[16]

1. Cordus was an unknown writer of epics: the *Theseid* (analogous to the *Aeneid*) was the work he gave at public recitations. *Telephus* and *Orestes* are tragedies—Euripides wrote two plays with these names—composed for a platform performance rather than the stage. In this whole catalogue J. is emphasizing the derivative, artificial, cliché-ridden nature of contemporary literature—a point also made by a list of hackneyed mythological references, which he takes obvious pleasure in debunking: a swipe at the allusive poets in the Alexandrian tradition, who dragged them in on every page, and were especially fond of periphrasis.

2. Pupils at school were often given the task of composing declamations, either to be put in the mouth of, or directed at, some great man of history. These exercises were known as *suasoriae*: examples of the Elder Seneca have survived. Sulla was Dictator from 82 to 78 B.C.

3. Gaius Lucilius (c. 180–c. 102 B.C.) was one of the earliest—and one of the greatest—Roman satirists. Protected by Scipio, he indulged in extremely outspoken social criticism, though his strictures, like J.'s, lacked moral coherence. Only fragments of his work survive.

4. Crispinus began his career as a fishmonger and was made an *eques* by Domitian. J. appears to have had some special grudge against him. He was from Memphis or Canopus in Egypt.

5. Sexual excess was commonly supposed in antiquity to produce an anaemic, washed-out appearance. For 'Caligula's competitions' see Suetonius, *Caligula*: 'Caligula gave . . . miscellaneous Games at Lyons, where he also held a competition in Greek and Latin oratory. The loser, it appears, had to present the winners with prizes and make speeches praising them; while those who failed miserably were forced to erase their entries with either sponges or their own tongues—at the threat of being thrashed and flung into the Rhone.'

6. The reference is to the Fall of Icarus: another sneer at ancient mythology, which in J.'s day had become no more than the lifeless stock-in-trade of every third-rate poet.

7. Locusta was a famous poisoner in Nero's reign. She dispatched the Emperor Claudius at Agrippina's orders, and also poisoned Britannicus for Nero himself. She was executed by Galba. See Suetonius, *Nero* 33 and Dio Cassius 64–3.

8. Professor J.P. Sullivan has pointed out to [translator Peter Green] that the removal of lines 85–6 from their present position in the MSS leaves a far more logical sentence structure behind. He is not, however, responsible for the decision to insert them after line 80. Such 'slipped-position' lines are by no means rare in Juvenal.

9. Originally clients were entertained by their patrons; later there was substituted the *sportula,* or little basket of food to carry away. Later still this was commuted to a financial dole.

10. The minimum property qualification for admission to the Equestrian Order was 400,000 sesterces. Originally a body of cavalry, the *equites* in Imperial times were largely identical with the rich nonsenatorial business community: 'burghers' or 'magnates' would be a fair equivalent. They held important posts in the civil service: the Prefecture of Egypt, for instance, was reserved for an *eques.*

11. Foreign slaves just imported had their feet chalked white by the dealer to distinguish them from from *vernae*, or home-bred slaves.

12. The consuls held office for a year, and under the Empire, as *consul suffectus,* for a few months only. The position carried no salary (though there was an inadequate expense account) and most consuls reckoned on recouping from their subsequent appointment to a provincial governorship.

13. The 'Egyptian pasha' was Tiberius Julius Alexander, a Jew who became a Roman *eques*; he rose to the rank of Prefect of Egypt, and may have become Praetorian Prefect as well (see E.G. Turner, *Journal of Roman Studies* 44 (1954), 54 ff.). J. manages to symbolize in him both the contempt he felt for the Jews and his perennial dislike of Egyptians—a not unnatural feeling, since Egypt was his place of exile.

14. Housman suggested, almost certainly correctly, that a line had dropped out of the text here, after line 131, in which the clients would be taken back to their patron's house. I have translated in accordance with this suggestion.

15. The text here is difficult. [Translator Peter Green] follows Housman (who supposes a line to have been lost after 156) and translates his conjectural restoration.

16. The Via Flaminia was, as it were, the Great North Road from Rome; the Via Latina branched off from its southern counterpart, the Via Appia. The aristocracy often had tombs beside the major arterial roads, and the closing lines hint clearly at the main target of J.'s satire. The tomb of the actor Paris lay beside the Via Flaminia; Domitian himself was buried by the Via

Latina. Yet—and coming after the reference to Lucilius himself this cannot but strike us as bathetic—J. is only going to attack those who are already dead. Highet (*Juvenal the Satirist* 56–8) points out (a) that most of his subjects are timeless; (b) that he may have been lying in order to protect himself; and (c) that he felt the past was truly important; that he 'saw the empire as one long continuous process of degeneration.'

Niccolò Machiavelli

(1469–1527)

Accounts of Niccolò Machiavelli's early life are vague, there being no mention of him in official until 1498, when he was nearly thirty. He was born in Florence on May 3, 1469. His father, Bernardo, a lawyer with a profitable estate, was well connected in Florence's political circles. This proved valuable later, when Niccolò needed an introduction into public service. His father also had a great love of scholarship and literature, especially the Latin classics, something that the two would share as Niccolò matured. It seems that Machiavelli received a typical education, learning Latin and Greek and studying the classical authors.

Machiavelli's first appearance on Florence's political scene was in 1498, when he became the Secretary of the Second Chancery of the city's ruling council. He had no previous political experience but his energy and enthusiasm, and his father's humanist intellectual connections, made him a favorite for the post. Within a month he was also appointed Secretary to the Council of Ten of War, the foreign policy arm of Florence's government. He would serve as an envoy in this position, traveling throughout Italy and Europe to talk with possible allies, transact business with the cities of the Florentine empire, and gather intelligence. In 1501, he married Marietta Corsini, who bore him seven children.

In his fourteen years as the Florentine secretary, Machiavelli interacted with and observed some of the most powerful men of the period, and from these meetings he gleaned the material for his later political writings. He visited the courts of Caterina Sforza, King Louis XII of France, Cesare Borgia, Pandolofo Petrucci, Pope Julius II, and Emperor Maximilian. He also became the confidante of Piero Soderini, who was named gonfaloniere, or head of the Florentine government, for life in 1502. The one coup in his diplomatic career was the surrender of Pisa to Florence in 1509 after a fifteen-year conflict. His glory days were to end, however, when the Medicis returned to power in 1512. They saw him only as Soderini's friend and banished him from Florence for a year. Adding to his misery was a false accusation of conspiracy against the new government, a charge resulting in imprisonment and torture on the rack to extract information. When Pope Leo X was elected in 1513, a general amnesty was granted to mark the occasion. Machiavelli was released, and he fled to the home outside Florence that he had inherited from his father.

Poor and out of a job, Machiavelli did some farming and mused on his future, bemoaning that he had only "knowledge of the state," and no occasion to use it. During this ten-year exile, he wrote poems, three comedic plays, and *Discourses upon the First Decade of Livy,* a critical examination of the writings of the Roman historian. He also wrote *The Prince*, a treatise on human behavior, foreign policy, and leadership. He dedicated *The Prince* to the Medicis, hoping to ingratiate himself and get some political work. But while that attempt did not succeed, his comedic plays brought him acclaim, and the Medicis eventually asked him to offer advice on the Florentine government. He was also commissioned to write a history of his native city and produced *Florentine History,* which he presented to Pope Clement VII in 1525.

His stint in the government would not last long. Rome fell, the Medicis were overthrown, and the Republic was restored in 1527. Machiavelli, despite his lifelong support of the Republic (as illustrated in his *Discourses*), was in the wrong place at the wrong time again. He was perceived as close to the Medicis and therefore incapable of playing a role in the new government. He did not have long to lament; he died a few days after the restoration of the Republic on June 20, 1527.

The Prince, Machiavelli's most famous work, was not published while he was alive. It probably circulated in manuscript form until 1532, when it was issued under the auspices of Clement. *The Prince* proved to be immensely popular, going through seven Italian editions in the next twenty years. It was placed on the Roman Catholic Church's "Index of Prohibited Books" (along with Machiavelli's other works), but this did little to dissuade readers, and the book was eventually translated into all the major European languages.

What is at first striking about *The Prince* is its matter-of-fact tone. Machiavelli discusses every topic, even the most brutal, in a clinical way. This tone is in large part responsible for his "evil" reputation, one that he himself fostered to shock his contemporaries. Ironically, in his everyday life he was a good citizen and father and treated his wife well. It is his endorsement of the use of cruelty, brutality, and deceit (in the name of preserving the state and the Prince's power) that has made his name synonymous with underhanded cunning.

The Prince is a thorough explication of how to obtain and maintain political power. It is divided into twenty-six chapters and begins with a dedication to Lorenzo Medici. In his dedication, Machiavelli sets out his purpose: to examine the conduct of great men and the aspects of princely rule. As a person of the lower classes, he claims to offer a unique perspective on the actions of the powerful, and he asks the Medicis to take pity on his plight. His aim is to please the Medici family in hopes of retaining a political role.

The Prince reviews the different types of principalities and armies, the character of the Prince, the behavior of the Prince as a military leader, and Italy's chaotic political situation. This last portion is an appeal to the Medici family to appoint someone who will lead the country out of its degradation. Although it would appear that Machiavelli's heart was beholden to the Republic, because of the terrible state of affairs in Italy he yearned for a princely figure to lead his country out of darkness. Machiavelli details the shortcomings and mistakes of rulers both past and present and suggests a model for effective government. To defend the principality, the prince should call on the citizenry, not foreign troops or mercenaries, he asserts, as the people have a stake in defending their own land and will not have a desire to turn on the leader. "There cannot be good laws where there are no good armies."

For the Prince himself, Machiavelli proposes these tools of power: the goodwill of the people, religion, "cruelty rather than mercy," and the controlled use of deception, brutality, and betrayal. He does not advocate the absence of a conscience, for a Prince cannot be counted among the great rulers in history if he continually performs cruel acts. Judicious cruelty will engender a type of fear that is empowering. "A Prince should inspire fear in such a way that if he does win love, he avoids hatred."

The Prince ends with a plea to the Medicis to find this Prince and rescue Italy from ruin. Italy looks to God for a savior, writes Machiavelli. And that redeemer, according to *The Prince*, will be a Medici. "Look how she prays to God to send someone to redeem her from these barbaric cruelties and insolence." This section is almost an afterthought, as *The Prince* solidly rejects the common belief in a moral basis of government that Christian thinkers had long proclaimed.

Some have suggested that *The Prince* is a satire warning of the dangers of allowing rulers to pursue power without restraint. From this perspective, Machiavelli the republican appears, exposing the machinations of tyranny so they can be fought. Today, *The Prince* is applied even to business and financial strategy.

However *The Prince* has been viewed (and misunderstood), it has served for almost 500 years as a blueprint for political behavior because of its clarity of purpose and straightforward prose. Machiavelli coldly dissected and elucidated a subject that previously had been left up to God and privileged bloodlines, and he did it so brilliantly that his tactics find their way onto modern best-seller lists and into twenty-first century boardrooms.

The Prince

CONTENTS

DEDICATION

TO THE MAGNIFICENT LORENZO DI PIERO DE' MEDICI

IT IS CUSTOMARY for such as seek a Prince's favour, to present themselves before him with those things of theirs which they themselves most value, or in which they perceive him chiefly to delight. Accordingly, we often see horses, armour, cloth of gold, precious stones, and the like costly gifts, offered to Princes as worthy of their greatness. Desiring in like manner to approach your Magnificence with some token of my devotion, I have found among my possessions none that I so much prize and esteem as a knowledge of the actions of great men, acquired in the course of a long experience of modern affairs and a continual study of antiquity. Which knowledge most carefully and patiently pondered over and sifted by me, and now reduced into this little book, I send to your Magnificence. And though I deem the work unworthy of your greatness, yet am I bold enough to hope that your courtesy will dispose you to accept it, considering that I can offer you no better gift than the means of mastering in a very brief time, all that in the course of so many years, and at the cost of so many hardships and dangers, I have learned, and know.

This work I have not adorned or amplified with rounded periods, swelling and high-flown language, or any other of those extrinsic attractions and allurements wherewith many authors are wont to set off and grace their writings; since it is my desire that it should either pass wholly unhonoured, or that the truth of its matter and the importance of its subject should alone recommend it.

Nor would I have it thought presumption that a person of very mean and humble station should venture to discourse and lay down rules concerning the government of Princes. For as those who make maps of countries place themselves low down in the plains to study the character of mountains and elevated lands, and place themselves high up on the mountains to get a better view of the plains, so in like manner to understand the People a man should be a Prince, and to have a clear notion of Princes he should belong to the People.

Let your Magnificence, then, accept this little gift in the spirit in which I offer it; wherein, if you diligently read and study it, you will recognize my extreme desire that you should attain to that eminence which Fortune and your own merits promise you. Should you from the height of your greatness some time turn your eyes to these humble regions, you will become aware how undeservedly I have to endure the keen and unremitting malignity of Fortune.

CHAPTER I

OF THE VARIOUS KINDS OF PRINCEDOM, AND OF THE WAYS IN WHICH THEY ARE ACQUIRED

ALL THE STATES and Governments by which men are or ever have been ruled, have been and are either Republics or Princedoms. Princedoms are either hereditary, in which the sovereignty is derived through an ancient line of ancestors, or they are new. New Princedoms are either wholly new, as that of Milan to Francesco Sforza; Or they are like limbs joined on to the hereditary possessions of the Prince who acquires them, as the Kingdom of Naples to the dominions of the King of Spain. The States thus acquired have either been used to live under a Prince or have been free; and he who acquires them does so either by his own arms or by the arms of others, and either by good fortune or by merit.

CHAPTER II

OF HEREDITARY PRINCEDOMS

OF REPUBLICS I shall not now speak, having elsewhere spoken of them at length. Here I shall treat exclusively of Princedoms, and, filling in the outline above traced out, shall proceed to examine how such States are to be governed and maintained.

I say, then, that hereditary States, accustomed to the family of their Prince, are maintained with far less difficulty than new States, since all that is required is that the Prince shall not depart from the usages of his ancestors, trusting for the rest to deal with events as they arise. So that if an hereditary Prince be of average address, he will always maintain himself in his Princedom, unless deprived of it by some extraordinary and irresistible force; and even if so deprived will recover it, should any, even the least, mishap overtake the usurper. We have in Italy an example of this in the Duke of Ferrara, who never could have withstood the attacks of the Venetians in 1484, nor those of Pope Julius in 1510, had not his authority in that State been consolidated by time. For since a Prince by birth has fewer occasions and less need to give offence, he ought to be better loved, and will naturally be popular with his subjects unless outrageous vices make him odious. Moreover, the very antiquity and continuance of his rule will efface the memories and causes which lead to innovation. For one change always leaves a dovetail into which another will fit.

CHAPTER III

OF MIXED PRINCEDOMS

BUT IN NEW Princedoms difficulties abound, And, first, if the Princedom be not wholly new, but joined on to the ancient dominions of the Prince, so as to form with them what may be termed a mixed Princedom, changes will come from a cause common to all new States, namely, that men, thinking to better their condition, are always ready to change masters, and in this expectation will take up arms against any ruler; wherein they deceive themselves, and find afterwards by experience that they are worse off than before. This again results naturally and necessarily from the circumstance that the Prince cannot avoid giving offence to his new subjects, either in respect of the troops he quarters on them, or of some other of the numberless vexations attendant on a new acquisition. And in this way you may find that you have enemies in all those whom you have injured in seizing the Princedom, yet cannot keep the friendship of those who helped you to gain it; since you can neither reward them as they expect, nor yet, being under obligations to them, use violent remedies against them. For however strong you may be in respect of your army, it is essential that in entering a new Province you should have the good will of its inhabitants.

Hence it happened that Louis XII of France, speedily gaining possession of Milan, as speedily lost it; and that on the occasion of its first capture, Lodovico Sforza was able with his own forces only to take it from him. For the very people who had opened the gates to the French King, when they found themselves deceived in their expectations and hopes of future benefits, could not put up with the insolence of their new ruler. True it is that when a State rebels and is again got under, it will not afterwards be lost so easily. For the Prince, using the rebellion as a pretext, will not scruple to secure himself by punishing the guilty, bringing the suspected to trial, and otherwise strengthening his position in the points where it was weak. So that if to recover Milan from the French it was enough on the first occasion that a Duke Lodovico should raise alarms on the frontiers, to wrest it from them a second time the whole world had to be ranged against them, and their armies destroyed and driven out of Italy. And this for the reasons above assigned. And yet, for a second time, Milan was lost to the King. The general causes of its first loss have been shown. It remains to note the causes of the second, and to point out the remedies which the French King had, or which might have been used by another in like circumstances to maintain his conquest more successfully than he did.

I say, then, that those States which upon their acquisition are joined on to the ancient dominions of the Prince who acquires them, are either of the same Province and tongue as the people of these dominions, or they are not. When they are, there is a great ease in retaining them, especially when they have not been accustomed to live in freedom. To hold them securely it is enough to have rooted out the line of the reigning Prince; because if in other respects the old condition of things be continued, and there be no discordance in their customs, men live peaceably with one another, as we see to have been the case in Brittany, Burgundy, Gascony, and Normandy, which have so long been united to France. For although there be some slight difference in their languages, their customs are similar, and they can easily get on together. He, therefore, who acquires such a State, if he mean to keep it, must see to two things; first, that the blood of the ancient line of Princes be destroyed; second, that no change be made in respect of laws or taxes; for in this way the newly acquired State speedily becomes incorporated with the hereditary.

But when States are acquired in a country differing in language, usages, and laws, difficulties multiply, and great good fortune, as well as address, is needed to overcome them. One of the best and most efficacious methods for dealing with such a State, is for the Prince who acquires it to go and dwell there in person, since this will tend to make his tenure more secure and lasting. This course has been followed by the Turk with regard to Greece, who, had he not, in addition to all his other precautions for securing that Province, himself come to live in it, could never have kept his hold of it. For when you are on the spot, disorders are detected in their beginnings and remedies can be readily applied; but when you are at a distance, they are not heard of until they have gathered strength and the case is past cure. Moreover, the Province in which you take up your abode is not pillaged by your officers; the people are pleased to have a ready recourse to their Prince; and have all the more reason if they are well disposed, to love, if disaffected, to fear him. A foreign enemy desiring to attack that State would be cautious how he did so. In short, where the Prince resides in person, it will be extremely difficult to oust him.

Another excellent expedient is to send colonies into one or two places, so that these may become, as it were, the keys of the Province; for you must either do this, or else keep up a numerous force of men-at-arms and foot soldiers. A Prince need not spend much on colonies. He can send them out and support them at little or no charge to himself, and the only persons to whom he gives offence are those whom he deprives of their fields and houses to bestow them on the new inhabitants. Those who are thus injured form but a small part of the community, and remaining scattered and poor can never become dangerous. All others being left unmolested, are in consequence easily quieted, and at the same time are afraid to make a false move, lest they share the fate of those who have been deprived of their possessions. In few words, these colonies cost less than soldiers, are more faithful, and give less offence, while those who are offended, being, as I have said, poor and dispersed, cannot hurt. And let it here be noted that men are either to be kindly treated, or utterly crushed, since they can revenge lighter injuries, but not graver. Wherefore the injury we do to a man should be of a sort to leave no fear of reprisals.

But if instead of colonies you send troops, the cost is vastly greater, and the whole revenues of the country are spent in guarding it; so that the gain becomes a loss, and much deeper offence is given; since in shifting the quarters of your soldiers from place to place the whole country suffers hardship, which as all feel, all are made enemies; and enemies who remaining, although vanquished, in their own homes, have power to hurt. In every way, therefore, this mode of defence is as disadvantageous as that by colonizing is useful.

The Prince who establishes himself in a Province whose laws and language differ from those of his own people, ought also to make himself the head and protector of his feebler neighbours, and endeavour to weaken the stronger, and must see that by no accident shall any other stranger as powerful as himself find an entrance there. For it will always happen that some such person will be called in by those of the Province who are discontented either through ambition or fear; as we see of old the Romans brought into Greece by the Aetolians, and in every other country that they entered, invited there by its inhabitants. And the usual course of things is that so soon as a formidable stranger enters a Province, all the weaker powers side with him, moved thereto by the ill-will they bear towards him who has hitherto kept them in subjection. So that in respect of these lesser powers, no trouble is needed to gain them over, for at once, together, and of their own accord, they throw in their lot with the government of the stranger. The new Prince, therefore, has only to see that they do not increase too much in strength, and with his own forces, aided by their good will, can easily subdue any who are powerful, so as to remain supreme in the Province. He who does not manage this matter well, will soon lose whatever he has gained, and while he retains it will find in it endless troubles and annoyances.

In dealing with the countries of which they took possession the Romans diligently followed the methods I have described. They planted colonies, conciliated weaker powers without adding to their strength, humbled the great, and never suffered a formidable stranger to acquire influence. A single example will suffice to show this. In Greece the Romans took the Achaians and Aetolians into their pay; the Macedonian monarchy was humbled; Antiochus was driven out. But the services of the Achaians and Aetolians never obtained for them any addition to their power; no persuasions on the part of Philip could induce the Romans to be his friends on the condition of sparing him humiliation; nor could all the power of Antiochus bring them to consent to his exercising any authority within that Province. And in thus acting the Romans did as all wise rulers should, who have to consider not only present difficulties but also future, against which they must use all diligence to provide; for these, if they be foreseen while yet remote, admit of easy remedy, but if their approach be awaited, are already past cure, the disorder having become hopeless; realizing what the physicians tell us of hectic fever, that in its beginning it is easy to cure, but hard to recognize; whereas, after a time, not having been detected and treated at the first, it becomes easy to recognize but impossible to cure.

And so it is with State affairs. For the distempers of a State being discovered while yet inchoate, which can only be done by a sagacious ruler, may easily be dealt with; but when, from not being observed, they are suffered to grow until they are obvious to every one, there is no longer any remedy. The Romans, therefore, foreseeing evils while they were yet far off, always provided against them, and never suffered them to take their course for the sake of avoiding war; since they knew that war is not so to be avoided, but is only postponed to the advantage of the other side. They chose, therefore, to make war with Philip and Antiochus in Greece, that they might not have to make it with them in Italy, although for a while they might have escaped both. This they did not desire, nor did the maxim *leave it to Time*, which the wise men of our own day have always on their lips, ever recommend itself to them. What they looked to enjoy were the fruits of their own valour and foresight. For Time, driving all things before it, may bring with it evil as well as good.

But let us now go back to France and examine whether she has followed any of those methods of which I have made mention. I shall speak of Louis and not of Charles, because from the former having held longer possession of Italy, his manner of acting is more plainly seen. You will find, then, that he has done the direct opposite of what he should have done in order to retain a foreign State.

King Louis was brought into Italy by the ambition of the Venetians, who hoped by his coming to gain for themselves a half of the State of Lombardy. I will not blame this coming, nor the part taken by the King, because, desiring to gain a footing in Italy, where he had no friends, but on the contrary, owing to the conduct of Charles, every door was shut against him, he was driven to accept such friendships as he could get. And his designs might easily have succeeded had he not made mistakes in other particulars of conduct.

By the recovery of Lombardy, Louis at once regained the credit which Charles had lost. Genoa made submission; the Florentines came to terms; the Marquis of Mantua, the Duke of Ferrara, the Bentivogli, the Countess of Forli, the Lords of Faenza, Pesaro, Rimini, Camerino, and Piombino, the citizens of Lucca, Pisa, and Siena, all came forward offering their friendship. The Venetians, who to obtain possession of a couple of towns in Lombardy had made the French King master of two-thirds of Italy, had now cause to repent the rash game they had played.

Let any one, therefore, consider how easily King Louis might have maintained his authority in Italy had he observed the rules which I have noted above, and secured and protected all those friends of his, who being weak, and fearful, some of the Church, some of the Venetians, were of necessity obliged to attach themselves to him, and with whose assistance, for they were many, he might readily have made himself safe against any other powerful State. But no sooner was he in Milan than he took a contrary course, in helping Pope Alexander to occupy Romagna; not perceiving that in seconding this enterprise he weakened himself by alienating friends and those who had thrown themselves into his arms, while he strengthened the Church by adding great temporal power to the spiritual power which of itself confers so mighty an authority. Making this first mistake, he was forced to follow it up, until at last, in order to curb the ambition of Pope Alexander, and prevent him becoming master of Tuscany, he was obliged to come himself into Italy.

And as though it were not enough for him to have aggrandized the Church and stripped himself of friends, he must needs in his desire to possess the Kingdom of Naples, divide it with the King of Spain; thus bringing into Italy, where before he had been supreme, a rival to whom the ambitious and discontented in that Province might have recourse. And whereas he might have left in Naples a King willing to hold as his tributary, he displaced him to make way for another strong enough to effect his expulsion. The wish to acquire is no doubt a natural and common sentiment, and when men attempt things within their power, they will always be praised rather than blamed. But when they persist in attempts that are beyond their power, mishaps and blame ensue. If France, therefore, with her own forces could have attacked Naples, she should have done so. If she could not, she ought not to have divided it. And if her partition of Lombardy with the Venetians may be excused as the means whereby a footing was gained in Italy, this other partition is to be condemned as not justified by the like necessity.

Louis, then, had made these five blunders. He had destroyed weaker States, he had strengthened a Prince already strong, he had brought into the country a very powerful stranger, he had not come to reside, and he had not sent colonies. And yet all these blunders might not have proved disastrous to him while he lived, had he not added to them a sixth in depriving the Venetians of their dominions. For had he neither aggrandized the Church, nor brought Spain into Italy, it might have been at once reasonable and necessary to humble the Venetians; but after committing himself to these other courses, he should never have consented to the ruin of Venice. For while the Venetians were powerful they would always have kept others back from an attempt on Lombardy, as well because they never would have agreed to that enterprise on any terms save of themselves being made its masters, as because others would never have desired to take it from France in order to hand it over to them, nor would ever have ventured to defy both. And if it be said that King Louis ceded Romagna to Alexander, and Naples to Spain in order to avoid war, I answer that for the reasons already given, you ought never to suffer your designs to be crossed in order to avoid war, since war is not so to be avoided, but is only deferred to your disadvantage. And if others should allege the King's promise to the Pope to undertake that enterprise on his behalf, in return for the dissolution of his marriage, and for the Cardinal's hat conferred on d'Amboise, I answer by referring to what I say further on concerning the faith of Princes and how it is to be kept.

King Louis, therefore, lost Lombardy from not following any one of the methods pursued by others who have taken Provinces with the resolve to keep them. Nor is this anything strange, but only what might reasonably and naturally, be looked for. And on this very subject I spoke to d'Amboise at Nantes, at the time when Duke Valentino, as Cesare Borgia, son to Pope Alexander, was vulgarly called, was occupying Romagna. For, on the Cardinal saying to me that the Italians did not understand war, I answered that the French did not understand statecraft, for had they done so, they never would have allowed the Church to grow so powerful. And the event shows that the aggrandizement of the Church and of Spain in Italy has been brought about by France, and that the ruin of France has been wrought by them. Whence we may draw the general axiom, which never or rarely errs, that *he who is the cause of another's greatness is himself undone*, since he must work either by address or force, each of which excites distrust in the person raised to power.

CHAPTER IV

WHY THE KINGDOM OF DARIUS, CONQUERED BY ALEXANDER, DID NOT, ON ALEXANDER'S DEATH, REBEL AGAINST HIS SUCCESSORS

ALEXANDER THE GREAT having achieved the conquest of Asia in a few years, and dying before he had well entered on possession, it might have been expected, having regard to the difficulty of preserving newly acquired States, that on his death the whole country would rise in revolt. Nevertheless, his successors were able to keep their hold, and found in doing so no other difficulty than arose from their own ambition and mutual jealousies.

If any one think this strange and ask the cause, I answer, that all the Princedoms of which we have record have been governed in one or other of two ways, either by a sole Prince, all others being his servants permitted by his grace and favour to assist in governing the kingdom as his ministers; or else, by a Prince with his Barons who hold their rank, not by the favour of a superior Lord, but by antiquity of blood, and who have States and subjects of their own who recognize them as their rulers and entertain for them a natural affection. States governed by a sole Prince and by his servants vest in him a more complete authority; because throughout the land none but he is recognized as sovereign, and if obedience be yielded to any others, it is yielded as to his ministers and officers for whom personally no special love is felt.

Of these two forms of government we have examples in our own days in the Turk and the King of France. The whole Turkish empire is governed by a sole Prince, all others being his slaves. Dividing his kingdom into *sandjaks*, he sends thither different governors whom he shifts and changes at his pleasure. The King of France, on the other hand, is surrounded by a multitude of nobles of ancient descent, each acknowledged and loved by subjects of his own, and each asserting a precedence in rank of which the King can deprive him only at his peril.

He, therefore, who considers the different character of these two States, will perceive that it would be difficult to gain possession of that of the Turk, but that once won it might be easily held. The obstacles to its conquest are that the invader cannot be called in by a native nobility, nor expect his enterprise to be aided by the defection of those whom the sovereign has around him. And this for the various reasons already given, namely, that all being slaves and under obligations they are not easily corrupted, or if corrupted can render little assistance, being unable, as I have already explained, to carry the people with them. Whoever, therefore, attacks the Turk must reckon on finding a united people, and must trust rather to his own strength than to divisions on the other side. But were his adversary once overcome and defeated in the field, so that he could not repair his armies, no cause for anxiety would remain, except in the family of the Prince; which being extirpated, there would be none else to fear; for since all beside are without credit with the people, the invader, as before his victory he had nothing to hope from them, so after it has nothing to dread.

But the contrary is the case in kingdoms governed like that of France, into which, because men who are discontented and desirous of change are always to be found, you may readily procure an entrance by gaining over some Baron of the Realm. Such persons, for the reasons already given, are able to open the way to you for the invasion of their country and to render its conquest easy. But afterwards the effort to hold your ground involves you in endless difficulties, as well in respect of those who have helped you, as of those whom you have overthrown. Nor will it be enough to have destroyed the family of the Prince, since all those other Lords remain to put themselves at the head of new movements; whom being unable either to content or to destroy, you lose the State whenever occasion serves them.

Now, if you examine the nature of the government of Darius, you will find that it resembled that of the Turk, and, consequently, that it was necessary for Alexander, first of all, to defeat him utterly and strip him of his dominions; after which defeat, Darius having died, the country, for the causes above explained, was permanently secured to Alexander. And had his successors continued united they might have enjoyed it undisturbed, since there arose no disorders in that kingdom save those of their own creating.

But kingdoms ordered like that of France cannot be retained with the same ease. Hence the repeated risings of Spain, Gaul, and Greece against the Romans, resulting from the number of small Princedoms of which these Provinces were made up. For while the memory of these lasted, the Romans could never think their tenure safe. But when that memory was worn out by the authority and long continuance of their rule, they gained a secure hold, and were able afterwards in their contests among themselves, each to carry with him some portion of these Provinces, according as each had acquired influence there; for these, on the extinction of the line of their old Princes, came to recognize no other Lords than the Romans.

Bearing all this in mind, no one need wonder at the ease wherewith Alexander was able to lay a firm hold on Asia, nor that Pyrrhus and many others found difficulty in preserving other acquisitions; since this arose, not from the less or greater merit of the conquerors, but from the different character of the States with which they had to deal.

CHAPTER V

HOW CITIES OR PROVINCES WHICH BEFORE THEIR ACQUISITION HAVE LIVED UNDER THEIR OWN LAWS ARE TO BE GOVERNED

WHEN A NEWLY acquired State has been accustomed, as I have said, to live under its own laws and in freedom, there are three methods whereby it may be held. The first is to destroy it; the second, to go and reside there in person; the third, to suffer it to live on under its own laws, subjecting it to a tribute, and entrusting its government to a few of the inhabitants who will keep the rest your friends. Such a Government, since it is the creature of the new Prince, will see that it cannot stand without his protection and support, and must therefore do all it can to maintain him; and a city accustomed to live in freedom, if it is to be preserved at all, is more easily controlled through its own citizens than in any other way.

We have examples of all these methods in the histories of the Spartans and the Romans. The Spartans held Athens and Thebes by creating oligarchies in these cities, yet lost them in the end. The Romans, to retain Capua, Carthage, and Numantia, destroyed them and never lost them. On the other hand, when they thought to hold Greece as the Spartans had held it, leaving it its freedom and allowing it to be governed by its own laws, they failed, and had to destroy many cities of that Province before they could secure it. For, in truth, there is no sure way of holding other than by destroying, and whomever becomes master of a City accustomed to live in freedom and does not destroy it, may reckon on being destroyed by it. For if it should rebel, it can always screen itself under the name of liberty and its ancient laws, which no length of time, nor any benefits conferred will ever cause it to forget; and do what you will, and take what care you may, unless the inhabitants be scattered and dispersed, this name, and the old order of things, will never cease to be remembered, but will at once be turned against you whenever misfortune overtakes you, as when Pisa rose against the Florentincs after a hundred years of servitude.

If, however, the newly acquired City or Province has been accustomed to live under a Prince, and his line is extinguished, it will be impossible for the citizens, used, on the one hand, to obey, and deprived, on the other, of their old ruler, to agree to choose a leader from among themselves; and as they know not how to live as freemen, and are therefore slow to take up arms, a stranger may readily gain them over and attach them to his cause. But in Republics there is a stronger vitality, a fiercer hatred, a keener thirst for revenge. The memory of their former freedom will not let them rest; so that the safest course is either to destroy them, or to go and live in them.

CHAPTER VI

OF NEW PRINCEDOMS WHICH A PRINCE ACQUIRES WITH HIS OWN ARMS AND BY MERIT

LET NO MAN marvel if in what I am about to say concerning Princedoms wholly new, both as regards the Prince and the form of Government, I cite the highest examples. For since men for the most part follow in the footsteps and imitate the actions of others, and yet are unable to adhere exactly to those paths which others have taken, or attain to the virtues of those whom they would resemble, the wise man should always follow the roads that have been trodden by the great, and imitate those who have most excelled, so that if he cannot reach their perfection, he may at least acquire something of its savour. Acting in this like the skilful archer, who seeing that the object he would hit is distant, and knowing the range of his bow, takes aim much above the destined mark; not designing that his arrow should strike so high, but that flying high it may alight at the point intended.

I say, then, that in entirely new Princedoms where the Prince himself is new, the difficulty of maintaining possession varies with the greater or less ability of him who acquires possession. And, because the mere fact of a private person rising to be a Prince presupposes either merit or good fortune, it will be seen that the presence of one or other of these two conditions lessens, to some extent, many difficulties. And yet, he who is less beholden to Fortune has often in the end the better success; and it may be for the advantage of a Prince that, from his having no other territories, he is obliged to reside in person in the State which he has acquired.

Looking first to those who have become Princes by their merit and not by their good fortune, I say that the most excellent among them are Moses, Cyrus, Romulus, Theseus, and the like. And though perhaps I ought not to name Moses, he being merely an instrument for carrying out the Divine commands, he is still to be admired for those qualities which made him worthy to converse with God. But if we consider Cyrus and the others who have acquired or founded kingdoms, they will all be seen to be admirable. And if their actions and the particular institutions of which they were the authors be studied, they will be found not to differ from those of Moses, instructed though he was by so great a teacher. Moreover, on examining their lives and actions, we shall see that they were debtors to Fortune for nothing beyond the opportunity which enabled them to shape things as they pleased, without which the force of their spirit would have been spent in vain; as on the other hand, opportunity would have offered itself in vain, had the capacity for turning it to account been wanting. It was necessary, therefore, that Moses should find the children of Israel in bondage in Egypt, and oppressed by the Egyptians, in order that they might be disposed to follow him, and so escape from their servitude. It was fortunate for Romulus that he found no home in Alba, but was exposed at the time of his birth, to the end that he might become king and founder of the City of Rome. It was necessary that Cyrus should find the Persians discontented with the rule of the Medes, and the Medes enervated and effeminate from a prolonged peace. Nor could Theseus have displayed his great qualities had he not found the Athenians disunited and dispersed. But while it was their opportunities that made these men fortunate, it was their own merit that enabled them to recognize these opportunities and turn them to account, to the glory and prosperity of their country.

IT SHOULD BE BORNE IN MIND THAT THE TEMPER OF THE MULTITUDE IS FICKLE, AND THAT WHILE IT IS EASY TO PERSUADE THEM OF A THING, IT IS HARD TO FIX THEM IN THAT PERSUASION.

They who come to the Princedom, as these did, by virtuous paths, acquire with difficulty, but keep with ease. The difficulties which they have in acquiring arise mainly from the new laws and institutions which they are forced to introduce in founding and securing their government. And let it be noted that there is no more delicate matter to take in hand, nor more dangerous to conduct, nor more doubtful in its success, than to set up as a leader in the introduction of changes. For he who innovates will have for his enemies all those who are well off under the existing order of things, and only lukewarm supporters in those who might be better off under the new. This lukewarm temper arises partly from the fear of adversaries who have the laws on their side, and partly from the incredulity of mankind, who will never admit the merit of anything new, until they have seen it proved by the event. The result, however, is that whenever the enemies of change make an attack, they do so with all the zeal of partisans, while the others defend themselves so feebly as to endanger both themselves and their cause.

But to get a clearer understanding of this part of our subject, we must look whether these innovators can stand alone, or whether they depend for aid upon others; in other words, whether to carry out their ends they must resort to entreaty, or can prevail by force. In the former case they always fare badly and bring nothing to a successful issue; but when they depend upon their own resources and can employ force, they seldom fail. Hence it comes that all armed Prophets have been victorious, and all unarmed Prophets have been destroyed.

For, besides what has been said, it should be borne in mind that the temper of the multitude is fickle, and that while it is easy to persuade them of a thing, it is hard to fix them in that persuasion. Wherefore, matters should be so ordered that when men no longer believe of their own accord, they may be compelled to believe by force. Moses, Cyrus, Theseus, and Romulus could never have made their ordinances be observed for any length of time had they been unarmed, as was the case, in our own days, with the Friar Girolamo Savonarola, whose new institutions came to nothing so soon as the multitude began to waver in their faith; since he had not the means to keep those who had been believers steadfast in their belief, or to make unbelievers believe.

Such persons, therefore, have great difficulty in carrying out their designs; but all their difficulties are on the road, and may be overcome by courage. Having conquered these, and coming to be held in reverence, and having destroyed all who were jealous of their influence, they remain powerful, safe, honoured, and prosperous.

To the great examples cited above, I would add one other, of less note indeed, but assuredly bearing some proportion to them, and which may stand for all others of a like character. I mean the example of Hiero the Syracusan. He from a private station rose to be Prince of Syracuse, and he too was indebted to Fortune only for his opportunity. For the Syracusans being oppressed, chose him to be their Captain, which office he so discharged as deservedly to be made their King. For even while a private citizen his merit was so remarkable, that one who writes of him says, he lacked nothing that a King should have save the Kingdom. Doing away with the old army, he organized a new, abandoned existing alliances and assumed new allies, and with an army and allies of his own, was able on that foundation to build what superstructure he pleased; having trouble enough in acquiring, but none in preserving what he had acquired.

CHAPTER VII

OF NEW PRINCEDOMS ACQUIRED BY THE AID OF OTHERS AND BY GOOD FORTUNE

THEY WHO FROM a private station become Princes by mere good fortune, do so with little trouble, but have much trouble to maintain themselves. They meet with no hindrance on their way, being carried as it were on wings to their destination, but all their difficulties overtake them when they alight. Of this class are those on whom States are conferred either in return for money, or through the favour of him who confers them; as it happened to many in the Greek cities of Ionia and the Hellespont to be made Princes by Darius, that they might hold these cities for his security and glory; and as happened in the case of those Emperors who, from privacy, attained the Imperial dignity by corrupting the army. Such Princes are wholly dependent on the favour and fortunes of those who have made them great, than which supports none could be less stable or secure; and they lack both the knowledge and the power that would enable them to maintain their position. They lack the knowledge, because unless they have great parts and force of character, it is not to be expected that having always lived in a private station they should have learned how to command. They lack the power, since they cannot look for support from attached and faithful troops. Moreover, States suddenly acquired, like all else that is produced and that grows up rapidly, can never have such root or hold as that the first storm which strikes them shall not overthrow them; unless, indeed, as I have said already, they who thus suddenly become Princes have a capacity for learning quickly how to defend what Fortune has placed in their lap, and can lay those foundations after they rise which by others are laid before.

Of each of these methods of becoming a Prince, namely, by merit and by good fortune, I shall select an instance from times within my own recollection, and shall take the cases of Francesco Sforza and Cesare Borgia. By suitable measures and singular ability, Francesco Sforza rose from privacy to be Duke of Milan, preserving with little trouble what it cost him infinite efforts to gain. On the other hand, Cesare Borgia, vulgarly spoken of as Duke Valentino, obtained his Princedom through the favourable fortunes of his father, and with these lost it, although, so far as in him lay, he used every effort and practised every expedient that a prudent and able man should, who desires to strike root in a State given him by the arms and fortune of another. For, as I have already said, he who does not lay his foundations at first, may, if he be of great parts, succeed in laying them afterwards, though with inconvenience to the builder and risk to the building. And if we consider the various measures taken by Duke Valentino, we shall perceive how broad were the foundations he had laid whereon to rest his future power.

These I think it not superfluous to examine, since I know not what lessons I could teach a new Prince, more useful than the example of his actions. And if the measures taken by him did not profit him in the end, it was through no fault of his, but from the extraordinary and extreme malignity of Fortune.

In his efforts to aggrandize the Duke his son, Alexander VI had to face many difficulties, both immediate and remote. In the first place, he saw no way to make him Lord of any State which was not a State of the Church, while, if he sought to take for him a State belonging to the Church, he knew that the Duke of Milan and the Venetians would withhold their consent; Faenza and Rimini being already under the protection of the latter. Further, he saw that the arms of Italy and those more especially of which he might have availed himself, were in the hands of men who had reason to fear his aggrandizement, that is, of the Orsini, the Colonnesi, and their followers. These therefore he could not trust. It was consequently necessary that the existing order of things should be changed, and the States of Italy thrown into confusion, in order that he might safely make himself master of some part of them; and this became easy for him when he found that the Venetians, moved by other causes, were plotting to bring the French once more into Italy. This design he accordingly did not oppose, but furthered by annulling the first marriage of the French King.

King Louis therefore came into Italy at the instance of the Venetians, and with the consent of Pope Alexander, and no sooner was he in Milan than the Pope got troops from him to aid him in his enterprise against Romagna, which Province, moved by the reputation of the French arms, at once submitted. After thus obtaining possession of Romagna, and after quelling the Colonnesi, Duke Valentino was desirous to follow up and extend his conquests. Two causes, however, held him back, namely, the doubtful fidelity of his own forces, and the waywardness of France. For he feared that the Orsini, of whose arms he had made use, might fail him, and not merely prove a hindrance to further acquisitions, but take from him what he had gained, and that the King might serve him the same turn. How little he could count on the Orsini was made plain when, after the capture of Faenza, he turned his arms against Bologna, and saw how reluctantly they took part in that enterprise. The King's mind he understood, when, after seizing on the Dukedom of Urbino, he was about to attack Tuscany; from which design Louis compelled him to desist. Whereupon the Duke resolved to depend no longer on the arms or fortune of others. His first step, therefore, was to weaken the factions of the Orsini and Colonnesi in Rome. Those of their following who were of good birth, he gained over by making them his own gentlemen, assigning them a liberal provision, and conferring upon them commands and appointments suited to their rank; so that in a few months their old partisan attachments died out, and the hopes of all rested on the Duke alone.

He then awaited an occasion to crush the chiefs of the Orsini, for those of the house of Colonna he had already scattered, and a good opportunity presenting itself, he turned it to the best account. For when the Orsini came at last to see that the greatness of the Duke and the Church involved their ruin, they assembled a council at Magione in the Perugian territory, whence resulted the revolt of Urbino, commotions in Romagna, and an infinity of dangers to the Duke, all of which he overcame with the help of France. His credit thus restored, the Duke trusting no longer either to the French or to any other foreign aid, that he might not have to confront them openly, resorted to stratagem, and was so well able to dissemble his designs, that the Orsini, through the mediation of Signor Paolo (whom he failed not to secure by every friendly attention, furnishing him with clothes, money, and horses), were so won over as to be drawn in their simplicity into his hands at Sinigaglia. When the leaders were thus disposed of, and their followers made his friends, the Duke had laid sufficiently good foundations for his future power, since he held all Romagna together with the Dukedom of Urbino, and had ingratiated himself with the entire population of these States, who now began to see that they were well off.

And since this part of his conduct merits both attention and imitation, I shall not pass it over in silence. After the Duke had taken Romagna, finding that it had been ruled by feeble Lords, who thought more of plundering than correcting their subjects, and gave them more cause for division than for union, so that the country was overrun with robbery, tumult, and every kind of outrage, he judged it necessary, with a view to render it peaceful and obedient to his authority, to provide it with a good government. Accordingly he set over it Messer Remiro d'Orco, a stern and prompt ruler, who being entrusted with the fullest powers, in a very short time, and with much credit to himself, restored it to tranquillity and order. But afterwards apprehending that such unlimited authority might become odious, the Duke decided that it was no longer needed, and established in the centre of the Province a civil Tribunal, with an excellent President, in which every town was represented by its advocate. And knowing that past severities had generated ill-feeling against himself, in order to purge the minds of the people and gain their good-will, he sought to show them that any cruelty which had been done had not originated with him, but in the harsh disposition of his minister. Availing himself of the pretext which this afforded, he one morning caused Remiro to be beheaded, and exposed in the market place of Cesena with a block and bloody axe by his side. The barbarity of which spectacle at once astounded and satisfied the populace.

But, returning to the point whence we diverged, I say that the Duke, finding himself fairly strong and in a measure secured against present dangers, being furnished with arms of his own choosing and having to a great extent got rid of those which, if left near him, might have caused him trouble, had to consider, if he desired to follow up his conquests, how he was to deal with France, since he saw he could expect no further support from King Louis, whose eyes were at last opened to his mistake. He therefore began to look about for new alliances, and to waver in his adherence to the French, then occupied with their expedition into the kingdom of Naples against the Spaniards, at that time laying siege to Gaeta; his object being to secure himself against France; and in this he would soon have succeeded had Alexander lived.

Such was the line he took to meet present exigencies. As regards the future, he had to apprehend that a new Head of the Church might not be his friend, and might even seek to deprive him of what Alexander had given. This he thought to provide against in four ways. First, by exterminating all who were of kin to those Lords whom he had despoiled of their possessions, that they might not become instruments in the hands of a new Pope. Second, by gaining over all the Roman nobles, so as to be able with their help to put a bridle, as the saying is, in the Pope's mouth. Third, by bringing the College of Cardinals, so far as he could, under his control. And fourth, by establishing his authority so firmly before his father's death, as to be able by himself to withstand the shock of a first onset.

Of these measures, at the time when Alexander died, he had already effected three, and had almost carried out the fourth. For of the Lords whose possessions he had usurped, he had put to death all whom he could reach, and very few had escaped. He had gained over the Roman nobility, and had the majority in the College of Cardinals on his side.

As to further acquisitions, his design was to make himself master of Tuscany. He was already in possession of Perugia and Piombino, and had assumed the protectorship of Pisa, on which city he was about to spring; taking no heed of France, as indeed he no longer had occasion, since the French had been deprived of the kingdom of Naples by the Spaniards under circumstances which made it necessary for both nations to buy his friendship. Pisa taken, Lucca and Siena would soon have yielded, partly through jealousy of Florence, partly through fear, and the position of the Florentines must then have been desperate.

Had he therefore succeeded in these designs, as he was succeeding in that very year in which Alexander died, he would have won such power and reputation that he might afterwards have stood alone, relying on his own strength and resources, without being beholden to the power and fortune of others. But Alexander died five years from the time he first unsheathed the sword, leaving his son with the State of Romagna alone consolidated, with all the rest unsettled, between two powerful hostile armies, and sick almost to death. And yet such were the fire and courage of the Duke, he knew so well how men must either be conciliated or crushed, and so solid were the foundations he had laid in that brief period, that had these armies not been upon his back, or had he been in sound health, he must have surmounted every difficulty.

How strong his foundations were may be seen from this, that Romagna waited for him for more than a month; and that although half dead, he remained in safety in Rome, where though the Baglioni, the Vitelli, and the Orsini came to attack him, they met with no success. Moreover, since he was able if not to make whom he liked Pope, at least to prevent the election of any whom he disliked, had he been in health at the time when Alexander died, all would have been easy for him. But he told me himself on the day on which Julius II was created, that he had foreseen and provided for everything else that could happen on his father's death, but had never anticipated that when his father died he too should be at death's-door.

Taking all these actions of the Duke together, I can find no fault with him; nay, it seems to me reasonable to put him forward, as I have done, as a pattern for all such as rise to power by good fortune and the help of others. For with his great spirit and high aims he could not act otherwise than he did, and nothing but the shortness of his father's life and his own illness prevented the success of his designs. Whoever, therefore, on entering a new Princedom, judges it necessary to rid himself of enemies, to conciliate friends, to prevail by force or fraud, to make himself feared yet not hated by his subjects, respected and obeyed by his soldiers, to crush those who can or ought to injure him, to introduce changes in the old order of things, to be at once severe and affable, magnanimous and liberal, to do away with a mutinous army and create a new one, to maintain relations with

Kings and Princes on such a footing that they must see it for their interest to aid him, and dangerous to offend, can find no brighter example than in the actions of this Prince.

The one thing for which he may be blamed was the creation of Pope Julius II, in respect of whom he chose badly. Because, as I have said already, though he could not secure the election he desired, he could have prevented any other; and he ought never to have consented to the creation of any one of those Cardinals whom he had injured, or who on becoming Pope would have reason to fear him; for fear is as dangerous an enemy as resentment. Those whom he had offended were, among others, San Pietro ad Vincula, Colonna, San Giorgio, and Ascanio; all the rest, excepting d'Amboise and the Spanish Cardinals (the latter from their connexion and obligations, the former from the power he derived through his relations with the French Court), would on assuming the Pontificate have had reason to fear him. The Duke, therefore, ought, in the first place, to have laboured for the creation of a Spanish Pope; failing in which, he should have agreed to the election of d'Amboise, but never to that of San Pietro ad Vincula. And he deceives himself who believes that with the great, recent benefits cause old wrongs to be forgotten.

The Duke, therefore, erred in the part he took in this election; and his error was the cause of his ultimate downfall.

CHAPTER VIII

OF THOSE WHO BY THEIR CRIMES COME TO BE PRINCES

BUT SINCE FROM privacy a man may also rise to be a Prince in one or other of two ways, neither of which can be referred wholly either to merit or to fortune, it is fit that I notice them here, though one of them may fall to be discussed more fully in treating of Republics.

The ways I speak of are, first, when the ascent to power is made by paths of wickedness and crime; and second, when a private person becomes ruler of his country by the favour of his fellow-citizens. The former method I shall make clear by two examples, one ancient, the other modern, without entering further into the merits of the matter, for these, I think, should be enough for any one who is driven to follow them.

Agathocles the Sicilian came, not merely from a private station, but from the very dregs of the people, to be King of Syracuse. Son of a potter, through all the stages of his fortunes he led a foul life. His vices, however, were conjoined with so great vigour both of mind and body, that becoming a soldier, he rose through the various grades of the service to be Praetor of Syracuse. Once established in that post, he resolved to make himself Prince, and to hold by violence and without obligation to others the authority which had been spontaneously entrusted to him. Accordingly, after imparting his design to Hamilcar, who with the Carthaginian armies was at that time waging war in Sicily, he one morning assembled the people and senate of Syracuse as though to consult with them on matters of public moment, and on a preconcerted signal caused his soldiers to put to death all the senators, and the wealthiest of the commons. These being thus got rid of, he assumed and retained possession of the sovereignty without opposition on the part of the people; and although twice defeated by the Carthaginians, and afterwards besieged, he was able not only to defend his city, but leaving a part of his forces for its protection, to invade Africa with the remainder, and so in a short time to raise the siege of Syracuse, reducing the Carthaginians to the utmost extremities, and compelling them to make terms whereby they abandoned Sicily to him and confined themselves to Africa.

Whoever examines this man's actions and achievements will discover little or nothing in them which can be ascribed to Fortune, seeing, as has already been said, that it was not through the favour of any, but by the regular steps of the military service, gained at the cost of a thousand hardships and hazards, he reached the princedom which he afterwards maintained by so many daring and dangerous enterprises. Still, to slaughter fellow citizens, to betray friends, to be devoid of honour, pity, and religion, cannot be counted as merits, for these are means which may lead to power, but which confer no glory. Wherefore, if in respect of the valour with which he encountered and extricated himself from difficulties, and the constancy of his spirit in supporting and conquering adverse fortune, there seems no reason to judge him inferior to the greatest captains that have ever lived, his unbridled cruelty and inhumanity, together with his countless crimes, forbid us to number him with the greatest men; but, at any rate, we cannot attribute to Fortune or to merit what he accomplished without either.

In our own times, during the papacy of Alexander VI, Oliverotto of Fermo, who some years before had been left an orphan, and had been brought up by his maternal uncle Giovanni Fogliani, was sent while still a lad to serve under Paolo Vitelli, in the expectation that a thorough training under that commander might qualify him for high rank as a soldier. After the death of Paolo, he served under his brother Vitellozzo, and in a very short time, being of a quick wit, hardy and resolute, he became one of the first soldiers of his company. But thinking it beneath him to serve under others, with the countenance of the Vitelleschi and the connivance of certain citizens of Fermo who preferred the slavery to the freedom of their country, he formed the design to seize on that town.

He accordingly wrote to Giovanni Fogliani that after many years of absence from home, he desired to see him and his native city once more, and to look a little into the condition of his patrimony; and as his one endeavour had been to make himself a name, in order that his fellow citizens might see that his time had not been mis-spent, he proposed to return honourably attended by a hundred horsemen from among his own friends and followers; and he begged Giovanni graciously to arrange for his reception by the citizens of Fermo with corresponding marks of distinction, as this would be creditable not only to himself, but also to the uncle who had brought him up.

Giovanni accordingly did not fail in any proper attention to his nephew, but caused him to be splendidly received by his fellow-citizens, and lodged him in his house; where Oliverotto having passed some days, and made the necessary arrangements for carrying out his wickedness, gave a formal banquet, to which he invited his uncle and all the first men of Fermo. When the repast and the other entertainments proper to such an occasion had come to an end, Oliverotto artfully turned the conversation to matters of grave interest, by speaking of the greatness of Pope Alexander and Cesare his son, and of their enterprises; and when Giovanni and the others were replying to what he said, he suddenly rose up, observing that these were matters to be discussed in a more private place, and so withdrew to another chamber; whither his uncle and all the other citizens followed him, and where they had no sooner seated themselves, than soldiers rushing out from places of concealment put Giovanni and all the rest to death.

HENCE WE MAY LEARN THE LESSON THAT ON SEIZING A STATE, THE USURPER SHOULD MAKE HASTE TO INFLICT WHAT INJURIES HE MUST, AT A STROKE, THAT HE MAY NOT HAVE TO RENEW THEM DAILY . . .

After this butchery, Oliverotto mounted his horse, rode through the streets, and besieged the chief magistrate in the palace, so that all were constrained by fear to yield obedience and accept a government of which he made himself the head. And all who from being disaffected were likely to stand in his way, he put to death, while he strengthened himself with new ordinances, civil and military, to such purpose, that for the space of a year during which he retained the Princedom, he not merely kept a firm hold of the city, but grew formidable to all his neighbours. And it would have been as impossible to unseat him as it was to unseat Agathocles, had he not let himself be overreached by Cesare Borgia on the occasion when, as has already been told, the Orsini and Vitelli were entrapped at Sinigaglia; where he too being taken, one year after the commission of his parricidal crime, was strangled along with Vitellozzo, whom he had assumed for his master in villany as in valour.

It may be asked how Agathocles and some like him, after numberless acts of treachery and cruelty, have been able to live long in their own country in safety, and to defend themselves from foreign enemies, without being plotted against by their fellow-citizens, whereas, many others, by reason of their cruelty, have failed to maintain their position even in peaceful times, not to speak of the perilous times of war. I believe that this results from cruelty being well or ill employed. Those cruelties we may say are well employed, if it be permitted to speak well of things evil, which are done once for all under the necessity of self-preservation, and are not afterwards persisted in, but so far as possible modified to the advantage of the governed. Ill-employed cruelties, on the other hand, are those which from small beginnings increase rather than diminish with time. They who follow the first of these methods, may, by the grace of God and man, find, as did Agathocles, that their condition is not desperate; but by no possibility can the others maintain themselves.

Hence we may learn the lesson that on seizing a state, the usurper should make haste to inflict what injuries he must, at a stroke, that he may not have to renew them daily, but be enabled by their discontinuance to reassure men's minds, and afterwards win them over by benefits. Whosoever, either through timidity or from following bad counsels, adopts a contrary course, must keep the sword always drawn, and can put no trust in his subjects, who suffering from continued and constantly renewed severities, will never yield him their confidence. Injuries, therefore, should be inflicted all at once, that their ill savour being less lasting may the less offend; whereas, benefits should be conferred little by little, that so they may be more fully relished.

But, before all things, a Prince should so live with his subjects that no vicissitude of good or evil fortune shall oblige him to alter his behaviour; because, if a need to change come through adversity, it is then too late to resort to severity; while any leniency you may use will be thrown away, for it will be seen to be compulsory and gain you no thanks.

CHAPTER IX

OF THE CIVIL PRINCEDOM

I COME NOW to the second case, namely, of the leading citizen who, not by crimes or violence, but by the favour of his fellow-citizens is made Prince of his country. This may be called a Civil Princedom, and its attainment depends not wholly on merit, nor wholly on good fortune, but rather on what may be termed a *fortunate astuteness*. I say then that the road to this Princedom lies either through the favour of the people or of the nobles. For in every city are to be found these two opposed humours having their origin in this, that the people desire not to be domineered over or oppressed by the nobles, while the nobles desire to oppress and domineer over the people. And from these two contrary appetites there arises in cities one of three results, a Princedom, or Liberty, or Licence. A Princedom is created either by the people or by the nobles, according as one or other of these factions has occasion for it. For when the nobles perceive that they cannot withstand the people, they set to work to magnify the reputation of one of their number, and make him their Prince, to the end that under his shadow they may be enabled to indulge their desires. The people, on the other hand, when they see that they cannot make head against the nobles, invest a single citizen with all their influence and make him Prince, that they may have the shelter of his authority.

He who is made Prince by the favour of the nobles, has greater difficulty to maintain himself than he who comes to the Princedom by aid of the people, since he finds many about him who think themselves as good as he, and whom, on that account, he cannot guide or govern as he would. But he who reaches the Princedom by the popular support, finds himself alone, with none, or but a very few about him who are not ready to obey. Moreover, the demands of the nobles cannot be satisfied with credit to the Prince, nor without injury to others, while those of the people well may, the aim of the people being more honourable than that of the nobles, the latter seeking to oppress, the former not to be oppressed. Add to this, that a Prince can never secure himself against a disaffected people, their number being too great, while he may against a disaffected nobility, since their number is small. The worst that a Prince need fear from a disaffected people is, that they may desert him, whereas when the nobles are his enemies he has to fear not only that they may desert him, but also that they may turn against him; because, as they have greater craft and foresight, they always choose their time to suit their safety, and seek favour with the side they think will win. Again, a Prince must always live with the same people, but need not always live with the same nobles, being able to make and unmake these from day to day, and give and take away their authority at his pleasure.

But to make this part of the matter clearer, I say that as regards the nobles there is this first distinction to be made. They either so govern their conduct as to bind themselves wholly to your fortunes, or they do not. Those who so bind themselves, and who are not grasping, should be loved and honoured. As to those who do not so bind themselves, there is this further distinction. For the most part they are held back by pusillanimity and a natural defect of courage, in which case you should make use of them, and of those among them more especially who are prudent, for they will do you honour in prosperity, and in adversity give you no cause for fear. But where they abstain from attaching themselves to you of set purpose and for ambitious ends, it is a sign that they are thinking more of themselves than of you, and against such men a Prince should be on his guard, and treat them as though they were declared enemies, for in his adversity they will always help to ruin him.

He who becomes a Prince through the favour of the people should always keep on good terms with them; which it is easy for him to do, since all they ask is not to be oppressed. But he who against the will of the people is made a Prince by the favour of the nobles, must, above all things, seek to conciliate the people, which he readily may by taking them under his protection. For since men who are well treated by one whom they expected to treat them ill, feel the more beholden to their benefactor, the people will at once become better disposed to such a Prince when he protects them, than if he owed his Princedom to them.

There are many ways in which a Prince may gain the good-will of the people, but, because these vary with circumstances, no certain rule can be laid down respecting them, and I shall, therefore, say no more about them. But this is the sum of the matter, that it is essential for a Prince to be on a friendly footing with his people, since, otherwise, he will have no resource in adversity. Nabis, Prince of Sparta, was attacked by the whole hosts of Greece, and by a Roman army flushed with victory, and defended his country and crown against them; and when danger approached, there were but few of his subjects against whom he needed to guard himself, whereas had the people been hostile, this would not have been enough.

And what I affirm let no one controvert by citing the old saw that '*he who builds on the people builds on mire,*' for that may be true of a private citizen who presumes on his favour with the people, and counts on being rescued by them when overpowered by his enemies or by the magistrates. In such cases a man may often find himself deceived, as happened to the Gracchi in Rome, and in Florence to Messer Giorgio Scali. But when he who builds on the people is a Prince capable of command, of a spirit not to be cast down by ill-fortune, who, while he animates the whole community by his courage and hearing, neglects no prudent precaution, he will not find himself betrayed by the people, but will be seen to have laid his foundations well.

The most critical juncture for Princedoms of this kind, is at the moment when they are about to pass from the popular to the absolute form of government: and as these Princes exercise their authority either directly or through the agency of the magistrates, in the latter case their position is weaker and more hazardous, since they are wholly in the power of those citizens to whom the magistracies are entrusted, who can, and especially in difficult times, with the greatest ease deprive them of their authority, either by opposing, or by not obeying them. And in times of peril it is too late for a Prince to assume to himself an absolute authority, for the citizens and subjects who are accustomed to take their orders from the magistrates, will not when dangers threaten take them from the Prince, so that at such seasons there will always be very few in whom he can trust. Such Princes, therefore, must not build on what they see in tranquil times when the citizens feel the need of the State. For then every one is ready to run, to promise, and, danger of death being remote, even to die for the State. But in troubled times, when the State has need of its citizens, few of them are to be found. And the risk of the experiment is the greater in that it can only be made once. Wherefore, a wise Prince should devise means whereby his subjects may at all times, whether favourable or adverse, feel the need of the State and of him, and then they will always be faithful to him.

CHAPTER X

HOW THE STRENGTH OF ALL PRINCEDOMS SHOULD BE MEASURED

IN EXAMINING THE character of these Princedoms, another circumstance has to be considered, namely, whether the Prince is strong enough, if occasion demands, to stand alone, or whether he needs continual help from others. To make the matter clearer, I pronounce those to be able to stand alone who, with the men and money at their disposal, can get together an army fit to take the field against any assailant; and, conversely I judge those to be in constant need of help who cannot take the field against their enemies, but are obliged to retire behind their walls, and to defend themselves there. Of the former I have already spoken, and shall speak again as occasion may require. As to the latter there is nothing to be said, except to exhort such Princes to strengthen and fortify the towns in which they dwell, and take no heed of the country outside. For whoever has thoroughly fortified his town, and put himself on such a footing with his subjects as I have already indicated and shall hereafter speak of, will always be attacked with much circumspection; for men are always averse to enterprises that are attended with difficulty, and it is impossible not to foresee difficulties in attacking a Prince whose town is strongly fortified and who is not hated by his subjects.

The towns of Germany enjoy great freedom. Having little territory, they render obedience to the Emperor only when so disposed, fearing neither him nor any other neighbouring power. For they are so fortified that it is plain to every one that it would be a tedious and difficult task to reduce them, since all of them are protected by moats and suitable ramparts, are well supplied with artillery, and keep their public magazines constantly stored with victual, drink and fuel, enough to last them for a year. Besides which, in order to support the poorer class of citizens without public loss, they lay in a common stock of materials for these to work on for a year, in the handicrafts which are the life and sinews of such cities, and by which the common people live. Moreover, they esteem military exercises and have many regulations for their maintenance.

A Prince, therefore, who has a strong city, and who does not make himself hated, can not be attacked, or should he be so, his assailant will come badly off; since human affairs are so variable that it is almost impossible for any one to keep an army posted in leaguer for a whole year without interruption of some sort. Should it be objected that if the citizens have possessions outside the town, and see them burned, they will lose patience, and that self-interest, together with the hardships of a protracted siege, will cause them to forget their loyalty; I answer that a capable and courageous Prince will always overcome these difficulties, now, by holding out hopes to his subjects that the evil will not be of long continuance; now, by exciting their fears of the enemy's cruelty; and, again, by dexterously silencing those who seem to him too forward in their complaints. Moreover, it is to be expected that the enemy will burn and lay waste the country immediately on their arrival, at a time when men's minds are still heated and resolute for defence. And for this very reason the Prince ought the less to fear, because after a few days, when the first ardour has abated, the injury is already done and suffered, and cannot be undone; and the people will now, all the more readily, make common cause with their Prince from his seeming to be under obligations to them, their houses having been burned and their lands wasted in his defence. For it is the nature of men to incur obligation as much by the benefits they render as by those they receive.

Wherefore, if the whole matter be well considered, it ought not to be difficult for a prudent Prince, both at the outset and afterwards, to maintain the spirits of his subjects during a siege; provided always that victuals and the other means of defence do not run short.

CHAPTER XI

OF ECCLESIASTICAL PRINCEDOMS

IT NOW ONLY remains for me to treat of Ecclesiastical Princedoms, all the difficulties in respect of which precede their acquisition. For they are acquired by merit or good fortune, but are maintained without either; being upheld by the venerable ordinances of Religion, which are all of such a nature and efficacy that they secure the authority of their Princes in whatever way they may act or live. These Princes alone have territories which they do not defend, and subjects whom they do not govern; yet their territories are not taken from them through not being defended, nor are their subjects concerned at not being governed, or led to think of throwing off their allegiance; nor is it in their power to do so. Accordingly these Princedoms alone are secure and happy. But inasmuch as they are sustained by agencies of a higher nature than the mind of man can reach, I forbear to speak of them: for since they are set up and supported by God himself, he would be a rash and presumptuous man who should venture to discuss them.

Nevertheless, should any one ask me how it comes about that the temporal power of the Church, which before the time of Alexander was looked on with contempt by all the Potentates of Italy, and not only by those so styling themselves, but by every Baron and Lordling however insignificant, has now reached such a pitch of greatness that the King of France trembles before it, and that it has been able to drive him out of Italy and to crush the Venetians; though the causes be known, it seems to me not superfluous to call them in some measure to recollection.

Before Charles of France passed into Italy, that country was under the control of the Pope, the Venetians, the King of Naples, the Duke of Milan, and the Florentines. Two chief objects had to be kept in view by all these powers: first, that no armed foreigner should be allowed to invade Italy; second, that no one of their own number should be suffered to extend his territory. Those whom it was especially needed to guard against, were the Pope and the Venetians. To hold back the Venetians it was necessary that all the other States should combine, as was done for the defence of Ferrara; while to restrain the Pope, use was made of the Roman Barons, who being divided into two factions, the Orsini and Colonnesi, had constant cause for feud with one another, and standing with arms in their hands under the very eyes of the Pontiff, kept the Popedom feeble and insecure.

And although there arose from time to time a courageous Pope like Sixtus, neither his prudence nor his good fortune could free him from these embarrassments. The cause whereof was the shortness of the lives of the Popes. For in the ten years, which was the average duration of a Pope's life, he could barely succeed in humbling one of these factions; so that if, for instance, one Pope had almost exterminated the Colonnesi, he was followed by another, who being the enemy of the Orsini had no time to rid himself of them, but so far from completing the destruction of the Colonnesi, restored them to life. This led to the temporal authority of the Popes being little esteemed in Italy.

Then came Alexander VI, who more than any of his predecessors showed what a Pope could effect with money and arms, achieving by the instrumentality of Duke Valentino, and by taking advantage of the coming of the French into Italy, all those successes which I have already noticed in speaking of the actions of the Duke. And although his object was to aggrandize, not the Church but the Duke, what he did turned to the advantage of the Church, which after his death, and after the Duke had been put out of the way, became the heir of his labours.

After him came Pope Julius, who found the Church strengthened by the possession of the whole of Romagna, and the Roman Barons exhausted and their factions shattered under the blows of Pope Alexander. He found also a way opened for the accumulation of wealth, which before the time of Alexander no one had followed. These advantages Julius not only used but added to. He undertook the conquest of Bologna, the overthrow of the Venetians, and the expulsion of the French from Italy; in all which enterprises he succeeded, and with the greater glory to himself in that whatever he did, was done to strengthen the Church and not to aggrandize any private person. He succeeded, moreover, in keeping the factions of the Orsini and Colonnesi within the same limits as he found them; and, though some seeds of insubordination may still have been left among them, two causes operated to hold them in check; first, the great power of the Church, which overawed them, and second, their being without Cardinals, who had been the cause of all their disorders. For these factions while they have Cardinals among them can never be at rest, since it is they who foment dissension both in Rome and out of it, in which the Barons are forced to take part, the ambition of the Prelates thus giving rise to tumult and discord among the Barons.

His Holiness, Pope Leo, has consequently found the Papacy most powerful; and from him we may hope, that as his predecessors made it great with arms, he will render it still greater and more venerable by his benignity and other countless virtues.

CHAPTER XII

HOW MANY DIFFERENT KINDS OF SOLDIERS THERE ARE, AND OF MERCENARIES

HAVING SPOKEN PARTICULARLY of all the various kinds of Princedom whereof at the outset I proposed to treat, considered in some measure what are the causes of their strength and weakness, and pointed out the methods by which men commonly seek to acquire them, it now remains that I should discourse generally concerning the means for attack and defence of which each of these different kinds of Princedom may make use.

I have already said that a Prince must lay solid foundations, since otherwise he will inevitably be destroyed. Now the main foundations of all States, whether new, old, or mixed, are good laws and good arms. But since you cannot have the former without the latter, and where you have the latter, are likely to have the former, I shall here omit all discussion on the subject of laws, and speak only of arms.

I say then that the arms wherewith a Prince defends his State are either his own subjects, or they are mercenaries, or they are auxiliaries, or they are partly one and partly another. Mercenaries and auxiliaries are at once useless and dangerous, and he who holds his State by means of mercenary troops can never be solidly or securely seated. For such troops are disunited, ambitious, insubordinate, treacherous, insolent among friends, cowardly before foes, and without fear of God or faith with man. Whenever they are attacked defeat follows; so that in peace you are plundered by them, in war by your enemies. And this because they have no tie or motive to keep them in the field beyond their paltry pay, in return for which it would be too much to expect them to give their lives. They are ready enough, therefore, to be your soldiers while you are at peace, but when war is declared they make off and disappear. I ought to have little difficulty in getting this believed, for the present ruin of Italy is due to no other cause than her having for many years trusted to mercenaries, who though heretofore they may have helped the fortunes of some one man, and made a show of strength when matched with one another, have always revealed themselves in their true colours so soon as foreign enemies appeared. Hence it was that Charles of France was suffered to conquer Italy *with chalk;* and he who said our sins were the cause, said truly, though it was not the sins he meant, but those which I have noticed. And as these were the sins of Princes, they it is who have paid the penalty.

> THE MAIN FOUNDATIONS OF ALL STATES, WHETHER NEW, OLD, OR MIXED, ARE GOOD LAWS AND GOOD ARMS.

But I desire to demonstrate still more clearly the untoward character of these forces. Captains of mercenaries are either able men or they are not. If they are, you cannot trust them, since they will always seek their own aggrandizement, either by overthrowing you who are their master, or by the overthrow of others contrary to your desire. On the other hand, if your captain be not an able man the chances are you will be ruined. And if it be said that whoever has arms in his hands will act in the same way whether he be a mercenary or no, I answer that when arms have to be employed by a Prince or a Republic, the Prince ought to go in person to take command as captain, the Republic should send one of her citizens, and if he prove incapable should change him, but if he prove capable should by the force of the laws confine him within proper bounds. And we see from experience that both Princes and Republics when they depend on their own arms have the greatest success, whereas from employing mercenaries nothing but loss results. Moreover, a Republic trusting to her own forces, is with greater difficulty than one which relies on foreign arms brought to yield obedience to a single citizen. Rome and Sparta remained for ages armed and free. The Swiss are at once the best armed and the freest people in the world.

Of mercenary arms in ancient times we have an example in the

Carthaginians, who at the close of their first war with Rome, were well nigh ruined by their hired troops, although these were commanded by Carthaginian citizens. So too, when, on the death of Epaminondas, the Thebans made Philip of Macedon captain of their army, after gaining a victory for them, he deprived them of their liberty. The Milanese, in like manner, when Duke Filippo died, took Francesco Sforza into their pay to conduct the war against the Venetians. But he, after defeating the enemy at Caravaggio, combined with them to overthrow the Milanese, his masters. His father too while in the pay of Giovanna, Queen of Naples, suddenly left her without troops, obliging her, in order to save her kingdom, to throw herself into the arms of the King of Aragon.

And if it be said that in times past the Venetians and the Florentines have extended their dominions by means of these arms, and that their captains have served them faithfully, without seeking to make themselves their masters, I answer that in this respect the Florentines have been fortunate, because among those valiant captains who might have given them cause for fear, some have not been victorious, some have had rivals, and some have turned their ambition in other directions.

Among those not victorious, was Giovanni Acuto, whose fidelity, since he was unsuccessful, was not put to the proof: but any one may see, that had he been victorious the Florentines must have been entirely in his hands. The Sforzas, again, had constant rivals in the Bracceschi, so that the one following was a check upon the other; moreover, the ambition of Francesco was directed against Milan, while that of Braccio was directed against the Church and the kingdom of Naples. Let us turn, however, to what took place lately. The Florentines chose for their captain Paolo Vitelli, a most prudent commander, who had raised himself from privacy to the highest renown in arms. Had he been successful in reducing Pisa, none can deny that the Florentines would have been completely in his power, for they would have been ruined had he gone over to their enemies, while if they retained him they must have submitted to his will.

Again, as to the Venetians, if we consider the growth of their power, it will be seen that they conducted their affairs with glory and safety so long as their subjects of all ranks, gentle and simple alike, valiantly bore arms in their wars; as they did before they directed their enterprises landwards. But when they took to making war by land, they forsook those methods in which they excelled and were content to follow the customs of Italy.

At first, indeed, in extending their possessions on the mainland, having as yet but little territory and being held in high repute, they had not much to fear from their captains; but when their territories increased, which they did under Carmagnola, they were taught their mistake. For as they had found him a most valiant and skilful leader when, under his command, they defeated the Duke of Milan, and, on the other hand, saw him slack in carrying on the war, they made up their minds that no further victories were to be had under him; and because, through fear of losing what they had gained, they could not discharge him, to secure themselves against him they were forced to put him to death. After him they have had for captains, Bartolommeo of Bergamo, Roberto of San Severino, the Count of Pitigliano, and the like, under whom their danger has not been from victories, but from defeats; as, for instance, at Vaila, where they lost in a single day what it had taken the efforts of eight hundred years to acquire. For the gains resulting from mercenary arms are slow, and late, and inconsiderable, but the losses sudden and astounding.

And since these examples have led me back to Italy, which for many years past has been defended by mercenary arms, I desire to go somewhat deeper into the matter, in order that the causes which led to the adoption of these arms being seen, they may the more readily be corrected. You are to understand, then, that when in these later times the Imperial control began to be rejected by Italy, and the temporal power of the Pope to be more thought of, Italy suddenly split up into a number of separate States. For many of the larger cities took up arms against their nobles, who, with the favour of the Emperor, had before kept them in subjection, and were supported by the Church with a view to add to her temporal authority: while in many others of these cities, private citizens became rulers. Hence Italy, having passed almost entirely into the hands of the Church and of certain Republics, the former made up of priests, the latter of citizens unfamiliar with arms, began to take foreigners into her pay.

The first who gave reputation to this service was Alberigo of Conio in Romagna, from whose school of warlike training descended, among others, Braccio and Sforza, who in their time were the arbiters of Italy; after whom came all those others who down to the present hour have held similar commands, and to whose merits we owe it that our country has been overrun by Charles, plundered by Louis, wasted by Ferdinand, and insulted by the Swiss.

The first object of these mercenaries was to bring foot soldiers into disrepute, in order to enhance the merit of their own followers; and this they did, because lacking territory of their own and depending on their profession for their support, a few foot soldiers gave them no importance, while for a large number they were unable to provide. For these reasons they had recourse to horsemen, a less retinue of whom was thought to confer distinction, and could be more easily maintained. And the matter went to such a length, that in an army of twenty thousand men, not two thousand foot soldiers were to be found. Moreover, they spared no endeavour to relieve themselves and their men from fatigue and danger, not killing one another in battle, but making prisoners who were afterwards released without ransom. They would attack no town by night; those in towns would make no sortie by night against a besieging army. Their camps were without rampart or trench. They had no winter campaigns. All which arrangements were sanctioned by their military rules, contrived by them, as I have said already, to escape fatigue and danger; but the result of which has been to bring Italy into servitude and contempt.

CHAPTER XIII

OF AUXILIARY, MIXED, AND NATIONAL ARMS

THE SECOND SORT of unprofitable arms are auxiliaries, by whom I mean, troops brought to help and protect you by a potentate whom you summon to your aid; as when in recent times, Pope Julius II observing the pitiful behaviour of his mercenaries at the enterprise of Ferrara, betook himself to auxiliaries, and arranged with Ferdinand of Spain to be supplied with horse and foot soldiers.

Auxiliaries may be excellent and useful soldiers for themselves, but are always hurtful to him who calls them in; for if they are defeated, he is undone, if victorious, he becomes their prisoner. Ancient histories abound with instances of this, but I shall not pass from the example of Pope Julius, which is still fresh in men's minds. It was the height of rashness for him, in his eagerness to gain Ferrara, to throw himself without reserve into the arms of a stranger. Nevertheless, his good fortune came to his rescue, and he had not to reap the fruits of his ill-considered conduct. For after his auxiliaries were defeated at Ravenna, the Swiss suddenly descended and, to their own surprise and that of every one else, swept the victors out of the country, so that, he neither remained a prisoner with his enemies, they being put to flight, nor with his auxiliaries, because victory was won by other arms than theirs. The Florentines, being wholly without soldiers of their own, brought ten thousand French men-at-arms to the siege of Pisa, thereby incurring greater peril than at any previous time of trouble. To protect himself from his neighbours, the Emperor of Constantinople summoned ten thousand Turkish soldiers into Greece, who, when the war was over, refused to leave, and this was the beginning of the servitude of Greece to the Infidel.

Let him, therefore, who would deprive himself of every chance of success, have recourse to auxiliaries, these being far more dangerous than mercenary arms, bringing ruin with them ready made. For they are united, and wholly under the control of their own officers; whereas, before mercenaries, even after gaining a victory, can do you hurt, longer time and better opportunities are needed; because, as they are made up of separate companies, raised and paid by you, he whom you place in command cannot at once acquire such authority over them as will be injurious to you. In short, with mercenaries your greatest danger is from their inertness and cowardice, with auxiliaries from their valour. Wise Princes, therefore, have always eschewed these arms, and trusted rather to their own, and have preferred defeat with the latter to victory with the former, counting that as no true victory which is gained by foreign aid.

I shall never hesitate to cite the example of Cesare Borgia and his actions. He entered Romagna with a force of auxiliaries, all of them French men-at-arms, with whom he took Imola and Forli. But it appearing to him afterwards that these troops were not to be trusted, he had recourse to mercenaries from whom he thought there would be less danger, and took the Orsini and Vitelli into his pay. But finding these likewise while under his command to be fickle, false, and treacherous, he got rid of them, and fell back on troops of his own raising. And we may readily discern the difference between these various kinds of arms, by observing the different degrees of reputation in which the Duke stood while he depended upon the French alone, when he took the Orsini and Vitelli into his pay, and when he fell back on his own troops and his own resources; for we find his reputation always increasing, and that he was never so well thought of as when every one perceived him to be sole master of his own forces.

I am unwilling to leave these examples, drawn from what has taken place in Italy and in recent times; and yet I must not omit to notice the case of Hiero of Syracuse, who is one of those whom I have already named. He, as I have before related, being made captain of their armies by the Syracusans, saw at once that a force of mercenary soldiers, supplied by men resembling our Italian *condottieri*, was not serviceable; and as he would not retain and could not disband them, he caused them all to be cut to pieces, and afterwards made war with native soldiers only, without other aid.

And here I would call to mind a passage in the Old Testament as bearing on this point. When David offered himself to Saul to go forth and fight Goliath the

Philistine champion, Saul to encourage him armed him with his own armour, which David, so soon as he had put it on, rejected, saying that with these untried arms he could not prevail, and that he chose rather to meet his enemy with only his sling and his sword. In a word, the armour of others is too wide, or too strait for us; it falls off us, or it weighs us down.

Charles VII, the father of Louis XI, who by his good fortune and valour freed France from the English, saw this necessity of strengthening himself with a national army, and drew up ordinances regulating the service both of men-at-arms and of foot soldiers throughout his kingdom. But afterwards his son, King Louis, did away with the national infantry, and began to hire Swiss mercenaries. Which blunder having been followed by subsequent Princes, has been the cause, as the result shows, of the dangers into which the kingdom of France has fallen; for, by enhancing the reputation of the Swiss, the whole of the national troops of France have been deteriorated. For from their infantry being done away with, their men-at-arms are made wholly dependent on foreign assistance, and being accustomed to co-operate with the Swiss, have grown to think they can do nothing without them. Hence the French are no match for the Swiss, and without them cannot succeed against others.

The armies of France, then, are mixed, being partly national and partly mercenary. Armies thus composed are far superior to mere mercenaries or mere auxiliaries, but far inferior to forces purely national. And this example is in itself conclusive, for the realm of France would be invincible if the military ordinances of Charles VII had been retained and extended. But from want of foresight men make changes which relishing well at first do not betray their hidden venom, as I have already observed respecting hectic fever. Nevertheless, the ruler is not truly wise who cannot discern evils before they develop themselves, and this is a faculty given to few.

If we look for the causes which first led to the overthrow of the Roman Empire, they will be found to have had their source in the employment of Gothic mercenaries, for from that hour the strength of the Romans began to wane and all the virtue which went from them passed to the Goths. And, to be brief, I say that without national arms no Princedom is safe, but on the contrary is wholly dependent on Fortune, being without the strength that could defend it in adversity. And it has always been the deliberate opinion of the wise, that nothing is so infirm and fleeting as a reputation for power not founded upon a national army, by which I mean one composed of subjects, citizens, and dependants, all others being mercenary or auxiliary.

The methods to be followed for organizing a national army may readily be ascertained, if the rules above laid down by me, and by which I abide, be well considered, and attention be given to the manner in which Philip, father of Alexander the Great, and many other Princes and Republics have armed and disposed their forces.

CHAPTER XIV

OF THE DUTY OF A PRINCE IN RESPECT OF MILITARY AFFAIRS

A PRINCE, THEREFORE, should have no care or thought but for war, and for the regulations and training it requires, and should apply himself exclusively to this as his peculiar province; for war is the sole art looked for in one who rules, and is of such efficacy that it not merely maintains those who are born Princes, but often enables men to rise to that eminence from a private station; while, on the other hand, we often see that when Princes devote themselves rather to pleasure than to arms, they lose their dominions. And as neglect of this art is the prime cause of such calamities, so to be a proficient in it is the surest way to acquire power. Francesco Sforza, from his renown in arms, rose from privacy to be Duke of Milan, while his descendants, seeking to avoid the hardships and fatigues of military life, from being Princes fell back into privacy. For among other causes of misfortune which your not being armed brings upon you, it makes you despised, and this is one of those reproaches against which, as shall presently be explained, a Prince ought most carefully to guard.

A PRINCE, THEREFORE, OUGHT NEVER TO ALLOW HIS ATTENTION TO BE DIVERTED FROM WARLIKE PURSUITS, AND SHOULD OCCUPY HIMSELF WITH THEM EVEN MORE IN PEACE THAN IN WAR.

Between an armed and an unarmed man no proportion holds, and it is contrary to reason to expect that the armed man should voluntarily submit to him who is unarmed, or that the unarmed man should stand secure among armed retainers. For with contempt on one side, and distrust on the other, it is impossible that men should work well together. Wherefore, as has already been said, a Prince who is ignorant of military affairs, besides other disadvantages, can neither be respected by his soldiers, nor can he trust them. A Prince, therefore, ought never to allow his attention to be diverted from warlike pursuits, and should occupy himself with them even more in peace than in war. This he can do in two ways, by practice or by study.

As to the practice, he ought, besides keeping his soldiers well trained and disciplined, to be constantly engaged in the chase, that he may inure his body to hardships and fatigue, and gain at the same time a knowledge of places, by observing how the mountains slope, the valleys open, and the plains spread; acquainting himself with the characters of rivers and marshes, and giving the greatest attention to this subject. Such knowledge is useful to him in two ways; for first, he learns thereby to know his own country, and to understand better how it may be defended; and next, from his familiar acquaintance with its localities, he readily comprehends the character of other districts when obliged to observe them for the first time. For the hills, valleys, plains, rivers, and marshes of Tuscany, for example, have a certain resemblance to those elsewhere; so that from a knowledge of the natural features of that province, similar knowledge in respect of other provinces may readily be gained. The Prince who is wanting in this kind of knowledge, is wanting in the first qualification of a good captain, for by it he is taught how to surprise an enemy, how to choose an encampment, how to lead his army on a march, how to array it for battle, and how to post it to the best advantage for a siege.

Among the commendations which Philopoemon, Prince of the Achaians, has received from historians is this—that in times of peace he was always thinking of methods of warfare, so that when walking in the country with his friends he would often stop and talk with them on the subject. 'If the enemy,' he would say, 'were posted on that hill, and we found ourselves here with our army, which of us would have the better position? How could we most safely and in the best order advance to meet them? If we had to retreat, what direction should we take? If they retired, how should we pursue?' In this way he put to his friends, as he went along, all the contingencies that can befall an army. He listened to their opinions, stated his own, and supported them with reasons; and from his being constantly occupied with such meditations, it resulted, that when in actual command no complication could ever present itself with which he was not prepared to deal.

As to the mental training of which we have spoken, a Prince should read histories, and in these should note the actions of great men, observe how they conducted themselves in their wars, and examine the causes of their victories and defeats, so as to avoid the latter and imitate them in the former. And above all, he should, as many great men of past ages have done, assume for his models those persons who before his time have been renowned and celebrated, whose deeds and achievements he should constantly keep in mind, as it is related that Alexander the Great sought to resemble Achilles, Caesar Alexander, and Scipio Cyrus. And any one who reads the life of this last-named hero, written by Xenophon, recognizes afterwards in the life of Scipio, how much this imitation was the source of his glory, and how nearly in his chastity, affability, kindliness, and generosity, he conformed to the character of Cyrus as Xenophon describes it.

A wise Prince, therefore, should pursue such methods as these, never resting idle in times of peace, but strenuously seeking to turn them to account, so that he may derive strength from them in the hour of danger, and find himself ready should Fortune turn against him, to resist her blows.

CHAPTER XV

OF THE QUALITIES IN RESPECT OF WHICH MEN, AND MOST OF ALL PRINCES, ARE PRAISED OR BLAMED

IT NOW REMAINS for us to consider what ought to be the conduct and bearing of a Prince in relation to his subjects and friends. And since I know that many have written on this subject, I fear it may be thought presumptuous in me to write of it also; the more so, because in my treatment of it I depart from the views that others have taken.

But since it is my object to write what shall be useful to whosoever understands it, it seems to me better to follow the real truth of things than an imaginary view of them. For many Republics and Princedoms have been imagined that were never seen or known to exist in reality. And the manner in which we live, and that in which we ought to live, are things so wide asunder, that he who quits the one to betake himself to the other is more likely to destroy than to save himself, since any one who would act up to a perfect standard of goodness in everything, must be ruined among so many who are not good. It is essential, therefore, for a Prince who desires to maintain his position, to have learned how to be other than good, and to use or not to use his goodness as necessity requires.

Laying aside, therefore, all fanciful notions concerning a Prince, and considering those only that are true, I say that all men when they are spoken of, and Princes more than others from their being set so high, are characterized by some one of those qualities which attach either praise or blame. Thus one is accounted liberal, another miserly (which word I use, rather than *avaricious,* to denote the man who is too sparing of what is his own, *avarice* being the disposition to take wrongfully what is another's); one is generous, another greedy; one cruel, another tender-hearted; one is faithless, another true to his word; one effeminate and cowardly, another high-spirited and courageous; one is courteous, another haughty; one impure, another chaste; one simple, another crafty; one firm, another facile; one grave, another frivolous; one devout, another unbelieving; and the like. Every one, I know, will admit that it would be most laudable for a Prince to be endowed with all of the above qualities that are reckoned good; but since it is impossible for him to possess or constantly practise them all, the conditions of human nature not allowing it, he must be discreet enough to know how to avoid the infamy of those vices that would deprive him of his government, and, if possible, be on his guard also against those which might not deprive him of it; though if he cannot wholly restrain himself, he may with less scruple indulge in the latter. He need never hesitate, however, to incur the reproach of those vices without which his authority can hardly be preserved; for if he well consider the whole matter, he will find that there may be a line of conduct having the appearance of virtue, to follow which would be his ruin, and that there may be another course having the appearance of vice, by following which his safety and well-being are secured.

CHAPTER XVI

OF LIBERALITY AND MISERLINESS

BEGINNING, THEN, WITH the first of the qualities above noticed, I say that it may be a good thing to be reputed liberal, but, nevertheless, that liberality without the reputation of it is hurtful; because, though it be worthily and rightly used, still if it be not known, you escape not the reproach of its opposite vice. Hence, to have credit for liberality with the world at large, you must neglect no circumstance of sumptuous display; the result being, that a Prince of a liberal disposition will consume his whole substance in things of this sort, and, after all, be obliged, if he would maintain his reputation for liberality, to burden his subjects with extraordinary taxes, and to resort to confiscations and all the other shifts whereby money is raised. But in this way he becomes hateful to his subjects, and growing impoverished is held in little esteem by any. So that in the end, having by his liberality offended many and obliged few, he is worse off than when he began, and is exposed to all his original dangers. Recognizing this, and endeavouring to retrace his steps, he at once incurs the infamy of miserliness.

A Prince, therefore, since he cannot without injury to himself practise the virtue of liberality so that it may be known, will not, if he be wise, greatly concern himself though he be called miserly. Because in time he will come to be regarded as more and more liberal, when it is seen that through his parsimony his revenues are sufficient; that he is able to defend himself against any who make war on him; that he can engage in enterprises against others without burdening his subjects; and thus exercise liberality towards all from whom he does not take, whose number is infinite, while he is miserly in respect of those only to whom he does not give, whose number is few.

In our own days we have seen no Princes accomplish great results save those who have been accounted miserly. All others have been ruined. Pope Julius II, after availing himself of his reputation for liberality to arrive at the Papacy, made no effort to preserve that reputation when making war on the King of France, but carried on all his numerous campaigns without levying from his subjects a single extraordinary tax, providing for the increased expenditure out of his long-continued savings. Had the present King of Spain been accounted liberal, he never could have engaged or succeeded in so many enterprises.

A Prince, therefore, if he is enabled thereby to forbear from plundering his subjects, to defend himself, to escape poverty and contempt, and the necessity of becoming rapacious, ought to care little though he incur the reproach of miserliness, for this is one of those vices which enable him to reign.

And should any object that Cæsar by his liberality rose to power, and that many others have been advanced to the highest dignities from their having been liberal and so reputed, I reply, 'Either you are already a Prince or you seek to become one; in the former case liberality is hurtful, in the latter it is very necessary that you be thought liberal; Cæsar was one of those who sought the sovereignty of Rome; but if after obtaining it he had lived on without retrenching his expenditure, he must have ruined the Empire.' And if it be further urged that many Princes reputed to have been most liberal have achieved great things with their armies, I answer that a Prince spends either what belongs to himself and his subjects, or what belongs to others; and that in the former case he ought to be sparing, but in the latter ought not to refrain from any kind of liberality. Because for a Prince who leads his armies in person and maintains them by plunder, pillage, and forced contributions, dealing as he does with the property of others this liberality is necessary, since otherwise he would not be followed by his soldiers. Of what does not belong to you or to your subjects you should, therefore, be a lavish giver, as were Cyrus, Cæsar, and Alexander; for to be liberal with the property of others does not take from your reputation, but adds to it. What injures you is to give away what is your own. And there is no quality so self-destructive as liberality; for while you practise it you lose the means whereby it can be practised, and become poor and despised, or else, to avoid poverty, you become rapacious and hated. For liberality leads to one or other of these two results, against which, beyond all others, a Prince should guard.

Wherefore it is wiser to put up with the name of being miserly, which breeds ignominy, but without hate, than to be obliged, from the desire to be reckoned liberal, to incur the reproach of rapacity, which breeds hate as well as ignominy.

CHAPTER XVII

OF CRUELTY AND CLEMENCY, AND WHETHER IT IS BETTER TO BE LOVED OR FEARED

PASSING TO THE other qualities above referred to, I say that every Prince should desire to be accounted merciful and not cruel. Nevertheless, he should be on his guard against the abuse of this quality of mercy. Cesare Borgia was reputed cruel, yet his cruelty restored Romagna, united it, and brought it to order and obedience; so that if we look at things in their true light, it will be seen that he was in reality far more merciful than the people of Florence, who, to avoid the imputation of cruelty, suffered Pistoja to be torn to pieces by factions.

A Prince should therefore disregard the reproach of being thought cruel where it enables him to keep his subjects united and obedient. For he who quells disorder by a very few signal examples will in the end be more merciful than he who from too great leniency permits things to take their course and so to result in rapine and bloodshed; for these hurt the whole State, whereas the severities of the Prince injure individuals only.

And for a new Prince, of all others, it is impossible to escape a name for cruelty, since new States are full of dangers. Wherefore Virgil, by the mouth of Dido, excuses the harshness of her reign on the plea that it was new, saying:—

A fate unkind, and newness in my reign
Compel me thus to guard a wide domain.

Nevertheless, the new Prince should not be too ready of belief, nor too easily set in motion; nor should he himself be the first to raise alarms; but should so temper prudence with kindliness that too great confidence in others shall not throw him off his guard, nor groundless distrust render him insupportable.

And here comes in the question whether it is better to be loved rather than feared, or feared rather than loved. It might perhaps be answered that we should wish to be both; but since love and fear can hardly exist together, if we must choose between them, it is far safer to be feared than loved. For of men it may generally be affirmed that they are thankless, fickle, false, studious to avoid danger, greedy of gain, devoted to you while you are able to confer benefits upon them, and ready, as I said before, while danger is distant, to shed their blood, and sacrifice their property, their lives, and their children for you; but in the hour of need they turn against you. The Prince, therefore, who without otherwise securing himself builds wholly on their professions is undone. For the friendships which we buy with a price, and do not gain by greatness and nobility of character, though they be fairly earned are not made good, but fail us when we have occasion to use them.

Moreover, men are less careful how they offend him who makes himself loved than him who makes himself feared. For love is held by the tie of obligation, which, because men are a sorry breed, is broken on every whisper of private interest; but fear is bound by the apprehension of punishment which never relaxes its grasp.

Nevertheless a Prince should inspire fear in such a fashion that if he do not win love he may escape hate. For a man may very well be feared and yet not hated, and this will be the case so long as he does not meddle with the property or with the women of his citizens and subjects. And if constrained to put any to death, he should do so only when there is manifest cause or reasonable justification. But, above all, he must abstain from the property of others. For men will sooner forget the death of their father than the loss of their patrimony. Moreover, pretexts for confiscation are never to seek, and he who has once begun to live by rapine always finds reasons for taking what is not his; whereas reasons for shedding blood are fewer, and sooner exhausted.

But when a Prince is with his army, and has many soldiers under his command, he must needs disregard the reproach of cruelty, for without such a reputation in its Captain, no army can be held together or kept under any kind of control. Among other things remarkable in Hannibal this has been noted, that having a very great army, made up of men of many different nations and brought to fight in a foreign country, no dissension ever arose among the soldiers themselves, nor any mutiny against their leader, either in his good or in his evil fortunes. This we can only ascribe to the transcendent cruelty, which, joined with numberless great qualities, rendered him at once venerable and terrible in the eyes of his soldiers; for without this reputation for cruelty these other virtues would not have produced the like results.

Unreflecting writers, indeed, while they praise his achievements, have condemned the chief cause of them; but that his other merits would not by themselves have been so efficacious we may see from the case of Scipio, one of the greatest Captains, not of his own time only but of all times of which we have record, whose armies rose against him in Spain from no other cause than his too great leniency in allowing them a freedom inconsistent with military strictness. With which weakness Fabius Maximus taxed him in the Senate House, calling him the corrupter of the Roman soldiery. Again, when the Locrians were shamefully outraged by one of his lieutenants, he neither avenged them, nor punished the insolence of his officer; and this from the natural easiness of his disposition. So that it was said in the Senate by one who sought to excuse him, that there were many who knew better how to refrain from doing wrong themselves than how to correct the wrong-doing of others. This temper, however, must in time have marred the name and fame even of Scipio, had he continued in it, and retained his command. But living as he did under the control of the Senate, this hurtful quality was not merely disguised, but came to be regarded as a glory.

Returning to the question of being loved or feared, I sum up by saying, that since his being loved depends upon his subjects, while his being feared depends upon himself, a wise Prince should build on what is his own, and not on what rests with others. Only, as I have said, he must do his utmost to escape hatred.

CHAPTER XVIII

HOW PRINCES SHOULD KEEP FAITH

EVERYONE UNDERSTANDS HOW praiseworthy it is in a Prince to keep faith, and to live uprightly and not craftily. Nevertheless, we see from what has taken place in our own days that Princes who have set little store by their word, but have known how to overreach men by their cunning, have accomplished great things, and in the end got the better of those who trusted to honest dealing.

Be it known, then, that there are two ways of contending, one in accordance with the laws, the other by force; the first of which is proper to men, the second to beasts. But since the first method is often ineffectual, it becomes necessary to resort to the second. A Prince should, therefore, understand how to use well both the man and the beast. And this lesson has been covertly taught by the ancient writers, who relate how Achilles and many others of these old Princes were given over to be brought up and trained by Chiron the Centaur; since the only meaning of their having for instructor one who was half man and half beast is, that it is necessary for a Prince to know how to use both natures, and that the one without the other has no stability.

HE OUGHT NOT TO QUIT GOOD COURSES IF HE CAN HELP IT, BUT SHOULD KNOW HOW TO FOLLOW EVIL COURSES IF HE MUST.

But since a Prince should know how to use the beast's nature wisely, he ought of beasts to choose both the lion and the fox; for the lion cannot guard himself from the toils, nor the fox from wolves. He must therefore be a fox to discern toils, and a lion to drive off wolves.

To rely wholly on the lion is unwise; and for this reason a prudent Prince neither can nor ought to keep his word when to keep it is hurtful to him and the causes which led him to pledge it are removed. If all men were good, this would not be good advice, but since they are dishonest and do not keep faith with you, you, in return, need not keep faith with them; and no prince was ever at a loss for plausible reasons to cloak a breach of faith. Of this numberless recent instances could be given, and it might be shown how many solemn treaties and engagements have been rendered inoperative and idle through want of faith in Princes, and that he who was best known to play the fox has had the best success.

It is necessary, indeed, to put a good colour on this nature, and to be skilful in simulating and dissembling. But men are so simple, and governed so absolutely by their present needs, that he who wishes to deceive will never fail in finding willing dupes. One recent example I will not omit. Pope Alexander VI had no care or thought but how to deceive, and always found material to work on. No man ever had a more effective manner of asseverating, or made promises with more solemn protestations, or observed them less. And yet, because he understood this side of human nature, his frauds always succeeded.

It is not essential, then, that a Prince should have all the good qualities which I have enumerated above, but it is most essential that he should seem to have them; I will even venture to affirm that if he has and invariably practises them all, they are hurtful, whereas the appearance of having them is useful. Thus, it is well to seem merciful, faithful, humane, religious, and upright, and also to be so; but the mind should remain so balanced that were it needful not to be so, you should be able and know how to change to the contrary.

And you are to understand that a Prince, and most of all a new Prince, cannot observe all those rules of conduct in respect whereof men are accounted good, being often forced, in order to preserve his Princedom, to act in opposition to good faith, charity, humanity, and religion. He must therefore keep his mind ready to shift as the winds and tides of Fortune turn, and, as I have already said, he ought not to quit good courses if he can help it, but should know how to follow evil courses if he must.

A Prince should therefore be very careful that nothing ever escapes his lips which is not replete with the five qualities above named, so that to see and hear him, one would think him the embodiment of mercy, good faith, integrity, humanity, and religion. And there is no virtue which it is more necessary for him to seem to possess than this last; because men in general judge rather by the eye than by the hand, for every one can see but few can touch. Every one sees what you seem, but few know what you are, and these few dare not oppose themselves to the opinion of the many who have the majesty of the State to back them up.

Moreover, in the actions of all men, and most of all of Princes, where there is no tribunal to which we can appeal, we look to results. Wherefore if a Prince succeeds in establishing and maintaining his authority, the means will always be judged honourable and be approved by every one. For the vulgar are always taken by appearances and by results, and the world is made up of the vulgar, the few only finding room when the many have no longer ground to stand on.

A certain Prince of our own days, whose name it is as well not to mention, is always preaching peace and good faith, although the mortal enemy of both; and both, had he practised them as he preaches them, would, oftener than once, have lost him his kingdom and authority.

CHAPTER XIX

THAT A PRINCE SHOULD SEEK TO ESCAPE CONTEMPT AND HATRED

HAVING NOW SPOKEN of the chief of the qualities above referred to, the rest I shall dispose of briefly with these general remarks, that a Prince, as has already in part been said, should consider how he may avoid such courses as would make him hated or despised; and that whenever he succeeds in keeping clear of these, he has performed his part, and runs no risk though he incur other infamies.

A Prince, as I have said before, sooner becomes hated by being rapacious and by interfering with the property and with the women of his subjects, than in any other way. From these, therefore, he should abstain. For so long as neither their property nor their honour is touched, the mass of mankind live contentedly, and the Prince has only to cope with the ambition of a few, which can in many ways and easily be kept within bounds.

A Prince is despised when he is seen to be fickle, frivolous, effeminate, pusillanimous, or irresolute, against which defects he ought therefore most carefully to guard, striving so to bear himself that greatness, courage, wisdom, and strength may appear in all his actions. In his private dealings with his subjects his decisions should be irrevocable, and his reputation such that no one would dream of overreaching or cajoling him.

The Prince who inspires such an opinion of himself is greatly esteemed, and against one who is greatly esteemed conspiracy is difficult; nor, when he is known to be an excellent Prince and held in reverence by his subjects, will it be easy to attack him. For a Prince is exposed to two dangers, from within in respect of his subjects, from without in respect of foreign powers. Against the latter he will defend himself with good arms and good allies, and if he have good arms he will always have good allies; and when things are settled abroad, they will always be settled at home, unless disturbed by conspiracies; and even should there be hostility from without, if he has taken those measures, and has lived in the way I have recommended, and if he never abandons hope, he will withstand every attack; as I have said was done by Nabis the Spartan.

As regards his own subjects, when affairs are quiet abroad, he has to fear they may engage in secret plots; against which a Prince best secures himself when he escapes being hated or despised, and keeps on good terms with his people; and this, as I have already shown at length, it is essential he should do. Not to be hated or despised by the body of his subjects, is one of the surest safeguards that a Prince can have against conspiracy. For he who conspires always reckons on pleasing the people by putting the Prince to death; but when he sees that instead of pleasing he will offend them, he cannot summon courage to carry out his design. For the difficulties that attend conspirators are infinite, and we know from experience that while there have been many conspiracies, few of them have succeeded.

He who conspires cannot do so alone, nor can he assume as his companions any save those whom he believes to be discontented; but so soon as you impart your design to a discontented man, you supply him with the means of removing his discontent, since by betraying you he can procure for himself every advantage; so that seeing on the one hand certain gain, and on the other a doubtful and dangerous risk, he must either be a rare friend to you, or the mortal enemy of his Prince, if he keep your secret.

To put the matter shortly, I say that on the side of the conspirator there are distrust, jealousy, and dread of punishment to deter him, while on the side of the Prince there are the laws, the majesty of the throne, the protection of friends and of the government to defend him; to which if the general good-will of the people be added, it is hardly possible that any should be rash enough to conspire. For while in ordinary cases, the conspirator has ground for fear only before the execution of his villainy, in this case he has also cause to fear after the crime has been perpetrated, since he has the people for his enemy, and is thus cut off from every hope of shelter.

Of this, endless instances might be given, but I shall content myself with one that happened within the recollection of our fathers. Messer Annibale Bentivoglio, Lord of Bologna and grandfather of the present Messer Annibale, was conspired against and murdered by the Canneschi, leaving behind none belonging to him save Messer Giovanni, then an infant in arms. Immediately upon the murder, the people rose and put all the Canneschi to death. This resulted from the general good-will with which the House of the Bentivogli was then regarded in Bologna; which feeling was so strong, that when upon the death of Messer Annibale no one was left who could govern the State, there being reason to believe that a descendant of the family (who up to that time had been thought to be the son of a smith) was living in Florence, the citizens of Bologna came there for him, and entrusted him with the government of their city; which he retained until Messer Giovanni was old enough to govern.

To be brief, a Prince has little to fear from conspiracies when his subjects are well disposed towards him; but when they are hostile and hold him in detestation, he has then reason to fear everything and every one. And well ordered States and wise Princes have provided with extreme care that the nobility shall not be driven to desperation, and that the commons shall be kept satisfied and contented; for this is one of the most important matters that a Prince has to look to.

Among the well ordered and governed Kingdoms of our day is that of France, wherein we find an infinite number of wise institutions, upon which depend the freedom and the security of the King, and of which the most important are the Parliament and its authority. For he who gave its constitution to this Realm, knowing the ambition and arrogance of the nobles, and judging it necessary to bridle and restrain them, and on the other hand knowing the hatred, originating in fear, entertained against them by the commons, and desiring that they should be safe, was unwilling that the responsibility for this should rest on the King; and to relieve him of the ill-will which he might incur with the nobles by favouring the commons, or with the commons by favouring the nobles, appointed a third party to be arbitrator, who without committing the King, might depress the nobles and uphold the commons. Nor could there be any better, wiser, or surer safeguard for the King and the Kingdom. And hence we may draw another notable lesson, namely, that Princes should devolve on others those matters that entail responsibility, and reserve to themselves those that relate to grace and favour. And again I say that a Prince should esteem the great, but must not make himself odious to the people.

To some it may perhaps appear, that if the lives and deaths of many of the Roman Emperors be considered, they offer examples opposed to the views expressed by me; since we find that some among them who had always lived good lives, and shown themselves possessed of great qualities, were nevertheless deposed and even put to death by their subjects who had conspired against them.

In answer to such objections, I shall examine the characters of several Emperors, and show that the causes of their downfall were in no way different from those which I have indicated. In doing this I shall submit for consideration such matters only as must strike every one who reads the history of these times; and it will be enough for my purpose to take those Emperors who reigned from the time of Marcus the Philosopher to the time of Maximinus, who were, inclusively, Marcus, Commodus his son, Pertinax, Julianus, Severus, Caracalla his son, Macrinus, Heliogabalus, Alexander, and Maximinus.

In the first place, then, we have to note that while in other Princedoms the Prince has only to contend with the ambition of the nobles and the insubordination of the people, the Roman Emperors had a further difficulty to encounter in the cruelty and rapacity of their soldiers, which were so distracting as to cause the ruin of many of these Princes. For it was hardly possible for them to satisfy both the soldiers and the people; the latter loving peace and therefore preferring sober Princes, while the former preferred a Prince of a warlike spirit, however harsh, haughty, or rapacious; being willing that he should exercise these qualities against the people, as the means of procuring for themselves double pay, and indulging their greed and cruelty.

Whence it followed that those Emperors who had not inherited or won for themselves such authority as enabled them to keep both people and soldiers in check, were always ruined. The most of them, and those especially who came to the Empire new and without experience, seeing the difficulty of dealing with these conflicting humours, set themselves to satisfy the soldiers, and made little account of offending the people. And for them this was a necessary course to take; for as Princes cannot escape being hated by some, they should, in the first place, endeavour not to be hated by a class; failing in which, they must do all they can to escape the hatred of that class which is the stronger. Wherefore those Emperors who, by reason of their newness, stood in need of extraordinary support, sided with the soldiery rather than with the people; a course which turned out advantageous or otherwise, according as the Prince knew, or did not know, how to maintain his authority over them.

From the causes indicated it resulted that Marcus, Pertinax, and Alexander, being Princes of a temperate disposition, lovers of justice, enemies of cruelty, gentle, and kindly, had all, save Marcus, an unhappy end. Marcus alone lived and died honoured in the highest degree; and this because he had succeeded to the Empire by right of inheritance, and not through the favour either of the soldiery or of the people; and also because, being endowed with many virtues which made him revered, he kept, while he lived, both factions within bounds, and was never either hated or despised.

But Pertinax was chosen Emperor against the will of the soldiery, who being accustomed to a licentious life under Commodus, could not tolerate the stricter discipline to which his successor sought to bring them back. And having thus made himself hated, and being at the same time despised by reason of his advanced age, he was ruined at the very outset of his reign.

And here it is to be noted that hatred is incurred as well on account of good actions as of bad; for which reason, as I have already said, a Prince who would maintain his authority is often compelled to be other than good. For when the class, be it the people, the soldiers, or the nobles, on whom you judge it necessary to rely for your support, is corrupt, you must needs adapt yourself to its humours, and satisfy these, in which case virtuous conduct will only prejudice you.

Let us now come to Alexander, who was so just a ruler that among the praises ascribed to him it is recorded, that, during the fourteen years he held the Empire, no man was ever put to death by him without trial. Nevertheless, being accounted effeminate, and thought to be governed by his mother, he fell into contempt, and the army conspiring against him, slew him.

When we turn to consider the characters of Commodus, Severus, and Caracalla, we find them all to have been most cruel and rapacious Princes, who to satisfy the soldiery, scrupled not to inflict every kind of wrong upon the people. And all of them, except Severus, came to a bad end. But in Severus there was such strength of character, that, keeping the soldiers his friends, he was able, although he oppressed the people, to reign on prosperously to the last; because his great qualities made him so admirable in the eyes both of the people and the soldiers, that the former remained in a manner amazed and awestruck, while the latter were respectful and contented.

And because his actions, for one who was a new Prince, were thus remarkable, I will point out shortly how well he understood to play the part both of the lion and of the fox, each of which natures, as I have observed before, a Prince should know how to assume.

Knowing the indolent disposition of the Emperor Julianus, Severus persuaded the army which he commanded in Illyria that it was their duty to go to Rome to avenge the death of Pertinax, who had been slain by the Pretorian guards. Under this pretext, and without disclosing his design on the Empire, he put his army in march, and reached Italy before it was known that he had set out. On his arrival in Rome, the Senate, through fear, elected him Emperor and put Julianus to death. After taking this first step, two obstacles still remained to his becoming sole master of the Empire; one in Asia, where Niger who commanded the armies of the East had caused himself to be proclaimed Emperor; the other in the West, where Albinus, who also aspired to the Empire, was in command. And as Severus judged it dangerous to declare open war against both, he resolved to proceed against Niger by arms, and against Albinus by artifice. To the latter, accordingly, he wrote, that having been chosen Emperor by the Senate, he desired to share the dignity with him; that he therefore sent him the title of Cæsar, and in accordance with a resolution of the Senate assumed him as his colleague. All which statements Albinus accepted as true. But so soon as Severus had defeated and slain Niger, and restored tranquillity in the East, returning to Rome he complained in the Senate that Albainus, all unmindful of the favours he had received from him, had treacherously sought to destroy him; for which cause he was compelled to go and punish his ingratitude. Whereupon he set forth to seek Albinus in Gaul, where he at once deprived him of his dignities and his life.

Whoever, therefore, examines carefully the actions of this Emperor, will find in him all the fierceness of the lion and all the craft of the fox, and will note how he was feared and respected by the people, yet not hated by the army, and will not be surprised that though a new man, he was able to maintain his hold of so great an Empire. For the splendour of his reputation always shielded him from the odium which the people might otherwise have conceived against him by reason of his cruelty and rapacity.

Caracalla, his son, was likewise a man of great parts, endowed with qualities that made him admirable in the sight of the people, and endeared him to the army, being of a warlike spirit, most patient of fatigue, and contemning all luxury in food and every other effeminacy. Nevertheless, his ferocity and cruelty were so extravagant and unheard of (he having put to death a vast number of the inhabitants of Rome at different times, and the whole of those of Alexandria at a stroke), that he came to be detested by all the world, and so feared even by those whom he had about him, that at the last he was slain by a centurion in the midst of his army.

And here let it be noted that deaths like this which are the result of a deliberate and fixed resolve, cannot be escaped by Princes, since any one who disregards his own life can effect them. A Prince, however, needs the less to fear them as they are seldom attempted. The only precaution he can take is to avoid doing grave wrong to any of those who serve him, or whom he has near him as officers of his Court, a precaution which Caracalla neglected in putting to a shameful death the brother of this centurion, and in using daily threats against the man himself whom he nevertheless retained as one of his bodyguard. This, as the event showed, was a rash and fatal course.

We come next to Commodus, who, as he took the Empire by hereditary right, ought to have held it with much ease. For being the son of Marcus, he had only to follow in his father's footsteps to content both the people and the soldiery. But being of a cruel and brutal nature, to sate his rapacity at the expense of the people, he sought support from the army, and indulged it in every kind of excess. On the other hand, by an utter disregard of his dignity, in frequently descending into the arena to fight with gladiators, and by other base acts wholly unworthy of the Imperial station, he became contemptible in the eyes of the soldiery; and being on the one hand hated, on the other despised, was at last conspired against and murdered.

The character of Maximinus remains to be touched upon. He was of a very warlike disposition, and on the death of Alexander, of whom we have already spoken, was chosen Emperor by the army who had been displeased with the effeminacy of that Prince. But this dignity he did not long enjoy, since two causes concurred to render him at once odious and contemptible; the one the baseness of his origin, he having at one time herded sheep in Thrace, a fact well known to all, and which led all to look on him with disdain; the other that on being proclaimed Emperor, delaying to repair to Rome and enter on possession of the Imperial throne, he incurred the reputation of excessive cruelty by reason of the many atrocities perpetrated by his prefects in Rome and other parts of the Empire. The result was that the whole world, stirred at once with scorn of his mean birth and with the hatred which the dread of his ferocity inspired, combined against him, Africa leading the way, the Senate and people of Rome and the whole of Italy following. In which conspiracy his own army joined. For they, being engaged in the siege of Aquileja and finding difficulty in reducing it, disgusted with his cruelty, and less afraid of him when they saw so many against him, put him to death.

I need say nothing of Heliogabalus, Macrinus, or Julianus, all of whom being utterly despicable, came to a speedy downfall, but shall conclude these remarks by observing, that the Princes of our own days are less troubled with the difficulty of having to make constant efforts to keep their soldiers in good humour. For though they must treat them with some indulgence, the need for doing so is soon over, since none of these Princes possesses a standing army which, like the armies of the Roman Empire, has strengthened with the growth of his government and the administration of his State. And if it was then necessary to satisfy the soldiers rather than the people, because the soldiers were more powerful than the people, now it is more necessary for all Princes, except the Turk and the Soldan, to satisfy the people rather than the soldiery, since the former are more powerful than the latter.

I except the Turk because he has always about him some twelve thousand foot soldiers and fifteen thousand horse, on whom depend the security and strength of his kingdom, and with whom he must needs keep on good terms, all regard for the people being subordinate. The government of the Soldan is similar, so that he too being wholly in the hands of his soldiers, must keep well with them without regard to the people.

And here you are to note that the State of the Soldan, while it is unlike all other Princedoms, resembles the Christian Pontificate in this, that it can neither be classed as new, nor as hereditary. For the sons of a Soldan who dies do not succeed to the kingdom as his heirs, but he who is elected to the post by those who have authority to make such elections. And this being the ancient and established order of things, the Princedom cannot be accounted new; since none of the difficulties that attend new Princedoms are found in it. For although the Prince be new, the institutions of the State are old, and are so contrived that the elected

Prince is accepted as though he were an hereditary Sovereign.

But returning to the matter in hand, I say that whoever reflects on the above reasoning will see that either hatred or contempt was the ruin of the Emperors whom I have named; and will also understand how it happened that some taking one way and some the opposite, one only by each of these roads came to a happy, and all the rest to an unhappy end. Because for Pertinax and Alexander, they being new Princes, it was useless and hurtful to try to imitate Marcus, who was an hereditary Prince; and similarly for Caracalla, Commodus, and Maximinus it was a fatal error to imitate Severus, since they lacked the qualities that would have enabled them to tread in his footsteps.

In short, a Prince new to the Princedom cannot imitate the actions of Marcus, nor is it necessary that he should imitate all those of Severus; but he should borrow from Severus those parts of his conduct which are needed to serve as a foundation for his government, and from Marcus those suited to maintain it, and render it glorious when once established.

CHAPTER XX

WHETHER FORTRESSES, AND CERTAIN OTHER EXPEDIENTS TO WHICH PRINCES OFTEN HAVE RECOURSE, ARE PROFITABLE OR HURTFUL

TO GOVERN MORE securely some Princes have disarmed their subjects, others have kept the towns subject to them divided by factions; some have fostered hostility against themselves, others have sought to gain over those who at the beginning of their reign were looked on with suspicion; some have built fortresses, others have dismantled and destroyed them; and though no definite judgment can be pronounced respecting any of these methods, without regard to the special circumstances of the State to which it is proposed to apply them, I shall nevertheless speak of them in as comprehensive a way as the nature of the subject will admit.

It has never chanced that any new Prince has disarmed his subjects. On the contrary, when he has found them unarmed he has always armed them. For the arms thus provided become yours, those whom you suspected grow faithful, while those who were faithful at the first, continue so, and from your subjects become your partisans. And though all your subjects cannot be armed, yet if those of them whom you arm be treated with marked favour, you can deal more securely with the rest. For the difference which those whom you supply with arms perceive in their treatment, will bind them to you, while the others will excuse you, recognizing that those who incur greater risk and responsibility merit greater rewards. But by disarming, you at once give offence, since you show your subjects that you distrust them, either as doubting their courage, or as doubting their fidelity, each of which imputations begets hatred against you. Moreover, as you cannot maintain yourself without arms you must have recourse to mercenary troops. What these are I have already shown, but even if they were good, they could never avail to defend you, at once against powerful enemies abroad and against subjects whom you distrust. Wherefore, as I have said already, new Princes in new Princedoms have always provided for their being armed; and of instances of this History is full.

But when a Prince acquires a new State, which thus becomes joined on like a limb to his old possessions, he must disarm its inhabitants, except such of them as have taken part with him while he was acquiring it, and even these, as time and occasion serve, he should seek to render soft and effeminate; and he must so manage matters that all the arms of the new State shall be in the hands of his own soldiers who have served under him in his ancient dominions.

Our forefathers, even such among them as were esteemed wise, were wont to say that '*Pistoja was to be held by feuds, and Pisa by fortresses*,' and on this principle used to promote dissensions in various subject towns with a view to retain them with less effort. At a time when Italy was in some measure in equilibrium, this may have been a prudent course to follow; but at the present day it seems impossible to recommend it as a general rule of policy. For I do not believe that divisions purposely caused can ever lead to good; on the contrary, when an enemy approaches, divided cities are lost at once, for the weaker faction will always side with the invader, and the other will not be able to stand alone.

The Venetians, influenced as I believe by the reasons above mentioned, fostered the factions of Guelf and Ghibelline in the cities subject to them; and though they did not suffer blood to be shed, fomented their feuds, in order that the citizens having their minds occupied with these disputes might not conspire against them. But this, as we know, did not turn out to their advantage, for after their defeat at Vaila, one of the two factions, suddenly taking courage, deprived them of the whole of their territory.

Moreover methods like these argue weakness in a Prince, for under a strong government such divisions would never be permitted, since they are profitable only in time of peace as an expedient whereby subjects may be more easily managed; but when war breaks out their insufficiency is demonstrated.

Doubtless, Princes become great by vanquishing difficulties and opposition, and Fortune, on that account, when she desires to aggrandize a new Prince, who has more need than an hereditary Prince to win reputation, causes enemies to spring up, and urges them on to attack him, to the end that he may have opportunities to overcome them, and make his ascent by the very ladder which they have planted. For which reason, many are of the opinion that a wise Prince, when he has the occasion, ought dexterously to promote hostility to himself in certain quarters, in order that his greatness may be enhanced by crushing it.

Princes, and new Princes especially, have found greater fidelity and helpfulness in those whom, at the beginning of their reign, they have held in suspicion, than in those who at the outset have enjoyed their confidence; and Pandolfo Petrucci, Lord of Siena, governed his State by the instrumentality of those whom he had at one time distrusted, in preference to all others. But on this point it is impossible to lay down any general rule, since the course to be followed varies with the circumstances. This only I will say, that those men who at the beginning of a reign have been hostile, if of a sort requiring support to maintain them, may always be won over by the Prince with much ease, and are the more bound to serve him faithfully because they know that they have to efface by their conduct the unfavourable impression he had formed of them; and in this way a Prince always obtains better help from them, than from those who serving him in too complete security neglect his affairs.

And since the subject suggests it, I must not fail to remind the Prince who acquires a new State through the favour of its inhabitants, to weigh well what were the causes which led those who favoured him to do so; and if it be seen that they have acted not from any natural affection for him, but merely out of discontent with the former government, that he will find the greatest difficulty in keeping them his friends, since it will be impossible for him to content them. Carefully considering the cause of this, with the aid of examples taken from times ancient and modern, he will perceive that it is far easier to secure the friendship of those who being satisfied with things as they stood, were for that very reason his enemies, than of those who sided with him and aided him in his usurpation only because they were discontented.

It has been customary for Princes, with a view to hold their dominions more securely, to build fortresses which might serve as a curb and restraint on such as have designs against them, and as a safe refuge against a first onset. I approve this custom, because it has been followed from the earliest times. Nevertheless, in our own days, Messer Niccolò Vitelli thought it prudent to dismantle two fortresses in Città di Castello in order to secure that town: and Guido Ubaldo, Duke of Urbino, on returning to his dominions, whence he had been driven by Cesare Borgia, razed to their foundations the fortresses throughout the Dukedom, judging that if these were removed, it would not again be so easily lost. A like course was followed by the Bentivogli on their return to Bologna.

Fortresses, therefore, are useful or no, according to circumstances, and if in one way they benefit, in another they injure you. We may state the case thus: the Prince who is more afraid of his subjects than of strangers ought to build fortresses, while he who is more afraid of strangers than of his subjects, should leave them alone. The citadel built by Francesco Sforza in Milan, has been, and will hereafter prove to be, more dangerous to the House of Sforza than any other disorder of that State. So that, on the whole, the best fortress you can have, is in not being hated by your subjects. If they hate you no fortress will save you; for when once the people take up arms, foreigners are never wanting to assist them.

Within our own time it does not appear that fortresses have been of service to any Prince, unless to the Countess of Forlì after her husband Count Girolamo was murdered; for by this means she was able to escape the first onset of the insurgents, and awaiting succour from Milan, to recover her State; the circumstances of the times not allowing any foreigner to lend assistance to the people. But afterwards, when she was attacked by Cesare Borgia, and the people, out of hostility to her, took part with the invader, her fortresses were of little avail. So that, both on this and on the former occasion, it would have been safer for her to have had no fortresses, than to have had her subjects for enemies.

All which considerations taken into account, I shall applaud him who builds fortresses, and him who does not; but I shall blame him who, trusting in them, reckons it a light thing to be held in hatred by his people.

CHAPTER XXI

HOW A PRINCE SHOULD BEAR HIMSELF SO AS TO ACQUIRE REPUTATION

NOTHING MAKES A Prince so well thought of as to undertake great enterprises and give striking proofs of his capacity.

Among the Princes of our time Ferdinand of Aragon, the present King of Spain, may almost be accounted a new Prince, since from one of the weakest he has become, for fame and glory, the foremost King in Christendom. And if you consider his achievements you will find them all great and some extraordinary.

In the beginning of his reign he made war on Granada, which enterprise was the foundation of his power. At first he carried on the war leisurely, without fear of interruption, and kept the attention and thoughts of the Barons of Castile so completely occupied with it, that they had no time to think of changes at home. Meanwhile he insensibly acquired reputation among them and authority over them. With the money of the Church and of his subjects he was able to maintain his armies, and during the prolonged contest to lay the foundations of that military discipline which afterwards made him so famous. Moreover, to enable him to engage in still greater undertakings, always covering himself with the cloak of religion, he had recourse to what may be called *pious cruelty*, in driving out and clearing his Kingdom of the Moors; than which exploit none could be more wonderful or uncommon. Using the same pretext he made war on Africa, invaded Italy, and finally attacked France; and being thus constantly busied in planning and executing vast designs, he kept the minds of his subjects in suspense and admiration, and occupied with the results of his actions, which arose one out of another in such close succession as left neither time nor opportunity to oppose them.

Again, it greatly profits a Prince in conducting the internal government of his State, to follow striking methods, such as are recorded of Messer Bernabò of Milan, whenever the remarkable actions of any one in civil life, whether for good or for evil, afford him occasion; and to choose such ways of rewarding and punishing as cannot fail to be much spoken of. But above all, he should strive by all his actions to inspire a sense of his greatness and goodness.

A Prince is likewise esteemed who is a stanch friend and a thorough foe, that is to say, who without reserve openly declares for one against another, this being always a more advantageous course than to stand neutral. For supposing two of your powerful neighbours come to blows, it must either be that you have, or have not, reason to fear the one who comes off victorious. In either case it will always be well for you to declare yourself, and join in frankly with one side or other. For should you fail to do so you are certain, in the former of the cases put, to become the prey of the victor to the satisfaction and delight of the vanquished, and no reason or circumstance that you may plead will avail to shield or shelter you; for the victor dislikes doubtful friends, and such as will not help him at a pinch; and the vanquished will have nothing to say to you, since you would not share his fortunes sword in hand.

When Antiochus, at the instance of the Aetolians, passed into Greece in order to drive out the Romans, he sent envoys to the Achaians, who were friendly to the Romans, exhorting them to stand neutral. The Romans, on the other hand, urged them to take up arms on their behalf. The matter coming to be discussed in the Council of the Achaians, the legate of Antiochus again urged neutrality, whereupon the Roman envoy answered—'Nothing can be less to your advantage than the course which has been recommended as the best and most useful for your State, namely, to refrain from taking any part in our war, for by standing aloof you will gain neither favour nor fame, but remain the prize of the victor.' And it will always happen that he who is not your friend will invite you to neutrality, while he who is your friend will call on you to declare yourself openly in arms. Irresolute Princes, to escape immediate danger, commonly follow the neutral path, in most instances to their destruction. But when you pronounce valiantly in favour of one side or other, if he to whom you give your adherence conquers, although he be powerful and you are at his mercy, still he is under obligations to you, and has become your friend; and none are so lost to shame as to destroy with manifest ingratitude, one who has helped them. Besides which, victories are never so complete that the victor can afford to disregard all considerations whatsoever, more especially considerations of justice. On the other hand, if he with whom you take part should lose, you will always be favourably regarded by him; while he can he will aid you, and you become his companion in a cause which may recover.

In the second case, namely, when both combatants are of such limited strength that whichever wins you have no cause to fear, it is all the more prudent for you to take a side, for you will then be ruining the one with the help of the other, who were he wise would endeavour to save him. If he whom you help conquers, he remains in your power, and with your aid he cannot but conquer.

And here let it be noted that a Prince should be careful never to join with one stronger than himself in attacking others, unless, as already said, he be driven to it by necessity. For if he whom you join prevails, you are at his mercy; and Princes, so far as in them lies, should avoid placing themselves at the mercy of others. The Venetians, although they might have declined the alliance, joined with France against the Duke of Milan, which brought about their ruin. But when an alliance cannot be avoided, as was the case with the Florentines when the Pope and Spain together led their armies to attack Lombardy, a Prince, for the reasons given, must take a side. Nor let it be supposed that any State can choose for itself a perfectly safe line of policy. On the contrary, it must reckon on every course which it may take being doubtful; for it happens in all human affairs that we never seek to escape one mischief without falling into another. Prudence therefore consists in knowing how to distinguish degrees of disadvantage, and in accepting a less evil as a good.

Again, a Prince should show himself a patron of merit, and should honour those who excel in every art. He ought accordingly to encourage his subjects by enabling them to pursue their callings, whether mercantile, agricultural, or any other, in security, so that this man shall not be deterred from beautifying his possessions from the apprehension that they may be taken from him, or that other refrain from opening a trade through fear of taxes; and he should provide rewards for those who desire so to employ themselves, and for all who are disposed in any way to add to the greatness of his City or State.

He ought, moreover, at suitable seasons of the year to entertain the people with festivals and shows. And because all cities are divided into guilds and companies, he should show attention to these societies, and sometimes take part in their meetings; offering an example of courtesy and munificence, but always maintaining the dignity of his station, which must under no circumstances be compromised.

CHAPTER XXII

OF THE SECRETARIES OF PRINCES

THE CHOICE OF Ministers is a matter of no small moment to a Prince. Whether they shall be good or no depends on his prudence, so that the readiest conjecture we can form of the character and sagacity of a Prince, is from seeing what sort of men he has about him. When they, are at once capable and faithful, we may always account him wise, since he has known to recognize their merit and to retain their fidelity. But if they be otherwise, we must pronounce unfavourably of him, since he has committed a first fault in making this selection.

There was none who knew Messer Antonio of Venafro as Minister of Pandolfo Petrucci, Lord of Siena, but thought Pandolfo a most prudent ruler in having him for his servant. And since there are three scales of intelligence, one which understands by itself, a second which understands what is shown it by others, and a third which understands neither by itself nor on the showing of others, the first of which is most excellent, the second good, but the third worthless, we must needs admit that if Pandolfo was not in the first of these degrees, he was in the second; for when one has the judgment to discern the good from the bad in what another says or does, though he be devoid of invention, he can recognize the merits and demerits of his servant, and will commend the former while he corrects the latter. The servant cannot hope to deceive such a master, and will continue good.

As to how a Prince is to know his Minister, this unerring rule may be laid down. When you see a Minister thinking more of himself than of you, and in all his actions seeking his own ends, that man can never be a good Minister or one that you can trust. For he who has the charge of the State committed to him, ought not to think of himself, but only of his Prince, and should never bring to the notice of the latter what does not directly concern him. On the other band, to keep his Minister good, the Prince should be considerate of him, dignifying him, enriching him, binding him to himself by benefits, and sharing with him the honours as well as the burthens of the State, so that the abundant honours and wealth bestowed upon him may divert him from seeking them at other hands; while the great responsibilities wherewith he is charged may lead him to dread change, knowing that he cannot stand alone without his master's support. When Prince and Minister are upon this footing they can mutually trust one another; but when the contrary is the case, it will always fare ill with one or other of them.

CHAPTER XXIII

THAT FLATTERERS SHOULD BE SHUNNED

ONE ERROR INTO which Princes, unless very prudent or very fortunate in their choice of friends, are apt to fall, is of so great importance that I must not pass it over. I mean in respect of flatterers. These abound in Courts, because men take such pleasure in their own concerns, and so deceive themselves with regard to them, that they can hardly escape this plague; while even in the effort to escape it there is risk of their incurring contempt.

For there is no way to guard against flattery but by letting it be seen that you take no offence in hearing the truth: but when every one is free to tell you the truth respect falls short. Wherefore a prudent Prince should follow a middle course, by choosing certain discreet men from among his subjects, and allowing them alone free leave to speak their minds on any matter on which he asks their opinion, and on none other. But he ought to ask their opinion on everything, and after hearing what they have to say, should reflect and judge for himself. And with these counsellors collectively, and with each of them separately, his hearing should be such, that each and all of them may know that the more freely they declare their thoughts the better they will be liked. Besides these, the Prince should hearken to no others, but should follow the course determined on, and afterwards adhere firmly to his resolves. Whoever acts otherwise is either undone by flatterers, or from continually vacillating as opinions vary, comes to be held in light esteem.

FOR HE WHO HAS THE CHARGE OF THE STATE COMMITTED TO HIM, OUGHT NOT TO THINK OF HIMSELF, BUT ONLY OF HIS PRINCE.

With reference to this matter, I shall cite a recent instance. Father Luke, who is attached to the Court of the present Emperor Maximilian, in speaking of his Majesty told me, that he seeks advice from none, yet never has his own way; and this from his following a course contrary to that above recommended. For being of a secret disposition, he never discloses his intentions to any, nor asks their opinion; and it is only when his plans are to be carried out that they begin to be discovered and known, and at the same time they begin to be thwarted by those he has about him, when he being facile gives way. Hence it happens that what he does one day, he undoes the next; that his wishes and designs are never fully ascertained; and that it is impossible to build on his resolves.

A Prince, therefore, ought always to take counsel, but at such times and seasons only as he himself pleases, and not when it pleases others; nay, he should discourage every one from obtruding advice on matters on which it is not sought. But he should be free in asking advice, and afterwards, as regards the matters on which he has asked it, a patient hearer of the truth, and even displeased should he perceive that any one, from whatever motive, keeps it back.

But those who think that every Prince who has a name for prudence owes it to the wise counsellors he has around him, and not to any merit of his own, are certainly mistaken; since it is an unerring rule and of universal application that a Prince who is not wise himself cannot be well advised by others, unless by chance he surrender himself to be wholly governed by some one adviser who happens to be supremely prudent; in which case he may, indeed, be well advised; but not for long, since such an adviser will soon deprive him of his Government. If he listen to a multitude of advisers, the Prince who is not wise will never have consistent counsels, nor will he know of himself how to reconcile them. Each of his counsellors will study his own advantage, and the Prince will be unable to detect or correct them. Nor could it well be otherwise, for men will always grow rogues on your hands unless they find themselves under a necessity to be honest.

Hence it follows that good counsels, whencesoever they come, have their origin in the prudence of the Prince, and not the prudence of the Prince in wise counsels.

CHAPTER XXIV

WHY THE PRINCES OF ITALY HAVE LOST THEIR STATES

THE LESSONS ABOVE taught if prudently followed will make a new Prince seem like an old one, and will soon seat him in his place more firmly and securely than if his authority had the sanction of time. For the actions of a new Prince are watched much more closely than those of an hereditary Prince; and when seen to be good are far more effectual than antiquity of blood in gaining men over and attaching them to his cause. For men are more nearly touched by things present than by things past, and when they find themselves well off as they are, enjoy their felicity and seek no further; nay, are ready to do their utmost in defence of the new Prince, provided he be not wanting to himself in other respects. In this way there accrues to him a twofold glory, in having laid the foundations of the new Princedom, and in having strengthened and adorned it with good laws and good arms, with faithful friends and great deeds; as, on the other hand, there is a double disgrace in one who has been born to a Princedom losing it by his own want of wisdom.

And if we contemplate those Lords who in our own times have lost their dominions in Italy, such as the King of Naples, the Duke of Milan, and others, in the first place we shall see, that in respect of arms they have, for reasons already dwelt on, been all alike defective; and next, that some of them have either had the people against them, or if they have had the people with them, have not known how to secure themselves against their nobles. For without such defects as these, States powerful enough to keep an army in the field are never overthrown.

Philip of Macedon, not the father of Alexander the Great, but he who was vanquished by Titus Quintius, had no great State as compared with the strength of the Romans and Greeks who attacked him. Nevertheless, being a

Prince of a warlike spirit, and skilful in gaining the good will of the people and in securing the fidelity of the nobles, he maintained himself for many years against his assailants, and in the end, though he lost some towns, succeeded in saving his Kingdom.

Let those Princes of ours, therefore, who, after holding them for a length of years, have lost their dominions, blame not Fortune but their own inertness. For never having reflected in tranquil times that there might come a change (and it is human nature when the sea is calm not to think of storms), when adversity overtook them, they thought not of defence but only of escape, hoping that their people, disgusted with the arrogance of the conqueror, would some day recall them.

This course may be a good one to follow when all others fail, but it were the height of folly, trusting to it, to abandon every other; since none would wish to fall on the chance of some one else being found to lift him up. It may not happen that you are recalled by your people, or if it happen, it gives you no security. It is an ignoble resource, since it does not depend on you for its success; and those modes of defence are alone good, certain and lasting, which depend upon yourself and your own worth.

CHAPTER XXV

WHAT FORTUNE CAN EFFECT IN HUMAN AFFAIRS, AND HOW SHE MAY BE WITHSTOOD

I AM NOT ignorant that many have been and are of the opinion that human affairs are so governed by Fortune and by God, that men cannot alter them by any prudence of theirs, and indeed have no remedy against them; and for this reason have come to think that it is not worth while to labour much about anything, but that they must leave everything to be determined by chance.

Often when I turn the matter over, I am in part inclined to agree with this opinion, which has had the readier acceptance in our own times from the great changes in things which we have seen, and every day see happen contrary to all human expectation. Nevertheless, that our free will be not wholly set aside, I think it may be the case that Fortune is the mistress of one half our actions, and yet leaves the control of the other half, or a little less, to ourselves. And I would liken her to one of those wild torrents which, when angry, overflow the plains, sweep away trees and houses, and carry off soil from one bank to throw it down upon the other. Every one flees before them, and yields to their fury without the least power to resist. And yet, though this be their nature, it does not follow that in seasons of fair weather, men cannot, by constructing weirs and moles, take such precautions as will cause them when again in flood to pass off by some artificial channel, or at least prevent their course from being so uncontrolled and destructive. And so it is with Fortune, who displays her might where there is no organized strength to resist her, and directs her onset where she knows that there is neither barrier nor embankment to confine her.

And if you look at Italy, which has been at once the seat of these changes and their cause, you will perceive that it is a field without embankment or barrier. For if, like Germany, France, and Spain, it had been guarded with sufficient skill, this inundation, if it ever came upon us, would never have wrought the violent changes which we have witnessed.

This I think enough to say generally touching resistance to Fortune. But confining myself more closely to the matter in hand, I note that one day we see a Prince prospering and the next day overthrown, without detecting any change in his nature or character. This, I believe, comes chiefly from a cause already dwelt upon, namely, that a Prince who rests wholly on Fortune is ruined when she changes. Moreover, I believe that he will prosper most whose mode of acting best adapts itself to the character of the times; and conversely that he will be unprosperous, with whose mode of acting the times do not accord. For we see that men in these matters which lead to the end that each has before him, namely, glory and wealth, proceed by different ways, one with caution, another with impetuosity, one with violence, another with sublety, one with patience, another with its contrary; and that by one or other of these different courses each may succeed.

Again, of two who act cautiously, you shall find that one attains his end, the other not, and that two of different temperament, the one cautious, the other impetuous, are equally successful. All which happens from no other cause than that the character of the times accords or does not accord with their methods of acting. And hence it comes, as I have already said, that two operating differently arrive at the same result, and two operating similarly, the one succeeds and the other not. On this likewise depend the vicissitudes of Fortune. For if to one who conducts himself with caution and patience, time and circumstances are propitious, so that his method of acting is good, he goes on prospering; but if these change he is ruined, because he does not change his method of acting.

For no man is found so prudent as to know how to adapt himself to these changes, both because he cannot deviate from the course to which nature inclines him, and because, having always prospered while adhering to one path, he cannot be persuaded that it would be well for him to forsake it. And so when occasion requires the cautious man to act impetuously, he cannot do so and is undone: whereas, had he changed his nature with time and circumstances, his fortune would have been unchanged.

Pope Julius II proceeded with impetuosity in all his undertakings, and found time and circumstances in such harmony with his mode of acting that be always obtained a happy result. Witness his first expedition against Bologna, when Messer Giovanni Bentivoglio was yet living. The Venetians were not favourable to the enterprise; nor was the King of Spain. Negotiations respecting it with the King of France were still open. Nevertheless, the Pope with his worried hardihood and impetuosity marched in person on the expedition, and by this movement brought the King of Spain and the Venetians to a check, the latter through fear, the former from his eagerness to recover the entire Kingdom of Naples; at the same time, he dragged after him the King of France, who, desiring to have the Pope for an ally in humbling the Venetians, on finding him already in motion saw that he could not refuse him his soldiers without openly offending him. By the impetuosity of his movements, therefore, Julius effected what no other Pontiff endowed with the highest human prudence could. For had he, as any other Pope would have done, put off his departure from Rome until terms had been settled and everything duly arranged, he never would have succeeded. For the King of France would have found a thousand pretexts to delay him, and the others would have menaced him with a thousand alarms. I shall not touch upon his other actions, which were all of a like character, and all of which had a happy issue, since the shortness of his life did not allow him to experience reverses. But if times had overtaken him, tendering a cautious line of conduct necessary, his ruin must have ensued, since he never could have departed from those methods to which nature inclined him.

To be brief, I say that since Fortune changes and men stand fixed in their old ways, they are prosperous so long as there is congruity between them, and the reverse when there is not. Of this, however, I am well persuaded, that it is better to be impetuous than cautious. For Fortune is a woman who to be kept under must be beaten and roughly handled: and we see that she suffers herself to be more readily mastered by those who so treat her than by those who are more timid in their approaches. And always, like a woman, she favours the young, because they are less scrupulous and fiercer, and command her with greater audacity.

CHAPTER XXVI

AN EXHORTATION TO LIBERATE ITALY FROM THE BARBARIANS

TURNING OVER IN my mind all the matters which have above been considered, and debating with myself whether in Italy at the present hour the times are such as might serve to confer honour on a new Prince, and whether a fit opportunity now offers for a prudent and valiant leader to bring about changes glorious for himself and beneficial to the whole Italian people, it seems to me that so many conditions combine to further such an enterprise, that I know of no time so favourable to it as the present. And if, as I have said, it was necessary in order to display the valour of Moses that the children of Israel should be slaves in Egypt, and to know the greatness and courage of Cyrus that the Persians should be oppressed by the Medes, and to illustrate the excellence of Theseus that the Athenians should be scattered and divided, so at this hour, to prove the worth of some Italian hero, it was required that Italy should be brought to her present abject condition, to be more a slave than the Hebrew, more oppressed than the Persian, more disunited than the Athenian, without a head, without order, beaten, spoiled, torn in pieces, over-run and abandoned to destruction in every shape.

But though, heretofore, glimmerings may have been discerned in this man or that, whence it might be conjectured that he was ordained by God for her redemption, nevertheless it has afterwards been seen in the further course of his actions that Fortune has disowned him; so that our country, left almost without life, still waits to know who it is that is to heal her bruises, to put an end to the devastation and plunder of Lombardy, to the exactions and imposts of Naples and Tuscany, and to stanch those wounds of hers which long neglect has changed into running sores.

We see how she prays God to send some one to rescue her from these barbarous cruelties and oppressions. We see too how ready and eager she is to follow any standard were there only some one to raise it. But at present we see no one except in your illustrious House (pre-eminent by its virtues and good fortune, and favoured by God and by the Church whose headship it now holds), who could undertake the part of a deliverer.

But for you this will not be too hard a task, if you keep before your eyes the lives and actions of those whom I have named above. For although these men were singular and extraordinary, after all they were but men, not one of whom had so great an opportunity as now presents itself to you. For their undertakings were not more just than this, nor more easy, nor was God more their friend than yours. The justice of the cause is conspicuous; for that war is just which is necessary, and those arms are sacred from which we derive our only hope. Everywhere there is the strongest disposition to engage in this cause; and where the disposition is strong the difficulty cannot be great, provided you follow the methods observed by those whom I have set before you as models.

But further, we see here extraordinary and unexampled proofs of Divine favour. The sea has been divided; the cloud has attended you on your way; the rock has flowed with water; the manna has rained from heaven; everything has concurred to promote your greatness. What remains to be done must be done by you; since in order not to deprive us of our free will and such share of glory as belongs to us, God will not do everything himself.

Nor is it to be marvelled at if none of those Italians I have named has been able to effect what we hope to see effected by your illustrious House; or that amid so many revolutions and so many warlike movements it should always appear as though the military virtues of Italy were spent; for this comes from her old system being defective, and from no one being found among us capable to strike out anew. Nothing confers such honour on the reformer of a State, as do the new laws and institutions which he devises; for these when they stand on a solid basis and have a greatness in their scope, make him admired and venerated. And in Italy material is not wanting for improvement in every form. If the head be weak the limbs are strong, and we see daily in single combats, or where few are engaged, how superior are the strength, dexterity, and intelligence of Italians. But when it comes to armies, they are nowhere, and this from no other reason than the defects of their leaders. For those who are skilful in arms will not obey, and every one thinks himself skilful, since hitherto we have had none among us so raised by merit or by fortune above his fellows that they should yield him the palm. And hence it happens that for the long period of twenty years, during which so many wars have taken place, whenever there has been an army purely Italian it has always been beaten. To this testify, first Taro, then Alessandria, Capua, Genoa, Vaila, Bologna, Mestri.

If then your illustrious House should seek to follow the example of those great men who have delivered their country in past ages, it is before all things necessary, as the true foundation of every such attempt, to be provided with national troops, since you can have no braver, truer, or more faithful soldiers; and although every single man of them be good, collectively they will be better, seeing themselves commanded by their own Prince, and honoured and esteemed by him. That you may be able, therefore, to defend yourself against the foreigner with Italian valour, the first step is to provide yourself with an army such as this.

And although the Swiss and the Spanish infantry are each esteemed formidable, there are yet defects in both, by reason of which troops trnd these are matters in reforming which the new Prince acquires reputation and importance.

This opportunity then, for Italy at last to look on her deliverer, ought not to be allowed to pass away. With what love he would be received in all those Provinces which have suffered from the foreign inundation, with what thirst for vengeance, with what fixed fidelity, with what devotion, and what tears, no words of mine can declare. What gates would be closed against him? What people would refuse him obedience? What jealousy would stand in his way? What Italian but would yield him homage? This barbarian tyranny stinks in all nostrils.

Let your illustrious House therefore take upon itself this enterprise with all the courage and all the hopes with which a just cause is undertaken; so that under your standard this our country may be ennobled, and under your auspices be fulfilled the words of Petrarch:—

Brief will be the strife
When valour arms against barbaric rage;
For the bold spirit of the bygone age
Still warms Italian hearts with life.

François Rabelais

(1495?–1553)

François Rabelais was born at Chinon in Touraine somewhere between 1483 and 1500; 1495 is the year most frequently used. His father Antoine was mentioned as a vine grower, an apothecary, a tavern owner, or a lawyer. He was thought to have owned a small estate called La Deviniere.

It is generally believed that when Rabelais was nine he was sent to a convent in Seuilly to be trained as a monk. He continued his education at La Baumette near Angers, meeting the brothers Du Bellay and Geoffroy d'Estissac, key figures in his later life. Rabelais was ordained as a priest at the Franciscan monastery of Fontenay-le Comte and by 1519, he had attained a position of civic and religious leadership in the community. In 1524, with the help of d'Estissac, who had become the Bishop of Mailezias, Rabelais was allowed to shift from the Franciscan to the Benedictine order and moved to Maillezias where he lived and studied for the next six years.

Rabelais never grew fond of his new order (he later satirized the Benedictines) and in 1530, he left the Benedictines to become a secular priest and in his own words, "wandered around for sometime about the world." Later that year he enrolled in the University of Montpellier, where he studied medicine and received a bachelor's degree in two months. He began to vary his activities, lecturing on Galen and Hippocrates, appearing as an actor in the farce, *The Man Who Married a Dumb Wife,* and creating a fermented fish sauce in the style of *garum*, which he passed on to the famous writer, Etienne Dolet. He is also thought to have fathered three children (one of whom died in infancy) by an unknown widow. François and Junie were given their father's name and legitimized by Pope Paul IV in 1540.

Rabelais moved to Lyons in 1532 and was caught up in the city's enlightened and vibrant culture. It was at this time and place that he discovered his true passion—writing—and perhaps pondered the stories of Gargantua and Pantagruel, giants popularized in the Middle Ages. Inspired by the success of an anonymous popular chapbook, *Le Grandes et inestimables chronicques du grant et enorme géant Gargantua* (which Rabelais is believed to have edited), he published, under the anagramatic pseudonym Alcofribas Nasier, his first novel, *Pantagruel,* a fanciful epic about a giant and his cronies. The novel is shorter and less complex than some of his later work, but nothing of this quality had been issued before in French in any similar genre. Rabelais exhibited his delight of language, his mastery of comic situation, monologue, dialogue, and action, as well as his exquisite touch as a fantastic storyteller. Within the setting of a mock-heroic, gallant romance, he ridicules the complicated reasoning patterns of the Jesuits, the scholastics, and the neo-Aristotelians to name a few.

"One inch of joy surmounts of grief a span, Because to laugh is proper to the man."

This successful novel was followed by the *Pantagrueline Prognostication*, a parody of the almanacs—astrological predications that were strongly influencing the Renaissance movement. He then resumed his wanderings in 1534 when his friend, Jean du Bellay, now Bishop of Paris, asked him to be his personal physician. In 1535 he published *Gargantua,* which addressed religious and intellectual persecution. In it he mocks the Sorbonne and promotes evangelism. A theological college founded in 1257 by Robert Sorbon, the Sorbonne had the ability to approve or disapprove of publications and suggest censure or banning of works. Rabelais frequently ran afoul of what the Sorbonne believed was appropriate literature; he was formally censored by the Sorbonne in 1543.

Sometime in 1546 Rabelais issued Book 3 in Paris, in his own name and under his own profession, a daring move considering his previous censure. Book 3, *The Third Book of the Heroic Deeds and Sayings of the Good Pantagruel,* was markedly different from the previous two. It contains no mention of giants, the text is aimed at a more educated public, and its evangelism is more overt than his past works. Book 3's theme is Panurge's desire to marry and his search for advice (in the form of thirteen consultations) on whether or not he should wed. Despite the title, the book contains *no* heroic deeds and very little plot. Panurge decides at the end of Book 3 to cross the seas and consult the oracle of the Divine Bottle, a story that comprises a large part of Book 4.

Rabelais then went to Rome as Du Bellay's personal physician and stayed on for at least four years. Upon his return to France, his works were bestowed the royal privilege of protection for ten years before or after the date of the pronouncement.

In January 1551, Rabelais was awarded two nonresident curacies. A year later, he published Book 4 under his own name, the last written work attributed to him. The fourth book tells of the voyage to seek the Divine Bottle and the curious creatures, people, and places that the main characters encounter. The story is dominated by satire, fantasy, and comedic elements. Pantagruel evolves into a more pious and learned man, becoming an almost joyous stoic, yet realizing that man is a tactile creature whose body matters as much as his soul.

On January 9, 1553, Rabelias resigned both curacies and died later that year. He was buried in Paris's Saint-Paul-des-Champs.

Pantagruel opens with an imaginary genealogy that begins just after Cain and Abel and flows down to Gargantua to Pantagruel. In *Gargantua*, Rabelais continues in the vein of mock-romance, telling the life story of the giant Gargantua, Pantagruel's father. He pokes fun at heraldry, scholastic pedagogy, and Charles V's imperialist designs of world conquest.

Rabelais is prolific in his use of "bawdy" language, especially in the Pantagruel-Gargantua books, one example being his utilization of twelve synonyms for excrement in the final section of Book 4. Yet Panurge decides at the end of this obscene diatribe that excrement is something rare and pleasant, a thing to be hailed with drink. Rejoice in what links body and mind, what makes us human, the bridge between dead and alive matter. His fascination with defecation, sexual practices and organs, eating, and drinking is a reaffirmation of the human condition, as these acts and conditions are harbingers of fertility, vitality, and growth. The base references—the slinging of dung, the urine soaking, the curses hurled and the 303 epithets describing the male sexual organ in the third book—are meant to induce laughter and levity. With his doctor's sensibility, Rabelais was comfortable with this material, feeling that acknowledging basic human functions and desires brought readers together.

Voltaire labled Rabelais "the drunken poet" and his work defies all labels. There are humanist aspects in *Pantagruel* and *Gargantua,* as they make forays into education, religion, and war and peace. But the main goal of his first two books is to inspire laughter and even outrage, and to introduce amazing new characters and scenarios to French Literature. He was a poet invested in the realm of learned men and their jokes and he delighted in toying with and expanding on this humor and all its possibilities. "'Tis true that it brings forth to you no birth, Of any value, but in point of mirth." This man—who was a country doctor, a lawyer, a priest, a teacher, and a monk all in one lifetime—has also written some of the most vulgar (and funny) passages ever to be published in the French language. Where was the inspiration for this gross, robust humor? Perhaps it was Rabelais' own fertile imagination combined with his profound humanist education, which gave him the freedom to embark on his fantastical literary journeys. He persisted with his writing despite occasional financial hardship, career and locale changes, and censorship. Rabelais wrote unique comic tales full of wonderful wordplay and imagery, earning himself a place amongst the great geniuses in world literature.

The Life of Gargantua and the Heroic Deeds of Pantagruel

THE LIFE OF GARGANTUA

BOOK I

CHAPTER 17

HOW GARGANTUA PAID HIS WELCOME TO THE PARISIANS, AND HOW HE TOOK AWAY THE GREAT BELLS OF OUR LADY'S CHURCH

Some few days after that they had refreshed themselves, he went to see the city, and was beheld of everybody there with great admiration; for the people of Paris are so sottish, so badot, so foolish and fond by nature, that a juggler, a carrier of indulgences, a sumpter-horse, or mule with cymbals or tinkling bells, a blind fiddler in the middle of a cross lane, shall draw a greater confluence of people together than an evangelical preacher. And they pressed so hard upon him, that he was constrained to rest himself upon the towers of our Lady's church. At which place, seeing so many about him, he said with a loud voice, "I believe that these buzzards will have me to pay them here my welcome hither, and my Proficiat: it is but good reason. I will now give them their wine, but it shall be only in sport." Then smiling, he untied his fair braguette, and made such flood that he drowned two hundred and sixty thousand four hundred and eighteen, besides the women and little children. Some, nevertheless, of the company escaped by mere speed of foot, who, when they were at the higher end of the university, sweating, coughing, spitting, and out of breath, they began to swear and curse, some in good hot earnest, and others in jest: Carimari, carimara; golynoly, golynolo. By my sweet Sanctesse, we are washed in sport, a sport truly to laugh at—in French, Par ris, for which that city hath been ever since called Paris; whose name formerly was Leucetia, as Strabo testifieth, lib. quarto, from the Greek word, λευκοτη, whiteness, because of the white skins of the ladies of that place. And forasmuch as at this imposition of a new name, all the people that were there swore, every one by the Sancts of his parish, the Parisians, which are patched up of all nations, and all pieces of countries, are by nature both good jurors and good jurists, and somewhat overweening; whereupon Joanninus de Barrauco, libro do copiositate reverentiarum, thinks that they are called Parisians from the Greek word παρρσια, which signifies boldness and liberty of speech.

This done, he considered the great bells which were in the said towers, and made them sound very harmoniously. Which whilst he was doing, it came into his mind, that they would serve very well for tingling tantans and ringing campanels to hang about his mare's neck, when she should be sent back to his father, as he intended to do, loaded with Brie cheese and fresh herring. And, indeed, he forthwith carried them to his lodging. In the meanwhile there came a master beggar of the friars of St. Anthony, to demand in his canting way the usual benevolence of some hoggish stuff, who, that he might be heard afar off, and to make the bacon he was in quest of shake in the very chimneys, made account to filch them away privily. Nevertheless, he left them behind him very honestly, not for that they were too hot, but that they were somewhat too heavy for his carriage. This was not he of Bourg, for he was too good a friend of mine.

All the city was risen up in sedition, they being, as you know, upon any slight occasion, so ready to uproars; and insurrectious, that foreign nations wonder at the patience of the kings of France, who do not, by good justice, restrain them from such tumultuous courses, seeing the manifold inconveniences which thence arise from day to day. Would to God I knew the shop wherein are forged these divisions and factious combinations, that I might bring them to light in the confraternities of my parish! Believe for a truth, that the place wherein the people gathered together was called Nesle, where then was, but now is no more, the Oracle of Leucetia. There was the case proposed, and the inconvenience shelved of the transporting of the bells. After they had well argued pro and con, they concluded in Baralipton, that they should send the oldest and most sufficient of the faculty unto Gargantua, to signify to him the great and horrible prejudice they sustained by the want of those bells. And notwithstanding the good reasons given in by some of the university, why this charge was titter for an crater than a sophister, there was chosen for this purpose on, master Janotus de Bragmardo.

CHAPTER 18

HOW JANOTUS THE BRAGMARDO WAS SENT TO GARGANTUA TO RECOVER THE GREAT BELLS

Master Janotus, with his hair cut round like a dish, à la Cæsarine, in his most antic accoutrement, liripipionated with a graduate's hood; and having sufficiently antidoted his stomach with oven-marmalades, that is, bread and holy water of the cellar, transported himself to the lodging of Gargantua, driving before him three red muzzled beadles, and dragging after him five or six artless masters, all thoroughly bedaggled with the mire of the streets. At their entry, Ponocrates met them, who was afraid, seeing them so disguised, and thought they had been some maskers out of their wits, which moved him to inquire of one of the said artless masters of the company, what this mummery meant? It was answered him, that they desired to have their bells restored to them. As soon as Ponocrates heard that, he ran in all haste to carry the news unto Gargantua, that he might be ready to answer them, and speedily resolve what was to be done. Gargantua, being advertised hereof, called apart his schoolmaster Ponocrates, Philotimus steward of his house, Gymnastes his esquire, and Eudemon, and very summarily conferred with them, both of what he should do, and what answer he should give. They were all of opinion that they should bring them unto the goblet office, which is the buttery, and there make them drink like roysters, and line their jackets soundly. And that this cougher might not be puffed up with vain-glory, by thinking the bells were restored at his request, they sent, whilst he was chopining and plying the pot, for the mayor of the city, the rector of the faculty, and the vicar of the church, unto whom they resolved to deliver the bells, before the sophister had propounded his commission. After that, in their hearing, he should pronounce his gallant oration, which was done; and they being come, the sophister was brought into a full hall, and began as followeth, in coughing.

CHAPTER 19

THE HARANGUE OF MASTER JANOTUS DE BRAGMARDO, FOR THE RECOVERY OF THE BELLS

"Hem, hem, gudday Sirs, gudday. Et vobis, my masters. It were but reason that you should restore to us our bells; for we have great need of them. Here, hem, aihfuhash! We have oftentimes heretofore refused good money for them of those of London, in Cahors, yea and of those of Bourdeaux in Brie, who would have bought them for the substantific quality of the elementary complexion, which is intronificated in the terrestreity of their quidditative nature, to extraneize the blasting mists and whirlwinds upon our vines, indeed not ours, but these round about us. For if we lose the piot and liquor of the grape, we lose all, both sense and law. If you restore them unto its at my request, I shall gain by it six basketfuls of sausages, and a fine pair of breeches, which will do my legs a great deal of good, or else they will not keep their promise to me. Ho by gob, Domine, a pair of breeches is good, et vir sapiens non abhorrebit eam. If a, ha, a pair of breeches is not so easily got; I have experience of it myself. Consider, *Domine*, I have been these eighteen days in matagrabolising this brave speech. *Reddite quæ sunt Cæsaris Cæsari, et quæ sunt Dei Deo. Ibi jacet lepus*. By my faith, *Domine*, if you will sup with me in *cameris charitatis nos faciemus bonum cherubin. Ego occidi unum porcum et ego habet bonum vino*: but of good wine we cannot make bad Latin. Well, *departe Dei date nobis bellas nostras*. Hold, I give you in the name of the faculty, a *Sermones de Utino*, that *utinam* you would give us our bells. *Vultis etiam pardonos? Per diem vos habebitis, et nihil payabitis*.

"O, Sir *Domine, Bellagivaminor nobis; verily est bonum urbis*. They are useful to everybody. If they fit your mare well, so do they do our faculty; *quæ comparata est jumentis insipientibus, et similis facta est eis, Psalmo nescio quo*. Yet did I quote it in my note-book, *et est unum bonum Achilles*, a good defending argument. *Hem, hem, hem, haickhash*! For I prove unto you that you should give me them. *Ego sic argumentor. Omnis bella (clocha) bellabilis in Bellerio bellando, bellans bellativo, bellare facit, bellabiliter bellantes. Parisius habet bellas; ergo gluc*, Ha, ha, ha. This is spoken to some purpose. It is *in Tertio Primæ*, in *Darii*, or else where. By my soul, I have seen the time that I could play the devil in arguing, but now I am much failed, and hence forward want nothing but a cup of good wine, a good bed, my back to the fire, my front to the table, and a good deep dish. *Hei Domine*, I beseech you, *in nomine Patris, Filii et Spiritus Sancti, Amen*, to restore unto us our bells; and God keep you from evil, and our Lady from health, *qui vivit et regnat per omnia secula seculorum, Amen. Hem, hashchehhawksash qzrchremhemhash*!

"*Verum enim vero, quandoquidem, dubio procul, ædepol, quoniam, ità certè, meus Deus fidius*; a town without bells is like a blind man without a staff, an ass without a crupper, and a cow without cymbals. Therefore be assured, until you have restored them unto us, we will never leave crying after you, like a blind man that hath lost his staff, braying like an ass without a crupper, and making a noise like a cow without cymbals. A certain Latinisator, dwelling near the hospital, said once, producing the authority of one Taponus,—I lie, it was Pontanus the secular poet,—who wished those bells had been made of feathers, and the clapper a fox tail, to the end that they might have begot a chronicle in the bowels of his brain, when he was about the composing of his carminiformal lines: But *Nac petetin petetac, tic, torche, lorgne, or rot kipipur kippipot put pantse malf*, he was declared an heretic. We make them as of wax. And no more saith the deponent. *Valete et plaudite. Calepinus recensui.*"

Miguel de Cervantes

(1547–1616)

Miguel de Cervantes Saavedra was born in Alcalá de Henares, a town twenty miles from Madrid, around September 29, 1547. He was the fourth of seven children, the son of banker-surgeon Don Rodrigo, a jack of all lesser medical trades such as bone setting, apothecary needs, and bloodletting. There might have been some minor gentry in Cervantes' lineage (though not nearly enough to legitimize Cervantes' nobleman pose); his mother, Leonor de Cortinas, descended from Jews who converted to Christianity.

The family was nomadic and there is little information about his early years, though it is clear that the family remained nowhere long enough for Cervantes to receive any formal education. He is placed in Madrid at fourteen, in Seville at seventeen, and then again in Madrid at nineteen. He had developed a passion for literature and enjoyed attending the theater when he could afford it. He had been an erstwhile pupil of Juan Lopez de Hoyos, the humanist schoolmaster and poet aficionado. Lopez de Hoyos published a memorial volume of poems after the death of Queen Isabella in 1569, and included four by Cervantes, to whom he referred as "my own dear and beloved disciple."

That same year Cervantes set off for Italy, serving as a chamberlain in the house of Cardinal Giulio Acquaviva in Rome. He enlisted as a private in the Spanish Infantry regiment in Naples, was assigned to the ship *Marquesa*, and in 1571 saw his first action in the Gulf of Lepanto near Corinth when his unit attacked the Turks. In the intense battle, Cervantes was shot in the left hand and twice in the chest. He referred to these wounds as "stars lighting one to heaven and to fame"; his left hand was permanently disabled "to the greater glory of his right." He recuperated in Messina, rejoined the army for three more years, and then was granted a discharge and allowed to return to Spain. He set sail on the

Sol, in September 1575, with reference letters from Don Juan and the Duke de Sessa in his pocket. His younger brother Rodrigo, who had served in the army with Cervantes, was also on board.

Cervantes never reached Spain. The *Sol* was hijacked on September 20 by three Barbary corsairs; he and his brother were sold into slavery to a Greek trader named Dali Mami, who hoped to ransom the brothers. Mami picked the wrong men to capture, as it took their family three years to raise enough money to rescue one of the brothers and Cervantes gallantly allowed his brother to go free. The letters Cervantes carried also added to the price on his head so he may have been considered a more lucrative prospect. He unsuccessfully attempted to escape several times. Finally, in 1580, the money was raised to bring him home and he arrived in Spain without further incident. This harrowing and adventurous period of his life would provide rich material for several of his works, notably "The Captive's Tale" in *Don Quixote*, and two plays set in Algiers: *El Trato de Angel* and *Los Banos de Algiers*.

Cervantes' next six years were a sharp contrast to the previous six. He lived in Madrid, wrote plays that were performed and well received (*La Numancia* and *El Trato de Angel*), and penned the novel *La Galatea*, a celebration of an Arcadian shepherdess named Galatea. It is said that the inspiration for the charming Galatea was Catalina de Salaza y Palacio, the eighteen-year-old daughter of a landed gentleman. This new love ended his affair with Ana de Villafranca, with whom he had a daughter, Isabel, his only child. Cervantes and Catalina were married on December 12, 1584, and moved to her hometown of Isquivia.

Cervantes' father soon died, leaving little behind. Needing to support his mother, sister, and brothers, Cervantes had to secure a steady income, as his writing career was not financially rewarding. He became a purveyor and tax collector, two occupations for which he had no talent. He was a terrible record-keeper and an incompetent administrator. He was sent to prison in 1597 when a bank to which he entrusted tax monies folded. It was during this prison stay that he began Part One of the *Ingenious Gentleman Don Quixote de la Mancha*.

When *Don Quixote* appeared in 1605, issued by publisher Juan de la Cuesta, it was an instant and resounding success. It went into several editions that year and was distributed in Brussels, France, and Italy. Yet Cervantes made a bad business decision; he sold the publishing rights to Part One outright, and was unable to make any further money after the first version was issued. Incredible fame came his way, but wealth did not follow.

Yet this success signaled the beginning of the most productive part of his career. After the return of Philip III in 1609, Cervantes and his family moved to Madrid. Three years later he published the *12 Novelas Exemplares*. The prologue has the only known physical description of the author: "of aquiline countenance, with dark brown hair, smooth, clear brow, merry eyes, and hooked but well-proportioned nose, his beard is silver . . . large moustache, small mouth with teeth neither big or little . . ."

In an attempt to attract a wider audience for his plays—he had lost hope of ever seeing them staged—Cervantes had eight of them published along with eight comedic skits in *Ocho comedias y ocho entremeses nuevos*. Around this time, he began Part Two of *Don Quixote*. While he was still working to compile the second part of his masterpiece, another writer known only by the pseudonym Alonso Fernandez de Avellaneda published a phony volume entitled *Second Tome of the Ingenious Gentleman Don Quixote de la Mancha*. Cervantes had no legal recourse (there were no copyright laws at the time), so he urgently worked to complete the true second part and *Don Quixote, Part Two* debuted in 1615. It was lauded as richer and more profound than the original and enjoyed the same success and rapid-fire issuance of editions.

Apparently, the sprint to finish the real version and the piracy on his masterwork took its toll on Cervantes. He was exhausted and depressed. He died in Madrid on April 23, 1616, a year after completing his finest work.

Don Quixote, a novel that parodies the chivalrous romances that preceded it, has an unusual premise. An elderly man has read so many of these knightly tales that he believes that they have occurred. "This gentleman gave himself up to the reading of books of knight errantry, he loved and enjoyed it so much that he almost entirely forgot his living and even care of his estate. He spent nights reading from twilight till daybreak and the days from dawn till dark; and from so much reading and so little sleep, his brain dried up and he lost his wits." He decides to become a knight-errant and to go out and live his own romantic adventure.

In Part Two of *Don Quixote*, Don Quixote and his sidekick Sancho have become like husband and wife, enduring these false challenges while snapping at each other, bickering and disbelieving the other's versions of their own experiences. Chapters 36–41 have the two being used as pawns in an elaborate practical joke staged by the duke and duchess who prey on Don Quixote's madness and Sancho's vices. Visiting the duke's garden is "The Distressed Duenna," who relates that she (really an actress hired by the duke and duchess) needs Don Quixote and Sancho's services to reverse a spell that has given her handmaidens beards of many hues. After Sancho's plea that he be let out of this one trip because of his mistrust of duennas, the men agree to go off to right the wrong on a wooden "magical" horse steered by a peg in the horse's forehead. They are blindfolded, to save them altitude dizziness, and "set off," actually going nowhere but convinced by sound and heat effects that they have traveled far. They find a note at the "end" of their journey, telling them they have concluded the adventure of the Countess Trifaldi (the Distressed Duenna) and the beards have been removed.

These chapters illustrate how Don Quixote's life has become a true fantasy story in which others control him and the action for their own amusement. It is now a satire within a satire and now even Sancho, who appeared to be the voice (or the at least the presence) of reason in Part I, has now become a dream-weaver himself.

This little episode does give Don Quixote and Sancho a bit of satisfaction at having "completed" a task set before them, and at having justified the onlookers' faith in them. Don Quixote is a man up for any challenge, with a firm belief in his own rightness and virtue. His steadfastness and moral passion is noble because it is turned outward, and used to help others. He fails, is duped, is made sport of, but because of his state of mind and belief in some higher calling, he remains undaunted and undeterred. In looking at Cervantes' own tumultuous life, it appears that he has put no small measure of his own will and spirit into his most famous character.

Don Quixote

CHAPTER XXXVI

WHEREIN IS RECORDED THE STRANGE AND INCONCEIVABLE ADVENTURE OF THE ILL-USED DUENNA, OR THE COUNTESS OF TRIFALDI; AND LIKEWISE SANCHO PANZA'S LETTER TO HIS WIFE TERESA PANZA.

THE WHOLE CONTRIVANCE of the former adventure was the work of the duke's steward, a man of humorous and facetious turn of mind. He it was who composed the verses, instructed a page to perform the part of Dulcinea, and personated himself the shade of Merlin. Assisted by the duke and duchess, he now prepared another scene still more entertaining than the former.

The next day the duchess inquired of Sancho if he had begun his penance for the relief of his unhappy lady. "By my faith, I have," said he, "for last night I gave myself five lashes." The duchess desired to know how he had given them. "With the palm of my hand," said he. "That," replied the duchess, "is rather clapping than whipping, and I am of opinion Signor Merlin will not be so easily satisfied. My good Sancho must get a rod of briers or of whipcord, that the strokes may be followed by sufficient smarting; for letters written in blood cannot be disputed, and the deliverance of a great lady like Dulcinea is not to be purchased with a song." "Give me, then, madam, some rod or bough," quoth Sancho, "and I will use it, if it does not smart too much; for I would have your ladyship know that, though I am a clown, my flesh has more of the cotton than of the rush, and there is no reason why I should flay myself for other folks' gain." "Fear not," answered the duchess, "it shall be my care to provide you with a whip that shall suit you exactly, and agree with the tenderness of your flesh as if it were its own brother." "But now, my dear lady," quoth Sancho, "you must know that I have written a letter to my wife Teresa Panza, giving her an account of all that has befallen me since I parted from her:—here it is in my bosom, and it wants nothing but the name on the outside. I wish your discretion would read it, for methinks it is written like a governor—I mean in the manner that governors ought to write." "And who indited it?" demanded the duchess. "Who should indite it but I myself, sinner as I am?" replied Sancho. "And did you write it too?" said the duchess. "No, indeed," answered Sancho, "for I can neither read nor write, though I can set my mark." "Let us see it," said the duchess, "for I dare say it shows the quality and extent of your genius." Sancho took the letter out of his bosom, unsealed it, and the duchess having taken it, read as follows:

SANCHO PANZA'S LETTER TO HIS WIFE TERESA PANZA.

"If I have been finely lashed, I have been finely mounted up; if I have got a good government, it has cost me many good lashes. This, my dear Teresa, thou canst not understand at present; another time thou wilt. Thou must know, Teresa, that I am determined that thou shalt ride in thy coach, which is somewhat to the purpose; for all other ways of going are no better than creeping upon all fours, like a cat. Thou shalt be a governor's wife: see then whether anybody will dare to tread on thy heels. I here send thee a green hunting suit, which my lady duchess gave me: fit it up so that it may serve our daughter for a jacket and petticoat. They say in this country that my master Don Quixote is a sensible madman and a pleasant fool, and that I am not a whit behind him. We have been in Montesinos' cave, and the sage Merlin, the wizard, has pitched upon me to disenchant the Lady Dulcinea del Toboso, who among you is called Aldonza Lorenzo. When I have given myself three thousand and three hundred lashes, lacking five, she will be as free from enchantment as the mother that bore her. Say nothing of this to anybody; for, bring your affairs into council, and one will cry it is white, another it is black. A few days hence I shall go to the government, whither I go with a huge desire to get money; and I am told it is the same with all new governors. I will first see how matters stand, and send thee word whether or not thou shalt come to me. Dapple is well, and sends thee his hearty service; part with him I will not, though I were made the great Turk. The duchess, my mistress kisses thy hands a thousand times over; return her two thousand; for, as my master says, nothing is cheaper than civil words. God has not been pleased to throw in my way another portmanteau, and another hundred crowns, as once before; but take no heed, my dear Teresa, for he that has the game in his hand need not mind the loss of a trick—the government will make up for all. One thing only troubles me: I am told if I once try it I shall eat my very fingers after it; and if so, it will not be much of a bargain: though, indeed, the crippled and maimed enjoy a petty-canonry in the alms they receive; so that, one way or another, thou art sure to be rich and happy. God send it may be so—as He easily can, and keep me for thy sake.

"Thy husband, the governor,

"SANCHO PANZA.

"From this Castle, the 20th of July, 1614"

The duchess, having read the letter, said to Sancho, "In two things the good governor is a little out of the way: the one in saying, or insinuating, that this government is conferred on him on account of the lashes he is to give himself; whereas he cannot deny, for he knows it well, that, when my lord duke promised it to him, nobody dreamt of lashes; the other is, that he appears to be covetous, and I hope no harm may come of it; for avarice bursts the bag, and the covetous governor doeth ungoverned justice." "Truly, madam, that is not my meaning," replied Sancho; "and, if your highness does not like this letter, it is but tearing it, and writing a new one, which, mayhap, may prove worse, if left to thy mending." "No, no," replied the duchess, "this is a very good one, and the duke shall see it."

They then repaired to a garden, where they were to dine that day; and there Sancho's letter was shown to the duke, who read it with great pleasure. After dinner, as Sancho was entertaining the company with some of his relishing conversation, they suddenly heard the dismal sound of an unbraced drum, accompanied by a fife. All were surprised at this martial and doleful harmony, especially Don Quixote, who was so agitated that he could scarcely keep his seat. As for Sancho, it is enough to say that fear carried him to his usual refuge, which was the duchess's side, or the skirts of her petticoat; for the sounds which they heard were truly dismal and melancholy. While they were thus held in suspense, two young men, clad in mourning robes trailing upon the ground, entered the garden, each of them beating a great drum, covered also with black; and with these a third, playing on the fife, in mourning like the rest. These were followed by a person of gigantic stature, not dressed, but rather enveloped, in a robe of the blackest dye, the train whereof was of a moderate length, and over it he wore a broad black belt, in which was slung a mighty cimeter enclosed within a sable scabbard. His face was covered by a thin black veil, through which might be discovered a long beard, white as snow. He marched forward, regulating his steps to the sound of the drums, with much gravity and stateliness. In short, his dark robe, his enormous bulk, his solemn deportment, and the funereal gloom of his figure, together with his attendants, might well produce the surprise that appeared on every countenance.

With all imaginable respect and formality he approached and knelt down before the duke, who received him standing, and would in nowise suffer him to speak till he rose up. The monstrous apparition, then rising, lifted up his veil, and exposed to view his fearful length of beard—the longest, whitest, and most luxuriant that ever human eyes beheld; then, fixing his eyes on the duke, in a voice grave and sonorous he said, "Most high and potent lord, my name is Trifaldin of the White Beard, and I am squire to the Countess Trifaldi, otherwise called the Afflicted Duenna, from whom I bear a message to your highness, requesting that you will be pleased to give her ladyship permission to approach, and relate to your Magnificence the unhappy and wonderful circumstances of her misfortune. But, first, she desires to know whether the valorous and invincible knight, Don Quixote de la Mancha, resides at this time in your castle; for in quest of him she has travelled on foot, and fasting, from the kingdom of Candaya to this your territory; an exertion miraculous and incredible, were it not wrought by enchantment. She is now at the outward gate of this castle, and only waits your highness's invitation to enter."

Having said this, he hemmed, stroked his beard from top to bottom, and with much gravity and composure stood expecting the duke's answer, which was to this effect: "Worthy Trifaldin of the White Beard, long since have we been apprised of the afflictions of my lady the Countess Trifaldi, who, through the malice of enchanters, is too truly called the Dolorous Duenna: tell her, therefore, stupendous squire, that she may enter, and that the valiant knight Don Quixote de la Mancha is here present, from whose generous assistance she may safely promise herself all the redress she requires. Tell her also that, if my aid be necessary, she may command my services, since, as a knight, I am bound to protect all women, more especially injured and afflicted matrons like her ladyship." Trifaldin, on receiving the duke's answer, bent one knee to the ground; then giving a signal to his musical attendants, he retired with the same solemnity as he had entered, leaving all in astonishment at the majesty of his figure and deportment.

The duke, then turning to Don Quixote, said, "It is evident, Sir Knight, that neither the clouds of malice nor of ignorance can obscure the light of your valor and virtue: six days have scarcely elapsed since you have honored this castle with your presence, and, behold, the afflicted and oppressed flock hither in quest of you from far distant countries; not in coaches, or upon dromedaries, but on foot, and fasting!—such is their confidence in the strength of that arm, the fame whereof spreads over the whole face of the earth." "I wish, my lord duke," answered Don Quixote, "that holy person, who but a few days since expressed himself with so much acrimony against knight-errant, were now here, that he might have ascertained, with his own eyes, whether or not such knights were necessary in the world; at least he would be forced to acknowledge that the afflicted and disconsolate, in extraordinary cases and in overwhelming calamities, fly not for relief to the houses of scholars, nor to village priests, nor to the country gentleman who never travels out of sight of his own domain, nor to the lazy courtier, who rather inquires after news to tell again than endeavors to perform deeds worthy of being related by others. No: remedy for the injured, support for the distressed, protection for damsels, and consolation for widows, are nowhere so readily to be found as among knights-errant; and I give infinite thanks to Heaven that I may endure in so honorable a vocation. Let the afflicted lady come forward and make known her request, and, be it whatever it may, she may rely on the strength of this arm, and the resolute courage of my soul."

CHAPTER XXXVII

IN WHICH IS CONTINUED THE FAMOUS ADVENTURE OF THE AFFLICTED DUENNA.

THE DUKE AND duchess were extremely delighted to find Don Quixote wrought up into a mood so favorable to their design; but Sancho was not so well satisfied. "I should be sorry," said he, "that this Madam Duenna should lay any stumbling-block in the way of my promised government; for I have heard an apothecary of Toledo, who talked like any goldfinch, say that no good ever comes of meddling with duennas. Odds my life! what an enemy to them was that apothecary! If, then, duennas of every quality and condition are troublesome and impertinent, what must those be who come in the doldrums? which seems to be the case with this same Countess Three-skirts, or Three-tails—for skirts and tails, in my country, are all one." "Hold thy peace, Sancho," said Don Quixote; "for as this lady duenna comes in quest of me from so remote a country, she cannot be one of those who fall under that apothecary's displeasure. Besides, thou must have noticed that this lady is a countess; and when countesses serve as duennas, it must be as attendants upon queens and empresses; having houses of their own, where they command, and are served by other duennas." "Yes, in sooth, so it is," said Donna Rodriguez (who was present); "and my lady duchess has duennas in her service who might have been countesses themselves had it pleased fortune; but 'laws go on kings' errands'; and let no one speak ill of duennas, especially of maiden ones; for, though I am not of that number, yet I can easily conceive the advantage a maiden duenna has over one that is a widow. But let them take heed, for he who attempts to clip us will be left with the shears in his hand."

"For all that," replied Sancho, "there is still so much to be sheared about your duennas, as my barber tells me, that it is better not to stir the rice though it burn to the pot." "These squires," quoth Donna Rodriguez, "are our sworn enemies; and being, as it were, evil spirits that prowl about ante-chambers, continually watching us the hours they are not at their beads—which are not a few—they can find no other pastime than reviling us, and will dig our bones only to give another death-blow to our reputations. But let me tell these jesters that, in spite of their flouts, we shall live in the world—ay, and in the best families too, though we starve for it, and cover our delicate or not delicate bodies with black weeds, as dunghills are sometimes covered with tapestry on a procession day. Foul slanderers!—by my faith, if I were allowed, and the occasion required it, I would prove to all here present, and to the whole world besides, that there is no virtue that is not contained in a duenna." "I am of opinion," quoth the duchess, "that my good Donna Rodriguez is very much in the right; but she must wait for a more proper opportunity to finish the debate, and confute and confound the calumnies of that wicked apothecary, and also to root out the ill opinion which the great Sancho Panza fosters in his breast." "I care not to dispute with her," quoth Sancho, "for, ever since the fumes of government have got into my head, I have given up all my squireship notions, and care not a fig for all the duennas in the world."

This dialogue about duennas would have continued, had not the sound of the drum and fife announced the approach of the afflicted lady. The duchess asked the duke whether it would not be proper for him to go and meet her, since she was a countess, and a person of quality. "Look you," quoth Sancho, before the duke could answer, "in regard to her being a countess, it is fitting your highness should go to receive her, but, inasmuch as she is a duenna, I am of opinion you should not stir a step." "Who desires thee to intermeddle in this matter, Sancho?" said Don Quixote. "Who, sir," answered Sancho, "but I myself? have I not a right to intermeddle, being a squire who has learned the rules of good manners in the school of your worship? Have I not had the flower of courtesy for my master, who has often told me that one may as well lose the game by a card too much as a card too little; and a word is enough to the wise." "Sancho is right," quoth the duke; "but let us see what kind of a countess this is, and then we shall judge what courtesy is due to her." The drums and fife now advanced as before—but here the author ended this short chapter, and began another with the continuation of the same adventure, which is one of the most remarkable in the history.

CHAPTER XXXVIII

WHICH CONTAINS THE ACCOUNT GIVEN BY THE AFFLICTED DUENNA OF HER MISFORTUNES.

THE DOLEFUL MUSICIANS were followed by twelve duennas, in two ranks, clad in large mourning robes, seemingly of milled serge, and covered with white veils of thin muslin that almost reached to their feet. Then came the Countess Trifaldi herself, led by her squire Trifaldin of the White Beard. She was clad in a robe of the finest serge, which, had it been napped, each grain would have been of the size of a good ronceval pea. The train, or tail (call it by either name), was divided into three separate portions, and supported by three pages, and spread out, making a regular mathematical figure with three angles; whence it was conjectured she obtained the name of Trifaldi, or Three-skirts. Indeed, Benengeli says that was the fact; her real name being Countess of Lobuna, or Wolf-land, from the multitude of wolves produced in that earldom; and, had they been foxes instead of wolves, she would have been styled Countess Zorruna, according to the custom of those nations for the great to take their titles from the things, with which the country most abounded. This great countess, however, was induced, from the singular form of her garments, to exchange her original title of Lobuna for that of Trifaldi. The twelve duennas, with the lady, advanced slowly in procession, having their faces covered with black veils—not transparent, like that of the squire Trifaldin, but so thick that nothing could be seen through them.

On the approach of this battalion of duennas, the duke, duchess, Don Quixote, and all the other spectators, rose from their seats; and now the attendant duennas halted, and separating, opened a passage through which their afflicted lady, still led by the squire Trifaldin, advanced towards the noble party, who stepped some dozen paces forward to receive her. She then cast herself on her knees, and, with a voice rather harsh and coarse than clear and delicate, said, "I entreat your graces will not condescend to so much courtesy to this your valet—I mean your handmaid; for my mind, already bewildered with affliction, will only be still more confounded. Alas! my unparalleled misfortune has seized and carried off my understanding, I know not whither; but surely it must be to a great distance, for the more I seek it the farther it seems from me." "He must be wholly destitute of understanding, lady countess," quoth the duke, "who could not discern your merit by your person, which alone claims all the cream of courtesy and all the flower of well-bred ceremony." Then raising her by the hand, he led her to a chair close by the duchess, who also received her with much politeness.

During the ceremony Don Quixote was silent, and Sancho dying with impatience to see the face of the Trifaldi, or of some one of her many duennas; but it was impossible till they chose to unveil themselves. All was expectation, and not a whisper was heard, till at length the afflicted lady began in these words: "Confident I am, most potent lord, most beautiful lady, and most discreet spectators, that my most unfortunate miserableness will find, in your generous and compassionate natures, a most merciful sanctuary; for so doleful and dolorous is my wretched state that it is sufficient to mollify marble, to soften adamant, and melt down the steel of the hardest hearts. But, before the rehearsal of my misfortunes is commenced on the public stage of your hearing faculties, I earnestly desire to be informed whether this noble circle be adorned by that renownedissimo knight, Don Quixote de la Manchissima, and his squirissimo Panza." "That same Panza," said Sancho, before any other could answer, "stands here before you, and also Don Quixotissimo; and therefore, most dolorous duennissima, say what you willissima; for we are all ready to be your most humble servantissimos."

Upon this Don Quixote stood up, and, addressing himself to the doleful countess, he said, "If your misfortunes, afflicted lady, can admit of remedy from the valor or fortitude of a knight-errant, the little all that I possess shall be employed in your service. I am Don Quixote de la Mancha, whose function it is to relieve every species of distress; you need not, therefore, madam, implore benevolence, nor have recourse to preambles, but plainly, and without circumlocution, declare your grievances, for you have auditors who will bestow commiseration if not redress." On hearing this, the afflicted duenna attempted to throw herself at Don Quixote's feet—in truth she did so, and struggling to kiss them, said, "I prostrate myself, O invincible knight! before these feet and legs, which are the bases and pillars of knight-errantry, and will kiss these feet, whose steps lead to the end and termination of my misfortunes! O valorous knight-errant, whose true exploits surpass and obscure the fabulous beats of the Amadises, Esplandians, and Belianises of old!"

Then, leaving Don Quixote, she turned to Sancho Panza, and taking him by the hand, said, "O thou, the most trusty squire that ever served knight-errant in present or in past ages, whose goodness is of greater extent than that beard of my usher Trifaldin; well mayest thou boast that, in serving Don Quixote, thou dost serve, in epitome, all the knights-errant that ever shone in the annals of chivalry. I conjure thee, by thy natural benevolence and inviolable fidelity, to intercede with thy lord in my behalf, that the light of his favor may forthwith shine upon the humblest and unhappiest of countesses." To which Sancho answered, "Whether my goodness, Madam Countess, be or be not as long and as broad as your squire's beard, is no concern of mine: so that my soul be well bearded and whiskered when it departs this life, I care little or nothing for beards here below: but without all this coaxing and beseeching, I will put in a word for you to my master, who I know has a kindness for me; besides, just now he stands in need of me about a certain business; so, take my word for it, he shall do what he can for you. Now pray unload your griefs, madam; let us hear all you have to say, and leave us to manage the matter."

The duke and duchess could scarcely preserve their gravity on seeing this adventure take so pleasant a turn, and were highly pleased with the ingenuity and good management of the Countess Trifaldi, who returning to her seat, thus began her tale of sorrow: "The famous kingdom of Candaya, which lies between the great Taprobana and the South Sea, two leagues beyond Cape Camorin, had for its queen the Lady Donna Maguncia, widow of King Archipiela, who died leaving the Infanta Antonomasia, their only child, heiress to the crown. This princess was brought up and educated under my care and instruction, I being the eldest and chief of the duennas in the household of her royal mother. Now, in process of time the young Antonomasia arrived at the age of fourteen, with such perfection of beauty that nature could not raise it a pitch higher; and, what is more, discretion itself was but a child to her; for she was as discreet as fair, and she was the fairest creature living; and so she still remains, if the envious fates and hard-hearted destinies have not cut short her thread of life. But sure they have not done it; for Heaven would never permit that so much injury should be done to the earth as to lop off prematurely the loveliest branch that ever adorned the garden of the world. Her wondrous beauty, which my feeble tongue can never sufficiently extol, attracted innumerable adorers; and princes of her own, and every other nation, became her slaves. Among the rest, a private cavalier of the court had the audacity to aspire to that earthly heaven; confiding in his youth, his gallantry, his sprightly and happy wit, with numerous other graces and qualifications. Indeed, I must confess to your highnesses—though with reverence be it spoken—he could touch the guitar to a miracle. He was, besides, a poet and a fine dancer, and had so rare a talent for making bird-cages that he might have gained his living by it in case of need. So many parts and elegant endowments were sufficient to have moved a mountain, much more the tender heart of a virgin. But all his graces and accomplishments would have proved ineffectual against the virtue of my beautiful charge, had not the robber and ruffian first artfully contrived to make a conquest of me. The assassin and barbarous vagabond began with endeavoring to obtain my good-will and suborn my inclination, that I might betray my trust, and deliver up to him the keys of the fortress I guarded. In short, he so plied me with toys and trinkets, and so insinuated himself into my soul, that I was bewitched. But that which chiefly brought me down, and levelled me with the ground, was a copy of verses which I heard him sing one night under my window; and if I remember right, the words were these:

"'The tyrant fair whose beauty sent
    The throbbing mischief to my heart,
The more my anguish to augment,
    Forbids me to reveal the smart.'

"The words of this song were to me so many pearls, and his voice was sweeter than honey; and many a time since have I thought, reflecting on the evils I incurred, that poets—at least, your amorous poets—should be banished from all good and well-regulated commonwealths; for, instead of composing pathetic verses like those of the Marquis of Mantua, which make women and children weep, they exercise their skill in soft strokes and tender touches, which pierce the soul, and, entering the body like lightning, consume all within, while the garment is left unsinged. Another time he sang:

"'Come, death, with gently-stealing pace,
And take me unperceived away,
Nor let me see thy wished-for face,
Lest joy my fleeting life should stay.'

"Thus was I assailed with these and such-like couplets, that astonish, and when chanted, are bewitching. But when our poets deign to compose a kind of verses much in fashion with us, called roundelays—good Heaven! they are no sooner heard than the whole frame is in a state of emotion; the soul is seized with a kind of quaking, a titillation of the fancy, a pleasing delirium of all the senses! I therefore say again, most noble auditors, that such versifiers deserve to be banished to the Isle of Lizards; though, in truth, the blame lies chiefly with the simpletons who commend, and the idiots who suffer themselves to be deluded by such things; and had I been a wise and discreet duenna, the nightly chanting of his verses would not have moved me, nor should I have lent an ear to such expressions as 'Dying I live; in ice I burn; I shiver in flames; in despair I hope; I fly, yet stay'; with other flimflams of the like stamp, of which such kind of writings are full. Then again, when they promise to bestow on us the phoenix of Arabia, the crown of Ariadne, the ringlets of Apollo, the pearls of the South Sea, the gold of Tiber, and the balsam of Pencaya, how beautiful are their pens! how liberal in promises which they cannot perform! But, woe is me, unhappy wretch! Whither do I stray? What madness impels me to dwell on the faults of others, who have so many of mine own to answer for? Woe is me again, miserable creature! No, it was not his verses that vanquished me, but my own weakness; music did not subdue me; no, it was my own levity, my ignorance and lack of caution that melted me down, that opened the way and smoothed the passage for Don Clavijo;—for that is the name of the treacherous cavalier. Thus being made the go-between, the wicked man was often in the chamber of the—not by him, but by me—betrayed Antonomasia, as her lawful spouse; for, sinner as I am, never would I have consented unless he had been her true husband that he should have come within the shadow of her shoe-string! No, no; marriage must be the forerunner of any business of this kind undertaken by me. The only mischief in the affair was that they were ill-sorted, Don Clavijo being but a private gentleman, and the Infanta Antonomasia, as I have already said, heiress of the kingdom.

"For some time this intercourse, enveloped in the sagacity of my circumspection, was concealed from every eye. At length circumstances occurred which I feared might lead to a discovery; we laid our three heads together, and determined that before their indiscretion should come to light, Don Clavijo should demand Antonomasia in marriage before the vicar, in virtue of a contract signed and given him by the infanta herself to be his wife, and so worded by wit, that the force of Samson could not have broken through it. Our plan was immediately carried into execution; the vicar examined the contract, took the lady's confession, and she was placed in the custody of an honest alguazil." "Bless me!" said Sancho, "alguazils too, and poets, and songs, and roundelays, in Candaya! I swear the world is the same everywhere! But pray get on, good Madam Trifaldi, for it grows late, and I am on thorns till I know the end of this long story." "I shall be brief," answered the countess.

CHAPTER XXXIX

WHEREIN THE DUENNA TRIFALDI CONTINUES HER STUPENDOUS AND MEMORABLE HISTORY.

EVERY WORD UTTERED by Sancho was the cause of much delight to the duchess, and disgust to Don Quixote, who having commanded him to hold his peace, the afflicted lady went on. "After many questions and answers," said she, "the infanta stood firm to her engagement, without varying a tittle from her first declaration; the vicar, therefore, confirmed their union as lawful man and wife, which so affected the Queen Donna Maguncia, mother to the Infanta Antonomasia, that three days after we buried her." "She died, then, I suppose?" quoth Sancho. "Assuredly," replied the squire Trifaldin; "in Candaya we do not bury the living, but the dead." "Nevertheless, Master Squire," said Sancho, "it has happened before now that people only in a swoon have been buried for dead; and methinks Queen Maguncia ought rather to have swooned than died in good earnest; for while there is life there is hope; and the young lady's offence was not so much out of the way that her mother should have taken it so to heart. Had she married one of her pages, or some serving-man of the family, as I have been told many have done, it would have been a bad business and past cure; but as she made choice of a well-bred young cavalier of such good parts, faith and troth, though mayhap it was foolish, it was no such mighty matter: for, as my master says, who is here present and will not let me lie, bishops are made out of learned men, and why may not kings and emperors be made out of cavaliers—especially if they be errant?" "Thou art in the right, Sancho," said Don Quixote; "for a knight-errant with but two grains of good luck is next in the order of promotion to the greatest lord in the world. But let the afflicted lady proceed; for I fancy the bitter part of this hitherto sweet story is still behind." "Bitter!" answered the countess—"ay, and so bitter that, in comparison, wormwood is sweet and rue savory!

HEREUPON THE AFFLICTED LADY AND THE REST OF THE DUENNAS LIFTED UP THE VEILS WHICH HAD HITHERTO CONCEALED THEM, AND DISCOVERED THEIR FACES PLANTED WITH BEARDS OF ALL COLORS, BLACK, BROWN, WHITE, AND PIEBALD!

"The queen being really dead, and not in a swoon, we buried her; and scarcely had we covered her with earth and pronounced the last farewell, when, '*Quis talia fando temperet a lacrymis*?'—lo, upon the queen's sepulchre who should appear, mounted on a wooden horse, but her cousin-german, the giant Malambruno! Yes, that cruel necromancer came expressly to avenge the death of his cousin, and to chastise the presumptuous Don Clavijo and the foolish Antonomasia, both of whom, by his cursed art, he instantly transformed—she into a monkey of brass, and him into a frightful crocodile of some strange metal; fixing upon them at the same time a plate of metal, engraven with Syriac characters; which being first rendered into the Candayan, and now into the Castilian language, have this meaning: 'These two presumptuous lovers shall not regain their pristine form till the valorous Manchegan engages with me in single combat; since for his mighty arm alone have the destinies reserved the achievement of that stupendous adventure.' No sooner was the wicked deed performed, than out he drew from its scabbard a dreadful cimeter, and taking me by the hair of my head, he seemed preparing to cut my throat, or whip off my head at a blow! Though struck with horror, and almost speechless, trembling and weeping, I begged for mercy in such moving tones and melting words that I at last prevailed on him to stop the cruel execution which he meditated. In short, he ordered into his presence all the duennas of the palace, being those you see here present—and, after having expatiated on our fault, inveighed against duennas, their wicked plots and worse intrigues, and reviled all for the crime of which I alone was guilty, he said, though he would vouchsafe to spare our lives, he would inflict on us a punishment that should be a lasting shame. At the same instant, we all felt the pores of our faces open, and a sharp pain all over them like the pricking of needle-points; upon which we clapped our hands to our faces, and found them in the condition you shall now behold."

Hereupon the afflicted lady and the rest of the duennas lifted up the veils which had hitherto concealed them, and discovered their faces planted with beards of all colors, black, brown, white, and piebald! The duke and duchess viewed the spectacle with surprise, and Don Quixote, Sancho, and the rest were all lost in amazement.

"Thus," continued Trifaldi, "hath that wicked and evil-minded felon Malambruno punished us!—covering our soft and delicate faces with these rugged bristles. Would to Heaven he had struck off our heads with his huge cimeter, rather than have obscured the light of our countenances with such an odious cloud! Whither, noble lords and lady,—Oh that I could utter what I have now to say with rivers of tears! but alas, the torrent is spent, and excess of grief has left our eyes without moisture, and as dry as beards of corn!—whither, I say, can a duenna go, whose chin is covered with a beard? What relation will own her? What charitable person will show her compassion or afford her relief? Even at the best, when the grain of her skin is the smoothest, and her face tortured and set off with a thousand different washes and ointments—with all this, how seldom does she meet with good-will from either man or woman? What then will become of her when her face is become a forest? O duennas! my dear partners in misfortune and companions in grief! in an evil hour were we brought into the world! Oh!"—here, being overcome with the strong sense of her calamity, she fell into a swoon.

CHAPTER XL

WHICH TREATS OF MATTERS RELATING AND APPERTAINING TO THIS ADVENTURE, AND TO THIS MEMORABLE HISTORY.

VERY GRATEFUL OUGHT all who delight in histories of this kind to be to the original author of the present work, Cid Hamet, for his punctilious regard for truth, in allowing no circumstance to escape his pen, and the curious exactness with which he notes and sets down everything just as it happened, nothing, however minute, being omitted! He lays open the inmost thoughts, speaks for the silent, clears up doubts, resolves arguments; in fine, satisfies, to the smallest particle, the most acute and inquisitive minds. O most incomparable author! O happy Don Quixote! O famous Dulcinea! O facetious Sancho Panza! Jointly and severally may ye live through endless ages, for the delight and recreation of mankind!

The history then proceeds to relate that when Sancho saw the afflicted lady faint away, he said, "Upon the word of an honest man, and by the blood of all my ancestors, the Panzas, I swear I never heard or saw, nor has my master ever told me, nor did such an adventure as this ever enter into his thoughts! A thousand devils take thee—not to say curse thee, Malambruno, for an enchanter and giant! Couldst thou, beast! hit upon no other punishment for these poor sinners, than clapping beards upon them? Had it not been better (for them I am sure it would) to have whipt off half their noses, though they had snuffled for it, than to have covered their faces with scrubbing-brushes! And what is worse, I'll wager a trifle that they have not wherewithal to pay for shaving." "That is true, indeed, sir," answered one of the twelve: "we have not wherewithal to satisfy the barber, and therefore, as a shaving shift some of us lay on plasters of pitch, which being pulled off with a jerk, take up roots and all, and thereby free us of this stubble for a while. As for the women who, in Candaya, go about from house to house to take off the superfluous hairs of the body, and trim the eyebrows, and do other private jobs for ladies, we, the duennas of her ladyship, would never have anything to do with them; for they are, most of them, no better than they should be; and therefore, if we are not relieved by Signor Don Quixote, with beards we shall live, and with beards be carried to our graves." "I would pluck off my own in the land of the Moors," said Don Quixote, "if I failed to deliver you from yours."

"Ah, valorous knight!" cried the Trifaldi, at that moment recovering from her fainting fit, "the sweet tinkling of that promise reached my hearing faculty, and restored me to life. Once again, then, illustrious knight-errant and invincible hero! let me beseech that your gracious promises may be converted into deeds." "The business shall not sleep with me," answered Don Quixote; "therefore say, madam, what I am to do, and you shall soon be convinced of my readiness to serve you." "Be it known, then, to you, sir," replied the afflicted dame, "that from this place to the kingdom of Candaya, by land, is computed to be about five thousand leagues, one or two more or less; but, through the air in a direct line, it is three thousand two hundred and twenty-seven. You are likewise to understand that Malambruno told me that, whenever fortune should direct me to the knight who was to be our deliverer, he would send him a steed—not like the vicious jades let out for hire, for it should be that very wooden horse upon which Peter of Provence carried off the fair Magalona. This horse is governed by a peg in his forehead, which serves instead of a bridle, and he flies as swiftly through the air as if the devil himself was switching him. This famous steed, tradition reports to have been formed by the cunning hand of Merlin the enchanter, who sometimes allowed him to be used by his particular friends, or those who paid him handsomely; and he it was who lent him to his friend, the valiant Peter, when, as I said before, he stole the fair Magalona; whisking her through the air behind him on the crupper, and leaving all that beheld him from the earth gaping with astonishment. Since the time of Peter to the present moment, we know of none that have mounted him; but this we know, that Malambruno, by his art, has now got possession of him, and by this means posts about to every part of the world. To-day he is here, to-morrow in France, and the next day in Potosi; and the best of it is, that this same horse neither eats nor sleeps, nor wants shoeing; and, without wings, he ambles so smoothly that in his most rapid flight the rider may carry in his hand a cup full of water without spilling a drop! No wonder, then, that the fair Magalona took such delight in riding him."

"As for easy going," quoth Sancho, "commend me to my Dapple, though he is no highflyer; but by land I will match him against all the amblers in the world." The gravity of the company was disturbed for a moment by Sancho's observation; but the unhappy lady proceeded: "Now, this horse," said she, "if it be Malambruno's intention that our misfortunes should have an end, will be here this very evening; for he told me that the sign by which I should be assured of my having arrived in the presence of my deliverer, would be his sending me the horse thither with all convenient dispatch." "Pray," quoth Sancho, "how many will that same horse carry?" "Two persons," answered the lady, "one in the saddle, and the other on the crupper; and generally these two persons are the knight and his squire, when there is no stolen damsel in the case." "I would fain know," quoth Sancho, "by what name he is called." "His name," answered the Trifaldi, "is not the same as the horse of Bellerophon, which was the Pegasus; nor is he called Bucephalus, like that of Alexander the Great; nor Brilladore, like that of Orlando Furioso; nor is it Bayarte, which belonged to Reynaldos of Montalvan; nor Frontino which was the steed of Rogero; nor is it Boötes, nor Pyrois—names given, it is said, to the horses of the sun; neither is he called Orelia, like the horse which the unfortunate Roderigo, the last king of the Goths in Spain, mounted in that battle wherein he lost his kingdom and his life."

"I will venture a wager," quoth Sancho, "since they have given him none of these famous and well known names, neither have they given him that of my master's horse Rozinante, which in fitness goes beyond all the names you have mentioned." "It is very true," answered the bearded lady; "yet the name he bears is correct and significant, for he is called Clavileno el Aligero; whereby his miraculous peg, his wooden frame, and extraordinary speed, are all curiously expressed: so that, in respect of his name, he may vie with the renowned Rozinante." "I dislike not his name," replied Sancho; "but with what bridle or what halter is he guided?" "I have already told you," answered the Trifaldi, "that he is guided by a peg, which the rider turning this way and that, makes him go either aloft in the air, or else sweeping, and, as it were, brushing the earth, or in the middle region: a course which the discreet and wise generally endeavor to keep." "I have a mighty desire to see him," quoth Sancho; "but to think I will get upon him, either in the saddle or behind upon the crupper, is to look for pears upon an elm-tree. It were a jest, indeed, for me, who can hardly sit upon my own Dapple, though upon a pannel softer than silk, to think of bestriding a wooden crupper, without either pillow or cushion! In faith, I do not intend to flay myself to unbeard the best lady in the land. Let every one shave or shear as he likes best; I have no mind for so long a journey: my master may travel by himself. Besides, I have nothing to do with it—I am not wanted for the taking off these beards, as well as the business of my lady Dulcinea." "Indeed, my friend, you are," said the Trifaldi; "and so much need is there of your kind help, that without it nothing can be done." "In the name of all the saints in heaven!" quoth Sancho, "what have squires to do with their masters' adventures? Are we always to share the trouble, and they to reap all the glory? Body o' me! it might be something if the writers who recount their adventures would but set down in their books, 'such a knight achieved such an adventure, with the help of such a one, his squire, without whom the devil a bit could he have done it.' I say it would be something if we had our due; but, instead of this, they coolly tell us that 'Don Paralipomenon of the Three Stars finished the notable adventure of the six goblins,' and the like, without once mentioning his squire any more than if he had been a thousand miles off; though mayhap he, poor devil, was in the thick of it all the while! In truth, my good lord and lady, I say again, my master may manage this adventure by himself; and much good may it do him. I will stay with my lady duchess here, and perhaps when he comes back he may find Madam Dulcinea's business pretty forward; for I intend at my leisure whiles to lay it on to some purpose, so that I shall not have a hair to shelter me."

"Nevertheless, honest Sancho," quoth the duchess, "if your company be really necessary, you will not refuse to go; indeed, all good people will make it their business to entreat you; for piteous, truly, would it be that, through your groundless fears, these poor ladies should remain in this unseemly plight." "Odds my life!" exclaimed Sancho, "were this piece of charity undertaken for modest maidens, or poor charity-girls, a man might engage to undergo something; but to take all this trouble to rid duennas of their beards!—plague take them!—I had rather see the whole finical and squeamish tribe bearded, from the highest to the lowest of them!" "You seem to be upon bad terms with duennas, friend Sancho," said the duchess, "and of the same mind as the Toledan apothecary; but in truth you are in the wrong; for I have duennas in my family who might serve as models to all duennas; and here is my Donna Rodriguez, who will not allow me to say otherwise." "Your excellency may say what you please," said Rodriguez; "but Heaven knows the truth of everything; and, good or bad, bearded or smooth, such as we are, our mothers brought us forth like other women; and, since God has cast us into the world, He knows why and wherefore; and upon His mercy I rely, and not upon anybody's beard whatever."

"Enough, Signora Rodriguez," quoth Don Quixote; "as for you, Lady Trifaldi, and your persecuted friends, I trust that Heaven will speedily look with a pitying eye upon your sorrows, and that Sancho will do his duty, in obedience to my wishes. Would that Clavileno were here, and on his back Malambruno himself! for I am confident no razor would more easily shave your ladyship's beards than my sword shall shave off Malambruno's head from his shoulders. If Heaven in its wisdom permits the wicked to prosper, it is but for a time." "Ah, valorous knight!" exclaimed the afflicted lady, "may all the stars of the celestial regions regard your excellency with eyes of benignity, and impart strength to your arm and courage to your heart, to be the shield and refuge of the reviled and oppressed duennian order, abominated by apothecaries, calumniated by squires, and scoffed at by pages! Scorn betake the wretch who, in the flower of her age, doth not rather profess herself a nun than a duenna! Forlorn and despised as we are, although our descent were to be traced in a direct line from Hector of Troy himself, our ladies would not cease to 'thee' and 'thou' us, were they to be made queens for their condescension. O giant Malambruno! who, though an enchanter, art punctual in thy promises, send us the incomparable Clavileno, that our misfortunes may cease; for if the heats come on, and these beards of ours remain, woe be to us!" The Trifaldi uttered this with so much pathos that she drew tears from the eyes of all present; and so much was the heart of Sancho moved, that he secretly resolved to accompany his master to the far part of the world, if that would contribute to remove the bristles which deformed those venerable faces.

CHAPTER XLI

OF THE ARRIVAL OF CLAVILENO, WITH THE CONCLUSION OF THIS PROLIX ADVENTURE.

EVENING NOW CAME on, which was the time when the famous horse Clavileno was expected to arrive, whose delay troubled Don Quixote much, being apprehensive that, by its not arriving, either he was not the knight for whom this adventure was reserved, or that Malambruno had not the courage to meet him in single combat. But lo, on a sudden, four savages entered the garden, all clad in green ivy, and bearing on their shoulders a large wooden horse! They set him upon his legs on the ground and one of the savages said, "Let the knight mount who has the courage to bestride this wondrous machine." "Not I," quoth Sancho; "for neither have I courage, nor am I a knight." "And let the squire, if he has one," continued the savage, "mount the crupper, and trust to valorous Malambruno; for no other shall do him harm. Turn but the pin on his forehead, and he will rush through the air to the spot where Malambruno waits; and to shun the danger of a lofty flight, let the eyes of riders be covered till the neighing of the horse shall give the signal of his completed journey." Having thus spoken, he left Clavileno, and with courteous demeanor departed with his companions.

The afflicted lady no sooner perceived the horse than, almost with tears, addressing herself to Don Quixote, "Valorous knight!" said she, "Malambruno has kept his word; here is the horse; our beards are increasing, and every one of us, with every hair of them, entreat and conjure you to shave and shear us. Mount, therefore, with your squire behind you, and give a happy beginning to your journey." "Madam," said Don Quixote, "I will do it with all my heart, without waiting for either cushion or spurs, so great is my desire to see your ladyship and these your unfortunate friends shaven and clean." "That will not I," quoth Sancho, "either with a bad or good will, or anywise; and if this shaving cannot be done without my mounting that crupper, let my master seek some other squire, or these madams some other barber; for, being no wizard, I have no stomach for these journeys. What will my islanders say when they hear that their governor goes riding upon the wind? Besides, it is three thousand leagues from here to Candaya,—what if the horse should tire upon the road, or the giant be fickle and change his mind? Seven years, at least, it would take us to travel home, and by that time I should have neither island or islanders that would own me! No, no, I know better things; I know, too, that delay breeds danger, and when they bring you a heifer, be ready with the rope. These gentlewomen's beards must excuse me;—faith! St. Peter is well at Rome; and so am I too, in this house, where I am made much of, and, through the noble master thereof, hope to see myself a governor."

"Friend Sancho," said the duke, "your island neither floats nor stirs, and therefore it will keep till your return; indeed, so fast is it rooted in the earth, that three good pulls would not tear it from its place; and, as you know that all officers of any value are obtained by some service or other consideration, what I expect in return for this government I have conferred upon you, is only that you attend your master on this memorable occasion; and, whether you return upon Clavileno with the expedition his speed promises, or be it your fortune to return on foot, like a pilgrim, from house to house and from inn to inn,—however it may be, you will find your island where you left it, and your islanders with the same desire to receive you for their governor. My good-will is equally unchangeable; and to doubt that truth, Signor Sancho, would be a notorious injury to the inclination I have to serve you." "Good your worship, say no more," quoth Sancho; "I am a poor squire, and my shoulders cannot bear the weight of so much kindness. Let my master mount, let my eyes be covered, and good luck go with us. But tell me, when we are aloft, may I not say my prayers and entreat all the saints and angels to help me?" "Yes, surely," answered the Trifaldi, "you may invoke whomsoever you please; for Malambruno is a Christian, and performs his enchantments with great discretion and much precaution." "Well, let us away," quoth Sancho, "and Heaven prosper us!" "Since the memorable business of the fulling-mill," said Don Quixote, "I have never seen thee, Sancho, in such trepidation; and were I superstitious, as some people, this extraordinary fear of thine would a little discourage me. But come hither, friend; for, with the leave of these nobles, I would speak a word or two with thee in private."

Don Quixote then drew Sancho aside among some trees out of hearing, and, taking hold of both his hands, said to him, "Thou seest, my good Sancho, the long journey we are about to undertake; the period of our return is uncertain, and Heaven alone knows what leisure or convenience our affairs may admit during our absence; I earnestly beg, therefore, now that opportunity serves, thou wilt retire to thy chamber, as if to fetch something necessary for the journey, and there in a trice give thyself, if it be but five hundred lashes, in part of the three thousand and three hundred for which thou art pledged; for work well begun is half ended." "By my soul," quoth Sancho, "your worship is stark mad! I am just going to gallop a thousand leagues upon a bare board, and you would have me first flay my body!—verily, verily, your worship is out of all reason. Let us go and shave these duennas, and on my return I promise to make such dispatch in getting out of debt, that your worship shall be contented,—can I say more?" "With that promise," said Don Quixote, "I feel somewhat comforted, and believe thou wilt perform it; for, though thou art not over-wise, thou art true blue in thy integrity." "I am not blue, but brown," quoth Sancho; "but though I were a mixture of both, I would make good my promise."

The knight and squire now returned to the company; and as they were preparing to mount Clavileno, Don Quixote said, "Hoodwink thyself, Sancho, and get up: he that sends for us from countries so remote cannot surely intend to betray us, for he would gain little glory by deceiving those who confide in him. And supposing the success of the adventure should not be equal to our hopes, yet of the glory of so brave an attempt no malice can deprive us." "Let us be gone, sir," quoth Sancho, "for the beards and tears of these ladies have pierced my heart, and I shall not eat to do me good till I see them smooth again. Mount, sir, and hoodwink first, for if I am to have the crupper, your worship, who sits in the saddle, must get up first." "That is true," replied Don Quixote; and, pulling a handkerchief out of his pocket, he requested the afflicted lady to place the bandage over his eyes; but it was no sooner done than he uncovered them again, saying, "I remember to have read in the 'Æneid' of Virgil, that the fatal wooden horse dedicated by the Greeks to their tutelary goddess Minerva, was filled with armed knights, who by that stratagem got admittance into Troy, and wrought its downfall. Will it not, therefore, be prudent, before I trust myself upon Clavileno, to examine what may be in his body?" "There is no need of that," said the Trifaldi; "for I am confident Malambruno has nothing in him of the traitor: your worship may mount him without fear, and should any harm ensue, let the blame fall on me alone."

Don Quixote, now considering that to betray any further doubts would be a reflection on his courage, vaulted at once into the saddle. He then tried the pin, which he found would turn very easily; stirrups he had none, so that, with his legs dangling, he looked like a figure in some Roman triumph woven in Flemish tapestry.

Very slowly, and much against his will, Sancho then got up behind, fixing himself as well as he could upon the crupper; and finding it very deficient in softness, he humbly begged the duke to accommodate him, if possible, with some pillow or cushion, even though it were from the duchess's state sofa, or from one of the page's beds, as the horse's crupper seemed rather to be of marble than of wood; but the Trifaldi, interfering, assured him that Clavileno would not endure any more furniture upon him; but that, by sitting sideways, as women ride, he would find himself greatly relieved. Sancho followed her advice; and, after taking leave of the company he suffered his eyes to be covered. But soon after he raised the bandage, and looking sorrowfully at his friends, begged them, with a countenance of woe, to assist him at that perilous crisis with a few *Paternosters* and *Ave Marias*, as they hoped for the same charity from others when in the like extremity. "What, then!" said Don Quixote, "art thou a thief in the hands of the executioner, and at the point of death, that thou hast recourse to such prayers? Dastardly wretch without a soul! dost thou not know that the fair Magalona sat in the same place, and, if there be truth in history, alighted from it, not into the grave, but into the throne of France? And do not I sit by thee—I that may vie with the valorous Peter, who pressed this very seat that I now press? Cover, cover thine eyes, heartless animal, and publish not thy shame—at least in my presence." "Hoodwink me, then," answered Sancho; "but, since I must neither pray myself, nor beg others to do it for me, no wonder if I am afraid that we may be followed by a legion of devils, who may watch their opportunity to fly away with us."

They were now blindfolded, and Don Quixote feeling himself firmly seated, put his hand to the peg, upon which all the duennas, and the whole company, raised their voices at once, calling out, "Speed you well, valorous knight! Heaven guide thee, undaunted squire! now you fly aloft!—see how they cut the air more swiftly than an arrow! how they mount and soar, and astonish the world below! Steady, steady, valorous Sancho! you seem to reel and totter in your seat—beware of falling; for, should you drop from that tremendous height, your fall would be more terrible than that of Phaeton!" Sancho, hearing all this, pressed closer to his master, and, grasping him fast, said, "How can they say, sir, that we are got so high, when we hear them as plain as if they were close by us?" "Take no heed of that, Sancho," said Don Quixote, "for in these extraordinary flights, to see or hear a thousand leagues is nothing. But squeeze me not quite so hard, good Sancho, or thou wilt unhorse me. In truth, I see not why thou shouldst be so alarmed, for I can safely swear, an easier-paced steed I never rode in all my life: faith, it goes as glibly as if it did not move at all! Banish fear, my friend; the business goes on swimmingly, with a gale fresh and far behind us." "Gad, I think so too!" quoth Sancho, "for I feel the wind here, as if a thousand pairs of bellows were puffing at my back." And, indeed, this was the fact, as sundry large bellows were just then pouring upon them an artificial storm; in truth, so well was this adventure managed and contrived, that nothing was wanting to make it complete. Don Quixote now feeling the wind, "Without doubt," said he, "we have now reached the second region of the air, where the hail and snow are formed; thunder and lightning are engendered in the third region; and, if we go on mounting at this rate, we shall soon be in the region of fire; and how to manage this peg I know not, so as to avoid mounting to where we shall be burnt alive."

Just at that time some flax, set on fire at the end of a long cane, was held near their faces; the warmth of which being felt, "May I be hanged," said Sancho, "if we are not already there, or very near it, for half my beard is singed off—I have a huge mind, sir, to peep out and see whereabouts we are." "Heaven forbid such rashness!" said Don Quixote: "remember the true story of the licentiate Toralvo, who was carried by devils, hoodwinked, riding on a cane, with his eyes shut, and in twelve hours reached Rome, where, lighting on the Tower of Nona, he saw the tumult, witnessed the assault and death of the Constable of Bourbon, and the next morning returned to Madrid, where he gave an account of all that he had seen. During his passage through the air, he said that a devil told him to open his eyes, which he did, and found himself, as he thought, so near the body of the moon that he could have laid hold of it with his hand; but that he durst not look downwards to the earth, lest his brain should turn. Therefore, Sancho, let us not run the risk of uncovering in such a place, but rather trust to him who has taken charge of us, as he will be responsible: perhaps we are just now soaring aloft to a certain height, in order to come souse down upon the kingdom of Candaya, like a hawk upon a heron; and, though it seems not more than half an hour since we left the garden, doubtless we have travelled through an amazing space." "As to that I can say nothing," quoth Sancho Panza; "I can only say that if Madam Magalona was content to ride upon this crupper without a cushion, her flesh could not have been the tenderest in the world."

... THROUGH A CREVICE I LOOKED DOWN, AND THERE I SAW (HEAVEN BLESS US!) THE EARTH SO FAR OFF THAT IT LOOKED TO ME NO BIGGER THAN A GRAIN OF MUSTARD-SEED ...

This conversation between the two heroes was overheard by the duke and duchess, and all who were in the garden, to their great diversion; and, being now disposed to finish the adventure, they applied some lighted flax to Clavileno's tail; upon which, his body being full of combustibles, he instantly blew up with a prodigious report, and threw his riders to the ground. The Trifaldi, with the whole bearded squadron of duennas, vanished, and all that remained in the garden were laid stretched on the ground as if in a trance. Don Quixote and Sancho got upon their legs in but an indifferent plight, and looking round, were amazed to find themselves to the same garden with such a number of people strewed about them on all sides; but their wonder was increased when, on a huge lance sticking in the earth, they beheld a sheet of white parchment attached to it by silken strings, whereon was written in letters of gold, the following words:

> "The renowned knight, Don Quixote de la Mancha, has achieved the stupendous adventure of Trifaldi the Afflicted and her companions in grief only by attempting it. Malambruno is satisfied, his wrath is appeased, the beards of the unhappy have vanished, and Don Clavijo and Antonomasia have recovered their pristine state. When the squirely penance shall be completed, then shall the white dove, delivered from the cruel talons of the pursuing hawks, be enfolded in the arms of her beloved turtle: such is the will of Merlin, prince of enchanters."

Don Quixote having read the prophetic decree, and perceiving at once that it referred to the disenchantment of Dulcinea, he expressed his gratitude to Heaven for having, with so much ease, performed so great an exploit, whereby many venerable females had been happily rescued from disgrace. He then went to the spot where the duke and duchess lay on the ground, and, taking the duke by the arm, he said, "Courage, courage, my good lord; the adventure is over without damage to the bars, as you will find by that record." The duke gradually, as if awaking from a sound sleep, seemed to recover his senses, as did the duchess and the rest of the party; expressing, at the same time, so much wonder and affright that what they feigned so well seemed almost reality to themselves.

Though scarcely awake, the duke eagerly looked at the scroll, and, having read it, with open arms embraced Don Quixote, declaring him to be the bravest of knights. Sancho looked all about for the afflicted duenna, to see what kind of face she had when beardless, and whether she was now as goodly to the sight as her stately presence seemed to promise; but he was told that, when Clavileno came tumbling down in the flames through the air, the Trifaldi, with her whole train, vanished, with not a beard to be seen among them—every hair was gone, root and branch!

The duchess inquired of Sancho how he had fared during that long voyage. "Why, truly, madam," answered he, "I have seen wonders; for as we were passing through the region of fire, as my master called it, I had, you must know, a mighty mind to take a peep; and though my master would not consent to it, I, who have an itch to know everything, and a hankering after what is forbidden, could not help, softly and unperceived, shoving the cloth a little aside, when through a crevice I looked down, and there I saw (Heaven bless us!) the earth so far off that it looked to me no bigger than a grain of mustard-seed, and the men that walked upon it little bigger than hazel-nuts!—only think, then, what a height we must have been!" "Take care what you say, friend," said the duchess; "had it been so, you could not have seen the earth nor the people upon it: a hazel-nut, good man, would have covered the whole earth." "Like enough," said Sancho, "but for all that, I had a side view of it, and saw it all." "Take heed, Sancho," said the duchess, "for one cannot see the whole of anything by a side view." "I know nothing about views," replied Sancho; "I only know that your ladyship should remember that, since we flew by enchantment, by enchantment I might see the whole earth, and all the men upon it, in whatever way I looked; and, if your ladyship will not credit that, neither will you believe me when I tell you that, thrusting up the kerchief close to my eyebrows, I found myself so near to heaven that it was not above a span and a half from me (bless us all! what a place it is for bigness!) and it so fell out that we passed close by the place where the seven little she-goats are kept; and, by my faith, having been a goatherd in my youth, I no sooner saw them than I longed to play with them awhile; and had I not done it, I verily believe I should have died; so what did I, but, without saying a word, softly slide down from Clavileno, and play with the sweet little creatures, which are like so many violets, for almost three-quarters of an hour; and all the while Clavileno seemed not to move from the place, nor stir a jot."

"And while honest Sancho was diverting himself with the goats," quoth the duke, "how did Signor Don Quixote amuse himself?" To which the knight answered, "As these and such-like concerns are out of the order of nature, I do not wonder at Sancho's assertions; for my own part, I can truly say I neither looked up nor down, and saw neither heaven nor earth, nor sea nor sands. It is nevertheless certain that I was sensible of our passing through the region of air, and even touched upon that of fire; but that we passed beyond it I cannot believe; for, the fiery region lying between the sphere of the moon and the uppermost region of the air, we could not reach that heaven where the seven goats are which Sancho speaks of, without being burnt; and since we were not burnt, either Sancho lies or Sancho dreams." "I neither lie nor dream," answered Sancho; "only ask me the marks of these same goats, and by them you may guess whether I speak the truth or not." "Tell us what they were, Sancho," quoth the duchess. "Two of them," replied Sancho, "are green, two carnation, two blue, and one motley-colored." "A new kind of goats are those," said the duke; "in our region of the earth we have none of such colors." "The reason is plain," quoth Sancho; "your highness will allow that there must be some difference between the goats of heaven and those of earth." "Prithee, Sancho," said the duke, "was there a he-goat among them?" "Not one, sir," answered Sancho; "and I was told that none are suffered to pass beyond the horns of the moon."

They did not choose to question Sancho any more concerning his journey, perceiving him to be in the humor to ramble all over the heavens, and tell them of all that was passing there, without having stirred a foot from the place where he mounted.

Thus concluded the adventure of the Afflicted Duenna, which furnished the duke and duchess with a subject of mirth, not only at the time, but for the rest of their lives, and Sancho something to relate had he lived for ages. "Sancho," said Don Quixote (whispering him in the ear); "if thou wouldst have us credit all thou hast told us of heaven, I expect thee to believe what I saw in Montesinos' cave—I say no more."

Ben Jonson

(1573–1637)

Ben Jonson is considered second only to Shakespeare in English Jacobean drama in his career that spanned three decades. During the reigns of Elizabeth I and James I, he wrote more than thirty plays, as many masques (allegorical plays performed by masked actors), and four books of poetry. Jonson never knew his father, who died two months before Jonson was born in June 1573. (Jonson dropped the *h* in his last name to distinguish himself, though it took until 1840 for the printers to stop inserting it.)

Despite his modest background as the stepson of a bricklayer, Jonson was fortunate enough to attend Westminster School, a prestigious academy. His intelligence and literary talents were noted by his tutors, but he was unable to continue at school. He joined his stepfather's trade and then traveled to the Netherlands as part of the Protestant Hollanders who were defending their religious and political rights against Spanish and Catholic rule. After a successful stint as a soldier (rumor has it he fought and killed an enemy soldier in a duel), Jonson returned to London and married Anne Lewis in 1592 (or 1594).

During their marriage they had two children, a daughter (who only lived six months) and a son, whom Jonson called his "best piece of poetry." Sadly, the boy was stricken by the plague and did not live past the age of seven. Jonson entered the dramatic arts in 1597, but did not seem content reciting other men's words, so he collaborated on a play, *The Isle of Dogs,* which was regarded as seditious and slanderous. It landed him in jail, where he met Philip Henslowe. Henslowe encouraged Jonson to join his (and Shakespeare's) theatre company when they were both released from jail.

The following year saw Jonson's first dramatic triumph with the premiere of *Every Man in His Humour*, a play written in the style of Latin Comedy. Apparently Shakespeare appeared in this performance at the Globe. Jonson made some money off the play and proceeded to spend it around town. He abandoned acting and lived off the penning of masques for the court. But his temper got him in trouble, and he became involved in a sword duel with an actor, Gabriel Spencer, in which he was the victor and Spencer the victim. He was put in prison for murder, and there he converted to Roman Catholicism. Because of his conversion, he was released after pleading "benefit of clergy." He was branded on his thumb so he could be identified as a repeat offender if he was accused of murder again. All his life, he bore this felon's mark.

After another year of debt and jail again, Jonson wrote *Every Man Out of His Humour.* The play made more enemies than profits when it was performed, so Jonson did a bold thing: he had the play published to allow people to read and judge it as poetry or literature separate from its interpretation on stage. His move paid off—the published version was very popular and went through three editions in its first year. In this play, Jonson caricatured Marston, a fellow playwright, and fired the first shot in what became known as the War of the Theatres. Jonson and Marston attacked and counterattacked with their plays, Jonson writing *Cynthia's Revels* and *The Poetaster.* Feelings were soothed when Marston included a tribute to Jonson in his play *The Malcontent.*

In 1606, Jonson completed *Volpone,* the stage play that is considered his finest work. It was first presented by Shakespeare's company, The King's Men, and signaled a return to theatrical glory for Jonson. It also marked his move to writing in a more serious vein, examining the morals and the ethics of the Elizabethan age and finding them lacking.

In the last thirty years of his career, Jonson shifted back and forth between masque and play writing, and writing poetry. He wrote four major plays between 1609 and 1616: *Epicoene, The Alchemist, Bartholomew Fair,* and *The Devil Is an Ass.* He returned to writing masques for the court and nondramatic poetry for nine years until 1625. He then penned a flurry of plays: *The Staple of News, The New Inn* (1629), *The Magnetic Lady* (1632), and *The Tale of the Tub,* finished in 1633.

With Shakespeare's death in 1616, Jonson had become the accepted head of the poetic guild. He was given an honorary degree at Oxford in 1619 and was chosen poet laureate of England, a post that came with a pension of a hundred pounds a year. He needed the money, for he had made little off his work and saved even less. He was in bad shape physically, morbidly obese, and in 1628 had suffered a stroke. He did continue to write (indeed, two of his plays were finished after 1628), but he never fully recovered from the stroke. He lived alone (his wife and children died before him) and struggled with paralysis and poverty. He died on August 6, 1637, at the age of sixty-five, and was buried in Westminster Abbey, his tomb bears the famous epitaph; "O rare Ben Johnson."

Volpone is considered Jonson's masterwork, a departure from his early lighter comedies and a work that draws on his knowledge of classical Roman drama. The plot involves legacy-hunting and the theme is that of the servant's being wiser than the master, both staples of Latin drama. An old, rich, single, childless man pretends to be dying to see how the suitors for his estate will behave and what they will bestow upon him to curry favor.

"I have no wife, no parent, child, ally/To give my substance to; but whom I make/must be my heir; . . ./This draws new clients daily to my house,/Women and men of every sex and age,/That bring me presents, send me plate, coin, jewels,/With hope that when I die (which they expect/Each greedy minute) it shall then return/Tenfold upon them."

In true Roman comic tradition, the servant Mosca (Italian for "fly," as in a parasite who lives off the host) is the brains behind the plot and brings Volpone these legacy-seekers bearing gifts. (The three male heir-hopefuls are named after predatory birds.) Mosca also plays each of them against one another to keep everyone off balance. Voltore (vulture) brings a silver plate and offers his legal services to Volpone later in court; Corbaccio (raven) brings him "a bag of bright chequeens"; and Corvino (crow) even offers his wife, Celia, as a sacrifice.

These characters are willing to lie, cheat, and debase themselves to be party to Volpone's fortune, allowing Jonson to populate his satire of humanity. He points to the effect that money has had on values and institutions. These people are willing to trade in their cherished traditions and relationships for gold. It is in a sense a moral comedy, for the wicked are revealed and punished. Jonson also parodies the law with the shark Voltore and his willingness to twist the truth to argue in Volpone's favor in court. Jonson attacks the money lust that was prevalent in London and the corrupt court system where he himself had spent so much time. All the characters in this play except Celia, Bonario, and Peregrine are corrupt and mercenary. Mosca connives to be made the sole heir. He is unmasked at the end by the judges and taken away to "first, then be whipt;/Then live perpetual prisoner in our galleys." After assaulting Celia and lying under oath in court, Volpone is also sentenced to jail. He is spared the whip, but is forced to languish in prison and reflect on his horrible deeds.

In *Volpone*, Jonson presented a new form of comedy, one that combined satirical and moral elements but was also entertaining and witty. The play tackled social issues: the danger of elevating gold above God, one's family, and one's values. Jonson succeeded on all fronts with *Volpone*. He expressed his outrage at the moral backsliding he saw in London, he created a whole new type of fable in poetic verse, and he sold some tickets.

"In all his poems still hath been this measure/To mix profit with your pleasure."

Volpone

DRAMATIS PERSONAE[1]

VOLPONE, a magnifico.
MOSCA, his parasite.
VOLTORE, an advocate.
CORBACCIO, an old gentleman.
CORVINO, a merchant.
BONARIO, son to Corbaccio.
SIR POLITIC WOULD-BE, a knight.
PEREGRINE, a gentleman traveller.
NANO, a dwarf.
CASTRONE, an eunuch.
ANDROGYNO, an hermaphrodite.
GREGE (or Mob)
COMMENDATORI, officers of justice.
MERCATORI, three merchants.
AVOCATORI, four magistrates.
NOTARIO, the register.
LADY WOULD-BE, Sir Politic's wife.
CELIA, Corvino's wife.
SERVITORI, SERVANTS, two WAITING-WOMEN, &c.

SCENE—VENICE

The Argument

*V*OLPONE, childless, rich, feigns sick, despairs,
*O*ffers his state to hopes of several heirs,
*L*ies languishing: his parasite receives
*P*resents of all, assures, deludes; then weaves
*O*ther cross plots, which ope themselves, are told.
*N*ew tricks for safety are sought; they thrive: when, bold,
*E*ach tempts th' other again, and all are sold.

Prologue

Now, luck yet send us, and a little wit
   Will serve to make our play hit;
According to the palates of the season,
   There is rhyme, not empty of reason.
This we were bid to credit from our poet,
   Whose true scope, if you would know it,
In all his poems still hath been this measure,
   To mix profit with your pleasure;
And not as some, whose throats their envy failing,
   Cry hoarsely, "All he writes is railing:"
And when his plays come forth, think they can flout them,
   With saying, he was a year about them.
To this there needs no lie, but this his creature,
   Which was two months since no feature:
And though he dares give them five lives to mend it,
   'T is known, five weeks fully penn'd it,
From his own hand, without a coadjutor,
   Novice, journeyman, or tutor.
Yet thus much I can give you as a token
   Of his play's worth, no eggs are broken,
Nor quaking custards with fierce teeth affrighted,
   Wherewith your rout are so delighted;
Nor hales he in a gull,[2] old ends reciting,
   To stop gaps in his loose writing;
With such a deal of monstrous and fore'd action,
   As might make Bethlem[3] a faction:

Nor made he his play for jests stol'n from each table,
But makes jests to fit his fable;
And so presents quick comedy refin'd,
As best critics have design'd;
The laws of time, place, persons he observeth,
From no needful rule he swerveth.
All gall and copperas[4] from his ink he draineth,
Only a little salt remaineth,
Wherewith he'll rub your cheeks, till, red with laughter,
They shall look fresh a week after.

ACT I

SCENE I—A ROOM IN VOLPONE'S HOUSE

Enter VOLPONE, MOSCA.

VOLPONE: Good morning to the day; and next, my gold!
Open the shrine, that I may see my saint. [MOSCA *withdraws the curtain, and discovers piles of gold, plate, jewels, etc.*]
Hail the world's soul, and mine! More glad than is
The teeming earth to see the long'd-for sun
Peep through the horns of the celestial Ram,
Am I, to view thy splendour dark'ning his;
That lying here, amongst my other hoards,
Show'st like a flame by night, or like the day
Struck out of chaos, when all darkness fled
Unto the centre.[5] O thou son of Sol,
But brighter than thy father, let me kiss,
With adoration, thee, and every relic
Of sacred treasure in this blessed room.
Well did wise poets, by thy glorious name,
Tide that age which they would have the best;
Thou being the best of things, and far transcending
All style of joy, in children, parents, friends,

Or any other waking dream on earth:
Thy looks when they to Venus did ascribe,
They should have given her twenty thousand Cupids;
Such are thy beauties and our loves! Dear saint,
Riches, the dumb god, that giv'st all men tongues,
That canst do nought, and yet mak'st men do all things;
The price of souls; even hell, with thee to boot,
Is made worth heaven. Thou art virtue, fame,
Honour, and all things else. Who can get thee,
He shall be noble, valiant, honest, wise—
MOS.: And what he will, sir. Riches are in fortune
A greater good than wisdom is in nature.
VOLPONE: True, my beloved Mosca. Yet I glory
More in the cunning purchase of my wealth,
Than in the glad possession, since I gain
No common way; I use no trade, no venture;
I wound no earth with ploughshares, I fat no beasts
To feed the shambles; have no mills for iron,
Oil, corn, or men, to grind them into powder;
I blow no subtle glass, expose no ships
To threat'nings of the furrow-faced sea;
I turn no monies in the public bank,
No usure private.
MOS.: No, sir, nor devour
Soft prodigals. You shall ha' some will swallow
A melting heir as glibly as your Dutch
Will pills of butter, and ne'er purge for it;
Tear forth the fathers of poor families
Out of their beds, and coffin them alive
In some kind clasping prison, where their bones
May be forthcoming, when the flesh is rotten:
But your sweet nature doth abhor these courses;
You loathe the widow's or the orphan's tears
Should wash your pavements, or their piteous cries
Ring in your roofs, and beat the air for vengeance.
VOLP.: Right, Mosca; I do loathe it.
MOS.: And, besides, sir,

You are not like the thresher that doth stand
With a huge flail, watching a heap of corn,
And, hungry, dares not taste the smallest grain,
But feeds on mallows, and such bitter herbs;
Nor like the merchant, who hath fill'd his vaults
With Romagnia, rich and Candian[6] wines,
Yet drinks the lees of Lombard's vinegar:
You will not lie in straw, whilst moths and worms
Feed on your sumptuous hangings and soft beds;
You know the use of riches, and dare give now
From that bright heap, to me, your poor observer,
Or to your dwarf, or your hermaphrodite,
Your eunuch, or what other household trifle
Your pleasure allows maintenance—
VOL.: Hold thee, Mosca,
Take of my hand; thou strik'st on truth in all,
And they are envious term thee parasite.
Call forth my dwarf, my eunuch, and my fool,
And let 'em make me sport.

[*Exit* MOSCA.]

What should I do,
But cocker[7] up my genius, and live free
To all delights my fortune calls me to?
I have no wife, no parent, child, ally,
To give my substance to; but whom I make
Must be my heir; and this makes men observe[8] me:
This draws new clients daily to my house,
Women and men of every sex and age,
That bring me presents, send me plate, coin, jewels,
With hope that when I die (which they expect
Each greedy minute) it shall then return
Tenfold upon them; whilst some, covetous
Above the rest, seek to engross me whole,
And counter-work the one unto the other,
Contend in gifts, as they would seem in love:
All which I suffer, playing with their hopes,
And am content to coin 'em into profit,

And look upon their kindness, and take more,
And look on that; still bearing them in hand,[9]
Letting the cherry knock against their lips,
And draw it by their mouths, and back again—
How now!

SCENE II—THE SAME

To him re-enter MOSCA, *with* NANO, ANDROGYNO, *and* CASTRONE.

NAN.: "Now, room for fresh gamesters, who do will you to know,
They do bring you neither play nor university show;
And therefore do intreat you that whatsoever they rehearse,
May not fare a whit the worse, for the false pace of the verse.
If you wonder at this, you will wonder more ere we pass,
For know, here[10] is inclos'd the soul of Pythagoras,
That juggler divine, as hereafter shall follow;
Which soul, fast and loose, sir, came first from Apollo,
And was breath'd into Aethalides, Mercurius his son,
Where it had the gift to remember all that ever was done.
From thence it fled forth, and made quick transmigration
To goldy-lock'd Euphorbus, who was kill'd in good fashion,
At the siege of old Troy, by the cuckold of Sparta.
Hermotimus was next (I find it in my charta).
To whom it did pass, where no sooner it was missing,
But with one Pyrrhus of Delos it learn'd to go a-fishing;
And thence did it enter the sophist of Greece.
From Pythagore, she went into a beautiful piece,
Hight Aspasia, the meretrix; and the next toss of her
Was again of a whore, she became a philosopher,
Crates the cynick, as itself doth relate it:
Since kings, knights, and beggars, knaves, lords, and fools gat it,
Besides ox and ass, camel, mule, goat, and brock,[11]
In all which it hath spoke, as in the cobbler's cock.[12]
But I come not here to discourse of that matter,
Or his one, two, or three, or his great oath, BY QUATER![13]

His musics, his trigon,[14] his golden thigh,
Or his telling how elements shift; but I
Would ask, how of late thou hast suffer'd translation,
And shifted thy coat in these days of reformation.
AND.: Like one of the reform'd, a fool, as you see,
Counting all old doctrine heresy.
NAN.: But not on thine own forbid meats hast thou ventur'd?
AND.: On fish, when first a Carthusian I enter'd.
NAN.: Why, then thy dogmatical silence hath left thee?
AND.: Of that an obstreperous lawyer bereft me.
NAN.: O wonderful change, when sir lawyer forsook thee!
For Pythagore's sake, what body then took thee?
AND.: A good dull mule.
NAN.: And how! by that means
Thou wert brought to allow of the eating of beans?
AND.: Yes.
NAN.: But from the mule into whom didst thou pass?
AND.: Into a very strange beast, by some writers call'd an ass;
By others a precise,[15] pure, illuminate brother
Of those devour flesh, and sometimes one another;
And will drop you forth a libel, or a sanctifi'd lie,
Betwixt every spoonful of a nativity-pie.[16]
NAN.: Now quit thee, for heaven, of that profane nation.
And gently report thy next transmigration.
AND.: To the same that I am.
NAN.: A creature of delight,
And, what is more than a fool, an hermaphrodite!
Now, prithee, sweet soul, in all thy variation,
Which body wouldst thou choose to keep up thy station?
AND.: Troth, this I am in: even here would I tarry.
NAN.: 'Cause here the delight of each sex thou canst vary?
AND.: Alas, those pleasures be stale and forsaken;
No, 'tis your fool wherewith I am so taken,
The only one creature that I can call blessed;
For all other forms I have prov'd most distressed.
NAN.: Spoke true, as thou wert in Pythagoras still.
This learned opinion we celebrate will,

Fellow eunuch, as behoves us, with all our wit and art,
To dignify that whereof ourselves are so great and special a part."
VOLP.: Now, very, very pretty! Mosca, this
Was thy invention?
MOS.: If it please my patron,
Not else.
VOLP.: It doth, good Mosca.
MOS.: Then it was, sir.
[NANO *and* CASTRONE *sing.*]
SONG.
"Fools, they are the only nation
Worth men's envy or admiration;
Free from care or sorrow-taking,
Selves and others merry making:
All they speak or do is sterling.
Your fool he is your great man's darling,
And your ladies' sport and pleasure;
Tongue and bauble are his treasure,
E'en his face begetteth laughter,
And he speaks truth free from slaughter;[17]
He's the grace of every feast,
And sometimes the chiefest guest;
Hath his trencher[18] and his stool,
When wit waits upon the fool.
O, who would not be
He, he, he?"
[*One knocks without.*]
VOLP.: Who's that? Away! Look, Mosca.
Fool, begone!
[*Exeunt* NANO, CAST. *and* ANDRO.]
MOS.: 'T is Signior Voltore, the advocate;
I know him by his knock.
VOLP.: Fetch me my gown,
My furs and night-caps; say my couch is changing
And let him entertain himself awhile
Without i' th' gallery.
[*Exit* MOSCA.]

Now, now my clients
Begin their visitation! Vulture, kite,
Raven, and gorcrow,[19] all my birds of prey,
That think me turning carcase, now they come:
I am not for 'em yet.
[*Re-enter* MOSCA, *with the gown, etc.*]
How now! the news?
MOS.: A piece of plate, sir.
VOLP.: Of what bigness?
MOS.: Huge,
Massy, and antique, with your name inscrib'd,
And arms engraven.
VOLP.: Good! and not a fox
Stretcht on the earth, with fine delusive sleights,
Mocking a gaping crow? ha, Mosca!
MOS.: Sharp, sir.
VOLP. Give me my furs.
[*Puts on his sick dress.*]
Why dost thou laugh so, man?
MOS.: I cannot choose, sir, when I apprehend
What thoughts he has without now, as he walks:
That this might be the last gift he should give
That this would fetch you; if you died to-day,
And gave him all, what he should be to-morrow;
What large return would come of all his ventures;
How he should worshipp'd be, and reverenc'd;
Ride with his furs, and foot cloths; waited on
By herds of fools and clients; have clear way
Made for his mule, as letter'd as himself,
Be call'd the great and learned advocate:
And then concludes, there's nought impossible.
VOLP.: Yes, to be learned, Mosca.
MOS.: O, no: rich
Implies it. Hood an ass with reverend purple,
So you can hide his two ambitious[20] ears,
And he shall pass for a cathedral doctor.
VOLP.: My caps, my caps, good Mosca. Fetch him in.

MOS.: Stay, sir; your ointment for your eyes.
VOLP.: That's true;
Dispatch, dispatch: I long to have possession
Of my new present.
MOS.: That, and thousands more,
I hope to see you lord of.
VOLP.: Thanks, kind Mosca.
MOS.: And that, when I am lost in blended dust,
And hundreds such as I am, in succession—
VOLP.: Nay, that were too much, Mosca.
MOS.: You shall live
Still to delude these harpies.
VOLP.: Loving Mosca!
'T is well: my pillow now, and let him enter.
[*Exit* MOSCA.]
Now, my feign'd cough, my phthisic,[21] and my gout,
My apoplexy, palsy, and catarrhs,
Help, with your forced functions, this my posture,
Wherein, this three year, I have milk'd their hopes.
He comes; I hear him—Uh! [*coughing*] uh! uh! uh! O—

SCENE III—THE SAME

VOLPONE*; re-enter* MOSCA, *introducing* VOLTORE *with a piece of plate.*

MOS.: You still are what you were, sir. Only you,
Of all the rest, are he commands his love,
And you do wisely to preserve it thus,
With early visitation, and kind notes
Of your good meaning to him, which, I know,
Cannot but come most grateful. Patron! sir!
Here's Signior Voltore is come—
VOLP.: [*Faintly.*] What say you?
MOS.: Sir, Signior Voltore is come this morning
To visit you.
VOLP.: I thank him.

MOS.: And hath brought
A piece of antique plate, bought of St. Mark,[22]
With which he here presents you.

VOLP.: He is welcome.
Pray him to come more often.

MOS.: Yes.

VOLT.: What says he?

MOS.: He thanks you, and desires you see him often.

VOLP.: Mosca,

MOS.: My patron!

VOLP.: Bring him near, where is he?
I long to feel his hand.

MOS.: The plate is here, sir.

VOLT.: How fare you, sir?

VOLP.: I thank you, Signior Voltore;
Where is the plate? mine eyes are bad.

VOLT.: [*putting it into his hands.*] I'm sorry
To see you still thus weak.

MOS.: [*Aside.*] That he's not weaker.

VOLP.: You are too munificent.

VOLT.: No, sir; would to heaven
I could as well give health to you, as that plate!

VOLP.: You give, sir, what you can; I thank you. Your love
Hath taste in this, and shall not be unanswer'd:
I pray you see me often.

VOLT.: Yes, I shall, sir.

VOLP.: Be not far from me.

MOS.: Do you observe that, sir?

VOLP.: Hearken unto me still; it will concern you.

MOS.: You are a happy man, sir; know your good.

VOLP.: I cannot now last long—

MOS.: [*Aside.*] You are his heir, sir.

VOLT.: [*Aside.*] Am I?

VOLP.: I feel me going: Uh! uh! uh! uh!
I'm sailing to my port. Uh! uh! uh! uh!
And I am glad I am so near my haven.

MOS.: Alas, kind gentleman! Well, we must all go—

VOLT.: But, Mosca—
MOS.: Age will conquer.
VOLT.: Prithee, hear me;
Am I inscrib'd his heir for certain?
MOS.: Are you!
I do beseech you, sir, you will vouchsafe
To write me i' your family. All my hopes
Depend upon your worship: I am lost
Except the rising sun do shine on me.
VOLT.: It shall both shine, and warm thee, Mosca.
MOS.: Sir,
I am a man that hath not done your love
All the worst offices: here I wear your keys,
See all your coffers and your caskets lock'd,
Keep the poor inventory of your jewels,
Your plate, and monies; am your steward, sir,
Husband your goods here.
VOLT.: But am I sole heir?
MOS.: Without a partner, sir: confirm'd this morning:
The wax is warm yet, and the ink scarce dry
Upon the parchment.
VOLT.: Happy, happy me!
By what good chance, sweet Mosca?
MOS.: Your desert, sir;
I know no second cause.
VOLT.: Thy modesty
Is loath to know it; well, we shall requite it.
MOS.: He ever lik'd your course, sir; that first took him.
I oft have heard him say how he admir'd
Men of your large profession, that could speak
To every cause, and things mere contraries,
Till they were hoarse again, yet all be law;
That, with most quick agility, could turn,
And return; make knots, and undo them;
Give forked counsel; take provoking gold
On either hand, and put it up; these men,
He knew, would thrive with their humility.

And, for his part, he thought he should be blest
To have his heir of such a suff'ring spirit,
So wise, so grave, of so perplex'd a tongue,
And loud withal, that would not wag, nor scarce
Lie still, without a fee; when every word
Your worship but lets fall, is a chequin![23]—
[*Another knocks.*]
Who's that? one knocks; I would not have you seen, sir.
And yet—pretend you came and went in haste;
I'll fashion an excuse—and, gentle sir,
When you do come to swim in golden lard,
Up to the arms in honey, that your chin
Is borne up stiff with fatness of the flood,
Think on your vassal; but remember me:
I ha' not been your worst of clients.
VOLT.: Mosca!—
MOS.: When will you have your inventory brought, sir?
Or see a copy of the will?—Anon!
I'll bring them to you, sir. Away, begone,
Put business i' your face.
[*Exit* VOLTORE.]
VOLP.: [*Springing up.*] Excellent Mosca!
Come hither, let me kiss thee.
MOS.: Keep you still, sir.
Here is Corbaccio.
VOLP.: Set the plate away:
The vulture's gone, and the old raven's come.

SCENE IV—THE SAME

MOSCA, VOLPONE.

MOS.: Betake you to your silence, and your sleep.
Stand there and multiply. [*Putting the plate to the rest.*] Now we shall see
A wretch who is indeed more impotent
Than this can feign to be; yet hopes to hop

Over his grave.

[*Enter* CORBACCIO.]

Signior Corbaccio!

You're very welcome, sir.

CORB.: How does your patron?

MOS.: Troth, as he did, sir; no amends.

CORB.: What! mends he?

MOS.: No, sir: he's rather worse.

CORB.: That's well. Where is he?

MOS.: Upon his couch, sir, newly fall'n asleep.

CORB.: Does be sleep well?

MOS.: No wink, sir, all this night,

CORB.: Nor yesterday; but slumbers.[24] Good! he should take
Some counsel of physicians: I have brought him
An opiate here, from mine own doctor.

MOS.: He will not hear of drugs.

CORB.: Why? I myself
Stood by while 't was made, saw all th' ingredients;
And know it cannot but most gently work:
My life for his, 't is but to make him sleep.

VOLP.: [*Aside.*] Ay, his last sleep, if he would take it.

MOS.: Sir,
He has no faith in physic.

CORB.: Say you, say you?

MOS.: He has no faith in physic: he does think
Most of your doctors are the greater danger,
And worse disease, t' escape. I often have
Heard him protest that your physician
Should never be his heir.

CORB.: Not I his heir?

MOS.: Not your physician, sir.

CORB.: O, no, no, no,
I do not mean it.

MOS.: No, sir, nor their fees
He cannot brook: he says they flay a man
Before they kill him.

CORB.: Right, I do conceive you.

MOS.: And then they do it by experiment;
For which the law not only doth absolve 'em,
But gives them great reward: and he is loth
To hire his death so.
CORB.: It is true, they kill
With as much licence as a judge.
MOS.: Nay, more;
For he but kills, sir, where the law condemns,
And these can kill him too.
CORB.: Ay, or me;
Or any man. How does his apoplex?
Is that strong on him still?
MOS.: Most violent.
His speech is broken, and his eyes are set,
His face drawn longer than 't was wont—
CORB.: How! how!
Stronger than he was wont?
MOS.: No, sir; his face
Drawn longer than 't was wont.
CORB.: O, good!
MOS.: His mouth
Is ever gaping, and his eyelids hang.
CORB.: Good.
MOS.: A freezing numbness stiffens all his joints,
And makes the colour of his flesh like lead.
CORB.: 'T is good.
MOS.: His pulse beats slow, and dull.
CORB.: Good symptoms still.
MOS.: And from his brain—
CORB.: Ha? How? Not from his brain?
MOS.: Yes, sir, and from his brain—
CORB.: I conceive you; good.
MOS.: Flows a cold sweat, with a continual rheum,
Forth the resolved corners of his eyes.
CORB.: Is 't possible? Yet I am better, ha!
How does he with the swimming of his head?
MOS.: O, sir, 't is past the scotomy;[25] he now

Hath lost his feeling, and hath left to snort:
You hardly can perceive him, that he breathes.
CORB.: Excellent, excellent! sure I shall outlast him:
This makes me young again, a score of years.
MOS.: I was a-coming for you, sir.
CORB.: Has he made his will?
What has he giv'n me?
MOS.: No, sir.
CORB.: Nothing! ha?
MOS.: He has not made his will, sir.
CORB.: Oh, oh, oh!
What then did Voltore, the lawyer, here?
MOS.: He smelt a carcase, sir, when he but heard
My master was about his testament;
As I did urge him to it for your good—
CORB.: He came unto him, did he? I thought so.
MOS.: Yes, and presented him this piece of plate.
CORB.: To be his heir?
MOS.: I do not know, sir.
CORB.: True:
I know it too.
MOS.: [*Aside.*] By your own scale, sir.
CORB.: Well,
I shall prevent him yet. See, Mosca, look,
Here I have brought a bag of bright chequins,
Will quite lay down his plate.
MOS: [*taking the bag.*] Yea, marry, sir.
This is true physic, this your sacred medicine;
No talk of opiates to this great elixir!
CORB.: 'T is *auram palpabile*, if not *potabile*.[26]
MOS: It shall be minister'd to him in his bowl.
CORB.: Ay, do, do, do.
MOS: Most blessed cordial!
This will recover him.
CORB.: Yes, do, do, do.
MOS.: I think it were not best, sir.
CORB.: What?

MOS.: To recover him.

CORB.: O, no, no, no; by no means.

MOS.: Why, sir, this
Will work some strange effect, if he but feel it.

CORB.: 'T is true, therefore forbear; I'll take my venture:
Give me 't again.

MOS: At no hand: pardon me:
You shall not do yourself that wrong, sir. I
Will so advise you, you shall have it all.

CORB.: How?

MOS: All, sir; 't is your right, your own; no man
Can claim a part: 't is yours without a rival,
Decreed by destiny.

CORB.: How, how, good Mosca?

MOS.: I'll tell you, sir. This fit he shall recover,—

CORB.: I do conceive you.

MOS: And on first advantage
Of his gain'd sense, will I re-importune him
Unto the making of his testament:
And show him this. [*Pointing to the money.*]

CORB.: Good, good.

MOS.: 'T is better yet,
If you will hear, sir.

CORB.: Yes, with all my heart.

MOS.: Now would I counsel you, make home with speed;
There, frame a will; whereto you shall inscribe
My master your sole heir.

CORB.: And disinherit
My son?

MOS: O, sir, the better: for that colour[27]
Shall make it much more taking.

CORB.: O, but colour?

MOS.: This will, sir, you shall send it unto me.
Now, when I come to inforce, as I will do,
Your cares, your watchings, and your many prayers,
Your more than many gifts, your this day's present,
And last, produce your will; where, without thought,

Or least regard, unto your proper issue,
A son so brave, and highly meriting,
The stream of your diverted love hath thrown you
Upon my master, and made him your heir;
He cannot be so stupid, or stone-dead,
But out of conscience and mere gratitude—
CORB.: He must pronounce me his?
MOS.: 'T is true.
CORB.:
This plot
Did I think on before.
MOS.: I do believe it.

WHAT A RARE PUNISHMENT IS AVARICE TO ITSELF!

CORB.: Do you not believe it?
MOS.: Yes, sir,
CORB.: Mine own project.
MOS.: Which, when he hath done, sir—
CORB.: Publish'd me his heir?
MOS.: And you so certain to survive him—
CORB.: Ay.
MOS.: Being so lusty a man—
CORB.: 'T is true.
MOS.: Yes, sir—
CORB.: I thought on that too. See, how he should be
The very organ to express my thoughts!
MOS.: You have not only done yourself a good—
CORB.: But multipli'd it on my son.
MOS.: 'T is right, sir.
CORB.: Still, my invention.
MOS.: 'Las, sir! heaven knows,
It hath been all my study, all my care,
(I e'en grow gray withal,) how to work things—
CORB.: I do conceive, sweet Mosca.
MOS.: You are he
For whom I labour here.
CORB.: Ay, do, do, do:
I'll straight about it. [*Going.*]
MOS.: [*Aside.*] Rook go with you,[28] raven!

CORB.: I know thee honest.
MOS.: You do lie, sir!
CORB.: And—
MOS.: Your knowledge is no better than your ears, sir.
CORB.: I do not doubt to be a father to thee.
MOS.: Nor I to gull my brother of his blessing.
CORB.: I may ha' my youth restor'd to me, why not?
MOS.: Your worship is a precious ass!
CORB.: What sayst thou?
MOS.: I do desire your worship to make haste, sir.
CORB.: 'T is done, 't is done; I go. [*Exit.*]
VOLP.: [*leaping from his couch.*] O, I shall burst!
Let out my sides, let out my sides—
MOS.: Contain
Your flux of laughter, sir: you know this hope
Is such a bait, it covers any hook.
VOLP.: O, but thy working, and thy placing it!
I cannot hold; good rascal, let me kiss thee:
I never knew thee in so rare a humour.
MOS.: Alas, sir, I but do as I am taught;
Follow your grave instructions; give them words;
Pour oil into their ears, and send them hence.
VOLP.: 'T is true, 't is true. What a rare punishment
Is avarice to itself!
MOS.: Ay, with our help, sir.
VOLP.: So many cares, so many maladies,
So many fears attending on old age.
Yea, so often call'd on, as no wish
Can be more frequent with 'em, their limbs taint,
Their senses dull, their seeing, hearing, going,
All dead before them; yea, their very teeth,
Their instruments of eating, failing them:
Yet this is reckon'd life! Nay, here was one,
Is now gone home, that wishes to live longer!
Feels not his gout, nor palsy; feigns himself
Younger by scores of years, flatters his age
With confident belying it, hopes he may

With charms like Aeson,[29] have his youth restor'd;
And with these thoughts so battens, as if fate
Would be as easily cheated on as he,
And all turns air! Who's that there, now? a third!
[*Another knocks.*]

MOS.: Close, to your couch again; I hear his voice.
It is Corvino, our spruce merchant.

VOLP.: [*Lies down as before.*] Dead.[30]

MOS.: Another bout, sir, with your eyes [*anointing them*]. Who's there?

SCENE V—THE SAME

MOSCA, VOLPONE. *Enter* CORVINO.

MOS.: Signior Corvino! come most wish'd for! O,
How happy were you, if you knew it, now!

CORV.: Why? what? wherein?

MOS.: The tardy hour is come, sir.

CORV.: He is not dead?

MOS.: Not dead, sir, but as good;
He knows no man.

CORV.: How shall I do then?

MOS.: Why, sir?

CORV.: I have brought him here a pearl.

MOS.: Perhaps he has
So much remembrance left as to know you, sir:
He still calls on you; nothing but your name
Is in his mouth. Is your pearl orient,[31] sir?

CORV.: Venice was never owner of the like.

VOLP.: [*Faintly.*] Signior Corvino!

MOS.: Hark!

VOLP.: Signior Corvino.

MOS.: He calls you; step and give it him—He's here, sir.
And he has brought you a rich pearl.

CORV.: How do you, sir?

Tell him it doubles the twelve carat.

MOS.: Sir,

He cannot understand, his hearing's gone;
And yet it comforts him to see you—

CORV.: Say

I have a diamond for him, too.

MOS.: Best show 't, sir;

Put it into his hand: 't is only there
He apprehends: he has his feeling yet.
See how he grasps it!

CORV.: 'Las, good gentleman!

How pitiful the sight is!

MOS.: Tut, forget, sir.

The weeping of an heir should still be laughter
Under a visor.

CORV.: Why, am I his heir?

MOS.: Sir, I am sworn, I may not show the will
Till he be dead; but here has been Corbaccio,
Here has been Voltore, here were others too,
I cannot number 'em, they were so many;
All gaping here for legacies: but I,
Taking the vantage of his naming you,
Signior Corvino, *Signior Corvino*, took
Paper, and pen, and ink, and there I ask'd him
Whom he would have his heir! *Corvino*. Who
Should be executor? *Corvino*. And
To any question he was silent to,
I still interpreted the nods he made,
Through weakness, for consent: and sent home th' others,
Nothing bequeath'd them, but to cry and curse.

CORV.: O, my dear Mosca. [*They embrace.*] Does he not perceive us?

MOS.: No more than a blind harper. He knows no man,
No face of friend, nor name of any servant,
Who 't was that fed him last, or gave him drink:
Not those he hath begotten, or brought up,
Can he remember.

CORV.: Has he children?

MOS.: Bastards,
Some dozen, or more, that he begot on beggars,
Gypsies, and Jews, and black-moors, when he was drunk.
Knew you not that, sir? 't is the common fable,
The dwarf, the fool, the eunuch, are all his;
He's the true father of his family,
In all save me:—but he has giv'n 'em nothing.
CORV.: That's well, that's well! Art sure he does not hear us?
MOS.: Sure, sir! why, look you, credit your own sense. [*Shouts in* VOLP.*'s ear.*]
The pox approach, and add to your diseases,
If it would send you hence the sooner, sir,
For your incontinence, it hath deserv'd it
Throughly and throughly, and the plague to boot!—
You may come near, sir—Would you would once close
Those filthy eyes of yours, that flow with slime
Like two frog-pits; and those same hanging cheeks,
Cover'd with hide instead of skin—Nay, help, sir[32]—
That look like frozen dish-clouts set on end!
CORV.: Or like an old smok'd wall, on which the rain
Ran down in streaks!
MOS.: Excellent, sir! speak out:
You may be louder yet; a culverin[33]
Discharged in his ear would hardly bore it.
CORV.: His nose is like a common sewer, still running.
MOS.: 'T is good! And what his mouth?
CORV.: A very draught.[34]
MOS.: O, stop it up—
CORV.: By no means.
MOS.: Pray you, let me:
Faith I could stifle him rarely with a pillow
As well as any woman that should keep him.
CORV.: Do as you will; but I'll begone.
MOS.: Be so;
It is your presence makes him last so long.
CORV.: I pray you use no violence.

MOS.: No, sir! why?
Why should you be thus scrupulous, pray you, sir?
CORV.: Nay, at your discretion.
MOS.: Well, good sir, be gone.
CORV.: I will not trouble him now to take my pearl.
MOS.: Puh! nor your diamond. What a needless care
Is this afflicts you? Is not all here yours?
Am not I here, whom you have made your creature?
That owe my being to you?
CORV.: Grateful Mosca!
Thou art my friend, my fellow, my companion,
My partner, and shalt share in all my fortunes.
MOS.: Excepting one.
CORV.: What's that?
MOS.: Your gallant wife, sir.
[*Exit* CORV.]
Now is he gone: we had no other means
To shoot him hence but this.
VOLP.: My divine Mosca!
Thou hast to-day outgone thyself Who's there?
[*Another knocks.*]
I will be troubled with no more. Prepare
Me music, dances, banquets, all delights;
The Turk is not more sensual in his pleasures
Than will Volpone. [*Exit* MOSCA.] Let me see; a pearl!
A diamond! plate! chequins! Good morning's purchase.[35]
Why, this is better than rob churches, yet;
Or fat, by eating, once a month, a man—
[*Re-enter* MOSCA.]
Who is 't?
MOS.: The beauteous Lady Would-be, sir,
Wife to the English knight, Sir Politic Would-be,
(This is the style, sir, is directed me)
Hath sent to know how you have slept to-night,
And if you would be visited?
VOLP.: Not now:
Some three hours hence.

MOS.: I told the squire[36] so much.
VOLP.: When I am high with mirth and wine; then, then:
'Fore heaven, I wonder at the desperate valour
Of the bold English, that they dare let loose
Their wives to all encounters!
MOS.: Sir, this knight
Had not his name for nothing, he is *politic*,
And knows, howe'er his wife affect strange airs,
She hath not yet the face to be dishonest:
But had she Signior Corvino's wife's face—
VOLP.: Hath she so rare a face?
MOS.: O, sir, the wonder,
The blazing star of Italy! a wench
Of the first year, a beauty ripe as harvest!
Whose skin is whiter than a swan all over,
Than silver, snow, or lilies; a soft lip,
Would tempt you to eternity of kissing!
And flesh that melteth in the touch to blood!
Bright as your gold, and lovely as your gold!
VOLP.: Why had not I known this before?
MOS.: Alas, sir,
Myself but yesterday discover'd it.
VOLP.: How might I see her?
MOS.: O, not possible;
She's kept as warily as is your gold;
Never does come abroad, never takes air
But at a windore.[37] All her looks are sweet,
As the first grapes or cherries, and are watch'd
As near as they are.
VOLP. I must see her.
MOS.: Sir,
There is a guard of ten spies thick upon her,
All his whole household; each of which is set
Upon his fellow, and have all their charge,
When he goes out, when he comes in, examin'd.
VOLP.: I will go see her, though but at her window.
MOS.: In some disguise then.

VOLP.: That is true; I must
Maintain mine own shape still the same: we'll think.

[*Exeunt.*]

ACT II

SCENE I—ST. MARK'S PLACE; A RETIRED CORNER BEFORE CORVINO'S HOUSE

Enter SIR POLITIC WOULD-BE *and* PEREGRINE.

SIR P.: Sir, to a wise man, all the world's his soil:
It is not Italy, nor France, nor Europe,
That must bound me, if my fates call me forth.
Yet I protest, it is no salt[38] desire
Of seeing countries, shifting a religion,
Nor any disaffection to the state
Where I was bred, and unto which I owe
My dearest plots, hath brought me out, much less
That idle, antique, stale, grey-headed project
Of knowing men's minds and manners, with Ulysses!
But a peculiar humour of my wife's
Laid for this height[39] of Venice, to observe,
To quote,[40] to learn the language, and so forth—
I hope you travel, sir, with licence?
PER.: Yes.
SIR P.: I dare the safelier converse—How long, sir,
Since you left England?
PER.: Seven weeks.
SIR P.: So lately!
You have not been with my lord ambassador?
PER.: Not yet, sir.
SIR P.: Pray you, what news, sir, vents our climate?
I heard last night a most strange thing reported
By some of my lord's followers, and I long

To hear how 't will be seconded.
PER.: What was 't, sir?
SIR P.: Marry, sir, of a raven that should build
In a ship royal of the king's.
PER.: [*Aside.*] This fellow,
Does he gull me, trow? or is gull'd? Your name, sir?
SIR P.: My name is Politic Would-be.
PER.: [*Aside.*] O, that speaks him.
A knight, sir?
SIR P.: A poor knight, sir.
PER.: Your lady
Lies[41] here in Venice, for intelligence
Of tires and fashions, and behaviour,
Among the courtesans? The fine Lady Would-be?
SIR P.: Yes, sir; the spider and the bee ofttimes
Suck from one flower.
PER.: Good Sir Politic,
I cry you mercy; I have heard much of you:
'T is true, sir, of your raven.
SIR P.: On your knowledge?
PER.: Yes, and your lion's whelping in the Tower.
SIR P.: Another whelp![42]
PER.: Another, sir.
SIR P.: Now heaven!
What prodigies be these? The fires at Berwick!
And the new star! These things concurring, strange,
And full of omen! Saw you those meteors?
PER.: I did, sir.
SIR P.: Fearful! Pray you, sir, confirm me,
Were there three porpoises seen above the bridge,
As they give out?
PER.: Six, and a sturgeon, sir.
SIR P.: I am astonish'd.
PER.: Nay, sir, be not so;
I'll tell you a greater prodigy than these.
SIR P.: What should these things portend?
PER.: The very day

(Let me be sure) that I put forth from London,
There was a whale discover'd in the river,
As high as Woolwich, that had waited there,
Few know how many months, for the subversion
Of the Stode fleet.

SIR P.: Is 't possible? Believe it,
'T was either sent from Spain, or the archduke's:
Spinola's whale,[43] upon my life, my credit!
Will they not leave these projects? Worthy sir,
Some other news.

PER.: Faith, Stone the fool is dead,
And they do lack a tavern fool extremely.

SIR P.: Is Mass Stone dead?

PER.: He's dead, sir; why, I hope
You thought him not immortal? [*Aside.*] O, this knight,
Were he well known, would be a precious thing
To fit our English stage: he that should write
But such a fellow, should be thought to feign
Extremely, if not maliciously.

SIR P.: Stone dead!

PER.: Dead—Lord! how deeply, sir, you apprehend it!
He was no kinsman to you?

SIR P.: That I know of.
Well! that same fellow was an unknown fool.

PER.: And yet you knew him, it seems?

SIR P.: I did so. Sir,
I knew him one of the most dangerous heads
Living within the state, and so I held him.

PER.: Indeed, sir?

SIR P.: While he liv'd, in action,
He has receiv'd weekly intelligence,
Upon my knowledge, out of the Low Countries,
For all parts of the world, in cabbages;
And those dispens'd again to ambassadors,
In oranges, musk-melons, apricots,
Lemons, pome-citrons, and such-like; sometimes
In Colchester oysters, and your Selsey cockles.

PER.: You make me wonder.
SIR P.: Sir, upon my knowledge.
Nay, I've observ'd him, at your public ordinary,
Take his advertisement[44] from a traveller,
A conceal'd statesman, in a trencher of meat;
And instantly, before the meal was done,
Convey an answer in a tooth-pick.
PER.: Strange!
How could this be, sir?
SIR P.: Why, the meat was cut
So like his character, and so laid as he
Must easily read the cipher.
PER.: I have heard,
He could not read, sir.
SIR P.: So 't was given out,
In policy, by those that did employ him:
But he could read, and had your languages,
And to 't, as sound a noddle—
PER.: I have heard, sir,
That your baboons were spies, and that they were
A kind of subtle nation near to China.
SIR P.: Ay, ay, your Mamaluchi.[45] Faith, they had
Their hand in a French plot or two; but they
Were so extremely giv'n to women, as
They made discovery of all: yet I
Had my advices here, on Wednesday last,
From one of their own coat, they were return'd,
Made their relations, as the fashion is,
And now stand fair for fresh employment.
PER.: [*Aside.*] Heart!
This Sir Pol will be ignorant of nothing—
It seems, sir, you know all.
SIR P.: Not all, sir; but
I have some general notions. I do love
To note and to observe: though I live out,
Free from the active torrent, yet I'd mark
The currents and the passages of things

For mine own private use; and know the ebbs
And flows of state.
PER.: Believe it, sir, I hold
Myself in no small tie[46] unto my fortunes,
For casting me thus luckily upon you,
Whose knowledge, if your bounty equal it,
May do me great assistance, in instruction
For my behaviour, and my bearing, which
Is yet so rude and raw.
SIR P.: Why? came you forth
Empty of rules for travel?
PER.: Faith, I had
Some common ones, from out that vulgar grammar,
Which he that cri'd Italian to me, taught me.
SIR P.: Why, this it is that spoils all our brave bloods,
Trusting our hopeful gentry unto pedants,
Fellows of outside, and mere bark. You seem
To be a gentleman of ingenuous race:—
I not profess it, but my fate hath been
To be, where I have been consulted with,
In this high kind, touching some great men's sons,
Persons of blood and honour—
PER.: Who be these, sir?

SCENE II.

To them enter MOSCA *and* NANO *disguised, followed by persons with materials for erecting a stage.*

MOS.: Under that window, there 't must be. The same.
SIR P.: Fellows, to mount a bank. Did your instructor
In the dear tongues, never discourse to you
Of the Italian mountebanks?[47]
PER.: Yes, sir.
SIR P.: Why,
Here shall you see one.

PER.: They are quacksalvers,
Fellows that live by venting oils and drugs.
SIR P.: Was that the character he gave you of them?
PER.: As I remember.
SIR P.: Pity his ignorance.
They are the only knowing men of Europe!
Great general scholars, excellent physicians,
Most admir'd statesmen, profest favourites
And cabinet counsellors to the greatest princes;
The only languag'd men of all the world!
PER.: And, I have heard, they are most lewd[48] impostors;
Made all of terms and shreds; no less beliers
Of great men's favours, than their own vile medicines;
Which they will utter upon monstrous oaths;
Selling that drug for twopence, ere they part,
Which they have valu'd at twelve crowns before.
SIR P.: Sir, calumnies are answer'd best with silence.
Yourself shall judge—Who is it mounts, my friends?
MOS.: Scoto of Mantua,[49] sir.
SIR P.: Is 't he? Nay, then
I'll proudly promise, sir, you shall behold.
Another man than has been phant'sied[50] to you.
I wonder yet, that he should mount his bank,
Here in this nook, that has been wont t' appear
In face of the Piazza!—Here he comes.
[*Enter* VOLPONE, *disguised as a mountebank Doctor, and followed by a crowd of people.*]
VOLP.: Mount, zany. [*To* NANO.]
MOS.: Follow, follow, follow, follow!
SIR P.: See how the people follow him! he's a man
May write ten thousand crowns in bank here. Note,
[VOLPONE *mounts the stage.*]
Mark but his gesture:—I do use to observe
The state he keeps in getting up.
PER.: 'T is worth it, sir.

VOLP.: "Most noble gentlemen, and my worthy patrons! It may seem strange that I, your Scoto Mantuano, who was ever wont to fix my bank in the face of the public Piazza, near the shelter of the Portico to the Procuratia, should now, after eight months' absence from this illustrious city of Venice, humbly retire myself into an obscure nook of the Piazza."

SIR P.: Did not I now object the same?

PER.: Peace, sir.

VOLP.: "Let me tell you: I am not, as your Lombard proverb saith, cold on my feet; or content to part with my commodities at a cheaper rate than I am accustom'd: look not for it. Nor that the calumnious reports of that impudent detractor, and shame to our profession (Alessandro Buttone, I mean), who gave out, in public, I was condemn'd *a' sforzato*[51] to the galleys, for poisoning the Cardinal Bembo's cook, hath at all attach'd, much less dejected me. No, no, worthy gentlemen; to tell you true, I cannot endure to see the rabble of these ground *ciarlitani*,[52] that spread their cloaks on the pavement, as if they meant to do feats of activity, and then come in lamely, with their mouldy tales out of Boccaccio, like stale Tabarin,[53] the fabulist: some of them discoursing their travels, and of their tedious captivity in the Turk's galleys, when, indeed, were the truth known, they were the Christian's galleys, where very temperately they eat bread, and drunk water, as a wholesome penance, enjoin'd them by their confessors, for base pilferies."

SIR P.: Note but his bearing, and contempt of these.

VOLP.: "These turdy-facy-nasty-paty-lousy-fartical rogues, with one poor groat's-worth of unprepar'd antimony, finely wrapt up in several *scartoccios*,[54] are able, very well, to kill their twenty a week, and play; yet these meagre, starv'd spirits, who have half stopt the organs of their minds with earthy oppilations,[55] want not their favourers among your shrivell'd salad-eating artisans, who are overjoy'd that they may have their half pe'rth of physic; though it purge 'em into another world, 't makes no matter."

SIR P.: Excellent! ha' you heard better language, sir?

VOLP.: "Well, let 'em go. And, gentlemen, honourable gentlemen, know, that for this time, our bank, being thus removed from the clamours of the *canaglia*[56] shall be the scene of pleasure and delight; for I have nothing to sell, little or nothing to sell."

SIR P.: I told you, sir, his end.

PER.: You did so, sir.

VOLP.: "I protest, I, and my six servants, are not able to make of this precious liquor so fast as it is fetch'd away from my lodging by gentlemen of your city; strangers of the Terra-firma;[57] worshipful merchants; ay, and senators too: who, ever since my arrival, have detain'd me to their uses, by their splendidous liberalities. And worthily; for, what avails your rich man to have his magazines stuft with *moscadelli*, or of the purest grape, when his physicians prescribe him, on pain of death, to drink nothing but water cocted[58] with aniseeds? O health! health! the blessing of the rich! the riches of the poor! who can buy thee at too dear a rate, since there is no enjoying this world without thee? Be not then so sparing of your purses, honourable gentlemen, as to abridge the natural course of life—"

PER.: You see his end.

SIR P.: Ay, is 't not good?

VOLP.: "For when a humid flux, or catarrh, by the mutability of air, falls from your head into an arm or shoulder, or any other part; take you a ducket, or your chequin of gold, and apply to the place affected: see what good effect it can work. No, no, 't is this blessed *unguento*,[59] this rare extraction, that hath only power to disperse all malignant humours, that proceed either of hot, cold, moist, or windy causes—"

PER.: I would he had put in dry too.

SIR P.: Pray you observe.

VOLP.: "To fortify the most indigest and crude stomach, ay, were it of one that, through extreme weakness, vomited blood, applying only a warm napkin to the place, after the unction and fricace;[60]—for the *vertigine*[61] in the head, putting but a drop into your nostrils, likewise behind the ears; a most sovereign and approv'd remedy; the *mal caduco*,[62] cramps, convulsions, paralyses, epilepsies, *tremorcordia*, retir'd nerves, ill vapours of the spleen, stoppings of the liver, the stone, the strangury, *hernia ventosa*, *iliaca passio*;[63] stops a *dysenteria* immediately; easeth the torsion[64] of the small guts; and cures *melancholia hypocondriaca*, being taken and appli'd, according to my printed receipt. [*Pointing to his bill and his glass.*] For this is the physician, this the medicine; this counsels, this cures; this gives the direction, this works the effect; and, in sum, both together may be term'd an abstract of the theoric and practic in the Aesculapian art. 'T will cost you eight crowns. And,—Zan Fritada, prithee sing a verse extempore in honour of it."

SIR P.: How do you like him, sir?

PER.: Most strangely, I!

SIR P.: Is not his language rare?

PER.: But alchemy,

I never heard the like; or Broughton's books.[65]

[NANO *sings.*]
Had old Hippocrates, or Galen,
That to their books put med'cines all in,
But known this secret, they had never
(Of which they will be guilty ever)
Been murderers of so much paper,
Or wasted many a hurtless taper;
No Indian drug had e'er been fam'd,
Tobacco, sassafras not nam'd;
Ne yet of guacum one small stick, sir,
Nor Raymund Lully's[66] great elixir.
Ne had been known the Danish Gonswart,[67]
Or Paracelsus,[68] with his long sword.

PER.: All this, yet, will not do; eight crowns is high.

VOLP.: "No more—Gentlemen, if I had but time to discourse to you the miraculous effects of this my oil, surnam'd Oglio del Scoto; with the countless catalogue of those I have cur'd of th' aforesaid, and many more diseases; the patents and privileges of all the princes and commonwealths of Christendom; or but the depositions of those that appear'd on my part, before the signiory of the Sanita and most learned College of Physicians; where I was authoris'd, upon notice taken of the admirable virtues of my medicaments, and mine own excellency in matter of rare and unknown secrets, not only to disperse them publicly in this famous city, but in all the territories, that happily joy under the government of the most pious and magnificent states of Italy. But may some other gallant fellow say, 'O, there be divers that make profession to have as good, and as experimented receipts as yours:' indeed, very many have assay'd, like apes, in imitation of that, which is really and essentially in me, to make of this oil; bestow'd great cost in furnaces, stills, alembics,[69] continual fires, and preparation of the ingredients (as indeed there goes to it six hundred several simples, besides some quantity of human fat, for the conglutination, which we buy of the anatomists), but when these practitioners come to the last decoction, blow, blow, puff, puff, and all flies in fumo:[70] ha, ha, ha! Poor wretches! I rather

> I RATHER PITY THEIR FOLLY AND INDISCRETION, THAN THEIR LOSS OF TIME AND MONEY; FOR THOSE MAY BE RECOVER'D BY INDUSTRY: BUT TO BE A FOOL BORN, IS A DISEASE INCURABLE.

pity their folly and indiscretion, than their loss of time and money; for those may be recover'd by industry: but to be a fool born, is a disease incurable.

"For myself, I always from my youth have endeavour'd to get the rarest secrets, and book them, either in exchange, or for money; I spar'd nor cost nor labour, where anything was worthy to be learned. And, gentlemen, honourable gentlemen, I will undertake, by virtue of chymical art, out of the honourable hat that covers your head, to extract the four elements; that is to say, the fire, air, water, and earth, and return you your felt without burn or stain. For, whilst others have been at the *ballo*,[71] I have been at my book; and am now past the craggy paths of study, and come to the flowery plains of honour and reputation."

SIR P.: I do assure you, sir, that is his aim.

VOLP.: "But to our price—"

PER.: And that withal, Sir Pol.

VOLP.: "You all know, honourable gentlemen, I never valu'd this *ampulla*, or vial, at less than eight crowns; but for this time, I am content to be depriv'd of it for six; six crowns is the price, and less in courtesy I know you cannot offer me; take it or leave it, howsoever, both it and I am at your service. I ask you not as the value of the thing, for then I should demand of you a thousand crowns, so the Cardinals Montalto, Fernese, the great Duke of Tuscany, my gossip,[72] with divers other princes, have given me; but I despise money. Only to show my affection to you, honourable gentlemen, and your illustrious state here, I have neglected the messages of these princes, mine own offices, fram'd my journey hither, only to present you with the fruits of my travels.—Tune your voices once more to the touch of your instruments, and give the honourable assembly some delightful recreation."

PER.: What monstrous and most painful circumstance
Is here, to get some three or four gazettes,[73]
Some threepence i' the whole! for that 't will come to.

[NANO *sings*.]
You that would last long, list to my song,
Make no more coil, but buy of this oil.
Would you be ever fair and young?
Stout of teeth, and strong of tongue?
Tart of palate? quick of ear?
Sharp of sight? of nostril clear?
Moist of hand? and light of foot?

Or, I will come nearer to 't,
Would you live free from all diseases?
Do the act your mistress pleases,
Yet fright all aches from your bones?
Here's a med'cine for the nones.[74]

VOLP.: "Well, I am in a humour at this time to make a present of the small quantity my coffer contains; to the rich in courtesy, and to the poor for God's sake. Wherefore now mark: I ask'd you six crowns; and six crowns, at other times, you have paid me; you shall not give me six crowns, nor five, nor four, nor three, nor two, nor one; nor half a ducat; no, nor a *moccinigo*.[75] Sixpence it will cost you, or six hundred pound—expect no lower price, for, by the banner of my front, I will not bate a bagatine,[76]—that I will have, only, a pledge of your loves, to carry something from amongst you, to show I am not contemn'd by you. Therefore, now, toss your handkerchiefs, cheerfully, cheerfully; and be advertis'd, that the first heroic spirit that deigns to grace me with a handkerchief, I will give it a little remembrance of something beside, shall please it better than if I had presented it with a double pistolet."[77]

PER.: Will you be that heroic spark, Sir Pol?
[CELIA, *at the window, throws down her handkerchief.*]
O, see! the windore has prevented[78] you.

VOLP.: "Lady, I kiss your bounty; and for this timely grace you have done your poor Scoto of Mantua, I will return you, over and above my oil, a secret of that high and inestimable nature, shall make you for ever enamour'd on that minute, wherein your eye first descended on so mean, yet not altogether to be despis'd, an object. Here is a powder conceal'd in this paper, of which, if I should speak to the worth, nine thousand volumes were but as one page, that page as a line, that line as a word; so short is this pilgrimage of man (which some call life) to the expressing of it. Would I reflect on the price? Why, the whole world is but as an empire, that empire as a province, that province as a bank, that bank as a private purse to the purchase of it. I will only tell you; it is the powder that made Venus a goddess (given her by Apollo), that kept her perpetually young, clear'd her wrinkles, firm'd her gums, fill'd her skin, colour'd her hair; from her deriv'd to Helen, and at the sack of Troy unfortunately lost: till now, in this our age, it was as happily recover'd, by a studious antiquary, out of some ruins of Asia, who sent a moiety of it to the court of France (but much sophisticated), wherewith the ladies there now colour their hair. The rest, at this present, remains with me;

extracted to a quintessence: so that, wherever it but touches, in youth it perpetually preserves, in age restores the complexion; seats your teeth, did they dance like virginal jacks,[79] firm as a wall: makes them white as ivory, that were black as—"

SCENE III—THE SAME

To them enter CORVINO.

COR.: Spite o' the devil, and my shame! come down here;
Come down!—No house but mine to make your scene?
Signior Flaminio, will you down, sir? down?
What, is my wife your Franciscina, sir?
No windores on the whole Piazza, here,
To make your properties, but mine? but mine?
[*Beats away* VOLPONE, NANO*, etc.*]
Heart! ere to-morrow I shall be new christen'd,
And called the Pantalone di Besogniosi,[80]
About the town.
PER.: What should this mean, Sir Pol?
SIR P.: Some trick of state, believe it; I will home.
PER.: It may be some design on you.
SIR P.: I know not.
I'll stand upon my guard.
PER.: It is your best, sir.
SIR P.: This three weeks, all my advices, all my letters.
They have been intercepted.
PER.: Indeed, sir!
Best have a care.
SIR P.: Nay, so I will.
PER.: This knight,
I may not lose him, for my mirth, till night.

[*Exeunt.*]

SCENE IV—A ROOM IN VOLPONE'S HOUSE

Enter VOLPONE, MOSCA.

VOLP.: O, I am wounded!
MOS.: Where, sir?
VOLP.: Not without;
Those blows were nothing: I could bear them ever.
But angry Cupid, bolting from her eyes,
Hath shot himself into me like a flame;
Where now he flings about his burning heat,
As in a furnace an ambitious fire
Whose vent is stopt. The fight is all within me.
I cannot live, except thou help me, Mosca;
My liver melts, and I, without the hope
Of some soft air from her refreshing breath,
Am but a heap of cinders.
MOS.: 'Las, good sir,
Would you had never seen her!
VOLP.: Nay, would thou
Hadst never told me of her!
MOS.: Sir, 't is true;
I do confess I was unfortunate,
And you unhappy; but I 'm bound in conscience,
No less than duty, to effect my best
To your release of torment, and I will, sir.
VOLP.: Dear Mosca, shall I hope?
MOS.: Sir, more than dear,
I will not bid you to despair of aught
Within a human compass.
VOLP.: O, there spoke
My better angel. Mosca, take my keys,
Gold, plate, and jewels, all 's at thy devotion;[81]
Employ them how thou wilt: nay, coin me too:
So thou in this but crown my longings, Mosca.
MOS.: Use but your patience.
VOLP.: So I have.

MOS.: I doubt not.
To bring success to your desires.
VOLP.: Nay, then,
I not repent me of my late disguise.
MOS.: If you can horn him, sir, you need not.
VOLP.: True:
Besides, I never meant him for my heir.
Is not the colour o' my beard and eyebrows
To make me known?
MOS.: No jot.
VOLP.: I did it well.
MOS.: So well, would I could follow you in mine,
With half the happiness! and yet I would
Escape your epilogue.[82]
VOLP.: But were they gull'd
With a belief that I was Scoto?
MOS.: Sir,
Scoto himself could hardly have distinguish'd!
I have not time to flatter you now; we'll part:
And as I prosper, so applaud my art.

[*Exeunt.*]

SCENE V—A ROOM IN CORVINO'S HOUSE

Enter CORVINO, *with his sword in his hand, dragging in* CELIA.

CORV.: Death of mine honour, with the city's fool!
A juggling, tooth-drawing, prating mountebank,
And at a public windore! where, whilst he,
With his strain'd action, and his dole of faces,[83]
To his drug-lecture draws your itching ears,
A crew of old, unmarri'd, noted lechers,
Stood leering up like satyrs: and you smile
Most graciously, and fan your favours forth,
To give your hot spectators satisfaction!
What, was your mountbank their call? their whistle?

Or were you enamour'd on his copper rings,
His saffron jewel, with the toad-stone in 't,
Or his embroid'red suit, with the cope-stitch,
Made of a hearse cloth? or his old tilt-feather?
Or his starch'd beard! Well, you shall have him, yes!
He shall come home, and minister unto you
The fricace for the mother.[84] Or, let me see,
I think you'd rather mount; would you not mount?
Why, if you'll mount, you may; yes, truly, you may!
And so you may be seen, down to the foot.
Get you a cittern,[85] Lady Vanity,
And be a dealer with the virtuous man;
Make one. I'll but protest myself a cuckold,
And save your dowry. I'm a Dutchman, I!
For if you thought me an Italian,
You would be damn'd ere you did this, you whore!
Thou 'dst tremble to imagine that the murder
Of father, mother, brother, all thy race,
Should follow, as the subject of my justice.

CEL.: Good sir, have patience.

CORV.: What couldst thou propose[86]
Less to thyself, than in this heat of wrath,
And stung with my dishonour, I should strike
This steel into thee, with as many stabs
As thou wert gaz'd upon with goatish eyes?

CEL.: Alas, sir, be appeas'd! I could not think
My being at the windore should more now
Move your impatience than at other times.

CORV.: No! not to seek and entertain a parley
With a known knave, before a multitude!
You were an actor with your handkerchief,
Which he most sweetly kist in the receipt,
And might, no doubt, return it with a letter,
And point the place where you might meet; your sister's,
Your mother's, or your aunt's might serve the turn.

CEL.: Why, dear sir, when do I make these excuses,
Or ever stir abroad, but to the church?

And that so seldom—
CORV.: Well, it shall be less;
And thy restraint before was liberty,
To what I now decree: and therefore mark me.
First, I will have this bawdy light damm'd up;[87]
And till 't be done, some two or three yards off,
I'll chalk a line; o'er which if thou but chance
To set thy desp'rate foot, more hell, more horror,
More wild remorseless rage shall seize on thee,
Than on a conjuror that had heedless left
His circle's safety ere his devil was laid.
Then here's a lock which I will hang upon thee,
And, now I think on 't, I will keep thee backwards;
Thy lodging shall be backwards: thy walks backwards;
Thy prospect, all be backwards; and no pleasure,
That thou shalt know but backwards: nay, since you force
My honest nature, know, it is your own,
Being too open, makes me use you thus:
Since you will not contain your subtle nostrils
In a sweet room, but they must snuff the air
Of rank and sweaty passengers. [*Knock within.*] One knocks.
Away, and be not seen, pain of thy life;
Nor look toward the windore; if thou dost—
Nay, stay, hear this—let me not prosper, whore,
But I will make thee an anatomy,
Dissect thee mine own self, and read a lecture
Upon thee to the city, and in public.
Away!—

[*Exit* CELIA.]

[*Enter* SERVANT.]

Who's there?
SER.: 'T is Signior Mosca, sir.

SCENE VI—THE SAME

CORVINO. *Enter* MOSCA.

CORVINO: Let him come in. His master's dead; there's yet
Some good to help the bad.—My Mosca, welcome!
I guess your news.
MOS.: I fear you cannot, sir.
CORV.: Is 't not his death?
MOS.: Rather the contrary.
CORV.: Not his recovery?
MOS.: Yes, sir.
CORV.: I am curs'd,
I am bewitch'd, my crosses meet to vex me.
How? how? how? how?
MOS.: Why, sir, with Scoto's oil;
Corbaccio and Voltore brought of it,
Whilst I was busy in an inner room—
CORV.: Death! that damn'd mountebank! but for the law
Now, I could kill the rascal: 't cannot be
His oil should have that virtue. Ha' not I
Known him a common rogue, come fiddling in
To the *osteria*,[88] with a tumbling whore,
And, when he has done all his forc'd tricks, been glad
Of a poor spoonful of dead wine, with flies in 't?
It cannot be. All his ingredients
Are a sheep's gall, a roasted bitch's marrow,
Some few sod[89] earwigs, pounded caterpillars,
A little capon's grease, and fasting spittle:[90]
I know them to a dram.
MOS.: I know not, sir;
But some on 't, there, they pour'd into his ears,
Some in his nostrils, and recover'd him;
Applying but the fricace.[91]
CORV.: Pox o' that fricace!
MOS.: And since, to seem the more officious
And flatt'ring of his health, there, they have had,
At extreme fees, the college of physicians
Consulting on him, how they might restore him;
Where one would have a cataplasm[92] of spices,
Another a flay'd ape clapp'd to his breast,

A third would have it a dog, a fourth an oil,
With wild cats' skins: at last, they all resolv'd
That to preserve him, was no other means
But some young woman must be straight sought out,
Lusty, and full of juice, to sleep by him;
And to this service most unhappily,
And most unwillingly, am I now employ'd,
Which here I thought to pre-acquaint you with,
For your advice, since it concerns you most;
Because I would not do that thing might cross
Your ends, on whom I have my whole dependence, sir;
Yet, if I do it not they may delate[93]
My slackness to my patron, work me out
Of his opinion; and there all your hopes,
Ventures, or whatsoever, are all frustrate!
I do but tell you, sir. Besides, they are all
Now striving who shall first present him; therefore—
I could entreat you, briefly conclude somewhat;
Prevent 'em if you can.
CORV.: Death to my hopes,
This is my villanous fortune! Best to hire
Some common courtesan.
MOS.: Ay, I thought on that, sir;
But they are all so subtle, full of art—
And age again doting and flexible,
So as—I cannot tell—we may, perchance,
Light on a quean may cheat us all.
CORV.: 'T is true.
MOS.: No, no: it must be one that has no tricks, sir,
Some simple thing, a creature made unto it;[94]
Some wench you may command. Ha' you no kinswoman?
Gods so—Think, think, think, think, think, think, think, sir.
One o' the doctors offer'd there his daughter.
CORV.: How!
MOS.: Yes, Signior Lupo, the physician.
CORV.: His daughter!
MOS.: And a virgin, sir. Why, alas,

He knows the state of 's body, what it is:
That nought can warm his blood, sir, but a fever;
Nor any incantation raise his spirit:
A long forgetfulness hath seiz'd that part.
Besides, sir, who shall know it? Some one or two—

CORV.: I pray thee give me leave. [*Walks aside.*] If any man
But I had had this luck—The thing in 't self,
I know, is nothing—Wherefore should not I
As well command my blood and my affections
As this dull doctor? In the point of honour,
The cases are all one of wife and daughter.

MOS.: [*Aside.*] I hear him coming.[95]

CORV.: She shall do 't: 't is done.
Slight! if this doctor, who is not engag'd,
Unless 't be for his counsel, which is nothing,
Offer his daughter, what should I, that am
So deeply in? I will prevent him: Wretch!
Covetous wretch!—Mosca, I have determin'd.

MOS.: How, sir?

CORV.: We'll make all sure. The party you wot of
Shall be mine own wife, Mosca.

MOS.: Sir, the thing,
But that I would not seem to counsel you,
I should have motion'd to you, at the first:
And make your count, you have cut all their throats.
Why, 't is directly taking a possession!
And in his next fit, we may let him go.
'T is but to pull the pillow from his head,
And he is throttled: it had been done before
But for your scrupulous doubts.

CORV.: Ay, a plague on 't,
My conscience fools my wit! Well, I'll be brief,
And so be thou, lest they should be before us.
Go home, prepare him, tell him with what zeal
And willingness I do it: swear it was
On the first hearing, as thou mayst do, truly,
Mine own free motion.

MOS.: Sir, I warrant you,
I'll so possess him with it, that the rest
Of his starv'd clients shall be banish'd all;
And only you receiv'd. But come not, sir,
Until I send, for I have something else
To ripen for your good, you must not know 't.
CORV.: But do not you forget to send now.
MOS.: Fear not. [*Exit.*]

SCENE VII—THE SAME

CORVINO.

CORV.: Where are you, wife? My Celia! wife! [*Enter* CELIA.]—What, blubb'ring?
Come, dry those tears. I think thou thought'st me in earnest;
Ha! by this light I talk'd so but to try thee:
Methinks, the lightness of the occasion
Should have confirm'd thee. Come, I am not jealous.
CEL.: No?
CORV.: Faith I am not, I, nor never was;
It is a poor unprofitable humour.
Do not I know, if women have a will,
They'll do 'gainst all the watches o' the world,
And that the fiercest spies are tam'd with gold?
Tut, I am confident in thee, thou shalt see 't;
And see I'll give thee cause too, to believe it.
Come kiss me. Go, and make thee ready straight,
In all thy best attire, thy choicest jewels,
Put 'em all on, and, with 'em, thy best looks
We are invited to a solemn feast,
At old Volpone's, where it shall appear
How far I am free from jealousy or fear.

[*Exeunt.*]

ACT III

SCENE I—A STREET

Enter MOSCA.

MOS.: I fear I shall begin to grow in love
With my dear self, and my most prosp'rous parts,
They do so spring and burgeon; I can feel
A whimsy in my blood: I know not how,
Success hath made me wanton. I could skip
Out of my skin now, like a subtle snake,
I am so limber. O! your parasite
Is a most precious thing, dropt from above,
Not bred 'mongst clods and clodpoles, here on earth.
I muse, the mystery[96] was not made a science,
It is so liberally protest! Almost
All the wise world is little else, in nature,
But parasites or sub-parasites. And yet
I mean not those that have your bare town-art,
To know who's fit to feed them; have no house,
No family, no care, and therefore mould
Tales for men's ears, to bait that sense; or get
Kitchen-invention, and some stale receipts
To please the belly, and the groin; nor those,
With their court dog-tricks, that can fawn and fleet,
Make their revenue out of legs[97] and faces,
Echo my lord, and lick away a moth:
But your fine elegant rascal, that can rise
And stoop, almost together, like an arrow;
Shoot through the air as nimbly as a star;
Turn short as doth a swallow; and be here,
And there, and here, and yonder, all at once;
Present to any humour, all occasion;
And change a visor swifter than a thought!
This is the creature had the art born with him;
Toils not to learn it, but doth practise it

Out of most excellent nature: and such sparks
Are the true parasites, others but their zanies.

SCENE II—THE SAME

MOSCA. *Enter* BONARIO.

Who's this? Bonario, old Corbaccio's son?
The person I was bound to seek. Fair sir,
You are happ'ly met.
BON.: That cannot be by thee.
MOS.: Why, sir?
BON.: Nay, pray thee know thy way, and leave me:
I would be loth to interchange discourse
With such a mate[98] as thou art.
MOS.: Courteous sir,
Scorn not my poverty.
BON.: Not I, by heaven;
But thou shalt give me leave to hate thy baseness.
MOS.: Baseness!
BON.: Ay; answer me, is not thy sloth
Sufficient argument? thy flattery?
Thy means of feeding?
MOS.: Heaven be good to me!
These imputations are too common, sir,
And easily stuck on virtue when she's poor.
You are unequal[99] to me, and however
Your sentence may be righteous, yet you are not,
That, ere you know me, thus proceed in censure:
St. Mark bear witness 'gainst you, 't is inhuman. [*Weeps.*]
BON.: [*Aside.*] What! does he weep? the sign is soft and good:
I do repent me that I was so harsh.
MOS.: 'T is true, that, sway'd by strong necessity,
I am enforc'd to eat my careful bread
With too much obsequy; 't is true, beside,
That I am fain to spin mine own poor raiment

Out of my mere observance, being not born
To a free fortune but that I have done
Base offices, in rending friends asunder,
Dividing families, betraying counsels,
Whisp'ring false lies, or mining men with praises,
Train'd their credulity with perjuries,
Corrupted chastity, or am in love
With mine own tender case, but would not rather
Prove the most rugged and laborious course,
That might redeem my present estimation,
Let me here perish, in all hope of goodness.

BON.: [*Aside.*] This cannot be a personated passion—
I was as to blame, so to mistake thy nature;
Prithee forgive me: and speak out thy business.

MOS.: Sir, it concerns you; and though I may seem
At first to make a main offence in manners,
And in my gratitude unto my master,
Yet for the pure love which I bear all right,
And hatred of the wrong, I must reveal it.
This very hour your father is in purpose
To disinherit you—

BON.: How!

MOS.: And thrust you forth,
As a mere stranger to his blood: 't is true, sir.
The work no way engageth me, but as
I claim an interest in the general state
Of goodness and true virtue, which I hear
T' abound in you; and for which mere respect,
Without a second aim, sir, I have done it.

BON.: This tale hath lost thee much of the late trust
Thou hadst with me; it is impossible.
I know not how to lend it any thought,
My father should be so unnatural.

MOS.: It is a confidence that well becomes
Your piety; and form'd, no doubt, it is
From your own simple innocence: which makes
Your wrong more monstrous and abhorr'd. But, sir,

I now will tell you more. This very minute,
It is, or will be doing; and if you
Shall be but pleas'd to go with me, I'll bring you,
I dare not say where you shall see, but where
Your ear shall be a witness of the deed;
Hear yourself written bastard, and protest
The common issue of the earth.
BON.: I'm maz'd!
MOS.: Sir, if I do it not, draw your just sword,
And score your vengeance on my front and face;
Mark me your villain: you have too much wrong,
And I do suffer for you, sir. My heart
Weeps blood in anguish—
BON.: Lead; I follow thee.

[*Exeunt.*]

SCENE III—A ROOM IN VOLPONE'S HOUSE

Enter VOLPONE, NANO, ANDROGYNO, CASTRONE.

VOLP.: Mosca stays long, methinks—Bring forth your sports,
And help to make the wretched time more sweet.
NAN.: "Dwarf, fool, and eunuch, well met here we be.
A question it were now, whether of us three,
Being all the known delicates of a rich man,
In pleasing him, claim the precedency can?"
CAS.: "I claim for myself."
AND.: "And so doth the fool."
NAN.: "'T is foolish indeed: let me set you both to school.
First for your dwarf, he's little and witty,
And everything, as it is little, is pretty;
Else why do men say to a creature of my shape,
So soon as they see him, 'It's a pretty little ape'?
And why a pretty ape, but for pleasing imitation
Of greater men's actions, in a ridiculous fashion?
Beside, this feat[100] body of mine doth not crave

Half the meat, drink, and cloth, one of your bulks will have.
Admit your fool's face be the mother of laughter,
Yet, for his brain, it must always come after:
And though that do feed him, it's a pitiful case,
His body is beholding to such a bad face."
[*One knocks.*]

VOLP.: Who's there? My couch; away! look! Nano, see:
[*Exeunt* AND. *and* CAS.]
Give me my caps first—go, inquire. [*Exit* NANO.] Now, Cupid
Send it be Mosca, and with fair return!

NAN.: [*within.*] It is the beauteous madam—

VOLP.: Would-be—is it?

NAN.: The same.

VOLP.: Now torment on me! Squire her in;
For she will enter, or dwell here for ever:
Nay, quickly. [*Retires to his couch.*] That my fit were past! I fear
A second hell too, that my loathing this
Will quite expel my appetite to the other:
Would she were taking now her tedious leave.
Lord, how it threats me what I am to suffer!

SCENE IV—THE SAME

To him enter NANO, LADY POLITIC WOULD-BE.

LADY P.: I thank you, good sir. Pray you signify
Unto your patron I am here—This band
Shows not my neck enough,—I trouble you, sir;
Let me request you bid one of my women
Come hither to me. In good faith, I am drest
Most favourably to-day! It is no matter:
'T is well enough.
[*Enter 1st Waiting-woman.*]
Look, see these petulant things,
How they have done this!

VOLP.: [*Aside.*] I do feel the fever

Ent'ring in at mine ears; O, for a charm,
To fright it hence!
LADY P.: Come nearer: is this curl
In his right place, or this? Why is this higher
Than all the rest? You ha' not wash'd your eyes yet!
Or do they not stand even i' your head?
Where is your fellow? Call her. [*Exit 1st Woman.*]
NAN.: Now, St. Mark
Deliver us! anon she'll beat her women,
Because her nose is red. [*Re-enter 1st with 2nd Woman.*]
LADY P.: I pray you view
This tire,[101] forsooth: are all things apt, or no?
1ST WOM.: One hair a little here sticks out, forsooth.
LADY P.: Does 't so, forsooth! and where was your dear sight,
When it did so, forsooth! What now! bird-ey'd?[102]
And you, too? Pray you, both approach and mend it.
Now, by that light I muse you're not asham'd!
I, that have preach'd these things so oft unto you,
Read you the principles, argu'd all the grounds,
Disputed every fitness, every grace,
Call'd you to counsel of so frequent dressings—
NAN.: [*Aside.*] More carefully than of your fame or honour.
LADY P.: Made you acquainted what an ample dowry
The knowledge of these things would be unto you,
Able alone to get you noble husbands
At your return: and you thus to neglect it!
Besides, you seeing what a curious nation
Th' Italians are, what will they say of me?
"The English lady cannot dress herself."
Here's a fine imputation to our country!
Well, go your ways, and stay i' the next room.
This fucus[103] was too coarse too; it's no matter—
Good sir, you'll give 'em entertainment?
[*Exeunt* NANO *and Waiting-women.*]
VOLP.: The storm comes toward me.
LADY P.: [*Goes to the couch.*] How does my Volpone?
VOLP.: Troubl'd with noise, I cannot sleep; I dreamt

That a strange fury ent'red now my house,
And, with the dreadful tempest of her breath,
Did cleave my roof asunder.
LADY P.: Believe me, and I
Had the most fearful dream, could I remember 't—
VOLP.: [*Aside.*] Out on my fate! I have given her the occasion
How to torment me: she will tell me hers.
LADY P.: Methought the golden mediocrity,
Polite, and delicate—
VOLP.: O, if you do love me,
No more: I sweat, and suffer, at the mention
Of any dream; feel how I tremble yet.
LADY P.: Alas, good soul! the passion of the heart.
Seed-pearl were good now, boil'd with syrup of apples,
Tincture of gold, and coral, citron-pills,
Your elecampane[104] root, myrobalanes[105]—
VOLP.: Ay me, I have ta'en a grasshopper by the wing!
LADY P.: Burnt silk and amber. You have muscadel
Good i' the house—
VOLP: You will not drink, and part?
LADY P.: No, fear not that. I doubt we shall not get
Some English saffron, half a dram would serve;
Your sixteen cloves, a little musk, dried mints;
Bugloss, and barley-meal
VOLP.: [*Aside.*] She's in again
Before I feign'd diseases, now I have one.
LADY P.: And these appli'd with a right scarlet cloth.
VOLP.: [*Aside.*]Another flood of words! a very torrent!
LADY P.: Shall I, sir, make you a poultice?
VOLP.: No, no, no.
I'm very well, you need prescribe no more.
LADY P.: I have a little studied physic; but now
I'm all for music, save, i' the forenoons,
An hour or two for painting, I would have
A lady, indeed, to have all letters and arts,
Be able to discourse, to write, to paint,
But principal, as Plato holds, your music,

And so does wise Pythagoras, I take it,
Is your true rapture: when there is concent,[106]
In face, in voice, and clothes: and is, indeed,
Our sex's chiefest ornament.
VOLP.: The poet
As old in time as Plato, and as knowing,
Says that your highest female grace is silence.
LADY P.: Which of your poets? Petrarch, or Tasso, or Dante?
Guarim? Ariosto? Aretine?
Cieco di Hadria? I have read them all,
VOLP.: [*Aside.*] Is everything a cause to my destruction?
LADY P.: I think I have two or three of 'em about me.
VOLP.: [*Aside.*]The sun, the sea, will sooner both stand still
Than her eternal tongue! nothing can scape it.
LADY P.: Here's Pastor Fido—
VOLP.: [*Aside.*] Profess obstinate silence;
That's now my safest.
LADY P.: All our English writers,
I mean such as are happy in th' Italian,
Will deign to steal out of this author, mainly;
Almost as much as from Montagnié:
He has so modern and facile a vein,
Fitting the time, and catching the court-ear!
Your Petrarch is more passionate, yet he,
In days of sonnetting, trusted 'em with much:
Dante is hard, and few can understand him.
But for a desperate wit, there's Aretine;
Only his pictures are a little obscene—
You mark me not.
VOLP.: Alas, my mind's perturb'd.
LADY P.: Why, in such cases, we must cure ourselves,
Make use of our philosophy—
VOLP.: Oh me!
LADY P.: And as we find our passions do rebel,
Encounter them with reason, or divert 'em,
By giving scope unto some other humour
Of lesser danger: as, in politic bodies,

There's nothing more doth overwhelm the judgment,
And cloud the understanding, than too much
Settling and fixing, and, as 't were, subsiding
Upon one object. For the incorporating
Of these same outward things, into that part
Which we call mental, leaves some certain faeces
That stop the organs, and, as Plato says,
Assassinate our knowledge.
VOLP.: [*Aside.*] Now, the spirit
Of patience help me!
LADY P.: Come, in faith, I must
Visit you more a days; and make you well:
Laugh and be lusty.
VOLP.: [*Aside.*] My good angel save me!
LADY P.: There was but one sole man in all the world
With whom I e'er could sympathise; and he
Would lie you, often,[107] three, four hours together
To hear me speak; and be sometime so rapt,
As he would answer me quite from the purpose,
Like you, and you are like him, just. I'll discourse,
An 't be but only, sir, to bring you asleep,
How we did spend our time and loves together,
For some six years.
VOLP.: Oh, oh, oh, oh, oh, oh!
LADY P.: For we were coaetanei,[108] and brought up—
VOLP.: Some power, some fate, some fortune rescue me!

SCENE V—THE SAME

To them enter MOSCA.

MOS.: God save you, madam!
LADY P.: Good sir.
VOLP.: Mosca! welcome,
Welcome to my redemption.
MOS.: Why, sir?

VOLP.: Oh,
Rid me of this my torture, quickly, there;
My madam with the everlasting voice:
The bells, in time of pestilence, ne'er made
Like noise, or were in that perpetual motion!
The cock-pit comes not near it. All my house,
But now, steam'd like a bath with her thick breath,
A lawyer could not have been heard; nor scarce
Another woman, such a hail of words
She has let fall. For hell's sake, rid her hence.

MOS.: Has she presented?

VOLP.: Oh, I do not care;
I'll take her absence upon any price,
With any loss.

MOS.: Madam—

LADY P.: I ha' brought your patron
A toy, a cap here, of mine own work.

MOS.: 'T is well.
I had forgot to tell you I saw your knight
Where you would little think it—

LADY P.: Where?

MOS.: Marry,
Where yet, if you make haste, you may apprehend him,
Rowing upon the water in a gondole,
With the most cunning courtesan of Venice.

LADY P.: Is 't true?

MOS.: Pursue 'em, and believe your eyes:
Leave me to make your gift. [*Exit* LADY P. *hastily.*] I knew 't would take:
For, lightly, they that use themselves most licence,
Are still most jealous.

VOLP.: Mosca, hearty thanks
For thy quick fiction, and delivery of me.
Now to my hopes, what sayst thou?
[*Re-enter* LADY P. WOULD-BE.]

LADY P.: But do you hear, sir?—

VOLP.: Again! I fear a paroxysm.

LADY P.: Which way
Row'd they together?
MOS.: Toward the Rialto.
LADY P.: I pray you lend me your dwarf.
MOS.: I pray you take him.
[*Exit* LADY P.] Your hopes, sir, are like happy blossoms, fair,
And promise timely fruit, if you will stay
But the maturing; keep you at your couch,
Corbaccio will arrive straight, with the will;
When he is gone, I'll tell you more. [*Exit.*]
VOLP.: My blood,
My spirits are return'd; I am alive:
And, like your wanton gamester at primero,
Whose thought had whisper'd to him, not go less,
Methinks I lie, and draw—for an encounter.[109]

SCENE VI—THE SAME

Enter MOSCA, BONARIO.

MOS.: Sir, here conceal'd [*opening a door*] you may hear all. But, pray you,
Have patience, sir; [*One knocks.*] the same 's your father knocks:
I am compell'd to leave you. [*Exit.*]
BON.: Do so—Yet
Cannot my thought imagine this a truth. [*Goes in.*]

SCENE VII—THE SAME

Enter MOSCA, CORVINO, CELIA—

MOS.: Death on me! you are come too soon, what meant you?
Did not I say I would send?
CORV.: Yes, but I fear'd
You might forget it, and then they prevent us.

MOS.: Prevent! [*Aside.*] Did e'er man haste so for his horns?
A courtier would not ply it so for a place.
—Well, now there is no helping it, stay here;
I'll presently return. [*Exit.*]
CORV.: Where are you, Celia?
You know not wherefore I have brought you hither?
CEL.: Not well, except you told me.
CORV.: Now I will:
Hark hither. [*They retire to one side.*] [*Re-enter* MOSCA.]
MOS.: [*to* BONARIO] Sir, your father hath sent word,
It will be half an hour ere he come;
And therefore, if you please to walk the while
Into that gallery—at the upper end,
There are some books to entertain the time:
And I'll take care no man shall come unto you, sir.
BON.: Yes. I will stay there—[*Aside.*] I do doubt this fellow. [*Exit.*]
MOS.: [*Looking after him.*] There; he is far enough; he can hear nothing:
And for his father, I can keep him off.
[*Goes to* VOLPONE'S *couch, opens the curtains, and whispers to him.*]
CORV.: Nay, now, there is no starting back, and therefore,
Resolve upon it: I have so decreed.
It must be done. Nor would I move 't afore,
Because I would avoid all shifts and tricks,
That might deny me.
CEL.: Sir, let me beseech you,
Affect not these strange trials; if you doubt
My chastity, why, lock me up for ever;
Make me the heir of darkness. Let me live
Where I may please your fears, if not your trust.
CORV.: Believe it, I have no such humour, I.
All that I speak I mean; yet I'm not mad;
Not horn-mad, you see? Go to, show yourself
Obedient, and a wife.
CEL.: O heaven!
CORV.: I say it,
Do so.
CEL.: Was this the train?[110]

CORV.: I've told you reasons;
What the physicians have set down; how much
It may concern me; what my engagements are;
My means, and the necessity of those means
For my recovery: wherefore, if you be
Loyal and mine, be won, respect my venture.
CEL.: Before your honour?
CORV.: Honour! tut, a breath:
There's no such thing in nature; a mere term
Invented to awe fools. What is my gold
The worse for touching, clothes for being look'd on?
Why, this 's no more. An old decrepit wretch,
That has no sense, no sinew; takes his meat
With others' fingers: only knows to gape
When you do scald his gums; a voice, a shadow;
And what can this man hurt you?
CEL.: [*Aside.*] Lord! what spirit
Is this hath ent'red him?
CORV.: And for your fame,
That's such a jig; as if I would go tell it,
Cry it on the Piazza! Who shall know it
But he that cannot speak it, and this fellow,
Whose lips are i' my pocket? Save yourself,
(if you'll proclaim 't, you may,) I know no other
Should come to know it.
CEL.: Are heaven and saints then nothing?
Will they be blind or stupid?
CORV.: How!
CEL.: Good sir,
Be jealous still, emulate them; and think
What hate they burn with toward every sin.
CORV.: I grant you: if I thought it were a sin
I would not urge you. Should I offer this
To some young Frenchman, or hot Tuscan blood
That had read Aretine, conn'd all his prints,
Knew every quirk within lust's labyrinth,
And were profest critic in lechery;

And I would look upon him, and applaud him,
This were a sin: but here, 't is contrary,
A pious work, mere charity for physic,
And honest polity, to assure mine own.
CEL.: O heaven! canst thou suffer such a change?
VOLP.: Thou art mine honour, Mosca, and my pride,
My joy, my tickling, my delight! Go bring 'em.
MOS.: [*Advancing.*] Please you draw near, sir.
CORV.: Come on, what—
You will not be rebellious? By that light—
MOS.: Sir, Signior Corvino, here, is come to see you.
VOLP.: Oh!
MOS.: And hearing of the consultation had,
So lately, for your health, is come to offer,
Or rather, sir, to prostitute—
CORV.: Thanks, sweet Mosca.
MOS.: Freely, unask'd, or unintreated—
CORV.: Well.
MOS.: As the true fervent instance of his love,
His own most fair and proper wife; the beauty
Only of price in Venice—
CORV.: 'T is well urg'd.
MOS.: To be your comfortress, and to preserve you.
VOLP.: Alas, I am past, already! Pray you, thank him
For his good care and promptness; but for that,
'T is a vain labour e'en to fight 'gainst heaven;
Applying fire to stone—uh, uh, uh, uh! [*Coughing.*]
Making a dead leaf grow again. I take
His wishes gently, though; and you may tell him
What I have done for him: marry, my state is hopeless.
Will him to pray for me; and to use his fortune
With reverence when he comes to 't.
MOS.: Do you hear, sir?
Go to him with your wife.
CORV.: Heart of my father!
Wilt thou persist thus? Come, I pray thee, come.
Thou seest 't is nothing, Celia. By this hand

I shall grow violent. Come, do 't, I say.
CEL.: Sir, kill me, rather: I will take down poison,
Eat burning coals, do anything—
CORV.: Be damn'd!
Heart, I will drag thee hence home by the hair;
Cry thee a strumpet through the streets; rip up
Thy mouth unto thine ears; and slit thy nose,
Like a raw rochet![111]—Do not tempt me; come,
Yield, I am loth—Death! I will buy some slave
Whom I will kill, and bind thee to him alive;
And at my windore hang you forth, devising
Some monstrous crime, which I, in capital letters,
Will eat into thy flesh with aquafortis,
And burning cor'sives,[112] on this stubborn breast.
Now, by the blood thou hast incens'd, I'll do it!
CEL.: Sir, what you please, you may; I am your martyr.
CORV.: Be not thus obstinate, I ha' not deserv'd it:
Think who it is intreats you. Prithee, sweet;—
Good faith, thou shalt have jewels, gowns, attires,
What thou wilt think, and ask. Do but go kiss him.
Or touch him but. For my sake. At my suit—
This once. No! not! I shall remember this.
Will you disgrace me thus? Do you thirst my undoing?
MOS.: Nay, gentle lady, be advis'd.
CORV.: No, no.
She has watch'd her time. God's precious, this is scurvy,
'T is very scurvy; and you are—
MOS.: Nay, good sir.
CORV.: An arrant locust—by heaven, a locust!—
Whore, crocodile, that hast thy tears prepar'd,
Expecting how thou 'lt bid 'em flow—
MOS.: Nay, pray you, sir!
She will consider.
CEL.: Would my life would serve
To satisfy—
CORV.: 'Sdeath! if she would but speak to him,
And save my reputation, 't were somewhat;

But spitefully to affect my utter ruin!
MOS.: Ay, now you have put your fortune in her hands.
Why i' faith, it is her modesty, I must quit her.
If you were absent, she would be more coming;
I know it: and dare undertake for her,
What woman can before her husband? Pray you,
Let us depart and leave her here.
CORV.: Sweet Celia,
Thou mayest redeem all yet; I'll say no more:
If not, esteem yourself as lost. Nay, stay there.
[*Exit with* MOSCA.]
CEL.: O God, and his good angels! whither, whither,
Is shame fled human breasts? that with such case,
Men dare put off your honours, and their own?
Is that, which ever was a cause of life,
Now plac'd beneath the basest circumstance,
And modesty an exile made, for money?
VOLP.: Ay, in Corvino, and such earth-fed minds,
[*He leaps from his couch.*]
That never tasted the true heaven of love.
Assure thee, Celia, he that would sell thee,
Only for hope of gain, and that uncertain,
He would have sold his part of Paradise
For ready money, had he met a cope-man.[113]
Why art thou maz'd to see me thus reviv'd?
Rather applaud thy beauty's miracle;
'T is thy great work, that hath, not now alone,
But sundry times rais'd me, in several shapes,
And, but this morning, like a mountebank,
To see thee at thy windore: ay, before
I would have left my practice, for thy love,
In varying figures, I would have contended
With the blue Proteus, or the horned flood.[114]
Now art thou welcome.
CEL.: Sir!
VOLP.: Nay, fly me not,
Nor let thy false imagination

That I was bed-rid, make thee think I am so:
Thou shalt not find it. I am now as fresh,
As hot, as high, and in as jovial plight
As, when, in that so celebrated scene,
At recitation of our comedy,
For entertainment of the great Valois,[115]
I acted young Antinous; and attracted
The eyes and ears of all the ladies present,
To admire each graceful gesture, note, and footing.
[*Sings.*]

SONG[116]

Come, my Celia, let us prove
While we can, the sports of love,
Time will not be ours for ever,
He, at length, our good will sever;
Spend not then his gifts in vain:
Suns that set rime rise again;
But if once we lose this light,
'T is with us perpetual night.
Why should we defer our joys?
Fame and rumour are but toys.
Cannot we delude the eyes
Of a few poor household spies?
Or his easier ears beguile,
Thus removed by our wile?
'T is no sin love's fruits to steal;
But the sweet thefts to reveal:
To be taken, to be seen,
These have crimes accounted been.

CEL.: Some serene[117] blast me, or dire lightning strike
This my offending face!

VOLP.: Why droops my Celia?
Thou hast, in place of a base husband found
A worthy lover: use thy fortune well,
With secrecy and pleasure. See, behold,
What thou art queen of; not in expectation,
As I feed others: but possess'd and crown'd.

See, here, a rope of pearl; and each more orient
Than the brave Aegyptian queen carous'd:
Dissolve and drink 'em.[118] See, a carbuncle,
May put out both the eyes of our St. Mark;
A diamond would have bought Lollia Paulina,[119]
When she came in like stair-light, hid with jewels
That were the spoils of provinces; take these
And wear, and lose 'em; yet remains an earring
To purchase them again, and this whole state.
A gem but worth a private patrimony
Is nothing; we will eat such at a meal.
The heads of parrots, tongues of nightingales,
The brains of peacocks, and of estriches,
Shall be our food, and, could we get the phoenix,
Though nature lost her kind, she were our dish.

CEL.: Good sir, these things might move a mind affected
With such delights; but I, whose innocence
Is all I can think wealthy, or worth th' enjoying,
And which, once lost, I have nought to lose beyond it,
Cannot be taken with these sensual baits:
If you have conscience—

VOLP.: 'T is the beggar's virtue;
If thou hast wisdom, hear me, Celia.
Thy baths shall be the juice of July-flowers,
Spirit of roses, and of violets,
The milk of unicorns, and panthers' breath
Gather'd in bags, and mix'd with Cretan wines.
Our drink shall be prepared gold and amber;
Which we will take until my roof whirl round
With the vertigo: and my dwarf shall dance,
My eunuch sing, my fool make up the antic,
Whilst we, in changed shapes, act Ovid's tales,
Thou, like Europa now, and I like Jove,
Then I like Mars, and thou like Erycine:
So of the rest, till we have quite run through,
And wearied all the fables of the gods.
Then will I have thee in more modern forms,

Attired like some sprightly dame of France,
Brave Tuscan lady, or proud Spanish beauty;
Sometimes unto the Persian sophy's[120] wife;
Or the grand signior's mistress; and for change,
To one of our most artful courtesans,
Or some quick Negro, or cold Russian;
And I will meet thee in as many shapes:
Where we may so transfuse our wand'ring souls
Out at our lips, and score up sums of pleasures,
[*Sings.*] That the curious shall not know
How to tell them as they flow;
And the envious, when they find
What their number is, be pin'd.

CEL.: If you have ears that will be pierc'd—or eyes
That can be open'd—a heart that may be touch'd—
Or any part that yet sounds man about you—
If you have touch of holy saints—or heaven—
Do me the grace to let me scape:—if not,
Be bountiful and kill me. You do know,
I am a creature, hither ill betray'd,
By one whose shame I would forget it were:
If you will deign me neither of these graces,
Yet feed your wrath, sir, rather than your lust,
(It is a vice comes nearer manliness,)
And punish that unhappy crime of nature,
Which you miscall my beauty: flay my face,
Or poison it with ointments for seducing
Your blood to this rebellion. Rub these hands
With what may cause an eating leprosy,
E'en to my bones and marrow: anything
That may disfavour me, save in my honour—
And I will kneel to you, pray for you, pay down
A thousand hourly vows, sir, for your health;
Report, and think you virtuous—

VOLP.: Think me cold,
Frozen, and impotent, and so report me?
That I had Nestor's hernia,[121] thou wouldst think.

I do degenerate, and abuse my nation,
To play with opportunity thus long;
I should have done the act, and then have parley'd.
Yield, or I'll force thee. [*Seizes her.*]
CEL.: O! just God!
VOLP.: In vain—
BON.: [*leaps out from where* MOSCA *had placed him.*] Forbear, foul ravisher! libidinous swine!
Free the forc'd lady, or thou diest, impostor.
But that I'm loth to snatch thy punishment
Out of the hand of justice, thou shouldst yet
Be made the timely sacrifice of vengeance,
Before this altar and this dross, thy idol—
Lady, let's quit the place, it is the den
Of villany; fear nought, you have a guard:
And he ere long shall meet his just reward.
[*Exeunt* BON. *and* CEL.]
VOLP.: Fall on me, roof, and bury me in ruin!
Become my grave, that wert my shelter! O!
I am unmask'd, unspirited, undone,
Betray'd to beggary, to infamy—

SCENE VIII—THE SAME

VOLPONE. *Enter MOSCA, wounded and bleeding.*

MOS.: Where shall I run, most wretched shame of men,
To beat out my unlucky brains?
VOLP.: Here, here.
What! dost thou bleed?
MOS.: O, that his well-driv'n sword
Had been so courteous to have cleft me down
Unto the navel, ere I liv'd to see
My life, my hopes, my spirits, my patron, all
Thus desperately engaged by my error!
VOLP.: Woe on thy fortune!
MOS.: And my follies, sir.

VOLP.: Thou hast made me miserable.
MOS.: And myself, sir.
Who would have thought he would have heark'ned so?
VOLP.: What shall we do?
MOS.: I know not; if my heart
Could expiate the mischance, I'd pluck it out.
Will you be pleas'd to hang me, or cut my throat?
And I'll requite you, sir. Let's die like Romans,[122]
Since we have liv'd like Grecians.
[*They knock without.*]
VOLP.: Hark! who's there?
I hear some footing; officers, the saffi,[123]
Come to apprehend us! I do feel the brand
Hissing already at my forehead; now
Mine ears are boring.
MOS.: To your couch, sir, you,
Make that place good, however. [VOLPONE *lies down as before.*] Guilty men
Suspect what they deserve still. Signior Corbaccio!

SCENE IX—THE SAME

To them enter CORBACCIO.

CORB.: Why, how now, Mosca?
MOS.: O, undone, amaz'd, sir.
Your son, I know not by what accident,
Acquainted with your purpose to my patron,
Touching your will, and making him your heir,
Ent'red our house with violence, his sword drawn,
Sought for you, called you wretch, unnatural,
Vow'd he would kill you.
CORB.: Me!
MOS.: Yes, and my patron.
CORB.: This act shall disinherit him indeed:
Here is the will.
MOS.: 'T is well, sir.

CORB.: Right and well:
Be you as careful now for me.
[*Enter* VOLTORE *behind.*]
MOS.: My life, sir,
Is not more tender'd; I am only yours.
CORB.: How does he? Will he die shortly, think'st thou?
MOS.: I fear
He'll outlast May.
CORB.: To-day?
MOS.: No, last out May, sir.
CORB.: Couldst thou not gi' him a dram?
MOS.: O, by no means, sir.
CORB.: Nay, I'll not bid you.
VOLT.: [*coming forward.*] This is a knave, I see.
MOS.: [*Aside, seeing* VOLT.]
How! Signior Voltore! did he hear me?
VOLT.: Parasite!
MOS.: Who's that?—O, sir, most timely welcome—
VOLT.: Scarce,
To the discovery of your tricks, I fear.
You are his, *only*? And mine also, are you not?
MOS.: Who? I, sir!
VOLT.: You, sir. What device is this
About a will?
MOS.: A plot for you, sir.
VOLT.: Come,
Put not your foists[124] upon me; I shall scent 'em.
MOS.: Did you not hear it?
VOLT.: Yes, I hear Corbaccio
Hath made your patron there his heir.
MOS.: 'T is true,
By my device, drawn to it by my plot,
With hope—
VOLT.: Your patron should reciprocate?
And you have promis'd?
MOS.: For your good I did, sir.
Nay, more, I told his son, brought, hid him here,

Where he might hear his father pass the deed;
Being persuaded to it by this thought, sir,
That the unnaturalness, first, of the act,
And then his father's oft disclaiming in him,
(Which I did mean t' help on), would sure enrage him
To do some violence upon his parent,
On which the law should take sufficient hold,
And you be stated in a double hope.
Truth be my comfort, and my conscience,
My only aim was to dig you a fortune
Out of these two rotten sepulchres—
VOLT.: I cry thee mercy, Mosca.
MOS.: —Worth your patience,
And your great merit, sir. And see the change!
VOLT.: Why, what success?
MOS.: Most hapless! you must help, sir.
Whilst we expected th' old raven, in comes
Corvino's wife, sent hither by her husband—
VOLT.: What, with a present?
MOS.: No, sir, on visitation;
(I'll tell you how anon;) and staying long,
The youth he grows impatient, rushes forth,
Seizeth the lady, wounds me, makes her swear
(Or he would murder her, that was his vow)
T' affirm my patron to have done her rape:
Which how unlike it is, you see! and hence,
With that pretext he's gone, t' accuse his father,
Defame my patron, defeat you—
VOLT.: Where 's her husband?
Let him be sent for straight.
MOS.: Sir, I'll go fetch him.
VOLT.: Bring him to the Scrutineo.[125]
MOS.: Sir, I will.
VOLT.: This must be stopt.
MOS.: O you do nobly, sir.
Alas, 't was labour'd all, sir, for your good;
Nor was there want of counsel in the plot:

But Fortune can, at any time, o'erthrow
The projects of a hundred learned clerks, sir.
CORB.: [*Listening.*] What's that?
VOLT.: Wilt please you, sir, to go along?
[*Exit* CORBACCIO, *followed by* VOLTORE.]
Patron, go in, and pray for our success.
VOLP.: [*Rising from his couch.*] Need makes devotion: heaven your labour bless!

[*Exeunt.*]

ACT IV

SCENE 1—A STREET

Enter SIR POLITIC WOULD-BE, PEREGRINE.

SIR P.: I told you, sir, it was a plot; you see
What observation is! You mention'd[126] me
For some instructions: I will tell you, sir,
(Since we are met here in this height of Venice,)
Some few particulars I have set down,
Only for this meridian, fit to be known
Of your crude traveller; and they are these.
I will not touch, sir, at your phrase, or clothes,
For they are old.
PER.: Sir, I have better.
SIR P.: Pardon,
I meant, as they are themes.
PER.: O, sir, proceed:
I'll slander you no more of wit, good sir.
SIR P.: First, for your garb,[127] it must be grave and serious,
Very reserv'd and lockt; not tell a secret
On any terms, not to your father; scarce
A fable, but with caution: make sure choice
Both of your company and discourse; beware

You never speak a truth—
PER.: How!
SIR P.: Not to strangers,
For those be they you must converse with most;
Others I would not know, sir, but at distance
So as I still might be a saver in them:
You shall have tricks else past upon you hourly.
And then, for your religion, profess none,
But wonder at the diversity of all;
And, for your part, protest, were there no other
But simply the laws o' th' land, you could content you.
Nick Machiavel and Monsieur Bodin,[128] both
Were of this mind. Then must you learn the use
And handling of your silver fork at meals,
The metal of your glass; (these are main matters
With your Italian;) and to know the hour
When you must eat your melons and your figs.
PER.: Is that a point of state too?
SIR P.: Here it is:
For your Venetian, if he see a man
Preposterous in the least, he has him straight;
He has; he strips him. I'll acquaint you, sir.
I now have liv'd here 't is some fourteen months:
Within the first week of my landing here,
All took me for a citizen of Venice,
I knew the forms so well—
PER.: [*Aside.*] And nothing else.
SIR P.: I had read Contarene,[129] took me a house,
Dealt with my Jews to furnish it with movables—
Well, if I could but find one man, one man
To mine own heart, whom I durst trust, I would—
PER.: What, what, sir?
SIR P.: Make him rich; make him a fortune:
He should not think again. I would command it.
PER.: As how?
SIR P.: With certain projects that I have;
Which I may not discover.[130]

PER.: [*Aside.*] If I had
But one to wager with, I would lay odds now,
He tells me instantly.
SIR P.: One is, and that
I care not greatly who knows, to serve the state
Of Venice with red herrings for three years,
And at a certain rate, from Rotterdam,
Where I have correspondence. There 's a letter,
Sent me from one o' th' states, and to that purpose:
He cannot write his name, but that's his mark.
PER.: He is a chandler?
SIR P.: No, a cheesemonger.
There are some others too with whom I treat
About the same negotiation;
And I will undertake it: for 't is thus.
I'll do 't with ease, I have cast it all. Your hoy[131]
Carries but three men in her, and a boy;
And she shall make me three returns a year:
So if there come but one of three, I save;
If two, I can defalk:[132]—but this is now,
If my main project fail.
PER.: Then you have others?
SIR P.: I should be loth to draw the subtle air
Of such a place, without my thousand aims.
I'll not dissemble, sir: where'er I come,
I love to be considerative; and 't is true,
I have at my free hours thought upon
Some certain goods unto the state of Venice,
Which I do call my Cautions; and, sir, which
I mean, in hope of pension, to propound
To the Great Council, then unto the Forty,
So to the Ten.[133] My means are made already—
PER.: By whom?
SIR P.: Sir, one that though his place be obscure,
Yet he can sway, and they will hear him. He 's
A *commandadore*.
PER.: What! a common serjeant?

SIR P.: Sir, such as they are, put it in their mouths,
What they should say, sometimes; as well as greater:
I think I have my notes to show you—
[*Searching his pockets.*]
PER.: Good sir.
SIR P.: But you shall swear unto me, on your gentry,
Not to anticipate—
PER.: I, sir!
SIR P.: Nor reveal
A circumstance—My paper is not with me.
PER.: O, but you can remember, sir.
SIR P.: My first is
Concerning tinder-boxes. You must know,
No family is here without its box.
Now, sir, it being so portable a thing,
Put case, that you or I were ill affected
Unto the state, sir; with it in our pockets,
Might not I go into the Arsenal,
Or you come out again, and none the wiser?
PER.: Except yourself, sir.
SIR P.: Go to, then. I therefore
Advertise to the state, how fit it were
That none but such as were known patriots,
Sound lovers of their country, should be suffer'd
T' enjoy them in their houses; and even those
Seal'd at some office, and at such a bigness
As might not lurk in pockets.
PER.: Admirable!
SIR P.: My next is, how t' inquire, and be resolv'd
By present demonstration, whether a ship,
Newly arriv'd from Soria,[134] or from
Any suspected part of all the Levant,[135]
Be guilty of the plague: and where they use
To lie out forty, fifty days, sometimes,
About the Lazaretto, for their trial;
I'll save that charge and loss unto the merchant,
And in an hour clear the doubt.

PER.: Indeed, sir!

SIR P.: Or—I will lose my labour.

PER.: My faith, that's much.

SIR P.: Nay, sir, conceive me. It will cost me in onions,
Some thirty livres—

PER.: Which is one pound sterling.

SIR P.: Beside my waterworks: for this I do, sir.
First, I bring in your ship 'twixt two brick wails;
But those the state shall venture. On the one
I strain me a fair tarpauling, and in that
I stick my onions, cut in halves; the other
Is full of loopholes, out of which I thrust
The noses of my bellows; and those bellows
I keep, with waterworks, in perpetual motion,
Which is the easiest matter of a hundred.
Now, sir, your onion, which doth naturally
Attract th' infection, and your bellows blowing
The air upon him, will show instantly,
By his chang'd colour, if there be contagion;
Or else remain as fair as at the first.
Now it is known, 't is nothing.

PER.: You are right, sir.

SIR P.: I would I had my note.

PER.: Faith, so would I:
But you ha' done well for once, sir.

SIR P.: Were I false
Or would be made so, I could show you reasons
How I could sell this state now to the Turk,
Spite of their galleys, or their—
[*Examining his papers.*]

PER.: Pray you, Sir Pol.

SIR P.: I have 'em not about me.

PER.: That I fear'd.
They are there, sir?

SIR P.: No, this is my diary,
Wherein I note my actions of the day.

PER.: Pray you let 's see, sir. What is here? *Notandum*,[136]

[*Reads.*]
"A rat had gnawn my spur-leathers; notwithstanding,
I put on new, and did go forth; but first
I threw three beans over the threshold. Item,
I went and bought two toothpicks, whereof one
I burst immediately, in a discourse
With a Dutch merchant, 'bout *ragion' del stato*.[137]
From him I went and paid a *moccinigo*
For piecing my silk stockings; by the way
I cheapen'd[138] sprats; and at St. Mark's I urin'd."
'Faith these are politic notes!

SIR P.: Sir, I do slip
No action of my life, but thus I quote[139] it.

PER.: Believe me, it is wise!

SIR P.: Nay, sir, read forth.

SCENE II—THE SAME

Enter, at a distance, LADY POLITIC WOULD-BE, NANO, *2 Waiting-women.*

LADY P.: Where should this loose knight be, trow? Sure he's hous'd.

NAN.: Why, then he's fast.

LADY P.: Ay, he plays both[140] with me.
I pray you stay. This heat will do more harm
To my complexion than his heart is worth.
(I do not care to hinder, but to take him.)
How it comes off! [*Rubbing her cheeks.*]

1ST WOM.: My master's yonder.

LADY P.: Where?

2ND WOM.: With a young gentleman.

LADY P.: That same's the party:
In man's apparel! Pray you, sir, jog my knight:
I will be tender to his reputation,
However he demerit.

SIR P.: [*seeing her*] My lady!

PER.: Where?

SIR P.: 'T is she indeed, sir; you shall know her. She is,
Were she not mine, a lady of that merit,
For fashion and behaviour; and for beauty
I durst compare—

PER.: It seems you are not jealous,
That dare commend her.

SIR P.: Nay, and for discourse—

PER.: Being your wife, she cannot miss that.

SIR P.: [*introducing* PER.] Madam,
Here is a gentleman, pray you, use him fairly;
He seems a youth, but he is—

LADY P.: None.

SIR P.: Yes one
Has put his face as soon into the world—

LADY P.: You mean, as early? But to-day?

SIR P. : How's this?

LADY P.: Why, in this habit, sir; you apprehend me.
Well, Master Would-be, this doth not become you;
I had thought the odour, sir, of your good name
Had been more precious to you; that you would not
Have done this dire massacre on your honour;
One of your gravity, and rank besides!
But knights, I see, care little for the oath
They make to ladies; chiefly their own ladies.

SIR P.: Now, by my spurs, the symbol of my knighthood—

PER.: [*Aside.*] Lord, how his brain is humbl'd for an oath!

SIR P.: I reach[141] you not.

LADY P.: Right, sir, your polity
May bear it through thus. Sir, a word with you.
[*To* PER.]
I would be loth to contest publicly
With any gentlewoman, or to seem
Froward, or violent, as the courtier says;
It comes too near rusticity in a lady,
Which I would shun by all means: and however
I may deserve from Master Would-be, yet

T' have one fair gentlewoman thus be made
The unkind instrument to wrong another,
And one she knows not, ay, and to persever;
In my poor judgment, is not warranted
From being a solecism in our sex,
If not in manners.

PER.: How is this!

SIR P.: Sweet madam,
Come nearer to your aim.

LADY P.: Marry, and will, sir.
Since you provoke me with your impudence,
And laughter of your light land-syren here,
Your Sporus,[142] your hermaphrodite—

PER.: What's here?
Poetic fury and historic storms!

SIR P.: The gentleman, believe it, is of worth
And of our nation.

LADY P.: Ay, your Whitefriars nation[143]
Come, I blush for you, Master Would-be, I;
And am asham'd you should ha' no more forehead
Than thus to be the patron, or St. George,
To a lewd harlot, a base fricatrice,[144]
A female devil, in a male outside.

SIR P.: Nay,
An you be such a one, I must bid adieu
To your delights. The case appears too liquid. [*Exit.*]

LADY P.: Ay, you may carry 't clear, with you state-face!
But for your carnival concupiscence,
Who here is fled for liberty of conscience,
From furious persecution of the marshal,
Her will I disc'ple.[145]

PER.: This is fine, i' faith!
And do you use this often? Is this part
Of your wit's exercise, 'gainst you have occasion?
Madam—

LADY P.: Go to, sir.

PER.: Do you hear me, lady?

Why, if your knight have set you to beg shirts,
Or to invite me home, you might have done it
A nearer way by far.
LADY P.: This cannot work you
Out of my snare.
PER.: Why, am I in it, then?
Indeed your husband told me you were fair,
And so you are; only your nose inclines,
That side that 's next the sun, to the queen-apple.[146]
LADY P.: This cannot be endur'd by any patience.

SCENE III—THE SAME

To them enter MOSCA.

MOS.: What is the matter, madam?
LADY P.: If the senate
Right not my quest in this, I will protest 'em
To all the world no aristocracy.
MOS.: What is the injury, lady?
LADY P.: Why, the callet[147]
You told me of, here I have ta'en disguis'd.
MOS.: Who? this! what means your ladyship? The creature
I mention'd to you is apprehended now,
Before the senate; you shall see her—
LADY P.: Where?
MOS.: I'll bring you to her. This young gentleman,
I saw him land this morning at the port.
LADY P.: Is 't possible! how has my judgment wander'd?
Sir, I must, blushing, say to you, I have err'd;
And plead your pardon.
PER.: What, more changes yet!
LADY P.: I hope you ha' not the malice to remember
A gentlewoman's passion. If you stay
In Venice here, please you to use me, sir—
MOS.: Will you go, madam?

LADY P.: Pray you, sir, use me; in faith,
The more you see me the more I shall conceive
You have forgot our quarrel.
[*Exeunt* LADY WOULD-BE, MOSCA, NANO*, and Waiting-women.*]
PER.: This is rare!
Sir Politic Would-be? No, Sir Politic Bawd,
To bring me thus acquainted with his wife!
Well, wise Sir Pol, since you have practis'd thus
Upon my freshman-ship, I'll try your salt-head,[148]
What proof it is against a counter-plot.

[*Exit.*]

SCENE IV—THE SCRUTINEO

Enter VOLTORE, CORBACCIO, CORVINO, MOSCA.

VOLT.: Well, now you know the carriage of the business,
Your constancy is all that is requir'd
Unto the safety of it.
MOS.: Is the lie
Safely convey'd amongst us? Is that sure?
Knows every man his burden?
CORV.: Yes.
MOS.: Then shrink not.
CORV.: But knows the advocate the truth?
MOS.: O, sir,
By no means; I devis'd a formal tale,
That salv'd your reputation. But be valiant, sir.
CORV.: I fear no one but him that this his pleading
Should make him stand for a co-heir—
MOS.: Co-halter!
Hang him; we will but use his tongue, his noise,
As we do croaker's[149] here.
CORV.: Ay, what shall he do?
MOS.: When we ha' done, you mean?
CORV.: Yes.

MOS.: Why, we'll think;
Sell him for mummia:[150] he's half dust already—
Do you not smile, [*to* VOLTORE] to see this buffalo,[151]
How he doth sport it with his head? [*Aside.*] I should,
If all were well and past—Sir, [*to* CORBACCIO] only you
Are he that shall enjoy the crop of all,
And these not know for whom they toil.
CORB.: Ay, peace.
MOS.: [*turning to* CORVINO.]
But you shall eat it. [*Aside.*] Much!—Worshipful sir, [*to* VOLTORE.]
Mercury sit upon your thund'ring tongue,
Or the French Hercules, and make your language
As conquering as his club, to beat along,
As with a tempest, flat, our adversaries;
But much more yours, sir.
VOLT.: Here they come, ha' done.
MOS.: I have another witness, if you need, sir, I can produce.
VOLT.: Who is it?
MOS.: Sir, I have her.

SCENE V—THE SAME

Enter 4 Avocatori, and take their seats, BONARIO, CELIA, *Notario, Commandadori, Saffi, and other Officers of Justice.*

1ST AVOC.: The like of this the senate never heard of.
2ND AVOC.: 'T will come most strange to them when we report it.
4TH AVOC.: The gentlewoman has been ever held
Of unreproved name.
3RD AVOC.: So has the youth.
4TH AVOC.: The more unnatural part that of his father.
2ND AVOC.: More of the husband.
1ST AVOC.: I not know to give
His act a name, it is so monstrous!
4TH AVOC.: But the impostor, he's a thing created.
T' exceed example!

1ST AVOC.: And all after-times!

2ND AVOC.: I never heard a true voluptuary
Describ'd but him.

3RD AVOC.: Appear yet those were cited?

NOT.: All but the old magnifico, Volpone.

1ST AVOC.: Why is not he here?

MOS: Please your fatherhoods,
Here is his advocate: himself's so weak,
So feeble—

4TH AVOC.: Who are you?

BON.: His parasite,
His knave, his pander. I beseech the court
He may be forc'd to come, that your grave eyes
May bear strong witness of his strange impostures.

VOLT.: Upon my faith and credit with your virtues.
He is not able to endure the air.

2ND AVOC.: Bring him.

3RD AVOC.: We will see him.

4TH AVOC.: Fetch him.

VOLT.: Your fatherhoods' fit pleasures be obey'd;

[*Exeunt Officers.*]

But sure, the sight will rather move your pities
Than indignation. May it please the court,
In the mean time, he may be heard in me.
I know this place most void of prejudice,
And therefore crave it, since we have no reason
To fear our truth should hurt our cause.

3RD AVOC.: Speak free.

VOLT.: Then know, most honour'd fathers, I must now
Discover to your strangely abus'd ears,
The most prodigious and most frontless piece
Of solid impudence, and treachery,
That ever vicious nature yet brought forth
To shame the state of Venice. This lewd woman,
That wants no artificial looks or tears
To help the vizor she has now put on,
Hath long been known a close adulteress

To that lascivious youth there; not suspected,
I say, but known, and taken in the act
With him; and by this man, the easy husband,
Pardon'd; whose timeless bounty makes him now
Stand here, the most unhappy, innocent person,
That ever man's own goodness made accus'd.
For these not knowing how to owe a gift
Of that dear grace, but with their shame; being plac'd
So above all powers of their gratitude,
Began to hate the benefit; and in place
Of thanks, devise t' extirp the memory
Of such an act: wherein I pray your fatherhoods
To observe the malice, yea, the rage of creatures
Discover'd in their evils: and what heart
Such take, ev'n from their crimes:—but that anon
Will more appear—This gentleman, the father,
Hearing of this foul fact, with many others,
Which daily struck at his too tender ears,
And griev'd in nothing more than that he could not
Preserve himself a parent (his son's ills
Growing to that strange flood), at last decreed
To disinherit him.

1ST AVOC.: These be strange turns!

2ND AVOC.: The young man's fame was ever fair and honest.

VOLT.: So much more full of danger is his vice,
That can beguile so, under shade of virtue.
But, as I said, my honour'd sires, his father
Having this settled purpose, by what means
To him betray'd, we know not, and this day
Appointed for the deed; that parricide,
I cannot style him better, by confederacy
Preparing this his paramour to be there,
Ent'red Volpone's house (who was the man,
Your fatherhoods must understand, design'd
For the inheritance), there sought his father:—
But with what purpose sought he him, my lords?
I tremble to pronounce it, that a son

Unto a father, and to such a father,
Should have so foul, felonious intent!
It was to murder him: when being prevented
By his more happy absence, what then did he?
Not check his wicked thoughts; no, now new deeds;
(Mischief doth never end where it begins)
An act of horror, fathers! He dragg'd forth
The aged gentleman that had there lain bedrid
Three years and more, out of his innocent couch,
Naked upon the floor; there left him; wounded
His servant in the face; and with this strumpet,
The stale[152] to his forg'd practice, who was glad
To be so active,—(I shall here desire
Your fatherhoods to note but my collections,
As most remarkable,—) thought at once to stop
His father's ends, discredit his free choice
In the old gentleman, redeem themselves,
By laying infamy upon this man,
To whom, with blushing, they should owe their lives.

1ST AVOC.: What proofs have you of this?

BON.: Most honour'd fathers,
I humbly crave there be no credit given
To this man's mercenary tongue.

2ND AVOC.: Forbear.

BON.: His soul moves in his fee.

3RD AVOC.: O, sir.

BON.: This fellow,
For six sols[153] more would plead against his Maker.

1ST AVOC.: You do forget yourself

VOLT.: Nay, nay, grave fathers,
Let him have scope: can any man imagine
That he will spare his accuser, that would not
Have spar'd his parent?

1ST AVOC.: Well, produce your proofs.

CEL.: I would I could forget I were a creature.

VOLT.: Signior Corbaccio!

[CORBACCIO *comes forward.*]

4TH AVOC.: What is he?

VOLT.: The father.

2ND AVOC.: Has he had an oath?

NOT.: Yes.

CORB.: What must I do now?

NOT.: Your testimony's crav'd.

CORB.: Speak to the knave?
I'll ha' my mouth first stopt with earth; my heart
Abhors his knowledge: I disclaim in[154] him.

1ST AVOC.: But for what cause?

CORB.: The mere portent of nature!
He is an utter stranger to my loins.

BON.: Have they made you to this?

CORB.: I will not hear thee,
Monster of men, swine, goat, wolf, parricide!
Speak not, thou viper.

BON.: Sir, I will sit down,
And rather wish my innocence should suffer
Than I resist the authority of a father.

VOLT.: Signior Corvino!
[CORVINO *comes forward.*]

2ND AVOC.: This is strange.

1ST AVOC.: Who's this?

NOT.: The husband.

4TH AVOC.: Is he sworn?

NOT.: He is.

3RD AVOC.: Speak then.

CORV.: This woman, please your fatherhoods, is a whore,
Of most hot exercise, more than a partridge,
Upon record—

1ST AVOC.: No more.

CORV.: Neighs like a jennet.[155]

NOT.: Preserve the honour of the court.

CORV.: I shall,
And modesty of your most reverend ears.
And yet I hope that I may say, these eyes
Have seen her glu'd unto that piece of cedar,

That fine well timber'd gallant: and that here
The letters may be read, thorough the horn,[156]
That make the story perfect.
MOS.: Excellent! sir.
CORV.: [*Aside to* MOSCA.]
There is no shame in this now, is there?
MOS.: None.
CORV.: Or if I said, I hop'd that she were onward
To her damnation, if there be a hell
Greater than whore and woman, a good Catholic
May make the doubt.
3RD AVOC.: His grief hath made him frantic.
1ST AVOC.: Remove him hence.
2ND AVOC.: Look to the woman.
[CELIA *swoons.*]
CORV.: Rare!
Prettily feign'd again!
4TH AVOC.: Stand from about her.
1ST AVOC.: Give her the air.
3RD AVOC.: [*To* MOSCA.] What can you say?
MOS.: My wound,
May it please your wisdoms, speaks for me, receiv'd
In aid of my good patron, when he mist
His sought-for father, when that well-taught dame
Had her cue giv'n her to cry out, "A rape!"
BON.: O most laid[157] impudence! Fathers—
3RD AVOC.: Sir, be silent;
You had your hearing free, so must they theirs.
2ND AVOC.: I do begin to doubt th' imposture here.
4TH AVOC.: This woman has too many moods.
VOLT.: Grave fathers,
She is a creature of a most profest
And prostituted lewdness.
CORV.: Most impetuous,
Unsatisfi'd, grave fathers!
VOLT.: May her feignings
Not take your wisdoms: but this day she baited

A stranger, a grave knight, with her loose eyes,
And more lascivious kisses. This man saw 'em
Together on the water, in a gondola.
MOS.: Here is the lady herself, that saw them too,
Without; who then had in the open streets
Pursu'd them, but for saving her knight's honour.
1ST AVOC.: Produce that lady.
2ND AVOC.: Let her come.
[*Exit* MOSCA.]
4TH AVOC.: These things,
They strike with wonder.
3RD AVOC.: I am turn'd a stone.

SCENE VI—THE SAME

To them re-enter MOSCA *with* LADY WOULD-BE.

MOS.: Be resolute, madam.
LADY P.: Ay, this same is she.
[*Pointing to* CELIA.]
Out, thou chameleon harlot! now thine eyes
Vie tears with the hyena. Dar'st thou look
Upon my wronged face? I cry your pardons,
I fear I have forgettingly transgrest
Against the dignity of the court—
2ND AVOC.: No, madam.
LADY P.: And been exorbitant—
2ND AVOC.: You have not, lady.
4TH AVOC.: These proofs are strong.
LADY P.: Surely, I had no purpose
To scandalize your honours, or my sex's.
3RD AVOC.: We do believe it.
LADY P.: Surely you may believe it.
2ND AVOC.: Madam, we do.
LADY P.: Indeed you may; my breeding
Is not so coarse—

4TH AVOC.: We know it.
LADY P.: To offend
With pertinacy—
3RD AVOC.: Lady—
LADY P.: Such a presence!
No surely.
1ST AVOC.: We will think it.
LADY P.: You may think it.
1ST AVOC.: Let her o'ercome. What witnesses have you,
To make good your report?
BON.: Our consciences.
CEL.: And heaven, that never fails the innocent.
1ST AVOC.: These are no testimonies.
BON.: Not in your courts,
Where multitude and clamour overcomes.
1ST AVOC.: Nay, then you do wax insolent.
VOLPONE [*brought in, as impotent*].
VOLT.: Here, here,
The testimony comes that will convince,
And put to utter dumbness their bold tongues!
See here, grave fathers, here's the ravisher,
The rider on men's wives, the great impostor,
The grand voluptuary! Do you not think
These limbs should affect venery? or these eyes
Covet a concubine? Pray you mark these hands;
Are they not fit to stroke a lady's breasts?
Perhaps he doth dissemble!
BON.: So he does.

THEIR SHAME, EV'N IN THEIR CRADLES, FLED THEIR FACES.

VOLT.: Would you ha' him tortur'd?
BON.:
I would have him prov'd.
VOLT.: Best try him then with goads, or burning irons;
Put him to the strappado:[158] I have heard
The rack hath cur'd the gout; faith, give it him,
And help him of a malady; be courteous.
I'll undertake, before these honour'd fathers,

He shall have yet as many left diseases,
As she has known adulterers, or thou strumpets.
O, my most equal hearers, if these deeds,
Acts of this bold and most exorbitant strain,
May pass with suff'rance, what one citizen
But owes the forfeit of his life, yea, fame,
To him that dares traduce him? Which of you
Are safe, my honour'd fathers? I would ask,
With leave of your grave fatherhoods, if their plot
Have any face or colour like to truth?
Or if, unto the dullest nostril here,
It smell not rank, and most abhorred slander?
I crave your care of this good gentleman,
Whose life is much endanger'd by their fable;
And as for them, I will conclude with this,
That vicious persons, when they're hot, and flesh'd
In impious acts, their constancy[159] abounds:
Damn'd deeds are done with greatest confidence.

1ST AVOC.: Take 'em to custody, and sever them.

2ND AVOC.: 'T is pity two such prodigies should live.

1ST AVOC.: Let the old gentleman be return'd with care.

[*Exeunt Officers with* VOLPONE.]

I'm sorry our credulity wrong'd him.

4TH AVOC.: These are two creatures!

3RD AVOC.: I've an earthquake in me.

2ND AVOC.: Their shame, ev'n in their cradles, fled their faces.

4TH AVOC.: [*To* VOLT.] You have done a worthy service to the state, sir,
In their discovery.

1ST AVOC.: You shall hear, ere night,
What punishment the court decrees upon 'em.

[*Exeunt Avocat., Not., and Officers with* BONARIO *and* CELIA.]

VOLT.: We thank your fatherhoods. How like you it?

MOS.: Rare.
I'd ha' your tongue, sir, tipt with gold for this;
I'd ha' you be the heir to the whole city;
The earth I'd have want men ere you want living:

They're bound to erect your statue in St. Mark's.
Signior Corvino, I would have you go
And show yourself that you have conquer'd.
CORV.: Yes.
MOS.: It was much better that you should profess
Yourself a cuckold thus, than that the other
Should have been prov'd.
CORV.: Nay, I consider'd that:
Now it is her fault.
MOS.: Then it had been yours.
CORV.: True; I do doubt this advocate still.
MOS.: I' faith.
You need not, I dare ease you of that care.
CORV.: I trust thee, Mosca. [*Exit.*]
MOS.: As your own soul, sir.
CORB.: Mosca!
MOS.: Now for your business, sir.
CORB.: How! ha' you business?
MOS.: Yes, yours, sir.
CORB.: O, none else?
MOS.: None else, not I.
CORB.: Be careful then.
MOS.: Rest you with both your eyes, sir.
CORB: Dispatch it.
MOS.: Instantly.
CORB.: And look that all,
Whatever, be put in, jewels, plate, moneys,
Household stuff, bedding, curtains.
MOS.: Curtain-rings, sir:
Only the advocate's fee must be deducted.
CORB.: I'll pay him now; you'll be too prodigal.
MOS: Sir, I must tender it.
CORB.: Two chequins is well.
MOS.: No, six, sir.
CORB.: 'T is too much.
MOS.: He talk'd a great while;
You must consider that, sir.

CORB.: Well, there's three—

MOS.: I'll give it him.

CORB.: Do so, and there's for thee. [*Exit.*]

MOS.: [*Aside.*] Bountiful bones! What horrid strange offence
Did he commit 'gainst nature, in his youth,
Worthy this age?—You see, sir, [*To* VOLT.] how I work
Unto your ends; take you no notice.

VOLT.: No,
I'll leave you.

MOS.: All is yours, the devil and all,
Good advocate!—Madam, I'll bring you home.

LADY P.: No, I'll go see your patron.

MOS.: That you shall not:
I'll tell you why. My purpose is to urge
My patron to reform his will, and for
The zeal you 've shown to-day, whereas before
You were but third or fourth, you shall be now
Put in the first; which would appear as begg'd
If you were present. Therefore—

LADY P.: You shall sway me.

[*Exeunt.*]

ACT V

SCENE 1—A ROOM IN VOLPONE'S HOUSE

Enter VOLPONE.

VOLP.: Well, I am here, and all this brunt is past.
I ne'er was in dislike with my disguise
Till this fled moment: here 't was good, in private;
But in your public,—*cavè*[160] whilst I breathe.
'Fore God, my left leg 'gan to have the cramp.
And I apprehended straight some power had struck me
With a dead palsy. Well! I must be merry,

And shake it off. A many of these fears
Would put me into some villanous disease,
Should they come thick upon me: I'll prevent 'em.
Give me a bowl of lusty wine, to fright
This humour from my heart. [*Drinks.*] Hum, hum, hum!
'T is almost gone already; I shall conquer.
Any device now of rare ingenious knavery,
That would possess me with a violent laughter,
Would make me up again. [*Drinks again.*] So, so, so, so!
This heat is life; 't is blood by this time:—Mosca!

SCENE II—THE SAME

VOLPONE. *Enter* MOSCA.

MOS.: How now, sir? Does the day look clear again?
Are we recover'd, and wrought out of error,
Into our way, to see our path before us?
Is our trade free once more?
VOLP.: Exquisite Mosca!
MOS.: Was it not carri'd learnedly?
VOLP.: And stoutly:
Good wits are greatest in extremities.
MOS.: It were folly beyond thought to trust
Any grand act unto a cowardly spirit.
You are not taken with it enough, methinks.
VOLP.: O, more than if I had enjoy'd the wench:
The pleasure of all woman-kind 's not like it.
MOS.: Why, now you speak, sir. We must here be fix'd;
Here we must rest; this is our masterpiece;
We cannot think to go beyond this.
VOLP.: True,
Thou hast play'd thy prize, my precious Mosca.
MOS.: Nay, sir,
To gull the court—
VOLP.: And quite divert the torrent

Upon the innocent.
MOS.: Yes, and to make
So rare a music out of discords—
VOLP.: Right.
That yet to me 's the strangest, how thou 'st borne it!
That these, being so divided 'mongst themselves,
Should not scent somewhat, or in me or thee,
Or doubt their own side.
MOS.: True, they will not see 't.
Too much light blinds 'em, I think. Each of 'em
Is so possest and stuft with his own hopes
That anything unto the contrary,
Never so true, or never so apparent,
Never so palpable, they will resist it—
VOLP.: Like a temptation of the devil.
MOS.: Right, sir.
Merchants may talk of trade, and your great signiors
Of land that yields well; but if Italy
Have any glebe[161] more fruitful than these fellows,
I am deceiv'd. Did not your advocate rare?
VOLP.: O—"My most honour'd fathers, my grave fathers,
Under correction of your fatherhoods,
What face of truth is here? If these strange deeds
May pass, most honour'd fathers"—I had much ado
To forbear laughing.
MOS.: It seem'd to me, you sweat, sir.
VOLP.: In troth, I did a little.
MOS.: But confess, sir,
Were you not daunted?
VOLP.: In good faith, I was
A little in a mist, but not dejected;
Never but still myself.
MOS.: I think it, sir.
Now, so truth help me, I must needs say this, sir,
And out of conscience for your advocate,
He has taken pains, in faith, sir, and deserv'd,
In my poor judgment, I speak it under favour,

Not to contrary you, sir, very richly—
Well—to be cozen'd.
VOLP.: Troth, and I think so too,
By that I heard him in the latter end.
MOS.: O, but before, sir: had you heard him first
Draw it to certain heads, then aggravate,
Then use his vehement figures—I look'd still
When he would shift a shirt;[162] and doing this
Out of pure love, no hope of gain—
VOLP.: 'T is right.
I cannot answer him, Mosca, as I would,
Not yet; but for thy sake, at thy entreaty,
I will begin, even now—to vex 'em all,
This very instant.
MOS.: Good sir.
VOLP.: Call the dwarf
And eunuch forth.
MOS.: Castrone, Nano! [*Enter* CASTRONE *and* NANO.]
NANO.: Here.
VOLP.: Shall we have a jig now?
MOS.: What you please, sir.
VOLP.: Go,
Straight give out about the streets, you two,
That I am dead; do it with constancy,
Sadly,[163] do you hear? Impute it to the grief
Of this late slander.
[*Exeunt* CAST. *and* NANO.]
MOS.: What do you mean, sir?
VOLP.: O,
I shall have instantly my Vulture, Crow,
Raven, come flying hither, on the news,
To peck for carrion, my she-wolf, and all,
Greedy, and full of expectation—
MOS.: And then to have it ravish'd from their mouths!
VOLP.: 'T is true. I will ha' thee put on a gown,
And take upon thee, as thou wert mine heir;
Show 'em a will. Open that chest, and reach

Forth one of those that has the blanks; I'll straight
Put in thy name.
MOS.: It will be rare, sir. [*Gives him a paper.*]
VOLP.: Ay,
When they e'en gape, and find themselves deluded—
MOS.: Yes.
VOLP.: And thou use them scurvily! Dispatch,
Get on thy gown.
MOS.: [*Putting on a gown.*] But what, sir, if they ask
After the body?
VOLP.: Say, it was corrupted.
MOS.: I'll say it stunk, sir; and was fain to have it
Coffin'd up instantly, and sent away.
VOLP.: Anything; what thou wilt. Hold, here's my will.
Get thee a cap, a count-book, pen and ink,
Papers afore thee; sit as thou wert taking
An inventory of parcels. I'll get up
Behind the curtain, on a stool, and hearken:
Sometime peep over, see how they do look,
With what degrees their blood doth leave their faces.
O, 't will afford me a rare meal of laughter!
MOS.: [*Putting on a cap, and setting out the table, &c.*]
Your advocate will turn stark dull upon it.
VOLP.: It will take off his oratory's edge.
MOS.: But your clarissimo, old roundback, he
Will crump you like a hog-louse, with the touch.[164]
VOLP.: And what Corvino?
MOS.: O, sir, look for him,
To-morrow morning, with a rope and dagger,
To visit all the streets; he must run mad,
My lady too, that came into the court,
To bear false witness for your worship—
VOLP.: Yes,
And kiss'd me 'fore the fathers, when my face
Flow'd all with oils—
MOS.: And sweat, sir. Why, your gold
Is such another med'cine, it dries up

All those offensive savours: it transforms
The most deformed, and restores them lovely,
As 't were the strange poetical girdle.[165] Jove
Could not invent t' himself a shroud more subtle
To pass Acrisius'[166] guards. It is the thing
Makes all the world her grace, her youth, her beauty.
VOLP.: I think she loves me.
MOS.: Who? The lady, sir?
She's jealous of you.
VOLP.: Dost thou say so?
[*Knocking within.*]
MOS.: Hark.
There's some already.
VOLP.: Look.
MOS.: It is the Vulture;
He has the quickest scent.
VOL.: I'll to my place,
Thou to thy posture. [*Goes behind the curtain.*]
MOS.: I am set.
VOLP.: But, Mosca,
Play the artificer now, torture 'em rarely.

SCENE III—THE SAME

MOSCA. *Enter* VOLTORE.

VOLT.: How now, my Mosca?
MOS.: [*Writing.*] "Turkey carpets, nine—"
VOLT.: Taking an inventory! that is well.
MOS.: "Two suits of bedding, tissue—"
VOLT.: Where's the will?
Let me read that the while.
[*Enter Servants with* CORBACCIO *in a chair.*]
CORB.: So, set me down,
And get you home.
[*Exeunt Servants.*]

VOLT.: Is he come now, to trouble us?

MOS.: "Of cloth of gold, two more—"

CORB.: Is it done, Mosca?

MOS.: "Of several velvets, eight—"

VOLT.: I like his care.

CORB.: Dost thou not hear?

[*Enter* CORVINO.]

CORV.: Ha! is the hour come, Mosca?

VOLP.: Ay, now they muster.

[*Peeps from behind a traverse.*]

CORV.: What does the advocate here,
Or this Corbaccio?

CORB.: What do these here?

[*Enter L*ADY POL. WOULD-BE.]

LADY P.: Mosca!
Is his thread spun?

MOS.: "Eight chests of linen—"

VOLP.: O,
My fine Dame Would-be, too!

CORV.: Mosca, the will,
That I may show it these, and rid 'em hence.

MOS.: "Six chests of diaper, four of damask."—There.

[*Gives them the will carelessly, over his shoulder.*]

CORB.: Is that the will?

MOS.: "Down-beds, and bolsters—"

VOLP.: Rare!
Be busy still. Now they begin to flutter:
They never think of me. Look, see, see, see!
How their swift eyes run over the long deed,
Unto the name, and to the legacies,
What is bequeath'd them there—

MOS.: "Ten suits of hangings—"

VOLP.: Ay, in their garters, Mosca. Now their hopes
Are at the gasp.

VOLT.: Mosca the heir.

CORB.: What's that?

VOLP.: My advocate is dumb; look to my merchant,

He 's heard of some strange storm, a ship is lost,
He faints; my lady will swoon. Old glazen-eyes,
He hath not reach'd his despair yet.
CORB.: All these
Are out of hope; I am, sure, the man.
[*Takes the will.*]
CORV.: But, Mosca—
MOS.: "Two cabinets—"
CORV.: Is this in earnest?
MOS.: "One
Of ebony—"
CORV.: Or do you but delude me?
MOS.: "The other, mother of pearl."—I'm very busy,
Good faith, it is a fortune thrown upon me—
"Item, one salt of agate"—not my seeking.
LADY P.: Do you hear, sir?
MOS.: "A perfum'd box"—Pray you forbear,
You see I'm troubl'd—"made of an onyx—"
LADY P.: How!
MOS.: To-morrow or next day, I shall be at leisure
To talk with you all.
CORV.: Is this my large hope's issue?
LADY P.: Sir, I must have a fairer answer.
MOS.: Madam!
Marry, and shall: pray you, fairly quit my house.
Nay, raise no tempest with your looks; but hark you,
Remember what your ladyship off'red me
To put you in an heir; go to, think on it:
And what you said e'en your best madams did
For maintenance; and why not you? Enough.
Go home, and use the poor Sir Pol, your knight well,
For fear I tell some riddles; go, be melancholic.
[*Exit* LADY WOULD-BE.]
VOLP.: O, my fine devil!
CORV.: Mosca, pray you a word.
MOS.: Lord! will not you take your dispatch hence yet?
Methinks, of all, you should have been th' example.

Why should you stay here? With what thought, what promise?
Hear you; do you not know, I know you an ass,
And that you would most fain have been a wittol[167]
If fortune would have let you? that you are
A declar'd cuckold, on good terms? This pearl,
You'll say, was yours? right: this diamond?
I'll not deny 't, but thank you. Much here else?
It may be so. Why, think that these good works
May help to hide your bad. I'll not betray you;
Although you be but extraordinary,
And have it only in fide, it sufficeth:
Go home, be melancholy too, or mad.

[*Exit* CORVINO.]

VOLP.: Rare Mosca! how his villany becomes him!
VOLT.: Certain he doth delude all these for me.
CORB.: Mosca the heir!
VOLP.: O, his four eyes have found it.
CORB.: I am cozen'd, cheated, by a parasite slave;
Harlot,[168] th' hast gull'd me.
MOS.: Yes, sir. Stop your mouth,
Or I shall draw the only tooth is left,
Are not you he, that filthy covetous wretch,
With the three legs, that here, in hope of prey,
Have, any time this three years, snuff'd about,
With your most grov'ling nose, and would have hir'd
Me to the pois'ning of my patron, sir?
Are not you he that have to-day in court
Profess'd the disinheriting of your son?
Perjur'd yourself? Go home, and die, and stink;
If you but croak a syllable, all comes out:
Away, and call your porters! [*Exit* CORBACCIO] Go, go, stink.
VOLP.: Excellent varlet!
VOLT.: Now, my faithful Mosca,
I find thy constancy—
MOS.: Sir!
VOLT.: Sincere.
MOS.: [*Writing.*]"A table

Of porphyry"—I marle[169] you'll be thus troublesome.

VOLT.: Nay, leave off now, they are gone.

MOS.: Why, who are you?
What! who did send for you? O, cry you mercy,
Reverend sir! Good faith, I am griev'd for you,
That any chance of mine should thus defeat
Your (I must needs say) most deserving travails:
But I protest, sir, it was cast upon me,
And I could almost wish to be without it,
But that the will o' the dead must be observ'd.
Marry, my joy is that you need it not;
You have a gift, sir (thank your education),
Will never let you want, while there are men,
And malice, to breed causes.[170] Would I had
But half the like, for all my fortune, sir!
If I have any suits, as I do hope,
Things being so easy and direct, I shall not,
I will make bold with your obstreperous aid,
Conceive me—for your fee, sir. In mean time,
You that have so much law, I know ha' the conscience
Not to be covetous of what is mine. Good sir,
I thank you for my plate; 't will help
To set up a young man. Good faith, you look
As you were costive; best go home and purge, sir.

[*Exit* VOLTORE.]

VOLP.: [*Comes from behind the curtain.*]
Bid him eat lettuce[171] well. My witty mischief,
Let me embrace thee. O that I could now
Transform thee to a Venus!—Mosca, go,
Straight take my habit of clarissimo,[172]
And walk the streets; be seen, torment 'em more:
We must pursue, as well as plot. Who would
Have lost this feast?

MOS.: I doubt it will lose them.

VOLP.: O, my recovery shall recover all.
That I could now but think on some disguise
To meet 'em in, and ask 'em questions:

How I would vex 'em still at every turn!
MOS.: Sir, I can fit you.
VOLP.: Canst thou?
MOS.: Yes, I know
One o' the commandadori, sir, so like you;
Him will I straight make drunk, and bring you his habit.
VOLP.: A rare disguise, and answering thy brain!
O, I will be a sharp disease unto 'em.
MOS.: Sir, you must look for curses—
VOLP.: Till they burst;
The Fox fares ever best when he is curst.

[*Exeunt.*]

SCENE IV—A HALL IN SIR POLITIC'S HOUSE

Enter PEREGRINE *disguised and 3 Mercatori.*

PER.: Am I enough disguis'd?
1ST MER.: I warrant you.
PER.: All my ambition is to fright him only.
2ND MER.: If you could ship him away, 't were excellent.
3RD MER.: To Zant, or to Aleppo![173]
PER.: Yes, and ha' his
Adventures put i' th' Book of Voyages,
And his gull'd story regist'red for truth.
Well, gentlemen, when I am in a while,
And that you think us warm in out discourse,
Know your approaches.
1ST MER.: Trust it to our care.

[*Exeunt Merchants.*]

[*Enter Waiting-woman.*]
PER.: Save you, fair lady! Is Sir Pol within?
WOM.: I do not know, sir.
PER.: Pray you say unto him
Here is a merchant, upon earnest business,
Desires to speak with him.

WOM.: I will see, sir.

[*Exit.*]

PER.: Pray you.
I see the family is all female here.
[*Re-enter Waiting-woman.*]
WOM.: He says, sir, he has weighty affairs of state
That now require him whole; some other time
You may possess him.
PER.: Pray you say again,
If those require him whole, these will exact him,
Whereof I bring him tidings. [*Exit Woman.*] What might be
His grave affair of state now! How to make
Bolognian sausages here in Venice, sparing
One o' th' ingredients?
WOM.: Sir, he says, he knows
By your word "tidings," that you are no statesman,
And therefore wills you stay.
PER.: Sweet, pray you return him;
I have not read so many proclamations,
And studied them for words, as he has done—
But—here he deigns to come.

[*Exit Woman.*]

[*Enter* SIR POLITIC.]
SIR P.: Sir, I must crave
Your courteous pardon. There hath chanc'd today
Unkind disaster 'twixt my lady and me;
And I was penning my apology,
To give her satisfaction, as you came now
PER.: Sir, I am griev'd I bring you worse disaster:
The gentleman you met at th' port to-day,
That told you he was newly arriv'd—
SIR P.: Ay, was
A fugitive punk?
PER.: No, sir, a spy set on you:
And he has made relation to the senate,
That you protest to him to have a plot
To sell the State of Venice to the Turk.

SIR P.: O me!

PER.: For which warrants are sign'd by this time
To apprehend you, and to search your study
For papers—

SIR P.: Alas, sir, I have none, but notes
Drawn out of play-books—

PER.: All the better, sir.

SIR P.: And some essays. What shall I do?

PER.: Sir, best
Convey yourself into a sugar-chest;
Or, if you could lie round, a frail[174] were rare;
And I could send you aboard.

SIR P.: Sir, I but talk'd so,
For discourse sake merely.
[*They knock without.*]

PER.: Hark! they are there.

SIR P.: I am a wretch, a wretch!

PER.: What will you do, sir?
Have you ne'er a currant-butt[175] to leap into?
They'll put you to the rack; you must be sudden.

SIR P.: Sir, I have an engine[176]—

3RD MER.: [*Within.*] Sir Politic Would-be!

2ND MER.: [*Within.*] Where is he?

SIR P.: That I have thought upon before time.

PER.: What is it?

SIR P.: I shall ne'er endure the torture.
Marry, it is, sir, of a tortoise-shell,
Fitted for these extremities: pray you, sir, help me.
Here I've a place, sir, to put back my legs,
Please you to lay it on, sir, [*Lies down while* PER. *places the shell upon him.*]—with this cap,
And my black gloves. I'll lie, sir, like a tortoise,
Till they are gone.

PER.: And call you this an engine?

SIR P.: Mine own device—Good sir, bid my wife's women
To burn my papers.

[*Exit* PER.]

[*The three Merchants rush in.*]

1ST MER.: Where is he hid?

3RD MER.: We must,
And will sure find him.

2ND MER.: Which is his study?

[*Re-enter* PEREGRINE.]

1ST MER.: What
Are you, sir?

PER.: I'm a merchant, that came here
To look upon this tortoise.

3RD MER.: How!

1ST MER.: St. Mark!
What beast is this?

PER.: It is a fish.

2ND MER.: Come out here!

PER.: Nay, you may strike him, sir, and tread upon him;
He'll bear a cart.

1ST MER.: What, to run over him?

PER.: Yes, sir.

3RD MER.: Let's jump upon him.

2ND MER.: Can he not go?

PER.: He creeps, sir.

1ST MER.: Let's see him creep.

PER.: No, good sir, you will hurt him.

2ND MER.: Heart, I will see him creep, or prick his guts.

3RD MER.: Come out here!

PER.: Pray you, sir, creep a little.

1ST MER.: Forth.

2ND MER.: Yet further.

PER.: Good sir!—Creep.

2ND MER.: We'll see his legs.

[*They pull off the shell and discover him.*]

3RD MER.: Gods so, he has garters!

1ST MER.: Ay, and gloves!

2ND MER.: Is this
Your fearful tortoise?

PER.: [*Discovering himself.*] Now, Sir Pol, we're even;

For your next project I shall be prepar'd:
I am sorry for the funeral of your notes, sir.
1ST MER.: 'T were a rare motion[177] to be seen in
Fleet-street.
2ND MER.: Ay, in the Term.
1ST MER.: Or Smithfield, in the fair.
3RD MER.: Methinks 't is but a melancholic sight.
PER.: Farewell, most politic tortoise!
[*Exeunt* PER. *and Merchants.*]
[*Re-enter Waiting-woman.*]
SIR P.: Where's my lady?
Knows she of this?
WOM.: I know not, sir.
SIR P.: Enquire—
O, I shall be the fable of all feasts,
The freight of the gazetti,[178] ship-boys' tale;
And, which is worst, even talk for ordinaries.
WOM.: My lady's come most melancholic home,
And says, sir, she will straight to sea, for physic.
SIR P.: And I, to shun this place and clime for ever,
Creeping with house on back, and think it well
To shrink my poor head in my politic shell.
[*Exeunt.*]

SCENE V—A ROOM IN VOLPONE'S HOUSE

Enter MOSCA *in the habit of a clarissimo, and* VOLPONE *in that of a commandadore.*

VOLP.: Am I then like him?
MOS.: O, sir, you are he;
No man can sever you.
VOLP.: Good.
MOS.: But what am I?
VOLP.: 'Fore heaven, a brave clarissimo; thou becom'st it!
Pity thou wert not born one.

MOS.: [*Aside.*] If I hold
My made one, 't will be well.
VOLP.: I'll go and see
What news first at the court.

[*Exit*]

MOS.: Do so. My Fox
Is out of his hole, and ere he shall re-enter,
I'll make him languish in his borrow'd case,[179]
Except he come to composition with me—
Androgyno, Castrone, Nano!
[*Enter* ANDROGYNO, CASTRONE, *and* NANO.]
ALL.: Here.
MOS.: Go, recreate yourselves abroad; go, sport—

[*Exeunt.*]

So, now I have the keys, and am possest.
Since he will needs be dead afore his time,
I'll bury him, or gain by 'm: I'm his heir,
And so will keep me, till he share at least.
To cozen him of all, were but a cheat
Well plac'd; no man would construe it a sin:
Let his sport pay for 't. This is call'd the Fox-trap.

[*Exit.*]

SCENE VI—A STREET

Enter CORBACCIO, CORVINO.

CORB.: They say the court is set.
CORV.: We must maintain
Our first tale good, for both our reputations.
CORB.: Why, mine's no tale: my son would there have kill'd me.
CORV.: That's true, I had forgot:—mine is, I'm sure.
But for your will, sir.
CORB.: Ay, I'll come upon him
For that hereafter, now his patron's dead.
[*Enter* VOLPONE.]

VOLP.: Signior Corvino! and Corbaccio! sir,
Much joy unto you.
CORV.: Of what?
VOLP.: The sudden good
Dropt down upon you—
CORB.: Where?
VOLP.: And none knows how,
From old Volpone, sir.
CORB.: Out, arrant knave!
VOLP.: Let not your too much wealth, sir, make you furious.
CORB.: Away, thou varlet.
VOLP.: Why, sir?
CORB.: Dost thou mock me?
VOLP.: You mock the world, sir; did you not change wills?
CORB.: Out, harlot!
VOLF.: O! belike you are the man,
Signior Corvino? Faith, you carry it well;
You grow not mad withal; I love your spirit:
You are not over-leaven'd with your fortune.
You should ha' some would swell now, like a wine-fat,
With such an autumn—Did he gi' you all, sir?
CORB.: Avoid, you rascal!
VOLP.: Troth, your wife has shown
Herself a very woman; but you are well,
You need not care, you have a good estate,
To bear it out, sir, better by this chance:
Except Corbaccio have a share.
CORB.: Hence, varlet.
VOLP.: You will not be acknown, sir; why, 't is wise.
Thus do all gamesters, at all games, dissemble:
No man will seem to win. [*Exeunt* CORVINO *and* CORBACCIO.] Here comes my vulture,
Heaving his beak up i' the air, and snuffing.

SCENE VII—THE SAME

VOLPONE. *Enter* VOLTORE.

VOLT.: Outstript thus, by a parasite! a slave,
Would run on errands, and make legs for crumbs!
Well, what I'll do—

VOLP.: The court stays for your worship.
I e'en rejoice, sir, at your worship's happiness,
And that it fell into so learned hands,
That understand the fing'ring—

VOLT.: What do you mean?

VOLP.: I mean to be a suitor to your worship,
For the small tenement, out of reparations,[180]
That, at the end of your long row of houses,
By the Piscaria: it was, in Volpone's time,
Your predecessor, ere he grew diseas'd,
A handsome, pretty, custom'd[181] bawdy-house
As any was in Venice, none disprais'd;
But fell with him: his body and that house
Decay'd together.

VOLT.: Come, sir, leave your prating.

VOLP.: Why, if your worship give me but your hand
That I may ha' the refusal, I have done.
'T is a mere toy to you, sir; candle-rents;[182]
As your learn'd worship knows—

VOLT.: What do I know?

VOLP.: Marry, no end of your wealth, sir; God decrease it!

VOLT.: Mistaking knave! what, mock'st thou my misfortune?

[*Exit.*]

VOLP.: His blessing on your heart, sir; would 't were more!—
Now to my first again, at the next corner.

[*Exit.*]

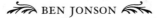

SCENE VIII—THE SCRUTINEO

Enter CORBACCIO *and* CORVINO;—(MOSCA *passant*.)

CORB.: See, in our habit![183] see the impudent varlet!

CORV.: That I could shoot mine eyes at him, like gun-stones!

[*Enter* VOLPONE.]

VOLP.: But is this true, sir, of the parasite?

CORB.: Again, t' afflict us! monster!

VOLP.: In good faith, sir,
I'm heartily griev'd, a beard of your grave length
Should be so over-reach'd. I never brook'd
That parasite's hair; methought his nose should cozen:[184]
There still was somewhat in his look, did promise
The bane of a clarissimo.

CORB.: Knave—

VOLP.: Methinks
Yet you, that are so traded i' the world,
A witty merchant, the fine bird, Corvino,
That have such moral emblems on your name,
Should not have sung your shame, and dropt your cheese,
To let the Fox laugh at your emptiness.

CORV.: Sirrah, you think the privilege of the place,
And your red saucy cap, that seems to me
Nail'd to your jolt-head with those two chequins,
Can warrant your abuses; come you hither:
You shall perceive, sir, I dare beat you; approach.

VOLP.: No haste, sir, I do know your valour well,
Since you durst publish what you are, sir.

CORV.: Tarry,
I'd speak with you.

VOLP.: Sir, sir, another time—

CORV.: Nay, now.

VOLP.: O lord, sir! I were a wise man,
Would stand the fury of a distracted cuckold.

[MOS. *walks by them.*]

CORB.: What, come again!

VOLP.: Upon 'em, Mosca; save me.
CORB.: The air's infected where he breathes.
CORV.: Let's fly him.

[*Exeunt* CORV. *and* CORB.]

VOLP.: Excellent basilisk! turn upon the vulture.

SCENE IX—THE SAME

MOSCA, VOLPONE. *Enter* VOLTORE.

VOLT.: Well, flesh-fly, it is summer with you now;
Your winter will come on.
MOS.: Good advocate,
Prithee not rail, nor threaten out of place thus;
Thou 'lt make a solecism, as madam says.
Get you a biggin[185] more; your brain breaks loose.

[*Exit.*]

VOLT.: Well sir.
VOLP.: Would you ha' me beat the insolent slave,
Throw dirt upon his first good clothes?
VOLT.: This same
Is doubtless some familiar.
VOLP.: Sir, the court,
In troth, stays for you. I am mad, a mule
That never read Justinian, should get up,
And ride an advocate. Had you no quirk
To avoid gullage, sir, by such a creature?
I hope you do but jest; he has not done 't
This 's but confederacy to blind the rest.
You are the heir?
VOLT.: A strange, officious,
Troublesome knave! thou dost torment me.
VOLP.: I know—
It cannot be, sir, that you should be cozen'd;
'T is not within the wit of man to do it;
You are so wise, so prudent; and 't is fit

That wealth and wisdom still should go together.

[*Exeunt.*]

SCENE X—THE SAME

Enter 4 Avocatori, Notario, BONARIO, CELIA, CORBACCIO, CORVINO, *Commandadori, [Saffi, etc.]*

1ST AVOC.: Are all the parties here?

NOT.: All but th' advocate.

2ND AVOC.: And here he comes.

[*Enter* VOLTORE *and* VOLPONE.]

1ST AVOC.: Then bring them forth to sentence.

VOLT.: O, my most honour'd fathers, let your mercy
Once win upon your justice, to forgive—
I am distracted—

VOLP.: [*Aside.*] What will he do now?

VOLT.: O,
I know not which t' address myself to first;
Whether your fatherhoods, or these innocents—

CORV.: [*Aside.*] Will he betray himself?

VOLT.: Whom equally
I have abus'd, out of most covetous ends—

CORV.: The man is mad!

CORB.: What's that?

CORV.: He is possest.

VOLT.: For which, now struck in conscience, here I prostrate
Myself at your offended feet, for pardon.

1ST, 2ND AVOC.: Arise.

CEL.: O heaven, how just thou art!

VOLP.: I'm caught
I' mine own noose—

CORV.: [*To* CORBACCIO.] Be constant, sir; nought now
Can help but impudence.

1ST AVOC.: Speak forward.

COM.: Silence!

VOLT.: It is not passion in me, reverend fathers,
But only conscience, conscience, my good sires,
That makes me now tell truth. That parasite,
That knave, hath been the instrument of all.

1ST AVOC.: Where is that knave? Fetch him.

VOLP.: I go.

[*Exit.*]

CORV.: Grave fathers,
This man 's distracted; he confest it now:
For, hoping to be old Volpone's heir,
Who now is dead—

3RD AVOC.: How!

2ND AVOC.: Is Volpone dead?

CORV.: Dead since, grave fathers.

BON.: O sure vengeance!

1ST AVOC.: Stay,
Then he was no deceiver?

VOLT.: O no, none: This parasite, grave fathers.

CORV.: He does speak
Out of mere envy, 'cause the servant's made
The thing he gap'd for. Please your fatherhoods,
This is the truth, though I'll not justify
The other, but he may be some-deal faulty.

VOLT.: Ay, to your hopes, as well as mine, Corvino:
But I'll use modesty.[186] Pleaseth your wisdoms,
To view these certain notes, and but confer[187] them;
And as I hope favour, they shall speak clear truth.

CORV.: The devil has ent'red him!

BON.: Or bides in you.

4TH AVOC.: We have done ill, by a public officer
To send for him, if he be heir.

2ND AVOC.: For whom?

4TH AVOC.: Him that they call the parasite.

3RD AVOC.: 'T is true,
He is a man of great estate, now left.

4TH AVOC.: Go you, and learn his name, and say the court
Entreats his presence here, but to the clearing

Of some few doubts.

[*Exit Notary.*]

2ND AVOC.: This same 's a labyrinth!

1ST AVOC.: Stand you unto your first report?

CORV.: My state,
My life, my fame—

BON.: Where is 't?

CORV.: Are at the stake.

1ST AVOC.: Is yours so too?

CORB.: The advocate's a knave,
And has a forked tongue—

2ND AVOC.: Speak to the point.

CORB.: So is the parasite too.

1ST AVOC.: This is confusion.

VOLT.: I do beseech your fatherhoods, read but those—
[*Giving them papers.*]

CORV.: And credit nothing the false spirit hath writ:
It cannot be but he's possest, grave fathers.

[*The scene closes.*]

SCENE XI—A STREET

Enter VOLPONE.

VOLP.: To make a snare for mine own neck! and run
My head into it, wilfully! with laughter!
When I had newly scap'd, was free and clear,
Out of mere wantonness! O, the dull devil
Was in this brain of mine when I devis'd it,
And Mosca gave it second; he must now
Help to sear up this vein, or we bleed dead.
[*Enter* NANO, ANDROGYNO*, and* CASTRONE.]
How now! Who let you loose? Whither go you now?
What, to buy gingerbread, or to drown kitlings?

NAN.: Sir, Master Mosca call'd us out of doors,
And bid us all go play, and took the keys.

AND.: Yes.
VOLP.: Did Master Mosca take the keys? Why, so!
I'm farther in. These are my fine conceits!
I must be merry, with a mischief to me!
What a vile wretch was I, that could not bear
My fortune soberly? I must ha' my crochets,[188]
And my conundrums! Well, go you, and seek him:
His meaning may be truer than my fear.
Bid him, he straight come to me to the court;
Thither will I, and, if 't be possible,
Unscrew my advocate, upon new hopes:
When I provok'd him, then I lost myself.

[*Exeunt.*]

SCENE XII—THE SCRUTINEO

Avocatori, BONARIO, CELIA, CORBACCIO, CORVINO*, Commandadori, Saffi, etc., as before.*

1ST AVOC.: These things can ne'er be reconcil'd. [*Showing the papers.*]
He here
Professeth that the gentleman was wrong'd,
And that the gentlewoman was brought thither,
Forc'd by her husband, and there left.
VOLT.: Most true.
CEL.: How ready is heaven to those that pray!
1ST AVOC.: But that
Volpone would have ravish'd her, he holds
Utterly false, knowing his impotence.
CORV.: Grave fathers, he's possest; again, I say,
Possest: nay, if there be possession, and
Obsession, he has both.
3RD AVOC.: Here comes our officer.
[*Enter* VOLPONE.]
VOLP.: The parasite will straight be here, grave fathers.
4TH AVOC.: You might invent some other name, sir varlet.

3RD AVOC.: Did not the notary meet him?

VOLP.: Not that I know.

4TH AVOC.: His coming will clear all.

2ND AVOC.: Yet it is misty.

VOLT.: May 't please your fatherhoods—

VOLP.: [*whispers* VOLT.] Sir, the parasite
Will'd me to tell you that his master lives;
That you are still the man; your hopes the same;
And this was only a jest—

VOLT.: How?

VOLP.: Sir, to try
If you were firm, and how you stood affected.

VOLT.: Art sure he lives?

VOLP.: Do I live, sir?

VOLT.: O me!
I was too violent.

VOLP.: Sir, you may redeem it.
They said you were possest; fall down, and seem so:
I'll help to make it good. [VOLTORE *falls.*] God bless the man!—
Stop your wind hard, and swell—See, see, see, see!
He vomits crooked pins! His eyes are set,
Like a dead hare's hung in a poulter's shop!
His mouth's running away! Do you see, signior?
Now it is in his belly.

CORV.: Ay, the devil!

VOLP.: Now in his throat.

CORV.: Ay, I perceive it plain.

VOLP.: 'T will out, 't will out! stand clear. See where it flies,
In shape of a blue toad, with a bat's wings!
Do you not see it, sir?

CORB.: What? I think I do.

CORV.: 'T is too manifest.

VOLP.: Look! he comes t' himself.

VOLT.: Where am I?

VOLP.: Take good heart, the worst is past, sir.
You're dispossest.

1ST AVOC.: What accident is this!

2ND AVOC.: Sudden and full of wonder!

3RD AVOC.: If he were
Possest, as it appears, all this is nothing.

CORV.: He has been often subject to these fits.

1ST AVOC.: Show him that writing:—do you know it, sir?

VOLP.: [*Whispers* VOLT.] Deny it, sir, forswear it; know it not.

VOLT.: Yes, I do know it well, it is my hand;
But all that it contains is false.

BON.: O practice![189]

2ND AVOC.: What maze is this!

1ST AVOC.: Is he not guilty then,
Whom you there name the parasite?

VOLT.: Grave fathers,
No more than his good patron, old Volpone.

4TH AVOC.: Why, he is dead.

VOLT.: O no, my honour'd fathers,
He lives—

1ST AVOC.: How! lives?

VOLT.: Lives.

2ND AVOC.: This is subtler yet!

3RD AVOC.: You said he was dead.

VOLT.: Never.

3RD AVOC.: You said so.

CORV.: I heard so.

4TH AVOC.: Here comes the gentleman; make him way.

[*Enter* MOSCA.]

3RD AVOC.: A stool.

4TH AVOC.: [*Aside.*] A proper man; and were Volpone dead,
A fit match for my daughter.

3RD AVOC.: Give him way.

VOLP.: [*Aside to* MOS.] Mosca, I was a'most lost; the advocate
Had betray'd all; but now it is recover'd;
All's on the hinge again—Say I am living.

MOS: What busy knave is this!—Most reverend fathers,
I sooner had attended your grave pleasures,
But that my order for the funeral
Of my dear patron did require me—

VOLP.: [*Aside.*] Mosca!

MOS.: Whom I intend to bury like a gentleman.

VOLP.: [*Aside.*] Ay, quick, and cozen me of all.

2ND AVOC.: Still stranger!
More intricate!

1ST AVOC.: And come about again!

4TH AVOC.: [*Aside.*] It is a match, my daughter is bestow'd.

MOS.: [*Aside to* VOLP.] Will you gi' me half?

VOLP.: First I'll be hang'd.

MOS.: I know
Your voice is good, cry not so loud.

1ST AVOC.: Demand
The advocate—Sir, did you not affirm
Volpone was alive?

VOLP.: Yes, and he is;
This gent'man told me so—[*Aside to* MOS.] Thou shalt have half.

MOS.: Whose drunkard is this same? Speak, some that know him:
I never saw his face—[*Aside to* VOLP.] I cannot now
Afford it you so cheap.

VOLP.: No!

1ST AVOC.: What say you?

VOLT.: The officer told me.

VOLP.: I did, grave fathers,
And will maintain he lives, with mine own life,
And that this creature [*Points to* MOSCA.] told me. [*Aside.*]—I was born
With all good stars my enemies.

MOS.: Most grave fathers,
If such an insolence as this must pass
Upon me, I am silent: 't was not this
For which you sent, I hope.

2ND AVOC.: Take him away.

VOLP.: Mosca!

3RD AVOC.: Let him be whipt.

VOLP.: Wilt thou betray me?
Cozen me?

3RD AVOC.: And taught to bear himself
Toward a person of his rank.

4TH AVOC.: Away.
[*The Officers seize* VOLPONE.]
MOS.: I humbly thank your fatherhoods.
VOLP.: Soft, soft: [*Aside.*] Whipt!
And lose all that I have! If I confess,
It cannot be much more.
4TH AVOC.: Sir, are you married?
VOLP.: They'll be alli'd anon; I must be resolute;
The Fox shall here uncase.
[*Puts off his disguise.*]
MOS.: Patron!
VOLP.: Nay, now
My ruin shall not come alone; your match
I'll hinder sure: my substance shall not glue you,
Nor screw you into a family.
MOS.: Why, patron!
VOLP.: I am Volpone, and this is my knave;
[*Pointing to* MOSCA.]
This [*to* VOLT.], his own knave; this [*to* CORB.], avarice's fool;
This [*to* CORV.], a chimera of wittol, fool, and knave:
And, reverend fathers, since we all can hope
Nought but a sentence, let 's not now despair it.
You hear me brief.
CORV.: May it please your fatherhoods—
COM.: Silence.
1ST AVOC.: The knot is now undone by miracle.
2ND AVOC.: Nothing can be more clear.
3RD AVOC.: Or can more prove
These innocent.
1ST AVOC.: Give 'em their liberty.
BON.: Heaven could not long let such gross crimes be hid.
2ND AVOC.: If this be held the highway to get riches,
May I be poor!
3RD AVOC.: This 's not the gain, but torment.
1ST AVOC.: These possess wealth, as sick men possess fevers,
Which trulier may be said to possess them.
2ND AVOC.: Disrobe that parasite.

CORV. MOS.: Most honour'd fathers—

1ST AVOC.: Can you plead aught to stay the course of justice?
If you can, speak.

CORV. VOLT.: We beg favour.

CEL.: And mercy.

1ST AVOC.: You hurt your innocence, suing for the guilty.
Stand forth; and first the parasite. You appear
T' have been the chiefest minister, if not plotter,
In all these lewd impostures, and now, lastly,
Have with your impudence abus'd the court,
And habit of a gentleman of Venice,
Being a fellow of no birth or blood:
For which our sentence is, first, then be whipt;
Then live perpetual prisoner in our galleys.

VOLP.: I thank you for him.

MOS.: Bane to thy wolfish nature!

1ST AVOC.: Deliver him to the saffi. [MOSCA *is carried out.*] Thou, Volpone,
By blood and rank a gentleman, canst not fall
Under like censure; but our judgment on thee
Is, that thy substance all be straight confiscate
To the hospital of the Incurabili:
And since the most was gotten by imposture,
By feigning lame, gout, palsy, and such diseases,
Thou art to lie in prison, cramp'd with irons,
Till thou be'st sick and lame indeed. Remove him.

VOLP.: This is called mortifying of a Fox.

[*He is taken from the Bar.*]

1ST AVOC.: Thou, Voltore, to take away the scandal
Thou hast giv'n all worthy men of thy profession,
Art banish'd from their fellowship, and our state.
Corbaccio!—bring him near. We here possess
Thy son of all thy state, and confine thee
To the monastery of San Spirito;
Where, since thou knew'st not how to live well here,
Thou shalt be learn'd to die well.

CORB.: Ha! what said he?

COM.: You shall know anon, sir.
1ST AVOC.: Thou, Corvino, shalt
Be straight embark'd from thine own house, and row'd
Round about Venice, through the Grand Canal,
Wearing a cap, with fair long ass's ears,
Instead of horns! and so to mount, a paper
Pinn'd on thy breast, to the Berlina.[190]
CORV.: Yes,
And have mine eyes beat out with stinking fish,
Bruis'd fruit, and rotten eggs—'t is well. I'm glad
I shall not see my shame yet.
1ST AVOC. And to expiate
Thy wrongs done to thy wife, thou art to send her
Home to her father, with her dowry trebled:
And these are all your judgments.
ALL.: Honour'd fathers—
1ST AVOC.: Which may not be revok'd. Now you begin,
When crimes are done and past, and to be punish'd,
To think what your crimes are. Away with them!
Let all that see these vices thus rewarded,
Take heart, and love to study 'em. Mischiefs feed
Like beasts, till they be fat, and then they bleed.

[*Exeunt.*]

VOLPONE: [*Comes forward.*]
"The seasoning of a play is the applause.
Now, though the Fox be punish'd by the laws,
He yet doth hope, there is no suff'ring due,
For any fact[191] which he hath done 'gainst you;
If there be, censure him; here he doubtful stands:
If not, fare jovially, and clap your hands."

[*Exit.*]

1. Many of the characters' names are in Italian, and their translations are the names of animals—Volpone: fox; Mosca: fly; Voltore: vulture; Corbaccio: raven; Corvino: crow. Bonario means "good-natured"; Nano means "dwarf"; Castrone means "gelding"; and Androgyno means "man-woman," from the Greek.
2. *gull*] an imposition, a trick.

3. *Bethlem*] or Bedlam, popular name for the Hospital of St. Mary of Bethlehem, the London insane asylum.
4. *copperas*] green vitriol, used in making ink.
5. *centre*] center of the earth.
6. *Romagnia ... Candian*] Romagna is a district in northern Italy on the Adriatic Sea; Candia is the isle of Crete.
7. *cocker*] to pamper.
8. *observe*] pay obsequious attention to.
9. *bearing ... hand*] deceiving them by false hopes.
10. *here*] in Androgyno.
11. *brock*] badger.
12. *cock*] This interlude is based on Lucian's dialogue between a cobbler and a cock.
13. *Quater*] quatre, the four in dice.
14. *trigon*] a triangular lyre.
15. *precise*] puritanical.
16. *nativity-pie*] Christmas-pie.
17. *free from slaughter*] with impunity.
18. *trencher*] plate.
19. *gorcrow*] carrion crow.
20. *ambitious*] also a reference to the word's etymological sense of "moving round."
21. *phthisic*] phthisis, a progressively wasting or consumptive condition.
22. *bought of St. Mark*] at one of the goldsmith's shops beside St. Mark's.
23. *chequin*] zechin, or zecchino, an Italian gold coin.
24. *slumbers*] dozes.
25. *scotomy*] imperfect sight, with giddiness.
26. aurum palpabile ... potabile] palpable, material gold, if not aurum potabile, or drinkable gold, which was the elixir.
27. *colour*] circumstance or appearance.
28. *Rook go with you*] May you be rooked, or cheated.
29. *Aeson*] Jason's father, who was restored to life by the charm of Medea the witch.
30. *Dead*] "Pretend that I'm dead."
31. *orient*] brilliant or lustrous, and therefore precious.
32. *Nay, help, sir*] said to Corvino, asking for his help in the abuse.
33. *culverin*] cannon.
34. *draught*] cesspool.
35. *purchase*] booty.
36. *squire*] messenger.
37. *windore*] window.
38. *salt*] frivolous.
39. *height*] latitude.
40. *To quote*] to make note of.
41. *Lies*] stays.
42. *Another whelp!*] A lion is recorded to have been born in the Tower of London, Aug. 5, 1604, the first born in captivity in England.
43. *was either sent ... Spinola's whale*] Sir Politic believes the whale's presence in the Thames River is some Spanish plot, perhaps directed by Archduke Albert, who ruled the Spanish Netherlands in the name of Philip II, or General Ambrosio Spinola, leader of the Spanish armies in Holland.
44. *advertisement*] information.
45. *Mamaluchi*] Italian form of mamelukes, slaves and warriors originally from Asia Minor, who for many years controlled the throne of Egypt.
46. *tie*] obligation.
47. *mountebanks*] from the Italian monta in banco, "to mount the bench," they were part street performer and part patent-medicine salesman.

48. *lewd*] ignorant.
49. *Scoto of Mantua*] a real performer, juggler and magician who visited England and performed before Queen Elizabeth.
50. *phant'sied*] described, misrepresented.
51. a' sforzato] to hard labor.
52. ciarlitani] petty charlatans, imposters.
53. *Tabarin*] a French charlatan of the early seventeenth century, whose jests were published.
54. scartoccios] folds of paper.
55. *oppilations*] obstructions.
56. canaglia] rabble.
57. *Terra-firma*] Continental possessions of Venice.
58. *cocted*] boiled.
59. unguento] ointment.
60. *fricace*] an oil to be rubbed in.
61. vertigine] dizziness.
62. mal caduco] epilepsy.
63. hernia ventosa, iliaca passio] gassy hernia, cramps of the small intestine.
64. *torsion*] twisting.
65. *Broughton's books*] Hugh Broughton, a Puritan divine and rabbinical scholar.
66. *Raymond Lully*] a Spanish mystic philosopher (ca. 1235-1316).
67. *Gonswart*] unidentified.
68. *Paracelsus*] famous 16th-century German doctor, who carried his familiar Spirits in the handle of his sword.
69. *alembics*] distilleries, also retorts.
70. *in fumo*] in smoke.
71. ballo] ball; dancing.
72. *gossip*] literally god-parent; usually, familiar friend.
73. *gazettes*] small Venetian coins.
74. *for the nones*] for the purpose.
75. moccinigo] a coin used in Venice, worth about ninepence.
76. *bagatine*] an Italian coin worth about one-third of a farthing.
77. *pistolet*] a Spanish coin.
78. *prevented*] anticipated.
79. *virginal jacks*] small pieces of wood to which were attached the quills which struck the strings of the virginal.
80. *Pantalone di Besogniosi*] Italian for "Fool of the Beggars."
81. *at thy devotion*] at your service.
82. *your epilogue*] i.e., the beating from Corvino.
83. *faces*] grimaces.
84. *fricace for the mother*] massage for the womb.
85. *cittern*] a kind of guitar.
86. *propose*] expect.
87. *bawdy light damm'd up*] i.e., brick up the window.
88. osteria] inn.
89. *sod*] boiled.
90. *fasting spittle*] spit from a hungry man.
91. *Applying but the fricace*] All they had to do was rub it in.
92. *cataplasm*] poultice.
93. *delate*] denounce, complain of.
94. *made unto it*] prepared for it.
95. *coming*] into the trap.
96. *mystery*] craft, profession.
97. *legs*] bows.

98. *mate*] fellow.
99. *unequal*] unfair.
100. *feat*] neatly made.
101. *tire*] head-dress.
102. *bird-ey'd*] sharp-sighted.
103. *fucus*] face paint.
104. *elecampane*] horse-heal, a medicinal herb.
105. *myrobalanes*] an astringent kind of plum.
106. *concent*] harmony.
107. *Would lie you, often*] Would often lie.
108. *coaetanei*] of the same age.
109. *not go less ... encounter*] primero was the early form of the card game ombre; "go less," "draw" and "encounter" are phrases used in the game.
110. *"Was this the train?"*] "Was this what you had in mind all the time?"
111. *rochet*] a kind of fish.
112. *aquafortis ... cor'sives*] acids and corrosives.
113. *cope-man*] buyer, merchant.
114. *blue Proteus, or the horned flood*] Proteus was a sea god who could take any shape at will; horned flood refers to the river god Achelous, who fought with Hercules, first in the shape of a river, then as a snake, then as a bull—hence "horned flood."
115. *Valois*] Henry of Valois, Duke of Anjou, the newly crowned King Henry III of France, was entertained with splendid festivities when he visited Venice in 1574.
116. The opening lines of the song are taken from Catullus.
117. *serene*] mist from heaven; malignant influence.
118. *Aegyptian queen ... drink 'em*] Supposedly, Cleopatra dissolved a precious pearl in wine, which she and Antony drank at a banquet.
119. *Lollia Paulina*] the wife of a Roman governor famed for the brilliance and costliness of her jewels.
120. *Persian sophy*] the Shah of Persia.
121. *Nestor's hernia*] from Juvenal's sixth satire; senile impotence.
122. *die like Romans*] i.e., by suicide.
123. *saffi*] bailiff's attendants.
124. *foists*] tricks, deceits, but also bad smells.
125. *Scrutineo*] Senate House, or court of law.
126. *mention'd*] asked.
127. *garb*] bearing, demeanor.
128. *Nic. Machiavel ... Bodin*] Niccolò Machiavelli (1469-1527), the Italian statesman, politician and philosopher, and Jean Bodin, a French political philosopher, who advocated religious tolerance.
129. *Contarene*] Contarini, author of a book on Venetian government.
130. *discover*] disclose, reveal.
131. *hoy*] a small passenger sloop.
132. *defalk*] cut off, reduce.
133. *Great Council ... the Ten*] increasingly lofty legislative bodies of the Venetian government.
134. *Soria*] Syria.
135. *Levant*] Middle East.
136. Notandum] take special note.
137. ragion' del state] "reason of state," politics.
138. *cheapen'd*] bargained for.
139. *quote*] note.
140. *he plays both*] both "fast and loose."
141. *reach*] understand.

142. *Sporus*] one of Nero's favorite catamites, whom he dressed in drag and married.
143. *Whitefriars nation*] a disreputable part of London, inhabited by prostitutes.
144. *fricatrice*] prostitute.
145. *disc'ple*] discipline.
146. *your now ... queen-apple*] her nose is red.
147. *callet*] prostitute.
148. *salt-head*] salaciousness, lasciviousness.
149. *croaker's*] Corbaccio's.
150. *mummia*] a medicine; supposedly made from the oozing from mummies.
151. *buffalo*] an allusion to a cuckold's horns.
152. *The stale*] The decoy.
153. *six sols*] three pence.
154. *disclaim in him*] disown him.
155. *jennet*] mare in heat.
156. *the horn*] of the cuckold.
157. *laid*] well-contrived.
158. *strappado*] a form of torture in which a man's hands were tied behind his back and he was hoisted by his wrists on a gallows, the usual result being the dislocation of his shoulders.
159. *constancy*] boldness.
160. cavè] Latin for "beware," "watch out."
161. *glebe*] soil.
162. *shift a shirt*] change his shirt (because he had sweated so much over his speech).
163. *Sadly*] Seriously.
164. *Will crump ... touch*] There was a kind of louse that would curl (crump) up when touched.
165. *poetical girdle*] The girdle of Venus made any wearer irresistibly beautiful.
166. *Acrisius*] the father of Danaë, who locked her up in a tower.
167. *wittol*] a pimp for his own wife.
168. *Harlot*] frequently used of both sexes, here meaning "scoundrel."
169. *marle*] marvel.
170. *causes*] lawsuits.
171. *lettuce*] thought to have a soporific effect.
172. *clarissimo*] patrician.
173. *Zant . . . Aleppo*] Zakynthos (Zant) is an Ionian island; Aleppo is in Syria.
174. *frail*] rush basket.
175. *currant butt*] cask for holding currants.
176. *engine*] contrivance.
177. *motion*] show.
178. *The freight of the gazetti*] The theme of the newspapers.
179. *his borrow'd case*] his disguise.
180. *out of reparations*] out of repair.
181. *custom'd*] well-frequented.
182. *candle-rents*] trivial things (to a rich man).
183. *in our habit*] dressed like us.
184. *cozen*] swindle.
185. *biggin*] barrister's cap.
186. *modesty*] moderation.
187. *confer*] compare.
188. *crochets*] perverse conceits odd fancies.
189. *practice*] conspiracy.
190. *Berlina*] pillory.
191. *fact*] deed

Molière

(Jean-Baptiste Poquelin)

(1622–1673)

Jean-Baptiste Poquelin was born around 1622. His mother, Marie Cresse, was a moderately wealthy and cultured woman from a upper-middle-class background (who died when Jean-Baptiste was ten). His father was in the retail upholstery business and was appointed a furnisher of the royal household in 1631. In 1636, Jean-Baptiste was sent to the College de Clermont, an aristocratic school where he was tutored in rhetoric and logic by the Jesuits and was introduced to Roman comedies.

His interest in the dramatic arts grew, and rather than join his father in the family business he chose to pursue the theatrical life. This career choice was an astonishing one considering that acting was thought no better than pimping or stealing at that time. He chose a stage name, Molière, perhaps to spare his family the embarrassment of having an actor among them. He became acquainted with Madeline Begart, a talented actress who urged him to establish a theater company (Illustre-Théâtre) with four of her siblings. Molière married Madeline's nineteen-year-old sister Armande (though some accounts say it was her daughter) when he was forty; they had three children together, though only one survived into adulthood. The marriage was not a happy one, supposedly due to Armande's wandering eye.

The Illustre-Théâtre was not an instant success and in 1654 Molière went to jail twice for failing to pay rent and debt on properties. The troupe set out to tour the provinces in the south and southeast of France, an exile that would last thirteen years and allow Molière to hone his skills as an actor, director, stage manager, and writer. By 1657, the company had moved to Rouen and caught the eye of Phillippe, brother of King Louis XIV, who gave them a bit of money and suggested they relocate to Paris.

The move proved to be the right one for Molière and his company; on October 24, 1658, after a tepid reception to a performance of a Cornielle play, the group improvised one of Molière's little "entertainments," which was a bit livelier. The play, *Le Docteur Amouveur* (*The Amorous Doctor*), was warmly received, especially by Louis XIV and his brother Phillippe, the Duke. Phillippe offered to sponsor the troupe. The troupe would appear at the Palais-Royal Théâtre and perform Molière's comedies under the auspices of the Duke for seven years, after which they became the King's Troupe exclusively in 1665. The royal label was useful when Molière's work inspired outrage in the clergy, the nobility, or the upper-middle classes. Although his plays are now considered comically brilliant, during his time the reaction was mixed. Some were considered so scandalous and dangerous to venerable institutions (such as marriage) that the authorities closed them down. While the royal name and protection were helpful, the royal financial support was less dependable and the company often had to rely solely on their own box office take to survive.

During the next fifteen years, Molière produced about two comedies a year, firmly establishing him as France's greatest dramatist. All of these plays are viewed as masterworks of comedy: *The Affected Young Ladies* (1659), *The School for Wives* (1663), *Tartuffe* or *The Hypocrite* (1664), *The Misanthrope* (1666), *The Miser* (1669), *The Bourgeois Gentleman* (1670), *The Blue Stockings* (1672), and *The Imaginary Invalid* (1673).

During the last half of his life, Molière was afflicted with tuberculosis. He struggled to continue writing and performing, especially during his last four years, from 1669 to 1673. He spent those years apart from his wife in his house in Auteil on a strict milk diet. In an ironic twist, during the performance of *The Imaginary Invalid*, a play about a healthy hypochondriac that satirizes the medical profession, he collapsed on stage. He was brought back home, where died later that night. Because he was an actor, an unsuitable profession in the eyes of the Church and one which he did not renounce on his deathbed, he was refused last rites and buried without formal ceremony at sunset on February 21, 1673. For a man who had sought to be a tragic actor but had succeeded in comedy, it was a truly tragic end.

Molière was not a preacher disguised as a comedian. He did not design his plays so that his characters were mouthpieces for his own opinions on religion, politics, or marriage. The actor in him influenced his writing; he wrote to see and hear his actors (and himself) burst forth in a volley of words and emotions. He enjoyed bizarre characters and over-the-top emoting. Some say that he sacrificed plot for action and vitality. His portrayals of certain points of view are not judgmental but are, rather, just a representation of a style of thinking. This holds true for one of his funniest works, *The Bourgeois Gentleman*. By making Monsieur Jourdain the object of farce and ridicule as he attempts to better his station, Molière succeeds in poking fun at both the upper middle class and those who enviously aspire to it. Monsieur Jourdain seeks to rise from his common station, to speak the foreign language of the upper class and be one of them. Yet even as he butchers this mannerly way of speaking, he is not an object of scorn but of pity. "Good heavens! For more than forty years, I've been speaking prose without knowing it." Molière does not pit one group against another but tars all with the same brush. Jourdain's wife is the voice of reason in the play, trying to steer her husband away from his foolish quest. Where her husband tumbles and trips over his new vocabulary, she is a well-spoken commoner and the comic foil for his ill-fated plot. Her sharp tongue cuts its way through all the well-turned phrases of the gentlemen who are after her daughter's hand. When Jourdain tries to find only gentlemen to court his daughter, the mother interjects: "What your daughter needs is a husband who suits her, and she would much better have an honorable man who is rich and handsome than some ugly gentleman without a penny." It is not that the gentlemen have more money, it is the breeding that Jourdain is after.

In seeking to better parts of himself, Jourdain only succeeds in making a parody of his whole self. Now the group from which he came thinks him a fool, and the people he is trying to fit in with think him a buffoon. He is tricked at the end of the play into thinking that he has attained a certain status for his daughter when in reality everything remains the same. Yet the light touch and antic language Molière employs makes the viewer feel protective toward Jourdain and comfortable with his delusion. A marriage, a happy ending for all, with no one the wiser. "Of all human follies there's none could be greater / Than trying to render our fellow-men better."

The Bourgeois Gentleman

DRAMATIS PERSONNAE

MONSIEUR JOURDAIN—the bourgeois
MADAME JOURDAIN—wife to *M. JOURDAIN*
LUCILE—daughter to *M. JOURDAIN*
CLÉONTE—in love with Lucile
DORIMÈNE—a marchioness
DORANTE—a count, Dorimène's lover
NICOLE—a maid-servant to *M. JOURDAIN*
COVIELLE—servant to *CLÉONTE*
MUSIC MASTER
MUSIC MASTER'S PUPIL
DANCING MASTER
FENCING MASTER
PHILOSOPHY MASTER
MASTER TAILOR
JOURNEYMAN TAILOR
LACKEYS
The scene is in Paris, in M. Jourdain's house

ACT I.

Scene I.

MUSIC MASTER, a PUPIL of the MUSIC MASTER (Composing at a table in the middle of the stage), a WOMAN SINGER, two MEN SINGERS, a DANCING MASTER, and DANCERS.

MUSIC MASTER. [*To the musicians*] Here, step into this hall, and sit there till he comes.

DANCING MASTER. [*To the dancers*] And you too, on this side.

MUSIC MASTER. [*To his pupil*] Is it done?

PUPIL. Yes.

MUSIC MASTER. Let's see . . . . 'Tis mighty well.

DANCING MASTER. Is it anything new?

MUSIC MASTER. Yes, 'tis an air for a serenade, which I set him to compose here while we wait till our gentleman's awake.

DANCING MASTER. May one see what it is?

MUSIC MASTER. You will hear it, with the dialogue, when he comes. He won't be long.

DANCING MASTER. We have no want of business, either of us, at present.

MUSIC MASTER. 'Tis true, we have found a man here, just such a one as we both of us want. This same Monsieur Jourdain is a sweet income, with his visions of nobility and gallantry which he has got into his noddle, and it would be well for your capers and my crotchets, were all the world like him.

DANCING MASTER. Not altogether so well; I wish, for his sake, that he were better skilled than he is in the things we give him.

MUSIC MASTER. It is true he understands 'em ill, but he pays for 'em well. And that's what our art has more need of at present than of anything else.

DANCING MASTER. For my part, I own it to you, I regale a little upon glory. I am sensible of applause, and think it a very grievous punishment in the liberal arts to display one's self to fools and to expose our compositions to the barbarous judgment of the stupid. Talk no more of it, there is a pleasure in working for persons who are capable of relishing the delicacies of an art, who know how to give a kind reception to the beauties of a work, and, by titillating approbation, regale you for your labour. Yes, the most agreeable recompense one can receive for the things one does is to see them understood, to see 'em caressed with an applause that does you honour. There's nothing, in my opinion, which pays us better than this for all our fatigues. And the praises of connoisseurs give an exquisite delight.

MUSIC MASTER. I grant it, and I relish them as well as you. There is nothing certainly that tickles more than the applause you speak of, but one cannot live upon this incense. Sheer praises won't make a man easy. There must be something solid mixed withal, and the best method of praising is to praise with the open hand. This indeed is one whose understanding is very shallow, who speaks of everything awry, and cross of the grain, and never applauds but in contradiction to sense. But his money sets his judgment right. He has discernment in his purse. His praises are current coin; and this ignorant commoner is more worth to us, as you see, than that grand witty lord who introduced us here.

DANCING MASTER. There's something of truth in what you say; but I find you lean a little too much towards the pelf. And mere interest is something so base that an honest man should never discover an attachment to it.

MUSIC MASTER. For all that, you decently receive the money our spark gives you.

DANCING MASTER. Certainly; but I don't place all my happiness in that: and I wish that, with his fortune, he had also some good taste of things.

MUSIC MASTER. I wish the same; 'tis what we both labour at as much as we can. But, however, he gives us the opportunity of making ourselves known in the world; and he'll pay for others what others praise for him.

DANCING MASTER. Here he comes.

Scene II.

M. JOURDAIN (in a nightgown and cap), PUPIL, DANCING MASTER, Music MASTER, SINGERS, DANCERS, LACKEYS.

M. JOURDAIN. Well, gentlemen? What have you there? Will you let me see your little drollery?

DANCING MASTER. How? What little drollery?

M. JOURDAIN. Why the—how do you call that thing? your prologue, or dialogue of songs and dancing.

DANCING MASTER. Ha, ha!

MUSIC MASTER. You see we are ready.

M. JOURDAIN. I have made you wait a little, but 'tis because I am to be dressed out to-day like your people of quality; and my hosier has sent me a pair of silk stockings which I thought I should never have got on.

MUSIC MASTER. We are here only to wait your leisure.

M. JOURDAIN. I desire you'll both stay till they have brought me my clothes, that you may see me.

DANCING MASTER. As you please.

M. JOURDAIN. You shall see me most exactly equipped from head to foot.

MUSIC MASTER. We don't doubt it.

M. JOURDAIN. I have had this Indian thing made up for me.

DANCING MASTER. 'Tis very handsome.

M. JOURDAIN. My tailor tells me that people of quality go thus in a morning.

MUSIC MASTER. It fits you to a miracle.

M. JOURDAIN. Why, ho! Fellow there! both my fellows!

FIRST LACKEY. Your pleasure, sir?

M. JOURDAIN. [*To the* MUSIC *and* DANCING MASTERS] What say you of my liveries?

DANCING MASTER. They are magnificent.

M. JOURDAIN. [*Half-opens his gown and reveals a tight pair of breeches of scarlet velvet, and a green velvet jacket*] Here again is a kind of dishabille to perform my exercises in a morning.

MUSIC MASTER. 'Tis gallant.

M. JOURDAIN. Lackey!

FIRST LACKEY. Sir?

M. JOURDAIN. T'other lackey!

SECOND LACKEY. Sir?

M. JOURDAIN. [*Taking off his gown*] Hold my gown. [*To the* MUSIC *and* DANCING MASTERS] Do you like me so?

DANCING MASTER. Mighty well; nothing can be better.

M. JOURDAIN. Now for your affair a little.

MUSIC MASTER. I should be glad first to let you hear an air [*Pointing to his pupil*] he has just composed for the serenade which you gave me orders about. He is one of my pupils, who has an admirable talent for these sort of things.

M. JOURDAIN. Yes, but that should not have been put to a pupil to do; you were not too good for that business yourself.

MUSIC MASTER. You must not let the name of pupil impose upon you, sir. These sort of pupils know as much as the greatest masters, and the air is as good as can be made. Hear it only.

M. JOURDAIN. [*To his servants*] Give me my gown that I may hear the better.—Stay, I believe I shall be better without the gown.—No, give it me again, it will do better.

MUSICIAN.

> I languish night and day, nor sleeps my pain,
> Since those fair eyes imposed the rigorous chain;
> But tell me, Iris, what dire fate attends
> Your enemies, if thus you treat your friends?

M. JOURDAIN. This song seems to me a little upon the dismal; it inclines one to sleep; I should be glad you could enliven it a little here and there.

MUSIC MASTER. 'Tis necessary, sir, that the air should be suited to the words.

M. JOURDAIN. I was taught one perfectly pretty some time ago. Stay—um—how is it?

DANCING MASTER. In good troth, I don't know.

M. JOURDAIN. There's lamb in it.

DANCING MASTER. Lamb?

M. JOURDAIN. Yes—Ho!

I thought my dear Namby
As gentle as fair-o:
I thought my dear Namby
As mild as a lamb-y.
Oh dear, oh dear, oh dear-o!
For now the sad scold is a thousand times told,
More fierce than a tiger or bear-o.

Isn't it pretty?

MUSIC MASTER. The prettiest in the world.

DANCING MASTER. And you sing it well.

M. JOURDAIN. Yet I never learnt music.

MUSIC MASTER. You ought to learn it, sir, as you do dancing. They are two arts which have a strict connection one with the other.

DANCING MASTER. And which open the human mind to see the beauty of things.

M. JOURDAIN. What, do people of quality learn music too?

MUSIC MASTER. Yes, sir.

M. JOURDAIN. I'll learn it then. But I don't know how I shall find time. For, besides the fencing master who teaches me, I have also got me a philosophy master, who is to begin this morning.

MUSIC MASTER. Philosophy is something; but music, sir, music—

DANCING MASTER. Music and dancing—music and dancing, that is all that's necessary.

MUSIC MASTER. There's nothing so profitable in a state as music.

DANCING MASTER. There's nothing so necessary for men as dancing.

MUSIC MASTER. A state cannot subsist without music.

DANCING MASTER. Without dancing, a man can do nothing.

MUSIC MASTER. All the disorders, all the wars one sees in the world, happen only from not learning music.

DANCING MASTER. All the disasters of mankind, all the fatal misfortunes that histories are replete with, the blunders of politicians, the miscarriages of great commanders, all this comes from want of skill in dancing.

M. JOURDAIN. How so?

MUSIC MASTER. Does not war proceed from want of concord amongst men?

M. JOURDAIN. That's true.

MUSIC MASTER. And if all men learnt music, would not that be a means of keeping them better in tune, and of seeing universal peace in the world?

M. JOURDAIN. You're in the right.

DANCING MASTER. When a man has been guilty of a defect in his conduct—be it in the affairs of his family, or in the government of the state, or in the command of an army—don't we always say, such a one has made a false step in such an affair?

M. JOURDAIN. Yes, we say so.

DANCING MASTER. And can making a false step proceed from anything but not knowing how to dance?

M. JOURDAIN. 'Tis true, and you are both in the right.

DANCING MASTER. This is to let you see the excellence and advantage of dancing and music.

M. JOURDAIN. I now comprehend it.

MUSIC MASTER. Will you see each of our compositions?

M. JOURDAIN. Yes.

MUSIC MASTER. I have told you already that this is a slight essay which I formerly made upon the different passions that may be expressed by music.

M. JOURDAIN. Very well.

MUSIC MASTER. [*To the* MUSICIANS] Here, come forward. [*To* M. JOURDAIN] You are to imagine with yourself that they are dressed like shepherds.

M. JOURDAIN. Why always shepherds? One sees nothing but such stuff everywhere.

MUSIC MASTER. When we are to introduce persons as speaking in music, 'tis necessary to probability that we give in to the pastoral way. Singing has always been appropriated to shepherds; and it is by no means natural in dialogue that princes or citizens should sing their passions.

M. JOURDAIN. Be it so, be it so. Let's see.

[*Dialogue in music between a Woman and two Men*]

WOMAN.

The heart that must tyrannic love obey,
A thousand fears and cares oppress.
Sweet are those sighs and languishments, they say;
Say what they will for me,
Nought is so sweet as liberty.

FIRST MAN.

Nothing so sweet as love's soft fire,
Which can two glowing hearts inspire
With the same life, the same desire.
The loveless swain no happiness can prove.
From life take soothing love,
All pleasure you remove.

SECOND MAN.

Sweet were the wanton archer's sway,
Would all with constancy obey;
But, cruel fate!
No nymph is true:
The faithless sex more worthy of our hate,
To love should bid eternally adieu.

FIRST MAN.

Pleasing heat!

WOMAN.

Freedom blest!

SECOND MAN.

Fair deceit!

FIRST MAN.

O how I love thee!

WOMAN.

How I approve thee!

SECOND MAN.

I detest!

FIRST MAN.

Against love's ardour quit this mortal hate.

WOMAN.

Shepherd, myself I bind here,
To show a faithful mate.

SECOND MAN.

Alas! but where to find her?

WOMAN.

Our glory to retrieve,
My heart I here bestow.

SECOND MAN.

But, nymph, can I believe
That heart no change will know?

WOMAN.

Let experience decide,
Who loves best of the two.

SECOND MAN.

And the perjured side
May vengeance pursue.

ALL THREE.

Then let us kindle soft desire,
Let us fan the amorous fire.
Ah! how sweet it is to love,
When hearts united constant prove!

M. JOURDAIN. Is this all?

MUSIC MASTER. Yes.

M. JOURDAIN. I find 'tis very concise, and there are some little sayings in it pretty enough.

DANCING MASTER. You have here, for my composition, a little essay of the finest movements, and the most beautiful attitudes with which a dance can possibly be varied.

M. JOURDAIN. Are they shepherds too?

DANCING MASTER. They're what you please. [*To the* DANCERS] Hola!

ACT II.

Scene I.

MONSIEUR JOURDAIN, MUSIC MASTER, DANCING MASTER, FOOT-BOY.

M. JOURDAIN. This is none of your stupid things, and these same fellows flutter it away bravely.

MUSIC MASTER. When the dance is mixed with the music, it will have a greater effect still, and you will see something gallant in the little entertainment we have prepared for you.

M. JOURDAIN. That's however for by and by; and the person for whom I have ordered all this, is to do me the honour of dining with me here.

DANCING MASTER. Everything's ready.

MUSIC MASTER. But in short, sir, this is not enough, 'tis necessary such a person as you, who live great and have an inclination to things that are handsome, should have a concert of music at your house every Wednesday, or every Thursday.

M. JOURDAIN. Why so? Have people of quality?

MUSIC MASTER. Yes, sir.

M. JOURDAIN. I'll have one then. Will it be fine?

MUSIC MASTER. Certainly. You must have three voices, a treble, a counter-tenor, and bass, which must be accompanied with a bass-viol, a theorbo-lute, and a harpsichord for the thorough-bass, with two violins to play the symphonies.

M. JOURDAIN. You must add also a trumpet-marine. The trumpet-marine is an instrument that pleases me, and is very harmonious.

MUSIC MASTER. Leave us to manage matters.

M. JOURDAIN. However, don't forget by and by to send the musicians to sing at table.

MUSIC MASTER. You shall have everything you should have.

M. JOURDAIN. But above all, let the entertainment be fine.

MUSIC MASTER. You will be pleased with it, and, amongst other things, with certain minuets you will find in it.

M. JOURDAIN. Ay, the minuets are my dance; and I have a mind you should see me dance 'em. Come, master.

DANCING MASTER. Your hat, sir, if you please. [M. JOURDAIN *takes off his foot-boy's hat, and puts it on over his own nightcap; upon which his master takes him by the hand and makes him dance to a minuet-air which he sings*]

Tol, lol, lol, lol, lol, lol,
Tol, lol, lol,
twice;
Tol, lol, lol; tol, lol.

In time, if you please,
Tol, lol,
the right leg.
Tol, lol, lol.
Don't shake your shoulders so much.
Tol, lol, lol, lol, lol.
Why, your arms are out of joint.
Tol, lol, lol, lol, tol.
Hold up your head. Turn out your toes.
Tol, lol, lol.
Your body erect.

M. JOURDAIN. Heh?

MUSIC MASTER. Admirably well performed.

M. JOURDAIN. Now I think of it, teach me how I must bow to salute a marchioness; I shall have occasion for it by and by.

DANCING MASTER. How you must bow to salute a marchioness?

M. JOURDAIN. Yes, a marchioness whose name is Dorimène.

DANCING MASTER. Give me your hand.

M. JOURDAIN. No. You need only to do it, I shall remember it easily.

DANCING MASTER. If you would salute her with a great deal of respect, you must first of all make a bow and fall back, then advancing towards her, bow thrice, and at the last bow down to her very knees.

M. JOURDAIN. Do it a little. [*After the* DANCING MASTER *has made three bows*] Right.

Scene II.

M. JOURDAIN, MUSIC MASTER, DANCING MASTER, a LACKEY.

LACKEY. Sir, your fencing master is here.

M. JOURDAIN. Bid him come in that he may give me a lesson. [*To the* MUSIC *and* DANCING MASTERS] I'd have you stay and see me perform.

Scene III.

M. JOURDAIN, FENCING MASTER, MUSIC MASTER, DANCING MASTER, a LACKEY (holding two foils).

FENCING MASTER. [*Taking the two foils out of the* LACKEY*'s hand, and giving one to* M. JOURDAIN] Come, sir, your salute. Your body straight. A little bearing upon the left thigh. Your legs not so much astraddle. Your feet both on a line. Your wrist opposite to your hip. The point of your sword over-against your shoulder. Your arm not quite so much extended. Your left hand on a level with your eye. Your left shoulder more square. Hold up your head. Your look bold. Advance. Your body steady. Beat carte, and push carte. One, two. Recover. Again with it, your foot firm. One, two. Leap back. When you make a pass, sir, 'tis necessary your sword should disengage first, and your body make as small a mark as possible. One, two. Come, beat tierce, and push the same. Advance. Your body firm. Advance. Quit after that manner. One, two. Recover. Repeat the same. One, two. Leap back. Parry, sir, parry. [*The* FENCING MASTER *gives him two or three home-thrusts, crying, "Parry"*]

M. JOURDAIN. Ugh!

MUSIC MASTER. You do wonders.

FENCING MASTER. I have told you already—the whole secret of arms consists but in two things, in giving and not receiving. And as I showed you t'other day by demonstrative reason, it is impossible you should receive if you know how to turn your adversary's sword from the line of your body; which depends only upon a small motion of your wrist, either inward, or outward.

M. JOURDAIN. At that rate therefore, a man without any courage is sure to kill his man and not to be killed.

FENCING MASTER. Certainly. Don't you see the demonstration of it?

M. JOURDAIN. Yes.

FENCING MASTER. By this one may see of what consideration such persons as we should be esteemed in a state, and how highly the science of arms excels all the other useless sciences, such as dancing, music, and—

DANCING MASTER. Soft and fair, Monsieur *Sa, sa*. Don't speak of dancing but with respect.

MUSIC MASTER. Pray learn to treat the excellence of music in a handsomer manner.

FENCING MASTER. You're merry fellows, to pretend to compare your sciences with mine.

MUSIC MASTER. Do but see the importance of the creature!

DANCING MASTER. The droll animal there, with his leathern stomacher!

FENCING MASTER. My little master skipper, I shall make you skip as you should do. And you, my little master scraper, I shall make you sing to some tune.

DANCING MASTER. Monsieur Tick-tack, I shall teach you your trade.

M. JOURDAIN. [*To the* DANCING MASTER] Are you bewitched to quarrel with him, who understands tierce and carte, who knows how to kill a man by demonstrative reason?

DANCING MASTER. I laugh at his demonstrative reason, and his tierce and his carte.

M. JOURDAIN. [*To the* DANCING MASTER] Softly, I say.

FENCING MASTER. [*To the* DANCING MASTER] How? Master Impertinence!

M. JOURDAIN. Nay, my dear fencing master!

DANCING MASTER. [*To the* FENCING MASTER] How? You great dray-horse!

M. JOURDAIN. Nay, my dancing master.

FENCING MASTER. If I lay my—

M. JOURDAIN. [*To the* FENCING MASTER] Gently.

DANCING MASTER. If I lay my clutches on you—

M. JOURDAIN. Easily.

FENCING MASTER. I shall curry you with such an air—

M. JOURDAIN. [*To the* FENCING MASTER] For goodness' sake.

DANCING MASTER. I shall drub you after such a manner—

M. JOURDAIN. [*To the* DANCING MASTER] I beseech you.

MUSIC MASTER. Let us teach him a little how to speak.

M. JOURDAIN. [*To the* MUSIC MASTER] Lack-a-day, be quiet.

Scene IV.

PHILOSOPHY MASTER, M. JOURDAIN, MUSIC MASTER, DANCING MASTER, FENCING MASTER, a LACKEY.

M. JOURDAIN. Hola, Monsieur Philosopher, you are come in the nick of time with your philosophy. Come, and make peace a little amongst these people here.

PHILOSOPHY MASTER. What's to do? What's the matter, gentlemen?

M. JOURDAIN. They have put themselves into such a passion about the preference of their professions as to call names, and would come to blows.

PHILOSOPHY MASTER. O fie, gentlemen, what need was there of all this fury? Have you not read the learned treatise upon anger, composed by Seneca?

Is there anything more base and shameful than this passion, which makes a savage beast of a man? And should not reason be master of all our commotions?

DANCING MASTER. How, sir? Why he has just now been abusing us both, in despising dancing which is my employment and music which is his profession.

PHILOSOPHY MASTER. A wise man is above all foul language that can be given him, and the grand answer one should make to all affronts is moderation and patience.

FENCING MASTER. They had both the assurance to compare their professions to mine.

PHILOSOPHY MASTER. Should this disturb you? Men should not dispute about vainglory and rank; that which perfectly distinguishes one from another is wisdom and virtue.

DANCING MASTER. I maintained to him that dancing was a science to which one cannot do sufficient honour.

MUSIC MASTER. And I, that music is one of those that all ages have revered.

FENCING MASTER. And I maintained against 'em both that the science of defence is the finest and most necessary of all sciences.

PHILOSOPHY MASTER. And what becomes of philosophy, then? You are all three very impertinent fellows, methinks, to speak with this arrogance before me; and impudently to give the name of science to things that one ought not to honour even with the name of art, that can't be comprised but under the name of a pitiful trade of gladiator, ballad-singer, and morris-dancer.

FENCING MASTER. Out, ye dog of a philosopher.

MUSIC MASTER. Hence, ye scoundrel of a pedant.

DANCING MASTER. Begone, ye arrant pedagogue. [*The* PHILOSOPHER *falls upon them, they all three lay him on.*]

PHILOSOPHY MASTER. How? Varlets as you are—

M. JOURDAIN. Monsieur Philosopher!

PHILOSOPHY MASTER. Infamous dogs! Rogues! Insolent curs!

M. JOURDAIN. Monsieur Philosopher!

FENCING MASTER. Plague on the animal!

M. JOURDAIN. Gentlemen!

PHILOSOPHY MASTER. Impudent villains!

M. JOURDAIN. Monsieur Philosopher!

DANCING MASTER. Deuce take the pack-saddled ass!

M. JOURDAIN. Gentlemen!

PHILOSOPHY MASTER. Profligate vermin!

M. JOURDAIN. Monsieur Philosopher!

MUSIC MASTER. The devil take the impertinent puppy!

M. JOURDAIN. Gentlemen!

PHILOSOPHY MASTER. Knaves! Ragamuffins! Traitors! Impostors!

M. JOURDAIN. Monsieur Philosopher! Gentlemen! Monsieur Philosopher! Gentlemen! Monsieur Philosopher! [*The four masters beat each other out.*]

Scene V.

M. JOURDAIN, a LACKEY.

M. JOURDAIN. Nay, beat your hearts out if you will, I shall neither meddle nor make with you, I shan't spoil my gown to part you. I should be a great fool to thrust myself among them, and receive some blow that might do me a mischief.

Scene VI.

PHILOSOPHY MASTER, M. JOURDAIN, a LACKEY.

PHILOSOPHY MASTER. [*Setting his band right*] Now to our lesson.

M. JOURDAIN. Ah! Sir, I'm sorry for the blows they have given you.

PHILOSOPHY MASTER. 'Tis nothing at all. A philosopher knows how to receive things in a proper manner; and I'll compose a satire against 'em, in the manner of Juvenal, that shall cut 'em most gloriously. Let that pass. What have you a mind to learn?

M. JOURDAIN. Everything I can, for I have all the desire in the world to be a scholar, and it vexes me that my father and mother had not made me study all the sciences when I was young.

PHILOSOPHY MASTER. 'Tis a very reasonable sentiment. *Nam, sine doctrinâ vita est quasi mortis imago*. You understand that, and are acquainted with Latin, without doubt?

M. JOURDAIN. Yes; but act as if I were not acquainted with it. Explain me the meaning of that.

PHILOSOPHY MASTER. The meaning of it is, that without learning, life is as it were an image of death.

M. JOURDAIN. That same Latin's in the right.

PHILOSOPHY MASTER. Have you not some principles, some rudiments of science?

M. JOURDAIN. Oh! yes, I can read and write.

PHILOSOPHY MASTER. Where would you please to have us begin? Would you have me teach you logic?

M. JOURDAIN. What may that same logic be?

PHILOSOPHY MASTER. It's that which teaches us the three operations of the mind.

M. JOURDAIN. What are those three operations of the mind?

PHILOSOPHY MASTER. The first, the second, and the third. The first is to conceive well, by means of universals. The second, to judge well, by means of categories. The third, to draw the conclusion right, by means of figures: Barbara, Celarent, Darii, Ferio, Baralipton, etc.

M. JOURDAIN. These words are too crabbed. This logic does not suit me by any means. Let's learn something else that's prettier.

PHILOSOPHY MASTER. Will you learn morality?

M. JOURDAIN. Morality?

PHILOSOPHY MASTER. Yes.

M. JOURDAIN. What means morality?

PHILOSOPHY MASTER. It treats of happiness, teaches men to moderate their passions, and—

M. JOURDAIN. No, no more of that. I'm as choleric as the devil, and there's no morality holds me; I will have my belly full of passion whenever I have a mind to it.

PHILOSOPHY MASTER. Would you learn physics?

M. JOURDAIN. What is it that physics treat of?

PHILOSOPHY MASTER. Physics are what explain the principles of things natural and the properties of bodies; which discourse of the nature of elements, of metals, of minerals, of stones, of plants, and animals, and teach us the cause of all the meteors; the rainbow, *ignes fatui*, cornets, lightnings, thunder, thunder-bolts, rain, snow, hail, winds, and whirlwinds.

M. JOURDAIN. There's too much hurly-burly in this, too much confusion.

PHILOSOPHY MASTER. What would you have me teach you then?

M. JOURDAIN. Teach me orthography.

PHILOSOPHY MASTER. With all my heart.

M. JOURDAIN. Afterwards you may teach me the almanack, to know when there's a moon, and when not.

PHILOSOPHY MASTER. Be it so. To pursue this thought of yours right and treat this matter like a philosopher, we must begin, according to the order of things, with an exact knowledge of the nature of letters and the different manner of pronouncing them. And on this head I am to tell you that letters are divided into vowels, called vowels because they express the voice: and into consonants, so called because they sound with the vowels and only mark the different articulations of the voice. There are five vowels or voices, A, E, I, O, U.

M. JOURDAIN. I understand all that.

PHILOSOPHY MASTER. The vowel A is formed by opening the mouth very wide, A.

M. JOURDAIN. A, A. Yes.

PHILOSOPHY MASTER. The vowel E is formed by drawing the under-jaw a little nearer to the upper, A, E.

M. JOURDAIN. A, E. A, E. In troth it is. How pretty that is!

PHILOSOPHY MASTER. And the vowel I, by bringing the jaws still nearer one to the other, and stretching the two corners of the mouth towards the ears, A, E, I.

M. JOURDAIN. A, E, I, I, I, I. 'Tis true. Long live learning!

PHILOSOPHY MASTER. The vowel O is formed by re-opening the jaws and drawing the lips near at the two corners, the upper and the under, O.

M. JOURDAIN. O, O. There's nothing more just, A, E, I, O, I, O. 'Tis admirable! I, O, I, O.

PHILOSOPHY MASTER. The opening of the mouth makes exactly a little ring, which resembles an O.

M. JOURDAIN. O, O, O. You're right, O. How fine a thing it is but to know something!

PHILOSOPHY MASTER. The vowel U is formed by bringing the teeth near together without entirely joining them, and pouting out both your lips, bringing them also near together without absolutely joining 'em, U.

M. JOURDAIN. U, U. There's nothing more true, U.

PHILOSOPHY MASTER. Your two lips pout out as if you were making faces. Whence it comes that if you would do that to anybody and make a jest of him, you need say nothing to him but U.

M. JOURDAIN. U, U. It's true. Ah! why did not I study sooner, that I might have known all this!

PHILOSOPHY MASTER. To-morrow we shall take a view of the other letters, which are the consonants.

M. JOURDAIN. Is there anything as curious in them, as in these?

PHILOSOPHY MASTER. Doubtless. The consonant D, for example, is pronounced by clapping the tip of your tongue above the upper teeth, DE.

M. JOURDAIN. DE, DE. 'Tis so. Oh! charming things! charming things!

PHILOSOPHY MASTER. The F, in leaning the upper teeth upon the lower lip, EF.

M. JOURDAIN. EF, EF. 'Tis truth. Ah! father and mother o' mine, how do I owe you a grudge!

PHILOSOPHY MASTER. And the R, in carrying the tip of the tongue up to the roof of your mouth; so that being grazed upon by the air which bursts out with a force, it yields to it, and returns always to the same part, making a kind of trill, R, ra.

M. JOURDAIN. R, r, ra. R, r, r, r, r, ra. That's true. What a clever man are you! And how have I lost time! R, r, r, ra.

PHILOSOPHY MASTER. I will explain to you all these curiosities to the bottom.

M. JOURDAIN. Pray do. But now, I must commit a secret to you. I'm in love with a person of great quality, and I should be glad you would help me to write something to her in a short *billet-doux*, which I'll drop at her feet.

PHILOSOPHY MASTER. Very well.

M. JOURDAIN. That will be very gallant, won't it?

PHILOSOPHY MASTER. Without doubt. Is it verse that you would write to her?

M. JOURDAIN. No, no, none of your verse.

PHILOSOPHY MASTER. You would only have prose?

M. JOURDAIN. No, I would neither have verse nor prose.

PHILOSOPHY MASTER. It must be one or t'other.

M. JOURDAIN. Why so?

PHILOSOPHY MASTER. Because, sir, there's nothing to express one's self by, but prose, or verse.

M. JOURDAIN. Is there nothing then but prose, or verse?

PHILOSOPHY MASTER. No, sir, whatever is not prose, is verse; and whatever is not verse, is prose.

M. JOURDAIN. And when one talks, what may that be then?

PHILOSOPHY MASTER. Prose.

M. JOURDAIN. How? When I say, Nicole, bring me my slippers, and give me my nightcap, is that prose?

PHILOSOPHY MASTER. Yes, sir.

M. JOURDAIN. On my conscience, I have spoken prose above these forty years without knowing anything of the matter; and I have all the obligations in the world to you for informing me of this. I would therefore put into a letter to her: Beautiful marchioness, your fair eyes make me die with love; but I would have this placed in a gallant manner; and have a gentle turn.

PHILOSOPHY MASTER. Why, add that the fire of her eyes has reduced your heart to ashes: that you suffer for her night and day all the torments—

M. JOURDAIN. No, no, no, I won't have all that—I'll have nothing but what I told you. Beautiful marchioness, your fair eyes make me die with love.

PHILOSOPHY MASTER. You must by all means lengthen the thing out a little.

M. JOURDAIN. No, I tell you, I'll have none but those very words in the letter: but turned in a modish way, ranged handsomely as they should be. I desire you'd show me a little, that I may see the different manners in which one may place them.

PHILOSOPHY MASTER. One may place them first of all as you said: Beautiful marchioness, your fair eyes make me die for love. Or suppose: For love die me make, beautiful marchioness, your fair eyes. Or perhaps: Your eyes fair, for love me make, beautiful marchioness, die. Or suppose: Die your fair eyes, beautiful marchioness, for love me make. Or however: Me make your eyes fair die, beautiful marchioness, for love.

M. JOURDAIN. But of all these ways, which is the best?

PHILOSOPHY MASTER. That which you said: Beautiful marchioness, your fair eyes make me die for love.

M. JOURDAIN. Yet at the same time, I never studied it, and I made the whole of it at the first touch. I thank you with all my heart, and desire you would come in good time to-morrow.

PHILOSOPHY MASTER. I shall not fail. [*Exit*]

Scene VII.

M. JOURDAIN, a LACKEY.

M. JOURDAIN. [*To his* LACKEY] What? Are my clothes not come yet?

LACKEY. No, sir.

M. JOURDAIN. This cursed tailor makes me wait unreasonably, considering it's a day I have so much business in. I shall go mad. A quartan ague wring this villain of a tailor. D—l take the tailor. A plague choke the tailor. If I had him but here now, this detestable tailor, this dog of a tailor, this traitor of a tailor, I—

Scene VIII.

M. JOURDAIN, MASTER TAILOR, JOURNEYMAN TAILOR (bringing a suit of clothes for M. JOURDAIN), a LACKEY.

M. JOURDAIN. Oh! You're there. I was going to be in a passion with you.

MASTER TAILOR. I could not possibly come sooner, and I set twenty fellows to work at your clothes.

M. JOURDAIN. You have sent me a pair of silk hose so tight that I had all the difficulty in the world to get 'em on, and there are two stitches broke in 'em.

MASTER TAILOR. They'll grow rather too large.

M. JOURDAIN. Yes, if I break every day a loop or two. You have made me a pair of shoes too, that pinch me execrably.

MASTER TAILOR. Not at all, Sir.

M. JOURDAIN. How, not at all?

MASTER TAILOR. No, they don't pinch you at all.

M. JOURDAIN. I tell you they do hurt me.

MASTER TAILOR. You fancy so.

M. JOURDAIN. I fancy so because I feel it. There's a fine reason indeed.

MASTER TAILOR. Hold, stay, here's one of the handsomest suits at court, and the best-matched. 'Tis a masterly work to invent a grave suit of clothes that should not be black, and I'll give the cleverest tailor in town six trials to equal it.

M. JOURDAIN. What a deuce have we here? You have put the flowers downwards.

MASTER TAILOR. Why, you did not tell me you would have 'em upwards.

M. JOURDAIN. Was there any need to tell you of that?

MASTER TAILOR. Yes, Certainly. All the people of quality wear 'em in that way.

M. JOURDAIN. Do people of quality wear the flowers downwards?

MASTER TAILOR. Yes, sir.

M. JOURDAIN. Oh, 'tis very well, then.

MASTER TAILOR. If you please I'll put 'em upwards.

M. JOURDAIN. No, no.

MASTER TAILOR. YOU need only say the word.

M. JOURDAIN. No, I tell you, you have done right. Do you think my clothes will fit me?

MASTER TAILOR. A pretty question! I defy a painter with his pencil to draw you anything that shall fit more exact. I have a fellow at home who, for fitting a pair of breeches, is the greatest genius in the world; another who, for the cut of a doublet, is the hero of the age.

M. JOURDAIN. Are the peruke and feather as they should be?

MASTER TAILOR. Everything's well.

M. JOURDAIN. [*Looking earnestly at the* TAILOR*'s clothes*] Ah, hah! Monsieur Tailor, here's my stuff of the last suit you made for me. I know it very well.

MASTER TAILOR. The stuff appeared to me so handsome, that I had a mind to cut a coat out of it for myself.

M. JOURDAIN. Yes, but you should not have cabbaged it out of mine.

MASTER TAILOR. Will you put on your clothes?

M. JOURDAIN, Yes, give 'em to me.

MASTER TAILOR. Stay; the matter must not go so. I have brought men along with me to dress you to music; these sort of suits are put on with ceremony. So ho? come in there, you.

Scene IX.

M. JOURDAIN, MASTER TAILOR, JOURNEYMAN TAILORS (dancing), a LACKEY.

MASTER TAILOR. Put on this suit of the gentleman's, in the manner you do to people of quality.

[*Two of the tailors pull off his straight breeches made for his exercises, and two others his waistcoat; then they put on his new suit to music, and* M. JOURDAIN *walks amongst them to show them his clothes to see whether they fit or no.*]

JOURNEYMAN TAILOR. My dear gentleman, please to give the tailor's men something to drink.

M. JOURDAIN. How do you call me?

JOURNEYMAN TAILOR. My dear gentleman.

M. JOURDAIN. "My dear gentleman!" See what it is to dress like people of quality. You may go clothed like a commoner all your days, and they'll never call you "my dear gentleman." [*Gives them something*] Stay, there's for "my dear gentleman."

JOURNEYMAN TAILOR. My lord, we are infinitely obliged to you.

M. JOURDAIN. My lord! Oh, ho! My lord! Stay, friend; "my lord" deserves something, "my lord" is none o' your pretty words. Hold, there, "my lord" gives you that.

JOURNEYMAN TAILOR. My lord, we shall go drink your grace's health.

M. JOURDAIN. Your grace! oh, oh, oh! stay, don't go. Your grace, to me! [*Aside*] I'faith if he goes as far as highness, he'll empty my purse. [*Aloud*] Hold, there's for "my grace."

JOURNEYMAN TAILOR. My lord, we most humbly thank your grace for your liberality.

M. JOURDAIN. He did very well; I was going to give him all.

ACT III.

Scene I.

M. JOURDAIN and his two LACKEYS.

M. JOURDAIN. Follow me, that I may go and show my clothes a little through the town; and especially take care, both of you, to walk immediately at my heels, that people may plainly see you belong to me.

LACKEYS. Yes, sir.

M. JOURDAIN. Call me Nicole, that I may give her some directions. You need not go—here she comes.

Scene II.

M. JOURDAIN, NICOLE, two LACKEYS.

M. JOURDAIN. Nicole?

NICOLE. Your pleasure, sir?

M. JOURDAIN. Harkee.

NICOLE. [*Laughing*] Ha, ha, ha, ha, ha.

M. JOURDAIN. Who do ye laugh at?

NICOLE. Ha, ha, ha, ha, ha, ha.

M. JOURDAIN. What does this slut mean?

NICOLE. Ha, ha, ha. How you are bedizened! Ha, ha, ha.

M. JOURDAIN. How's that?

NICOLE. Oh! oh! my stars! ha, ha, ha, ha, ha.

M. JOURDAIN. What a jade is here! What! do ye make a jest of me?

NICOLE. No, no, sir, I should be very sorry to do so. Ha, ha, ha, ha, ha, ha.

M. JOURDAIN. I shall give ye a slap o' the chops, if you laugh any more.

NICOLE. Sir, I cannot help it. Ha, ha, ha, ha, ha, ha.

M. JOURDAIN. Won't ye have done?

NICOLE. Sir, I ask your pardon; but you are so comical, that I cannot hold from laughing. Ha, ha, ha.

M. JOURDAIN. Do but see the insolence!

NICOLE. You are so thoroughly droll there! Ha, ha.

M. JOURDAIN. I shall—

NICOLE. I beg you would excuse me. Ha, ha, ha, ha.

M. JOURDAIN. Hold, if you laugh again the least in the world, I protest and swear I'll give ye such a box o' the ear as ye never had in your life.

NICOLE. Well, sir, I have done; I won't laugh any more.

M. JOURDAIN. Take care you don't. You must clean out against by and by—

NICOLE. Ha, ha.

M. JOURDAIN. You must clean out as it should be—

NICOLE. Ha, ha.

M. JOURDAIN. I say, you must go clean out the hall, and—

NICOLE. Ha, ha.

M. JOURDAIN. Again?

NICOLE. [*Tumbles down with laughing*] Hold, sir, beat me rather, and let me laugh my belly-full, that will do me more good. Ha, ha, ha, ha.

M. JOURDAIN. I shall run mad!

NICOLE. For goodness' sake, sir, I beseech you let me laugh. Ha, ha, ha.

M. JOURDAIN. If I take you in hand—

NICOLE. Si-ir, I shall bu-urst, if I do—not laugh. Ha, ha, ha.

M. JOURDAIN. But did ever anybody see such a jade as that, who insolently laughs in my face, instead of receiving my orders!

NICOLE. What would you have me do, sir?

M. JOURDAIN. Why, take care to get ready my house for the company that's to come by and by.

NICOLE. [*Getting up*] Ay, i'fakins, I've no more inclination to laugh; all your company makes such a litter here that the very word's enough to put one in an ill humour.

M. JOURDAIN. What! I ought to shut my doors against all the world for your sake?

NICOLE. You ought at least to shut it against certain people.

Scene III.

MME. JOURDAIN, M. JOURDAIN, NICOLE, two LACKEYS.

MME. JOURDAIN. Ah, hah! Here's some new story. What means this, husband, this same equipage? D'ye despise the world, that you harness yourself out in this manner? Have you a mind to make yourself a laughing-stock wherever ye go?

M. JOURDAIN. None but fools, wife, will laugh at me.

MME. JOURDAIN. In truth, people have not stayed thus long to laugh; 'tis a good while ago that your ways have furnished all the world with a laugh.

M. JOURDAIN. Who is that "all the world," pray?

MME. JOURDAIN. That "all the world" is a world perfectly in the right, and much wiser than yourself. For my part, I am shocked at the life you lead. I don't know what to call our house. One would swear 'twere carnival here all the year round; and from break o'day, for fear there should be any respite, there's nothing to be heard here but an uproar of fiddles and songsters which disturb the whole neighbourhood.

NICOLE. Madame says right. I shall never see my things set to rights again for that gang of folks that you bring to the house. They ransack every quarter of the town with their feet for dirt to bring here; and poor Frances is e'en almost slaved off her legs with scrubbing of the floors, which your pretty masters come to daub as regularly as the day comes.

M. JOURDAIN. Hey-day! our maid Nicole! you have a pretty nimble tongue of your own for a country-wench.

MME. JOURDAIN. Nicole's in the right, and she has more sense than you have. I should be glad to know what you think to do with a dancing master, at your age?

NICOLE. And with a lubberly fencing master, that comes here with his stamping to shake the whole house, and tear up all the pavement of the hall.

M. JOURDAIN. Peace, our maid, and our wife.

MME. JOURDAIN. What! will you learn to dance against the time you'll have no legs?

NICOLE. What! have you a mind to murder somebody?

M. JOURDAIN. Hold your prate; I tell you you are ignorant creatures, both of you, and don't know the advantage of all this.

MME. JOURDAIN. You ought much rather to think of marrying your daughter, who is of age to be provided for.

M. JOURDAIN. I shall think of marrying my daughter when a suitable match presents itself; but I shall think too of learning the *belles sciences*.

NICOLE. I've heard say further, madame, that to pin the basket, he has got him a philosophy master to-day.

M. JOURDAIN. Very well. I've a mind to have wit, and to know how to reason upon things with your genteel people.

MME. JOURDAIN. Won't you go to school one of these days, and be whipped at your age?

M. JOURDAIN. Why not? Would I were whipped this very instant before all the world, so I did but know what they learn at school!

NICOLE. Yes, forsooth, that would be a mighty advantage t'ye.

M. JOURDAIN. Without doubt.

MME. JOURDAIN. This is all very necessary to the management of your house.

M. JOURDAIN. Certainly. You talk, both of you, like asses, and I'm ashamed of your ignorance. [*To* MME. JOURDAIN] For example, do you know, you, what it is you now speak?

MME. JOURDAIN. Yes, I know that what I speak is very right, and that you ought to think of living in another manner.

M. JOURDAIN. I don't talk of that. I ask you what the words are that you now speak?

MME. JOURDAIN. They are words that have a good deal of sense in them, and your conduct is by no means such.

M. JOURDAIN. I don't talk of that, I tell you. I ask you, what is that I now speak to you, which I say this very moment.

MME. JOURDAIN. Mere stuff.

M. JOURDAIN. Pshaw, no, 'tis not that. That which we both of us say, the language we speak this instant?

MME. JOURDAIN. Well?

M. JOURDAIN. How is it called?

MME. JOURDAIN. 'Tis called just what you please to call it.

M. JOURDAIN. 'Tis prose, you ignorant creature.

MME. JOURDAIN. Prose?

M. JOURDAIN. Yes, prose. Whatever is prose, is not verse; and whatever is not verse, is prose. Now, see what it is to study. And you, [*To* NICOLE] do you know very well how you must do to say U?

NICOLE. How?

M. JOURDAIN. Yes. What is it you do when you say U?

NICOLE. What?

M. JOURDAIN. Say U a little, to try.

NICOLE. Well, U.

M. JOURDAIN. What is it you do?

NICOLE. I say U.

M. JOURDAIN. Yes, but when you say U, what is it you do?

NICOLE. I do as you bid me.

M. JOURDAIN. O! what a strange thing it is to have to do with brutes! You pout out your lips, and bring your under-jaw to your upper, U, d'ye see? I make a mouth, U.

NICOLE. Yes, that's fine.

MME. JOURDAIN. 'Tis admirable!

M. JOURDAIN. 'Tis quite another thing, had but you seen O, and DE, DE, and EF, EF.

MME. JOURDAIN. What is all this ridiculous stuff?

NICOLE. What are we the better for all this?

M. JOURDAIN. It makes one mad, to see these ignorant women.

MME. JOURDAIN. Go, go, you should send all these folks apacking with their silly stuff.

NICOLE. And especially that great lubberly fencing master, who fills all my house with dust.

M. JOURDAIN. Hey-day! This fencing master sticks strangely in thy stomach. I'll let thee see thy impertinence presently. [*He orders the foils to be brought, and gives one to* NICOLE] Stay, reason demonstrative, the line of the body. When they push in carte one need only do so; and when they push in tierce one need only do so. This is the way never to be killed; and is not that clever to be upon sure grounds, when one has an encounter with anybody? There, push at me a little, to try.

NICOLE. Well, how?[NICOLE *gives him several thrusts*]

M. JOURDAIN. Gently! Hold! Oh! Softly; deuce take the hussy.

NICOLE. You bid me push.

M. JOURDAIN. Yes, but you push me in tierce before you push in carte, and you have not patience while I parry.

MME. JOURDAIN. You are a fool, husband, with all these whims, and this is come to you since you have taken upon you to keep company with quality.

M. JOURDAIN. When I keep company with quality, I show my judgment; and that's much better than herding with your bourgeoisie.

MME. JOURDAIN. Yes, truly, there's a great deal to be got by frequenting your nobility; and you have made fine work with that count you are so bewitched with.

M. JOURDAIN. Peace, take care what you say. Do you well know, wife, that you don't know whom you speak of when you speak of him? He's a man of more importance than you think of; a nobleman of consideration at court, who speaks to the king just for all the world as I speak to you. Is it not a thing that does me great honour, that you see a person of that quality come so often to my house, who calls me his dear friend and treats me as if I were his equal? He has more kindness for me than one would ever imagine, and he caresses me in such a manner before all the world that I myself am perfectly confounded at it.

WHATEVER IS PROSE, IS NOT VERSE; AND WHATEVER IS NOT VERSE, IS PROSE. NOW, SEE WHAT IT IS TO STUDY.

MME. JOURDAIN. Yes, he has a great kindness for you, and caresses you; but he borrows your money of you.

M. JOURDAIN. Well, and is it not a great honour to me to lend money to a man of that condition? And can I do less for a lord who calls me his dear friend?

MME. JOURDAIN. And what is it this lord does for you?

M. JOURDAIN. Things that would astonish you if you did but know 'em.

MME. JOURDAIN. And what may they be?

M. JOURDAIN. Peace, I can't explain myself. 'Tis sufficient that if I have lent him money, he'll pay it me honestly, and that before 'tis long.

MME. JOURDAIN. Yes, stay you for that.

M. JOURDAIN. Certainly. Did he not tell me so?

MME. JOURDAIN. Yes, yes, and he won't fail to disappoint you.

M. JOURDAIN. He swore to me on the faith of a gentleman.

MME. JOURDAIN. A mere song.

M. JOURDAIN. Hey! You are mighty obstinate, wife of mine; I tell you he will keep his word with me, I am sure of it.

MME. JOURDAIN. And I am sure that he will not, and all the court he makes to you is only to cajole you.

M. JOURDAIN. Hold your tongue. Here he comes.

MME. JOURDAIN. That's all we shall have of him. He comes perhaps to borrow something more of you; the very sight of him gives me my dinner.

M. JOURDAIN. Hold your tongue, I say.

Scene IV.

DORANTE, M. JOURDAIN, MME. JOURDAIN, NICOLE.

DORANTE. My dear friend, Monsieur Jourdain, how do you do?

M. JOURDAIN. Very well, sir, to do you what little service I can.

DORANTE. And Madame Jourdain there, how does she do?

MME. JOURDAIN. Madame Jourdain does as well as she can.

DORANTE. Hah! Monsieur Jourdain, you're dressed the most genteelly in the world!

M. JOURDAIN. As you see.

DORANTE. You have a very fine air with that dress, and we have ne'er a young fellow at court that's better made than you.

M. JOURDAIN. He, he.

MME. JOURDAIN. [*Aside*] He scratches him where it itches.

DORANTE. Turn about. 'Tis most gallant.

MME. JOURDAIN. [*Aside*] Yes, as much of the fool behind as before.

DORANTE. 'Faith, Monsieur Jourdain, I was strangely impatient to see you. You're the man in the world I most esteem, and I was talking of you again this morning at the king's levee.

M. JOURDAIN. You do me a great deal of honour, sir. [*To* MME. JOURDAIN] At the king's levee!

DORANTE. Come, be covered.

M. JOURDAIN. Sir, I know the respect I owe you.

DORANTE. Lack-a-day, be covered; no ceremony, pray, between us two.

M. JOURDAIN. Sir—

DORANTE. Put on your hat, I tell you, Monsieur Jourdain; you are my friend.

M. JOURDAIN. Sir, I am your humble servant.

DORANTE. I won't be covered, if you won't.

M. JOURDAIN. [*Puts on his hat*] I choose rather to be unmannerly than troublesome.

DORANTE. I am your debtor, you know.

MME. JOURDAIN. [*Aside*] Yes, we know it but too well.

DORANTE. You have generously lent me money upon several occasions, and have obliged me, most certainly, with the best grace in the world.

M. JOURDAIN. You jest, sir.

DORANTE. But I know how to repay what is lent me, and to be grateful for the favours done me.

M. JOURDAIN. I don't doubt it, sir.

DORANTE. I'm willing to get out of your books, and came hither to make up our accounts together.

M. JOURDAIN. [*Aside to* MME. JOURDAIN] Well, you see your impertinence, wife.

DORANTE. I'm one who love to be out of debt as soon as I can.

M. JOURDAIN. [*Aside to* MME. JOURDAIN] I told you so.

DORANTE. Let's see a little what 'tis I owe you.

M. JOURDAIN. [*Aside to* MME. JOURDAIN] You there, with your ridiculous suspicions.

DORANTE. Do you remember right all the money you have lent me?

M. JOURDAIN. I believe so. I made a little memorandum of it. Here it is. Let you have at one time two hundred louis d'or.

DORANTE. 'Tis true.

M. JOURDAIN. Another time, six-score.

DORANTE. Yes.

M. JOURDAIN. And another time a hundred and forty.

DORANTE. You are right.

M. JOURDAIN. These three articles make four hundred and sixty louis d'or, which come to five thousand and sixty livres.

DORANTE. The account is very right. Five thousand and sixty livres.

M. JOURDAIN. One thousand eight hundred and thirty-two livres to your plume-maker.

DORANTE. Just.

M. JOURDAIN. Two thousand seven hundred and four-score livres to your tailor.

DORANTE. 'Tis true.

M. JOURDAIN. Four thousand three hundred and seventy-nine livres, twelve sols, and eight deniers to your tradesman.

DORANTE. Very well. Twelve sols, eight deniers. The account is just.

M. JOURDAIN. And a thousand seven hundred and forty-eight livres, seven sols, four deniers to your saddler.

DORANTE. 'Tis all true. What does that come to?

M. JOURDAIN. Sum total, fifteen thousand eight hundred livres.

DORANTE. The sum total, and just. Fifteen thousand and eight hundred livres. To which add two hundred pistoles, which you are going to lend me, that will make exactly eighteen thousand francs, which I shall pay you the first opportunity.

MME. JOURDAIN. [*Aside to* M. JOURDAIN] Well, did I not guess how 'twould be!

M. JOURDAIN. [*Aside to* MME. JOURDAIN] Peace.

DORANTE. Will it incommode you to lend me what I tell you?

M. JOURDAIN. Oh! no.

MME. JOURDAIN. [*Aside to* M. JOURDAIN] This man makes a mere milch cow of you.

M. JOURDAIN. [*Aside to* MME. JOURDAIN] Hold your tongue.

DORANTE. If this will incommode you, I'll seek it elsewhere.

M. JOURDAIN. No, sir.

MME. JOURDAIN. [*Aside to* M. JOURDAIN] He'll ne'er be satisfied till he has ruined you.

M. JOURDAIN. [*Aside to* MME. JOURDAIN] Hold your tongue, I tell you.

DORANTE. You need only tell me if this puts you to any straits.

M. JOURDAIN. Not at all, sir.

MME. JOURDAIN. [*Aside to* M. JOURDAIN] 'Tis a true wheedler.

M. JOURDAIN. [*Aside to* MME. JOURDAIN] Hold your tongue then.

MME. JOURDAIN. [*Aside to* M. JOURDAIN] He'll drain you to the last farthing.

M. JOURDAIN. [*Aside to* MME. JOURDAIN] Will you hold your tongue?

DORANTE. I've a good many people would be glad to lend it me, but as you are my very good friend, I thought I should wrong you if I asked it of anybody else.

M. JOURDAIN. 'Tis too much honour, sir, you do me. I'll go fetch what you want.

MME. JOURDAIN. [*Aside to* M. JOURDAIN] What! going to lend him still more?

M. JOURDAIN. [*Aside to* MME. JOURDAIN] What can I do? Would you have me refuse a man of that rank, who spoke of me this morning at the king's levee?

MME. JOURDAIN. [*Aside to* M. JOURDAIN] Go, you're a downright dupe.

Scene V.

DORANTE, MME. JOURDAIN, NICOLE.

DORANTE. You seem to me very melancholy. What ails you, Madame Jourdain?

MME. JOURDAIN. My head's bigger than my fist, even if it is not swelled.

DORANTE. Where is Mademoiselle your daughter that I don't see her?

MME. JOURDAIN. Mademoiselle my daughter is pretty well where she is.

DORANTE. How does she go on?

MME. JOURDAIN. She goes on her two legs.

DORANTE. Won't you come with her, one of these days, and see the ball, and the play that's acted at court?

MME. JOURDAIN. Yes, truly, we've a great inclination to laugh, a great inclination to laugh have we.

DORANTE. I fancy, Madame Jourdain, you had a great many sparks in your younger years, being so handsome and good-humoured as you were.

MME. JOURDAIN. Tredame, sir! what, is Madame Jourdain grown decrepit, and does her head totter already with a palsy?

DORANTE. Odso, Madame Jourdain, I ask your pardon. I was not thinking that you are young. I'm very often absent. Pray excuse my impertinence.

Scene VI.

M. JOURDAIN, MME. JOURDAIN, DORANTE, NICOLE.

M. JOURDAIN. [*To* DORANTE] Here's two hundred pieces for you, hard money.

DORANTE. I do assure you, Monsieur Jourdain, I am absolutely yours; and I long to do you service at court.

M. JOURDAIN. I'm infinitely obliged to you.

DORANTE. If Madame Jourdain inclines to see the royal diversion, I'll get her the best places in the ballroom.

MME. JOURDAIN. Madame Jourdain kisses your hand.

DORANTE. [*Aside to* M. JOURDAIN] Our pretty marchioness, as I informed you in my letter, will be here by and by to partake of your ball and collation; I brought her, at last, to consent to the entertainment you design to give her.

M. JOURDAIN. Let us draw to a distance a little, for a certain reason.

DORANTE. 'Tis eight days since I saw you, and I gave you no tidings of the diamond you put into my hands to make her a present of, as from you; but the reason was, I had all the difficulty in the world to conquer her scruples, and 'twas no longer ago than to-day, that she resolved to accept of it.

M. JOURDAIN. How did she like it?

DORANTE. Marvellously; and I am much deceived if the beauty of this diamond has not an admirable effect upon her.

M. JOURDAIN. Grant it, kind Heaven!

MME. JOURDAIN. [*To* NICOLE] When he's once with him, he can never get rid of him.

DORANTE. I made her sensible in a proper manner of the richness of the present and the strength of your passion.

M. JOURDAIN. These kindnesses perfectly overwhelm me; I am in the greatest confusion in the world to see a person of your quality demean himself on my account as you do.

DORANTE. You jest sure. Does one ever stop at such sort of scruples among friends? And would not you do the same thing for me, if occasion offered?

M. JOURDAIN. Oh! certainly, and with all my soul.

MME. JOURDAIN. [Aside *to* NICOLE] How the sight of him torments me!

DORANTE. For my part, I never mind anything when a friend is to be served; and when you imparted to me the ardent passion you had entertained for the agreeable marchioness, with whom I was acquainted, you see that I made an immediate offer of my service.

M. JOURDAIN. 'Tis true, these favours are what confound me.

MME. JOURDAIN. [*To* NICOLE] What! will he never be gone?

NICOLE. They are mighty great together.

DORANTE. You've taken the right way to smite her. Women, above all things, love the expense we are at on their account; and your frequent serenades, your continual entertainments, that sumptuous firework she saw on the water, the diamond she received by way of present from you, and the regale you are now preparing—all this speaks much better in favour of your passion than all the things you yourself could possibly have said to her.

M. JOURDAIN. There's no expense I would not be at, if I could by that means find the way to her heart. A woman of quality has powerful charms for me, and 'tis an honour I would purchase at any rate.

MME. JOURDAIN. [Aside *to* NICOLE] What can they have to talk of so long together? Go softly, and listen a little.

DORANTE. By and by you will enjoy the pleasure of seeing her at your ease; your eyes will have full time to be satisfied.

M. JOURDAIN. To be at full liberty, I have ordered matters so that my wife shall dine with my sister, where she'll pass the whole afternoon.

DORANTE. You have done wisely, for your wife might have perplexed us a little. I have given the proper orders for you to the cook, and for everything necessary for the ball. 'Tis of my own invention; and provided the execution answers the plan, I am sure 'twill be—

M. JOURDAIN. [*Perceives that* NICOLE *listens, and gives her a box on the ear*] Hey, you're very impertinent. [*To* DORANTE] Let us go if you please.

Scene VII.

MME. JOURDAIN, NICOLE.

NICOLE. I'faith, curiosity has cost me something; but I believe there's a snake in the grass, for they were talking of some affair which they were not willing you should be present at.

MME. JOURDAIN. This is not the first time, Nicole, that I have had suspicions of my husband. I am the most deceived person in the world, or there is some amour in agitation, and I am labouring to discover what it should be. But let's think of my daughter. You know the love Cléonte has for her. He is a man who hits my fancy, and I have a mind to favour his addresses and help him to Lucile, if I can.

NICOLE. In truth, madame, I am the most ravished creature in the world, to find you in these sentiments; for if the master hits your taste, the man hits mine no less; and I could wish our marriage might be concluded under favour of theirs.

MME. JOURDAIN. Go, and talk with him about it, as from me, and tell him to come to me presently, that we may join in demanding my daughter of my husband.

NICOLE. I fly, madame, with joy, and I could not have received a more agreeable commission. [*Alone*] I believe I shall very much rejoice their hearts.

Scene VIII.

CLÉONTE, COVIELLE, NICOLE.

NICOLE. Hah, most luckily met. I'm an ambassadress of joy, and I come—

CLÉONTE. Be gone, ye perfidious slut, and don't come to amuse me with thy traitorous speeches.

NICOLE. Is it thus you receive—

CLÉONTE. Be gone, I tell thee, and go directly and inform thy false mistress, that she never more, while she lives, shall impose upon the too simple Cléonte.

NICOLE. What whim is this? My dear Covielle, tell me a little what does this mean.

COVIELLE. Thy dear Covielle, wicked minx? Away quickly out of my sight, hussy, and leave me at quiet.

NICOLE. What! dost thou, too—

COVIELLE. Out o' my sight, I tell thee, and talk not to me, for thy life.

NICOLE. [*Aside*] Hey-day! What gadfly has stung 'em both? Well, I must march and inform my mistress of this pretty piece of history.

Scene IX.

CLÉONTE, COVIELLE.

CLÉONTE. What! treat a lover in this manner; and a lover the most constant, the most passionate of all lovers!

COVIELLE. 'Tis a horrible trick they have served us both.

CLÉONTE. I discover all the ardour for her, all the tenderness one can imagine. I love nothing in the world but her, have nothing in my thoughts besides her. She is all my care, all my desire, all my joy, I speak of nought but her, think of nought but her, dream of nought but her, I breathe only for her, my heart lives wholly in her; and this is the worthy recompense of such a love! I am two days without seeing her, which are to me two horrible ages; I meet her accidentally, my heart feels all transported at the sight; joy sparkles in my face; I fly to her with ecstasy, and the faithless creature turns away her eyes, and brushes hastily by me, as if she had never seen me in her life!

COVIELLE. I say the same as you do.

CLÉONTE. Is it possible to see anything, Covielle, equal to this perfidy of the ungrateful Lucile?

COVIELLE. Or to that, sir, of the villainous jade Nicole?

CLÉONTE. After so many ardent sacrifices of sighs and vows that I have made to her charms!

COVIELLE. After so much assiduous sneaking, cares, and services that I have paid her in the kitchen!

CLÉONTE. So many tears that I have shed at her feet!

COVIELLE. So many buckets of water that I have drawn for her!

CLÉONTE. Such ardour as I have shown, in loving her more than myself!

COVIELLE. So much heat as I have endured, in turning the spit in her place!

CLÉONTE. She flies me with disdain!

COVIELLE. She turns her back upon me with impudence!

CLÉONTE. This is a perfidy worthy the greatest punishment.

COVIELLE. This a treachery that deserves a thousand boxes o' the ear.

CLÉONTE. Prithee, never think to speak once more to me in her favour.

COVIELLE. I, sir? Marry, Heaven forbid.

CLÉONTE. Never come to excuse the action of this perfidious woman.

COVIELLE. Fear it not.

CLÉONTE. No, d'ye see, all discourses in her defence will signify nothing.

COVIELLE. Who dreams of such a thing?

CLÉONTE. I'm determined to continue my resentment against her, and break off all correspondence.

COVIELLE. I give my consent.

CLÉONTE. This same count that visits her, pleases perhaps her eye; and her fancy, I see plainly, is dazzled with quality. But I must, for my own honour, prevent the triumph of her inconstancy. I'll make as much haste as she can do towards the change which I see she's running into, and won't leave her all the glory of quitting me.

COVIELLE. 'Tis very well said, and for my share, I enter into all your sentiments.

CLÉONTE. Second my resentments, and support my resolutions against all the remains of love that may yet plead for her. I conjure thee, say all the ill things of her thou canst. Paint me her person so as to make her despicable; and, in order to disgust me, mark me out well all the faults thou canst find in her.

COVIELLE. She, sir? A pretty mawkin, a fine piece to be so much enamoured with. I see nothing in her but what's very indifferent, and you might find a hundred persons more deserving of you. First of all she has little eyes.

CLÉONTE. That's true, she has little eyes; but they are full of fire, the most sparkling, the most piercing in the world, the most striking that one shall see.

COVIELLE. She has a wide mouth.

CLÉONTE. Yes; but one sees such graces in it, as one does not see in other mouths, and the sight of that mouth inspires desire: 'tis the most attractive, the most amorous in the world.

COVIELLE. As to her height, she's not tall.

CLÉONTE. No; but she's easy, and well-shaped.

COVIELLE. She affects a negligence in speaking and acting.

CLÉONTE. 'Tis true; but all this has a gracefulness in her, and her ways are engaging; they have I don't know what charms that insinuate into our hearts.

COVIELLE. As to her wit—

CLÉONTE. Ah! Covielle, she has the most refined, the most delicate turn of wit.

COVIELLE. Her conversation—

CLÉONTE. Her conversation is charming.

COVIELLE. She's always grave.

CLÉONTE. Would you have flaunting pleasantry, a perpetual profuse mirth? And d'ye see anything more impertinent than those women who are always upon the giggle?

COVIELLE. But in short, she is the most capricious creature in the world.

CLÉONTE. Yes, she is capricious, I grant ye, but everything sits well upon fine women; we bear with everything from the fair.

COVIELLE. Since that's the case, I see plainly you desire always to love her.

CLÉONTE. I! I should love death sooner; and I am now going to hate her as much as ever I loved her.

COVIELLE. But how, if you think her so perfect?

CLÉONTE. Therein shall my vengeance be more glaring; therein shall I better display the force of my resolution in hating her, quitting her, most beautiful as she is; most charming, most amiable, as I think her. Here she is.

Scene X.

LUCILE, CLÉONTE, COVIELLE, NICOLE.

NICOLE. [*To* LUCILE] For my part, I was perfectly shocked at it.

LUCILE. It can be nothing else, Nicole, but what I said. But there he comes.

CLÉONTE. [*To* COVIELLE] I won't so much as speak to her.

COVIELLE. I'll follow your example.

LUCILE. What means this, Cléonte, what's the matter with you?

NICOLE. What ails thee, Covielle?

LUCILE. What trouble has seized you?

NICOLE. What cross humour possesses thee?

LUCILE. Are you dumb, Cléonte?

NICOLE. Hast thou lost thy speech, Covielle?

CLÉONTE. The abandoned creature!

COVIELLE. Oh! the Judas!

LUCILE. I see very well that the late meeting has disordered your mind.

CLÉONTE. [*To* COVIELLE] O, ho! She sees what she has done.

NICOLE. The reception of this morning has made thee take snuff.

COVIELLE. [*To* CLÉONTE] She has guessed where the shoe pinches.

LUCILE. Is it not true, Cléonte, that this is the reason of your being out of humour?

CLÉONTE. Yes, perfidious maid, that is it, since I must speak; and I can tell you that you shall not triumph, as you imagine, by your unfaithfulness, that I shall be beforehand in breaking with you, and you won't have the credit of discarding me. I shall, doubtless, have some difficulty in conquering the passion I have for you: 'twill cause me uneasiness; I shall suffer for a while; but I shall compass my point, and I would sooner stab myself to the heart than have the weakness of returning to you.

COVIELLE. [*To* NICOLE] As says the master, so says the man.

LUCILE. Here's a noise indeed about nothing. I'll tell you, Cléonte, the reason that made me avoid joining you this morning.

CLÉONTE. [*Endeavouring to go to avoid* LUCILE] No, I'll hear nothing.

NICOLE. [*To* COVIELLE] I'll let thee into the cause that made us pass you so quick.

COVIELLE. [*Endeavouring to go to avoid* NICOLE] I will hear nothing.

LUCILE. [*Following* CLÉONTE] Know that this morning—

CLÉONTE. [*Walks about without regarding* LUCILE] No, I tell you.

NICOLE. [*Following* COVIELLE] Learn that—

COVIELLE. [*Walks about likewise without regarding* NICOLE] No, traitress.

LUCILE. Hear me.

CLÉONTE. Not a bit.

NICOLE. Let me speak.

COVIELLE. I'm deaf.

LUCILE. Cléonte!

CLÉONTE. No.

NICOLE. Covielle!

COVIELLE. No.

LUCILE. Stay.

CLÉONTE. Idle stuff.

NICOLE. Hear me.

COVIELLE. No such thing.

LUCILE. One moment.

CLÉONTE. Not at all.

NICOLE. A little patience.

COVIELLE. A fiddle-stick.

LUCILE. Two words.

CLÉONTE. No, 'tis over.

NICOLE. One word.

COVIELLE. No more dealings.

LUCILE. [*Stopping*] Well, since you won't hear me, keep your opinion, and do what you please.

NICOLE. [*Stopping likewise*] Since that's thy way, e'en take it all just as it pleases thee.

CLÉONTE. Let's know the subject then of this fine reception.

LUCILE. [*Going in her turn to avoid* CLÉONTE] I've no longer an inclination to tell it.

COVIELLE. Let us a little into this history.

NICOLE. [*Going likewise in her turn to avoid* COVIELLE] I won't inform thee now, not I.

CLÉONTE. [*Following* LUCILE] Tell me—

LUCILE. No, I'll tell you nothing.

COVIELLE. [*Following* NICOLE] Say—

NICOLE. No, I say nothing.

CLÉONTE. For goodness' sake.

LUCILE. No, I tell you.

COVIELLE. Of all charity.

NICOLE. Not a bit.

CLÉONTE. I beseech you.

LUCILE. Let me alone.

COVIELLE. I conjure thee.

NICOLE. Away with thee.

CLÉONTE. Lucile!

LUCILE. No.

COVIELLE. Nicole!

NICOLE. Not at all.

CLÉONTE. For Heaven's sake.

LUCILE. I will not.

COVIELLE. Speak to me.

NICOLE. Not a word.

CLÉONTE. Clear up my doubts.

LUCILE. No, I'll do nothing towards it.

COVIELLE. Cure my mind.

NICOLE. No, 'tis not my pleasure.

CLÉONTE. Well, since you are so little concerned to ease me of my pain, and to justify yourself as to the unworthy treatment my passion has received from you, ungrateful creature, 'tis the last time you shall see me, and I am going far from you to die of grief and love.

COVIELLE. [*To* NICOLE] And I'll follow his steps.

LUCILE. [*To* CLÉONTE*, who is going*] Cléonte!

NICOLE. [*To* COVIELLE, *who follows his master*] Covielle!

CLÉONTE. [*Stopping*] Hey?

COVIELLE. [*Likewise stopping*] Your pleasure?

LUCILE. Whither do you go?

CLÉONTE. Where I told you.

COVIELLE. We go to die.

LUCILE. Do you go to die, Cléonte?

CLÉONTE. Yes, cruel, since you will have it so.

LUCILE. I? I have you die?

CLÉONTE. Yes, you would.

LUCILE. Who told you so?

CLÉONTE. [*Going up to* LUCILE] Would you not have it so, since you would not clear up my suspicions?

LUCILE. Is that my fault? Would you but have given me the hearing, should I not have told you that the adventure you make such complaints about was occasioned this morning by the presence of an old aunt who will absolutely have it that the mere approach of a man is a dishonour to a girl, who is perpetually lecturing us upon this head, and represents to us all mankind as so many devils, whom one ought to avoid.

NICOLE. [*To* COVIELLE] There's the whole secret of the affair.

CLÉONTE. Don't you deceive me, Lucile?

COVIELLE. [*To* NICOLE] Dost thou not put a trick upon me?

LUCILE. [*To* CLÉONTE] There's nothing more true.

NICOLE. [*To* COVIELLE] 'Tis the very thing, as it is.

COVIELLE. [*To* CLÉONTE] Shall we surrender upon this?

CLÉONTE. Ah, Lucile, what art have you to calm my passions with a single word! How easily do we suffer ourselves to be persuaded by those we love!

COVIELLE. How easily is one wheedled by these plaguey animals!

Scene XI.

MME. JOURDAIN, CLÉONTE, LUCILE, COVIELLE, NICOLE.

MME JOURDAIN. I am very glad to see you, Cléonte, and you are here apropos. My husband's acoming; catch your opportunity quick, and demand Lucile in marriage.

CLÉONTE. Ah, madame, how sweet is that word, how it flatters my wishes! Could I receive an order more charming? a favour more precious?

Scene XII.

CLÉONTE, M. JOURDAIN, MME. JOURDAIN, LUCILE, COVIELLE, NICOLE.

CLÉONTE. Sir, I was not willing to employ any other person to make a certain demand of you which I have long intended. It concerns me sufficiently to undertake it in my own person; and, without farther circumlocution, I shall inform you that the honour of being your son-in-law is an illustrious favour which I beseech you to grant me.

M. JOURDAIN. Before I give you an answer, sir, I desire you would tell me whether you are a gentleman.

CLÉONTE. Sir, the generality of people don't hesitate much on this question. People speak out bluff, and with ease. They make no scruple of taking this title upon 'em, and custom now-a-days seems to authorise the theft. For my part, I confess to you, my sentiments in this matter are somewhat more delicate. I look upon all imposture as unworthy an honest man, and that there is cowardice in denying what Heaven has made us; in tricking ourselves out, to the eyes of the world, in a stolen title; in desiring to put ourselves off for what we are not. I am undoubtedly born of parents who have held honourable employments. I have had the honour of six years' service in the army; and I find myself of consequence enough to hold a tolerable rank in the world; but for all this I won't give myself a name, which others in my place would think they might pretend to, and I'll tell you frankly that I am no gentleman.

M. JOURDAIN. Your hand, sir; my daughter is no wife for you.

CLÉONTE. How?

M. JOURDAIN. You are no gentleman, you shan't have my daughter.

MME. JOURDAIN. What would you be at then with your gentlemen? D'ye think we sort of people are of the line of St. Louis?

M. JOURDAIN. Hold your tongue, wife, I see you're acoming.

MME. JOURDAIN. Are we either of us otherwise descended than of plain citizens?

M. JOURDAIN. There's a scandalous reflection for you!

MME. JOURDAIN. And was not your father a tradesman as well as mine?

YOUR DAUGHTER SHOULD HAVE A HUSBAND THAT'S PROPER FOR HER, AND AN HONEST MAN WHO IS RICH AND WELL MADE WOULD BE MUCH BETTER FOR HER THAN A GENTLEMAN WHO IS DEFORMED AND A BEGGAR.

M. JOURDAIN. Plague take the woman! She never has done with this. If your father was a tradesman, so much was the worse for him; but as for mine, they are numskulls that say he was. All that I have to say to you is that I will have a gentleman for my son-in-law.

MME. JOURDAIN. Your daughter should have a husband that's proper for her, and an honest man who is rich and well made would be much better for her than a gentleman who is deformed and a beggar.

NICOLE. That's very true. We have a young squire in our town who is the most awkward looby, the veriest driveller that I ever set eyes on.

M. JOURDAIN. Hold your prate, Madame Impertinence. You are always thrusting yourself into conversation. I've means sufficient for my daughter, and want nothing but honour, and I will have her a marchioness.

MME. JOURDAIN. A marchioness!

M. JOURDAIN. Yes, a marchioness.

MME. JOURDAIN. Marry, Heaven preserve me from it!

M. JOURDAIN. 'Tis a determined thing.

MME. JOURDAIN. 'Tis what I shall never consent to. Matches with people above one are always subject to grievous inconveniences. I don't like that a son-in-law should have it in his power to reproach my daughter with her parents, or that she should have children who should be ashamed to call me grandmother. Should she come and visit me with the equipage of a grand lady and, through inadvertency, miss curtsying to some of the neighbourhood, they would not fail, presently, saying a hundred idle things. Do but see, would they say, this lady marchioness, what haughty airs she gives herself. She's the daughter of Monsieur Jourdain, who was over and above happy, when she was a little one, to play children's play with us. She was not always so lofty as she is now; and her two grandfathers sold cloth near St. Innocent's Gate. They amassed great means for their children, which they are paying for now, perhaps very dear, in the other world. People don't generally grow so rich by being honest. I won't have all these tittle-tattle stories; in one word, I'll have a man who shall be beholden to me for my daughter, and to whom I can say: Sit you down there, son-in-law, and dine with me.

M. JOURDAIN. See there the sentiments of a little soul, to desire always to continue in a mean condition. Let me have no more replies; my daughter shall be a marchioness in spite of the world; and if you put me in a passion, I'll make her a duchess.

Scene XIII.

MME. JOURDAIN, LUCILE, CLÉONTE, NICOLE, COVIELLE.

MME. JOURDAIN. Cléonte, don't be discouraged by all this. [*To* LUCILE] Follow me, daughter, and come tell your father resolutely that if you have not him, you won't marry anybody at all.

Scene XIV.

CLÉONTE, COVIELLE.

COVIELLE. You have made a pretty piece of work of it with your fine sentiments.

CLÉONTE. What wouldst thou have me do? I have a scrupulousness in this case that no precedents can conquer.

COVIELLE. You're in the wrong to be serious with such a man as that. Don't you see that he's a fool? And would it cost you anything to accommodate yourself to his chimeras?

CLÉONTE. You're in the right; but I did not dream it was necessary to bring your proofs of nobility, to be son-in-law to Monsieur Jourdain.

COVIELLE. [*Laughing*] Ha, ha, ha.

CLÉONTE. What d'ye laugh at?

COVIELLE. At a thought that's come into my head to play our spark off and help you to obtain what you desire.

CLÉONTE. How?

COVIELLE. The thought is absolutely droll.

CLÉONTE. What is it?

COVIELLE. There was a certain masquerade performed a little while ago, which comes in here the best in the world; and which I intend to insert into a piece of roguery I design to make for our coxcomb. This whole affair looks a little like making a joke of him; but with him we may hazard everything. There's no need here to study finesse so much—he's a man who will play his part to a wonder, and will easily give in to all the sham tales we shall take in our heads to tell him. I have actors, I have habits all ready, only let me alone.

CLÉONTE. But inform me of it.

COVIELLE. I am going to let you into the whole of it. Let's retire; there he comes.

Scene XV.

M. JOURDAIN (alone).

M. JOURDAIN. What a deuce can this mean? They have nothing but great lords to reproach me with; and I for my part see nothing so fine as keeping company with your great lords; there's nothing but honour and civility among 'em, and I would it had cost me two fingers of a hand to have been born a count or a marquis.

Scene XVI.

M. JOURDAIN, a LACKEY.

LACKEY. Sir, here's the count, and a lady whom he's handing in.

M. JOURDAIN. Good lack-a-day, I have some orders to give. Tell 'em that I'm acoming in a minute.

Scene XVII.

DORIMÈNE, DORANTE, a LACKEY.

LACKEY. My master says that he's acoming in a minute.

Scene XVIII.

DORIMÈNE, DORANTE.

DORANTE. 'Tis very well.

DORIMÈNE. I don't know, Dorante; I take a strange step herein suffering you to bring me to a house where I know nobody.

DORANTE. What place then, madame, would you have a lover choose to entertain you in, since, to avoid clamour, you neither allow of your own house nor mine?

DORIMÈNE. But you don't mention that I am every day insensibly engaged to receive too great proofs of your passion. In vain do I refuse things, you weary me out of resistance, and you have a civil kind of obstinacy which makes me come gently into whatsoever you please. Frequent visits commenced, declarations came next, which drew after them serenades and entertainments, which were followed by presents. I opposed all these things, but you are not disheartened, and you become master of my resolutions step by step. For my part, I can answer for nothing hereafter, and I believe in the end you will bring me to matrimony, from which I stood so far aloof.

DORANTE. Faith, madame, you ought to have been there already. You are a widow, and depend upon nobody but yourself. I am my own master, and love you more than my life. What does it stick at, then, that you should not, from this day forward, complete my happiness?

DORIMÈNE. Lack-a-day, Dorante, there must go a great many qualities on both sides, to make people live happily together; and two of the most reasonable persons in the world have often much ado to compose a union to both their satisfactions.

DORANTE. You're in the wrong, madame, to represent to yourself so many difficulties in this affair; and the experience you have had concludes nothing for the rest of the world.

DORIMÈNE. In short, I always abide by this. The expenses you put yourself to for me disturb me for two reasons; one is, they engage me more than I could wish; and the other is, I'm sure (no offence to you!) that you can't do this but you must incommode yourself, and I would not have you do that.

DORANTE. Fie, madame, these are trifles, and 'tis not by that—

DORIMÈNE. I know what I say; and, amongst other things, the diamond you forced me to take, is of value—

DORANTE. Nay, madame, pray don't enhance the value of a thing my love thinks unworthy of you: and permit—Here's the master of the house.

Scene XIX.

M. JOURDAIN, DORIMÈNE, DORANTE.

M. JOURDAIN. [*After having made two bows, finding himself too near* DORIMÈNE] A little farther, madame.

DORIMÈNE. How?

M. JOURDAIN. One step, if you please.

DORIMÈNE. What then?

M. JOURDAIN. Fall back a little for the third.

DORANTE. Monsieur Jourdain, madame, knows the world.

M. JOURDAIN. Madame, 'tis a very great honour that I am fortunate enough to be so happy, but to have the felicity that you should have the goodness to grant me the favour, to do me the honour, to honour me with the favour of your presence; and had I also the merit to merit a merit like yours, and that Heaven—envious of my good—had granted me—the advantage of being worthy—of—

DORANTE. Monsieur Jourdain, enough of this; my lady does not love great compliments, and she knows you are a man of wit. [*Aside to* DORIMÈNE] 'Tis a downright bourgeois, ridiculous enough, as you see, in his whole behaviour.

DORIMÈNE. [*Aside to* DORANTE] It is not very difficult to perceive it.

DORANTE. Madame, this is a very good friend of mine.

M. JOURDAIN. 'Tis too much honour you do me.

DORANTE. A very polite man.

DORIMÈNE. I have a great esteem for him.

M. JOURDAIN. I have done nothing yet, madame, to merit this favour.

DORANTE. [*Aside to* M. JOURDAIN] Take good care however not to speak to her of the diamond you gave her.

M. JOURDAIN. [*Aside to* DORANTE] Mayn't I ask her only how she likes it?

DORANTE. [*Aside to* M. JOURDAIN] How! Take special care you don't. 'Twould be villainous of you; and to act like a man of gallantry, you should make as if it were not you who made the present. [*Aloud*] Monsieur Jourdain, madame, says that he's in raptures to see you at his house.

DORIMÈNE. He does me a great deal of honour.

M. JOURDAIN. [*To* DORANTE] How am I obliged to you, sir, for speaking to her in that manner on my account!

DORANTE. [*Aside to* M. JOURDAIN] I have had a most terrible difficulty to get her to come hither.

M. JOURDAIN. [*To* DORANTE] I don't know how to thank you enough for it.

DORANTE. He says, madame, that he thinks you the most charming person in the world.

DORIMÈNE. 'Tis a great favour he does me.

M. JOURDAIN. Madame, it's you who do the favours, and—

DORANTE. Let's think of eating.

Scene XX.

M. JOURDAIN, DORIMÈNE, DORANTE, a LACKEY.

LACKEY. Everything is ready, sir.

DORANTE. Come, then, let us sit down to table; and fetch the musicians.

ACT IV.

Scene I.

DORIMÈNE, MONSIEUR JOURDAIN, DORANTE, three MUSICIANS, LACKEYS.

DORIMÈNE. How, Dorante? Why here's a most magnificent repast!

M. JOURDAIN. You are pleased to banter, madame; I would it were more worthy of your acceptance. [DORIMÈNE, M. JOURDAIN, DORANTE, and three MUSICIANS *sit down at the table*]

DORANTE. Monsieur Jourdain, madame, is in the right in what he says, and he obliges me in paying you, after so handsome a manner, the honours of his house. I agree with him that the repast is not worthy of you. As it was myself who ordered it, and I am not so clearly sighted in these affairs as certain of our friends, you have here no very learned feast; and you will find incongruities of good cheer in it, some barbarisms of good taste. Had our friend Damis had a hand here, everything had been done by rule; elegance and erudition would have run through the whole, and he would not have failed exaggerating all the regular pieces of the repast he gave you, and force you to own his great capacity in the science of good eating; he would have told you of bread *de rive*, with the golden kissing-crust, raised too all round with a crust that crumples tenderly in your teeth; of wine with a velvet sap, heightened with a smartness not too overpowering; of a breast of mutton stuffed with parsley; of a loin of veal *de rivière*, thus long, white, delicate, and which is a true almond paste between the teeth; of your partridges heightened with a surprising *goût*; and then by way of farce or entertainment, of a soup with jelly broth, fortified with a young plump turkey-pout, cantoned with pigeons, and garnished with white onions married to succory. But, for my part, I confess to you my ignorance; and, as Monsieur Jourdain has very well said, I wish the repast were more worthy of your acceptance.

DORIMÈNE. I make no other answer to this compliment than eating as I do.

M. JOURDAIN. Ah! what pretty hands are there!

DORIMÈNE. The hands are so so, Monsieur Jourdain; but you mean to speak of the diamond, which is very pretty.

M. JOURDAIN. I, madame? Marry, Heaven forbid I should speak of it; I should not act like a gentleman of gallantry, and the diamond is a very trifle.

DORIMÈNE. You are wondrous nice.

M. JOURDAIN. You have too much goodness—

DORANTE. [*Having made signs to* M. JOURDAIN] Come, give some wine to Monsieur Jourdain, and to those gentlemen who will do us the favour to sing us a catch.

DORIMÈNE. You give a wondrous relish to the good cheer by mixing music with it; I am admirably well regaled here.

M. JOURDAIN. Madame, it is not—

DORANTE. Monsieur Jourdain, let us listen to these gentlemen, they'll entertain us with something better than all we can possibly say.

FIRST AND SECOND MUSICIANS. [*Together, each with a glass in his hand*]

Put it round, my dear Phyllis, invert the bright glass;
    Oh what charms to the crystal those fingers impart!
You and Bacchus combined, all resistance surpass,
    And with passion redoubled have ravished my heart.
        'Twixt him, you, and me, my charmer, my fair,
        Eternal affection let's swear.
At the touch of those lips how he sparkles more bright!
    And his touch, in return, those lips does embellish:
I could quaff 'em all day, and drink bumpers all night.
What longing each gives me, what gusto, what relish!
        'Twixt him, You, and me, my charmer, my fair,
        Eternal affection let's swear.

SECOND AND THIRD MUSICIANS. [*Together*]

Since time flies so nimbly away,
    Come drink, my dear boys, drink about;
Let's husband him well while we may,
    For life may be gone before the mug's out.
When Charon has got us aboard,
    Our drinking and wooing are past;
We ne'er to lose time can afford,
    For drinking's a trade not always to last.
Let your puzzling rogues in the schools,
    Dispute of the *bonum* of man;
Philosophers dry are but fools
    The secret is this: drink, drink off your can.
When Charon has got us aboard,
    Our drinking and wooing are past;

We ne'er to lose time can afford,
For drinking's a trade not always to last.

ALL THREE. [*Together*]

Why bob there! some wine, boys! come fill the glass, fill,
Round and round let it go, till we bid it stand still.

DORIMÈNE. I don't think anything can be better sung; and 'tis extremely fine.

M. JOURDAIN. I see something here though, madame, much finer.

DORIMÈNE. Hey! Monsieur Jourdain is more gallant than I thought he was.

DORANTE. How, madame! who do you take Monsieur Jourdain for?

M. JOURDAIN. I wish she would take me for what I could name.

DORIMÈNE. Again?

DORANTE. [*To* DORIMÈNE] You don't know him.

M. JOURDAIN. She shall know me whenever she pleases.

DORIMÈNE. Oh! Too much.

DORANTE. He's one who has a repartee always at hand. But you don't see, madame, that Monsieur Jourdain eats all the pieces you have touched.

DORIMÈNE. Monsieur Jourdain is a man that I am charmed with.

M. JOURDAIN. If I could charm your heart, I should be—

Scene II.

MME. JOURDAIN, M. JOURDAIN, DORIMÈNE, DORANTE, SINGERS, LACKEYS.

MME. JOURDAIN. Hey-day! why here's a jolly company of you, and I see very well you did not expect me. It was for this pretty affair, then, Monsieur Husband o' mine, that you were in such a violent hurry to pack me off to dine with my sister; I just now found a play-house below, and here I find a dinner fit for a wedding. Thus it is you spend your money, and thus it is you feast the ladies in my absence, and present 'em with music and a play, whilst I'm sent abroad in the meantime.

DORANTE. What do you mean, Madame Jourdain? and what's your fancy to take it into your head that your husband spends his money, and that 'tis he who entertains my lady? Know, pray, that 'tis I do it, that he only lends me his house, and that you ought to consider a little better what you say.

M. JOURDAIN. Yes, Madame Impertinence, 'tis the count that presents the lady with all this, who is a person of quality. He does me the honour to borrow my house, and is pleased to let me be with him.

MME. JOURDAIN. 'Tis all stuff, this. I know what I know.

DORANTE. Madame Jourdain, take your best spectacles, take 'em.

MME. JOURDAIN. I've no need of spectacles, sir, I see clear enough; I've smelt things out a great while ago, I am no ass. 'Tis base in you, who are a great lord, to lend a helping hand, as you do, to the follies of my husband. And you, madame, who are a great lady, 'tis neither handsome nor honest in you to sow dissension in a family, and to suffer my husband to be in love with you.

DORIMÈNE. What can be the meaning of all this? Go, Dorante, 'tis wrong in you to expose me to the silly visions of this raving woman.

DORANTE. Madame, why madame, where are you running?

M. JOURDAIN. Madame—My lord, make my excuses to her and endeavour to bring her back.

Scene III.

MME. JOURDAIN, M. JOURDAIN, LACKEYS.

M. JOURDAIN. [*To* MME. JOURDAIN] Ah! impertinent creature as you are, these are your fine doings; you come and affront me in the face of all the world, and drive people of quality away from my house.

MME. JOURDAIN. I value not their quality.

M. JOURDAIN. [LACKEYS *take away the table*] I don't know what hinders me, you plaguy hussy, from splitting your skull with the fragments of the feast you came here to disturb.

MME. JOURDAIN. [*Going*] I despise all this. I defend my own rights, and I shall have all the wives on my side.

M. JOURDAIN. You do well to get out of the way of my fury.

Scene IV.

M. JOURDAIN (alone).

She came here at a most unlucky time. I was in the humour of saying fine things, and never did I find myself so witty. What have we got here?

Scene V.

M. JOURDAIN, COVIELLE (in disguise).

COVIELLE. Sir, I don't know whether I have the honour to be known to you.

M. JOURDAIN. No, sir.

COVIELLE. I have seen you when you were not above thus tall.

M. JOURDAIN. Me?

COVIELLE. Yes. You were one of the prettiest children in the world; and all the ladies used to take you in their arms to kiss you.

M. JOURDAIN. To kiss me?

COVIELLE. Yes, I was an intimate friend of the late gentleman your father.

M. JOURDAIN. Of the late gentleman my father!

COVIELLE. Yes. He was a very honest gentleman.

M. JOURDAIN. What is't you say?

COVIELLE. I say that he was a very honest gentleman.

M. JOURDAIN. My father?

COVIELLE. Yes.

M. JOURDAIN. Did you know him very well?

COVIELLE. Certainly.

M. JOURDAIN. And did you know him for a gentleman?

COVIELLE. Without doubt.

M. JOURDAIN. I don't know then what the world means.

COVIELLE. How?

M. JOURDAIN. There is a stupid sort of people who would face me down that he was a tradesman.

COVIELLE. He a tradesman? 'Tis mere scandal; he never was one. All that he did was, that he was very obliging, very officious, and as he was a great connoisseur in stuffs, he used to pick them up everywhere, have 'em carried to his house, and gave 'em to his friends for money.

M. JOURDAIN. I'm very glad of your acquaintance, that you may bear witness that my father was a gentleman.

COVIELLE. I'll maintain it in the face of all the world.

M. JOURDAIN. You will oblige me. What business brings you here?

COVIELLE. Since my acquaintance with the late gentleman your father, honest gentleman, as I was telling you, I have travelled round the world.

M. JOURDAIN. Round the world?

COVIELLE. Yes.

M. JOURDAIN. I fancy 'tis a huge way off, that same country.

COVIELLE. Most certainly. I have not been returned from these tedious travels of mine but four days. And because I have all interest in everything that concerns you, I come to tell you the best news in the world.

M. JOURDAIN. What?

COVIELLE. You know that the son of the Great Turk is here.

M. JOURDAIN. I? No.

COVIELLE. How? He has a most magnificent train. All the world goes to see him, and he has been received in this country as a person of importance.

M. JOURDAIN. In troth, I did not know that.

COVIELLE. What is of advantage to you in this affair is that he is in love with your daughter.

M. JOURDAIN. The son of the Great Turk?

COVIELLE. Yes, and wants to be your son-in-law.

M. JOURDAIN. My son-in-law, the son of the Great Turk?

COVIELLE. The son of the Great Turk your son-in-law. As I have been to see him, and perfectly understand his language, he held a conversation with me; and after some other discourse, says he to me: "Acciam croc soler, onch alla moustaph gidelum amanahem varahini oussere carbulath." That is to say, "Have you not seen a young handsome person, who is the daughter of Monsieur Jourdain, a gentleman of Paris?"

M. JOURDAIN. The son of the Great Turk said that of me?

COVIELLE. Yes, as I made answer to him that I knew you particularly well, and that I had seen your daughter. Ah, says he to me, "Marababa sahem"; that is to say, "Ah! how am I enamoured with her!"

M. JOURDAIN. "Marababa sahem" means: "Ah! how am I enamoured with her?"

COVIELLE. Yes.

M. JOURDAIN. Marry, you did well to tell me so, for as for my part, I should never have believed that "Marababa sahem" had meant, "Ah! how am I enamoured with her!" 'Tis an admirable language, this same Turkish!

COVIELLE. More admirable than one can believe. Do you know very well what is the meaning of "Cacaramouchen"?

M. JOURDAIN. "Cacaramouchen"? No.

COVIELLE. 'Tis as if you should say, "My dear soul."

M. JOURDAIN. "Cacaramouchen" means, "My dear soul?"

COVIELLE. Yes.

M. JOURDAIN. Why, 'tis very wonderful! "Cacaramouchen—my dear soul." Would one ever have thought it? I am perfectly confounded at it.

COVIELLE. In short, to finish my embassy, he comes to demand your daughter in marriage; and to have a father-in-law who should be suitable to him, he designs to make you a Mamamouchi, which is a certain grand dignity of his country.

M. JOURDAIN. Mamamouchi?

COVIELLE. Yes, Mamamouchi; that is to say, in our language, a Paladin. Paladin is your ancient—Paladin, in short—there's nothing in the world more noble than this; and you will rank with the grandest lord upon earth.

M. JOURDAIN. The son of the Great Turk does me a great deal of honour, and I desire you would carry me to him, to return him my thanks.

COVIELLE. How? Why he's just acoming hither.

M. JOURDAIN. Is he acoming hither?

COVIELLE. Yes. And he brings all things along with him for the ceremony of your dignity.

M. JOURDAIN. He's main hasty.

COVIELLE. His love will suffer no delay.

M. JOURDAIN. All that perplexes me, in this case, is that my daughter is an obstinate hussy who has took into her head one Cléonte, and vows she'll marry no person besides him.

COVIELLE. She'll change her opinion when she sees the son of the Grand Turk; and then there happens here a very marvellous adventure, that is, that the son of the Grand Turk resembles this Cléonte, with a trifling difference. I just now came from him, they showed him me; and the love she bears for one may easily pass to the other, and—I hear him coming; there he is.

Scene VI.

CLÉONTE (dressed as a Turk), three PAGES (bearing CLÉONTE's Turkish waistcoat), M. JOURDAIN, COVIELLE.

CLÉONTE. Ambousahim oqui boraf, Iordina, salamalequi.

COVIELLE. [*To* M. JOURDAIN] That is to say, Monsieur Jourdain, "May your heart be all the year like a rose-tree in flower!" These are obliging ways of speaking in that country.

M. JOURDAIN. I am His Turkish Highness's most humble servant.

COVIELLE. Carigar camboto oustin moraf.

CLÉONTE. Oustin yoc catamalequi basum base alla moran.

COVIELLE. He says, "Heaven give you the strength of lions and the prudence of serpents!"

M. JOURDAIN. His Turkish Highness does me too much honour; and I wish him all manner of prosperity.

COVIELLE. Ossa binamin sadoc babally oracaf ouram.

CLÉONTE. Bel-men.

COVIELLE. He says that you should go quickly with him to prepare yourself for the ceremony, in order afterwards to see your daughter and to conclude the marriage.

M. JOURDAIN. So many things in two words?

COVIELLE. Yes, the Turkish language is much in that way; it says a great deal in a few words. Go quickly where he desires you.

Scene VII.

COVIELLE (alone).

COVIELLE. Ha, ha, ha. I'faith, this is all absolutely droll. What a dupe! Had he had his part by heart, he could not have played it better. O, ho!

Scene VIII.

DORANTE, COVIELLE.

COVIELLE. I beseech you, sir, lend us a helping hand here, in a certain affair which is in agitation.

DORANTE. Ah! ah! Covielle, who could have known thee? How art thou trimmed out there!

COVIELLE. You see, ha, ha!

DORANTE. What do ye laugh at?

COVIELLE. At a thing, sir, that well deserves it.

DORANTE. What?

COVIELLE. I could give you a good many times, sir, to guess the stratagem we are making use of with Monsieur Jourdain, to bring him over to give his daughter to my master.

DORANTE. I don't at all guess the stratagem, but I guess it will not fail of its effect, since you undertake it.

COVIELLE. I know, sir, you are not unacquainted with the animal.

DORANTE. Tell me what it is.

COVIELLE. Be at the trouble of withdrawing a little farther off, to make room for what I see acoming. You will see one part of the story whilst I give you a narration of the rest.

Scene IX.

THE TURKISH CEREMONY

The MUFTI, DERVISHES, TURKS (assisting the MUFTI), SINGERS, and DANCERS.

Six TURKS enter gravely, two and two, to the sound of instruments. They bear three carpets, with which they dance in several figures, and then lift them up very high. THE TURKS, singing, pass under the carpets and range themselves on each side of the stage. The MUFTI, accompanied by DERVISHES, closes the march.

Then THE TURKS spread the carpets on the ground and kneel down upon them, the MUFTI and the DERVISHES standing in the middle of them; while the MUFTI invokes Mahomet in dumb contortions and grimaces, THE TURKS prostrate themselves to the ground, singing "Allah," raising their hands to heaven, singing "Allah", and so continuing alternately to the end of the invocation, when they all rise up, singing "Allah hu-akbar."

Scene X.

MUFTI, DERVISHES, TURKS (who sing and dance), M. JOURDAIN (dressed in Turkish style, his head shaved, without turban or saber).

MUFTI. [*To* M. JOURDAIN]
If thou understandest,
Answer,
If thou dost not understand,
Hold thy peace, hold thy peace.

I am Mufti,
    Thou! who thou art
I don't know:
    Hold thy peace, hold thy peace.

Scene XI.

MUFTI, DERVISHES, TURKS (who sing and dance).

MUFTI. Say, Turk, who is this,
    An Anabaptist, an Anabaptist?
THE TURKS. No.
MUFTI. A Zwinglian?
THE TURKS. No.
MUFTI. A Coffite?
THE TURKS. No.
MUFTI. A Hussite? A Morist? A Fronist?
THE TURKS. No, no, no.
MUFTI. No, no, no. Is he a Pagan?
THE TURKS. No.
MUFTI. A Lutheran?
THE TURKS. No.
MUFTI. A Puritan?
THE TURKS. No.
MUFTI. A Brahmin? A Moffian? A Zurian?
THE TURKS. No, no, no.
MUFTI. No, no, no. A Mahometan, a Mahometan?
THE TURKS. There you have it, there you have it.
MUFTI. How is he called? How is he called?
THE TURKS. Jourdain, Jourdain.
MUFTI. [*Dancing*] Jourdain! Jourdain!
THE TURKS. Jourdain, Jourdain.
MUFTI.
    To Mahomet for Jourdain
    I pray night and day,
    That he would make a Paladin
    Of Jourdain, of Jourdain.

Give him a turban, and give a sabre,
With a galley and a brigantine,
To defend Palestine.
To Mahomet for Jourdain
I pray night and day.

[*To* THE TURKS] Is Jourdain a good Turk?

THE TURKS. That he is, that he is.

MUFTI. [*Singing and dancing*]

Hou la ba, ba la chou, ba la ba, ba la da.

THE TURKS.

Hou la ba, ba la chou, ba la ba, ba la da.

Scene XII.

TURKS (who sing and dance).

Scene XIII.

MUFTI, DERVISHES, M. JOURDAIN, TURKS (who sing and dance).

The MUFTI returns with the State Turban, which is of an immeasurable largeness, garnished with lighted wax candles, four or five rows deep, accompanied by two DERVISHES, bearing the Koran, with comic caps garnished also with lighted candles.

The two other DERVISHES lead up M. JOURDAIN and place him on his knees with his hands to the ground so that his back, on which the Koran is placed, may serve for a desk to the MUFTI, who makes a second burlesque invocation, knitting his eyebrows, striking his hands sometimes upon the Koran, and tossing over the leaves with precipitation, after which, lifting up his hands, and crying with a loud voice, *Hoo.*

During this second invocation the assistant TURKS, bowing down and raising themselves alternately, sing likewise,

HOO, HOO, HOO.

M. JOURDAIN. [*After they have taken the Koran off his back*] Ouf!

MUFTI. [*To* M. JOURDAIN] Thou wilt not be a knave?

THE TURKS. No, no, no.

MUFTI. Not be a thief?

THE TURKS. No, no, no.

MUFTI. [*To* THE TURKS] Give the turban.

THE TURKS. [*Putting the turban on* M. JOURDAIN*'s head*]

Thou wilt not be a knave?

No, no, no.

Not be a thief?

No, no, no.

Give the turban.

MUFTI. [*Giving the sabre to* M. JOURDAIN]

Be brave, be no scoundrel,

Take the sabre.

THE TURKS. [*Drawing their sabres*]

Be brave, be no scoundrel,

Take the sabre.

[THE TURKS*, dancing, strike* M. JOURDAIN *several times with their sabres, to music*]

MUFTI.

Give, give

The bastonade.

THE TURKS.

Give, give

The bastonade.

[THE TURKS*, dancing, give* M. JOURDAIN *several strokes with a cudgel, to music*]

MUFTI.

Don't think it a shame,

This is the last affront.

THE TURKS.

Don't think it a shame,

This is the last affront.

[*The* MUFTI *begins a third invocation. The* DERVISHES *support him with great respect, after which* THE TURKS*, singing and dancing round the* MUFTI*, retire with him and lead off* M. JOURDAIN.]

ACT V.

Scene I.

MME. JOURDAIN, M. JOURDAIN.

MME. JOURDAIN. Bless us all! Mercy upon us! What have we got here? What a figure! What! dressed to go a-mumming, and is this a time to go masked? Speak therefore, what does this mean? Who has trussed you up in this manner?

M. JOURDAIN. Do but see the impertinent slut, to speak after this manner to a Mamamouchi.

MME. JOURDAIN. How's that?

M. JOURDAIN. Yes, you must show me respect now I am just made a Mamamouchi.

MME. JOURDAIN. What d'ye mean with your Mamamouchi?

M. JOURDAIN. Mamamouchi, I tell you. I am a Mamamouchi.

MME. JOURDAIN. What beast is that?

M. JOURDAIN. Mamamouchi, that is to say, in our language, a Paladin.

MME. JOURDAIN. A Paladin? Are you of an age to be a morris-dancer?

M. JOURDAIN. What an ignoramus! I say, Paladin. Tis a dignity of which I have just now gone through the ceremony.

MME. JOURDAIN. What ceremony then?

M. JOURDAIN. Mahometa per Jordina.

MME. JOURDAIN. What does that mean?

M. JOURDAIN. Jordina, that is to say, Jourdain.

MME. JOURDAIN. Well, how Jourdain?

M. JOURDAIN. Voler far un Paladina de Jordina.

MME. JOURDAIN. What?

M. JOURDAIN. Dar turbanta con galera.

MME. JOURDAIN. What's the meaning of that?

M. JOURDAIN. Per deffender Palestina.

MME. JOURDAIN. What is it you would say?

M. JOURDAIN. Dara, dara, bastonnara.

MME. JOURDAIN. What is this same jargon?

M. JOURDAIN. Non tener honta, questa star l'ultima affronta.

MME. JOURDAIN. What in the name of wonder can all this be?

M. JOURDAIN. [*Singing and dancing*]

Hou la ba, ba la chou, ba la ba, ba la da. [*Falls down to the ground*]

MME. JOURDAIN. Alas and well-a-day! My husband is turned fool.

M. JOURDAIN. [*Getting up and walking off*] Peace! insolence, show respect to Monsieur Mamamouchi.

MME. JOURDAIN. [*Alone*] How could he lose his senses? I must run and prevent his going out. [*Seeing* DORIMÈNE *and* DORANTE] So, so, here come the rest of our gang. I see nothing but vexation on all sides.

Scene II.

DORANTE, DORIMÈNE.

DORANTE. Yes, madame, you'll see the merriest thing that can be seen; and I don't believe it's possible, in the whole world, to find another man so much a fool as this here. And besides, madame, we must endeavour to promote Cléonte's amour and to countenance his masquerade. He's a very pretty gentleman and deserves that one should interest one's self in his favour.

DORIMÈNE. I've a very great value for him, and he deserves good fortune.

DORANTE. Besides, we have here, madame, an entertainment that will suit us, and which we ought not to suffer to be lost; and I must by all means see whether my fancy will succeed.

DORIMÈNE. I saw there magnificent preparations, and these are things, Dorante, I can no longer suffer. Yes, I'm resolved to put a stop, at last, to your profusions; and to break off all the expenses you are at on my account, I have determined to marry you out of hand. This is the real secret of the affair, and all these things end, as you know, with marriage.

DORANTE. Ah! madame, is it possible you should form so kind a resolution in my favour?

DORIMÈNE. I only do it to prevent you from ruining yourself; and without this, I see plainly that before 'tis long you won't be worth a groat.

DORANTE. How am I obliged to you, madame, for the care you take to preserve my estate! 'Tis entirely at your service, as well as my heart, and you may use both of 'em just in the manner you please.

DORIMÈNE. I shall make a proper use of them both. But here comes your man; an admirable figure.

Scene III.

M. JOURDAIN, DORANTE, DORIMÈNE.

DORANTE. Sir, my lady and I are come to pay our homage to your new dignity, and to rejoice with you at the marriage you are concluding betwixt your daughter and the son of the Grand Turk.

M. JOURDAIN. [*Bowing first in the Turkish manner*] Sir, I wish you the force of serpents and the wisdom of lions.

DORIMÈNE. I was exceeding glad to be one of the first, sir, who should come and congratulate you upon the high degree of glory to which you are raised.

M. JOURDAIN. Madame, I wish your rose-tree may flower all the year round; I am infinitely obliged to you for interesting yourselves in the honour that's paid me; and I am greatly rejoiced to see you returned hither, that I may make my most humble excuses for the impertinence of my wife.

DORIMÈNE. That's nothing at all, I can excuse a commotion of this kind in her; your heart ought to be precious to her, and 'tis not at all strange the possession of such a man as you are should give her some alarms.

M. JOURDAIN. The possession of my heart is a thing you have entirely gained.

DORANTE. You see, madame, that Monsieur Jourdain is none of those people whom prosperity blinds, and that he knows, in all his grandeur, how to own his friends.

DORIMÈNE. 'Tis the mark of a truly generous soul.

DORANTE. Where is His Turkish Highness? We should be glad, as your friends, to pay our devoirs to him.

M. JOURDAIN. There he comes, and I have sent to bring my daughter to join hands with him.

Scene IV.

M. JOURDAIN, DORIMÈNE, DORANTE, CLÉONTE (dressed as a Turk).

DORANTE. [*To* CLÉONTE] Sir, we come to compliment Your Highness, as friends of the gentleman your father-in-law, and to assure you, with respect, of our most humble services.

M. JOURDAIN. Where's the dragoman, to tell him who you are and make him understand what you say? You shall see that he'll answer you, and he speaks Turkish marvellously. Hola! there; where the deuce is he gone? [*To* CLÉONTE] Stref, strif, strof, straf.

The gentleman is a

grande segnore, grande segnore, grande segnore;

and madame is a

granda dama, granda dama.

[*Seeing he cannot make himself be understood*] Lack-a-day! [*To* CLÉONTE] Sir, he be a French Mamamouchi, and madame a French Mamamouchess. I can't speak plainer. Good, here's the dragoman.

Scene V.

M. JOURDAIN, DORIMÈNE, CLÉONTE (dressed as a Turk), COVIELLE (in disguise).

M. JOURDAIN. Where do you run? We can say nothing without you. [*Pointing to* CLÉONTE] Inform him a little that the gentleman and lady are persons of great quality who come to pay their compliments to him, as friends of mine, and to assure him of their services. [*To* DORIMÈNE *and* DORANTE] You shall see how he will answer.

COVIELLE. Alabala crociam, acci boram alabamen.

CLÉONTE. Catalequi tubal ourin soter amalouchan.

M. JOURDAIN. [*To* DORIMÈNE *and* DORANTE] Do ye see?

COVIELLE. He says that the rain of prosperity waters, at all seasons, the garden of your family.

M. JOURDAIN. I told you that he speaks Turkish.

DORANTE. This is admirable.

Scene VI.

LUCILE, CLÉONTE, M. JOURDAIN, DORIMÈNE, DORANTE, COVIELLE.

M. JOURDAIN. Come, daughter, come nearer, and give the gentleman your hand who does you the honour of demanding you in marriage.

LUCILE. What's the matter, father, how are you dressed here? What! are you playing a comedy?

M. JOURDAIN. No, no, 'tis no comedy, 'tis a very serious affair; and the most honourable for you that possibly can be wished. [*Pointing to* CLÉONTE] This is the husband I bestow upon you.

LUCILE. Upon me, father?

M. JOURDAIN. Yes, upon you. Come, take him by the hand, and thank Heaven for your good fortune.

LUCILE. I won't marry.

M. JOURDAIN. I'll make you; am I not your father?

LUCILE. I won't do it.

M. JOURDAIN. Here's a noise indeed! Come, I tell you. Your hand here.

LUCILE. No, father, I've told you before that there's no power can oblige me to take any other husband than Cléonte; and I am determined upon all extremities rather than— [*Discovering* CLÉONTE] 'Tis true that you are my father; I owe you absolute obedience; and you may dispose of me according to your pleasure.

M. JOURDAIN. Hah, I am charmed to see you return so readily to your duty; and it is a pleasure to me to have my daughter obedient.

Scene VII.

MME. JOURDAIN, CLÉONTE, M. JOURDAIN, LUCILE, DORANTE, DORIMÈNE, COVIELLE.

MME. JOURDAIN. How, how, what does this mean? They tell me you design to marry your daughter to a mummer.

M. JOURDAIN. Will you hold your tongue, impertinence? You're always coming to mix your extravagances with everything; there's no possibility of teaching you common sense.

MME. JOURDAIN. 'Tis you whom there's no teaching to be wise, and you go from folly to folly. What's your design, what would you do with this flock of people?

M. JOURDAIN. I design to marry my daughter to the son of the Grand Turk.

MME. JOURDAIN. To the son of the Grand Turk?

M. JOURDAIN. [*Pointing to* COVIELLE] Make your compliments to him by the dragoman there.

MME. JOURDAIN. I have nothing to do with the dragoman, and I shall tell him plainly to his face that he shall have none of my daughter.

M. JOURDAIN. Will you hold your tongue once more?

DORANTE. What, Madame Jourdain, do you oppose such an honour as this? Do you refuse His Turkish Highness for a son-in-law?

MME. JOURDAIN. Lack-a-day, sir, meddle you with your own affairs.

DORIMÈNE. 'Tis a great honour, 'tis by no means to be rejected.

MME. JOURDAIN. Madame, I desire you too not to give yourself any trouble about what no ways concerns you.

DORANTE. 'Tis the friendship we have for you that makes us interest ourselves in what is of advantage to you.

MME. JOURDAIN. I shall easily excuse your friendship.

DORANTE. There's your daughter consents to her father's pleasure.

MME. JOURDAIN. My daughter consent to marry a Turk?

DORANTE. Certainly.

MME. JOURDAIN. Can she forget Cléonte?

DORANTE. What would one not do to be a great lady?

MME. JOURDAIN. I would strangle her with my own hands, had she done such a thing as this.

M. JOURDAIN. Here's tittle-tattle in abundance. I tell you this marriage shall be consummated.

MME. JOURDAIN. And I tell you that it shall not be consummated.

M. JOURDAIN. What a noise is here?

LUCILE. Mother!

MME. JOURDAIN. Go, you are a pitiful hussy.

M. JOURDAIN. [*To* MME. JOURDAIN] What! do you scold her for being obedient to me?

MME. JOURDAIN. Yes, she belongs to me as well as you.

COVIELLE. [*To* MME. JOURDAIN] Madame.

MME. JOURDAIN. What would you say to me, you?

COVIELLE. One word.

MME. JOURDAIN. I've nothing to do with your word.

COVIELLE. [*To* M. JOURDAIN] Sir, would she hear me but one word in private, I'll promise you to make her consent to what you have a mind.

MME. JOURDAIN. I won't consent to it.

COVIELLE. Only hear me.

MME. JOURDAIN. No.

M. JOURDAIN. [*To* MME. JOURDAIN] Give him the hearing.

MME. JOURDAIN. No, I won't hear him.

M. JOURDAIN. He'll tell you—

MME. JOURDAIN. He shall tell me nothing.

M. JOURDAIN. Do but see the great obstinacy of the woman! Will it do you any harm to hear him?

COVIELLE. Only hear me; you may do what you please afterwards.

MME. JOURDAIN. Well, what?

COVIELLE. [*Aside to* MME. JOURDAIN] We have made signs to you, madame, this hour. Don't you see plainly that all is done purely to accommodate ourselves to the visions of your husband; that we are imposing upon him under this disguise, and that it is Cléonte himself who is the son of the Great Turk?

MME. JOURDAIN. [*Aside to* COVIELLE] Oh, oh?

COVIELLE. [*Aside to* MME. JOURDAIN] And that 'tis me, Covielle, who am the dragoman?

MME. JOURDAIN. [*Aside to* COVIELLE] Oh! in that case, I give up.

COVIELLE. [*Aside to* MME. JOURDAIN] Don't seem to know anything of the matter.

MME. JOURDAIN. [*Aloud*] Yes, 'tis all done, I consent to the marriage.

M. JOURDAIN. Ay, all the world submits to reason. [*To* MME. JOURDAIN] You would not hear him. I knew he would explain to you what the son of the Great Turk is.

MME. JOURDAIN. He has explained it to me sufficiently, and I'm satisfied with it. Let us send for a notary.

DORANTE. 'Tis well said. And, Madame Jourdain, that you may set your mind perfectly at rest, and that you should this day quit all jealousy which you may have entertained of the gentleman your husband, my lady and I shall make use of the same notary to marry us.

MME. JOURDAIN. I consent to that too.

M. JOURDAIN. [*Aside to* DORANTE] 'Tis to make her believe.

DORANTE. [*Aside to* M. JOURDAIN] We must by all means amuse her a little with this pretence.

M. JOURDAIN. Good, good. [*Aloud*] Let somebody go for the notary.

DORANTE. In the meantime, till he comes and has drawn up the contracts, let us see our entertainment, and give His Turkish Highness the diversion of it.

M. JOURDAIN. Well advised; come let us take our places.

MME. JOURDAIN. And Nicole?

M. JOURDAIN. I give her to the dragoman; and my wife, to whosoever pleases to take her.

COVIELLE. Sir, I thank you. [*Aside*] If it's possible to find a greater fool than this, I'll go and publish it in Rome.

Jonathan Swift

(1667–1745)

In Dublin, on the 30th of November of the year 1667, an impoverished widow named Abigail Erick Smith gave birth to a son. Named Jonathan for his seven-months-dead father—a cousin of the poet John Dryden, who, years later, would write to the now grown-up Jonathan, "Cousin Swift, you will never be a poet," a slight that Swift never forgave—he would spend his earliest years in near poverty. Nonetheless, his nurse doted on him, taking young Jonathan with her when she returned to her home in Whitehaven. When she came back to Dublin, three-year-old Jonathan could already read. Shortly thereafter, his mother returned to her own family in Leicestershire, leaving him in the custody of his uncle. Though educated at Ireland's best schools—first Kilkenny and then Trinity—Swift famously observed, "I am not of this vile country; I am an Englishman."

Complaints, in fact, are a commonplace observation by Swift about his early life. His comment about the "vile treatment by his closest relatives" no doubt refers to his uncle's decision to send him to Trinity (rather than his preferred choice, Oxford), where he received, in his own words, "the education of a dog."

In 1689, in escape from the havoc wrought by the arrival of James II in Ireland, Swift departed to his mother's family in Leicestershire. There he found employment first as a secretary, then as a tutor in the household of the wealthy Sir William Temple. He also met Esther Johnson, whom he named "Stella" and who would be perhaps Swift's closest friend until her death. His *Journal to Stella* (based on letters to both Esther Johnson and her friend, Rebecca Dingley) remains one of the richest sources of information about Swift's interior thoughts. Swift continued his education in England, receiving a Master's degree (he left Ireland with only his baccalaureate) in order to qualify for a position in the protestant Church of Ireland. He was ordained in 1694, and, with Temple's help, was able to secure a position as a clergyman at Kilroot, near Belfast. As he remained somewhat lacking in the normal degree of affection for one's native land, Swift was able to persuade Church authorities to grant him license for non-residence at Kilroot (while still receiving the "prebend" or salary). Two years passed before he received it, but he then returned to Leicestershire, and Temple.

In 1699 Temple died, leaving Swift 100 pounds, and effectively a position as his literary executor; Swift was to receive the profits of any of Temple's posthumous publications. He applied for a position as secretary to Lord Berkeley, hoping for a well-paying appointment, but was thwarted by a rival. He instead became Vicar of Laracor, and, in 1701, received his degree of Doctor of Divinity.

In 1704, Swift finally published, in a single volume, *Battle of the Books,* and a work he had begun even earlier, *Tale of a Tub*. The former was a scathing attack on pedantic scholarship; the latter a satire on religion, especially religious fanaticism. It was just this sort of fanaticism—and a hostility to the Whig policies that he believed showed hostility to the Church—that provided the raw material for a number of pamphlets Swift produced in the early 1700s, including "An Argument Against Abolishing Christianity" and the "Letter Concerning the Sacramental Test." In the meantime, Ireland retained its repulsive character for Swift, and he spent as much time as possible in England, developing friendships with Joseph Addison, Sir Richard Steele, William Congreve, and Alexander Pope. His opposition to the Whigs brought him into contact with the Tories, for whom he engaged in some political pamphleteering (not least because by doing so he hoped to improve his chances for social and material betterment). However, his inability to subscribe to an orthodoxy he did not possess once again prevented his advancement; friends who delighted in his intellect and wit were nonetheless not disposed to help . . . and Swift's already prickly temper was not improved by the experience.

In 1713 Queen Anne appointed Swift dean of St. Patrick's Cathedral in Dublin. It was not a warm welcome when he assumed office. Then Queen Anne died, George I took power, and the Tory ministry was replaced. Swift retired to his Dublin Cathedral (and aside from two trips back to England between 1726 and 1727, he was to live out his life in Ireland). There, he became involved in a "triangle" with Stella and the daughter of a Dublin merchant, Esther Vanhomrigh, who had followed him from London to Ireland. It is this Esther who becomes the "Vanessa" of his writings. There is no proof of any marriage between Stella and Swift, yet she viewed "Vanessa" as "the other woman." There are many theories and stories surrounding these three, but no clear evidence of their true relationship exists.

It is around this time that Swift first turns his pen to the defense of his until-now-not-very-well-loved home island, publishing pseudonymous pamphlets including, in 1720, a vicious denunciation of all things made in England, the "Proposal for the Universal Use of Irish Manufactures," and, four years later, the "Drapier's Letters."

It is also now that Swift began work on another book, the most famous—and greatest—satire in English literature, whose object, Swift admitted in a 1725 letter to Alexander Pope, was "to vex the world, not to divert it." He wanted it to be known, once and for all time, that he "hated and detested that animal called man." *Gulliver's Travels* was published in 1726, and was an immediate and massive success. "Perhaps," wrote Sir Walter Scott, "no work ever exhibited such general attractions for all classes." Voltaire was so taken with it that he became the driving force behind its translation into French.

"A Modest Proposal for Preventing the Children of Poor People in Ireland from Being a Burden to Their Parents or Country, and for Making Them Beneficial to the Public" was published in 1729. No better example can be found of Swift's by-now-complete misanthropy than this faux serious policy paper proposing that England's colonial policy toward Ireland be taken to its logical conclusion: Irish babies, in the *Proposal*, are not a drain on society's wealth, but a source of ready protein. He writes, "I have been assured by a very knowing American of my acquaintance in London, that a young healthy child well nursed is at a year old a most delicious, nourishing, and wholesome food, whether stewed, roasted, baked, or boiled; and I make no doubt that it will equally serve in a fricassee or a ragout . . ."

Among the many advantages—Swift cites half a dozen specifically—is that the policy, once implemented, would become a great inducement to marriage, for "men would become as fond of their wives during the time of their pregnancy as they are now of their mares in foal . . ." An attack on both English venality and Irish passivity, written with remarkable economy, savagery, and irony, it may be the most cited satirical essay in history. Nearly two hundred years after its publication, H.L. Mencken wrote of Swift, "He was simply a premature and lonely forerunner of the modern age—a Voltaire born in the wrong country and a couple of generations too soon . . . When he regarded *Homo sapiens* he did not see a god with a few lamentable defects; he saw a poor worm with no virtues at all, but only a crushing burden of follies, weaknesses, and imbecilities. He saw a coward and an idiot, a fraud and a scoundrel."

Jonathan Swift died on October 19, 1745. He was not quite seventy-eight years old, and had suffered more than two-thirds of his life from bouts of vertigo and ringing in the ears—a disease diagnosed retroactively as Meuniere's Disease, an affliction of the inner ear. Dozens of Swift's letters attest to the grief the disease caused him, finally convincing him that he was in danger of losing his sanity. His epitaph reads, in part: *Ubi Saeva Indignatio Ulterius Cor Lacerare Nequit Abi Viator* ("He has gone where fierce indignation can lacerate his heart no more") . . . but perhaps more telling is Swift's last will and testament, which specified a bequest to establish an Irish hospital for "ideots & lunaticks." No nation, he added, "wanted it so much."

A Modest Proposal for Preventing the Children of Poor People in Ireland from Being a Burden to Their Parents or Country, and for Making Them Beneficial to the Public.

IT IS A melancholy object to those who walk through this great town or travel in the country, when they see the streets, the roads, and cabin doors, crowded with beggars of the female sex, followed by three, four, or six children, all in rags and importuning every passenger for an alms. These mothers, instead of being able to work for their honest livelihood, are forced to employ all their time in strolling to beg sustenance for their helpless infants; who as they grow up either turn thieves for want of work, or leave their dear native country to fight for the pretender in Spain,[1] or sell themselves to the Barbadoes.

I think it is agreed by all parties that this prodigious number of children in the arms, or on the backs, or at the heels of their mothers, and frequently of their fathers, is in the present deplorable state of the kingdom a very great additional grievance; and therefore whoever could find out a fair, cheap, and easy method of making these children sound useful members of the commonwealth, would deserve so well of the public as to have his statue set up for a preserver of the nation.

But my intention is very far from being confined to provide only for the children of professed beggars; it is of a much greater extent, and shall take in the whole number of infants at a certain age who are born of parents in effect as little able to support them as those who demand our charity in the streets.

As to my own part, having turned my thoughts for many years upon this important subject, and maturely weighed the several schemes of our projectors,

I have always found them grossly mistaken in their computation. It is true, a child just dropped from its dam, may be supported by her milk for a solar year, with little other nourishment; at most not above the value of 2*s*., which the mother may certainly get, or the value in scraps by her lawful occupation of begging; and it is exactly at one year old that I propose to provide for them in such a manner as instead of being a charge upon their parents or the parish, or wanting food and raiment for the rest of their lives, they shall on the contrary contribute to the feeding, and partly to the clothing, of many thousands.

There is likewise another great advantage in my scheme, that it will prevent those voluntary abortions, and that horrid practice of women murdering their bastard children, alas, too frequent among us! sacrificing the poor innocent babes I doubt more to avoid the expense than the shame, which would move tears and pity in the most savage and inhuman breast.

The number of souls in this kingdom being usually reckoned one million and a half, of these I calculate there may be about 200,000 couple whose wives are breeders; from which number I subtract 30,000 couple who are able to maintain their own children, (although I apprehend there cannot be so many, under the present distresses of the kingdom;) but this being granted, there will remain 170,000 breeders. I again subtract 50,000 for those women who miscarry, or whose children die by accident or disease within the year. There only remain 120,000 children of poor parents annually born. The question therefore is, how this number shall be reared and provided for? which as I have already said under the present situation of affairs is utterly impossible by all the methods hitherto proposed. For we can neither employ them in handicraft or agriculture; we neither build houses (I mean in the country) nor cultivate land; they can very seldom pick up a livelihood by stealing, till they arrive at six years old, except where they are of towardly parts; although I confess they learn the rudiments much earlier; during which time, they can however be properly looked upon only as probationers; as I have been informed by a principal gentleman in the county of Cavan, who protested to me that he never knew above one or two instances under the age of six, even in a part of the kingdom so renowned for the quickest proficiency in that art.

I am assured by our merchants, that a boy or a girl before twelve years old is no saleable commodity; and even when they come to this age they will not yield above 3*l*. or 3*l*. 2*s*. 6*d*. at most on the exchange; which cannot turn to account either to the parents or kingdom, the charge of nutriment and rags having been at least four times that value.

I shall now, therefore humbly propose my own thoughts, which I hope will not be liable to the least objection.

I have been assured by a very knowing American of my acquaintance in London, that a young healthy child well nursed is at a year old a most delicious, nourishing, and wholesome food, whether stewed, roasted, baked, or boiled; and I make no doubt that it will equally serve in a fricassee or a ragout.

I do therefore humbly offer it to public consideration that of the 120,000 children already computed, 20,000 may be reserved for breed, whereof only one-fourth part to be males; which is more than we allow to sheep, black cattle or swine; and my reason is, that these children are seldom the fruits of marriage, a circumstance not much regarded by our savages, therefore one male will be sufficient to serve four females. That the remaining 100,000 may at a year old, be offered in sale to the persons of quality and fortune through the kingdom; always advising the mother to let them suck plentifully in the last month, so as to render them plump and fat for a good table. A child will make two dishes at an entertainment for friends; and when the family dines alone, the fore or hind quarter will make a reasonable dish, and seasoned with a little pepper or salt will be very good boiled on the fourth day, especially in winter.

A YOUNG HEALTHY CHILD WELL NURSED IS AT A YEAR OLD A MOST DELICIOUS, NOURISHING, AND WHOLESOME FOOD, WHETHER STEWED, ROASTED, BAKED, OR BOILED; AND I MAKE NO DOUBT THAT IT WILL EQUALLY SERVE IN A FRICASSEE OR A RAGOUT.

I have reckoned upon a medium that a child just born will weigh 12 pounds, and in a solar year, if tolerably nursed, will increase to 28 pounds.

I grant this food will be somewhat dear, and therefore very proper for landlords, who, as they have already devoured most of the parents, seem to have the best title to the children.

Infant's flesh will be in season throughout the year, but more plentifully in March, and a little before and after: for we are told by a grave author, an eminent French physician, that fish being a prolific diet, there are more children born in Roman catholic countries about nine months after Lent than at any other season; therefore, reckoning a year after Lent, the markets will be more glutted than usual, because the number of popish infants is at least three to one in this kingdom: and therefore it will have one other collateral advantage, by lessening the number of papists among us.

I have already computed the charge of nursing a beggar's child (in which list I reckon all cottagers, labourers, and four-fifths of the farmers) to be about 2*s*. per annum, rags included; and I believe no gentleman would repine to give 10*s*. for the carcass of a good fat child, which as I have said will make four dishes of excellent nutritive meat, when he has only some particular friend or his own family to dine with him. Thus the squire will learn to be a good landlord, and grow popular among his tenants; the mother will have 8*s*. net profit, and be fit for work till she produces another child.

Those who are more thrifty (as I must confess the times require) may flay the carcass; the skin of which artificially dressed will make admirable gloves for ladies, and summer boots for fine gentlemen.

As to our city of Dublin, shambles may be appointed for this purpose in the most convenient parts of it, and butchers we may be assured will not be wanting; although I rather recommend buying the children alive than dressing them hot from the knife as we do roasting pigs.

A very worthy person, a true lover of his country and whose virtues I highly esteem, was lately pleased in discoursing on this matter to offer a refinement upon my scheme. He said that many gentlemen of this kingdom, having of late destroyed their deer, he conceived that the want of venison might be well supplied by the bodies of young lads and maidens, not exceeding 14 years of age nor under 12; so great a number of both sexes in every country being now ready to starve for want of work and service; and these to be disposed of by their parents if alive, or otherwise by their nearest relations. But with due deference to so excellent a friend and so deserving a patriot, I cannot be altogether in his sentiments; for as to the males, my American acquaintance assured me, from frequent experience, that their flesh was generally tough and lean, like that of our schoolboys by continual exercise, and their taste disagreeable; and to fatten them would not answer the charge. Then as to the females, it would I think with humble submission be a loss to the public, because they soon would become breeders themselves: and besides, it is not improbable that some scrupulous people might be apt to censure such a practice, (although indeed very unjustly,) as a little bordering upon cruelty; which, I confess, has always been with me the strongest objection against any project, how well soever intended.

But in order to justify my friend, he confessed that this expedient was put into his head by the famous Psalmanazar,[2] a native of the island Formosa, who came from thence to London about twenty years ago; and in conversation told my friend, that in his country when any young person happened to be put to death, the executioner sold the carcass to persons of quality as a prime dainty; and that in his time the body of a plump girl of 15, who was crucified for an attempt to poison the emperor, was sold to his imperial majesty's prime minister of state, and other great mandarins of the court, in joints from the gibbet, at 400 crowns. Neither indeed can I deny, that if the same use were made of several plump young girls in this town, who without one single groat to their fortunes cannot stir abroad without a chair, and appear at playhouse and assemblies in foreign fineries which they never will pay for, the kingdom would not be the worse.

Some persons of a desponding spirit are in great concern about that vast number of poor people, who are aged, diseased, or maimed, and I have been desired to employ my thoughts what course may be taken to ease the nation of so grievous an encumbrance. But I am not in the least pain upon that matter, because it is very well known that they are every day dying and rotting by cold and famine, and filth and vermin, as fast as can be reasonably expected. And as to the young labourers they are now in almost as hopeful a condition; they cannot get work, and consequently pine away for want of nourishment, to a degree that if at any time they are accidentally hired to common labour, they have not strength to perform it; and thus the country and themselves are happily delivered from the evils to come.

I have too long digressed and therefore shall return to my subject. I think the advantages by the proposal which I have made, are obvious and many as well as of the highest importance.

For first, as I have already observed, it would greatly lessen the number of papists, with whom we are yearly over-run, being the principal breeders of the nation as well as our most dangerous enemies; and who stay at home on purpose to deliver the kingdom to the pretender, hoping to take their advantage by the absence of so many good protestants, who have chosen rather to leave their country than stay at home and pay tithes against their conscience to an episcopal curate.

Secondly, The poorer tenants will have something valuable of their own, which by law may be made liable to distress and help to pay their landlord's rent, their corn and cattle being already seized, and money a thing unknown.

Thirdly, Whereas the maintenance of 100,000 children, from two years old and upward, cannot be computed at less than 10*s*. a-piece per annum, the nation's stock will be thereby increased 50,000*l*. per annum, beside the profit of a new dish introduced to the tables of all gentlemen of fortune in the kingdom who have any refinement in taste. And the money will circulate among ourselves, the goods being entirely of our own growth and manufacture.

Fourthly, The constant breeders, beside the gain of 8*s*. sterling per annum by the sale of their children, will be rid of the charge of maintaining them after the first year.

Fifthly, This food would likewise bring great custom to taverns; where the vintners will certainly be so prudent as to procure the best receipts for dressing it to perfection, and consequently have their houses frequented by all the fine gentlemen, who justly value themselves upon their knowledge in good eating: and a skilful cook, who understands how to oblige his guests, will contrive to make it as expensive as they please.

Sixthly, This would be a great inducement to marriage, which all wise nations have either encouraged by rewards or enforced by laws and penalties. It would increase the care and tenderness of mothers toward their children, when they were sure of a settlement for life to the poor babes, provided in some sort by the public, to their annual profit or expense. We should see an honest emulation among the married women, which of them could bring the fattest child to the market. Men would become as fond of their wives during the time of their pregnancy as they are now of their mares in foal, their cows in calf, their sows when they are ready to farrow; nor offer to beat or kick them (as is too frequent a practice) for fear of a miscarriage.

Many other advantages might be enumerated. For instance, the addition of some thousand carcasses in our exportation of barreled beef, the propagation of swine's flesh, and improvement in the art of making good bacon, so much wanted among us by the great destruction of pigs, too frequent at our table; which are no way comparable in taste or magnificence to a well-grown, fat, yearling child, which roasted whole will make a considerable figure at a lord mayor's feast or any other public entertainment. But this and many others I omit, being studious of brevity.

Supposing that 1000 families in this city would be constant customers for infants' flesh, beside others who might have it at merry-meetings, particularly at weddings and christenings, I compute that Dublin would take off annually about 20,000 carcasses; and the rest of the kingdom (where probably they will be sold somewhat cheaper) the remaining 80,000.

I can think of no one objection that will possibly be raised against this proposal, unless it should be urged that the number of people will be thereby much lessened in the kingdom. This I freely own, and it was indeed one principal design in offering it to the world. I desire the reader will observe, that I calculate my remedy for this one individual kingdom of Ireland and for no other that ever was, is, or I think ever can be upon earth. Therefore let no man talk to me of other expedients: of taxing our absentees at 5*s*. a pound: of using neither clothes nor household furniture except what is of our own growth and manufacture: of utterly rejecting the materials and instruments that promote foreign luxury: of curing the expensiveness of pride, vanity, idleness, and gaming in our women: of introducing a vein of parsimony, prudence, and temperance: of learning to love our country, in the want of which we differ even from LAPLANDERS and the inhabitants of TOPINAMBOO: of quitting our animosities and factions, nor acting any longer like the Jews, who were murdering one another at the very moment their city was taken: of being a little cautious not to sell our country and conscience for nothing: of teaching landlords to have at least one degree of mercy toward their tenants: lastly, of putting a spirit of honesty, industry, and skill into our shopkeepers; who, if a resolution could now be taken to buy only our native goods, would immediately unite to cheat and exact upon us in the price, the measure, and the goodness, nor could ever yet be brought to make one fair proposal of just dealing though often and earnestly invited to it.

Therefore I repeat, let no man talk to me of these and the like expedients, till he has at least some glimpse of hope that there will be ever some hearty and sincere attempt to put them in practice.

But as to myself, having been wearied out for many years with offering vain, idle, visionary thoughts, and at length utterly despairing of success I fortunately fell upon this proposal; which, as it is wholly new, so it has something solid and real, of no expense and little trouble, full in our own power and whereby we can incur no danger in disobliging ENGLAND. For this kind of commodity will not bear exportation, the flesh being of too tender a consistence to admit a long continuance in salt, although perhaps I could name a country which would be glad to eat up our whole nation without it.

After all, I am not so violently bent upon my own opinion as to reject any offer proposed by wise men, which shall be found equally innocent, cheap, easy, and effectual. But before something of that kind shall be advanced in contradiction to my scheme, and offering a better, I desire the author or authors will be pleased maturely to consider two points. First, as things now stand, how they will be able to find food and raiment for 100,000 useless mouths and backs. And secondly, there being a round million of creatures in human figure throughout this kingdom, whose whole subsistence put into a common stock would leave them in debt 2,000,000*l*. sterling, adding those who are beggars by profession to the bulk of farmers, cottagers, and labourers, with the wives and children who are beggars in effect; I desire those politicians who dislike my overture, and may perhaps be so bold as to attempt an answer, that they will first ask the parents of these mortals, whether they would not at this day think it a great happiness to have been sold for food at a year old in the manner I prescribe, and thereby have avoided such a perpetual scene of misfortunes as they have since gone through by the oppression of landlords, the impossibility of paying rent without money or trade, the want of common sustenance, with neither house nor clothes to cover them from the inclemencies of the weather, and the most inevitable prospect of entailing the like or greater miseries upon their breed for ever.

I profess, in the sincerity of my heart, that I have not the least personal interest in endeavouring to promote this necessary work, having no other motive than the public good of my country, by advancing our trade, providing for infants, relieving the poor, and giving some pleasure to the rich. I have no children by which I can propose to get a single penny; the youngest being nine years old, and my wife past childbearing.

1. pretender in Spain] James Francis Edward Stuart (1688–1766), son of the deposed James II of England and claimant to the British throne. During his exile, he distinguished himself fighting for the French in the fighting for the Spanish Succession (1701–1714).

2. *Psalmanazar*] George Psalmanazar (c. 1679–1763), French literary imposter who "translated" the Church of England catechism and a book about Formosa (Taiwan) into "Formosan," a language he invented.

Alexander Pope

(1688–1744)

Alexander Pope was born on May 21, 1688, in London to Roman Catholic, middle-class parents. His father (who, along with Alexander's mother, was over forty years old) had prospered as a wholesale linen merchant and retired soon after Alexander's birth. The family was forced to move from London in 1700 by a statute requiring Catholics to live at least ten miles from London or Westminster. They relocated to Binfield, finding a community of Catholic families who were to figure prominently in Pope's later life. There, he met John Caryll, who would later urge him to write *The Rape of the Lock,* and Martha Blount, a woman to whom he often dedicated poetry and left the bulk of his estate. But while he bonded with other Catholics, his religion also put him out of reach of formal education. He received tutoring at home by priests and also attended Catholic schools (which, while illegal, existed in a few places) at Twyford, near Winchester, and at Hyde Park in London. Mostly, though, he was self-educated at home.

Tuberculosis of the bone, the disease that would become his lifelong affliction (he would turn the phrase and refer to "this long disease, my life"), became apparent when Pope was twelve. Over time, it caused some deformity; Sir Joshua Reynolds described him as "about four feet six high, very humpbacked and deformed." He suffered from constant headaches, shortness of breath, and blinding pain in his bones and muscles. It was a struggle to walk for long periods and do any normal physical activity, so he turned all of his energy toward cerebral exertions, namely reading and writing.

Pope's faith denied him opportunities, his health ruled out most occupations, and his appearance closed off many of life's pleasures so the youth turned to poetry, something well within his grasp. "As yet a child, nor yet a fool to fame/I lisp'd in numbers, for the numbers came." His parents encouraged his teenage "rhimes" and they provided financial support for him to follow his dream.

Pope was a voracious reader of Latin, Greek, French, and Italian and he taught himself aspects of these languages. He would also attempt to mimic the style of poets he admired. Pope was lucky enough to know some influential neighbors who introduced him to established writers, some former members of John Dryden's circle, notably William Wycherly, Henry Cromwell, and William Walsh. By 1705, when Pope was just seventeen, his "Pastorals" were on paper and being reviewed by these and other great literary minds. Two of these men brought "Pastorals" to the attention of Jacob Tonson—a leading poetry publisher—who published them in 1708 in his *Poetical Miscellanies.* By then, Pope was hard at work on a poem about the craft of writing; this piece became "An Essay on Criticism," which debuted in 1711. From this stunning verse poem sprang some of the most famous epigrams of our time: "To err is human, to forgive, divine," "A little learning is a dangerous thing," and "Fools rush in where angels fear to tread." Echoes of Horace, Boileau, and Quintilian are clearly heard in these verbal gems, yet to claim that they are derivative is to discount Pope's triumph in capturing the essence of one hundred years of critical thinking and illustrating how nature can be conveyed through art.

Pope's success brought him money, new friends, and a new outlet for expression: *The Spectator*, a journal that commented on public behavior and ethics using satire and witty finger-wagging. Influenced by a desire to mend a rift between two Catholic families with which he was acquainted, Pope published *The Rape of the Lock,* a potent satirical poem about the feud that started over a clipping of hair. Two cantos of the poem appeared in 1712, five in 1715. He wrote of this escalated quarrel in a mock-epic manner, treating the dispute as if it were the Greek-Trojan War, borrowing a bit from Homer. Using this approach reveals the participants and the society in which they moved as ridiculous, which was assuredly Pope's aim. The story is as follows: Lord Petre snipped off a lock of Arabella Fermor's hair and caused an estrangement between two previously close families. Lord Petre may have been a suitor of Arabella's, or there may have been some turmoil under the surface of this tight-knit group that the trivial incident uncovered.

The genius of the poem is its use of recurrent devices from the traditional epics to heighten the "drama." A standard trait of the epic is the hero/heroine's journey to the underworld; Pope includes this as a mock-heroic element in Canto IV: "No cheerful breeze this sullen region knows/The dreaded *East* is all the wind that blows/Here in a grotto, shelter'd close from air . . ." Another standard contrivance, the epic feast, is employed in Canto III: "Hither the Heroes and Nymphs resort/To taste awhile the Pleasures of a Court/In various Talk th' instructive Hours they past, Who gave a *Ball,* or paid the *Visit* last."

Although the poem made a big splash when it appeared, it read differently when Lord Petre chose another to wed, Catherine Warmsley, an heiress seven years younger and richer than Arabella. The language lives on but the buzz had died down by the time Pope revised the poem in 1717. Lord Petre had passed on due to smallpox and Arabella had married.

Pope and his parents moved from Binfield to Cheswick in 1716. His father died in 1716 and two years later he and his mother leased a villa on the Thames at Twickenham, where he would spend the remainder of his life.

During the next five years, Pope not only became the most celebrated poet of his day, he also repositioned the poet's place in the world. He had become what no other poet had been until now: independent and financially successful. As he himself said: "live and thrive/Indebted to no Prince or Peer alive." He could look upon lords as friends rather than patrons. He published *Works* in 1717. He published the great labor of his literary life, his translation of Homer's *Iliad* in a six-volume set, in 1720. Pope, Elijah Fenton, and William Broome translated *The Odyssey* and issued it in 1725. Both translations earned him 10,000 pounds. Yet with success comes criticism, which seemed unrelenting in Pope's case. His colorful personality and attacks on his perceived enemies didn't help. He also had a nasty habit of lying—about authorship of particularly vicious and licentious pieces, and about his ancestry. He was not one to give credit to friends or collaborators.

The caviling crescendo was reached with his edition of Shakespeare, amended to address contemporary tastes, which was soundly denounced by the scholar Lewis Theobald in his own book, *Shakespeare Restored*. Pope had tried to endure the vitriol with silence but he decided to retaliate and defend his stance (which he felt echoed civilized society). He published *The Dunciad,* a parody of the *Iliad* (dedicated to Jonathan Swift), which contains a character, the son of the Goddess of Dullness, modeled after Theobald.

For the next fifteen years until his death in 1744 at the age of fifty-six, Pope perfected his form as a satirist, publishing at least eleven poems adapting Horatian themes to current issues. He also reissued *The Dunciad* in 1743, substituting Colley Cibber, the poet laureate and recent foil, for the former nemesis Theobald. Yet it is his earlier work, his astounding command of iambic pentameter to craft such exquisite rhyming couplets, that makes him one of the most exceptional linguistic technicians and artists in the history of poetry.

TO MRS. ARABELLA FERMOR

MADAM,

IT WILL BE vain to deny that I have some Value for this Piece, since I dedicate it to You. Yet You may bear me Witness, it was intended only to divert a few young Ladies, who have good Sense and good Humour enough, to laugh not only at their Sex's little unguarded Follies, but at their own. But as it was communicated with the Air of a Secret, it soon found its Way into the World. An imperfect Copy having been offered to a Bookseller, You had the Good-Nature for my Sake to consent to the Publication of one more correct: This I was forced to before I had executed half my Design, for the *Machinery* was entirely wanting to compleat it.

The *Machinery*, Madam, is a term invented by the Criticks, to signify that Part which the Deities, Angels, or Daemons, are made to act in a Poem: For the ancient Poets are in one Respect like many modern Ladies: Let an Action be never so trivial in itself, they always make it appear of the utmost Importance. These Machines I determin'd to raise on a very new and odd Foundation, the *Rosicrucian* Doctrine of Spirits.

I know how disagreeable it is to make use of hard Words before a Lady: but 'tis so much the Concern of a Poet to have his Works understood, and particularly by your Sex, that You must give me leave to explain two or three difficult Terms.

The *Rosicrucians* are a People I must bring You acquainted with. The best Account I know of them is in a French Book called *Le Comte de Gabalis*, which both in its Title and Size is so like a Novel, that many of the Fair Sex have read it for one by Mistake. According to these Gentlemen the four Elements are inhabited by Spirits, which they call *Sylphs*, *Gnomes*, *Nymphs*, and *Salamanders*. The *Gnomes*, or Daemons of Earth, delight in Mischief: but the *Sylphs*, whose Habitation is Air, are the best-conditioned Creatures imaginable. For they say, any Mortals may enjoy the most intimate Familiarities with these gentle Spirits, upon a Condition very easy to all true *Adepts*, an inviolate Preservation of Chastity.

As to the following Canto's, all the Passages of them are as Fabulous, as the Vision at the Beginning, or the Transformation at the End; (except the Loss of your Hair, which I always name with Reverence.) The Human Persons are as Fictitious as the Airy ones; and the Character of *Belinda*, as it is now manag'd, resembles You in nothing but in Beauty.

If this Poem had as many Graces as there are in Your Person, or in Your Mind, yet I could never hope it should pass thro' the World half so Uncensured as You have done. But let its Fortune be what it will, mine is happy enough, to have given me this Occasion of assuring You that I am, with the truest Esteem,

Madam,
Your most Obedient
Humble Servant,
A. POPE.

The Rape of the Lock

CANTO I

WHAT DIRE OFFENCE from am'rous Causes springs,
What mighty Contests rise from trivial Things,
I sing—This verse to Caryll, Muse! is due;
This, ev'n *Belinda* may vouchsafe to view:

Slight is the Subject, but not so the Praise,
If She inspire, and He approve, my Lays.

Say what strange Motive, Goddess! cou'd compel
A well-bred *Lord* t' assault a gentle *Belle?*
Oh say what stranger Cause, yet unexplor'd,
Cou'd make a gentle *Belle* reject a *Lord?*
In tasks so bold, can little Men engage,
And in soft Bosoms, dwell such mighty Rage?

Sol through white Curtains shot a tim'rous Ray,
And ope'd those Eyes that must eclipse the Day:
Now Lap-dogs give themselves the rouzing Shake,
And sleepless Lovers, just at Twelve, awake:
Thrice rung the Bell, the Slipper knock'd the Ground,
And the press'd Watch return'd a silver sound,
Belinda still her downy Pillow prest,
Her guardian *Sylph* prolong'd the balmy rest.
'Twas he had summon'd to her silent Bed
The Morning Dream that hover'd o'er her Head.
A Youth more glitt'ring than a *Birth-night Beau*
(That ev'n in slumber caus'd her Cheek to glow)
Seem'd to her Ear his winning Lips to lay,
And thus in Whispers said, or seemed to say.

Fairest of Mortals, thou distinguish'd Care
Of thousand bright Inhabitants of Air!
If e'er one Vision touch'd thy infant Thought,
Of all the Nurse and all the Priest have taught,
Of airy Elves by Moonlight Shadows seen,
The silver Token, and the Circled Green,
Or Virgins visited by Angel-pow'rs
With Golden Crowns and Wreaths of heav'nly Flow'rs;
Hear and believe! thy own Importance know,
Nor bound thy narrow Views to things below.
Some secret Truths, from Learned Pride conceal'd,
To Maids alone and Children are reveal'd:

What tho' no Credit doubting Wits may give?
The Fair and Innocent shall still believe.
Know then, unnumber'd Spirits round thee fly,
The light *Militia* of the lower sky:
These, tho' unseen, are ever on the Wing,
Hang o'er the *Box*, and hover round the *Ring*.
Think what an Equipage thou hast in Air,
And view with scorn *Two Pages* and a *Chair*.
As now your own, our Beings were of old,
And once inclos'd in Woman's beauteous Mold;
Thence, by a soft Transition, we repair
From earthly Vehicles to these of Air.
Think not, when Woman's transient Breath is fled,
That all her Vanities at once are dead.
Succeeding Vanities she still regards,
And tho' she plays no more, o'erlooks the Cards.
Her joy in gilded Chariots, when alive,
And love of *Ombre*, after Death survive.
For when the Fair in all their Pride expire,
To their first Elements the Souls retire:
The Sprites of fiery Termagants in Flame
Mount up, and take a *Salamander's* name.
Soft yielding Minds to Water glide away,
And sip, with *Nymphs*, their elemental Tea.
The graver Prude sinks downward to a *Gnome*,
In search of Mischief still on Earth to roam.
The light Coquettes in *Sylphs* aloft repair,
And sport and flutter in the Fields of Air.

Know further yet; Whoever fair and chaste
Rejects Mankind, is by some *Sylph* embrac'd:
For Spirits, freed from mortal Laws, with ease
Assume what Sexes and what Shapes they please.
What guards the Purity of melting Maids,
In Courtly Balls, and Midnight Masquerades,
Safe from the treach'rous Friend, the daring Spark,
The Glance by Day, the Whisper in the Dark;

When kind Occasion prompts their warm Desires,
When Music softens, and when Dancing fires?
'Tis but their *Sylph*, the wise Celestials know,
Tho' *Honour* is the Word with Men below.

Some Nymphs there are, too conscious of their Face,
For Life predestin'd to the *Gnomes*' Embrace.
Who swell their Prospects and exalt their Pride,
When Offers are disdain'd, and Love deny'd.
Then gay Ideas crowd the vacant Brain,
While Peers and Dukes, and all their sweeping Train,
And Garters, Stars, and Coronets appear,
And in soft sounds, *Your Grace* salutes their Ear.
'Tis these that early taint the Female Soul,
Instruct the eyes of young *Coquettes* to roll,
Teach Infant Checks a bidden Blush to know,
And little Hearts to flutter at a *Beau*.

Oft when the World imagine Women stray,
The *Sylphs* through Mystic mazes guide their Way.
Thro' all the giddy Circle they pursue,
And old Impertinence expel by new.
What tender Maid but must a Victim fall
To one Man's Treat, but for another's Ball?
When *Florio* speaks, what Virgin could withstand,
If gentle *Damon* did not squeeze her Hand?
With varying Vanities, from ev'ry Part,
They shift the moving Toyshop of their Heart;
Where Wigs with Wigs, with Sword-knots Sword-knots strive,
Beaux banish Beaux, and Coaches Coaches drive.
This erring Mortals Levity may call,
Oh blind to Truth! the *Sylphs* contrive it all.

Of these am I, who thy Protection claim,
A watchful Sprite, and *Ariel* is my Name.
Late, as I rang'd the crystal Wilds of Air,

In the clear Mirror of thy ruling *Star*
I saw, alas! some dread Event impend,
Ere to the Main this morning's Sun descend,
But Heav'n reveals not what, or how, or where:
Warn'd by thy *Sylph*, oh pious Maid beware!
This to disclose is all thy Guardian can.
Beware of all, but most beware of Man!

He said: when *Shock*, who thought she slept too long,
Leap'd up, and wak'd his Mistress with his Tongue.
'Twas then, *Belinda!* if Report say true,
Thy Eyes first open'd on a *Billet-doux*;
Wounds, *Charms*, and *Ardors*, were no sooner read,
But all the Vision vanish'd from thy Head.

And now, unveil'd, the *Toilet* stands display'd,
Each Silver Vase in mystic Order laid.
First, rob'd in White, the Nymph intent adores
With Head uncover'd, the *Cosmetic* Pow'rs.
A heav'nly Image in the Glass appears,
To that she bends, to that her Eyes she rears;
Th' inferior Priestess, at her Altar's side,
Trembling, begins the sacred Rites of Pride.
Unnumber'd Treasures ope at once, and here
The various Off'rings of the World appear;
From each she nicely culls with curious Toil,
And decks the Goddess with the glitt'ring Spoil.
This Casket *India's* glowing Gems unlocks,
And all *Arabia* breathes from yonder Box.
The Tortoise here and Elephant unite,
Transform'd to *Combs*, the speckled and the white.
Here Files of Pins extend their shining Rows,
Puffs, Powders, Patches, Bibles, Billet-doux.
Now awful Beauty puts on all its Arms;
The Fair each moment rises in her Charms,
Repairs her Smiles, awakens ev'ry Grace,
And calls forth all the Wonders of her Face;

Sees by Degrees a purer Blush arise,
And keener Lightnings quicken in her Eyes.
The busy *Sylphs* surround their darling Care;
These set the Head, and those divide the Hair,
Some fold the Sleeve, whilst others plait the Gown
And *Betty*'s prais'd for labours not her own.

CANTO II

NOT WITH MORE Glories, in th' Ethereal Plain,
The Sun first rises o'er the purpled Main,
Than issuing forth, the Rival of his Beams
Launch'd on the Bosom of the Silver *Thames*.
Fair Nymphs, and well-drest Youths around her shone,
But ev'ry Eye was fix'd on her alone.
On her white Breast a sparkling *Cross* she wore,
Which *Jews* might kiss, and Infidels adore.
Her lively Looks a sprightly Mind disclose,
Quick as her Eyes, and as unfix'd as those:
Favours to none, to all she Smiles extends,
Oft she rejects, but never once offends.
Bright as the Sun, her Eyes the Gazers strike,
And, like the Sun, they shine on all alike.
Yet graceful Ease, and Sweetness void of Pride,
Might hide her Faults, if *Belles* had Faults to hide:
If to her share some Female Errors fall,
Look on her Face, and you'll forget 'em all.

This Nymph, to the Destruction of Mankind,
Nourish'd two Locks which graceful hung behind
In equal Curls, and well conspir'd to deck
With shining Ringlets the smooth Iv'ry Neck.
Love in these Labyrinths his Slaves detains,
And mighty Hearts are held in slender Chains.
With hairy sprindges we the Birds betray,
Slight lines of Hair surprise the Finny Prey,

Fair Tresses Man's Imperial Race insnare,
And Beauty draws us with a single Hair.

Th' Advent'rous *Baron* the bright Locks admir'd,
He saw, he wish'd, and to the Prize aspir'd:
Resolv'd to win, he meditates the way,
By Force to ravish, or by Fraud betray;
For when Success a Lover's Toil attends,
Few ask, if Fraud or Force attain'd his Ends.

For this, ere *Phoebus* rose, he had implor'd
Propitious Heav'n, and ev'ry Pow'r ador'd,
But chiefly *Love*—to *Love* an Altar built,
Of twelve vast *French* Romances, neatly gilt.
There lay three Garters, half a Pair of Gloves,
And all the Trophies of his former Loves.
With tender *Billet-doux* he lights the Pyre,
And breathes three am'rous Sighs to raise the Fire.
Then prostrate falls, and begs with ardent Eyes
Soon to obtain, and long possess the Prize:
The Pow'rs gave Ear, and granted half his Pray'r,
The rest, the Winds dispers'd in empty Air.

But now secure the painted Vessel glides,
The Sun-beams trembling on the floating Tydes,
While melting Musick steals upon the Sky,
And soften'd Sounds along the Waters die.
Smooth flow the Waves, the Zephyrs gently play,
Belinda smil'd, and all the World was gay.
All but the *Sylph*—With careful Thoughts opprest,
Th' impending Woe sat heavy on his Breast.
He summons straight his Denizens of Air;
The lucid Squadrons round the Sails repair:
Soft o'er the Shrouds Aerial Whispers breath,
That seem'd but Zephyrs to the Train beneath.
Some to the Sun their Insect-Wings unfold,
Waft on the Breeze, or sink in Clouds of Gold.

Transparent Forms, too fine for mortal Sight,
Their fluid Bodies half dissolv'd in Light.
Loose to the Wind their airy Garments flew,
Thin glitt'ring Textures of the filmy Dew;
Dipt in the richest Tincture of the Skies,
Where Light disports in ever-mingling Dies,
While ev'ry Beam new transient Colours flings,
Colours that change whene'er they wave their Wings.
Amid the Circle, on the gilded mast,
Superiour by the Head, was *Ariel* plac'd
His Purple Pinions op'ning to the Sun,
He rais'd his Azure Wand, and thus begun.

Ye *Sylphs* and *Sylphids*, to your Chief give ear,
Fays, *Fairies*, *Genii*, *Elves*, and *Daemons* hear!
Ye know the Spheres and various Tasks assign'd
By Laws Eternal to th' Aerial Kind.
Some in the Fields of purest *Aether* play,
And bask and whiten in the Blaze of Day.
Some guide the Course of wand'ring Orbs on high,
Or roll the Planets through the boundless Sky.
Some less refin'd, beneath the Moon's pale Light
Pursue the Stars that shoot athwart the Night;
Or suck the Mists in grosser Air below,
Or dip their Pinions in the painted Bow,
Or brew fierce Tempests on the wintry Main,
Or o'er the Glebe distil the kindly Rain.
Others on Earth o'er human Race preside,
Watch all their Ways, and all their Actions guide:
Of these the Chief the Care of Nations own,
And guard with Arms Divine the *British Throne*.

Our humbler Province is to tend the Fair,
Not a less pleasing, tho' less glorious Care.
To save the Powder from too rude a Gale,
Nor let th' imprison'd Essences exhale;
To draw fresh Colours from the vernal Flow'rs,

To steal from Rainbows ere they drop in Show'rs
A brighter Wash; to curl their waving Hairs,
Assist their Blushes, and inspire their Airs;
Nay oft, in Dreams, Invention we bestow,
To change a *Flounce*, or add a *Furbelo!*

This Day, black Omens threat the brightest Fair
That e'er deserv'd a watchful Spirit's Care;
Some dire Disaster, or by Force, or Slight,
But what, or where, the Fates have wrapt in Night.
Whether the Nymph shall break *Diana's* law,
Or some frail *China* jar receive a Flaw,
Or stain her Honour, or her new Brocade,
Forget her Pray'rs, or miss a Masquerade,
Or lose her Heart, or Necklace, at a Ball;
Or whether Heav'n has doom'd that *Shock* must fall.
Haste then ye Spirits! to your Charge repair;
The flutt'ring Fan be *Zephyretta's* Care;
The Drops to thee, *Brillante*, we consign;
And, *Momentilla*, let the Watch be thine;
Do thou, *Crispissa*, tend her fav'rite Lock;
Ariel himself shall be the guard of *Shock*.

To Fifty chosen *Sylphs*, of special Note,
We trust th' important Charge, the *Petticoat*:
Oft have we known that sev'nfold Fence to fail,
Tho' stiff with Hoops, and arm'd with Ribs of Whale.
Form a strong Line about the Silver Bound,
And guard the wide Circumference around.

Whatever Spirit, careless of his Charge,
His Post neglects, or leave the Fair at large,
Shall feel sharp Vengeance soon o'ertake his Sins,
Be stop'd in *Vials*, or transfixt with *Pins*;
Or plung'd in Lakes of bitter *Washes* lie,
Or wedg'd whole Ages in a *Bodkin's* Eye:
Gums and *Pomatums* shall his Flight restrain,

While clog'd he beats his silken Wings in vain;
Or Alom-*Stypticks* with contracting Pow'r
Shrink his thin Essence like a rivell'd Flower.
Or, as *Ixion* fix'd, the Wretch shall feel
The giddy Motion of the whirling Mill,
Midst Fumes of burning Chocolate shall glow,
And tremble at the Sea that froths below!

He spoke; the Spirits from the Sails descend;
Some, Orb in Orb, around the Nymph extend,
Some thread the mazy Ringlets of her Hair,
Some hang upon the Pendants of her Ear;
With beating Hearts the dire Event they wait,
Anxious, and trembling for the Birth of Fate.

CANTO III

CLOSE BY THOSE Meads for ever crown'd with Flow'rs,
Where *Thames* with Pride surveys his rising Tow'rs,
There stands a Structure of Majestic Fame,
Which from the neighb'ring *Hampton* takes its Name.
Here *Britain's* Statesmen oft the Fall foredoom
Of foreign Tyrants, and of Nymphs at home;
Here Thou, great *Anna!* whom three Realms obey,
Dost sometimes Counsel take—and sometimes *Tea*.

Hither the Heroes and the Nymphs resort,
To taste awhile the Pleasures of a Court;
In various Talk th' instructive Hours they past,
Who gave a *Ball*, or paid the *Visit* last:
One speaks the Glory of the *British Queen*,
And one describes a charming *Indian Screen*;
A third interprets Motions, Looks, and Eyes;
At every Word a Reputation dies.
Snuff, or the *Fan*, supply each Pause of Chat,
With singing, laughing, ogling, *and all that*.

Mean while, declining from the Noon of Day,
The Sun obliquely shoots his burning Ray;
The hungry judges soon the Sentence sign,
And Wretches hang that Jury-men may Dine;
The Merchant from th' *Exchange* returns in Peace,
And the long Labours of the Toilet cease.
Belinda now, whom Thirst of Fame invites,
Burns to encounter two adventrous Knights,
At *Ombre* singly to decide their Doom;
And swells her Breast with Conquests yet to come.
Straight the three Bands prepare in Arms to join,
Each Band the number of the Sacred Nine.
Soon as she spreads her Hand, th' Aerial Guard
Descend, and sit on each important Card:
First *Ariel* perch'd upon a *Matadore*,
Then each, according to the Rank they bore;
For *Sylphs*, yet mindful of their ancient Race,
Are, as when women, wond'rous fond of Place.

Behold, four *Kings*, in Majesty rever'd,
With hoary Whiskers and a forky Beard;
And four fair *Queens* whose Hands sustain a Flow'r,
Th' expressive Emblem of their softer Pow'r;
Four *Knaves* in Garbs succinct, a trusty Band;
Caps on their heads, and Halberds in their hand;
And particolour'd Troops, a shining Train,
Draw forth to combat on the Velvet Plain.

The skilful Nymph reviews her Force with Care;
Let Spades be Trumps! she said, and Trumps they were.

Now move to War her Sable *Matadores*,
In show like Leaders of the swarthy *Moors*.
Spadillio first, unconquerable Lord!
Let off two captive Trumps, and swept the Board.
As many more *Manillio* forc'd to yield,
And march'd a Victor from the verdant Field.

Him *Basto* follow'd, but his Fate more hard
Gain'd but one Trump and one *Plebeian* card.
With his broad Sabre next, a Chief in Years,
The hoary Majesty of *Spades* appears;
Puts forth one manly Leg, to sight reveal'd,
The rest, his many-colour'd Robe conceal'd.
The Rebel-*Knave*, that dares his Prince engage,
Proves the just Victim of his Royal Rage.
Ev'n mighty *Pam*, that Kings and Queens o'erthrew,
And mow'd down Armies in the Fights of *Lu*,
Sad Chance of War! now, destitute of Aid,
Falls undistinguish'd by the Victor *Spade!*

Thus far both Armies to *Belinda* yield;
Now to the *Baron* Fate inclines the Field.
His warlike *Amazon* her Host invades,
Th' Imperial Consort of the Crown of *Spades*.
The *Club's* black Tyrant first her Victim dy'd,
Spite of his haughty Mien, and barb'rous Pride:
What boots the Regal Circle on his Head,
His Giant Limbs, in State unwieldy spread;
That long behind he trails his pompous Robe,
And of all Monarchs only grasps the Globe?

The *Baron* now his *Diamonds* pours apace;
Th' embroider'd *King* who shows but half his Face,
And his refulgent *Queen*, with Pow'rs combin'd,
Of broken Troops an easy Conquest find.
Clubs, *Diamonds*, *Hearts*, in wild Disorder seen,
With Throngs promiscuous strew the level Green.
Thus when dispers'd a routed Army runs,
Of *Asia's* Troops, and *Afric's* Sable Sons,
With like Confusion different Nations fly,
In various Habits, and of various Dye,
The pierc'd Battalions dis-united fall,
In Heaps on Heaps; one Fate o'erwhelms them all.

The *Knave* of *Diamonds* tries his wily Arts,
And wins (oh shameful Chance!) the *Queen* of *Hearts*.
At this, the Blood the Virgin's Cheek forsook,
A livid Paleness spreads o'er all her Look;
She sees, and trembles at th' approaching Ill,
Just in the Jaws of Ruin, and *Codille*.
And now (as oft in some distemper'd State)
On one nice *Trick* depends the gen'ral Fate,
An *Ace* of Hearts steps forth: The *King* unseen
Lurk'd in her Hand, and mourn'd his captive *Queen*.
He springs to Vengeance with an eager Pace,
And falls like Thunder on the prostrate *Ace*.
The Nymph exulting fills with Shouts the Sky;
The Walls, the Woods, and long Canals reply.

Oh thoughtless Mortals! ever blind to Fate,
Too soon dejected, and too soon elate!
Sudden these Honours shall be snatch'd away,
And curs'd for ever this Victorious Day.

For lo! the Board with Cups and Spoons is crown'd,
The Berries crackle, and the Mill turns round;
On shining Altars of *Japan* they raise
The silver Lamp, and fiery Spirits blaze:
From silver Spouts the grateful Liquors glide,
And *China's* earth receives the smoking Tyde.
At once they gratify their Scent and Taste,
While frequent Cups prolong the rich Repast.
Strait hover round the Fair her Airy Band;
Some, as she sipp'd, the fuming Liquor fann'd,
Some o'er her Lap their careful Plumes display'd,
Trembling, and conscious of the rich Brocade.
Coffee (which makes the Politician wise,
And see through all things with his half-shut Eyes)
Sent up in Vapours to the *Baron's* Brain
New Stratagems, the radiant Lock to gain.
Ah cease rash Youth! desist e'er 'tis too late,

Fear the just Gods, and think of *Scylla's* Fate!
Chang'd to a Bird, and sent to flit in Air,
She dearly pays for *Nisus'* injur'd Hair!

But when to Mischief Mortals bend their Will,
How soon they find fit Instruments of Ill!
Just then, *Clarissa* drew with tempting Grace
A two-edg'd Weapon from her shining Case;
So Ladies in Romance assist their Knight,
Present the Spear, and arm him for the Fight.
He takes the Gift with rev'rence, and extends
The little Engine on his Fingers' Ends;
This just behind *Belinda's* Neck he spread
As o'er the fragrant Steams she bends her Head:
Swift to the Lock a thousand Sprights repair,
A thousand Wings, by turns, blow back the Hair;
And thrice they twitch'd the Diamond in her Ear,
Thrice she look'd back, and thrice the Foe drew near.
Just in that instant, anxious *Ariel* sought
The close Recesses of the Virgin's thought;
As on the Nosegay in her Breast reclin'd,
He watch'd th' Ideas rising in her Mind,
Sudden he view'd, in spite of all her Art,
An Earthly Lover lurking at her Heart.
Amaz'd, confus'd, he found his Power expir'd,
Resign'd to Fate, and with a Sigh retir'd.

The *Peer* now spreads the glittering *Forfex* wide,
T' inclose the Lock; now joins it, to divide.
Ev'n then, before the fatal Engine clos'd,
A wretched *Sylph* too fondly interpos'd;
Fate urged the Sheers, and cut the *Sylph* in twain,
(But Airy Substance soon unites again)
The meeting Points the sacred Hair dissever
From the fair Head, for ever and for ever!

Then flash'd the living Lightnings from her Eyes,
And Screams of Horror rend th' affrighted Skies.
Not louder Shrieks to pitying Heav'n are cast,
When Husbands, or when Lapdogs breath their last,
Or when rich *China* Vessels, fal'n from high,
In glitt'ring Dust and painted Fragments lie!

Let Wreaths of Triumph now my Temples twine,
(The Victor cry'd) the glorious Prize is mine!
While Fish in Streams, or Birds delight in Air,
Or in a Coach and Six the *British* Fair,
As long as *Atalantis* shall be read,
Or the small Pillow grace a Lady's Bed,
While *Visits* shall be paid on solemn Days,
When num'rous Wax-lights in bright Order blaze,
While Nymphs take Treats, or Assignations give,
So long my Honour, Name, and Praise shall live!

What Time would spare, from Steel receives its date,
And Monuments, like Men, submit to Fate!
Steel cou'd the Labour of the Gods destroy,
And strike to Dust th' Imperial Tow'rs of *Troy*;
Steel cou'd the Works of mortal Pride confound,
And hew Triumphal Arches to the Ground.
What Wonder then, fair Nymph! thy Hair shou'd feel
The conqu'ring Force of unresisted Steel?

CANTO IV

BUT ANXIOUS CARES the pensive Nymph oppress'd,
And secret Passions labour'd in her Breast.
Not youthful Kings in Battle seiz'd alive,
Not scornful Virgins who their Charms survive,
Not ardent Lovers robb'd of all their Bliss,
Not ancient Ladies when refus'd a Kiss,

Not Tyrants fierce that unrepenting die,
Not *Cynthia* when her *Manteau's* pinn'd awry,
E'er felt such Rage, Resentment, and Despair,
As Thou, sad Virgin! for thy ravish'd Hair.

For, that sad moment, when the *Sylphs* withdrew,
And *Ariel* weeping from *Belinda* flew,
Umbriel, a dusky, melancholy Sprite,
As ever sully'd the fair Face of Light,
Down to the Central Earth, his proper Scene,
Repair'd to search the gloomy Cave of *Spleen*.

Swift on his sooty Pinions flits the *Gnome*,
And in a Vapour reach'd the dismal Dome.
No cheerful Breeze this sullen Region knows,
The dreaded *East* is all the Wind that blows.
Here in a Grotto, shelter'd close from Air,
And screen'd in Shades from Day's detested Glare,
She sighs for ever on her pensive Bed,
Pain at her Side, and *Megrim* at her Head.

Two Handmaids wait the Throne: Alike in Place,
But diff'ring far in Figure and in Face.
Here stood *Ill-nature* like an *ancient Maid*,
Her wrinkled form in *Black* and *White* array'd;
With store of Pray'rs, for Mornings, Nights, and Noons,
Her Hand is fill'd; her Bosom with Lampoons.

There *Affectation* with a sickly Mien,
Shows in her Cheek the Roses of Eighteen,
Practis'd to Lisp, and hang the Head aside,
Faints into Airs, and languishes with Pride;
On the rich Quilt sinks with becoming Woe,
Wrapt in a Gown, for Sickness, and for Show.
The Fair ones feel such Maladies as these,
When each new Night-Dress gives a new Disease.

A constant *Vapour* o'er the Palace flies;
Strange Phantoms rising as the Mists arise;
Dreadful, as Hermits' Dreams in haunted Shades,
Or bright, as Visions of expiring Maids.
Now glaring Fiends, and Snakes on rolling Spires,
Pale Spectres, gaping Tombs, and Purple Fires:
Now Lakes of liquid Gold, *Elysian* Scenes,
And Crystal Domes, and Angels in Machines.

Unnumber'd Throngs, on ev'ry side are seen,
Of Bodies chang'd to various forms by *Spleen*.
Here living *Teapots* stand, one Arm held out,
One bent; the Handle this, and that the Spout:
A Pipkin there like *Homer's Tripod* walks;
Here sighs a Jar, and there a Goose-pye talks;
Men prove with Child, as pow'rful Fancy works,
And Maids turn'd Bottels, call aloud for Corks.

Safe past the *Gnome* through this fantastic Band,
A Branch of healing *Spleenwort* in his Hand.
Then thus addrest the Pow'r—Hail wayward Queen;
Who rule the Sex to Fifty from Fifteen,
Parent of Vapors and of Female Wit,
Who give th' *Hysteric* or *Poetic* Fit,
On various Tempers act by various ways,
Make some take Physic, others scribble Plays;
Who cause the Proud their Visits to delay,
And send the Godly in a Pett, to pray.
A Nymph there is, that all thy Pow'r disdains,
And thousands more in equal Mirth maintains.
But oh! if e'er thy *Gnome* could spoil a Grace,
Or raise a Pimple on a beauteous Face,
Like Citron-Waters Matrons' Cheeks inflame,
Or change Complexions at a losing Game;
If e'er with airy Horns I planted Heads,
Or rumpled Petticoats, or tumbled Beds,
Or caus'd Suspicion when no Soul was rude,

Or discompos'd the Head-Dress of a Prude,
Or e'er to costive Lap-Dog gave Disease,
Which not the Tears of brightest Eyes could ease:
Hear me, and touch *Belinda* with Chagrin;
That single Act gives half the World the Spleen.

The Goddess with a discontented Air
Seems to reject him, tho' she grants his Pray'r.
A wond'rous Bag with both her Hands she binds,
Like that where once *Ulysses* held the Winds;
There she collects the Force of Female Lungs,
Sighs, Sobs, and Passions, and the War of Tongues.
A Vial next she fills with fainting Fears,
Soft Sorrows, melting Griefs, and flowing Tears.
The *Gnome* rejoycing bears her Gift away,
Spreads his black Wings, and slowly mounts to Day.

Sunk in *Thalestris'* Arms the Nymph he found,
Her Eyes dejected, and her Hair unbound.
Full o'er their Heads the swelling Bag he rent,
And all the Furies issu'd at the Vent.
Belinda burns with more than mortal Ire,
And fierce *Thalestris* fans the rising Fire.
O wretched Maid! she spread her Hands, and cry'd,
(While *Hampton's* Ecchoes, wretched Maid reply'd)
Was it for this you took such constant Care
The *Bodkin*, *Comb*, and *Essence* to prepare;
For this your Locks in Paper-Durance bound,
For this with tort'ring Irons wreath'd around!
For this with Fillets strain'd your tender Head,
And bravely bore the double Loads of Lead?
Gods! shall the Ravisher display your Hair,
While the Fops envy, and the Ladies stare!
Honour forbid! at whose unrivall'd Shrine
Ease, Pleasure, Virtue, All, our Sex resign.
Methinks already I your Tears survey,
Already hear the horrid Things they say,

Already see you a degraded Toast,
And all your Honour in a Whisper lost!
How shall I, then, your hapless Fame defend?
'Twill then be Infamy to seem your Friend!
And shall this Prize, th' inestimable Prize,
Expos'd through Crystal to the gazing Eyes,
And heighten'd by the Diamond's circling Rays,
On that Rapacious Hand for ever blaze?
Sooner shall Grass in *Hide-Park Circus* grow,
And Wits take Lodgings in the sound of *Bow*;
Sooner let Earth, Air, Sea, to *Chaos* fall,
Men, Monkeys, Lap-dogs, Parrots, perish all!

She said; then raging to Sir *Plume* repairs,
And bids her *Beau* demand the precious Hairs:
(Sir *Plume*, of *Amber Snuff-box* justly vain,
And the nice Conduct of a *Clouded Cane*)
With earnest Eyes and round unthinking Face,
He first the Snuff-box open'd, then the Case,
And thus broke out—"My Lord, why, what the Devil!
"Z——ds! damn the Lock! 'fore Gad, you must be civil!
"Plague on't! 'tis past a Jest—nay, prithee, Pox!
"Give her the Hair"—he spoke, and rapp'd his Box.

It grieves me much (replied the Peer again)
Who speaks so well shou'd ever speak in vain.
But by this Lock, this sacred Lock I swear,
(Which never more shall join its parted Hair;
Which never more its Honours shall renew,
Clipp'd from the lovely Head where late it grew)
That while my Nostrils draw the vital Air,
This Hand, which won it, shall for ever wear.
He spoke, and speaking, in proud Triumph spread
The long-contended Honours of her Head.

But *Umbriel*, hateful *Gnome!* forbears not so;
He breaks the Vial whence the Sorrows flow.

Then see! the Nymph in beauteous Grief appears,
Her Eyes half-languishing, half-drown'd in Tears;
On her heav'd Bosom hung her drooping Head,
Which, with a Sigh, she rais'd; and thus she said.

For ever curs'd be this detested Day,
Which snatch'd my best, my fav'rite Curl away!
Happy! ah ten times happy had I been,
If *Hampton-Court* these Eyes had never seen!
Yet am not I the first mistaken Maid,
By love of *Courts* to num'rous Ills betray'd.
Oh had I rather unadmir'd remain'd
In some lone Isle, or distant *Northern* land;
Where the gilt *Chariot* never mark'd the way,
Where none learn *Ombre*, none e'er taste *Bohea!*
There kept my Charms conceal'd from mortal Eye,
Like Roses that in Desarts bloom and die.
What mov'd my Mind with youthful Lords to rome?
O had I stay'd, and said my Pray'rs at home!
'Twas this the Morning *Omens* did foretel;
Thrice from my trembling Hand the *Patch-box* fell;
The tott'ring *China* shook without a Wind,
Nay, *Poll* sate mute, and *Shock* was most Unkind!
A *Sylph* too warn'd me of the Threats of Fate,
In mystic Visions, now believ'd too late!
See the poor Remnants of these slighted Hairs!
My Hands shall rend what ev'n thy Rapine spares.
These, in two sable Ringlets taught to break,
Once gave new Beauties to the snowy Neck.
The Sister-Lock now sits uncouth, alone,
And in its Fellow's Fate foresees its own;
Uncurl'd it hangs, the fatal Sheers demands;
And tempts once more thy sacrilegious Hands.
Oh hadst thou, Cruel! been content to seize
Hairs less in sight, or any Hairs but these!

CANTO V

SHE SAID: THE pitying Audience melt in Tears,
But *Fate* and *Jove* had stopp'd the *Baron's* Ears.
In vain *Thalestris* with Reproach assails,
For who can move when fair *Belinda* fails?
Not half so fix'd the *Trojan* could remain,
While *Anna* begg'd and *Dido* rag'd in vain.
Then grave *Clarissa* graceful wav'd her Fan;
Silence ensu'd, and thus the Nymph began.

Say, why are Beauties prais'd and honour'd most,
The Wise Man's Passion, and the Vain Man's Toast?
Why deck'd with all that Land and Sea afford,
Why Angels call'd, and Angel-like ador'd?
Why round our Coaches crowd the white-gloved Beaux,
Why bows the Side-box from its inmost Rows?
How vain are all these Glories, all our Pains,
Unless good Sense preserve what Beauty gains:
That Men may say, when we the Front-box grace,
Behold the first in Virtue as in Face!
Oh! if to dance all Night, and dress all Day,
Charm'd the Small-pox, or chas'd old Age away;
Who would not scorn what Housewife's Cares produce,
Or who would learn one earthly Thing of Use?
To patch, nay ogle, might become a Saint,
Nor could it sure be such a Sin to paint.
But since, alas! frail Beauty must decay,
Curl'd or uncurl'd, since Locks will turn to grey;
Since painted, or not painted, all shall fade,
And she who scorns a Man, must die a Maid,
What then remains but well our Pow'r to use,
And keep good Humour still whate'er we lose?
And trust me, dear! good Humour can prevail,
When Airs, and Flights, and Screams, and Scolding fail.
Beauties in vain their pretty Eyes may roll;
Charms strike the Sight, but Merit wins the Soul.

So spoke the Dame, but no Applause ensu'd;
Belinda frown'd, *Thalestris* call'd her Prude.
To Arms, to Arms! the fierce Virago cries,
And swift as Lightning to the Combate flies.
All side in Parties, and begin th' Attack;
Fans clap, Silks rustle, and tough Whalebones crack;
Heroes and Heroins Shouts confus'dly rise,
And base, and treble Voices strike the Skies.
No common Weapons in their Hands are found,
Like Gods they fight, nor dread a mortal Wound.

So when bold *Homer* makes the Gods engage,
And heav'nly Breasts with human Passions rage;
'Gainst *Pallas*, *Mars*; *Latona*, *Hermes*, Arms;
And all *Olympus* rings with loud Alarms.
Jove's Thunder roars, Heav'n trembles all around;
Blue *Neptune* storms, the bellowing Deeps resound;
Earth shakes her nodding Tow'rs, the Ground gives way,
And the pale Ghosts start at the Flash of Day!

Triumphant *Umbriel* on a Sconce's Height
Clapp'd his glad Wings, and sate to view the Fight,
Propp'd on their Bodkin Spears the Sprites survey
The growing Combat, or assist the Fray.

While through the Press enrag'd *Thalestris* flies,
And scatters Death around from both her Eyes,
A *Beau* and *Witling* perish'd in the Throng,
One dy'd in *Metaphor*, and one in *Song*.
O cruel Nymph! a living death I bear,
Cried *Dapperwit*, and sunk beside his Chair.
A mournful Glance Sir *Fopling* upwards cast,
Those eyes are made so killing—was his last:
Thus on *Meander's* flow'ry Margin lies
Th' expiring Swan, and as he sings he dies.

As bold Sir *Plume* had drawn *Clarissa down*,
Chloe stepp'd in, and kill'd him with a Frown;
She smil'd to see the doughty Hero slain,
But at her Smile, the Beau reviv'd again.

Now *Jove* suspends his golden Scales in Air,
Weighs the Men's Wits against the Lady's Hair;
The doubtful Beam long nods from side to side;
At length the Wits mount up, the Hairs subside.

See fierce *Belinda* on the *Baron* flies,
With more than usual Lightning in her Eyes:
Nor fear'd the Chief th' unequal Fight to try,
Who sought no more than on his Foe to die.
But this bold Lord, with manly Strength endu'd,
She with one Finger and a Thumb subdu'd:
Just where the Breath of Life his Nostrils drew,
A charge of *Snuff* the wily Virgin threw;
The *Gnomes* direct, to ev'ry Atome just,
The pungent Grains of titillating Dust,
Sudden, with starting Tears each Eye o'erflows,
And the high Dome re-ecchoes to his Nose.

Now meet thy Fate, incens'd *Belinda* cry'd,
And drew a deadly *Bodkin* from her Side.
(The same, his ancient Personage to deck,
Her great great Grandsire wore about his Neck
In three *Seal-Rings*; which after melted down,
Form'd a vast *Buckle* for his Widow's Gown:
Her infant Grandame's *Whistle* next it grew,
The Bells she jingled, and the *Whistle* blew;
Then in a *Bodkin* grac'd her Mother's hairs,
Which long she wore, and now *Belinda* wears.)

Boast not my Fall (he cry'd) insulting Foe!
Thou by some other shalt be laid as low.

Nor think, to die dejects my lofty Mind.
All that I dread, is leaving you behind!
Rather than so, ah let me still survive,
And burn in *Cupid's* Flames—but burn alive.

Restore the Lock! she cries; and all around
Restore the Lock! the Vaulted Roofs rebound.
Not fierce *Othello* in so loud a Strain
Roar'd for the Handkerchief that caus'd his Pain.
But see how oft Ambitious Aims are cross'd,
And Chiefs contend 'till all the Prize is lost!
The Lock, obtain'd with Guilt, and kept with Pain,
In ev'ry place is sought, but sought in vain:
With such a Prize no Mortal must be blest,
So Heav'n decrees! with Heav'n who can contest?

Some thought it mounted to the Lunar Sphere,
Since all things lost on Earth, are treasur'd there.
There Heroes' Wits are kept in pond'rous Vases,
And Beaux' in *Snuff-boxes* and *Tweezer-cases*.
There broken Vows, and Death-bed Alms are found,
And Lovers' Hearts with Ends of Riband bound;
The Courtier's Promises, and Sick Man's Pray'rs,
The Smiles of Harlots, and the Tears of Heirs,
Cages for Gnats, and Chains to Yoak a Flea;
Dried Butterflies, and Tomes of Casuistry.

But trust the Muse—she saw it upward rise,
Tho' marked by none but quick Poetic eyes:
(So *Rome's* great Founder to the Heav'ns withdrew,
To *Proculus* alone confess'd in view.)
A sudden Star, it shot through liquid Air,
And drew behind a radiant *Trail of Hair*.
Not *Berenice's* Locks first rose so bright,
The Skies bespangling with dishevel'd Light.
The *Sylphs* behold it kindling as it flies,
And pleas'd pursue its Progress through the Skies.

This the *Beau-monde* shall from the *Mall* survey,
And hail with *Musick* its propitious Ray.
This the blest Lover shall for *Venus* take,
And send up Vows from *Rosamonda's* Lake.
This *Partridge* soon shall view in cloudless Skies,
When next he looks through *Gallilæo's* Eyes;
And hence th' Egregious Wizard shall foredoom
The fate of *Louis*, and the fall of *Rome*.

Then cease, bright Nymph! to mourn the ravish'd Hair
Which adds new Glory to the shining Sphere!
Not all the Tresses that fair Head can boast
Shall draw such Envy as the Lock you lost.
For, after all the Murders of your Eye,
When, after Millions slain, yourself shall die;
When those fair Suns shall set, as set they must,
And all those Tresses shall be laid in dust;
This *Lock*, the Muse shall consecrate to fame,
And 'midst the stars inscribe *Belinda's* Name!

Voltaire

(François–Marie Arouet)

(1694–1778)

Voltaire (pen name of François-Marie Arouet) is called the Father of the French Revolution—the leading apostle of freedom and justice of the eighteenth century. He is the author of more than fifty plays, numerous historical, philosophical, and scientific works, and scores of critical pamphlets.

"I was born with two feet in the grave," Voltaire once said. He was such a tiny, sickly baby that the nurse did not expect him to survive; formal baptism was held off for several months. This raises some confusion about actual birth dates; two possibilities are February 20 and November 20, 1694. He was the last of five children born to François and Marie Arouet, though Voltaire himself said he was convinced that his mother's husband was not his real father. His mother died when he was seven.

François, who was a lawyer and notary, insisted that the young Voltaire study law and enrolled him in the Jesuit College of Louis-le-Grand in 1704. Voltaire excelled in his studies, won many academic prizes (in spite of his disdain for the Jesuit teachings), and honed his skill as a writer. He aspired to be a poet, but his father urged him to press on with his law studies. He humored his father but continued to entertain secret literary aspirations. Voltaire began moving in aristocratic circles, in a society known as the Temple, which had dukes, princes, and poets as members.

Voltaire began to write satirical verse, and thought his chance at fame was to become a tragic poet. His father, trying to redirect his son's ambitions, sent Voltaire to Paris twice in three years, but to no avail. When he returned from the second in 1715, he stirred up trouble by writing libelous lampoons of the regent.

(Appointed by the government, the regent had enormous power and acted on the king's behalf if the king could not serve because he was underage or in poor health.) Voltaire was imprisoned in the Bastille on May 17, 1717, and remained there for eleven months, where he worked on his tragedy *Oedipe* and began his poem "L'Herrade."

When he was released, he changed his name to Aurot de Voltaire. His tragedy *Oedipe* premiered in November 1718 in Paris, where he was welcomed back as a talented tragic poet. But he could not stay out of trouble. He continued to taunt the aristocrats, and soon left France for England. He stayed in England for three years and immersed himself in English literature, reading Bacon, Milton, Newton, Shakespeare, and Locke. He enjoyed the freedom and tolerance of England but he eventually wanted to return home. He was allowed back into his native country in 1729 and stayed until 1733, when *English Letters* and the satirical poem "Temple du Goût" brought another wave of persecution. This would become the pattern of his life.

Luckily, for Voltaire, when the police ransacked his home seeking evidence of authorship, he was in Lorraine as the guest of the Marquise du Châtelet, a woman who would play an invigorating and supportive role in Voltaire's life for the next sixteen years. She was bright, interested in mathematics, philosophy, and science, and did her own translations and commentary. In this productive relationship, Voltaire produced six plays, two poems, and a paper on metaphysics and worked on two other essays.

When his nemesis the regent died, Voltaire returned to Paris. In 1748, his "Poème de Fontanay" was warmly received and he was made the royal histographer, following in the footsteps of the great playwrights Racine and Corneille. In 1746, he was elected to the Academie Française. Despite having achieved respectability, he continued to dabble in satire and found it expedient to keep on the move throughout France. Sadly, in 1749, his friend the Marquise du Châtelet died in childbirth after a brief romance with the poet Saint Lambert. It was a tragic end to a relationship that had been a source of support and inspiration for fifteen years. Mourning his loss, Voltaire returned to their home in Paris.

Frederick the Great had been trying to lure Voltaire to his intellectual academy in Potsdam, Germany, and it again seemed a good time to escape Paris. There he finished his most ambitious historical work, *Siècle de Louis XIV.* Yet the good times did not last for long: Voltaire managed once again to alienate his hosts, this time by writing a piece entitled "Diatribe du Doctor Akakia," criticizing the director of the academy. Voltaire fled Prussia (after being arrested and searched in Frankfurt) and hid out in Geneva for a year. It was there, in 1759 that he wrote *Candide*. Although he enjoyed the more tolerant atmosphere in Switzerland, he did not see eye to eye with the Calvinists, who were repelled by his ownership and operation of a private theater.

In 1759, Voltaire bought a chateau in Ferney, in France near the Swiss border, where he would live until his death. Ferney soon evolved into an intellectual community, as Voltaire produced even more influential plays, papers, pamphlets, and letters. He was welcomed back to Paris in 1778 but fell gravely ill. On his deathbed he refused the Roman Catholic sacraments of extreme unction and confession; he was subsequently denied burial in Paris. His body was placed in the abbey of Scellières in Champagne. Thirteen years later it was brought back to Paris to be buried at the Pantheon, the resting place of heroes of French culture.

Candide is an unusual work: a witty novel that addresses a most serious subject—the ordeal of suffering. Voltaire presents the vexing question: If God is omnipotent and benevolent, then why didn't He fashion a more perfect world? If He is all-knowing, why doesn't He use this knowledge to better the plight of man?

In 1755, while Voltaire was in Postsdam, a horrifying earthquake struck Lisbon, Portugal, resulting in the death of more than 30,000 people. This disaster had a huge impact on Voltaire's already pessimistic worldview. He no longer put his complete faith in a benign being who would guide man through a safe existence and who would reward virtue. Accident played a larger role in life than he had previously imagined and man was almost helpless against the vagaries of chance.

The catastrophic earthquake, coupled with the beginning of the Seven Years War in Europe, led Voltaire to believe that blind optimism was a fool's dream best abandoned. Previously, he had been an admirer of the philosophy of Baron Gottfried Wilhelm von Leibniz, who espoused the propositions that God is beneficent and created the best possible world. Extending therefrom is the concept that evil does indeed exist but what is right and moral will eventually emerge victorious. There is a divine plan, and one cannot judge isolated parts of this grand design. Leibnitz suggested that nature moves in an orderly way, that its laws are immutable and any deviation would upset the balance of the universe.

Voltaire ultimately rejected these ideas. His education and experiences had provided him with ample reason to call Leibniz "a bit of a charlatan," (*un peu charlatan*).

Thus the novel *Candide* is fashioned out of Voltaire's new way of thinking and is a direct attack on Leibniz's philosophy. He takes his hero, Candide, out of a utopian environment and thrusts him into the cold without food or hope of shelter. Candide endures torture, horrors beyond his imagination, and concludes, "This is not the best of all possible worlds," turning Leibniz's dictum on its head. The phrase "all's well" echoes time and again in *Candide* and becomes a cruel joke as the painful events around the main characters unfold. After surviving an unending parade of mass acts of cruelty and intolerance, Candide ends up living on a farm, poor, married to a woman he once desired but who now has turned ugly and shrewish. He and his philosophizing friends Pangloss and Martin conclude that "to work without reason . . . is the only way to make life bearable." They (and Voltaire) realize that the pursuit of wider knowledge and happiness is not life's goal. Rather than trying to puzzle out the greater meaning of life, we must stop wishing for it in vain, as evil cannot be understood or conquered. Find the meaning in work—"cultivate our garden," as Candide remarks at the close of the novel—and life will gain some definition.

Candide

CONTENTS

CHAPTER I

HOW CANDIDE WAS BROUGHT UP IN A MAGNIFICENT CASTLE, AND HOW HE WAS EXPELLED THENCE

IN A CASTLE OF Westphalia, belonging to the Baron of Thunder-ten-Tronckh, lived a youth, whom nature had endowed with the most gentle manners. His countenance was a true picture of his soul. He combined a true judgment with simplicity of spirit, which was the reason, I apprehend, of his being called Candide. The old servants of the family suspected him to have been the son of the Baron's sister, by a good, honest gentleman of the neighborhood, whom that young lady would never marry because he had been able to prove only seventy-one quarterings, the rest of his genealogical tree having been lost through the injuries of time.

The Baron was one of the most powerful lords in Westphalia, for his castle had not only a gate, but windows. His great hall, even, was hung with tapestry. All the dogs of his farmyards formed a pack of hounds at need; his grooms were his huntsmen; and the curate of the village was his grand almoner. They called him "My Lord," and laughed at all his stories.

The Baron's lady weighed about three hundred and fifty pounds, and was therefore a person of great consideration, and she did the honours of the house with a dignity that commanded still greater respect. Her daughter Cunegonde was seventeen years of age, fresh-coloured, comely, plump, and desirable. The Baron's son seemed to be in every respect worthy of his father. The Preceptor Pangloss[1] was the oracle of the family, and little Candide heard his lessons with all the good faith of his age and character.

Pangloss was professor of metaphysico-theologico-cosmolo-nigology. He proved admirably that there is no effect without a cause, and that, in this best of all possible worlds, the Baron's castle was the most magnificent of castles, and his lady the best of all possible Baronesses.

"It is demonstrable," said he, "that things cannot be otherwise than as they are; for all being created for an end, all is necessarily for the best end. Observe, that the nose has been formed to bear spectacles—thus we have spectacles. Legs are visibly designed for stockings—and we have stockings. Stones were made to be hewn, and to construct castles—therefore my lord has a magnificent castle; for the greatest baron in the province ought to be the best lodged. Pigs were made to be eaten—therefore we eat pork all the year round. Consequently they who assert that all is well have said a foolish thing, they should have said all is for the best."

Candide listened attentively and believed innocently; for he thought Miss Cunegonde extremely beautiful, though he never had the courage to tell her so. He concluded that after the happiness of being born Baron of Thunder-ten-Tronckh, the second degree of happiness was to be Miss Cunegonde, the third that of seeing her every day, and the fourth that of hearing Master Pangloss, the greatest philosopher of the whole province, and consequently of the whole world.

One day Cunegonde, while walking near the castle, in a little wood which they called a park, saw between the bushes, Dr. Pangloss giving a lesson in experimental natural philosophy to her mother's chamber-maid, a little brown wench, very pretty and very docile. As Miss Cunegonde had a great disposition for the sciences, she breathlessly observed the repeated experiments of which she was a witness; she clearly perceived the force of the Doctor's reasons, the effects, and the causes; she turned back greatly flurried, quite pensive, and filled with the desire to be learned; dreaming that she might well be *sufficient reason* for young Candide, and he for her.

She met Candide on reaching the castle and blushed; Candide blushed also; she wished him good morrow in a faltering tone, and Candide spoke to her without knowing what he said. The next day after dinner, as they went from table, Cunegonde and Candide found themselves behind a screen; Cunegonde let fall her handkerchief, Candide picked it up, she took him innocently by the hand, the youth as innocently kissed the young lady's hand with particular vivacity, sensibility, and grace; their lips met, their eyes sparkled, their knees trembled, their hands strayed. Baron Thunder-ten-Tronckh passed near the screen and beholding this cause and effect chased Candide from the castle with great kicks on the backside; Cunegonde fainted away; she was boxed on the ears by the Baroness, as soon as she came to herself; and all was consternation in this most magnificent and most agreeable of all possible castles.

CHAPTER II

WHAT BECAME OF CANDIDE AMONG THE BULGARIANS

CANDIDE, DRIVEN FROM terrestrial paradise, walked a long while without knowing where, weeping, raising his eyes to heaven, turning them often towards the most magnificent of castles which imprisoned the purest of noble young ladies. He lay down to sleep without supper, in the middle of a field between two furrows. The snow fell in large flakes. Next day Candide, all benumbed, dragged himself towards the neighbouring town which was called Waldberghofftrarbkdikdorff, having no money, dying of hunger and fatigue, he stopped sorrowfully at the door of an inn. Two men dressed in blue observed him.

"Comrade," said one, "here is a well-built young fellow, and of proper height."

They went up to Candide and very civilly invited him to dinner.

"Gentlemen," replied Candide, with a most engaging modesty, "you do me great honour, but I have not wherewithal to pay my share."

"Oh, sir," said one of the blues to him, "people of your appearance and of your merit never pay anything; are you not five feet five inches high?"

"Yes, sir, that is my height," answered he, making a low bow.

"Come, sir, seat yourself; not only will we pay your reckoning, but we will never suffer such a man as you to want money; men are only born to assist one another."

"You are right," said Candide; "this is what I was always taught by Mr. Pangloss, and I see plainly that all is for the best."

They begged of him to accept a few crowns. He took them, and wished to give them his note; they refused; they seated themselves at table.

"Love you not deeply?"

"Oh yes," answered he; "I deeply love Miss Cunegonde."

"No," said one of the gentlemen, "we ask you if you do not deeply love the King of the Bulgarians?"

"Not at all," said he; "for I have never seen him."

"What! he is the best of kings, and we must drink his health."

"Oh! very willingly, gentlemen," and he drank.

"That is enough," they tell him. "Now you are the help, the support, the defender, the hero of the Bulgarians. Your fortune is made, and your glory is assured."

Instantly they fettered him, and carried him away to the regiment. There he was made to wheel about to the right, and to the left, to draw his rammer, to return his rammer, to present, to fire, to march, and they gave him thirty blows with a cudgel. The next day he did his exercise a little less badly, and he received but twenty blows. The day following they gave him only ten, and he was regarded by his comrades as a prodigy.

"MY FRIEND," SAID THE ORATOR TO HIM, "DO YOU BELIEVE THE POPE TO BE ANTI-CHRIST?" "I HAVE NOT HEARD IT," ANSWERED CANDIDE; "BUT WHETHER HE BE, OR WHETHER HE BE NOT, I WANT BREAD."

Candide, all stupefied, could not yet very well realise how he was a hero. He resolved one fine day in spring to go for a walk, marching straight before him, believing that it was a privilege of the human as well as of the animal species to make use of their legs as they pleased. He had advanced two leagues when he was overtaken by four others, heroes of six feet, who bound him and carried him to a dungeon. He was asked which he would like the best, to be whipped six-and-thirty times through all the regiment, or to receive at once twelve balls of lead in his brain. He vainly said that human will is free, and that he chose neither the one nor the other. He was forced to make a choice; he determined, in virtue of that gift of God called liberty, to run the gauntlet six-and-thirty times. He bore this twice. The regiment was composed of two thousand men; that composed for him four thousand strokes, which laid bare all his muscles and nerves, from the nape of his neck quite down to his rump. As they were going to proceed to a third whipping, Candide, able to bear no more, begged as a favour that they would be so good as to shoot him. He obtained this favour; they bandaged his eyes, and bade him kneel down. The King of the Bulgarians passed at this moment and ascertained the nature of the crime. As he had great talent, he understood from all that he learnt of Candide that he was a young metaphysician, extremely ignorant of the things of this world, and he accorded him his pardon with a clemency which will bring him praise in all the journals, and throughout all ages.

An able surgeon cured Candide in three weeks by means of emollients taught by Dioscorides. He had already a little skin, and was able to march when the King of the Bulgarians gave battle to the King of the Abares.[2]

CHAPTER III

HOW CANDIDE MADE HIS ESCAPE FROM THE BULGARIANS, AND WHAT AFTERWARDS BECAME OF HIM

THERE WAS NEVER anything so gallant, so spruce, so brilliant, and so well disposed as the two armies. Trumpets, fifes, hautboys, drums, and cannon made music such as Hell itself had never heard. The cannons first of all laid flat about six thousand men on each side; the muskets swept away from this best of worlds nine or ten thousand ruffians who infested its surface. The bayonet was also a *sufficient reason* for the death of several thousands. The whole might amount to thirty thousand souls. Candide, who trembled like a philosopher, hid himself as well as he could during this heroic butchery.

At length, while the two kings were causing Te Deum to be sung each in his own camp, Candide resolved to go and reason elsewhere on effects and causes. He passed over heaps of dead and dying, and first reached a neighbouring village; it was in cinders, it was an Abare village which the Bulgarians had burnt according to the laws of war. Here, old men covered with wounds, beheld their wives, hugging their children to their bloody breasts, massacred before their faces; there, their daughters, disembowelled and breathing their last after having satisfied the natural wants of Bulgarian heroes; while others, half burnt in the flames, begged to be despatched. The earth was strewed with brains, arms, and legs.

Candide fled quickly to another village; it belonged to the Bulgarians; and the Abarian heroes had treated it in the same way. Candide, walking always over palpitating limbs or across ruins, arrived at last beyond the seat of war, with a few provisions in his knapsack, and Miss Cunegonde always in his heart. His provisions failed him when he arrived in Holland; but having heard that everybody was rich in that country, and that they were Christians, he did not doubt but he should meet with the same treatment from them as he had met with in the Baron's castle, before Miss Cunegonde's bright eyes were the cause of his expulsion thence.

He asked alms of several grave-looking people, who all answered him, that if he continued to follow this trade they would confine him to the house of correction, where he should be taught to get a living.

The next he addressed was a man who had been haranguing a large assembly for a whole hour on the subject of charity. But the orator, looking askew, said:

"What are you doing here? Are you for the good cause?"

"There can be no effect without a cause," modestly answered Candide; "the whole is necessarily concatenated and arranged for the best. It was necessary for me to have been banished from the presence of Miss Cunegonde, to have afterwards run the gauntlet, and now it is necessary I should beg my bread until I learn to earn it; all this cannot be otherwise."

"My friend," said the orator to him, "do you believe the Pope to be Anti-Christ?"

"I have not heard it," answered Candide; "but whether he be, or whether he be not, I want bread."

"Thou dost not deserve to eat," said the other. "Begone, rogue; begone, wretch; do not come near me again."

The orator's wife, putting her head out of the window, and spying a man that doubted whether the Pope was Anti-Christ, poured over him a full . . . Oh, heavens! to what excess does religious zeal carry the ladies.

A man who had never been christened, a good Anabaptist, named James, beheld the cruel and ignominious treatment shown to one of his brethren, an unfeathered biped with a rational soul, he took him home, cleaned him, gave him bread and beer, presented him with two florins, and even wished to teach him the manufacture of Persian stuffs which they make in Holland. Candide, almost prostrating himself before him, cried:

"Master Pangloss has well said that all is for the best in this world, for I am infinitely more touched by your extreme generosity than with the inhumanity of that gentleman in the black coat and his lady."

The next day, as he took a walk, he met a beggar all covered with scabs, his eyes diseased, the end of his nose eaten away, his mouth distorted, his teeth black, choking in his throat, tormented with a violent cough, and spitting out a tooth at each effort.

CHAPTER IV

HOW CANDIDE FOUND HIS OLD MASTER PANGLOSS, AND WHAT HAPPENED TO THEM

CANDIDE, YET MORE moved with compassion than with horror, gave to this shocking beggar the two florins which he had received from the honest Anabaptist James. The spectre looked at him very earnestly, dropped a few tears, and fell upon his neck. Candide recoiled in disgust.

"Alas!" said one wretch to the other, "do you no longer know your dear Pangloss?"

"What do I hear? You, my dear master! you in this terrible plight! What misfortune has happened to you? Why are you no longer in the most magnificent of castles? What has become of Miss Cunegonde, the pearl of girls, and nature's masterpiece?"

"I am so weak that I cannot stand," said Pangloss.

Upon which Candide carried him to the Anabaptist's stable, and gave him a crust of bread. As soon as Pangloss had refreshed himself a little:

"Well," said Candide, "Cunegonde?"

"She is dead," replied the other.

Candide fainted at this word; his friend recalled his senses with a little bad vinegar which he found by chance in the stable. Candide reopened his eyes.

"Cunegonde is dead! Ah, best of worlds, where art thou? But of what illness did she die? Was it not for grief, upon seeing her father kick me out of his magnificent castle?

"No," said Pangloss, "she was ripped open by the Bulgarian soldiers, after having been violated by many; they broke the Baron's head for attempting to defend her; my lady, her mother, was cut in pieces; my poor pupil was served just in the same manner as his sister; and as for the castle, they have not left one stone upon another, not a barn, nor a sheep, nor a duck, nor a tree; but we have had our revenge, for the Abates have done the very same thing to a neighbouring barony, which belonged to a Bulgarian lord."

At this discourse Candide fainted again; but coming to himself, and having said all that it became him to say, inquired into the cause and effect, as well as into the *sufficient reason* that had reduced Pangloss to so miserable a plight.

"Alas!" said the other, "it was love; love, the comfort of the human species, the preserver of the universe, the soul of all sensible beings, love, tender love."

"Alas!" said Candide, "I know this love, that sovereign of hearts, that soul of our souls; yet it never cost me more than a kiss and twenty kicks on the backside. How could this beautiful cause produce in you an effect so abominable?"

Pangloss made answer in these terms: "Oh, my dear Candide, you remember Paquette, that pretty wench who waited on our noble baroness; in her arms I tasted the delights of paradise, which produced in me those hell torments with which you see me devoured; she was infected with them, she is perhaps dead of them. This present Paquette received of a learned Grey Friar, who had traced it to its source; he had had it of an old countess, who half received it from a cavalry captain, who owed it to a marchioness, who took it from a page, who had received it from a Jesuit, who when a novice had it in a direct line from one of the companions of Christopher Columbus.[3] For my part I shall give it to nobody. I am dying."

"Oh, Pangloss!" cried Candide, "what a strange genealogy! Is not the Devil the original stock of it?"

"Not at all," replied this great man, "it was a thing unavoidable, a necessary ingredient in the best of worlds; for if Columbus had not in an island of America caught this disease, which contaminates the source of life, frequently even hinders generation, and which is evidently opposed to the great end of nature, we should have neither chocolate nor cochineal. We are also to observe that upon our continent, this distemper is like religious controversy, confined to a particular spot. The Turks, the Indians, the Persians, the Chinese, the Siamese, the Japanese, know nothing of it; but there is a sufficient reason for believing that they will know it in their turn in a few centuries. In the meantime, it has made marvellous progress among us, especially in those great armies composed of honest well-disciplined hirelings, who decide the destiny of states; for we may safely affirm that when an army of thirty thousand men fights another of an equal number, there are about twenty thousand of them p—x—d on each side."

"Well, this is wonderful!" said Candide, "but you must get cured."

"Alas! how can I?" said Pangloss, "I have not a farthing, my friend, and all over the globe there is no letting of blood or taking a glister, without paying, or somebody paying for you."

These last words determined Candide; he went and flung himself at the feet of the charitable Anabaptist James, and gave him so touching a picture of the state to which his friend was reduced, that the good man did not scruple to take Dr. Pangloss into his house, and had him cured at his expense. In the cure Pangloss lost only an eye and an ear. He wrote well, and knew arithmetic perfectly. The Anabaptist James made him his bookkeeper. At the end of two months, being obliged to go to Lisbon about some mercantile affairs, he took the two philosophers with him in his ship. Pangloss explained to him how everything was so constituted that it could not be better. James was not of this opinion.

"It is more likely," said he, "mankind have a little corrupted nature, for they were not born wolves, and they have become wolves; God has given them neither cannon of four-and-twenty pounders, nor bayonets; and yet they have made cannon and bayonets to destroy one another. Into this account I might throw not only bankrupts, but Justice which seizes on the effects of bankrupts to cheat the creditors."

"All this was indispensable," replied the one-eyed doctor, "for private misfortunes make the general good, so that the more private misfortunes there are the greater is the general good."

While he reasoned, the sky darkened, the winds blew from the four quarters, and the ship was assailed by a most terrible tempest within sight of the port of Lisbon.

CHAPTER V

TEMPEST, SHIPWRECK, EARTHQUAKE, AND WHAT BECAME OF DOCTOR PANGLOSS, CANDIDE, AND JAMES THE ANABAPTIST

HALF DEAD OF that inconceivable anguish which the rolling of a ship produces, one-half of the passengers were not even sensible of the danger. The other half shrieked and prayed. The sheets were rent, the masts broken, the vessel gaped. Work who would, no one heard, no one commanded. The Anabaptist being upon deck bore a hand; when a brutish sailor struck him roughly and laid him sprawling; but with the violence of the blow he himself tumbled head foremost overboard, and stuck upon a piece of the broken mast. Honest James ran to his assistance, hauled him up, and from the effort he made was precipitated into the sea in sight of the sailor, who left him to perish, without deigning to look at him. Candide drew near and saw his benefactor, who rose above the water one moment and was then swallowed up for ever. He was just going to jump after him, but was prevented by the philosopher Pangloss, who demonstrated to him that the Bay of Lisbon had been made on purpose for the Anabaptist to be drowned. While he was proving this *a priori*, the ship foundered; all perished except Pangloss, Candide, and that brutal sailor who had drowned the good Anabaptist. The villain swam safety to the shore, while Pangloss and Candide were borne thither upon a plank.

As soon as they recovered themselves a little they walked toward Lisbon. They had some money left, with which they hoped to save themselves from starving, after they had escaped drowning. Scarcely had they reached the city, lamenting the death of their benefactor, when they felt the earth tremble under their feet. The sea swelled and foamed in the harbour, and beat to pieces the vessels riding at anchor. Whirlwinds of fire and ashes covered the streets and public places; houses fell, roofs were flung upon the pavements, and the pavements were scattered. Thirty thousand inhabitants of all ages and sexes were crushed under the ruins.[4] The sailor, whistling and swearing, said there was booty to be gained here.

"What can be the *sufficient reason* of this phenomenon?" said Pangloss.

"This is the Last Day!" cried Candide.

The sailor ran among the ruins, facing death to find money; finding it, he took it, got drunk, and having slept himself sober, purchased the favours of the first good-natured wench whom he met on the ruins, of the destroyed houses, and in the midst of the dying and the dead. Pangloss pulled him by the sleeve.

"My friend," said he, "this is not right. You sin against the *universal reason;* you choose your time badly."

"S'blood and fury!" answered the other; "I am a sailor and born at Batavia. Four times have I trampled upon the crucifix in four voyages to Japan;[5] a fig for thy universal reason."

Some falling stones had wounded Candide. He lay stretched in the street covered with rubbish.

"Alas!" said he to Pangloss, "get me a little wine and oil; I am dying."

"This concussion of the earth is no new thing," answered Pangloss. "The city of Lima, in America, experienced the same convulsions last year; the same cause, the same effects; there is certainly a train of sulphur under ground from Lima to Lisbon."

"Nothing more probable," said Candide; "but for the love of God a little oil and wine."

"How, probable?" replied the philosopher. "I maintain that the point is capable of being demonstrated."

Candide fainted away, and Pangloss fetched him some water from a neighbouring fountain. The following day they rummaged among the ruins and found provisions, with which they repaired their exhausted strength. After this they joined with others in relieving those inhabitants who had escaped death. Some, whom they had succoured, gave them as good a dinner as they could in such disastrous circumstances; true, the repast was mournful, and the company moistened their bread with tears; but Pangloss consoled them, assuring them that things could not be otherwise.

"For," said he, "all that is is for the best. If there is a volcano at Lisbon it cannot be elsewhere. It is impossible that things should be other than they are; for everything is right."

A little man dressed in black, Familiar of the Inquisition, who sat by him, politely took up his word and said:

"Apparently, then, sir, you do not believe in original sin; for if all is for the best there has then been neither Fall nor punishment."

"I humbly ask your Excellency's pardon," answered Pangloss, still more politely; "for the Fall and curse of man necessarily entered into the system of the best of worlds."

CANDIDE, TERRIFIED, AMAZED, DESPERATE, ALL BLOODY, ALL PALPITATING, SAID TO HIMSELF: "IF THIS IS THE BEST OF POSSIBLE WORLDS, WHAT THEN ARE THE OTHERS?"

"Sir," said the Familiar, "you do not then believe in liberty?"

"Your Excellency will excuse me," said Pangloss; "liberty is consistent with absolute necessity, for it was necessary we should be free; for, in short, the determinate will—"

Pangloss was in the middle of his sentence, when the Familiar beckoned to his footman, who gave him a glass of wine from Porto or Oporto.

CHAPTER VI

HOW THE PORTUGUESE MADE A BEAUTIFUL AUTO-DA-FÉ, TO PREVENT ANY FURTHER EARTHQUAKES; AND HOW CANDIDE WAS PUBLICLY WHIPPED

AFTER THE EARTHQUAKE had destroyed three-fourths of Lisbon, the sages of that country could think of no means more effectual to prevent utter ruin than to give the people a beautiful *auto-da-fé*;[6] for it had been decided by the University of Coimbra, that the burning of a few people alive by a slow fire, and with great ceremony, is an infallible secret to hinder the earth from quaking.

In consequence hereof, they had seized on a Biscayner, convicted of having married his godmother, and on two Portuguese, for rejecting the bacon which larded a chicken they were eating;[7] after dinner, they came and secured Dr. Pangloss, and his disciple Candide, the one for speaking his mind, the other for having listened with an air of approbation. They were conducted to separate apartments, extremely cold, as they were never incommoded by the sun. Eight days after they were dressed in *san-benitos*[8] and their heads ornamented with paper mitres. The mitre and *san-benito* belonging to Candide were painted with reversed flames and with devils that had neither tails nor claws; but Pangloss's devils had claws and tails and the flames were upright. They marched in procession thus habited and heard a very pathetic sermon, followed by fine church music. Candide was whipped in cadence while they were singing; the Biscayner, and the two men who had refused to eat bacon, were burnt; and Pangloss was hanged, though that was not the custom. The same day, the earth sustained a most violent concussion.

Candide, terrified, amazed, desperate, all bloody, all palpitating, said to himself:

"If this is the best of possible worlds, what then are the others? Well, if I had been only whipped I could put up with it, for I experienced that among the Bulgarians; but oh, my dear Pangloss! thou greatest of philosophers, that I should have seen you hanged, without knowing for what! Oh, my dear Anabaptist, thou best of men, that thou should'st have been drowned in the very harbour! Oh, Miss Cunegonde, thou pearl of girls! that thou should'st have had thy belly ripped open!"

Thus he was musing, scarce able to stand, preached at, whipped, absolved, and blessed, when an old woman accosted him saying:

"My son, take courage and follow me."

CHAPTER VII

HOW THE OLD WOMAN TOOK CARE OF CANDIDE, AND HOW HE FOUND THE OBJECT HE LOVED

CANDIDE DID NOT take courage, but followed the old woman to a decayed house, where she gave him a pot of pomatum to anoint his sores, showed him a very neat little bed, with a suit of clothes hanging up, and left him something to eat and drink.

"Eat, drink, sleep," said she, "and may our lady of Atocha,[9] the great St. Anthony of Padua, and the great St. James of Compostela, receive you under their protection. I shall be back to-morrow."

Candide, amazed at all he had suffered and still more with the charity of the old woman, wished to kiss her hand.

"It is not my hand you must kiss," said the old woman; "I shall be back to-morrow. Anoint yourself with the pomatum, eat and sleep."

Candide, notwithstanding so many disasters, ate and slept. The next morning the old woman brought him his breakfast, looked at his back, and rubbed it herself with another ointment; in like manner she brought him his dinner; and at night she returned with his supper. The day following she went through the very same ceremonies.

"Who are you?" said Candide; "who has inspired you with so much goodness? What return can I make you?"

The good woman made no answer; she returned in the evening, but brought no supper.

"Come with me," she said, "and say nothing."

She took him by the am, and walked with him about a quarter of a mile into the country; they arrived at a lonely house, surrounded with gardens and canals. The old woman knocked at a little door, it opened, she led Candide up a private staircase into a small apartment richly furnished. She left him on a brocaded sofa, shut the door and went away. Candide thought himself in a dream; indeed, that he had been dreaming unluckily all his life, and that the present moment was the only agreeable part of it all.

The old woman returned very soon, supporting with difficulty a trembling woman of a majestic figure, brilliant with jewels, and covered with a veil.

"Take off that veil," said the old woman to Candide.

The young man approaches, he raises the veil with a timid hand. Oh! what a moment! what surprise! he believes he beholds Miss Cunegonde? he really sees her! it is herself! His strength fails him, he cannot utter a word, but drops at her feet. Cunegonde falls upon the sofa. The old woman supplies a smelling bottle; they come to themselves and recover their speech. As they began with broken accents, with questions and answers interchangeably interrupted with sighs, with tears, and cries, the old woman desired they would make less noise and then she left them to themselves.

"What, is it you?" said Candide, "you live? I find you again in Portugal? then you have not been ravished? then they did not rip open your belly as Doctor Pangloss informed me?"

"Yes, they did," said the beautiful Cunegonde; "but those two accidents are not always mortal."

"But were your father and mother killed?"

"It is but too true," answered Cunegonde, in tears.

"And your brother?"

"My brother also was killed."

"And why are you in Portugal? and how did you know of my being here? and by what strange adventure did you contrive to bring me to this house?"

"I will tell you all that," replied the lady, "but first of all let me know your history, since the innocent kiss you gave me and the kicks which you received."

Candide respectfully obeyed her, and though he was still in a surprise, though his voice was feeble and trembling, though his back still pained him, yet he gave her a most ingenuous account of everything that had befallen him since the moment of their separation. Cunegonde lifted up her eyes to heaven; shed tears upon hearing of the death of the good Anabaptist and of Pangloss; after which she spoke as follows to Candide, who did not lose a word and devoured her with his eyes.

CHAPTER VIII

THE HISTORY OF CUNEGONDE

"I WAS IN bed and fast asleep when it pleased God to send the Bulgarians to our delightful castle of Thunder-ten-Tronckh; they slew my father and brother, and cut my mother in pieces. A tall Bulgarian, six feet high, perceiving that I had fainted away at this sight, began to ravish me; this made me recover; I regained my senses, I cried, I struggled, I bit, I scratched, I wanted to tear out the tall Bulgarian's eyes—not knowing that what happened at my father's house was the usual practice of war. The brute gave me a cut in the left side with his hanger, and the mark is still upon me.

"Ah! I hope I shall see it," said honest Candide.

"You shall," said Cunegonde, "but let us continue."

"Do so," replied Candide.

Thus she resumed the thread of her story:

"A Bulgarian captain came in, saw me all bleeding, and the soldier not in the least disconcerted. The captain flew into a passion at the disrespectful behaviour of the brute, and slew him on my body. He ordered my wounds to be dressed, and took me to his quarters as a prisoner of war. I washed the few shirts that he had, I did his cooking; he thought me very pretty—he avowed it; on the other hand, I must own he had a good shape, and a soft and white skin; but he had little or no mind or philosophy, and you might see plainly that he had never been instructed by Doctor Pangloss. In three months' time, having lost all his money, and being grown tired of my company, he sold me to a Jew, named Don Issachar, who traded to Holland and Portugal, and had a strong passion for women. This Jew was much attached to my person, but could not triumph over it; I resisted him better than the Bulgarian soldier. A modest woman may be ravished once, but her virtue is strengthened by it. In order to render me more tractable, he brought me to this country house. Hitherto I had imagined that nothing could equal the beauty of Thunder-ten-Tronckh Castle; but I found I was mistaken.

"The Grand Inquisitor, seeing me one day at Mass, stared long at me, and sent to tell me that he wished to speak on private matters. I was conducted to his palace, where I acquainted him with the history of my family, and he represented to me how much it was beneath my rank to belong to an Israelite. A proposal was then made to Don Issachar that he should resign me to my lord. Don Issachar, being the court banker, and a man of credit, would hear nothing of it. The Inquisitor threatened him with an *auto-da-fé*. At last my Jew, intimidated, concluded a bargain, by which the house and myself should belong to both in common; the Jew should have for himself Monday, Wednesday, and Saturday, and the Inquisitor should have the rest of the week. It is now six months since this agreement was made. Quarrels have not been wanting, for they could not decide whether the night from Saturday to Sunday belonged to the old law or to the new. For my part, I have so far held out against both, and I verily believe that this is the reason why I am still beloved.

"At length, to avert the scourge of earthquakes, and to intimidate Don Issachar, my Lord Inquisitor was pleased to celebrate an *auto-da-fé*. He did me the honour to invite me to the ceremony. I had a very good seat, and the ladies were served with refreshments between Mass and the execution. I was in truth seized with horror at the burning of those two Jews, and of the honest Biscayner who had married his godmother; but what was my surprise, my fright, my trouble, when I saw in a *san-benito* and mitre a figure which resembled that of Pangloss! I rubbed my eyes, I looked at him attentively; I saw him hanged; I fainted. Scarcely had I recovered my senses than I saw you stripped, stark naked, and this was the height of my horror, consternation, grief, and despair. I tell you, truthfully, that your skin is yet whiter and of a more perfect colour than that of my Bulgarian captain. This spectacle redoubled all the feelings which overwhelmed and devoured me. I screamed out, and would have said, 'Stop, barbarians!' but my voice failed me, and my cries would have been useless after you had been severely whipped. How is it possible, said I, that the beloved Candide and the wise Pangloss should both be at Lisbon, the one to receive a hundred lashes, and the other to be hanged by the Grand Inquisitor, of whom I am the well-beloved? Pangloss most cruelly deceived me when he said that everything in the world is for the best.

"Agitated, lost, sometimes beside myself, and sometimes ready to die of weakness, my mind was filled with the massacre of my father, mother, and brother, with the insolence of the ugly Bulgarian soldier, with the stab that he gave me, with my servitude under the Bulgarian captain, with my hideous Don Issachar, with my abominable Inquisitor, with the execution of Doctor Pangloss, with the grand Miserere to which they whipped you, and especially with the kiss I gave you behind the screen the day that I had last seen you. I praised God for bringing you back to me after so many trials, and I charged my old woman to take care of you, and to conduct you hither as soon as possible. She has executed her commission perfectly well; I have tasted the inexpressible pleasure of seeing you again, of hearing you, of speaking with you. But you must be hungry, for myself, I am famished; let us have supper."

They both sat down to table, and, when supper was over, they placed themselves once more on the sofa; where they were when Signor Don Issachar arrived. It was the Jewish Sabbath, and Issachar had come to enjoy his rights, and to explain his tender love.

CHAPTER IX

WHAT BECAME OF CUNEGONDE, CANDIDE, THE GRAND INQUISITOR, AND THE JEW

THIS ISSACHAR WAS the most choleric Hebrew that had ever been seen in Israel since the Captivity in Babylon.

"What!" said he, "thou bitch of a Galilean, was not the Inquisitor enough for thee? Must this rascal also share with me?"

In saying this he drew a long poniard which he always carried about him; and not imagining that his adversary had any arms he threw himself upon Candide; but our honest Westphalian had received a handsome sword from the old woman along with the suit of clothes. He drew his rapier, despite his gentleness, and laid the Israelite stone dead upon the cushions at Cunegonde's feet.

"Holy Virgin!" cried she, "what will become of us? A man killed in my apartment! If the officers of justice come, we are lost!"

"Had not Pangloss been hanged," said Candide, "he would give us good counsel in this emergency, for he was a profound philosopher. Failing him let us consult the old woman."

She was very prudent and commenced to give her opinion when suddenly another little door opened. It was an hour after midnight, it was the beginning of Sunday. This day belonged to my lord the Inquisitor. He entered, and saw the whipped Candide, sword in hand, a dead man upon the floor, Cunegonde aghast, and the old woman giving counsel.

At this moment, the following is what passed in the soul of Candide, and how he reasoned:

If this holy man call in assistance, he will surely have me burnt; and Cunegonde will perhaps be served in the same manner; he was the cause of my being cruelly whipped; he is my rival; and, as I have now begun to kill, I will kill away, for there is no time to hesitate. This reasoning was clear and instantaneous; so that without giving time to the Inquisitor to recover from his surprise, he pierced him through and through, and cast him beside the Jew.

"Yet again!" said Cunegonde, "now there is no mercy for us, we are excommunicated, our last hour has come. How could you do it? you, naturally so gentle, to slay a Jew and a prelate in two minutes!"

"My beautiful young lady," responded Candide, "when one is a lover, jealous and whipped by the Inquisition, one stops at nothing."

The old woman then put in her word, saying:

"There are three Andalusian horses in the stable with bridles and saddles, let the brave Candide get them ready; madame has money, jewels; let us therefore mount quickly on horseback, though I can sit only on one buttock; let us set out for Cadiz. It is the finest weather in the world, and there is great pleasure in travelling in the cool of the night."

Immediately Candide saddled the three horses, and Cunegonde, the old woman and he, travelled thirty miles at a stretch. While they were journeying, the Holy Brotherhood entered the house; my lord the Inquisitor was interred in a handsome church, and Issachar's body was thrown upon a dunghill.

Candide, Cunegonde, and the old woman had now reached the little town of Avacena in the midst of the mountains of the Sierra Morena, and were speaking as follows in a public inn.

CHAPTER X

IN WHAT DISTRESS CANDIDE, CUNEGONDE, AND THE OLD WOMAN ARRIVED AT CADIZ; AND OF THEIR EMBARKATION

"WHO WAS IT that robbed me of my money and jewels?" said Cunegonde, all bathed in tears. "How shall we live? What shall we do? Where find Inquisitors or Jews who will give me more?"

"Alas!" said the old woman, "I have a shrewd suspicion of a reverend Grey Friar who stayed last night in the same inn with us at Badajos. God preserve me from judging rashly, but he came into our room twice, and he set out upon his journey long before us."

"Alas!" said Candide, "dear Pangloss has often demonstrated to me that the goods of this world are common to all men, and that each has an equal right to them. But according to these principles the Grey Friar ought to have left us enough to carry us through our journey. Have you nothing at all left, my dear Cunegonde?"

"Not a farthing," said she.

"What then must we do?" said Candide.

"Sell one of the horses," replied the old woman. "I will ride behind Miss Cunegonde though I can hold myself only on one buttock and we shall reach Cadiz."

In the same inn there was a Benedictine prior who bought the horse for a cheap price. Candide, Cunegonde, and the old woman, having passed through Lucena, Chillas, and Lebrixa, arrived at length at Cadiz. A fleet was there getting ready, and troops assembling to bring to reason the reverend Jesuit Fathers of Paraguay, accused of having made one of the native tribes in the neighborhood of San Sacrament revolt against the Kings of Spain and Portugal. Candide having been in the Bulgarian service, performed the military exercise before the general of this little army with so graceful an address, with so intrepid an air, and with such agility and expedition, that he was given the command of a company of foot. Now, he was a captain! He set sail with Miss Cunegonde, the old woman, two valets, and the two Andalusian horses, which had belonged to the Grand Inquisitor of Portugal.

During their voyage they reasoned a good deal on the philosophy of poor Pangloss.

"We are going into another world," said Candide; "and surely it must be there that all is for the best. For I must confess there is reason to complain a little of what passeth in our world in regard to both natural and moral philosophy.

"I love you with all my heart," said Cunegonde; "but my soul is still full of fright at that which I have seen and experienced."

"All will be well," replied Candide; "the sea of this new world is already better than our European sea; it is calmer, the winds more regular. It is certainly the New World which is the best of all possible worlds.

"God grant it," said Cunegonde; "but I have been so horribly unhappy there that my heart is almost closed to hope."

"You complain," said the old woman; "alas! you have not known such misfortunes as mine."

Cunegonde almost broke out laughing, finding the good woman very amusing, for pretending to have been as unfortunate as she.

"Alas!" said Cunegonde, "my good mother, unless you have been ravished by two Bulgarians, have received two deep wounds in your belly, have had two castles demolished, have had two mothers cut to pieces before your eyes, and two of your lovers whipped at an *auto-da-fé*, I do not conceive how you could be more unfortunate than I. Add that I was born a baroness of seventy-two quarterings—and have been a cook!"

"Miss," replied the old woman, "you do not know my birth; and were I to show you my backside, you would not talk in the manner but would suspend your judgment."

This speech having raised extreme curiosity in the minds of Cunegonde and Candide, the old woman spoke to them as follows.

CHAPTER XI

HISTORY OF THE OLD WOMAN

"I HAD NOT always bleared eyes and red eyelids; neither did my nose always touch my chin; nor was I always a servant. I am the daughter of Pope Urban X.[10] and of the Princess of Palestrina. Until the age of fourteen I was brought up in a palace, to which all the castles of your German barons would scarcely have served for stables; and one of my robes was worth more than all the magnificence of Westphalia. As I grew up I improved in beauty, wit, and every graceful accomplishment, in the midst of pleasures, hopes, and respectful homage. Already I inspired love. My throat was formed, and such a throat! white, firm, and shaped like that of the Venus of Medici; and what eyes! what eyelids! what black eyebrows! such flames darted from my dark pupils that they eclipsed the scintillation of the stars—as I was told by the poets in our part of the world. My waiting women, when dressing and undressing me, used to fall into an ecstasy, whether they viewed me before or behind; how glad would the gentlemen have been to perform that office for them!

"I was affianced to the most excellent Prince of Massa Carara. Such a prince! as handsome as myself, sweet-tempered, agreeable, brilliantly witty, and sparkling with love. I loved him as one loves for the first time—with idolatry, with transport. The nuptials were prepared. There was surprising pomp and magnificence; there were *fêtes*, carousals, continual *opera bouffe*; and all Italy composed sonnets in my praise, though not one of them was passable. I was just upon the point of reaching the summit of bliss, when an old marchioness who had been mistress to the Prince, my husband, invited him to drink chocolate with her. He died in less than two hours of most terrible convulsions. But this is only a bagatelle. My mother, in despair, and scarcely less afflicted than myself, determined to absent herself for some time from so fatal a place. She had a very fine estate in the neighbourhood of Gaeta. We embarked on board a galley of the country which was gilded like the great altar of St. Peter's at Rome. A Sallee corsair swooped down and boarded us. Our men defended themselves like the Pope's soldiers; they flung themselves upon their knees, and threw down their arms, begging of the corsair an absolution *in articulo mortis*.

"Instantly they were stripped as bare as monkeys; my mother, our maids of honour, and myself were all served in the same manner. It is amazing with what expedition those gentry undress people. But what surprised me most was, that they thrust their fingers into the part of our bodies which the generality of women suffer no other instrument but pipes to enter. It appeared to me a very strange kind of ceremony; but thus one judges of things when one has not seen the world. I afterwards learnt that it was to try whether we had concealed any diamonds. This is the practice established from time immemorial, among civilised nations that scour the seas. I was informed that the very religious Knights of Malta never fail to make this search when they take any Turkish prisoners of either sex. It is a law of nations from which they never deviate.

"I need not tell you how great a hardship it was for a young princess and her mother to be made slaves and carried to Morocco. You may easily imagine all we had to suffer on board the pirate vessel. My mother was still very handsome; our maids of honour, and even our waiting women, had more charms than are to be found in all Africa. As for myself, I was ravishing, was exquisite, grace itself, and I was a virgin! I did not remain so long; this flower, which had been reserved for the handsome Prince of Massa Carara, was plucked by the corsair captain. He was an abominable negro, and yet believed that he did me a great deal of honour. Certainly the Princess of Palestrina and myself must have been very strong to go through all that we experienced until our arrival at Morocco. But let us pass on; these are such common things as not to be worth mentioning.

"Morocco swam in blood when we arrived. Fifty sons of the Emperor Muley-Ismael[11] had each their adherents; this produced fifty civil wars, of blacks against blacks, and blacks against tawnies, and tawnies against tawnies, and mulattoes against mulattoes. In short it was a continual carnage throughout the empire.

"No sooner were we landed, than the blacks of a contrary faction to that of my captain attempted to rob him of his booty. Next to jewels and gold we were the most valuable things he had. I was witness to such a battle as you have never seen in your European climates. The northern nations have not that heat in their blood, nor that raging lust for women, so common in Africa. It seems that you Europeans have only milk in your veins; but it is vitriol, it is fire which runs in those of the inhabitants of Mount Atlas and the neighbouring countries. They fought with the fury of the lions, tigers, and serpents of the country, to see who should have us. A Moor seized my mother by the right arm, while my captain's lieutenant held her by the left; a Moorish soldier had hold of her by one leg, and one of our corsairs held her by the other. Thus almost all our women were drawn in quarters by four men. My captain concealed me behind him; and with his drawn scimitar cut and slashed every one that opposed his fury. At length I saw all our Italian women, and my mother herself, torn, mangled, massacred, by the monsters who disputed over them. The slaves, my companions, those who had taken them, soldiers, sailors, blacks, whites, mulattoes, and at last my captain, all were killed, and I remained dying on a heap of dead. Such scenes as this were transacted through an extent of three hundred leagues—and yet they never missed the five prayers a day ordained by Mahomet.

"With difficulty I disengaged myself from such a heap of slaughtered bodies, and crawled to a large orange tree on the bank of a neighbouring rivulet, where I fell, oppressed with fright, fatigue, horror, despair, and hunger. Immediately after, my senses, overpowered, gave themselves up to sleep, which was yet more swooning than repose. I was in this state of weakness and insensibility, between life and death, when I felt myself pressed by something that moved upon my body. I opened my eyes, and saw a white man, of good countenance, who sighed, and who said between his teeth: '*O che sciagura d'essere senza coglioni!*'"[12]

CHAPTER XII

THE ADVENTURES OF THE OLD WOMAN CONTINUED

"ASTONISHED AND DELIGHTED to hear my native language, and no less surprised at what this man said, I made answer that there were much greater misfortunes than that of which he complained. I told him in a few words of the horrors which I had endured, and fainted a second time. He carried me to a neighbouring house, put me to bed, gave me food, waited upon me, consoled me, flattered me; he told me that he had never seen any one so beautiful as I, and that he never so much regretted the loss of what it was impossible to recover.

"'I was born at Naples,' said he, 'there they geld two or three thousand children every year; some die of the operation, others acquire a voice more beautiful than that of women, and others are raised to offices of state.[13] This operation was performed on me with great success and I was chapel musician to madam, the Princess of Palestrina.'

"'To my mother!' cried I.

"'Your mother!' cried he, weeping. 'What! can you be that young princess whom I brought up until the age of six years, and who promised so early to be as beautiful as you?'

"'It is I, indeed; but my mother lies four hundred yards hence, torn in quarters, under a heap of dead bodies.'

"I told him all my adventures, and he made me acquainted with his; telling me that he had been sent to the Emperor of Morocco by a Christian power, to conclude a treaty with that prince, in consequence of which he was to be furnished with military stores and ships to help to demolish the commerce of other Christian Governments.

A HUNDRED TIMES I WAS UPON THE POINT OF KILLING MYSELF; BUT STILL I LOVED LIFE.

"'My mission is done,' said this honest eunuch; 'I go to embark for Ceuta, and will take you to Italy. *Ma che sciagura d'essere senza coglioni!*"

"I thanked him with tears of commiseration; and instead of taking me to Italy he conducted me to Algiers, where he sold me to the Dey. Scarcely was I sold, than the plague which had made the tour of Africa, Asia, and Europe, broke out with great malignancy in Algiers. You have seen earthquakes; but pray, miss, have you ever had the plague?"

"Never," answered Cunegonde.

"If you had," said the old woman, "you would acknowledge that it is far more terrible than an earthquake. It is common in Africa, and I caught it. Imagine to yourself the distressed situation of the daughter of a Pope, only fifteen years old, who, in less than three months, had felt the miseries of poverty and slavery, had been ravished almost every day, had beheld her mother drawn in quarters, had experienced famine and war, and was dying of the plague in Algiers. I did not die, however, but my eunuch, and the Dey, and almost the whole seraglio of Algiers perished.

"As soon as the first fury of this terrible pestilence was over, a sale was made of the Dey's slaves; I was purchased by a merchant, and carried to Tunis; this man sold me to another merchant, who sold me again to another at Tripoli; from Tripoli I was sold to Alexandria, from Alexandria to Smyrna, and from Smyrna to Constantinople. At length I became the property of an Aga of the Janissaries, who was soon ordered away to the defence of Azof, then besieged by the Russians.

"The Aga, who was a very gallant man, took his whole seraglio with him, and lodged us in a small fort on the Palus Méotides, guarded by two black eunuchs and twenty soldiers. The Turks killed prodigious numbers of the

Russians, but the latter had their revenge. Azof was destroyed by fire, the inhabitants put to the sword, neither sex nor age was spared; until there remained only our little fort, and the enemy wanted to starve us out. The twenty Janissaries had sworn they would never surrender. The extremities of famine to which they were reduced, obliged them to eat our two eunuchs, for fear of violating their oath. And at the end of a few days they resolved also to devour the women.

"We had a very pious and humane Iman, who preached an excellent sermon, exhorting them not to kill us all at once.

"'Only cut off a buttock of each of those ladies,' said he, 'and you'll fare extremely well; if you must go to it again, there will be the same entertainment a few days hence; heaven will accept of so charitable an action, and send you relief.'

"He had great eloquence; he persuaded them; we underwent this terrible operation. The Iman applied the same balsam to us, as he does to children after circumcision; and we all nearly died.

"Scarcely had the Janissaries finished the repast with which we had furnished them, than the Russians came in flat-bottomed boats; not a Janissary escaped. The Russians paid no attention to the condition we were in. There are French surgeons in all parts of the world; one of them who was very clever took us under his care—he cured us; and as long as I live I shall remember that as soon as my wounds were healed he made proposals to me. He bid us all be of good cheer, telling us that the like had happened in many sieges, and that it was according to the laws of war.

"As soon as my companions could walk, they were obliged to set out for Moscow. I fell to the share of a Boyard who made me his gardener, and gave me twenty lashes a day. But this nobleman having in two years' time been broke upon the wheel along with thirty more Boyards for some broils at court, I profited by that event; I fled. I traversed all Russia; I was a long time an inn-holder's servant at Riga, the same at Rostock, at Vismar, at Leipzig, at Cassel, at Utrecht, at Leyden, at the Hague, at Rotterdam. I waxed old in misery and disgrace, having only one-half of my posteriors, and always remembering I was a Pope's daughter. A hundred times I was upon the point of killing myself; but still I loved life. This ridiculous foible is perhaps one of our most fatal characteristics; for is there anything more absurd than to wish to carry continually a burden which one can always throw down? to detest existence and yet to cling to one's existence? in brief, to caress the serpent which devours us, till he has eaten our very heart?

"In the different countries which it has been my lot to traverse, and the numerous inns where I have been servant, I have taken notice of a vast number of people who held their own existence in abhorrence, and yet I never knew of more than eight who voluntarily put an end to their misery; three negroes, four Englishmen, and a German professor named Robek.[14] I ended by being servant to the Jew, Don Issachar, who placed me near your presence, my fair lady. I am determined to share your fate, and have been much more affected with your misfortunes than with my own. I would never even have spoken to you of my misfortunes, had you not piqued me a little, and if it were not customary to tell stories on board a ship in order to pass away the time. In short, Miss Cunegonde, I have had experience, I know the world; therefore I advise you to divert yourself, and prevail upon each passenger to tell his story; and if there be one of them all, that has not cursed his life many a time, that has not frequently looked upon himself as the unhappiest of mortals, I give you leave to throw me headforemost into the sea."

CHAPTER XIII

HOW CANDIDE WAS FORCED AWAY FROM FAIR CUNEGONDE AND THE OLD WOMAN

THE BEAUTIFUL CUNEGONDE having heard the old woman's history, paid her all the civilities due to a person of her rank and merit. She likewise accepted her proposal, and engaged all the passengers, one after the other, to relate their adventures; and then both she and Candide allowed that the old woman was in the tight.

"It is a great pity," said Candide, "that the sage Pangloss was hanged contrary to custom at an *auto-da-fé*; he would tell us most amazing things in regard to the physical and moral evils that overspread earth and sea, and I should be able, with due respect, to make a few objections."

While each passenger was recounting his story, the ship made her way. They landed at Buenos Ayres. Cunegonde, Captain Candide, and the old woman, waited on the Governor, Don Fernando d'Ibaraa, y Figueora, y Mascarenes, y Lampourdos, y Souza. This nobleman had a stateliness becoming a person who bore so many names. He spoke to men with so noble a disdain, carried his nose so loftily, raised his voice so unmercifully, assumed so imperious an air, and stalked with such intolerable pride, that those who saluted him were strongly inclined to give him a good drubbing. Cunegonde appeared to him the most beautiful he had ever met. The first thing he did was to ask whether she was not the captain's wife. The manner in which he asked the question alarmed Candide; he durst not say she was his wife, because indeed she was not; neither durst he say she was his sister, because it was not so; and although this obliging lie had been formerly much in favour among the ancients, and although it could be useful to the moderns, his soul was too pure to betray the truth.

"Miss Cunegonde," said he, "is to do me the honour to marry me, and we beseech your excellency to deign to sanction our marriage."

Don Fernando d'Ibaraa, y Figueora, y Mascarenes, y Lampourdos, y Souza, turning up his moustachios, smiled mockingly, and ordered Captain Candide to go and review his company. Candide obeyed, and the Governor remained alone with Miss Cunegonde. He declared his passion, protesting he would marry her the next day in the face of the church, or otherwise, just as should be agreeable to herself. Cunegonde asked a quarter of an hour to consider of it, to consult the old woman, and to take her resolution.

The old woman spoke thus to Cunegonde:

"Miss, you have seventy-two quarterings, and not a farthing; it is now in your power to be wife to the greatest lord in South America, who has very beautiful moustachios. Is it for you to pique yourself upon inviolable fidelity? You have been ravished by Bulgarians; a Jew and an Inquisitor have enjoyed your favours. Misfortune gives sufficient excuse. I own, that if I were in your place, I should have no scruple in marrying the Governor and in making the fortune of Captain Candide."

While the old woman spoke with all the prudence which age and experience gave, a small ship entered the port on board of which were an Alcalde and his alguazils, and this was what had happened.

As the old woman had shrewdly guessed, it was a Grey Friar who stole Cunegonde's money and jewels in the town of Badajos, when she and Candide were escaping. The Friar wanted to sell some of the diamonds to a jeweller; the jeweller knew them to be the Grand Inquisitor's. The Friar before he was hanged confessed he had stolen them. He described the persons, and the route they had taken. The flight of Cunegonde and Candide was already known. They were traced to Cadiz. A vessel was immediately sent in pursuit of them. The vessel was already in the port of Buenos Ayres. The report spread that the Alcalde was going to land, and that he was in pursuit of the murderers of my lord the Grand Inquisitor. The prudent old woman saw at once what was to be done.

"You cannot run away," said she to Cunegonde, "and you have nothing to fear, for it was not you that killed my lord; besides the Governor who loves you will not suffer you to be ill-treated; therefore stay."

She then ran immediately to Candide.

"Fly," said she, "or in an hour you will be burnt."

There was not a moment to lose; but how could he part from Cunegonde, and where could he flee for shelter?

CHAPTER XIV

HOW CANDIDE AND CACAMBO WERE RECEIVED BY THE JESUITS OF PARAGUAY

CANDIDE HAD BROUGHT such a valet with him from Cadiz, as one often meets with on the coasts of Spain and in the American colonies. He was a quarter Spaniard, born of a mongrel in Tucuman; he had been singing-boy, sacristan, sailor, monk, pedlar, soldier, and lackey. His name was Cacambo, and he loved his master, because his master was a very good man. He quickly saddled the two Andalusian horses.

"Come, master, let us follow the old woman's advice; let us start, and run without looking behind us."

Candide shed tears.

"Oh! my dear Cunegonde! must I leave you just at a time when the Governor was going to sanction our nuptials? Cunegonde, brought to such a distance what will become of you?"

"She will do as well as she can," said Cacambo; "the women are never at a loss, God provides for them, let us run."

"Whither art thou carrying me? Where shall we go? What shall we do without Cunegonde?" said Candide.

"By St. James of Compostela," said Cacambo, "you were going to fight against the Jesuits; let us go to fight for them; I know the road well, I'll conduct you to their kingdom, where they will be charmed to have a captain that understands the Bulgarian exercise. You'll make a prodigious fortune; if we cannot find our account in one world we shall in another. It is a great pleasure to see and do new things."

"You have before been in Paraguay, then?" said Candide.

"Ay, sure," answered Cacambo, "I was servant in the College of the Assumption, and am acquainted with the government of the good Fathers as well as I am with the streets of Cadiz. It is an admirable government. The kingdom is upwards of three hundred leagues in diameter, and divided into thirty provinces; there the Fathers possess all, and the people nothing; it is a masterpiece of reason and justice. For my part I see nothing so divine as the Fathers who here make war upon the kings of Spain and Portugal, and in Europe confess those kings; who here kill Spaniards, and in Madrid send them to heaven; this delights me, let us push forward. You are going to be the happiest of mortals. What pleasure will it be to those Fathers to hear that a captain who knows the Bulgarian exercise has come to them!"

As soon as they reached the first barrier, Cacambo told the advanced guard that a captain wanted to speak with my lord the Commandant. Notice was given to the main guard, and immediately a Paraguayan officer ran and laid himself at the feet of the Commandant, to impart this news to him. Candide and Cacambo were disarmed, and their two Andalusian horses seized. The strangers were introduced between two files of musketeers; the Commandant was at the further end, with the three-cornered cap on his head, his gown tucked up, a sword by his side, and a spontoon[15] in his hand. He beckoned, and straightway the new-comers were encompassed by four-and-twenty soldiers. A sergeant told them they must wait, that the Commandant could not speak to them, and that the reverend Father Provincial does not suffer any Spaniard to open his month but in his presence, or to stay above three hours in the province.

"And where is the reverend Father Provincial?" said Cacambo.

"He is upon the parade just after celebrating mass," answered the sergeant, "and you cannot kiss his spurs till three hours hence."

"However," said Cacambo, "the captain is not a Spaniard, but a German. He is ready to perish with hunger as well as myself; cannot we have something for breakfast, while we wait for his reverence?"

The sergeant went immediately to acquaint the Commandant with what he had heard.

"God be praised!" said the reverend Commandant. "since he is a German, I may speak to him; take him to my arbour."

Candide was at once conducted to a beautiful summer-house, ornamented with a very pretty colonnade of green and gold marble, and with trellises, enclosing parraquets, humming-birds, fly-birds, guinea-hens, and all other rare birds. An excellent breakfast was provided in vessels of gold; and while the Paraguayans were eating maize out of wooden dishes, in the open fields and exposed to the heat of the sun, the reverend Father Commandant retired to his arbour.

He was a very handsome young man, with a full face, white skin but high in colour; be had an arched eyebrow, a lively eye, red ears, vermilion lips, a bold air, but such a boldness as neither belonged to a Spaniard nor a Jesuit. They returned their arms to Candide and Cacambo, and also the two Andalusian horses; to whom Cacambo gave some oats to eat just by the arbour, having an eye upon them all the while for fear of a surprise.

Candide first kissed the hem of the Commandant's robe, then they sat down to table.

"You are, then, a German?" said the Jesuit to him in that language.

"Yes, reverend Father," answered Candide.

As they pronounced these words they looked at each other with great amazement, and with such an emotion as they could not conceal.

"And from what part of Germany do you come?" said the Jesuit.

"I am from the dirty province of Westphalia," answered Candide; "I was born in the Castle of Thunder-ten-Tronckh."

"Oh! Heavens! is it possible?" cried the Commandant.

"What a miracle!" cried Candide.

"Is it really you?" said the Commandant.

"It is not possible!" said Candide.

They drew back; they embraced; they shed rivulets of tears.

"What, is it you, reverend Father? You, the brother of the fair Cunegonde! You, that was slain by the Bulgarians! You, the Baron's son! You, a Jesuit in Paraguay! I must confess this is a strange world that we live in. Oh, Pangloss! Pangloss! how glad you would be if you had not been hanged!"

The Commandant sent away the negro slaves and the Paraguayans, who served them with liquors in goblets of rock-crystal. He thanked God and St. Ignatius a thousand times; he clasped Candide in his arms; and their faces were all bathed with tears.

"You will he more surprised, more affected, and transported," said Candide, "when I tell you that Cunegonde, your sister, whom you believe to have been ripped open, is in perfect health."

"Where?"

"In your neighborhood, with the Governor of Buenos Ayres; and I was going to fight against you."

Every word which they uttered in this long conversation but added wonder to wonder. Their souls fluttered on their tongues, listened in their ears, and sparkled in their eyes. As they were Germans, they sat a good while at table, waiting for the reverend Father Provincial, and the Commandant spoke to his dear Candide as follows.

CHAPTER XV

HOW CANDIDE KILLED THE BROTHER OF HIS DEAR CUNEGONDE

"I SHALL HAVE ever present to my memory the dreadful day, on which I saw my father and mother killed, and my sister ravished. When the Bulgarians retired, my dear sister could not be found; but my mother, my father, and myself, with two maid-servants and three little boys all of whom had been slain, were put in a hearse, to be conveyed for interment to a chapel belonging to the Jesuits, within two leagues of our family seat. A Jesuit sprinkled us with some holy water; it was horribly salt; a few drops of it fell into my eyes; the father perceived that my eyelids stirred a little; he put his hand upon my heart and felt it beat. I received assistance, and at the end of three weeks I recovered. You know, my dear Candide, I was very pretty but I grew up much prettier, and the reverend Father Didrie,[16] Superior of that House, conceived the tenderest friendship for me; he gave me the habit of the order, some years after I was sent to Rome. The Father General needed new levies of voting German-Jesuits. The sovereigns of Paraguay admit as few Spanish Jesuits as possible; they prefer those of other nations as being more subordinate to their commands. I was judged fit by the reverend Father-General to go and work in this vineyard. We set out—a Pole, a Tyrolese, and myself. Upon my arrival I was honoured with a sub-deaconship and a lieutenancy. I am to-day colonel and priest. We shall give a warm reception to the King of Spain's troops; I will answer for it that they shall be excommunicated and well beaten. Providence sends you here to assist us. But is it, indeed, true that my dear sister Cunegonde is in the neighbourhood, with the Governor of Buenos Ayres?"

Candide assured him on oath that nothing was more true, and their tears began afresh.

The Baron could not refrain from embracing Candide; he called him his brother, his saviour.

"Ah! perhaps," said he, "we shall together, my dear Candide, enter the town as conquerors, and recover my sister Cunegonde."

"That is all I want," said Candide, "for I intended to marry her, and I still hope to do so."

"You insolent!" replied the Baron, "would you have the impudence to marry my sister who has seventy-two quarterings! I find thou hast the most consummate effrontery to dare to mention so presumptuous a design!"

Candide, petrified at this speech, made answer:

"Reverend Father, all the quarterings in the world signify nothing; I rescued your sister from the arms of a Jew and of an Inquisitor; she has great obligations to me, she wishes to marry me; Master Pangloss always told me that all men are equal, and certainly I will marry her."

"We shall see that, thou scoundrel!" said the Jesuit Baron de Thunder-ten-Tronckh, and that instant struck him across the face with the flat of his sword. Candide in an instant drew his rapier, and plunged it up to the hilt in the Jesuit's belly; but in pulling it out reeking hot, he burst into tears.

"Good God!" said he, "I have killed my old master, my friend, my brother-in-law! I am the best-natured creature in the world, and yet I have already killed three men, and of these three two were priests."

Cacambo, who stood sentry by the door of the arbour, ran to him.

"We have nothing more for it than to sell our lives as dearly as we can," said his master to him, "without doubt some one will soon enter the arbour, and we must die sword in hand."

Cacambo, who had been in a great many scrapes in his lifetime, did not lose his head; he took the Baron's Jesuit habit, put it on Candide, gave him the square cap, and made him mount on horseback. All this was done in the twinkling of an eye.

"Let us gallop fast, master, everybody will take you for a Jesuit, going to give directions to your men, and we shall have passed the frontiers before they will be able to overtake us."

He flew as he spoke these words, crying out aloud in Spanish:

"Make way, make way, for the reverend Father Colonel."

CHAPTER XVI

ADVENTURES OF THE TWO TRAVELLERS, WITH TWO GIRLS, TWO MONKEYS, AND THE SAVAGES CALLED OREILLONS

CANDIDE AND HIS valet had got beyond the barrier, before it was known in the camp that the German Jesuit was dead. The wary Cacambo had taken care to fill his wallet with bread, chocolate, bacon, fruit, and a few bottles of wine. With their Andalusian horses they penetrated into an unknown country, where they perceived no beaten track. At length they came to a beautiful meadow intersected with purling rills. Here our two adventurers fed their horses. Cacambo proposed to his master to take some food, and he set him an example.

"How can you ask me to eat ham," said Candide, "after killing the Baron's son, and being doomed never more to see the beautiful Cunegonde? What will it avail me to spin out my wrenched days and drag them far from her in remorse and despair? And what will the *Journal of Trevoux*[17] say?"

While he was thus lamenting his fate, he went on eating. The sun went down. The two wanderers heard some little cries which seemed to be uttered by women. They did not know whether they were cries of pain or joy; but they started up precipitately with that inquietude and alarm which every little thing inspires in an unknown country. The noise was made by two naked girls, who tripped along the mead, while two monkeys were pursuing them and biting their buttocks. Candide was moved with pity; he had learned to fire a gun in the Bulgarian service, and he was so clever at it, that he could hit a filbert in a hedge without touching a leaf of the tree. He took up his double-barrelled Spanish fusil, let it off, and killed the two monkeys.

"God be praised! My dear Cacambo, I have rescued those two poor creatures from a most perilous situation. If I have committed a sin in killing an Inquisitor and a Jesuit, I have made ample amends by saving the lives of these girls. Perhaps they are young ladies of family; and this adventure may procure us great advantages in this country."

He was continuing, but stopped short when he saw the two girls tenderly embracing the monkeys, bathing their bodies in tears, and rending the air with the most dismal lamentations.

"Little did I expect to see such good-nature," said he at length to Cacambo, who made answer:

"Master, you have done a fine thing now; you have slain the sweethearts of those two young ladies."

"The sweethearts! Is it possible? You are jesting, Cacambo, I can never believe it!"

"Dear master," replied Cacambo; "you are surprised at everything. Why should you think it so strange that in some countries there are monkeys which insinuate themselves into the good graces of the ladies; they are a fourth part human, as I am a fourth part Spaniard."

"Alas!" replied Candide, "I remember to have heard Master Pangloss say, that formerly such accidents used to happen; then these mixtures were productive of Centaurs, Fauns, and Satyrs; and that many of the ancients had seen such monsters, but I looked upon the whole as fabulous."

"You ought now to be convinced," said Cacambo, "that it is the truth, and you see what use is made of those creatures, by persons that have not had a proper education; all I fear is that those ladies will play us some ugly trick."

These sound reflections induced Candide to leave the meadow and to plunge into a wood. He supped there with Cacambo; and after cursing the Portuguese inquisitor, the Governor of Buenos Ayres, and the Baron, they fell asleep on moss. On awaking they felt that they could not move; for during the night the Oreillons, who inhabited that country, and to whom the ladies had denounced them, had bound them with cords made of the bark of trees. They were encompassed by fifty naked Oreillons, armed with bows and arrows, with clubs and flint hatchets. Some were making a large cauldron boil, others were preparing spits, and all cried:

"A Jesuit! a Jesuit! we shall be revenged, we shall have excellent cheer, let us eat the Jesuit, let us eat him tip!"

"I told you, my dear master," cried Cacambo sadly, "that those two girls would play us some ugly trick."

Candide seeing the cauldron and the spits, cried:

"We are certainly going to be either roasted or boiled. Ah! what would Master Pangloss say, were he to see how pure nature is formed? Everything is right, may be, but I declare it is very hard to have lost Miss Cunegonde and to be put upon a spit by Oreillons."

Cacambo never lost his head.

"Do not despair," said he to the disconsolate Candide, "I understand a little of the jargon of these people, I will speak to them."

"Be sure," said Candide. "to represent to them how frightfully inhuman it is to cook men, and how very un-Christian."

"Gentlemen," said Cacambo, "you reckon you are to-day going to feast upon a Jesuit. It is all very well, nothing is more unjust than thus to treat your enemies. Indeed, the law of nature teaches us to kill our neighbour, and such is the practice all over the world. If we do not accustom ourselves to eating them, it is because we have better fare. But you have not the same resources as we; certainly it is much better to devour your enemies than to resign to the crows and rooks the fruits of your victory. But, gentlemen, surely you would not choose to eat your friends. You believe that you are going to spit a Jesuit, and he is your defender. It is the enemy of your enemies that you are going to roast. As for myself, I was born in your country; this gentleman is my master, and, far from being a Jesuit, he has just killed one, whose spoils he wears; and thence comes your mistake. To convince you of the truth of what I say, take his habit and carry it to the first barrier of the Jesuit kingdom, and inform yourselves whether my master did not kill a Jesuit officer. It will not take you long, and you can always eat us if you find that I have lied to you. But I have told you the truth. You are too well acquainted with the principles of public law, humanity, and justice not to pardon us."

The Oreillons found this speech very reasonable. They deputed two of their principal people with all expedition to inquire into the truth of the matter; these executed their commission like men of sense, and soon returned with good news. The Oreillons untied their prisoners, showed them all sorts of civilities, offered them girls, gave them refreshment, and reconducted them to the confines of their territories, proclaiming with great joy:

"He is no Jesuit! He is no Jesuit!"

Candide could not help being surprised at the cause of his deliverance.

"What people!" said he; "what men! what manners! If I had not been so lucky as to run Miss Cunegonde's brother through the body, I should have been devoured without redemption. But, after all, pure nature is good, since these people, instead of feasting upon my flesh, have shown me a thousand civilities, when they learned I was not a Jesuit."

CHAPTER XVII

ARRIVAL OF CANDIDE AND HIS VALET AT EL DORADO, AND WHAT THEY SAW THERE

"YOU SEE," SAID Cacambo to Candide, as soon as they had reached the frontiers of the Oreillons, "that this hemisphere is not better than the others, take my word for it; let us go back to Europe by the shortest way."

"How go back?" said Candide, "and where shall we go? to my own country? The Bulgarians and the Abares are slaying all; to Portugal? there I shall be burnt; and if we abide here we are every moment in danger of being spitted. But how can I resolve to quit a part of the world where my dear Cunegonde resides?"

"Let us turn towards Cayenne," said Cacambo, "there we shall find Frenchmen, who wander all over the world; they may assist us; God will perhaps have pity on us."

It was not easy to get to Cayenne; they knew vaguely in which direction to go, but rivers, precipices, robbers, savages, obstructed them all the way. Their horses died of fatigue. Their provisions were consumed; they fed a whole month upon wild fruits, and found themselves at last near a little river bordered with cocoa trees, which sustained their lives and their hopes.

Cacambo, who was as good a counsellor as the old woman, said to Candide:

"We are able to hold out no longer; we have walked enough. I see an empty canoe near the river-side; let us fill it with cocoanuts, throw ourselves into it, and go with the current; a river always leads to some inhabited spot. If we do not find pleasant things we shall at least find new things."

"With all my heart," said Candide. "Let us recommend ourselves to Providence."

They rowed a few leagues, between banks, in some places flowery, in others barren; in some parts smooth, in others rugged. The stream ever widened, and at length lost itself under an arch of frightful rocks which reached to the sky. The two travellers had the courage to commit themselves to the current. The river, suddenly contracting at this place, whirled them along with a dreadful noise and rapidity. At the end of four-and-twenty hours they saw daylight again, but their canoe was dashed to pieces against the rocks. For a league they had to creep from rock to rock, until at length they discovered an extensive plain, bounded by inaccessible mountains. The country was cultivated as much for pleasure as for necessity. On all sides the useful was also the beautiful. The roads were covered, or rather adorned, with carriages of a glittering form and substance, in which were men and women of surprising beauty, drawn by large red sheep which surpassed in fleetness the finest coursers of Andalusia, Tetuan, and Mequinez.[18]

"Here, however, is a country," said Candide, "which is better than Westphalia."

He stepped out with Cacambo towards the first village which he saw. Some children dressed in tattered brocades played at quoits on the outskirts. Our travellers from the other world amused themselves by looking on. The quoits were large round pieces, yellow, red, and green, which cast a singular lustre! The travellers picked a few of them off the ground; this was of gold, that of emeralds, the other of rubies—the least of them would have been the greatest ornament on the Mogul's throne.

"Without doubt," said Cacambo, "these children must be the king's sons that are playing at quoits!"

The village schoolmaster appeared at this moment and called them to school.

"There," said Candide, "is the preceptor of the royal family."

The little truants immediately quitted their game, leaving the quoits on the ground with all their other playthings. Candide gathered them up, ran to the master, and presented them to him in a most humble manner, giving him to understand by signs that their royal highnesses had forgotten their gold and jewels. The schoolmaster, smiling, flung them upon the ground; then, looking at Candide with a good deal of surprise, went about his business.

The travellers, however, took care to gather up the gold, the rubies, and the emeralds.

"Where are we?" cried Candide. "The king's children in this country must be well brought up, since they are taught to despise gold and precious stones."

Cacambo was as much surprised as Candide. At length they drew near the first house in the village. It was built like an European palace. A crowd of people pressed about the door, and there were still more in the house. They heard most agreeable music, and were aware of a delicious odour of cooking. Cacambo went up to the door and heard they were talking Peruvian; it was his mother tongue, for it is well known that Cacambo was born in Tucuman, in a village where no other language was spoken.

"I will be your interpreter here," said he to Candide; "let us go in, it is a public-house."

Immediately two waiters and two girls, dressed in cloth of gold, and their hair tied up with ribbons, invited them to sit down to table with the landlord. They served four dishes of soup, each garnished with two young parrots; a boiled condor[19] which weighed two hundred pounds; two roasted monkeys, of excellent flavour; three hundred humming-birds in one dish, and six hundred fly-birds in another; exquisite ragouts; delicious pastries; the whole served up in dishes of a kind of rock-crystal. The waiters and girls poured out several liqueurs drawn from the sugar-cane.

Most of the company were chapmen and waggoners, all extremely polite; they asked Cacambo a few questions with the greatest circumspection, and answered his in the most obliging manner.

As soon as dinner was over. Cacambo believed as well as Candide that they might well pay their reckoning by laying down two of those large gold pieces which they had picked up. The landlord and landlady shouted with laughter and held their sides. When the fit was over:

"Gentlemen," said the landlord, "it is plain you are strangers, and such guests we are not accustomed to see; pardon us therefore for laughing when you offered us the pebbles from our highroads in payment of your reckoning. You doubtless have not the money of the country; but it is not necessary to have any money at all to dine in this house. All hostelries established for the convenience of commerce are paid by the government. You have fared but very indifferently because this is a poor village; but everywhere else, you will be received as you deserve."

Cacambo explained this whole discourse with great astonishment to Candide, who was as greatly astonished to hear it.

"What sort of a country then is this," said they to one another; "a country unknown to all the rest of the world, and where nature is of a kind so different from ours? It is probably the country where all is well; for there absolutely must be one such place. And, whatever Master Pangloss might say, I often found that things went very ill in Westphalia."

CHAPTER XVIII

WHAT THEY SAW IN THE COUNTRY OF EL DORADO

CACAMBO EXPRESSED HIS curiosity to the landlord, who made answer:

"I am very ignorant, but not the worse on that account. However, we have in this neighbourhood an old man retired from Court who is the most learned and most communicative person in the kingdom."

At once he took Cacambo to the old man. Candide acted now only a second character, and accompanied his valet. They entered a very plain house, for the door was only of silver, and the ceilings were only of gold, but wrought in so elegant a taste as to vie with the richest. The antechamber, indeed, was only encrusted with rubies and emeralds, but the order in which everything was arranged made amends for this great simplicity.

The old man received the strangers on his sofa, which was stuffed with humming-birds' feathers, and ordered his servants to present them with liqueurs in diamond goblets; after which he satisfied their curiosity in the following terms:

"I am now one hundred and seventy-two years old, and I learnt of my late father, Master of the Horse to the King, the amazing revolutions of Peru, of which he had been an eyewitness. The kingdom we now inhabit is the ancient country of the Incas, who quitted it very imprudently to conquer another part of the world, and were at length destroyed by the Spaniards.

"More wise by far were the princes of their family, who remained in their native country; and they ordained, with the consent of the whole nation, that none of the inhabitants should ever be permitted to quit this little kingdom; and this has preserved our innocence and happiness. The Spaniards have had a confused notion of this country, and have called it *El Dorado*; and an Englishman, whose name was Sir Walter Raleigh, came very near it about a hundred years ago; but being surrounded by inaccessible rocks and precipices, we have hitherto been sheltered from the rapaciousness of European nations, who have an inconceivable passion for the pebbles and dirt of our land, for the sake of which they would murder us to the last man."

The conversation was long; it turned chiefly on their form of government, their manners, their women, their public entertainments, and the arts. At length Candide, having always had a taste for metaphysics, made Cacambo ask whether there was any religion in that country.

The old man reddened a little.

"How then," said he, "can you doubt it? Do you take us for ungrateful wretches?"

Cacambo humbly asked, "What was the religion in El Dorado?"

The old man reddened again.

"Can there be two religions?" said he. "We have, I believe, the religion of all the world; we worship God night and morning."

"Do you worship but one God?" said Cacambo, who still acted as interpreter in representing Candide's doubts.

"Surely," said the old man, "there are not two, nor three, nor four. I must confess the people from your side of the world ask very extraordinary questions."

Candide was not yet tired of interrogating the good old man; he wanted to know in what manner they prayed to God in El Dorado.

"We do not pray to Him," said the worthy sage; "we have nothing to ask of Him; He has given us all we need, and we return Him thanks without ceasing."

Candide having a curiosity to see the priests asked where they were. The good old man smiled.

"My friend," said he, "we are all priests. The King and all the head, of families sing solemn canticles of thanksgiving every morning, accompanied by five or six thousand musicians."

"What! have you no monks who teach, who dispute, who govern, who cabal, and who burn people that are not of their opinion?"

"We must be mad, indeed, if that were the case," said the old man; "here we are all of one opinion, and we know not what you mean by monks."

During this whole discourse Candide was in raptures, and he said to himself:

"This is vastly different from Westphalia and the Baron's castle. Had our friend Pangloss seen El Dorado he would no longer have said that the castle of Thunder-ten-Tronckh was the finest upon earth. It is evident that one must travel.

After this long conversation the old man ordered a coach and six sheep to be got ready, and twelve of his domestics to conduct the travellers to Court.

"Excuse me," said he, "if my age deprives me of the honour of accompanying you. The King will receive you in a manner that cannot displease you; and no doubt you will make an allowance for the customs of the country, if some things should not be to your liking."

Candide and Cacambo got into the coach, the six sheep flew, and in less than four hours they reached the King's palace situated at the extremity of the capital. The portal was two hundred and twenty feet high, and one hundred wide; but words are wanting to express the materials of which it was built. It is plain such materials must have prodigious superiority over those pebbles and sand which we call gold and precious stones.

Twenty beautiful damsels of the King's guard received Candide and Cacambo as they alighted from the coach, conducted them to the bath, and dressed them in robes woven of the down of humming-birds; after which the great crown officers, of both sexes, led them to the King's apartment, between two files of musicians, a thousand on each side. When they drew near to the audience chamber Cacambo asked one of the great officers in what way he should pay his obeisance to his Majesty; whether they should throw themselves upon their knees or on their stomachs; whether they should put their hands upon their heads or behind their backs; whether they should lick the dust off the floor; in a word, what was the ceremony?

"The custom," said the great officer, "is to embrace the King, and to kiss him on each cheek."

Candide and Cacambo threw themselves round his Majesty's neck. He received them with all the goodness imaginable, and politely invited them to supper.

While waiting they were shown the city, and saw the public edifices raised as high as the clouds, the market places ornamented with a thousand columns, the fountains of spring water, those of rose water, those of liqueurs drawn from sugar-cane, incessantly flowing into the great squares, which were paved with a kind of precious stone, which gave off a delicious fragrancy like that of cloves and cinnamon. Candide asked to see the court of justice, the parliament. They told him they had none, and that they were strangers to lawsuits. He asked if they had any prisons, and they answered no. But what surprised him most and gave him the greatest pleasure was the palace of sciences, where he saw a gallery two thousand feet long and filled with instruments employed in mathematics and physics.

After rambling about the city the whole afternoon, and seeing but a thousandth part of it, they were reconducted to the royal palace, where Candide sat down to table with his Majesty, his valet Cacambo, and several ladies. Never was there a better entertainment, and never was more wit shown at a table than that which fell from his Majesty. Cacambo explained the King's *bon-mots* to Candide, and notwithstanding they were translated they still appeared to be *bon-mots*. Of all the things that surprised Candide this was not the least.

They spent a month in this hospitable place. Candide frequently said to Cacambo:

"I own, my friend, once more that the castle where I was born is nothing in comparison with this; but, after all, Miss Cunegonde is not here, and you have, without doubt, some mistress in Europe. If we abide here we shall only be upon a footing with the rest, whereas, if we return to our old world, only with twelve sheep laden with the pebbles of El Dorado, we shall be richer than all the kings in Europe. We shall have no more Inquisitors to fear, and we may easily recover Miss Cunegonde."

This speech was agreeable to Cacambo; mankind are so fond of roving, of making a figure in their own country, and of boasting of what they have seen in their travels, that the two happy ones resolved to be no longer so, but to ask his Majesty's leave to quit the country.

"You are foolish," said the King. "I am sensible that my kingdom is but a small place, but when a person is comfortably settled in any part he should abide there. I have not the right to detain strangers. It is a tyranny which neither our manners nor our laws permit. All men are free. Go when you wish, but the going will be very difficult. It is impossible to ascend that rapid river on which you came as by a miracle, and which runs under vaulted rocks. The mountains which surround my kingdom are ten thousand feet high, and as steep as walls; they are each over ten leagues in breadth, and there is no other way to descend them than by precipices. However, since you absolutely wish to depart, I shall give orders to my engineers to construct a machine that will convey you very safely. When we have conducted you over the mountains no one can accompany you further, for my subjects have made a vow never to quit the kingdom, and they are too wise to break it. Ask me besides anything that you please."

"We desire nothing of your Majesty," says Candide, "but a few sheep laden with provisions, pebbles, and the earth of this country."

The King laughed.

"I cannot conceive," said he, "what pleasure you Europeans find in our yellow clay, but take as much as you like, and great good may it do you."

At once he gave directions that his engineers should construct a machine to hoist up these two extraordinary men out of the kingdom. Three thousand good mathematicians went to work; it was ready in fifteen days, and did not cost more than twenty million sterling in the specie of that country. They placed Candide and Cacambo on the machine. There were two great red sheep saddled and bridled to ride upon as soon as they were beyond the mountains, twenty pack-sheep laden with provisions, thirty with presents of the curiosities of the country, and fifty with gold, diamonds, and precious stones. The King embraced the two wanderers very tenderly.

Their departure, with the ingenious manner in which they and their sheep were hoisted over the mountains, was a splendid spectacle. The mathematicians took their leave after conveying them to a place of safety, and Candide had no other desire, no other aim, than to present his sheep to Miss Cunegonde.

"Now," said he, "we are able to pay the Governor of Buenos Ayres if Miss Cunegonde can be ransomed. Let us journey towards Cayenne. Let us embark, and we will afterwards see what kingdom we shall be able to purchase."

CHAPTER XIX

WHAT HAPPENED TO THEM AT SURINAM AND HOW CANDIDE GOT ACQUAINTED WITH MARTIN

OUR TRAVELLERS SPENT the first day very agreeably. They were delighted with possessing more treasure than all Asia, Europe, and Africa could scrape together. Candide, in his raptures, cut Cunegonde's name on the trees. The second day two of their sheep plunged into a morass, where they and their burdens were lost; two more died of fatigue a few days after; seven or eight perished with hunger in a desert; and others subsequently fell down precipices. At length, after travelling a hundred days, only two sheep remained. Said Candide to Cacambo:

"My friend, you see how perishable are the riches of this world; there is nothing solid but virtue, and the happiness of seeing Cunegonde once more.

"I grant all you say," said Cacambo, "but we have still two sheep remaining, with more treasure than the King of Spain will ever have; and I see a town which I take to be Surinam, belonging to the Dutch. We are at the end of all our troubles, and at the beginning of happiness."

As they drew near the town, they saw a negro stretched upon the ground, with only one moiety of his clothes, that is, of his blue linen drawers; the poor man had lost his left leg and his right hand.

"Good God!" said Candide in Dutch, "what art thou doing there, friend, in that shocking condition?"

"I am waiting for my master, Mynheer Vanderdendur, the famous merchant," answered the negro.

"Was it Mynheer Vanderdendur," said Candide, "that treated thee thus?"

"Yes, sir," said the negro, "it is the custom. They give us a pair of linen drawers for our whole garment twice a year. When we work at the sugar-canes, and the mill snatches hold of a finger, they cut off the hand; and when we attempt to run away, they cut off the leg; both cases have happened to me. This is the price at which you eat sugar in Europe. Yet when my mother sold me for ten patagons on the coast of Guinea, she said to me: 'My dear child, bless our fetiches, adore them for ever; they will make thee live happily; thou hast the honour of being the slave of our lords, the whites, which is making the fortune of thy father and mother.' Alas! I know not whether I have made their fortunes; this I know, that they have not made mine. Dogs, monkeys, and parrots art a thousand times less wretched than I. The Dutch fetiches, who have converted me, declare every Sunday that we are all of us children of Adam—blacks as well as whites. I am not a genealogist, but if these preachers tell truth, we are all second cousins. Now, you must agree, that it is impossible to treat one's relations in a more barbarous manner."

"Oh, Pangloss!" cried Candide, "thou hadst not guessed at this abomination; it is the end. I must at last renounce thy optimism."

"What is this optimism?" said Cacambo.

"Alas!" said Candide, "it is the madness of maintaining that everything is right when it is wrong."

Looking at the negro, he shed tears, and weeping, he entered Surinam.

The first thing they inquired after was whether there was a vessel in the harbour which could be sent to Buenos Ayres. The person to whom they applied was a Spanish sea-captain, who offered to agree with them upon reasonable terms. He appointed to meet them at a public-house, whither Candide and the faithful Cacambo went with their two sheep, and awaited his coming.

Candide, who had his heart upon his lips, told the Spaniard all his adventures, and avowed that he intended to elope with Miss Cunegonde.

"Then I will take good care not to carry you to Buenos Ayres," said the seaman. "I should be hanged, and so would you. The fair Cunegonde is my lord's favourite mistress."

This was a thunderclap for Candide; he wept for a long while. At last he drew Cacambo aside.

"Here, my dear friend," said he to him, "this thou must do. We have, each of us in his pocket, five or six millions in diamonds; you are more clever than I; you must go and bring Miss Cunegonde from Buenos Ayres. If the Governor makes any difficulty, give him a million; if he will not relinquish her, give him two; as you have not killed an Inquisitor, they will have no suspicion of you; I'll get another ship, and go and wait for you at Venice; that's a free country, where there is no danger either from Bulgarians, Abates, Jews, or Inquisitors."

Cacambo applauded this wise resolution. He despaired at parting from so good a master, who had become his intimate friend; but the pleasure of serving him prevailed over the pain of leaving him. They embraced with tears; Candide charged him not to forget the good old woman. Cacambo set out that very same day. This Cacambo was a very honest fellow.

Candide stayed some time longer in Surinam, waiting for another captain to carry him and the two remaining sheep to Italy. After he had hired domestics, and purchased everything necessary for a long voyage, Mynheer Vanderdendur, captain of a large vessel, came and offered his services.

THE VILLAINY OF MANKIND PRESENTED ITSELF BEFORE HIS IMAGINATION IN ALL ITS DEFORMITY, AND HIS MIND WAS FILLED WITH GLOOMY IDEAS.

"How much will you charge," said he to this man. "to carry me straight to Venice—me, my servants, my baggage, and these two sheep?"

The skipper asked ten thousand piastres. Candide did not hesitate.

"Oh! oh!" said the prudent Vanderdendur to himself, "this stranger gives ten thousand piastres unhesitatingly! He must be very rich."

Returning a little while after, he let him know that upon second consideration, he could not undertake the voyage for less than twenty thousand piastres.

"Well, you shall have them," said Candide.

"Ay!" said the skipper to himself, "this man agrees to pay twenty thousand piastres with as much ease as ten."

He went back to him again, and declared that he could not carry him to Venice for less than thirty thousand piastres.

"Then you shall have thirty thousand," replied Candide.

"Oh! oh!" said the Dutch skipper once more to himself, "thirty thousand piastres are a trifle to this man; surely these sheep must be laden with an immense treasure; let us say no more about it. First of all, let him pay down the thirty thousand piastres; then we shall see."

Candide sold two small diamonds, the least of which was worth more than what the skipper asked for his freight. He paid him in advance. The two sheep were put on board. Candide followed in a little boat to join the vessel in the roads. The skipper seized his opportunity, set sail, and put out to sea, the wind favouring him. Candide, dismayed and stupefied, soon lost sight of the vessel.

"Alas!" said he, "this is a trick worthy of the old world!"

He put back, overwhelmed with sorrow, for indeed he had lost sufficient to make the fortune of twenty monarchs. He waited upon the Dutch magistrate, and in his distress he knocked over loudly at the door. He entered and told his adventure, raising his voice with unnecessary vehemence. The magistrate began by fining him ten thousand piastres for making a noise; then he listened patiently, promised to examine into his affair at the skipper's return, and ordered him to pay ten thousand piastres, for the expense of the hearing.

This drove Candide to despair; he had, indeed, endured misfortunes a thousand times worse; the coolness of the magistrate and of the skipper who had robbed him, roused his choler and flung him into a deep melancholy. The villainy of mankind presented itself before his imagination in all its deformity, and his mind was filled with gloomy ideas. At length hearing that a French vessel was ready to set sail for Bordeaux, as he had no sheep laden with diamonds to take along with him he hired a cabin at the usual price. He made it known in the town that he would pay the passage and board and give two thousand piastres to any honest man who would make the voyage with him, upon condition that this man was the most dissatisfied with his state, and the most unfortunate in the whole province.

Such a crowd of candidates presented themselves that a fleet of ships could hardly have held them. Candide being desirous of selecting from among the best, marked out about one-twentieth of them who seemed to be sociable men, and who all pretended to merit his preference. He assembled them at his inn, and gave them a supper on condition that each took an oath to relate his history faithfully, promising to choose him who appeared to be most justly discontented with his state, and to bestow some presents upon the rest.

They sat until foul o'clock in the morning. Candide, in listening to all their adventures, was reminded of what the old woman had said to him in their voyage to Buenos Ayres, and of her wager that there was not a person on board the ship but had met with very great misfortunes. He dreamed of Pangloss at every adventure told to him.

"This Pangloss," said he, "would be puzzled to demonstrate his system. I wish that he were here. Certainly, if all things are good, it is in El Dorado and not in the rest of the world.

At length he made choice of a poor man of letters, who had worked ten years for the booksellers of Amsterdam. He judged that there was not in the whole world a trade which could disgust one more.

This philosopher was an honest man; but he had been robbed by his wife, beaten by his son, and abandoned by his daughter who got a Portuguese to run away with her. He had just been deprived of a small employment, on which he subsisted; and he was persecuted by the preachers of Surinam, who took him for a Socinian. We must allow that the others were at least as wretched as he; but Candide hoped that the philosopher would entertain him during the voyage. All the other candidates complained that Candide had done them great injustice; but he appeased them by giving one hundred piastres to each.

CHAPTER XX

WHAT HAPPENED AT SEA TO CANDIDE AND MARTIN

THE OLD PHILOSOPHER, whose name was Martin, embarked then with Candide for Bordeaux. They had both seen and suffered a great deal; and if the vessel had sailed from Surinam to Japan, by the Cape of Good Hope, the subject of moral and natural evil would have enabled them to entertain one another during the whole voyage.

Candide, however, had one great advantage over Martin, in that he always hoped to see Miss Cunegonde; whereas Martin had nothing at all to hope.

Besides, Candide was possessed of money and jewels, and though he had lost one hundred large red sheep, laden with the greatest treasure upon earth; though the knavery of the Dutch skipper still sat heavy upon his mind; yet when he reflected upon what he had still left, and when he mentioned the name of Cunegonde, especially towards the latter end of a repast, he inclined to Pangloss's doctrine.

"But you, Mr. Martin," said he to the philosopher, "what do you think of all this? what are your ideas on moral and natural evil?"

"Sir," answered Martin, "our priests accused me of being a Socinian, but the real fact is I am a Manichean."[20]

"You jest," said Candide; "there are no longer Manicheans in the world."

"I am one," said Martin. "I cannot help it; I know not how to think otherwise."

"Surely you must be possessed by the devil," said Candide.

"He is so deeply concerned in the affairs of this world," answered Martin, "that he may very well be in me, as well as in everybody else; but I own to you that when I cast an eye on this globe, or rather on this little ball, I cannot help thinking that God has abandoned it to some malignant being. I except, always, El Dorado. I scarcely ever knew a city that did not desire the destruction of a neighbouring city, nor a family that did not wish to exterminate some other family. Everywhere the weak execrate the powerful, before whom they cringe; and the powerful beat them like sheep whose wool and flesh they sell. A million regimented assassins, from one extremity of Europe to the other, get their bread by disciplined depredation and murder, for want of more honest employment. Even in those cities which seem to enjoy peace, and where the arts flourish, the inhabitants are devoured by more envy, care, and uneasiness than are experienced by a besieged town. Secret griefs are more cruel than public calamities. In a word, I have seen so much and experienced so much that I am a Manichean."

"There are, however, some things good," said Candide.

"That may be," said Martin; "but I know them not."

In the middle of this dispute they heard the report of cannon; it redoubled every instant. Each took out his glass. They saw two ships in close fight about three miles off. The wind brought both so near to the French vessel that our travellers had the pleasure of seeing the fight at their ease. At length one let off a broadside, so low and so truly aimed, that the other sank to the bottom. Candide and Martin could plainly perceive a hundred men on the deck of the sinking vessel; they raised their hands to heaven and uttered terrible outcries, and the next moment were swallowed up by the sea.

"Well," said Martin, "this is how men treat one another."

"It is true," said Candide; "there is something diabolical in this affair."

While speaking, he saw he knew not what, of a shining red, swimming close to the vessel. They put out the longboat to see what it could be; it was one of his sheep! Candide was more rejoiced at the recovery of this one sheep than he had been grieved at the loss of the hundred laden with the large diamonds of El Dorado.

The French captain soon saw that the captain of the victorious vessel was a Spaniard, and that the other was a Dutch pirate, and the very same one who had robbed Candide. The immense plunder which this villain had amassed, was buried with him in the sea, and out of the whole only one sheep was saved.

"You see," said Candide to Martin, "that crime is sometimes punished. This rogue of a Dutch skipper has met with the fate he deserved."

"Yes," said Martin; "but why should the passengers be doomed also to destruction? God has punished the knave, and the devil has drowned the rest."

The French and Spanish ships continued their course, and Candide continued his conversation with Martin. They disputed fifteen successive days, and on the last of those fifteen days, they were as far advanced as on the first. But, however, they chatted, they communicated ideas, they consoled each other. Candide caressed his sheep.

"Since I have found thee again," said he, "I may likewise chance to find my Cunegonde."

CHAPTER XXI

CANDIDE AND MARTIN, REASONING, DRAW NEAR THE COAST OF FRANCE

AT LENGTH THEY descried the coast of France.

"Were you ever in France, Mr. Martin?" said Candide.

"Yes," said Martin, "I have been in several provinces. In some one-half of the people are fools, in others they are too cunning; in some they are weak and simple, in others they affect to be witty; in all, the principal occupation is love, the next is slander, and the third is talking nonsense."

"But, Mr. Martin, have you seen Paris?"

"'Yes, I have. All these kinds are found there. It is a chaos—a confused multitude, where everybody seeks pleasure and scarcely any one finds it, at least as it appeared to me. I made a short stay there. On my arrival I was robbed of all I had by pickpockets at the fair of St. Germain. I myself was taken for a robber and was imprisoned for eight days, after which I served as corrector of the press to gain the money necessary for my return to Holland on foot. I knew the whole scribbling rabble, the party rabble, the fanatic rabble. It is said that there are very polite people in that city, and I wish to believe it."

"For my part, I have no curiosity to see France," said Candide. "You may easily imagine that after spending a month at El Dorado I can desire to behold nothing upon earth but Miss Cunegonde. I go to await her at Venice. We shall pass through France on our way to Italy. Will you bear me company?"

"With all my heart," said Martin. "It is said that Venice is fit only for its own nobility, but that strangers meet with a very good reception if they have a good deal of money. I have none of it; you have, therefore I will follow you all over the world."

"But do you believe," said Candide, "that the earth was originally a sea, as we find it asserted in that large book belonging to the captain?"

"I do not believe a word of it," said Martin, "any more than I do of the many ravings which have been published lately."

"But for what end, then, has this world been formed?" said Candide.

"To plague us to death," answered Martin.

"Are you not greatly surprised," continued Candide, "at the love which these two girls of the Oreillons had for those monkeys, of which I have already told you?"

"Not at all," said Martin. "I do not see that that passion was strange. I have seen so many extraordinary things that I have ceased to be surprised."

"Do you believe," said Candide, "that men have always massacred each other as they do to-day, that they have always been liars, cheats, traitors, ingrates, brigands, idiots, thieves, scoundrels, gluttons, drunkards, misers, envious, ambitious, bloody-minded, calumniators, debauchees, fanatics, hypocrites, and fools?"

"Do you believe," said Martin, "that hawks have always eaten pigeons when they have found them?"

"Yes, without doubt," said Candide.

"Well, then," said Martin, "if hawks have always had the same character why should you imagine that men may have changed theirs?"

"Oh!" said Candide, "there is a vast deal of difference, for free will—"

And reasoning thus they arrived at Bordeaux.

CHAPTER XXII

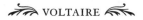

WHAT HAPPENED IN FRANCE TO CANDIDE AND MARTIN

CANDIDE STAYED IN Bordeaux no longer than was necessary for the selling of a few of the pebbles of El Dorado, and for hiring a good chaise to hold two passengers; for he could not travel without his Philosopher Martin. He was only vexed at parting with his sheep, which he left to the Bordeaux Academy of Sciences, who set as a subject for that year's prize, "to find why this sheep's wool was red;" and the prize was awarded to a learned man of the North, who demonstrated by A plus B minus C divided by Z, that the sheep must be red, and die of the rot.

Meanwhile, all the travellers whom Candide met in the inns along his route, said to him, "We go to Paris." This general eagerness at length gave him, too, a desire to see this capital; and it was not so very great a *détour* from the road to Venice.

He entered Paris by the suburb of St. Marceau, and fancied that he was in the dirtiest village of Westphalia.

Scarcely was Candide arrived at his inn, than he found himself attacked by a slight illness, caused by fatigue. As he had a very large diamond on his finger, and the people of the inn had taken notice of a prodigiously heavy box among his baggage, there were two physicians to attend him, though he had never sent for them, and two devotees who warmed his broths.

"I remember," Martin said, "also to have been sick at Paris in my first voyage; I was very poor, thus I bad neither friends, devotees, nor doctors, and I recovered."

However, what with physic and bleeding, Candide's illness became serious. A parson of the neighborhood came with great meekness to ask for a bill for the other world payable to the bearer. Candide would do nothing for him; but the devotees assured him it was the new fashion. He answered that he was not a man of fashion. Martin wished to throw the priest out of the window. The priest swore that they would not bury Candide. Martin swore that he would bury the priest if he continued to be troublesome. The quarrel grew heated. Martin took him by the shoulders and roughly turned him out of doors; which occasioned great scandal and a law-suit.

Candide got well again, and during his convalescence he had very good company to sup with him. They played high. Candide wondered why it was that the ace never came to him; but Martin was not at all astonished.

Among those who did him the honours of the town was a little Abbé of Perigord, one of those busybodies who are ever alert, officious, forward, fawning, and complaisant; who watch for strangers in their passage through the capital, tell them the scandalous history of the town, and offer them pleasure at all prices. He first took Candide and Martin to La Comédie, where they played a new tragedy. Candide happened to be seated near some of the fashionable wits. This did not prevent his shedding tears at the well-acted scenes. One of these critics at his side said to him between the acts:

"Your tears are misplaced; that is a shocking actress; the actor who plays with her is yet worse; and the play is still worse than the actors. The author does not know a word of Arabic, yet the scene is in Arabia; moreover he is a man that does not believe in innate ideas; and I will bring you, to-morrow, twenty pamphlets written against him."[21]

"How many dramas have you in France, sir?" said Candide to the Abbé.

"Five or six thousand."

"What a number!" said Candide. "How many good?"

"Fifteen or sixteen," replied the other.

"What a number!" said Martin.

Candide was very pleased with an actress who played Queen Elizabeth in a somewhat insipid tragedy[22] sometimes acted.

"That actress," said he to Martin, "pleases me much; she has a likeness to Miss Cunegonde; I should be very glad to wait upon her."

The Perigordian Abbé offered to introduce him. Candide, brought up in Germany, asked what was the etiquette, and how they treated queens of England in France.

"It is necessary to make distinctions," said the Abbé. "In the provinces one takes them to the inn; in Paris, one respects them when they are beautiful, and throws them on the highway when they are dead."[23]

"Queens on the highway!" said Candide.

"Yes, truly," said Martin, "the Abbé is right. I was in Paris when Miss Monime passed, as the saying is, from this life to the other. She was refused what people call the *honours of sepulture*—that is to say, of rotting with all the beggars of the neighbourhood in an ugly cemetery; she was interred all alone by her company at the comer of the Rue de Bourgogne, which ought to trouble her much, for she thought nobly."

"That was very uncivil," said Candide.

"What would you have?" said Martin; "these people are made thus. Imagine all contradictions, all possible incompatibilities—you will find them in the government, in the law-courts, in the churches, in the public shows of this droll nation."

"Is it true that they always laugh in Paris?" said Candide.

"Yes," said the Abbé, "but it means nothing, for they complain of everything with great fits of laughter; they even do the most detestable things while laughing."

"Who," said Candide, "is that great pig who spoke so ill of the piece at which I wept, and of the actors who gave me so much pleasure?"

"He is a bad character," answered the Abbé, "who gains his livelihood by saying evil of all plays and of all books. He hates whatever succeeds, as the eunuchs hate those who enjoy; he is one of the serpents of literature who nourish themselves on dirt and spite; he is a *folliculaire*."

"What is a *folliculaire*?" said Candide.

"It is," said the Abbé, "a pamphleteer—a Fréron."[24]

Thus Candide, Martin, and the Perigordian conversed on the staircase, while watching every one go out after the performance.

"Although I am eager to see Cunegonde again," said Candide, "I should like to sup with Miss Clairon, for she appears to me admirable."

The Abbé was not the man to approach Miss Clairon, who saw only good company.

"She is engaged for this evening," he said, "but I shall have the honour to take you to the house of a lady of quality, and there you will know Paris as if you had lived in it for years."

Candide, who was naturally curious, let himself be taken to this lady's house, at the end of the Faubourg St. Honoré. The company was occupied in playing faro; a dozen melancholy punters held each in his hand a little pack of cards; a bad record of his misfortunes. Profound silence reigned; pallor was on the faces of the punters, anxiety on that of the banker, and the hostess, sitting near the unpitying banker, noticed with lynx-eyes all the doubled and other increased stakes, as each player dog's-eared his cards; she made them turn down the edges again with severe, but polite attention; she showed no vexation for fear of losing her customers. The lady insisted upon being called the Marchioness of Parolignac. Her daughter, aged fifteen, was among the punters, and notified with a covert glance the cheatings of the poor people who tried to repair the cruelties of fate. The Perigordian Abbé, Candide and Martin entered; no one rose, no one saluted them, no one looked at them; all were profoundly occupied with their cards.

"The Baroness of Thunder-ten-Tronckh was more polite," said Candide.

However, the Abbé whispered to the Marchioness, who half rose, honoured Candide with a gracious smile, and Martin with a condescending nod; she gave a seat and a pack of cards to Candide, who lost fifty thousand francs in two deals, after which they supped very gaily, and every one was astonished that Candide was not moved by his loss; the servants said among themselves, in the language of servants:

"Some English lord is here this evening."

The supper passed at first like most Parisian suppers, in silence, followed by a noise of words which could not be distinguished, then with pleasantries of which most were insipid, with false news, with bad reasoning, a little politics, and much evil speaking; they also discussed new books.

"Have you seen," said the Perigordian Abbé, "the romance of Sieur Gauchat, doctor of divinity?"[25]

"Yes," answered one of the guests, "but I have not been able to finish it. We have a crowd of silly writings, but all together do not approach the impertinence of 'Gauchat, Doctor of Divinity.' I am so satiated with the great number of detestable books with which we are inundated that I am reduced to punting at faro."

"And the *Mélanges* of Archdeacon Trublet,[26] what do you say of that?" said the Abbé.

"Ah!" said the Marchioness of Parolignac, "the wearisome mortal! How curiously he repeats to you all that the world knows! How heavily he discusses that which is not worth the trouble of lightly remarking upon! How, without wit, he appropriates the wit of others! How he spoils what he steals! How he disgusts me! But he will disgust me no longer—it is enough to have read a few of the Archdeacon's pages."

There was at table a wise man of taste, who supported the Marchioness. They spoke afterwards of tragedies; the lady asked why there were tragedies which were sometimes played and which could not be read. The man of taste explained very well how a piece could have some interest, and have almost no merit; he proved in few words that it was not enough to introduce one or two of those situations which one finds in all romances, and which always seduce the spectator, but that it was necessary to be new without being odd, often sublime and always natural, to know the human heart and to make it speak; to be a great poet without allowing any person in the piece to appear to be a poet; to know language perfectly—to speak it with purity, with continuous harmony and without rhythm ever taking anything from sense.

"Whoever," added he, "does not observe all these rules can produce one or two tragedies, applauded at a theatre, but he will never be counted in the ranks of good writers. There are very few good tragedies; some are idylls in dialogue, well written and well rhymed, others political reasonings which loll to sleep, or amplifications which repel; others demoniac dreams in barbarous style, interrupted in sequence, with long apostrophes to the gods, because they do not know how to speak to men, with false maxims, with bombastic commonplaces!"

Candide listened with attention to this discourse, and conceived a great idea of the speaker, and as the Marchioness had taken care to place him beside her, he leaned towards her and took the liberty of asking who was the man who had spoken so well.

"He is a scholar," said the lady, "who does not play, whom the Abbé sometimes brings to supper; he is perfectly at home among tragedies and books, and he has written a tragedy which was hissed, and a book of which nothing has ever been seen outside his bookseller's shop excepting the copy which he dedicated to me."

"The great man!" said Candide. "He is another Pangloss!"

Then, turning towards him, he said:

"Sir, you think doubtless that all is for the best in the moral and physical world, and that nothing could be otherwise than it is?"

"I, sir!" answered the scholar, "I know nothing of all that; I find that all goes awry with me; that no one knows either what is his rank, nor what is his condition, what he does nor what he ought to do; and that except supper, which is always gay, and where there appears to be enough concord, all the rest of the time is passed in impertinent quarrels; Jansenist against Molinist, Parliament against the Church, men of letters against men of letters, courtesans against courtesans, financiers against the people, wives against husbands, relatives against relatives—it is eternal war."

"I have seen the worst," Candide replied. "But a wise man, who since has had the misfortune to be hanged, taught me that all is marvellously well; these are but the shadows on a beautiful picture."

"Your hanged man mocked the world," said Martin. "The shadows are horrible blots."

"They are men who make the blots," said Candide, "and they cannot be dispensed with."

"It is not their fault then," said Martin.

Most of the printers, who understood nothing of this language, drank, and Martin reasoned with the scholar, and Candide related some of his adventures to his hostess.

After supper the Marchioness took Candide into her boudoir, and made him sit upon a sofa.

"Ah, well!" said she to him, "you love desperately Miss Cunegonde of Thunder-ten-Tronckh?"

"Yes, madame," answered Candide.

The Marchioness replied to him with a tender smile:

"You answer me like a young man from Westphalia. A Frenchman would have said, 'It is true that I have loved Miss Cunegonde, but seeing you, madame, I think I no longer love her.'"

"Alas! madame," said Candide, "I will answer you as you wish."

"Your passion for her," said the Marchioness, "commenced by picking up her handkerchief. I wish that you would pick up my garter."

"With all my heart," said Candide. And he picked it up.

"But I wish that you would put it on," said the lady.

And Candide put it on.

"You see," said she, "you are a foreigner. I sometimes make my Parisian lovers languish for fifteen days, but I give myself to you the first night because one must do the honours of one's country to a young man from Westphalia."

The lady having perceived two enormous diamonds upon the hands of the young foreigner praised them with such good faith that from Candide's fingers they passed to her own.

Candide, returning with the Perigordian Abbé, felt some remorse in having been unfaithful to Miss Cunegonde. The Abbé sympathised in his trouble; he had had but a light part of the fifty thousand francs lost at play and of the value of the two brilliants, half given, half extorted. His design was to profit as much as he could by the advantages which the acquaintance of Candide could procure for him. He spoke much of Cunegonde, and Candide told him that he should ask forgiveness of that beautiful one for his infidelity when he should see her in Venice.

The Abbé redoubled his politeness and attentions, and took a tender interest in all that Candide said, in all that he did, in all that he wished to do.

"And so, sir, you have a rendezvous at Venice?"

"Yes, monsieur Abbé," answered Candide. "It is absolutely necessary that I go to meet Miss Cunegonde."

And then the pleasure of talking of that which he loved induced him to relate, according to his custom, part of his adventures with the fair Westphalian.

"I believe," said the Abbé, "that Miss Cunegonde has a great deal of wit, and that she writes charming letters?"

"I have never received any from her," said Candide, "for being expelled from the castle on her account I had not an opportunity for writing to her. Soon after that I heard she was dead; then I found her alive; then I lost her again; and last of all, I sent an express to her two thousand five hundred leagues from here, and I wait for an answer."

The Abbé listened attentively, and seemed to be in a brown study. He soon took his leave of the two foreigners after a most tender embrace. The following day Candide received, on awaking, a letter couched in these terms:

"My very dear love, for eight days I have been ill in this town. I learn that you are here. I would fly to your arms if I could but move. I was informed of your passage at Bordeaux, where I left faithful Cacambo and the old woman, who are to follow me very soon. The Governor of Buenos Ayres has taken all, but there remains to me your heart. Come! your presence will either give me life or kill me with pleasure."

This charming, this unhoped-for letter transported Candide with an inexpressible joy, and the illness of his dear Cunegonde overwhelmed him with grief. Divided between those two passions, he took his gold and his diamonds and hurried away, with Martin, to the hotel where Miss Cunegonde was lodged. He entered her room trembling, his heart palpitating, his voice sobbing; he wished to open the curtains of the bed, and asked for a light.

"Take care what you do," said the servant-maid; "the light hurts her," and immediately she drew the curtain again.

"My dear Cunegonde," said Candide, weeping, "how are you? If you cannot see me, at least speak to me."

"She cannot speak," said the maid.

The lady then put a plump hand out from the bed, and Candide bathed it with his tears and afterwards filled it with diamonds, leaving a bag of gold upon the easy chair.

In the midst of these transports in came an officer, followed by the Abbé and a file of soldiers.

"There," said he, "are the two suspected foreigners," and at the same time he ordered them to be seized and carried to prison.

"Travellers are not treated thus in El Dorado," said Candide.

"I am more a Manichean now than ever," said Martin.

"But pray, sir, where are you going to carry us?" said Candide.

"To a dungeon," answered the officer.

Martin, having recovered himself a little, judged that the lady who acted the part of Cunegonde was a cheat, that the Perigordian Abbé was a knave who had imposed upon the honest simplicity of Candide, and that the officer was another knave whom they might easily silence.

Candide, advised by Martin and impatient to see the real Cunegonde, rather than expose himself before a court of justice, proposed to the officer to give him three small diamonds, each worth about three thousand pistoles.

"Ah, sir," said the man with the ivory baton, "had you committed all the imaginable crimes you would be to me the most honest man in the world. Three diamonds! Each worth three thousand pistoles! Sir, instead of carrying you to jail I would lose my life to serve you. There are orders for arresting all foreigners, but leave it to me. I have a brother at Dieppe in Normandy! I'll conduct you thither, and if you have a diamond to give him he'll take as much care of you as I would."

"And why," said Candide, "should all foreigners be arrested?"

"It is," the Perigordian Abbé then made answer, "because a poor beggar of the country of Atrébatie[27] heard some foolish things said. This induced him to commit a parricide, not such as that of 1610 in the month of May,[28] but such as that of 1594 in the month of December,[29] and such as others which have been committed in other years and other months by other poor devils who had heard nonsense spoken."

The officer then explained what the Abbé meant.

"Ah, the monsters!" cried Candide. "What horror among a people who dance and sing! Is there no way of getting quickly out of this country where monkeys provoke tigers? I have seen no bears in my country, but men I have beheld nowhere except in El Dorado. In the name of God, sir, conduct me to Venice, where I am to await Miss Cunegonde."

"I can conduct you no further than lower Normandy," said the officer.

Immediately he ordered his irons to be struck off, acknowledged himself mistaken, sent away his men, set out with Candide and Martin for Dieppe, and left them in the care of his brother.

There was then a small Dutch ship in the harbour. The Norman, who by the virtue of three more diamonds had become the most subservient of men, put Candide and his attendants on board a vessel that was just ready to set sail for Portsmouth in England.

This was not the way to Venice, but Candide thought he had made his way out of hell, and reckoned that he would soon have an opportunity for resuming his journey.

CHAPTER XXIII

CANDIDE AND MARTIN TOUCHED UPON THE COAST OF ENGLAND, AND WHAT THEY SAW THERE

"AH, PANGLOSS! PANGLOSS! Ah, Martin! Martin! Ah, my dear Cunegonde, what sort of a world is this?" said Candide on board the Dutch ship.

"Something very foolish and abominable," said Martin.

"You know England? Are they as foolish there as in France?"

"It is another kind of folly," said Martin. "You know that these two nations are at war for a few acres of snow in Canada,[30] and that they spend over this beautiful war much more than Canada is worth. To tell you exactly, whether there are more people fit to send to a madhouse in one country than the other, is what my imperfect intelligence will not permit. I only know in general that the people we are going to see are very atrabilious."

Talking thus they arrived at Portsmouth. The coast was lined with crowds of people, whose eyes were fixed on a fine man kneeling, with his eyes bandaged, on board one of the men of war in the harbour. Four soldiers stood opposite to this man; each of them fired three balls at his head, with all the calmness in the world; and the whole assembly went away very well satisfied.

"What is all this?" said Candide; "and what demon is it that exercises his empire in this country?"

He then asked who was that fine man who had been killed with so much ceremony. They answered, he was an Admiral.[31]

"And why kill this Admiral?"

"It is because he did not kill a sufficient number of men himself. He gave battle to a French Admiral; and it has been proved that he was not near enough to him."

"But," replied Candide, "the French Admiral was as far from the English Admiral."

"There is no doubt of it; but in this country it is found good, from time to time, to kill one Admiral to encourage the others."

THERE IS NO DOUBT OF IT; BUT IN THIS COUNTRY IT IS FOUND GOOD, FROM TIME TO TIME, TO KILL ONE ADMIRAL TO ENCOURAGE THE OTHERS.

Candide was so shocked and bewildered by what he saw and heard, that he would not set foot on shore, and he made a bargain with the Dutch skipper (were he even to rob him like the

Surinam captain) to conduct him without delay to Venice.

The skipper was ready in two days. They coasted France; they passed in sight of Lisbon, and Candide trembled. They passed through the Straits, and entered the Mediterranean. At last they landed at Venice.

"God be praised!" said Candide, embracing Martin. "It is here that I shall see again my beautiful Cunegonde. I trust Cacambo as myself. All is well, all will be well, all goes as well as possible."

CHAPTER XXIV

OF PAQUETTE AND FRIAR GIROFLÉE

UPON THEIR ARRIVAL at Venice, Candide went to search for Cacambo at every inn and coffeehouse, and among all the ladies of pleasure, but to no purpose. He sent every day to inquire on all the ships that came in. But them was no news of Cacambo.

"What!" said he to Martin, "I have had time to voyage from Surinam to Bordeaux, to go from Bordeaux to Paris, from Paris to Dieppe, from Dieppe to Portsmouth, to coast along Portugal and Spain, to cross the whole Mediterranean, to spend some months, and yet the beautiful Cunegonde has not arrived! Instead of her I have only met a Parisian wench and a Perigordian Abbé. Cunegonde is dead without doubt, and there is nothing for me but to die. Alas! how much better it would have been for me to have remained in the paradise of El Dorado than to come back to this cursed Europe! You are in the right, my dear Martin; all is misery and illusion."

He fell into a deep melancholy, and neither went to see the opera, nor any of the other diversions of the Carnival; nay, he was proof against the temptations of all the ladies.

"You are in truth very simple," said Martin to him, "if you imagine that a mongrel valet, who has five or six millions in his pocket, will go to the other end of the world to seek your mistress and bring her to you to Venice. If he find her, he will keep her to himself; if he do not find her he will get another. I advise you to forget your valet Cacambo and your mistress Cunegonde."

Martin was not consoling. Candide's melancholy increased; and Martin continued to prove to him that there was very little virtue or happiness upon earth, except perhaps in El Dorado, where nobody could gain admittance.

While they were disputing on this important subject and waiting for Cunegonde, Candide saw a young Theatin friar in St. Mark's Piazza, holding a girl on his am. The Theatin looked fresh-coloured, plump, and vigorous; his eyes were sparkling, his air assured, his look lofty, and his step bold. The girl was very pretty, and sang; she looked amorously at her Theatin, and from time to time pinched his fat cheeks.

"At least you will allow me," said Candide to Martin, "that these two are happy. Hitherto I have met with none but unfortunate people in the whole habitable globe, except in El Dorado; but as to this pair, I would venture to lay a wager that they are very happy."

"I lay you they are not," said Martin.

"We need only ask them to dine with us," said Candide, "and you will see whether I am mistaken."

Immediately he accosted them, presented his compliments, and invited them to his inn to eat some macaroni, with Lombard partridges, and caviare, and to drink some Montepulciano, Lachryme Christi, Cyprus and Samos wine. The girl blushed, the Theatin accepted the invitation and she followed him, casting her eyes on Candide with confusion and surprise, and dropping a few tears. No sooner had she set foot in Candide's apartment than she cried out:

"Ah! Mr. Candide does not know Paquette again."

Candide had not viewed her as yet with attention, his thoughts being entirely taken up with Cunegonde; but recollecting her as she spoke.

"Alas!" said he, "my poor child, it is you who reduced Doctor Pangloss to the beautiful condition in which I saw him?"

"Alas! it was I, sir, indeed," answered Paquette. "I see that you have heard all. I have been informed of the frightful disasters that befell the family of my lady Baroness, and the fair Cunegonde. I swear to you that my fate has been scarcely less sad. I was very innocent when you knew me. A Grey Friar, who was my confessor, easily seduced me. The consequences were terrible. I was obliged to quit the castle some time after the Baron had sent you away with kicks on the backside. If a famous surgeon had not taken compassion on me, I should have died. For some time I was this surgeon's mistress, merely out of gratitude. His wife, who was mad with jealousy, beat me every day unmercifully; she was a fury. The surgeon was one of the ugliest of men, and I the most wretched of women, to be continually beaten for a man I did not love. You know, sir, what a dangerous thing it is for an ill-natured woman to be married to a doctor. Incensed at the behaviour of his wife, he one day gave her so effectual a remedy to cure her of a slight cold, that she died two hours after, in most horrid convulsions. The wife's relations prosecuted the husband; he took flight, and I was thrown into jail. My innocence would not have saved me if I had not been good-looking. The judge set me free, on condition that he succeeded the surgeon. I was soon supplanted by a rival, turned out of doors quite destitute, and obliged to continue this abominable trade, which appears so pleasant to you men, while to us women it is the utmost abyss of misery. I have come to exercise the profession at Venice. Ah! sir, if you could only imagine what it is to be obliged to caress indifferently an old merchant, a lawyer, a monk, a gondolier, an abbé, to be exposed to abuse and insults, to be often reduced to borrowing a petticoat, only to go and have it raised by a disagreeable man; to be robbed by one of what one has earned from another; to be subject to the extortions of the officers of justice; and to have in prospect only a frightful old age, a hospital, and a dung-hill; you would conclude that I am one of the most unhappy creatures in the world."[32]

Paquette thus opened her heart to honest Candide, in the presence of Martin, who said to his friend:

"You see that already I have won half the wager."

Friar Giroflée stayed in the dining-room, and drank a glass or two of wine while he was waiting for dinner.

"But," said Candide to Paquette, "you looked so gay and content when I met you; you sang and you behaved so lovingly to the Theatin, that you seemed to me as happy as you pretend to be now the reverse."

"Ah! sir," answered Paquette, "this is one of the miseries of the trade. Yesterday I was robbed and beaten by an officer; yet to-day I must put on good humour to please a friar."

Candide wanted no more convincing; he owned that Martin was in the right. They sat down to table with Paquette and the Theatin; the repast was entertaining; and towards the end they conversed with all confidence.

"Father," said Candide to the Friar, "you appear to me to enjoy a state that all the world might envy; the flower of health shines in your face. Your expression makes plain your happiness; you have a very pretty girl for your recreation, and you seem well satisfied with your state as a Theatin."

"My faith, sir," said Friar Giroflée, "I wish that all the Theatins were at the bottom of the sea. I have been tempted a hundred times to set fire to the convent, and go and become a Turk. My parents forced me at the age of fifteen to put on this detestable habit, to increase the fortune of a cursed elder brother, whom God confound. Jealousy, discord, and fury, dwell in the convent. It is true I have preached a few bad sermons that have brought me in a little money, of which the prior stole half, while the rest serves to maintain my girls; but when I return at night to the monastery, I am ready to dash my head against the walls of the dormitory; and all my fellows are in the same case."

Martin turned towards Candide with his usual coolness.

"Well," said he, "have I not won the whole wager?"

Candide gave two thousand piastres to Paquette, and one thousand to Friar Giroflée.

"I'll answer for it," said he, "that with this they will be happy."

"I do not believe it at all," said Martin; "you will, perhaps, with these piastres only render them the more unhappy."

"Let that be as it may," said Candide, "but one thing consoles me. I see that we often meet with those whom we expected never to see more; so that, perhaps, as I have found my red sheep and Paquette, it may well be that I shall also find Cunegonde."

"I wish," said Martin, "she may one day make you very happy; but I doubt it very much."

"You are very hard of belief," said Candide.

"I have lived," said Martin.

"You see those gondoliers," said Candide, "are they not perpetually singing?"

"You do not see them," said Martin, "at home with their wives and brats. The Doge has his troubles, the gondoliers have theirs. It is true that, all things considered, the life of a gondolier is preferable to that of a Doge; but I believe the difference to be so trifling that it is not worth the trouble of examining."

"People talk," said Candide, "of the Senator Pococurante, who lives in that fine palace on the Brenta, where he entertains foreigners in the politest manner. They pretend that this man has never felt any uneasiness."

"I should be glad to see such a rarity," said Martin.

Candide immediately sent to ask the Lord Pococurante permission to wait upon him the next day.

CHAPTER XXV

THE VISIT TO LORD POCOCURANTE, A NOBLE VENETIAN

CANDIDE AND MARTIN went in a gondola on the Brenta, and arrived at the palace of the noble Signor Pococurante. The gardens, laid out with taste, were adorned with fine marble statues. The palace was beautifully built. The master of the house was a man of sixty, and very rich. He received the two travellers with polite indifference, which put Candide a tittle out of countenance, but was not at all disagreeable to Martin.

First, two pretty girls, very neatly dressed, served them with chocolate, which was frothed exceedingly well. Candide could not refrain from commending their beauty, grace, and address.

"They are good enough creatures," said the Senator. "I make them lie with me sometimes, for I am very tired of the ladies of the town, of their coquetries, of their jealousies, of their quarrels, of their humours, of their pettinesses, of their prides, of their follies, and of the sonnets which one must make, or have made, for them. But after all, these two girls begin to weary me."

After breakfast, Candide walking into a long gallery was surprised by the beautiful pictures. He asked, by what master were the two first.

"They are by Raphael," said the Senator. "I bought them at a great price, out of vanity, some years ago. They are said to be the finest things in Italy, but they do not please me at all. The colours are too dark, the figures are not sufficiently rounded, nor in good relief; the draperies in no way resemble stuffs. In a word, whatever may be said, I do not find there a true imitation of nature. I only care for a picture when I think I see nature itself; and there are none of this sort. I have a great many pictures, but I prize them very little."

While they were waiting for dinner Pococurante ordered a concert. Candide found the music delicious.

"This noise," said the Senator, "may amuse one for half an hour; but if it were to last longer it would grow tiresome to everybody, though they durst not own it. Music, to-day, is only the art of executing difficult things, and that which is only difficult cannot please long. Perhaps I should be fonder of the opera if they had not found the secret of making of it a monster which shocks me. Let who will go to see bad tragedies set to music, where the scenes are contrived for no other end than to introduce two or three songs ridiculously out of place, to show off an actress's voice. Let who will, or who can, die away with pleasure at the sight of an eunuch quavering the *rôle* of Caesar, or of Cato, and strutting awkwardly upon the stage. For my part I have long since renounced those paltry entertainments which constitute the glory of modern Italy, and are purchased so dearly by sovereigns."

Candide disputed the point a little, but with discretion. Martin was entirely of the Senator's opinion.

They sat down to table, and after an excellent dinner they went into the library. Candide, seeing a Homer magnificently bound, commended the virtuoso on his good taste.

"There," said he, "is a book that was once the delight of the great Pangloss, the best philosopher in Germany."

"It is not mine," answered Pococurante coolly. "They used at one time to make me believe that I took a pleasure in reading him. But that continual repetition of battles, so extremely like one another; those gods that are always active without doing anything decisive; that Helen who is the cause of the war, and who yet scarcely appears in the piece; that Troy, so long besieged without being taken; all these together caused me great weariness. I have sometimes asked learned men whether they were not as weary as I of that work. Those who were sincere have owned to me that the poem made them fall asleep; yet it was necessary to have it in their library as a monument of antiquity, or like those rusty medals which are no longer of use in commerce."

"But your Excellency does not think thus of Virgil?" said Candide.

"I grant," said the Senator, "that the second, fourth, and sixth books of his *Æneid* are excellent, but as for his pious Æneas, his strong Cloanthus, his friend Achates, his little Ascanius, his silly King Latinus, his bourgeois Amata, his insipid Lavinia, I think there can be nothing more flat and disagreeable. I prefer Tasso a good deal, or even the soporific tales of Ariosto."

"May I presume to ask you, sir," said Candide, "whether you do not receive a great deal of pleasure from reading Horace?"

"There are maxims in this writer," answered Pococurante, "from which a man of the world may reap great benefit, and being written in energetic verse they are more easily impressed upon the memory. But I care little for his journey to Brundusium, and his account of a bad dinner, or of his low quarrel between one Rupilius whose words he says were full of poisonous filth, and another whose language was imbued with vinegar. I have read with much distaste his indelicate verses against old women and witches; nor do I see any merit in telling his friend Mæcenas that if he will but rank him in the choir of lyric poets, his lofty head shall touch the stars. Fools admire everything in an author of reputation. For my part, I read only to please myself. I like only that which serves my purpose."

Candide, having been educated never to judge for himself, was much surprised at what he heard. Martin found there was a good deal of reason in Pococurante's remarks.

"Oh! here is Cicero," said Candide. "Here is the great man whom I fancy you are never tired of reading."

"I never read him," replied the Venetian. "What is it to me whether he pleads for Rabirius or Cluentius? I try causes enough myself; his philosophical works seem to me better, but when I found that he doubted of everything, I concluded that I knew as much as he, and that I had no need of a guide to learn ignorance."

"Ha! here are four-score volumes of the Academy of Sciences," cried Martin. "Perhaps there is something valuable in this collection."

"BUT IS THERE NOT A PLEASURE," SAID CANDIDE, "IN CRITICISING EVERYTHING, IN POINTING OUT FAULTS WHERE OTHERS SEE NOTHING BUT BEAUTIES?"

"There might be," said Pococurante, "if only one of those rakers of rubbish had shown how to make pins; but in all these volumes there is nothing but chimerical systems, and not a single useful thing."

"And what dramatic works I see here," said Candide, "in Italian, Spanish, and French."

"Yes," replied the Senator, "there are three thousand, and not three dozen of them good for anything. As to those collections of sermons, which altogether are not worth a single page of Seneca, and those huge volumes of theology, you may well imagine that neither I nor any one else ever opens them."

Martin saw some shelves filled with English books.

"I have a notion," said he, "that a Republican must be greatly pleased with most of these books, which are written with a spirit of freedom."

"Yes," answered Pococurante, "it is noble to write as one thinks; this is the privilege of humanity. In all our Italy we write only what we do not think; those who inhabit the country of the Cæsars and the Antoninuses dare not acquire a single idea without the permission of a Dominican friar. I should be pleased with the liberty which inspires the English genius if passion and party spirit did not corrupt all that is estimable in this precious liberty."

Candide, observing a Milton, asked whether he did not look upon this author as a great man.

"Who?" said Pococurante, "that barbarian, who writes a long commentary in ten books of harsh verse on the first chapter of Genesis; that coarse imitator of the Greeks, who disfigures the Creation, and who, while Moses represents the Eternal producing the world by a word, makes the Messiah take a great pair of compasses from the armoury of heaven to circumscribe His work? How can I have any esteem for a writer who has spoiled Tasso's hell and the devil, who transforms Lucifer sometimes into a toad and other times into a pigmy, who makes him repeat the same things a hundred times, who makes him dispute on theology, who, by a serious imitation of Ariosto's comic invention of firearms, represents the devils cannonading in heaven? Neither I nor any man in Italy could take pleasure in those melancholy extravagances; and the marriage of Sin and Death, and the snakes brought forth by Sin, are enough to turn the stomach of any one with the least taste, and his long description of a pest-house is good only for a grave-digger. This obscure, whimsical, and disagreeable poem was despised upon its first publication, and I only treat it now as it was treated in its own country by contemporaries. For the matter of that I say what I think, and I care very little whether others think as I do."

Candide was grieved at this speech, for he had a respect for Homer and was fond of Milton.

"Alas!" said he softly to Martin, "I am afraid that this man holds our German poets in very great contempt."

"There would not be much harm in that," said Martin.

"Oh! what a superior man," said Candide below his breath. "What a great genius is this Pococurante! Nothing can please him."

After their survey of the library they went down into the garden, where Candide praised its several beauties.

"I know of nothing in so bad a taste," said the master. "All you see here is merely trifling. After to-morrow I will have it planted with a nobler design."

"Well," said Candide to Martin when they had taken their leave, "you will agree that this is the happiest of mortals, for he is above everything he possesses.

"But do you not see," answered Martin, "that he is disgusted with all he possesses? Plato observed a long while ago that those stomachs are not the best that reject all sorts of food."

"But is there not a pleasure," said Candide, "in criticising everything, in pointing out faults where others see nothing but beauties?"

"That is to say," replied Martin, "that there is some pleasure in having no pleasure."

"Well, well," said Candide, "I find that I shall be the only happy man when I am blessed with the sight of my dear Cunegonde."

"It is always well to hope," said Martin.

However, the days and the weeks passed. Cacambo did not come, and Candide was so overwhelmed with grief that he did not even reflect that Paquette and Friar Giroflée did not return to thank him.

CHAPTER XXVI

OF A SUPPER WHICH CANDIDE AND MARTIN TOOK WITH SIX STRANGERS, AND WHO THEY WERE[33]

ONE EVENING THAT Candide and Martin were going to sit down to supper with some foreigners who lodged in the same inn, a man whose complexion was as black as soot, came behind Candide, and taking him by the arm, said:

"Get yourself ready to go along with us; do not fail."

Upon this he turned round and saw—Cacambo! Nothing but the sight of Cunegonde could have astonished and delighted him more. He was on the point of going mad with joy. He embraced his dear friend.

"Cunegonde is here, without doubt; where is she? Take me to her that I may die of joy in her company."

"Cunegonde is not here," said Cacambo, "she is at Constantinople."

"Oh, heavens! at Constantinople! But were she in China I would fly thither; let us be off."

"We shall set out after supper," replied Cacambo. "I can tell you nothing more; I am a slave, my master awaits me, I must serve him at table; speak not a word, eat, and then get ready."

Candide, distracted between joy and grief, delighted at seeing his faithful agent again, astonished at finding him a slave, filled with the fresh hope of recovering his mistress, his heart palpitating, his understanding confused, sat down to table with Martin, who saw all these scenes quite unconcerned, and with six strangers who had come to spend the Carnival at Venice.

Cacambo waited at table upon one of the strangers; towards the end of the entertainment he drew near his master, and whispered in his ear:

"Sire, your Majesty may start when you please, the vessel is ready."

On saying these words he went out. The company in great surprise looked at one another without speaking a word, when another domestic approached his master and said to him:

"Sire, your Majesty's chaise is at Padua, and the boat is ready."

The master gave a nod and the servant went away. The company all stared at one another again, and their surprise redoubled. A third valet came up to a third stranger, saying:

"Sire, believe me, your Majesty ought not to stay here any longer. I am going to get everything ready."

And immediately he disappeared. Candide and Martin did not doubt that this was a masquerade of the Carnival. Then a fourth domestic said to a fourth master:

"Your Majesty may depart when you please."

Saying this he went away like the rest. The fifth valet said the same thing to the fifth master. But the sixth valet spoke differently to the sixth stranger, who sat near Candide. He said to him:

"Faith, Sire, they will no longer give credit to your Majesty nor to me, and we may perhaps both of us be put in jail this very night. Therefore I will take care of myself. Adieu."

The servants being all gone, the six strangers, with Candide and Martin, remained in a profound silence. At length Candide broke it.

"Gentlemen," said he, "this is a very good joke indeed, but why should you all be kings? For me I own that neither Martin nor I is a king."

Cacambo's master then gravely answered in Italian:

"I am not at all joking. My name is Achmet III. I was Grand Sultan many years. I dethroned my brother; my nephew dethroned me, my viziers were beheaded, and I am condemned to end my days in the old Seraglio. My nephew, the great Sultan Mahmoud, permits me to travel sometimes for my health, and I am come to spend the Carnival at Venice."

A young man who sat next to Achmet, spoke then as follows:

"My name is Ivan. I was once Emperor of all the Russias, but was dethroned in my cradle. My parents were confined in prison and I was educated there; yet I am sometimes allowed to travel in company with persons who act as guards; and I am come to spend the Carnival at Venice."

The third said:

"I am Charles Edward, King of England; my father has resigned all his legal rights to me. I have fought in defence of them; and above eight hundred of my adherents have been hanged, drawn, and quartered. I have been confined in prison; I am going to Rome, to pay a visit to the King, my father, who was dethroned as well as myself and my grandfather, and I am come to spend the Carnival at Venice."

The fourth spoke thus in his turn:

"I am the King of Poland; the fortune of war has stripped me of my hereditary dominions; my father underwent the same vicissitudes; I resign myself to Providence in the same manner as Sultan Achmet, the Emperor Ivan, and King Charles Edward, whom God long preserve; and I am come to the Carnival at Venice."

The fifth said:

"I am King of Poland also; I have been twice dethroned; but Providence has given me another country, where I have done more good than all the Sarmatian kings were ever capable of doing on the banks of the Vistula; I resign myself likewise to Providence, and am come to pass the Carnival at Venice."

It was now the sixth monarch's turn to speak:

"Gentlemen," said he, "I am not so great a prince as any of you; however, I am a king. I am Theodore, elected King of Corsica; I had the title of Majesty, and now I am scarcely treated as a gentleman. I have coined money, and now am not worth a farthing; I have had two secretaries of state, and now I have scarce a valet; I have seen myself on a throne, and I have seen myself upon straw in a common jail in London. I am afraid that I shall meet with the same treatment here though, like your majesties, I am come to see the Carnival at Venice."

The other five kings listened to this speech with generous compassion. Each of them gave twenty sequins to King Theodore to buy him clothes and linen; and Candide made him a present of a diamond worth two thousand sequins.

"Who can this private person be," said the five kings to one another, "who is able to give, and really has given, a hundred times as much as any of us?"

Just as they rose from table, in came four Serene Highnesses, who had also been stripped of their territories by the fortune of war, and were come to spend the Carnival at Venice. But Candide paid no regard to these newcomers, his thoughts were entirely employed on his voyage to Constantinople, in search of his beloved Cunegonde.

CHAPTER XXVII

CANDIDE'S VOYAGE TO CONSTANTINOPLE

THE FAITHFUL CACAMBO had already prevailed upon the Turkish skipper, who was to conduct the Sultan Achmet to Constantinople, to receive Candide and Martin on his ship. They both embarked after having made their obeisance to his miserable Highness.

"You see," said Candide to Martin on the way, "we supped with six dethroned kings, and of those six there was one to whom I gave charity. Perhaps there are many other princes yet more unfortunate. For my part I have only lost a hundred sheep; and now I am flying into Cunegonde's arms. My dear Martin, yet once more Pangloss was right; all is for the best."

"I wish it," answered Martin.

"But," said Candide, "it was a very strange adventure we met with at Venice. It has never before been seen or heard that six dethroned kings have supped together at a public inn."

"It is not more extraordinary," said Martin, "than most of the things that have happened to us. It is a very common thing for kings to be dethroned; and as for the honour we have had of supping in their company, it is a trifle not worth our attention."

No sooner had Candide got on board the vessel than he flew to his old valet and friend Cacambo, and tenderly embraced him.

"Well," said he, "what news of Cunegonde? Is she still a prodigy of beauty? Does she love me still? How is she? Thou hast doubtless bought her a palace at Constantinople?"

"My dear master," answered Cacambo, "Cunegonde washes dishes on the banks of the Propontis, in the service of a prince, who has very few dishes to wash; she is a slave in the family of an ancient sovereign named Ragotsky,[34] to whom the Grand Turk allows three crowns a day in his exile. But what is worse still is, that she has lost her beauty and has become horribly ugly."

"Well, handsome or ugly," replied Candide, "I am a man of honour, and it is my duty to love her still. But how came she to be reduced to so abject a state with the five or six millions that you took to her?"

"Ah!" said Cacambo, "was I not to give two millions to Señor Don Fernando d'Ibaraa, y Figueora, y Mascarenes, y Lampourdos, y Souza, Governor of Buenos Ayres, for permitting Miss Cunegonde to come away? And did not a corsair bravely rob us of all the rest? Did not this corsair carry us to Cape Matapan, to Milo, to Nicaria, to Samos, to Petra, to the Dardanelles, to Marmora, to Scutari? Cunegonde and the old woman serve the prince I now mentioned to you, and I am slave to the dethroned Sultan."

"What a series of shocking calamities!" cried Candide. "But after all, I have some diamonds left; and I may easily pay Cunegonde's ransom. Yet it is a pity that she is grown so ugly."

Then, turning towards Martin: "Who do you think," said he, "is most to be pitied—the Sultan Achmet, the Emperor Ivan, King Charles Edward, or I?"

"How should I know!" answered Martin. "I must see into your hearts to be able to tell."

"Ah!" said Candide, "if Pangloss were here, he could tell."

"I know not," said Martin, "in what sort of scales your Pangloss would weigh the misfortunes of mankind and set a just estimate on their sorrows. All that I can presume to say is, that there are millions of people upon earth who have a hundred times more to complain of than King Charles Edward, the Emperor Ivan, or the Sultan Achmet."

"That may well be," said Candide.

In a few days they reached the Bosphorus, and Candide began by paying a very high ransom for Cacambo. Then without losing time, he and his companions went on board a galley, in order to search on the banks of the Propontis for his Cunegonde, however ugly she might have become.

Among the crew there were two slaves who rowed very badly, and to whose bare shoulders the Levantine captain would now and then apply blows from a bull's pizzle. Candide, from a natural impulse, looked at these two slaves more attentively than at the other oarsmen, and approached them with pity. Their features though greatly disfigured, had a slight resemblance to those of Pangloss and the unhappy Jesuit and Westphalian Baron, brother to Miss Cunegonde. This moved and saddened him. He looked at them still more attentively.

"Indeed," said he to Cacambo, "if I had not seen Master Pangloss hanged, and if I had not had the misfortune to kill the Baron, I should think it was they that were rowing."

At the names of the Baron and of Pangloss, the two galley-slaves uttered a loud cry, held fast by the seat, and let drop their oars. The captain ran up to them and redoubled his blows with the bull's pizzle.

"Stop! stop! sir," cried Candide. "I will give you what money you please."

"What! it is Candide!" said one of the slaves.

"What! it is Candide!" said the other.

"Do I dream?" cried Candide; "am I awake? or am I on board a galley? Is this the Baron whom I killed? Is this Master Pangloss whom I saw hanged?"

"It is we! it is we!" answered they.

"Well! is this the great philosopher?" said Martin.

"Ah! captain," said Candide, "what ransom will you take for Monsieur de Thunder-ten-Tronckh, one of the first barons of the empire, and for Monsieur Pangloss, the profoundest metaphysician in Germany?"

"Dog of a Christian," answered the Levantine captain, "since these two dogs of Christian slaves are barons and metaphysicians, which I doubt not are high dignities in their country, you shall give me fifty thousand sequins."

"You shall have them, sir. Carry me back at once to Constantinople, and you shall receive the money directly. But no; carry me first to Miss Cunegonde."

Upon the first proposal made by Candide, however, the Levantine captain had already tacked about, and made the crew ply their oars quicker than a bird cleaves the air.

Candide embraced the Baron and Pangloss a hundred times.

"And how happened it, my dear Baron, that I did not kill you? And, my dear Pangloss, how came you to life again after being hanged? And why are you both in a Turkish galley?"

"And it is true that my dear sister is in this country?" said the Baron.

"Yes," answered Cacambo.

"Then I behold, once more, my dear Candide," cried Pangloss.

Candide presented Martin and Cacambo to them; they embraced each other, and all spoke at once. The galley flew; they were already in the port. Instantly Candide sent for a Jew, to whom he sold for fifty thousand sequins a diamond worth a hundred thousand, though the fellow swore to him by Abraham that he could give him no more. He immediately paid the ransom for the Baron and Pangloss. The latter threw himself at the feet of his deliverer, and bathed them with his tears; the former thanked him with a nod, and promised to return him the money on the first opportunity.

"But is it indeed possible that my sister can be in Turkey?" said he.

"Nothing is more possible," said Cacambo, "since she scours the dishes in the service of a Transylvanian prince."

Candide sent directly for two Jews and sold them some more diamonds, and then they all set out together in another galley to deliver Cunegonde from slavery.

CHAPTER XXVIII

WHAT HAPPENED TO CANDIDE, CUNEGONDE, PANGLOSS, MARTIN, ETC.

"I ASK YOUR pardon once more," said Candide to the Baron, "your pardon, reverend father, for having run you through the body."

"Say no more about it," answered the Baron. "I was a little too hasty, I own, but since you wish to know by what fatality I came to be a galley-slave I will inform you. After I had been cured by the surgeon of the college of the wound you gave me, I was attacked and carried off by a party of Spanish troops, who confined me in prison at Buenos Ayres at the very time my sister was setting out thence. I asked leave to return to Rome to the General of my Order. I was appointed chaplain to the French Ambassador at Constantinople. I had not been eight days in this employment when one evening I met with a young Ichoglan, who was a very handsome fellow. The weather was warm. The young man wanted to bathe, and I took this opportunity of bathing also. I did not know that it was a capital crime for a Christian to be found naked with a young Mussulman. A cadi ordered me a hundred blows on the soles of the feet, and condemned me to the galleys. I do not think there ever was a greater act of injustice. But I should be glad to know how my sister came to be scullion to a Transylvanian prince who has taken shelter among the Turks."

"But you, my dear Pangloss," said Candide, "how can it be that I behold you again?"

"It is true," said Pangloss, "that you saw me hanged. I should have been burnt, but you may remember it rained exceedingly hard when they were going to roast me; the storm was so violent that they despaired of lighting the fire, so I was hanged because they could do no better. A surgeon purchased my body, carried me home, and dissected me. He began with making a crucial incision on me from the navel to the clavicula. One could not have been worse hanged than I was. The executioner of the Holy Inquisition was a sub-deacon, and knew how to burn people marvellously well, but he was not accustomed to hanging. The cord was wet and did not slip properly, and besides it was badly tied; in short, I still drew my breath, when the crucial incision made me give such a frightful scream that my surgeon fell flat upon his back, and imagining that he had been dissecting the devil he ran away, dying with fear, and fell down the staircase in his flight. His wife, hearing the noise, flew from the next room. She saw me stretched out upon the table with my crucial incision. She was seized with yet greater fear than her husband, fled, and tumbled over him. When they came to themselves a little, I heard the wife say to her husband: 'My dear, how could you take it into your head to dissect a heretic? Do you not know that these people always have the devil in their bodies? I will go and fetch a priest this minute to exorcise him.' At this proposal I shuddered, and mustering up what little courage I had still remaining I cried out aloud, 'Have mercy on me!' At length the Portuguese barber plucked up his spirits. He sewed up my wounds; his wife even nursed me. I was upon my legs at the end of fifteen days. The barber found me a place as lackey to a knight of Malta who was going to Venice, but finding that my master had no money to pay me my wages I entered the service of a Venetian merchant, and went with him to Constantinople. One day I took it into my head to step into a mosque, where I saw an old Iman and a very pretty young devotee who was saying her paternosters. Her bosom was uncovered, and between her breasts she had a beautiful bouquet of tulips, roses, anemones, ranunculus, hyacinths, and auriculas. She dropped her bouquet; I picked it up, and presented it to her with a profound reverence. I was so long in delivering it that the Iman began to get angry, and seeing that I was a Christian he called out for help. They carried me before the cadi, who ordered me a hundred lashes on the soles of the feet and sent me to the galleys. I was chained to the very same galley and the same bench as the young Baron. On board this galley there were four voting men from Marseilles, five Neapolitan priests, and two monks from Corfu, who told us similar adventures happened daily. The Baron maintained that he had suffered greater injustice than I, and I insisted that it was far more innocent to take up a bouquet and place it again on a woman's bosom than to be found stark naked with an Ichoglan. We were continually disputing, and received twenty lashes with a bull's pizzle when the concatenation of universal events brought you to our galley, and you were good enough to ransom us."

"Well, my dear Pangloss," said Candide to him, "when you had been hanged, dissected, whipped, and were tugging at the oar, did you always think that everything happens for the best?"

"I am still of my first opinion," answered Pangloss, "for I am a philosopher and I cannot retract, especially as Leibnitz could never be wrong; and besides, the pre-established harmony is the finest thing in the world, and so is his *plenum* and *materia subtilis*."

CHAPTER XXIX

HOW CANDIDE FOUND CUNEGONDE AND THE OLD WOMAN AGAIN

WHILE CANDIDE, THE Baron, Pangloss, Martin, and Cacambo were relating their several adventures, were reasoning on the contingent or non-contingent events of the universe, disputing on effects and causes, on moral and physical evil, on liberty and necessity, and on the consolations a slave may feel even on a Turkish galley, they arrived at the house of the Transylvanian prince on the banks of the Propontis. The first objects which met their sight were Cunegonde and the old woman hanging towels out to dry.

The Baron paled at this sight. The tender, loving Candide, seeing his beautiful Cunegonde embrowned, with blood-shot eyes, withered neck, wrinkled cheeks, and rough, red arms, recoiled three paces, seized with horror, and then advanced out of good manners. She embraced Candide and her brother; they embraced the old woman, and Candide ransomed them both.

There was a small farm in the neighbourhood which the old woman proposed to Candide to make a shift with till the company could be provided for in a better manner. Cunegonde did not know she had grown ugly, for nobody had told her of it; and she reminded Candide of his promise in so positive a tone that the good man durst not refuse her. He therefore intimated to the Baron that he intended marrying his sister.

"I will not suffer," said the Baron, "such meanness on her part, and such insolence on yours; I will never be reproached with this scandalous thing; my sister's children would never be able to enter the church in Germany. No; my sister shall only marry a baron of the empire."

Cunegonde flung herself at his feet, and bathed them with her tears; still he was inflexible.

"Thou foolish fellow," said Candide; "I have delivered thee out of the galleys, I have paid thy ransom, and thy sister's also; she was a scullion, and is very ugly, yet I am so condescending as to marry her; and dost thou pretend to oppose the match? I should kill thee again, were I only to consult my anger."

"Thou mayest kill me again," said the Baron, "but thou shalt not marry my sister, at least whilst I am living."

CHAPTER XXX

THE CONCLUSION

AT THE BOTTOM of his heart Candide had no wish to marry Cunegonde. But the extreme impertinence of the Baron determined him to conclude the match, and Cunegonde pressed him so strongly that he could not go from his word. He consulted Pangloss, Martin, and the faithful Cacambo. Pangloss drew up an excellent memorial, wherein he proved that the Baron had no right over his sister, and that according to all the laws of the empire, she might marry

Candide with her left hand. Martin was for throwing the Baron into the sea; Cacambo decided that it would be better to deliver him up again to the captain of the galley, after which they thought to send him back to the General Father of the Order at Rome by the first ship. This advice was well received, the old woman approved it; they said not a word to his sister; the thing was executed for a little money, and they had the double pleasure of entrapping a Jesuit, and punishing the pride of a German baron.

It is natural to imagine that after so many disasters Candide married, and living with the philosopher Pangloss, the philosopher Martin, the prudent Cacambo, and the old woman, having besides brought so many diamonds from the country of the ancient Incas, must have led a very happy life. But he was so much imposed upon by the Jews that he had nothing left except his small farm; his wife became uglier every day, more peevish and unsupportable; the old woman was infirm and even more fretful than Cunegonde. Cacambo, who worked in the garden, and took vegetables for sale to Constantinople, was fatigued with hard work, and cursed his destiny. Pangloss was in despair at not shining in some German university. For Martin, he was firmly persuaded that he would be as badly off elsewhere, and therefore bore things patiently. Candide, Martin, and Pangloss sometimes disputed about morals and metaphysics. They often saw passing under the windows of their farm boats full of Effendis, Pashas, and Cadis, who were going into banishment to Lemnos, Mitylene, or Erzeroum. And they saw other Cadis, Pashas, and Effendis coming to supply the place of the exiles, and afterwards exiled in their turn. They saw heads decently impaled for presentation to the Sublime Porte. Such spectacles as these increased the number of their dissertations; and when they did not dispute time hung so heavily upon their hands, that one day the old woman ventured to say to them:

"I want to know which is worse, to be ravished a hundred times by negro pirates, to have a buttock cut off, to run the gauntlet among the Bulgarians, to be whipped and hanged at an *auto-da-fé*, to be dissected, to row in the galleys—in short, to go through all the miseries we have undergone, or to stay here and have nothing to do?"

"It is a great question," said Candide.

This discourse gave rise to new reflections, and Martin especially concluded that man was born to live either in a state of distracting inquietude or of lethargic disgust. Candide did not quite agree to that, but he affirmed nothing. Pangloss owned that he had always suffered horribly, but as he had once asserted that everything went wonderfully well, he asserted it still, though he no longer believed it.

What helped to confirm Martin in his detestable principles, to stagger Candide more than ever, and to puzzle Pangloss, was that one day they saw Paquette and Friar Giroflée land at the farm in extreme misery. They had soon squandered their three thousand piastres, parted, were reconciled, quarrelled again, were thrown into gaol, had escaped, and Friar Giroflée had at length become Turk. Paquette continued her trade wherever she went, but made nothing of it.

"I foresaw," said Martin to Candide, "that your presents would soon be dissipated, and only make them the more miserable. You have rolled in millions of money, you and Cacambo; and yet you are not happier than Friar Giroflée and Paquette."

"Ha!" said Pangloss to Paquette, "Providence has then brought you amongst us again, my poor child! Do you know that you cost me the tip of my nose, an eye, and an ear, as you may see? What a world is this!"

And now this new adventure set them philosophising more than ever.

In the neighbourhood there lived a very famous Dervish who was esteemed the best philosopher in all Turkey, and they went to consult him. Pangloss was the speaker.

"Master," said he, "we come to beg you to tell why so strange an animal as man was made."

"With what meddlest thou?" said the Dervish; "is it thy business?"

"But, reverend father," said Candide, "there is horrible evil in this world."

"What signifies it," said the Dervish, "whether there be evil or good? When his highness sends a ship to Egypt, does he trouble his head whether the mice on board are at their ease or not?"

"What, then, must we do?" said Pangloss.

"Hold your tongue," answered the Dervish.

"I was in hopes," said Pangloss, "that I should reason with you a little about causes and effects, about the best of possible worlds, the origin of evil, the nature of the soul, and the pre-established harmony."

At these words, the Dervish shut the door in their faces.

During this conversation, the news was spread that two Viziers and the Mufti had been strangled at Constantinople, and that several of their friends had been impaled. This catastrophe made a great noise for some hours. Pangloss, Candide, and Martin, returning to the little farm, saw a good old man taking the fresh air at his door under an orange bower. Pangloss, who was as inquisitive as he was argumentative, asked the old man what was the name of the strangled Mufti.

"I do not know," answered the worthy man, "and I have not known the name of any Mufti, nor of any Vizier. I am entirely ignorant of the event you mention; I presume in general that they who meddle with the administration of public affairs die sometimes miserably, and that they deserve it; but I never trouble my head about what is transacting at Constantinople; I content myself with sending there for sale the fruits of the garden which I cultivate."

Having said these words, he invited the strangers into his house; his two sons and two daughters presented them with several sorts of sherbet, which they made themselves, with Kaimak enriched with the candied peel of citrons, with oranges, lemons, pine-apples, pistachio-nuts, and Mocha coffee unadulterated with the bad coffee of Batavia or the American islands. After which the two daughters of the honest Mussulman perfumed the strangers' beards.

"You must have a vast and magnificent estate," said Candide to the Turk.

"I have only twenty acres," replied the old man; "I and my children cultivate them; our labour preserves us from three great evils—weariness, vice, and want."

Candide, on his way home, made profound reflections on the old man's conversation.

"This honest Turk," said he to Pangloss and Martin, "seems to be in a situation far preferable to that of the six kings with whom we had the honour of supping."

"Grandeur," said Pangloss, "is extremely dangerous according to the testimony of philosophers. For, in short, Eglon, King of Moab, was assassinated by Ehud; Absalom was hung by his hair, and pierced with three darts; King Nadab, the son of Jeroboam, was killed by Baasa; King Ela by Zimri; Ahaziah by Jehu; Athaliah by Jehoiada; the Kings Jehoiakim, Jeconiah, and Zedekiah were led into captivity. You know how perished Croesus, Astyages, Darius, Dionysius of Syracuse, Pyrrhus, Perseus, Hannibal, Jugurtha, Ariovistus, Cæsar, Pompey, Nero, Otho, Vitellius, Domitian, Richard II of England, Edward II, Henry VI, Richard III, Mary Stuart, Charles I, the three Henrys of France, the Emperor Henry IV! You know—"

"LET US WORK," SAID MARTIN, "WITHOUT DISPUTING; IT IS THE ONLY WAY TO RENDER LIFE TOLERABLE."

"I know also," said Candide, "that we must cultivate our garden."

"You are right," said Pangloss, "for when man was first placed in the Garden of Eden, he was put there *ut operaretur eum*, that he might cultivate it; which shows that man was not born to be idle."

"Let us work," said Martin, "without disputing; it is the only way to render life tolerable."

The whole little society entered into this laudable design, according to their different abilities. Their little plot of land produced plentiful crops. Cunegonde was, indeed, very ugly, but she became an excellent pastry cook; Paquette worked at embroidery; the old woman looked after the linen. They were all, not excepting Friar Giroflée, of some service or other; for he made a good joiner, and became a very honest man.

Pangloss sometimes said to Candide:

"There is a concatenation of events in this best of all possible worlds: for if you had not been kicked out of a magnificent castle for love of Miss Cunegonde: if you had not been put into the Inquisition: if you had not walked over America: if you had not stabbed the Baron: if you had not lost all your sheep from the fine country of El Dorado: you would not be here eating preserved citrons and pistachio-nuts."

"All that is very well," answered Candide, "but let us cultivate our garden."

NOTES TO THE TEXT

1. The name Pangloss is derived from two Greek words signifying "all" and "language."

2. The Abares were a tribe of Tartars settled on the shores of the Danube, who later dwelt in part of Circassia.

3. Venereal disease was said to have been first brought from Hispaniola, in the West Indies, by some followers of Columbus who were later employed in the siege of Naples. From this latter circumstance it was at one time known as the Neapolitan disease.

4. The great earthquake of Lisbon happened on the first of November, 1755.

5. Such was the aversion of the Japanese to the Christian faith that they compelled Europeans trading with their islands to trample on the cross, renounce all marks of Christianity, and swear that it was not their religion. See chap. xi. of the voyage to Laputa in Swift's *Gulliver's Travels*.

6. This *auto-da-fé* actually took place, some months after the earthquake, on June 20, 1756.

7. The rejection of bacon convicting them, of course, of being Jews, and therefore fitting victims for an *auto-da-fé*.

8. The *san-benito* was a kind of loose overgarment painted with flames, figures of devils, the victim's own portrait, etc., worn by persons condemned to death by the Inquisition when going to the stake on the occasion of an *auto-da-fé*. Those who expressed repentance for their errors wore a garment of the same kind covered with flames directed downwards, while that worn by Jews, sorcerers, and renegades bore a St. Andrew's cross before and behind.

9. "This Notre-Dame is of wood; every year she weeps on the day of her *fête*, and the people weep also. One day the preacher, seeing a carpenter with dry eyes, asked him how it was that he did not dissolve in tears when the Holy Virgin wept. 'Ah, my reverend father,' replied he, 'it is I who refastened her in her niche yesterday. I drove three great nails through her behind; it is then she would have wept if she had been able.'"—Voltaire, *Mélanges*.

10. The following posthumous note of Voltaire's was first added to M. Beuchot's edition of his works issued in 1829; "See the extreme discretion of the author; them has not been up to the present any Pope named Urban X.; he feared to give a bastard to a known Pope. What circumspection! What delicacy of conscience!" The last Pope Urban was the eighth, and he died in 1644.

11. Muley-Ismael was Emperor of Morocco from 1672 to 1727, and was a notoriously cruel tyrant.

12. "Oh, what a misfortune to be an eunuch!"

13. Carlo Broschi, called Farinelli, an Italian singer, born at Naples in 1705, without being exactly Minister, governed Spain under Ferdinand VI.; he died in 1782. He has been made one of the chief persons in one of the comic operas of MM. Auber and Scribe.

14. Jean Robeck, a Swede, who was born in 1672, will be found mentioned in Rousseau's *Nouvelle Héloïse*. He drowned himself in the Weser at Bremen in 1729, and was the author of a Latin treatise on voluntary death, first printed in 1735.

15. A spontoon was a kind of half-pike, a military weapon carried by officers of infantry and used as a medium for signalling orders to the regiment.

16. Later Voltaire substituted the name of the Father Croust for that of Didrie. Of Croust he said in the *Dictionnaire Philosophique* that he was "the most brutal of the Society."

17. By the *Journal of Trevoux* Voltaire meant a critical periodical printed by the Jesuits at Trevoux under the title of *Mémoires pour servir à l'Histoire des Sciences et des Beaux-Arts*. It existed from 1701 until 1767, during which period its title underwent many changes.

18. It has been suggested that Voltaire, in speaking of red sheep, referred to the llama, a South American ruminant allied to the camel. These animals are sometimes of a reddish colour, and were notable as pack-carriers and for their fleetness.

19. The first English translator curiously gives "a tourene of bouilli that weighed two hundred pounds," as the equivalent of "*un contour bouilli qui pesait deux cent livres*." The French editor of the 1869 reprint points out that the South American vulture, or condor, is meant; the name of this bird, it may be added, is taken from *cuntur,* that given it by the aborigines.

20. *Socinians*; followers of the teaching of Lalius and Faustus Socinus (16th century), which denied the doctrine of the Trinity, the deity of Christ, the personality of the devil, the native and total depravity of man, the vicarious atonement and eternal punishment. The Socinians are now represented by the Unitarians. *Manicheans*; followers of Manes or Manichaeus (3rd century), a Persian who maintained that there are two principles, the one good and the other evil, each equally powerful in the government of the world.

21. In the 1759 editions, in place of the following long passage from here to page 385, line 21, there was only the following: "'Sir,' said the Perigordian Abbé to him, 'have you noticed that young person who has so roguish a face and so fine a figure? You may have her for ten thousand francs a month, and fifty thousand crowns in diamonds.' 'I have only a day or two to give her,' answered Candide, 'because I have a rendezvous at Venice.' In the evening after supper the insinuating Perigordian redoubled his politeness and attentions."

22. The play referred to is supposed to be "Le Comte d'Essex," by Thomas Corneille.

23. In France actors were at one time looked upon as excommunicated persons, not worthy of burial in holy ground or with Christian rites. In 1730 the "honours of sepulture" were refused to Mademoiselle Lecouvreur (doubtless the Miss Monime of this passage). Voltaire's miscellaneous works contain a paper on the matter.

24. Élie-Catherine Fréron was a French critic (1719-1776) who incurred the enmity of Voltaire. In 1752 Fréron, in *Lettres sur quelques écrits du temps*, wrote pointedly of Voltaire as one who chose to be all things to all men, and Voltaire retaliated by references such as these in *Candide*.

25. Gabriel Gauchat (1709-1779), French ecclesiastical writer, was author of a number of works on religious subjects.

26. Nicholas Charles Joseph Trublet (1697-1770) was a French writer whose criticism of Voltaire was revenged in passages such as this one in *Candide*, and one in the *Pauvre Diable* beginning:

> L'abbé Trublet avait alors le rage
> D'être à Paris un petit personnage.

27. Damiens, who attempted the life of Louis XV. in 1757, was born at Arras, capital of Artois (Atrébatie).

28. On May 14, 1610, Ravaillac assassinated Henry VI.

29. On December 27, 1594, Jean Châtel attempted to assassinate Henry IV.

30. This same curiously inept criticism of the war which cost France her American provinces occurs in Voltaire's *Memoirs*, wherein he says, "In 1756 England made a piratical war upon France for some acres of snow." See also his *Précis du Siècle de Louis XV*.

31. Admiral Byng was shot on March 14, 1757.

32. Commenting upon this passage, M. Sarcey says admirably: "All is there! In those ten lines Voltaire has gathered all the griefs and all the terrors of these creatures; the picture is admirable for its truth and power! But do you not feel the pity and sympathy of the painter? Here irony becomes sad, and in a way an avenger. Voltaire cries out with horror against the society which throws some of its members into such an abyss. He has his 'Bartholomew' fever; we tremble with him through contagion."

33. The following particulars of the six monarchs may prove not uninteresting. Achmet III (*b*. 1673, *d*. 1739) was dethroned in 1730. Ivan VI (*b*. 1740, *d*. 1762) was dethroned in 1741. Charles Edward Stuart, the Pretender (*b*. 1720, *d*. 1788). Auguste III (*b*. 1696, *d*. 1763). Stanislaus (*b*. 1682, *d*. 1766). Theodore (*b*. 1690, *d*. 1755). It will be observed that, although quite impossible for the six kings ever to have met, five of them might have been made to do so without any anachronism.

34. François Leopold Ragotsky (1676-1735).

The Marquis de Sade

(Comte Donatien-Alphonse-François de Sade)

(1740–1814)

The table of contents for this anthology contains some of the most famous names in all of literature—names that have even added adjectives to the language: "Machiavellian" for cunning; "Swiftian" for satiric; "Rabelaisian" for ribald. Only one, however, can claim ownership of a noun. A mere twenty years after the death of Comte Donatien-Alphonse-François de Sade, a dictionary first defined *sadism* as the deliberate enjoyment of the infliction of pain. The Marquis' fame—or, more correctly, infamy—had been well-earned.

Sade was born June 2, 1740, to Jean-Baptiste de Sade and his wife Marie-Eléonore de Maillé at the Condé Palace in Paris. On his father's side, Sade descended from a noble family who had held titles in Provence for nearly 500 years. His mother was distantly related to the royal family and hoped that her son would develop a friendship with Louis Joseph de Bourbon, the Prince de Condé. Sent away at age four (a fight with his prospective—and royal—playmate is the likely reason) to Provence, Sade spent the next six years living at a family estate in Saumane in the custody of his uncle, the Abbe dé Sade. There he was tutored by Jacques-François Amblet, who would become Sade's lifelong companion. Amblet accompanied Sade when he returned to Paris to begin his schooling at Louis-le-Grand, a Jesuit school, where he failed to distinguish himself academically. Nonetheless, in 1754, the fourteen-year-old Sade was admitted to the elite training academy for the King's Light Cavalry, and commissioned as an officer in the King's Own Foot Guards a year later. During the Seven Years War (1756–1763) Sade saw combat, was promoted twice, and, in 1763, departed the King's service with the rank of Captain in the Burgundy Cavalry.

Life in Paris for the former soldier was a whirlwind of balls, plays, and sexual assignations. But despite his growing attraction to the actresses and prostitutes who frequented what would someday be called Paris's demimonde, on May 17, 1763, Sade acceded to the wishes of his family and married Renée-Pelagie de Montreuil. For the next twenty-seven years, her somewhat-bizarre loyalty to Sade would never flag, though not for lack of provocation. Five months after his wedding, the newlywed husband was arrested for unspecified "excesses" committed on a Parisian prostitute. Released a month later, he was exiled from Paris. Granted the right to return the following April, he immediately returned to form, and by November, the police were explicitly warning brothel keepers to keep their charges away from such a potentially dangerous customer.

In 1768, the Marquis—Sade had inherited the title upon the death of his father the previous year—brought a prostitute to his already notorious rented house in Arcueil for the purpose of flogging, cutting, sodomizing, and otherwise abusing her. When the woman escaped and brought charges, the Marquis was again imprisoned, continuing a cycle that would recur throughout his life. He was released from prison into exile at his chateau, La Coste, in 1772, where he poisoned a troupe of prostitutes with an overdose of Spanish Fly. Sade was convicted of attempted murder and sodomy (probably at the behest of his mother-in-law; Madame de Montreuil was understandably annoyed at the Marquis for seducing her younger daughter Anne-Prospère) and imprisoned. He escaped and returned to La Coste in 1775, hiring a group of young domestics to serve as sex slaves. When they complained to the authorities, Sade fled to Italy. Arrested in 1777 on the sodomy-and-poisoning charge from 1772, he was convicted and began an incarceration that would last for the next thirteen years, first at Vincennes, then at the Bastille, and finally at the insane asylum at Charenton, from which he was released by the Revolutionary Government in 1790.

He spent the next three years as a relatively free man (calling himself Citizen Louis Sade) until 1793, when he was arrested—again—during the Reign of Terror. For the only time in his life, however, the arrest was not for sexual criminality, but for his aristocratic background. Escaping virtually certain execution by a matter of weeks when Robespierre's overthrow ended the Terror, Sade was released in 1794. For the next seven years, the Marquis lived as a free, if impoverished, man. But by 1801, his pornographic writings attracted the attention of the government of Napoleon Bonaparte, and Sade was imprisoned for the final time, first at Saint Pelagie prison, and then at the asylum at Charenton, where he would spend the last eleven years of his life.

During one of his many tours of the French penal system, Sade's wife pled for his release, asking that the authorities "... not judge him from his writings, but rather judge him by his deeds." Had the Marquis de Sade bequeathed the world nothing but his deeds, his life would scarcely be worth remarking. But the words that he committed to paper—*The 120 Days of Sodom*, *Philosophy of the Bedroom*, *Juliet: Or the Triumph of Vice,* the stories and plays, and the thousands of letters, virtually all composed during his long stays in prison—reveal both a brilliant and debauched mind. *Justine: Or the Misfortunes of Virtue* (the title and form disclose the author's intention to parody Samuel Richardson's 1740 novel *Pamela: Or Virtue Rewarded*) was begun while Sade was a prisoner in the Bastille and published in 1791, during one of Sade's brief periods of freedom. *Justine* (it is perhaps too much of a coincidence that Catherine Trillet, one of the domestics hired in 1775 at La Coste, was called "Justine" by Sade) tells the story of two sisters. One, the title character, is completely virtuous, "a charming creature whose naïve graces and delicate traits are beyond our power to describe;" the other, her sister Juliet, is as depraved as Sade himself. Justine is sexually tortured, imprisoned in a monastery where she is repeatedly raped by the monks, accused of murder, and finally struck by a lightning bolt that kills her.

Juliet (who would feature in the complementary novel, *Juliet: Or the Triumph of Vice,* six years later) becomes a courtesan, destroys the lives of innumerable men, prospers, and ends her days in a nunnery. The narrator's claim that the novel's moral is that "true happiness is to be found nowhere but virtue's womb" is perhaps the most ironic phrase in literature. *Justine* is—for those of a certain taste—a classic piece of erotica, but more significantly a satire worthy of Swift at his most scabrous: a fevered drama showing self-restraint to be a violation of the "natural" desire to inflict and receive pain.

Is *Justine* pornography or parable? Was de Sade "the freest spirit that has yet existed" in the words of Guillaume Appollinaire who famously dubbed him "The Divine Marquis?" Or, are the writings, as critic and scholar Roger Shattuck has it, a "return to barbarism?" Perhaps it is best—and possibly inevitable, when speaking of the author of some of the longest novels ever written—to give the last word to the Marquis himself. His self-description, included in his last will and testament, reads in part "... imperious, choleric, irascible, extreme in everything, with a dissolute imagination the like of which has never been seen ... Kill me again or take me as I am, for I will not change."

Justine:
Or the Misfortunes of Virtue

Monsieur de Bressac had the charm of a youth and the most attractive countenance too; if there were some defects in his figure or his features, it was because they had a rather too pronounced tendency toward that nonchalance, that softness which properly belongs only to women; it seemed that, in lending him the attributes of the feminine sex, Nature had introduced its tastes to him as well. . . . Yet what a soul lurked behind those effeminate graces! All the vices which characterize the villain's genius were to be encountered in his: never had wickedness, vindictiveness, cruelty, atheism, debauchery, contempt for all duties and principally those out of which Nature is said to fashion our delights, never had all these qualities been carried to such an extreme. In the midst of all his faults predominated another: Monsieur de Bressac detested his aunt. The Marquise did everything conceivable to restore her nephew to the paths of virtue; perhaps she put too much rigorousness into her attempts; the result, however, was that the Count, further inflamed by that rigor's effects, only more impetuously gave himself up to his predilections, and the poor Marquise gained nothing from her persecutions but his redoubled hate.

"Do not imagine," the Count would often tell me, "that it is of her own accord my aunt acts in all that concerns you, Thérèse; believe me, were it not for my constant badgering she would quickly forget what she has promised to do for you. She would have you feel indebted to her, but all she has done is owing exclusively to me; yes, Thérèse, exactly, it is to me alone you are beholden, and the thanks I expect from you should appear the more disinterested, for although you've a pretty face, it is not, and you know it very well, after your favors I aspire; no, Thérèse, the services I await from you are of a radically different sort, and when you are well convinced of what I have accomplished in behalf of your tranquility, I hope I will find what I think I have the right to expect from your spirit."

So obscure were these speeches I knew not how to answer: however, reply to him I did, on a chance, as it were, and perhaps with too great a facility. Must I confess it? Alas! yes; to conceal my shortcomings would be to wrong your confidence and poorly to respond to the interest my misfortunes have quickened in you. Hear then, Madame, of the one deliberate fault with which I have to reproach myself. . . . What am I saying, a fault? It was a folly, an extravagance. . . . there has never been one equal to it; but at least it is not a crime, it is merely a mistake, for which I alone have been punished, and of which it surely does not seem that the equitable hand of Heaven had to make use in order to plunge me into the abyss which yawned beneath me soon afterward. Whatever the foul treatment to which Comte de Bressac had exposed me the first day I had met him, it had, all the same, been impossible to see him so frequently without feeling myself so drawn toward him by an insuperable and instinctive tenderness. Despite all my recollections of his cruelty, all my thoughts upon his disinclinations towards women, upon the depravity of his tastes, upon the gulf which separated us morally, nothing in the world was able to extinguish this nascent passion, and had the Count called upon me to lay down my life, I would have sacrificed it for him a thousand times over. He was far from suspecting my sentiments. . . . he was far, the ungrateful one, from divining the cause of the tears I shed every day; nevertheless, it was out of the question for him to be in doubt of my eagerness to fly to do his every bidding, to please him in every possible way, it could not have been he did not glimpse, did not have some inkling of my attentions; doubtless, because they were instinctive, they were also mindless, and went to the point to serving his errors, of serving them as far as decency permitted, and always of hiding them from his aunt. This behavior had in some sort won me his confidence, and all that came from him was so precious to me, I was so blinded by the little his heart offered me, that I sometimes had the weakness to believe he was not indifferent to me. But how promptly his excessive disorders disabused me: they were such that even his health was affected. I several times took the liberty to represent to him the dangers of his conduct, he would hear me out patiently, then end by telling me that one does not break oneself of the vice he cherished.

"Ah, Thérèse!" he exclaimed one day, full of enthusiasm, "if only you knew this fantasy's charms, if only you could understand what one experiences from the sweet illusion of being no more than a woman! incredible inconsistency! one abhors that sex, yet one wishes to imitate it! Ah! how sweet it is to succeed, Thérèse, how delicious it is to be a slut to everyone who would have to do with you and carrying delirium and prostitution to their ultimate period, successively, in the very same day, to be the mistress of a porter, a marquis, a valet, a friar, to be the beloved of each one after the other, caressed, envied, menaced, beaten, sometimes victorious in their arms, sometimes a victim and at their feet, melting them with caresses, reanimating them with excesses. . . . Oh no, Thérèse, you do not understand what is this pleasure for a mind constructed like mine. . . . But, morals aside, if you were able to imagine this divine whimsy's physical sensations, there is no withstanding it, it is a titillation so lively, it is of so piquant a voluptuousness. . . one becomes giddy, one ceases to reason, stammers; a thousand kisses one more tender than the next do not inflame us with an ardor in any way approaching the drunkenness into which the agent plunges us; enlaced in his arms, our mouth glued to his, we would that our entire being were incorporated into his; we would not make but a single being with him; if we dare complain, 'tis of being neglected; we would have him, more robust than Hercules, enlarge us, penetrate us; we would have that precious semen shot blazing to the depths of our entrails, cause, by its heat and its strength, our own to leap forth into his hands. . . . Do not suppose, Thérèse, we are made like other men; 'tis an entirely different structure we have; and, in creating us, Heaven has ornamented the altars at which our Celadons sacrifice with that very same sensitive membrane which lines your temple of Venus; we are, in that sector, as certainly women as you are in your generative sanctuary; not one of your pleasures is unknown to us, there is not one we do not know how to enjoy, but we have in addition to them our own, and it is this delicious combination which makes us of all men on earth the most sensitive to pleasure, the best created to experience it; it is this enchanting combination which renders our tastes incorrigible, which would turn us into enthusiasts and frenetics were one to have the stupidity to punish us. . . which makes us worship, unto the grave itself, the charming God who enthralls us."

Thus the Count expressed himself, celebrating his eccentricities; when I strove to speak to him of the Being to whom he owed everything, and of the grief such disorders caused his respectable aunt, I perceived nothing in him but spleen and ill-humor and especially impatience at having to see, in such hands and for so long, riches which, he would say, already ought to belong to him; I saw nothing but the most inveterate hatred for that so gentle woman, nothing but the most determined revolt against every natural sentiment. It would then be true that when in one's tastes one has been able so formally to transgress that law's sacred instinct, the necessary consequence of this original crime is a frightful penchant to commit every other.

Sometimes I employed the means Religion provides; almost always comforted by it, I attempted to insinuate its sweetness into this perverse creature's soul, more or less certain he could be restrained by those bonds were I to succeed in having him strike at the lure; but the Count did not long tolerate my use of such weapons. A declared enemy of our most holy mysteries, a stubborn critic of the purity of our dogmas, an impassioned antagonist of the idea of a Supreme Being's existence, Monsieur de Bressac, instead of letting himself be converted by me, sought rather to work my corruption.

"All religions start from a false premise, Thérèse," he would say; "each supposes as necessary the worship of a Creator, but that creator never existed. In this connection, put yourself in mind of the sound precepts of that certain Coeur-de-fer who, you told me, used to labor over your mind as I do; nothing more just, nor more precise, than that man's principles, and the degradation in which we have the stupidity to keep him does not deprive him of the right to reason well.

"If all Nature's productions are the resultant effects of the laws whereof she is captive; if her perpetual action and reaction supposed the motion necessary to her essence, what becomes of the sovereign master fools gratuitously give her? that is what your sagacious instructor said to you, dear girl. What, then, are religions if not the restraint wherewith the tyranny of the mightier sought to enslave the weaker? Motivated by that design, he dared say to him whom he claimed the right to dominate, that a God had forged the irons with which cruelty manacled him; and the latter, bestialized by his misery, indistinctly believed everything the former wished. Can religions, born of these rogueries, merit respect? Is there one of them, Thérèse, which does not bear the stamp of imposture and of stupidity? What do I descry in them all? Mysteries which cause reason to shudder, dogmas which outrage Nature, grotesque ceremonies which simply inspire derision and disgust. But if amongst them all there were one which most particularly deserves our scold and hatred, O Thérèse, is it not that barbaric law of the Christianity into which both of us were born? Is there any more odious? one which so spurs both the heart and mind to revolt? How is it that rational men are still able to lend any credence to the obscure mutterings, to the alleged miracles of that appalling cult's vile originator? Has there ever existed a rowdy scoundrel more worth of public indignation! What is he more than a leprous Jew who, born of a slut and a soldier in the world's meanest stews, dared fob himself off for the spokesman of him who, they say, created the universe! With such lofty pretensions, you will have to admit, Thérèse, at least a few credentials are necessary. But what are those of this ridiculous Ambassador? What is he going to do to prove his mission? Is the earth's face going to be changed? are the plagues which beset it going to be annihilated? is the sun going to shine upon it by night as well as by day? vices will soil it no more? Are we going to see happiness reign at last? . . .

Not at all; it is through hocus-pocus, antic capers, and puns that God's envoy announces himself to the world; it is in the elegant society of manual laborers, artisans, and streetwalkers that Heaven's minister comes to manifest his grandeur; it is by drunken carousing with these, bedding with those, that God's friend, God himself, comes to bend the toughened sinner to his laws; it is by inventing nothing for his farces but what can satisfy either his lewdness or his gourmand's guts that the knavish fellow demonstrates his mission; however all that may be, he makes his fortune; a few beef-witted satellites gravitate toward the villain; a sect is formed; this crowd's dogmas manage to seduce some Jews; slaves of the Roman power, they joyfully embrace a religion which, ridding them of their shackles, makes them subject to none but a metaphysical tyranny. Their motives becomes evident, their indocility unveils itself, the seditious louts are arrested; their captain perishes, but of a death doubtless much too merciful for his species of crime, and through an unpardonable lapse in intelligence, this uncouth boor's disciples are allowed to disperse instead of being slaughtered cheek to jowl with their leader. Fanaticism gets minds in its grip, women shriek, fools scrape and scuffle, imbeciles believe, and lo! the most contemptible of beings, the most maladroit quacksalver, the clumsiest imposter ever to have made his entrance, there he is: behold! God, there's God's little boy, his papa's peer; and now all his dreams are consecrated! and now all his epigrams are become dogmas! and all his blunders mysteries! His fabulous father's breast opens to receive him and that Creator, once upon a time simple, of a sudden becomes compound, triple, to humor his son, this lad so worthy of his greatness; but does that sacred God stick to that? No, surely not, his celestial might is going to bestow many another and greater favor. At the beck and call of a priest, of, that is to say, a strange fellow foul with lies, the great God, creator of all we behold, is going to abase himself to the point of descending ten or twelve million times every morning in a morsel of wheat paste; this the faithful devour and assimilate, and God Almighty is lugged to the bottom of their intestines where he is speedily transmuted into the vilest excrements, and all that for the satisfaction of the tender son, odious inventor of this monstrous impiety which had it beginnings in a cabaret supper. He spake, and it was ordained. He said: this bread you see will be my flesh; you will digest it as such; now, I am God; hence, God will be digested by you; hence, the Creator of Heaven and Earth will be changed, because I have spoken, into the vilest stuff the body of man can exhale, and man will eat his God, because this God is good and because he is omnipotent. However, these blatherings increase; their growth is attributed to their authenticity, their greatness, their sublimity to the puissance of him who introduced them, while in truth the commonest causes double their existence, for the credit error acquires never proved anything but the presence of swindlers on the one side and of idiots on the other. This infamous religion finally arrives on the throne, and it is a weak, cruel, ignorant and fanatical emperor who, enveloping it in the royal mantle, soils the four corners of the earth with it. O Thérèse, what weight are these arguments to carry with an inquiring and philosophic mind? Is the sage able to see anything in this appalling heap of fables but the disgusting fruit of a few men's imposture and the diddled credulity of a vast number? had God willed it that we have some religion or other, and had he been truly powerful or, to frame it more suitably, had there truly been a God, would it have been by these absurd means he would have imparted his instructions to us? Would it have been through the voice of a contemptible bandit he would have shown how it were necessary to serve him? Were he supreme, were he mighty, were he just, were he good, this God you tell me about, would it be through enigmas and buffooneries he would wish to teach me to serve and know him? Sovereign mover of the stars and the heart of man, may he not instruct us by employing the one or convince us by graving himself in the other? Let him, one of these days, upon the Sun indite the law, writ out in letters of fire, the law as he wants us to understand it, in the version that pleases him; then from one end of the universe to the other, all mankind will read it, will behold it at once, and thereafter will be guilty if they obey it not. But to indicate his desires nowhere but in some unknown corner of Asia; to select for witnesses the most crafty and visionary of people, for alter ego the meanest artisan, the most absurd, him of the greatest rascality; to frame his doctrine so confusedly it is impossible to make it out; to limit knowledge of it to a small group of individuals; to leave the others in error and to punish them for remaining there. . . . Why, no, Thérèse, no, these atrocities are not what we want for our guidance; I should prefer to die a thousand deaths rather than believe them. When atheism will wish for martyrs, let it designate them; my blood is ready to be shed. Let us detest these horrors, Thérèse; let the most steadfast outrages cement the scorn which is patently their due. . . . My eyes were barely open when I began to loathe these coarse reveries; very early I made it a law unto myself to trample them in the dust, I took oath to return to them never more; if you would be happy, imitate me; as do I, hate, abjure, profane the foul object of this dreadful cult; and this cult too, created for illusion, made like him to be reviled by everyone who pretends to wisdom."

"Oh! Monsieur, " I responded, weeping, "you would deprive an unfortunate of her fondest hope were you to wither in her heart this religion which is her whole comfort. Firmly attached to its teachings, absolutely convinced that all the blows leveled against it are nothing but libertinage's effects and the passions', am I to sacrifice, to blasphemies, to sophistries horrible to me, my heart's sweetest sustenance?"

I added a thousand other arguments to this one, they merely caused the Count to laugh, and his captious principles, nourished by a more male eloquence, supported by readings and studies I, happily, had never performed, daily attacked my own principles, without shaking them. Madame de Bressac, that woman filled with piety and virtue, was not unaware her nephew justified his wild behavior with every one of the day's paradoxes; she too often shuddered upon hearing them; and as she condescended to attribute somewhat more good sense to me than to her other women, she would sometimes take me aside and speak of her chagrin.

Meanwhile, her nephew, champing at the bit had reached the point where he no longer bothered to hid his malign intentions; not only had he surrounded his aunt with all of that dangerous *canaille* which served his pleasures, but he had even carried boldness so far as to declare to her, in my presence, that were she to take it into her head to frustrate his appetite, he would convince her of their charm by practicing them before her very eyes.

I trembled; I beheld this conduct with horror. I strove to rationalize my reactions by attributing their origin to personal motives, for I wished to stifle the unhappy passion which burned in my soul; but is love an illness to be cured? All I endeavored to oppose to it merely fanned its flames, and the perfidious Count never appeared more lovable to me than when I had assembled before me everything which ought to have induced me to hate him.

I had remained four years in this household unrelentingly persecuted by the same sorrows, forever consoled by the same sweetnesses, when this abominable man, finally believing himself sure of me, dared disclose his infamous schemes. We were in the country at the time, I alone attended upon the Marquise, her fist maid-in-waiting had obtained leave to remain in Paris through the summer to look after some of her husband's business. One evening shortly after I had retired, and as I was taking some air upon the balcony of my room, being unable to bring myself to go to bed because of the extreme heat, I suddenly heard the Count knock; he wished to have a word or two with me. Alas! the moment that cruel author of my ills accorded me of his presence were too precious for me to dare refuse him one; he enters, carefully closed the door and flings himself into an armchair.

"Listen to me, Thérèse," and there is a note of embarrassment in his voice, "I have things of the greatest importance to say to you; swear to me you will never reveal any of them."

"Monsieur," I reply, "do you think me capable of abusing your confidence?"

"You have no idea what you would be risking were you to prove to me I had made a mistake in trusting you!"

"The most frightful of all my woes should be to lose your trust, I have no need of greater meaces...."

"Ah the, Thérèse, I have condemned my aunt to die ... and it is your hand I must employ."

"My hand!" I cried, recoiling in fright, "have you been able, Monsieur, to conceive such projects? ... no, dispose of my life if you must, but imagine not you will ever obtain from me the horror you propose."

"Hear me, Thérèse," says the Count, reasoning with me calmly, "I indeed foresaw your distaste for the idea but, as you have wit and verve, I flattered myself with the belief I could vanquish your feelings ... could prove to you that this crime, which seems to you of such enormity, is, at bottom, a very banal affair.

"Two misdeeds present themselves, Thérèse, to your not very philosophic scrutiny: the destruction of a creature bearing a resemblance to us, and the evil with which this destruction is augmented when the said creature is one of our near kinsmen. With regard to the crime of destroying one's fellow, be persuaded, dear girl, it is purely hallucinatory; man has not been accorded the power to destroy; he has at best the capacity to alter forms but lacks that required to annihilate them: well, every form is of equal worth in Nature's view; nothing is lost in the immense melting pot where variations are wrought: all the material masses which fall into it spring incessantly forth in other shapes, and whatsoever be our interventions in this process, not one of them, needless to say, outrages her, not one is capable of offending her. Our depredations revive her power; they stimulate her energy, but no one attenuates her; she is neither impeded nor thwarted by any.... Why! what difference does it make to her creative hand if this mass of flesh today wearing the conformation of a bipedal individual is reproduced tomorrow in the guise of a handful of centipedes? Dare one say that the construction of this two-legged animal costs her any more than that of an earthworm, and that she should take a greater interest in the one than in the other? If then the degree of attachment, or rather of indifference, is the same, what can it be to her if, by one man's sword, another man is trans-speciated into a fly or a blade of grass? When they will have convinced me of the sublimity of our species, when they will have demonstrated to me that it is really so important to Nature, that her laws are necessarily violated by this transmutation, then I will be able to believe that murder is a crime; but when the most thoughtful and sober study has proven to me that everything that vegetates upon this globe is of equal value in her eyes, I shall never concede that the alteration of one of these creatures in a thousand others can in any sense upset her intentions or sort ill with her desires. I say to myself: all men, all animals, all plants growing, feeding, destroying and reproducing themselves by the same means, never undergoing a real death, but a simply variation in what modifies them; all, I say, appearing today in one form and several years or hours later in another, all may, at the will of the being who wishes to move them, change a thousand thousand times in a single day, without one of Nature's directives being affected for one instant—what do I say? without this transmuter having done anything but good, since, by dismantling the individuals whose basic components again become necessary to Nature, he does naught by this action, improperly qualified as criminal, but render her creative energy of which she is necessarily deprived by him who, through brutish indifference, dares not to undertake any shuffling, as it were, of the deck.... O Thérèse, it is man's pride alone erects murder as a crime. This vain creature, imagining himself the most sublime of the globe's inhabitants, its most essential, takes his departure from this false principle in order to affirm that the deed which results in his undoing can be nothing but an infamy; but his vanity, his lunacy alter the laws of Nature not one jot; no person exists who in the depths of his heart does not feel the most vehement desire to be rid of those by whom he is hampered, troubled, or whose death may be of some advantage to him; and do you suppose, Thérèse, that the difference between this desire and its effect is very great? Now, if these impressions come to us from Nature, can it be presumed they irritate her? Would she inspire in us what would cause her downfall? Ah, be at ease, dear girl, we experience nothing that does not serve her; all the impulses she puts in us are the agents of her decrees; man's passions are but the means she employs to attain her ends. If she stands in need of more individuals, she inspires lust in us and behold! there are creations; when destructions become necessary to her, she inserts vengeance, avarice, lechery, ambition into our hearts and lo! you have murders; but she has not ceased to labor in her own behalf, and whatever we do, there can be no question of it, we are unthinking instruments of her caprices.

"Ah, no, Thérèse, no! Nature does not leave in our hands the possibility of committing crimes which would conflict with her economy; has it ever been known to happen that the weakest were able to offend the mightiest? What are we in comparison to her? Can she, when she created us, have placed in us what would be capable of hurting her? Can that idiotic supposition consort with the sublime and sure manner in which we see her attain her ends? Ah! were murder not one of the human actions which best fulfilled her intentions, would she permit the doing of murder? May to imitate then be to injure her? Can she be incensed to see man do to his brethren what she herself does to him every day? Since it is proven that she cannot reproduce without destructions, is it not to act in harmony with her wishes to multiply them unceasingly? The man who moves in this direction, who plunges ahead with all possible zeal, will incontestably be the one who serves her best, since it will be he who most co-operates with the schemes she manifests constantly. The primary and most beautiful of Nature's qualities is motion, which agitates her at all times, but this motion is simply a perpetual consequence of crimes, she conserves it by means of crimes only; the person who most nearly resembles her, and therefore the most perfect being, necessarily will be the one whose most active agitation will become the cause of many crimes; whereas, I repeat, the inactive or indolent person, that is to say, the virtuous person, must be in her eyes—how may there be any doubt of it?—the least perfect since he tends only to apathy, to lethargy, to that inactivity which would immediately plunge everything back into chaos were his star to be in the ascendant. Equilibrium must be preserved; it can only be preserved by crimes; therefore, crimes serve Nature; if they serve her, if she demands them, if she desires them, can they offend her? And who else can be offended if she is not?

"But my aunt is the creature I am going to destroy.... Oh, Thérèse, in a philosopher's view how frivolous are these consanguinary ties! Forgive me, but I do not even wish to discuss them, so futile are they. These contemptible chains, fruit of our laws and our political institutions—can they mean anything to Nature?

"Desert your prejudices, Thérèse, leave them behind, and serve me; your fortune is made."

"Oh Monsieur!" I replied, terrified by the Comte de Bressac, "your mind invents this theory of an impassive, indifferent Nature; deign rather to heed your heart, and you will hear it condemn all of libertinage's false reasonings. Is not that heart, to whose tribunal I recommend you , the sanctuary where this Nature you outrage wished to be heard and respected? If she engraves upon it the extreme horror of the crime you mediate, will you grant me it is a damnable one? Passions, I know, are blinding you at the present moment, but once they subside, how will you not be torn by remorse? The greater your sensitivity, the more cruelly shall it sting you.... Oh Monsieur! preserve, respect this tender, invaluable friend's life; sacrifice it not; you would perish of despair! Every day ... at every instant you would be visited by the image of this cherished aunt, she whom your unthinking rage would have hurled into her tomb; you would hear her plaintive voice still pronouncing those sweet names that were your childhood's joy; she would be present during your waking hours and appear to torture you in your dreams; she would open with her bloodstained fingers the wounds wherewith you would have mutilated her; thereafter not one happy moment would shine for you while you dwelt upon this earth; you would become a stranger to pleasures; your every idea would be of trouble; a celestial arm, whose might you do not appreciate, would avenge the days you would have obliterated, by envenoming your own, and without having tasted happiness from your felonies, you would be slain by mortal sorrow for having dared accomplish them."

As I uttered those words tears returned to my eyes, I sank to my knees before the Count; by all that is most holy I did implore him to let fade into oblivion an infamous aberration I swore to him all my life I would conceal.... But I did not know the man with whom I was dealing; I knew not to what point passions had enthroned crime in that perverse soul. The Count rose and spoke in a voice of ice.

"I see very well I was mistaken, Thérèse," said he. "I regret it, perhaps as much on your account as on my own; no matter, I shall discover other means, and it will be much you shall have lost without your mistress gaining anything."

The threat changed all my ideas; by not accepting the criminal role proposed to me, I was exposing myself to great personal risk and my protectress was infallibly to perish; by consenting to be his accomplice, I would shield myself from the Count's wrath and would assuredly save his aunt; an instant's reflection convinced me I should agree to everything. But as so rapid a reversal would have appeared suspicious, I strove to delay my capitulation; I obliged the Count to repeat his sophistries often; little by little I took on an air of not knowing what to reply: Bressac believed me vanquished; I justified my weakness by the potency of his art and in the end I surrendered. The Count sprang into my arms. Ah, how I should have been overjoyed had his movement been inspired by another motive.... What is it I am saying? The time had passed: his horrible conduct, his barbarous designs had annihilated all the feelings my weakling heart had dared conceive, and I saw in him nothing but a monster....

"You are the first woman I have ever held in my arms," said the Count, "and truly, it is with all my soul.... You are delicious, my child; a gleam of wisdom seems to have penetrated into your mind! That this charming mind has lain in darkness for so long! Incredible."

Next, we came to facts. In two or three days, as soon, that is, as an opportunity presented itself, I was to drop a dose of poison—Bressac gave me the package that contained it—into the cup of chocolate Madame customarily took in the morning. The Count assured my immunity against all consequences and directly I consummated the deed, handed me a contract providing me with an annuity of two thousand crowns; he signed these promises without characterizing the state in which I was to enjoy their benefits; we separated.

In the midst of all this, something most singular occurred something all too able to reveal the atrocious soul of the monster with whom I had to deal; I must not interrupt myself for a moment for, no doubt, you are awaiting the denouement of the adventure in which I had become involved.

Two days following the conclusion of our criminal pact, the Count learned that an uncle, upon whose succession he had not in the least counted, had just left him an income of eighty thousand pounds . . . . "O Heaven!" I said to myself upon hearing the news, "is it then in thuswise celestial justice punished the basest conspiracy!" And straightway repenting this blasphemy spoken against Providence, I cast myself upon my knees and implored the Almighty's forgiveness, and happily supposed that this unexpected development should at least change the Count's plans . . . . What was my error!

"Ah, my dear Thérèse," he said that same evening, having run to my room, "how prosperity does rain down upon me! Often I have told you so: the idea of a crime or an execution is the surest means to attract good fortune; none exists save for villains."

"What!" I responded, "this unhoped for bounty does not persuade you, Monsieur, patiently to await the death you wished to hasten?"

"Wait?" the Count replied sharply, "I do not intend to wait two minutes, Thérèse; are you not aware I am twenty-eight? Well, it is hard to wait at my age . . . . No, let this affect our scheme not in the slightest, give me the comfort of seeing everything brought to an end before the time comes for us to return to Paris . . . . Tomorrow, at the very latest the day after tomorrow, I beseech you. There has been delay enough: the hour approaches for the payment of the first quarter of your annuity . . . for performing the act which guarantees you the money . . . . "

As best I could, I disguised the fright this desperate eagerness inspired in me, and I renewed my resolution of the day before, well persuaded that if I were not to execute the horrible crime I had engaged to commit, the Count would soon notice I was playing a trick upon him and that, if I were to warn Madame de Bressac, whatever would be her reaction to the project's disclosure, the young Count, observing himself deceived one way or another, would promptly resort to more certain methods which, causing his aunt equally to perish, would also expose me to all her nephew's vengeance. There remained the alternative of consulting the law, but nothing in the world could have induced me to adopt it; I decided to forewarn the Marquise; of all possible measures, that seemed the best, and I elected it.

"Madame," I said to her on the morrow of my last interview with the Count, "Madame, I have something of the highest importance to reveal, but however vital its interest to you, I shall not broach it unless, beforehand, you give me your word of honor to bear no resentment against your nephew for what Monsieur has had the audacity to concert.... You will act, Madame, you will take the steps prudence enjoins, but you will say not a word. Deign to give me your promise; else I am silent."

Madame de Bressac, who thought it was but a question of some of her nephew's everyday extravagances, bound herself by the oath I demanded, and I disclosed everything. The unhappy woman burst into tears upon learning of the infamy .... "The monster!" she cried, "have I ever done anything that was not for his good? Had I wished to thwart his vices, or correct them, what other motive than his own happiness could have constrained me to severity! And is it not thanks to me he inherits this legacy his uncle has just left him? Ah, Thérèse, Thérèse, prove to me that it is true, this project ... put me in a way that will prevent me from doubting; I need all that may aid in extinguishing the sentiments my unthinking heart dares yet preserve for the monster .... " And then I brought the package of poison into view; it were difficult to furnish better proof; yet the Marquise wised to experiment with it; we made a dog swallow a light dose, shut up the animal, and at the end of two hours it was dead after being seized by frightful convulsions. Any lingering doubt by now dispelled, Madame de Bressac came to a decision; she bade me give her the rest of the poison and immediately sent a courier with a letter to the Duc de Sonzeval, related to her, asking him to go directly, but in secrecy, to the Secretary of State, and to expose the atrocity of a nephew whose victim she might at any moment become; to provide himself with a *lettre de cachet;* to make all possible haste to come and deliver her from the wretch who had so cruelly plotted to take her life.

But the abominable crime was to be consummated; some inconceivable permission must have been granted by Heaven that virtue might be made to yield to villainy's oppressions: the animal upon which we had experiment revealed everything to the Count: he heard it howling; I knowing of his aunt's fondness for the beast, he asked what had been done to it; those to whom he spoke knew nothing of the matter and made him no clear answer; from this moment, his suspicions began to take shape; he uttered not a word, but I saw that he was disquieted; I mentioned his state to the Marquise, she became further upset, but could think of nothing to do save urge the courier to make yet greater haste, and, if possible, still more carefully to hide the purpose of his mission. She advised her nephew that she was writing to Paris to beg the Duc de Sonzeval to waste not a moment to take up the matter of the recently deceased uncle's inheritance for if no one were to appear to claim it, there was litigation to be feared; she added that she had requested the Duke to come and have her a complete account of the affair, in order that she might learn whether or not she and her nephew would be obliged to make a journey to Paris. Too skillful a physiognomist to fail to notice the embarrassment in this aunt's face, to fail to notice the embarrassment in his aunt's face, to fail to observe, as well, some confusion written upon mine, the count smiled at everything and was no less on his guard. Under the pretext of taking a promenade, he leaves the château; he lies in wait for the courier at a place the man must inevitably pass. The messenger, far more a creature of the Count than his aunt's trustworthy minion, raises no objections when his master demands to see the dispatches he is carrying, and Bressac, once convinced of what no doubt he calls my treachery, gives the courier a hundred *louis*, together with instructions never to appear again at the Marquise's. He returns to the château, rage in his heart; however, he restrains himself; he encounters me, as usual he cajoles me, asks whether it shall not be tomorrow, points out it is essential the deed be performed before the Duke's arrival, then goes to bed with a tranquil air about which nothing is to remarked. At the time I knew nothing, I was the dupe of everything. Were the appalling crime to be committed—as the Count's actions informed me later—he would of course have to commit it himself; but I did not know how; I conjectured much; what good would it do to tell you what I imagined? Rather, let us move ahead to the cruel manner in which I was punished for not having wished to undertake the thing. On the day after the messenger was intercepted, Madame drank her chocolate as she always did, dressed, seemed agitated, and sat down at table; scarcely was I out of the dining room when the Count accosted me.

"Thérèse," and nothing could have been more phlegmatic than his manner as he spoke, "I have found a more reliable method than the one I proposed to attain our objectives, but numerous details are involved, and I dare not come so often to your room; at precisely five o'clock be at the corner of the park, I'll join you, we will take a walk together in the woods; while on our promenade I'll explain it all."

I wish to affirm, Madame, that, whether because of the influence of Providence, whether owing to an excessive candor, whether to blindness, nothing gave me a hint of the terrible misery awaiting me; I believed myself so safe, thanks to the Marquise's secret arrangements, that I never for a moment imagined that the Count had been able to discover them; nevertheless I was not entirely at ease.

"Le parjure est vertu quand on promit le crime," one of our tragic poets has said; but perjury is always odious to a delicate and sensitive spirit which finds itself compelled to resort to it. My role embarrassed me.

However that may be, I came to the rendezvous; the count was not late in getting there; he came up to me very gay and easy and we set off into the forest; the while he but laughed banteringly and jested as was his habit when we were together. When I sought to guide the conversation to the subject which he had desired to discuss, he told me to wait yet a little, he said he feared we might be observed, it did not seem to him we were in a safe enough place; very gradually, without my perceiving, it we approached the four trees to which I had been so cruelly bound long ago. Upon seeing the place, a quiver ran through me: all the horror of my fate rose up before my eyes, and fancy whether my terror was not doubled when I caught sight of the preparations which had been made in that horrible place. Ropes hung from one of the trees; huge mastiffs were leashed to each of the other three and seemed to be waiting for nothing but me in order to fall to sating the hunger announced by their gaping foam-flecked jaws; one of the count's favorites guarded them.

Whereupon the perfidious creature ceased to employ all but the very foulest epithets.

"Scum," quoth he, "do you recognized that bush whence I dragged you like wild beast only to spare a life you deserved to lose? Do you recognized these trees unto which I threatened to lash you were you ever to give me cause to repent my kindness? Why did you agree to perform the task I demanded, if you intended to betray me to my aunt? and how could you imagine it was virtue you served by imperiling the freedom of him to whom you owe all your happiness? By necessity placed between two crimes, why have you chosen the more abominable?"

"Alas! I did not choose the less . . . "

"But you should have refused," the Count continued, in his rage seizing one of my arms and shaking me furiously, "yes, certainly, refused, and not consented to betray me."

Then Monsieur de Bressac told me how he had gone about the interception of Madame's messages, and how the suspicion had been born which had led him to decide to stop them.

"What has your duplicity done for you, unworthy creature? You have risked your life without having saved my aunt's: the die is cast, upon my return to the château I will find a fortune awaiting me, but you must perish; before you expire you must learn that the virtuous road is not always the safest, and that there are circumstances in this world when complicity in crime is preferable to informing." And without giving me time to reply, without giving evidence of the least pity for the frightful situation I was in, he dragged me toward the tree destined for me and by which his valet stood expectantly. "Here she is," he said, "the creature who wanted to poison my aunt and who may already have committed the terrible crime in spite of my efforts to prevent it; no doubt, it would have been better to have put her into the hands of justice, but the law would have taken away her life, and I prefer to leave it to her in order that she may have longer to suffer."

The two villains then lay hands on me, in an instant they strip me naked. "Pretty buttocks," said the count in a tone of cruelest irony, brutally handling those objects, "superb flesh . . . excellent lunch for the dogs." When no article of clothing is left upon me, I am secured to the tree by a rope attached around my waist; so that I may defend myself as best I can, my arms are left free, and enough slack is provide for me to advance or retreat about two yards. The arrangements completed, the Count, very much moved steps up to have a look at my expression, he turns and passes around me; his savage way of handling me seems to say that his murderous fingers would like to dispute the rage of his mastiff's steel teeth . . . .

"Come," says he to his lieutenant, "free the animals, the time has arrived."

They are loosed, the Count excites them, all three fling themselves upon my poor body, one would think they were sharing it in such wise that not one of its parts would be exempt from assault; in vain I drive them back, they bite and tear me with renewed fury, and throughout this horrible scene, Bressac, the craven Bressac, as if my torments had ignited his perfidious lust ... the beastly man gives himself up , while he regards me, to his companion's criminal caresses.

"Enough," said he after several minutes had gone by, "that will do. Tie up the dogs and let's abandon this creature to her sweet fate.

"Well indeed, Thérèse," says he as he severs my bonds, "virtue is not to be practiced at some expense; a pension of two thousand crowns, would that not have been worth more than the bites you are covered with?"

But in my state I can scarcely hear him; I slump to the foot of the tree and am about to lose consciousness.

"It is most generous of me to save your life," continues the traitor whom my sufferings inflame, "at least take good care how you make use of this favor...."

Then he orders me to get up, dress, and quit the place at once. As my blood is flowing everywhere, in order that my few clothes, the only clothes I have, not be stained, I gather some grass to wipe myself; Bressac paces to and fro, much more preoccupied with his thoughts than concerned with me.

My swollen flesh, the blood that continues to stream from my multiple wounds, the atrocious pain I am enduring, everything makes the operation of dressing well nigh impossible; never once does the dishonest man who has just put me into this horrible state ... him for whom I once would have sacrificed my life, never once does he deign to show me the least hint of sympathy. When at length I am ready:

"Go wherever you wish," says he; "you must have some money left, I will not take it from you, but beware of reappearing at anyone of my houses in the city or the country: there are two excellent reasons for not doing so: you may just as well know, first of all, that the affair you thought finished is not at all over. They informed you that the law was done with you; they told you what is not true; the warrant for your arrest still holds, the case is still warm: you were left in this situation so that your conduct might be observed. In the second place, you are going to pass, insofar as the public is concerned, for the Marquise's murderer; if she yet breaths, I am going to see to it she carries this notion into the grave, the entire household will share it; and there you have two trials till to face instead of one: instead of a vile usurer, you have for an adversary a rich and powerful who is determined to hound you into Hell itself if you misuse the life his compassion leaves to you."

"Oh Monsieur!" was my response, "whatever have been your severities with me, fear not that I will retaliate; I thought myself obliged to take steps against you when it was a question of your aunt's life; but where only the unhappy Thérèse is involved, I shall never do anything. Adieu, Monsieur, may your crimes render you as happy as your cruelties have made me to suffer; and no matter what the fate reserved to me by Heaven, while it shall prolong my deplorable life, I shall only employ my days in uttering prayers for you."

The Count raised his head; he could not avoid glancing at me upon hearing these words, and, as he beheld me quavering and covered with tears and doubtless was afraid lest he be moved by what he saw, the cruel one went away, and I saw him nevermore.

Entirely delivered unto my agony, I fell back again and lay by the tree; there, giving fee reign to my hurt, I made the forest resound with my groans; I pressed my stricken frame against the earth, and shed upon the sward all my tears.

"O my God," I cried out, "Thou has so willed it; it was grained in Thy eternal decrees that the innocent were to fall unto the guilty and were to be their prey: dispose of me, O Lord, I am yet far away from what Thou didst suffer for us; may those I endure, as I adore Thee, render me worthy someday of what rewards Thou keepeth for the lowly, when he hath Thee before him in his tribulations, and let his anguishes be unto Thy greater glorification!"

Night was closing: it was almost beyond my power to move; I was scarcely able to stand erect; I cast my eyes upon the thicket where four years earlier I had slept a night when I had been in circumstances almost as unhappy! I dragged myself along as best I could, and having reached the very same spot, tormented by my still bleeding wounds, overwhelmed by my mind's anxieties and the sorrow of my heart, I passed the cruelest night imaginable.

Jane Austen

(1775–1817)

Jane Austen was born in December 16, 1775, in the Hampshire village of Stevenson where her father, the Reverend George Austen, was rector. Jane was the seventh of eight children (six boys and two girls); her only sister, Cassandra, was her closest friend. Their mother had remarked that the sisters were so close that if "Cassandra were going to have her head cut off, that Jane would insist on having hers cut off as well."

Unfortunately for literary history, this intimacy gave Cassandra the right, after Jane's death, to destroy any of Jane's letters that she felt were too private for public consumption.

Women in this era who belonged to the upper middle class, as Jane and Cassandra did, remained at home until they married. Neither Austen sister ever married so neither daughter ever moved out of the home. Jane's days seemed to have been filled with helping out at home. The Austens had their own dairy, brewed their own ale, and baked their own bread. As with the characters in Jane's novels, spare time was spent sewing, receiving visits from friends and relatives, and attending parties and balls. The extended Austen family was huge, with aunts, nieces, uncles, nephews, and cousins dropping in to enjoy Jane's wit and charm.

Jane and her sister had little more than five years of formal schooling between them. In 1782, they were sent to a Mrs. Cowley to be tutored, but that did not prove effective. After a year, the girls returned to their parents' home; the Abbey School was subsequently chosen. The sisters remained there until 1787 and then continued their education at home using their father's vast library. Reverend Austin had been a Fellow at St. John's College before taking his vows and fostered in his children a zest for learning. The family's favorite pastime was acting, turning their barn into a theater and staging plays with neighbors and relatives.

Jane started writing in her early teens: verses, short novels, and plays to entertain her family—twenty-one in all between 1787 to 1795. They reveal an analytical mind experimenting with parody of popular literary genres, mostly sentimental fiction. *Lady Susan*, an epistolary novella, emerged from this flurry of literary inspiration. These early efforts introduce Jane's gift: the arch observation of women in familial and societal circles.

In 1796, Jane's first romantic relationship was recorded, a bond with a handsome young Irishman named Tom Lefroy, who was staying nearby in his uncle's parish. This ended when he was sent back to Ireland. She accepted a marriage proposal from Harris Biggs-Wither, the twenty-one-year-old heir of a Hampshire family. After a good night's rest, Jane changed her mind. There may have been other entanglements during her lifetime, especially during a conspicuous gap in her correspondence between May 1801 and September 1804 (letters were burned by her protective sister).

After residing twenty-five years in her beloved Stevenson, Jane was forced to relocate with her ailing father to Bath. There she completed *Northanger Abbey* (then titled *Susan*) and sold it for ten dollars to a publisher who never issued it. Reverend Austen passed away in 1805, and after four years at different residences, the three Austen women settled in Southampton. In 1809, Jane's brother Edward provided them with a sizable cottage on his land at Chawton in Hampshire, which was close to Stevenson. This return to her native countryside seems to have given Jane a renewed zeal to write, and the following years would prove to be her most fruitful.

Settled into this bucolic setting, Jane set about drafting *Sense and Sensibility* and *Pride and Prejudice*. *Sense and Sensibility* was published anonymously in 1811 and was well received. The *Critical Review* and *Quarterly Review*—the most respected literary reviews of the day—praised her balance of "instruction and amusement." She began *Mansfield Park* just as *Pride and Prejudice* was published in January 1813, once again anonymously. *Mansfield Park* was issued in 1814 and *Emma* in 1815 (though dated 1816). By the time *Emma* was released, Jane Austen was a famous author, albeit an anonymous one. Of the novel's heroine, she said, "I am going to take a heroine whom none but myself will much like." The most important review of this novel came from Sir Walter Scott (in the *Quarterly Review* in March 1816), who lauded "this nameless author" as a master of the modern novel, praising "the talent for describing the involvement and feelings of characters of ordinary life."

Yet for all her critical and literary success, physically Jane was in decline. At the time she was thought to have been suffering from "bile" (bile is secreted in the liver and passes to the gallbadder, which in turn transports it to the small intestine or stores it. When this process doesn't work properly, symptoms such as weakness, nausea, and fever occur). Modern medical knowledge suggests that Jane had Addison's disease, which is characterized by similar symptoms. In one last burst of energy, she finished *Sandition*, a self-deprecating satire on health retreats and invalidism. In April 1817, she made her will (leaving almost all of her estate to Cassandra) and by May was so ill that she was moved to Winchester under the care of an expert surgeon. Jane Austen died on July 18, 1817, and was buried in Winchester Cathedral.

Her brother Henry revealed her authorship to the world upon the publication of *Northanger Abbey* and *Persuasion* in a "Biographical Notice of the Author." He drew a loving portrait of his sister, celebrating Jane's sharp mind and sterling character and quoting her final words, "I want nothing but death."

Novels in the form of exchanges of letters were hugely popular in mid-eighteenth-century Britain, but had fallen out of favor by the time Jane Austen began writing *Lady Susan,* sometime between 1794 and 1805. Not published until 1871, as part of the *Memoir of Jane Austen* written by her nephew, James Edward Austen-Leigh, the book—Austen's only epistolary novel, and the only one not published during her lifetime—remained untitled until Austen-Leigh named it for its eponymous main character, the utterly amoral, though beautiful, Lady Susan Vernon.

"Amoral" scarcely does Lady Susan justice; she verges on the sociopathic in her determination to win at the marriage game, both for herself and for her daughter, Frederica. Lying, cheating, pretending to a humility she doesn't feel and a kindness she doesn't understand, Lady Susan attempts to force her daughter into a marriage with a man she despises, while juggling two potential suitors herself—one of them her sister-in-law's brother. Some have suggested that the model for the irredeemable Lady Susan was a Mrs. Craven, a vindictive society matron well known to the Austens; others have seen in her a model for Mary Crawford in *Mansfield Park*. Comparisons have been made between this novel and *Les Liasions Dangereuses* in terms of the depth of cruelty and manipulation of the main characters.

Lady Susan cannot be called a bizarre departure from the author's previous work since it is one of the first things that Jane Austen had written, but it can be considered an aberration with respect to the depth of the main character's villainy. There is plenty of cruelty in Austen's later writing is but most of it is hypocritical and sanctimonious rather than bald-faced. The character of Lady Susan is more extreme than what we have come to expect from Jane Austen. She is a blatant adulteress, fresh from an affair with the host of the family with whom she has been staying. She details her schemes to her confidantes and revels in each twist and turn that these plans bring her. Within the character's wickedness there is also a vitality, an energy that seems to be missing from Austen's later heroines. Lady Susan is Machiavellian, but there is a magnetic quality to her plotting, and the other characters are simply not as interesting as she is. It doesn't seem a sin to root for Lady Susan.

What emerges from these portraits is Austen's dislike of London and city living, and of people who aspire to a more worldly life. Perhaps *Lady Susan* was Austen's display of her grasp of social malice and machinations. Done once, perhaps she decided to temper her writings. Austen had a malicious streak, as revealed in her letters, but these are aspects that her "good" heroines have never displayed. After reviewing *Lady Susan*, she may have decided that she preferred a more subdued portrayal of social interaction. The corrupt world is infinitely more enticing than the good one in this novella, and that missing balance is what Austen finally attained in her later works. Even at the young age of twenty, Jane Austen realized that the reading public would prefer that in battle good and evil be more evenly matched.

LADY SUSAN

I.

LADY SUSAN VERNON TO MR. VERNON.

Langford, Dec.

MY DEAR BROTHER,—I can no longer refuse myself the pleasure of profiting by your kind invitation when we last parted of spending some weeks with you at Churchhill, and, therefore, if quite convenient to you and Mrs. Vernon to receive me at present, I shall hope within a few days to be introduced to a sister whom I have so long desired to be acquainted with. My kind friends here are most affectionately urgent with me to prolong my stay, but their hospitable and cheerful dispositions lead them too much into society for my present situation and state of mind; and I impatiently look forward to the hour when I shall be admitted into your delightful retirement.

I long to be made known to your dear little children, in whose hearts I shall be very eager to secure an interest. I shall soon have need for all my fortitude, as I am on the point of separation from my own daughter. The long illness of her dear father prevented my paying her that attention which duty and affection equally dictated, and I have too much reason to fear that the governess to whose care I consigned her was unequal to the charge. I have therefore resolved on placing her at one of the best private schools in town, where I shall have an opportunity of leaving her myself in my way to you. I am determined, you see, not to be denied admittance at Churchhill. It would indeed give me most painful sensations to know that it were not in your power to receive me.

Your most obliged and affectionate Sister,
S. VERNON.

II.

LADY SUSAN VERNON TO MRS. JOHNSON.

Langford.

You were mistaken, my dear Alicia, in supposing me fixed at this place for the rest of the winter: it grieves me to say how greatly you were mistaken, for I have seldom spent three months more agreeably than those which have just flown away. At present, nothing goes smoothly; the females of the family are united against me. You foretold how it would be when I first came to Langford, and Mainwaring is so uncommonly pleasing that I was not without apprehensions for myself. I remember saying to myself, as I drove to the house, 'I like this man, pray Heaven no harm come of it!' But I was determined to be discreet, to bear in mind my being only four months a widow, and to be as quiet as possible: and I have been so, my dear creature; I have admitted no one's attentions but Mainwaring's. I have avoided all general flirtation whatever; I have distinguished no creature besides, of all the numbers resorting hither, except Sir James Martin, on whom I bestowed a little notice, in order to detach him from Miss Mainwaring; but, if the world could know my motive *there* they would honour me. I have been called an unkind mother, but it was the sacred impulse of maternal affection, it was the advantage of my daughter that led me on; and if that daughter were not the greatest simpleton on earth, I might have been rewarded for my exertions as I ought.

Sir James did make proposals to me for Frederica; but Frederica, who was born to be the torment of my life, chose to set herself so violently against the match that I thought it better to lay aside the scheme for the present. I have more than once repented that I did not marry him myself; and were he but one degree less contemptibly weak I certainly should: but I must own myself rather romantic in that respect, and that riches only will not satisfy me. The event of all this is very provoking: Sir James is gone, Maria highly incensed, and Mrs. Mainwaring insupportably jealous; so jealous, in short, and so enraged against me, that, in the fury of her temper, I should not be surprised at her appealing to her guardian, if she had the liberty of addressing him: but there your husband stands my friend; and the kindest, most amiable action of his life was his throwing her off for ever on her marriage. Keep up his resentment, therefore, I charge you. We are now in a sad state; no house was ever more altered; the whole party are at war, and Mainwaring scarcely dares speak to me. It is time for me to be gone; I have therefore determined on leaving them, and shall spend, I hope, a comfortable day with you in town within this week. If I am as little in favour with Mr. Johnson as ever, you must come to me at 10 Wigmore Street; but I hope this may not be the case, for as Mr. Johnson, with all his faults, is a man to whom that great word 'respectable' is always given, and I am known to be so intimate with his wife, his slighting me has an awkward look.

I take London in my way to that insupportable spot, a country village; for I am really going to Churchhill. Forgive me, my dear friend, it is my last resource. Were there another place in England open to me I would prefer it. Charles Vernon is my aversion, and I am afraid of his wife. At Churchhill, however, I must remain till I have something better in view. My young lady accompanies me to town, where I shall deposit her under the care of Miss Summers, in Wigmore Street, till she becomes a little more reasonable. She will make good connections there as the girls are all of the best families. The price is immense, and much beyond what I can ever attempt to pay.

Adieu, I will send you a line as soon as I arrive in town.

Yours ever,
S. VERNON.

III.

MRS. VERNON TO LADY DE COURCY.

Churchhill.

My dear Mother,—I am very sorry to tell you that it will not be in our power to keep our promise of spending our Christmas with you; and we are prevented that happiness by a circumstance which is not likely to make us any amends. Lady Susan, in a letter to her brother-in-law, has declared her intention of visiting us almost immediately; and as such a visit is in all probability merely an affair of convenience, it is impossible to conjecture its length. I was by no means prepared for such an event, nor can I now account for her ladyship's conduct; Langford appeared so exactly the place for her in every respect, as well from the elegant and expensive style of living there, as from her particular attachment to Mr. Mainwaring, that I was very far from expecting so speedy a distinction, though I always imagined from her increasing friendship for us since her husband's death that we should, at some future period, be obliged to receive her. Mr. Vernon, I think, was a great deal too kind to her when he was in Staffordshire; her behaviour to him, independent of her general character, has been so inexcusably artful and ungenerous since our marriage was first in agitation that no one less amiable and mild than himself could have overlooked it all; and though, as his brother's widow, and in narrow circumstances, it was proper to render her pecuniary assistance, I cannot help thinking his pressing invitation to her to visit us at Churchhill perfectly unnecessary. Disposed, however, as he always is to think the best of everyone, her display of grief, and professions of regret, and general resolutions of prudence, were sufficient to soften his heart and make him really confide in her sincerity; but, as for myself, I am still unconvinced, and plausibly as her ladyship has now written, I cannot make up my mind till I better understand her real meaning in coming to us. You may guess, therefore, my dear madam, with what feelings I look forward to her arrival. She will have occasion for all those attractive powers for which she is celebrated to gain any share of my regard; and I shall certainly endeavour to guard myself against their influence, if not accompanied by something more substantial. She expresses a most eager desire of being acquainted with me, and makes very gracious mention of my children, but I am not quite weak enough to suppose a woman who has behaved with inattention, if not with unkindness to her own child, should be attached to any of mine. Miss Vernon is to be placed at a school in London before her mother comes to us, which I am glad of, for her sake and my own. It must be to her advantage to be separated from her mother, and a girl of sixteen who has received so wretched an education, could not be a very desirable companion here. Reginald has long wished, I know, to see the captivating Lady Susan, and we shall depend on his joining our party soon. I am glad to hear that my father continues so well; and am, with best love, &c,

CATHERINE VERNON.

IV.

MR. DE COURCY TO MRS. VERNON.

Parklands.

My dear Sister,—I congratulate you and Mr. Vernon on being about to receive into your family the most accomplished coquette in England. As a very distinguished flirt I have always been taught to consider her, but it has lately fallen in my way to hear some particulars of her conduct at Langford, which prove that she does not confine herself to that sort of honest flirtation which satisfies most people, but aspires to the more delicious gratification of making a whole family miserable. By her behaviour to Mr. Mainwaring she gave jealousy and wretchedness to his wife, and by her attentions to a young man previously attached to Mr. Mainwaring's sister deprived an amiable girl of her lover.

I learnt all this from Mr. Smith, now in this neighbourhood (I have dined with him, at Hurst and Wilford), who is just come from Langford where he was a fortnight with her ladyship, and who is therefore well qualified to make the communication.

What a woman she must be! I long to see her, and shall certainly accept your kind invitation, that I may form some idea of those bewitching powers which can do so much—engaging at the same time, and in the same house, the affections of two men, who were neither of them at liberty to bestow them—and all this without the charm of youth! I am glad to find Miss Vernon does not accompany her mother to Churchhill, as she has not even manners to recommend her; and, according to Mr. Smith's account, is equally dull and proud. Where pride and stupidity unite there can be no dissimulation worthy notice, and Miss Vernon shall be consigned to unrelenting contempt; but by all that I can gather Lady Susan possesses a degree of captivating deceit which it must be pleasing to witness and detect. I shall be with you very soon, and am ever,

Your affectionate Brother,
R. DE COURCY.

V.

LADY SUSAN VERNON TO MRS. JOHNSON.

Churchhill.

I received your note, my dear Alicia, just before I left town, and rejoice to be assured that Mr. Johnson suspected nothing of your engagement the evening before. It is undoubtedly better to deceive him entirely, and since he will be stubborn he must be tricked. I arrived here in safety, and have no reason to complain of my reception from Mr. Vernon; but I confess myself not equally satisfied with the behaviour of his lady. She is perfectly well-bred, indeed, and has the air of a woman of fashion, but her manners are not such as can persuade me of her being prepossessed in my favour. I wanted her to be delighted at seeing me. I was as amiable as possible on the occasion, but all in vain. She does not like me. To be sure when we consider that I *did* take some pains to prevent my brother-in-law's marrying her, this want of cordiality is not very surprising, and yet it shows illiberal and vindictive spirit to resent a project which influenced me six years ago, and which never succeeded at last.

I am sometimes disposed to repent that I did not let Charles buy Vernon Castle, when we were obliged to sell it; but it was a trying circumstance, especially as the sale took place exactly at the time of his marriage; and everybody ought to respect the delicacy of those feelings which could not endure that my husband's dignity should be lessened by his younger brother's having possession of the family estate. Could matters have been so arranged as to prevent the necessity of our leaving the castle, could we have lived with Charles and kept him single, I should have been very far from persuading my husband to dispose of it elsewhere; but Charles was on the point of marrying Miss De Courcy, and the event has justified me. Here are children in abundance, and what benefit could have accrued to me from his purchasing Vernon? My having prevented it may perhaps have given his wife an unfavourable impression, but where there is a disposition to dislike, a motive will never be wanting; and as to money matters it has not withheld him from being very useful to me. I really have a regard for him, he is so easily imposed upon! The house is a good one, the furniture fashionable, and everything announces plenty and elegance. Charles is very rich I am sure; when a man has once got his name in a banking-house he rolls in money; but they do not know what to do with it, keep very little company, and never go to London but on business. We shall be as stupid as possible. I mean to win my sister-in-law's heart through the children; I know all their names already, and am going to attach myself with the greatest sensibility to one in particular, a young Frederic, whom I take on my lap and sigh over for his dear uncle's sake.

Poor Mainwaring! I need not tell you how much I miss him, how perpetually he is in my thoughts. I found a dismal letter from him on my arrival here, full of complaints of his wife and sister, and lamentations on the cruelty of his fate. I passed off the letter as his wife's, to the Vernons, and when I write to him it must be under cover to you.

Ever yours,
S. VERNON.

VI.

MRS. VERNON TO MR. DE COURCY.

Churchhill.

Well, my dear Reginald, I have seen this dangerous creature, and must give you some description of her, though I hope you will soon be able to form your own judgment. She is really excessively pretty; however you may choose to question the allurements of a lady no longer young, I must, for my own part, declare that I have seldom seen so lovely a woman as Lady Susan. She is delicately fair, with fine grey eyes and dark eyelashes; and from her appearance one would not suppose her more than five and twenty, though she must in fact be ten years older. I was certainly not disposed to admire her, though always hearing she was beautiful; but I cannot help feeling that she possesses an uncommon union of symmetry, brilliancy, and grace. Her address to me was so gentle, frank, and even affectionate, that, if I had not known how much she has always disliked me for marrying Mr. Vernon, and that we had never met before, I should have imagined her an attached friend. One is apt, I believe, to connect assurance of manner with coquetry, and to expect that an impudent address will naturally attend an impudent mind; at least I was myself prepared for an improper degree of confidence in Lady Susan; but her countenance is absolutely sweet, and her voice and manner winningly mild. I am sorry it is so, for what is this but deceit? Unfortunately, one knows her too well. She is clever and agreeable, has all that knowledge of the world which makes conversation easy, and talks very well, with a happy command of language, which is too often used, I believe, to make black appear white. She has already almost persuaded me of her being warmly attached to her daughter, though I have been so long convinced to the contrary. She speaks of her with so much tenderness and anxiety, lamenting so bitterly the neglect of her education, which she represents however as wholly unavoidable, that I am forced to recollect how many successive springs her ladyship spent in town, while her daughter was left in Staffordshire to the care of servants, or a governess very little better, to prevent my believing what she says.

If her manners have so great an influence on my resentful heart, you may judge how much more strongly they operate on Mr. Vernon's generous temper. I wish I could be as well satisfied as he is, that it was really her choice to leave Langford for Churchhill; and if she had not stayed there for months before she discovered that her friend's manner of living did not suit her situation or feelings,

I might have believed that concern for the loss of such a husband as Mr. Vernon, to whom her own behaviour was far from unexceptionable, might for a time make her wish for retirement. But I cannot forget the length of her visit to the Mainwarings, and when I reflect on the different mode of life which she led with them from that to which she must now submit, I can only suppose that the wish of establishing her reputation by following though late the path of propriety, occasioned her removal from a family where she must in reality have been particularly happy. Your friend Mr. Smith's story, however, cannot be quite correct, as she corresponds regularly with Mrs. Mainwaring. At any rate it must be exaggerated. It is scarcely possible that two men should be so grossly deceived by her at once.

Yours, &c.,
CATHERINE VERNON.

VII.

LADY SUSAN VERNON TO MRS. JOHNSON.

Churchhill.

My dear Alicia,—You are very good in taking notice of Frederica, and I am grateful for it as a mark of your friendship; but as I cannot have any doubt of the warmth of your affection, I am far from exacting so heavy a sacrifice. She is a stupid girl, and has nothing to recommend her. I would not, therefore, on my account, have you encumber one moment of your precious time by sending for her to Edward Street, especially as every visit is so much deducted from the grand affair of education, which I really wish to have attended to while she remains at Miss Summers'. I want her to play and sing with some portion of taste and a good deal of assurance, as she has my hand and arm and a tolerable voice. I was so much indulged in my infant years that I was never obliged to attend to anything, and consequently am without the accomplishments which are now necessary to finish a pretty woman. Not that I am an advocate for the prevailing fashion of acquiring a perfect knowledge of all languages, arts, and sciences. It is throwing time away to be mistress of French, Italian, and German: music, singing, and drawing, &c., will gain a woman some applause, but will not add one lover to her list—grace and manner, after all, are of the greatest importance. I do not mean, therefore, that Frederica's acquirements should be more than superficial, and I flatter myself that she will not remain long enough at school to understand anything thoroughly. I hope to see her the wife of Sir James within a twelvemonth. You know on what I ground my hope, and it is certainly a good foundation, for school must be very humiliating to a girl of Frederica's age. And, by-the-by, you had better not invite her any more on that account, as I wish her to find her situation as unpleasant as possible. I am sure of Sir James at any time, and could make him renew his application by a line. I shall trouble you meanwhile to prevent his forming any other attachment when he comes to town. Ask him to your house occasionally, and talk to him of Frederica, that he may not forget her. Upon the whole, I commend my own conduct in this affair extremely, and regard it as a very happy instance of circumspection and tenderness. Some mothers would have insisted on their daughter's accepting so good an offer on the first overture; but I could not reconcile it to myself to force Frederica into a marriage from which her heart revolted, and instead of adopting so harsh a measure merely propose to make it her own choice, by rendering her thoroughly uncomfortable till she does accept him—but enough of this tiresome girl. You may well wonder how I contrive to pass my time here, and for the first week it was insufferably dull. Now, however, we begin to mend, our party is enlarged by Mrs. Vernon's brother, a handsome young man, who promises me some amusement. There is something about him which rather interests me, a sort of sauciness and familiarity which I shall teach him to correct. He is lively, and seems clever, and when I have inspired him with greater respect for me than his sister's kind offices have implanted, he may be an agreeable flirt. There is exquisite pleasure in subduing an insolent spirit, in making a person predetermined to dislike acknowledge one's superiority. I have disconcerted him already by my calm reserve, and it shall be my endeavour to humble the pride of these self-important De Courcys still lower, to convince Mrs. Vernon that her sisterly cautions have been bestowed in vain, and to persuade Reginald that she has scandalously belied me. This project will serve at least to amuse me, and prevent my feeling so acutely this dreadful separation from you and all whom I love.

Yours ever,

S. VERNON.

VIII.

MRS. VERNON TO LADY DE COURCY.

Churchhill.

My dear Mother,—You must not expect Reginald back again for some time. He desires me to tell you that the present open weather induces him to accept Mr. Vernon's invitation to prolong his stay in Sussex, that they may have some hunting together. He means to send for his horses immediately, and it is impossible to say when you may see him in Kent. I will not disguise my sentiments on this change from you, my dear mother, though I think you had better not communicate them to my father, whose excessive anxiety about Reginald would subject him to an alarm which might seriously affect his health and spirits. Lady Susan has certainly contrived, in the space of a fortnight, to make my brother like her. In short, I am persuaded that his continuing here beyond the time originally fixed for his return is occasioned as much by a degree of fascination towards her, as by the wish of hunting with Mr. Vernon, and of course I cannot receive that pleasure from the length of his visit which my brother's company would otherwise give me. I am, indeed, provoked at the artifice of this unprincipled woman; what stronger proof of her dangerous abilities can be given than this perversion of Reginald's judgment, which when he entered the house was so decidedly against her? In his last letter he actually gave me some particulars of her behaviour at Langford, such as he received from a gentleman who knew her perfectly well, which, if true, must raise abhorrence against her, and which Reginald himself was entirely disposed to credit. His opinion of her, I am sure, was as low as of any woman in England; and when he first came it was evident that he considered her as one entitled neither to delicacy nor respect, and that he felt she would be delighted with the attentions of any man inclined to flirt with her. Her behaviour, I confess, has been calculated to do away with such an idea; I have not detected the smallest impropriety in it—nothing of vanity, of pretension, of levity; and she is altogether so attractive that I should not wonder at his being delighted with her, had he known nothing of her previous to this personal acquaintance; but, against reason, against conviction, to be so well pleased

> IT IS THROWING TIME AWAY TO BE MISTRESS OF FRENCH, ITALIAN, AND GERMAN: MUSIC, SINGING, AND DRAWING, &C., WILL GAIN A WOMAN SOME APPLAUSE, BUT WILL NOT ADD ONE LOVER TO HER LIST . . .

with her, as I am sure he is, does really astonish me. His admiration was at first very strong, but no more than was natural, and I did not wonder at his being much struck by the gentleness and delicacy of her manners; but when he has mentioned her of late it has been in terms of more extraordinary praise; and yesterday he actually said that he could not be surprised at any effect produced on the heart of man by such loveliness and such abilities; and when I lamented, in reply, the badness of her disposition, he observed that whatever might have been her errors they were to be imputed to her neglected education and early marriage, and that she was altogether a wonderful woman. This tendency to excuse her conduct, or to forget it, in the warmth of admiration, vexes me; and if I did not know that Reginald is too much at home at Churchhill to need an invitation for lengthening his visit, I should regret Mr. Vernon's giving him any. Lady Susan's intentions are of course those of absolute coquetry, or a desire of universal admiration; I cannot for a moment imagine that she has anything more serious in view; but it mortifies me to see a young man of Reginald's sense duped by her at all.

I am, &c.,
CATHERINE VERNON.

IX.

MRS. JOHNSON TO LADY S. VERNON.

Edward Street.

My dearest Friend—I congratulate you on Mr. De Courcy's arrival, and I advise you by all means to marry him; his father's estate is, we know, considerable, and I believe certainly entailed. Sir Reginald is very infirm, and not likely to stand in your way long. I hear the young man well spoken of; and though no one can really deserve you, my dearest Susan, Mr. De Courcy may be worth having. Mainwaring will storm of course, but you may easily pacify him; besides, the most scrupulous point of honour could not require you to wait for *his* emancipation. I have seen Sir James; he came to town for a few days last week, and called several times in Edward Street. I talked to him about you and your daughter, and he is so far from having forgotten you, that I am sure he would marry either of you with pleasure. I gave him hopes of Frederica's relenting, and told him a great deal of her improvements. I scolded him for making love to Maria Mainwaring;

he protested that he had been only in joke, and we both laughed heartily at her disappointment; and, in short, were very agreeable. He is as silly as ever.

Yours faithfully,
ALICIA.

X.

LADY SUSAN VERNON TO MRS. JOHNSON.

Churchhill.

I am much obliged to you, my dear friend, for your advice respecting Mr. De Courcy, which I know was given with the full conviction of its expediency, though I am not quite determined on following it. I cannot easily resolve on anything so serious as marriage; especially as I am not at present in want of money, and might perhaps, till the old gentleman's death, be very little benefited by the match. It is true that I am vain enough to believe it within my reach. I have made him sensible of my power, and can now enjoy the pleasure of triumphing over a mind prepared to dislike me, and prejudiced against all my past actions. His sister, too, is, I hope, convinced how little the ungenerous representations of anyone to the disadvantage of another will avail when opposed by the immediate influence of intellect and manner. I see plainly that she is uneasy at my progress in the good opinion of her brother, and conclude that nothing will be wanting on her part to counteract me; but having once made him doubt the justice of her opinion of me, I think I may defy her. It has been delightful to me to watch his advances towards intimacy, especially to observe his altered manner in consequence of my repressing by the cool dignity of my deportment his insolent approach to direct familiarity. My conduct has been equally guarded from the first, and I never behaved less like a coquette in the whole course of my life, though perhaps my desire of dominion was never more decided. I have subdued him entirely by sentiment and serious conversation, and made him, I may venture to say, at least *half* in love with me, without the semblance of the most commonplace flirtation. Mrs. Vernon's consciousness of deserving every sort of revenge that it can be in my power to inflict for her ill-offices could alone enable her to perceive that I am actuated by any design in behaviour so gentle and unpretending. Let her think and act as she chooses, however. I have never yet found that the advice of a sister could prevent a young man's being in love if he chose. We are advancing now to some kind of confidence, and in short are likely to be engaged in a sort of platonic friendship. On my side you may be sure of its never being more, for if I were not attached to another person as much as I can be to anyone, I should make a point of not bestowing my affection on a man who had dared to think so meanly of me. Reginald has a good figure and is not unworthy the praise you have heard given him, but is still greatly inferior to our friend at Langford. He is less polished, less insinuating than Mainwaring, and is comparatively deficient in the power of saying those delightful things which put one in good humour with oneself and all the world. He is quite agreeable enough, however, to afford me amusement, and to make many of those hours pass very pleasantly which would otherwise be spent in endeavouring to overcome my sister-in-law's reserve, and listening to the insipid talk of her husband. Your account of Sir James is most satisfactory, and I mean to give Miss Frederica a hint of my intentions very soon.

Yours, &c.,
S. VERNON.

XI.

MRS. VERNON TO LADY DE COURCY.

Churchhill.

I really grow quite uneasy, my dearest mother, about Reginald, from witnessing the very rapid increase of Lady Susan's influence. They are now on terms of the most particular friendship, frequently engaged in long conversations together; and she has contrived by the most artful coquetry to subdue his judgment to her own purposes. It is impossible to see the intimacy between them so very soon established without some alarm, though I can hardly suppose that Lady Susan's plans extend to marriage. I wish you could get Reginald home again on any plausible pretence; he is not at all disposed to leave us, and I have given him as many hints of my father's precarious state of health as common decency will allow me to do in my own house. Her power over him must now be boundless, as she has entirely effaced all his former ill-opinion, and persuaded him not merely to forget but to justify her conduct. Mr. Smith's account of her proceedings at

Langford, where he accused her of having made Mr. Mainwaring and a young man engaged to Miss Mainwaring distractedly in love with her, which Reginald firmly believed when he came here, is now, he is persuaded, only a scandalous invention. He has told me so with a warmth of manner which spoke his regret at having believed the contrary himself. How sincerely do I grieve that she ever entered this house! I always looked forward to her coming with uneasiness; but very far was it from originating in anxiety for Reginald. I expected a most disagreeable companion for myself, but could not imagine that my brother would be in the smallest danger of being captivated by a woman with whose principles he was so well acquainted, and whose character he so heartily despised. If you can get him away it will be a good thing.

Yours, &c.,
CATHERINE VERNON.

XII.

SIR REGINALD DE COURCY TO HIS SON.

Parklands.

I know that young men in general do not admit of any enquiry even from their nearest relations into affairs of the heart, but I hope, my dear Reginald, that you will be superior to such as allow nothing for a father's anxiety, and think themselves privileged to refuse him their confidence and slight his advice. You must be sensible that as an only son, and the representative of an ancient family, your conduct in life is most interesting to your connections; and in the very important concern of marriage especially, there is everything at stake—your own happiness, that of your parents, and the credit of your name. I do not suppose that you would deliberately form an absolute engagement of that nature without acquainting your mother and myself, or at least, without being convinced that we should approve of your choice; but I cannot help fearing that you may be drawn in, by the lady who has lately attached you, to a marriage which the whole of your family, far and near, must highly reprobate. Lady Susan's age is itself a material objection, but her want of character is one so much more serious, that the difference of even twelve years becomes in comparison of small amount. Were you not blinded by a sort of fascination, it would be ridiculous in me to repeat the instances of great misconduct on her side so very generally known.

Her neglect of her husband, her encouragement of other men, her extravagance and dissipation, were so gross and notorious that no one could be ignorant of them at the time, nor can now have forgotten them. To our family she has always been represented in softened colours by the benevolence of Mr. Charles Vernon, and yet, in spite of his generous endeavours to excuse her, we know that she did, from the most selfish motives, take all possible pains to prevent his marriage with Catherine.

My years and increasing infirmities make me very desirous of seeing you settled in the world, To the fortune of a wife, the goodness of my own will make me indifferent, but her family and character must be equally unexceptionable. When your choice is fixed so that no objection can be made to it, then I can promise you a ready and cheerful consent; but it is my duty to oppose a match which deep art only could render possible, and must in the end make wretched. It is possible her behaviour may arise only from vanity, or the wish of gaining the admiration of a man whom she must imagine to be particularly prejudiced against her; but it is more likely that she should aim at something further. She is poor, and may naturally seek an alliance which must be advantageous to herself; you know your own rights, and that it is out of my power to prevent your inheriting the family estate. My ability of distressing you during my life would be a species of revenge to which I could hardly stoop under any circumstances.

I honestly tell you my sentiments and intentions: I do not wish to work on your fears, but on your sense and affection. It would destroy every comfort of my life to know that you were married to Lady Susan Vernon; it would be the death of that honest pride with which I have hitherto considered my son; I should blush to see him, to hear of him, to think of him. I may perhaps do no good but that of relieving my own mind by this letter, but I felt it my duty to tell you that your partiality for Lady Susan is no secret to your friends, and to warn you against her. I should be glad to hear your reasons for disbelieving Mr. Smith's intelligence; you had no doubt of its authenticity a month ago. If you can give me your assurance of having no design beyond enjoying the conversation of a clever woman for a short period, and of yielding admiration only to her beauty and abilities, without being blinded by them to her faults, you will restore me to happiness; but, if you cannot do this, explain to me, at least, what has occasioned so great an alteration in your opinion of her!

I am, &c., &c.,

REGINALD DE COURCY.

XIII.

LADY DE COURCY TO MRS. VERNON.

Parklands.

My dear Catherine,—Unluckily I was confined to my room when your last letter came, by a cold which affected my eyes so much as to prevent my reading it myself, so I could not refuse your father when he offered to read it to me, by which means he became acquainted, to my great vexation, with all your fears about your brother. I had intended to write to Reginald myself as soon as my eyes would let me, to point out, as well as I could, the danger of an intimate acquaintance, with so artful a woman as Lady Susan, to a young man of his age, and high expectations. I meant, moreover, to have reminded him of our being quite alone now, and very much in need of him to keep up our spirits these long winter evenings. Whether it would have done any good can never be settled now, but I am excessively vexed that Sir Reginald should know anything of a matter which we foresaw would make him so uneasy, He caught all your fears the moment he had read your letter, and I am sure he has not had the business out of his head since. He wrote by the same post to Reginald a long letter full of it all, and particularly asking an explanation of what he may have heard from Lady Susan to contradict the late shocking reports. His answer came this morning, which I shall enclose to you, as I think you will like to see it. I wish it was more satisfactory; but it seems written with such a determination to think well of Lady Susan, that his assurances as to marriage, &c., do not set my heart at ease. I say all I can, however, to satisfy your father, and he is certainly less uneasy since Reginald's letter. How provoking it is, my dear Catherine, that this unwelcome guest of yours should not only prevent our meeting this Christmas, but be the occasion of so much vexation and trouble! Kiss the dear children for me.

Your affectionate mother,
C. DE COURCY.

XIV.

MR. DE COURCY TO SIR REGINALD.

Churchhill.

My dear Sir,—I have this moment received your letter, which has given me more astonishment than I ever felt before. I am to thank my sister, I suppose, for having represented me in such a light as to injure me in your opinion, and give you all this alarm. I know not why she should choose to make herself and her family uneasy by apprehending an event which no one but herself, I can affirm, would ever have thought possible. To impute such a design to Lady Susan would be taking from her every claim to that excellent understanding which her bitterest enemies have never denied her; and equally low must sink my pretensions to common sense if I am suspected of matrimonial views in my behaviour to her. Our difference of age must be an insuperable objection, and I entreat you, my dear father, to quiet your mind, and no longer harbour a suspicion which cannot be more injurious to your own peace than to our understandings. I can have no other view in remaining with Lady Susan, than to enjoy for a short time (as you have yourself expressed it) the conversation of a woman of high intellectual powers. If Mrs. Vernon would allow something to my affection for herself and her husband in the length of my visit, she would do more justice to us all; but my sister is unhappily prejudiced beyond the hope of conviction against Lady Susan. From an attachment to her husband, which in itself does honour to both, she cannot forgive the endeavours at preventing their union, which have been attributed to selfishness in Lady Susan; but in this case, as well as in many others, the world has most grossly injured that lady, by supposing the worst where the motives of her conduct have been doubtful. Lady Susan had heard something so materially to the disadvantage of my sister as to persuade her that the happiness of Mr. Vernon, to whom she was always much attached, would be wholly destroyed by the marriage. And this circumstance, while it explains the true motives of Lady Susan's conduct, and removes all the blame which has been so lavished on her, may also convince us how little the general report of anyone ought to be credited; since no character, however upright, can escape the malevolence of slander. If my sister, in the security of retirement, with as little opportunity as inclination to do evil, could not avoid censure, we must not rashly condemn those who, living in the world and surrounded with temptations, should be accused of errors which they are known to have the power of committing.

I blame myself severely for having so easily believed the slanderous tales invented by Charles Smith to the prejudice of Lady Susan, as I am now convinced how greatly they have traduced her. As to Mrs. Mainwaring's jealousy it was totally his own invention, and his account of her attaching Miss Mainwaring's lover was scarcely better founded. Sir James Martin had been drawn in by that young lady to pay her some attention; and as he is a man of fortune, it was easy to see *her* views extended to marriage. It is well known that Miss M. is absolutely on the catch for a husband, and no one therefore can pity her for losing, by the superior attractions of another woman, the chance of being able to make a worthy man completely wretched. Lady Susan was far from intending such a conquest, and on finding how warmly Miss Mainwaring resented her lover's defection, determined, in spite of Mr. and Mrs. Mainwaring's most urgent entreaties, to leave the family. I have reason to imagine she did receive serious proposals from Sir James, but her removing to Langford immediately on the discovery of his attachment, must acquit her on that article with any mind of common candour. You will, I am sure, my dear Sir, feel the truth of this, and will hereby learn to do justice to the character of a very injured woman. I know that Lady Susan in coming to Churchhill was governed only by the most honourable and amiable intentions; her prudence and economy are exemplary, her regard for Mr. Vernon equal even to *his* deserts; and her wish of obtaining my sister's good opinion merits a better return than it has received. As a mother she is unexceptionable; her solid affection for her child is shown by placing her in hands where her education will be properly attended to; but because she has not the blind and weak partiality of most mothers, she is accused of wanting maternal tenderness. Every person of sense, however, will know how to value and commend her well-directed affection, and will join me in wishing that Frederica Vernon may prove more worthy than she has yet done of her mother's tender care. I have now, my dear father, written my real sentiments of Lady Susan; you will know from this letter how highly I admire her abilities, and esteem her character; but if you are not equally convinced by my full and solemn assurance that your fears have been most idly created, you will deeply mortify and distress me.

I am, &c., &c.,
R. DE COURCY.

XV.

MRS. VERNON TO LADY DE COURCY.

Churchhill.

My dear Mother,—I return you Reginald's letter, and rejoice with all my heart that my father is made easy by it: tell him so, with my congratulations; but, between ourselves, I must own it has only convinced *me* of my brother's having no *present* intention of marrying Lady Susan, not that he is in no danger of doing so three months hence. He gives a very plausible account of her behaviour at Langford; I wish it may be true, but his intelligence must come from herself, and I am less disposed to believe it than to lament the degree of intimacy subsisting between them implied by the discussion of such a subject. I am sorry to have incurred his displeasure, but can expect nothing better while he is so very eager in Lady Susan's justification. He is very severe against me indeed, and yet I hope I have not been hasty in my judgment of her. Poor woman! though I have reasons enough for my dislike, I cannot help pitying her at present, as she is in real distress, and with too much cause. She had this morning a letter from the lady with whom she has placed her daughter, to request that Miss Vernon might be immediately removed, as she had been detected in an attempt to run away. Why, or whither she intended to go, does not appear; but, as her situation seems to have been unexceptionable, it is a sad thing, and of course highly distressing to Lady Susan. Frederica must be as much as sixteen, and ought to know better; but from what her mother insinuates, I am afraid she is a perverse girl. She has been sadly neglected, however, and her mother ought to remember it. Mr. Vernon set off for London as soon as she had determined what should be done. He is, if possible, to prevail on Miss Summers to let Frederica continue with her; and if he cannot succeed, to bring her to Churchhill for the present, till some other situation can be found for her. Her ladyship is comforting herself meanwhile by strolling along the shrubbery with Reginald, calling forth all his tender feelings, I suppose, on this distressing occasion. She has been talking a great deal about it to me. She talks vastly well; I am afraid of being ungenerous, or I should say, *too* well to feel so very deeply; but I will not look for faults; she may be Reginald's wife! Heaven forbid it! but why should I be quicker-sighted than anyone else? Mr. Vernon declares that he never saw deeper distress than hers, on the receipt of the letter; and is his judgment inferior to mine? She was very unwilling that Frederica should be allowed to come to Churchhill, and justly enough, as it seems a sort of reward to behaviour deserving very differently; but it was impossible to take her anywhere else, and she is not to remain here long. 'It will be absolutely necessary,' said she, 'as you, my dear sister, must be sensible, to treat my daughter with some severity while she is here; a most painful necessity, but I will *endeavour* to submit to it. I am afraid I have often been too indulgent, but my poor Frederica's temper could never bear opposition well: you must support and encourage me; you must urge the necessity of reproof if you see me too lenient.' All this sounds very reasonably. Reginald is so incensed against the poor silly girl! Surely it is not to Lady Susan's credit that he should be so bitter against her daughter; his idea of her must be drawn from the mother's description. Well, whatever may be his fate, we have the comfort of knowing that we have done our utmost to save him. We must commit the event to a higher power.

Yours ever, &c.
CATHERINE VERNON.

XVI.

LADY SUSAN TO MRS. JOHNSON.

Churchhill.

Never, my dearest Alicia, was I so provoked in my life as by a letter this morning from Miss Summers. That horrid girl of mine has been trying to run away. I had not a notion of her being such a little devil before, she seemed to have all the Vernon milkiness; but on receiving the letter in which I declared my intention about Sir James, she actually attempted to elope; at least, I cannot otherwise account for her doing it. She meant, I suppose, to go to the Clarks in Staffordshire, for she has no other acquaintances. But she shall be punished, she *shall* have him. I have sent Charles to town to make matters up if he can, for I do not by any means want her here. If Miss Summers will not keep her, you must find me out another school, unless we can get her married immediately. Miss S. writes word that she could not get the young lady to assign any cause for her extraordinary conduct, which confirms me in my own previous explanation of it. Frederica is too shy, I think, and too much in awe of me to tell tales, but if the mildness of her uncle should get anything out of her, I am not afraid. I trust I shall be able to make my story as good as hers. If I am vain of anything, it is of my eloquence. Consideration and esteem as surely follow command of language as admiration waits on beauty, and here I have opportunity enough for the exercise of my talent, as the chief of my time is spent in conversation.

Reginald is never easy unless we are by ourselves, and when the weather is tolerable, we pace the shrubbery for hours together. I like him on the whole very well; he is clever and has a good deal to say, but he is sometimes impertinent and troublesome. There is a sort of ridiculous delicacy about him which requires the fullest explanation of whatever he may have heard to my disadvantage, and is never satisfied till he thinks he has ascertained the beginning and end of everything. This is one sort of love, but I confess it does not particularly recommend itself to me. I infinitely prefer the tender and liberal spirit of Mainwaring, which, impressed with the deepest conviction of my merit, is satisfied that whatever I do must be right; and look with a degree of contempt on the inquisitive and doubtful fancies of that heart which seems always debating on the reasonableness of its emotions. Mainwaring is indeed, beyond all compare, superior to Reginald—superior in everything but the power of being with me! Poor fellow! he is much distracted by jealousy, which I am not sorry for, as I know no better support of love. He has been teazing me to allow of his coming into this country, and lodging somewhere near *incog.*; but I forbade everything of the kind. Those women are inexcusable who forget what is due to themselves, and the opinion of the world.

Yours ever,
S. VERNON.

XVII.

MRS. VERNON TO LADY DE COURCY.

Churchhill.

My dear Mother,—Mr. Vernon returned on Thursday night, bringing his niece with him. Lady Susan had received a line from him by that day's post, informing her that Miss Summers had absolutely refused to allow of Miss Vernon's continuance in her academy; we were therefore prepared for her arrival, and expected them impatiently the whole evening. They came while we were at tea, and I never saw any creature look so frightened as Frederica when she entered the room. Lady Susan, who had been shedding tears before, and showing great agitation at the idea of the meeting, received her with perfect self-command, and without betraying the least tenderness of spirit. She hardly spoke to her, and on Frederica's bursting into tears as soon as we were seated, took her out of the room, and did not return for some time. When she did, her eyes looked very red, and she was as much agitated as before. We saw no more of her daughter. Poor Reginald was beyond measure concerned to see his fair friend in such distress, and watched her with so much tender solicitude, that I, who occasionally caught her observing his countenance with exultation, was quite out of patience. This pathetic representation lasted the whole evening, and so ostentatious and artful a display has entirely convinced me that she did in fact feel nothing. I am more angry with her than ever since I have seen her daughter; the poor girl looks so unhappy that my heart aches for her. Lady Susan is surely too severe, for Frederica does not seem to have the sort of temper to make severity necessary. She looks perfectly timid, dejected, and penitent. She is very pretty, though not so handsome as her mother, nor at all like her. Her complexion is delicate, but neither so fair nor so blooming as Lady Susan's, and she has quite the Vernon cast of countenance, the oval face and mild dark eyes, and there is peculiar sweetness in her look when she speaks either to her uncle or me, for as we behave kindly to her we have of course engaged her gratitude.

Her mother has insinuated that her temper is intractable, but I never saw a face less indicative of any evil disposition than hers; and from what I can see of the behaviour of each to the other, the invariable severity of Lady Susan and the silent dejection of Frederica, I am led to believe as heretofore that the former has no real love for her daughter, and has never done her justice or treated her affectionately. I have not been able to have any conversation with my niece; she is shy, and I think I can see that some pains are taken to prevent her being much with me. Nothing satisfactory transpires as to her reason for running away. Her kind-hearted uncle, you may be sure, was too fearful of distressing her to ask many questions as they travelled. I wish it had been possible for me to fetch her instead of him. I think I should have discovered the truth in the course of a thirty-mile journey. The small pianoforte has been removed within these few days, at Lady Susan's request, into her dressing-room, and Frederica spends great part of the day there, practising as it is called; but I seldom hear any noise when I pass that way; what she does with herself there I do not know. There are plenty of books, but it is not every girl who has been running wild the first fifteen years of her life, that can or will read. Poor creature! the prospect from her window is not very instructive, for that room overlooks the lawn, you know, with the shrubbery on one side, where she may see her mother walking for an hour together in earnest conversation with Reginald. A girl of Frederica's age must be childish indeed, if such things do not strike her. Is it not inexcusable to give such an example to a daughter? Yet Reginald still thinks Lady Susan the best of mothers, and still condemns Frederica as a worthless girl! He is convinced that her attempt to run away proceeded from no justifiable cause, and had no provocation. I am sure I cannot say that it *had*, but while Miss Summers declares that Miss Vernon showed no signs of obstinacy or perverseness during her whole stay in Wigmore Street, till she was detected in this scheme, I cannot so readily credit what Lady Susan has made him, and wants to make me believe, that it was merely an impatience of restraint and a desire of escaping from the tuition of masters which brought on the plan of an elopement. O Reginald, how is your judgment enslaved! He scarcely dares even allow her to be handsome, and when I speak of her beauty, replies only that her eyes have no brilliancy! Sometimes he is sure she is deficient in understanding, and at others that her temper only is in fault. In short, when a person is always to deceive, it is impossible to be consistent. Lady Susan finds it necessary that Frederica should be to blame, and probably has sometimes judged it expedient to excuse her of ill-nature and sometimes to lament her want of sense. Reginald is only repeating after her ladyship.

I remain, &c., &c.,
CATHERINE VERNON.

XVIII.

FROM THE SAME TO THE SAME.

Churchhill.

My dear Mother,—I am very glad to find that my description of Frederica Vernon has interested you, for I do believe her truly deserving of your regard; and when I have communicated a notion which has recently struck me, your kind impressions in her favour will, I am sure, be heightened. I cannot help fancying that she is growing partial to my brother. I so very often see her eyes fixed on his face with a remarkable expression of pensive admiration. He is certainly very handsome; and yet more, there is an openness in his manner that must be highly prepossessing, and I am sure she feels it so. Thoughtful and pensive in general, her countenance always brightens into a smile when Reginald says anything amusing; and, let the subject be ever so serious that he may be conversing on, I am much mistaken if a syllable of his uttering escapes her. I want to make him sensible of all this, for we know the power of gratitude on such a heart as his; and could Frederica's artless affection detach him from her mother, we might bless the day which brought her to Churchhill. I think, my dear mother, you would not disapprove of her as a daughter. She is extremely young, to be sure, has had a wretched education, and a dreadful example of levity in her mother; but yet I can pronounce her disposition to be excellent, and her natural abilities very good. Though totally without accomplishments, she is by no means so ignorant as one might expect to find her, being fond of books and spending the chief of her time in reading. Her mother leaves her more to herself than she did, and I have her with me as much as possible, and have taken great pains to overcome her timidity. We are very good friends, and though she never opens her lips before her mother, she talks enough when alone with me to make it clear that, if properly treated by Lady Susan, she would always appear to much greater advantage. There cannot be a more gentle, affectionate heart; or more obliging manners, when acting without restraint; and her little cousins are all very fond of her.

Your affectionate Daughter,
C. VERNON

XIX.

LADY SUSAN TO MRS. JOHNSON.

Churchhill.

You will be eager, I know, to hear something further of Frederica, and perhaps may think me negligent for not writing before. She arrived with her uncle last Thursday fortnight, when, of course, I lost no time in demanding the cause of her behaviour; and soon found myself to have been perfectly right in attributing it to my own letter. The prospect of it frightened her so thoroughly, that, with a mixture of true girlish perverseness and folly, she resolved on getting out of the house and proceeding directly by the stage to her friends, the Clarkes; and had really got as far as the length of two streets in her journey when she was fortunately missed, pursued, and overtaken. Such was the first distinguished exploit of Miss Frederica Vernon; and, if we consider that it was achieved at the tender age of sixteen, we shall have room for the most flattering prognostics of her future renown. I am excessively provoked, however, at the parade of propriety which prevented Miss Summers from keeping the girl; and it seems so extraordinary a piece of nicety, considering my daughter's family connections, that I can only suppose the lady to be governed by the fear of never getting her money. Be that as it may, however, Frederica is returned on my hands; and, having nothing else to employ her, is busy in pursuing the plan of romance begun at Langford. She is actually falling in love with Reginald De Courcy! To disobey her mother by refusing an unexceptionable offer is not enough; her affections must also be given without her mother's approbation. I never saw a girl of her age bid fairer to be the sport of mankind. Her feelings are tolerably acute, and she is so charmingly artless in their display as to afford the most reasonable hope of her being ridiculous, and despised by every man who sees her.

Artlessness will never do in love matters; and that girl is born a simpleton who has it either by nature or affectation. I am not yet certain that Reginald sees what she is about, nor is it of much consequence. She is now an object of indifference to him, and she would be one of contempt were he to understand her emotions. Her beauty is much admired by the Vernons, but it has no effect on him. She is in high favour with her aunt altogether, because she is so little like myself, of course. She is exactly the companion for Mrs. Vernon, who dearly loves to be first, and to have all the sense and all the wit of the conversation to herself: Frederica will never eclipse her. When she first came I was at some pains to prevent her seeing much of her aunt; but I have relaxed, as I believe I may depend on her observing the rules I have laid down for their discourse. But do not imagine that with all this lenity I have for a moment given up my plan of her marriage. No; I am unalterably fixed on this point, though I have not yet quite decided on the manner of bringing it about. I should not choose to have the business brought on here, and canvassed by the wise heads of Mr. and Mrs. Vernon; and I cannot just now afford to go to town. Miss Frederica must therefore wait a little.

Yours ever,
S. VERNON

XX.

MRS. VERNON TO LADY DE COURCY.

Churchhill.

We have a very unexpected guest with us at present, my dear mother: he arrived yesterday. I heard a carriage at the door, as I was sitting with my children while they dined; and supposing I should be wanted, left the nursery soon afterwards, and was half-way down stairs, when Frederica, as pale as ashes, came running up, and rushed by me into her own room. I instantly followed, and asked her what was the matter. 'Oh!' said she, 'he is come—Sir James is come, and what shall I do?' This was no explanation; I begged her to tell me what she meant. At that moment we were interrupted by a knock at the door: it was Reginald, who came, by Lady Susan's direction, to call Frederica down. 'It is Mr. De Courcy!' said she, colouring violently. 'Mamma has sent for me; I must go.' We all three went down together; and I saw my brother examining the terrified face of Frederica with surprise. In the breakfast-room we found Lady Susan, and a young man of gentlemanlike appearance, whom she introduced by the name of Sir James Martin—the very person, as you may remember, whom it was said she had been at pains to detach from Miss Mainwaring; but the conquest, it seems, was not designed for herself, or she has since transferred it to her daughter; for Sir James is now desperately in love with Frederica, and with full encouragement from mamma. The poor girl, however, I am sure, dislikes him; and though his person and address are very well, he appears, both to Mr. Vernon and me, a very weak young man. Frederica looked so shy, so confused, when we entered the room, that I felt for her exceedingly. Lady Susan behaved with great attention to her visitor; and yet I thought I could perceive that she had no particular pleasure in seeing him. Sir James talked a great deal, and made many civil excuses to me for the liberty he had taken in coming to Churchhill—mixing more frequent laughter with his discourse than the subject required—said many things over and over again, and told Lady Susan three times that he had seen Mrs. Johnson a few evenings before. He now and then addressed Frederica, but more frequently her mother. The poor girl sat all this time without opening her lips—her eyes cast down, and her colour varying every instant; while Reginald observed all that passed in perfect silence. At length Lady Susan, weary, I believe, of her situation, proposed walking; and we left the two gentlemen together, to put on our pelisses. As we went upstairs Lady Susan begged permission to attend me for a few moments in my dressing-room, as she was anxious to speak with me in private. I led her thither accordingly, and as soon as the door was closed, she said: 'I was never more surprised in my life than by Sir James's arrival, and the suddenness of it requires some apology to you, my dear sister; though to *me*, as a mother, it is highly flattering. He is so extremely attached to my daughter that he could not exist longer without seeing her. Sir James is a young man of an amiable disposition and excellent character; a little too much of the rattle, perhaps, but a year or two will rectify *that*: and he is in other respects so very eligible a match for Frederica, that I have always observed his attachment with the greatest pleasure; and am persuaded that you and my brother will give the alliance your hearty approbation. I have never before mentioned the likelihood of its taking place to anyone, because I thought that whilst Frederica continued at school it had better not be known to exist; but now, as I am convinced that Frederica is too old ever to submit to school confinement, and have, therefore, begun to consider her union with Sir James as not very distant, I had intended within a few days to acquaint yourself and Mr. Vernon with the whole business. I am sure, my dear sister, you will excuse my remaining silent so long, and agree with me that such circumstances, while they continue from any cause in suspense, cannot be too cautiously concealed. When you have the happiness of bestowing your sweet little Catherine, some years hence, on a man who in connection and character is alike unexceptionable, you will know what I feel now; though, thank Heaven, you cannot have all my reasons for rejoicing in such an event. Catherine will be amply provided for, and not, like my Frederica, indebted to a fortunate establishment for the comforts of life.' She concluded by demanding my congratulations. I gave them somewhat awkwardly, I believe; for, in fact, the sudden disclosure of so important a matter took from me the power of speaking with any clearness. She thanked me, however, most affectionately, for my kind concern in the welfare of herself and daughter; and then said: 'I am not apt to deal in professions, my dear Mrs. Vernon, and I never had the convenient talent of affecting sensations foreign to my heart; and therefore I trust you will believe me when I declare, that much as I had heard in your praise before I knew you, I had no idea that I should ever love you as I now do; and I must further say that your friendship towards me is more particularly gratifying because I have reason to believe that some attempts were made to prejudice you against me. I only wish that they, whoever they are, to whom I am indebted for such kind intentions, could see the terms on which we now are together, and understand the real affection we feel for each other; but I will not detain you any longer. God bless you, for your goodness to me and my girl, and continue to you all your present happiness.' What can one say of such a woman, my dear mother? Such earnestness, such solemnity of expression! and yet I cannot help suspecting the truth of everything she says. As for Reginald, I believe he does not know what to make of the matter. When Sir James came, he appeared all astonishment and perplexity; the folly of the young man and the confusion of Frederica entirely engrossed him; and though a little private discourse with Lady Susan has since had its effect, he is still hurt, I am sure, at her allowing of such a man's attentions to her daughter. Sir James invited himself with great composure to remain here a few days—hoped we would not think it odd, was aware of its being very impertinent, but he took the liberty of a relation; and concluded by wishing, with a laugh, that he might be really one very soon. Even Lady Susan seemed a little disconcerted by this forwardness; in her heart I am persuaded she sincerely wished him gone. But something must be done for this poor girl, if her feelings are such as both I and her uncle believe them to be. She must not be sacrificed to policy or ambition, and she must not be left to suffer from the dread of it. The girl whose heart can distinguish Reginald De Courcy, deserves, however he may slight her, a better fate than to be Sir James Martin's wife. As soon as I can get her alone, I will discover the real truth; but she seems to wish to avoid me. I hope this does not proceed from anything wrong, and that I shall not find out I have thought too well of her. Her behaviour to Sir James certainly speaks the greatest consciousness and embarrassment, but I see nothing in it more like encouragement. Adieu, my dear mother.

ARTLESSNESS WILL NEVER DO IN LOVE MATTERS; AND THAT GIRL IS BORN A SIMPLETON WHO HAS IT EITHER BY NATURE OR AFFECTATION.

Yours, &c.
C. VERNON.

XXI.

MISS VERNON TO MR. DE COURCY.

Sir,—I hope you will excuse this liberty; I am forced upon it by the greatest distress, or I should be ashamed to trouble you. I am very miserable about Sir James

Martin, and have no other way in the world of helping myself but by writing to you, for I am forbidden even speaking to my uncle and aunt on the subject; and this being the case, I am afraid my applying to you will appear no better than equivocation, and as if I attended to the letter and not the spirit of mamma's commands. But if you do not take my part and persuade her to break it off, I shall be half distracted, for I cannot bear him. No human being but *you* could have any chance of prevailing with her. If you will, therefore, have the unspeakably great kindness of taking my part with her, and persuading her to send Sir James away, I shall be more obliged to you than it is possible for me to express. I always disliked him from the first: it is not a sudden fancy, I assure you, sir; I always thought him silly and impertinent and disagreeable, and now he is grown worse than ever. I would rather work for my bread than marry him. I do not know how to apologise enough for this letter; I know it is taking so great a liberty. I am aware how dreadfully angry it will make mamma, but I remember the risk.

I SHALL EVER DESPISE THE MAN WHO CAN BE GRATIFIED BY THE PASSION WHICH HE NEVER WISHED TO INSPIRE, NOR SOLICITED THE AVOWAL OF.

I am, Sir, your most humble servant,
F. S. V.

XXII.

LADY SUSAN TO MRS. JOHNSON.

Churchhill.

This is insufferable! My dearest friend, I was never so enraged before, and must relieve myself by writing to you, who I know will enter into all my feelings. Who should come on Tuesday but Sir James Martin! Guess my astonishment, and vexation—for, as you well know, I never wished him to be seen at Churchhill. What a pity that you should not have known his intentions! Not content with coming, he actually invited himself to remain here a few days, I could have poisoned him! I made the best of it, however, and told my story with great success to Mrs. Vernon, who, whatever might be her real sentiments, said nothing in opposition to mine. I made a point also of Frederica's behaving civilly to Sir James, and gave her to understand that I was absolutely determined on her marrying him. She said something of her misery, but that was all. I have for some time been more particularly resolved on the match from seeing the rapid increase of her affection for Reginald, and from not feeling secure that a knowledge of such affection might not in the end awaken a return. Contemptible as a regard founded only on compassion must make them both in my eyes, I felt by no means assured that such might not be the consequence. It is true that Reginald had not in any degree grown cool towards me; but yet he has lately mentioned Frederica spontaneously and unnecessarily, and once said something in praise of her person. *He* was all astonishment at the appearance of my visitor, and at first observed Sir James with an attention which I was pleased to see not unmixed with jealousy; but unluckily it was impossible for me really to torment him, as Sir James, though extremely gallant to me, very soon made the whole party understand that his heart was devoted to my daughter. I had no great difficulty in convincing De Courcy, when we were alone, that I was perfectly justified, all things considered, in desiring the match; and the whole business seemed most comfortably arranged. They could none of them help perceiving that Sir James was no Solomon; but I had positively forbidden Frederica complaining to Charles Vernon or his wife, and they had therefore no pretence for interference; though my impertinent sister, I believe, wanted only opportunity for doing so. Everything, however, was going on calmly and quietly; and, though I counted the hours of Sir James's stay, my mind was entirely satisfied with the posture of affairs. Guess, then, what I must feel at the sudden disturbance of all my schemes; and that, too, from a quarter where I had least reason to expect it. Reginald came this morning into my dressing-room with a very unusual solemnity of countenance, and after some preface informed me in so many words that he wished to reason with me on the impropriety and unkindness of allowing Sir James Martin to address my daughter contrary to her inclinations. I was all amazement. When I found that he was not to be laughed out of his design, I calmly begged an explanation, and desired to know by what he was impelled, and by whom commissioned, to reprimand me. He then told me, mixing in his speech a few insolent compliments and ill-timed expressions of tenderness, to which I listened with perfect indifference, that my daughter had acquainted him with some circumstances concerning herself, Sir James, and me which had given him great uneasiness. In short, I found that she had in the first place actually written to him to request his interference, and that, on receiving her letter, he had conversed with her on the subject of it, in order to understand the particulars, and to assure himself of her real wishes. I have not a doubt but that the girl took this opportunity of making downright love to him. I am convinced of it by the manner in which he spoke of her. Much good may such love do him! I shall ever despise the man who can be gratified by the passion which he never wished to inspire, nor solicited the avowal of. I shall always detest them both. He can have no true regard for me, or he would not have listened to her; and *she*, with her little rebellious heart and indelicate feelings, to throw herself into the protection of a young man with whom she has scarcely ever exchanged two words before! I am equally confounded at *her* impudence and *his* credulity. How dared he believe what she told him in my disfavour! Ought he not to have felt assured that I must have unanswerable motives for all that I had done? Where was his reliance on my sense and goodness then? Where the resentment which true love would have dictated against the person defaming me—that person, too, a chit, a child, without talent or education, whom he had been always taught to despise? I was calm for some time; but the greatest degree of forbearance may be overcome, and I hope I was afterwards sufficiently keen. He endeavoured, long endeavoured, to soften my resentment; but that woman is a fool indeed who, while insulted by accusation, can be worked on by compliments. At length he left me, as deeply provoked as myself; and he showed his anger more. I was quite cool, but he gave way to the most violent indignation; I may therefore expect it will the sooner subside, and perhaps his may be vanished for ever, while mine will be found still fresh and implacable. He is now shut up in his apartment, whither I heard him go on leaving mine. How unpleasant, one would think, must be his reflections! but some people's feelings are incomprehensible. I have not yet tranquillised myself enough to see Frederica. *She* shall not soon forget the occurrences of this day; she shall find that she has poured forth her tender tale of love in vain, and exposed herself for ever to the contempt of the whole world, and the severest resentment of her injured mother.

Your affectionate!
S. VERNON.

XXIII.

MRS. VERNON TO LADY DE COURCY.

Churchhill.

Let me congratulate you, my dearest mother! The affair which has given us so much anxiety is drawing to a happy conclusion. Our prospect is most delightful, and since matters have now taken so favourable a turn, I am quite sorry that I ever imparted my apprehensions to you; for the pleasure of learning that the danger is over is perhaps dearly purchased by all that you have previously suffered. I am so much agitated by delight that I can scarcely hold a pen; but am determined to send you a few short lines by James, that you may have some explanation of what must so greatly astonish you, as that Reginald should be returning to Parklands. I was sitting about half-an-hour ago with Sir James in the breakfast parlour, when my brother called me out of the room. I instantly saw that something was the matter; his complexion was raised, and he spoke with great emotion; you know his eager manner, my dear mother, when his mind is interested. 'Catherine,' said he, 'I am going home to-day: I am sorry to leave you, but I must go: it is a great while since I have seen my father and mother. I am going to send James forward with my hunters immediately; if you have any letter, therefore, he can take it. I shall not be at home myself till Wednesday or Thursday, as I shall go through London, where I have business; but before I leave you,' he continued, speaking in a lower tone, and with still greater energy, 'I must warn you of one thing—do not let Frederica Vernon be made unhappy by that Martin. He wants to marry her; her mother promotes the match, but she cannot endure the idea of it. Be assured that I speak from the fullest conviction of the truth of what I say; I know that Frederica is made wretched by Sir James's continuing here. She is a sweet girl, and deserves a better fate. Send him away immediately; he is only a fool: but what her mother can mean, Heaven only knows! Good bye,' he added, shaking my hand with earnestness; 'I do not know when you will see me again; but remember what I tell you of Frederica; you *must* make it your business to see justice done her. She is an amiable girl, and has a very superior mind to what we have given her credit for.' He then left me, and ran upstairs. I would not try to stop him, for I know what his feelings must be. The nature of mine, as I listened to him, I need not attempt to describe; for a minute or two I remained in the same spot, overpowered by wonder of a most agreeable sort indeed; yet it required some consideration to be tranquilly happy. In about ten minutes after my return to the parlour Lady Susan entered the room. I concluded, of course, that she and Reginald had been quarrelling; and looked with anxious curiosity for a confirmation of my belief in her face. Mistress of deceit, however, she appeared perfectly unconcerned, and after chatting on indifferent subjects for a short time, said to me, 'I find from Wilson that we are going to lose Mr. De Courcy—is it true that he leaves Churchhill this morning?' I replied that it was. 'He told us nothing of all this last night,' said she, laughing, 'or even this morning at breakfast; but perhaps he did not know it himself. Young men are often hasty in their resolutions, and not more sudden in forming than unsteady in keeping them. I should not be surprised if he were to change his mind at last, and not go.' She soon afterwards left the room. I trust, however, my dear mother, that we have no reason to fear an alteration of his present plan; things have gone too far. They must have quarrelled, and about Frederica, too. Her calmness astonishes me. What delight will be yours in seeing him again; in seeing him still worthy your esteem, still capable of forming your happiness! When I next write I shall be able to tell you that Sir James is gone, Lady Susan vanquished, and Frederica at peace. We have much to do, but it shall be done. I am all impatience to hear how this astonishing change was effected. I finish as I began, with the warmest congratulations.

Yours ever, &c.,
CATH. VERNON.

XXIV.

FROM THE SAME TO THE SAME.

Churchhill.

Little did I imagine, my dear mother, when I sent off my last letter, that the delightful perturbation of spirits I was then in would undergo so speedy, so melancholy a reverse. I never can sufficiently regret that I wrote to you at all. Yet who could have foreseen what has happened? My dear mother, every hope which made me so happy only two hours ago has vanished. The quarrel between Lady Susan and Reginald is made up, and we are all as we were before. One point only is gained. Sir James Martin is dismissed. What are we now to look forward to? I am indeed disappointed; Reginald was all but gone, his horse was ordered and all but brought to the door; who would not have felt safe? For half an hour I was in momentary expectation of his departure. After I had sent off my letter to you, I went to Mr. Vernon, and sat with him in his room talking over the whole matter, and then determined to look for Frederica, whom I had not seen since breakfast. I met her on the stairs, and saw that she was crying. 'My dear aunt,' said she, 'he is going—Mr. De Courcy is going, and it is all my fault. I am afraid you will be very angry with me, but indeed I had no idea it would end so.' 'My love,' I replied, 'do not think it necessary to apologise to me on that account. I shall feel myself under an obligation to anyone who is the means of sending my brother home, because, recollecting myself, 'I know my father wants very much to see him. But what is it you have done to occasion all this?' She blushed deeply as she answered: 'I was so unhappy about Sir James that I could not help—I have done something very wrong, I know; but you have not an idea of the misery I have been in: and mamma had ordered me never to speak to you or my uncle about it, and—' 'You therefore spoke to my brother to engage his interference,' said I, to save her the explanation. 'No, but I wrote to him—I did indeed, I got up this morning before it was light, and was two hours about it; and when my letter was done I thought I never should have courage to give it. After breakfast, however, as I was going to my room, I met him in the passage, and then, as I knew that everything must depend on that moment, I forced myself to give it. He was so good as to take it immediately. I dared not look at him, and ran away directly. I was in such a fright I could hardly breathe. My dear aunt, you do not know how miserable I have been.' 'Frederica,' said I, 'you ought to have told me all your distresses. You would have found in me a friend always ready to assist you. Do you think that your uncle or I should not have espoused your cause as warmly as my brother?' 'Indeed, I did not doubt your kindness,' said she, colouring again, 'but I thought Mr. De Courcy could do anything with my mother; but I was mistaken: they have had a dreadful quarrel about it, and he is going away. Mamma will never forgive me, and I shall be worse off than ever.' 'No, you shall not,' I replied; 'in such a point as this your mother's prohibition ought not to have prevented your speaking to me on the subject. She has no right to make you unhappy, and she shall *not* do it. Your applying, however, to Reginald can be productive only of good to all parties. I believe it is best as it is. Depend upon it that you shall not be made unhappy any longer.' At that moment how great was my astonishment at seeing Reginald come out of Lady Susan's dressing-room. My heart misgave me instantly. His confusion at seeing me was very evident. Frederica immediately disappeared. 'Are you going?' I said; 'you will find Mr. Vernon in his own room.' 'No, Catherine,' he replied, 'I am not going. Will you let me speak to you a moment?' We went into my room. 'I find,' he continued, his confusion increasing as he spoke, 'that I have been acting with my usual foolish impetuosity. I have entirely misunderstood Lady Susan, and was on the point of leaving the house under a false impression of her conduct. There has been some very great mistake; we have been all mistaken, I fancy. Frederica does not know her mother. Lady Susan means nothing but her good, but she will not make a friend of her. Lady Susan does not always know, therefore, what will make her daughter happy. Besides, I could have no right to interfere. Miss Vernon was mistaken in applying to me. In short, Catherine, everything has gone wrong, but it is now all happily settled. Lady Susan, I believe, wishes to speak to you about it, if you are at leisure.' 'Certainly,' I replied, deeply sighing at the recital of so lame a story. I made no comments, however, for words would have been vain.

Reginald was glad to get away, and I went to Lady Susan, curious, indeed, to hear her account of it. 'Did I not tell you,' said she with a smile, 'that your brother would not leave us after all?' 'You did, indeed,' replied I very gravely; 'but I flattered myself you would be mistaken.' 'I should not have hazarded such an opinion,' returned she, 'if it had not at that moment occurred to me that his resolution of going might be occasioned by a conversation in which we had been this morning engaged, and which had ended very much to his dissatisfaction, from our not rightly understanding each other's meaning. This idea struck me at the moment, and I instantly determined that an accidental dispute, in which I might probably be as much to blame as himself, should not deprive you of your brother. If you remember, I left the room almost immediately. I was resolved to lose no time in clearing up those mistakes as far as I could. The case was this—Frederica had set herself violently against marrying Sir James.' 'And can your ladyship wonder that she should?' cried I with some warmth; 'Frederica has an excellent understanding, and Sir James has none!' 'I am at least very far from regretting it, my dear sister,' said she; 'on the contrary, I am grateful for so favourable a sign of my daughter's sense. Sir James is certainly below par (his boyish manners make him appear worse); and had Frederica possessed the penetration and the abilities which I could have wished in my daughter, or had I even known her to possess as much as she does, I should not have been anxious for the match.' 'It is odd that you should alone be ignorant of your daughter's sense!' 'Frederica never does justice to herself; her manners are shy and childish, and besides she is afraid of me. During her poor father's life she was a spoilt child; the severity which it has since been necessary for me to show has alienated her affection; neither has she any of that brilliancy of intellect, that genius or vigour of mind which will force itself forward.' 'Say rather that she has been unfortunate in her education!' 'Heaven knows, my dearest Mrs. Vernon, how fully I am aware of that; but I would wish to forget every circumstance that might throw blame on the memory of one whose name is sacred with me.' Here she pretended to cry; I was out of patience with her. 'But what,' said I, 'was your ladyship going to tell me about your disagreement with my brother?' 'It originated in an action of my daughter's, which equally marks her want of judgment and the unfortunate dread of me I have been mentioning—she wrote to Mr. De Courcy.' 'I know she did; you had forbidden her speaking to Mr. Vernon or to me on the cause of her distress; what could she do, therefore, but apply to my brother?' 'Good God!' she exclaimed, 'what an opinion you must have of me! Can you possibly suppose that I was aware of her unhappiness? that it was my object to make my own child miserable, and that I had forbidden her speaking to you on the subject from a fear of your interrupting the diabolical scheme? Do you think me destitute of every honest, every natural feeling? Am I capable of consigning *her* to everlasting misery whose welfare it is my first earthly duty to promote? The idea is horrible!' 'What, then, was your intention when you insisted on her silence?' 'Of what use, my dear sister, could be any application to you, however the affair might stand? Why should I subject you to entreaties which I refused to attend to myself? Neither for your sake nor for hers, nor for my own, could such a thing be desirable. When my own resolution was taken I could not wish for the interference, however friendly, of another person. I was mistaken, it is true, but I believed myself right.' 'But what was this mistake to which your ladyship so often alludes? from whence arose so astonishing a misconception of your daughter's feelings? Did you not know that she disliked Sir James?' 'I knew that he was not absolutely the man she would have chosen, but I was persuaded that her objections to him did not arise from any perception of his deficiency. You must not question me, however, my dear sister, too minutely on this point,' continued she, taking me affectionately by the hand; 'I honestly own that there is something to conceal. Frederica makes me very unhappy! Her applying to Mr. De Courcy hurt me particularly.' 'What is it you mean to infer,' said I, 'by this appearance of mystery? If you think your daughter at all attached to Reginald, her objecting to Sir James could not less deserve to be attended to than if the cause of her objecting had been a consciousness of his folly; and why should your ladyship, at any rate, quarrel with my brother for an interference which, you must know, it is not in his nature to refuse when urged in such a manner?'

'His disposition, you know, is warm, and he came to expostulate with me; his compassion all alive for this ill-used girl, this heroine in distress! We misunderstood each other: he believed me more to blame than I really was; I considered his interference less excusable than I now find it. I have a real regard for him, and was beyond expression mortified to find it, as I thought, so ill bestowed. We were both warm, and of course both to blame. His resolution of leaving Churchhill is consistent with his general eagerness. When I understood his intention, however, and at the same time began to think that we had been perhaps equally mistaken in each other's meaning, I resolved to have an explanation before it was too late. For any member of your family I must always feel a degree of affection, and I own it would have sensibly hurt me if my acquaintance with Mr. De Courcy had ended so gloomily. I have now only to say further, that as I am convinced of Frederica's having a reasonable dislike to Sir James, I shall instantly inform him that he must give up all hope of her. I reproach myself for having even, though innocently, made her unhappy on that score. She shall have all the retribution in my power to make; if she value her own happiness as much as I do, if she judge wisely, and command herself as she ought, she may now be easy. Excuse me, my dearest sister, for thus trespassing on your time, but I owe it to my own character; and after this explanation I trust I am in no danger of sinking in your opinion.' I could have said, 'Not much, indeed!' but I left her almost in silence. It was the greatest stretch of forbearance I could practise. I could not have stopped myself had I begun. Her assurance! her deceit! but I will not allow myself to dwell on them; they will strike you sufficiently. My heart sickens within me. As soon as I was tolerably composed I returned to the parlour. Sir James's carriage was at the door, and he, merry as usual, soon afterwards took his leave. How easily does her ladyship encourage or dismiss a lover! In spite of this release, Frederica still looks unhappy: still fearful, perhaps, of her mother's anger; and though dreading my brother's departure, jealous, it may be, of his staying. I see how closely she observes him and Lady Susan, poor girl! I have now no hope for her. There is not a chance of her affection being returned. He thinks very differently of her from what he used to do; he does her some justice, but his reconciliation with her mother precludes every dearer hope. Prepare, my dear mother, for the worst! The probability of their marrying is surely heightened! He is more securely hers than ever. When that wretched event takes place, Frederica must belong wholly to us. I am thankful that my last letter will precede this by so little, as every moment that you can be saved from feeling a joy which leads only to disappointment is of consequence.

Yours ever, &c.
CATHERINE VERNON.

XXV.

LADY SUSAN TO MRS. JOHNSON.

Churchhill.

I call on you, dear Alicia, for congratulations: I am my ownself, gay and triumphant! When I wrote to you the other day I was, in truth, in high irritation, and with ample cause. Nay, I know not whether I ought to be quite tranquil now, for I have had more trouble in restoring peace than I ever intended to submit to—a spirit, too, resulting from a fancied sense of superior integrity, which is peculiarly insolent! I shall not easily forgive him, I assure you. He was actually on the point of leaving Churchhill! I had scarcely concluded my last, when Wilson brought me word of it. I found, therefore, that something must be done; for I did not choose to leave my character at the mercy of a man whose passions are so violent and so revengeful. It would have been trifling with my reputation to allow of his departing with such an impression in my disfavour; in this light, condescension was necessary. I sent Wilson to say that I desired to speak with him before he went; he came immediately. The angry emotions which had marked every feature when we last parted were partially subdued. He seemed astonished at the summons, and looked as if half wishing and half fearing to be softened by what I might say. If my countenance expressed what I aimed at, it was composed and dignified; and yet, with a degree of pensiveness which might convince him that I was not quite happy. 'I beg your pardon, sir, for the liberty I have taken in sending for you,' said I: 'but as I have just learnt your intention of leaving this place to-day, I feel it my duty to entreat that you will not on my account shorten your visit here even an hour. I am perfectly aware that after what has passed between us it would ill suit the feelings of either to remain longer in the same house: so very great, so total a change from the intimacy of friendship must render any future intercourse the severest punishment; and your resolution of quitting Churchhill is undoubtedly in unison with our situation, and with those lively feelings which I know you to possess. But, at the same time, it is not for me to suffer such a sacrifice as it must be to leave relations to whom you are so much attached, and are so dear. My remaining here cannot give that pleasure to Mr. and Mrs. Vernon which your society must; and my visit has already perhaps been too long. My removal, therefore, which must, at any rate, take place soon, may, with perfect convenience, be hastened; and I make it my particular request that I may not in any way be instrumental in separating a family so affectionately attached to each other. Where I go is of no consequence to anyone; of very little to myself; but you are of importance to all your connections.' Here I concluded, and I hope you will be satisfied with my speech. Its effect on Reginald justifies some portion of vanity, for it was no less favourable than instantaneous. Oh, how delightful it was to watch the variations of his countenance while I spoke! to see the struggle between returning tenderness and the remains of displeasure. There is something agreeable in feelings so easily worked on; not that I envy him their possession, nor would, for the world, have such myself; but they are very convenient when one wishes to influence the passions of another. And yet this Reginald, whom a very few words from me softened at once into the utmost submission, and rendered more tractable, more attached, more devoted than ever, would have left me in the first angry swelling of his proud heart without deigning to seek an explanation. Humbled as he now is, I cannot forgive him such an instance of pride, and am doubtful whether I ought not to punish him by dismissing him at once after this reconciliation, or by marrying and teazing him for ever. But these measures are each too violent to be adopted without some deliberation; at present my thoughts are fluctuating between various schemes. I have many things to compass: I must punish Frederica, and pretty severely too, for her application to Reginald; I must punish him for receiving it so favourably, and for the rest of his conduct. I must torment my sister-in-law for the insolent triumph of her look and manner since Sir James has been dismissed; for, in reconciling Reginald to me, I was not able to save that ill-fated young man; and I must make myself amends for the humiliation to which I have stooped within these few days. To effect all this I have various plans. I have also an idea of being soon in town; and whatever may be my determination as to the rest, I shall probably put *that* project in execution; for London will be always the fairest field of action, however my views may be directed; and at any rate I shall there be rewarded by your society, and a little dissipation, for a ten weeks' penance at Churchhill. I believe I owe it to my character to complete the match between my daughter and Sir James after having so long intended it. Let me know your opinion on this point. Flexibility of mind, a disposition easily biassed by others, is an attribute which you know I am not very desirous of obtaining; nor has Frederica any claim to the indulgence of her notions at the expense of her mother's inclinations. Her idle love for Reginald, too! It is surely my duty to discourage such romantic nonsense. All things considered, therefore, it seems incumbent on me to take her to town and marry her immediately to Sir James. When my own will is effected contrary to his, I shall have some credit in being on good terms with Reginald, which at present, in fact, I have not; for though he is still in my power, I have given up the very article by which our quarrel was produced, and at best the honour of victory is doubtful. Send me your opinion on all these matters, my dear Alicia, and let me know whether you can get lodgings to suit me within a short distance of you.

Your most attached
S. VERNON.

XXVI.

MRS. JOHNSON TO LADY SUSAN.

Edward Street.

I am gratified by your reference, and this is my advice: that you come to town yourself, without loss of time, but that you leave Frederica behind. It would surely be much more to the purpose to get yourself well established by marrying Mr. De Courcy, than to irritate him and the rest of his family by making her marry Sir James. You should think more of yourself and less of your daughter. She is not of a disposition to do you credit in the world, and seems precisely in her proper place at Churchhill, with the Vernons. But you are fitted for society, and it is shameful to have you exiled from it. Leave Frederica, therefore, to punish herself for the plague she has given you, by indulging that romantic tender-heartedness which will always ensure her misery enough, and come to London as soon as you can. I have another reason for urging this: Mainwaring came to town last week, and has contrived, in spite of Mr. Johnson, to make opportunities of seeing me. He is absolutely miserable about you, and jealous to such a degree of De Courcy that it would be highly unadvisable for them to meet at present. And yet, if you do not allow him to see you here, I cannot answer for his not committing some great imprudence—such as going to Churchhill, for instance, which would be dreadful! Besides, if you take my advice, and resolve to marry De Courcy, it will be indispensably necessary to you to get Mainwaring out of the way; and you only can have influence enough to send him back to his wife. I have still another motive for your coming: Mr. Johnson leaves London next Tuesday; he is going for his health to Bath, where, if the waters are favourable to his constitution and my wishes, he will be laid up with the gout many weeks. During his absence we shall be able to chuse our own society, and to have true enjoyment. I would ask you to Edward Street, but that once he forced from me a kind of promise never to invite you to my house; nothing but my being in the utmost distress for money should have extorted it from me. I can get you, however, a nice drawing-room apartment in Upper Seymour Street, and we may be always together there or here; for I consider my promise to Mr. Johnson as comprehending only (at least in his absence) your not sleeping in the house. Poor Mainwaring gives me such histories of his wife's jealousy. Silly woman to expect constancy from so charming a man! but she always was silly—intolerably so in marrying him at all, she the heiress of a large fortune and he without a shilling: one title, I know, she might have had, besides baronets. Her folly in forming the connection was so great that, though Mr. Johnson was her guardian, and I do not in general share *his* feelings, I never can forgive her.

Adieu. Yours ever,
ALICIA.

XXVII.

MRS. VERNON TO LADY DE COURCY.

Churchhill.

This letter, my dear mother, will be brought you by Reginald. His long visit is about to be concluded at last, but I fear the separation takes place too late to do us any good. She is going to London to see her particular friend, Mrs. Johnson. It was at first her intention that Frederica should accompany her, for the benefit of masters, but we overruled her there. Frederica was wretched in the idea of going, and I could not bear to have her at the mercy of her mother; not all the masters in London could compensate for the ruin of her comfort. I should have feared, too, for her health, and for everything but her principles—there I believe she is not to be injured by her mother, or her mother's friends; but with those friends she must have mixed (a very bad set, I doubt not), or have been left in total solitude, and I can hardly tell which would have been worse for her. If she is with her mother, moreover, she must, alas! in all probability be with Reginald, and that would be the greatest evil of all. Here we shall in time be in peace, and our regular employments, our books and conversations, with exercise, the children, and every domestic pleasure in my power to procure her, will, I trust, gradually overcome this youthful attachment. I should not have a doubt of it were she slighted for any other woman in the world than her own mother. How long Lady Susan will be in town, or whether she returns here again, I know not. I could not be cordial in my invitation, but if she chuses to come no want of cordiality on my part will keep her away. I could not help asking Reginald if he intended being in London this winter, as soon as I found her ladyship's steps would be bent thither; and though he professed himself quite undetermined, there was something in his look and voice as he spoke which contradicted his words. I have done with lamentation; I look upon the event as so far decided that I resign myself to it in despair. If he leaves you soon for London everything will be concluded.

Your affectionate, &c.,
C. VERNON.

XXVIII.

MRS. JOHNSON TO LADY SUSAN.

Edward Street.

My dearest Friend,—I write in the greatest distress; the most unfortunate event has just taken place. Mr. Johnson has hit on the most effectual manner of plaguing us all. He had heard, I imagine, by some means or other, that you were soon to be in London, and immediately contrived to have such an attack of the gout as must at least delay his journey to Bath, if not wholly prevent it. I am persuaded the gout is brought on or kept off at pleasure; it was the same when I wanted to join the Hamiltons to the Lakes; and three years ago, when *I* had a fancy for Bath, nothing could induce him to have a gouty symptom.

I am pleased to find that my letter had so much effect on you, and that De Courcy is certainly your own. Let me hear from you as soon as you arrive, and in particular tell me what you mean to do with Mainwaring. It is impossible to say when I shall be able to come to you; my confinement must be great. It is such an abominable trick to be ill here instead of at Bath that I can scarcely command myself at all. At Bath his old aunts would have nursed him, but here it all falls upon me; and he bears pain with such patience that I have not the common excuse for losing my temper.

Yours ever,
ALICIA.

XXIX.

LADY SUSAN VERNON TO MRS. JOHNSON.

Upper Seymour Street.

My dear Alicia,—There needed not this last fit of the gout to make me detest Mr. Johnson, but now the extent of my aversion is not to be estimated. To have you confined as nurse in his apartment! My dear Alicia, of what a mistake were you guilty in marrying a man of his age! just old enough to be formal, ungovernable, and to have the gout; too old to be agreeable, too young to die. I arrived last night about five, had scarcely swallowed my dinner when Mainwaring made his appearance. I will not dissemble what real pleasure his sight afforded me, nor how strongly I felt the contrast between his person and manners and those of Reginald, to the infinite disadvantage of the latter. For an hour or two I was even staggered in my resolution of marrying him, and though this was too idle and nonsensical an idea to remain long on my mind, I do not feel very eager for the conclusion of my marriage, nor look forward with much impatience to the time when Reginald, according to our agreement, is to be in town. I shall probably put off his arrival under some pretence or other. He must not come till Mainwaring is gone. I am still doubtful at times as to marrying; if the old man would die I might not hesitate, but a state of dependance on the caprice of Sir Reginald will not suit the freedom of my spirit; and if I resolve to wait for that event, I shall have excuse enough at present in having been scarcely ten months a widow. I have not given Mainwaring any hint of my intention, or allowed him to consider my acquaintance with Reginald as more than the commonest flirtation, and he is tolerably appeased. Adieu, till we meet; I am enchanted with my lodgings.

Yours ever,
S. VERNON.

XXX.

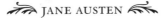

LADY SUSAN VERNON TO MR. DE COURCY.

Upper Seymour Street.

I have received your letter, and though I do not attempt to conceal that I am gratified by your impatience for the hour of meeting, I yet feel myself under the necessity of delaying that hour beyond the time originally fixed. Do not think me unkind for such an exercise of my power, nor accuse me of instability without first hearing my reasons. In the course of my journey from Churchhill I had ample leisure for reflection on the present state of our affairs, and every review has served to convince me that they require a delicacy and cautiousness of conduct to which we have hitherto been too little attentive. We have been hurried on by our feelings to a degree of precipitation which ill accords with the claims of our friends or the opinion of the world. We have been unguarded in forming this hasty engagement, but we must not complete the imprudence by ratifying it while there is so much reason to fear the connection would be opposed by those friends on whom you depend. It is not for us to blame any expectations on your father's side of your marrying to advantage; where possessions are so extensive as those of your family, the wish of increasing them, if not strictly reasonable, is too common to excite surprise or resentment. He has a right to require a woman of fortune in his daughter-in-law, and I am sometimes quarrelling with myself for suffering you to form a connection so imprudent; but the influence of reason is often acknowledged too late by those who feel like me. I have now been but a few months a widow, and, however little indebted to my husband's memory for any happiness derived from him during a union of some years, I cannot forget that the indelicacy of so early a second marriage must subject me to the censure of the world, and incur, what would be still more insupportable, the displeasure of Mr. Vernon. I might perhaps harden myself in time against the injustice of general reproach, but the loss of *his* valued esteem I am, as you well know, ill-fitted to endure; and when to this may be added the consciousness of having injured you with your family, how am I to support myself? With feelings so poignant as mine, the conviction of having divided the son from his parents would make me, even with you, the most miserable of beings. It will surely, therefore, be advisable to delay our union—to delay it till appearances are more promising—till affairs have taken a more favourable turn. To assist us in such a resolution I feel that absence will be necessary. We must not meet. Cruel as this sentence may appear, the necessity of pronouncing it, which can alone reconcile it to myself, will be evident to you when you have considered our situation in the light in which I have found myself imperiously obliged to place it. You may be—you must be—well assured that nothing but the strongest conviction of duty could induce me to wound my own feelings by urging a lengthened separation, and of insensibility to yours you will hardly suspect me. Again, therefore, I say that we ought not, we must not, yet meet. By a removal for some months from each other we shall tranquillise the sisterly fears of Mrs. Vernon, who, accustomed herself to the enjoyment of riches, considers fortune as necessary everywhere, and whose sensibilities are not of a nature to comprehend ours. Let me hear from you soon—very soon. Tell me that you submit to my arguments, and do not reproach me for using such. I cannot bear reproaches: my spirits are not so high as to need being repressed. I must endeavour to seek amusement, and fortunately many of my friends are in town; amongst them the Mainwarings; you know how sincerely I regard both husband and wife.

I am, very faithfully yours,
S. VERNON.

XXXI.

LADY SUSAN TO MRS. JOHNSON.

Upper Seymour Street.

My dear Friend,—That tormenting creature, Reginald, is here. My letter, which was intended to keep him longer in the country, has hastened him to town. Much as I wish him away, however, I cannot help being pleased with such a proof of attachment. He is devoted to me, heart and soul. He will carry this note himself, which is to serve as an introduction to you, with whom he longs to be acquainted. Allow him to spend the evening with you, that I may be in no danger of his returning here. I have told him that I am not quite well, and must be alone; and should he call again there might be confusion, for it is impossible to be sure of servants. Keep him, therefore, I entreat you, in Edward Street. You will not find him a heavy companion, and I allow you to flirt with him as much as you like. At the same time, do not forget my real interest; say all that you can to convince him that I shall be quite wretched if he remains here; you know my reasons—propriety, and so forth. I would urge them more myself, but that I am impatient to be rid of him, as Mainwaring comes within half an hour. Adieu!

S. VERNON.

XXXII.

MRS. JOHNSON TO LADY SUSAN.

Edward Street.

My dear Creature,—I am in agonies, and know not what to do. Mr. De Courcy arrived just when he should not. Mrs. Mainwaring had that instant entered the house, and forced herself into her guardian's presence, though I did not know a syllable of it till afterwards, for I was out when both she and Reginald came, or I should have sent him away at all events; but *she* was shut up with Mr. Johnson, while *he* waited in the drawing-room for me. She arrived yesterday in pursuit of her husband, but perhaps you know this already from himself. She came to this house to entreat my husband's interference, and before I could be aware of it, everything that you could wish to be concealed was known to him, and unluckily she had wormed out of Mainwaring's servant that he had visited you every day since your being in town, and had just watched him to your door herself! What could I do? Facts are such horrid things! All is by this time known to De Courcy, who is now alone with Mr. Johnson. Do not accuse me; indeed, it was impossible to prevent it. Mr. Johnson has for some time suspected De Courcy of intending to marry you, and would speak with him alone as soon as he knew him to be in the house. That detestable Mrs. Mainwaring, who, for your comfort, has fretted herself thinner and uglier than ever, is still here, and they have been all closeted together. What can be done? At any rate, I hope he will plague his wife more than ever. With anxious wishes,

Yours faithfully,
ALICIA.

XXXIII.

LADY SUSAN TO MRS. JOHNSON.

Upper Seymour Street.

This eclaircissement is rather provoking. How unlucky that you should have been from home! I thought myself sure of you at seven! I am undismayed however. Do not torment yourself with fears on my account; depend on it, I can make my story good with Reginald. Mainwaring is just gone; he brought me the news of his wife's arrival. Silly woman, what does she expect by such manœuvres? Yet I wish she had stayed quietly at Langford. Reginald will be a little enraged at first, but by tomorrow's dinner, everything will be well again.

Adieu!
S. V.

XXXIV.

MR. DE COURCY TO LADY SUSAN.

—Hotel.

I write only to bid you farewell, the spell is removed; I see you as you are. Since we parted yesterday, I have received from indisputable authority such a history of you as must bring the most mortifying conviction of the imposition I have been under, and the absolute necessity of an immediate and eternal separation from you. You cannot doubt to what I allude. Langford! Langford! that word will be sufficient. I received my information in Mr. Johnson's house, from Mrs. Mainwaring herself. You know how I have loved you; you can intimately judge of my present feelings, but I am not so weak as to find indulgence in describing them to a woman who will glory in having excited their anguish, but whose affection they have never been able to gain.

R. DE COURCY.

XXXV.

LADY SUSAN TO MR. DE COURCY.

Upper Seymour Street.

I will not attempt to describe my astonishment in reading the note this moment received from you. I am bewildered in my endeavours to form some rational conjecture of what Mrs. Mainwaring can have told you to occasion so extraordinary a change in your sentiments. Have I not explained everything to you with respect to myself which could bear a doubtful meaning, and which the ill-nature of the world had interpreted to my discredit? What can you *now* have heard to stagger your esteem for me? Have I ever had a concealment from you? Reginald, you agitate me beyond expression, I cannot suppose that the old story of Mrs. Mainwaring's jealousy can be revived again, or at least be *listened* to again. Come to me immediately, and explain what is at present absolutely incomprehensible. Believe me the single word of Langford is not of such potent intelligence as to supersede the necessity of more. If we *are* to part, it will at least be handsome to take your personal leave—but I have little heart to jest; in truth, I am serious enough; for to be sunk, though but for an hour, in your esteem is a humiliation to which I know not how to submit. I shall count every minute till your arrival.

S. V.

XXXVI.

MR. DE COURCY TO LADY SUSAN.

—Hotel.

Why would you write to me? Why do you require particulars? But, since it must be so, I am obliged to declare that all the accounts of your misconduct during the life, and since the death of Mr. Vernon, which had reached me, in common with the world in general, and gained my entire belief before I saw you, but which you, by the exertion of your perverted abilities, had made me resolved to disallow, have been unanswerably proved to me; nay more, I am assured that a connection, of which I had never before entertained a thought, has for some time existed, and still continues to exist, between you and the man whose family you robbed of its peace in return for the hospitality with which you were received into it; that you have corresponded with him ever since your leaving Langford; not with his wife, but with him, and that he now visits you every day. Can you, dare you deny it? and all this at the time when I was an encouraged, an accepted lover! From what have I not escaped! I have only to be grateful. Far from me be all complaint, every sigh of regret. My own folly had endangered me, my preservation I owe to the kindness, the integrity of another; but the unfortunate Mrs. Mainwaring, whose agonies while she related the past seemed to threaten her reason, how is *she* to be consoled! After such a discovery as this, you will scarcely affect further wonder at my meaning in bidding you adieu. My understanding is at length restored, and teaches no less to abhor the artifices which had subdued me than to despise myself for the weakness on which their strength was founded.

R. DE COURCY.

XXXVII.

LADY SUSAN TO MR. DE COURCY.

Upper Seymour Street.

I am satisfied, and will trouble you no more when these few lines are dismissed. The engagement which you were eager to form a fortnight ago is no longer compatible with your views, and I rejoice to find that the prudent advice of your parents has not been given in vain. Your restoration to peace will, I doubt not, speedily follow this act of filial obedience, and I flatter myself with the hope of surviving my share in this disappointment.

S. V.

XXXVIII.

MRS. JOHNSON TO LADY SUSAN VERNON.

Edward Street.

I am grieved, though I cannot be astonished at your rupture with Mr. De Courcy; he has just informed Mr. Johnson of it by letter. He leaves London, he says, to-day. Be assured that I partake in all your feelings, and do not be angry if I say that our intercourse, even by letter, must soon be given up. It makes me miserable; but

Mr.Johnson vows that if I persist in the connection, he will settle in the country for the rest of his life, and you know it is impossible to submit to such an extremity while any other alternative remains. You have heard of course that the Mainwarings are to part, and I am afraid Mrs. M. will come home to us again; but she is still so fond of her husband, and frets so much about him, that perhaps she may not live long. Miss Mainwaring is just come to town to be with her aunt, and they say that she declares she will have Sir James Martin before she leaves London again. If I were you, I would certainly get him myself. I had almost forgot to give you my opinion of Mr. De Courcy; I am really delighted with him; he is full as handsome, I think, as Mainwaring, and with such an open, good-humoured countenance, that one cannot help loving him at first sight. Mr. Johnson and he are the greatest friends in the world. Adieu, my dearest Susan, I wish matters did not go so perversely. That unlucky visit to Langford! but I dare say you did all for the best, and there is no defying destiny.

Your sincerely attached,
ALICIA.

XXXIX.

LADY SUSAN TO MRS. JOHNSON.

Upper Seymour Street.

My dear Alicia,—I yield to the necessity which parts us. Under circumstances you could not act otherwise. Our friendship cannot be impaired by it, and in happier times, when your situation is as independent as mine, it will unite us again in the same intimacy as ever. For this I shall impatiently wait, and meanwhile can safely assure you that I never was more at ease, or better satisfied with myself and everything about me than at the present hour. Your husband I abhor, Reginald I despise, and I am secure of never seeing either again. Have I not reason to rejoice? Mainwaring is more devoted to me than ever; and were we at liberty, I doubt if I could resist even matrimony offered by *him*. This event, if his wife live with you, it may be in your power to hasten. The violence of her feelings, which must wear her out, may be easily kept in irritation. I rely on your friendship for this. I am now satisfied that I never could have brought myself to marry Reginald, and am equally determined that Frederica never *shall*. To-morrow, I shall fetch her from Churchhill, and let Maria Mainwaring tremble for the consequence. Frederica shall be Sir James's wife before she quits my house, and *she* may whimper, and the Vernons may storm, I regard them not. I am tired of submitting my will to the caprices of others; of resigning my own judgment in deference to those to whom I owe no duty, and for whom I feel no respect; I have given up too much, have been too easily worked on, but Frederica shall now feel the difference. Adieu, dearest of friends; may the next gouty attack be more favourable! and may you always regard me as unalterably yours,

S. VERNON.

XL.

LADY DE COURCY TO MRS. VERNON.

My dear Catherine,—I have charming news for you, and if I had not sent off my letter this morning you might have been spared the vexation of knowing of Reginald's being gone to London, for he is returned. Reginald is returned, not to ask our consent to his marrying Lady Susan, but to tell us they are parted for ever. He has been only an hour in the house, and I have not been able to learn particulars, for he is so very low that I have not the heart to ask questions, but I hope we shall soon know all. This is the most joyful hour he has ever given us since the day of his birth. Nothing is wanting but to have you here, and it is our particular wish and entreaty that you would come to us as soon as you can. You have owed us a visit many long weeks; I hope nothing will make it inconvenient to Mr. Vernon; and pray bring all my grandchildren; and your dear niece is included, of course; I long to see her. It has been a sad, heavy winter hitherto, without Reginald, and seeing nobody from Churchhill. I never found the season so dreary before; but this happy meeting will make us young again. Frederica runs much in my thoughts, and when Reginald has recovered his usual good spirits (as I trust he soon will) we will try to rob him of his heart once more, and I am full of hopes of seeing their hands joined at no great distance.

Your affectionate mother,
C. DE COURCY.

XLI.

MRS. VERNON TO LADY DE COURCY.

Churchhill.

My dear Mother,—Your letter has surprised me beyond measure! Can it be true that they are really separated—and for ever? I should be overjoyed if I dared depend on it, but after all that I have seen how can one be secure? And Reginald really with you! My surprise is the greater because on Wednesday, the very day of his coming to Parklands, we had a most unexpected and unwelcome visit from Lady Susan, looking all cheerfulness and good humour, and seeming more as if she were to marry him when she got to London than as if parted from him for ever. She stayed nearly two hours, was as affectionate and agreeable as ever, and not a syllable, not a hint was dropped, of any disagreement or coolness between them. I asked her whether she had seen my brother since his arrival in town; not, as you may suppose, with any doubt of the fact, but merely to see how she looked. She immediately answered, without any embarrassment, that he had been kind enough to call on her on Monday; but she believed he had already returned home, which I was very far from crediting. Your kind invitation is accepted by us with pleasure, and on Thursday next we and our little ones will be with you. Pray heaven, Reginald may not be in town again by that time! I wish we could bring dear Frederica too, but I am sorry to say that her mother's errand hither was to fetch her away; and, miserable as it made the poor girl, it was impossible to detain her. I was thoroughly unwilling to let her go, and so was her uncle; and all that could be urged we did urge; but Lady Susan declared that as she was now about to fix herself in London for several months, she could not be easy if her daughter were not with her for masters, &c. Her manner, to be sure, was very kind and proper, and Mr. Vernon believes that Frederica will now be treated with affection. I wish I could think so too. The poor girl's heart was almost broke at taking leave of us. I charged her to write to me very often, and to remember that if she were in any distress we should be always her friends. I took care to see her alone, that I might say all this, and I hope made her a little

> MAINWARING IS MORE DEVOTED TO ME THAN EVER; AND WERE WE AT LIBERTY, I DOUBT IF I COULD RESIST EVEN MATRIMONY OFFERED BY HIM. THIS EVENT, IF HIS WIFE LIVE WITH YOU, IT MAY BE IN YOUR POWER TO HASTEN.

more comfortable; but I shall not be easy till I can go to town and judge of her situation myself. I wish there were a better prospect than now appears of the match which the conclusion of your letter declares your expectations of. At present, it is not very likely.

Yours ever, &c.,
C. VERNON.

CONCLUSION.

This correspondence, by a meeting between some of the parties, and a separation between the others, could not, to the great detriment of the Post-Office revenue, be continued any longer. Very little assistance to the State could be derived from the epistolary intercourse of Mrs. Vernon and her niece; for the former soon perceived, by the style of Frederica's letters, that they were written under her mother's inspection! and therefore, deferring all particular enquiry till she could make it personally in London, ceased writing minutely or often. Having learnt enough, in the meanwhile, from her open-hearted brother, of what had passed between him and Lady Susan to sink the latter lower than ever in her opinion, she was proportionably more anxious to get Frederica removed from such a mother, and placed under her own care; and, though with little hope of success, was resolved to leave nothing unattempted that might offer a chance of obtaining her sister-in-law's consent to it. Her anxiety on the subject made her press for an early visit to London; and Mr. Vernon, who, as it must already have appeared, lived only to do whatever he was desired, soon found some accommodating business to call him thither. With a heart full of the matter, Mrs. Vernon waited on Lady Susan shortly after her arrival in town, and was met with such an easy and cheerful affection, as made her almost turn from her with horror. No remembrance of Reginald, no consciousness of guilt, gave one look of embarrassment; she was in excellent spirits, and seemed eager to show at once by every possible attention to her brother and sister her sense of their kindness, and her pleasure in their society. Frederica was no more altered than Lady Susan; the same restrained manners, the same timid look in the presence of her mother as heretofore, assured her aunt of her situation being uncomfortable, and confirmed her in the plan of altering it. No unkindness, however, on the part of Lady Susan appeared. Persecution on the subject of Sir James was entirely at an end; his name merely mentioned to say that he was not in London; and indeed, in all her conversation, she was solicitous only for the welfare and improvement of her daughter, acknowledging, in terms of grateful delight, that Frederica was now growing every day more and more what a parent could desire. Mrs. Vernon, surprised and incredulous, knew not what to suspect, and, without any change in her own views, only feared greater difficulty in accomplishing them. The first hope of anything better was derived from Lady Susan's asking her whether she thought Frederica looked quite as well as she had done at Churchhill, as she must confess herself to have sometimes an anxious doubt of London's perfectly agreeing with her. Mrs. Vernon, encouraging the doubt, directly proposed her niece's returning with them into the country. Lady Susan was unable to express her sense of such kindness, yet knew not, from a variety of reasons, how to part with her daughter; and as, though her own plans were not yet wholly fixed, she trusted it would ere long be in her power to take Frederica into the country herself, concluded by declining entirely to profit by such unexampled attention. Mrs. Vernon persevered, however, in the offer of it, and though Lady Susan continued to resist, her resistance in the course of a few days seemed somewhat less formidable. The lucky alarm of an influenza decided what might not have been decided quite so soon. Lady Susan's maternal fears were then too much awakened for her to think of anything but Frederica's removal from the risk of infection; above all disorders in the world she most dreaded the influenza for her daughter's constitution!

Frederica returned to Churchhill with her uncle and aunt; and three weeks afterwards, Lady Susan announced her being married to Sir James Martin. Mrs. Vernon was then convinced of what she had only suspected before, that she might have spared herself all the trouble of urging a removal which Lady Susan had doubtless resolved on from the first. Frederica's visit was nominally for six weeks, but her mother, though inviting her to return in one or two affectionate letters, was very ready to oblige the whole party by consenting to a prolongation of her stay, and in the course of two months ceased to write of her absence, and in the course of two more to write to her at all. Frederica was therefore fixed in the family of her uncle and aunt till such time as Reginald De Courcy could be talked, flattered, and finessed into an affection for her which, allowing leisure for the conquest of his attachment to her mother, for his abjuring all future attachments, and detesting the sex, might be reasonably looked for in the course of a twelvemonth. Three months might have done it in general, but Reginald's feelings were no less lasting than lively. Whether Lady Susan was or was not happy in her second choice, I do not see how it can ever be ascertained; for who would take her assurance of it on either side of the question? The world must judge from probabilities; she had nothing against her but her husband, and her conscience. Sir James may seem to have drawn a harder lot than mere folly merited; I leave him, therefore, to all the pity that anybody can give him. For myself, I confess that *I* can pity only Miss Mainwaring; who, coming to town, and putting herself to an expense in clothes which impoverished her for two years, on purpose to secure him, was defrauded of her due by a woman ten years older than herself.

FINIS.

Nikolai Vasilievich Gogol

(1809–1852)

Dramatist, novelist, and the enormously influential founder of nineteenth-century Russian realism, Nikolai Gogol was born March 20, 1809, in the town of Sorochintsy in Poltava Province (now Ukraine, but then a part of the Russian Empire). Gogol's parents were Ukrainian Cossacks and lower-ranking members of the gentry, though some have speculated that they changed their original family name, Ianovskii, to claim noble Cossack ancestry. In 1821, they sent twelve-year-old Nikolai to school at Nezhin, where his first stories appeared, exhibiting in a raw form the writing talent that would someday make him Russia's most famous writer and an inspiration to talents as disparate as Tolstoy and Dostoyevsky.

Gogol moved to Russia's capital, St. Petersburg, when he was nineteen years old in 1828. There, in his first attempt to find an audience for his work, he arranged for the self-publication of his poem "Hanz Küchelgarten." Critics savaged it so badly that Gogol bought and destroyed all copies of the poem. Depressed by the experience, he planned a trip to America, but did not follow through. Instead, he took—perhaps "embezzled" is a better word—money that was intended to pay the outstanding mortgage on the Gogol family farm. With it, he toured Germany. Returning to St. Petersburg, Gogol joined the civil service as low-level bureaucrat and, with the debacle of "Hanz Küchelgarten" behind him, started to write short stories.

His first book, *Evenings on a Farm Near Dikanka* (*Vechera na khutore bliz Dikanki*), a collection of stories based on Ukrainian folklore, was published in 1831. That same year, the now-celebrated young writer became friends with the more established poets Vasily Zhukovsky and more significantly, Aleksandr

Pushkin, who would remain a powerful influence on Gogol until Pushkin's death in 1837. Though Gogol would briefly become an assistant professor of medieval history at St. Petersburg University in 1834, he would live the rest of his life as a writer—one of the most famous and occasionally notorious in the entire Russian Empire.

As if to say farewell to teaching once and for all, Gogol published two story collections in 1835. The first, *Mirgorod,* includes both "Old-World Landowners," a relatively affectionate satire of rural Russian society, and "Taras Bulba," a rousing and bloody heroic tale of the Ukrainian Cossacks. The second, *Arabeski* (sometimes titled *St. Petersburg Tales*), is best remembered for "Diary of a Madman" (*Zapiski Sumassshedshego*), whose eponymous civil-servant hero plunges into megalomania, and ends his days in a lunatic asylum.

A year later, Gogol published his first play, *The Inspector General,* in Pushkin's famous literary journal *Sovremennik* (*The Contemporary*). The play's protagonist, Khlestakov, is an innocuous stranger mistaken by locals in a small town for a government inspector whom they must bribe to hide the town's corruption—a situation he eagerly exploits. First produced on the stage in St. Petersburg, this acidulous satire of greed and corrupt officialdom legendarily evoked the following comment from the tzar: "Gets at everyone, and most of all at me!" Believing discretion the better part of valor, particularly valor in the face of the tzar of all the Russias (the world's leading autocrat), Gogol swiftly decamped for Switzerland, Germany, and Italy, settling for a time in Rome.

While in Rome, Gogol wrote two works with which his name would forever be linked. In the short story "The Overcoat" (*Shinel*), protagonist Akakii Akakievich saves money to buy a sumptuous new overcoat, which is stolen by thieves almost immediately. Akakii Akakievich pleads for help from a general, who so frightens the hero that he dies almost immediately thereafter, returning as a ghost to attack the general and steal his overcoat. But it is the novel *Dead Souls* (*Mertvye Dushi*) that would become Gogol's best-known work and one of the greatest of all Russian novels. Supposedly inspired by Pushkin, *Dead Souls* tells the story of Pavel Ivanovich Chichikov, a charming con-man with a scheme to purchase certain property on the cheap, property that owners will be eager to sell in order to avoid paying taxes, property on which he can borrow sufficient capital to buy an estate. The property in question is, of course, serfs—"souls"—who have died, but whose deaths have not been recorded by the census. A powerful satire of a slaveholding society, and a work of enormous picaresque charm, *Dead Souls* was to be both Gogol's most lasting achievement, and, indirectly, his doom.

While in Rome, Gogol also published *Selected Passages from Correspondence with Friends*, thirty-two pieces extolling the orthodox church and the tzarist autocracy. The *Passages* prompted the far more famous *Letter to Gogol*, a response by critic Vissarion Belinsky, who expressed the betrayal felt by Russian liberals toward a man they felt embodied progressive thought. He also expressed that betrayal so frankly, in fact, that the *Letter* could not be published until 1906. In 1848, beset by former friends anxious about his creative powers (lacking since he began the sequel to *Dead Souls*) and more and more obsessed by religious feeling, Gogol made a pilgrimage to the Holy Land. He returned and fell under the spell of a fanatic orthodox priest, Matvey Konstantinovsky, who forced Gogol to destroy—on February 24, 1852—the by-now complete second part of *Dead Souls* as expiation for having written the first part. Ten days later, having refused all food as part of his mortification of the flesh, Gogol died.

"The Nose," written by Gogol in 1836, is a surrealistic (no other word will do) story. "Like any self-respecting Russian artisan, Ivan Yakovlevich [a barber] was a terrible drunkard" who chooses a loaf of bread with onion for his breakfast one morning, and finds in it a nose. And not just any nose, but the nose of a man, Kovalyov, whose face Ivan has been shaving "every Wednesday and Sunday" for years. Yakovlevich is a drunkard, but he is cold sober as he attempts to rid himself of the unwanted appendage by throwing it off a bridge. Meanwhile, the nose's rightful owner, Major Kovalyov, embarks on a quest to recapture his runaway proboscis, for his only purpose in coming to St. Petersburg is to improve his social standing, which is possible without an arm or leg, or even an ear perhaps, but "without a nose a man is, goodness knows what . . ."

Kovalyov meets his own nose, wearing a gold-embroidered uniform, doeskin breeches, a sword, and plumed hat, and is snubbed. Fearful that the runaway appendage might leave town, he advertises in the newspaper, offering a reward for its return. He recovers the nose, but cannot persuade it to adhere to its former position. The physician hired to return the nose to its proper place fails, and then offers to buy the nose himself. An absurdist satire of a society organized around the appurtenances of rank, "The Nose" is a comic classic.

A year before he published "The Nose," Gogol wrote in "The Diary of a Madman" "Another reason the moon is such a tender globe its that people just cannot live on it any more, and all that's left alive there are noses. This is also why we cannot see our own noses—they're all on the moon."

The Nose

CHAPTER I

On March 25th there took place, in Petersburg, an extraordinarily strange occurrence. The barber Ivan Yakovlevich, who lives on Voznesensky Avenue (his family name has been lost and even on his signboard, where a gentleman is depicted with a lathered cheek and the inscription "Also bloodletting," there is nothing else)—the barber Ivan Yakovlevich woke up rather early and smelled fresh bread. Raising himself slightly in bed he saw his spouse, a rather respectable lady who was very fond of drinking coffee, take some newly baked loaves out of the oven.

"I won't have any coffee to-day, Praskovya Osipovna," said Ivan Yakovlevich. "Instead, I would like to eat a bit of hot bread with onion." (That is to say, Ivan Yakovlevich would have liked both the one and the other, but he knew that it was quite impossible to demand two things at once, for Praskovya Osipovna very much disliked such whims.) "Let the fool eat the bread; all the better for me," the wife thought to herself, "there will be an extra cup of coffee left." And she threw a loaf onto the table.

For the sake of propriety Ivan Yakovlevich put a tailcoat on over his shirt and, sitting down at the table, poured out some salt, got two onions ready, picked up a knife and, assuming a meaningful expression, began to slice the bread. Having cut the loaf in two halves, he looked inside and to his astonishment saw something white. Ivan Yakovlevich poked it carefully with the knife and felt it with his finger. "Solid!" he said to himself. "What could it be?"

He stuck in his finger and extracted—a nose! Ivan Yakovlevich was dumbfounded. He rubbed his eyes and felt the object: a nose, a nose indeed, and a familiar one at that. Ivan Yakovlevich's face expressed horror. But this horror was nothing compared to the indignation which seized his spouse.

"You beast, where did you cut off a nose?" she shouted angrily "Scoundrel! drunkard! I'll report you to the police myself. What a ruffian! I have already heard from three people that you jerk their noses about so much when shaving that it's a wonder they stay in place."

But Ivan Yakovlevich was more dead than alive. He recognized the nose as that of none other than Collegiate Assessor Kovalyov, whom he shaved every Wednesday and Sunday.

"Hold on, Praskovya Osipovna! I shall put it in a corner, after I've wrapped it in a rag: let it lie there for a while, and later I'll take it away."

"I won't even hear of it. That I should allow a cut-off nose to lie about in my room? You dry stick! All he knows is how to strop his razor, but soon he'll be in no condition to carry out his duty, the rake, the villain! Am I to answer for you to the police? You piece of filth, you blockhead! Away with it! Away! Take it anywhere you like! Out of my sight with it!"

Ivan Yakovlevich stood there as though bereft of senses. He thought and thought—and really did not know what to think. "The devil knows how it happened," he said at last, scratching behind his ear with his hand. "Was I drunk or wasn't I when I came home yesterday, I really can't say. Whichever way you look at it, this is an impossible occurrence. After all, bread is something baked, and a nose is something altogether different. I can't make it out at all."

Ivan Yakovlevich fell silent. The idea that the police might find the nose in his possession and bring a charge against him drove him into a complete frenzy. He was already visualizing the scarlet collar, beautifully embroidered with silver, the saber—and he trembled all over. At last he got out his underwear and boots, pulled on all these tatters and, followed by rather weighty exhortations from Praskovya Osipovna, wrapped the nose in a rag and went out into the street.

He wanted to shove it under something somewhere, either into the hitching-post by the gate—or just drop it as if by accident and then turn off into a side street. But as bad luck would have it, he kept running into people he knew, who at once would ask him, "Where are you going?" or "Whom are you going to shave so early?", so that Ivan Yakovlevich couldn't find the right moment. Once he actually did drop it, but a policeman some distance away pointed to it with his halberd and said: "Pick it up—you've dropped something there," and Ivan Yakovlevich was obliged to pick up the nose and hide it in his pocket. He was seized with despair, all the more so as the number of people in the street constantly increased when the shops began to open.

He decided to go to St. Isaac's Bridge—might he not just manage to toss it into the Neva? But I am somewhat to blame for having so far said nothing about Ivan Yakovlevich, in many ways a respectable man.

Like any self-respecting Russian artisan, Ivan Yakovlevich was a terrible drunkard. And although every day he shaved other people's chins his own was ever unshaven. Ivan Yakovlevich's tailcoat (Ivan Yakovlevich never wore a frock-coat) was piebald, that is to say, it was all black but dappled with brownish-yellow and gray; the collar was shiny, and in place of three of the buttons hung just the ends of thread. Ivan Yakovlevich was a great cynic, and when Collegiate Assessor Kovalyov told him while being shaved, "Your hands, Ivan Yakovlevich, always stink," Ivan Yakovlevich would reply with the question, "Why should they stink?" "I don't know, my dear fellow," the Collegiate Assessor would say, "but they do," and Ivan Yakovlevich, after taking a pinch of snuff, would, in retaliation, lather all over his cheeks and under his nose, and behind his ear, and under his chin—in other words, wherever his fancy took him.

This worthy citizen now found himself on St. Isaac's Bridge. To begin with, he took a good look around, then leaned on the railings as though to look under the bridge to see whether or not there were many fish swimming about, and surreptitiously tossed down the rag containing the nose. He felt as though all of a sudden a ton had been lifted off him: Ivan Yakovlevich even smirked. Instead of going to shave some civil servants' chins he set off for an establishment bearing a sign "Snacks and Tea" to order a glass of punch when he suddenly noticed, at the end of the bridge, a police officer of distinguished appearance, with wide sideburns, wearing a three-cornered hat and with a sword. His heart sank: the officer was wagging his finger at him and saying, "Step this way, my friend."

Knowing the etiquette, Ivan Yakovlevich removed his cap while still some way off, and approaching with alacrity said, "I wish your honor good health."

"No, no, my good fellow, not 'your honor.' Just you tell me, what were you doing over there, standing on the bridge?"

"Honestly, sir, I've been to shave someone and only looked to see if the river were running fast."

"You're lying, you're lying. This won't do. Just be so good as to answer."

"I am ready to shave your worship twice a week, or even three times, and no complaints," replied Ivan Yakovlevich.

"No, my friend, all that's nonsense. I have three barbers who shave me and deem it a great honor, too. Just be so good as to tell me, what were you doing over there?"

Ivan Yakovlevich turned pale. . . . But here the whole episode becomes shrouded in mist, and of what happened subsequently absolutely nothing is known.

CHAPTER II

Collegiate Assessor Kovalyov woke up rather early and made a "b-rr-rr" sound with his lips as he was wont to do on awakening, although he could not have explained the reason for it. Kovalyov stretched and asked for the small mirror standing on the table. He wanted to have a look at the pimple which had, the evening before, appeared on his nose. But to his extreme amazement he saw that he had, in the place of his nose, a perfectly smooth surface. Frightened, Kovalyov called for some water and rubbed his eyes with a towel: indeed, no nose! He ran his hand over himself to see whether or not he was asleep. No, he didn't think so. The Collegiate Assessor jumped out of bed and shook himself—no nose! He at once ordered his clothes to be brought to him, and flew off straight to the chief of police.

In the meantime something must be said about Kovalyov, to let the reader see what sort of man this collegiate assessor was. Collegiate assessors who receive their rank on the strength of scholarly diplomas can by no means be equated with those who make the rank in the Caucasus. They are two entirely different breeds. Learned collegiate assessors . . . But Russia is such a wondrous land that if you say something about one collegiate assessor all the collegiate assessors from Riga to Kamchatka will not fail to take it as applying to them, too. The same is true of all our ranks and titles. Kovalyov belonged to the Caucasus variety of collegiate assessors. He had only held that rank for two years and therefore could not forget it for a moment; and in order to lend himself added dignity and weight he never referred to himself as collegiate assessor but always as major. "Listen, my dear woman," he would usually say on meeting in the street a woman selling shirt fronts, "come to my place, my apartment is on Sadovaya; just ask where Major Kovalyov lives, anyone will show you." And if the woman he met happened to be a pretty one, he would also give some confidential instructions, adding, "You just ask, lovey, for Major Kovalyov's apartment."—That is why we, too, will henceforth refer to this collegiate assessor as Major.

Major Kovalyov was in the habit of taking a daily stroll along Nevsky Avenue. The collar of his dress shirt was always exceedingly clean and starched. His sidewhiskers were of the kind you can still see on provincial and district surveyors, or architects (provided they are Russians), as well as on those individuals who perform various police duties, and in general on all those men who have full rosy cheeks and are very good at boston; these sidewhiskers run along the middle of the cheek straight up to the nose. Major Kovalyov wore a great many cornelian seals, some with crests and others with Wednesday, Thursday, Monday, etc., engraved on them. Major Kovalyov had come to Petersburg on business, to wit, to look for a post befitting his rank; if he could arrange it, that of a vice-governor; otherwise, that of a procurement officer in some important government department. Major Kovalyov was not averse to getting married, but only in the event that the bride had a fortune of two hundred thousand. And therefore the reader can now judge for himself what this major's state was when he saw, in the place of a fairly presentable and moderate-sized nose, a most ridiculous flat and smooth surface.

As bad luck would have it, not a single cab showed up in the street, and he was forced to walk, wrapped up in his cloak, his face covered with a handkerchief, pretending that his nose was bleeding. "But perhaps I just imagined all this—a nose cannot disappear in this idiotic way." He stepped into a coffee-house just in order to look at himself in a mirror. Fortunately, there was no one there. Serving boys were sweeping the rooms and arranging the chairs; some of them, sleepy-eyed, were bringing out trays of hot turnovers; yesterday's papers, coffee-stained, lay about on tables and chairs. "Well, thank God, there is no one here," said the major. "Now I can have a look." Timidly he approached the mirror and glanced at it. "Damnation! How disgusting!" he exclaimed after spitting. "If at least there were something in place of the nose, but there's nothing!"

Biting his lips with annoyance, he left the coffee-house and decided, contrary to his habit, not to look or to smile at anyone. Suddenly he stopped dead in his tracks before the door of a house. An inexplicable phenomenon took place before his very eyes: a carriage drew up to the entrance; the doors opened; a gentleman in uniform jumped out, slightly stooping, and ran up the stairs. Imagine the horror and at the same time the amazement of Kovalyov when he recognized that it was his own nose! At this extraordinary sight everything seemed to whirl before his eyes; he felt that he could hardly keep on his feet. Trembling all over as though with fever, he made up his mind, come what may, to await the gentleman's return to the carriage. Two minutes later the Nose indeed came out. He was wearing a gold-embroidered uniform with a big stand-up collar and doeskin breeches; there was a sword at his side. From his plumed hat one could infer that he held the rank of a state councillor. Everything pointed to his being on the way to pay a call. He looked right and left, shouted to his driver, "Bring the carriage round," got in and was driven off.

Poor Kovalyov almost went out of his mind. He did not even know what to think of this strange occurrence. Indeed, how could a nose which as recently as yesterday had been on his face and could neither ride nor walk—how could it be in uniform? He ran after the carriage, which fortunately had not gone far but had stopped before the Kazan Cathedral.

He hurried into the cathedral, made his way past the ranks of old beggar-women with bandaged faces and two slits for their eyes, whom he used to make such fun of, and went inside. There were but few worshippers there: they all stood by the entrance. Kovalyov felt so upset that be was in no condition to pray and searched with his eyes for the gentleman in all the church corners. At last he saw him standing to one side. The Nose had completely hidden his face in his big stand-up collar and was praying in an attitude of utmost piety.

"How am I to approach him?" thought Kovalyov. "From everything, from his uniform, from his hat, one can see that he is a state councillor. I'll be damned if I know how to do it."

He started clearing his throat, but the Nose never changed his devout attitude and continued his genuflections.

"My dear sir," said Kovalyov, forcing himself to take courage, "my dear sir . . ."

"What is it you desire?" said the Nose turning round.

"It is strange, my dear sir . . . I think . . . you ought to know your place. And all of a sudden I find you—and where? In church. You'll admit . . ."

TWO MINUTES LATER THE NOSE INDEED CAME OUT. HE WAS WEARING A GOLD-EMBROIDERED UNIFORM WITH A BIG STAND-UP COLLAR AND DOE-SKIN BREECHES; THERE WAS A SWORD AT HIS SIDE. FROM HIS PLUMED HAT ONE COULD INFER THAT HE HELD THE RANK OF A STATE COUNCILLOR.

"Excuse me, I cannot understand what you are talking about. . . . Make yourself clear."

"How shall I explain to him?" thought Kovalyov and, emboldened, began: "Of course, I . . . however, I am a major. For me to go about without my nose, you'll admit, is unbecoming. It's all right for a peddler woman who sells peeled oranges on Voskresensky Bridge, to sit without a nose. But since I'm expecting—and besides, having many acquaintances among the ladies—Mrs. Chekhtaryova, a state councillor's wife, and others . . . Judge for yourself . . . I don't know, my dear sir . . ." (Here Major Kovalyov shrugged his shoulders.) "Forgive me, if one were to look at this in accordance with rules of duty and honor . . . you yourself can understand . . . ."

"I understand absolutely nothing," replied the Nose. "Make yourself more clear."

"My dear sir," said Kovalyov with a sense of his own dignity, "I don't know how to interpret your words . . . The whole thing seems to me quite obvious . . . Or do you wish . . . After all, you are my own nose!"—

The Nose looked at the major and slightly knitted his brows.

"You are mistaken, my dear sir, I exist in my own right. Besides, there can be no close relation between us. Judging by the buttons on your uniform, you must be employed in the Senate or at least in the Ministry of Justice. As for me, I am in the scholarly line."

Having said this, the Nose turned away and went back to his prayers.

Kovalyov was utterly flabbergasted. He knew not what to do or even what to think. Just then he heard the pleasant rustle of a lady's dress: an elderly lady, all in lace, had come up near him and with her, a slim one, in a white frock which agreeably outlined her slender figure, and in a straw-colored hat, light as a cream-puff. Behind them, a tall footman with huge sidewhiskers and a whole dozen collars, stopped and opened a snuff-box.

Kovalyov stepped closer, pulled out the cambric collar of his dress shirt, adjusted his seals hanging on a golden chain and, smiling in all directions, turned his attention to the ethereal young lady who, like a spring flower, bowed her head slightly and put her little white hand with its translucent fingers to her forehead. The smile on Kovalyov's face grew even wider when from under her hat he caught a glimpse of her little round dazzling-white chin and part of her cheek glowing with the color of the first rose of spring. But suddenly he sprang back as though scalded. He remembered that there was absolutely nothing in the place of his nose, and tears came to his eyes. He turned round, intending without further ado to tell the gentleman in uniform that he was merely pretending to be a state councillor, that he was a rogue and a cad and nothing more than his, the major's, own nose. . . . But the Nose was no longer there; he had managed to dash off, probably to pay another call.

This plunged Kovalyov into despair. He went back, stopped for a moment under the colonnade and looked carefully, this way and that, for the Nose to turn up somewhere. He remembered quite well that the latter had a plumed hat and a gold-embroidered uniform, but he had not noticed his overcoat, or the color of his carriage or of his horses, not even whether he had a footman at the back, and if so in what livery. Moreover, there was such a multitude of carriages dashing back and forth and at such speed that it was difficult to tell them apart; but even if he did pick one of them out, he would have no means of stopping it. The day was fine and sunny. There were crowds of people on Nevsky Avenue. A whole flowery cascade of ladies poured over the sidewalk, all the way down from Police Bridge to Anichkin Bridge. Here came a court councillor he knew, and was used to addressing as lieutenant-colonel, especially in the presence of strangers. Here, too, was Yarygin, a head clerk in the Senate, a great friend of his, who invariably lost at boston when he went up eight. Here was another major who had won his assessorship in the Caucasus, waving to Kovalyov to join him. . . .

"O hell!" said Kovalyov. "Hey, cabby, take me straight to the chief of police!"

Kovalyov got into the cab and kept shouting to the cabman, "Get going as fast as you can."

"Is the chief of police at home?" he called out as he entered the hall.

"No, sir," answered the doorman, "he has just left."

"You don't say."

"Yes," added the doorman, "he has not been gone long, but he's gone. Had you come a minute sooner perhaps you might have found him in."

Without removing the handkerchief from his face, Kovalyov got back into the cab and in a voice of despair shouted, "Drive on!"

"Where to?" asked the cabman.

"Drive straight ahead!"

"What do you mean straight ahead? There is a turn here. Right or left?"

This question nonplussed Kovalyov and made him think again. In his plight the first thing for him to do was to apply to the Police Department, not because his case had anything to do directly with the police, but because they could act much more quickly than any other institution; while to seek satisfaction from the superiors of the department by which the Nose claimed to be employed would be pointless because from the Nose's own replies it was obvious that this fellow held nothing sacred, and that he was capable of lying in this case, too, as he had done when he had assured Kovalyov that they had never met. Thus Kovalyov was on the point of telling the cabman to take him to the Police Department when the thought again occurred to him that this rogue and swindler, who had already treated him so shamelessly during their first encounter, might again seize his first chance to slip out of town somewhere, and then all search would be futile or might drag on, God forbid, a whole month. Finally, it seemed, heaven itself brought him to his senses. He decided to go straight to the newspaper office and, before it was too late, place an advertisement with a detailed description of the Nose's particulars, so that anyone coming across him could immediately deliver him or at least give information about his whereabouts. And so, his mind made up, he told the cabby to drive to the newspaper office, and all the way down to it kept whacking him in the back with his fist, saying, "Faster, you villain! faster, you rogue!"—"Ugh, mister!" the cabman would say, shaking his head and flicking his reins at the horse whose coat was as long as a lapdog's. At last the cab drew up to a stop, and Kovalyov, panting, ran into a small reception room where a gray-haired clerk in an old tailcoat and glasses sat at a table and, pen in his teeth, counted newly brought in coppers.

"Who accepts advertisements here?" cried Kovalyov. "Ah, good morning!"

"How do you do," said the gray-haired clerk, raising his eyes for a moment and lowering them again to look at the neat stacks of money.

"I should like to insert—"

"Excuse me. Will you wait a moment," said the clerk as he wrote down a figure on a piece of paper with one hand and moved two beads on the abacus with the fingers of his left hand. A liveried footman, whose appearance suggested his sojourn in an aristocratic house, and who stood by the table with a note in his hand, deemed it appropriate to demonstrate his savoir-faire: "Would you believe it, sir, this little mutt is not worth eighty kopecks, that is, I wouldn't even give eight kopecks for it; but the countess loves it, honestly she does—and so whoever finds it will get one hundred rubles! To put it politely, just as you and I are talking, people's tastes differ: if you're a hunter, keep a pointer or a poodle; don't grudge five hundred, give a thousand, but then let it be a good dog."

The worthy clerk listened to this with a grave expression while at the same time trying to count the number of letters in the note brought to him. All around stood a great many old women, salespeople and house porters with notes. One of them offered for sale a coachman of sober conduct; another, a little-used carriage brought from Paris in 1814; still others, a nineteen-year-old serf girl experienced in laundering work and suitable for other kinds of work; a sound droshky with one spring missing; a young and fiery dappled-gray horse seventeen years old; turnip and radish seed newly received from London; a summer residence with all the appurtenances—to wit, two stalls for horses and a place for planting a grove of birches or firs; there was also an appeal to those wishing to buy old boot soles, inviting them to appear for final bidding every day between eight and three o'clock. The room in which this entire company was crowded was small, and the air in it was extremely thick; but Collegiate Assessor Kovalyov was not in a position to notice the smell, because he kept his handkerchief pressed to his face and because his nose itself was goodness knows where.

"My dear sir, may I ask you . . . It is very urgent," he said at last with impatience.

"Presently, presently! Two rubles forty-three kopecks! Just a moment! One ruble sixty-four kopecks," recited the gray-haired gentleman, tossing the notes into the faces of the old women and the house porters. "What can I do for you?" he said at last, turning to Kovalyov.

"I wish . . . ," said Kovalyov. "There has been a swindle or a fraud . . . I still can't find out. I just wish to advertise that whoever hands this scoundrel over to me will receive an adequate reward."

"Allow me to inquire, what is your name?"

"What do you want my name for? I can't give it to you. I have many acquaintances: Mrs. Chekhtaryova, the wife of a state councillor; Pelageya Grigoryevna Podtochina, the wife of a field officer . . . What if they suddenly were to find out? Heaven forbid! You can simply write down: a collegiate assessor or, still better, a person holding the rank of major."

"And was the runaway your household serf?"

"What do you mean, household serf? That wouldn't be such a bad swindle! The runaway was . . . my nose. . . ."

"Hmm! what a strange name! And did this Mr. Nosov rob you of a big sum?"

"My nose, I mean to say—You've misunderstood me. My nose, my very own nose has disappeared goodness knows where. The devil must have wished to play a trick on me!"

"But how did it disappear? I don't quite understand it."

"Well, I can't tell you how, but the main thing is that it is now gallivanting about town and calling itself a state councillor. And that is why I am asking you to advertise that whoever apprehends it should deliver it to me immediately and without delay. Judge for yourself. How, indeed, can I do without such a conspicuous part of my body? It isn't like some little toe which I put into my boot, and no one can see whether it is there or not. On Thursdays I call at the house of Mrs. Chekhtaryova, a state councillor's wife. Mrs. Podtochina, Pelageya Grigoryevna, a field officer's wife, and her very pretty daughter, are also very good friends of mine, and you can judge for yourself how can I now . . . I can't appear at their house now."

The clerk thought hard, his lips pursed tightly in witness thereof.

"No, I can't insert such an advertisement in the papers," he said at last after a long silence.

"How so? Why?"

"Well, the paper might lose its reputation. If everyone were to write that his nose had run away, why . . . As it is, people say that too many absurd stories and false rumors are printed."

"But why is this business absurd? I don't think it is anything of the sort."

"That's what you think. But take last week, there was another such case. A civil servant came in, just as you have, bringing a note, was billed two rubles seventy-three kopecks, and all the advertisement consisted of was that a black-coated poodle had run away. Doesn't seem to amount to much, does it now? But it turned out to be a libel. This so-called poodle was the treasurer of I don't recall what institution."

"But I am not putting in an advertisement about a poodle—it's about my very own nose; that is, practically the same as about myself."

"No, I can't possibly insert such an advertisement."

"But when my nose actually has disappeared!"

"If it has disappeared, then it's a doctor's business. They say there are people who can fix you up with any nose you like. However, I observe that you must be a man of gay disposition and fond of kidding in company."

"I swear to you by all that is holy! Perhaps, if it comes to that, why I'll show you."

"Why trouble yourself?" continued the clerk, taking a pinch of snuff. "However, if it isn't too much trouble," he added, moved by curiosity, "I'd like to have a look."

The collegiate assessor removed the handkerchief from his face.

"Very strange indeed!" said the clerk. "It's absolutely flat, like a pancake fresh off the griddle. Yes, incredibly smooth."

"Well, will you go on arguing after this? You see yourself that you can't refuse to print my advertisement. I'll be particularly grateful and am very glad that this opportunity has given me the pleasure of making your acquaintance. . . ." The major, as we can see, decided this time to use a little flattery.

"To insert it would be easy enough, of course," said the clerk, "but I don't see any advantage to you in it. If you really must, give it to someone who wields a skillful pen and let him describe this as a rare phenomenon of nature and publish this little item in *The Northern Bee*" (here he took another pinch of snuff) "for the benefit of the young" (here he wiped his nose), "or just so, as a matter of general interest."

The collegiate assessor felt completely discouraged. He dropped his eyes to the lower part of the paper where theatrical performances were announced. His face was about to break out into a smile as he came across the name of a pretty actress, and his hand went to his pocket to check whether he had a blue note, because in his opinion field officers ought to sit in the stalls—but the thought of his nose spoiled it all.

The clerk himself seemed to be moved by Kovalyov's embarrassing situation. Wishing at least to ease his distress he deemed it appropriate to express his sympathy in a few words: "I really am grieved that such a thing happened to you. Wouldn't you care for a pinch of snuff? It dispels headaches and melancholy; it's even good for hemorrhoids." With those words the clerk offered Kovalyov his snuff-box, rather deftly snapping open the lid which pictured a lady in a hat.

This unpremeditated action made Kovalyov lose all patience. "I can't understand how you find this a time for jokes," he said angrily. "Can't you see that I lack the very thing one needs to take snuff? To hell with your snuff! I can't bear the sight of it now, even if you offered me some *râpé* itself, let alone your wretched Berezin's." After saying this he left the newspaper office, deeply vexed, and went to visit the district police inspector, a man with a passion for sugar. In his house the entire parlor, which served also as the dining room, was stacked with sugar loaves which local tradesmen brought to him out of friendship. At the moment his cook was pulling off the inspector's regulation topboots; his sword and all his military trappings were already hanging peacefully in the corners, and his three-year-old son was reaching for his redoubtable three-cornered hat, while the inspector himself was preparing to taste the fruits of peace after his day of warlike, martial pursuits.

Kovalyov came in at the moment when the inspector had just stretched, grunted and said, "Oh, for a couple of hours' good snooze!" It was therefore easy to see that the collegiate assessor had come at quite the wrong time. And I wonder whether he would have been welcome even if he had brought several pounds of tea or a piece of cloth. The police inspector was a great patron of all arts and manufactures, but he preferred a bank note to everything else. "This is the thing," he would usually say. "There can be nothing better than it—it doesn't ask for food, it doesn't take much space, it'll always fit into a pocket, and if you drop it it won't break."

The inspector received Kovalyov rather coolly and said that after dinner was hardly the time to conduct investigations, that nature itself intended that man should rest a little after a good meal (from this the collegiate assessor could see that the aphorisms of the ancient sages were not unknown to the police inspector), that no real gentleman would allow his nose to be pulled off, and that there were many majors in this world who hadn't even decent underwear and hung about in all sorts of disreputable places.

This last was too close for comfort. It must be observed that Kovalyov was extremely quick to take offense. He could forgive whatever was said about himself, but never anything that referred to rank or title. He was even of the opinion that in plays one could allow references to junior officers, but that there should be no criticism of field officers. His reception by the inspector so disconcerted him that he tossed his head and said with an air of dignity, spreading his arms slightly: "I confess that after such offensive remarks on your part, I've nothing more to add. . . ." and left the room.

He came home hardly able to stand on his feet. It was already dusk. After all this fruitless search his apartment appeared to him melancholy or extraordinarily squalid. Coming into the entrance hall he caught sight of his valet Ivan who, lying on his back on the soiled leather sofa, was spitting at the ceiling and rather successfully hitting one and the same spot. Such indifference on the man's part infuriated him; he struck him on the forehead with his hat, saying, "You pig, always doing something stupid!"

Ivan jumped up abruptly and rushed to take off his cloak.

Entering his room the major, tired and sad, sank into an armchair and at last, after several sighs, said:

"O Lord, O Lord! What have I done to deserve such misery? Had I lost an arm or a leg, it would not have been so bad; had I lost my ears, it would have been bad enough but nevertheless bearable; but without a nose a man is goodness knows what; he's not a bird, he's not a human being; in fact, just take him and throw him out the window! And if at least it had been chopped off in battle or in a duel, or if I myself had been to blame; but it disappeared just like that, with nothing, nothing at all to show for it. But no, it can't be," he added after some thought. "It's unbelievable that a nose should disappear; absolutely unbelievable. I must be either dreaming or just imagining it. Maybe, somehow, by mistake instead of water I drank the vodka which I rub on my chin after shaving. That fool Ivan didn't take it away and I probably gulped it down."—To satisfy himself that he was not drunk the major pinched himself so hard that he cried out. The pain he felt fully convinced him that he was wide awake. He stealthily approached the mirror and at first half-closed his eyes, thinking that perhaps the nose would appear in its proper place; but the same moment he sprang back exclaiming, "What a caricature of a face!"

It was indeed incomprehensible. If a button, a silver spoon, a watch, or some such thing had disappeared—but to disappear, and for whom to disappear? and besides in his own apartment, too! . . . After considering all the circumstances, Major Kovalyov was inclined to think that most likely it was the fault of none other than the field officer's wife, Mrs. Podtochina, who wanted him to marry her daughter. He, too, liked to flirt with her but avoided a final showdown. And when the field officer's wife told him point-blank that she wanted to marry her daughter off to him, he eased off on his attentions, saying that he was still young, that he had to serve another five years when he would be exactly forty-two. And so the field officer's wife, presumably in revenge, had decided to put a curse on him and hired for this purpose some old witchwomen, because it was impossible even to suppose that the nose had been simply cut off: no one had entered his room; the barber, Ivan Yakovlevich, had shaved him as recently as Wednesday and throughout that whole day and even on Thursday his nose was all there—he remembered and knew it very well. Besides, he would have felt the pain and no doubt the wound could not have healed so soon and be as smooth as a pancake. Different plans of action occurred to him: should he formally summons Mrs. Podtochina to court or go to her himself and expose her in person? His reflections were interrupted by light breaking through all the cracks in the door, which told him that Ivan had lit the candle in the hall. Soon Ivan himself appeared, carrying it before him and brightly illuminating the whole room. Kovalyov's first gesture was to snatch his handkerchief and cover the place where his nose had been only the day before, so that indeed the silly fellow would not stand there gaping at such an oddity in his master's strange appearance.

Barely had Ivan gone into his cubbyhole when an unfamiliar voice was heard in the hall saying, "Does Collegiate Assessor Kovalyov live here?"

"Come in. Major Kovalyov is here," said Kovalyov, jumping up quickly and opening the door.

In came a police officer of handsome appearance with sidewhiskers that were neither too light nor too dark, and rather full cheeks, the very same who at the beginning of this story was standing at the end of St. Isaac's Bridge.

"Did you happen to mislay your nose?"

"That's right."

"It has been recovered."

"What are you saying!" exclaimed Major Kovalyov. He was tongue-tied with joy. He stared at the police officer standing in front of him, on whose full lips and cheeks the trembling light of the candle flickered. "How?"

"By an odd piece of luck—he was intercepted on the point of leaving town. He was about to board a stagecoach and leave for Riga. He even had a passport made out a long time ago in the name of a certain civil servant. Strangely enough, I also at first took him for a gentleman. But fortunately I had my glasses with me and I saw at once that it was a nose. You see, I am nearsighted and when you stand before me all I can see is that you have a face, but I can't make out if you have a nose or a beard or anything. My mother-in-law, that is, my wife's mother, can't see anything, either."

Kovalyov was beside himself. "Where is it? Where? I'll run there at once."

"Don't trouble yourself. Knowing that you need it I have brought it with me. And the strange thing is that the chief villain in this business is that rascally barber from Voznesensky Street who is now in a lockup. I have long suspected him of drunkenness and theft, and as recently as the day before yesterday he stole a dozen buttons from a certain shop. Your nose is quite in order."—With these words the police officer reached into his pocket and pulled out a nose wrapped up in a piece of paper.

"That's it!" shouted Kovalyov. "That's it, all right! Do join me in a little cup of tea today."

"I would consider it a great pleasure, but I simply can't: I have to drop in at a mental asylum. . . . All food prices have gone up enormously. . . .I have my mother-in-law, that's my wife's mother, living with me, and my children; the eldest is particularly promising, a very clever lad, but we haven't the means to educate him."

Kovalyov grasped his meaning and, snatching up a red banknote from the table, thrust it into the hands of the inspector who, clicking his heels, went out the door. Almost the very same instant Kovalyov heard his voice out in the street where he was admonishing with his fist a stupid peasant who had driven his cart onto the boulevard.

After the police officer had left, the collegiate assessor remained for a few minutes in a sort of indefinable state and only after several minutes recovered the capacity to see and feel: his unexpected joy had made him lose his senses. He carefully took the newly found nose in both his cupped hands and once again examined it thoroughly.

"That's it, that's it, all right," said Major Kovalyov. "Here on the left side is the pimple which swelled up yesterday." The major very nearly laughed with joy.

But there is nothing enduring in this world, and that is why even joy is not as keen in the moment that follows the first; and a moment later it grows weaker still and finally merges imperceptibly into one's usual state of mind, just as a ring on the water, made by the fall of a pebble, merges finally into the smooth surface. Kovalyov began to reflect and realized that the whole business was not yet over: the nose was found but it still had to be affixed, put in its proper place.

"And what if it doesn't stick?"

At this question, addressed to himself, the major turned pale.

Seized by unaccountable fear, he rushed to the table and drew the looking-glass closer, to avoid affixing the nose crookedly. His hands trembled. Carefully and deliberately, he put it in its former place. O horror! the nose wouldn't stick. . . . He carried it to his mouth, warmed it slightly with his breath, and again brought it to the smooth place between his two cheeks; but the nose just wouldn't stay on.

"Well, come on, come on, you fool!" he kept saying to it. But the nose was as though made of wood and plopped back on the table with a strange corklike sound. The major's face was twisted in convulsion. "Won't it really grow on?" he said fearfully. But no matter how many times he tried to fit it in its proper place, his efforts were unsuccessful as before.

He called Ivan and sent him for the doctor who occupied the best apartment on the first floor of the same house. The doctor was a fine figure of a man; he had beautiful pitch-black sidewhiskers, a fresh, healthy wife, ate raw apples first thing in the morning, and kept his mouth extraordinarily clean, rinsing it every morning for nearly three quarters of an hour and polishing his teeth with five different kinds of little brushes. The doctor came at once. After asking him how long ago the mishap had occurred, he lifted Major Kovalyov's face by the chin and flicked him with his thumb on the very spot where the nose used to be, so that the major had to throw his head back with such force that he hit the back of it against the wall. The doctor said this didn't matter and, suggesting that he move a little away from the wall, told him first to bend his head to the right, and, after feeling the spot where the nose had been, said "Hmm!" Then he told him to bend his head to the left and said "Hmm!"; and in conclusion he again flicked him with his thumb so that Major Kovalyov jerked his head like a horse whose teeth are being examined. Having carried out this test, the doctor shook his head and said: "No, can't be done. You'd better stay like this, or we might make things even worse. Of course, it can be stuck on. I daresay, I could do it right now for you, but I assure you it'll be worse for you."

"I like that! How am I to remain without a nose?" said Kovalyov. "It couldn't possibly be worse than now. This is simply a hell of a thing! How can I show myself anywhere in such a scandalous state? I have acquaintances in good society; why, this evening, now, I am expected at parties in two houses. I know many people: Mrs. Chekhtaryova, a state councillor's wife, Mrs. Podtochina, a field officer's wife . . . although after what she's done now I'll have nothing more to do with her except through the police. I appeal to you," pleaded Kovalyov, "is there no way at all? Fix it on somehow, even if not very well, just so it stays on; in an emergency, I could even prop it up with my hand. And besides, I don't dance, so I can't do any harm by some careless movement. As regards my grateful acknowledgment of your visits, be assured that as far as my means allow. . . ."

"Would you believe it," said the doctor in a voice that was neither loud nor soft but extremely persuasive and magnetic, "I never treat people out of self-interest. This is against my principles and my calling. It is true that I charge for my visits, but solely in order not to offend by my refusal. Of course I could affix your nose; but I assure you on my honor, if you won't take my word for it, that it will be much worse. Rather, let nature take its course. Wash the place more often with cold water, and I assure you that without a nose you'll be as healthy as if you had one. As for the nose itself, I advise you to put the nose in a jar with alcohol, or, better still, pour into the jar two tablespoonfuls of aqua fortis and warmed-up vinegar—and then you can get good money for it. I'll buy it myself, if you don't ask too much."

"No, no! I won't sell it for anything!" exclaimed Major Kovalyov in desperation. "Let it rather go to blazes!"

"Excuse me!" said the doctor, bowing himself out, "I wanted to be of some use to you. . . . Never mind! At least you saw my good will." Having said this the doctor left the room with a dignified air. Kovalyov didn't even notice his face and in his benumbed state saw nothing but the cuffs of his snow-white shirt peeping out of the sleeves of his black tailcoat.

The very next day he decided, before lodging a complaint, to write to Mrs. Podtochina requesting her to restore him his due without a fight. The letter ran as follows:

> Dear Madam Alexandra Grigoryevna,
>
> I fail to understand your strange behavior. Be assured that, acting in this way, you gain nothing and certainly will not force me to marry your daughter. Believe me that the incident with my nose is fully known to me, just as is the fact that you—and no one else—are the principal person involved. Its sudden

detachment from its place, its flight and its disguise, first as a certain civil servant, then at last in its own shape, is nothing other than the result of a spell cast by you or by those who engage like you in such noble pursuits. I for my part deem it my duty to forewarn you that if the abovementioned nose is not back in its place this very day I shall be forced to resort to the defense and protection of the law.

Whereupon I have the honor to remain, with my full respect,

Your obedient servant
Platon Kovalyov

Dear Sir
Platon Kuzmich,

Your letter came as a complete surprise to me. I frankly confess that I never expected it, especially as regards your unjust reproaches. I beg to inform you that I never received in my house the civil servant you mention, neither in disguise nor in his actual shape. It is true that Filipp Ivanovich Potanchikov had been visiting me. And though he did indeed seek my daughter's hand, being himself of good sober conduct and great learning, I never held out any hopes to him. You also mention your nose. If by this you mean that I wanted to put your nose out of joint, that is, to give you a formal refusal, then I am surprised to hear you mention it, for I, as you know, was of the exactly opposite opinion, and if you now seek my daughter in marriage in the lawful way, I am ready to give you immediate satisfaction, for this has always been the object of my keenest desire, in the hope of which I remain always at your service,

Alexandra Podtochina

"No," said Kovalyov, after he had read the letter. "She certainly isn't guilty. Impossible! The letter is written in a way no person guilty of a crime can write."—The collegiate assessor was an expert in this matter, having been sent several times to take part in a judicial investigation while still serving in the Caucasus.—"How then, how on earth could this have happened? The devil alone can make it out," he said at last in utter dejection.

In the meantime rumors about this extraordinary occurrence had spread all over the capital and, as is usual in such cases, not without some special accretions. In those days the minds of everybody were particularly inclined toward things extraordinary: not long before, the whole town had shown an interest in experiments with the effects of hypnotism. Moreover, the story of the dancing chairs in Konyushennaya Street was still fresh in memory, and one should not be surprised therefore that soon people began saying that Collegiate Assessor Kovalyov's nose went strolling along Nevsky Avenue at precisely three o'clock. Throngs of curious people came there every day. Someone said that the Nose was in Junker's store: and such a crowd and jam was created outside Junker's that the police had to intervene. One profit-seeker of respectable appearance, with sidewhiskers, who sold a variety of dry pastries at the entrance to a theater, had specially constructed excellent, sturdy wooden benches, on which he invited the curious to mount for eighty kopecks apiece. One veteran colonel made a point of leaving his house earlier than usual and with much difficulty made his way through the crowd, but to his great indignation saw in the window of the shop instead of the nose an ordinary woollen undershirt and a lithograph showing a young girl straightening her stocking and a dandy, with a lapeled waistcoat and a small beard, peeping at her from behind a tree—a picture which had been hanging in the same place for more than ten years. Moving away he said with annoyance, "How can they confound the people by such silly and unlikely rumors?"—Then a rumor went round that Major Kovalyov's nose was out for a stroll, not on Nevsky Avenue but in Taurida Gardens, that it had been there for ages; that when Khosrev-Mirza lived there he marveled greatly at this strange freak of nature. Some students from the Surgical Academy went there. One aristocratic, respectable lady, in a special letter to the Superintendent of the Gardens, asked him to show her children this rare phenomenon, accompanied, if possible, with an explanation edifying and instructive for the young.

All the men about town, the *habitués* of society parties, who liked to amuse ladies and whose resources had by that time been exhausted, were extremely glad of all these goings-on. A small percentage of respectable and well-meaning people were extremely displeased. One gentleman said indignantly that he could not understand how in this enlightened age such senseless stories could spread and that he was surprised at the government failure to take heed of it. This gentleman apparently was one of those gentlemen who would like to embroil the government in everything, even in their daily quarrels with their wives. After that . . . but here again the whole incident is shrouded in fog, and what happened afterwards is absolutely unknown.

CHAPTER III

Utterly nonsensical things happen in this world. Sometimes there is absolutely no rhyme or reason in them: suddenly the very nose which had been going around with the rank of a state councillor and created such a stir in the city, found itself again, as though nothing were the matter, in its proper place, that is to say, between the two cheeks of Major Kovalyov. This happened on April 7th. Waking up and chancing to look in the mirror, he sees—his nose! He grabbed it with his hand—his nose indeed! "Aha!" said Kovalyov, and in his joy he very nearly broke into a barefooted dance round the room, but Ivan's entry stopped him. He told Ivan to bring him some water to wash in and, while washing, glanced again at the mirror—his nose! Drying himself with his towel, he again glanced at the mirror—his nose!

"Take a look, Ivan, I think there's a pimple on my nose," he said, and in the meantime thought, "How awful if Ivan says: 'Why, no sir, not only there is no pimple but also the nose itself is gone!'"

But Ivan said: "Nothing, sir, no pimple—your nose is fine!"

"That's great, damn it!" the major said to himself, snapping his fingers. At that moment the barber Ivan Yakovlevich peeped in at the door but as timidly as a cat which had just been whipped for stealing lard.

"First you tell me—are your hands clean?" Kovalyov shouted to him before he had approached.

"They are."

"You're lying."

"I swear they are, sir."

"Well, we'll see."

Kovalyov sat down. Ivan Yakovlevich draped him with a napkin and instantly, with the help of a shaving brush, transformed his chin and part of his cheek into the whipped cream served at merchants' namesday parties. "Well, I never!" Ivan Yakovlevich said to himself, glancing at his nose, and then cocked his head on the other side and looked at it sideways: "Look at that! just you try and figure that out," he continued and took a good look at his nose. At last, gently, with the greatest care imaginable, he raised two fingers to grasp it by the tip. Such was Ivan Yakovlevich's method.

"Now, now, now, look out there!" cried Kovalyov. Dumbfounded and confused as never before in his life, Ivan Yakovlevich let his hands drop. At last he began cautiously tickling him with the razor under the chin, and although it wasn't at all handy for him and difficult to shave without holding on to the olfactory portion of the face, nevertheless, somehow bracing his gnarled thumb against the cheek and the lower jaw, he finally overcame all obstacles and finished shaving him.

When everything was ready, Kovalyov hastened to dress, hired a cab and went straight to the coffee-house. Before he was properly inside the door he shouted, "Boy, a cup of chocolate!" and immediately made for the mirror: the nose was there. He turned round cheerfully and looked ironically, slightly screwing up one eye, at two military gentlemen one of whom had a nose no bigger than a waistcoat button. After that he set off for the office of the department where he was trying to obtain the post of a vice-governor or, failing that, of a procurement officer. Passing through the reception room, he glanced in the mirror: the nose was there. Then he went to visit another collegiate assessor or major, a great wag, to whom he often said in reply to various derisive remarks: "Oh, come off it, I know you, you're a kidder." On the way there he thought: "If the major doesn't explode with laughter on seeing me, it's a sure sign that everything is in its proper place." The collegiate assessor did not explode. "That's great, that's great, damn it!" Kovalyov thought to himself. On the street he met Mrs. Podtochina, the field officer's wife, together with her daughter, bowed to them and was hailed with joyful exclamations, and so everything was all right, no part of him was missing. He talked with them a very long time and, deliberately taking out his snuff-box, right in front of them kept stuffing his nose with snuff at both entrances for a very long time, saying to himself: "So much for you, you women, you stupid hens! I won't marry the daughter all the same. Anything else, *par amour*—by all means." And from that time on, Major Kovalyov went strolling about as though nothing had happened, both on Nevsky Avenue, and in the theaters, and everywhere. And his nose too, as though nothing had happened, stayed on his face, betraying no sign of having played truant. And thereafter Major Kovalyov was always seen in good humor, smiling, running after absolutely all the pretty ladies, and once even stopping in front of a little shop in Gostinny Dvor and buying himself the ribbon of some order, goodness knows why, for he hadn't been decorated with any order.

That is the kind of affair that happened in the northern capital of our vast empire. Only now, on second thoughts, can we see that there is much that is improbable in it. Without speaking of the fact that the supernatural detachment of the nose and its appearance in various places in the guise of a state councillor is indeed strange, how is it that Kovalyov did not realize that one does not advertise for one's nose through the newspaper office? I do not mean to say that advertising rates appear to me too high: that's nonsense, and I am not at all one of those mercenary people. But it's improper, embarrassing, not nice! And then again—how did the nose come to be in a newly baked loaf, and how about Ivan Yakovlevich? . . . No, this is something I can't understand, positively can't understand. But the strangest, the most incomprehensible thing of all, is how authors can choose such subjects. I confess that this is quite inconceivable; it is indeed . . . no, no, I just can't understand it at all! In the first place, there is absolutely no benefit in it for the fatherland; in the second place . . . but in the second place, there is no benefit either. I simply don't know what to make of it. . . .

And yet, in spite of it all, though, of course, we may assume this and that and the other, perhaps even . . . And after all, where aren't there incongruities?—But all the same, when you think about it, there really is something in all this. Whatever anyone says, such things happen in this world; rarely, but they do.

Mark Twain

(Samuel Langhorne Clemens)

(1835–1910)

"There was things that he stretched but he mainly told the truth."
—*The Adventures of Huckleberry Finn*

The name Mark Twain first appeared as the byline of a humorous travel piece on February 3, 1863, in Nevada's *Virginia City Territorial Enterprise*. The name is actually river slang for "two fathoms," water that is almost too rough to steer through. Thus was born the pen persona of Samuel Langhorne Clemens, then a twenty-seven-year-old reporter.

Born on November 30, 1835, in Florida, Missouri, Samuel Clemens was the sixth child of John Marshall and Jane Lampton Clemens. When he was four, his family moved to nearby Hannibal where his father set up a dry goods and grocery store and became involved in local politics. It was there, on the banks of the Mississippi River, that Clemens would absorb the wondrous and often dangerous aspects of river life—steamboats, heelboats, gamblers, roving stevedores, and the rough raft travelers. After his father died in 1847, Samuel pitched in on weekends and during the summer to support the family. He took jobs ranging from delivery boy and grocery boy to blacksmith's assistant.

A year later, he quit school and began working full-time as a printer's apprentice. His brother, Orion, had begun a newspaper (the *Hannibal Journal*) and Clemens went to work for him as a compositor and a contributor, using the name Rambler as a byline. Clemens's first piece in his own name, a comical sketch called "The Dandy Frightening the Squatter," appeared in a humorous Boston publication called *The Carpet-Bag* when he was sixteen.

Orion's newspaper did not fare well, so Clemens took to the road at seventeen. He would live his life on and off that road for the next seventeen years. He worked as a printer in New York, Philadelphia, and Washington. He went to South America to do some travel writing but abandoned that project after five letters home. He apprenticed on a steamboat for four years, calling that time "the most carefree of my life." He became a licensed steamboat pilot but his career was cut short by the start of the Civil War.

The information on Clemens's whereabouts during the war is hazy, but he did team up with his brother for a three-week stagecoach trip to the West after Orion had been named to a post in the Nevada Territory (as recompense for his service to Abraham Lincoln during the 1860 presidential campaign). Clemens unsuccessfully tried gold and silver prospecting and stock speculation before landing a real job as a writer for the *Territorial Enterprise,* where his alter ego, Mark Twain, was born. In 1865, he wrote "The Celebrated Jumping Frog of Calaveras County." The short story ran in the Saturday press but was reprinted nationally. This tall tale is written in the Southern twang of Twain's youth and was his first critical and commercial triumph.

Until he settled down and married Olivia Langdon in 1870, Twain worked as a travel writer, playing the keen-eyed Westerner, humorously satirizing the tourists who looked to guidebooks for what to think, to feel, and to look for when abroad. These arch observations, written in letters for Horace Greeley's *New York Tribune,* became his first book, *The Innocents Abroad or The New Pilgrim's Progress*.

In 1871, Twain and his wife moved to Hartford, Connecticut; they resided there for the next twenty years and had three daughters. These years with Olivia and family would prove to be the most prolific and happiest of Twain's life. In 1872 *Roughing It* was published, and *The Gilded Age* came out in 1873. Twain hit the lecture circuit, mesmerizing audiences with his outrageous wit, wild exaggerations, and biting satire. He chronicled his steamboat experiences for the *Atlantic Monthly* in 1875, which he later expanded on in *Life on the Mississippi*, an evocation of a bygone world. He then wrote to his childhood friends, asking them to share with him their memories of Hannibal, which he merged with his own recollections (and a healthy dose of fiction) to create the novel *The Adventures of Tom Sawyer*. The portrait of youth's resiliency and of a pre–Civil War town on the Mississippi has made the novel an enduring classic for both children and adults.

During 1878 and 1879, Twain and his family went traveling. Their walking tour through the Black Forest inspired *A Tramp Abroad* (1880). A year later, in *The Prince and the Pauper* Twain once again used boyhood adventures to express social criticism, and also mocked monarchies. Twain's finest achievement was to come during this period, when he published *The Adventures of Huckleberry Finn* in 1885. Huck, though poor, uneducated, and unrefined, is a shrewd, cheerful, and compassionate boy who embarks on a long journey down the Mississippi River with a runaway slave named Jim. Huck's eventual acceptance of the varied types of people he meets during this escapade is a sharp contrast to the continuing thread of man's cruelty to man that runs through the whole book.

Twain had a love for financial speculation that his literary success did not quell, and he once again had a bad spate of luck in the late 1880s with his investment in a typesetting machine. The machine was useless, and the success of *Grant's Memoirs* in 1885 did little to help improve his financial status. Twain was forced to sell his house in Hartford and take his family traveling in Europe. His own publishing firm issued *The American Claimant* in 1892 and *Tom Sawyer Abroad* in 1894, yet neither book sold well and Twain and his company soon went bankrupt. His friend Henry Huttleson Rogers, an executive at the Standard Oil Company, took over the management of his assets. The publication of *The Tragedy of Pudd'nhead Wilson* (1894), *Personal Recollections of Joan of Arc* (1895), and *Following the Equator* (1897), coupled with proceeds from his lectures, allowed Twain to regain his financial footing. While lecturing in London in 1895, Twain learned that his eldest daughter, Susy, had died. Despite this setback, the family remained overseas for five more years, until they learned that their youngest daughter, Jane, was incurably ill.

In the autumn of 1903, Twain and his family relocated near Florence, Italy. His wife, whose normally robust health had been failing in recent years, became very ill and passed away. For a man who had suffered so much grief in the recent past, this was the cruelest blow. He expressed his loneliness, pessimism, and sorrow in two works, *Extracts From Adam's Diary* and *Eve's Diary.* He began dictating his autobiography in 1906, parts of which appeared in periodicals. He earned enough money from this endeavor to fund the construction of new a house in Redding, Connecticut, which he named Stormfield. The house was finished in 1908. He died there on April 10, 1910.

The essays and stories in this anthology, "English as She Is Taught," "Fenimore Cooper's Literary Offenses," "Marjorie Fleming, the Wonder Child," "In Defense of Harriet Shelley," "A Medieval Romance," "The Story of the Good Little Boy," and "The Grateful Poodle and Sequel," embrace subjects as varied as grammar, romance, and deception in the Middle Ages, a boy who could do no wrong, a biography of Percy Shelley, James Fenimore Cooper's literary failings, and a little Irish girl genius. In the first three essays Twain is alternately exasperated and amazed at what will be accepted as good writing, criticism ("The Shelley biography is a literary cake-walk"), or storytelling. "English as She Is Taught" is a diatribe against an American school system that tries to cram information into its pupils without laying a foundation on which the children can absorb and understand it. He uses hilarious examples from a book of malapropisms assembled by an English teacher and sent to himself: "*Equestrian*: one who asks questions"; "*Parasite*: a kind of umbrella."

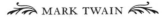

Twain does not have to do much in this essay to prove his point; just listing these excerpts is enough to convey his message. He goes the same route in "Fenimore Cooper's Literary Offenses," except that the author he is denigrating is a lauded, famous one, not a school-age child. He disagrees with the description of Cooper's tales as works of art; Twain finds that "Cooper's art has some defects." In fact Cooper's work violates eighteen of Twain's nineteen "rules governing literary art." Two of those broken rules are that "a tale shall accomplish something and arrive somewhere," and that "the personages in a tale shall be alive, except in the case of corpses, and that the reader shall be able to tell corpses from the other." Twain may have been turning the critic's knife on another writer to avenge his own wounds. Whatever the case, he savages Cooper's books and leaves no room for doubt about his feelings toward Cooper's efforts. Yet he throws him a bone at the end: "Counting these out, what is left is Art, I think we all must admit that."

"Marjorie Fleming, the Wonder Child" is an enigmatic essay regarding an eight-year-old Irish girl with an extraordinary intelligence. She apparently could quote Shakespeare, spent quality time with Sir Walter Scott, and wrote prolifically in her journals, which Twain quotes in the piece. Twain attacks the child-genius cult by engaging in treacly, sarcastic praise for the girl when detailing her supposed achievements and the public's adoration of her. He devotes ten pages to painfully delineating almost her every thought and deed, commenting on each with derision: "Frank? Yes, Marjorie was that. And during the brief moment that she enchanted this dull earth with her presence she was the bewitchingest speller and punctuator in all of Christendom." No kid-glove treatment here; Twain spares not the precocious child nor the adults who exalt these rare tots.

"In Defense of Harriet Shelley" is a lengthy testimonial to the innocence of Percy Bysshe Shelley's wife, Harriet, and her noble behavior in the face of his callowness and infidelity. Twain savages Professor Dowden, Shelley's biographer, for being unfair to Harriet by smearing her memory with rumor, gossip, conjecture, and innuendo. Shelley betrays his wife, yet it is the wife who is blamed for "forcing" her husband into the arms of another woman with her seemingly hostile household changes. Twain asserts that Harriet is "free of all offense as far as we have historical facts for guidance, and upbriads Dowden for holding her unforgivably responsible for her husband's innocent action deserting her and taking up with another woman." Twain's essay is a literary exercise. He scrutinizes passages from the biography and taking issue with specific points, questions the biographer's choices and conclusions. Even though Twain himself was capable of stretching the truth from time to time to make things interesting, he detested this practice in what he saw as serious writing. Write from the facts or don't write at all, is the message of this piece.

"A Medieval Romance" is a parody of chivalric tales. The daughter of a lord is made to pose as a boy from birth to inherit her uncle's title, throne, and fortune. Wackiness ensues when the daughter of the uncle falls in love with the imposter. Twain takes the typical knight's tale and turns it on its head, with an especially delicious twist at the end.

A reactionary parable, "The Story of the Good Little Boy" illustrates the folly of elevating the good and obedient child at the expense of the mischievous and skeptical child. These children may be rascals but they will grow up to be true and brave men, unlike Jacob Blivens of the "Good Little Boy." The boy cannot understand why his straight-arrow behavior is not noticed and rewarded as promised in the Sunday school books. The ruffians he has met and scolded have always had fun and were not punished for their bad deeds or pranks, even when he tried to warn them or turn them in. It does not end well for Jacob, and it just goes to show: you can't believe everything you read.

Mark Twain's stories and essays are so varied in topic, genre, and structure that it is impossible to summarize in a few brief paragraphs the many forms his short works assume. Yet all his works, from essay to mock parable, arise out of a similar style: very folksy, often addressing the reader directly, and professing to tell it like it is. His manner is plain spoken, picturesque yet direct. "The difference between the right word and almost the right word, Twain said, "is the difference between lightning and the lightning bug." Twain was an emotional writer, not concerned with whether the targets of his indignant opposition actually existed. He was the anti-romantic, the anti-idealist, living up to his role as an American of the New West with only disdain for the backward ways of Old Europe. By expressing his ideas as ferocious jokes he gets his point across but blunted the sting. Well, somewhat.

English as She Is Taught

In the appendix to Croker's *Boswell's Johnson* one finds this anecdote:

> *Cato's Soliloquy*.—One day Mrs. Gastrel set a little girl to repeat to him [Dr. Samuel Johnson] Cato's Soliloquy, which she went through very correctly. The Doctor, after a pause, asked the child:
>
> "What was to bring Cato to an end?"
>
> She said it was a knife.
>
> "No, my dear, it was not so."
>
> "My aunt Polly said it was a knife."
>
> "Why, Aunt Polly's knife *may do,* but it was a *dagger,* my dear."
>
> He then asked her the meaning of "bane and antidote," which she was unable to give. Mrs. Gastrel said:
>
> "You cannot expect so young a child to know the meaning of such words."
>
> He then said:
>
> "My dear, how many pence are there in *sixpence*?"
>
> "I cannot tell, sir," was the half-terrified reply.
>
> On this, addressing himself to Mrs. Gastrel, he said:
>
> "Now, my dear lady, can anything be more ridiculous than to teach a child Cato's Soliloquy, who does not know how many pence there are in sixpence?"

In a lecture before the Royal Geographical Society Professor Ravenstein quoted the following list of frantic questions, and said that they had been asked in an examination:

> Mention all the names of places in the world derived from Julius Cæsar or Augustus Cæsar.
>
> Where are the following rivers: Pisuerga, Sakaria, Guadalete, Jalon, Mulde?
>
> All you know of the following: Machacha, Pilmo, Schebulos,

Crivoscia, Basecs, Mancikert, Taxhem, Citeaux, Meloria, Zutphen.

The highest peaks of the Karakorum range.

The number of universities in Prussia.

Why are the tops of mountains continually covered with snow [*sic*]?

Name the length and breadth of the streams of lava which issued from the Skaptar Jokul in the eruption of 1783.

That list would oversize nearly anybody's geographical knowledge. Isn't it reasonably possible that in our schools many of the questions in all studies are several miles ahead of where the pupil is?—that he is set to struggle with things that are ludicrously beyond his present reach, hopelessly beyond his present strength? This remark in passing, and by way of text; now I come to what I was going to say.

I have just now fallen upon a darling literary curiosity. It is a little book, a manuscript compilation, and the compiler sent it to me with the request that I say whether I think it ought to be published or not. I said, Yes; but as I slowly grow wise I briskly grow cautious; and so, now that the publication is imminent, it has seemed to me that I should feel more comfortable if I could divide up this responsibility with the public by adding them to the court. Therefore I will print some extracts from the book, in the hope that they may make converts to my judgment that the volume has merit which entitles it to publication.

As to its character. Every one has sampled "English as She Is Spoke" and "English as She Is Wrote"; this little volume furnishes us an instructive array of examples of "English as She Is Taught" in the public schools of—well, this country. The collection is made by a teacher in those schools, and all the examples in it are genuine; none of them have been tampered with, or doctored in any way. From time to time, during several years, whenever a pupil has delivered himself of anything peculiarly quaint or toothsome in the course of his recitations, this teacher and her associates have privately set that thing down in a memorandum-book; strictly following the original, as to grammar, construction, spelling, and all; and the result is this literary curiosity.

The contents of the book consist mainly of answers given by the boys and girls to questions, said answers being given sometimes verbally, sometimes in writing. The subjects touched upon are fifteen in number: I. Etymology; II. Grammar; III. Mathematics; IV. Geography; V. "Original"; VI. Analysis; VII. History; VIII. "Intellectual"; IX. Philosophy; X. Physiology; XI. Astronomy; XII. Politics; XIII. Music; XIV. Oratory; XV. Metaphysics.

You perceive that the poor little young idea has taken a shot at a good many kinds of game in the course of the book. Now as to results. Here are some quaint definitions of words. It will be noticed that in all of these instances the sound of the word, or the look of it on paper, has misled the child:

Aborigines, a system of mountains.
Alias, a good man in the Bible.
Amenable, anything that is mean.
Ammonia, the food of the gods.
Assiduity, state of being an acid.
Auriferous, pertaining to an orifice.
Capillary, a little caterpillar.
Corniferous, rocks in which fossil corn is found.
Emolument, a headstone to a grave.
Equestrian, one who asks questions.
Eucharist, one who plays euchre.
Franchise, anything belonging to the French.
Idolater, a very idol person.
Ipecac, a man who likes a good dinner.
Irrigate, to make fun of.
Mendacious, what can be mended.
Mercenary, one who feels for another.
Parasite, a kind of umbrella.
Parasite, the murder of an infant.
Publican, a man who does his prayers in public.
Tenacious, ten acres of land.

Here is one where the phrase "publicans and sinners" has got mixed up in the child's mind with politics, and the result is a definition which takes one in a sudden and unexpected way:

Republican, a sinner mentioned in the Bible.

Also in Democratic newspapers now and then. Here are two where the mistake has resulted from sound assisted by remote fact:

Plagiarist, a writer of plays.

Demagogue, a vessel containing beer and other liquids.

I cannot quite make out what it was that misled the pupil in the following instances; it would not seem to have been the sound of the word, nor the look of it in print:

Asphyxia, a grumbling, fussy temper.
Quarternions, a bird with a flat beak and no bill, living in New Zealand.
Quarternions, the name given to a style of art practiced by the Phœnicians.
Quarternions, a religious convention held every hundred years.
Sibilant, the state of being idiotic.
Crosier, a staff carried by the Deity.

In the following sentences the pupil's ear has been deceiving him again:

The marriage was illegible.
He was totally dismasted with the whole performance.
He enjoys riding on a philosopher.
She was very quick at repertoire.
He prayed for the waters to subsidize.
The leopard is watching his sheep.
They had a strawberry vestibule.

Here is one which—well, now, how often we do slam right into the truth without ever suspecting it:

The men employed by the Gas Company go around and speculate the meter.

Indeed they do, dear; and when you grow up, many and many's the time you will notice it in the gas bill. In the following sentences the little people have some information to convey, every time; but in my case they fail to connect: the light always went out on the keystone word:

The coercion of some things is remarkable; as bread and molasses.

> Her hat is contiguous because she wears it on one side.
>
> He preached to an egregious congregation.
>
> The captain eliminated a bullet through the man's heart.
>
> You should take caution and be precarious.
>
> The supercilious girl acted with vicissitude when the perennial time came.

That last is a curiously plausible sentence; one seems to know what it means, and yet he knows all the time that he doesn't. Here is an odd (but entirely proper) use of a word, and a most sudden descent from a lofty philosophical altitude to a very practical and homely illustration:

> We should endeavor to avoid extremes—like those of wasps and bees.

And here—with "zoological" and "geological" in his mind, but not ready to his tongue—the small scholar has innocently gone and let out a couple of secrets which ought never to have been divulged in any circumstances:

> There are a good many donkeys in theological gardens.
>
> Some of the best fossils are found in theological cabinets.

Under the head of "Grammar" the little scholars furnish the following information:

> Gender is the distinguishing nouns without regard to sex.
>
> A verb is something to eat.
>
> Adverbs should always be used as adjectives and adjectives as adverbs.
>
> Every sentence and name of God must begin with a caterpillar.

"Caterpillar" is well enough, but capital letter would have been stricter. The following is a brave attempt at a solution, but it failed to liquify:

> When they are going to say some prose or poetry before they say the poetry or prose they must put a semicolon just after the introduction of the prose or poetry.

The chapter on "Mathematics" is full of fruit. From it I take a few samples—mainly in an unripe state.

> A straight line is any distance between two places.
>
> Parallel lines are lines that can never meet until they run together.
>
> A circle is a round straight line with a hole in the middle.
>
> Things which are equal to each other are equal to anything else.
>
> To find the number of square feet in a room you multiply the room by the number of the feet. The product is the result.

Right you are. In the matter of geography this little book is unspeakably rich. The questions do not appear to have applied the microscope to the subject, as did those quoted by Professor Ravenstein; still, they proved plenty difficult enough without that. These pupils did not hunt with a microscope, they hunted with a shot-gun; this is shown by the crippled condition of the game they brought in:

> America is divided into the Passiffic slope and the Mississippi valey.
>
> North America is separated by Spain.
>
> America consists from north to south about five hundred miles.
>
> The United States is quite a small country compared with some other countrys, but is about as industrious.
>
> The capital of the United States is Long Island.
>
> The five seaports of the U. S. are Newfunlan and Sanfrancisco.
>
> The principal products of the U. S. is earthquakes and volcanoes.
>
> The Alaginnies are mountains in Philadelphia.
>
> The Rocky Mountains are on the western side of Philadelphia.
>
> Cape Hateras is a vast body of water surrounded by land and flowing into the Gulf of Mexico.
>
> Mason and Dixon's line is the Equater.
>
> One of the leading industries of the United States is mollasses, book-covers, numbers, gas, teaching, lumber, manufacturers, paper-making, publishers, coal.
>
> In Austria the principal occupation is gathering Austrich feathers.
>
> Gibraltar is an island built on a rock.
>
> Russia is very cold and tyrannical.
>
> Sicily is one of the Sandwich Islands.

Hindoostan flows through the Ganges and empties into the Mediterranean Sea.

Ireland is called the Emigrant Isle because it is so beautiful and green.

The width of the different zones Europe lies in depend upon the surrounding country.

The imports of a country are the things that are paid for, the exports are the things that are not.

Climate lasts all the time and weather only a few days.

The two most famous volcanoes of Europe are Sodom and Gomorrah.

The chapter headed "Analysis" shows us that the pupils in our public schools are not merely loaded up with those showy facts about geography, mathematics, and so on, and left in that incomplete state; no, there's machinery for clarifying and expanding their minds. They are required to take poems and analyze them, dig out their common sense, reduce them to statistics, and reproduce them in a luminous prose translation which shall tell you at a glance what the poet was trying to get at. One sample will do. Here is a stanza from "The Lady of the Lake," followed by the pupil's impressive explanation of it:

Alone, but with unbated zeal,
The horseman plied with scourge and steel;
For jaded now and spent with toil,
Embossed with foam and dark with soil,
While every gasp with sobs he drew,
The laboring stag strained full in view.

The man who rode on the horse performed the whip and an instrument made of steel alone with strong ardor not diminishing, for, being tired from the time passed with hard labor overworked with anger and ignorant with weariness, while every breath for labor he drew with cries full of sorrow, the young deer made imperfect who worked hard filtered in sight.

I see, now, that I never understood that poem before. I have had glimpses of its meaning, in moments when I was not as ignorant with weariness as usual, but this is the first time the whole spacious idea of it ever filtered in sight. If I were a public-school pupil I would put those other studies aside and stick to analysis; for, after all, it is the thing to spread your mind.

We come now to historical matters, historical remains, one might say. As one turns the pages he is impressed with the depth to which one date has been driven into the American child's head—1492. The date is there, and it is there to stay. And it is always at hand, always deliverable at a moment's notice. But the Fact that belongs with it? That is quite another matter. Only the date itself is familiar and sure: its vast Fact has failed of lodgment. It would appear that whenever you ask a public-school pupil when a thing—anything, no matter what—happened, and he is in doubt, he always rips out his 1492. He applies it to everything, from the landing of the ark to the introduction of the horse-car. Well, after all, it is our first date, and so it is right enough to honor it, and pay the public schools to teach our children to honor it:

> George Washington was born in 1492.
>
> Washington wrote the Declaration of Independence in 1492.
>
> St. Bartholemew was massacred in 1492.
>
> The Brittains were the Saxons who entered England in 1492 under Julius Cæsar.
>
> The earth is 1492 miles in circumference.

To proceed with "History":

> Christopher Columbus was called the Father of his Country.
>
> Queen Isabella of Spain sold her watch and chain and other millinery so that Columbus could discover America.
>
> The Indian wars were very desecrating to the country.
>
> The Indians pursued their warfare by hiding in the bushes and then scalping them.
>
> Captain John Smith has been styled the father of his country. His life was saved by his daughter Pochahantas.
>
> The Puritans found an insane asylum in the wilds of America.
>
> The Stamp Act was to make everybody stamp all materials so they should be null and void.
>
> Washington died in Spain almost broken-hearted. His remains were taken to the cathedral in Havana.

Gorilla warfare was where men rode on gorillas.

John Brown was a very good insane man who tried to get fugitives slaves into Virginia. He captured all the inhabitants, but was finally conquered and condemned to his death. The Confederasy was formed by the fugitive slaves.

Alfred the Great reigned 872 years. He was distinguished for letting some buckwheat cakes burn, and the lady scolded him.

Henry Eight was famous for being a great widower haveing lost several wives.

Lady Jane Grey studied Greek and Latin and was beheaded after a few days.

John Bright is noted for an incurable disease.

Lord James Gordon Bennett instigated the Gordon Riots.

The Middle Ages come in between antiquity and posterity.

Luther introduced Christianity into England a good many thousand years ago. His birthday was November 1883. He was once a Pope. He lived at the time of the Rebellion of Worms.

Julius Cæsar is noted for his famous telegram dispatch I came I saw I conquered.

Julius Cæsar was really a very great man. He was a very great soldier and wrote a book for beginners in the Latin.

Cleopatra was caused by the death of an asp which she dissolved in a wine cup.

The only form of government in Greece was a limited monkey.

The Persian war lasted about 500 years.

Greece had only 7 wise men.

Socrates . . . destroyed some statues and had to drink Shamrock.

Here is a fact correctly stated; and yet it is phrased with such ingenious infelicity that it can be depended upon to convey misinformation every time it is uncarefully read:

> By the Salic law no woman or descendant of a woman could occupy the throne.

To show how far a child can travel in history with judicious and diligent boosting in the public school, we select the following mosaic:

Abraham Lincoln was born in Wales in 1599.

In the chapter headed "Intellectual" I find a great number of most interesting statements. A sample or two may be found not amiss:

Bracebridge Hall was written by Henry Irving.

Snow Bound was written by Peter Cooper.

The House of the Seven Cables was written by Lord Bryant.

Edgar A. Poe was a very curdling writer.

Cotton Mather was a writer who invented the cotten gin and wrote histories.

Beowulf wrote the Scriptures.

Ben Johnson survived Shakspeare in some respects.

In the Canterbury Tale it gives account of King Alfred on his way to the shrine of Thomas Bucket.

Chaucer was the father of English pottery.

Chaucer was a bland verse writer of the third century.

Chaucer was succeeded by H. Wads. Longfellow an American Writer. His writings were chiefly prose and nearly one hundred years elapsed.

Shakspere translated the Scriptures and it was called St. James because he did it.

In the middle of the chapter I find many pages of information concerning Shakespeare's plays, Milton's works, and those of Bacon, Addison, Samuel Johnson, Fielding, Richardson, Sterne, Smollett, De Foe, Locke, Pope, Swift, Goldsmith, Burns, Cowper, Wordsworth, Gibbon, Byron, Coleridge, Hood, Scott, Macaulay, George Eliot, Dickens, Bulwer, Thackeray, Browning, Mrs. Browning, Tennyson, and Disraeli—a fact which shows that into the restricted stomach of the public-school pupil is shoveled every year the blood, bone, and viscera of a gigantic literature, and the same is there digested and disposed of in a most successful and characteristic and gratifying public-school way. I have space for but a trifling few of the results:

Lord Byron was the son of an heiress and a drunken man.

Wm. Wordsworth wrote the Barefoot Boy and Imitations on Immortality.

Gibbon wrote a history of his travels in Italy. This was original.

George Eliot left a wife and children who mourned greatly for his genius.

George Eliot Miss Mary Evans Mrs. Cross Mrs. Lewis was the greatest female poet unless George Sands is made an exception of.

Bulwell is considered a good writer.

Sir Walter Scott Charles Bronte Alfred the Great and Johnson were the first great novelists.

Thomas Babington Makorlay graduated at Harvard and then studied law, he is raised to the peerage as baron in 1557 and died in 1776.

Here are two or three miscellaneous facts that may be of value, if taken in moderation:

Homer's writings are Homer's Essays Virgil the Aneid and Paradise lost some people say that these poems were not written by Homer but by another man of the same name.

A sort of sadness kind of shone in Bryant's poems.

Holmes is a very profligate and amusing writer.

When the public-school pupil wrestles with the political features of the Great Republic, they throw him sometimes:

A bill becomes a law when the President vetoes it.

The three departments of the government is the President rules the world, the governor rules the State, the mayor rules the city.

The first conscientious Congress met in Philadelphia.

The Constitution of the United States was established to ensure domestic hostility.

Truth crushed to earth will rise again. As follows:

The Constitution of the United States is that part of the book at the end which nobody reads.

And here she rises once more and untimely. There should be a limit to public-school instruction; it cannot be wise or well to let the young find out everything:

> Congress is divided into civilized half civilized and savage.

Here are some results of study in music and oratory:

> An interval in music is the distance on the keyboard from one piano to the next.
>
> A rest means you are not to sing it.
>
> Emphasis is putting more distress on one word than another.

The chapter on "Physiology" contains much that ought not to be lost to science:

> Physillogigy is to study about your bones stummick and vertebry.
>
> Occupations which are injurious to health are carbolic acid gas which is impure blood.
>
> We have an upper and a lower skin. The lower skin moves all the time and the upper skin moves when we do.
>
> The body is mostly composed of water and about one half is avaricious tissue.
>
> The stomach is a small pear-shaped bone situated in the body.
>
> The gastric juice keeps the bones from creaking.
>
> The Chyle flows up the middle of the backbone and reaches the heart where it meets the oxygen and is purified.
>
> The salivary glands are used to salivate the body.
>
> In the stomach starch is changed to cane sugar and cane sugar to sugar cane.
>
> The olfactory nerve enters the cavity of the orbit and is developed into the special sense of hearing.
>
> The growth of a tooth begins in the back of the mouth and extends to the stomach.
>
> If we were on a railroad track and a train was coming the train would deafen our ears so that we couldn't see to get off the track.

If, up to this point, none of my quotations have added flavor to the Johnsonian anecdote at the head of this article, let us make another attempt:

> The theory that intuitive truths are discovered by the light of nature originated from St. John's interpretation of a passage in the Gospel of Plato.
>
> The weight of the earth is found by comparing a mass of known lead with that of a mass of unknown lead.
>
> To find the weight of the earth take the length of a degree on a meridian and multiply by 62½ pounds.
>
> The spheres are to each other as the squares of their homologous sides.
>
> A body will go just as far in the first second as the body will go plus the force of gravity and that's equal to twice what the body will go.
>
> Specific gravity is the weight to be compared weight of an equal volume of or that is the weight of a body compared with the weight of an equal volume.
>
> The law of fluid pressure divide the different forms of organized bodies by the form of attraction and the number increased will be the form.
>
> Inertia is that property of bodies by virtue of which it cannot change its own condition of rest or motion. In other words it is the negative quality of passiveness either in recoverable latency or insipient latescence.

If a laugh is fair here, not the struggling child, nor the unintelligent teacher—or rather the unintelligent Boards, Committees, and Trustees—are the proper target for it. All through this little book one detects the signs of a certain probable fact—that a large part of the pupil's "instruction" consists in cramming him with obscure and wordy "rules" which he does not understand and has no time to understand. It would be as useful to cram him with brickbats; they would at least stay. In a town in the interior of New York, a few years ago, a gentleman set forth a mathematical problem and proposed to give a prize to every public-school pupil who should furnish the correct solution of it. Twenty-two of the brightest boys in the public schools entered the contest. The problem was not a very difficult one for pupils of their mathematical rank and standing, yet they all failed—by a hair—through one trifling mistake or another. Some searching questions were asked, when it turned out that these lads were as glib as parrots with the "rules," but could not reason out a single rule or explain the principle underlying it. Their memories had been stocked, but not their understandings. It was a case of brickbat culture, pure and simple.

There are several curious "compositions" in the little book, and we must make room for one. It is full of naïveté, brutal truth, and unembarrassed directness, and is the funniest (genuine) boy's composition I think I have ever seen:

ON GIRLS

Girls are very stuck up and dignefied in their maner and be have your. They think more of dress than anything and like to play with dowls and rags. They cry if they see a cow in a far distance and are afraid of guns. They stay at home all the time and go to church on Sunday. They are al-ways sick. They are al-ways funy and making fun of boy's hands and they say how dirty. They cant play marbels. I pity them poor things. They make fun of boys and then turn round and love them. I dont beleave they ever kiled a cat or anything. They look out every nite and say oh ant the moon lovely. Thir is one thing I have not told and that is they al-ways now their lessons bettern boys.

From Mr. Edward Charming's recent article in *Science:*

The marked difference between the books now being produced by French, English, and American travelers, on the one hand, and German explorers, on the other, is too great to escape attention. That difference is due entirely to the fact that in school and university the German is taught, in the first place to see, and in the second place to understand what he does see.

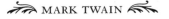

Fenimore Cooper's Literary Offenses

The Pathfinder and *The Deerslayer* stand at the head of Cooper's novels as artistic creations. There are others of his works which contain parts as perfect as are to be found in these, and scenes even more thrilling. Not one can be compared with either of them as a finished whole.

The defects in both of these tales are comparatively slight. They were pure works of art. — *Prof. Lounsbury*.

The five tales reveal an extraordinary fulness of invention. . . . One of the very greatest characters in fiction, "Natty Bumppo." . . . The craft of the woodsman, the tricks of the trapper, all the delicate art of the forest, were familiar to Cooper from his youth up. — *Prof. Brander Matthews*.

Cooper is the greatest artist in the domain of romantic fiction yet produced by America. — *Wilkie Collins*.

IT SEEMS TO me that it was far from right for the Professor of English Literature in Yale, the Professor of English Literature in Columbia, and Wilkie Collins, to deliver opinions on Cooper's literature without having read some of it. It would have been much more decorous to keep silent and let persons talk who have read Cooper.

Cooper's art has some defects. In one place in *Deerslayer*, and in the restricted space of two-thirds of a page, Cooper has scored 114 offences against literary art out of a possible 115. It breaks the record.

There are nineteen rules governing literary art in the domain of romantic fiction—some say twenty-two. In *Deerslayer* Cooper violated eighteen of them. These eighteen require:

1. That a tale shall accomplish something and arrive somewhere. But the *Deerslayer* tale accomplishes nothing and arrives in the air.

2. They require that the episodes of a tale shall be necessary parts of the tale, and shall help to develop it. But as the *Deerslayer* tale is not a tale, and accomplishes nothing and arrives nowhere, the episodes have no rightful place in the work, since there was nothing for them to develop.

3. They require that the personages in a tale shall be alive, except in the case of corpses, and that always the reader shall be able to tell the corpses from the others. But this detail has often been overlooked in the *Deerslayer* tale.

4. They require that the personages in a tale, both dead and alive, shall exhibit a sufficient excuse for being there. But this detail also has been overlooked in the *Deerslayer* tale.

5. They require that when the personages of a tale deal in conversation, the talk shall sound like human talk, and be talk such as human beings would be likely to talk in the given circumstances, and have a discoverable meaning, also a discoverable purpose, and a show of relevancy, and remain in the neighborhood of the subject in hand, and be interesting to the reader, and help out the tale, and stop when the people cannot think of anything more to say. But this requirement has been ignored from the beginning of the *Deerslayer* tale to the end of it.

6. They require that when the author describes the character of a personage in his tale, the conduct and conversation of that personage shall justify said description. But this law gets little or no attention in the *Deerslayer* tale, as "Natty Bumppo's" case will amply prove.

7. They require that when a personage talks like an illustrated, gilt-edged, tree-calf, hand-tooled, seven-dollar Friendship's Offering in the beginning of a paragraph, he shall not talk like a negro minstrel in the end of it. But this rule is flung down and danced upon in the *Deerslayer* tale.

8. They require that crass stupidities shall not be played upon the reader as "the craft of the woodsman, the delicate art of the forest," by either the author or the people in the tale. But this rule is persistently violated in the *Deerslayer* tale.

9. They require that the personages of a tale shall confine themselves to possibilities and let miracles alone; or, if they venture a miracle, the author must so plausibly set it forth as to make it look possible and reasonable. But these rules are not respected in the *Deerslayer* tale.

10. They require that the author shall make the render feel a deep interest in the personages of his tale and in their fate; and that he shall make the reader love the good people in the tale and hate the bad ones. But the reader of the *Deerslayer*

tale dislikes the good people in it, is indifferent to the others, and wishes they would all get drowned together.

11. They require that the characters in a tale shall be so clearly defined that the reader can tell beforehand what each will do in a given emergency. But in the *Deerslayer* tale this rule is vacated.

In addition to these large rules there are some little ones. These require that the author shall

12. *Say* what he is proposing to say, not merely come near it.

13. Use the right word, not its second cousin.

14. Eschew surplusage.

15. Not omit necessary details.

16. Avoid slovenliness of form.

17. Use good grammar.

18. Employ a simple and straightforward style.

Even these seven are coldly and persistently violated in the *Deerslayer* tale.

Cooper's gift in the way of invention was not a rich endowment; but such as it was he liked to work it, he was pleased with the effects, and indeed he did some quite sweet things with it. In his little box of stage properties he kept six or eight cunning devices, tricks, artifices for his savages and woodsmen to deceive and circumvent each other with, and he was never so happy as when he was working these innocent things and seeing them go. A favorite one was to make a moccasined person tread in the tracks of the moccasined enemy and thus hide his own trail.

Cooper wore out barrels and barrels of moccasins in working that trick. Another stage-property that he pulled out of his box pretty frequently was his broken twig. He prized his broken twig above all the rest of his effects, and worked it the hardest. It is a restful chapter in any book of his when somebody doesn't step on a dry twig and alarm all the reds and whites for two hundred yards around. Every time a Cooper person is in peril, and absolute silence is worth four dollars a minute, he is sure to step on a dry twig. There may be a hundred handier things to step on, but that wouldn't satisfy Cooper. Cooper requires him to turn out and find a dry twig; and if he can't do it, go and borrow one. In fact the Leather Stocking Series ought to have been called the Broken Twig Series.

EVERY TIME A COOPER PERSON IS IN PERIL, AND ABSOLUTE SILENCE IS WORTH FOUR DOLLARS A MINUTE, HE IS SURE TO STEP ON A DRY TWIG.

I am sorry there is not room to put in a few dozen instances of the delicate art of the forest, as practiced by Natty Bumppo and some of the other Cooperian experts. Perhaps we may venture two or three samples. Cooper was a sailor—a naval officer; yet he gravely tells us how a vessel, driving toward a lee shore in a gale, is steered for a particular spot by her skipper because he knows of an *undertow* there which will hold her back against the gale and save her. For just pure woodcraft, or sailor craft, or whatever it is, isn't that neat? For several years Cooper was daily in the society of artillery, and he ought to have noticed that when a cannon-ball strikes the ground it either buries itself or skips a hundred feet or so; skips again a hundred feet or so—and so on, till it finally gets tired and rolls. Now in one place he loses some "females"—as he always calls women—in the edge of a wood near a plain at night in a fog, on purpose to give Bumppo a chance to show off the delicate art of the forest before the reader. These mislaid people are hunting for a fort. They hear a cannon-blast, and a cannon-ball presently comes rolling into the wood and stops at their feet. To the females this suggests nothing. The case is very different with the admirable Bumppo. I wish I may never know peace again if he doesn't strike out promptly and follow the track of that cannon-ball across the plain through the dense fog and find the fort. Isn't it a daisy? If Cooper had any real knowledge of Nature's ways of doing things, he had a most delicate art in concealing the fact. For instance: one of his acute Indian experts, Chingachgook (pronounced Chicago, I think), has lost the trail of a person he is tracking through the forest. Apparently that trail is hopelessly lost. Neither you nor I could ever have guessed out the way to find it. It was very different with Chicago. Chicago was not stumped for long. He turned a running stream out of its course, and there, in the slush in its old bed, were that person's moccasin tracks. The current did not wash them away, as it would have done in all other like cases—no, even the eternal laws of Nature have to vacate when Cooper wants to put up a delicate job of woodcraft on the reader.

We must be a little wary when Brander Matthews tells us that Cooper's books "reveal an extraordinary fulness of invention." As a rule, I am quite willing to accept Brander Matthews's literary judgments and applaud his lucid and graceful phrasing of them; but that particular statement needs to be taken with a few tons of salt. Bless your heart, Cooper hadn't any more invention than a horse; and I don't mean a high-class horse, either; I mean a clothes-horse. It would be very difficult to find a real, clever "situation" in Cooper's books; and still more difficult to find one of any kind which he has failed to tender absurd by his handling of it. Look at the episodes of "the caves;" and at the celebrated scuffle between Magua and those others on the table-land a few days later; and at Hurry Harry's queer water-transit from the castle to the ark; and at Deerslayer's half hour with his first corpse; and at the quarrel between Hurry Harry and Deerslayer later; and at—but choose for yourself; you can't go amiss.

If Cooper had been an observer, his inventive faculty would have worked better, not more interestingly, but more rationally, more plausibly. Cooper's proudest creations in the way of "situations" suffer noticeably from the absence of the observer's protecting gift. Cooper's eye was splendidly inaccurate. Cooper seldom saw anything correctly. He saw nearly all things as through a glass eye, darkly. Of course a man who cannot see the commonest little everyday matters accurately is working at a disadvantage when he is constructing a "situation." In the *Deerslayer* tale Cooper has a stream which is fifty feet wide, where it flows out of a lake; it presently narrows to twenty as it meanders along for no good reason, and yet, when a stream acts like that it ought to be required to explain itself. Fourteen pages later the width of the brook's outlet from the lake has suddenly shrunk thirty feet, and become "the narrowest part of the stream." This shrinkage is not accounted for. The stream has bends in it, a sure indication that it has alluvial banks, and cuts them; yet these bends are only thirty and fifty feet long. If Cooper had been a nice and punctilious observer he would have noticed that the bends were oftener nine hundred feet long than short of it.

Cooper made the exit of that stream fifty feet wide in the first place, for no particular reason; in the second place, he narrowed it to less than twenty to accommodate some Indians. He bends a "sapling" to the form of an arch over this narrow passage, and conceals six Indians in its foliage. They are "laying" for a settler's scow or ark which is coming up the stream on its way to the lake; it is being hauled against the stiff current by a rope whose stationary end is anchored in the lake; its rate of progress cannot be more than a mile an hour. Cooper describes the ark, but pretty obscurely. In the matter of dimensions "it was little more than a modern canal boat." Let us guess, then, that it was about 140 feet long. It was of "greater breadth than common." Let us guess, then, that it was about sixteen feet wide. This leviathan had been prowling down bends which were but a third as long as itself, and scraping between banks where it had only two feet of space to spare on each side. We cannot too much admire this miracle. A low-roofed log dwelling occupies "two-thirds of the ark's length"—a dwelling ninety feet long and sixteen feet wide, let us say—a kind of vestibule train. The dwelling has two rooms—each forty-five feet long and sixteen feet wide, let us guess. One of them is the bed-room of the Hutter girls, Judith and Hetty; the other is the parlor, in the day time, at night it is papa's bed chamber. The ark is arriving at the stream's exit, now, whose width has been reduced to less than twenty feet to accommodate the Indians—say to eighteen. There is a foot to spare on each side of the boat. Did the Indians notice that there was going to be a tight squeeze? Did they notice that they could make money by climbing down out of that arched sapling and just stepping aboard when the ark scraped by? No; other Indians would have noticed these things, but Cooper's Indians never notice anything. Cooper thinks they are marvellous creatures for noticing, but he was almost always in error about his Indians. There was seldom a sane one among them.

The ark is 140 feet long; the dwelling is 90 feet long. The idea of the Indians is to drop softly and secretly from the arched sapling to the dwelling as the ark creeps along under it at the rate of a mile an hour, and butcher the family. It will take the ark a minute and a half to pass under. It will take the 90-foot dwelling a minute to pass under. Now, then, what did the six Indians do? It would take you thirty years to guess, and even then you would have to give it up, I believe. Therefore, I will tell you what the Indians did. Their chief, a person of quite extraordinary intellect for a Cooper Indian, warily watched the canal boat as it squeezed along under him, and when he had got his calculations fined down to exactly the right shade, as he judged, he let go and dropped. And missed the house! That is actually what he did. He missed the house, and landed in the stern of the scow. It was not much of a fall, yet it knocked him silly. He lay there unconscious. If the house had been 97 feet long, he would have made the trip. The fault was Cooper's, not his. The error lay in the construction of the house. Cooper was no architect.

There still remained in the roost five Indians. The boat has passed under and is now out of their reach. Let me explain what the five did—you would not be able to reason it out for yourself. No. 1 jumped for the boat, but fell in the water astern of it. Then No. 2 jumped for the boat, but fell in the water still further astern of it. Then No. 3 jumped for the boat, and fell a good way astern of it. Then No. 4 jumped for the boat, and fell in the water away astern. Then even No. 5 made a jump for the boat—for he was a Cooper Indian. In the matter of intellect, the difference between a Cooper Indian and the Indian that stands in front of the cigar shop is not spacious. The scow episode is really a sublime burst of invention; but it does not thrill, because the inaccuracy of the details throws a sort of air of fictitiousness and general improbability over it. This comes of Cooper's inadequacy as an observer.

The reader will find some examples of Cooper's high talent for inaccurate observation in the account of the shooting match in *The Pathfinder*. "A common wrought nail was driven lightly into the target, its head having been first touched with paint." The color of the paint is not stated—an important omission, but Cooper deals freely in important omissions. No, after all, it was not an important omission; for this nail head is a hundred yards from the marksman and could not be seen by them at that distance no matter what its color might be. How far can the best eyes see a common house fly? A hundred yards? It is quite impossible. Very well, eyes that cannot see a house fly that is a hundred yards away cannot see an ordinary nail head at that distance, for the size of the two objects is the same. It takes a keen eye to see a fly or a nail head at fifty yards—one hundred and fifty feet. Can the reader do it?

The nail was lightly driven, its head painted, and game called. Then the Cooper miracles began. The bullet of the first marksman chipped an edge of the nail head; the next man's bullet drove the nail a little way into the target and removed all the paint. Haven't the miracles gone far enough now? Not to suit Cooper; for the purpose of this whole scheme is to show off his prodigy, Deerslayer-Hawkeye-Long-Rifle-Leather-Stocking-Pathfinder-Bumppo before the ladies.

> "Be all ready to clench it, boys!" cried out Pathfinder, stepping into his friend's tracks the instant they were vacant. "Never mind a new nail; I can see that, though the paint is gone, and what I can see, I can hit at a hundred yards, though it were only a mosquitoe's eye. Be ready to clench!"
>
> The rifle cracked, the bullet sped its way and the head of the nail was buried in the wood, covered by the piece of flattened lead.

There, you see, is a man who could hunt flies with a rifle, and command a ducal salary in a Wild West show to-day, if we had him back with us.

The recorded feat is certainly surprising, just as it stands; but it is not surprising enough for Cooper. Cooper adds a touch. He has made Pathfinder do this miracle with another man's rifle, and not only that, but Pathfinder did not have even the advantage of loading it himself. He had everything against him, and yet he made that impossible shot, and not only made it, but did it with absolute confidence, saying, "Be ready to clench." Now a person like that would have undertaken that same feat with a brickbat, and with Cooper to help he would have achieved it, too.

Pathfinder showed off handsomely that day before the ladies. His very first feat was a thing which no Wild West show can touch. He was standing with the group of marksmen, observing—a hundred yards from the target, mind: one Jasper raised his rifle and drove the centre of the bull's-eye. Then the quartermaster fired. The target exhibited no result this time. There was a laugh. "It's a dead miss" said Major Lundie. Pathfinder waited an impressive moment or two, then said in that calm, indifferent, know-it-all way of his, "No, Major—he has covered Jasper's bullet, as will be seen if anyone will take the trouble to examine the target."

Wasn't it remarkable! How *could* he see that little pellet fly through the air and enter that distant bullet-hole? Yet that is what he did; for nothing is impossible to a Cooper person. Did any of those people have any deep-seated doubts about this thing? No; for that would imply sanity, and these were all Cooper people.

> The respect for Pathfinder's skill and for his *quickness* and *accuracy* of sight (the italics are mine) was so profound and general, that the instant he made this declaration the spectators began to distrust their own opinions, and a dozen rushed to the target in order to ascertain the fact. There, sure enough, it is found that the quartermaster's bullet had gone through the hole made by Jasper's, and that, too, so accurately as to require a minute examination to be certain of the circumstance, which, however, was soon clearly established by discovering one bullet over the other in the stump against which the target was placed.

They made a "minute" examination; but never mind, how could they know that there were two bullets in that hole without digging the latest one out? for neither probe nor eyesight could prove the presence of any more than one bullet. Did they dig? No; as we shall see. It is the Pathfinder's turn now; he steps out before the ladies, takes aim, and fires.

But alas! here is a disappointment; an incredible, an unimaginable disappointment—for the target's aspect is unchanged; there is nothing there but that same old bullet hole!

> "If one dared to hint at such a thing," cried Major Duncan, "I should say that the Pathfinder has also missed the target."

As nobody had missed it yet, the "also" was not necessary; but never mind about that, for the Pathfinder is going to speak.

> "No, no, Major," said he, confidently, "that *would* be a risky declaration. I didn't load the piece, and can't say what was in it, but if it was lead, you will find the bullet driving down those of the Quartermaster and Jasper, else is not my name Pathfinder."
>
> A shout from the target announced the truth of this assertion.

Is the miracle sufficient as it stands? Not for Cooper. The Pathfinder speaks again, as he "now slowly advances towards the stage occupied by the females:"

> "That's not all, boys, that's not all; if you find the target touched at all, I'll own to a miss. The quartermaster cut the wood, but you'll find no wood cut by that last messenger."

The miracle is at last complete. He knew—doubtless *saw*—at the distance of a hundred yards—that his bullet had passed into the hole *without fraying the edges*. There were now three bullets in that one hole—three bullets imbedded processionally in the body of the stump back of the target. Everybody knew this—somehow or other—and yet nobody had dug any of them out to make sure. Cooper is not a close observer, but he is interesting. He is certainly always that, no matter what happens. And he is more interesting when he is not noticing what he is about than when he is. This is a considerable merit.

The conversations in the Cooper books have a curious sound in our modern ears. To believe that such talk really ever came out of people's mouths would be to believe that there was a time when time was of no value to a person who thought he had something to say; when it was the custom to spread a two-minute remark out to ten; when a man's mouth was a rolling-mill, and busied itself all day long in turning four-foot pigs of thought into thirty-foot bars of conversational railroad iron by attenuation; when subjects were seldom faithfully stuck to, but the talk wandered all around and arrived nowhere; when conversations consisted mainly of irrelevances, with here and there a relevancy, a relevancy with an embarrassed look, as not being able to explain how it got there.

Cooper was certainly not a master in the construction of dialogue. Inaccurate observation defeated him here as it defeated him in so many other enterprises of his. He even failed to notice that the man who talks corrupt English six days in the week must and will talk it on the seventh, and can't help himself. In the *Deerslayer* story he lets Deerslayer talk the showiest kind of book talk sometimes, and at other times the basest of base dialects. For instance, when some one asks him if he has a sweetheart, and if so, where she abides, this is his majestic answer:

> "She's in the forest—hanging from the boughs of the trees, in a soft rain—in the dew on the open grass—the clouds that float about in the blue heavens—the birds that sing in the woods—the sweet springs where I slake my thirst—and in all the other glorious gifts that come from God's Providence!"

And he preceded that, a little before, with this:

> "It consarns me as all things that touches a fri'nd consarns a fri'nd."

And this is another of his remarks:

> "If I was Injin born, now, I might tell of this, or carry in the scalp and boast of the expl'ite afore the whole tribe; or if my inimy had only been a bear"—and so on.

We cannot imagine such a thing as a veteran Scotch Commander-in-Chief comporting himself in the field like a windy melodramatic actor, but Cooper could. On one occasion Alice and Cora were being chased by the French through a fog in the neighborhood of their father's fort:

> *Point de quartier aux coquins*!" cried an eager pursuer, who seemed to direct the operations of the enemy.
>
> "Stand firm and be ready, my gallant 60ths!" suddenly exclaimed a voice above them; "wait to see the enemy; fire low, and sweep the glacis."
>
> "Father! father!" exclaimed a piercing cry from out of the mist; "it is I! Alice! thy own Elsie! spare, O! save your daughters!"
>
> "Hold!" shouted the former speaker, in the awful tones of parental agony, the sound reaching even to the woods, and rolling back in solemn echo. "'Tis she! God has restored me my

> children! Throw open the sally-port; to the field, 60ths, to the field; pull not a trigger, lest ye kill my lambs! Drive off these dogs of France with your steel."

Cooper's word-sense was singularly dull. When a person has a poor ear for music he will flat and sharp right along without knowing it. He keeps near the tune, but it is not the tune. When a person has a poor ear for words, the result is a literary flatting and sharping; you perceive what he is intending to say, but you also perceive that he doesn't *say* it. This is Cooper. He was not a word-musician. His ear was satisfied with the *approximate* word. I will furnish some circumstantial evidence in support of this charge. My instances are gathered from half a dozen pages of the tale called *Deerslayer*. He uses "verbal," for "oral"; "precision," for "facility"; "phenomena," for "marvels"; "necessary," for "predetermined"; "unsophisticated," for "primitive"; "preparation," for "expectancy"; "rebuked," for "subdued"; "dependent on," for "resulting from"; "fact," for "condition"; "fact," for "conjecture"; "precaution," for "caution"; "explain," for "determine"; "mortified," for "disappointed"; "meretricious," for "factitious"; "materially," for "considerably"; "decreasing," for "deepening"; "increasing," for "disappearing"; "embedded," for "enclosed"; "treacherous," for "hostile"; "stood," for "stooped"; "softened," for "replaced"; "rejoined," for "remarked"; "situation," for "condition"; "different," for "differing"; "insensible", for "unsentient"; "brevity," for "celerity"; "distrusted," for "suspicious"; "mental imbecility," for "imbecility"; "eyes," for "sight"; "counteracting," for "opposing"; "funeral obsequies," for "obsequies."

There have been daring people in the world who claimed that Cooper could write English, but they are all dead now—all dead but Lounsbury. I don't remember that Lounsbury makes the claim in so many words, still he makes it, for he says that *Deerslayer* is a "pure work of art." Pure, in that connection, means faultless—faultless in all details—and language is a detail. If Mr. Lounsbury had only compared Cooper's English with the English which he writes himself—but it is plain that he didn't; and so it is likely that he imagines until this day that Cooper's is as clean and compact as his own. Now I feel sure, deep down in my heart, that Cooper wrote about the poorest English that exists in our language, and that the English of *Deerslayer* is the very worst that even Cooper ever wrote.

I may be mistaken, but it does seem to me that *Deerslayer* is not a work of art in any sense; it does seem to me that it is destitute of every detail that goes to the making of a work of art; in truth, it seems to me that *Deerslayer* is just simply a literary *delerium tremens*.

A work of art? It has no invention; it has no order, system, sequence, or result; it has no lifelikeness, no thrill, no stir, no seeming of reality; its characters are confusedly drawn, and by their acts and words they prove that they are not the sort of people the author claims that they are; its humor is pathetic; its pathos is funny; its conversations are—oh! indescribable; its love-scenes odious; its English a crime against the language.

Counting these out, what is left is Art. I think we must all admit that.

Marjorie Fleming, the Wonder Child

Marjorie has been in her tiny grave a hundred years; and still the tears fall for her, and will fall. What an intensely human little creature she was! How vividly she lived her small life; how impulsive she was; how sudden, how tempestuous, how tender, how loving, how sweet, how loyal, how rebellious, how repentant, how wise, how unwise, how bursting with fun, how frank, how free, how honest, how innocently bad, how natively good, how charged with quaint philosophies, how winning, how precious, how adorable—and how perennially and indestructibly interesting! And all this exhibited, proved, and recorded before she reached the end of her ninth year and "fell on sleep."

Geographically considered, the lassie was a Scot; but in fact she had no frontiers, she was the world's child, she was the human race in little. It is one of the prides of my life that the first time I ever heard her name it came from the lips of Dr. John Brown—his very own self—Dr. John Brown of Edinburgh—Dr. John Brown of *Rab and His Friends*—Dr. John Brown of the beautiful face and the sweet spirit, whose friends loved him with a love that was worship—Dr. John Brown, who was Marjorie's biographer, and who clasped an aged hand that has caressed Marjorie's fifty years before, thus linking me with that precious child by an unbroken chain of handshakes, for I had shaken hands with Dr. John. This was in Edinburgh thirty-six years ago. He gave my wife his little biography of Marjorie, and I have it yet.

Is Marjorie known in America? No—at least to only a few. When Mr. L. MacBean's new and enlarged and charming biography* of her was published five years ago it was sent over here in sheets, the market not being large enough to justify recomposing and reprinting it on our side of the water. I find that there are even cultivated Scotchmen among us who have not heard of Marjorie Fleming.

She was born in Kirkcaldy in 1803, and she died when she was eight years and eleven months old. By the time she was five years old she was become a devourer of various kinds of literature—both heavy and light—and was also become a quaint and free-spoken and charming little thinker and philosopher whose views were a delightful jumble of first-hand cloth of gold and second-hand rags.

When she was six she opened up that rich mine, her journals, and continued to work it by spells during the remainder of her brief life. She was a pet of Walter Scott, from the cradle, and when he could have her society for a few hours he was content, and required no other. Her little head was full of noble passages from Shakespeare and other favorites of hers, and the fact that she could deliver them with moving effect is proof that her elocution was a born gift with her, and not a mechanical reproduction of somebody else's art, for a child's parrot-work does not move. When she was a little creature of seven years, Sir Walter Scott "would read ballads to her in his own glorious way, the two getting wild with excitement over them; and he would take her on his knee and make her repeat Constance's speeches in *King John* till he swayed to and fro, sobbing his fill." [Dr. John Brown.]

SHE WAS MADE OUT OF THUNDER-STORMS AND SUNSHINE, AND NOT EVEN HER LITTLE PERFUNCTORY PIETIES AND SHOP-MADE HOLINESS COULD SQUELCH HER SPIRITS OR PUT OUT HER FIRES FOR LONG.

"Sobbing his fill"—that great man—over that little thing's inspired interpretations. It is a striking picture; there is no mate to it. Sir Walter Scott said of her:

"She's the most extraordinary creature I ever met with, and her repeating of Shakespeare overpowers me as nothing else does."

She spent the whole of her little life in a Presbyterian heaven; yet she was not affected by it; she could not have been happier if she had been in another heaven.

* *Marjorie Fleming*. By L. MacBean G.P. Putnam's Sons Publishers, London and New York. Permission to use the extracts quoted from Marjorie's Journals has been granted me by the publishers.

She was made out of thunder-storms and sunshine, and not even her little perfunctory pieties and shop-made holiness could squelch her spirits or put out her fires for long. Under pressure of a pestering sense of duty she heaves a shovelful of trade godliness into her journal every little while, but it does not offend, for none of it is her own; it is all borrowed, it is a convention, a custom of her environment, it is the most innocent of hypocrisies, and this tainted butter of hers soon gets to be as delicious to the reader as are the stunning and worldly sincerities she splatters around it every time her pen takes a fresh breath. The adorable child! she hasn't a discoverable blemish in her make-up anywhere.

Marjorie's first letter was written before she was six years old; it was to her cousin, Isa Keith, a young lady of whom she was passionately fond. It was done in a sprawling hand, ten words to the page—and in those foolscap days a page was a spacious thing:

> "My Dear Isa—
>
> "I now sit down on my botom to answer all the kind & beloved letters which you was so so good as to write to me. This is the first time I ever wrote a letter in my Life.
>
> "Miss Potune, a lady of my acquaintance, praises me dreadfully. I repeated something out of Deen Swift & she said I was fit for the stage, & you may thing I was primmed up with majestick Pride, but upon my word I felt myself turn a little birsay–birsay is a word which is a word that William composed which is as you may suppose a little enraged. This horid fat Simpliton says that my Aunt is beautifull which is intirely impossible for that is not her nature."

Frank? Yes, Marjorie was that. And during the brief moment that she enchanted this dull earth with her presence she was the bewitchingest speller and punctuator in all of Christendom.

The average child of six "prints" its correspondence in rickety and reeling Roman capitals, or dictates to mamma, who puts the little chap's message on paper. The sentences are labored, repetitious, and slow: there are but three or four of them; they deal in information solely, they contain no ideas, they venture no judgments, no opinions; they inform papa that the cat has had kittens again; that Mary has a new doll that can wink; that Tommy has lost his top; and will papa come soon and bring the writer something nice? But with Marjorie it is different.

She needs no amanuensis, she puts her message on paper herself; and not in weak and tottering Roman capitals, but in a thundering hand that can be heard a mile and be read across the square without glasses. And she doesn't have to study, and puzzle, and search her head for something to say; no, she had only to connect the pen with the paper and turn on the current; the words spring forth at once, and go chasing after each other like leaves dancing down a stream. For she has a faculty, has Marjorie! Indeed yes; when she sits down on her botom to do a letter, there isn't going to be any lack of materials, nor of fluency, and neither is her letter going to be wanting in pepper, or vinegar, or vitriol, or any of the other condiments employed by genius to save a literary work of art from flatness and vapidity. And as for judgments and opinions, they are as commodiously in her line as they are in the Lord Chief Justice's. They have weight, too, and are convincing: for instance, for thirty-six years they have damaged that horid Simpliton in my eyes; and, more than that, they have even imposed upon me—and most unfairly and unwarrantably—an aversion to the horrid fat Simpliton's name; a perfectly innocent name, and yet, because of the prejudice against it with which this child has poisoned my mind for a generation I cannot see "Potune" on paper and keep my gorge from rising.

In her journals Marjorie changes her subject whenever she wants to—and that is pretty often. When the deep moralities pay her a passing visit she registers them. Meantime if a cherished love passage drifts across her memory she shoves it into the midst of the moralities—it is nothing to her that it may not feel at home there:

> "We should not be happy at the death of our fellow creatures, for they love life like us love your neighbor & he will love you Bountifulness and Mercifulness are always rewarded, In my travels I met a handsome lad names Charles Balfour Esge [Esqr.] and from him I got offers of marage—ofers of marage did I say? nay plainly [he] loved me. Goodness does not belong to the wicked but badness dishonor befals wickedness but not virtue, no disgrace befals virtue perciverence overcomes almost al difficulties no I am rong in saying almost I should say always as it is so perciverence is a virtue my Csosin says pacience is a cristain virtue, which is true."

She is not copying these profundities out of a book, she is getting them out of her memory; her spelling shows that the book is not before her. The easy and effortless flow of her talk is a marvellous thing in a baby of her age. Her interests are as wide and varied as a grown person's: she discusses all sorts of books, and fearlessly delivers judgment upon them; she examines whosoever crosses the field of her vision, and again delivers a verdict; she dips into religion and history, and even into politics; she takes a shy at the news of the day, and comments upon it; and now and then she drops into poetry—into rhyme, at any rate.

Marjorie would not intentionally mislead anyone, but she has just been making a remark which moves me to hoist a danger-signal for the protection of the modern reader. It is this one: *"In my travels."* Naturally we are apt to clothe a word with its present-day meaning—the meaning we are used to, the meaning we are familiar with; and so—well, you get the idea: some words that are giants to-day were very small dwarfs a century ago, and if we are not careful to take that vast enlargement into account when we run across them in the literatures of the past, they are apt to convey to us a distinctly wrong impression. To-day, when a person says *"in my travels"* he means that he has been around the globe nineteen or twenty times, and we so understand him; and so, when Marjorie says it, it startles us for a moment, for it gives us the impression that *she* has been around it fourteen or fifteen times; whereas, such is not at all the case. She had travelled prodigiously for *her* day, but not for ours. She had "travelled" altogether, three miles by land and eight by water—per ferry-boat. She is fairly and justly proud of it, for it is the exact equivalent, in grandeur and impressiveness, in the case of a child of our day, to two trips across the Atlantic and a thousand miles by rail.

> "In the love novels all the heroins are very desperate Isabella will not allow me to speak about lovers and heroins, and tiss too refined for my taste a loadstone is a curious thing indeed it is true Heroic love doth never win disgrace this is my maxum and I will follow it forever Miss Eguards [Edgeworth] tails are very good particularly some that are very much adopted for youth as Lazy Lawrence Tarelton False Key &c &c Persons of the parlement house are as I think caled Advocakes Mr. Cay and Mr. Crakey has that honour. This has been a very mild winter. Mr. Banestors Budget is to-night I hope it will be a good one. A great many authors have expressed themselfes too sentimentaly .... The Mercandile Afares are in a perilous situation sickness & a delicante frame I have not & I do not know what it is, but

> Ah me perhaps I shall have it, Grandure reigns in Edinburgh. . . . Tomson is a beautifull author and Pope but nothing is like Shakespear of which I have a little knoledge of. An unfortunate death James the 5 had for he died of greif Macbeth is a pretty composition but awful one Macbeth is so bad & wicked, but Lady Macbeth is so hardened in guilt she does not mind her sins & faults No.
>
> ". . . A sailor called here to say farewell, it must be dreadful to leave his native country where he might get a wife or perhaps me, for I love him very much & with all my heart, but O I forgot Isabella forbid me to speak about love. . . . I wish everybody would follow her example & be as good as pious & virtious as she is & they would get husbands soon enough, love is a papithatick [pathetic] thing as well as troublesome & tiresome but O Isabella forbid me to speak about it."

But the little rascal can't *keep* her from speaking about it, because it is her supreme interest in life; her heart is not capacious enough to hold all the product that is engendered by the ever-recurring inflaming spectacle of man-creatures going by, and the surplus is obliged to spill over; Isa's prohibitions are no sufficient dam for such a discharge.

> "Love I think is the fasion for everybody is marring [marrying]. . . . Yesterday a marrade man named Mr. John Balfour Esg [Esq.] offered to kiss me, & offered to marry me though the man was espused [espoused], & his wife was present & said he must ask her permission but he did not, I think he was ashamed or confounded before 3 gentlman Mr. Jobson and two Mr. Kings."

I must make room here for another of Marjorie's second-hand high-morality outbreaks. They give me a sinful delight which I ought to grieve at, I suppose, but I can't seem to manage it:

> "James Macary is to be transported for murder in the flower of his youth O passion is a terrible thing for it leads people from sin to sin at last it gets so far as to come to greater crimes than

> we thought we could comit and it must be dreadful to leave his native country and his friends and to be so disgraced and affronted."

That is Marjorie talking shop, dear little diplomat—to please and comfort mamma and Isa, no doubt.

This wee little child has a marvellous range of interests. She reads philosophies, novels, baby books, histories, the mighty poets—reads them with burning interest, and frankly and freely criticises them all; she revels in storms, sunsets, cloud effects, scenery of a mountain, plain, ocean, and forest, and all the other wonders of nature, and sets down her joy in them all; she loves people, she detests people, according to mood and circumstances, and delivers her opinion of them, sometimes seasoned with attar of roses, sometimes with vitriol; in games, and all kinds of childish play she is an enthusiast; she adores animals, adores them all; none is too forlorn to fail of favor in her friendly eyes, no creature so humble that she cannot find something in it on which to lavish her caressing worship.

> "I am going to-morrow to a delightfull place, Braehead by name, belonging to Mrs. Crraford [Crauford], where this is ducks cocks hens bobblyjocks 2 dogs 2 cats and swine which is delightful. I think it is shocking to think that the dog and cat should bear them and they are drowned after all."

She is a dear child, a bewitching little scamp; and never dearer, I think, than when the devil has had her in possession and she is breaking her stormy little heart over the remembrance of it:

> "I confess I have been very more like a little young divil than a creature for when Isabella went up stairs to teach me religion and my multiplication and to be good and all my other lessons I stamped with my foot and threw my new hat which she had made on the ground and was sulky and was dreadfully passionate, but she never whiped me but said Marjory go into another room and think what a great crime you are committing letting your temper git the better of you. But I went so sulkily that the devil got the better of me but she never never whips me so that I think I would be the better of it & the next time that I behave

> ill I think she should do it for she never does it. . . . Isabella has given me praise for checking my temper for I was sulky even when she was kneeling an whole hour teaching me to write."

The wise Isabella, the sweet and patient Isabella! It is just a hundred years down (May, 1909) since the grateful child made that golden picture of you and laid your good heart bare for distant generations to see and bless; a hundred years—but if the picture endures a thousand it will still bring you the blessing, and with it the reverent homage that is your due. You had the seeing eye and the wise head. A fool would have punished Marjorie and wrecked her, but you held your hand, as knowing that when her volcanic fires went down she would repent, and grieve, and punish herself, and be saved.

I HAVE ADORED HER BECAUSE SHE DETESTED THAT ODIOUS AND CONFUSING AND UNVANQUISHABLE AND UNLEARNABLE AND SHAMELESS INVENTION, THE MULTIPLICATION TABLE . . .

Sometimes when Marjorie was miraculously good, she got a penny for it, and once she got an entire sixpence, she recognized that it was wealth. This wealth brought joy to her heart. Why? Because she could spend it on somebody else! We who know Marjorie would know that without being told it. I am sorry—often sorry, often grieved—that I was not there and looking over her shoulder when she was writing down her valued penny rewards: I would have said, "Save that scrap of manuscript, dear; make a will, and leave it to your posterity, to save them from want when penury shall threaten them; a day will come when it will be worth a thousand guineas, and a later day will come when it will be worth five thousand; here you are, rejoicing in copper farthings, and don't know that your magic pen is showering gold coin all over the paper." But I was not there to say it; those who were there did not think to say it; and so there is not a line of that quaint precious cacography in existence to-day.

I have adored Marjorie for six-and-thirty years; I have adored her in detail, I have adored the whole of her; but above all other details—just a little above all the other details—I have adored her because she detested that odious and confusing and unvanquishable and unlearnable and shameless invention, the multiplication table:

> "I am now going to tell you the horible and wretched plaege [plague] that my multiplication gives me you can't conceive it

> the most Devilish thing is 8 times 8 & 7 times 7 it is what nature itself cant endure."

I stand reverently uncovered in the presence of that holy verdict.

Here is that person again whom I so dislike—and for no reason at all except that my Marjorie doesn't like her:

> "Miss Potune is very fat she pretends to be very learned she says she saw a stone that dropt from the skies, but she is a good christian."

Of course, stones have fallen from the skies, but I don't believe this horid fat Simpliton had ever seen one that had done it; but even if she had, it was none of her business, and she could have been better employed than in going around exaggerating it and carrying on about it and trying to make trouble with a little child that had never done *her* any harm.

> ". . . The Birds do chirp the Lambs do leap and Nature is clothed with the garments of green yellow, and white, purple, and red.

> ". . . There is a book that is called the Newgate Calendar that contains all the Murders: all the Murders did I say, nay all the Theft & Forgeries that ever were committed and fills me with horror & consternation."

Marjorie is a diligent little student, and her education is always storming along and making great time and lots of noise:

> "Isabella this morning taught me some Franch words one of which is bon saur the interpretation is good morning."

It slanders Isabella, but slander is not intentional. The main thing to notice is that big word, "interpretation." Not many children of Marjorie's age can handle a five syllable team in that easy and confident way. It is observable that she frequently employs words of an imposingly formidable size, and is manifestly quite familiar with them and not at all afraid of them.

> "Isa is teaching me to make Simecolings nots of interrigations periods & commas &c. As this is Sunday I will meditate uppon senciable & Religious subjects first I should be very thankful I am not a beggar as many are."

That was the "first." She didn't get to her second subject, but got side-tracked by a saner interest, and used her time to better purpose.

> "It is melancholy to think, that I have so many talents, & many there are that have not had the attention paid to them that I have, & yet they contrive to be better then me.
>
> ". . . Isabella is far too indulgent to me & even the Miss Crafords say that they wonder at her patience with me & it is indeed true for my temper is a bad one."

The daring child wrote a (synopsized) history of Mary Queen of Scots and five of the royal Jameses in rhyme—but never mind, we have no room to discuss it here. Nothing that was entirely beyond her literary jurisdiction; if it had occurred to her that the laws of Rome needed codifying she would have taken a chance at it.

Here is a sad note:

> "My religion is greatly falling off because I don't pray with so much attention when I am saying my prayers and my character is lost a-mong the Breahead people I hope I will be religious again but as for regaining my character I despare of it."

When religion and character go, they leave a large vacuum. But there are ways to fill it:

> "I've forgot to say, but I've four lovers, the other one is Harry Watson, a very delightful boy. . . . James Keith hardly ever Spoke to me, he said Girl! make less noise. . . . Craky Hall . . . I walked to that delightfull place with a delightfull young man beloved by all his friends and espacialy by me his loveress but I must not talk any longer about him for Isa said it is not proper

for to speak of gentalman but I will never forget him. . . .

> "The Scythians tribe live very coarsely for a Gluton Introdused to Arsaces the Captain of the Army, 1 man who Dressed hair and another man who was a good cook but Arsaces said that he would keep 1 for brushing his horses tail and the other to fead his pigs. . . .
>
> "On Saturday I expected no less than three well-made bucks, the names of whom is here advertised. Mr. Geo Crakey [Cragie], and Wm. Keith and Jn. Keith—the first is the funniest of every one of them. Mr. Crakey and I walked to Craky-Hall [Craigiehall] hand in hand in Innocence and matitation sweet thinking on the kind love which flows in our tender hearted mind which is overflowing with majestic pleasure no one was ever so polite to me in the hole state of my existence. Mr. Craky you must know is a great Buck ad pretty good-looking."

For a purpose, I wish the reader to take careful note of these statistics:

> "I am going to tell you of a melancholy story. A young turkie of 2 or 3 months old, would you believe it, the father broke its leg, & he killed another! I think he ought to be transported or hanged."

Marjorie wrote some verses about this tragedy—I think. I cannot be quite certain it is this one, for in the verses there are three deaths, whereas these statistics do no furnish so many. Also in the statistics the father of the deceased is indifferent about the loss he has sustained, whereas in the verses he is not. Also in the third verse, the *mother,* too, exhibits feeling, whereas in the two closing verses of the poem she—at least she seems to be she—is indifferent. At least it looks like indifference to me, and I believe it *is* indifference:

> "Three turkeys fair their last have
> breathed,
> And now this world forever leaved;
> Their father, and their mother too,

They sighed and weep as well as you;
Indeed, the rats their bones have
    cranched.
Into eternity theire launched.
A direful death indeed they had,
As wad put any parent mad;
But she was more than usual calm,
She did not give a single dam."

The naughty little scamp! I mean, for not leaving out the *l* in the word "calm," so as to perfect the rhyme. It seems a pity to damage with a lame rhyme a couplet that is otherwise without a blemish.

Marjorie wrote four journals. She began the first one in January, 1809, when she was jus six years old, and finished it five months later, in June.

She began the second in the following month, and finished it six months afterward (January, 1810), when she was just seven.

She began the third one in April, 1810, and finished it in the autumn.

She wrote the fourth in the winter of 1810-11, and the last entry in it bears date July 19, 1811, and she died exactly five months later, December 19th, aged eight years and eleven months. It contains her rhymed Scottish histories.

Let me quote from Dr. John Brown:

> The day before her death, Sunday, she sat up in bed, worn and thin, her eye gleaming as with the light of a coming world, and with a tremulous, old voice repeated a long poem by Burns—heavy with the shadow of death, and lit with the fantasy of the judgment seat—the publican's prayer in paraphrase, beginning:
>
> " 'Why am I loth to leave this earthly
>   scene?
>   Have I so found it full of pleasing
>   charms?
>   Some drops of joy, with draughts of ill
>   between,
>   Some gleams of sunshine 'mid renewing
>   storms.'

"It is more affecting than we care to say to read her mother's and Isabella Keith's letters written immediately after her death. Old and withered, tattered and pale, they are now; but when you read them, how quick, how throbbing with life and love! How rich in that language of affection which only women, and Shakespeare, and Luther can use—that power of detaining the soul over the beloved object and its loss."

Fifty years after Marjorie's death her sister, writing to Dr. Brown, said:

"My mother was struck by the patient quietness manifested by Marjorie during this illness, unlike her ardent, impulsive nature; but love and poetic feeling were unquenched. When Dr. Johnstone rewarded her submissiveness with a sixpence, the request speedily followed that she might get out ere New-Year's Day came. When asked why she was so desirous of getting out, she immediately rejoined: 'Oh, I am so anxious to buy something with my sixpence for my dear Isa Keith.' Again, when lying very still, her mother asked her if there was anything she wished: 'Oh yes, if you would just leave the room door open a wee bit, and play the *Land o' the Leal*, and I will lie and *think* and enjoy myself' (this is just as stated to me by her mother and mine). Well, the happy day came, alike to parents and child, when Marjorie was allowed to come forth from the nursery to the parlor. It was Sabbath evening, and after tea. My father, who idolized this child, and never afterward in my hearing mentioned her name, took her in his arms; and while walking her up and down the room she said: 'Father, I will repeat something to you; what would you like?' He said, 'Just choose for yourself, Maidie.' She hesitated for a moment between the paraphrase, 'Few are thy days and full of woe,' and the lines of Burns already quoted but decided on the latter; a remarkable choice for a child. The repeating of these lines seemed to stir up the depths of feeling in her soul. She asked to be allowed to write a poem. There was a doubt whether it would be right to allow her, in case of hurting her eyes. She pleaded earnestly, 'Just this once'; the point was yielded, her slate given her, and with great

> rapidity she wrote an address of fourteen lines. 'To my loved cousin on the author's recovery.'"

The cousin was Isa Keith.

> "She went to bed apparently well, awoke in the middle of the night with the old cry of woe to a mother's heart, 'My head, my head!' Three days of dire malady, 'water in the head,' followed, and the end came."

In Defense of Harriet Shelley

I

I have committed sins, of course; but I have not committed enough of them to entitle me to the punishment of reduction to the bread and water of ordinary literature during six years when I might have been living on the fat diet spread for the righteous in Professor Dowden's *Life of Shelley*, if I had been justly dealt with.

During these six years I have been living a life of peaceful ignorance. I was not aware that Shelley's first wife was unfaithful to him, and that that was why he deserted her and wiped the stain from his sensitive honor by entering into soiled relations with Godwin's young daughter. This was all new to me when I heard it lately, and was told that the proofs of it were in this book, and that this book's verdict is accepted in the girls' colleges of America and its view taught in their literary classes.

In each of these six years multitudes of young people in our country have arrived at the Shelley-reading age. Are these six multitudes unacquainted with this life of Shelley? Perhaps they are; indeed, one may feel pretty sure that the great bulk of them are. To these, then, I address myself, in the hope that some account of this romantic historical fable and the fabulist's manner of constructing and adorning it may interest them.

First, as to its literary style. Our negroes in America have several ways of entertaining themselves which are not found among the whites anywhere. Among these inventions of theirs is one which is particularly popular with them. It is a competition in elegant deportment. They hire a hall and bank the spectators' seats in rising tiers along the two sides, leaving all the middle stretch of the floor free. A cake is provided as a prize for the winner in the competition, and a bench of experts in deportment is appointed to award it. Sometimes there are as many as fifty contestants, male and female, and five hundred spectators. One at a time the contestants enter, clothed regardless of expense in what each considers the perfection of style and taste, and walk down the vacant central space and back again with that multitude of critical eyes on them. All that the competitor knows of fine airs and graces he throws into his carriage, all that he knows of seductive expression he throws into his countenance. He may use all the helps he can devise: watch-chain to twirl with his fingers, cane to do graceful things with, snowy handkerchief to flourish and get artful effects out of, shiny new stovepipe hat to assist in his courtly bows; and the colored lady may have a fan to work up *her* effects with, and smile over and blush behind, and she may add other helps, according to her judgment. When the review by individual detail is over, a grand review of all the contestants in procession follows, with all the airs and graces and all the bowings and smirkings on exhibition at once, and this enables the bench of experts to make the necessary comparisons and arrive at a verdict. The successful competitor gets the prize which I have before mentioned, and an abundance of applause and envy along with it. The negroes have a name for this grave deportment tournament; a name taken from the prize contended for. They call it a Cake-Walk.

The Shelley biography is a literary cake-walk. The ordinary forms of speech are absent from it. All the pages, all the paragraphs, walk by sedately, elegantly, not to say mincingly, in their Sunday-best, shiny and sleek, perfumed, and with *boutonnières* in their buttonholes; it is rare to find even a chance sentence that has forgotten to dress. If the book wishes to tell us that Mary Godwin, child of sixteen, had known afflictions, the fact saunters forth in this nobby outfit: "Mary was herself not unlearned in the lore of pain"—meaning by that that she had not always traveled on asphalt; or, as some authorities would frame it, that she had "been there herself," a form which, while preferable to the book's form, is still not to be recommended. If the book wishes to tell us that Harriet Shelley hired a wet-nurse, that commonplace fact gets turned into a dancing-master, who does his professional bow before us in pumps and knee-breeches, with his fiddle under one arm and his crush-hat under the other, thus: "The beauty of Harriet's motherly relation to her babe was marred in Shelley's eyes by the introduction into his house of a hireling nurse to whom was delegated the mother's tenderest office."

This is perhaps the strangest book that has seen the light since Frankenstein. Indeed, it is a Frankenstein itself; a Frankenstein with the original infirmity supplemented by a new one; a Frankenstein with the reasoning faculty wanting. Yet it believes it can reason, and is always trying. It is not content to leave a mountain of fact standing in the clear sunshine, where the simplest reader can perceive its form, its details, and its relation to the rest of the landscape, but thinks it must help him examine it and understand it; so its drifting mind settles upon it with that intent, but always with one and the same result: there is a change of temperature and the mountain is hid in a fog. Every time it sets up a premise and starts to reason from it, there is a surprise in store for the reader. It is strangely near-sighted, cross-eyed, and purblind. Sometimes when a mastodon walks across the field of its vision it takes it for a rat; at other times it does not see it at all.

The materials of this biographical fable are facts, rumors, and poetry. They are connected together and harmonized by the help of suggestion, conjecture, innuendo, perversion, and semi-suppression.

The fable has a distinct object in view, but this object is not acknowledged in set words. Percy Bysshe Shelley has done something which in the case of other men is called a grave crime; it must be shown that in his case it is not that, because he does not think as other men do about these things.

Ought not that to be enough, if the fabulist is serious? Having proved that a crime is not a crime, was it worth while to go on and fasten the responsibility of a crime which was not a crime upon somebody else? What is the use of hunting down and holding to bitter account people who are responsible for other people's innocent acts?

Still, the fabulist thinks it a good idea to do that. In his view Shelley's first wife, Harriet, free of all offense as far as we have historical facts for guidance, must be held unforgivably responsible for her husband's innocent act in deserting her and taking up with another woman.

Any one will suspect that this task has its difficulties. Any one will divine that nice work is necessary here, cautious work, wily work, and that there is entertainment to be had in watching the magician do it. There is indeed entertainment in watching him. He arranges his facts, his rumors, and his poems on his table in full view of the house, and shows you that everything is there—no deception, everything fair and aboveboard. And this is apparently true, yet there is a defect, for some of his best stock is hid in an appendix-basket behind the door, and you do not come upon it until the exhibition is over and the enchantment of your mind accomplished—as the magician thinks.

There is an insistent atmosphere of candor and fairness about this book which is engaging at first, then a little burdensome, then a trifle fatiguing, then progressively suspicious, annoying, irritating, and oppressive. It takes one some little time to find out that phrases which seem intended to guide the reader aright are there to mislead him; that phrases which seem intended to throw light are there to throw darkness; that phrases which seem intended to interpret a fact are there to misinterpret it; that phrases which seem intended to forestall prejudice are there to create it; that phrases which seem antidotes are poisons in disguise. The naked facts arrayed in the book establish Shelley's guilt in that one episode which disfigures his otherwise superlatively lofty and beautiful life; but the historian's careful and methodical misinterpretation of them transfers the responsibility to the wife's shoulders—as he persuades himself. The few meager facts of Harriet Shelley's life, as furnished by the book, acquit her of offense; but by calling in the forbidden helps of rumor, gossip, conjecture, insinuation, and innuendo he destroys her character and rehabilitates Shelley's—as he believes. And in truth his unheroic work has not been barren of the results he aimed at; as witness the assertion made to me that girls in the colleges of America are taught that Harriet Shelley put a stain upon her husband's honor, and that that was what stung him into repurifying himself by deserting her and his child and entering into scandalous relations with a school-girl acquaintance of his.

If that assertion is true, they probably use a reduction of this work in those colleges, maybe only a sketch outlined from it. Such a thing as that could be harmful and misleading. They ought to cast it out and put the whole book in its place. It would not deceive. It would not deceive the janitor.

All of this book is interesting on account of the sorcerer's methods and the attractiveness of some of his characters and the repulsiveness of the rest, but no part of it is so much so as are the chapters wherein he tries to think he thinks he sets forth the causes which led to Shelley's desertion of his wife in 1814.

Harriet Westbrook was a school-girl sixteen years old. Shelley was teeming with advanced thought. He believed that Christianity was a degrading and selfish superstition, and he had a deep and sincere desire to rescue one of his sisters from it. Harriet was impressed by his various philosophies and looked upon him as an intellectual wonder—which indeed he was. He had an idea that she could give him valuable help in his scheme regarding his sister; therefore he asked her to correspond with him. She was quite willing. Shelley was not thinking of love, for he was just getting over a passion for his cousin, Harriet Grove, and just getting well steeped in one for Miss Hitchener, a school-teacher. What might happen to Harriet Westbrook before the letter-writing was ended did not enter his mind. Yet an older person could have made a good guess at it, for in person Shelley was as beautiful as an angel, he was frank, sweet, winning, unassuming, and so rich in unselfishness, generosities, and magnanimities that he made his whole generation seem poor in these great qualities by comparison. Besides, he was in distress. His college had expelled him for writing an atheistical pamphlet and afflicting the reverend heads of the university with it, his rich father and grandfather had closed their purses against him, his friends were cold. Necessarily, Harriet fell in love with him; and so deeply, indeed, that there was no way for Shelley to save her from suicide but to marry her. He believed himself to blame for this state of things, so the marriage took place. He was pretty fairly in love with Harriet, although he loved Miss Hitchener better. He wrote and explained the case to Miss Hitchener after the wedding, and he could not have been franker or more naïve and less stirred up about the circumstance if the matter in issue had been a commercial transaction involving thirty-five dollars.

Shelley was nineteen. He was not a youth, but a man. He had never had any youth. He was an erratic and fantastic child during eighteen years, then he stepped into manhood, as one steps over a door-sill. He was curiously mature at nineteen in his ability to do independent thinking on the deep questions of life and to arrive at sharply definite decisions regarding them, and stick to them—stick to them and stand by them at cost of bread, friendships, esteem, respect, and approbation.

For the sake of his opinions he was willing to sacrifice all these valuable things, and did sacrifice them; and went on doing it, too, when he could at any moment have made himself rich and supplied himself with friends and esteem by compromising with his father, at the moderate expense of throwing overboard one or two indifferent details of his cargo of principles.

He and Harriet eloped to Scotland and got married. They took lodgings in Edinburgh of a sort answerable to their purse, which was about empty, and there their life was a happy one and grew daily more so. They had only themselves for company, but they needed no additions to it. They were as cozy and contented as birds in a nest. Harriet sang evenings or read aloud; also she studied and tried to improve her mind, her husband instructing her in Latin. She was very beautiful, she was modest, quiet, genuine, and, according to her husband's testimony, she had no fine-lady airs or aspirations about her. In Matthew Arnold's judgment, she was "a pleasing figure."

The pair remained five weeks in Edinburgh, and then took lodgings in York, where Shelley's college-mate, Hogg, lived. Shelley presently ran down to London, and Hogg took this opportunity to make love to the young wife. She repulsed him, and reported the fact to her husband when he got back. It seems a pity that Shelley did not copy this creditable conduct of hers some time or other when under temptation, so that we might have seen the author of his biography hang the miracle in the skies and squirt rainbows at it.

At the end of the first year of marriage—the most trying year for any young couple, for then the mutual failings are coming one by one to light, and the necessary adjustments are being made in pain and tribulation—Shelley was able to recognize that his marriage venture had been a safe one. As we have seen, his love for his wife had begun in a rather shallow way and with not much force, but now it was become deep and strong, which entitles his wife to a broad credit mark, one may admit. He addresses a long and loving poem to her, in which both passion and worship appear:

Exhibit A

O thou
Whose dear love gleamed upon the gloomy path
Which this lone spirit travelled,
. . . .
. . . wilt thou not turn
Those spirit-beaming eyes and look on me,
Until I be assured that Earth is Heaven
And Heaven is Earth?
. . . .
Harriet! let death all mortal ties dissolve,
But ours shall not be mortal.

Shelley also wrote a sonnet to her in August of this same year in celebration of her birthday:

Exhibit B

Ever as now with Love and Virtue's glow
    May thy unwithering soul not cease to burn,
Still may thine heart with those pure thoughts o'erflow
    Which force from mine such quick and warm return.

Was the girl of seventeen glad and proud and happy? We may conjecture that she was.

That was the year 1812. Another year passed—still happily, still successfully—a child was born in June, 1813, and in September, three months later, Shelley addresses a poem to this child, Ianthe, in which he points out just when the little creature is most particularly dear to him:

Exhibit C

Dearest when most thy tender traits express
The image of thy mother's loveliness.

Up to this point the fabulist counsel for Shelley and prosecutor of his young wife has had easy sailing, but now his trouble begins, for Shelley is getting ready to make some unpleasant history for himself, and it will be necessary to put the blame of it on the wife.

Shelley had made the acquaintance of a charming gray-haired, young-hearted Mrs. Boinville, whose face "retained a certain youthful beauty"; she lived at Bracknell, and had a young daughter named Cornelia Turner, who was equipped with many fascinations. Apparently these people were sufficiently sentimental. Hogg says of Mrs. Boinville:

> "The greater part of her associates were odious. I generally found there two or three sentimental young butchers, an eminently philosophical tinker, and several very unsophisticated medical practitioners or medical students, all of low origin and vulgar and offensive manners. They sighed, turned up their eyes, retailed philosophy, such as it was," etc.

Shelley moved to Bracknell, July 27th (this is still 1813) purposely to be near this unwholesome prairie-dogs' nest. The fabulist says: "It was the entrance into a world more amiable and exquisite than he had yet known."

"In this acquaintance the attraction was mutual"—and presently it grew to be very mutual indeed, between Shelley and Cornelia Turner, when they got to studying the Italian poets together. Shelley, "responding like a tremulous instrument to every breath of passion or of sentiment," had his chance here. It took only four days for Cornelia's attractions to begin to dim Harriet's. Shelley arrived on the 27th of July; on the 31st he wrote a sonnet to Harriet in which "one detects already the little rift in the lover's lute which had seemed to be healed or never to have gaped at all when the later and happier sonnet to Ianthe was written"—in September, we remember:

Exhibit D

EVENING. TO HARRIET

O thou bright Sun! Beneath the dark blue line
Of western distance that sublime descendest,
And, gleaming lovelier as thy beams decline,
Thy million hues to every vapor lendest,
And over cobweb, lawn, and grove, and stream
Sheddest the liquid magic of thy light,
Till calm Earth, with the parting splendor bright,
Shows like the vision of a beauteous dream;
What gazer now with astronomic eye
Could coldly count the spots within thy sphere?
Such were thy lover, Harriet, could he fly
The thoughts of all that makes his passion dear,
And turning senseless from thy warm caress
Pick flaws in our close-woven happiness.

I cannot find the "rift"; still it may be there. What the poem *seems* to say is, that a person would be coldly ungrateful who could consent to count and consider little spots and flaws in such a warm, great, satisfying sun as Harriet is. It is a "little rift which had seemed to be healed, *or* never to have gaped at all." That is, "one *detects*" a little rift which perhaps had never existed. How does one do that? How does one see the invisible? It is the fabulist's secret; he knows how to detect what does not exist, he knows how to see what is not seeable; it is his gift, and he works it many a time to poor dead Harriet Shelley's deep damage.

"As yet, however, if there was a speck upon Shelley's happiness it was no more than a speck"—meaning the one which one detects where "it may never have gaped at all"—"nor had Harriet cause for discontent."

Shelley's Latin instructions to his wife had ceased. "From a teacher he had now become a pupil." Mrs. Boinville and her young married daughter Cornelia were teaching him Italian poetry; a fact which warns one to receive with some caution that other statement that Harriet had no "cause for discontent."

Shelley had stopped instructing Harriet in Latin, as before mentioned. The biographer thinks that the busy life in London some time back, and the intrusion of the baby, account for this. These were hindrances, but were there no others? He is always overlooking a detail here and there that might be valuable in helping us understand a situation. For instance, when a man has been hard at work at the Italian poets with a pretty woman, hour after hour, and responding like a tremulous instrument to every breath of passion or of sentiment in the mean time, that man is dog-tired when he gets home, and he *can't* teach his wife Latin; it would be unreasonable to expect it.

Up to this time we have submitted to having Mrs. Boinville pushed upon us as ostensibly concerned in these Italian lessons, but the biographer drops her now, of his own accord. Cornelia "perhaps" is sole teacher. Hogg says she was a prey to a kind of sweet melancholy, arising from causes purely imaginary; she required consolation, and found it in Petrarch. He also says, "Bysshe entered at once fully into her views and caught the soft infection, breathing the tenderest and sweetest melancholy, as every true poet ought."

Then the author of the book interlards a most stately and fine compliment to Cornelia, furnished by a man of approved judgment who knew her well "in later years." It is a very good compliment indeed, and she no doubt deserved it in her "later years," when she had for generations ceased to be sentimental and lackadaisical, and was no longer engaged in enchanting young husbands and sowing sorrow for young wives. But why is that compliment to that old gentlewoman intruded there? Is it to make the reader believe she was well-chosen and safe society for a young, sentimental husband? The biographer's device was not well planned. That old person was not present—it was her other self that was there, her young, sentimental, melancholy, warm-blooded self, in those early sweet times before antiquity had cooled her off and mossed her back.

"In choosing for friends such women as Mrs. Newton, Mrs. Boinville, and

Cornelia Turner, Shelley gave good proof of his insight and discrimination." That is the fabulist's opinion—Harriet Shelley's is not reported.

Early in August, Shelley was in London trying to raise money. In September he wrote the poem to the baby, already quoted from. In the first week of October Shelley and family went to Warwick, then to Edinburgh, arriving there about the middle of the month.

"Harriet was happy." Why? The author furnishes a reason, but hides from us whether it is history or conjecture; it is because *"the babe had borne the journey well."* It has all the aspect of one of his artful devices—flung in in his favorite casual way—the way he has when he wants to draw one's attention away from an obvious thing and amuse it with some trifle that is less obvious but more useful—in a history like this. The obvious thing is, that Harriet was happy because there was much territory between her husband and Cornelia Turner now; and because the perilous Italian lessons were taking a rest; and because, if there chanced to be any respondings like a tremulous instrument to every breath of passion or of sentiment in stock in these days, she might hope to get a share of them herself; and because, with her husband liberated, now, from the fetid fascinations of that sentimental retreat so pitilessly described by Hogg, who also dubbed it "Shelley's paradise" later, she might hope to persuade him to stay away from it permanently; and because she might also hope that his brain would cool, now, and his heart become healthy, and both brain and heart consider the situation and resolve that it would be a right and manly thing to stand by this girl wife and her child and see that they were honorably dealt with, and cherished and protected and loved by the man that had promised these things, and so be made happy and kept so. And because, also—may we conjecture this?—we may hope for the privilege of taking up our cozy Latin lessons again, that used to be so pleasant, and brought us so near together—so near, indeed, that often our heads touched, just as heads do over Italian lessons; and our hands met in casual and unintentional, but still most delicious and thrilling little contacts and momentary clasps, just as they inevitably do over Italian lessons. Suppose one should say to any young wife: "I find that your husband is poring over the Italian poets and being instructed in the beautiful

> THE BABY BORE THE JOURNEY WELL, AND THAT THAT WAS WHY THE YOUNG WIFE WAS HAPPY. THAT ACCOUNTS FOR TWO PER CENT. OF THE HAPPINESS, BUT IT WAS NOT RIGHT TO IMPLY THAT IT ACCOUNTED FOR THE OTHER NINETY-EIGHT ALSO.

Italian language by the lovely Cornelia Robinson"—would that cozy picture fail to rise before her mind? would its possibilities fail to suggest themselves to her? would there be a pang in her heart and a blush on her face? or, on the contrary, would the remark give her pleasure, make her joyous and gay? Why, one needs only to make the experiment—the result will not be uncertain.

However, we learn—by authority of deeply reasoned and searching conjecture—that the baby bore the journey well, and that that was why the young wife was happy. That accounts for two per cent. of the happiness, but it was not right to imply that it accounted for the other ninety-eight also.

Peacock, a scholar, poet, and friend of the Shelleys, was of their party when they went away. He used to laugh at the Boinville menagerie, and "was not a favorite." One of the Boinville group, writing to Hogg, said, "The Shelleys have made an addition to their party in the person of a cold scholar, who, I think, has neither taste nor feeling. This, Shelley will perceive sooner or later, for his warm nature craves sympathy." True, and Shelley will fight his way back there to get it—there will be no way to head him off.

Toward the end of November it was necessary for Shelley to pay a business visit to London, and he conceived the project of leaving Harriet and the baby in Edinburgh with Harriet's sister, Eliza Westbrook, a sensible, practical maiden lady about thirty years old, who had spent a great part of her time with the family since the marriage. She was an estimable woman, and Shelley had had reason to like her, and did like her; but along about this time his feeling toward her changed. Part of Shelley's plan, as he wrote Hogg, was to spend his London evenings with the Newtons—members of the Boinville Hysterical Society. But, alas, when he arrived early in December, that pleasant game was partially blocked, for Eliza and the family arrived *with* him. We are left destitute of conjectures at this point by the biographer, and it is my duty to supply one. I chance the conjecture that it was Eliza who interfered with that game. I think she tried to do what she could toward modifying the Boinville connection, in the interest of her young sister's peace and honor.

If it was she who blocked that game, she was not strong enough to block the next one. Before the month and year were out—no date given, let us call it Christmas—Shelley and family were nested in a furnished house in Windsor, "at no great distance from the Boinvilles"—these decoys still residing at Bracknell.

What we need, now, is a misleading conjecture. We get it with characteristic promptness and depravity:

> But Prince Athanase found not the aged Zonoras, the friend of his boyhood, in any wanderings to Windsor. Dr. Lind had died a year since, and with his death Windsor must have lost, for Shelley, its chief attraction.

Still, not to mention Shelley's wife, there was Bracknell, at any rate. While Bracknell remains, all solace is not lost. Shelley is represented by this biographer as doing a great many careless things, but to my mind this hiring a furnished house for three months in order to be with a man who has been dead a year, is the carelessest of them all. One feels for him—that is but natural, and does us honor besides—yet one is vexed, for all that. He could have written and asked about the aged Zonoras before taking the house. He may not have had the address, but that is nothing—any postman would know the aged Zonoras; a dead postman would remember a name like that.

And yet, why throw a rag like this to us ravening wolves? Is it seriously supposable that we will stop to chew it and let our prey escape? No, we are getting to expect this kind of device, and to give it merely a sniff for certainty's sake and then walk around it and leave it lying. Shelley was not after the aged Zonoras; he was pointed for Cornelia and the Italian lessons, for his warm nature was craving sympathy.

II

The year 1813 is just ended now, and we step into 1814.

To recapitulate, how much of Cornelia's society has Shelley had, thus far? Portions of August and September, and four days of July. That is to say, he has had opportunity to enjoy it, more or less, during that brief period. Did he want some more of it? We must fall back upon history, and then go to conjecturing.

> In the early part of the year 1814, Shelley was a frequent visitor at Bracknell.

"Frequent" is a cautious word, in this author's mouth; the very cautiousness of it, the vagueness of it, provokes suspicion; it makes one suspect that this frequency was more frequent than the mere common every-day kinds of frequency which one is in the habit of averaging up with the unassuming term "frequent."

I think so because they fixed up a bedroom for him in the Boinville house. One doesn't need a bedroom if one is only going to run over now and then in a disconnected way to respond like a tremulous instrument to every breath of passion or of sentiment and rub up one's Italian poetry a little.

The young wife was not invited, perhaps. If she was, she most certainly did not come, or she would have straightened the room up; the most ignorant of us knows that a wife would not endure a room in the condition in which Hogg found this one when he occupied it one night. Shelley was away—why, nobody can divine. Clothes were scattered about, there were books on every side: "Wherever a book could be laid was an open book turned down on its face to keep its place." It seems plain that the wife was not invited. No, not that; I think she was invited, but said to herself that she could not bear to go there and see another young woman touching heads with her husband over an Italian book and making thrilling hand-contacts with him accidentally.

As remarked, he was a frequent visitor there, "where he found an easeful resting-place in the house of Mrs. Boinville—the white-haired Maimuna—and of her daughter, Mrs. Turner." The aged Zonoras was deceased, but the white-haired Maimuna was still on deck, as we see. "Three charming ladies entertained the mocker (Hogg) with cups of tea, late hours, Wieland's Agathon, sighs and smiles, and the celestial manna of refined sentiment." "Such," says Hogg, "were the delights of Shelley's paradise in Bracknell."

The white-haired Maimuna presently writes to Hogg:

> I will not have you despise home-spun pleasures. Shelley is making a trial of them with us—

A trial of them. It may be called that. It was March 11, and he had been in the house a month. She continues:

> Shelley "likes them so well that he is resolved to leave off rambling—"

But he has *already* left it off. He has been there a month.

> "And begin a course of them himself."

But he has already begun it. He has been at it a *month*. He likes it so well that he has forgotten all about his wife, as a letter of his reveals.

> Seriously, I think his mind and body want rest.

Yet he has been resting both for a month, with Italian, and tea, and manna of sentiment, and late hours, and every restful thing a young husband could need for the refreshment of weary limbs and a sore conscience, and a nagging sense of shabbiness and treachery.

> His journeys after what he has never found have racked his purse and his tranquillity. He is resolved to take a little care of the former, in pity to the latter, which I applaud, and shall second with all my might.

But she does not say whether the young wife, a stranger and lonely yonder, wants another woman and her daughter Cornelia to be lavishing so much inflamed interest on her husband or not. That young wife is always silent—we are never allowed to hear from her. She must have opinions about such things, she cannot be indifferent, she must be approving or disapproving, surely she would speak if she were allowed—even to-day and from her grave she would, if she could, I think—but we get only the other side, they keep her silent always.

> He has deeply interested us. In the course of your intimacy he must have made you feel what we now feel for him. He is seeking a house close to us—

Ah! he is not close enough yet, it seems—

> and if he succeeds we shall have an additional motive to induce you to come among us in the summer.

The reader would puzzle a long time and not guess the biographer's comment upon the above letter. It is this:

> These sound like words of a considerate and judicious friend.

That is what he thinks. That is, it is what he thinks he thinks. No, that is not quite it: it is what he thinks he can stupefy a particularly and unspeakably dull reader into thinking it is what he thinks. He makes that comment with the knowledge that Shelley is in love with this woman's daughter, and that it is because of the fascinations of these two that Shelley has deserted his wife—for this month, considering all the circumstances, and his new passion, and his employment of the time, amounted to desertion; that is its rightful name. We cannot know how the wife regarded it and felt about it; but if she could have read the letter which Shelley was writing to Hogg four or five days later, we could guess her thought and how she felt. Hear him:

> I have been staying with Mrs. Boinville for the last month; I have escaped, in the society of all that philosophy and friendship combine, from the dismaying solitude of myself.

It is fair to conjecture that he was feeling ashamed.

> They have revived in my heart the expiring flame of life. I have felt myself translated to a paradise which has nothing of mortality but its transitoriness; my heart sickens at the view of that necessity which will quickly divide me from the delightful tranquillity of this happy home—for it has become my home.
>
> . . .
>
> Eliza is still with us—not here!—but will be with me when the infinite malice of destiny forces me to depart.

Eliza is she who blocked that game—the game in London—the one where we were purposing to dine every night with one of the "three charming ladies" who fed tea and manna and late hours to Hogg at Bracknell.

Shelley could send Eliza away, of course; could have cleared her out long ago if so minded, just as he had previously done with a predecessor of hers whom he had first worshiped and then turned against; but perhaps she was useful there as a thin excuse for staying away himself.

> I am now but little inclined to contest this point. I certainly hate her with all my heart and soul. . .
>
> It is a sight which awakens an inexpressible sensation of disgust and horror, to see her caress my poor little Ianthe, in whom

> I may hereafter find the consolation of sympathy. I sometimes feel faint with the fatigue of checking the overflowings of my unbounded abhorrence for this miserable wretch. But she is no more than a blind and loathsome worm, that cannot see to sting.
>
> I have begun to learn Italian again. . . Cornelia assists me in this language. Did I not once tell you that I thought her cold and reserved? She is the reverse of this, as she is the reverse of everything bad. She inherits all the divinity of her mother. . . . I have sometimes forgotten that I am not an inmate of this delightful home—that a time will come which will cast me again into the boundless ocean of abhorred society.
>
> I have written nothing but one stanza, which has no meaning, and that I have only written in thought:
>
> Thy dewy looks sink in my breast;
> Thy gentle words stir poison there;
> Thou hast disturbed the only rest
> That was the portion of despair.
> Subdued to duty's hard control,
> I could have borne my wayward lot:
> The chains that bind this ruined soul
> Had cankered then, but crushed it not.
>
> This is the vision of a delirious and distempered dream, which passes away at the cold clear light of morning. Its surpassing excellence and exquisite perfections have no more reality than the color of an autumnal sunset.

Then it did not refer to his wife. That is plain; otherwise he would have said so. It is well that he explained that it has no meaning, for if he had not done that, the previous soft references to Cornelia and the way he has come to feel about her now would make us think she was the person who had inspired it while teaching him how to read the warm and ruddy Italian poets during a month.

The biography observes that portions of this letter "read like the tired moaning of a wounded creature." Guesses at the nature of the wound are permissible; we will hazard one.

Read by the light of Shelley's previous history, his letter seems to be the cry of a tortured conscience. Until this time it was a conscience that had never felt a pang or known a smirch. It was the conscience of one who, until this time, had never done a dishonorable thing, or an ungenerous, or cruel, or treacherous thing, but was now doing all of these, and was keenly aware of it. Up to this time Shelley had been master of his nature, and it was a nature which was as beautiful and as nearly perfect as any merely human nature may be. But he was drunk now, with a debasing passion, and was not himself. There is nothing in his previous history that is in character with the Shelley of this letter. He had done boyish things, foolish things, even crazy things, but never a thing to be ashamed of. He had done things which one might laugh at, but the privilege of laughing was limited always to the thing itself; you could not laugh at the motive back of it—that was high, that was noble. His most fantastic and quixotic acts had a purpose back of them which made them fine, often great, and made the rising laugh seem profanation and quenched it; quenched it, and changed the impulse to homage. Up to this time he had been loyalty itself, where his obligations lay—treachery was new to him; he had never done an ignoble thing—baseness was new to him; he had never done an unkind thing—that also was new to him.

This was the author of that letter, this was the man who had deserted his young wife and was lamenting, because he must leave another woman's house which had become a "home" to him, and go away. Is he lamenting *mainly* because he must go back to his wife and child? No, the lament is mainly for what he is to leave behind him. The physical comforts of the house? No, in his life he had never attached importance to such things. Then the thing which he grieves to leave is narrowed down to a person—to the person whose "dewy looks" had sunk into his breast, and whose seducing words had "stirred poison there."

He was ashamed of himself, his conscience was upbraiding him. He was the slave of a degrading love; he was drunk with his passion, the real Shelley was in temporary eclipse. This is the verdict which his previous history must certainly deliver upon this episode, I think.

One must be allowed to assist himself with conjectures like these when trying to find his way through a literary swamp which has so many misleading finger-boards up as this book is furnished with.

We have now arrived at a part of the swamp where the difficulties and perplexities are going to be greater than any we have yet met with—where, indeed, the finger-boards are multitudinous, and the most of them pointing diligently in the wrong direction. We are to be told by the biography why Shelley deserted his wife and child and took up with Cornelia Turner and Italian. It was not on account of Cornelia's sighs and sentimentalities and tea and manna and late hours and soft and sweet and industrious enticements; no, it was because "his happiness in his home had been wounded and bruised almost to death."

It had been wounded and bruised almost to death in this way:

1st. Harriet persuaded him to set up a carriage.

2d. After the intrusion of the baby, Harriet stopped reading aloud and studying.

3d. Harriet's walks with Hogg "commonly conducted us to some fashionable bonnet-shop."

4th. Harriet hired a wet-nurse.

5th. When an operation was being performed upon the baby, "Harriet stood by, narrowly observing all that was done, but, to the astonishment of the operator, betraying not the smallest sign of emotion."

6th. Eliza Westbrook, sister-in-law, was still of the household.

The evidence against Harriet Shelley is all in; there is no more. Upon these six counts she stands indicted of the crime of driving her husband into that sty at Bracknell; and this crime, by these helps, the biographical prosecuting attorney has set himself the task of proving upon her.

Does the biographer *call* himself the attorney for the prosecution? No, only to himself, privately; publicly he is the passionless, disinterested, impartial judge on the bench. He holds up his judicial scales before the world, that all may see; and it all tries to look so fair that a blind person would sometimes fail to see him slip the false weights in.

Shelley's happiness in his home had been wounded and bruised almost to death, first, because Harriet had persuaded him to set up a carriage. I cannot discover that any evidence is offered that she asked him to set up a carriage. Still, if she did, was it a heavy offense? Was it unique? Other young wives had committed it before, others have committed it since. Shelley had dearly loved her in those London days; possibly he set up the carriage gladly to please her; affectionate young husbands do such things. When Shelley ran away with another girl, by and by, this girl persuaded him to pour the price of many carriages and many horses down the bottomless well of her father's debts, but this impartial judge finds no fault with that. Once she appeals to Shelley to raise money—necessarily by borrowing, there was no other way—to pay her father's debts with at a time when Shelley was in danger of being arrested and imprisoned for his own debts; yet the good judge finds no fault with her even for this.

First and last, Shelley emptied into that rapacious mendicant's lap a sum which cost him—for he borrowed it at ruinous rates—from eighty to one hundred thousand dollars. But it was Mary Godwin's papa, the supplications were often sent through Mary, the good judge is Mary's strenuous friend, so Mary gets no censures. On the Continent *Mary rode in her private carriage*, built, as Shelley boasts, "by one of the best makers in Bond Street," yet the good judge makes not even a passing comment on this iniquity. Let us throw out Count No. 1 against Harriet Shelley as being far-fetched and frivolous.

Shelley's happiness in his home had been wounded and bruised almost to death, secondly, because Harriet's studies "had dwindled away to nothing, Bysshe had ceased to express any interest in them." At what time was this? It was when Harriet "had fully recovered from the fatigue of her first effort of maternity, . . . and was now in full force, vigor, and effect." Very well, the baby was born two days before the close of June. It took the mother a month to get back her full force, vigor, and effect; this brings us to July 27th and the deadly Cornelia. If a wife of eighteen is studying with her husband and he gets smitten with another woman, isn't he likely to lose interest in his wife's studies for *that* reason, and is not his wife's interest in her studies likely to languish for the *same* reason? Would not the mere sight of those books of hers sharpen the pain that is in her heart? This sudden breaking down of a mutual intellectual interest of two years' standing is coincident with Shelley's re-encounter with Cornelia; and we are allowed to gather from that time forth for nearly two months he did all his studying in that person's society. We feel at liberty to rule out Count No. 2 from the indictment against Harriet.

Shelley's happiness in his home had been wounded and bruised almost to death, thirdly, because Harriet's walks with Hogg commonly led to some fashionable bonnet-shop. I offer no palliation; I only ask why the dispassionate, impartial judge did not offer one himself—merely, I mean, to offset his leniency in a similar case or two where the girl who ran away with Harriet's husband was the shopper. There are several occasions where she interested herself with shopping—among them being walks which ended at the bonnet-shop—yet in none of these cases does she get a word of blame from the good judge, while in one of them he covers the deed with a justifying remark, she doing the shopping that time to find easement for her mind, her child having died.

Shelley's happiness in his home had been wounded and bruised almost to death, fourthly, by the introduction there of a wet-nurse. The wet-nurse was introduced at the time of the Edinburgh sojourn, immediately after Shelley had been enjoying the two months of study with Cornelia which broke up his wife's studies and destroyed his personal interest in them. Why, by this time, nothing that Shelley's wife could do would have been satisfactory to him, for he was in love with another woman, and was never going to be contented again until he got back to her. If he had been still in love with his wife it is not easily conceivable that he would care much who nursed the baby, provided the baby was well nursed. Harriet's jealousy was assuredly voicing itself now, Shelley's conscience was assuredly nagging him, pestering him, persecuting him. Shelley needed excuses for his altered attitude toward his wife; Providence pitied him and sent the wet-nurse. If Providence had sent him a cotton doughnut it would have answered just as well; all he wanted was something to find fault with.

Shelley's happiness in his home had been wounded and bruised almost to death, fifthly, because Harriet narrowly watched a surgical operation which was being performed upon her child, and, "to the astonishment of the operator," who was watching Harriet instead of attending to his operation, she betrayed "not the smallest sign of emotion." The author of this biography was not ashamed to set down that exultant slander. He was apparently not aware that it was a small business to bring into his court a witness whose name he does not know, and whose character and veracity there is none to vouch for, and allow him to strike this blow at the motherheart of this friendless girl. The biographer says, "We may not infer from this that Harriet did not feel"—why put it in, then?—"but we learn that those about her could believe her to be hard and insensible." Who were those who were about her? Her husband? He hated her now, because he was in love elsewhere. Her sister? Of course that is not charged. Peacock? Peacock does not testify. The wet-nurse? She does not testify. If any others were there we have no mention of them. "Those about her" are reduced to one person—her husband. Who reports the circumstance? It is Hogg. Perhaps he was there—we do not know. But if he was, he still got his information at second hand, as it was the operator who noticed Harriet's lack of emotion, not himself. Hogg is not given to saying kind things when Harriet is his subject. He may have said them the time that he tried to tempt her to soil her honor, but after that he mentions her usually with a sneer. "Among those who were about her" was one witness well equipped to silence all tongues, abolish all doubts, set our minds at rest; one witness, not called, and not callable, whose evidence, if we could but get it, would outweigh the oaths of whole battalions of hostile Hoggs and nameless surgeons—the baby. I wish we had the baby's testimony; and yet if we had it it would not do us any good—a furtive conjecture, a sly insinuation, a pious "if" or two, would be smuggled in, here and there, with a solemn air of judicial investigation, and its positiveness would wilt into dubiety.

The biographer says of Harriet, "If words of tender affection and motherly pride proved the reality of love, then undoubtedly she loved her firstborn child." That is, if mere empty words can prove it, it stands proved—and in this way, without committing himself, he gives the reader a chance to infer that there isn't any extant evidence but words, and that he doesn't take much stock in them. How seldom he shows his hand! He is always lurking behind a non-committal "if" or something of that kind; always gliding and dodging around, distributing colorless poison here and there and everywhere, but always leaving himself in a position to say that his language will be found innocuous if taken to pieces and examined. He clearly exhibits a steady and never-relaxing purpose to make Harriet the scapegoat for her husband's first great sin—but it is in the general view that this is revealed, not in the details. His insidious literature is like blue water; you know what it is that makes it blue, but you cannot produce and verify any detail of the cloud of microscopic dust in it that does it. Your adversary can dip up a glassful and show you that it is pure white and you cannot deny it; and he can dip the lake dry, glass by glass, and show that every glassful is white, and prove it to any one's eye—and yet that lake *was* blue and you can swear it. This book is blue—with slander in solution.

Let the reader examine, for example, the paragraph of comment which immediately follows the letter containing Shelley's self-exposure which we have been considering. This is it. One should inspect the individual sentences as they go by, then pass them in procession and review the cake-walk as a whole:

> Shelley's happiness in his home, as is evident from this pathetic letter, had been fatally stricken; it is evident, also, that he knew where duty lay; he felt that his part was to take up his burden, silently and sorrowfully, and to bear it henceforth with the quietness of despair. But we can perceive that he scarcely possessed the strength and fortitude needful for success in such an attempt. And clearly Shelley himself was aware how perilous it was to accept that respite of blissful ease which he enjoyed in the Boinville household; for gentle voices and dewy looks and words of sympathy could not fail to remind him of an ideal of tranquillity or of joy which could never be his, and which he must henceforth sternly exclude from his imagination.

That paragraph commits the author in no way. Taken sentence by sentence it *asserts* nothing against anybody or in favor of anybody, pleads for nobody, accuses nobody. Taken detail by detail, it is as innocent as moonshine. And yet, taken as a whole, it is a design against the reader; its intent is to remove the feeling which the letter must leave with him if let alone, and put a different one in its place—to remove a feeling justified by the letter and substitute one not justified by it. The letter itself gives you no uncertain picture—no lecturer is needed to stand by with a stick and point out its details and let on to explain what they mean. The picture is the very clear and remorsefully faithful picture of a fallen and fettered angel who is ashamed of himself; an angel who beats his soiled wings and cries, who complains to the woman who enticed him that he *could* have borne his wayward lot, he *could* have stood by his duty if it had not been for her beguilements; an angel who rails at the "boundless ocean of abhorred society," and rages at his poor judicious sister-in-law. If there is any dignity about this spectacle it will escape most people.

Yet when the paragraph of comment is taken as a whole, the picture is full of dignity and pathos; we have before us a blameless and noble spirit stricken to the earth by malign powers, but not conquered; tempted, but grandly putting the temptation away; enmeshed by subtle coils, but sternly resolved to rend them and march forth victorious, at any peril of life or limb. Curtain—slow music.

Was it the purpose of the paragraph to take the bad taste of Shelley's letter out of the reader's mouth? If that was not it, good ink was wasted; without that, it has no relevancy—the multiplication table would have padded the space as rationally.

We have inspected the six reasons which we are asked to believe drove a man of conspicuous patience, honor, justice, fairness, kindliness, and iron firmness, resolution, and steadfastness, from the wife whom he loved and who loved him, to a refuge in the mephitic paradise of Bracknell. These are six infinitely little reasons; but there were six colossal ones, and these the counsel for the destruction of Harriet Shelley persists in not considering very important.

Moreover, the colossal six preceded the little six, and had done the mischief before they were born. Let us double-column the twelve; then we shall see at a glance that each little reason is in turn answered by a retorting reason of a size to overshadow it and make it insignificant:

1. Harriet sets up carriage.	1. CORNELIA TURNER.
2. Harriet stops studying.	2. CORNELIA TURNER.
3. Harriet goes to bonnet-shop.	3. CORNELIA TURNER.

4. Harriet takes a wet-nurse.	4. Cornelia Turner.
5. Harriet has too much nerve.	5. Cornelia Turner.
6. Detested sister-in-law.	6. Cornelia Turner.

As soon as we comprehend that Cornelia Turner and the Italian lessons happened *before* the little six had been discovered to be grievances, we understand why Shelley's happiness in his home had been wounded and bruised almost to death, and no one can persuade us into laying it on Harriet. Shelley and Cornelia are the responsible persons, and we cannot in honor and decency allow the cruelties which they practised upon the unoffending wife to be pushed aside in order to give us a chance to waste time and tears over six sentimental justifications of an offense which the six can't justify, nor even respectably assist in justifying.

Six? There were seven; but in charity to the biographer the seventh ought not to be exposed. Still, he hung it out himself, and not only hung it out, but thought it was a good point in Shelley's favor. For two years Shelley found sympathy and intellectual food and all that at home; there was enough for spiritual and mental support, but not enough for luxury; and so, at the end of the contented two years, this latter detail justifies him in going bag and baggage over to Cornelia Turner and supplying the rest of his need in the way of surplus sympathy and intellectual pie unlawfully. By the same reasoning a man in merely comfortable circumstances may rob a bank without sin.

III

It is 1814, it is the 16th of March, Shelley had written his letter, he has been in the Boinville paradise a month, his deserted wife is in her husbandless home. Mischief has been wrought. It is the biographer who concedes this. We greatly need some light on Harriet's side of the case now; we need to know how she enjoyed the month, but there is no way to inform ourselves; there seems to be a strange absence of documents and letters and diaries on that side. Shelley kept a diary, the approaching Mary Godwin kept a diary, her father kept one, her half-sister by marriage, adoption, and the dispensation of God kept one, and the entire tribe and all its friends wrote and received letters, and the letters were kept and are producible when this biography needs them; but there are only three or four scraps of Harriet's writing, and no diary. Harriet wrote plenty of letters to her husband—nobody knows where they are, I suppose; she wrote plenty of letters to other people—apparently they have disappeared, too. Peacock says she wrote good letters, but apparently interested people had sagacity enough to mislay them in time. After all her industry she went down into her grave and lies silent there—silent, when she has so much need to speak. We can only wonder at this mystery, not account for it.

No, there is no way of finding out what Harriet's state of feeling was during the month that Shelley was disporting himself in the Bracknell paradise. We have to fall back upon conjecture, as our fabulist does when he has nothing more substantial to work with. Then we easily conjecture that as the days dragged by Harriet's heart grew heavier and heavier under its two burdens—shame and resentment; the shame of being pointed at and gossiped about as a deserted wife, and resentment against the woman who had beguiled her husband from her and now kept him in a disreputable captivity. Deserted wives—deserted whether for cause or without cause—find small charity among the virtuous and the discreet. We conjecture that one after another the neighbors ceased to call; that one after another they got to being "engaged" when Harriet called; that finally they one after the other cut her dead on the street; that after that she stayed in the house daytimes, and brooded over her sorrows, and nighttimes did the same, there being nothing else to do with the heavy hours and the silence and solitude and the dreary intervals which sleep should have charitably bridged, but didn't.

Yes, mischief had been wrought. The biographer arrives at this conclusion, and it is a most just one. Then, just as you begin to half hope he is going to discover the cause of it and launch hot bolts of wrath at the guilty manufacturers of it, you have to turn away disappointed. You are disappointed, and you sigh. This is what he says—the italics are mine:

> However the mischief may have been wrought—*and at this day no one can wish to heap blame on any buried head*—

So it is poor Harriet, after all. Stern justice must take its course—justice tempered with delicacy, justice tempered with compassion, justice that pities a forlorn dead girl and refuses to strike her. Except in the back. Will not be ignoble and *say* the harsh thing, but only insinuate it. Stern justice knows about the carriage and the wet-nurse and the bonnet-shop and the other dark things that caused this sad mischief, and may not, *must* not blink them; so it delivers judgment where judgment belongs, but softens the blow by not seeming to deliver judgment at all. To resume—the italics are mine:

> However the mischief may have been wrought—and at this day no one can wish to heap blame on any buried head—*it is certain that some cause or causes of deep division between Shelley and his wife were in operation during the early part of the year 1814.*

This shows penetration. No deduction could be more accurate than this. There were indeed some causes of deep division. But next comes another disappointing sentence:

> To guess at the precise nature of these causes, in the absence of definite statement, were useless.

Why, he has already been guessing at them for several pages, and we have been trying to outguess him, and now all of a sudden he is tired of it and won't play any more. It is not quite fair to us. However, he will get over this by and by, when Shelley commits his next indiscretion and has to be guessed out of it at Harriet's expense.

"We may rest content with Shelley's own words"—in a Chancery paper drawn up by him three years later. They were these: "Delicacy forbids me to say more than that we were disunited by incurable dissensions."

As for me, I do not quite see why we should rest content with anything of the sort. It is not a very definite statement. It does not necessarily mean anything more than that he did not wish to go into the tedious details of those family quarrels. Delicacy could quite properly excuse him from saying, "I was in love with Cornelia all that time; my wife kept crying and worrying about it and upbraiding me and begging me to cut myself free from a connection which was wronging her and disgracing us both; and I being stung by these reproaches retorted with fierce and bitter speeches—for it is my nature to do that when I am stirred, especially if the target of them is a person whom I had greatly loved and respected before, as witness my various attitudes toward Miss Hitchener, the Gisbornes, Harriet's sister, and others—and finally I did not improve this state of things when I deserted my wife and spent a whole month with the woman who had infatuated me."

No, he could not go into those details, and we excuse him; but, nevertheless, we do not rest content with this bland proposition to puff away that whole long disreputable episode with a single meaningless remark of Shelley's.

We do admit that "it is certain that some cause or causes of deep division were in operation." We would admit it just the same if the grammar of the statement were as straight as a string, for we drift into pretty indifferent grammar ourselves when we are absorbed in historical work; but we have to decline to admit that we cannot guess those cause or causes.

But guessing is not really necessary. There is evidence attainable—evidence from the batch discredited by the biographer and set out at the back door in his appendix-basket; and yet a court of law would think twice before throwing it out, whereas it would be a hardy person who would venture to offer in such a place a good part of the material which is placed before the readers of this book as "evidence," and so treated by this daring biographer. Among some letters (in the appendix-basket) from Mrs. Godwin, detailing the Godwinian share in the Shelleyan events of 1814, she tells how Harriet Shelley came to her and her husband, agitated and weeping, to implore them to forbid Shelley the house, and prevent his seeing Mary Godwin.

> She related that last November he had fallen in love with Mrs. Turner and paid her such marked attentions Mr. Turner, the husband, had carried off his wife to Devonshire.

The biographer finds a technical fault in this: "the Shelleys were in *Edinburgh* in November." What of that? The woman is recalling a conversation which is more than two months old; besides, she was probably more intent upon the central and important fact of it than upon its unimportant date.

Harriet's quoted statement has some sense in it; for that reason, if for no other, it ought to have been put in the body of the book. Still, that would not have answered; even the biographer's enemy could not be cruel enough to ask him to let this real grievance, this compact and substantial and picturesque figure, this rawhead-and-bloody-bones, come striding in there among those pale shams, those rickety specters labeled WET-NURSE, BONNET-SHOP, and so on—no, the father of all malice could not ask the biographer to expose his pathetic goblins to a competition like that.

The fabulist finds fault with the statement because it has a technical error in it; and he does this at the moment that he is furnishing us an error himself, and of a graver sort. He says:

> If Turner carried off his wife to Devonshire he brought her back, and Shelley was staying with her and her mother on terms of cordial intimacy in March, 1814.

We accept the "cordial intimacy"—it was the very thing Harriet was complaining of—but there is nothing to show that it was Turner who brought his wife back. The statement is thrown in as if it were not only true, but was proof that Turner was not uneasy. Turner's *movements* are proof of nothing. Nothing but a statement from Turner's mouth would have any value here, and he made none.

Six days after writing his letter Shelley and his wife were together again for a moment—to get remarried according to the rites of the English Church.

Within three weeks the new husband and wife were apart again, and the former was back in his odorous paradise. This time it is the wife who does the deserting. She finds Cornelia too strong for her, probably. At any rate, she goes away with her baby and sister, and we have a playful fling at her from good Mrs. Boinville, the "mysterious spinner Maimuna"; she whose "face was as a damsel's face, and yet her hair was gray"; she of whom the biographer has said, "Shelley was indeed caught in an almost invisible thread spun around him, but unconsciously, by this subtle and benignant enchantress." The subtle and benignant enchantress writes to Hogg, April 18: "Shelley is again a widower; his beauteous half went to town on Thursday."

Then Shelley writes a poem—a chant of grief over the hard fate which obliges him now to leave his paradise and take up with his wife again. It seems to intimate that the paradise is cooling toward him; that he is warned off by acclamation; that he must not even venture to tempt with one last tear his friend Cornelia's ungentle mood, for her eye is glazed and cold and dares not entreat her lover to stay:

Exhibit E

Pause not! the time is past! Every voice cries "Away!"
Tempt not with one last tear thy friend's ungentle mood;
Thy lover's eye, so glazed and cold, dares not entreat thy stay:
Duty and dereliction guide thee back to solitude.
Back to the solitude of his now empty home, that is!
Away! away! to thy sad and silent home;
Pour bitter tears on its desolated hearth.

But he will have rest in the grave by and by. Until that time comes, the charms of Bracknell will remain in his memory, along with Mrs. Boinville's voice and Cornelia Turner's smile:

Thou in the grave shalt rest—yet, till the phantoms flee
Which that house and hearth and garden made dear to thee erewhile,
Thy remembrance and repentance and deep musings are not free
From the music of two voices and the light of one sweet smile.

We *cannot* wonder that Harriet could not stand it. Any of us would have left. We would not even stay with a cat that was in this condition. Even the Boinvilles could not endure it; and so, as we have seen, they gave this one notice.

> Early in May, Shelley was in London. He did not yet despair of reconciliation with Harriet, nor had he ceased to love her.

Shelley's poems are a good deal of trouble to his biographer. They are constantly inserted as "evidence," and they make much confusion. As soon as one of them has proved one thing, another one follows and proves quite a different thing. The poem just quoted shows that he was in love with Cornelia, but a month later he is in love with Harriet again, and there is a poem to prove it.

> In this piteous appeal Shelley declares that he has now no grief but one—the grief of having known and lost his wife's love.

Exhibit F

Thy look of love has power to calm
The stormiest passion of my soul.

But without doubt she had been reserving her looks of love a good part of the time for ten months, now—ever since he began to lavish his own on Cornelia Turner at the end of the previous July. He does really seem to have already forgotten Cornelia's merits in one brief month, for he eulogizes Harriet in a way which rules all competition out:

Thou only virtuous, gentle, kind,
Amid a world of hate.

He complains of her hardness, and begs her to make the concession of a "slight endurance"—of his waywardness, perhaps—for the sake of "a fellow-being's lasting weal." But the main force of his appeal is in his closing stanza, and is strongly worded:

O trust for once no erring guide!
  Bid the remorseless feeling flee;
'Tis malice, 'tis revenge, 'tis pride,
  'Tis anything but thee;
O deign a nobler pride to prove,
And pity if thou canst not love.

This is in May—apparently toward the end of it. Harriet and Shelley were corresponding all the time. Harriet got the poem—a copy exists in her own handwriting; she being the only gentle and kind person amid a world of hate, according to Shelley's own testimony in the poem, we are permitted to think that the daily letters would presently have melted that kind and gentle heart and brought about the reconciliation, if there had been time—but there wasn't; for in a very few days—in fact, before the 8th of June—Shelley was in love with *another* woman.

And so—perhaps while Harriet was walking the floor nights, trying to get *her* poem by heart—her husband was doing a fresh one—for the other girl—Mary Wollstonecraft Godwin—with sentiments like these in it:

Exhibit G

To spend years thus and be rewarded,
As thou, sweet love, requited me
When none were near.
. . . thy lips did meet
Mine tremblingly; . . .

Gentle and good and mild thou art,
Nor can I live if thou appear
Aught but thyself. . . .

And so on. "Before the close of June it was known and felt by Mary and Shelley that each was inexpressibly dear to the other." Yes, Shelley had found this child of sixteen to his liking, and had wooed and won her in the graveyard. But that is nothing; it was better than wooing her in her nursery, at any rate, where it might have disturbed the other children.

However, she was a child in years only. From the day that she set her masculine grip on Shelley he was to frisk no more. If she had occupied the only kind and gentle Harriet's place in March it would have been a thrilling spectacle to see her invade the Boinville rookery and read the riot act. That holiday of Shelley's would have been of short duration, and Cornelia's hair would have been as gray as her mother's when the services were over.

Hogg went to the Godwin residence in Skinner Street with Shelley on that 8th of June. They passed through Godwin's little debt-factory of a book-shop and went up-stairs hunting for the proprietor. Nobody there. Shelley strode about the room impatiently, making its crazy floor quake under him. Then a door "was partially and softly opened. A thrilling voice called, 'Shelley!' A thrilling voice answered, 'Mary!' And he darted out of the room like an arrow from the bow of the far-shooting King. A very young female, fair and fair-haired, pale, indeed, and with a piercing look, wearing a frock of tartan, an unusual dress in London at that time, had called him out of the room."

This is Mary Godwin, as described by Hogg. The thrill of the voices shows that the love of Shelley and Mary was already upward of a fortnight old; therefore it had been born within the month of May—born while Harriet was still trying to get her poem by heart, we think. I must not be asked how I know so much about that thrill; it is my secret. The biographer and I have private ways of finding out things when it is necessary to find them out and the customary methods fail.

Shelley left London that day, and was gone ten days. The biographer conjectures that he spent this interval with Harriet in Bath. It would be just like him. To the end of his days he liked to be in love with two women at once. He was more in love with Miss Hitchener when he married Harriet than he was with Harriet, and told the lady so with simple and unostentatious candor. He was more in love with Cornelia than he was with Harriet in the end of 1813 and the beginning of 1814, yet he supplied both of them with love poems of an equal temperature meantime; he loved Mary and Harriet in June, and while getting ready to run off with the one, it is conjectured that he put in his odd time trying to get reconciled to the other; by and by, while still in love with Mary, he will make love to her half-sister by marriage, adoption, and the visitation of God, through the medium of clandestine letters, and she will answer with letters that are for no eye but his own.

When Shelley encountered Mary Godwin he was looking around for another paradise. He had tastes of his own, and there were features about the Godwin establishment that strongly recommended it. Godwin was an advanced thinker and an able writer. One of his romances is still read, but his philosophical works, once so esteemed, are out of vogue now; their authority was already declining when Shelley made his acquaintance—that is, it was declining with the public, but not with Shelley. They had been his moral and political Bible, and they were that yet. Shelley the infidel would himself have claimed to be less a work of God than a work of Godwin. Godwin's philosophies had formed his mind and interwoven themselves into it and become a part of its texture; he regarded himself as Godwin's spiritual son. Godwin was not without self-appreciation; indeed, it may be conjectured that from his point of view the last syllable of his name was surplusage. He lived serene in his lofty world of philosophy, far above the mean interests that absorbed smaller men, and only came down to the ground at intervals to pass the hat for alms to pay his debts with, and insult the man that relieved him. Several of his principles were out of the ordinary. For example, he was opposed to marriage. He was not aware that his preachings from this text were but theory and wind; he supposed he was in earnest in imploring people to live together without marrying, until Shelley furnished him a working model of his scheme and a practical example to analyze, by applying the principle in his own family; the matter took a different and surprising aspect then. The late Matthew Arnold said that the main defect in Shelley's make-up was that he was destitute of the sense of humor. This episode must have escaped Mr. Arnold's attention.

But we have said enough about the head of the new paradise. Mrs. Godwin is described as being in several ways a terror; and even when her soul was in repose she wore green spectacles. But I suspect that her main unattractiveness was born of the fact that she wrote the letters that are out in the appendix-basket in the back yard—letters which are an outrage and wholly untrustworthy, for they say some kind things about poor Harriet and tell some disagreeable truths about her husband; and these things make the fabulist grit his teeth a good deal.

Next we have Fanny Godwin—a Godwin by courtesy only; she was Mrs. Godwin's natural daughter by a former friend. She was a sweet and winning girl, but she presently wearied of the Godwin paradise, and poisoned herself.

Last in the list is Jane (or Claire, as she preferred to call herself) Clairmont, daughter of Mrs. Godwin by a former marriage. She was very young and pretty and accommodating, and always ready to do what she could to make things pleasant. After Shelley ran off with her part-sister Mary, she became the guest of the pair, and contributed a natural child to their nursery—Allegra. Lord Byron was the father.

We have named the several members and advantages of the new paradise in Skinner Street, with its crazy book-shop underneath. Shelley was all right now, this was a better place than the other; more variety anyway, and more different kinds of fragrance. One could turn out poetry here without any trouble at all.

The way the new love-match came about was this: Shelley told Mary all his aggravations and sorrows and griefs, and about the wet-nurse and the bonnet-shop and the surgeon and the carriage, and the sister-in-law that blocked the London game, and about Cornelia and her mamma, and how they had turned him out of the house after making so much of him; and how he had deserted Harriet and then Harriet had deserted him, and how the reconciliation was working along and Harriet getting her poem by heart; and still he was not happy, and Mary pitied him, for she had had trouble herself. But I am not satisfied with this. It reads too much like statistics. It lacks smoothness and grace, and is too earthy and business-like. It has the sordid look of a trades-union procession out on strike. That is not the right form for it. The book does it better; we will fall back on the book and have a cake-walk:

> It was easy to divine that some restless grief possessed him; Mary herself was not unlearned in the lore of pain. His generous zeal in her father's behalf, his spiritual sonship to Godwin, his reverence for her mother's memory, were guarantees with Mary of his excellence.[1] The new friends could not lack subjects of discourse, and underneath their words about Mary's mother, and "Political Justice," and "Rights of Woman," were two young hearts, each feeling toward the other, each perhaps unaware, trembling in the direction of the other. The desire to assuage the suffering of one whose happiness has grown precious to us may become a hunger of the spirit as keen as any other, and this hunger now possessed Mary's heart; when her eyes rested unseen on Shelley, it was with a look full of the ardor of a "soothing pity."

Yes, that is better and has more composure. That is just the way it happened. He told her about the wet-nurse, she told him about political justice; he told her

1. What she was after was guarantees of his excellence. That he stood ready to desert his wife and child was one of them, apparently.

about the deadly sister-in-law, she told him about her mother; he told her about the bonnet-shop, she murmured back about the rights of woman; then he assuaged her, then she assuaged him; then he assuaged her some more, next she assuaged him some more; then they both assuaged one another simultaneously; and so they went on by the hour assuaging and assuaging and assuaging, until at last what was the result? They were in love. It will happen so every time.

> He had married a woman who, as he now persuaded himself, had never truly loved him, who loved only his fortune and his rank, and who proved her selfishness by deserting him in his misery.

I think that that is not quite fair to Harriet. We have no certainty that she knew Cornelia had turned him out of the house. He went back to Cornelia, and Harriet may have supposed that he was as happy with her as ever. Still, it was judicious to begin to lay on the whitewash, for Shelley is going to need many a coat of it now, and the sooner the reader becomes used to the intrusion of the brush the sooner he will get reconciled to it and stop fretting about it.

After Shelley's (conjectured) visit to Harriet at Bath—8th of June to 18th—"it seems to have been arranged that Shelley should henceforth join the Skinner Street household each day at dinner."

Nothing could be handier than this; things will swim along now.

> Although now Shelley was coming to believe that his wedded union with Harriet was a thing of the past, he had not ceased to regard her with affectionate consideration; he wrote to her frequently, and kept her informed of his whereabouts.

We must not get impatient over these curious inharmoniousnesses and irreconcilabilities in Shelley's character. You can see by the biographer's attitude toward them that there is nothing objectionable about them. Shelley was doing his best to make two adoring young creatures happy: he was regarding the one with affectionate consideration by mail, and he was assuaging the other one at home.

> Unhappy Harriet, residing at Bath, had perhaps never desired that the breach between herself and her husband should be irreparable and complete.

I find no fault with that sentence except that the "perhaps" is not strictly warranted. It should have been left out. In support—or shall we say extenuation?—of this opinion I submit that there is not sufficient evidence to warrant the uncertainty which it implies. The only "evidence" offered that Harriet was hard and proud and standing out against a reconciliation is a poem—the poem in which Shelley beseeches her to "bid the remorseless feeling flee" and "pity" if she "cannot love." We have just that as "evidence," and out of its meager materials the biographer builds a cobhouse of conjectures as big as the Coliseum; conjectures which convince him, the prosecuting attorney, but ought to fall far short of convincing any fair-minded jury.

Shelley's love poems may be very good evidence, but we know well that they are "good for this day and train only." We are able to believe that they spoke the truth for that one day, but we know by experience that they could not be depended on to speak it the next. The very supplication for a rewarming of Harriet's chilled love was followed so suddenly by the poet's plunge into an adoring passion for Mary Godwin that if it had been a check it would have lost its value before a lazy person could have gotten to the bank with it.

Hardness, stubbornness, pride, vindictiveness—these may sometimes reside in a young wife and mother of nineteen, but they are not charged against Harriet Shelley outside of that poem, and one has no right to insert them into her character on such shadowy "evidence" as that. Peacock knew Harriet well, and she has a flexible and persuadable look, as painted by him:

> Her manners were good, and her whole aspect and demeanor such manifest emanations of pure and truthful nature that to be once in her company was to know her thoroughly. She was fond of her husband, and accommodated herself in every way to his tastes. If they mixed in society, she adorned it; if they lived in retirement, she was satisfied; if they traveled, she enjoyed the change of scene.

"Perhaps" she had never desired that the breach should be irreparable and complete. The truth is, we do not even know that there was any breach at all at this time. We know that the husband and wife went before the altar and took a new oath on the 24th of March to love and cherish each other until death—and this may be regarded as a sort of reconciliation itself, and a wiping out of the old grudges. Then Harriet went away, and the sister-in-law removed herself from her society. That was in April. Shelley wrote his "appeal" in May, but the corresponding went right along afterward. We have a right to doubt that the subject of it was a "reconciliation," or that Harriet had any suspicion that she needed to be reconciled and that her husband was trying to persuade her to it—as the biographer has sought to make us believe, with his Coliseum of conjectures built out of a waste-basket of poetry. For we have "evidence" now—not poetry and conjecture. When Shelley had been dining daily in the Skinner Street paradise fifteen days and continuing the love-match which was already a fortnight old twenty-five days earlier, he forgot to write Harriet; forgot it the next day and the next. During four days Harriet got no letter from him. Then her fright and anxiety rose to expression-heat, and she wrote a letter to Shelley's publisher which seems to reveal to us that Shelley's letters to her had been the customary affectionate letters of husband to wife, and had carried no appeals for reconciliation and had not needed to:

> BATH (postmark July 7, 1814).
>
> MY DEAR SIR,—You will greatly oblige me by giving the inclosed to Mr. Shelley. I would not trouble you, but it is now four days since I have heard from him, which to me is an age. Will you write by return of post and tell me what has become of him? as I always fancy something dreadful has happened if I do not hear from him. If you tell me that he is well I shall not come to London, but if I do not hear from you or him I shall certainly come, as I cannot endure this dreadful state of suspense. You are his friend and you can feel for me.
>
> I remain yours truly,
>
> H.S.

Even without Peacock's testimony that "her whole aspect and demeanor were manifest emanations of a pure and truthful nature," we should hold this to be a truthful letter, a sincere letter, a loving letter; it bears those marks; I think it is also the letter of a person accustomed to receiving letters from her husband frequently, and that they have been of a welcome and satisfactory sort, too, this long time back—ever since the solemn remarriage and reconciliation at the altar most likely.

The biographer follows Harriet's letter with a conjecture. He conjectures that she "would now gladly have retraced her steps." Which means that it is proven that she had steps to retrace—proven by the poem. Well, if the poem is better evidence than the letter, we must let it stand at that.

Then the biographer attacks Harriet Shelley's honor—by authority of random and unverified gossip scavengered from a group of people whose very names make a person shudder: Mary Godwin, mistress of Shelley; her part-sister, discarded mistress of Lord Byron; Godwin, the philosophical tramp, who gathers his share of it from a shadow—that is to say, from a person whom he shirks out of naming. Yet the biographer dignifies this sorry rubbish with the name of "evidence."

Nothing remotely resembling a distinct charge from a named person professing to know is offered among this precious "evidence."

1. "Shelley *believed*" so and so.

2. Byron's discarded mistress says that Shelley told Mary Godwin so and so, and *Mary* told *her*.

3. "Shelley said" so and so—and later "admitted over and over again that he had been in error."

4. The unspeakable Godwin "wrote to Mr. Baxter" that he knew so and so "from unquestionable authority"—name not furnished.

How any man in his right mind could bring himself to defile the grave of a shamefully abused and defenseless girl with these baseless fabrications, this manufactured filth, is inconceivable. How any man, in his right mind or out of it, could sit down and coldly try to persuade anybody to believe it, or listen patiently to it, or, indeed, do anything but scoff at it and deride it, is astonishing.

The charge insinuated by these odious slanders is one of the most difficult of all offenses to prove; it is also one which no man has a right to mention even in a whisper about any woman, living or dead, unless he knows it to be true, and not even then unless he can also *prove* it to be true. There is no justification for the abomination of putting this stuff in the book.

Against Harriet Shelley's good name there is not one scrap of tarnishing evidence, and not even a scrap of evil gossip, that comes from a source that entitles it to a hearing.

On the credit side of the account we have strong opinions from the people who knew her best. Peacock says:

> I feet it due to the memory of Harriet to state my most decided conviction that her conduct as a wife was as pure, as

> true, as absolutely faultless, as that of any who for such conduct are held most in honor.

Thornton Hunt, who had picked and published slight flaws in Harriet's character, says, as regards this alleged large one:

> There is not a trace of evidence or a whisper of scandal against her before her voluntary departure from Shelley.

Trelawney says:

> I was assured by the evidence of the few friends who knew both Shelley and his wife—Hookham, Hogg, Peacock, and one of the Godwins—that Harriet was perfectly innocent of all offense.

What excuse was there for raking up a parcel of foul rumors from malicious and discredited sources and flinging them at this dead girl's head? Her very defenselessness should have been her protection. The fact that all letters to her or about her, with almost every scrap of her own writing, had been diligently mislaid, leaving her case destitute of a voice, while every pen-stroke which could help her husband's side had been as diligently preserved, should have excused her from being brought to trial. Her witnesses have all disappeared, yet we see her summoned in her grave-clothes to plead for the life of her character, without the help of an advocate, before a disqualified judge and a packed jury.

Harriet Shelley wrote her distressed letter on the 7th of July. On the 28th her husband ran away with Mary Godwin and her part-sister Claire to the Continent. He deserted his wife when her confinement was approaching. She bore him a child at the end of November, his mistress bore him another one something over two months later. The truants were back in London before either of these events occurred.

On one occasion, presently, Shelley was so pressed for money to support his mistress with that he went to his wife and got some money of his that was in her hands—twenty pounds. Yet the mistress was not moved to gratitude; for later, when the wife was troubled to meet her engagements, the mistress makes this entry in her diary:

> Harriet sends her creditors here; nasty woman. Now we shall have to change our lodgings.

The deserted wife bore the bitterness and obloquy of her situation two years and a quarter; then she gave up, and drowned herself. A month afterward the body was found in the water. Three weeks later Shelley married his mistress.

I must here be allowed to italicize a remark of the biographer's concerning Harriet Shelley:

> *That no act of Shelley's during the two years which immediately preceded her death tended to cause the rash act which brought her life to its close seems certain.*

Yet her husband had deserted her and her children, and was living with a concubine all that time! Why should a person attempt to write biography when the simplest facts have no meaning to him? This book is littered with as crass stupidities as that one—deductions by the page which bear no discoverable kinship to their premises.

The biographer throws off that extraordinary remark without any perceptible disturbance to his serenity; for he follows it with a sentimental justification of Shelley's conduct which has not a pang of conscience in it, but is silky and smooth and undulating and pious—a cake-walk with all the colored brethren at their best. There may be people who can read that page and keep their temper, but it is doubtful.

Shelley's life has the one indelible blot upon it but is otherwise worshipfully noble and beautiful. It even stands out indestructibly gracious and lovely from the ruck of these disastrous pages, in spite of the fact that they expose and establish his responsibility for his forsaken wife's pitiful fate—a responsibility which he himself tacitly admits in a letter to Eliza Westbrook, wherein he refers to his taking up with Mary Godwin as an act which Eliza "might excusably regard as the cause of her sister's ruin."

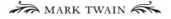

A Medieval Romance

CHAPTER I

THE SECRET REVEALED

It was night. Stillness reigned in the grand old feudal castle of Klugenstein. The year 1222 was drawing to a close. Far away up in the tallest of the castle's towers a single light glimmered. A secret council was being held there. The stern old lord of Klugenstein sat in a chair of state meditating. Presently he said, with a tender accent:

"My daughter!"

A young man of noble presence, clad from head to heel in knightly mail, answered:

"Speak, father!"

"My daughter, the time is come for the revealing of the mystery that hath puzzled all your young life. Know, then, that it had its birth in the matters which I shall now unfold. My brother Ulrich is the great Duke of Brandenburgh. Our father, on his deathbed, decreed that if no son were born to Ulrich, the succession should pass to my house, provided a son were born to me. And further, in case no son were born to either, but only daughters, then the succession should pass to Ulrich's daughter, if she proved stainless; if she did not, my daughter should succeed, if she retained a blameless name. And so I and my old wife here prayed fervently for the good boon of a son, but the prayer was vain. You were born to us. I was in despair. I saw the mighty prize slipping from my grasp, the splendid dream vanishing away. And I had been so hopeful! Five years had Ulrich lived in wedlock, and yet his wife had borne no heir of either sex.

"'But hold,' I said, 'all is not lost.' A saving scheme had shot athwart my brain. You were born at midnight. Only the leech, the nurse, and six waiting-women knew your sex. I hanged them every one before an hour had sped. Next morning all the barony went mad with rejoicing over the proclamation that a son was born to Klugenstein, an heir to mighty Brandenburgh! And well the secret has been kept. Your mother's own sister nursed your infancy, and from that time forward we feared nothing.

"When you were ten years old, a daughter was born to Ulrich. We grieved, but hoped for good results from measles, or physicians, or other natural enemies of infancy, but were always disappointed. She lived, she throve—Heaven's malison upon her! But it is nothing. We are safe. For, ha! ha! have we not a son? And is not our son the future duke? Our well-beloved Conrad, is it not so?—for woman of eight-and-twenty years as you are, my child, none other name than that hath ever fallen to *you!*

"Now it hath come to pass that age hath laid its hand upon my brother, and he waxes feeble. The cares of state do tax him sore. Therefore he wills that you shall come to him and be already duke—in act, though not yet in name. Your servitors are ready—you journey forth to-night.

"Now listen well. Remember every word I say. There is a law as old as Germany that if any woman sit for a single instant in the great ducal chair before she hath been absolutely crowned in presence of the people—SHE SHALL DIE! So heed my, words. Pretend humility. Pronounce your judgments from the Premier's chair, which stands at the *foot* of the throne. Do this until you are crowned and safe. It is not likely that your sex will ever be discovered; but still it is the part of wisdom to make all things as safe as may be in this treacherous earthly life."

"Oh, my father! is it for this my life hath been a lie! Was it that I might cheat my unoffending cousin of her rights? Spare me, father, spare your child!"

"What, hussy! Is this my reward for the august fortune my brain has wrought for thee? By the bones of my father, this puling sentiment of thine but ill accords with my humor. Betake thee to the duke instantly, and beware how thou meddlest with my purpose!"

Let this suffice of the conversation. It is enough for us to know that the prayers, the entreaties, and the tears of the gentle-natured girl availed nothing. They nor anything could move the stout old lord of Klugenstein. And so, at last, with a heavy heart, the daughter saw the castle gates close behind her, and found herself riding away in the darkness surrounded by a knightly array of armed vassals and a brave following of servants.

The old baron sat silent for many minutes after his daughter's departure, and then he turned to his sad wife, and said:

"Dame, our matters seem speeding fairly. It is full three months since I sent the shrewd and handsome Count Detzin on his devilish mission to my brother's daughter Constance. If he fail, we are not wholly safe; but if he do succeed, no power can bar our girl from being duchess, e'en though ill fortune should decree she never should be duke!"

"My heart is full of bodings; yet all may still be well."

"Tush, woman! Leave the owls to croak. To bed with ye, and dream of Brandenburgh and grandeur!"

CHAPTER II

FESTIVITY AND TEARS

Six days after the occurrences related in the above chapter, the brilliant capital of the Duchy of Brandenburgh was resplendent with military pageantry and noisy with the rejoicings of loyal multitudes, for Conrad, the young heir to the crown, was come. The old duke's heart was full of happiness, for Conrad's handsome person and graceful bearing had won his love at once. The great halls of the palace were thronged with nobles, who welcomed Conrad bravely; and so bright and happy did all things seem that he felt his fears and sorrows passing away and giving place to a comforting contentment.

But in a remote apartment of the palace a scene of a different nature was transpiring. By a window stood the duke's only child, the Lady Constance. Her eyes were red and swollen and full of tears. She was alone. Presently she fell to weeping anew, and said aloud:

"The villain Detzin is gone—has fled the dukedom! I could not believe it at first, but alas! it is too true. And I loved him so. I dared to love him though I knew the duke my father would never let me wed him. I loved him—but now I hate him! With all my soul I hate him! Oh, what is to become of me? I am lost, lost, lost! I shall go mad!

CHAPTER III

THE PLOT THICKENS

A few months drifted by. All men published the praises of the young Conrad's government and extolled the wisdom of his judgments, the mercifulness of his sentences, and the modesty with which he bore himself in his great office. The old duke soon gave everything into his hands, and sat apart and listened with proud satisfaction while his heir delivered the decrees of the crown from the seat of the premier. It seemed plain that one so loved and praised and honored of all men as Conrad was could not be otherwise than happy. But, strangely enough, he was not. For he saw with dismay that the Princess Constance had begun to love him! The love of the rest of the world was happy fortune for him, but this was freighted with danger! And he saw, moreover, that the delighted duke had discovered his daughter's passion likewise, and was already dreaming of a marriage. Every day somewhat of the deep sadness that had been in the princess's face faded away; every day hope and animation beamed brighter from her eye; and by and by even vagrant smiles visited the face that had been so troubled.

Conrad was appalled. He bitterly cursed himself for having yielded to the instinct that had made him seek the companionship of one of his own sex when he was new and a stranger in the palace—when he was sorrowful and yearned for a sympathy such as only women can give or feel. He now began to avoid his cousin. But this only made matters worse, for, naturally enough, the more he avoided her, the more she cast herself in his way. He marveled at this at first, and next it startled him. The girl haunted him; she hunted him; she happened upon him at all times and in all places, in the night as well as in the day. She seemed singularly anxious. There was surely a mystery somewhere.

This could not go on forever. All the world was talking about it. The duke was beginning to look perplexed. Poor Conrad was becoming a very ghost through dread and dire distress. One day as he was emerging from a private anteroom attached to the picture gallery Constance confronted him, and seizing both his hands in hers, exclaimed:

"Oh, why, do you avoid me? What have I done—what have I said, to lose your kind opinion of me—for surely I had it once? Conrad, do not despise me, but pity a tortured heart? I cannot, cannot hold the words unspoken longer, lest they kill me—I LOVE YOU, CONRAD! There, despise me if you must, but they *would* be uttered!"

Conrad was speechless. Constance hesitated a moment, and then, misinterpreting his silence, a wild gladness flamed in her eyes, and she flung her arms about his neck and said:

"You relent! you relent! You *can* love me—you *will* love me! Oh, say you will, my own, my worshiped Conrad!'"

Conrad groaned aloud. A sickly pallor overspread his countenance, and he trembled like an aspen. Presently, in desperation, he thrust the poor girl from him, and cried:

"You know not what you ask! It is forever and ever impossible!" And then he fled like a criminal and left the princess stupefied with amazement. A minute afterward she was crying and sobbing there, and Conrad was crying and sobbing in his chamber. Both were in despair. Both saw ruin staring them in the face.

By and by Constance rose slowly to her feet and moved away, saying:

"To think that he was despising my love at the very moment that I thought it was melting his cruel heart! I hate him! He spurned me—did this man—he spurned me from him like a dog!"

CHAPTER IV

THE AWFUL REVELATION

Time passed on. A settled sadness rested once more upon the countenance of the good duke's daughter. She and Conrad were seen together no more now. The duke grieved at this. But as the weeks wore away, Conrad's color came back to his cheeks and his old-time vivacity to his eye, and he administered the government with a clear and steadily ripening wisdom.

Presently a strange whisper began to be heard about the palace. It grew louder; it spread farther. The gossips of the city got hold of it. It swept the dukedom. And this is what the whisper said:

"The Lady Constance hath given birth to a child!"

When the lord of Klugenstein heard it, he swung his plumed helmet thrice around his head and shouted: "Long live Duke Conrad!—for lo, his crown is sure, from this day forward! Detzin has done his errand well, and the good scoundrel shall be rewarded!"

And he spread the tidings far and wide, and for eight-and-forty hours no soul in all the barony but did dance and sing, carouse and illuminate, to celebrate the great event, and all proud and happy at old Klugenstein's expense.

CHAPTER V

THE FRIGHTFUL CATASTROPHE

The trial was at hand. All the great lords and barons of Brandenburgh were assembled in the Hall of Justice in the ducal palace. No space was left unoccupied where there was room for a spectator to stand or sit. Conrad, clad in purple and ermine, sat in the premier's chair, and on either side sat the great judges of the realm. The old duke had sternly commanded that the trial of his daughter should proceed without favor, and then had taken to his bed broken-hearted. His days were numbered. Poor Conrad had begged, as for his very life, that he might be spared the misery of sitting in judgment upon his cousin's crime, but it did not avail.

The saddest heart in all that great assemblage was in Conrad's breast.

The gladdest was in his father's, for unknown to his daughter "Conrad," the old Baron Klugenstein was come, and was among the crowd of nobles triumphant in the swelling fortunes of his house.

After the heralds had made due proclamation and the other preliminaries had followed, the venerable Lord Chief Justice said: "Prisoner, stand forth!"

The unhappy princess rose and stood unveiled before the vast multitude. The Lord Chief Justice continued:

"Most noble lady, before the great judges of this realm it hath been charged and proven that out of holy wedlock your Grace hath given birth unto a child,; and by our ancient law the penalty is death excepting in one sole contingency, whereof his Grace the acting duke, our good Lord Conrad, will advertise you in his solemn sentence now; wherefore give heed."

Conrad stretched forth the reluctant sceptre, and in the self-same moment the womanly heart beneath his robe yearned pityingly toward the doomed prisoner, and the tears came into his eyes. He opened his lips to speak, but the Lord Chief Justice said quickly:

"Not there, your Grace, not there! It is not lawful to pronounce judgment upon any of the ducal line SAVE FROM THE DUCAL THRONE!"

A shudder went to the heart of poor Conrad, and a tremor shook the iron frame of his old father likewise. CONRAD HAD NOT BEEN CROWNED—dared he profane the throne? He hesitated and turned pale with fear. But it must be done. Wondering eyes were already upon him. They would be suspicious eyes if he hesitated longer. He ascended the throne. Presently he stretched forth the sceptre again, and said:

"Prisoner, in the name of our sovereign lord, Ulrich, Duke of Brandenburgh, I proceed to the solemn duty that hath devolved upon me. Give heed to my words. By the ancient law of the land, except you produce the partner of your guilt and deliver him up to the executioner, you must surely die. Embrace this opportunity—save yourself while yet you may. Name the father of your child!"

A solemn hush fell upon the great court—a silence so profound that men could hear their own hearts beat. Then the princess slowly turned, with eyes gleaming with hate, and pointing her finger straight at Conrad, said:

"Thou art the man!"

An appalling conviction of his helpless, hopeless peril struck a chill to Conrad's heart like the chill of death itself. What power on earth could save him! To disprove the charge, he must reveal that he was a woman; and for an uncrowned woman to sit in the ducal chair was death! At one and the same moment, he and his grim old father swooned and fell to the ground.

The remainder of this thrilling and eventful story will NOT be found in this or any other publication, either now or at any future time.

The truth is, I have got my hero (or heroine) into such a particularly close place that I do not see how I am ever going to get him (or her) out of it again—and therefore I will wash my hands of the whole business, and leave that person to get out the best way that offers—or else stay there. I thought it was going to be easy enough to straighten out that little difficulty, but it looks different now.

The Story of the Good Little Boy

Once there was a good little boy by the name of Jacob Blivens. He always obeyed his parents, no matter how absurd and unreasonable their demands were; and he always learned his book, and never was late at Sabbath-school. He would not play hookey, even when his sober judgment told him it was the most profitable thing he could do. None of the other boys could ever make that boy out, he acted so strangely. He wouldn't lie, no matter how convenient it was. He just said it was wrong to lie, and that was sufficient for him. And he was so honest that he was simply ridiculous. The curious ways that that Jacob had, surpassed everything. He wouldn't play marbles on Sunday, he wouldn't rob birds' nests, he wouldn't give hot pennies to organ-grinders' monkeys; he didn't seem to take any interest in any kind of rational amusement. So the other boys used to try to reason it out and come to an understanding of him, but they couldn't arrive at any satisfactory conclusion. As I said before, they could only figure out a sort of vague idea that he was "afflicted," and so they took him under their protection, and never allowed any harm to come to him.

This good little boy read all the Sunday-school books; they were his greatest delight. This was the whole secret of it. He believed in the good little boys they put in the Sunday-school books; he had every confidence in them. He longed to come across one of them alive once; but he never did. They all died before his time, maybe. Whenever he read about a particularly good one he turned over quickly to the end to see what became of him, because he wanted to travel thousands of miles and gaze on him; but it wasn't any use; that good little boy always died in the last chapter, and there was a picture of the funeral, with all his relations and the Sunday-school children standing around the grave in pantaloons that were too short, and bonnets that were too large, and everybody crying into handkerchiefs that had as much as a yard and a half of stuff in them. He was always headed off in this way. He never could see one of those good little boys on account of his always dying in the last chapter.

Jacob had a noble ambition to be put in a Sunday-school book. He wanted to be put in, with pictures representing him gloriously declining to lie to his mother, and her weeping for joy about it; and pictures representing him standing on the doorstep giving a penny to a poor beggar-woman with six children, and telling her to spend it freely, but not to be extravagant, because extravagance is a sin; and pictures of him magnanimously refusing to tell on the bad boy who always lay in wait for him around the corner as he came from school, and welted him over the head with a lath, and then chased him home, saying, "Hi! hi!" as he proceeded. That was the ambition of young Jacob Blivens. He wished to be put in a Sunday-school book. It made him feel a little uncomfortable sometimes when he reflected that the good little boys always died. He loved to live, you know, and this was the most unpleasant feature about being a Sunday-school-book boy. He knew it was not healthy to be good. He knew it was more fatal than consumption to be so supernaturally good as the boys in the books were; he knew that none of them had ever been able to stand it long, and it pained him to think that if they put him in a book he wouldn't ever see it, or even if they did get the book out before he died it wouldn't be popular without any picture of his funeral in the back part of it. It couldn't be much of a Sunday-school book that couldn't tell about the advice he gave to the community when he was dying. So at last, of course, he had to make up his mind to do the best he could under the circumstances—to live right, and hang on as long as he could, and have his dying speech all ready when his time came.

But somehow nothing ever went right with this good little boy; nothing ever turned out with him the way it turned out with the good little boys in the books. They always had a good time, and the bad boys had the broken legs; but in his case there was a screw loose somewhere, and it all happened just the other way. When he found Jim Blake stealing apples, and went under the tree to read to him about the bad little boy who fell out of a neighbor's apple tree and broke his arm, Jim fell out of the tree, too, but he fell on *him* and broke *his* arm, and Jim wasn't hurt at all. Jacob couldn't understand that. There wasn't anything in the books like it.

And once, when some bad boys pushed a blind man over in the mud, and Jacob ran to help him up and receive his blessing, the blind man did not give him any blessing at all, but whacked him over the head with his stick and said he would like to catch him shoving *him* again, and then pretending to help him up. This was not in accordance with any of the books. Jacob looked them all over to see.

One thing that Jacob wanted to do was to find a lame dog that hadn't any place to stay, and was hungry and persecuted, and bring him home and pet him and have that dog's imperishable gratitude. And at last he found one and was happy; and he brought him home and fed him, but when he was going to pet him the dog flew at him and tore all the clothes off him except those that were in front, and made a spectacle of him that was astonishing. He examined authorities, but he could not understand the matter. It was of the same breed of dogs that was in the books, but it acted very differently. Whatever this boy did he got into trouble. The very things the boys in the books got rewarded for turned out to be about the most unprofitable things he could invest in.

Once, when he was on his way to Sunday-school, he saw some bad boys starting off pleasuring in a sailboat. He was filled with consternation, because he knew from his reading that boys who went sailing on Sunday invariably got drowned. So he ran out on a raft to warn them, but a log turned with him and slid him into the river. A man got him out pretty soon, and the doctor pumped the water out of him, and gave him a fresh start with his bellows, but he caught cold and lay sick abed nine weeks. But the most unaccountable thing about it was that the bad boys in the boat had a good time all day, and then reached home alive and well in the most surprising manner. Jacob Blivens said there was nothing like these things in the books. He was perfectly dumfounded.

> THE VERY THINGS THE BOYS IN THE BOOKS GOT REWARDED FOR TURNED OUT TO BE ABOUT THE MOST UNPROFITABLE THINGS HE COULD INVEST IN.

When he got well he was a little discouraged, but he resolved to keep on trying anyhow. He knew that so far his experiences wouldn't do to go in a book, but he hadn't yet reached the allotted term of life for good little boys, and he hoped to be able to make a record yet if he could hold on till his time was fully up. If everything else failed he had his dying speech to fall back on.

He examined his authorities, and found that it was now time for him to go to sea as a cabin-boy. He called on a ship-captain and made his application, and when the captain asked for his recommendations he proudly drew out a tract and pointed to the word, "To Jacob Blivens, from his affectionate teacher." But the captain was a coarse, vulgar man, and he said, "Oh, that be blowed! *that* wasn't any proof that he knew how to wash dishes or handle a slush-bucket, and he guessed he didn't want him." This was altogether the most extraordinary thing that ever happened to Jacob in all his life. A compliment from a teacher, on a tract, had never failed to move the tenderest emotions of ship-captains, and open the way to all offices of honor and profit in their gift—it never had in any book that ever *he* had read. He could hardly believe his senses.

This boy always had a hard time of it. Nothing ever came out according to the authorities with him. At last, one day, when he was around hunting up bad little boys to admonish, he found a lot of them in the old iron-foundry fixing up a little joke on fourteen or fifteen dogs, which they had tied together in long procession, and were going to ornament with empty nitroglycerin cans made fast to their tails. Jacob's heart was touched. He sat down on one of those cans (for he never minded grease when duty was before him), and he took hold of the foremost dog by the collar, and turned his reproving eye upon wicked Tom Jones. But just at that moment Alderman McWelter, full of wrath, stepped in. All the bad boys ran away, but Jacob Blivens rose in conscious innocence and began one of those stately little Sunday-school-book speeches which always commence with "Oh, sir!" in dead opposition to the fact that no boy, good or bad, ever starts a remark with "Oh, sir." But the alderman never waited to hear the rest. He took Jacob Blivens by the ear and turned him around, and hit him a whack in the rear with the flat of his hand; and in an instant that good little boy shot out through the roof and soared away toward the sun, with the fragments of those fifteen dogs stringing after him like the tail of a kite. And there wasn't a sign of that alderman or that old iron-foundry left on the face of the earth; and, as for young Jacob Blivens, he never got a chance to make his last dying speech after all his trouble fixing it up, unless he made it to the birds; because, although the bulk of him came down all right in a tree-top in an adjoining county, the rest of him was apportioned around among four townships, and so they had to hold five inquests on him to find out whether he was dead or not, and how it occurred. You never saw a boy scattered so.

Thus perished the good little boy who did the best he could, but didn't come out according to the books. Every boy who ever did as he did prospered except him. His case is truly remarkable. It will probably never be accounted for.

The Grateful Poodle

One day a benevolent physician (who had read the books) having found a stray poodle suffering from a broken leg, conveyed the poor creature to his home, and after setting and bandaging the injured limb gave the little outcast its liberty again, and thought no more about the matter. But how great was his surprise, upon opening his door one morning, some days later, to find the grateful poodle patiently waiting there, and in its company another stray dog, one of whose legs, by some accident, had been broken. The kind physician at once relieved the distressed animal, nor did he forget to admire the inscrutable goodness and mercy of God, who had been willing to use so humble an instrument as the poor outcast poodle for the inculcating of, etc., etc., etc.

SEQUEL

The next morning the benevolent physician found the two dogs, beaming with gratitude, waiting at his door, and with them two other dogs-cripples. The cripples were speedily healed, and the four went their way, leaving the benevolent physician more overcome by pious wonder than ever. The day passed, the morning came. There at the door sat now the four reconstructed dogs, and with them four others requiring reconstruction. This day also passed, and another morning came; and now sixteen dogs, eight of them newly crippled, occupied the sidewalk, and the people were going around. By noon the broken legs were all set, but the pious wonder in the good physician's breast was beginning to get mixed with involuntary profanity. The sun rose once more, and exhibited thirty-two dogs, sixteen of them with broken legs, occupying the sidewalk and half of the street; the human spectators took up the rest of the room. The cries of the wounded, the songs of the healed brutes, and the comments of the onlooking citizens made great and inspiring cheer, but traffic was interrupted in that street. The good physician hired a couple of assistant surgeons and got through his benevolent work before dark, first taking the precaution to cancel his church-membership, so that he might express himself with the latitude which the case required.

But some things have their limits. When once more the morning dawned, and the good physician looked out upon a massed and far-reaching multitude of clamorous and beseeching dogs, he said, "I might as well acknowledge it, I have been fooled by the books; they only tell the pretty part of the story, and then stop. Fetch me the shotgun; this thing has gone along far enough."

He issued forth with his weapon, and chanced to step upon the tail of the original poodle, who promptly bit him in the leg. Now the great and good work which this poodle had been engaged in had engendered in him such a mighty and augmenting enthusiasm as to turn his weak head at last and drive him mad. A month later, when the benevolent physician lay in the death-throes of hydrophobia, he called his weeping friends about him, and said:

"Beware of the books. They tell but half of the story. Whenever a poor wretch asks you for help, and you feel a doubt as to what result may flow from your benevolence, give yourself the benefit of the doubt and kill the applicant."

And so saying he turned his face to the wall and gave up the ghost.

Ambrose Bierce

(1842–1914)

One of the best-known journalists of his generation, Ambrose Bierce was born on June 24, 1842, in Meigs County, Ohio, into a family of at least eight children (each with a first name beginning with the letter A). His father, Marcus, had a large home library and spent many hours with his books, giving some hint to the origin of young Ambrose's literary interests. After a year in high school, Bierce began working at age fifteen as a printer's apprentice on *The Northern Indianian*, which was known as an abolitionist paper.

In 1861, at the start of the Civil War, Bierce enlisted in Indiana's Ninth Regiment in response to President Lincoln's call for volunteers. In a stint that was supposed to last only three months, Bierce served as an officer in the Union army for three years, re-enlisting to act as sergeant of volunteers at battles such as Shiloh, Chickamauga, and Chattanooga. While in the army, he met a man who would be an influential figure in his life, General William Babcock Hazen, known as one of the toughest and most quarrelsome high Union officers. Looking for a loner who had a talent for map-sketching and wasn't afraid to take risks, Hazen chose Bierce in early 1863 to be a reconnaissance scout. Bierce rose to the occasion, happy to operate solo and have men depend on his accuracy and speed. It was during this period that he absorbed the experiences that would inspire his "war " (really anti-war) stories.

A bullet lodged in Bierce's head, behind his left ear, during the Battle of Kenesaw Mountain. He said "it crushed my skull like a broken walnut." He was sent back home to recover but rejoined his regiment and remained with it until Lee's surrender in April 1865. A year later, he followed his mentor Hazen (who was now employed as a cartographer) to San Francisco. After a brief time at the U.S. Treasury, he flipped a coin to choose between the army and journalism as a career path. The newspaper business won, and he began working at the *San Francisco Newsletter and California Advertiser* in 1868, writing what may have been the first regular humorous news column, "Town Crier." He perfected the barbed epigram, skewering many subjects and developing a wide following. He began to contribute to various periodicals and published his first short story, "The Haunted Valley," in 1871 in the *Overland Monthly*.

Bierce married Mollie Day the next year, and they took their honeymoon, funded by Molly's father, in England. Bierce wanted to test the London literary market, and the couple ended up living there for three years. In London he published, under pseudonyms, three volumes of essays and sketches: *The Fiends' Delight* (1872), *Nuggets and Dust Panned out of California* (1872), and *Cobwebs from an Empty Skull* (1874). He returned to San Francisco in 1875 more cultured, more experienced, and with a wider reputation. However, he had no job.

Eventually, Bierce was tapped for an editor's post at a new magazine, *The Argonaut*, but he and the owner did not get along and he left in 1879. He then became the editor-in-chief at *The Wasp* magazine from 1881 to 1887, where he issued *The Devil's Dictionary,* perhaps his wittiest work. He also was able to publish five of his early short stories and write *The Dance of Death* with Thomas A. Harcouth. When his tenure at *The Wasp* ended, Bierce was invited by William Randolph Hearst to join the *San Francisco Examiner* and revive his "Prattle" column, which he began writing at *The Wasp*.

Despite this professional high point, Bierce's personal life was not working out. Forced to live in the hills of San Francisco because of asthma, Bierce became estranged from Mollie and their three children. They separated and his oldest son, Day, died in a gunfight. This horrible event, coupled with slurs and rumors, was used by rival journalists to discredit Bierce. Undaunted, he continued to publish satirical pieces and short stories, issuing the now-famous collection *Tales of Soldiers and Civilians* (renamed *In the Midst of Life*) in 1891.

In 1896, his fiction career at an end, Bierce moved to Washington, D.C., to be the *Examiner*'s national columnist. He eventually bit the hand that fed him, satirizing Hearst's views on the Spanish-American War, but Hearst remained true to his star and put him out to pasture as the literary critic at *Cosmopolitan* magazine.

Bierce spent what were to be the last years of his life compiling and editing his own collected works with his publisher, Walter Neale. It took three years to assemble what grew to be a twelve-volume work, too expensive for the average reader and too complicated and museum-like for the reviewers to digest when it finally was published in 1912. Still, it is a literary treasure and a testament to an exceptional satirist and literary writer.

In 1913, at the age of 71, Bierce ceased writing altogether and went into the midst of the revolution in Mexico, "to seek the good, kind darkness." It is also said he went to fight alongside the famous bandit Pancho Villa. He supposedly mailed a letter from the city of Chihuahua, which was his last contact of any kind. "Death is not the end," the man nicknamed Bitter Bierce wrote; "there remains the litigation over the estate."

Ambrose Bierce reinvented the short story genre when he began his fiction career. He shortened the short story, and made it a sharper, more toned medium. His stories were similar to Poe's, but he usually went at least one step further in pathology and horror. No girls in peril, happy endings, dashing heroes in his work—only twisted and bizarre situations with mannerly narrators who have no sane perspective on what has occurred. In his war stories, it is almost incidental that the mortal conflict is raging, for it is the individual human incivilities that he chooses to dramatize, as in "Killed at Resaca," when a woman's idle comments send a man to a needless death.

Yet for all the gore, Bierce can be viewed as a successful comic writer, if you like your humor black with no sugar. His "humor noir" is an art. He paints a gruesome scene and inserts a glimmer of levity. Take the opening sentences in "Oil of Dog:" "My name is Boffer Bings. I was born of honest parents in one of the humbler walks of life, my father being a manufacturer of dog-oil and my mother having a small studio in the shadow of a village church where she disposed of unwanted babes." What breaks up the grisly atmosphere are the words "honest" and "studio," nice, normal descriptive words that are used here to strike ironic tones. The calm, detached delivery of mundane words or phrases amidst horror is also evident in the opening of "An Imperfect Conflagration": "Early one June morning in 1872 I murdered my father—an act that made a deep impression on me at the time." And in the first sentence in "My Favorite Murder": "Having murdered my mother under circumstances of singular atrocity, I was arrested and put upon my trial, which lasted seven years."

"The Boarded Window" has no such obvious satire. It involves a man named Murlock who believes his wife to be dead after a sudden fever and discovers he was mistaken when her last act is to defend him ("this unfaithful watcher") as he lay sleeping against a panther that burst through their window. He finds her mangled body with a part of the animal's ear in her mouth. The tension of the story is in the fact that he felt nothing when she "died." "He was surprised, too, that he did not weep; surely it is unkind not to weep for the dead." Bierce leaves the reader to guess Murlock's true intent and nature, as he does in most of his short horror stories.

Bierce lived and wrote as he wished. He enjoyed freedom from hypocrisy and conformity. He was fortunate to find a use for his talent and an audience: "My independence is my wealth; it is my literature. I have written to please myself, no matter who should be hurt."

Killed at Resaca

The best soldier of our staff was Lieutenant Herman Brayle, one of the two aides-de-camp. I don't remember where the general picked him up; from some Ohio regiment, I think; none of us had previously known him, and it would have been strange if we had, for no two of us came from the same State, nor even from adjoining States. The general seemed to think that a position on his staff was a distinction that should be so judiciously conferred as not to beget any sectional jealousies and imperil the integrity of that part of the country which was still an integer. He would not even choose officers from his own command, but by some jugglery at department headquarters obtained them from other brigades. Under such circumstances, a man's services had to be very distinguished indeed to be heard of by his family and the friends of his youth; and "the speaking trump of fame" was a trifle hoarse from loquacity, anyhow.

Lieutenant Brayle was more than six feet in height and of splendid proportions, with the light hair and gray-blue eyes which men so gifted usually find associated with a high order of courage. As he was commonly in full uniform, especially in action, when most officers are content to be less flamboyantly attired, he was a very striking and conspicuous figure. As to the rest, he had a gentleman's manners, a scholar's head, and a lion's heart. His age was about thirty.

We all soon came to like Brayle as much as we admired him, and it was with sincere concern that in the engagement at Stone's River—our first action after he joined us—we observed that he had one most objectionable and unsoldierly quality: he was vain of his courage. During all the vicissitudes and mutations of that hideous encounter, whether our troops were fighting in the open cotton fields, in the cedar thickets, or behind the railway embankment, he did not once take cover, except when sternly commanded to do so by the general, who usually had other things to think of than the lives of his staff officers—or those of his men, for that matter.

In every later engagement while Brayle was with us it was the same way. He would sit his horse like an equestrian statue, in a storm of bullets and grape, in the most exposed places—wherever, in fact, duty, requiring him to go, permitted him to remain—when, without trouble and with distinct advantage to his reputation for common sense, he might have been in such security as is possible on a battlefield in the brief intervals of personal inaction.

On foot, from necessity or in deference to his dismounted commander or associates, his conduct was the same. He would stand like a rock in the open when officers and men alike had taken to cover; while men older in service and years, higher in rank and of unquestionable intrepidity, were loyally preserving behind the crest of a hill lives infinitely precious to their country, this fellow would stand, equally idle, on the ridge, facing in the direction of the sharpest fire.

When battles are going on in open ground it frequently occurs that the opposing lines, confronting each other within a stone's throw for hours, hug the earth as closely as if they loved it. The line officers in their proper places flatten themselves no less, and the field officers, their horses all killed or sent to the rear, crouch beneath the infernal canopy of hissing lead and screaming iron without a thought of personal dignity.

In such circumstances the life of a staff officer of a brigade is distinctly "not a happy one," mainly because of its precarious tenure and the unnerving alternations of emotion to which he is exposed. From a position of that comparative security from which a civilian would ascribe his escape to a "miracle," he may be despatched with an order to some commander of a prone regiment in the front line—a person for the moment inconspicuous and not always easy to find without a deal of search among men somewhat preoccupied, and in a din in which question and answer alike must be imparted in the sign language. It is customary in such cases to duck the head and scuttle away on a keen run, an object of lively interest to some thousands of admiring marksmen. In returning—well, it is not customary to return.

Brayle's practice was different. He would consign his horse to the care of an orderly, he loved his horse,—and walk quietly away on his perilous errand with never a stoop of the back, his splendid figure, accentuated by his uniform, holding the eye with a strange fascination. We watched him with suspended breath, our hearts in our mouths. On one occasion of this kind, indeed, one of our number, an impetuous stammerer, was so possessed by his emotion that he shouted at me:

"I'll b-b-bet you t-two d-d-dollars they d-drop him b-b-before he g-gets to that d-d-ditch!"

I did not accept the brutal wager; I thought they would.

Let me do justice to a brave man's memory; in all these needless exposures of life there was no visible bravado nor subsequent narration. In the few instances when some of us had ventured to remonstrate, Brayle had smiled pleasantly and made some light reply, which, however, had not encouraged a further pursuit of the subject. Once he said:

"Captain, if ever I come to grief by forgetting your advice, I hope my last moments will be cheered by the sound of your beloved voice breathing into my ear the blessed words, I told you so.'"

We laughed at the captain—just why we could probably not have explained—and that afternoon when he was shot to rags from an ambuscade Brayle remained by the body for some time, adjusting the limbs with needless care—there in the middle of a road swept by gusts of grape and canister! It is easy to condemn this kind of thing, and not very difficult to refrain from imitation, but it is impossible not to respect, and Brayle was liked none the less for the weakness which had so heroic an expression. We wished he were not a fool, but he went on that way to the end, sometimes hard hit, but always returning to duty about as good as new.

Of course, it came at last; he who ignores the law of probabilities challenges an adversary that is seldom beaten. It was at Resaca, in Georgia, during the movement that resulted in the taking of Atlanta. In front of our brigade the enemy's line of earthworks ran through open fields along a slight crest. At each end of this open ground we were close up to him in the woods, but the clear ground we could not hope to occupy until night, when darkness would enable us to burrow like moles and throw up earth. At this point our line was a quarter-mile away in the edge of a wood. Roughly, we formed a semicircle, the enemy's fortified line being the chord of the arc.

"Lieutenant, go tell Colonel Ward to work up as close as he can get cover, and not to waste much ammunition in unnecessary firing. You may leave your horse."

When the general gave this direction we were in the fringe of the forest, near the right extremity of the arc. Colonel Ward was at the left. The suggestion to leave the horse obviously enough meant that Brayle was to take the longer line, through the woods and among the men. Indeed, the suggestion was needless; to go by the short route meant absolutely certain failure to deliver the message. Before anybody could interpose, Brayle had cantered lightly into the field and the enemy's works were in crackling conflagration.

"Stop that damned fool!" shouted the general.

A private of the escort, with more ambition than brains, spurred forward to obey, and within ten yards left himself and his horse dead on the field of honor.

Brayle was beyond recall, galloping easily along, parallel to the enemy and less than two hundred yards distant. He was a picture to see! His hat had been blown or shot from his head, and his long, blond hair rose and fell with the motion of his horse. He sat erect in the saddle, holding the reins lightly in his left hand, his right hanging carelessly at his side. An occasional glimpse of his handsome profile as he turned his head one way or the other proved that the interest which he took in what was going on was natural and without affectation.

HE COULD NOT GO FORWARD, HE WOULD NOT TURN BACK — HE STOOD AWAITING DEATH. IT DID NOT KEEP HIM LONG WAITING.

The picture was intensely dramatic, but in no degree theatrical. Successive scores of rifles spat at him viciously as he came within range, and our own line in the edge of the timber broke out in visible and audible defense. No longer regardful of themselves or their orders, our fellows sprang to their feet, and swarming into the open sent broad sheets of bullets against the blazing crest of the offending works, which poured an answering fire into their unprotected groups with deadly effect. The artillery on both sides joined the battle, punctuating the rattle and roar with deep, earth-shaking explosions and tearing the air with storms of screaming grape, which from the enemy's side splintered the trees and spattered them with blood, and from ours defiled the smoke of his arms with banks and clouds of dust from his parapet.

My attention had been for a moment drawn to the general combat, but now, glancing down the unobscured avenue between these two thunderclouds, I saw Brayle, the cause of the carnage. Invisible now from either side, and equally doomed by friend and foe, he stood in the shot-swept space, motionless, his face toward the enemy. At some little distance lay his horse. I instantly saw what had stopped him.

As topographical engineer I had, early in the day, made a hasty examination of the ground, and now remembered that at that point was a deep and sinuous gully, crossing half the field from the enemy's line, its general course at right angles to it. From where we now were it was invisible, and Brayle had evidently not known about it. Clearly, it was impassable. Its salient angles would have afforded him absolute security if he had chosen to be satisfied with the miracle already wrought in his favor and leapt into it. He could not go forward, he would not turn back—he stood awaiting death. It did not keep him long waiting.

By some mysterious coincidence, almost instantaneously as he fell, the firing ceased, a few desultory shots at long intervals serving rather to accentuate than break the silence. It was as if both sides had suddenly repented of their profitless crime. Four stretcher-bearers of ours, following a sergeant with a white flag, soon afterward moved unmolested into the field, and made straight for Brayle's body. Several Confederate officers and men came out to meet them, and with uncovered heads assisted them to take up their sacred burden. As it was borne toward us we heard beyond the hostile works fifes and a muffled drum—a dirge. A generous enemy honored the fallen brave.

Amongst the dead man's effects was a soiled Russia-leather pocketbook. In the distribution of mementoes of our friend, which the general, as administrator, decreed, this fell to me.

A year after the close of the war, on my way to California, I opened and idly inspected it. Out of an overlooked compartment fell a letter without envelope or address. It was in a woman's handwriting, and began with words of endearment, but no name.

It had the following date line: "San Francisco, Cal., July 9, 1862." The signature was "Darling," in marks of quotation. Incidentally, in the body of the text, the writer's full name was given—Marian Mendenhall.

The letter showed evidence of cultivation and good breeding, but it was an ordinary love letter, if a love letter can be ordinary. There was not much in it, but there was something. It was this:

"Mr. Winters, whom I shall always hate for it, has been telling that at some battle in Virginia, where he got his hurt, you were seen crouching behind a tree. I think he wants to injure you in my regard, which he knows the story would do if I believed it. I could bear to hear of my soldier lover's death, but not of his cowardice."

These were the words which on that sunny afternoon, in a distant region, had slain a hundred men. Is woman weak?

One evening I called on Miss Mendenhall to return the letter to her. I intended, also, to tell her what she had done—but not that she did it. I found her in a handsome dwelling on Rincon Hill. She was beautiful, well bred—in a word, charming.

"You knew Lieutenant Herman Brayle," I said, rather abruptly. "You know, doubtless, that he fell in battle. Among his effects was found this letter from you. My errand here is to place it in your hands."

She mechanically took the letter, glanced through it with deepening color, and then, looking at me with a smile, said:

"It is very good of you, though I am sure it was hardly worth while." She started suddenly and changed color. "This stain," she said, "is it—surely it is not—"

"Madam," I said, "pardon me, but that is the blood of the truest and bravest heart that ever beat."

She hastily flung the letter on the blazing coals. "Uh! I cannot bear the sight of blood!" she said. "How did he die?"

I had involuntarily risen to rescue that scrap of paper, sacred even to me, and now stood partly behind her. As she asked the question she turned her face about and slightly upward. The light of the burning letter was reflected in her eyes and touched her check with a tinge of crimson like the stain upon its page. I had never seen anything so beautiful as this detestable creature.

"He was bitten by a snake," I replied.

Oil of Dog

My name is Boffer Bings. I was born of honest parents in one of the humbler walks of life, my father being a manufacturer of dog-oil and my mother having a small studio in the shadow of the village church, where she disposed of unwelcome babes. In my boyhood I was trained to habits of industry; I not only assisted my father in procuring dogs for his vats, but was frequently employed by my mother to carry away the debris of her work in the studio. In performance of this duty I sometimes had need of all my natural intelligence for all the law officers of the vicinity were opposed to my mother's business. They were not elected on an opposition ticket, and the matter had never been made a political issue; it just happened so. My father's business of making dog-oil was, naturally, less unpopular, though the owners of missing dogs sometimes regarded him with suspicion, which was reflected, to some extent, upon me. My father had, as silent partners, all the physicians of the town, who seldom wrote a prescription which did not contain what they were pleased to designate as *Ol. can*. It is really the most valuable medicine ever discovered. But most persons are unwilling to make personal sacrifices for the afflicted, and it was evident that many of the fattest dogs in town had been forbidden to play with me—a fact which pained my young sensibilities, and at one time came near driving me to become a pirate.

Looking back upon those days, I cannot but regret, at times, that by indirectly bringing my beloved parents to their death I was the author of misfortunes profoundly affecting my future.

One evening while passing my father's oil factory with the body of a foundling from my mother's studio I saw a constable who seemed to be closely watching my movements. Young as I was, I had learned that a constable's acts, of whatever apparent character, are prompted by the most reprehensible motives, and I avoided him by dodging into the oilery by a side door which happened to stand ajar. I locked it at once and was alone with my dead. My father had retired for the night. The only light in the place came from the furnace, which glowed a deep, rich crimson under one of the vats, casting ruddy reflections on the walls. Within the cauldron the oil still rolled in indolent ebullition, occasionally pushing to the surface a piece of dog. Seating myself to wait for the constable to go away, I held the naked body of the foundling in my lap and tenderly stroked its short, silken hair. Ah, how beautiful it was! Even at that early age I was passionately fond of children, and as I looked upon this cherub I could almost find it in my heart to wish that the small, red wound upon its breast—the work of my dear mother—had not been mortal.

It had been my custom to throw the babes into the river which nature had thoughtfully provided for the purpose, but that night I did not dare to leave the oilery for fear of the constable. "After all," I said to myself, "it cannot greatly matter if I put it into this cauldron. My father will never know the bones from those of a puppy, and the few deaths which may result from administering another kind of oil for the incomparable *Ol. can.* are not important in a population which increases so rapidly." In short, I took the first step in crime and brought myself untold sorrow by casting the babe into the cauldron.

The next day, somewhat to my surprise, my father, rubbing his hands with satisfaction, informed me and my mother that he had obtained the finest quality of oil that was ever seen; that the physicians to whom he had shown samples had so pronounced it. He added that he had no knowledge as to how the result was obtained; the dogs had been treated in all respects as usual, and were of an ordinary breed. I deemed it my duty to explain—which I did, though palsied would have been my tongue if I could have foreseen the consequences. Bewailing their previous ignorance of the advantages of combining their industries, my parents at once took measures to repair the error. My mother removed her studio to a wing of the factory building and my duties in connection with the business ceased; I was no longer required to dispose of the bodies of the small superfluous, and there was no need of alluring dogs to their doom, for my father discarded them altogether, though they still had an honorable place in the name of the oil. So suddenly thrown into idleness, I might naturally have been expected to become vicious and dissolute, but I did not. The holy influence of my dear mother was ever about me to protect me from the temptations which beset youth, and my father was a deacon in a church. Alas, that through my fault these estimable persons should have come to so bad an end!

Finding a double profit in her business, my mother now devoted herself to it with a new assiduity. She removed not only superfluous and unwelcome babes to order, but went out into the highways and byways, gathering in children of a larger growth, and even such adults as she could entice to the oilery. My father, too, enamored of the superior quality of oil produced, purveyed for his vats with diligence and zeal. The conversion of their neighbors into dog-oil became, in short, the one passion of their lives—an absorbing and overwhelming greed took possession of their souls and served them in place of a hope in Heaven—by which, also, they were inspired.

So enterprising had they now become that a public meeting was held and resolutions passed severely censuring them. It was intimated by the chairman that any further raids upon the population would be met in a spirit of hostility. My poor parents left the meeting broken-hearted, desperate and, I believe, not altogether sane. Anyhow, I deemed it prudent not to enter the oilery with them that night, but slept outside in a stable.

At about midnight some mysterious impulse caused me to rise and peer through a window into the furnace-room, where I knew my father now slept. The fires were burning as brightly as if the following day's harvest had been expected to be abundant. One of the large cauldrons was slowly "walloping" with a mysterious appearance of self-restraint, as if it bided its time to put forth its full energy. My father was not in bed; he had risen in his night clothes and was preparing a noose in a strong cord. From the looks which he cast at the door of my mother's bedroom I knew too well the purpose that he had in mind. Speechless and motionless with terror, I could do nothing in prevention or warning. Suddenly the door of my mother's apartment was opened, noiselessly, and the two confronted each other, both apparently surprised. The lady, also, was in her night clothes, and she held in her right hand the tool of her trade, a long, narrow-bladed dagger.

She, too, had been unable to deny herself the last profit which the unfriendly action of the citizens and my absence had left her. For one instant they looked into each other's blazing eyes and then sprang together with indescribable fury. Round and round the room they struggled, the man cursing, the woman shrieking, both fighting like demons—she to strike him with the dagger, he to strangle her with his great bare hands. I know not how long I had the unhappiness to observe this disagreeable instance of domestic infelicity, but at last, after a more than usually vigorous struggle, the combatants suddenly moved apart.

My father's breast and my mother's weapon showed evidences of contact. For another instant they glared at each other in the most unamiable way; then my poor, wounded father, feeling the hand of death upon him, leaped forward, unmindful of resistance, grasped by dear mother in his arms, dragged her to the side of the boiling cauldron, collected all his failing energies, and sprang in with her! In a moment, both had disappeared and were adding their oil to that of the committee of citizens who had called the day before with an invitation to the public meeting.

Convinced that these unhappy events closed to me every avenue to an honorable career in that town, I removed to the famous city of Otumwee, where these memoirs are written with a heart full of remorse for a heedless act entailing so dismal a commercial disaster.

An Imperfect Conflagration

Early one June morning in 1872 I murdered my father—an act which made a deep impression on me at the time. This was before my marriage, while I was living with my parents in Wisconsin. My father and I were in the library of our home, dividing the proceeds of a burglary which we had committed that night. These consisted of household goods mostly, and the task of equitable division was difficult. We got on very well with the napkins, towels and such things, and the silverware was parted pretty nearly equally, but you can see for yourself that when you try to divide a single music-box by two without a remainder you will have trouble. It was that music-box which brought disaster and disgrace upon our family. If we had left it my poor father might now be alive.

It was a most exquisite and beautiful piece of workmanship—inlaid with costly woods and carven very curiously. It would not only play a great variety of tunes, but would whistle like a quail, bark like a dog, crow every morning at daylight whether it was wound up or not, and break the Ten Commandments. It was this last mentioned accomplishment that won my father's heart and caused him to commit the only dishonorable act of his life, though possibly he would have committed more if he had been spared: he tried to conceal that music-box from me, and declared upon his honor that he had not taken it, though I knew very well that, so far as he was concerned, the burglary had been undertaken chiefly for the purpose of obtaining it.

My father had the music-box hidden under his cloak; we had worn cloaks by way of disguise. He had solemnly assured me that he did not take it. I knew that he did, and knew something of which he was evidently ignorant; namely, that the box would crow at daylight and betray him if I could prolong the division of profits till that time. All occurred as I wished: as the gaslight began to pale in the library and the shape of the windows was seen dimly behind the curtains, a long cock-a-doodle-doo came from beneath the old gentleman's cloak, followed by a few bars of an aria from *Tannhäuser*, ending with a loud click. A small hand-axe, which we had used to break into the unlucky house, lay between us on the table; I picked it up. The old man, seeing that further concealment was useless, took the box from under his cloak and set it on the table. "Cut it in two if you prefer that plan," said he; "I tried to save it from destruction."

He was a passionate lover of music and could himself play the concertina with expression and feeling.

I said: "I do not question the purity of your motive: it would be presumptuous in me to sit in judgment on my father. But business is business, and with this axe I am going to effect a dissolution of our partnership unless you will consent in all future burglaries to wear a bell-punch."

"No," he said, after some reflection, "no, I could not do that; it would look like a confession of dishonesty. People would say that you distrusted me."

I could not help admiring his spirit and sensitiveness; for a moment I was proud of him and disposed to overlook his fault, but a glance at the richly jeweled music-box decided me, and, as I said, I removed the old man from this vale of tears. Having done so, I was a trifle uneasy. Not only was he my father—the author of my being—but the body would be certainly discovered. It was now broad daylight and my mother was likely to enter the library at any moment.

Under the circumstances, I thought it expedient to remove her also, which I did. Then I paid off all the servants and discharged them.

That afternoon I went to the chief of police, told him what I had done and asked his advice. It would be very painful to me if the facts became publicly known. My conduct would be generally condemned; the newspapers would bring it up against me if ever I should run for office. The chief saw the force of these considerations; he was himself an assassin of wide experience. After consulting with the presiding judge of the Court of Variable Jurisdiction he advised me to conceal the bodies in one of the book-cases, get a heavy insurance on the house and burn it down. This I proceeded to do.

In the library was a book-case which my father had recently purchased of some cranky inventor and had not filled. It was in shape and size something like the old-fashioned "wardrobes" which one sees in bed-rooms without closets, but opened all the way down, like a woman's night-dress. It had glass doors. I had recently laid out my parents and they were now rigid enough to stand erect; so I stood them in this book-case, from which I had removed the shelves. I locked them in and tacked some curtains over the glass doors. The inspector from the insurance office passed a half-dozen times before the case without suspicion.

> NOT ONLY WAS HE MY FATHER—THE AUTHOR OF MY BEING—BUT THE BODY WOULD BE CERTAINLY DISCOVERED. IT WAS NOW BROAD DAYLIGHT AND MY MOTHER WAS LIKELY TO ENTER THE LIBRARY AT ANY MOMENT. UNDER THE CIRCUMSTANCES, I THOUGHT IT EXPEDIENT TO REMOVE HER ALSO, WHICH I DID.

That night, after getting my policy, I set fire to the house and started through the woods to town, two miles away, where I managed to be found about the time the excitement was at its height. With cries of apprehension for the fate of my parents, I joined the rush and arrived at the fire some two hours after I had kindled it. The whole town was there as I dashed up. The house was entirely consumed, but in one end of the level bed of glowing embers, bolt upright and uninjured, was that book-case! The curtains had burned away, exposing the glass-doors, through which the fierce, red light illuminated the interior. There stood my dear father "in his habit as he lived," and at his side the partner of his joys and sorrows. Not a hair of them was singed, their clothing was intact. On their heads and throats the injuries which in the accomplishment of my designs I had been compelled to inflict were conspicuous. As in the presence of a miracle, the people were silent; awe and terror had stilled every tongue. I was myself greatly affected.

Some three years later, when the events herein related had nearly faded from my memory, I went to New York to assist in passing some counterfeit United States bonds. Carelessly looking into a furniture store one day, I saw the exact counterpart of that book-case. "I bought it for a trifle from a reformed inventor," the dealer explained. "He said it was fireproof, the pores of the wood being filled with alum under hydraulic pressure and the glass made of asbestos. I don't suppose it is really fireproof—you can have it at the price of an ordinary book-case."

"No," I said, "if you cannot warrant it fireproof I won't take it"—and I bade him good morning.

I would not have had it at any price: it revived memories that were exceedingly disagreeable.

My Favorite Murder

Having murdered my mother under circumstances of singular atrocity, I was arrested and put upon my trial, which lasted seven years. In charging the jury, the judge of the Court of Acquittal remarked that it was one of the most ghastly crimes that he had ever been called upon to explain away.

At this, my attorney rose and said:

"May it please your Honor, crimes are ghastly or agreeable only by comparison. If you were familiar with the details of my client's previous murder of his uncle you would discern in his later offense (if offense it may be called) something in the nature of tender forbearance and filial consideration for the feelings of the victim. The appalling ferocity of the former assassination was indeed inconsistent with any hypothesis but that of guilt; and had it not been for the fact that the honorable judge before whom he was tried was the president of a life insurance company that took risks on hanging, and in which my client held a policy, it is hard to see how he could decently have been acquitted. If your Honor would like to hear about it for instruction and guidance of your Honor's mind, this unfortunate man, my client, will consent to give himself the pain of relating it under oath."

The district attorney said: "Your Honor, I object. Such a statement would be in the nature of evidence, and the testimony in this case is closed. The prisoner's statement should have been introduced three years ago, in the spring of 1881."

"In a statutory sense," said the judge, "you are right, and in the Court of Objections and Technicalities you would get a ruling in your favor. But not in a Court of Acquittal. The objection is overruled."

"I except," said the district attorney.

"You cannot do that," the judge said. "I must remind you that in order to take an exception you must first get this case transferred for a time to the Court of Exceptions on a formal motion duly supported by affidavits. A motion to that effect by your predecessor in office was denied by me during the first year of this trial. Mr. Clerk, swear the prisoner."

The customary oath having been administered, I made the following statement, which impressed the judge with so strong a sense of the comparative triviality of the offense for which I was on trial that he made no further search for mitigating circumstances, but simply instructed the jury to acquit, and I left the court, without a stain on my reputation:

"I was born in 1856 in Kalamakee, Mich., of honest and reputable parents, one of whom Heaven has mercifully spared to comfort me in my later years. In 1867 the family came to California and settled near Nigger Head, where my father opened a road agency and prospered beyond the dreams of avarice. He was a reticent, saturnine man then, though his increasing years have now somewhat relaxed the austerity of his disposition, and I believe that nothing but his memory of the sad event for which I am now on trial prevents him from manifesting a genuine hilarity.

"Four years after we had set up the road agency an itinerant preacher came along, and having no other way to pay for the night's lodging that we gave him, favored us with an exhortation of such power that, praise God, we were all converted to religion. My father at once sent for his brother, the Hon. William Ridley of Stockton, and on his arrival turned over the agency to him, charging him nothing for the franchise nor plant—the latter consisting of a Winchester rifle, a sawed-off shotgun, and an assortment of masks made out of flour sacks. The family then moved to Ghost Rock and opened a dance house. It was called 'The Saints' Rest Hurdy-Gurdy,' and the proceedings each night began with prayer. It was there that my now sainted mother, by her grace in the dance, acquired the *sobriquet* of 'The Bucking Walrus.'

"In the fall of '75 I had occasion to visit Coyote, on the road to Mahala, and took the stage at Ghost Rock. There were four other passengers. About three miles beyond Nigger Head, persons whom I identified as my Uncle William and his two sons held up the stage. Finding nothing in the express box, they went through the passengers. I acted a most honorable part in the affair, placing myself in line with the others, holding up my hands and permitting myself to be deprived of forty dollars and a gold watch. From my behavior no one could have suspected that I knew the gentlemen who gave the entertainment. A few days later, when I went to Nigger Head and asked for the return of my money and watch my uncle and cousins swore they knew nothing of the matter, and they affected a belief that my father and I had done the job ourselves in dishonest violation of commercial good faith. Uncle William even threatened to retaliate by starting an opposition dance house at Ghost Rock. As 'The Saints' Rest' had become rather unpopular, I saw that this would assuredly ruin it and prove a paying enterprise, so I told my uncle that I was willing to overlook the past if he would take me into the scheme and keep the partnership a secret from my father. This fair offer he rejected, and I then perceived that it would be better and more satisfactory if he were dead.

"My plans to that end were soon perfected, and communicating them to my dear parents I had the gratification of receiving their approval. My father said he was proud of me, and my mother promised that although her religion forbade her to assist in taking human life I should have the advantage of her prayers for my success. As a preliminary measure looking to my security in case of detection I made an application for membership in that powerful order, the Knights of Murder, and in due course was received as a member of the Ghost Rock commandery. On the day that my probation ended I was for the first time permitted to inspect the records of the order and learn who belonged to it—all the rites of initiation having been conducted in masks. Fancy my delight when, in looking over the roll of membership, I found the third name to be that of my uncle, who indeed was junior vice-chancellor of the order! Here was an opportunity exceeding my wildest dreams—to murder I could add insubordination and treachery. It was what my good mother would have called 'a special Providence.'

"At about this time something occurred which caused my cup of joy, already full, to overflow on all sides, a circular cataract of bliss. Three men, strangers in that locality, were arrested for the stage robbery in which I had lost my money and watch. They were brought to trial and, despite my efforts to clear them and fasten the guilt upon three of the most respectable and worthy citizens of Ghost Rock, convicted on the clearest proof. The murder would now be as wanton and reasonless as I could wish.

"One morning I shouldered my Winchester rifle, and going over to my uncle's house, near Nigger Head, asked my Aunt Mary, his wife, if he were at home, adding that I had come to kill him. My aunt replied with her peculiar smile that so many gentlemen called on that errand and were afterward carried away without having performed it that I must excuse her for doubting my good faith in the matter. She said I did not look as if I would kill anybody, so, as a proof of good faith I leveled my rifle and wounded a Chinaman who happened to be passing the house. She said she knew whole families that could do a thing of that kind, but Bill Ridley was a horse of another color. She said, however, that I would find him over on the other side of the creek in the sheep lot; and she added that she hoped the best man would win.

"My Aunt Mary was one of the most fair-minded women that I have ever met.

"I found my uncle down on his knees engaged in skinning a sheep. Seeing that he had neither gun nor pistol handy I had not the heart to shoot him, so I approached him, greeted him pleasantly and struck him a powerful blow on the head with the butt of my rifle. I have a very good delivery and Uncle William lay down on his side, then rolled over on his back, spread out his fingers and shivered. Before he could recover the use of his limbs I seized the knife that he had been using and cut his hamstrings. You know, doubtless, that when you sever the *tendo Achillis* the patient has no further use of his leg; it is just the same as if he had no leg. Well, I parted them both, and when he revived he was at my service. As soon as he comprehended the situation, he said:

"'Samuel, you have got the drop on me and can afford to be generous. I have only one thing to ask of you, and that is that you carry me to the house and finish me in the bosom of my family.'

"I told him I thought that a pretty reasonable request and I would do so if he would let me put him into a wheat sack; he would be easier to carry that way and if we were seen by the neighbors *en route* it would cause less remark. He agreed to that, and going to the barn I got a sack. This, however, did not fit him; it was too short and much wider than he; so I bent his legs, forced his knees up against his breast and got him into it that way, tying the sack above his head. He was a heavy man and I had all that I could do to get him on my back, but I staggered along for some distance until I came to a swing that some of the children had suspended to the branch of an oak. Here I laid him down and sat upon him to rest, and the sight of the rope gave me a happy inspiration. In twenty minutes my uncle, still in the sack, swung free to the sport of the wind.

"I had taken down the rope, tied one end tightly about the month of the bag, thrown the other across the limb and hauled him up about five feet from the ground. Fastening the other end of the rope also about the mouth of the sack, I had the satisfaction to see my uncle converted into a large, fine pendulum. I must add that he was not himself entirely aware of the nature of the change that he had undergone in his relation to the exterior world, though in justice to a good man's memory I ought to say that I do not think he would in any case have wasted much of my time in vain remonstrance.

"Uncle William had a ram that was famous in all that region as a fighter. It was in a state of chronic constitutional indignation. Some deep disappointment in early life had soured its disposition and it had declared war upon the whole world. To say that it would butt anything accessible is but faintly to express the nature and scope of its military activity: the universe was its antagonist; its methods that of a projectile. It fought like the angels and devils, in midair, cleaving the atmosphere like a bird, describing a parabolic curve and descending upon its victim at just the exact angle of incidence to make the most of its velocity and weight. Its momentum, calculated in foot-tons, was something incredible. It had been seen to destroy a four year old bull by a single impact upon that animal's gnarly forehead. No stone wall had ever been known to resist its downward swoop; there were no trees tough enough to stay it; it would splinter them into matchwood and defile their leafy honors in the dust. This irascible and implacable brute—this incarnate thunderbolt—this monster of the upper deep, I had seen reposing in the shade of an adjacent tree, dreaming dreams of conquest and glory. It was with a view to summoning it forth to the field of honor that I suspended its master in the manner described.

"Having completed my preparations, I imparted to the avuncular pendulum a gentle oscillation, and retiring to cover behind a contiguous rock, lifted up my voice in a long rasping cry whose diminishing final note was drowned in a noise like that of a swearing cat, which emanated from the sack. Instantly that formidable sheep was upon its feet and had taken in the military situation at a glance. In a few moments it had approached, stamping, to within fifty yards of the swinging foeman, who, now retreating and anon advancing, seemed to invite the fray. Suddenly I saw the beast's head drop earthward as if depressed by the weight of its enormous horns; then a dim, white, wavy streak of sheep prolonged itself from that spot in a generally horizontal direction to within about four yards of a point immediately beneath the enemy. There it struck sharply upward, and before it had faded from my gaze at the place whence it had set out I heard a horrid thump and a piercing scream, and my poor uncle shot forward, with a slack rope higher than the limb to which he was attached. Here the rope tautened with a jerk, arresting his flight, and back he swung in a breathless curve to the other end of his arc. The ram had fallen, a heap of indistinguishable legs, wool and horns, but pulling itself together and dodging as its antagonist swept downward it retired at random, alternately shaking its head and stamping its fore-feet. When it had backed about the same distance as that from which it had delivered the assault it paused again, bowed its head as if in prayer for victory and again shot forward, dimly visible as before—a prolonging white streak with monstrous undulations, ending with a sharp ascension. Its Course this time was at a right angle to its former one, and its impatience so great that it struck the enemy before he had nearly reached the lowest point of his arc. In consequence he went flying round and round in a horizontal circle whose radius was about equal to half the length of the rope, which I forgot to say was nearly twenty feet long. His shrieks, *crescendo* in approach and *diminuendo* in recession, made the rapidity of his revolution more obvious to the ear than to the eye. He had evidently not yet been struck in a vital spot. His posture in the sack and the distance from the ground at which he hung compelled the ram to operate upon his lower extremities and the end of his back. Like a plant that has struck its root into some poisonous mineral, my poor uncle was dying slowly upward.

"After delivering its second blow the ram had not again retired. The fever of battle burned hot in its heart; its brain was intoxicated with the wine of strife. Like a pugilist who in his rage forgets his skill and fights ineffectively at half-arm's length, the angry beast endeavored to reach its fleeting foe by awkward vertical leaps as he passed overhead, sometimes, indeed, succeeding in striking him feebly, but more frequently overthrown by its own misguided eagerness. But as the impetus was exhausted and the man's circles narrowed in scope and diminished in speed, bringing him nearer to the ground, these tactics produced better results, eliciting a superior quality of screams, which I greatly enjoyed.

"Suddenly, as if the bugles had sung truce, the ram suspended hostilities and walked away, thoughtfully wrinkling and smoothing its great aquiline nose, and occasionally cropping a bunch of grass and slowly munching it. It seemed to have tired of war's alarms and resolved to beat the sword into a plowshare and cultivate the arts of peace. Steadily it held its course away from the field of fame until it had gained a distance of nearly a quarter of a mile. There it stopped and stood with its rear to the foe, chewing its cud and apparently half asleep. I observed, however, an occasional slight turn of its head, as if its apathy were more affected than real.

"Meantime Uncle William's shrieks had abated with his motion, and nothing was heard from him but long, low moans, and at long intervals my name, uttered in pleading tones exceedingly grateful to my ear. Evidently the man had not the faintest notion of what was being done to him, and was inexpressibly terrified. When Death comes cloaked in mystery he is terrible indeed. Little by little my uncle's oscillations diminished, and finally he hung motionless. I went to him and was about to give him the *coup de grâce*, when I heard and felt a succession of smart shocks which shook the ground like a series of light earthquakes, and turning in the direction of the ram, saw a long cloud of dust approaching me with inconceivable rapidity and alarming effect! At a distance of some thirty yards away it stopped short, and from the near end of it rose into the air what I at first thought a great white bird. Its ascent was so smooth and easy and regular that I could not realize its extraordinary celerity, and was lost in admiration of its grace. To this day the impression remains that it was a slow, deliberate movement, the ram—for it was that animal—being upborne by some power other than its own impetus, and supported through the successive stages of its flight with infinite tenderness and care. My eyes followed its progress through the air with unspeakable pleasure, all the greater by contrast with my former terror of its approach by land. Onward and upward the noble animal sailed, its head bent down almost between its knees, its fore-feet thrown back, its hinder legs trailing to rear like the legs of a soaring heron.

"At a height of forty or fifty feet, as fond recollection presents it to view, it attained its zenith and appeared to remain an instant stationary; then, tilting suddenly forward without altering the relative position of its parts, it shot downward on a steeper and steeper course with augmenting velocity, passed immediately above me with a noise like the rush of a cannon shot and struck my poor uncle almost squarely on the top of the head! So frightful was the impact that not only the man's neck was broken, but the rope too; and the body of the deceased, forced against the earth, was crushed to pulp beneath the awful front of that meteoric sheep! The concussion stopped all the clocks between Lone Hand and Dutch Dan's, and Professor Davidson, a distinguished authority in matters seismic, who happened to be in the vicinity, promptly explained that the vibrations were from north to southwest.

"Altogether, I cannot help thinking that in point of artistic atrocity my murder of Uncle William has seldom been excelled."

The Boarded Window

In 1830, only a few miles away from what is now the great city of Cincinnati lay an immense and almost unbroken forest. The whole region was sparsely settled by people of the frontier—restless souls who no sooner had hewn fairly habitable homes out of the wilderness and attained to that degree of prosperity which to-day we should call indigence than impelled by some mysterious impulse of their nature they abandoned all and pushed farther westward, to encounter new perils and privations in the effort to regain the meagre comforts which they had voluntarily renounced. Many of them had already forsaken that region for the remoter settlements, but among those remaining was one who had been of those first arriving. He lived alone in a house of logs surrounded on all sides by the great forest, of whose gloom and silence he seemed a part, for no one had ever known him to smile nor speak a needless word. His simple wants were supplied by the sale or barter of skins of wild animals in the river town, for not a thing did he grow upon the land which, if needful, he might have claimed by right of undisturbed possession. There were evidences of "improvement"—a few acres of ground immediately about the house had once been cleared of its trees, the decayed stumps of which were half concealed by the new growth that had been suffered to repair the ravage wrought by the ax. Apparently, the man's zeal for agriculture had burned with a failing flame, expiring in penitential ashes.

The little log house with its chimney of sticks, its roof of warping clapboards weighted with traversing poles and its "chinking" of clay, had a single door and, directly opposite, a window. The latter, however, was boarded up—nobody could remember a time when it was not. And none knew why it was so closed; certainly not because of the occupant's dislike of light and air, for on those rare occasions when a hunter had passed that lonely spot the recluse had commonly been seen sunning himself on his doorstep if heaven had provided sunshine for his need.

I fancy there are few persons living to-day who ever knew the secret of that window, but I am one, as you shall see.

The man's name was said to be Murlock. He was apparently seventy years old, actually about fifty. Something besides years had had a hand in his aging. His hair and long, full beard were white, his gray, lustreless eyes sunken, his face singularly seamed with wrinkles which appeared to belong to two intersecting systems. In figure he was tall and spare, with a stoop of the shoulders—a burden bearer. I never saw him; these particulars I learned from my grandfather, from whom also I got the man's story when I was a lad. He had known him when living nearby in that early day.

One day Murlock was found in his cabin, dead. It was not a time and place for coroners and newspapers, and I suppose it was agreed that he had died from natural causes or I should have been told, and should remember. I know only that with what was probably a sense of the fitness of things the body was buried near the cabin, alongside the grave of his wife, who had preceded him by so many years that local tradition had retained hardly a hint of her existence. That closes the final chapter of this true story—excepting, indeed, the circumstance that many years afterward, in company with an equally intrepid spirit, I penetrated to the place and ventured near enough to the ruined cabin to throw a stone against it, and ran away to avoid the ghost which every well-informed boy thereabout knew haunted the spot. But there is an earlier chapter—that supplied by my grandfather.

When Murlock built his cabin and began laying sturdily about with his ax to hew out a farm—the rifle, meanwhile, his means of support—he was young, strong, and full of hope. In that eastern country whence he came he had married, as was the fashion, a young woman in all ways worthy of his honest devotion, who shared the dangers and privations of his lot with a willing spirit and light heart. There is no known record of her name; of her charms of mind and person tradition is silent and the doubter is at liberty to entertain his doubt; but God forbid that I should share it! Of their affection and happiness there is abundant assurance in every added day of the man's widowed life; for what but the magnetism of a blessed memory could have chained that venturesome spirit to a lot like that?

One day Murlock returned from gunning in a distant part of the forest to find his wife prostrate with fever, and delirious. There was no physician within miles, no neighbor; nor was she in a condition to be left, to summon help. So he set about the task of nursing her back to health, but at the end of the third day she fell into unconsciousness and so passed away, with never a gleam of returning reason.

From what we know of a nature like this we may venture to sketch some of the details of the outline picture drawn by my grandfather. When convinced that she was dead, Murlock had sense enough to remember that the dead must be prepared for burial. In performance of this sacred duty he blundered now and again, did certain things incorrectly, and others which he did correctly were done over and over. His occasional failures to accomplish some simple and ordinary act filled him with astonishment, like that of a drunken man who wonders at the suspension of familiar natural laws. He was surprised, too, that he did not weep—surprised and a little ashamed; surely it is unkind not to weep for the dead. "To-morrow," he said aloud, "I shall have to make the coffin and dig the grave; and then I shall miss her, when she is no longer in sight; but now—she is dead, of course, but it is all right—it *must* be all right, somehow. Things cannot be so bad as they seem."

He stood over the body in the fading light, adjusting the hair and putting the finishing touches to the simple toilet, doing all mechanically, with soulless care. And still through his consciousness ran an undersense of conviction that all was right—that he should have her again as before, and everything explained. He had had no experience of grief; his capacity had not been enlarged by use. His heart could not contain it all, not his imagination rightly conceive it. He did not know he was so hard struck; *that* knowledge would come later, and never go. Grief is an artist of powers as various as the instruments upon which he plays his dirges for the dead, evoking some of the sharpest, shrillest notes, from others the low, grave chords that throb recurrent like the slow beating of a distant drum. Some natures it startles; some it stupefies. To one it comes like the stroke of an arrow, stinging all the sensibilities to a keener life; to another as the blow of a bludgeon, which in crushing benumbs. We may conceive Murlock to have been that way affected, for (and here we are upon surer ground than that of conjecture) no sooner had he finished his pious work than, sinking into a chair by the side of the table upon which the body lay, and noting how white the profile showed in the deepening gloom, he laid his arms upon the table's edge, and dropped his face into them, tearless yet and unutterably weary. At that moment came in through the open window a long, wailing sound like the cry of a lost child in the far deeps of the darkening wood! But the man did not move. Again, and nearer than before, sounded that unearthly cry upon his failing sense. Perhaps it was a wild beast: perhaps it was a dream. For Murlock was asleep.

Some hours later, as it afterward appeared, this unfaithful watcher awoke and lifting his head from his arms intently listened—he knew not why. There in the black darkness by the side of the dead, recalling all without a shock, he strained his eyes to see—he knew not what. His senses were all alert, his breath was suspended, his blood had stilled its tides as if to assist the silence. Who—what had awakened him, and where was it?

Suddenly the table shook beneath his arms, and at that same moment he heard, or fancied that he heard, a light, soft step—another—sounds as of bare feet upon the floor!

He was terrified beyond the power to cry out or move. Perforce he waited—waited there in the darkness through seeming centuries of such dread as one may know, yet live to tell. He tried vainly to speak the dead woman's name, vainly to stretch forth his hand across the table to learn if she were there. His throat was powerless, his arms and hands were like lead. Then occurred something most frightful. Some heavy body seemed hurled against the table with an impetus that pushed it against his breast so sharply as nearly to overthrow him, and at the same instant he heard and felt the fall of something upon the floor with so violent a thump that the whole house was shaken by the impact. A scuffling ensued, and a confusion of sounds impossible to describe. Murlock had risen to his feet. Fear had by excess forfeited control of his faculties. He flung his hands upon the table. Nothing was there!

There is a point at which terror may turn to madness; and madness incites to action. With no definite intent, from no motive but the wayward impulse of a madman, Murlock sprang to the wall, with a little groping, seized his loaded rifle, and without aim discharged it. By the flash which lit up the room with a vivid illumination, he saw an enormous panther dragging the dead woman toward the window, its teeth fixed in her throat. Then there were darkness blacker than before, and silence; and when he returned to consciousness the sun was high and the wood vocal with songs of birds.

The body lay near the window, where the beast had left it when frightened away by the flash and report of the rifle, The clothing was deranged, the long hair in disorder, the limbs lay anyhow. From the throat, dreadfully lacerated, had issued a pool of blood not yet entirely coagulated. The ribbon with which he had bound the wrists was broken; the hands were tightly clenched. Between the teeth was a fragment of the animal's ear.

The Lion and the Thorn

A Lion roaming through the forest got a thorn in his foot, and, meeting a Shepherd, asked him to remove it. The Shepherd did so, and the Lion, having just surfeited himself on another shepherd, went away without harming him. Some time afterward the Shepherd was condemned on a false accusation to be cast to the lions in the ampitheatre. When they were about to devour him, one of them said:

"This is the man who removed the thorn from my foot."

Hearing this, the others honorably abstained, and the claimant ate the Shepherd all himself.

A Revolt of the Gods

My father was a deodorizer of dead dogs, my mother kept the only shop for the sale of cats'-meat in my native city. They did not live happily; the difference in social rank was a chasm which could not be bridged by the vows of marriage. It was indeed an ill-assorted and most unlucky alliance; and as might have been foreseen it ended in disaster. One morning after the customary squabbles at breakfast, my father rose from the table, quivering and pale with wrath, and proceeding to the parsonage thrashed the clergyman who had performed the marriage ceremony. The act was generally condemned and public feeling ran so high against the offender that people would permit dead dogs to lie on their property until the fragrance was deafening rather than employ him; and the municipal authorities suffered one bloated old mastiff to utter itself from a public square in so clamorous an exhalation that passing strangers supposed themselves to be in the vicinity of a saw-mill. My father was indeed unpopular. During these dark days the family's sole dependence was on my mother's emporium for cats'-meat.

The business was profitable. In that city, which was the oldest in the world, the cat was an object of veneration. Its worship was the religion of a country. The multiplication and addition of cats were a perpetual instruction in arithmetic. Naturally, any inattention to the wants of a cat was punished with great severity in this world and the next; so my good mother numbered her patients by the hundred. Still, with an unproductive husband and seventeen children she had some difficulty in making both ends cats'-meat; and at last the necessity of increasing the discrepancy between the cost price and the selling price of her carnal wares drove her to an expedient which proved eminently disastrous: she conceived the unlucky notion of retaliating by refusing to sell cats'-meat until the boycott was taken off her husband.

On the day when she put this resolution into practice the shop was thronged with excited customers, and others extended in turbulent and restless masses up four streets, out of sight. Inside there was nothing but cursing, crowding, shouting and menace. Intimidation was freely resorted to—several of my younger brothers and sisters being threatened with cutting up for the cats—but my mother was as firm as a rock, and the day was a black one for Sardasa, the ancient and sacred city that was the scene of these events. The lock-out was vigorously maintained, and seven hundred and fifty thousand cats went to be hungry!

The next morning the city was found to have been placarded during the night with a proclamation of the Federated Union of Old Maids. This ancient and powerful order averred through its Supreme Executive Head that the boycotting of my father and the retaliatory lock-out of my mother were seriously imperiling the interests of religion. The proclamation went on to state that if the arbitration were not adopted by noon that day all the old maids of the federation would strike—and strike they did.

The next act of this unhappy drama was an insurrection of cats. These sacred animals, seeing themselves doomed to starvation, held a mass-meeting and marched in procession through the streets, swearing and spitting like fiends. This revolt of the gods produced such consternation that many pious persons died of fright and all business was suspended to bury them and pass terrifying resolutions.

Matters were now about as bad as it seemed possible for them to be. Meetings among representatives of the hostile interests were held, but no understanding was arrived at that would hold. Every agreement was broken as soon as made, and each element of the discord was frantically appealing to the people. A new horror was in store.

It will be remembered that my father was a deodorizer of dead dogs, but was unable to practice his useful and humble profession because no on would employ him. The dead dogs in consequence reeked rascally. Then they struck! From every vacant lot and public dumping ground, from every hedge and ditch and gutter and cistern, every crystal rill and the clabbered waters of all the canals and estuaries—from all the places, in short, which from time immemorial have been preempted by dead dogs and consecrated to the uses of them and their heirs and successors forever—they trooped innumerous, a ghastly crew! Their procession was a mile in length. Midway of the town it met the procession of cats in full song. The cats instantly exalted their backs and magnified their tails; the dead dogs uncovered their teeth as in life, and erected such of their bristles as still adhered to the skin.

The carnage that ensued was too awful for relation! The light of the sun was obscured by flying fur, and the battle was waged in the darkness, blindly and regardless. The swearing of the cats was audible miles away, while the fragrance of the dead dogs desolated seven provinces.

How the battle might have resulted it is impossible to say, but when it was at its fiercest the Federated Union of Old Maids came running down a side street and sprang into the thickest of the fray. A moment later my mother herself bore down upon the warring hosts, brandishing a cleaver, and laid about her with great freedom and impartiality. My father joined the fight, the municipal authorities engaged, and the general public, converging on the battle-field from all points of the compass, consumed itself in the center as it pressed in from the circumference. Last of all, the dead held a meeting in the cemetery and resolving on a general strike, began to destroy vaults, tombs, monuments, headstones, willows, angels, and young sheep in marble—everything they could lay their hands on. By nightfall the living and dead were alike exterminated, and where the ancient and sacred city of Sardasa had stood nothing remained but an excavation filled with dead bodies and building materials, shreds of cat and blue patches of decayed dog. The place is now a vast pool of stagnant water in the center of a desert.

The stirring events of those few days constituted my industrial education, and so well have I improved my advantages that I am now Chief of Misrule to the Dukes of Disorder, an organization numbering thirteen million American workingmen.

Oscar Wilde

(1854–1900)

Oscar Fingal O'Flahertie Wills Wilde was born in Dublin on October 16, 1854, to professional and literary parents. His father, Sir William Wilde, was Ireland's foremost ear and eye surgeon, an accomplished author who was knighted in 1864. His mother was both a poet and an authority on Celtic myth and folklore. Young Wilde was surrounded by intellectual curiosity at home and he often went with his father on trips to visit ruins and detail the local superstitions.

When Wilde was nine he was sent to attend the Portora Royal School at Enniskillen. After Portora, he went as a scholarship student to Trinity College in Dublin (1871–1874) and Magadalen College, Oxford (1874–1878), where he earned a degree with honors. He not only excelled at his studies but was thought of as a witty poseur with a talent for poetry. He won the Newdigate Prize in 1878 with his long poem *Ravenna*, written about a trip to the Italian city of Ravenna the previous year. In the poem he muses on the city's decline from greatness, a familiar theme and one that he would tragically follow in his own life.

Wilde was influenced by the ideas of John Ruskin and Walter Pater; namely, the importance of art in everyday existence and Pater's notion that life should be lived with an artistic intensity. Wilde wanted to be thought of as deep and complex but he also wanted to have the ability to shock and delight people. He dressed in a flamboyant manner and decorated his Oxford rooms with objets d'art.

Wilde moved to London in 1880; he began to dress almost in costume and soon gained a foothold in artistic and social circles. The magazine *Punch* took notice and satirized his act several times a month. Wilde took such reviews in stride, saying, "There is only one thing worse than being talked about, and that is not being talked about."

Referred to obliquely in a Gilbert and Sullivan play as the "fleshy poet,"

Wilde sought to capitalize on such notoriety by self-publishing a volume called *Poems* in 1881. Seen as a visionary of the Aesthetic movement in England, Wilde was asked to lecture in the United States and Canada in 1882. He arrived in New York, announcing that he had "nothing to declare but my genius." The press ridiculed his foppish poses and theatrical costumes of knee breeches, velvet jacket, and black silk stockings but Wilde pressed on, staying in America for one year and spreading his "gospel" to embrace beauty and art. Audiences were charmed and even the Colorado silver miners who had sniggered at his donning of a sunflower came away with some respect for Wilde after he drank the toughest of them under the table. He then returned to London and a more circumscribed life.

In 1884, he married Constance Mary Lloyd; with her money, he was able to buy a house in Chelsea. He reviewed books for the *Pall Mall Gazette* and edited *Woman's World* for two years. They had two sons, Cyril and Vyvyan. During this relaxed domestic period, Wilde began to grow as a writer, publishing *The Happy Prince and Other Tales*, a book of romantic allegories in the form of fairy tales.

In what would turn out to be the final decade of his life, Wilde wrote and published almost all of his major works. His one novel, *The Picture of Dorian Gray*, appeared in 1891, and combined elements of eerie Gothic novels and rich, hedonistic French fiction. The novel illustrated Wilde's contention that "There is no such thing as a moral or an immoral book. Books are well written, or badly written. That is all." The novel, in its first incarnation, was poorly received, almost vilified. It was called a "poisonous book" by the *Daily Chronicle*. A second, edited version caused few waves and was commended by W.B. Yeats and Sir Arthur Conan Doyle. A book of essays titled *Intentions* and two volumes of stories and fairy tales (*Lord Savile's Crime and Other Stories* and *A House of Pomegrantes*) also were published in 1891.

But Wilde's greatest accolades came with his social comedies—four in all—written and performed between 1892 and 1885. *Lady Windermere's Fan* premiered on February 20, 1892, at the St. James's Theatre and was seen to have revived the antiquated apparatus of French drama. His second social farce, *A Woman of No Importance* (1893), was hailed by the critic William Archer, who urged that Wilde's plays "must be taken on the very highest plane of modern English drama." His last two plays, *An Ideal Husband* and *The Importance of Being Earnest,* were produced in early 1895. With these he reached the pinnacle of his fame.

Exposing secrets and lies and the effect that these revelations have on the characters' lives are prominent themes in Wilde's work. Ironically, he would live out a similar scenario in his own life following these years of heady success. His close friendship with Lord Alfred Douglas, the son of the Marquess of Queensbury, riled the Marquess, who accused Wilde of being a sodomite. Wilde sued for libel but the Marquess was acquitted. On the same day of the ruling, Wilde was arrested on morals charges involving Lord Douglas. He was told by his friends to flee to Paris to escape the trial but he refused and was brought to court.

Despite brilliant, witty testimony and a hung jury in the first trial, Wilde lost his case in the second trial and was sentenced to two years' hard labor. He served his time at Reading Gaol, writing a recriminating essay about prison and his ties to Lord Douglas which took the form of a letter to Douglas (because *only* letters were allowed to be scripted in jail). This piece was published as *De Profundis*. When Wilde was set free, he was broke and broken. He went to Paris in an attempt to restore his career but only managed to issue *The Ballad of Reading Gaol,* a tale of murder and imprisonment, which came out under a pseudonym. Wilde died in Paris on November 30, 1900, a victim of an acute brain inflammation triggered by an ear infection. On his deathbed, he was received into the Roman Catholic Church, his final wish.

The Picture of Dorian Gray revolves around Dorian Gray, his complex and twisted relationship with Lord Henry Wotton, and a portrait of Dorian painted by Basil Hallward that sets the Gothic plot in motion. Dorian begins the story as a malleable, adventure-seeking young man who meets up with Lord Wotton, a hedonist whom Dorian adopts as a mentor. Under Wotton's Mephistophelean influence, Dorian's wish to remain forever young and beautiful is granted . . . at a price. Dorian starts out pursuing a life of pleasure but instead ends up leading a life of corruption and debauchery, committing ruthless acts and eventually murder. His painted portrait, kept under a cloth in his attic, reveals these gruesome changes even if his human visage does not. Wilde's Lord Wotton is a true aesthetic: none of the consequences of his behavior (his divorce, the suicide of one of Dorian's friends) have altered his pursuit of pleasure or his attitude toward his life.

Although outwardly he does not show it, Dorian has failed as an aesthetic, as he is suffering because of his selfish deeds. For him, there cannot be a purely aesthetic lifestyle without some sacrifice; living a life as a work of art has its costs, as Wilde himself later learned. Although Dorian's story does not have a happy ending, it does appear, in the final scenes, that Dorian has grown disgusted with his own debauchery as he takes a last look at the painting. The picture looks more evil than ever, with "a look of cunning and in the mouth, the curved wrinkle of the hypocrite." There is more blood coating the limbs in the portrait and Dorian is so unnerved that he toys with the idea of confessing his crime. He decides against it. He tries to destroy this "evidence" against him by slashing the portrait with the knife he earlier used on a victim, but only succeeds in eliminating himself. Perhaps this was Wilde's concession that there may be risks to a lifestyle which he himself espoused, a lesson which he was forced to learn in the sad drama that played out toward the end of his life.

The Picture of Dorian Gray

CHAPTER I

THE STUDIO WAS filled with the rich odour of roses, and when the light summer wind stirred amidst the trees of the garden there came through the open door the heavy scent of the lilac, or the more delicate perfume of the pink-flowering thorn.

From the corner of the divan of Persian saddlebags on which he was lying, smoking, as was his custom, innumerable cigarettes, Lord Henry Wotton could just catch the gleam of the honey-sweet and honey-coloured blossoms of a laburnum, whose tremulous branches seemed hardly able to bear the burden of a beauty so flame-like as theirs; and now and then the fantastic shadows of birds in flight flitted across the long tussore-silk curtains that were stretched in front of the huge window, producing a kind of momentary Japanese effect, and making him think of those pallid jade-faced painters of Tokio who, through the medium of an art that is necessarily immobile, seek to convey the sense of swiftness and motion. The sullen murmur of the bees shouldering their way through the long unmown grass, or circling with monotonous insistence round the dusty gilt horns of the straggling woodbine, seemed to make the stillness more oppressive. The dim roar of London was like the bourdon note of a distant organ.

In the centre of the room, clamped to an upright easel, stood the full-length portrait of a young man of extraordinary personal beauty, and in front of it, some little distance away, was sitting the artist himself, Basil Hallward, whose sudden disappearance some years ago caused, at the time, such public excitement, and gave rise to so many strange conjectures.

As the painter looked at the gracious and comely form he had so skillfully mirrored in his art, a smile of pleasure passed across his face, and seemed about to linger there. But he suddenly started up, and, closing his eyes, placed his fingers upon the lids, as though he sought to imprison within his brain some curious dream from which he feared he might awake.

"It is your best work, Basil, the best thing you have ever done," said Lord

Henry, languidly. "You must certainly send it next year to the Grosvenor. The Academy is too large and too vulgar. Whenever I have gone there, there have been either so many people that I have not been able to see the pictures, which was dreadful, or so many pictures that I have not been able to see the people, which was worse. The Grosvenor is really the only place."

"I don't think I shall send it anywhere," he answered, tossing his head back in that odd way that used to make his friends laugh at him at Oxford. "No: I won't send it anywhere."

Lord Henry elevated his eyebrows, and looked at him in amazement through the thin blue wreaths of smoke that curled up in such fanciful whorls from his heavy opium-tainted cigarette. "Not send it anywhere? My dear fellow, why? Have you any reason? What odd chaps you painters are! You do anything in the world to gain a reputation. As soon as you have one, you seem to want to throw it away. It is silly of you, for there is only one thing in the world worse than being talked about, and that is not being talked about. A portrait like this would set you far above all the young men in England, and make the old men quite jealous, if old men are ever capable of any emotion."

"I know you will laugh at me," he replied, "but I really can't exhibit it. I have put too much of myself into it."

Lord Henry stretched himself out on the divan and laughed.

"Yes, I knew you would; but it is quite true, all the same."

"Too much of yourself in it! Upon my word, Basil, I didn't know you were so vain; and I really can't see any resemblance between you, with your rugged strong face and your coal-black hair, and this young Adonis, who looks as if he was made out of ivory and rose-leaves. Why, my dear Basil, he is a Narcissus, and you—well, of course you have an intellectual expression, and all that. But beauty, real beauty, ends where an intellectual expression begins. Intellect is in itself a mode of exaggeration, and destroys the harmony of any face. The moment one sits down to think, one becomes all nose, or all forehead, or something horrid. Look at the successful men in any of the learned professions. How perfectly hideous they are! Except, of course, in the Church. But then in the Church they don't think. A bishop keeps on saying at the age of eighty what he was told to say when he was a boy of eighteen, and as a natural consequence he always looks absolutely delightful. Your mysterious young friend,

IT IS SILLY OF YOU, FOR THERE IS ONLY ONE THING IN THE WORLD WORSE THAN BEING TALKED ABOUT, AND THAT IS NOT BEING TALKED ABOUT.

whose name you have never told me, but whose picture really fascinates me, never thinks. I feel quite sure of that. He is some brainless, beautiful creature, who should be always here in winter when we have no flowers to look at, and always here in summer when we want something to chill our intelligence. Don't flatter yourself, Basil: you are not in the least like him."

"You don't understand me, Harry," answered the artist. "Of course I am not like him. I know that perfectly well. Indeed, I should be sorry to look like him. You shrug your shoulders? I am telling you the truth. There is a fatality about all physical and intellectual distinction, the sort of fatality that seems to dog through history the faltering steps of kings. It is better not to be different from one's fellows. The ugly and the stupid have the best of it in this world. They can sit at their ease and gape at the play. If they know nothing of victory, they are at least spared the knowledge of defeat. They live as we all should live, undisturbed, indifferent, and without disquiet. They neither bring ruin upon others, nor ever receive it from alien hands. Your rank and wealth, Harry; my brains, such as they are—my art, whatever it may be worth; Dorian Gray's good looks—we shall all suffer for what the gods have given us, suffer terribly."

"Dorian Gray? Is that his name?" asked Lord Henry, walking across the studio towards Basil Hallward.

"Yes, that is his name. I didn't intend to tell it to you."

"But why not?"

"Oh, I can't explain. When I like people immensely I never tell their names to any one. It is like surrendering a part of them. I have grown to love secrecy. It seems to be the one thing that can make modern life mysterious or marvellous to us. The commonest thing is delightful if one only hides it. When I leave town now I never tell my people where I am going. If I did, I would lose all my pleasure. It is a silly habit, I dare say, but somehow it seems to bring a great deal of romance into one's life. I suppose you think me awfully foolish about it?"

"Not at all," answered Lord Henry, "not at all, my dear Basil. You seem to forget that I am married, and the one charm of marriage is that it makes a life of deception absolutely necessary for both parties. I never know where my wife is, and my wife never knows what I am doing. When we meet—we do meet occasionally, when we dine out together, or go down to the Duke's—we tell each other the most absurd stories with the most serious faces. My wife is very good at it—much better, in fact, than I am. She never gets confused over her dates, and I always do. But when she does find me out, she makes no row at all. I sometimes wish she would; but she merely laughs at me."

"I hate the way you talk about your married life, Harry," said Basil Hallward, strolling towards the door that led into the garden. "I believe that you are really a very good husband, but that you are thoroughly ashamed of your own virtues. You are an extraordinary fellow. You never say a moral thing, and you never do a wrong thing. Your cynicism is simply a pose."

"Being natural is simply a pose, and the most irritating pose I know," cried Lord Henry, laughing; and the two young men went out into the garden together, and ensconced themselves on a long bamboo seat that stood in the shade of a tall laurel bush. The sunlight slipped over the polished leaves. In the grass, white daisies were tremulous.

After a pause, Lord Henry pulled out his watch. "I am afraid I must be going, Basil," he murmured, "and before I go, I insist on your answering a question I put to you some time ago."

"What is that?" said the painter, keeping his eyes fixed on the ground.

"You know quite well."

"I do not, Harry."

"Well, I will tell you what it is. I want you to explain to me why you won't exhibit Dorian Gray's picture. I want the real reason."

"I told you the real reason."

"No, you did not. You said it was because there was too much of yourself in it. Now, that is childish. "

"Harry," said Basil Hallward, looking him straight in the face, "every portrait that is painted with feeling is a portrait of the artist, not of the sitter. The sitter is merely the accident, the occasion. It is not he who is revealed by the painter; it is rather the painter who, on the coloured canvas, reveals himself. The reason I will not exhibit this picture is that I am afraid that I have shown in it the secret of my own soul."

Lord Henry laughed. "And what is that?" he asked.

"I will tell you," said Hallward; but an expression of perplexity came over his face.

"I am all expectation, Basil," continued his companion, glancing at him.

"Oh, there is really very little to tell, Harry," answered the painter; "and I am afraid you will hardly understand it. Perhaps you will hardly believe it."

Lord Henry smiled, and leaning down, plucked a pink-petalled daisy from the grass, and examined it. "I am quite sure I shall understand it," he replied, gazing intently at the little golden white-feathered disk, "and as for believing things, I can believe anything, provided that it is quite incredible."

The wind shook some blossoms from the trees, and the heavy lilac-blooms, with their clustering stars, moved to and fro in the languid air. A grasshopper began to chirrup by the wall, and like a blue thread a long thin dragon-fly floated past on its brown gauze wings. Lord Henry felt as if he could hear Basil Hallward's heart beating, and wondered what was coming.

"The story is simply this," said the painter after some time. "Two months ago I went to a crush at Lady Brandon's. You know we poor artists have to show ourselves in society from time to time, just to remind the public that we are not savages. With an evening coat and a white tie, as you told me once, anybody, even a stock-broker, can gain a reputation for being civilized. Well, after I had been in the room about ten minutes, talking to huge overdressed dowagers and tedious Academicians, I suddenly became conscious that some one was looking at me. I turned halfway round, and saw Dorian Gray for the first time. When our eyes met, I felt that I was growing pale. A curious sensation of terror came over me. I knew that I had come face to face with some one whose mere personality was so fascinating that, if I allowed it to do so, it would absorb my whole nature, my whole soul, my very art itself. I did not want any external influence in my life. You know yourself, Harry, how independent I am by nature. I have always been my own master; had at least always been so, till I met Dorian Gray. Then—but I don't know how to explain it to you. Something seemed to tell me that I was on the verge of a terrible crisis in my life. I had a strange feeling that Fate had in store for me exquisite joys and exquisite sorrows. I grew afraid, and turned to quit the room. It was not conscience that made me do so: it was a sort of cowardice. I take no credit to myself for trying to escape."

"Conscience and cowardice are really the same things, Basil. Conscience is the trade-name of the firm. That is all."

"I don't believe that, Harry, and I don't believe you do either. However, whatever was my motive—and it may have been pride, for I used to be very proud—I certainly struggled to the door. There, of course, I stumbled against Lady Brandon. 'You are not going to run away so soon, Mr. Hallward?' she screamed out. You know her curiously shrill voice?"

"Yes; she is a peacock in everything but beauty," said Lord Henry, pulling the daisy to bits with his long, nervous fingers.

"I could not get rid of her. She brought me up to Royalties, and people with Stars and Garters, and elderly ladies with gigantic tiaras and parrot noses. She spoke of me as her dearest friend. I had only met her once before, but she took it into her head to lionize me. I believe some picture of mine had made a great success at the time, at least had been chattered about in the penny newspapers, which is the nineteenth-century standard of immortality. Suddenly I found myself face to face with the young man whose personality had so strangely stirred me. We were quite close, almost touching. Our eyes met again. It was reckless of me, but I asked Lady Brandon to introduce me to him. Perhaps it was not so reckless, after all. It was simply inevitable. We would have spoken to each other without any introduction. I am sure of that. Dorian told me so afterwards. He, too, felt that we were destined to know each other."

"And how did Lady Brandon describe this wonderful young man?" asked his companion. "I know she goes in for giving a rapid *précis* of all her guests. I remember her bringing me up to a truculent and red-faced old gentleman covered all over with orders and ribbons, and hissing into my ear, in a tragic whisper which must have been perfectly audible to everybody in the room, the most astounding details. I simply fled. I like to find out people for myself. But Lady Brandon treats her guests exactly as an auctioneer treats his goods. She either explains them entirely away, or tells one everything about them except what one wants to know."

"Poor Lady Brandon! You are hard on her, Harry!" said Hallward, listlessly.

"My dear fellow, she tried to found a *salon*, and only succeeded in opening a restaurant. How could I admire her? But tell me, what did she say about Mr. Dorian Gray?"

"Oh, something like, 'Charming boy—poor dear mother and I absolutely inseparable. Quite forget what he does—afraid he—doesn't do anything—oh, yes, plays the piano—or is it the violin, dear Mr. Gray?' Neither of us could help laughing, and we became friends at once."

"Laughter is not at all a bad beginning for a friendship, and it is far the best ending for one," said the young lord, plucking another daisy.

Hallward shook his head. "You don't understand what friendship is, Harry," he murmured—"or what enmity is, for that matter. You like every one; that is to say, you are indifferent to every one."

"How horribly unjust of you!" cried Lord Henry, tilting his hat back, and looking up at the little clouds that, like ravelled skeins of glossy white silk, were drifting across the hollowed turquoise of the summer sky. "Yes; horribly unjust of you. I make a great difference between people. I choose my friends for their good looks, my acquaintances for their good characters, and my enemies for their good intellects. A man cannot be too careful in the choice of his enemies. I have not got one who is a fool. They are all men of some intellectual power, and consequently they all appreciate me. Is that very vain of me? I think it is rather vain."

"I should think it was, Harry. But according to your category I must be merely an acquaintance."

"My dear old Basil, you are much more than an acquaintance."

"And much less than a friend. A sort of brother, I suppose?"

"Oh, brothers! I don't care for brothers. My elder brother won't die, and my younger brothers seem never to do anything else."

"Harry!" exclaimed Hallward, frowning.

"My dear fellow, I am not quite serious. But I can't help detesting my relations. I suppose it comes from the fact that none of us can stand other people having the same faults as ourselves. I quite sympathize with the rage of the English democracy against what they call the vices of the upper orders. The masses feel that drunkenness, stupidity, and immorality should be their own special property, and that if any one of us makes an ass of himself he is poaching on their preserves. When poor Southwark got into the Divorce Court, their indignation was quite magnificent. And yet I don't suppose that ten cent of the proletariat live correctly. "

"I don't agree with a single word that you have said, and, what is more, Harry, I feel sure you don't either."

Lord Henry stroked his pointed brown beard, and tapped the toe of his patent-leather boot with a tasselled ebony cane. "How English you are Basil! That is the second time you have made that observation. If one puts forward an idea to a true Englishman—always a rash thing to do—he never dreams of considering whether the idea is right or wrong. The only thing he considers of any importance is whether one believes it oneself. Now, the value of an idea has nothing whatsoever to do with the sincerity of the man who expresses it. Indeed, the probabilities are that the more insincere the man is, the more purely intellectual will the idea be, as in that case it will not be coloured by either his wants, his desires, or his prejudices. However, I don't propose to discuss politics, sociology, or metaphysics with you. I like persons better than principles, and I like persons with no principles better than anything else in the world. Tell me more about Mr. Dorian Gray. How often do you see him?"

"Every day. I couldn't be happy if I didn't see him every day. He is absolutely necessary to me."

"How extraordinary! I thought you would never care for anything but your art."

"He is all my art to me now," said the painter, gravely. "I sometimes think,

Harry, that there are only two eras of any importance in the world's history. The first is the appearance of a new medium for art, and the second is the appearance of a new personality for art also. What the invention of oil-painting was to the Venetians, the face of Antinoüs was to late Greek sculpture, and the face of Dorian Gray will some day be to me. It is not merely that I paint from him, draw from him, sketch from him. Of course I have done all that. But he is much more to me than a model or a sitter. I won't tell you that I am dissatisfied with what I have done of him, or that his beauty is such that Art cannot express it. There is nothing that Art cannot express, and I know that the work I have done, since I met Dorian Gray, is good work, is the best work of my life. But in some curious way—I wonder will you understand me?—his personality has suggested to me an entirely new manner in art, an entirely new mode of style. I see things differently, I think of them differently. I can now recreate life in a way that was hidden from me before. 'A dream of form in days of thought'—who is it who says that? I forget; but it is what Dorian Gray has been to me. The merely visible presence of this lad—for he seems to me little more than a lad, though he is really over twenty—his merely visible presence—ah! I wonder can you realize all that that means? Unconsciously he defines for me the lines of a fresh school, a school that is to have in it all the passion of the romantic spirit, all the perfection of the spirit that is Greek. The harmony of soul and body—how much that is! We in our madness have separated the two, and have invented a realism that is vulgar, an ideality that is void. Harry! if you only knew what Dorian Gray is to me! You remember that landscape of mine, for which Agnew offered me such a huge price, but which I would not part with? It is one of the best things I have ever done. And why is it so? Because, while I was painting it, Dorian Gray sat beside me. Some subtle influence passed from him to me, and for the first time in my life I saw in the plain woodland the wonder I had always looked for, and always missed."

"Basil, this is extraordinary! I must see Dorian Gray."

Hallward got up from the seat, and walked up and down the garden. After some time he came back. "Harry," he said, "Dorian Gray is to me simply a motive in art. You might see nothing in him. I see everything in him. He is never more present in my work than when no image of him is there. He is a suggestion, as I have said, of a new manner. I find him in the curves of certain lines, in the loveliness and subtleties of certain colours. That is all."

"Then why won't you exhibit his portrait?" asked Lord Henry.

"Because, without intending it, I have put into it some expression of all this curious artistic idolatry, of which, of course, I have never cared to speak to him. He knows nothing about it. He shall never know anything about it. But the world might guess it; and I will not bare my soul to their shallow, prying eyes. My heart shall never be put under their microscope. There is too much of myself in the thing, Harry—too much of myself!"

"Poets are not so scrupulous as you are. They know how useful passion is for publication. Nowadays a broken heart will run to many editions."

"I hate them for it," cried Hallward. "An artist should create beautiful things, but should put nothing of his own life into them. We live in an age when men treat art as if it were meant to be a form of autobiography. We have lost the abstract sense of beauty. Some day I will show the world what it is; and for that reason the world shall never see my portrait of Dorian Gray."

"I think you are wrong, Basil, but I won't argue with you. It is only the intellectually lost who ever argue. Tell me, is Dorian Gray very fond of you?"

The painter considered for a few moments. "He likes me," he answered after a pause; "I know he likes me. Of course I flatter him dreadfully. I find a strange pleasure in saying things to him that I know I shall be sorry for having said. As a rule, he is charming to me, and we sit in the studio and talk of a thousand things. Now and then, however, he is horribly thoughtless, and seems to take a real delight in giving me pain. Then I feel, Harry, that I have given away my whole soul to some one who treats it as if it were a flower to put in his coat, a bit of decoration to charm his vanity, an ornament for a summer's day."

"Days in summer, Basil, are apt to linger," murmured Lord Henry. "Perhaps you will tire sooner than he will. It is a sad thing to think of, but there is no doubt that Genius lasts longer than Beauty. That accounts for the fact that we all take such pains to over-educate ourselves. In the wild struggle for existence, we want to have something that endures, and so we fill our minds with rubbish and facts, in the silly hope of keeping our place. The thoroughly well-informed man—that is the modern ideal. And the mind of the thoroughly well-informed man is a dreadful thing. It is like a bric-à-brac shop, all monsters and dust, with everything priced above its proper value. I think you will tire first, all the same. Some day you will look at your friend, and he will seem to you to be a little out of drawing, or you won't like his tone of colour, or something. You will bitterly reproach him in your own heart, and seriously think that he has behaved very badly to you. The next time he calls, you will be perfectly cold and indifferent. It will be a great pity, for it will alter you. What you have told me is quite a romance, a romance of art one might call it, and the worst of having a romance of any kind is that it leaves one so unromantic."

"Harry, don't talk like that. As long as I live, the personality of Dorian Gray will dominate me. You can't feel what I feel. You change too often."

"Ah, my dear Basil, that is exactly why I can feel it. Those who are faithful know only the trivial side of love: it is the faithless who know love's tragedies." And Lord Henry struck a light on a dainty silver case, and began to smoke a cigarette with a self-conscious and satisfied air, as if he had summed up the world in a phrase. There was a rustle of chirruping sparrows in the green lacquer leaves of the ivy, and the blue cloud-shadows chased themselves across the grass like swallows. How pleasant it was in the garden! And how delightful other people's emotions were!—much more delightful than their ideas, it seemed to him. One's own soul, and the passions of one's friends—those were the fascinating things in life. He pictured to himself with silent amusement the tedious luncheon that he had missed by staying so long with Basil Hallward. Had he gone to his aunt's, he would have been sure to have met Lord Goodbody there, and the whole conversation would have been about the feeding of the poor, and the necessity for model lodging-houses. Each class would have preached the importance of those virtues, for whose exercise there was no necessity in their own lives. The rich would have spoken on the value of thrift, and the idle grown eloquent over the dignity of labour. It was charming to have escaped all that! As he thought of his aunt, an idea seemed to strike him. He turned to Hallward, and said, "My dear fellow, I have just remembered."

"Remembered what, Harry?"

"Where I heard the name of Dorian Gray."

"Where was it?" asked Hallward, with a slight frown.

"Don't look so angry, Basil. It was at my aunt, Lady Agatha's. She told me she had discovered a wonderful young man, who was going to help her in the East End, and that his name was Dorian Gray. I am bound to state that she never told me he was good-looking. Women have no appreciation of good looks; at least, good women have not. She said that he was very earnest, and had a beautiful nature. I at once pictured to myself a creature with spectacles and lank hair, horribly freckled, and tramping about on huge feet. I wish I had known it was your friend."

"I am very glad you didn't, Harry."

"Why?"

"I don't want you to meet him."

"You don't want me to meet him?"

"No."

"Mr. Dorian Gray is in the studio, sir," said the butler, coming into the garden.

"You must introduce me now," cried Lord Henry, laughing.

The painter turned to his servant, who stood blinking in the sunlight. "Ask Mr. Gray to wait, Parker: I shall be in in a few moments." The man bowed, and went up the walk.

Then he looked at Lord Henry. "Dorian Gray is my dearest friend," he said. "He has a simple and beautiful nature. Your aunt was quite right in what she said of him. Don't spoil him. Don't try to influence him. Your influence would be bad. The world is wide, and has many marvellous people in it. Don't take away from me the one person who gives to my art whatever charm it possesses: my life as an artist depends on him. Mind, Harry, I trust you." He spoke very slowly, and the words seemed wrung out of him almost against his will.

"What nonsense you talk!" said Lord Henry, smiling, and, taking Hallward by the arm, he almost led him into the house.

CHAPTER II

AS THEY ENTERED they saw Dorian Gray. He was seated at the piano, with his back to them, turning over the pages of a volume of Schumann's "Forest Scenes." "You must lend me these, Basil," he cried. "I want to learn them. They are perfectly charming."

"That entirely depends on how you sit to-day, Dorian."

"Oh, I am tired of sitting, and I don't want a life-sized portrait of myself," answered the lad, swinging round on the music-stool, in a willful, petulant manner. When he caught sight of Lord Henry, a faint blush coloured his cheeks for a moment, and he started up. "I beg your pardon, Basil, but I didn't know you had any one with you."

"This is Lord Henry Wotton, Dorian, an old Oxford friend of mine. I have just been telling him what a capital sitter you were, and now you have spoiled everything."

"You have not spoiled my pleasure in meeting you, Mr. Gray," said Lord Henry, stepping forward and extending his hand. "My aunt has often spoken to me about you. You are one of her favourites, and, I am afraid, one of her victims also."

"I am in Lady Agatha's black books at present," answered Dorian, with a funny look of penitence. "I promised to go to a club in Whitechapel with her last Tuesday, and I really forgot all about it. We were to have played a duet together—three duets, I believe. I don't know what she will say to me. I am far too frightened to call."

"Oh, I will make your peace with my aunt. She is quite devoted to you. And I don't think it really matters about your not being there. The audience probably thought it was a duet. When Aunt Agatha sits down to the piano she makes quite enough noise for two people."

"That is very horrid to her, and not very nice to me," answered Dorian, laughing.

Lord Henry looked at him. Yes, he was certainly wonderfully handsome, with his finely-curved scarlet lips, his frank blue eyes, his crisp gold hair. There was something in his face that made one trust him at once. All the candour of youth was there, as well as all youth's passionate purity. One felt that he had kept himself unspotted from the world. No wonder Basil Hallward worshipped him.

"You are too charming to go in for philanthropy, Mr. Gray—far too charming." And Lord Henry flung himself down on the divan, and opened his cigarette-case.

The painter had been busy mixing his colours and getting his brushes ready. He was looking worried, and when he heard Lord Henry's last remark he glanced at him, hesitated for a moment, and then said, "Harry, I want to finish this picture to-day. Would you think it awfully rude of me if I asked you to go away?"

Lord Henry smiled, and looked at Dorian Gray. "Am I to go, Mr. Gray?" he asked.

"Oh, please don't, Lord Henry. I see that Basil is in one of his sulky moods; and I can't bear him when he sulks. Besides, I want you to tell me why I should not go in for philanthropy."

"I don't know that I shall tell you that, Mr. Gray. It is so tedious a subject that one would have to talk seriously about it. But I certainly shall not run away, now that you have asked me to stop. You don't really mind, Basil, do you? You have often told me that you liked your sitters to have some one to chat to."

Hallward bit his lip. "If Dorian wishes it, of course you must stay. Dorian's whims are laws to everybody, except himself."

Lord Henry took up his hat and gloves. "You are very pressing, Basil, but I am afraid I must go. I have promised to meet a man at the Orleans. Good-bye, Mr. Gray. Come and see me some afternoon in Curzon Street. I am nearly always at home at five o'clock. Write to me when you are coming. I should be sorry to miss you."

"Basil," cried Dorian Gray, "if Lord Henry Wotton goes I shall go too. You never open your lips while you are painting, and it is horribly dull standing on a platform and trying to look pleasant. Ask him to stay. I insist upon it."

"Stay, Harry, to oblige Dorian, and to oblige me," said Hallward, gazing intently at his picture. "It is quite true, I never talk when I am working, and never listen either, and it must be dreadfully tedious for my unfortunate sitters. I beg you to stay."

"But what about my man at the Orleans?"

The painter laughed. "I don't think there will be any difficulty about that. Sit down again, Harry. And now, Dorian, get up on the platform, and don't move about too much, or pay any attention to what Lord Henry says. He has a very bad influence over all his friends, with the single exception of myself."

Dorian Gray stepped up on the dais, with the air of a young Greek martyr, and made a little *moue* of discontent to Lord Henry, to whom he had rather taken a fancy. He was so unlike Basil. They made a delightful contrast. And he had such a beautiful voice. After a few moments he said to him, "Have you really a very bad influence, Lord Henry? As bad as Basil says?"

"There is no such thing as a good influence, Mr. Gray. All influence is immoral—immoral from the scientific point of view."

"Why?"

"Because to influence a person is to give him one's own soul. He does not think his natural thoughts, or burn with his natural passions. His virtues are not real to him. His sins, if there are such things as sins, are borrowed. He becomes an echo of some one else's music, an actor of a part that has not been written for him. The aim of life is self-development. To realize one's nature perfectly—that is what each of us is here for. People are afraid of themselves, nowadays. They have forgotten the highest of all duties, the duty that one owes to one's self. Of course they are charitable. They feed the hungry, and clothe the beggar. But their own souls starve, and are naked. Courage has gone out of our race. Perhaps we never really had it. The terror of society, which is the basis of morals, the terror of God, which is the secret of religion—these are the two things that govern us. And yet—"

"Just turn your head a little more to the right, Dorian, like a good boy," said the painter, deep in his work, and conscious only that a look had come into the lad's face that he had never seen there before.

"And yet," continued Lord Henry, in his low, musical voice, and with that graceful wave of the hand that was always so characteristic of him, and that he had even in his Eton days, "I believe that if one man were to live out his life fully and completely, were to give form to every feeling, expression to every thought, reality to every dream—I believe that the world would gain such a fresh impulse of joy that we would forget all the maladies of mediaevalism, and return to the Hellenic ideal—to something finer, richer, than the Hellenic ideal, it may be. But the bravest man amongst us is afraid of himself. The mutilation of the savage has its tragic survival in the self-denial that mars our lives. We are punished for our refusals. Every impulse that we strive to strangle broods in the mind, and poisons us. The body sins once, and has done with its sin, for action is a mode of purification. Nothing remains then but the recollection of a pleasure, or the luxury of a regret. The only way to get rid of a temptation is to yield to it. Resist it, and your soul grows sick with longing for the things it has forbidden to itself, with desire for what its monstrous laws have made monstrous and unlawful. It has been said that the great events of the world take place in the brain. It is in the brain, and the brain only, that the great sins of the world take place also. You, Mr. Gray, you yourself, with your rose-red youth and your rose-white boyhood, you have had passions that have made you afraid, thoughts that have filled you with terror, day-dreams and sleeping dreams whose mere memory might stain your cheek with shame."

"Stop!" faltered Dorian Gray, "stop! you bewilder me. I don't know what to say. There is some answer to you, but I cannot find it. Don't speak. Let me think. Or, rather, let me try not to think."

For nearly ten minutes he stood there, motionless, with parted lips, and eyes strangely bright. He was dimly conscious that entirely fresh influences were at work within him. Yet they seemed to him to have come really from himself. The few words that Basil's friend had said to him—words spoken by chance, no doubt, and with willful paradox in them—had touched some secret chord that had never been touched before, but that he felt was now vibrating and throbbing to curious pulses.

Music had stirred him like that. Music had troubled him many times. But music was not articulate. It was not a new world, but rather another chaos, that it created in us. Words! Mere words! How terrible they were! How clear, and vivid, and cruel! One could not escape from them. And yet what a subtle magic there was in them! They seemed to be able to give a plastic form to formless things, and to have a music of their own as sweet as that of viol or of lute. Mere words! Was there anything so real as words?

Yes; there had been things in his boyhood that he had not understood. He understood them now. Life suddenly became fiery-coloured to him. It seemed to him that he had been walking in fire. Why had he not known it?

With his subtle smile, Lord Henry watched him. He knew the precise psychological moment when to say nothing. He felt intensely interested. He was amazed at the sudden impression that his words had produced, and, remembering a book that he had read when he was sixteen, a book which had revealed to him much that he had not known before, he wondered whether Dorian Gray was passing through a similar experience. He had merely shot an arrow into the air. Had it hit the mark? How fascinating the lad was!

Hallward painted away with that marvellous bold touch of his, that had the true refinement and perfect delicacy that in art, at any rate, comes only from strength. He was unconscious of the silence.

"Basil, I am tired of standing," cried Dorian Gray, suddenly. "I must go out and sit in the garden. The air is stifling here."

"My dear fellow, I am so sorry. When I am painting, I can't think of anything else. But you never sat better. You were perfectly still. And I have caught the effect I wanted—the half-parted lips, and the bright look in the eyes. I don't know what Harry has been saying to you, but he has certainly made you have the most wonderful expression. I suppose he has been paying you compliments. You mustn't believe a word that he says."

"He has certainly not been paying me compliments. Perhaps that is the reason that I don't believe anything he has told me."

"You know you believe it all," said Lord Henry, looking at him with his dreamy, languorous eyes. "I will go out to the garden with you. It is horribly hot in the studio. Basil, let us have something iced to drink, something with strawberries in it."

"Certainly, Harry. Just touch the bell, and when Parker comes I will tell him what you want. I have got to work up this background, so I will join you later on. Don't keep Dorian too long. I have never been in better form for painting than I am to-day. This is going to be my masterpiece. It is my masterpiece as it stands."

Lord Henry went out to the garden, and found Dorian Gray burying his face in the great cool lilac-blossoms, feverishly drinking in their perfume as if it had been wine. He came close to him, and put his hand upon his shoulder. "You are quite right to do that," he murmured. "Nothing can cure the soul but the senses, just as nothing can cure the senses but the soul."

The lad started and drew back. He was bare-headed, and the leaves had tossed his rebellious curls and tangled all their gilded threads. There was a look of fear in his eyes, such as people have when they are suddenly awakened. His finely-chiselled nostrils quivered, and some hidden nerve shook the scarlet of his lips and left them trembling.

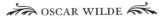

"Yes," continued Lord Henry, "that is one of the great secrets of life—to cure the soul by means of the senses, and the senses by means of the soul. You are a wonderful creation. You know more than you think you know, just as you know less than you want to know."

Dorian Gray frowned and turned his head away. He could not help liking the tall, graceful young man who was standing by him. His romantic olive-coloured face and worn expression interested him. There was something in his low, languid voice that was absolutely fascinating. His cool, white, flower-like hands, even, had a curious charm. They moved, as he spoke, like music, and seemed to have a language of their own. But he felt afraid of him, and ashamed of being afraid. Why had it been left for a stranger to reveal him to himself? He had known Basil Hallward for months, but the friendship between them had never altered him. Suddenly there had come some one across his life who seemed to have disclosed to him life's mystery. And, yet, what was there to be afraid of? He was not a schoolboy or a girl. It was absurd to be frightened.

"Let us go and sit in the shade," said Lord Henry. "Parker has brought out the drinks, and if you stay any longer in this glare you will be quite spoiled, and Basil will never paint you again. You really must not allow yourself to become sunburnt. It would be unbecoming."

"What can it matter?" cried Dorian Gray, laughing, as he sat down on the seat at the end of the garden.

"It should matter everything to you, Mr. Gray."

"Why?"

"Because you have the most marvellous youth, and youth is the one thing worth having."

"I don't feel that, Lord Henry."

"No, you don't feel it now. Some day, when you are old and wrinkled and ugly, when thought has seared your forehead with its lines, and passion branded your lips with its hideous fires, you will feel it, you will feel it terribly. Now, wherever you go, you charm the world. Will it always be so? . . . You have a wonderfully beautiful face, Mr. Gray. Don't frown. You have. And Beauty is a form of Genius—is higher, indeed, than Genius, as it needs no explanation. It is of the great facts of the world, like sunlight, or spring-time, or the reflection in dark waters of that silver shell we call the moon. It cannot be questioned. It has its divine right of sovereignty. It makes princes of those who have it. You smile? Ah! when you have lost it you won't smile. . . . People say sometimes that Beauty is only superficial. That may be so. But at least it is not so superficial as Thought is. To me, Beauty is the wonder of wonders. It is only shallow people who do not judge by appearances. The true mystery of the world is the visible, not the invisible. . . . Yes, Mr. Gray, the gods have been good to you. But what the gods give they quickly take away. You have only a few years in which to live really, perfectly, and fully. When your youth goes, your beauty will go with it, and then you will suddenly discover that there are no triumphs left for you, or have to content yourself with those mean triumphs that the memory of your past will make more bitter than defeats. Every month as it wanes brings you nearer to something dreadful. Time is jealous of you, and wars against your lilies and your roses. You will become sallow, and hollow-cheeked, and dull-eyed. You will suffer horribly. . . Ah! realize your youth while you have it. Don't squander the gold of your days, listening to the tedious, trying to improve the hopeless failure, or giving away your life to the ignorant, the common, and the vulgar. These are the sickly alms, the false ideals, of our age. Live! Live the wonderful life that is in you! Let nothing be lost upon you. Be always searching for new sensations. Be afraid of nothing. . . . A new Hedonism—that is what our century wants. You might be its visible symbol. With your personality there is nothing you could not do. The world belongs to you for a season. . . . The moment I met you I saw that you were quite unconscious of what you really are, of what you really might be. There was so much in you that charmed me that I felt I must tell you something about yourself. I thought how tragic it would be if you were wasted. For there is such a little time that your youth will last—such a little time. The common hill-flowers wither, but they blossom again. The laburnum will be as yellow next June as it is now. In a month there will be purple stars on the clematis, and year after year the green night of its leaves will hold its purple stars. But we never get back our youth. The pulse of joy that beats in us at twenty, becomes sluggish. Our limbs fail, our senses rot. We degenerate into hideous puppets, haunted by the memory of the passions of which we were too much afraid, and the exquisite temptations that we had not the courage to yield to. Youth! Youth! There is absolutely nothing in the world but youth!"

Dorian Gray listened, open-eyed and wondering. The spray of lilac fell from his hand upon the gravel. A furry bee came and buzzed round it for a moment.

Then it began to scramble all over the oval stellated globe of the tiny blossoms. He watched it with that strange interest in trivial things that we try to develop when things of high import make us afraid, or when we are stirred by some new emotion for which we cannot find expression, or when some thought that terrifies us lays sudden siege to the brain and calls on us to yield. After a time the bee flew away. He saw it creeping into the stained trumpet of a Tyrian convolvulus. The flower seemed to quiver, and then swayed gently to and fro.

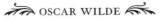

Suddenly the painter appeared at the door of the studio, and made staccato signs for them to come in. They turned to each other, and smiled.

"I am waiting," he cried. "Do come in. The light is quite perfect, and you can bring your drinks."

They rose up, and sauntered down the walk together. Two green-and-white butterflies fluttered past them, and in the pear-tree at the corner of the garden a thrush began to sing.

"You are glad you have met me, Mr. Gray," said Lord Henry, looking at him.

"Yes, I am glad now. I wonder shall I always be glad?"

"Always! That is a dreadful word. It makes me shudder when I hear it. Women are so fond of using it. They spoil every romance by trying to make it last for ever. It is a meaningless word, too. The only difference between a caprice and a life-long passion is that the caprice lasts a little longer."

As they entered the studio, Dorian Gray put his hand upon Lord Henry's arm. "In that case, let our friendship be a caprice," he murmured, flushing at his own boldness, then stepped up on the platform and resumed his pose.

Lord Henry flung himself into a large wicker arm-chair, and watched him. The sweep and dash of the brush on the canvas made the only sound that broke the stillness, except when, now and then, Hallward stepped back to look at his work from a distance. In the slanting beams that streamed through the open doorway the dust danced and was golden. The heavy scent of the roses seemed to brood over everything.

After about a quarter of an hour Hallward stopped painting, looked for a long time at Dorian Gray, and then for a long time at the picture, biting the end of one of his huge brushes, and frowning. "It is quite finished," he cried at last, and stooping down he wrote his name in long vermilion letters on the left-hand corner of the canvas.

Lord Henry came over and examined the picture. It was certainly a wonderful work of art, and a wonderful likeness as well.

"My dear fellow, I congratulate you most warmly," he said. "It is the finest portrait of modern times. Mr. Gray, come over and look at yourself. "

The lad started, as if awakened from some dream. "Is it really finished?" he murmured, stepping down from the platform.

"Quite finished," said the painter. "And you have sat splendidly to-day. I am awfully obliged to you."

"That is entirely due to me, " broke in Lord Henry. "Isn't it, Mr. Gray?"

Dorian made no answer, but passed listlessly in front of his picture and turned towards it. When he saw it he drew back, and his cheeks flushed for a moment with pleasure. A look of joy came into his eyes, as if he had recognized himself for the first time. He stood there motionless and in wonder, dimly conscious that Hallward was speaking to him, but not catching the meaning of his words. The sense of his own beauty came on him like a revelation. He had never felt it before. Basil Hallward's compliments had seemed to him to be merely the charming exaggerations of friendship. He had listened to them, laughed at them, forgotten them. They had not influenced his nature. Then had come Lord Henry Wotton with his strange panegyric on youth, his terrible warning of its brevity. That had stirred him at the time, and now, as he stood gazing at the shadow of his own loveliness, the full reality of the description flashed across him. Yes, there would be a day when his face would be wrinkled and wizen, his eyes dim and colourless, the grace of his figure broken and deformed. The scarlet would pass away from his lips, and the gold steal from his hair. The life that was to make his soul would mar his body. He would become dreadful, hideous, and uncouth.

As he thought of it, a sharp pang of pain struck through him like a knife, and made each delicate fibre of his nature quiver. His eyes deepened into amethyst, and across them came a mist of tears. He felt as if a hand of ice had been laid upon his heart.

"Don't you like it?" cried Hallward at last, stung a little by the lad's silence, not understanding what it meant.

"Of course he likes it," said Lord Henry. "Who wouldn't like it? It is one of the greatest things in modern art. I will give you anything you like to ask for it. I must have it."

"It is not my property, Harry."

"Whose property is it?"

"Dorian's, of course," answered the painter.

"He is a very lucky fellow."

"How sad it is!" murmured Dorian Gray, with his eyes still fixed upon his own portrait. "How sad it is! I shall grow old, and horrible, and dreadful. But this picture will remain always young. It will never be older than this particular day of June. . . . If it were only the other way! If it were I who was to be always young, and the picture that was to grow old! For that—for that—I would give everything! Yes, there is nothing in the whole world I would not give! I would give my soul for that!"

"You would hardly care for such an arrangement, Basil," cried Lord Henry, laughing. "It would be rather hard lines on your work."

"I should object very strongly, Harry," said Hallward.

Dorian Gray turned and looked at him. "I believe you would, Basil. You like your art better than your friends. I am no more to you than a green bronze figure. Hardly as much, I dare say."

The painter stared in amazement. It was so unlike Dorian to speak like that. What had happened? He seemed quite angry. His face was flushed and his cheeks burning.

"Yes," he continued, "I am less to you than your ivory Hermes or your silver Faun. You will like them always. How long will you like me? Till I have my first wrinkle, I suppose. I know, now, that when one loses one's good looks, whatever they may be, one loses everything. Your picture has taught me that. Lord Henry Wotton is perfectly right. Youth is the only thing worth having. When I find that I am growing old, I shall kill myself."

Hallward turned pale, and caught his hand. "Dorian! Dorian!" he cried, "don't talk like that. I have never had such a friend as you, and shall never have such another. You are not jealous of material things, are you?—you who are finer than any of them!"

"I am jealous of everything whose beauty does not die. I am jealous of the portrait you have painted of me. Why should it keep what I must lose? Every moment that passes takes something from me, and gives something to it. Oh, if it were only the other way! If the picture could change, and I could be always what I am now! Why did you paint it? It will mock me some day—mock me horribly!" The hot tears welled into his eyes; he tore his hand away, and, flinging himself on the divan, he buried his face in the cushions, as though he was praying.

"This is your doing, Harry," said the painter, bitterly.

Lord Henry shrugged his shoulders. "It is the real Dorian Gray—that is all."

"It is not."

"If it is not, what have I to do with it?"

"You should have gone away when I asked you," he muttered.

"I stayed when you asked me," was Lord Henry's answer.

"Harry, I can't quarrel with my two best friends at once, but between you both you have made me hate the finest piece of work I have ever done, and I will destroy it. What is it but canvas and colour? I will not let it come across our three lives and mar them."

Dorian Gray lifted his golden head from the pillow, and with pallid face and tear-stained eyes looked at him, as he walked over to the deal painting-table that was set beneath the high curtained window. What was he doing there? His fingers were straying about among the litter of tin tubes and dry brushes, seeking for something. Yes, it was for the long palette-knife, with its thin blade of lithe steel. He had found it at last. He was going to rip up the canvas.

With a stifled sob the lad leaped from the couch, and, rushing over to Hallward, tore the knife out of his hand, and flung it to the end of the studio. "Don't, Basil, don't!" he cried. "It would be murder!"

"I am glad you appreciate my work at last, Dorian," said the painter, coldly, when he had recovered from his surprise. "I never thought you would."

"Appreciate it? I am in love with it, Basil. It is part of myself. I feel that."

"Well, as soon as you are dry, you shall be varnished, and framed, and sent home. Then you can do what you like with yourself." And he walked across the room and rang the bell for tea. "You will have tea, of course, Dorian? And so will you, Harry? Or do you object to such simple pleasures?"

"I adore simple pleasures," said Lord Henry. "They are the last refuge of the complex. But I don't like scenes, except on the stage. What absurd fellows you are, both of you! I wonder who it was defined man as a rational animal. It was the most premature definition ever given. Man is many things, but he is not rational. I am glad he is not, after all: though I wish you chaps would not squabble over the picture. You had much better let me have it, Basil. This silly boy doesn't really want it, and I really do."

"If you let any one have it but me, Basil, I shall never forgive you!" cried Dorian Gray; "and I don't allow people to call me a silly boy."

"You know the picture is yours, Dorian. I gave it to you before it existed."

"And you know you have been a little silly, Mr. Gray, and that you don't really object to being reminded that you are extremely young."

"I should have objected very strongly this morning, Lord Henry."

"Ah! this morning! You have lived since then."

There came a knock at the door, and the butler entered with a laden tea-tray and set it down upon a small Japanese table. There was a rattle of cups and saucers and the hissing of a fluted Georgian urn. Two globe-shaped china dishes were brought in by a page. Dorian Gray went over and poured out the tea. The two men sauntered languidly to the table, and examined what was under the covers.

"Let us go to the theatre to-night," said Lord Henry. "There is sure to be something on, somewhere. I have promised to dine at White's, but it is only with an old friend, so I can send him a wire to say that I am ill, or that I am prevented from coming in consequence of a subsequent engagement. I think that would be a rather nice excuse: it would have all the surprise of candour."

"It is such a bore putting on one's dress-clothes," muttered Hallward. "And, when one has them on, they are so horrid."

"Yes," answered Lord Henry, dreamily, "the costume of the nineteenth century is detestable. It is so sombre, so depressing. Sin is the only real colour-element left in modern life."

"You really must not say things like that before Dorian, Harry."

"Before which Dorian? The one who is pouring out tea for us, or the one in the picture?"

"Before either."

"I should like to come to the theatre with you, Lord Henry," said the lad.

"Then you shall come; and you will come too, Basil, won't you?"

"I can't, really. I would sooner not. I have a lot of work to do."

"Well, then, you and I will go alone, Mr. Gray."

"I should like that awfully."

The painter bit his lip and walked over, cup in hand, to the picture. "I shall stay with the real Dorian," he said, sadly.

"Is it the real Dorian?" cried the original of the portrait, strolling across to him. "Am I really like that?"

"Yes; you are just like that."

"How wonderful, Basil!"

"At least you are like it in appearance. But it will never alter," sighed Hallward. "That is something."

"What a fuss people make about fidelity!" exclaimed Lord Henry. "Why, even in love it is purely a question for physiology. It has nothing to do with our own will. Young men want to be faithful, and are not; old men want to be faithless, and cannot: that is all one can say."

"Don't go to the theatre to-night, Dorian," said Hallward. "Stop and dine with me."

"I can't, Basil."

"Why?"

"Because I have promised Lord Henry Wotton to go with him."

"He won't like you the better for keeping your promises. He always breaks his own. I beg you not to go."

Dorian Gray laughed and shook his head.

"I entreat you."

The lad hesitated, and looked over at Lord Henry, who was watching them from the tea-table with an amused smile.

"I must go, Basil," he answered.

"Very well," said Hallward; and he went over and laid down his cup on the tray. "It is rather late, and, as you have to dress, you had better lose no time. Good-bye, Harry. Good-bye, Dorian. Come and see me soon. Come to-morrow."

"Certainly."

"You won't forget?"

"No, of course not," cried Dorian.

"And . . . Harry!"

"Yes, Basil?"

"Remember what I asked you, when we were in the garden this morning."

"I have forgotten it."

"I trust you."

"I wish I could trust myself," said Lord Henry, laughing. "Come, Mr. Gray, my hansom is outside, and I can drop you at your own place. Good-bye, Basil. It has been a most interesting afternoon."

As the door closed behind them, the painter flung himself down on a sofa, and a look of pain came into his face.

CHAPTER III

AT HALF-PAST twelve next day Lord Henry Wotton strolled from Curzon Street over to the Albany to call on his uncle, Lord Fermor, a genial if somewhat rough-mannered old bachelor, whom the outside world called selfish because it derived no particular benefit from him, but who was considered generous by Society as he fed the people who amused him. His father had been our ambassador at Madrid when Isabella was young, and Prim unthought of, but had retired from the Diplomatic Service in a capricious moment of annoyance on not being offered the Embassy at Paris, a post to which he considered that he was fully entitled by reason of his birth, his indolence, the good English of his despatches, and his inordinate passion for pleasure. The son, who had been his father's secretary, had resigned along with his chief, somewhat foolishly as was thought at the time, and on succeeding some months later to the title, had set himself to the serious study of the great aristocratic art of doing absolutely nothing. He had two large town houses, but preferred to live in chambers as it was less trouble, and took most of his meals at his club. He paid some attention to the management of his collieries in the Midland counties, excusing himself for this taint of industry on the ground that the one advantage of having coal was that it enabled a gentleman to afford the decency of burning wood on his own hearth. In politics he was a Tory, except when the Tories were in office, during which period he roundly abused them for being a pack of Radicals. He was a hero to his valet, who bullied him, and a terror to most of his relations, whom he bullied in turn. Only England could have produced him, and he always said that the country was going to the dogs. His principles were out of date, but there was a good deal to be said for his prejudices.

When Lord Henry entered the room, he found his uncle sitting in a rough shooting coat, smoking a cheroot and grumbling over *The Times*. "Well, Harry," said the old gentleman, "what brings you out so early? I thought you dandies never got up till two, and were not visible till five."

"Pure family affection, I assure you, Uncle George. I want to get something out of you."

"Money, I suppose," said Lord Fermor, making a wry face. "Well, sit down and tell me all about it. Young people, nowadays, imagine that money is everything."

"Yes," murmured Lord Henry, settling his button-hole in his coat; "and when they grow older they know it. But I don't want money. It is only people who pay their bills who want that, Uncle George, and I never pay mine. Credit is the capital of a younger son, and one lives charmingly upon it. Besides, I always deal with Dartmoor's tradesmen, and consequently they never bother me. What I want is information: not useful information, of course; useless information."

"Well, I can tell you anything that is in an English Blue-book, Harry, although those fellows nowadays write a lot of nonsense. When I was in the Diplomatic, things were much better. But I hear they let them in now by examination. What can you expect? Examinations, sir, are pure humbug from beginning to end. If a man is a gentleman, he knows quite enough, and if he is not a gentleman, whatever he knows is bad for him."

"Mr. Dorian Gray does not belong to Blue-books, Uncle George," said Lord Henry, languidly.

"Mr. Dorian Gray? Who is he?" asked Lord Fermor, knitting his bushy white eyebrows.

"That is what I have come to learn, Uncle George. Or rather, I know who he is. He is the last Lord Kelso's grandson. His mother was a Devereux, Lady Margaret Devereux. I want you to tell me about his mother. What was she like? Whom did she marry? You have known nearly everybody in your time, so you might have known her. I am very much interested in Mr. Gray at present. I have only just met him."

"Kelso's grandson!" echoed the old gentleman—"Kelso's grandson! . . . Of course. . . . I knew his mother intimately. I believe I was at her christening. She was an extraordinarily beautiful girl, Margaret Devereux, and made all the men frantic by running away with a penniless young fellow, a mere nobody, sir, a subaltern in a foot regiment, or something of that kind. Certainly. I remember the whole thing as if it happened yesterday. The poor chap was killed in a duel at Spa a few months after the marriage. There was an ugly story about it. They said Kelso got some rascally adventurer, some Belgian brute, to insult his son-in-law in public, paid him, sir, to do it, paid him, and that the fellow spitted his man as if he had been a pigeon. The thing was hushed up, but, egad, Kelso ate his chop alone at the club for some time afterwards. He brought his daughter back with him, I was told, and she never spoke to him again. Oh, yes; it was a bad business. The girl died too, died within a year. So she left a son, did she? I had forgotten that. What sort of boy is he? If he is like his mother he must be a good-looking chap."

"He is very good-looking," assented Lord Henry.

"I hope he will fall into proper hands," continued the old man. "He should have a pot of money waiting for him if Kelso did the right thing by him. His mother had money too. All the Selby property came to her, through her grandfather. Her grandfather hated Kelso, thought him a mean dog. He was, too. Came to Madrid once when I was there. Egad, I was ashamed of him. The Queen used to ask me about the English noble who was always quarrelling with the cabmen about their fares. They made quite a story of it. I didn't dare show my face at Court for a month. I hope he treated his grandson better than he did the jarvies."

"I don't know," answered Lord Henry. "I fancy that the boy will be well off. He is not of age yet. He has Selby, I know. He told me so. And . . . his mother was very beautiful?"

"Margaret Devereux was one of the loveliest creatures I ever saw, Harry. What on earth induced her to behave as she did, I never could understand. She could have married anybody she chose. Carlington was mad after her. She was romantic, though. All the women of that family were. The men were a poor lot, but, egad! the women were wonderful. Carlington went on his knees to her. Told me so himself. She laughed at him, and there wasn't a girl in London at the time who wasn't after him. And by the way, Harry, talking about silly marriages, what is this humbug your father tells me about Dartmoor wanting to marry an American? Ain't English girls good enough for him?"

"It is rather fashionable to marry Americans just now, Uncle George."

"I'll back English women against the world, Harry," said Lord Fermor, striking the table with his fist.

"The betting is on the Americans."

"They don't last, I am told," muttered his uncle.

"A long engagement exhausts them, but they are capital at a steeplechase. They take things flying. I don't think Dartmoor has a chance."

"Who are her people?" grumbled the old gentleman. "Has she got any?"

Lord Henry shook his head. "American girls are as clever at concealing their parents, as English women are at concealing their past," he said, rising to go.

"They are pork-packers, I suppose?"

"I hope so, Uncle George, for Dartmoor's sake. I am told that pork-packing is the most lucrative profession in America, after politics."

"Is she pretty?"

"She behaves as if she was beautiful. Most American women do. It is the secret of their charm."

"Why can't these American women stay in their own country? They are always telling us that it is the Paradise for women."

"It is. That is the reason why, like Eve, they are so excessively anxious to get out of it," said Lord Henry. "Good-bye, Uncle George. I shall be late for lunch, if I stop any longer. Thanks for giving me the information I wanted. I always like to know everything about my new friends, and nothing about my old ones."

"Where are you lunching, Harry?"

"At Aunt Agatha's. I have asked myself and Mr. Gray. He is her latest *protégé*."

"Humph! tell your Aunt Agatha, Harry, not to bother me any more with her charity appeals. I am sick of them. Why, the good woman thinks that I have nothing to do but to write cheques for her silly fads."

"All right, Uncle George, I'll tell her, but it won't have any effect. Philanthropic people lose all sense of humanity. It is their distinguishing characteristic."

The old gentleman growled approvingly, and rang the bell for his servant. Lord Henry passed up the low arcade into Burlington Street, and turned his steps in the direction of Berkeley Square.

So that was the story of Dorian Gray's parentage. Crudely as it had been told to him, it had yet stirred him by its suggestion of a strange almost modern romance. A beautiful woman risking everything for a mad passion. A few wild weeks of happiness cut short by a hideous, treacherous crime. Months of voiceless agony, and then a child born in pain. The mother snatched away by death, the boy left to solitude and the tyranny of an old and loveless man. Yes; it was an interesting background. It posed the lad, made him more perfect as it were. Behind every exquisite thing that existed, there was something tragic. Worlds had to be in travail, that the meanest flower might blow. . . . And how charming he had been at dinner the night before, as with startled eyes and lips parted in frightened pleasure he had sat opposite to him at the Club, the red candleshades staining to a richer rose the wakening wonder of his face. Talking to him was like playing upon an exquisite violin. He answered to every touch and thrill of the bow. . . . There was something terribly enthralling in the exercise of influence. No other activity was like it. To project one's soul into some gracious form, and let it tarry there for a moment; to hear one's own intellectual views echoed back to one with all the added music of passion and youth; to convey one's temperament into another as though it were a subtle fluid or a strange perfume: there was a real joy in that—perhaps the most satisfying joy left to us in an age so limited and vulgar as our own, an age grossly carnal in its pleasures, and grossly common in its aims. . . . He was a marvellous type, too, this lad, whom by so curious a chance he had met in Basil's studio, or could be fashioned into a marvellous type, at any rate. Grace was his, and the white purity of boyhood, and beauty such as old Greek marbles kept for us. There was nothing that one could not do with him. He could be made a Titan or a toy. What a pity it was that such beauty was destined to fade! . . . And Basil? From a psychological point of view, how interesting he was! The new manner in art, the fresh mode of looking at life, suggested so strangely by the merely visible presence of one who was unconscious of it all; the silent spirit that dwelt in dim woodland, and walked unseen in open field, suddenly showing herself, Dryad-like and not afraid, because in his soul who sought for her there had been wakened that wonderful vision to which alone are wonderful things revealed; the mere shapes and patterns of things becoming, as it were, refined, and gaining a kind of symbolical value, as though they were themselves patterns of some other and more perfect form whose shadow they made real: how strange it all was! He remembered something like it in history. Was it not Plato, the artist in thought, who had first analyzed it? Was it not Buonarotti who had carved it in the coloured marbles of a sonnet-sequence? But in our own century it was strange. . . . Yes; he would try to be to Dorian Gray what, without knowing it, the lad was to the painter who had fashioned the wonderful portrait. He would seek to dominate him—had already, indeed, half done so. He would make that wonderful spirit his own. There was something fascinating in this son of Love and Death.

Suddenly he stopped, and glanced up at the houses. He found that he had passed his aunt's some distance, and, smiling to himself, turned back. When he entered the somewhat sombre hall, the butler told him that they had gone in to lunch. He gave one of the footmen his hat and stick, and passed into the dining-room.

"Late as usual, Harry," cried his aunt, shaking her head at him.

He invented a facile excuse, and having taken the vacant seat next to her, looked round to see who was there. Dorian bowed to him shyly from the end of the table, a flush of pleasure stealing into his cheek. Opposite was the Duchess of Harley, a lady of admirable good-nature and good temper, much liked by every one who knew her, and of those ample architectural proportions that in women who are not Duchesses are described by contemporary historians as stoutness. Next to her sat, on her right, Sir Thomas Burden, a Radical member of Parliament, who followed his leader in public life, and in private life followed the best cooks, dining with the Tories, and thinking with the Liberals, in accordance with a wise and well-known rule. The post on her left was occupied by Mr. Erskine of Treadley, an old gentleman of considerable charm and culture, who had fallen, however, into bad habits of silence, having, as he explained once to Lady Agatha, said everything that he had to say before he was thirty. His own neighbour was Mrs. Vandeleur, one of his aunt's oldest friends, a perfect saint amongst women, but so dreadfully dowdy that she reminded one of a badly bound hymn-book. Fortunately for him she had on the other side Lord Faudel, a most intelligent middle-aged mediocrity, as bald as a Ministerial statement in the House of Commons, with whom she was conversing in that intensely earnest manner which is the one unpardonable error, as he remarked once himself, that all really good people fall into, and from which none of them ever quite escape.

"We are talking about poor Dartmoor, Lord Henry," cried the Duchess, nodding pleasantly to him across the table. "Do you think he will really marry this fascinating young person?"

"I believe she had made up her mind to propose to him, Duchess."

"How dreadful!" exclaimed Lady Agatha. "Really, some one should interfere."

"I am told, on excellent authority, that her father keeps an American dry-goods store," said Sir Thomas Burden, looking supercilious.

"My uncle has already suggested pork-packing, Sir Thomas."

"Dry-goods! What are American Dry-goods?" asked the Duchess, raising her large hands in wonder, and accentuating the verb.

"American novels," answered Lord Henry, helping himself to some quail.

The Duchess looked puzzled.

"Don't mind him, my dear," whispered Lady Agatha. "He never means anything that he says."

"When America was discovered," said the Radical member, and he began to give some wearisome facts. Like all people who try to exhaust a subject, he exhausted his listeners. The Duchess sighed, and exercised her privilege of interruption. "I wish to goodness it never had been discovered at all!" she exclaimed. "Really, our girls have no chance nowadays. It is most unfair."

"Perhaps, after all, America never has been discovered," said Mr. Erskine; "I myself would say that it had merely been detected."

"Oh! but I have seen specimens of the inhabitants," answered the Duchess, vaguely. "I must confess that most of them are extremely pretty. And they dress well, too. They get all their dresses in Paris. I wish I could afford to do the same."

"They say that when good Americans die they go to Paris," chuckled Sir Thomas, who had a large wardrobe of Humour's cast-off clothes.

"Really! And where do bad Americans go to when they die?" inquired the Duchess.

"They go to America," murmured Lord Henry.

Sir Thomas frowned. "I am afraid that your nephew is prejudiced against that great country," he said to Lady Agatha. "I have travelled all over it, in cars provided by the directors, who, in such matters, are extremely civil. I assure you that it is an education to visit."

"But must we really see Chicago in order to be educated?" asked Mr. Erskine, plaintively. "I don't feel up to the journey."

Sir Thomas waved his hand. "Mr. Erskine of Treadley has the world on his shelves. We practical men like to see things, not to read about them. The Americans are an extremely interesting people. They are absolutely reasonable. I think that is their distinguishing characteristic. Yes, Mr. Erskine, an absolutely reasonable people. I assure you there is no nonsense about the Americans."

"How dreadful!" cried Lord Henry. "I can stand brute force, but brute reason is quite unbearable. There is something unfair about its use. It is hitting below the intellect."

"I do not understand you," said Sir Thomas, growing rather red.

"I do, Lord Henry," murmured Mr. Erskine, with a smile.

"Paradoxes are all very well in their way. . . ." rejoined the Baronet.

"Was that a paradox?" asked Mr. Erskine. "I did not think so. Perhaps it was. Well, the way of paradoxes is the way of truth. To test Reality we must see it on the tight-rope. When the Verities become acrobats we can judge them."

"Dear me!" said Lady Agatha, "how you men argue! I am sure I never can make out what you are talking about. Oh! Harry, I am quite vexed with you. Why do you try to persuade our nice Mr. Dorian Gray to give up the East End? I assure you he would be quite valuable. They would love his playing."

"I want him to play to me," cried Lord Henry, smiling, and he looked down the table and caught a bright answering glance.

"But they are so unhappy in Whitechapel," continued Lady Agatha.

"I can sympathize with everything, except suffering," said Lord Henry, shrugging his shoulders. "I cannot sympathize with that. It is too ugly, too horrible, too distressing. There is something terribly morbid in the modern sympathy with pain. One should sympathize with the colour, the beauty, the joy of life. The less said about life's sores the better."

"Still, the East End is a very important problem," remarked Sir Thomas, with a grave shake of the head.

"Quite so," answered the young lord. "It is the problem of slavery, and we try to solve it by amusing the slaves."

The politician looked at him keenly. "What change do you propose, then?" he asked.

Lord Henry laughed. "I don't desire to change anything in England except the weather," he answered. "I am quite content with philosophic contemplation. But, as the nineteenth century has gone bankrupt through an over-expenditure of sympathy, I would suggest that we should appeal to Science to put us straight. The advantage of the emotions is that they lead us astray, and the advantage of Science is that it is not emotional."

"But we have such grave responsibilities," ventured Mrs. Vandeleur, timidly.

"Terribly grave," echoed Lady Agatha.

Lord Henry looked over at Mr. Erskine. "Humanity takes itself too seriously.

It is the world's original sin. If the caveman had known how to laugh, History would have been different."

"You are really very comforting," warbled the Duchess. "I have always felt rather guilty when I came to see your dear aunt, for I take no interest at all in the East End. For the future I shall be able to look her in the face without a blush."

"A blush is very becoming, Duchess," remarked Lord Henry.

"Only when one is young," she answered. "When an old woman like myself blushes, it is a very bad sign. Ah! Lord Henry, I wish you would tell me how to become young again."

He thought for a moment. "Can you remember any great error that you committed in your early days, Duchess?" he asked, looking at her across the table.

"A great many, I fear," she cried.

"Then commit them over again," he said, gravely. "To get back one's youth, one has merely to repeat one's follies."

"A delightful theory!" she exclaimed. "I must put it into practice."

"A dangerous theory!" came from Sir Thomas's tight lips. Lady Agatha shook her head, but could not help being amused. Mr. Erskine listened.

"Yes," he continued, "that is one of the great secrets of life. Nowadays most people die of a sort of creeping common sense, and discover when it is too late that the only things one never regrets are one's mistakes."

A laugh ran round the table.

He played with the idea, and grew willful; tossed it into the air and transformed it; let it escape and recaptured it; made it iridescent with fancy, and winged it with paradox. The praise of folly, as he went on, soared into a philosophy, and Philosophy herself became young, and catching the mad music of Pleasure, wearing, one might fancy, her wine-stained robe and wreath of ivy, danced like a Bacchante over the hills of life, and mocked the slow Silenus for being sober. Facts fled before her like frightened forest things. Her white feet trod the huge press at which wise Omar sits, till the seething grape-juice rose round her bare limbs in waves of purple bubbles, or crawled in red foam over the vat's black, dripping, sloping sides. It was an extraordinary improvisation. He felt that the eyes of Dorian Gray were fixed on him, and the consciousness that amongst his audience there was one whose temperament he wished to fascinate, seemed to give his wit keenness, and to lend colour to his imagination. He was brilliant, fantastic, irresponsible. He charmed his listeners out of themselves, and

TO GET BACK ONE'S YOUTH, ONE HAS MERELY TO REPEAT ONE'S FOLLIES.

they followed his pipe laughing. Dorian Gray never took his gaze off him, but sat like one under a spell, smiles chasing each other over his lips, and wonder growing grave in his darkening eyes.

At last, liveried in the costume of the age, Reality entered the room in the shape of a servant to tell the Duchess that her carriage was waiting. She wrung her hands in mock despair. "How annoying!" she cried. "I must go. I have to call for my husband at the club, to take him to some absurd meeting at Willis's Rooms, where he is going to be in the chair. If I am late he is sure to be furious, and I couldn't have a scene in this bonnet. It is far too fragile. A harsh word would ruin it. No, I must go, dear Agatha. Good-bye, Lord Henry, you are quite delightful, and dreadfully demoralizing. I am sure I don't know what to say about your views. You must come and dine with us some night. Tuesday? Are you disengaged Tuesday?"

"For you I would throw over anybody, Duchess," said Lord Henry with a bow.

"Ah! that is very nice, and very wrong of you," she cried; "so mind you come;" and she swept out of the room, followed by Lady Agatha and the other ladies.

When Lord Henry had sat down again, Mr. Erskine moved round, and taking a chair close to him, placed his hand upon his arm.

"You talk books away," he said; "why don't you write one?"

"I am too fond of reading books to care to write them, Mr. Erskine. I should like to write a novel certainly, a novel that would be as lovely as a Persian carpet and as unreal. But there is no literary public in England for anything except newspapers, primers, and encyclopaedias. Of all people in the world the English have the least sense of the beauty of literature. "

"I fear you are right," answered Mr. Erskine. "I myself used to have literary ambitions, but I gave them up long ago. And now, my dear young friend, if you will allow me to call you so, may I ask if you really meant all that you said to us at lunch?"

"I quite forget what I said," smiled Lord Henry. "Was it all very bad?"

"Very bad indeed. In fact I consider you extremely dangerous, and if anything happens to our good Duchess we shall all look on you as being primarily responsible. But I should like to talk to you about life. The generation into which I was born was tedious. Some day, when you are tired of London, come down to Treadley, and expound to me your philosophy of pleasure over some admirable Burgundy I am fortunate enough to possess."

"I shall be charmed. A visit to Treadley would be a great privilege. It has a perfect host, and a perfect library."

"You will complete it," answered the old gentleman, with a courteous bow. "And now I must bid good-bye to your excellent aunt. I am due at the Athenaeum. It is the hour when we sleep there."

"All of you, Mr. Erskine?"

"Forty of us, in forty arm-chairs. We are practicing for an English Academy of Letters."

Lord Henry laughed, and rose. "I am going to the Park," he cried.

As he was passing out of the door Dorian Gray touched him on the arm. "Let me come with you," he murmured.

"But I thought you had promised Basil Hallward to go and see him," answered Lord Henry.

"I would sooner come with you; yes, I feel I must come with you. Do let me. And you will promise to talk to me all the time? No one talks so wonderfully as you do."

"Ah! I have talked quite enough for to-day," said Lord Henry, smiling. "All I want now is to look at life. You may come and look at it with me, if you care to."

CHAPTER IV

ONE AFTERNOON, A month later, Dorian Gray was reclining in a luxurious arm-chair, in the little library of Lord Henry's house in Mayfair. It was, in its way, a very charming room, with its high panelled wainscoting of olive-stained oak, its cream-coloured frieze and ceiling of raised plaster-work, and its brick-dust felt carpet strewn with silk long-fringed Persian rugs. On a tiny satin-wood table stood a statuette by Clodion, and beside it lay a copy of "Les Cent Nouvelles," bound for Margaret of Valois by Clovis Eve, and powdered with the gilt daisies that Queen had selected for her device. Some large blue china jars and parrot-tulips were ranged on the mantelshelf, and through the small leaded panes of the window streamed the apricot-coloured light of a summer day in London.

Lord Henry had not yet come in. He was always late on principle, his principle being that punctuality is the thief of time. So the lad was looking rather sulky, as with listless fingers he turned over the pages of an elaborately-illustrated edition of "Manon Lescaut" that he had found in one of the bookcases. The formal monotonous ticking of the Louis Quatorze clock annoyed him. Once or twice he thought of going away.

At last he heard a step outside, and the door opened. "How late you are, Harry!" he murmured.

"I am afraid it is not Harry, Mr. Gray," answered a shrill voice.

He glanced quickly round, and rose to his feet. "I beg your pardon. I thought—"

"You thought it was my husband. It is only his wife. You must let me introduce myself. I know you quite well by your photographs. I think my husband has got seventeen of them."

"Not seventeen, Lady Henry?"

"Well, eighteen, then. And I saw you with him the other night at the Opera." She laughed nervously as she spoke, and watched him with her vague forget-me-not eyes. She was a curious woman, whose dresses always looked as if they had been designed in a rage and put on in a tempest. She was usually in love with somebody, and, as her passion was never returned, she had kept all her illusions. She tried to look picturesque, but only succeeded in being untidy. Her name was Victoria, and she had a perfect mania for going to church.

"That was at 'Lohengrin,' Lady Henry, I think?"

"Yes; it was at dear 'Lohengrin.' I like Wagner's music better than anybody's. It is so loud that one can talk the whole time without other people hearing what one says. That is a great advantage: don't you think so, Mr. Gray?"

The same nervous staccato laugh broke from her thin lips, and her fingers began to play with a long tortoise-shell paper-knife.

Dorian smiled, and shook his head: "I am afraid I don't think so, Lady Henry. I never talk during music—at least, during good music. If one hears bad music, it is one's duty to drown it in conversation."

"Ah! that is one of Harry's views, isn't it, Mr. Gray? I always hear Harry's views from his friends. It is the only way I get to know of them. But you must not think I don't like good music. I adore it, but I am afraid of it. It makes me too romantic. I have simply worshipped pianists—two at a time, sometimes, Harry tells me. I don't know what it is about them. Perhaps it is that they are foreigners. They all are, ain't they? Even those that are born in England become foreigners after a time, don't they? It is so clever of them, and such a compliment to art. Makes it quite cosmopolitan, doesn't it? You have never been to any of my parties, have you, Mr. Gray? You must come. I can't afford orchids, but I spare no expense in foreigners. They make one's rooms look so picturesque. But here is Harry!—Harry, I came in to look for you, to ask you something—I forget what it was—and I found Mr. Gray here. We have had such a pleasant chat about music. We have quite the same ideas. No; I think our ideas are quite different. But he has been most pleasant. I am so glad I've seen him."

"I am charmed, my love, quite charmed," said Lord Henry, elevating his dark crescent-shaped eyebrows and looking at them both with an amused smile. "So sorry I am late, Dorian. I went to look after a piece of old brocade in Wardour Street, and had to bargain for hours for it. Nowadays people know the price of everything, and the value of nothing."

"I am afraid I must be going," exclaimed Lady Henry, breaking an awkward silence with her silly sudden laugh. "I promised to drive with the Duchess. Good-bye, Mr. Gray. Good-bye Harry. You are dining out, I suppose? So am I. Perhaps I shall see you at Lady Thornbury's. "

"I dare say, my dear," said Lord Henry, shutting the door behind her, as, looking like a bird of paradise that had been out all night in the rain, she flitted out of the room, leaving a faint odour of frangipanni. Then he lit a cigarette, and flung himself down on the sofa.

"Never marry a woman with straw-coloured hair, Dorian," he said, after a few puffs.

"Why, Harry?"

"Because they are so sentimental."

"But I like sentimental people."

"Never marry at all, Dorian. Men marry because they are tired; women, because they are curious: both are disappointed."

"I don't think I am likely to marry, Harry. I am too much in love. That is one of your aphorisms. I am putting it into practice, as I do everything that you say."

"Who are you in love with?" asked Lord Henry, after a pause.

"With an actress," said Dorian Gray, blushing.

Lord Henry shrugged his shoulders. "That is a rather commonplace *début*."

"You would not say so if you saw her, Harry."

"Who is she?"

"Her name is Sibyl Vane."

"Never heard of her."

"No one has. People will some day, however. She is a genius."

"My dear boy, no woman is a genius. Women are a decorative sex. They never have anything to say, but they say it charmingly. Women represent the triumph of matter over mind, just as men represent the triumph of mind over morals."

"Harry, how can you?"

"My dear Dorian, it is quite true. I am analyzing women at present, so I ought to know. The subject is not so abstruse as I thought it was. I find that, ultimately, there are only two kinds of women, the plain and the coloured. The plain women are very useful. If you want to gain a reputation for respectability, you have merely to take them down to supper. The other women are very charming. They commit one mistake, however. They paint in order to try and look young. Our grandmothers painted in order to try and talk brilliantly. *Rouge* and *esprit* used to go together. That is all over now. As long as a woman can look ten years younger than her own daughter, she is perfectly satisfied. As for conversation, there are only five women in London worth talking to, and two of these can't be admitted into decent society. However, tell me about your genius. How long have you known her?"

"Ah! Harry, your views terrify me."

"Never mind that. How long have you known her?"

"About three weeks."

"And where did you come across her?"

"I will tell you, Harry; but you mustn't be unsympathetic about it. After all, it never would have happened if I had not met you. You filled me with a wild desire to know everything about life. For days after I met you, something seemed to throb in my veins. As I lounged in the Park, or strolled down Piccadilly, I used to look at every one who passed me, and wonder, with a mad curiosity, what sort of lives they led. Some of them fascinated me. Others filled me with terror. There was an exquisite poison in the air. I had a passion for sensations. . . . Well, one evening about seven o'clock, I determined to go out in search of some adventure. I felt that this grey, monstrous London of ours, with its myriads of people, its sordid sinners, and its splendid sins, as you once phrased it, must have something in store for me. I fancied a thousand things. The mere danger gave me a sense of delight. I remembered what you had said to me on that wonderful evening when we first dined together, about the search for beauty being the real secret of life. I don't know what I expected, but I went out and wandered eastward, soon losing my way in a labyrinth of grimy streets and black, grassless squares. About half-past eight I passed by an absurd little theatre, with great flaring gas-jets and gaudy play-bills. A hideous Jew, in the most amazing waistcoat I ever beheld in my life, was standing at the entrance, smoking a vile cigar. He had greasy ringlets, and an enormous diamond blazed in the centre of a soiled shirt. 'Have a box, my Lord?' he said, when he saw me, and he took off his hat with an air of gorgeous servility. There was something about him, Harry, that amused me. He was such a monster. You will laugh at me, I know, but I really went in and paid a whole guinea for the stage-box. To the present day I can't make out why I did so; and yet if I hadn't—my dear Harry, if I hadn't I should have missed the greatest romance of my life. I see you are laughing. It is horrid of you!"

"I am not laughing, Dorian; at least I am not laughing at you. But you should not say the greatest romance of your life. You should say the first romance of your life. You will always be loved, and you will always be in love with love. A *grande passion* is the privilege of people who have nothing to do. That is the one use of the idle classes of a country. Don't be afraid. There are exquisite things in store for you. This is merely the beginning."

"Do you think my nature so shallow?" cried Dorian Gray, angrily.

"No; I think your nature so deep."

"How do you mean?"

"My dear boy, the people who love only once in their lives are really the shallow people. What they call their loyalty, and their fidelity, I call either the lethargy of custom or their lack of imagination. Faithfulness is to the emotional life what consistency is to the life of the intellect—simply a confession of failure. Faithfulness! I must analyze it some day. The passion for property is in it. There are many things that we would throw away if we were not afraid that others might pick them up. But I don't want to interrupt you. Go on with your story."

"Well, I found myself seated in a horrid little private box, with a vulgar drop-scene staring me in the face. I looked out from behind the curtain, and surveyed the house. It was a tawdry affair, all Cupids and cornucopias, like a third-rate wedding-cake. The gallery and pit were fairly full, but the two rows of dingy stalls quite empty, and there was hardly a person in what I suppose they called the dress-circle. Women went about with oranges and ginger-beer, and there was a terrible consumption of nuts going on."

"It must have been just like the palmy days of the British Drama."

"Just like, I should fancy, and very depressing. I began to wonder what on earth I should do, when I caught sight of the play-bill. What do you think the play was, Harry?"

"I should think 'The Idiot Boy, or Dumb but Innocent.' Our fathers used to like that sort of piece, I believe. The longer I live, Dorian, the more keenly I feel that whatever was good enough for our fathers is not good enough for us. In art, as in politics, *les grandpéres ont toujours tort*."

"This play was good enough for us, Harry. It was 'Romeo and Juliet.' I must admit that I was rather annoyed at the idea of seeing Shakespeare done in such a wretched hole of a place. Still, I felt interested, in a sort of way. At any rate, I determined to wait for the first act. There was a dreadful orchestra, presided over by a young Hebrew who sat at a cracked piano, that nearly drove me away, but at last the drop-scene was drawn up, and the play began. Romeo was a stout elderly gentleman, with corked eyebrows, a husky tragedy voice, and a figure like a beer-barrel. Mercutio was almost as bad. He was played by the low-comedian, who had introduced gags of his own and was on most friendly terms with the pit. They were both as grotesque as the scenery, and that looked as if it had come out of a country-booth. But Juliet! Harry, imagine a girl, hardly seventeen years of age, with a little flower-like face, a small Greek head with plaited coils of dark-brown hair, eyes that were violet wells of passion, lips that were like the petals of a rose. She was the loveliest thing I had ever seen in my life. You said to me once that pathos left you unmoved, but that beauty, mere beauty, could fill your eyes with tears. I tell you, Harry, I could hardly see this girl for the mist of tears that came across me. And her voice—I never heard such a voice. It was very low at first, with deep mellow notes, that seemed to fall singly upon one's ear. Then it became a little louder, and sounded like a flute or a distant hautbois. In the garden-scene it had all the tremulous ecstasy that one hears just before dawn when nightingales are singing. There were moments, later on, when it had the wild passion of violins. You know how a voice can stir one. Your voice and the voice of Sibyl Vane are two things that I shall never forget. When I close my eyes, I hear them, and each of them says something different. I don't know which to follow. Why should I not love her? Harry, I do love her. She is everything to me in life. Night after night I go to see her play. One evening she is Rosalind, and the next evening she is Imogen. I have seen her die in the gloom of a Italian tomb, sucking the poison from her lover's lips. I have watched her wandering through the forest of Arden, disguised as a pretty boy in hose and doublet and dainty cap. She has been mad, and has come into the presence of a guilty king, and given him rue to wear, and bitter herbs to taste of. She has been innocent, and the black hands of jealousy have crushed her reed-like throat. I have seen her in every age and in every costume. Ordinary women never appeal to one's imagination. They are limited to their century. No glamour ever transfigures them. One knows their minds as easily as one knows their bonnets. One can always find them. There is no mystery in any of them. They ride in the Park in the morning, and chatter at tea-parties in the afternoon. They have their stereotyped smile, and their fashionable manner. They are quite obvious. But an actress! How different an actress is! Harry! why didn't you tell me that the one thing worth loving is an actress?"

"Because I have loved so many of them, Dorian."

"Oh, yes, horrid people with dyed hair and painted faces."

"Don't run down dyed hair and painted faces. There is an extraordinary charm in them, sometimes," said Lord Henry.

"I wish now I had not told you about Sibyl Vane."

"You could not have helped telling me, Dorian. All through your life you will tell me everything you do."

"Yes, Harry, I believe that is true. I cannot help telling you things. You have a curious influence over me. If I ever did a crime, I would come and confess it to you. You would understand me."

"People like you—the wilful sunbeams of life—don't commit crimes, Dorian. But I am much obliged for the compliment, all the same. And now tell me—reach me the matches, like a good boy: thanks:—what are your actual relations with Sibyl Vane?"

Dorian Gray leaped to his feet, with flushed cheeks and burning eye. "Harry! Sibyl Vane is sacred!"

"It is only the sacred things that are worth touching, Dorian," said Lord Henry, with a strange touch of pathos in his voice. "But why should you be annoyed? I suppose she will belong to you some day. When one is in love, one always begins by deceiving one's self, and one always ends by deceiving others. That is what the world calls a romance. You know her, at any rate, I suppose?"

"Of course I know her. On the first night I was at the theatre, the horrid old Jew came round to the box after the performance was over, and offered to take me behind the scenes and introduce me to her. I was furious with him, and told him that Juliet had been dead for hundreds of years, and that her body was lying in a marble tomb in Verona. I think, from his blank look of amazement, that he was under the impression that I had taken too much champagne, or something."

"I am not surprised."

"Then he asked me if I wrote for any of the newspapers. I told him I never even read them. He seemed terribly disappointed at that, and confided to me that all the dramatic critics were in a conspiracy against him, and that they were every one of them to be bought."

"I should not wonder if he was quite right there. But, on the other hand, judging from their appearance, most of them cannot be at all expensive."

"Well, he seemed to think that they were beyond his means," laughed

Dorian. "By this time, however, the lights were being put out in the theatre, and I had to go. He wanted me to try some cigars that he strongly recommended. I declined. The next night, of course, I arrived at the place again. When he saw me he made me a low bow, and assured me that I was a munificent patron of art. He was a most offensive brute, though he had an extraordinary passion for Shakespeare. He told me once, with an air of pride, that his five bankruptcies were entirely due to 'The Bard,' as he insisted on calling him. He seemed to think it a distinction."

"It was a distinction, my dear Dorian—a great distinction. Most people become bankrupt through having invested too heavily in the prose of life. To have ruined one's self over poetry is an honour. But when did you first speak to Miss Sibyl Vane?"

"The third night. She had been playing Rosalind. I could not help going round. I had thrown her some flowers, and she had looked at me; at least I fancied that she had. The old Jew was persistent. He seemed determined to take me behind, so I consented. It was curious my not wanting to know her, wasn't it?"

"No; I don't think so."

"My dear Harry, why?"

"I will tell you some other time. Now I want to know about the girl."

"Sibyl? Oh, she was so shy, and so gentle. There is something of a child about her. Her eyes opened wide in exquisite wonder when I told her what I thought of her performance, and she seemed quite unconscious of her power. I think we were both rather nervous. The old Jew stood grinning at the doorway of the dusty greenroom, making elaborate speeches about us both, while we stood looking at each other like children. He would insist on calling me 'My Lord,' so I had to assure Sibyl I that I was not anything of the kind. She said quite simply to me, 'You look more like a prince. I must call you Prince Charming.'"

"Upon my word, Dorian, Miss Sibyl knows how to pay compliments."

"You don't understand her, Harry. She regarded me merely as a person in a play. She knows nothing of life. She lives with her mother, a faded tired woman who played Lady Capulet in a sort of magenta dressing-wrapper on the first night, and looks as if she had seen better days."

"I know the look. It depresses me," murmured Lord Henry, examining his rings.

"The Jew wanted to tell me her history, but I said it did not interest me."

"You were quite right. There is always something infinitely mean about other people's tragedies."

"Sibyl is the only thing I care about. What is it to me where she came from? From her little head to her little feet, she is absolutely and entirely divine. Every night of my life I go to see her act, and every night she is more marvellous."

"That is the reason, I suppose, that you never dine with me now. I thought you must have some curious romance on hand. You have; but it is not quite what I expected."

"My dear Harry, we either lunch or sup together every day, and I have been to the Opera with you several times," said Dorian, opening his blue eyes in wonder.

"You always come dreadfully late."

"Well, I can't help going to see Sibyl play," he cried, "even if it is only for a single act. I get hungry for her presence; and when I think of the wonderful soul that is hidden away in that little ivory body, I am filled with awe."

"You can dine with me to-night, Dorian, can't you?"

He shook his head. "To-night she is Imogen," he answered, "and to-morrow night she will be Juliet."

"When is she Sibyl Vane?"

"Never."

"I congratulate you."

"How horrid you are! She is all the great heroines of the world in one. She is more than an individual. You laugh, but I tell you she has genius. I love her, and I must make her love me. You, who know all the secrets of life, tell me how to charm Sibyl Vane to love me! I want to make Romeo jealous. I want the dead lovers of the world to hear our laughter, and grow sad. I want a breath of our passion to stir their dust into consciousness, to wake their ashes into pain. My God, Harry, how I worship her!" He was walking up and down the room as he spoke. Hectic spots of red burned on his cheeks. He was terribly excited.

Lord Henry watched him with a subtle sense of pleasure. How different he was now from the shy, frightened boy he had met in Basil Hallward's studio. His nature had developed like a flower, had borne blossoms of scarlet flame. Out of its secret hiding-place had crept his Soul, and Desire had come to meet it on the way.

"And what do you propose to do?" said Lord Henry, at last.

"I want you and Basil to come with me some night and see her act. I have not the slightest fear of the result. You are certain to acknowledge her genius. Then we must get her out of the Jew's hands. She is bound to him for three years—at least for two years and eight months—from the present time. I shall have to pay him something, of course. When all that is settled, I shall take a West

End theatre and bring her out properly. She will make the world as mad as she has made me."

"That would be impossible, my dear boy."

"Yes, she will. She has not merely art, consummate art-instinct, in her, but she has personality also; and you have often told me that it is personalities, not principles, that move the age."

"Well, what night shall we go?"

"Let me see. To-day is Tuesday. Let us fix to-morrow. She plays Juliet to-morrow."

"All right. The Bristol at eight o'clock; and I will get Basil."

"Not eight, Harry, please. Half-past six. We must be there before the curtain rises. You must see her in the first act, where she meets Romeo."

"Half-past six! What an hour! It will be like having a meat-tea, or reading an English novel. It must be seven. No gentleman dines before seven. Shall you see Basil between this and then? Or shall I write to him?"

"Dear Basil! I have not laid eyes on him for a week. It is rather horrid of me, as he has sent me my portrait in the most wonderful frame, specially designed by himself, and, though I am a little jealous of the picture for being a whole month younger than I am, I must admit that I delight in it. Perhaps you better write to him. I don't want to see him alone. He says things that annoy me. He gives me good advice."

Lord Henry smiled. "People are very fond of giving away what they need most themselves. It is what I call the depth of generosity."

"Oh, Basil is the best of fellows, but he seems to me to be just a bit of a Philistine. Since I have known you, Harry, I have discovered that."

"Basil, my dear boy, puts everything that is charming in him into his work. The consequence is that he has nothing left for life but his prejudices, his principles, and his common sense. The only artists I have ever known, who are personally delightful, are bad artists. Good artists exist simply in what they make, and consequently are perfectly uninteresting in what they are. A great poet, a really great poet, is the most unpoetical of all creatures. But inferior poets are absolutely fascinating. The worse their rhymes are, the more picturesque they look. The mere fact of having published a book of second-rate sonnets makes a man quite irresistible. He lives the poetry that he cannot write. The others write the poetry that they dare not realize."

"I wonder is that really so, Harry?" said Dorian Gray, putting some perfume on his handkerchief out of a large gold-topped bottle that stood on the table. "It must be, if you say it. And now I am off. Imogen is waiting for me. Don't forget about to-morrow. Good-bye."

As he left the room, Lord Henry's heavy eyelids drooped, and he began to think. Certainly few people had ever interested him so much as Dorian Gray, and yet the lad's mad adoration of some one else caused him not the slightest pang of annoyance or jealousy. He was pleased by it. It made him a more interesting study. He had been always enthralled by the methods of natural science, but the ordinary subject-matter of that science had seemed to him trivial and of no import. And so he had begun by vivisecting himself, as he had ended by vivisecting others. Human life—that appeared to him the one thing worth investigating. Compared to it there was nothing else of any value. It was true that as one watched life in its curious crucible of pain and pleasure, one could not wear over one's face a mask of glass, nor keep the sulphurous fumes from troubling the brain and making the imagination turbid with monstrous fancies and misshapen dreams. There were poisons so subtle that to know their properties one had to sicken of them. There were maladies so strange that one had to pass through them if one sought to understand their nature. And, yet, what a great reward one received! How wonderful the whole world became to one! To note the curious hard logic of passion, and the emotional coloured life of the intellect—to observe where they met, and where they separated, at what point they were in unison, and at what point they were at discord—there was a delight in that! What matter what the cost was? One could never pay too high a price for any sensation.

He was conscious—and the thought brought a gleam of pleasure into his brown agate eyes—that it was through certain words of his, musical words said with musical utterance, that Dorian Gray's soul had turned to this white girl and bowed in worship before her. To a large extent the lad was his own creation. He had made him premature. That was something. Ordinary people waited till life disclosed to them its secrets, but to the few, to the elect, the mysteries of life were revealed before the veil was drawn away. Sometimes this was the effect of art, and chiefly of the art of literature, which dealt immediately with the passions and the intellect. But now and then a complex personality took the place and assumed the office of art, was indeed, in its way, a real work of art, Life having its elaborate masterpieces, just as poetry has, or sculpture, or painting.

Yes, the lad was premature. He was gathering his harvest while it was yet spring. The pulse and passion of youth were in him, but he was becoming self-conscious. It was delightful to watch him. With his beautiful face, and his beautiful soul, he was a thing to wonder at. It was no matter how it all ended, or was destined to end. He was like one of those gracious figures in a pageant or a play, whose joys seemed to be remote from one, but whose sorrows stir one's sense of beauty, and whose wounds are like red roses.

Soul and body, body and soul—how mysterious they were! There was animalism in the soul, and the body had its moments of spirituality. The senses could refine, and the intellect could degrade. Who could say where the fleshly impulse ceased, or the psychical impulse began? How shallow were the arbitrary definitions of ordinary psychologists! And yet how difficult to decide between the claims of the various schools! Was the soul a shadow seated in the house of sin? Or was the body really in the soul, as Giordano Bruno thought? The separation of spirit from matter was a mystery, and the union of spirit with matter was a mystery also.

He began to wonder whether we could ever make psychology so absolute a science that each little spring of life would be revealed to us. As it was, we always misunderstood ourselves, and rarely understood others. Experience was of no ethical value. It was merely the name men gave to their mistakes. Moralists had, as a rule, regarded it as a mode of warning, had claimed for it a certain ethical efficacy in the formation of character, had praised it as something that taught us what to follow and showed us what to avoid. But there was no motive power in experience. It was as little of an active cause as conscience itself. All that it really demonstrated was that our future would be the same as our past, and that the sin we had done once, and with loathing, we would do many times, and with joy.

It was clear to him that the experimental method was the only method by which one could arrive at any scientific analysis of the passions; and certainly Dorian Gray was a subject made to his hand, and seemed to promise rich and fruitful results. His sudden mad love for Sibyl Vane was a psychological phenomenon of no small interest. There was no doubt that curiosity had much to do with it, curiosity and the desire for new experiences; yet it was not a simple but rather a very complex passion. What there was in it of the purely sensuous instinct of boyhood had been transformed by the workings of the imagination, changed into something that seemed to the lad himself to be remote from sense, and was for that very reason all the more dangerous. It was the passions about whose origin we deceived ourselves that tyrannized most strongly over us. Our weakest motives were those of whose nature we were conscious. It often happened that when we thought we were experimenting on others we were really experimenting on ourselves.

While Lord Henry sat dreaming on these things, a knock came to the door, and his valet entered, and reminded him it was time to dress for dinner. He got up and looked out into the street. The sunset had smitten into scarlet gold the upper windows of the houses opposite. The panes glowed like plates of heated metal. The sky above was like a faded rose. He thought of his friend's young fiery-coloured life, and wondered how it was all going to end.

When he arrived home, about half-past twelve o'clock, he saw a telegram lying on the hall table. He opened it, and found it was from Dorian Gray. It was to tell him that he was engaged to be married to Sibyl Vane.

CHAPTER V

"MOTHER, MOTHER, I am so happy!" whispered the girl, burying her face in the lap of the faded, tired-looking woman who, with back turned to the shrill intrusive light, was sitting in the one arm-chair that their dingy sitting-room contained. "I am so happy!" she repeated, "and you must be happy too!"

Mrs. Vane winced, and put her thin bismuth-whitened hands on her daughter's head. "Happy!" she echoed, "I am only happy, Sibyl, when I see you act. You must not think of anything but your acting. Mr. Isaacs has been very good to us, and we owe him money."

The girl looked up and pouted. "Money, mother?" she cried, "what does money matter? Love is more than money."

"Mr. Isaacs has advanced us fifty pounds to pay off our debts, and to get a proper outfit for James. You must not forget that, Sybil. Fifty pounds is a very large sum. Mr. Isaacs has been most considerate."

"He is not a gentleman, mother, and I hate the way he talks to me," said the girl, rising to her feet, and going over to the window.

"I don't know how we could manage without him," answered the elder woman, querulously.

Sibyl Vane tossed her head and laughed. "We don't want him any more, mother. Prince Charming rules life for us now." Then she paused. A rose shook in her blood, and shadowed her cheeks. Quick breath parted the petals of her lips. They trembled. Some southern wind of passion swept over her, and stirred the dainty folds of her dress. "I love him," she said, simply.

"Foolish child! foolish child!" was the parrot-phrase flung in answer. The waving of crooked, false-jewelled fingers gave grotesqueness to the words.

The girl laughed again. The joy of a caged bird was in her voice. Her eyes caught the melody, and echoed it in radiance: then closed for a moment, as though to hide their secret. When they opened, the mist of a dream had passed across them.

Thin-lipped wisdom spoke at her from the worn chair, hinted at prudence, quoted from that book of cowardice whose author apes the name of common sense. She did not listen. She was free in her prison of passion. Her prince, Prince Charming, was with her. She had called on Memory to remake him. She had sent her soul to search for him, and it had brought him back. His kiss burned again upon her month. Her eyelids were warm with his breath.

Then Wisdom altered its method and spoke of espial and discovery. This young man might be rich. If so, marriage should be thought of. Against the shell of her ear broke the waves of worldly cunning. The arrows of craft shot by her. She saw the thin lips moving, and smiled.

Suddenly she felt the need to speak. The wordy silence troubled her. "Mother, mother," she cried, "why does he love me so much? I know why I love him. I love him because he is like what Love himself should be. But what does he see in me? I am not worthy of him. And yet—why, I cannot tell—though I feel so much beneath him, I don't feel humble. I feel proud, terribly proud. Mother, did you love my father as I love Prince Charming?"

The elder woman grew pale beneath the coarse powder that daubed her checks, and her dry lips twitched with a spasm of pain. Sibyl rushed to her, flung her arms round her neck, and kissed her. "Forgive me, mother. I know it pains you to talk about our father. But it only pains you because you loved him so much. Don't look so sad. I am as happy to-day as you were twenty years ago. Ah! let me be happy for ever!"

"My child, you are far too young to think of falling in love. Besides, what do you know of this young man? You don't even know his name. The whole thing is most inconvenient, and really, when James is going away to Australia, and I have so much to think of, I must say that you should have shown more consideration. However, as I said before, if he is rich . . ."

"Ah! mother, mother, let me be happy!"

Mrs. Vane glanced at her, and with one of those false theatrical gestures that so often become a mode of second nature to a stage-player, clasped her in her arms. At this moment the door opened, and a young lad with rough brown hair came into the room. He was thick-set of figure, and his hands and feet were large, and somewhat clumsy in movement. He was not so finely bred as his sister. One would hardly have guessed the close relationship that existed between them.

Mrs. Vane fixed her eyes on him, and intensified her smile. She mentally elevated her son to the dignity of all audience. She felt sure that the *tableau* was interesting.

"You might keep some of your kisses, for me, Sibyl, I think," said the lad, with a good-natured grumble.

"Ah! but you don't like being kissed, Jim," she cried. "You are a dreadful old bear." And she ran across the room and hugged him.

James Vane looked into his sister's face with tenderness. "I want you to come out with me for a walk, Sibyl. I don't suppose I shall ever see this horrid London again. I am sure I don't want to."

"My son, don't say such dreadful things," murmured Mrs. Vane, taking up a tawdry theatrical dress, with a sigh, and beginning to patch it. She felt a little disappointed that he had not joined the group. It would have increased the theatrical picturesqueness of the situation.

"Why not, mother? I mean it."

"You pain me, my son. I trust you will return from Australia in a position of affluence. I believe there is no society of any kind in the Colonies, nothing that I would call society; so when you have made your fortune you must come back and assert yourself in London."

"Society!" muttered the lad. "I don't want to know anything about that. I should like to make some money to take you and Sibyl off the stage. I hate it."

"Oh, Jim!" said Sibyl, laughing, "how unkind of you! But are you really going for a walk with me? That will be nice! I was afraid you were going to say good-bye to some of your friends—to Tom Hardy, who gave you the hideous pipe, or Ned Langton, who makes fun of you for smoking it. It is very sweet of you to let me have your last afternoon. Where shall we go? Let us go to the Park."

"I am too shabby," he answered, frowning. "Only swell people go to the Park."

"Nonsense, Jim," she whispered, stroking the sleeve of his coat.

He hesitated for a moment. "Very well," he said at last, "but don't be too long dressing." She danced out of the door. One could hear her singing as she ran upstairs. Her little feet pattered overhead.

He walked up and down the room two or three times. Then he turned to the still figure in the chair. "Mother, are my things ready?" he asked.

"Quite ready, James," she answered, keeping her eyes on her work. For some months past she had felt ill at ease when she was alone with this rough, stern son of hers. Her shallow secret nature was troubled when their eyes met. She used to wonder if he suspected anything. The silence, for he made no other observation, became intolerable to her. She began to complain. Women defend themselves by attacking, just as they attack by sudden and strange surrenders. "I hope you will be contented, James, with your sea-faring life," she said. "You must remember that it is your own choice. You might have entered a solicitor's office. Solicitors are a very respectable class, and in the country often dine with the best families."

"I hate officers, and I hate clerks," he replied. "But you are quite right. I have chosen my own life. All I say is, watch over Sibyl. Don't let her come to any harm. Mother, you must watch over her."

"James, you really talk very strangely. Of course I watch over Sibyl."

"I hear a gentleman comes every night to the theatre, and goes behind to talk to her. Is that right? What about that?"

"You are speaking about things you don't understand, James. In the profession we are accustomed to receive a great deal of most gratifying attention. I myself used to receive many bouquets at one time. That was when acting was really understood. As for Sibyl, I do not know at present whether her attachment is serious or not. But there is no doubt that the young man in question is a perfect gentleman. He is always most polite to me. Besides, he has the appearance of being rich, and the flowers he sends are lovely."

"You don't know his name, though," said the lad, harshly.

"No," answered his mother, with a placid expression in her face. "He has not yet revealed his real name. I think it is quite romantic of him. He is probably a member of the aristocracy."

James Vane bit his lip. "Watch over Sibyl, mother," he cried, "watch over her."

"My son, you distress me very much. Sibyl is always under my special care. Of course, if this gentleman is wealthy, there is no reason why she should not contract an alliance with him. I trust he is one of the aristocracy. He has all the appearance of it, I must say. It might be a most brilliant marriage for Sibyl. They would make a charming couple. His good looks are really quite remarkable; everybody notices them."

The lad muttered something to himself, and drummed on the window-pane with his coarse fingers. He had just turned round to say something, when the door opened, and Sibyl ran in.

"How serious you both are!" she cried. "What is the matter?"

"Nothing," he answered. "I suppose one must be serious sometimes. Good-bye mother; I will have my dinner at five o'clock. Everything is packed, except my shirts, so you need not trouble."

"Good-bye, my son," she answered, with a bow of strained stateliness.

She was extremely annoyed at the tone he had adopted with her, and there was something in his look that had made her feel afraid.

"Kiss me, mother," said the girl. Her flower-like lips touched the withered check, and warmed its frost.

"My child! my child!" cried Mrs. Vane, looking up to the ceiling in search of an imaginary gallery.

"Come, Sibyl," said her brother, impatiently. He hated his mother's affectations.

They went out into the flickering wind-blown sunlight, and strolled down the dreary Euston Road. The passersby glanced in wonder at the sullen, heavy youth, who, in coarse, ill-fitting clothes, was in the company of such a graceful, refined-looking girl. He was like a common gardener walking with a rose.

Jim frowned from time to time when he caught the inquisitive glance of some stranger. He had that dislike of being stared at which comes on geniuses late in life, and never leaves the commonplace. Sibyl, however, was quite unconscious of the effect she was producing. Her love was trembling in laughter on her lips. She was thinking of Prince Charming, and, that she might think of him all the more, she did not talk of him, but prattled on about the ship in which Jim was going to sail, about the gold he was certain to find, about the wonderful heiress whose life he was to save from the wicked, red-shirted bushrangers. For he was not to remain a sailor, or a super-cargo, or whatever he was going to be. Oh, no! A sailor's existence was dreadful. Fancy being cooped up in a horrid ship, with the hoarse, hump-backed waves trying to get in, and a black wind blowing the masts down, and tearing the sails into long screaming ribands! He was to leave the vessel at Melbourne, bid a polite good-bye to the captain, and go off at once to the gold-fields. Before a week was over he was to come across a large nugget of pure gold, the largest nugget that had ever been discovered, and bring it down to the coast in a waggon guarded by six mounted policemen. The bushrangers were to attack them three times, and be defeated with immense slaughter. Or, no. He was not to go to the gold-fields at all. They were horrid places, where men got intoxicated, and shot each other in bar-rooms, and used bad language. He was to be a nice sheep-farmer, and one evening, as he was riding home, he was to see the beautiful heiress being carried off by a robber on a black horse, and give chase, and rescue her. Of course she would fall in love with him, and he with her, and they would get married, and come home, and live in an immense house in

London. Yes, there were delightful things in store for him. But he must be very good, and not lose his temper, or spend his money foolishly. She was only a year older than he was, but she knew so much more of life. He must be sure, also, to write to her by every mail, and to say his prayers each night before he went to sleep. God was very good, and would watch over him. She would pray for him too, and in a few years he would come back quite rich and happy.

The lad listened sulkily to her, and made no answer. He was heart-sick at leaving home.

Yet it was not this alone that made him gloomy and morose. Inexperienced though he was, he had still a strong sense of danger of Sibyl's position. This young dandy who was making love to her could mean her no good. He was a gentleman, and he hated him for that, hated him through some curious race-instinct for which he could not account, and which for that reason was all the more dominant within him. He was conscious also of the shallowness and vanity of his mother's nature, and in that saw infinite peril for Sibyl and Sibyl's happiness. Children begin by loving their parents; as they grow older they judge them; sometimes they forgive them.

His mother! He had something on his mind to ask of her, something that he had brooded on for many months of silence. A chance phrase that he had heard at the theatre, a whispered sneer that had reached his ears one night as he waited at the stage-door, had set loose a train of horrible thoughts. He remembered it as if it had been the lash of a hunting-crop across his face. His brows knit together into a wedge-like furrow, and with a twitch of pain he bit his under-lip.

"You are not listening to a word I am saying, Jim," cried Sibyl, "and I am making the most delightful plans for your future. Do say something."

"What do you want me to say?"

"Oh! that you will be a good boy, and not forget us," she answered, smiling at him.

He shrugged his shoulders. "You are more likely to forget me, than I am to forget you, Sibyl."

She flushed. "What do you mean, Jim?" she asked.

"You have a new friend, I hear. Who is he? Why have you not told me about him? He means you no good."

"Stop, Jim!" she exclaimed. "You must not say anything against him. I love him."

"Why, you don't even know his name," answered the lad. "Who is he? I have a right to know."

"He is called Prince Charming. Don't you like the name? Oh! you silly boy! you should never forget it. If you only saw him, you would think him the most wonderful person in the world. Some day you will meet him: when you come back from Australia. You will like him so much. Everybody likes him, and I . . . love him. I wish you could come to the theatre to-night. He is going to be there, and I am to play Juliet. Oh! how I shall play it! Fancy, Jim, to be in love and play Juliet! To have him sitting there! To play for his delight! I am afraid I may frighten the company, frighten or enthrall them. To be in love is to surpass one's self. Poor dreadful Mr. Isaacs will be shouting 'genius' to his loafers at the bar. He has preached me as a dogma; to-night he will announce me as a revelation. I feel it. And it is all his, his only, Prince Charming, my wonderful lover, my god of graces. But I am poor beside him. Poor? What does that matter? When poverty creeps in at the door, love flies in through the window. Our proverbs want re-writing. They were made in winter, and it is summer now; spring-time for me, I think, a very dance of blossoms in blue skies."

"He is a gentleman," said the lad, sullenly.

"A Prince!" she cried, musically. "What more do you want?"

"He wants to enslave you."

"I shudder at the thought of being free."

"I want you to beware of him."

"To see him is to worship him, to know him is to trust him."

"Sibyl, you are mad about him."

She laughed, and took his arm. "You dear old Jim, you talk as if you were a hundred. Some day you will be in love yourself. Then you will know what it is. Don't look so sulky. Surely you should be glad to think that, though you are going away, you leave me happier than I have ever been before. Life has been hard for us both, terribly hard and difficult. But it will be different now. You are going to a new world, and I have found one. Here are two chairs; let us sit down and see the smart people go by."

They took their seats amidst a crowd of watchers. The tulip-beds across the road flamed like throbbing rings of fire. A white dust, tremulous cloud of orris-root it seemed, hung in the panting air. The brightly-coloured parasols danced and dipped like monstrous butterflies.

She made her brother talk of himself, his hopes, his prospects. He spoke slowly and with effort. They passed words to each other as players at a game pass counters. Sibyl felt oppressed. She could not communicate her joy. A faint smile curving that sullen mouth was all the echo she could win. After some time she became silent. Suddenly she caught a glimpse of golden hair and laughing lips, and in an open carriage with two ladies Dorian Gray drove past.

She started to her feet. "There he is!" she cried.

"Who?" said Jim Vane.

"Prince Charming," she answered, looking after the victoria.

He jumped up, and seized her roughly by the arm. "Show him to me. Which is he? Point him out. I must see him!" he exclaimed; but at that moment the Duke of Berwick's four-in-hand came between, and when it had left the space clear, the carriage had swept out of the Park.

"He is gone," murmured Sibyl, sadly. "I wish you had seen him."

"I wish I had, for as sure as there is a God in heaven, if he ever does you any wrong, I shall kill him."

She looked at him in horror. He repeated his words. They cut the air like a dagger. The people round began to gape. A lady standing close to her tittered.

"Come away, Jim; come away," she whispered. He followed her doggedly, as she passed through the crowd. He felt glad at what he had said.

When they reached the Achilles Statue she turned round. There was pity in her eyes that became laughter on her lips. She shook her head at him. "You are foolish, Jim, utterly foolish; a bad-tempered boy is all. How can you say such horrible things? You don't know what you are talking about. You are simply jealous and unkind. Ah! I wish you would fall in love. Love makes people good, and what you said was wicked."

"I am sixteen," he answered, "and I know what I am about. Mother is no help to you. She doesn't understand how to look after you. I wish now that I was not going to Australia at all. I have a great mind to chuck the whole thing up. I would, if my articles hadn't been signed."

"Oh, don't be so serious, Jim. You are like one of the heroes of those silly melodramas mother used to be so fond of acting in. I am not going to quarrel with you. I have seen him, and oh! to see him is perfect happiness. We won't quarrel. I know you would never harm any one I love, would you?"

"Not as long as you love him, I suppose," was the sullen answer.

"I shall love him for ever!" she cried.

"And he?"

"For ever, too!"

"He had better."

She shrank from him. Then she laughed and put her hand on his arm. He was merely a boy.

At the Marble Arch they hailed an omnibus, which left them close to their shabby home in the Euston Road. It was after five o'clock, and Sibyl had to lie down for a couple of hours before acting. Jim insisted that she should do so. He said that he would sooner part with her when their mother was not present. She would be sure to make a scene, and he detested scenes of every kind.

In Sibyl's own room they parted. There was jealousy in the lad's heart, and a fierce, murderous hatred of the stranger who, as it seemed to him, had come between them. Yet, when her arms were flung round his neck, and her fingers strayed through his hair, he softened, and kissed her with real affection. There were tears in his eyes as he went downstairs.

His mother was waiting for him below. She grumbled at his un-punctuality, as he entered. He made no answer, but sat down to his meagre meal. The flies buzzed round the table, and crawled over the stained cloth. Through the rumble of omnibuses, and the clatter of street-cabs, he could hear the droning voice devouring each minute that was left to him.

After some time, he thrust away his plate, and put his head in his hands. He felt that he had a right to know. It should have been told to him before, if it was as he suspected. Leaden with fear, his mother watched him. Words dropped mechanically from her lips. A tattered lace handkerchief twitched in her fingers. When the clock struck six, he got up, and went to the door. Then he turned back, and looked at her. Their eyes met. In hers he saw a wild appeal for mercy. It enraged him.

"Mother, I have something to ask you," he said. Her eyes wandered vaguely about the room. She made no answer. "Tell me the truth. I have a right to know. Were you married to my father?"

She heaved a deep sigh. It was a sigh of relief. The terrible moment, the moment that night and day, for weeks and months, she had dreaded, had come at last, and yet she felt no terror. Indeed in some measure of it was a disappointment to her. The vulgar distress of the question called for a direct answer. The situation had not been gradually led up to. It was crude. It reminded her of a bad rehearsal.

"No," she answered, wondering at the harsh simplicity of life.

"My father was a scoundrel then!" cried the lad, clenching his fists.

She shook her head. "I knew he was not free. We loved each other very much. If he had lived, he would have made provision for us. Don't speak against him, my son. He was your father, and a gentleman. Indeed he was highly connected."

An oath broke from his lips. "I don't care for myself," he exclaimed, "but don't let Sibyl. . . . It is a gentleman, isn't it, who is in love with her, or says he is? Highly connected, too, I suppose."

For a moment a hideous sense of humiliation came over the woman. Her head drooped. She wiped her eyes with shaking hands. "Sibyl has a mother," she murmured; "I had none."

The lad was touched. He went towards her, and stooping down he kissed her. "I am sorry if I have pained you by asking about my father," he said, "but I could not help it. I must go now. Good-bye. Don't forget that you will have only one child now to look after, and believe me that if this man wrongs my sister, I will find out who he is, track him down, and kill him like a dog. I swear it."

The exaggerated folly of the threat, the passionate gesture that accompanied it, the mad melodramatic words, made life seem more vivid to her. She was familiar with the atmosphere. She breathed more freely, and for the first time for many months she really admired her son. She would have liked to have continued the scene on the same emotional scale, but he cut her short. Trunks had to be carried down, and mufflers looked for. The lodging-house drudge bustled in and out. There was the bargaining with the cab-man. The moment was lost in vulgar details. It was with a renewed feeling of disappointment that she waved the tattered lace handkerchief from the window, as her son drove away. She was conscious that a great opportunity had been wasted. She consoled herself by telling Sibyl how desolate she felt her life would be, now that she had only one child to look after. She remembered the phrase. It had pleased her. Of the threat she said nothing. It was vividly and dramatically expressed. She felt that they would all laugh at it some day.

CHAPTER VI

"I SUPPOSE YOU have heard the news, Basil?" said Lord Henry that evening, as Hallward was shown into a little private room at the Bristol where dinner had been laid for three.

"No, Harry," answered the artist, giving his hat and coat to the bowing waiter. "What is it? Nothing about politics, I hope? They don't interest me. There is hardly a single person in the House of Commons worth painting; though many of them would be the better for a little whitewashing."

"Dorian Gray is engaged to be married," said Lord Henry, watching him as he spoke.

Halward started, and then frowned. "Dorian engaged to be married!" he cried. "Impossible!"

"It is perfectly true."

"To whom?"

"To some little actress or other."

"I can't believe it. Dorian is far too sensible."

"Dorian is far too wise not to do foolish things now and then, my dear Basil."

"Marriage is hardly a thing that one can do now and then, Harry."

"Except in America," rejoined Lord Henry, languidly. "But I didn't say he was married. I said he was engaged to be married. There is a great difference. I have a distinct remembrance of being married, but I have no recollection at all of being engaged. I am inclined to think that I never was engaged."

"But think of Dorian's birth, and position, and wealth. It would be absurd for him to marry so much beneath him."

"If you want to make him marry this girl tell him that, Basil. He is sure to do it, then. Whenever a man does a thoroughly stupid thing, it is always from the noblest motives."

"I hope the girl is good, Harry. I don't want to see Dorian tied to some vile creature, who might degrade his nature and ruin his intellect."

"Oh, she is better than good—she is beautiful," murmured Lord Henry, sipping a glass of vermouth and orange-bitters. "Dorian says she is beautiful; and he is not often wrong about things of that kind. Your portrait of him has quickened his appreciation of the personal appearance of other people. It has had that excellent effect, amongst others. We are to see her to-night, if that boy doesn't forget his appointment."

"Are you serious?"

"Quite serious, Basil. I should be miserable if I thought I should ever be more serious than I am at the present moment."

"But do you approve of it, Harry?" asked the painter, walking up and down the room, and biting his lip. "You can't approve of it, possibly. It is some silly infatuation."

"I never approve, or disapprove, of anything now. It is an absurd attitude to take towards life. We are not sent into the world to air our moral prejudices. I never take any notice of what common people say, and I never interfere with what charming people do. If a personality fascinates me, whatever mode of expression that personality selects is absolutely delightful to me. Dorian Gray falls in love with a beautiful girl who acts Juliet, and proposes to marry her. Why not? If he wedded Messalina he would be none the less interesting. You know I am not a champion of marriage. The real drawback to marriage is that it makes one unselfish. And unselfish people are colourless. They lack individuality. Still, there are certain temperaments that marriage makes more complex. They retain their egotism, and add to it many other egos. They are forced to have more than one life. They become more highly organized, and to be highly organized is, I should fancy, the object of man's existence. Besides, every experience is of value, and, whatever one may say against marriage, it is certainly an experience. I hope that Dorian Gray will make this girl his wife, passionately adore her for six months, and then suddenly become fascinated by some one else. He would be a wonderful study."

"You don't mean a single word of all that, Harry; you know you don't. If Dorian Gray's life were spoiled, no one would be sorrier than yourself. You are much better than you pretend to be."

Lord Henry laughed. "The reason we all like to think so well of others is that we are all afraid for ourselves. The basis of optimism is sheer terror. We think that we are generous because we credit our neighbour with the possession of those virtues that are likely to be a benefit to us. We praise the banker that we may overdraw our account, and find good qualities in the highwayman in the hope that he may spare our pockets. I mean everything that I have said. I have the greatest contempt for optimism. As for a spoiled life, no life is spoiled but one whose growth is arrested. If you want to mar a nature, you have merely to reform it. As for marriage, of course that would be silly, but there are other and more interesting bonds between men and women. I will certainly encourage them. They have the charm of being fashionable. But here is Dorian himself. He will tell you more than I can."

THE REAL DRAWBACK TO MARRIAGE IS THAT IT MAKES ONE UNSELFISH. AND UNSELFISH PEOPLE ARE COLOURLESS. THEY LACK INDIVIDUALITY.

"My dear Harry, my dear Basil, you must both congratulate me!" said the lad, throwing off his evening cape with its satin-lined wings, and shaking each of his friends by the hand in turn. "I have never been so happy. Of course it is sudden: all really delightful things are. And yet it seems to me to be the one thing I have been looking for all my life." He was flushed with excitement and pleasure, and looked extraordinarily handsome.

"I hope you will always be very happy, Dorian," said Hallward, "but I don't quite forgive you for not having let me know of your engagement. You let Harry know."

"And I don't forgive you for being late for dinner," broke in Lord Henry, putting his hand on the lad's shoulder, and smiling as he spoke. "Come, let us sit down and try what the new *chef* here is like, and then you will tell us how it all came about."

"There is really not much to tell," cried Dorian, as they took their seats at the small round table. "What happened was simply this. After I left you yesterday evening, Harry, I dressed, had some dinner at that little Italian restaurant in Rupert Street you introduced me to, and went down at eight o'clock to the theatre. Sibyl was playing Rosalind. Of course the scenery was dreadful, and the Orlando absurd. But Sibyl! You should have seen her! When she came on in her boy's clothes she was perfectly wonderful. She wore a moss-coloured velvet jerkin with cinnamon sleeves, slim brown cross-gartered hose, a dainty little green cap with a hawk's feather caught in a jewel, and a hooded cloak lined with dull red. She had never seemed to me more exquisite. She had all the delicate grace of that Tanagra figurine that you have in your studio, Basil. Her hair clustered round her face like dark leaves round a pale rose. As for her acting—well, you shall see her to-night. She is simply a born artist. I sat in the dingy box absolutely enthralled. I forgot that I was in London and in the nineteenth century. I was away with my love in a forest that no man had ever seen. After the performance was over I went behind, and spoke to her. As we were sitting together, suddenly there came into her eyes a look that I have never seen there before. My lips moved towards hers. We kissed each other. I can't describe to you what I felt at that moment. It seemed to me that all my life had been narrowed to one perfect point of rose-coloured joy. She trembled all over, and shook like a white narcissus. Then she flung herself on her knees and kissed my hands. I feel that I should not tell you all this, but I can't help it. Of course our engagement is a dead secret. She has not even told her own mother. I don't know what my guardians will say. Lord Radley is sure to be furious. I don't care. I shall be of age in less than a year, and then I can do what I like. I have been right, Basil, haven't I, to take my love out of poetry, and to find my wife in Shakespeare's plays? Lips that Shakespeare taught to speak have whispered their secret in my ear. I have had the arms of Rosalind around me, and kissed Juliet on the mouth."

"Yes, Dorian, I suppose you were right," said Hallward, slowly.

"Have you seen her to-day?" asked Lord Henry

Dorian Gray shook his head. "I left her in the forest of Arden, I shall find her in an orchard in Verona."

Lord Henry sipped his champagne in a meditative manner. "At what particular point did you mention the word marriage, Dorian? And what did she say in answer? Perhaps you forgot all about it."

"My dear Harry, I did not treat it as a business transaction, and I did not make any formal proposal. I told her that I loved her, and she said she was not worthy to be my wife. Not worthy! Why, the whole world is nothing to me compared with her."

"Women are wonderfully practical," murmured Lord Henry,—"much more practical than we are. In situations of that kind we often forget to say anything about marriage, and they always remind us."

Hallward laid his hand upon his arm. "Don't, Harry. You have annoyed Dorian. He is not like other men. He would never bring misery upon any one. His nature is too fine for that."

Lord Henry looked across the table. "Dorian is never annoyed with me," he answered. "I asked the question for the best reason possible, for the only reason, indeed, that excuses one for asking any question—simple curiosity. I have a theory that it is always the women who propose to us, and not we who propose to the women. Except, of course, in middle-class life. But then the middle classes are not modern."

Dorian Gray laughed, and tossed his head. "You are quite incorrigible, Harry; but I don't mind. It is impossible to be angry with you. When you see Sibyl Vane you will feel that the man who could wrong her would be a beast, a beast without a heart. I cannot understand how any one can wish to shame the thing he loves. I love Sibyl Vane. I want to place her on a pedestal of gold, and to see the world worship the woman who is mine. What is marriage? An irrevocable vow. You mock at it for that. Ah! don't mock. It is an irrevocable vow that I want to take. Her trust makes me faithful, her belief makes me good. When I am with her, I regret all that you have taught me. I become different from what you have known me to be. I am changed, and the mere touch of Sibyl Vane's, hand makes me forget you and all your wrong, fascinating, poisonous, delightful theories."

"And those are . . . ?" asked Lord Henry, helping himself to some salad.

"Oh, your theories about life, your theories about love, your theories about pleasure. All your theories, in fact, Harry."

"Pleasure is the only thing worth having a theory about," he answered, in his slow, melodious voice. "But I am afraid I cannot claim my theory as my own. It belongs to Nature, not to me. Pleasure is Nature's test, her sign of approval. When we are happy we are always good, but when we are good we are not always happy."

"Ah! but what do you mean by good?" cried Basil Hallward.

"Yes," echoed Dorian, leaning back in his chair, and looking at Lord Henry over the heavy clusters of purple-lipped irises that stood in the centre of the table, "what do you mean by good, Harry?"

"To be good is to be in harmony with one's self," he replied, touching the thin stem of his glass with his pale, fine-pointed fingers. "Discord is to be forced to be in harmony with others. One's own life—that is the important thing. As for the lives of one's neighbours, if one wishes to be a prig or a Puritan, one can flaunt one's moral views about them, but they are not one's concern. Besides, Individualism has really the higher aim. Modern morality consists in accepting the standard of one's age. I consider that for any man of culture to accept the standard of his age is a form of the grossest immorality."

"But, surely, if one lives merely for one's self, Harry, one pays a terrible price for doing so?" suggested the painter.

"Yes, we are overcharged for everything nowadays. I should fancy that the real tragedy of the poor is that they can afford nothing but self-denial. Beautiful sins, like beautiful things, are the privilege of the rich."

"One has to pay in other ways but money."

"What sort of ways, Basil?"

"Oh! I should fancy in remorse, in suffering, in . . . well, in the consciousness of degradation."

Lord Henry shrugged his shoulders. "My dear fellow, mediæval art is charming, but mediæval emotions are out of date. One can use them in fiction, of course. But then the only things that one can use in fiction are the things that one has ceased to use in fact. Believe me, no civilized man ever regrets a pleasure, and no uncivilized man ever knows what a pleasure is."

"I know what pleasure is," cried Dorian Gray. "It is to adore some one."

"That is certainly better than being adored," he answered, toying with some fruits. "Being adored is a nuisance. Women treat us just as Humanity treats its gods. They worship us, and are always bothering us to do something for them."

"I should have said that whatever they ask for they had first given to us," murmured the lad, gravely. "They create Love in our natures. They have a right to demand it back."

"That is quite true, Dorian," cried Hallward.

"Nothing is ever quite true," said Lord Henry.

"This is," interrupted Dorian. "You must admit, Harry, that women give to men the very gold of their lives."

"Possibly," he sighed, "but they invariably want it back in such very small change. That is the worry. Women, as some witty Frenchman once put it, inspire us with the desire to do masterpieces, and always prevent us from carrying them out."

"Harry, you are dreadful! I don't know why I like you so much."

"You will always like me, Dorian," he replied. "Will you have some coffee, you fellows?—Waiter, bring coffee, and *fine-champagne*, and some cigarettes. No: don't mind the cigarettes; I have some. Basil, I can't allow you to smoke cigars. You must have a cigarette. A cigarette is the perfect type of a perfect pleasure. It is exquisite, and it leaves one unsatisfied. What more can one want? Yes, Dorian, you will always be fond of me. I represent to you all the sins you have never had the courage to commit."

"What nonsense you talk, Harry!" cried the lad, taking a light from a fire-breathing silver dragon that the waiter had placed on the table. "Let us go down to the theatre. When Sibyl comes on the stage you will have a new ideal of life. She will represent something to you that you have never known."

"I have known everything," said Lord Henry, with a tired look in his eyes, "but I am always ready for a new emotion. I am afraid, however, that, for me at any rate, there is no such thing. Still, your wonderful girl may thrill me. I love acting. It is so much more real than life. Let us go. Dorian, you will come with me. I am so sorry, Basil, but there is only room for two in the brougham. You must follow us in a hansom."

They got up and put on their coats, sipping their coffee standing. The painter was silent and preoccupied. There was a gloom over him. He could not bear this marriage, and yet it seemed to him to be better than many other things that might have happened. After a few minutes, they all passed downstairs. He drove off by himself, as had been arranged, and watched the flashing lights of the little brougham in front of him. A strange sense of loss came over him. He felt that Dorian Gray would never again be to him all that he had been in the past. Life had come between them. . . . His eyes darkened, and the crowded, flaring streets became blurred to his eyes. When the cab drew up at the theatre, it seemed to him that he had grown years older.

CHAPTER VII

FOR SOME REASON or other, the house was crowded that night, and the fat Jew manager who met them at the door was beaming from ear to ear with an oily, tremulous smile. He escorted them to their box with a sort of pompous humility, waving his fat jewelled hands, and talking at the top of his voice. Dorian Gray loathed him more than ever. He felt as if he had come to look for Miranda and had been met by Caliban. Lord Henry, upon the other hand, rather liked him. At least he declared he did, and insisted on shaking him by the hand, and assuring him that he was proud to meet a man who had discovered a real genius and gone bankrupt over a poet. Hallward amused himself with watching the faces in the pit. The heat was terribly oppressive, and the huge sunlight flamed like a monstrous dahlia with petals of yellow fire. The youths in the gallery had taken off their coats and waistcoats and hung them over the side. They talked to each other across the theatre, and shared their oranges with the tawdry girls who sat beside them. Some women were laughing in the pit. Their voices were horribly shrill and discordant. The sound of the popping of corks came from the bar.

"What a place to find one's divinity in!" said Lord Henry.

"Yes!" answered Dorian Gray. "It was here I found her, and she is divine beyond all living things. When she acts you will forget everything. These common, rough people, with their coarse faces and brutal gestures, become quite different when she is on the stage. They sit silently and watch her. They weep and laugh as she wills them to do. She makes them as responsive as a violin. She spiritualizes them, and one feels that they are of the same flesh and blood as one's self."

"The same flesh and blood as one's self! Oh, I hope not!" exclaimed Lord Henry, who was scanning the occupants of the gallery through his opera-glass.

"Don't pay any attention to him, Dorian," said the painter. "I understand what you mean, and I believe in this girl. Any one you love must be marvellous, and any girl that has the effect you describe must be fine and noble. To spiritualize one's age—that is something worth doing. If this girl can give a soul to those who have lived without one, if she can create the sense of beauty in people whose lives have been sordid and ugly, if she can strip them of their selfishness and lend them tears for sorrows that are not their own, she is worthy of all your adoration, worthy of the adoration of the world. This marriage is quite right. I did not think so at first, but I admit it now. The gods made Sibyl Vane for you. Without her you would have been incomplete."

"Thanks, Basil," answered Dorian Gray, pressing his hand. "I knew that you would understand me. Harry is so cynical, he terrifies me. But here is the orchestra. It is quite dreadful, but it only lasts for about five minutes. Then the curtain rises, and you will see the girl to whom I am going to give all my life, to whom I have given everything that is good in me."

A quarter of an hour afterwards, amidst all extraordinary turmoil of applause, Sibyl Vane stepped on to the stage. Yes, she was certainly lovely to look at—one of the loveliest creatures, Lord Henry thought, that he had ever seen. There was something of the fawn in her shy grace and startled eyes. A faint blush, like the shadow of a rose in a mirror of silver, came to her cheeks as she glanced at the crowded, enthusiastic house. She stepped back a few paces, and her lips seemed to tremble. Basil Hallward leaped to his feet and began to applaud. Motionless, and as one in a dream, sat Dorian Gray, gazing at her. Lord Henry peered through his glasses, murmuring, "Charming! charming!"

The scene was the hall of Capulet's house, and Romeo in his pilgrim's dress had entered with Mercutio and his other friends. The band, such as it was, struck up a few bars of music, and the dance began. Through the crowd of ungainly, shabbily-dressed actors, Sibyl Vane moved like a creature from a finer world. Her body swayed, while she danced, as a plant sways in the water. The curves of her throat were the curves of a white lily. Her hands seemed to be made of cool ivory.

Yet she was curiously listless. She showed no sign of joy when her eyes rested on Romeo. The few words she had to speak—

> Good pilgrim, you do wrong your hand too much,
> Which mannerly devotion shows in this;
> For saints have hands that pilgrims' hands do touch,
> And palm to palm is holy palmers' kiss—

with the brief dialogue that follows, were spoken in a thoroughly artificial manner. The voice was exquisite, but from the point of view of tone it was absolutely false. It was wrong in colour. It took away all the life from the verse. It made the passion unreal.

Dorian Gray grew pale as he watched her. He was puzzled and anxious. Neither of his friends dared to say anything to him. She seemed to them to be absolutely incompetent. They were horribly disappointed.

Yet they felt that the true test of any Juliet is the balcony scene of the second act. They waited for that. If she failed there, there was nothing in her. She looked charming as she came out in the moonlight. That could not be denied. But the staginess of her acting was unbearable, and grew worse as she went on. Her gestures became absurdly artificial. She overemphasized everything that she had to say. The beautiful passage—

> Thou knowest the mask of night is on my face,
> Else would a maiden blush bepaint my cheek,
> For that which thou hast heard me speak to-night—

was declaimed with the painful precision of a school-girl who has been taught to recite by some second-rate professor of elocution. When she leaned over the balcony and came to those wonderful lines—

> Although I joy in thee,
> I have no joy of this contract to-night:
> It is too rash, too unadvised, too sudden;
> Too like the lightning, which doth cease to be
> Ere one can say, "It lightens." Sweet, good-night!
> This bud of love by summer's ripening breath
> May prove a beauteous flower when next we meet—

she spoke the words as though they conveyed no meaning to her. It was not nervousness. Indeed, so far from being nervous, she was absolutely self-contained. It was simply bad art. She was a complete failure.

Even the common, uneducated audience of the pit and gallery lost their interest in the play. They got restless, and began to talk loudly and to whistle. The Jew manager, who was standing at the back of the dress-circle, stamped and swore with rage. The only person unmoved was the girl herself.

When the second act was over there came a storm of hisses, and Lord Henry got up from his chair and put on his coat. "She is quite beautiful, Dorian, " he said, "but she can't act. Let us go."

"I am going to see the play through," answered the lad, in a hard, bitter voice. "I am awfully sorry that I have made you waste an evening, Harry. I apologize to you both."

"My dear Dorian, I should think Miss Vane was ill," interrupted Hallward. "We will come some other night."

"I wish she were ill," he rejoined. "But she seems to me to be simply callous and cold. She has entirely altered. Last night she was a great artist. This evening she is merely a commonplace, mediocre actress."

"Don't talk like that about any one you love, Dorian. Love is a more wonderful thing than Art."

"They are both simply forms of imitation," remarked Lord Henry. "But do let us go. Dorian, you must not stay here any longer. It is not good for one's morals to see bad acting. Besides, I don't suppose you will want your wife to act. So what does it matter if she plays Juliet like a wooden doll? She is very lovely, and if she knows as little about life as she does about acting, she will be a delightful experience. There are only two kinds of people who are really fascinating—people who know absolutely everything, and people who know absolutely nothing. Good heavens, my dear boy, don't look so tragic! The secret of remaining young is never to have an emotion that is unbecoming. Come to the club with Basil and myself. We will smoke cigarettes and drink to the beauty of Sibyl Vane. She is beautiful. What more can you want?"

"Go away, Harry," cried the lad. "I want to be alone. Basil, you must go. Ah! can't you see that my heart is breaking?" The hot tears came to his eyes. His lips trembled, and, rushing to the back of the box, he leaned up against the wall, hiding his face in his hands.

"Let us go, Basil," said Lord Henry, with a strange tenderness in his voice; and the two young men passed out together.

A few moments afterwards the footlights flared up, and the curtain rose on the third act. Dorian Gray went back to his seat. He looked pale, and proud, and indifferent. The play dragged on, and seemed interminable. Half of the audience went out, tramping in heavy boots, and laughing. The whole thing was a fiasco. The last act was played to almost empty benches. The curtain went down on a titter, and some groans.

As soon as it was over, Dorian Gray rushed behind the scenes into the greenroom. The girl was standing there alone, with a look of triumph on her face. Her eyes were lit with an exquisite fire. There was a radiance about her. Her parted lips were smiling over some secret of their own.

When he entered, she looked at him, and an expression of infinite joy came over her. "How badly I acted tonight, Dorian!" she cried.

"Horribly!" he answered, gazing at her in amazement—"horribly! It was dreadful. Are you ill? You have no idea what it was. You have no idea what I suffered."

The girl smiled. "Dorian," she answered, lingering over his name with long-drawn music in her voice, as though it were sweeter than honey to the red petals of her mouth—"Dorian, you should have understood. But you understand now, don't you?"

"Understand what?" he asked, angrily.

"Why I was so bad to-night. Why I shall always be bad. Why I shall never act well again."

He shrugged his shoulders. "You are ill, I suppose. When you are ill you shouldn't act. You make yourself ridiculous. My friends were bored. I was bored."

She seemed not to listen to him. She was transfigured with joy. An ecstasy of happiness dominated her.

"Dorian, Dorian," she cried, "before I knew you, acting was the one reality of my life. It was only in the theatre that I lived. I thought that it was all true. I was Rosalind one night, and Portia the other. The joy of Beatrice was my joy, and the sorrows of Cordelia were mine also. I believed in everything. The common people who acted with me seemed to me to be godlike. The painted scenes were my world. I knew nothing but shadows, and I thought them real. You came—oh, my beautiful love!—and you freed my soul from prison. You taught me what reality really is. To-night, for the first time in my life, I saw through the hollowness, the sham, the silliness of the empty pageant in which I had played. To-night, for the first time, I became conscious that the Romeo was hideous, and old, and painted, that the moonlight in the orchard was false, that the scenery was vulgar, and that the words I had to speak were unreal, were not my words, were not what I wanted to say. You had brought me something higher, something of which all art is but a reflection. You had made me understand what love really is. My love! My love! Prince Charming! Prince of life! I have grown sick of shadows. You are more to me than all art can ever be. What have I to do with the puppets of a play? When I came on to-night, I could not understand how it was that everything had gone from me. I thought that I was going to be wonderful. I found that I could do nothing. Suddenly it dawned on my soul what it all meant. The knowledge was exquisite to me. I heard them hissing, and I smiled. What could they know of love such as ours? Take me away, Dorian—take me away with you, where we can be quite alone. I hate the stage. I might mimic a passion that I do not feel, but I cannot mimic one that burns me like fire. Oh, Dorian, Dorian, you understand now what it signifies? Even if I could do it, it would be profanation for me to play at being in love. You have made me see that."

He flung himself down on the sofa, and turned away his face. "You have killed my love," he muttered.

She looked at him in wonder, and laughed. He made no answer. She came across to him, and with her little fingers stroked his hair. She knelt down and pressed his hands to her lips. He drew them away, and a shudder ran through him.

Then he leaped up, and went to the door. "Yes," he cried, "you have killed my love. You used to stir my imagination. Now you don't even stir my curiosity. You simply produce no effect. I loved you because you were marvellous, because you had genius and intellect, because you realized the dreams of great poets and gave shape and substance to the shadows of art. You have thrown it all away. You are shallow and stupid. My God! how mad I was to love you! What a fool I have been! You are nothing to me now. I will never see you again. I will never think of you. I will never mention your name. You don't know what you were to me, once. Why, once . . . Oh, I can't bear to think of it! I wish I had never laid eyes upon you! You have spoiled the romance of my life. How little you can know of love, if you say it mars your art! Without your art you are nothing. I would have made you famous, splendid, magnificent. The world would have worshipped you, and you would have borne my name. What are you now? A third-rate actress with a pretty face."

The girl grew white, and trembled. She clenched her hands together, and her voice seemed to catch in her throat. "You are not serious, Dorian?" she murmured. "You are acting."

"Acting! I leave that to you. You do it so well," he answered, bitterly.

She rose from her knees, and, with a piteous expression of pain in her face, came across the room to him. She put her hand upon his arm, and looked into his eyes. He thrust her back. "Don't touch me!" he cried.

A low moan broke from her, and she flung herself at his feet, and lay there like a trampled flower. "Dorian, Dorian, don't leave me!" she whispered. "I am so sorry I didn't act well. I was thinking of you all the time. But I will try—indeed, I will try. It came so suddenly across me, my love for you. I think I should never have known it if you had not kissed me—if we had not kissed each other. Kiss me again, my love. Don't go away from me. I couldn't bear it. Oh! don't go away from me. My brother . . . No; never mind. He didn't mean it. He was in jest. . . . But you, oh! can't you forgive me for to-night? I will work so hard, and try to improve. Don't be cruel to me because I love you better than anything in the world. After all, it is only once that I have not pleased you. But you are quite right, Dorian. I should have shown myself more of an artist. It was foolish of me; and yet I couldn't help it. Oh, don't leave me, don't leave me." A fit of passionate sobbing choked her. She crouched on the floor like a wounded thing, and Dorian Gray, with his beautiful eyes, looked down at her, and his chiselled lips curled in exquisite disdain. There is always something ridiculous about the emotions of people whom one has ceased to love. Sibyl Vane seemed to him to be absurdly melodramatic. Her tears and sobs annoyed him.

"I am going," he said at last, in his calm, clear voice. "I don't wish to be unkind, but I can't see you again. You have disappointed me."

She wept silently, and made no answer, but crept nearer. Her little hands stretched blindly out, and appeared to be seeking for him. He turned on his heel, and left the room. In a few moments he was out of the theatre.

Where he went to he hardly knew. He remembered wandering through dimly-lit streets, past gaunt black-shadowed archways and evil-looking houses. Women with hoarse voices and harsh laughter had called after him. Drunkards had reeled by cursing, and chattering to themselves like monstrous apes. He had seen grotesque children huddled upon doorsteps, and heard shrieks and oaths from gloomy courts.

As the dawn was just breaking he found himself close to Covent Garden. The darkness lifted, and, flushed with faint fires, the sky hollowed itself into a perfect pearl. Huge carts filled with nodding lilies rumbled slowly down the polished empty street. The air was heavy with the perfume of the flowers, and their beauty seemed to bring him an anodyne for his pain. He followed into the market, and watched the men unloading their waggons. A white-smocked carter offered him some cherries. He thanked him, wondered why he refused to accept any money for them, and began to eat them listlessly. They had been plucked at midnight, and the coldness of the moon had entered into them. A long line of boys carrying crates of striped tulips, and of yellow and red roses, defiled in front of him, threading their way through the huge jade-green piles of vegetables. Under the portico, with its grey sun-bleached pillars, loitered a troop of draggled bareheaded girls, waiting for the auction to be over. Others crowded round the swinging doors of the coffee-house in the Piazza. The heavy cart-horses slipped and stamped upon the rough stones, shaking their bells and trappings. Some of the drivers were lying asleep on a pile of sacks. Iris-necked, and pink-footed, the pigeons ran about picking up seeds.

After a little while, he hailed a hansom, and drove home. For a few moments he loitered upon the doorstep, looking round at the silent Square with its blank close-shuttered windows, and its staring blinds. The sky was pure opal now, and the roofs of the houses glistened like silver against it. From some chimney opposite a thin wreath of smoke was rising. It curled, a violet riband, through the nacre-coloured air.

In the huge gilt Venetian lantern, spoil of some Doge's barge, that hung from the ceiling of the great oak-panelled hall of entrance, lights were still burning from three flickering jets: thin blue petals of flame they seemed, rimmed with white fire. He turned them out, and, having thrown his hat and cape on the table, passed through the library towards the door of his bedroom, a large octagonal chamber on the ground floor that, in his new-born feeling for luxury, he had just had decorated for himself, and hung with some curious Renaissance tapestries that had been discovered stored in a disused attic at Selby Royal. As he was turning the handle of the door, his eye fell upon the portrait Basil Hallward had painted of him. He started back as if in surprise. Then he went on into his own room, looking somewhat puzzled. After he had taken the buttonhole out of his coat, he seemed to hesitate. Finally he came back, went over to the picture, and examined it. In the dim arrested light that struggled through the cream-coloured silk blinds, the face appeared to him to be a little changed. The expression looked different. One would have said that there was a touch of cruelty in the mouth. It was certainly strange.

He turned round, and, walking to the window, drew up the blind. The bright dawn flooded the room, and swept the fantastic shadows into dusky corners, where they lay shuddering. But the strange expression that he had noticed in the face of the portrait seemed to linger there, to be more intensified even. The quivering, ardent sunlight showed him the lines of cruelty round the mouth as clearly as if he had been looking into a mirror after he had done some dreadful thing.

He winced, and, taking up from the table an oval glass framed in ivory Cupids, one of Lord Henry's many presents to him, glanced hurriedly into its polished depths. No line like that warped his red lips. What did it mean?

He rubbed his eyes, and came close to the picture, and examined it again. There were no signs of any change when he looked into the actual painting, and yet there was no doubt that the whole expression had altered. It was not a mere fancy of his own. The thing was horribly apparent.

He threw himself into a chair, and began to think. Suddenly there flashed across his mind what he had said in Basil Hallward's studio the day the picture had been finished. Yes, he remembered it perfectly. He had uttered a mad wish that he himself might remain young, and the portrait grow old; that his own beauty might be untarnished, and the face on the canvas bear the burden of his passions and his sins; that the painted image might be seared with the lines of suffering and thought, and that he might keep all the delicate bloom and loveliness of his then just conscious boyhood. Surely his wish had not been fulfilled? Such things were impossible. It seemed monstrous even to think of them. And, yet, there was the picture before him, with the touch of cruelty in the mouth.

Cruelty! Had he been cruel? It was the girl's fault, not his. He had dreamed of her as a great artist, had given his love to her because he had thought her great.

Then she had disappointed him. She had been shallow and unworthy. And, yet, a feeling of infinite regret came over him, as he thought of her lying at his feet sobbing like a little child. He remembered with what callousness he had watched her. Why had he been made like that? Why had such a soul been given to him? But he had suffered also. During the three terrible hours that the play had lasted, he had lived centuries of pain, æon upon æon of torture. His life was well worth hers. She had marred him for a moment, if he had wounded her for an age. Besides, women were better suited to bear sorrow than men. They lived on their emotions. They only thought of their emotions. When they took lovers, it was merely to have some one with whom they could have scenes. Lord Henry had told him that, and Lord Henry knew what women were. Why should he trouble about Sibyl Vane? She was nothing to him now.

But the picture? What was he to say of that? It held the secret of his life, and told his story. It had taught him to love his own beauty. Would it teach him to loathe his own soul? Would he ever look at it again?

No; it was merely an illusion wrought on the troubled senses. The horrible night that he had passed had left phantoms behind it. Suddenly there had fallen upon his brain that tiny scarlet speck that makes men mad. The picture had not changed. It was folly to think so.

Yet it was watching him, with its beautiful marred face and its cruel smile. Its bright hair gleamed in the early sunlight. Its blue eyes met his own. A sense of infinite pity, not for himself, but for the painted image of himself, came over him. It had altered already, and would alter more. Its gold would wither into grey. Its red and white roses would die. For every sin that he committed, a stain would fleck and wreck its fairness. But he would not sin. The picture, changed or unchanged, would be to him the visible emblem of conscience. He would resist temptation. He would not see Lord Henry any more—would not, at any rate, listen to those subtle poisonous theories that in Basil Hallward's garden had first stirred within him the passion for impossible things. He would go back to Sibyl Vane, make her amends, marry her, try to love her again. Yes, it was his duty to do so. She must have suffered more than he had. Poor child! He had been selfish and cruel to her. The fascination that she had exercised over him would return. They would be happy together. His life with her would be beautiful and pure.

He got up from his chair, and drew a large screen right in front of the portrait, shuddering as he glanced at it. "How horrible!" he murmured to himself, and he walked across to the window and opened it. When he stepped out on to the grass, he drew a deep breath. The fresh morning air seemed to drive away all his sombre passions. He thought only of Sibyl. A faint echo of his love came back to him. He repeated her name over and over again. The birds that were singing in the dew-drenched garden seemed to be telling the flowers about her.

CHAPTER VIII

IT WAS LONG past noon when he awoke. His valet had crept several times on tiptoe into the room to see if he was stirring, and had wondered what made his young master sleep so late. Finally his bell sounded, and Victor came in softly with a cup of tea, and a pile of letters, on a small tray of old Sèvres china, and drew back the olive-satin curtains, with their shimmering blue lining, that hung in front of the three tall windows.

"Monsieur has well slept this morning," he said, smiling.

"What o'clock is it, Victor?" asked Dorian Gray, drowsily.

"One hour and a quarter, Monsieur."

How late it was! He sat up, and, having sipped some tea, turned over his letters. One of them was from Lord Henry, and had been brought by hand that morning. He hesitated for a moment, and then put it aside. The others he opened listlessly. They contained the usual collection of cards, invitations to dinner, tickets for private views, programmes of charity concerts, and the like, that are showered on fashionable young men every morning during the season. There was a rather heavy bill, for a chased silver Louis-Quinze toilet-set, that he had not yet had the courage to send on to his guardians, who were extremely old-fashioned people and did not realize that we live in an age when unnecessary things are our only necessities; and there were several very courteously worded communications from Jermyn Street money-lenders offering to advance any sum of money at a moment's notice and at the most reasonable rates of interest.

After about ten minutes he got up, and, throwing on an elaborate dressing-gown of silk-embroidered cashmere wool, passed into the onyx-paved bathroom. The cool water refreshed him after his long sleep. He seemed to have forgotten all that he had gone through. A dim sense of having taken part in some strange tragedy came to him once or twice, but there was the unreality of a dream about it.

As soon as he was dressed, he went into the library and sat down to a light French breakfast, that had been laid out for him on a small round table close to the open window. It was an exquisite day. The warm air seemed laden with spices. A bee flew in, and buzzed round the blue-dragon bowl that, filled with sulphur-yellow roses, stood before him. He felt perfectly happy.

Suddenly his eye fell on the screen that he had placed in front of the portrait, and he started.

"Too cold for Monsieur?" asked his valet, putting an omelette on the table. "I shut the window?"

Dorian shook his head. "I am not cold," he murmured.

Was it all true? Had the portrait really changed? Or had it been simply his own imagination that had made him see a look of evil where there had been a look of joy? Surely a painted canvas could not alter? The thing was absurd. It would serve as a tale to tell Basil some day. It would make him smile.

And, yet, how vivid was his recollection of the whole thing! First in the dim twilight, and then in the bright dawn, he had seen the touch of cruelty round the warped lips. He almost dreaded his valet leaving the room. He knew that when he was alone he would have to examine the portrait. He was afraid of certainty. When the coffee and cigarettes had been brought and the man turned to go, he felt a wild desire to tell him to remain. As the door was closing behind him he called him back. The man stood waiting for his orders. Dorian looked at him for a moment. "I am not at home to any one, Victor," he said, with a sigh. The man bowed and retired.

Then he rose from the table, lit a cigarette, and flung himself down on a luxuriously-cushioned couch that stood facing the screen. The screen was an old one, of gilt Spanish leather, stamped and wrought with a rather florid Louis-Quatorze pattern. He scanned it curiously, wondering if ever before it had concealed the secret of a man's life.

Should he move it aside, after all? Why not let it stay there? What was the use of knowing? If the thing was true, it was terrible. If it was not true, why trouble about it? But what if, by some fate or deadlier chance, eyes other than his spied behind, and saw the horrible change? What should he do if Basil Hallward came and asked to look at his own picture? Basil would be sure to do that. No; the thing had to be examined, and at once. Anything would be better than this dreadful state of doubt.

He got up, and locked both doors. At least he would be alone when he looked upon the mask of his shame. Then he drew the screen aside, and saw himself face to face. It was perfectly true. The portrait had altered.

As he often remembered afterwards, and always with no small wonder, he found himself at first gazing at the portrait with a feeling of almost scientific interest. That such a change should have taken place was incredible to him. And yet it was a fact. Was there some subtle affinity between the chemical atoms, that shaped themselves into form and colour on the canvas, and the soul that was within him? Could it be that what that soul thought, they realized?—that what it dreamed, they made true? Or was there some other, more terrible reason? He shuddered, and felt afraid, and, going back to the couch, lay there, gazing at the picture in sickened horror.

One thing, however, he felt that it had done for him. It had made him conscious how unjust, how cruel, he had been to Sibyl Vane. It was not too late to make reparation for that. She could still be his wife. His unreal and selfish love would yield to some higher influence, would be transformed into some nobler passion, and the portrait that Basil Hallward had painted of him would be a guide to him through life, would be to him what holiness is to some, and conscience to others, and the fear of God to us all. There were opiates for remorse, drugs that could lull the moral sense to sleep. But here was a visible symbol of the degradation of sin. Here was an ever-present sign of the ruin men brought upon their souls.

Three o'clock struck, and four, and the half-hour rang its double chime, but Dorian Gray did not stir. He was trying to gather up the scarlet threads of life, and to weave them into a pattern; to find his way through the sanguine labyrinth of passion through which he was wandering. He did not know what to do, or what to think. Finally, he went over to the table and wrote a passionate letter to the girl he had loved, imploring her forgiveness, and accusing himself of madness. He covered page after page with wild words of sorrow, and wilder words of pain. There is a luxury in self-reproach. When we blame ourselves we feel that no one else has a right to blame us. It is the confession, not the priest, that gives us absolution. When Dorian had finished the letter, he felt that he had been forgiven.

Suddenly there came a knock to the door, and he heard Lord Henry's voice outside. "My dear boy, I must see you. Let me in at once. I can't bear your shutting yourself up like this."

He made no answer at first, but remained quite still. The knocking still continued, and grew louder. Yes, it was better to let Lord Henry in, and to explain to him the new life he was going to lead, to quarrel with him if it became necessary to quarrel, to part if parting was inevitable. He jumped up, drew the screen hastily across the picture, and unlocked the door.

"I am so sorry for it all, Dorian," said Lord Henry, as he entered. "But you must not think too much about it."

"Do you mean about Sibyl Vane?" asked the lad.

"Yes, of course," answered Lord Henry, sinking into a chair, and slowly pulling off his yellow gloves. "It is dreadful, from one point of view; but it was not your fault. Tell me, did you go behind and see her, after the play was over?"

"Yes."

"I felt sure you had. Did you make a scene with her?"

"I was brutal, Harry—perfectly brutal. But it is all right now. I am not sorry for anything that has happened. It has taught me to know myself better."

"Ah, Dorian, I am so glad you take it in that way! I was afraid I would find you plunged in remorse, and tearing that nice curly hair of yours."

"I have got through all that," said Dorian, shaking his head, and smiling. "I am perfectly happy now I know what conscience is, to begin with. It is not what you told me it was. It is the divinest thing in us. Don't sneer at it, Harry, any more—at least not before me. I want to be good. I can't bear the idea of my soul being hideous."

"A very charming artistic basis for ethics, Dorian! I congratulate you on it. But how are you going to begin?"

"By marrying Sibyl Vane."

"Marrying Sibyl Vane!" cried Lord Henry, standing up, and looking at him in perplexed amazement. "But, my dear Dorian—"

"Yes, Harry, I know what you are going to say. Something dreadful about marriage. Don't say it. Don't ever say things of that kind to me again. Two days ago I asked Sibyl to marry me. I am not going to break my word to her. She is to be my wife."

"Your wife! Dorian! . . . Didn't you get my letter? I wrote to you this morning, and sent the note down, by my own man."

"Your letter? Oh, yes, I remember. I have not read it yet, Harry. I was afraid there might be something in it that I wouldn't like. You cut life to pieces with your epigrams."

"You know nothing then?"

"What do you mean?"

Lord Henry walked across the room, and, sitting down by Dorian Gray, took both his hands in his own, and held them tightly. "Dorian," he said, "my letter—don't be frightened—was to tell you that Sibyl Vane is dead."

A cry of pain broke from the lad's lips, and he leaped to his feet, tearing his hands away from Lord Henry's grasp. "Dead! Sibyl is dead! It is not true! It is a horrible lie! How dare you say it?"

"It is quite true, Dorian," said Lord Henry, gravely. "It is in all the morning papers. I wrote down to you to ask you not to see any one till I came. There will have to be an inquest, of course, and you must not be mixed up in it. Things like that make a man fashionable in Paris. But in London people are so prejudiced. Here, one should never make one's *début* with a scandal. One should reserve that to give an interest to one's old age. I suppose they don't know your name at the theatre? If they don't, it is all right. Did any one see you going round to her room? That is an important point."

Dorian did not answer for a few moments. He was dazed with horror. Finally he stammered, in a stifled voice, "Harry, did you say an inquest? What did you mean by that? Did Sibyl—? Oh, Harry, I can't bear it! But be quick. Tell me everything at once."

"I have no doubt it was not an accident, Dorian, though it must be put in that way to the public. It seems that as she was leaving the theatre with her mother, about half past twelve or so, she said she had forgotten something upstairs. They waited some time for her, but she did not come down again. They ultimately found her lying dead on the floor of her dressing-room. She had swallowed something by mistake, some dreadful thing they use at theatres. I don't know what it was, but it had either prussic acid or white lead in it. I should fancy it was prussic acid, as she seems to have died instantaneously."

"Harry, Harry, it is terrible!" cried the lad.

"Yes; it is very tragic, of course, but you must not get yourself mixed up in it. I see by *The Standard* that she was seventeen. I should have thought she was almost younger than that. She looked such a child, and seemed to know so little about acting. Dorian, you mustn't let this thing get on your nerves. You must come and dine with me, and afterwards we will look in at the Opera. It is a Patti night, and everybody will be there. You can come to my sister's box. She has got some smart women with her."

"So I have murdered Sibyl Vane," said Dorian Gray, half to himself—"murdered her as surely as if I had cut her little throat with a knife. Yet the roses are not less lovely for all that. The birds sing just as happily in my garden. And to-night I am to dine with you, and then go on to the Opera, and sup somewhere, I suppose, afterwards. How extraordinarily dramatic life is! If I had read all this in a book, Harry, I think I would have wept over it. Somehow, now that it has happened actually, and to me, it seems far too wonderful for tears. Here is the first passionate love-letter I have ever written in my life. Strange, that my first passionate love-letter should have been addressed to a dead girl. Can they feel, I wonder, those white silent people we call the dead? Sibyl! Can she feel, or know, or listen? Oh, Harry, how I loved her once! It seems years ago to me now. She was everything to me. Then came that dreadful night—was it really only last night?—when she played so badly, and my heart almost broke. She explained it all to me. It was terribly pathetic. But I was not moved a bit. I thought her shallow. Suddenly something happened that made me afraid. I can't tell you what it was, but it was terrible. I said I would go back to her. I felt I had done wrong. And now she is dead. My God! my God! Harry, what shall I do? You don't know the danger I am in, and there is nothing to keep me straight. She would have done that for me. She had no right to kill herself. It was selfish of her."

"My dear Dorian," answered Lord Henry, taking a cigarette from his case, and producing a gold-latten matchbox, "the only way a woman can ever reform a man is by boring him so completely that he loses all possible interest in life. If you had married this girl you would have been wretched. Of course you would have treated her kindly. One can always be kind to people about whom one cares nothing. But she would have soon found out that you were absolutely indifferent to her. And when a woman finds that out about her husband, she either becomes dreadfully dowdy, or wears very smart bonnets that some other woman's husband has to pay for. I say nothing about the social mistake, which would have been abject, which, of course, I would not have allowed, but I assure you that in any case the whole thing would have been an absolute failure."

"I suppose it would," muttered the lad, walking up and down the room, and looking horribly pale. "But I thought it was my duty. It is not my fault that this terrible tragedy has prevented my doing what was right. I remember your saying once that there is a fatality about good resolutions—that they are always made too late. Mine certainly were."

"Good resolutions are useless attempts to interfere with scientific laws. Their origin is pure vanity. Their result is absolutely *nil*. They give us, now and then, some of those luxurious sterile emotions that have a certain charm for the weak. That is all that can be said for them. They are simply cheques that men draw on a bank where they have no account."

"Harry," cried Dorian Gray coming over and sitting down beside him, "why is it that I cannot feel this tragedy as much as I want to? I don't think I am heartless. Do you?"

"You have done too many foolish things during the last fortnight to be enititled to give yourself that name, Dorian," answered Lord Henry, with his sweet, melancholy smile.

The lad frowned. "I don't like that explanation, Harry," he rejoined, "but I am glad you don't think I am heartless. I am nothing of the kind. I know I am not. And yet I must admit that this thing that has happened does not affect me as it should. It seems to me to be simply like a wonderful ending to a wonderful play. It has all the terrible beauty of a Greek tragedy, a tragedy in which I took a great part, but by which I have not been wounded."

"It is an interesting question," said Lord Henry, who found an exquisite pleasure in playing on the lad's unconscious egotism—"an extremely interesting question. I fancy that the true explanation is this. It often happens that the real tragedies of life occur in such an inartistic manner that they hurt us by their crude violence, their absolute incoherence, their absurd want of meaning, their entire lack of style. They affect us just as vulgarity affects us. They give us an impression of sheer brute force, and we revolt against that. Sometimes, however, a tragedy that possesses artistic elements of beauty crosses our lives. If these elements of beauty are real, the whole thing simply appeals to our sense of dramatic effect. Suddenly we find that we are no longer the actors, but the spectators of the play. Or rather we are both. We watch ourselves, and the mere wonder of the spectacle enthralls us. In the present case, what is it that has really happened? Some one has killed herself for love of you. I wish that I had ever had such an experience. It would have made me in love with love for the rest of my life. The people who have adored me—there have not been very many, but there have been some—have always insisted on living on, long after I had ceased to care for them, or they to care for me. They have become stout and tedious, and when I meet them they go in at once for reminiscences. That awful memory of woman! What a fearful thing it is! And what an utter intellectual stagnation it reveals! One should absorb the colour of life, but one should never remember its details. Details are always vulgar."

"I must sow poppies in my garden," sighed Dorian.

"There is no necessity," rejoined his companion. "Life has always poppies in her hands. Of course, now and then things linger. I once wore nothing but violets all through one season, as a form of artistic mourning for a romance that would not die. Ultimately, however, it did die. I forget what killed it. I think it was her proposing to sacrifice the whole world for me. That is always a dreadful moment. It fills one with the terror of eternity. Well—would you believe it?—a week ago, at Lady Hampshire's, I found myself seated at dinner next the lady in question, and she insisted on going over the whole thing again, and digging up the past, and taking up the future. I had buried my romance in a bed of asphodel. She dragged it out again, and assured me that I had spoiled her life. I am bound to state that she ate an enormous dinner, so I did not feel any anxiety. But what a lack of taste she showed! The one charm of the past is that it is the past. But women never know when the curtain has fallen. They always want a sixth act, and as soon as the interest of the play is entirely over they propose to continue it. If they were allowed their own way, every comedy would have a tragic ending, and every tragedy would culminate in a farce. They are charmingly artificial, but they have no sense of art. You are more fortunate than I am. I assure you, Dorian, that not one of the women I have known would have done for me what Sibyl Vane did for you. Ordinary women always console themselves. Some of them do it by going in for sentimental colours. Never trust a woman who wears mauve, whatever her age may be, or a woman over thirty-five who is fond of pink ribbons. It always means that they have a history. Others find a great consolation in suddenly discovering the good qualities of their husbands. They flaunt their conjugal felicity in one's face, as if it were the most fascinating of sins. Religion consoles some. Its mysteries have all the charm of a flirtation, a woman once told me; and I can quite understand it. Besides, nothing makes one so vain as being told that one is a sinner. Conscience makes egotists of us all. Yes; there is really no end to the consolations that women find in modern life. Indeed, I have not mentioned the most important one."

ONE SHOULD ABSORB THE COLOUR OF LIFE, BUT ONE SHOULD NEVER REMEMBER ITS DETAILS. DETAILS ARE ALWAYS VULGAR.

"What is that, Harry?" said the lad, listlessly.

"Oh, the obvious consolation. Taking some one else's admirer when one loses one's own. In good society that always whitewashes a woman. But really, Dorian, how different Sibyl Vane must have been from all the women one meets! There is something to me quite beautiful about her death. I am glad I am living in a century when such wonders happen. They make one believe in the reality of the things we all play with, such as romance, passion, and love."

"I was terribly cruel to her. You forget that."

"I am afraid that women appreciate cruelty, downright cruelty, more than anything else. They have wonderfully primitive instincts. We have emancipated them, but they remain slaves looking for their masters, all the same. They love being dominated. I am sure you were splendid. I have never seen you really and absolutely angry, but I can fancy how delightful you looked. And, after all, you said something to me the day before yesterday that seemed to me at the time to be merely fanciful, but that I see now was absolutely true, and it holds the key to everything."

"What was that, Harry?"

"You said to me that Sibyl Vane represented to you all the heroines of romance—that she was Desdemona one night, and Ophelia the other; that if she died as Juliet, she came to life as Imogen."

"She will never come to life again now," muttered the lad, burying his face in his hands.

"No, she will never come to life. She has played her last part. But you must think of that lonely death in the tawdry dressing-room simply as a strange lurid fragment from some Jacobean tragedy, as a wonderful scene from Webster, or Ford, or Cyril Tourneur. The girl never really lived, and so she has never really died. To you at least she was always a dream, a phantom that flitted through Shakespeare's plays and left them lovelier for its presence, a reed through which Shakespeare's music sounded richer and more full of joy. The moment she touched actual life, she marred it, and it marred her, and so she passed away. Mourn for Ophelia, if you like. Put ashes on your head because Cordeia was strangled. Cry out against Heaven because the daughter of Brabantio died. But don't waste your tears over Sibyl Vane. She was less real than they are."

There was a silence. The evening darkened in the room. Noiselessly, and with silver feet, the shadows crept in from the garden. The colours faded wearily out of things.

After some time Dorian Gray looked up. "You have explained me to myself, Harry," he murmured, with something of a sigh of relief. "I felt all that you have said, but somehow I was afraid of it, and I could not express it to myself. How well you know me! But we will not talk again of what has happened. It has been a marvellous experience. That is all. I wonder if life has still in store for me anything as marvellous."

"Life has everything in store for you, Dorian. There is nothing that you, with your extraordinary good looks, will not be able to do."

"But suppose, Harry, I became haggard, and old, and wrinkled? What then?"

"Ah, then," said Lord Henry, rising to go—"then, my dear Dorian, you would have to fight for your victories. As it is, they are brought to you. No, you must keep your good looks. We live in an age that reads too much to be wise, and that thinks too much to be beautiful. We cannot spare you. And now you had better dress, and drive down to the club. We are rather late, as it is."

"I think I shall join you at the Opera, Harry. I feel too tired to eat anything. What is the number of your sister's box?"

"Twenty-seven, I believe. It is on the grand tier. You will see her name on the door. But I am sorry you won't come and dine."

"I don't feel up to it," said Dorian, listlessly. "But I am awfully obliged to you for all that you have said to me. You are certainly my best friend. No one has ever understood me as you have."

"We are only at the beginning of our friendship, Dorian," answered Lord Henry, shaking him by the hand. "Good-bye. I shall see you before nine-thirty, I hope. Remember, Patti is singing."

As he closed the door behind him, Dorian Gray touched the bell, and in a few minutes Victor appeared with the lamps and drew the blinds down. He waited impatiently for him to go. The man seemed to take an interminable time over everything.

As soon as he had left, he rushed to the screen, and drew it back. No; there was no further change in the picture. It had received the news of Sibyl Vane's death before he had known of it himself. It was conscious of the events of life as they occurred. The vicious cruelty that marred the fine lines of the mouth had, no doubt, appeared at the very moment that the girl had drunk the poison, whatever it was. Or was it indifferent to results? Did it merely take cognizance of what passed within the soul? He wondered, and hoped that some day he would see the change taking place before his very eyes, shuddering as he hoped it.

Poor Sibyl! what a romance it had all been! She had often mimicked death on the stage. Then Death himself had touched her, and taken her with him. How had she played that dreadful last scene? Had she cursed him, as she died? No; she had died for love of him, and love would always be a sacrament to him now. She had atoned for everything, by the sacrifice she had made of her life. He would not think any more of what she had made him go through, on that horrible night at the theatre. When he thought of her, it would be as a wonderful tragic figure sent on to the world's stage to show the supreme reality of Love. A wonderful tragic figure? Tears came to his eyes as he remembered her childlike look and winsome fanciful ways and shy tremulous grace. He brushed them away hastily, and looked again at the picture.

He felt that the time had really come for making his choice. Or had his choice already been made? Yes, life had decided that for him—life, and his own infinite curiosity about life. Eternal youth, infinite passion, pleasures subtle and secret, wild joys and wilder sins—he was to have all these things. The portrait was to bear the burden of his shame: that was all.

A feeling of pain crept over him as he thought of the desecration that was in store for the fair face on the canvas. Once, in boyish mockery of Narcissus, he had kissed, or feigned to kiss, those painted lips that now smiled so cruelly at him. Morning after morning he had sat before the portrait wondering at its beauty, almost enamoured of it, as it seemed to him at times. Was it to alter now with every mood to which he yielded? Was it to become a monstrous and loathsome thing, to be hidden away in a locked room, to be shut out from the sunlight that had so often touched to brighter gold the waving wonder of its hair? The pity of it! the pity of it!

For a moment he thought of praying that the horrible sympathy that existed between him and the picture might cease. It had changed in answer to a prayer; perhaps in answer to a prayer it might remain unchanged. And, yet, who, that knew anything about Life, would surrender the chance of remaining always young, however fantastic that chance might be, or with what fateful consequences it might be fraught? Besides, was it really under his control? Had it indeed been prayer that had produced the substitution? Might there not be some curious scientific reason for it all? If thought could exercise its influence upon a living organism, might not thought exercise all influence upon dead and inorganic things? Nay, without thought or conscious desire, might not things external to ourselves vibrate in unison with our moods and passions, atom calling to atom in secret love or strange affinity? But the reason was of no importance. He would never again tempt by a prayer any terrible power. If the picture was to alter, it was to alter. That was all. Why inquire too closely into it?

For there would be a real pleasure in watching it. He would be able to follow his mind into its secret places. This portrait would be to him the most magical of mirrors. As it had revealed to him his own body, so it would reveal to him his own soul. And when winter came upon it, he would still be standing where spring trembles on the verge of summer. When the blood crept from its face, and left behind a pallid mask of chalk with leaden eyes, he would keep the glamour of boyhood. Not one blossom of his loveliness would ever fade. Not one pulse of his life would ever weaken. Like the gods of the Greeks, he would be strong, and fleet, and joyous. What did it matter what happened to the coloured image on the canvas? He would be safe. That was everything.

He drew the screen back into its former place in front of the picture, smiling as he did so, and passed into his bedroom, where his valet was already waiting for him. An hour later he was at the Opera, and Lord Henry was leaning over his chair.

CHAPTER IX

AS HE WAS sitting at breakfast next morning, Basil Hallward was shown into the room.

"I am so glad I have found you, Dorian," he said, gravely. "I called last night, and they told me you were at the Opera. Of course I knew that was impossible. But I wish you had left word where you had really gone to. I passed a dreadful evening, half afraid that one tragedy might be followed by another. I think you might have telegraphed for me when you heard of it first. I read of it quite by chance in a late edition of *The Globe*, that I picked up at the club. I came here at once, and was miserable at not finding you. I can't tell you how heart-broken I am about the whole thing. I know what you must suffer. But where were you? Did you go down and see the girl's mother? For a moment I thought of following you there. They gave the address in the paper. Somewhere in the Euston Road, isn't it? But I was afraid of intruding upon a sorrow that I could not lighten. Poor woman! What a state she must be in! And her only child, too! What did she say about it all?"

"My dear Basil, how do I know?" murmured Dorian Gray, sipping some pale-yellow wine from a delicate gold-beaded bubble of Venetian glass, and looking dreadfully bored. "I was at the Opera. You should have come on there. I met Lady Gwendolen, Harry's sister, for the first time. We were in her box. She is perfectly charming; and Patti sang divinely. Don't talk about horrid subjects. If one doesn't talk about a thing, it has never happened. It is simply expression, as Harry says, that gives reality to things. I may mention that she was not the woman's only child. There is a son, a charming fellow, I believe. But he is not on the stage. He is a sailor, or something. And now, tell me about yourself and what you are painting."

"You went to the Opera?" said Hallward, speaking very slowly, and with a strained touch of pain in his voice. "You went to the Opera while Sibyl Vane was lying dead in some sordid lodging? You can talk to me of other women being charming, and of Patti singing divinely, before the girl you loved has even the quiet of a grave to sleep in? Why, man, there are horrors in store for that little white body of hers!"

"Stop, Basil! I won't hear it!" cried Dorian, leaping to his feet. "You must not tell me about things. What is done is done. What is past is past."

"You call yesterday the past?"

"What has the actual lapse of time got to do with it? It is only shallow people who require years to get rid of an emotion. A man who is master of himself can end a sorrow as easily as he can invent a pleasure. I don't want to be at the mercy of my emotions. I want to use them, to enjoy them, and to dominate them."

"Dorian, this is horrible! Something has changed you completely. You look exactly the same wonderful boy who, day after day, used to come down to my studio to sit for his picture. But you were simple, natural, and affectionate then. You were the most unspoiled creature in the whole world. Now, I don't know what has come over you. You talk as if you had no heart, no pity in you. It is all Harry's influence. I see that."

The lad flushed up, and, going to the window, looked out for a few moments on the green, flickering, sun-lashed garden. "I owe a great deal to Harry, Basil," he said, at last—"more than I owe to you. You only taught me to be vain."

"Well, I am punished for that, Dorian—or shall be some day."

"I don't know what you mean, Basil," he exclaimed, turning round. "I don't know what you want. What do you want?"

"I want the Dorian Gray I used to paint," said the artist, sadly.

"Basil," said the lad, going over to him, and putting his hand on his shoulder, "you have come too late. Yesterday when I heard that Sibyl Vane had killed herself—"

"Killed herself! Good heavens! is there no doubt about that?" cried Hallward, looking up at him with an expression of horror.

"My dear Basil! Surely you don't think it was a vulgar accident? Of course she killed herself."

The elder man buried his face in his hands. "How fearful," he muttered, and a shudder ran through him.

"No," said Dorian Gray, "there is nothing fearful about it. It is one of the great romantic tragedies of the age. As a rule, people who act lead the most commonplace lives. They are good husbands, or faithful wives, or something tedious. You know what I mean—middle-class virtue, and all that kind of thing. How different Sibyl was! She lived her finest tragedy. She was always a heroine. The last night she played—the night you saw her—she acted badly because she had known the reality of love. When she knew its unreality, she died, as Juliet might have died. She passed again into the sphere of art. There is something of the martyr about her. Her death has all the pathetic uselessness of martyrdom, all its wasted beauty. But, as I was saying, you must not think I have not suffered. If you had come in yesterday at a particular moment—about half-past five, perhaps, or a quarter of six—you would have found me in tears. Even Harry, who was here, who brought me the news, in fact, had no idea what I was going through. I suffered immensely. Then it passed away. I cannot repeat an emotion. No one can, except sentimentalists. And you are awfully unjust, Basil. You come down here to console me. That is charming of you. You find me consoled, and you are furious. How like a sympathetic person! You remind me of a story Harry told me about a certain philanthropist who spent twenty years of his life in trying to get some grievance redressed, or some unjust law altered—I forget exactly what it was. Finally he succeeded, and nothing could exceed his disappointment. He had absolutely nothing to do, almost died of *ennui*, and became a confirmed misanthrope. And besides, my dear old Basil, if you really want to console me, teach me rather to forget what has happened, or to see it from a proper artistic point of view. Was it not Gautier who used to write about *la consolation des arts*? I remember picking up a little vellum-covered book in your studio one day and chancing on that delightful phrase. Well, I am not like that young man you told me of when we were down at Marlow together, the young man who used to say that yellow satin could console one for all the miseries of life. I love beautiful things that one can touch and handle. Old brocades, green bronzes, lacquer-work, carved ivories, exquisite surroundings, luxury, pomp, there is much to be got from all these. But the artistic temperament that they create, or at any rate reveal, is still more to me. To become the spectator of one's own life, as Harry says, is to escape the suffering of life. I know you are surprised at my talking to you like this. You have not realized how I have developed. I was a schoolboy when you knew me. I am a man now. I have new passions, new thoughts, new ideas. I am different, but you must not like me less. I am changed, but you must always be my friend. Of course I am very fond of Harry. But I know that you are better than he is. You are not stronger—you are too much afraid of life—but you are better. And how happy we used to be together! Don't leave me, Basil, and don't quarrel with me. I am what I am. There is nothing more to be said."

The painter felt strangely moved. The lad was infinitely dear to him, and his personality had been the great turning-point in his art. He could not bear the idea of reproaching him any more. After all, his indifference was probably merely a mood that would pass away. There was so much in him that was good, so much in him that was noble.

"Well, Dorian," he said, at length, with a sad smile, "I won't speak to you again about this horrible thing, after today. I only trust your name won't be mentioned in connection with it. The inquest is to take place this afternoon. Have they summoned you?"

Dorian shook his head, and a look of annoyance passed over his face at the mention of the word "inquest." There was something so crude and vulgar about everything of the kind. "They don't know my name," he answered.

"But surely she did?"

"Only my Christian name, and that I am quite sure she never mentioned to any one. She told me once that they were all rather curious to learn who I was, and that she invariably told them my name was Prince Charming. It was pretty of her. You must do me a drawing of Sibyl, Basil. I should like to have something more of her than the memory of a few kisses and some broken pathetic words."

"I will try and do something, Dorian, if it would please you. But you must come and sit to me yourself again. I can't get on without you."

"I can never sit to you again, Basil. It is impossible!" he exclaimed, starting back.

The painter stared at him. "My dear boy, what nonsense!" he cried. "Do you mean to say you don't like what I did of you? Where is it? Why have you pulled the screen in front of it? Let me look at it. It is the best thing I have ever done. Do take the screen away, Dorian. It is simply disgraceful of your servant hiding my work like that. I felt the room looked different as I came in."

"My servant has nothing to do with it, Basil. You don't imagine I let him arrange my room for me? He settles my flowers for me sometimes—that is all. No; I did it myself. The light was too strong on the portrait."

"Too strong! Surely not, my dear fellow? It is an admirable place for it. Let me see it." And Hallward walked towards the corner of the room.

A cry of terror broke from Dorian Gray's lips, and he rushed between the painter and the screen. "Basil," he said, looking very pale, "you must not look at it. I don't wish you to."

"Not look at my own work! you are not serious. Why shouldn't I look at it?" exclaimed Hallward, laughing.

"If you try to look at it, Basil, on my word of honour I will never speak to you again as long as I live. I am quite serious. I don't offer any explanation, and you are not to ask for any. But, remember, if you touch this screen, everything is over between us."

Hallward looked thunderstruck. He looked at Dorian Gray in absolute amazement. He had never seen him like this before. The lad was actually pallid with rage. His hands were clenched, and the pupils of his eyes were like disks of blue fire. He was trembling all over.

"Dorian!"

"Don't speak!"

"But what is the matter? Of course I won't look at it if you don't want me to," he said, rather coldly, turning on his heel, and going over towards the window. "But, really, it seems rather absurd that I shouldn't see my own work, especially as I am going to exhibit it in Paris in the autumn. I shall probably have to give it another coat of varnish before that so I must see it some day, and why not to-day?"

"To exhibit it! You want to exhibit it?" exclaimed Dorian Gray, a strange sense of terror creeping over him. Was the world going to be shown his secret? Were people to gape at the mystery of his life? That was impossible. Something—he did not know what—had to be done at once.

"Yes; I don't suppose you will object to that. Georges Petit is going to collect all my best pictures for a special exhibition in the Rue de Sèze, which will open the first week in October. The portrait will only be away a month. I should think you could easily spare it for that time. In fact, you are sure to be out of town. And if you keep it always behind a screen, you can't care much about it."

Dorian Gray passed his hand over his forehead. There were beads of perspiration there. He felt that he was on the brink of a horrible danger. "You told me a month ago that you would never exhibit it," he cried. "Why have you changed your mind? You people who go in for being consistent have just as many moods as others have. The only difference is that your moods are rather meaningless. You can't have forgotten that you assured me most solemnly that nothing in the world would induce you to send it to any exhibition. You told Harry exactly the same thing." He stopped suddenly, and a gleam of light came into his eyes. He remembered that Lord Henry had said to him once, half seriously and half in jest, "If you want to have a strange quarter of an hour, get Basil to tell you why he won't exhibit your picture. He told me why he wouldn't, and it was a revelation to me." Yes, perhaps Basil, too, had his secret. He would ask him and try.

"Basil," he said, coming over quite close, and looking him straight in the face, "we have each of us a secret. Let me know yours, and I shall tell you mine. What was your reason for refusing to exhibit my picture?"

The painter shuddered in spite of himself. "Dorian, if I told you, you might like me less than you do, and you would certainly laugh at me. I could not bear your doing either of those two things. If you wish me never to look at your picture again, I am content. I have always you to look at. If you wish the best work I have ever done to be hidden from the world, I am satisfied. Your friendship is dearer to me than any fame or reputation."

"No, Basil, you must tell me," insisted Dorian Gray. "I think I have a right to know." His feeling of terror had passed away, and curiosity had taken its place. He was determined to find out Basil Hallward's mystery.

"Let us sit down, Dorian," said the painter, looking troubled. "Let us sit down. And just answer me one question. Have you noticed in the picture something curious?—something that probably at first did not strike you, but that revealed itself to you suddenly?"

"Basil!" cried the lad, clutching the arms of his chair with trembling hands, and gazing at him with wild, startled eyes.

"I see you did. Don't speak. Wait till you hear what I have to say. Dorian, from the moment I met you, your personality had the most extraordinary influence over me. I was dominated, soul, brain, and power by you. You became to me the visible incarnation of that unseen ideal whose memory haunts us artists like an exquisite dream. I worshipped you. I grew jealous of every one to whom you spoke. I wanted to have you all to myself. I was only happy when I was with you. When you were away from me you were still present in my art. . . . Of course I never let you know anything about this. It would have been impossible. You would not have understood it. I hardly understood it myself. I only knew that I had seen perfection face to face, and that the world had become wonderful to my eyes—too wonderful, perhaps, for in such mad worships there is peril, the peril of losing them, no less than the peril of keeping them. . . . Weeks and weeks went on, and I grew more and more absorbed in you. Then came a new development. I had drawn you as Paris in dainty armour, and as Adonis with huntsman's cloak and polished boar-spear. Crowned with heavy lotus-blossoms you had sat on the prow of Adrian's barge, gazing across the green turbid Nile. You had leant over the still pool of some Greek woodland, and seen in the water's silent silver the marvel of your own face. And it had all been what art should be, unconscious, ideal, and remote. One day, a fatal day I sometimes think, I determined to paint a wonderful portrait of you as you actually are, not in the costume of dead ages, but in your own dress and in your own time. Whether it was the Realism of the method, or the mere wonder of your personality, thus directly presented to me without mist or veil, I cannot tell. But I know that as I worked at it, every flake and film of colour seemed to me to reveal my secret. I grew afraid that others would know of my idolatry. I felt, Dorian, that I had told too much, that I had put too much of myself into it. Then it was that I resolved never to allow the picture to be exhibited. You were a little annoyed; but then you did not realize all that it meant to me. Harry, to whom I talked about it, laughed at me. But I did not mind that. When the picture was finished, and I sat alone with it, I felt that I was right. . . . Well, after a few days the thing left my studio, and as soon as I had got rid of the intolerable fascination of its presence it seemed to me that I had been foolish in imagining that I had seen anything in it, more than that you were extremely good-looking and that I could paint. Even now I cannot help feeling that it is a mistake to think that the passion one feels in creation is ever really shown in the work one creates. Art is always more abstract than we fancy. Form and colour tell us of form and colour—that is all. It often seems to me that art conceals the artist far more completely than it ever reveals him. And so when I got this offer from Paris I determined to make your portrait the principal thing in my exhibition. It never occurred to me that you would refuse. I see now that you were right. The picture cannot be shown. You must not be angry with me, Dorian, for what I have told you. As I said to Harry, once, you are made to be worshipped."

Dorian Gray drew a long breath. The colour came back to his cheeks, and a smile played about his lips. The peril was over. He was safe for the time. Yet he could not help feeling infinite pity for the painter who had just made this strange confession to him, and wondered if he himself would ever be so dominated by the personality of a friend. Lord Henry had the charm of being very dangerous. But that was all. He was too clever and too cynical to be really fond of. Would there ever be some one who would fill him with a strange idolatry? Was that one of the things that life had in store?

"It is extraordinary to me, Dorian," said Hallward, "that you should have seen this in the portrait. Did you really see it?"

"I saw something in it," he answered, "something that seemed to me very curious."

"Well, you don't mind my looking at the thing now?"

Dorian shook his head. "You must not ask me that, Basil. I could not possibly let you stand in front of that picture."

"You will some day surely?"

"Never."

"Well, perhaps you are right. And now good-bye, Dorian. You have been the one person in my life who has really influenced my art. Whatever I have done that is good, I owe to you. Ah! you don't know what it cost me to tell you all that I have told you."

"My dear Basil," said Dorian, "what have you told me? Simply that you felt that you admired me too much. That is not even a compliment."

"It was not intended as a compliment. It was a confession. Now that I have made it, something seems to have gone out of me. Perhaps one should never put one's worship into words."

"It was a very disappointing confession."

"Why, what did you expect, Dorian? You didn't see anything else in the picture, did you? There was nothing else to see?"

"No; there was nothing else to see. Why do you ask? But you mustn't talk about worship. It is foolish. You and I are friends, Basil, and we must always remain so."

"You have got Harry," said the painter, sadly.

"Oh, Harry!" cried the lad, with a ripple of laughter. "Harry spends his days in saying what is incredible, and his evenings in doing what is improbable. Just the sort of life I would like to lead. But still I don't think I would go to Harry if I were in trouble. I would sooner go to you, Basil."

"You will sit to me again?"

"Impossible!"

"You spoil my life as an artist by refusing, Dorian. No man came across two ideal things. Few come across one."

"I can't explain it to you, Basil, but I must never sit to you again. There is something fatal about a portrait. It has a life of its own. I will come and have tea with you. That will be just as pleasant."

"Pleasanter for you, I am afraid," murmured Hallward, regretfully. "And now good-bye. I am sorry you won't let me look at the picture once again. But that can't be helped. I quite understand what you feel about it."

As he left the room, Dorian Gray smiled to himself. Poor Basil! how little he knew of the true reason! And how strange it was that, instead of having been forced to reveal his own secret, he had succeeded, almost by chance, in wrestling a secret from his friend! How much that strange confession explained to him! The painter's absurd fits of jealousy, his wild devotion, his extravagant panegyrics, his curious reticences—he understood them all now, and he felt sorry. There seemed to him to be something tragic in a friendship so coloured by romance.

He sighed, and touched the bell. The portrait must be hidden away at all costs. He could not run such a risk of discovery again. It had been mad of him to have allowed the thing to remain, even for an hour, in a room to which any of his friends had access.

CHAPTER X

WHEN HIS SERVANT entered, he looked at him steadfastly, and wondered if he had thought of peering behind the screen. The man was quite impassive, and waited for his orders. Dorian lit a cigarette, and walked over to the glass and glanced into it. He could see the reflection of Victor's face perfectly It was like a placid mask of servility. There was nothing to be afraid of, there. Yet he thought it best to be on his guard.

Speaking very slowly, he told him to tell the housekeeper that he wanted to see her, and then to go to the framemaker and ask him to send two of his men round at once. It seemed to him that as the man left the room his eyes wandered in the direction of the screen. Or was that merely his own fancy?

After a few moments, in her black silk dress, with old-fashioned thread mittens on her wrinkled hands, Mrs. Leaf bustled into the library. He asked her for the key of the schoolroom.

"The old schoolroom, Mr. Dorian?" she exclaimed. "Why, it is full of dust. I must get it arranged, and put straight before you go into it. It is not fit for you to see, sir. It is not, indeed."

"I don't want it put straight, Leaf. I only want the key."

"'Well, sir, you'll be covered with cobwebs if you go into it. Why, it hasn't been opened for nearly five years, not since his lordship died."

He winced at the mention of his grandfather. He had hateful memories of him. "That does not matter," he answered. "I simply want to see the place—that is all. Give me the key."

"And here is the key, sir," said the old lady, going over the contents of her bunch with tremulously uncertain hands. "Here is the key. I'll have it off the bunch in a moment. But you don't think of living up there, sir, and you so comfortable here?"

"No, no, " he cried, petulantly. "Thank you, Leaf. That will do."

She lingered for a few moments, and was garrulous over some detail of the household. He sighed, and told her to manage things as she thought best. She left the room, wreathed in smiles.

As the door closed, Dorian put the key in his pocket, and looked around the room. His eye fell on a large purple satin coverlet heavily embroidered with gold, a splendid piece of late seventeenth-century Venetian work that his grandfather had found in a convent near Bologna. Yes, that would serve to wrap the dreadful thing in. It had perhaps served often as a pall for the dead. Now it was to hide something that had a corruption of its own, worse than the corruption of death itself—something that would breed horrors and yet would never die. What the worm was to the corpse, his sins would be to the painted image on the canvas. They would mar its beauty, and eat away its grace. They would defile it, and make it shameful. And yet the thing would still live on. It would be always alive.

He shuddered, and for a moment he regretted that he had not told Basil the true reason why he had wished to hide the picture away. Basil would have helped him to resist Lord Henry's influence, and the still more poisonous influences that came from his own temperament. The love that he bore him—for it was really love—had nothing in it that was not noble and intellectual. It was not that mere physical admiration of beauty that is born of the senses, and that dies when the senses tire. It was such love as Michael Angelo had known, and Montaigne, and Winckelmann, and Shakespeare himself. Yes, Basil could have saved him. But it was too late now. The past could always be annihilated. Regret, denial, or forgetfulness could do that. But the future was inevitable. There were passions in him that would find their terrible outlet, dreams that would make the shadow of their evil real.

He took up from the couch the great purple-and-gold texture that covered it, and, holding it in his hands, passed behind the screen. Was the face on the canvas viler than before? It seemed to him that it was unchanged; and yet his loathing of it was intensified. Bold hair, blue eyes, and rose-red lips—they all were there. It was simply the expression that had altered. That was horrible in its cruelty. Compared to what he saw in it of censure or rebuke, how shallow Basil's reproaches about Sibyl Vane had been!—how shallow, and of what little account! His own soul was looking out at him from the canvas and calling him to judgment. A look of pain came across him, and he flung the rich pall over the picture. As he did so, a knock came to the door. He passed out as his servant entered.

"The persons are here, Monsieur."

He felt that the man must be got rid of at once. He must not be allowed to know where the picture was being taken to. There was something sly about him, and he had thoughtful, treacherous eyes. Sitting down at the writing-table, he scribbled a note to Lord Henry, asking him to send him round something to read, and reminding him that they were to meet at eight-fifteen that evening.

"Wait for an answer," he said, handing it to him, "and show the men in here."

In two or three minutes there was another knock, and Mr. Hubbard himself, the celebrated frame-maker of South Audley Street, came in with a somewhat rough-looking young assistant. Mr. Hubbard was a florid, red-whiskered little man, whose admiration for art was considerably tempered by the inveterate impecuniosity of most of the artists who dealt with him. As a rule, he never left his shop. He waited for people to come to him. But he always made an exception in favour of Dorian Gray. There was something about Dorian that charmed everybody. It was a pleasure even to see him.

"What can I do for you, Mr. Gray?" he said, rubbing his fat freckled hands. "I thought I would do myself the honour of coming round in person. I have just got a beauty of a frame, sir. Picked it up at a sale. Old Florentine. Came from Fonthill, I believe. Admirably suited for a religious subject, Mr. Gray."

"I am so sorry you have given yourself the trouble of coming round, Mr. Hubbard. I shall certainly drop in and look at the frame—though I don't go in much at present for religious art—but to-day I only want a picture carried to the top of the house for me. It is rather heavy, so I thought I would ask you to lend me a couple of your men."

"No trouble at all, Mr. Gray. I am delighted to be of any service to you. Which is the work of art, sir?"

"This," replied Dorian, moving the screen back. "Can you move it, covering and all, just as it is? I don't want it to get scratched going upstairs."

"There will be no difficulty, sir," said the genial frame-maker, beginning, with the aid of his assistant, to unhook the picture from the long brass chains by which it was suspended. "And, now, where shall we carry it to, Mr. Gray?"

"I will show you the way, Mr. Hubbard, if you will kindly follow me. Or perhaps you had better go in front. I am afraid it is right at the top of the house. We will go up by the front staircase, as it is wider."

He held the door open for them, and they passed out into the hall and began the ascent. The elaborate character of the frame had made the picture extremely bulky, and now and then, in spite of the obsequious protests of Mr. Hubbard, who had the true tradesman's spirited dislike of seeing a gentleman doing anything useful, Dorian put his hand to it so as to help them.

"Something of a load to carry, sir," gasped the little man, when they reached the top landing. And he wiped his shiny forehead.

"I am afraid it is rather heavy," murmured Dorian, as he unlocked the door that opened into the room that was to keep for him the curious secret of his life and hide his soul from the eyes of men.

He had not entered the place for more than four years—not, indeed, since he had used it first as a play-room when he was a child, and then as a study when he grew somewhat older. It was a large, well-proportioned room, which had been specially built by the last Lord Kelso for the use of the little grandson whom, for his strange likeness to his mother, and also for other reasons, he had always hated and desired to keep at a distance. It appeared to Dorian to have but little changed. There was the huge Italian *cassone*, with its fantastically-painted panels and its tarnished gilt mouldings, in which he had so often hidden himself as a boy. There the satinwood bookcase filled with his dog-eared schoolbooks. On the wall behind it was hanging the same ragged Flemish tapestry where a faded king and queen were playing chess in a garden, while a company of hawkers rode by, carrying hooded birds on their gauntleted wrists. How well he remembered it all! Every moment of his lonely childhood came back to him as he looked round. He recalled the stainless purity of his boyish life, and it seemed horrible to him that it was here the fatal portrait was to be hidden away. How little he had thought, in those dead days, of all that was in store for him!

But there was no other place in the house so secure from prying eyes as this. He had the key, and no one else could enter it. Beneath its purple pall, the face painted on the canvas could grow bestial, sodden, and unclean. What did it matter? No one could see it. He himself would not see it. Why should he watch the hideous corruption of his soul? He kept his youth—that was enough. And, besides, might not his nature grow finer, after all? There was no reason that the future should be so full of shame. Some one might come across his life, and purify him, and shield him from those sins that seemed to be already stirring in spirit and in flesh—those curious unpictured sins whose very mystery lent them their subtlety and their charm. Perhaps, some day, the cruel look would have passed away from the scarlet sensitive mouth, and he might show to the world Basil Hallward's masterpiece.

No; that was impossible. Hour by hour, and week by week, the thing upon the canvas was growing old. It might escape the hideousness of sin, but the hideousness of age was in store for it. The cheeks would become hollow or flaccid. Yellow crow's-feet would creep round the fading eyes and make them horrible. The hair would lose its brightness, the mouth would gape or droop, would be foolish or gross, as the mouths of old men are. There would be the wrinkled throat, the cold, blue-veined hands, the twisted body, that he remembered in the grandfather who had been so stern to him in his boyhood. The picture had to be concealed. There was no help for it.

"Bring it in, Mr. Hubbard, please," he said, wearily, turning round. "I am sorry I kept you so long. I was thinking of something else."

"Always glad to have a rest, Mr. Gray," answered the frame-maker, who was still gasping for breath. "Where shall we put it, sir?"

"Oh, anywhere. Here this will do. I don't want to have it hung up. Just lean it against the wall. Thanks."

"Might one look at the work of art, sir?"

Dorian started. "It would not interest you, Mr. Hubbard," he said, keeping his eye on the man. He felt ready to leap upon him and fling him to the ground if he dared to lift the gorgeous hanging that concealed the secret of his life. "I sha'n't trouble you any more now. I am much obliged for your kindness in coming round."

"Not at all, not at all, Mr. Gray. Ever ready to do anything for you, sir."

And Mr. Hubbard tramped downstairs, followed by the assistant, who glanced back at Dorian with a look of shy wonder in his rough, uncomely face. He had never seen any one so marvellous.

When the sound of their footsteps had died away, Dorian locked the door, and put the key in his pocket. He felt safe now. No one would ever look upon the horrible thing. No eye but his would ever see his shame.

On reaching the library he found that it was just after five o'clock, and that the tea had been already brought up. On a little table of dark perfumed wood thickly incrusted with nacre, a present from Lady Radley, his guardian's wife, a pretty professional invalid, who had spent the preceding winter in Cairo, was lying a note from Lord Henry, and beside it was a book bound in yellow paper, the cover slightly torn and the edges soiled. A copy of the third edition of *The St. James's Gazette* had been placed on the tea-tray. It was evident that Victor had returned. He wondered if he had met the men in the hall as they were leaving the house, and had wormed out of them what they had been doing. He would be sure to miss the picture—had no doubt missed it already, while he had been laying the tea-things. The screen had not been set back, and a blank space was visible on the wall. Perhaps some night he might find him creeping upstairs and trying to force the door of the room. It was a horrible thing to have a spy in one's house. He had heard of rich men who had been blackmailed all their lives by some servant who had read a letter, or overheard a conversation, or picked up a card with an address, or found beneath a pillow a withered flower or a shred of crumpled lace.

He sighed, and, having poured himself out some tea, opened Lord Henry's note. It was simply to say that he sent him round the evening paper, and a book that might interest him, and that he would be at the club at eight-fifteen. He opened *The St. James's* languidly, and looked through it. A red pencil-mark on the fifth page caught his eye. It drew attention to the following paragraph:

"Inquest On An Actress.—An inquest was held this morning at the Bell Tavern, Hoxton Road, by Mr. Danby, the District Coroner, on the body of Sibyl Vane, a young actress recently engaged at the Royal Theatre, Holborn. A verdict of death by misadventure was returned. Considerable sympathy was expressed for the mother of the deceased, who was greatly affected during the giving of her own evidence, and that of Dr. Birrell, who had made the post-mortem examination of the deceased."

He frowned, and, tearing the paper in two, went across the room and flung the pieces away. How ugly it all was! And how horribly real ugliness made things! He felt a little annoyed with Lord Henry for having sent him the report. And it was certainly stupid of him to have marked it with red pencil. Victor might have read it. The man knew more than enough English for that.

Perhaps he had read it, and had begun to suspect something. And, yet, what did it matter? What had Dorian Gray to do with Sibyl Vane's death? There was nothing to fear. Dorian Gray had not killed her.

His eye fell on the yellow book that Lord Henry had sent him. What was it, he wondered. He went towards the little pearl-coloured octagonal stand, that had always looked to him like the work of some strange Egyptian bees that wrought in silver, and taking up the volume, flung himself into an arm-chair, and began to turn over the leaves. After a few minutes he became absorbed. It was the strangest book that he had ever read. It seemed to him that in exquisite raiment, and to the delicate sound of flutes, the sins of the world were passing in dumb show before him. Things that he had dimly dreamed of were suddenly made real to him. Things of which he had never dreamed were gradually revealed.

It was a novel without a plot, and with only one character, being, indeed, simply a psychological study of a certain young Parisian, who spent his life trying to realize in the nineteenth century all the passions and modes of thought that belonged to every century except his own, and to sum up, as it were, in himself the various moods through which the world-spirit had ever passed, loving for their mere artificiality those renunciations that men have unwisely called virtue, as much as those natural rebellions that wise men still call sin. The style in which it was written was that curious jewelled style, vivid and obscure at once, full of *argot* and of archaisms, of technical expressions and of elaborate paraphrases, that characterizes the work of some of the finest artists of the French school of *Symbolistes*. There were in it metaphors as monstrous as orchids, and as subtle in colour. The life of the senses was described in the terms of mystical philosophy. One hardly knew at times whether one was reading the spiritual ecstasies of some mediæval saint or the morbid confessions of a modern sinner. It was a poisonous book. The heavy odour of incense seemed to cling about its pages and to trouble the brain. The mere cadence of the sentences, the subtle monotony of their music, so full as it was of complex refrains and movements elaborately repeated, produced in the mind of the lad, as he passed from chapter to chapter, a form of reverie, a malady of dreaming, that made him unconscious of the failing day and creeping shadows.

Cloudless, and pierced by one solitary star, a copper-green sky gleamed through the windows. He read on by its wan light till he could read no more. Then, after his valet had reminded him several times of the lateness of the hour, he got up, and, going into the next room, placed the book on the little Florentine table that always stood at his bedside, and began to dress for dinner.

It was almost nine o'clock before he reached the club, where he found Lord Henry sitting alone, in the morning-room, looking very much bored.

"I am so sorry, Harry," he cried, "but really it is entirely your fault. That book you sent me so fascinated me that I forgot how the time was going."

"Yes: I thought you would like it," replied his host, rising from his chair.

"I didn't say I liked it, Harry. I said it fascinated me. There is a great difference."

"Ah, you have discovered that?" murmured Lord Henry. And they passed into the dining-room.

CHAPTER XI

FOR YEARS, DORIAN Gray could not free himself from the influence of this book. Or perhaps it would be more accurate to say that he never sought to free himself from it. He procured from Paris no less than nine large-paper copies of the first edition, and had them bound in different colours, so that they might suit his various moods and the changing fancies of a nature over which he seemed, at times, to have almost entirely lost control. The hero, the wonderful young Parisian, in whom the romantic and the scientific temperaments were so strangely blended, became to him a kind of prefiguring type of himself. And, indeed, the whole book seemed to him to contain the story of his own life, written before he had lived it.

In one point he was more fortunate than the novel's fantastic hero. He never knew—never, indeed, had any cause to know—that somewhat grotesque dread of mirrors, and polished metal surfaces, and still water, which came upon the young Parisian so early in his life, and was occasioned by the sudden decay of a beauty that had once, apparently, been so remarkable. It was with an almost cruel joy—and perhaps in nearly every joy, as certainly in every pleasure, cruelty has its place—that he used to read the latter part of the book, with its really tragic, if somewhat overemphasized, account of the sorrow and despair of one who had himself lost what in others, and in the world, he had most dearly valued.

For the wonderful beauty that had so fascinated Basil Hallward, and many others besides him, seemed never to leave him. Even those who had heard the most evil things against him, and from time to time strange rumours about his mode of life crept through London and became the chatter of the clubs, could not believe anything to his dishonour when they saw him. He had always the look of one who had kept himself unspotted from the world. Men who talked grossly became silent when Dorian Gray entered the room. There was something in the purity of his face that rebuked them. His mere presence seemed to recall to them the memory of the innocence that they had tarnished. They wondered how one so charming and graceful as he was could have escaped the stain of an age that was at once sordid and sensual.

Often, on returning home from one of those mysterious and prolonged absences that gave rise to such strange conjecture among those who were his friends, or thought that they were so, he himself would creep upstairs to the locked room, open the door with the key that never left him now, and stand, with a mirror, in front of the portrait that Basil Hallward had painted of him, looking now at the evil and aging face on the canvas, and now at the fair young face that laughed back at him from the polished glass. The very sharpness of the contrast used to quicken his sense of pleasure. He grew more and more enamoured of his own beauty, more and more interested in the corruption of his own soul. He would examine with minute care, and sometimes with a monstrous and terrible delight, the hideous lines that seared the wrinkling forehead or crawled around the heavy sensual mouth, wondering sometimes which were the more horrible, the signs of sin or the signs of age. He would place his white hands beside the coarse bloated hands of the picture, and smile. He mocked the misshapen body and the failing limbs.

There were moments, indeed, at night, when, lying sleepless in his own delicately-scented chamber, or in the sordid room of the little ill-famed tavern near the Docks, which, under an assumed name, and in disguise, it was his habit to frequent, he would think of the ruin he had brought upon his soul, with a pity that was all the more poignant because it was purely selfish. But moments such as these were rare. That curiosity about life which Lord Henry had first stirred in him, as they sat together in the garden of their friend, seemed to increase with gratification. The more he knew, the more he desired to know. He had mad hungers that grew more ravenous as he fed them.

Yet he was not really reckless, at any rate in his relations to society. Once or twice every month during the winter, and on each Wednesday evening while the season lasted, he would throw open to the world his beautiful house and have the most celebrated musicians of the day to charm his guests with the wonders of their art. His little dinners, in the settling of which Lord Henry always assisted him, were noted as much for the careful selection and placing of those invited, as for the exquisite taste shown in the decoration of the table, with its subtle symphonic arrangements of exotic flowers, and embroidered cloths, and antique plate of gold and silver. Indeed, there were many, especially among the very young men, who saw, or fancied that they saw, in Dorian Gray the true realization of a type of which they had often dreamed in Eton or Oxford days, a type that was to combine something of the real culture of the scholar with all the grace and distinction and perfect manner of a citizen of the world. To them he seemed to be of the company of those whom Dante describes as having sought to "make themselves perfect by the worship of beauty." Like Gautier, he was one for whom "the visible world existed."

And, certainly, to him Life itself was the first, the greatest, of the arts, and for it all the other arts seemed to be but a preparation. Fashion, by which what is really fantastic becomes for a moment universal, and Dandyism, which, in its own way, is an attempt to assert the absolute modernity of beauty, had, of course, their fascination for him. His mode of dressing, and the particular styles that from time to time he affected, had their marked influence on the young exquisites of the Mayfair balls and Pall Mall club windows, who copied him in everything that he did, and tried to reproduce the accidental charm of his graceful, though to him only half-serious, fopperies.

For, while he was but too ready to accept the position that was almost immediately offered to him on his coming of age, and found, indeed, a subtle pleasure in the thought that he might really become to the London of his own day what to imperial Neronian Rome the author of the "Satyricon" once had been, yet in his inmost heart he desired to be something more than a mere *arbiter elegantiarum*, to be consulted on the wearing of a jewel, or the knotting of a necktie, or the conduct of a cane. He sought to elaborate some new scheme of life that would have its reasoned philosophy and its ordered principles, and find in the spiritualizing of the senses its highest realization.

The worship of the senses has often, and with much justice, been decried, men feeling a natural instinct of terror about passions and sensations that seem stronger than themselves, and that they are conscious of sharing with the less highly organized forms of existence. But it appeared to Dorian Gray that the true nature of the senses had never been understood, and that they had remained savage and animal merely because the world had sought to starve them into submission or to kill them by pain, instead of aiming at making them elements of a new spirituality, of which a fine instinct for beauty was to be the dominant characteristic. As he looked back upon man moving through History, he was haunted by a feeling of loss. So much had been surrendered! and to such little purpose! There had been mad wilful rejections, monstrous forms of self-torture and self-denial, whose origin was fear, and whose result was a degradation infinitely more terrible than that fancied degradation from which, in their ignorance, they had sought to escape, Nature, in her wonderful irony, driving out the anchorite to feed with the wild animals of the desert and giving to the hermit the beasts of the field as his companions.

Yes: there was to be, as Lord Henry had prophesied, a new Hedonism that was to recreate life, and to save it from that harsh, uncomely puritanism that is having, in our own day, its curious revival. It was to have its service of the intellect, certainly; yet, it was never to accept any theory or system that would involve the sacrifice of any mode of passionate experience. Its aim, indeed, was to be experience itself, and not the fruits of experience, sweet or bitter as they might be. Of the asceticism that deadens the senses, of the vulgar profligacy that dulls them, it was to know nothing. But it was to teach man to concentrate himself upon the moments of a life that is itself but a moment.

There are few of us who have not sometimes wakened before dawn, either after one of those dreamless nights that make us almost enamoured of death, or one of those nights of horror and misshapen joy, when through the chambers of the brain sweep phantoms more terrible than reality itself, and instinct with that vivid life that lurks in all grotesques, and that lends to Gothic art its enduring vitality, this art being, one might fancy, especially the art of those whose minds have been troubled with the malady of reverie. Gradually white fingers creep through the curtains, and they appear to tremble. In black fantastic shapes, dumb shadows crawl into the corners of the room, and crouch there. Outside, there is the stirring of birds among the leaves, or the sound of men going forth to their work, or the sigh and sob of the wind coming down from the hills, and wandering round the silent house, as though it feared to wake the sleepers, and yet must needs call forth sleep from her purple cave. Veil after veil of thin dusky gauze is lifted, and by degrees the forms and colours of things are restored to them, and we watch the dawn remaking the world in its antique pattern. The wan mirrors get back their mimic life. The flameless tapers stand where we had left them, and beside them lies the half-cut book that we had been studying, or the wired flower that we had worn at the ball, or the letter that we had been afraid to read, or that we had read too often. Nothing seems to us changed. Out of the unreal shadows of the night comes back the real life that we had known. We have to resume it where we had left off, and there steals over us a terrible sense of the necessity for the continuance of energy in the same wearisome round of stereotyped habits, or a wild longing, it may be, that our eyelids might open some morning upon a world that had been refashioned anew in the darkness for our pleasure, a world in which things would have fresh shapes and colours, and be changed, or have other secrets, a world in which the past would have little or no place, or survive, at any rate, in no conscious form of obligation or regret, the remembrance even of joy having its bitterness, and the memories of pleasure their pain.

It was the creation of such worlds as these that seemed to Dorian Gray to be the true object, or amongst the true objects, of life; and in his search for sensations that would be at once new and delightful, and possess that element of strangeness that is so essential to romance, he would often adopt certain modes of thought that he knew to be really alien to his nature, abandon himself to their subtle influences, and then, having, as it were, caught their colour and satisfied his intellectual curiosity, leave them with that curious indifference that is not incompatible with a real ardour of temperament, and that indeed, according to certain modern psychologists, is often a condition of it.

It was rumoured of him once that he was about to join the Roman Catholic communion; and certainly the Roman ritual had always a great attraction for him. The daily sacrifice, more awful really than all the sacrifices of the antique world, stirred him as much by its superb rejection of the evidence of the senses as by the primitive simplicity of its elements and the eternal pathos of the human tragedy that it sought to symbolize. He loved to kneel down on the cold marble pavement, and watch the priest, in his stiff flowered dalmatic, slowly and with white hands moving aside the veil of the tabernacle, or raising aloft the jewelled lantern-shaped monstrance with that pallid wafer that at times, one would fain think, is indeed the *"panis caelestis,"* the bread of angels, or, robed in the garments of the Passion of Christ, breaking the Host into the chalice, and smiting his breast for his sins. The fuming censers, that the grave boys, in their lace and scarlet, tossed into the air like great gilt flowers, had their subtle fascination for him. As he passed out, he used to look with wonder at the black confessionals, and long to sit in the dim shadow of one of them and listen to men and women whispering through the worn grating the true story of their lives.

But he never fell into the error of arresting his intellectual development by any formal acceptance of creed or system, or of mistaking, for a house in which to live, an inn that is but suitable for the sojourn of a night, or for a few hours of a night in which there are no stars and the moon is in travail. Mysticism, with its marvellous power of making common things strange to us, and the subtle antinomianism that always seems to accompany it, moved him for a season; and for a season he inclined to the materialistic doctrines of the *Darwinismus* movement in Germany and found a curious pleasure in tracing the thoughts and passions of men to some pearly cell in the brain, or some white nerve in the body, delighting in the conception of the absolute dependence of the spirit on certain physical conditions, morbid or healthy, normal or diseased. Yet, as has been said of him before, no theory of life seemed to him to be of any importance compared with life itself. He felt keenly conscious of how barren all intellectual speculation is when separated from action and experiment. He knew that the senses, no less than the soul, have their spiritual mysteries to reveal.

And so he would now study perfumes, and the secrets of their manufacture, distilling heavily-scented oils, and burning odorous gums from the East. He saw that there was no mood of the mind that had not its counterpart in the sensuous life, and set himself to discover their true relations, wondering what there was in frankincense that made one mystical, and in ambergris that stirred one's passions, and in violets that woke the memory of dead romances, and in musk that troubled the brain, and in champak that stained the imagination; and seeking often to elaborate a real psychology of perfumes, and to estimate the several influences of sweet-smelling roots, and scented pollen-laden flowers, of aromatic balms, and of dark and fragrant woods, of spikenard that sickens, of hovenia that makes men mad, and of aloes that are said to be able to expel melancholy from the soul.

At another time he devoted himself entirely to music, and in a long latticed room, with a vermilion-and-gold ceiling and walls of olive-green lacquer, he used to give curious concerts in which mad gypsies tore wild music from little zithers, or grave yellow-shawled Tunisians plucked at the strained strings of monstrous lutes, while grinning negroes beat monotonously upon copper drums, and, crouching upon scarlet mats, slim turbaned Indians blew through long pipes of reed or brass, and charmed, or feigned to charm, great hooded snakes and horrible horned adders. The harsh intervals and shrill discords of barbaric music stirred him at times when Schubert's grace, and Chopin's beautiful sorrows, and the mighty harmonies of Beethoven himself, fell unheeded on his ear. He collected together from all parts of the world the strangest instruments that could be found, either in the tombs of dead nations or among the few savage tribes that have survived contact with Western civilizations, and loved to touch and try them. He had the mysterious *juruparis* of the Rio Negro Indians, that women are not allowed to look at, and that even youths may not see till they have been subjected to fasting and scourging, and the earthen jars of the Peruvians that have the shrill cries of birds, and flutes of human bones such as Alfonso de Ovalle heard in Chili, and the sonorous green jaspers that are found near Cuzco and give forth a note of singular sweetness. He had painted gourds filled with pebbles that rattled when they were shaken; the long *clarin* of the Mexicans, into which the performer does not blow, but through which he inhales the air; the harsh *turc* of the Amazon tribes, that is sounded by the sentinels who sit all day long in high trees, and can be heard, it is said, at the distance of three leagues; the *teponaztli*, that has two vibrating tongues of wood, and is beaten with sticks that are smeared with an elastic gum obtained from the milky juice of plants; the *yotl*-bells of the Aztecs, that are hung in clusters like grapes; and a huge cylindrical drum, covered with the skins of great serpents, like the one that Bernal Diaz saw when he went with Cortes into the Mexican temple, and of whose doleful sound he has left us so vivid a description. The fantastic character of these instruments fascinated him, and he felt a curious delight in the thought that Art, like Nature, has her monsters, things of bestial shape and with hideous voices. Yet, after some time, he wearied of them, and would sit in his box at the Opera, either alone or with Lord Henry, listening in rapt pleasure to "Tannhäuser," and seeing in the prelude to that great work of art a presentation of the tragedy of his own soul.

On one occasion he took up the study of jewels, and appeared at a costume ball as Anne de Joyeuse, Admiral of France, in a dress covered with five hundred and sixty pearls. This taste enthralled him for years, and, indeed, may be said never to have left him. He would often spend a whole day settling and resettling in their cases the various stones that he had collected, such as the olive-green chrysoberyl that turns red by lamplight, the cymophane with its wire-like line of silver, the pistachio-coloured peridot, rose-pink and wine-yellow topazes, carbuncles of fiery scarlet with tremulous four-rayed stars, flame-red cinnamon-stones, orange and violet spinels, and amethysts with their alternate layers of ruby and sapphire. He loved the red gold of the sunstone, and the moonstone's pearly whiteness, and the broken rainbow of the milky opal. He procured from Amsterdam three emeralds of extraordinary size and richness of colour, and had a turquoise *de la vieille roche* that was the envy of all the connoisseurs.

He discovered wonderful stories, also, about jewels. In Alphonso's "Clericalis Disciplina" a serpent was mentioned with eyes of real jacinth, and in the romantic history of Alexander, the Conqueror of Emathia was said to have found in the vale of Jordan snakes "with collars of real emeralds growing on their backs." There was a gem in the brain of the dragon, Philostratus told us, and "by the exhibition of golden letters and a scarlet robe" the monster could be thrown into a magical sleep, and slain. According to the great alchemist, Pierre de Boniface, the diamond rendered a man invisible, and the agate of India made him eloquent. The cornelian appeased anger, and the hyacinth provoked sleep, and the amethyst drove away the fumes of wine. The garnet cast out demons, and the hydropicus deprived the moon of her colour. The selenite waxed and waned with the moon, and the meloceus, that discovers thieves, could be affected only by the blood of kids. Leonardus Camillus had seen a white stone taken from the brain of a newly-killed toad, that was a certain antidote against poison. The bezoar, that was found in the heart of the Arabian deer, was a charm that could cure the plague. In the nests of Arabian birds was the aspilates, that, according to Democritus, kept the wearer from any danger by fire.

The King of Ceilan rode through his city with a large ruby in his hand, as the ceremony of his coronation. The gates of the palace of John the Priest were "made of sardius, with the horn of the horned snake inwrought, so that no man might bring poison within." Over the gable were "two golden apples, in which were two carbuncles," so that the gold might shine by day, and the carbuncles by night. In Lodge's strange romance "A Margarite of America" it was stated that in the chamber of the queen one could behold "all the chaste ladies of the world, inchased out of silver, looking through fair mirrours of chrysolites, carbuncles, sapphires, and greene emeraults." Marco Polo had seen the inhabitants of Zipangu place rose-coloured pearls in the mouths of the dead. A sea-monster had been enamoured of the pearl that the diver brought to King Perozes, and had slain the thief, and mourned for seven moons over its loss. When the Huns lured the king into the great pit, he flung it away—Procopius tells the story—nor was it ever found again, though the Emperor Anastasius offered five hundred-weight of gold pieces for it. The King of Malabar had shown to a certain Venetian a rosary of three hundred and four pearls, one for every god that he worshipped.

When the Duke de Valentinois, son of Alexander VI, visited Louis XII of France, his horse was loaded with gold leaves, according to Brantôme, and his cap had double rows of rubies that threw out a great light. Charles of England had ridden in stirrups hung with four hundred and twenty-one diamonds. Richard II had a coat, valued at thirty thousand marks, which was covered with balas rubies. Hall described Henry VIII, on his way to the Tower previous to his coronation, as wearing "a jacket of raised gold, the placard embroidered with diamonds and other rich stones, and a great bauderike about his neck of large balasses." The favourites of James I wore earrings of emeralds set in gold filigrane. Edward II gave to Piers Gaveston a suit of red-gold armour studded with jacinths, a collar of gold roses set with turquoise-stones, and a skull-cap *parsemé* with pearls. Henry II wore jewelled gloves reaching to the elbow, and had a hawk-glove sewn with twelve rubies and fifty-two great orients. The ducal hat of Charles the Rash, the last Duke of Burgundy of his race, was hung with pear-shaped pearls, and studded with sapphires.

How exquisite life had once been! How gorgeous in its pomp and decoration! Even to read of the luxury of the dead was wonderful.

Then he turned his attention to embroideries, and to the tapestries that performed the office of frescoes in the chill rooms of the Northern nations of Europe. As he investigated the subject—and he always had an extraordinary faculty of becoming absolutely absorbed for the moment in whatever he took up—he was almost saddened by the reflection of the ruin that Time brought on beautiful and wonderful things. He, at any rate, had escaped that. Summer followed summer, and the yellow jonquils bloomed and died many times, and nights of horror repeated the story of their shame, but he was unchanged. No winter marred his face or stained his flower-like bloom. How different it was with material things! Where had they passed to? Where was the great crocus-coloured robe, on which the gods fought against the giants, that had been worked by brown girls for the pleasure of Athena? Where, the huge velarium that Nero had stretched across the Colosseum at Rome, that Titan sail of purple on which was represented the starry sky, and Apollo driving a chariot drawn by white gilt-reined steeds? He longed to see the curious table-napkins wrought for the Priest of the Sun, on which were displayed all the dainties and viands that could be wanted for a feast; the mortuary cloth of King Chilperic, with its three hundred golden bees; the fantastic robes that excited the indignation of the Bishop of Pontus, and were figured with "lions, panthers, bears, dogs, forests, rocks, hunters—all, in fact, that a painter can copy from nature;" and the coat that Charles of Orleans once wore, on the sleeves of which were embroidered the verses of a song beginning "*Madame, je suis tout joyeux*," the musical accompaniment of the words being wrought in gold thread, and each note, of square shape in those days, formed with four pearls. He read of the room that was prepared at the palace at Rheims for the use of Queen Joan of Burgundy, and was decorated with "thirteen hundred and twenty-one parrots, made in broidery, and blazoned with the king's arms, and five hundred and sixty-one butterflies, whose wings were similarly ornamented with the arms of the queen, the whole worked in gold." Catherine de Médicis had a mourning-bed made for her of black velvet powdered with crescents and suns. Its curtains were of damask, with leafy wreaths and garlands, figured upon a gold and silver ground, and fringed along the edges with broideries of pearls, and it stood in a room hung with rows of the queen's devices in cut black velvet upon cloth of silver. Louis XIV had gold embroidered caryatides fifteen feet high in his apartment. The state bed of Sobieski, King of Poland, was made of Smyrna gold brocade embroidered in turquoises with verses from the Koran. Its supports were of silver gilt, beautifully chased, and profusely set with enamelled and jewelled medallions. It had been taken from the Turkish camp before Vienna, and the standard of Mohammed had stood beneath the tremulous gilt of its canopy.

And so, for a whole year, he sought to accumulate the most exquisite specimens that he could find of textile and embroidered work, getting the dainty Delhi muslins, finely wrought with gold-thread palmates, and stitched over with iridescent beetles' wings; the Dacca gauzes, that from their transparency are known in the East as "woven air," and "running water," and "evening dew"; strange figured cloths from Java; elaborate yellow Chinese hangings; books bound in tawny satins or fair blue silks, and wrought with *fleurs de lys*, birds, and images; veils of *lacis* worked in Hungary point; Sicilian brocades, and stiff Spanish velets; Georgian work with its gilt coins, and Japanese *Foukousas* with their green-toned golds and their marvellously-plumaged birds.

He had a special passion, also, for ecclesiastical vestments, as indeed he had for everything connected with the service of the Church. In the long cedar chests that lined the west gallery of his house he had stored away many rare and beautiful specimens of what is really the raiment of the Bride of Christ, who must wear purple and jewels and fine linen that she may hide the pallid macerated body that is worn by the suffering that she seeks for, and wounded by self-inflicted pain. He possessed a gorgeous cope of crimson silk and gold-thread damask, figured with a repeating pattern of golden pomegranates set in six-petalled formal blossoms, beyond which on either side was the pine-apple device wrought in seed-pearls. The orphreys were divided into panels representing scenes from the life of the Virgin, and the coronation of the Virgin was figured in coloured silks upon the hood. This was Italian work of the fifteenth century. Another cope was of green velvet, embroidered with heart-shaped groups of acanthus-leaves, from which spread long-stemmed white blossoms, the details of which were picked out with silver thread and coloured crystals. The morse bore a seraph's head in gold-thread raised work. The orphreys were woven in a diaper of red and gold silk, and were starred with medallions of many saints and martyrs, among whom was St. Sebastian. He had chasubles, also, of amber-coloured silk, and blue silk and gold brocade, and yellow silk damask and cloth of gold, figured with representations of the Passion and Crucifixion of Christ, and embroidered with lions and peacocks and other emblems; dalmatics of white satin and pink silk damask, decorated with tulips and dolphins and *fleurs de lys*; altar frontals of crimson velvet and blue linen; and many corporals, chalice-veils, and sudaria. In the mystic offices to which such things were put, there was something that quickened his imagination.

For these treasures, and everything that he collected in his lovely house, were to be to him means of forgetfulness, modes by which he could escape, for a season, from the fear that seemed to him at times to be almost too great to be borne. Upon the walls of the lonely locked room where he had spent so much of his boyhood, he had hung with his own hands the terrible portrait whose changing features showed him the real degradation of his life, and in front of it had draped the purple-and-gold pall as a curtain. For weeks he would not go there, would forget the hideous painted thing, and get back his light heart, his wonderful joyousness, his passionate absorption in mere existence. Then, suddenly, some night he would creep out of the house, go down to dreadful places near Blue Gate Fields, and stay there, day after day, until he was driven away. On his return he would sit in front of the picture, sometimes loathing it and himself, but filled, at other times, with that pride of individualism that is half the fascination of sin, and smiling, with secret pleasure, at the misshapen shadow that had to bear the burden that should have been his own.

After a few years he could not endure to be long out of England, and gave up the villa that he had shared at Trouville with Lord Henry as well as the little white walled-in house at Algiers where they had more than once spent the winter. He hated to be separated from the picture that was such a part of his life, and was also afraid that during his absence some one might gain access to the room, in spite of the elaborate bars that he had caused to be placed upon the door.

He was quite conscious that this would tell them nothing. It was true that the portrait still preserved, under all the foulness and ugliness of the face, its marked likeness to himself; but what could they learn from that? He would laugh at any one who tried to taunt him. He had not painted it. What was it to him how vile and full of shame it looked? Even if he told them, would they believe it?

Yet he was afraid. Sometimes when he was down at his great house in Nottinghamshire, entertaining the fashionable voting men of his own rank who were his chief companions, and astounding the county by the wanton luxury and gorgeous splendour of his mode of life, he would suddenly leave his guests and rush back to town to see that the door had not been tampered with, and that the picture was still there. What if it should be stolen? The mere thought made him cold with horror. Surely the world would know his secret then. Perhaps the world already suspected it.

For, while he fascinated many, there were not a few who distrusted him. He was very nearly blackballed at a West End club of which his birth and social position fully entitled him to become a member, and it was said that on one occasion, when he was brought by a friend into the smoking-room of the Churchill, the Duke of Berwick and another gentleman got up in a marked manner and went out. Curious stories became current about him after he had passed his twenty-fifth year. It was rumoured that he had been seen brawling with foreign sailors in a low den in the distant parts of Whitechapel, and that he consorted with thieves and coiners and knew the mysteries of their trade. His extraordinary absences became notorious, and, when he used to reappear again in society, men would whisper to each other in corners, or pass him with a sneer, or look at him with cold searching eyes, as though they were determined to discover his secret.

Of such insolences and attempted slights he, of course, took no notice, and in the opinion of most people his frank debonnair manner, his charming boyish smile, and the infinite grace of that wonderful youth that seemed never to leave him, were in themselves a sufficient answer to the calumnies, for so they termed them, that were circulated about him. It was remarked, however, that some of those who had been most intimate with him appeared, after a time, to shun him. Women who had wildly adored him, and for his sake had braved all social censure and set convention at defiance, were seen to grow pallid with shame or horror if Dorian Gray entered the room.

Yet these whispered scandals only increased, in the eyes of many, his strange and dangerous charm. His great wealth was a certain element of security. Society, civilized society at least, is never very ready to believe anything to the detriment of those who are both rich and fascinating. It feels instinctively that manners are of more importance than morals, and, in its opinion, the highest respectability is of much less value than the possession of a good *chef*. And, after all, it is a very poor consolation to be told that the man who has given one a bad dinner, or poor wine, is irreproachable in his private life. Even the cardinal virtues cannot atone for half-cold *entrées*, as Lord Henry remarked once, in a discussion on the subject; and there is possibly a good deal to be said for his view. For the canons of good society are, or should be, the same as the canons of art. Form is absolutely essential to it. It should have the dignity of a ceremony, as well as its unreality, and should combine the insincere character of a romantic play with the wit and beauty that make such plays delightful to us. Is insincerity such a terrible thing? I think not. It is merely a method by which we can multiply our personalities.

Such, at any rate, was Dorian Gray's opinion. He used to wonder at the shallow psychology of those who conceive the Ego in man as a thing simple, permanent, reliable, and of one essence. To him, man was a being with myriad lives and myriad sensations, a complex multiform creature that bore within itself strange legacies of thought and passion, and whose very flesh was tainted with the monstrous maladies of the dead. He loved to stroll through the gaunt cold picture-gallery of his country house and look at the various portraits of those whose blood flowed in his veins. Here was Philip Herbert, described by Francis Osborne, in his "Memoires on the Reigns of Queen Elizabeth and King James," as one who was "caressed by the Court for his handsome face, which kept him not long company." Was it young Herbert's life that he sometimes led? Had some strange poisonous germ crept from body to body till it had reached his own? Was it some dim sense of that ruined grace that had made him so suddenly, and almost without cause, give utterance, in Basil Hallward's studio, to the mad prayer that had so changed his life? Here, in gold-embroidered red doublet, jewelled surcoat, and gilt-edged ruff and wrist-bands, stood Sir Anthony Sherard, with his silver-and-black armour piled at his feet. What had this man's legacy been? Had the lover of Giovanna of Naples bequeathed him some inheritance of sin and shame? Were his own actions merely the dreams that the dead man had not dared to realize? Here, from the fading canvas, smiled Lady Elizabeth Devereux, in her gauze hood, pearl stomacher, and pink slashed sleeves. A flower was in her right hand, and her left clasped an enamelled collar of white and damask roses. On a table by her side lay a mandolin and an apple. There were large green rosettes upon her little pointed shoes. He knew her life, and the strange stories that were told about her lovers. Had he something of her temperament in him? These oval heavy-lidded eyes seemed to look curiously at him. What of George Willoughby, with his powdered hair and fantastic patches? How evil he looked! The face was saturnine and swarthy, and the sensual lips seemed to be twisted with disdain. Delicate lace ruffles fell over the lean yellow hands that were so overladen with rings. He had been a macaroni of the eighteenth century, and the friend, in his youth, of Lord Ferrars. What of the second Lord Beckenham, the companion of the Prince Regent in his wildest days, and one of the witnesses at the secret marriage with Mrs. Fitzherbert? How proud and handsome he was, with his chestnut curls and insolent pose! What passions had he bequeathed? The world had looked upon him as infamous. He had led the orgies at Carlton House. The star of the Garter glittered upon his breast. Beside him hung the portrait of his wife, a pallid, thin-lipped woman in black. Her blood, also, stirred within him. How curious it all seemed! And his mother with her Lady Hamilton face, and her moist wine-dashed lips—he knew what he had got from her. He had got from her his beauty, and his passion for the beauty of others. She laughed at him in her loose Bacchante dress. There were vine leaves in her hair. The purple spilled from the cup she was holding. The carnations of the painting had withered, but the eyes were still wonderful in their depth and brilliancy of colour. They seemed to follow him wherever he went.

Yet one had ancestors in literature, as well as in one's own race, nearer perhaps in type and temperament, many of them, and certainly with an influence of which one was more absolutely conscious. There were times when it appeared to Dorian Gray that the whole of history was merely the record of his own life, not as he had lived it in act and circumstance, but as his imagination had created it for him, as it had been in his brain and in his passions. He felt that he had known them all, those strange terrible figures that had passed across the stage of the world and made sin so marvellous and evil so full of subtlety. It seemed to him that in some mysterious way their lives had been his own.

The hero of the wonderful novel that had so influenced his life had himself known this curious fancy. In the seventh chapter he tells how, crowned with laurel, lest lightning might strike him, he had sat, as Tiberius in a garden at Capri, reading the shameful books of Elephantis, while dwarfs and peacocks strutted round him and the flute-player mocked the swinger of the censer; and, as

Caligula, had caroused with the green-shirted jockeys in their stables, and supped in an ivory manger with a jewel-frontleted horse; and, as Domitian, had wandered through a corridor lined with marble mirrors, looking round with haggard eyes for the reflection of the dagger that was to end his days, and sick with that ennui, that terrible *taedium vitae*, that comes on those to whom life denies nothing; and had peered through a clear emerald at the red shambles of the Circus, and then, in a litter of pearl and purple drawn by silver-shod mules, been carried through the Street of Pomegranates to a House of Gold, and heard men cry on Nero Caesar as he passed by; and, as Elagabalus, had painted his face with colours, and plied the distaff among the women, and brought the Moon from Carthage, and given her in mystic marriage to the Sun.

Over and over again Dorian used to read this fantastic chapter, and the two chapters immediately following, in which, as in some curious tapestries or cunningly-wrought enamels, were pictured the awful and beautiful forms of those whom Vice and Blood and Weariness had made monstrous or mad: Filippo, Duke of Milan, who slew his wife, and painted her lips with a scarlet poison that her lover might suck death from the dead thing he fondled; Pietro Barbi, the Venetian, known as Paul the Second, who sought in his vanity to assume the title of Formosus, and whose tiara, valued at two hundred thousand florins, was bought at the price of a terrible sin; Gian Maria Visconti, who used hounds to chase living men, and whose murdered body was covered with roses by a harlot who had loved him; the Borgia on his white horse, with Fratricide riding beside him, and his mantle stained with the blood of Perotto; Pietro Riario, the young Cardinal Archbishop of Florence, child and minion of Sixtus IV, whose beauty was equalled only by his debauchery, and who received Leonora of Aragon in a pavilion of white and crimson silk, filled with nymphs and centaurs, and gilded a boy that he might serve at the feast as Ganymede or Hylas; Ezzelin, whose melancholy could be cured only by the spectacle of death, and who had a passion for red blood, as other men have for red wine—the son of the Fiend, as was reported, and one who had cheated his father at dice when gambling with him for his own soul; Giambattista Cibo, who in mockery took the name of Innocent, and into whose torpid veins the blood of three lads was infused by a Jewish doctor; Sigismondo Malatesta, the lover of Isotta, and the lord of Rimini, whose effigy was burned at Rome as the enemy of God and man, who strangled Polyssena with a napkin, and gave poison to Ginevra d'Este in a cup of emerald, and in honour of a shameful passion built a pagan church for Christian worship; Charles VI, who had so wildly adored his brother's wife that a leper had warned him of the insanity that was coming on him, and who, when his brain had sickened and grown strange, could only be soothed by Saracen cards painted with the images of Love and Death and Madness; and, in his trimmed jerkin and jewelled cap and acanthus-like curls, Grifonetto Baglioni, who slew Astorre with his bride, and Simonetto with his page, and whose comeliness was such that, as he lay dying in the yellow piazza of Perugia, those who had hated him could not choose but weep, and Atalanta, who had cursed him, blessed him.

There was a horrible fascination in them all. He saw them at night, and they troubled his imagination in the day. The Renaissance knew of strange manners of poisoning—poisoning by a helmet and a lighted torch, by an embroidered glove and a jewelled fan, by a gilded pomander and by an amber chain. Dorian Gray had been poisoned by a book. There were moments when he looked on evil simply as a mode through which he could realize his conception of the beautiful.

CHAPTER XII

IT WAS ON the ninth of November, the eve of his own thirty-eighth birthday, as he often remembered afterwards.

He was walking home about eleven o'clock from Lord Henry's, where he had been dining, and was wrapped in heavy furs, as the night was cold and foggy. At the corner of Grosvenor Square and South Audley Street a man passed him in the mist, walking very fast, and with the collar of his grey ulster turned up. He had a bag in his hand. Dorian recognized him. It was Basil Hallward. A strange sense of fear, for which he could not account, came over him. He made no sign of recognition, and went on quickly, in the direction of his own house.

But Hallward had seen him. Dorian heard him first stopping on the pavement and then hurrying after him. In a few moments his hand was on his arm.

"Dorian! What an extraordinary piece of luck! I have been waiting for you in your library ever since nine o'clock. Finally I took pity on your tired servant, and told him to go to bed, as he let me out. I am off to Paris by the midnight train, and I particularly wanted to see you before I left. I thought it was you, or rather your fur coat, as you passed me. But I wasn't quite sure. Didn't you recognize me?"

"In this fog, my dear Basil? Why, I can't even recognize Grosvenor Square. I believe my house is somewhere about here, but I don't feel at all certain about it. I am sorry you are going away, as I have not seen you for ages. But I suppose you will be back soon?"

"No: I am going to be out of England for six months. I intend to take a studio in Paris, and shut myself up till I have finished a great picture I have in my head. However, it wasn't about myself I wanted to talk. Here we are at your door. Let me come in for a moment. I have something to say to you."

"I shall be charmed. But won't you miss your train?" said Dorian Gray, languidly, as he passed up the steps and opened the door with his latch-key.

The lamp-light struggled out through the fog, and Hallward looked at his watch. "I have heaps of time," he answered. "The train doesn't go till twelve-fifteen, and it is only just eleven. In fact, I was on my way to the club to look for you, when I met you. You see, I sha'n't have any delay about luggage, as I have sent on my heavy things. All I have with me is in this bag, and I can easily get to Victoria in twenty minutes."

Dorian looked at him and smiled. "What a way for a fashionable painter to travel! A Gladstone bag, and an ulster! Come in, or the fog will get into the house. And mind you don't talk about anything serious. Nothing is serious nowadays. At least nothing should be."

Hallward shook his head, as he entered, and followed Dorian into the library. There was a bright wood fire blazing in the large open hearth. The lamps were lit, and an open Dutch silver spirit-case stood, with some siphons of soda-water and large cut-glass tumblers, on a little marqueterie table.

"You see your servant made me quite at home, Dorian. He gave me everything I wanted, including your best gold-tipped cigarettes. He is a most hospitable creature. I like him much better than the Frenchman you used to have. What has become of the Frenchman, by the bye?"

Dorian shrugged his shoulders. "I believe he married Lady Radley's maid, and has established her in Paris as an English dressmaker. *Anglomanie* is very fashionable over there now, I hear. It seems silly of the French, doesn't it? But—do you know?—he was not at all a bad servant. I never liked him, but I had nothing to complain about. One often imagines things that are quite absurd. He was really very devoted to me, and seemed quite sorry when he went away. Have another brandy-and-soda? Or would you like hock-and-seltzer? I always take hock-and-seltzer myself. There is sure to be some in the next room."

"Thanks, I won't have anything more," said the painter, taking his cap and coat off, and throwing them on the bag that he had placed in the corner. "And now my dear fellow, I want to speak to you seriously. Don't frown like that. You make it so much more difficult for me."

"What is it all about?" cried Dorian, in his petulant way, flinging himself down on the sofa. "I hope it is not about myself. I am tired of myself to-night. I should like to be somebody else."

"It is about yourself," answered Hallward, in his grave, deep voice, "and I must say it to you. I shall only keep you half an hour."

Dorian sighed, and lit a cigarette. "Half an hour!" he murmured.

"It is not much to ask of you, Dorian, and it is entirely for your own sake that I am speaking. I think it right that you should know that the most dreadful things are being said against you in London."

"I don't wish to know anything about them. I love scandals about other people, but scandals about myself don't interest me. They have not got the charm of novelty."

"They must interest you, Dorian. Every gentleman is interested in his good name. You don't want people to talk of you as something vile and degraded. Of course you have your position, and your wealth, and all that kind of thing. But position and wealth are not everything. Mind you, I don't believe these rumours at all. At least, I can't believe them when I see you. Sin is a thing that writes itself across a man's face. It cannot be concealed. People talk sometimes of secret vices. There are no such things. If a wretched man has a vice, it shows itself in the lines of his mouth, the droop of his eyelids, the moulding of his hands even. Somebody—I won't mention his name, but you know him—came to me last year to have his portrait done. I had never seen him before, and had never heard anything about him at the time, though I have heard a good deal since. He offered an extravagant price. I refused him. There was something in the shape of his fingers that I hated. I know now that I was quite right in what I fancied about him. His life is dreadful. But you, Dorian, with your pure, bright, innocent face, and your marvellous untroubled youth—I can't believe anything against you. And yet I see you very seldom, and you never come down to the studio now, and when I am away from you, and I hear all these hideous things that people are whispering about you, I don't know what to say. Why is it, Dorian, that a man like the Duke of Berwick leaves the room of a club when you enter it? Why is it that so many gentlemen in London will neither go to your house nor invite you to theirs? You used to be a friend of Lord Staveley. I met him at dinner last week. Your name happened to come up in conversation, in connection with the miniatures you have lent to the exhibition at the Dudley. Staveley curled his lip, and said that you might have the most artistic tastes, but that you were a man whom no pure-minded girl should be allowed to know, and whom no chaste woman should sit in the same room with. I reminded him that I was a friend of yours, and asked him what he meant. He told me. He told me right out before everybody. It was horrible! Why is your friendship so fatal to young men? There was that wretched boy in the Guards who committed suicide. You were his great friend. There was Sir Henry Ashton, who had to leave England, with a tarnished name. You and he were inseparable. What about Adrian Singleton, and his dreadful end? What about Lord Kent's only son, and his career? I met his father yesterday in St. James's Street. He seemed broken with shame and sorrow. What about the young Duke of Perth? What sort of life has he got now? What gentleman would associate with him?"

"Stop, Basil. You are talking about things of which you know nothing," said Dorian Gray, biting his lip, and with a note of infinite contempt in his voice. "You ask me why Berwick leaves a room when I enter it. It is because I know everything about his life, not because he knows anything about mine. With such blood as he has in his veins, how could his record be clean? You ask me about Henry Ashton and young Perth. Did I teach the one his vices, and the other his debauchery? If Kent's silly son takes his wife from the streets, what is that to me? If Adrian Singleton writes his friend's name across a bill, am I his keeper? I know how people chatter in England. The middle classes air their moral prejudices over their gross dinner-tables, and whisper about what they call the profligacies of their betters in order to try and pretend that they are in smart society, and on intimate terms with the people they slander. In this country it is enough for a man to have distinction and brains for every common tongue to wag against him. And what sort of lives do these people, who pose as being moral, lead themselves? My dear fellow, you forget that we are in the native land of the hypocrite."

"Dorian," cried Hallward, "that is not the question. England is bad enough I know, and English society is all wrong. That is the reason why I want you to be fine. You have not been fine. One has the right to judge of a man by the effect he has over his friends. Yours seem to lose all sense of honour, of goodness, of purity. You have filled them with a madness for pleasure. They have gone down into the depths. You led them there. Yes: you led them there, and yet you can smile, as you are smiling now. And there is worse behind. I know you and Harry are inseparable. Surely for that reason, if for none other, you should not have made his sister's name a by-word."

"Take care, Basil. You go too far."

"I must speak, and you must listen. You shall listen. When you met Lady Gwendolen, not a breath of scandal had ever touched her. Is there a single decent woman in London now who would drive with her in the Park? Why, even her children are not allowed to live with her. Then there are other stories—stories that you have been seen creeping at dawn out of dreadful houses and slinking in disguise into the foulest dens in London. Are they true? Can they be true? When I first heard them, I laughed. I hear them now, and they make me shudder. What about your country house, and the life that is led there? Dorian, you don't know what is said about you. I won't tell you that I don't want to preach to you. I remember Harry saying once that every man who turned himself into an amateur curate for the moment always began by saying that, and then proceeded to break his word. I do want to preach to you. I want you to lead such a life as will make the world respect you. I want you to have a clean name and a fair record. I want you to get rid of the dreadful people you associate with. Don't shrug your shoulders like that. Don't be so indifferent. You have a wonderful influence. Let it be for good, not for evil. They say that you corrupt every one with whom you become intimate, and that it is quite sufficient for you to enter a house, for shame of some kind to follow after. I don't know whether it is so or not. How should I know? But it is said of you. I am told things that it seems impossible to doubt. Lord Gloucester was one of my greatest friends at Oxford. He showed me a letter that his wife had written to him when she was dying alone in her villa at Mentone. Your name was implicated in the most terrible confession I ever read. I told him that it was absurd—that I knew you thoroughly and that you were incapable of anything of the kind. Know you? I wonder do I know you? Before I could answer that, I should have to see your soul."

"To see my soul!" muttered Dorian Gray, starting up from the sofa and turning almost white from fear.

"Yes," answered Hallward, gravely, and with deep-toned sorrow in his voice—"to see your soul. But only God can do that."

A bitter laugh of mockery broke from the lips of the younger man. "You shall see it yourself, to-night!" he cried, seizing a lamp from the table. "Come: it is your own handiwork. Why shouldn't you look at it? You can tell the world all about it afterwards, if you choose. Nobody would believe you. If they did believe you, they would like me all the better for it. I know the age better than you do, though you will prate about it so tediously. Come, I tell you. You have chattered enough about corruption. Now you shall look on it face to face."

There was the madness of pride in every word he uttered. He stamped his foot upon the ground in his boyish insolent manner. He felt a terrible joy at the thought that some one else was to share his secret, and that the man who had painted the portrait that was the origin of all his shame was to be burdened for the rest of his life with the hideous memory of what he had done.

"Yes," he continued, coming closer to him, and looking steadfastly into his stern eyes, "I shall show you my soul. You shall see the thing that you fancy only God can see."

Hallward started back. "This is blasphemy, Dorian!" he cried. "You must not say things like that. They are horrible, and they don't mean anything."

"You think so?" He laughed again.

"I know so. As for what I said to you to-night I said it for your good. You know I have been always a staunch friend to you."

"Don't touch me. Finish what you have to say."

A twisted flash of pain shot across the painter's face. He paused for a moment, and a wild feeling of pity came over him. After all, what right had he to pry into the life of Dorian Gray? If he had done a tithe of what was rumoured about him, how much he must have suffered! Then he straightened himself up, and walked over to the fireplace, and stood there, looking at the burning logs with their frost-like ashes and their throbbing cores of flame.

"I am waiting, Basil," said the young man, in a hard, clear voice.

He turned round. "What I have to say is this," he cried. "You must give me some answer to these horrible charges that are made against you. If you tell me that they are absolutely untrue from beginning to end, I shall believe you. Deny them, Dorian, deny them! Can't you see what I am going through? My God! don't tell me that you are bad, and corrupt, and shameful."

Dorian Gray smiled. There was a curl of contempt in his lips. "Come upstairs, Basil," he said, quietly. "I keep a diary of my life from day to day, and it never leaves the room in which it is written. I shall show it to you if you come with me."

"I shall come with you, Dorian, if you wish it. I see I have missed my train. That makes no matter. I can go to-morrow. But don't ask me to read anything to-night. All I want is a plain answer to my question."

"That shall be given to you upstairs. I could not give it here. You will not have to read long."

CHAPTER XIII

HE PASSED OUT of the room, and began the ascent, Basil Hallward following close behind. They walked softly, as men do instinctively at night. The lamp cast fantastic shadows on the wall and staircase. A rising wind made some of the windows rattle.

When they reached the top landing, Dorian set the lamp down on the floor, and taking out the key turned it in the lock. "You insist on knowing, Basil?" he asked, in a low voice.

"Yes."

"I am delighted," he answered, smiling. Then he added, somewhat harshly, "You are the one man in the world who is entitled to know everything about me. You have had more to do with my life than you think:" and, taking up the lamp, he opened the door and went in. A cold current of air passed them, and the light shot up for a moment in a flame of murky orange. He shuddered. "Shut the door behind you," he whispered, as he placed the lamp on the table.

Halward glanced round him, with a puzzled expression. The room looked as if it had not been lived in for years. A faded Flemish tapestry, a curtained picture, an old Italian *cassone*, and an almost empty bookcase—that was all that it seemed to contain, besides a chair and a table. As Dorian Gray was lighting a half-burned candle that was standing on the mantelshelf, he saw that the whole place was covered with dust, and that the carpet was in holes. A mouse ran scuffling behind the wainscoting. There was a damp odour of mildew.

"So you think that it is only God who sees the soul, Basil? Draw that curtain back, and you will see mine."

The voice that spoke was cold and cruel. "You are mad, Dorian, or playing a part," muttered Hallward, frowning.

"You won't? Then I must do it myself," said the young man; and he tore the curtain from its rod, and flung it on the ground.

An exclamation of horror broke from the painter's lips as he saw in the dim light the hideous face on the canvas grinning at him. There was something in its expression that filled him with disgust and loathing. Good heavens! it was Dorian Gray's own face that he was looking at! The horror, whatever it was, had not entirely spoiled that marvellous beauty. There was still some gold in the thinning hair and some scarlet on the sensual mouth. The sodden eyes had kept something of the loveliness of their blue, the noble curves had not yet completely passed away from chiselled nostrils and from plastic throat. Yes, it was Dorian himself. But who had done it? He seemed to recognize his own brushwork, and the frame was his own design. The idea was monstrous, yet he felt afraid. He seized the lighted candle, and held it to the picture. In the left-hand corner was his own name, traced in long letters of bright vermilion.

It was some foul parody, some infamous, ignoble satire. He had never done that. Still, it was his own picture. He knew it, and he felt as if his blood had changed in a moment from fire to sluggish ice. His own picture! What did it mean? Why had it altered? He turned, and looked at Dorian Gray with the eyes of a sick man. His mouth twitched, and his parched tongue seemed unable to articulate. He passed his hand across his forehead. It was dank with clammy sweat.

The young man was leaning against the mantelshelf, watching him with that strange expression that one sees on the faces of those who are absorbed in a play when some great artist is acting. There was neither real sorrow in it nor real joy. There was simply the passion of the spectator, with perhaps a flicker of triumph in his eyes. He had taken the flower out of his coat, and was smelling it, or pretending to do so.

"What does this mean?" cried Hallward, at last. His own voice sounded shrill and curious in his ears.

"Years ago, when I was a boy," said Dorian Gray, crushing the flower in his hand, "you met me, flattered me, and taught me to be vain of my good looks. One day you introduced me to a friend of yours, who explained to me the wonder of youth, and you finished a portrait of me that revealed to me the wonder of beauty. In a mad moment, that, even now, I don't know whether I regret or not, I made a wish, perhaps you would call it a prayer . . ."

"I remember it! Oh, how well I remember it! No! the thing is impossible. The room is damp. Mildew has got into the canvas. The paints I used had some wretched mineral poison in them. I tell you the thing is impossible."

"Ah, what is impossible?" murmured the young man, going over to the window, and leaning his forehead against the cold, mist-stained glass.

"You told me you had destroyed it."

"I was wrong. It has destroyed me."

"I don't believe it is my picture."

"Can't you see your ideal in it?" said Dorian, bitterly.

"My ideal, as you call it . . ."

"As you called it."

"There was nothing evil in it, nothing shameful. You were to me such an ideal as I shall never meet again. This is the face of a satyr."

"It is the face of my soul."

"Christ! what a thing I must have worshipped! It has the eyes of a devil."

"Each of us has Heaven and Hell in him, Basil," cried Dorian, with a wild gesture of despair.

Hallward turned again to the portrait, and gazed at it. "My God! if it is true," he exclaimed, "and this is what you have done with your life, why, you must be worse than those who talk against you fancy you to be!" He held the light up again to the canvas, and examined it. The surface seemed to be quite undisturbed, and as he had left it. It was from within, apparently, that the foulness and horror had come. Through some strange quickening of inner life the leprosies of sin were slowly eating the thing away. The rotting of a corpse in a watery grave was not so fearful.

His hand shook, and the candle fell from its socket on the floor, and lay there sputtering. He placed his foot on it and put it out. Then he flung himself into the rickety chair that was standing by the table and buried his face in his hands.

"Good God, Dorian, what a lesson! what an awful lesson!" There was no answer, but he could hear the young man sobbing at the window. "Pray, Dorian, pray," he murmured. "What is it that one was taught to say in one's boyhood? 'Lead us not into temptation. Forgive us our sins. Wash away our iniquities.' Let us say that together. The prayer of your pride has been answered. The prayer of your repentance will be answered also. I worshipped you too much. I am punished for it. You worshipped yourself too much. We are both punished."

Dorian Gray turned slowly around, and looked at him with tear-dimmed eyes. "It is too late, Basil," he faltered.

"It is never too late, Dorian. Let us kneel down and try if we cannot remember a prayer. Isn't there a verse somewhere, 'Though your sins be as scarlet, yet I will make them as white as snow'?"

"Those words mean nothing to me now."

"Hush! don't say that. You have done enough evil in your life. My God! don't you see that accursed thing leering at us?"

Dorian Gray glanced at the picture, and suddenly an uncontrollable feeling of hatred for Basil Hallward came over him, as though it had been suggested to him by the image on the canvas, whispered into his ear by those grinning lips. The mad passions of a hunted animal stirred within him, and he loathed the man who was seated at the table, more than in his whole life he had ever loathed anything. He glanced wildly around. Something glimmered on the top of the painted chest that faced him. His eye fell on it. He knew what it was. It was a knife that he had brought up, some days before, to cut a piece of cord, and had forgotten to take away with him. He moved slowly towards it, passing Hallward as he did so. As soon as he got behind him, he seized it, and turned round. Hallward stirred in his chair as if he was going to rise. He rushed at him, and dug the knife into the great vein that is behind the ear, crushing the man's head down on the table, and stabbing again and again.

There was a stifled groan, and the horrible sound of some one choking with blood. Three times the outstretched arms shot up convulsively, waving grotesque stiff-fingered hands in the air. He stabbed him twice more, but the man did not move. Something began to trickle on the floor. He waited for a moment, still pressing the head down. Then he threw the knife on the table, and listened.

He could hear nothing, but the drip, drip on the threadbare carpet. He opened the door and went out on the landing. The house was absolutely quiet. No one was about. For a few seconds he stood bending over the balustrade, and peering down into the black seething well of darkness. Then he took out the key and returned to the room, locking himself in as he did so.

The thing was still seated in the chair, straining over the table with bowed head, and humped back, and long fantastic arms. Had it not been for the red jagged tear in the neck, and the clotted black pool that was slowly widening on the table, one would have said that the man was simply asleep.

How quickly it had all been done! He felt strangely calm, and, walking over to the window, opened it, and stepped out on the balcony. The wind had blown the fog away, and the sky was like a monstrous peacock's tail, starred with myriads of golden eyes. He looked down, and saw the policeman going his rounds and flashing the long beam of his lantern on the doors of the silent houses. The crimson spot of a prowling hansom gleamed at the corner, and then vanished. A woman in a fluttering shawl was creeping slowly by the railings, staggering as she went. Now and then she stopped, and peered back. Once, she began to sing in a hoarse voice. The policeman strolled over and said something to her. She stumbled away, laughing. A bitter blast swept across the Square. The gas-lamps flickered, and became blue, and the leafless trees shook their black iron branches to and fro. He shivered, and went back, closing the window behind him.

Having reached the door, he turned the key, and opened it. He did not even glance at the murdered man. He felt that the secret of the whole thing was not to realize the situation. The friend who had painted the fatal portrait to which all his misery had been due, had gone out of his life. That was enough.

Then he remembered the lamp. It was a rather curious one of Moorish workmanship, made of dull silver inlaid with arabesques of burnished steel, and studded with coarse turquoises. Perhaps it might be missed by his servant, and questions would be asked. He hesitated for a moment, then he turned back and took it from the table. He could not help seeing the dead thing. How still it was! How horribly white the long hands looked! It was like a dreadful wax image.

Having locked the door behind him, he crept quietly downstairs. The woodwork creaked, and seemed to cry out as if in pain. He stopped several times, and waited. No: everything was still. It was merely the sound of his own footsteps.

When he reached the library, he saw the bag and coat in the corner. They must be hidden away somewhere. He unlocked a secret press that was in the wainscoting, a press in which he kept his own curious disguises, and put them into it. He could easily burn them afterwards. Then he pulled out his watch. It was twenty minutes to two.

He sat down, and began to think. Every year—every month, almost—men were strangled in England for what he had done. There had been a madness of murder in the air. Some red star had come too close to the earth. . . . And yet what evidence was there against him? Basil Hallward had left the house at eleven. No one had seen him come in again. Most of the servants were at Selby Royal. His valet had gone to bed. . . . Paris! Yes. It was to Paris that Basil had gone, and by the midnight train, as he had intended. With his curious reserved habits, it would be months before any suspicions would be aroused. Months! Everything could be destroyed long before then.

A sudden thought struck him. He put on his fur coat and hat, and went out into the hall. There he paused, hearing the slow heavy tread of the policeman on the pavement outside, and seeing the flash of the bull's-eye reflected in the window. He waited, and held his breath.

After a few moments he drew back the latch, and slipped out, shutting the door very gently behind him. Then he began ringing the bell. In about five minutes his valet appeared, half dressed, and looking very drowsy.

"I am sorry to have had to wake you up, Francis," he said, stepping in; "but I had forgotten my latch-key. What time is it?"

"Ten minutes past two, sir," answered the man, looking at the clock and blinking.

"Ten minutes past two? How horribly late! You must wake me at nine to-morrow. I have some work to do."

"All right, sir."

"Did any one call this evening?"

"Mr. Hallward, sir. He stayed here till eleven, and then he went away to catch his train."

"Oh! I am sorry I didn't see him. Did he leave any message?"

"No, sir, except that he would write to you from Paris, if he did not find you at the club."

"That will do, Francis. Don't forget to call me at nine to-morrow."

"No, sir."

The man shambled down the passage in his slippers.

Dorian Gray threw his hat and coat upon the table, and passed into the library. For a quarter of an hour he walked up and down the room biting his lip, and thinking. Then he took down the Blue Book from one of the shelves, and began to turn over the leaves. "Alan Campbell, 152, Hertford Street, Mayfair." Yes; that was the man he wanted.

CHAPTER XIV

AT NINE O'CLOCK in the next morning his servant came in with a cup of chocolate on a tray, and opened the shutters. Dorian was sleeping quite peacefully, lying on his right side, with one hand underneath his cheek. He looked like a boy who had been tired out with play, or study.

The man had to touch him twice on the shoulder before he woke, and as he opened his eyes a faint smiled passed across his lips, as though he had been lost in some delightful dream. Yet he had not dreamed at all. His night had been untroubled by any images of pleasure or of pain. But youth smiles without any reason. It is one of its chiefest charms.

He turned round, and, leaning upon his elbow, began to sip his chocolate. The mellow November sun came streaming into the room. The sky was bright, and there was a genial warmth in the air. It was almost like a morning in May.

Gradually the events of the preceding night crept with silent bloodstained feet into his brain, and reconstructed themselves there with terrible distinctness. He winced at the memory of all that he had suffered, and for a moment the same curious feeling of loathing for Basil Hallward, that had made him kill him as he sat in the chair, came back to him, and he grew cold with passion. The dead man was still sitting there, too, and in the sunlight now. How horrible that was! Such hideous things were for the darkness, not for the day.

He felt that if he brooded on what he had gone through he would sicken or grow mad. There were sins whose fascination was more in the memory than in the doing of them, strange triumphs that gratified the pride more than the passions, and gave to the intellect a quickened sense of joy, greater than any joy they brought, or could ever bring, to the senses. But this was not one of them. It was a thing to be driven out of the mind, to be drugged with poppies, to be strangled lest it might strangle one itself.

When the half-hour struck, he passed his hand across his forehead, and then got up hastily, and dressed himself with even more than his usual care, giving a good deal of attention to the choice of his necktie and scarfpin, and changing his rings more than once. He spent a long time also over breakfast, tasting the various dishes, talking to his valet about some new liveries that he was thinking of getting made for the servants at Selby, and going through his correspondence. At some of the letters he smiled. Three of them bored him. One he read several times over, and then tore up with a slight look of annoyance in his face. "That awful thing, a woman's memory!" as Lord Henry had once said.

After he had drunk his cup of black coffee, he wiped his lips slowly with a napkin, motioned to his servant to wait, and going over to the table sat down and wrote two letters. One he put in his pocket, the other he handed to the valet.

"Take this round to 152, Hertford Street, Francis, and if Mr. Campbell is out of town, get his address."

As soon as he was alone, he lit a cigarette, and began sketching upon a piece of paper, drawing first flowers, and bits of architecture, and then human faces. Suddenly he remarked that every face that he drew seemed to have a fantastic likeness to Basil Hallward. He frowned, and, getting up, went over to the bookcase and took out a volume at hazard. He was determined that he would not think about what had happened until it became absolutely necessary that he should do so.

When he had stretched himself on the sofa, he looked at the title-page of the book. It was Gautier's "Émaux et Camées," Charpentier's Japanese-paper edition, with the Jacquemart etching. The binding was of citron-green leather, with a design of gilt trellis-work and dotted pomegranates. It had been given to him by Adrian Singleton. As he turned over the pages his eye fell on the poem about the hand of Lacenaire, the cold yellow hand "*du supplice encore mal lavée*" with its downy red hairs and its "*doigts de faune*." He glanced at his own white taper fingers, shuddering slightly in spite of himself, and passed on till he came to those lovely stanzas upon Venice:—

"Sur une gamme chromatique,
Le sein de perles ruisselant,
La Vénus de l'Adriatique
Sort de l'eau son corps rose et blanc.

Les dômes, sur l'azur des ondes
Suivant la phrase au pur contour,
S'enflent comme des gorges rondes
Que souléve on soupir d'amour.

L'esquif aborde et me dépose,
Jetant son amarre au pilier,
Devant une façade rose,
Sur le marbre d'un escalier."

How exquisite they were! As one read them, one seemed to be floating down the green waterways of the pink and pearl city, seated in a black gondola with silver prow and trailing curtains. The mere lines looked to him like those straight lines of turquoise-blue that follow one as one pushes out to the Lido. The sudden flashes of colour reminded him of the gleam of the opal-and-iris-throated birds that flutter round the tall honey-combed Campanile, or stalk, with such stately grace, through the dim, dust-stained arcades. Leaning back with half-closed eyes, he kept saying over and over to himself:—

"Devant une façade rose,
Sur le marbre d'un escalier."

The whole of Venice was in those two lines. He remembered the autumn that he had passed there, and a wonderful love that had stirred him to mad, delightful follies. There was romance in every place. But Venice, like Oxford, had kept the background for romance, and, to the true romantic, background was everything, or almost everything. Basil had been with him part of the time, and had gone wild over Tintoret. Poor Basil! what a horrible way for a man to die!

He sighed, and took up the volume again, and tried to forget. He read of the swallows that fly in and out of the little café at Smyrna where the Hadjis sit counting their amber beads and the turbaned merchants smoke their long tasselled pipes and talk gravely to each other; he read of the Obelisk in the Place de la Concorde that weeps tears of granite in its lonely sunless exile, and longs to be back by the hot lotus-covered Nile, where there are Sphinxes, and rose-red ibises, and white vultures with gilded claws, and crocodiles, with small beryl eyes, that crawl over the green steaming mud; he began to brood over those verses which, drawing music from kiss-stained marble, tell of that curious statue that Gautier compares to a contralto voice, the "*monstre charmant*" that couches in the porphyry-room of the Louvre. But after a time the book fell from his hand. He grew nervous, and a horrible fit of terror came over him. What if Alan Campbell should be out of England? Days would elapse before he could come back. Perhaps he might refuse to come. What could he do then? Every moment was of vital importance.

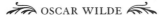

They had been great friends once, five years before—almost inseparable, indeed. Then the intimacy had come suddenly to an end. When they met in society now, it was only Dorian Gray who smiled: Alan Campbell never did.

He was an extremely clever young man, though he had no real appreciation of the visible arts, and whatever little sense of the beauty of poetry he possessed he had gained entirely from Dorian. His dominant intellectual passion was for science. At Cambridge he had spent a great deal of his time working in the Laboratory, and had taken a good class in the Natural Science Tripos of his year. Indeed, he was still devoted to the study of chemistry, and had a laboratory of his own, in which he used to shut himself up all day long, greatly to the annoyance of his mother, who had set her heart on his standing for Parliament and had a vague idea that a chemist was a person who made up prescriptions. He was an excellent musician, however, as well, and played both the violin and the piano better than most amateurs. In fact, it was music that had first brought him and Dorian Gray together—music and that indefinable attraction that Dorian seemed to be able to exercise whenever he wished, and indeed exercised often without being conscious of it. They had met at Lady Berkshire's the night that Rubinstein played there, and after that used to be always seen together at the Opera, and wherever good music was going on. For eighteen months their intimacy lasted. Campbell was always either at Selby Royal or in Grosvenor Square. To him, as to many others, Dorian Gray was the type of everything that is wonderful and fascinating in life. Whether or not a quarrel had taken place between them no one ever knew. But suddenly people remarked that they scarcely spoke when they met, and that Campbell seemed always to go away early from any party at which Dorian Gray was present. He had changed, too—was strangely melancholy at times, appeared almost to dislike hearing music, and would never himself play, giving as his excuse, when he was called upon, that he was so absorbed in science that he had no time left in which to practise. And this was certainly true. Every day he seemed to become more interested in biology, and his name appeared once or twice in some of the scientific reviews, in connection with certain curious experiments.

This was the man Dorian Gray was waiting for. Every second he kept glancing at the clock. As the minutes went by he became horribly agitated. At last he got up, and began to pace up and down the room, looking like a beautiful caged thing. He took long stealthy strides. His hands were curiously cold.

The suspense became unbearable. Time seemed to him to be crawling with feet of lead, while he by monstrous winds was being swept towards the jagged edge of some black cleft of precipice. He knew what was waiting for him there; saw it indeed, and, shuddering, crushed with dank hands his burning lids as though he would have robbed the very brain of sight, and driven the eyeballs back into their cave. It was useless. The brain had its own food on which it battened, and the imagination, made grotesque by terror, twisted and distorted as a living thing by pain, danced like some foul puppet on a stand, and grinned through moving masks. Then, suddenly, Time stopped for him. Yes: that blind, slow-breathing thing crawled no more, and horrible thoughts, Time being dead, raced nimbly on in front, and dragged a hideous future from its grave, and showed it to him. He stared at it. Its very horror made him stone.

At last the door opened, and his servant entered. He turned glazed eyes upon him.

"Mr. Campbell, sir," said the man.

A sigh of relief broke from his parched lips, and the colour came back to his cheeks.

"Ask him to come in at once, Francis." He felt that he was himself again. His mood of cowardice had passed away

The man bowed, and retired. In a few moments Alan Campbell walked in, looking very stern and rather pale, his pallor being intensified by his coal-black hair and dark eyebrows.

"Alan! this is kind of you. I thank you for coming."

"I had intended never to enter your house again, Gray. But you said it was a matter of life and death." His voice was hard and cold. He spoke with slow deliberation. There was a look of contempt in the steady searching gaze that he turned on Dorian. He kept his hands in the pockets of his Astrakhan coat, and seemed not to have noticed the gesture with which he had been greeted.

"Yes: it is a matter of life and death, Alan, and to more than one person. Sit down."

Campbell took a chair by the table, and Dorian sat opposite to him. The two men's eyes met. In Dorian's there was infinite pity. He knew that what he was going to do was dreadful.

After a strained moment of silence, he leaned across and said, very quietly, but watching the effect of each word upon the face of him he had sent for, "Alan, in a locked room at the top of this house, a room to which nobody but myself has access, a dead man is seated at a table. He has been dead ten hours now. Don't stir, and don't look at me like that. Who the man is, why he died, how he died, are matters that do not concern you. What you have to do is this—"

"Stop, Gray. I don't want to know anything further. Whether what you have told me is true or not true, doesn't concern me. I entirely decline to be mixed up in your life. Keep your horrible secrets to yourself. They don't interest me any more."

"Alan, they will have to interest you. This one will have to interest you. I am awfully sorry for you, Alan. But I can't help myself. You are the one man who is able to save me. I am forced to bring you into the matter. I have no option. Alan, you are scientific. You know about chemistry, and things of that kind. You have made experiments. What you have got to do is to destroy the thing that is upstairs—to destroy it so that not a vestige of it will be left. Nobody saw this person come into the house. Indeed, at the present moment he is supposed to be in Paris. He will not be missed for months. When he is missed, there must be no trace of him found here. You, Alan, you must change him, and everything that belongs to him, into a handful of ashes that I may scatter in the air."

"You are mad, Dorian."

"Ah! I was waiting for you to call me Dorian."

"You are mad, I tell you—mad to imagine that I would raise a finger to help you, mad to make this monstrous confession. I will have nothing to do with this matter, whatever it is. Do you think I am going to peril my reputation for you? What is it to me what devil's work you are up to?"

"It was suicide, Alan."

"I am glad of that. But who drove him to it? You, I should fancy."

"Do you still refuse to do this for me?"

"Of course I refuse. I will have absolutely nothing to do with it. I don't care what shame comes on you. You deserve it all. I should not be sorry to see you disgraced, publicly disgraced. How dare you ask me, of all men in the world, to mix myself up in this horror? I should have thought you knew more about people's characters. Your friend Lord Henry Wotton can't have taught you much about psychology, whatever else he has taught you. Nothing will induce me to stir a step to help you. You have come to the wrong man. Go to some of your friends. Don't come to me."

"Alan, it was murder. I killed him. You don't know what he had made me suffer. Whatever my life is, he had more to do with the making or the marring of it than poor Harry has had. He may not have intended it, the result was the same."

"Murder! Good God, Dorian, is that what you have come to? I shall not inform upon you. It is not my business. Besides, without my stirring in the matter, you are certain to be arrested. Nobody ever commits a crime without doing something stupid. But I will have nothing to do with it."

"You must have something to do with it. Wait, wait a moment; listen to me. Only listen, Alan. All I ask of you is to perform a certain scientific experiment. You go to hospitals and dead-houses, and the horrors that you do there don't affect you. If in some hideous dissecting-room or fetid laboratory you found this man lying on a leaden table with red gutters scooped out in it for the blood to flow through, you would simply look upon him as an admirable subject. You would not turn a hair. You would not believe that you were doing anything wrong. On the contrary, you would probably feel that you were benefiting the human race, or increasing the sum of knowledge in the world, or gratifying intellectual curiosity, or something of that kind. What I want you to do is merely what you have often done before. Indeed, to destroy a body must be far less horrible than what you are accustomed to work at. And, remember, it is the only piece of evidence against me. If it is discovered, I am lost; and it is sure to be discovered unless you help me."

"I have no desire to help you. You forget that. I am simply indifferent to the whole thing. It has nothing to do with me."

"Alan, I entreat you. Think of the position I am in. Just before you came I almost fainted with terror. You may know terror yourself some day. No! don't think of that. Look at the matter purely from the scientific point of view. You don't inquire where the dead things on which you experiment come from. Don't inquire now. I have told you too much as it is. But I beg of you to do this. We were friends once, Alan."

"Don't speak about those days, Dorian: they are dead."

"The dead linger sometimes. The man upstairs will not go away. He is sitting at the table with bowed head and outstretched arms. Alan! Alan! if you don't come to my assistance I am ruined. Why, they will hang me, Alan! Don't you understand? They will hang me for what I have done."

"There is no good in prolonging this scene. I absolutely refuse to do anything in the matter. It is insane of you to ask me."

"You refuse?"

"Yes."

"I entreat you, Alan."

"It is useless."

The same look of pity came into Dorian Gray's eyes. Then he stretched out his hand, took a piece of paper, and wrote something on it. He read it over twice, folded it carefully, and pushed it across the table. Having done this, he got up, and went over to the window.

Campbell looked at him in surprise, and then took up the paper, and opened it. As he read it, his face became ghastly pale, and he fell back in his chair. A horrible sense of sickness came over him. He felt as if his heart was beating itself to death in some empty hollow.

After two or three minutes of terrible silence, Dorian turned round, and came and stood behind him, putting his hand upon his shoulder.

"I am so sorry for you, Alan," he murmured, "but you leave me no alternative. I have a letter written already. Here it is. You see the address. If you don't help me, I must send it. If you don't help me, I will send it. You know what the result will be. But you are going to help me. It is impossible for you to refuse now. I tried to spare you. You will do me the justice to admit that. You were stern, harsh, offensive. You treated me as no man has ever dared to treat me—no living man, at any rate. I bore it all. Now it is for me to dictate terms."

Campbell buried his face in his hands, and a shudder passed through him.

"Yes, it is my turn to dictate terms, Alan. You know what they are. The thing is quite simple. Come, don't work yourself into this fever. The thing has to be done. Face it, and do it."

A groan broke from Campbell's lips, and he shivered all over. The ticking of the clock on the mantelpiece seemed to him to be dividing Time into separate atoms of agony, each of which was too terrible to be borne. He felt as if an iron ring was being slowly tightened round his forehead, as if the disgrace with which he was threatened had already come upon him. The hand upon his shoulder weighed like a hand of lead. It was intolerable. It seemed to crush him.

"Come, Alan, you must decide at once."

"I cannot do it," he said, mechanically, as though words could alter things.

"You must. You have no choice. Don't delay."

He hesitated a moment. "Is there a fire in the room upstairs?"

"Yes, there is a gas-fire with asbestos."

"I shall have to go home and get some things from the laboratory."

"No, Alan, you must not leave the house. Write out on a sheet of notepaper what you want, and my servant will take a cab and bring the things back to you."

Campbell scrawled a few lines, blotted them, and addressed the envelope to his assistant. Dorian took the note up and read it carefully. Then he rang the bell, and gave it to his valet, with orders to return as soon as possible, and to bring the things with him.

As the hall door shut, Campbell started nervously, and, having got up from the chair, went over to the chimney-piece. He was shivering with a kind of ague. For nearly twenty minutes, neither of the men spoke. A fly buzzed noisily about the room, and the ticking of the clock was like the beat of a hammer.

As the chime struck one, Campbell turned round, and, looking at Dorian Gray, saw that his eyes were filled with tears. There was something in the purity and refinement of that sad face that seemed to enrage him. "You are infamous, absolutely infamous!" he muttered.

"Hush, Alan: you have saved my life," said Dorian.

"Your life? Good heavens! what a life that is! You have gone from corruption to corruption, and now you have culminated in crime. In doing what I am going to do, what you force me to do, it is not of your life that I am thinking."

"Ah, Alan," murmured Dorian, with a sigh, "I wish you had a thousandth part of the pity for me that I have for you." He turned away as he spoke, and stood looking out at the garden. Campbell made no answer.

After about ten minutes a knock came to the door, and the servant entered, carrying a large mahogany chest of chemicals, with a long coil of steel and platinum wire and two rather curiously-shaped iron clamps. "Shall I leave the things here, sir?" he asked Campbell.

"Yes," said Dorian. "And I am afraid, Francis, that I have another errand for you. What is the name of the man at Richmond who supplies Selby with orchids?"

"Harden, sir."

"Yes—Harden. You must go down to Richmond at once, see Harden personally, and tell him to send twice as many orchids as I ordered, and to have as few white ones as possible. In fact, I don't want any white ones. It is a lovely day, Francis, and Richmond is a very pretty place, otherwise I wouldn't bother you about it."

"No trouble, sir. At what time shall I be back?"

Dorian looked at Campbell. "How long will your experiment take, Alan?" he said, in a calm, indifferent voice. The presence of a third person in the room seemed to give him extraordinary courage.

Campbell frowned, and bit his lip. "It will take about five hours," he answered.

"It will be time enough, then, if you are back at half-past seven, Francis. Or stay: just leave my things out for dressing. You can have the evening to yourself. I am not dining at home, so I shall not want you."

"Thank you, sir, " said the man, leaving the room.

"Now, Alan, there is not a moment to be lost. How heavy this chest is! I'll take it for you. You bring the other things." He spoke rapidly, and in an authoritative manner. Campbell felt dominated by him. They left the room together.

When they reached the top landing, Dorian took out the key and turned it in the lock. Then he stopped, and a troubled look came into his eyes. He shuddered. "I don't think I can go in, Alan," he murmured.

"It is nothing to me. I don't require you," said Campbell, coldly.

Dorian half opened the door. As he did so, he saw the face of his portrait leering in the sunlight. On the floor in front of it the torn curtain was lying. He remembered that the night before he had forgotten, for the first time in his life, to hide the fatal canvas, and was about to rush forward, when he drew back with a shudder.

What was that loathsome red dew that gleamed, wet and glistening, on one of the hands, as though the canvas had sweated blood? How horrible it was!—more horrible, it seemed to him for the moment, than the silent thing that he knew was stretched across the table, the thing whose grotesque misshapen shadow on the spotted carpet showed him that it had not stirred, but was still there, as he had left it.

He heaved a deep breath, opened the door a little wider, and with half-closed eyes and averted head walked quickly in, determined that he would not look even once upon the dead man. Then, stooping down, and taking up the gold-and-purple hanging, he flung it right over the picture.

There he stopped, feeling afraid to turn round, and his eyes fixed themselves on the intricacies of the pattern before him. He heard Campbell bringing in the heavy chest, and the irons, and the other things that he had required for his dreadful work. He began to wonder if he and Basil Hallward had ever met, and, if so, what they had thought of each other.

"Leave me now," said a stern voice behind him.

He turned and hurried out, just conscious that the dead man had been thrust back into the chair, and that Campbell was gazing into a glistening yellow face. As he was going downstairs he heard the key being turned in the lock.

It was long after seven when Campbell came back into the library. He was pale, but absolutely calm. "I have done what you asked me to do," he muttered.

"And now, good-bye. Let us never see each other again."

"You have saved me from ruin, Alan. I cannot forget that," said Dorian, simply.

As soon as Campbell left, he went upstairs. There was a horrible smell of nitric acid in the room. But the thing that had been sitting at the table was gone.

CHAPTER XV

THAT EVENING, AT eight-thirty, exquisitely dressed, and wearing a large buttonhole of Parma violets, Dorian Gray was ushered into Lady Narborough's drawing-room by bowing servants. His forehead was throbbing with maddened nerves, and he felt wildly excited, but his manner as he bent over his hostess's hand was as easy and graceful as ever. Perhaps one never seems so much at one's ease as when one has to play a part. Certainly no one looking at Dorian Gray that night could have believed that he had passed through a tragedy as horrible as any tragedy of our age. Those finely-shaped fingers could never have clutched a knife for sin, nor those smiling lips have cried out on God and goodness. He himself could not help wondering at the calm of his demeanour, and for a moment felt keenly the terrible pleasure of a double life.

It was a small party, got up rather in a hurry by Lady Narborough, who was a very clever woman, with what Lord Henry used to describe as the remains of really remarkable ugliness. She had proved an excellent wife to one of our most tedious ambassadors, and having buried her husband properly in a marble mausoleum, which she had herself designed, and married off her daughters to some rich, rather elderly men, she devoted herself now to the pleasures of French fiction, French cookery, and French *esprit* when she could get it.

Dorian was one of her especial favourites, and she always told him that she was extremely glad she had not met him in early life. "I know, my dear, I should have fallen madly in love with you," she used to say, "and thrown my bonnet right over the mills for your sake. It is most fortunate that you were not thought of at the time. As it was, our bonnets were so unbecoming, and the mills were so occupied in trying to raise the wind, that I never had even a flirtation with anybody. However, that was all Narborough's fault. He was dreadfully short-sighted, and there is no pleasure in taking a husband who never sees anything."

Her guests this evening were rather tedious. The fact was, as she explained to Dorian, behind a very shabby fan, one of her married daughters had come up quite suddenly to stay with her, and, to make matters worse, had actually brought her husband with her. "I think it is most unkind of her, my dear," she whispered. "Of course I go and stay with them every summer after I come from Homburg, but then an old woman like me must have fresh air sometimes, and besides, I really wake them up. You don't know what an existence they lead down there. It is pure unadulterated country life. They get up early, because they have so much to do, and go to bed early because they have so little to think about. There has not been a scandal in the neighbourhood since the time of Queen Elizabeth, and consequently they all fall asleep after dinner. You sha'n't sit next either of them. You shall sit by me, and amuse me."

Dorian murmured a graceful compliment, and looked round the room. Yes: it was certainly a tedious party. Two of the people he had never seen before, and the others consisted of Ernest Harrowden, one of those middle-aged mediocrities so common in London clubs who have no enemies, but are thoroughly disliked by their friends; Lady Ruxton, an overdressed woman of forty-seven, with a hooked nose, who was always trying to get herself compromised, but was so peculiarly plain that to her great disappointment no one would ever believe anything against her; Mrs. Erlynne, a pushing nobody, with a delightful lisp, and Venetian-red hair; Lady Alice Chapman, his hostess's daughter, a dowdy dull girl, with one of those characteristic British faces, that, once seen, are never remembered; and her husband, a red-cheeked, white-whiskered creature who, like so many of his class, was under the impression that inordinate joviality can atone for an entire lack of ideas.

HER CAPACITY FOR FAMILY AFFECTION IS EXTRAORDINARY. WHEN HER THIRD HUSBAND DIED, HER HAIR TURNED QUITE GOLD FROM GRIEF.

He was rather sorry he had come, till Lady Narborough, looking at the great ormolu gilt clock that sprawled in gaudy curves on the mauve-draped mantelshelf, exclaimed: "How horrid of Henry Wotton to be so late! I sent round to him this morning on chance, and he promised faithfully not to disappoint me."

It was some consolation that Harry was to be there, and when the door opened and he heard his slow musical voice lending charm to some insincere apology, he ceased to feel bored.

But at dinner he could not eat anything. Plate after plate went away untasted. Lady Narborough kept scolding him for what she called "an insult to poor Adolphe, who invented the *menu* specially for you," and now and then Lord Henry looked across at him, wondering at his silence and abstracted manner. From time to time the butler filled his glass with champagne. He drank eagerly, and his thirst seemed to increase.

"Dorian," said Lord Henry, at last, as the *chaudfroid* was being handed round, "what is the matter with you to-night? You are quite out of sorts."

"I believe he is in love," cried Lady Narborough, "and that he is afraid to tell me for fear I should be jealous. He is quite right. I certainly should."

"Dear Lady Narborough," murmured Dorian, smiling, "I have not been in love for a whole week—not, in fact, since Madame de Ferrol left town."

"How you men can fall in love with that woman!" exclaimed the old lady. "I really cannot understand it."

"It is simply because she remembers you when you were a little girl, Lady Narborough," said Lord Henry. "She is the one link between us and your short frocks."

"She does not remember my short frocks at all, Lord Henry. But I remember her very well at Vienna thirty years ago, and how *décolletée* she was then."

"She is still *décolletée*," he answered, taking an olive in his long fingers; "and when she is in a very smart gown she looks like an *édition de luxe* of a bad French novel. She is really wonderful, and full of surprises. Her capacity for family affection is extraordinary. When her third husband died, her hair turned quite gold from grief."

"How can you, Harry!" cried Dorian.

"It is a most romantic explanation," laughed the hostess. "But her third husband, Lord Henry! You don't mean to say Ferrol is the fourth?"

"Certainly, Lady Narborough."

"I don't believe a word of it."

"Well, ask Mr. Gray. He is one of her most intimate friends."

"Is it true, Mr. Gray?"

"She assures me so, Lady Narborough," said Dorian. "I asked her whether, like Marguerite de Navarre, she had their hearts embalmed and hung at her girdle. She told me she didn't, because none of them had had any hearts at all."

"Four husbands! Upon my word that is *trop de zèle*."

"*Trop d'audace*, I tell her," said Dorian.

"Oh! she is audacious enough for anything, my dear. And what is Ferrol like? I don't know him."

"The husbands of very beautiful women belong to the criminal classes," said Lord Henry, sipping his wine.

Lady Narborough hit him with her fan. "Lord Henry, I am not at all surprised that the world says that you are extremely wicked."

"But what world says that?" asked Lord Henry, elevating his eyebrows. "It can only be the next world. This world and I are on excellent terms."

"Everybody I know says you are very wicked," cried the old lady, shaking her head.

Lord Henry looked serious for some moments. "It is perfectly monstrous," he said, at last, "the way people go about nowadays saying things against one behind one's back that are absolutely and entirely true."

"Isn't he incorrigible?" cried Dorian, leaning forward in his chair.

"I hope so," said his hostess, laughing. "But really if you all worship Madame de Ferrol in this ridiculous way, I shall have to marry again so as to be in the fashion."

"You will never marry again, Lady Narborough," broke in Lord Henry. "You were far too happy. When a woman marries again it is because she detested her first husband. When a man marries again, it is because he adored his first wife. Women try their luck; men risk theirs."

"Narborough wasn't perfect," cried the old lady.

"If he had been, you would not have loved him, my dear lady," was the rejoinder. "Women love us for our defects. If we have enough of them they will forgive us everything, even our intellects. You will never ask me to dinner again, after saying this, I am afraid, Lady Narborough; but it is quite true."

"Of course it is true, Lord Henry. If we women did not love you for your defects, where would you all be? Not one of you would ever be married. You would be a set of unfortunate bachelors. Not, however, that that would alter you much. Nowadays all the married men live like bachelors, and all the bachelors like married men."

"*Fin de siècle*," murmured Lord Henry.

"*Fin du globe*," answered his hostess.

"I wish it were *fin du globe*," said Dorian, with a sigh. "Life is a great disappointment."

"Ah, my dear," cried Lady Narborough, putting on her gloves, "don't tell me that you have exhausted Life. When a man says that one knows that Life has exhausted him. Lord Henry is very wicked, and I sometimes wish that I had been; but you are made to be good—you look so good. I must find you a nice wife. Lord Henry, don't you think that Mr. Gray should get married?"

"I am always telling him so, Lady Narborough," said Lord Henry, with a bow.

"Well, we must look out for a suitable match for him. I shall go through Debrett carefully tonight, and draw out a list of all the eligible young ladies."

"With their ages, Lady Narborough?" asked Dorian.

"Of course, with their ages, slightly edited. But nothing must be done in a hurry. I want it to be what *The Morning Post* calls a suitable alliance, and I want you both to be happy."

"What nonsense people talk about happy marriages!" exclaimed Lord Henry. "A man can be happy with any woman, as long as he does not love her."

"Ah! what a cynic you are!" cried the old lady, pushing back her chair, and nodding to Lady Ruxton. "You must come and dine with me soon again. You are really an admirable tonic, much better than what Sir Andrew prescribes for me. You must tell me what people you would like to meet, though. I want it to be a delightful gathering."

"I like men who have a future, and women who have a past," he answered. "Or do you think that would make it a petticoat party?"

"I fear so," she said, laughing, as she stood up. "A thousand pardons, my dear Lady Ruxton," she added, "I didn't see you hadn't finished your cigarette."

"Never mind, Lady Narborough. I smoke a great deal too much. I am going to limit myself, for the future."

"Pray don't, Lady Ruxton," said Lord Henry. "Moderation is a fatal thing. Enough is as bad as a meal. More than enough is as good as a feast."

Lady Ruxton glanced at him curiously. "You must come and explain that to me some afternoon, Lord Henry. It sounds a fascinating theory," she murmured, as she swept out of the room.

"Now, mind you don't stay too long over your politics and scandal," cried Lady Narborough from the door. "If you do, we are sure to squabble upstairs."

The men laughed, and Mr. Chapman got up solemnly from the foot of the table and came up to the top. Dorian Gray changed his seat, and went and sat by Lord Henry. Mr. Chapman began to talk in a loud voice about the situation in the House of Commons. He guffawed at his adversaries. The word *doctrinaire*—word full of terror to the British mind—reappeared from time to time between his explosions. An alliterative prefix served as an ornament of oratory. He hoisted the Union Jack on the pinnacles of Thought. The inherited stupidity of the race—sound English common sense he jovially termed it—was shown to be the proper bulwark for Society.

A smile curved Lord Henry's lips, and he turned round and looked at Dorian.

"Are you better, my dear fellow?" he asked. "You seemed rather out of sorts at dinner."

"I am quite well, Harry. I am tired. That is all."

"You were charming last night. The little Duchess is quite devoted to you. She tells me she is going down to Selby."

"She has promised to come on the twentieth."

"Is Monmouth to be there too?"

"Oh, yes, Harry."

"He bores me dreadfully, almost as much as he bores her. She is very clever, too clever for a woman. She lacks the indefinable charm of weakness. It is the feet of clay that make the gold of the image precious. Her feet are very pretty, but they are not feet of clay. White porcelain feet, if you like. They have been through the fire, and what fire does not destroy, it hardens. She has had experiences."

"How long has she been married?" asked Dorian.

"An eternity, she tells me. I believe, according to the peerage, it is ten years, but ten years with Monmouth must have been like eternity, with time thrown in. Who else is coming?"

"Oh, the Willoughbys, Lord Rugby and his wife, our hostess, Geoffrey Clouston, the usual set. I have asked Lord Grotrian."

"I like him," said Lord Henry. "A great many people don't, but I find him charming. He atones for being occasionally somewhat over-dressed, by being always absolutely over-educated. He is a very modern type."

"I don't know if he will be able to come, Harry. He may have to go to Monte Carlo with his father."

"Ah! what a nuisance people's people are! Try and make him come. By the way, Dorian, you ran off very early last night. You left before eleven. What did you do afterwards? Did you go straight home?"

Dorian glanced at him hurriedly, and frowned. "No, Harry," he said at last, "I did not get home till nearly three."

"Did you go to the club?"

"Yes," he answered. Then he bit his lip. "No, I don't mean that. I didn't go to the club. I walked about. I forget what I did. . . . How inquisitive you are, Harry! You always want to know what one has been doing. I always want to forget what I have been doing. I came in at half past two, if you wish to know the exact time. I had left my latch-key at home, and my servant had to let me in. If you want any corroborative evidence on the subject you can ask him."

Lord Henry shrugged his shoulders. "My dear fellow, as if I cared! Let us go up to the drawing-room. No sherry, thank you, Mr. Chapman. Something has happened to you, Dorian. Tell me what it is. You are not yourself to-night."

"Don't mind me, Harry. I am irritable, and out of temper. I shall come round and see you to-morrow, or next day. Make my excuses to Lady Narborough. I sha'n't go upstairs. I shall go home. I must go home."

"All right, Dorian. I dare say I shall see you to-morrow at tea-time. The Duchess is coming."

"I will try to be there, Harry," he said, leaving the room. As he drove back to his own house he was conscious that the sense of terror he thought he had strangled had come back to him. Lord Henry's casual questioning had made him lose his nerves for the moment, and he wanted his nerve still. Things that were dangerous had to be destroyed. He winced. He hated the idea of even touching them.

Yet it had to be done. He realized that, and when he had locked the door of his library, he opened the secret press into which he had thrust Basil Hallward's coat and bag. A huge fire was blazing. He piled another log on it. The smell of the singeing clothes and burning leather was horrible. It took him three-quarters of an hour to consume everything. At the end he felt faint and sick, and having lit some Algerian pastilles in a pierced copper brazier, he bathed his hands and forehead with a cool musk-scented vinegar.

Suddenly he started. His eyes grew strangely bright, and he gnawed nervously at his upper-lip. Between two of the windows stood a large Florentine cabinet, made out of ebony, and inlaid with ivory and blue lapis. He watched it as though it were a thing that could fascinate and make afraid, as though it held something that he longed for and yet almost loathed. His breath quickened. A mad craving came over him. He lit a cigarette and then threw it away. His eyelids drooped till the long fringed lashes almost touched his cheek. But he still watched the cabinet. At last he got up from the sofa on which he had been lying, went over to it, and, having unlocked it, touched some hidden spring. A triangular drawer passed slowly out. His fingers moved instinctively towards it, dipped in, and closed on something. It was a small Chinese box of black and gold-dust lacquer, elaborately wrought, the sides patterned with curved waves, and the silken cords hung with round crystals and tasselled in plaited metal threads. He opened it. Inside was a green paste waxy in lustre, the odour curiously heavy and persistent.

He hesitated for some moments, with a strangely immobile smile upon his face. Then shivering, though the atmosphere of the room was terribly hot, he drew himself up, and glanced at the clock. It was twenty minutes to twelve. He put the box back, shutting the cabinet doors as he did so, and went into his bedroom.

As midnight was striking bronze blows upon the dusky air, Dorian Gray, dressed commonly, and with a muffler wrapped round his throat, crept quietly out of his house. In Bond Street he found a hansom with a good horse. He hailed it, and in a low voice gave the driver an address.

The man shook his head. "It is too far for me," he muttered.

"Here is a sovereign for you," said Dorian. "You shall have another if you drive fast."

"All right, sir," answered the man, "you will be there in an hour," and after his fare had got in he turned his horse round, and drove rapidly towards the river.

CHAPTER XVI

A COLD RAIN began to fall, and the blurred street-lamps looked ghastly in the dripping mist. The public-houses were just closing, and dim men and women were clustering in broken groups round their doors. From some of the bars came the sound of horrible laughter. In others, drunkards brawled and screamed.

Lying back in the hansom, with his hat pulled over his forehead, Dorian Gray watched with listless eyes the sordid shame of the great city, and now and then he repeated to himself the words that Lord Henry had said to him on the first day they had met, "To cure the soul by means of the senses, and the senses by means of the soul." Yes, that was the secret. He had often tried it, and would try it again now. There were opium-dens, where one could buy oblivion, dens of horror where the memory of old sins could be destroyed by the madness of sins that were new.

The moon hung low in the sky like a yellow skull. From time to time a huge misshapen cloud stretched a long arm across and hid it. The gas-lamps grew fewer, and the streets more narrow and gloomy. Once the man lost his way, and had to drive back half a mile. A steam rose from the horse as it splashed up the puddles. The side-windows of the hansom were clogged with a grey-flannel mist.

"To cure the soul by means of the senses, and the senses by means of the soul!" How the words rang in his ears! His soul, certainly, was sick to death. Was it true that the senses could cure it? Innocent blood had been spilt. What could atone for that? Ah! for that there was no atonement; but though forgiveness was impossible, forgetfulness was possible still, and he was determined to forget to stamp the thing out, to crush it as one would crush the adder that had stung one.

Indeed, what right had Basil to have spoken to him as he had done? Who had made him a judge over others? He had said things that were dreadful, horrible, not to be endured.

On and on plodded the hansom, going slower, it seemed to him, at each step. He thrust up the trap, and called to the man to drive faster. The hideous hunger for opium began to gnaw at him. His throat burned, and his delicate hands twitched nervously together. He struck at the horse madly with his stick. The driver laughed, and whipped up. He laughed in answer, and the man was silent.

The way seemed interminable, and the streets like the black web of some sprawling spider. The monotony became unbearable, and, as the mist thickened, he felt afraid.

Then they passed by lonely brickfields. The fog was lighter here, and he could see the strange bottle-shaped kilns with their orange fan-like tongues of fire. A dog barked as they went by, and far away in the darkness some wandering sea-gull screamed. The horse stumbled in a rut, then swerved aside, and broke into a gallop.

After some time they left the clay road, and rattled again over rough-paven streets. Most of the windows were dark, but now and then fantastic shadows were silhouetted against some lamp-lit blind. He watched them curiously. They moved like monstrous marionettes, and made gestures like live things. He hated them. A dull rage was in his heart. As they turned a corner a woman yelled something at them from an open door, and two men ran after the hansom for about a hundred yards. The driver beat at them with his whip.

It is said that passion makes one think in a circle. Certainly with hideous iteration the bitten lips of Dorian Gray shaped and reshaped those subtle words that dealt with soul and sense, till he had found in them the full expression, as it were, of his mood, and justified, by intellectual approval, passions that without such justification would still have dominated his temper. From cell to cell of his brain crept the one thought; and the wild desire to live, most terrible of all man's appetites, quickened into force each trembling nerve and fibre. Ugliness that had once been hateful to him because it made things real, became dear to him now for that very reason. Ugliness was the one reality. The coarse brawl, the loathsome den, the crude violence of disordered life, the very vileness of thief and outcast, were more vivid, in their intense actuality of impression, than all the gracious shapes of Art, the dreamy shadows of Song. They were what he needed for forgetfulness. In three days he would be free.

Suddenly the man drew up with a jerk at the top of a dark lane. Over the low roofs and jagged chimney-stacks of the houses rose the black masts of ships. Wreaths of white mist clung like ghostly sails to the yards.

"Somewhere about here, sir, ain't it?" he asked huskily through the trap.

Dorian started, and peered round. "This will do," he answered, and, having got out hastily, and given the driver the extra fare he had promised him, he walked quickly in the direction of the quay. Here and there a lantern gleamed at the stern of some huge merchantman. The light shook and splintered in the puddles. A red glare came from an outward-bound steamer that was coaling. The slimy pavement looked like a wet mackintosh.

He hurried on towards the left, glancing back now and then to see if he was being followed. In about seven or eight minutes he reached a small shabby house, that was wedged in between two gaunt factories. In one of the top-windows stood a lamp. He stopped, and gave a particular knock.

After a little time he heard steps in the passage, and the chain being unhooked. The door opened quietly, and he went in without saying a word to the squat misshapen figure that flattened itself into the shadow as he passed. At the end of the hall hung a tattered green curtain that swayed and shook in the gusty wind which had followed him in from the street. He dragged it aside, and entered a long, low room which looked as if it had once been a third-rate dancing-saloon. Shrill flaring gas-jets, dulled and distorted in the fly-blown mirrors that faced them, were ranged round the walls. Greasy reflectors of ribbed tin backed them, making quivering discs of light. The floor was covered with ochre-coloured sawdust, trampled here and there into mud, and stained with dark rings of spilt liquor. Some Malays were crouching by a little charcoal stove playing with bone counters, and showing their white teeth as they chattered. In one corner with his head buried in his arms, a sailor sprawled over a table, and by the tawdrily-painted bar that ran across one complete side stood two haggard women mocking an old man who was brushing the sleeves of his coat with an expression of disgust. "He thinks he's got red ants on him," laughed one of them, as Dorian passed by. The man looked at her in terror, and began to whimper.

At the end of the room there was a little staircase, leading to a darkened chamber. As Dorian hurried up its three ricketty steps, the heavy odour of opium met him. He heaved a deep breath, and his nostrils quivered with pleasure. When he entered, a young man with smooth yellow hair, who was bending over a lamp lighting a long thin pipe, looked up at him, and nodded in a hesitating manner.

"You here, Adrian?" muttered Dorian.

"Where else should I be?" he answered, listlessly. "None of the chaps will speak to me now."

"I thought you had left England."

"Darlington is not going to do anything. My brother paid the bill at last. George doesn't speak to me either. . . . I don't care," he added, with a sigh. "As long as one has this stuff, one doesn't want friends. I think I have had too many friends."

Dorian winced, and looked around at the grotesque things that lay in such fantastic postures on the ragged mattresses. The twisted limbs, the gaping mouths, the staring lustreless eyes, fascinated him. He knew in what strange heavens they were suffering, and what dull hells were teaching them the secret of some new joy. They were better off than he was. He was prisoned in thought. Memory, like a horrible malady, was eating his soul away. From time to time he seemed to see the eyes of Basil Hallward looking at him. Yet he felt he could not stay. The presence of Adrian Singleton troubled him. He wanted to be where no one would know who he was. He wanted to escape from himself.

"I am going on to the other place," he said, after a pause.

"On the wharf?"

"Yes."

"That mad-cat is sure to be there. They won't have her in this place now."

Dorian shrugged his shoulders. "I am sick of women who love one. Women who hate one are much more interesting. Besides, the stuff is better."

"Much the same."

"I like it better. Come and have something to drink. I must have something."

"I don't want anything," murmured the young man.

"Never mind."

Adrian Singleton rose up wearily, and followed Dorian to the bar. A half-caste, in a ragged turban and a shabby ulster, grinned a hideous greeting as he thrust a bottle of brandy and two tumblers in front of them. The women sidled up, and began to chatter. Dorian turned his back on them, and said something in a low voice to Adrian Singleton.

A crooked smile, like a Malay crease, writhed across the face of one of the women. "We are very proud to-night," she sneered.

"For God's sake don't talk to me," cried Dorian, stamping his foot on the ground. "What do you want? Money? Here it is. Don't ever talk to me again."

Two red sparks flashed for a moment in the woman's sodden eyes, then flickered out, and left them dull and glazed. She tossed her head, and raked the coins off the counter with greedy fingers. Her companion watched her enviously.

"It's no use," sighed Adrian Singleton. "I don't care to go back. What does it matter? I am quite happy here."

"You will write to me if you want anything, won't you?" said Dorian, after a pause.

"Perhaps."

"Good-night, then."

"Good-night," answered the young man, passing up the steps, and wiping his parched mouth with a handkerchief.

Dorian walked to the door with a look of pain in his face. As he drew the curtain aside a hideous laugh broke from the painted lips of the woman who had taken his money. "There goes the devil's bargain!" she hiccoughed, in a hoarse voice.

"Curse you!" he answered, "don't call me that."

She snapped her fingers. "Prince Charming is what you like to be called, ain't it?" she yelled after him.

The drowsy sailor leapt to his feet as she spoke, and looked wildly round. The sound of the shutting of the hall door fell on his ear. He rushed out as if in pursuit.

Dorian Gray hurried along the quay through the drizzling rain. His meeting with Adrian Singleton had strangely moved him, and he wondered if the ruin of that young life was really to be laid at his door, as Basil Hallward had said to him with such infamy of insult. He bit his lip, and for a few seconds his eyes grew sad. Yet, after all, what did it matter to him? One's days were too brief to take the burden of another's errors on one's shoulders. Each man lived his own life, and paid his own price for living it. The only pity was one had to pay so often for a single fault. One had to pay over and over again, indeed. In her dealings with man Destiny never closed her accounts.

There are moments, psychologists tell us, when the passion for sin, or for what the world calls sin, so dominates a nature, that every fibre of the body, as every cell of the brain, seems to be instinct with fearful impulses. Men and women at such moments lose the freedom of their will. They move to their terrible end as automatons move.

Choice is taken from them, and conscience is either killed, or, if it lives at all, lives but to give rebellion its fascination, and disobedience its charm. For all sins, as theologians weary not of reminding us, are sins of disobedience. When that high spirit, that morning-star of evil, fell from heaven, it was as a rebel that he fell.

Callous, concentrated on evil, with stained mind, and soul hungry for rebellion, Dorian Gray hastened on, quickening his step as he went, but as he darted aside into a dim archway, that had served him often as a short cut to the ill-famed place where he was going, he felt himself suddenly seized from behind, and before he had time to defend himself he was thrust back against the wall, with a brutal hand round his throat.

He struggled madly for life, and by a terrible effort wrenched the tightening fingers away. In a second he heard the click of a revolver, and saw the gleam of a polished barrel pointing straight at his head, and the dusky form of a short thick-set man facing him.

"What do you want?" he gasped.

"Keep quiet," said the man. "If you stir, I shoot you."

"You are mad. What have I done to you?"

"You wrecked the life of Sibyl Vane," was the answer, "and Sibyl Vane was my sister. She killed herself. I know it. Her death is at your door. I swore I would kill you in return. For years I have sought you. I had no clue, no trace. The two people who could have described you are dead. I knew nothing of you but the pet name she used to call you. I heard it tonight by chance. Make your peace with God, for to-night you are going to die."

Dorian Gray grew sick with fear. "I never knew her," he stammered. "I never heard of her. You are mad."

"You had better confess your sin, for as sure as I am James Vane, you are going to die." There was a horrible moment. Dorian did not know what to say or do. "Down on your knees!" growled the man. "I give you one minute to make your peace—no more. I go on board to-night for India, and I must do my job first. One minute. That's all."

Dorian's arms fell to his side. Paralyzed with terror, he did not know what to do. Suddenly a wild hope flashed across his brain. "Stop," he cried. "How long ago is it since your sister died? Quick, tell me!"

"Eighteen years," said the man. "Why do you ask me? What do years matter?"

"Eighteen years," laughed Dorian Gray, with a touch of triumph in his voice. "Eighteen years! Set me under the lamp and look at my face."

James Vane hesitated for a moment, not understanding what was meant. Then he seized Dorian Gray and dragged him from the archway.

Dim and wavering as was the windblown light, yet it served to show him the hideous error, as it seemed, into which he had fallen, for the face of the man he had sought to kill had all the bloom of boyhood, all the unstained purity of youth. He seemed little more than a lad of twenty summers, hardly older, if older indeed at all, than his sister had been when they had parted so many years ago. It was obvious that this was not the man who had destroyed her life.

He loosened his hold and reeled back. "My God! my God!" he cried, "and I would have murdered you!"

Dorian Gray drew a long breath. "You have been on the brink of committing a terrible crime, my man," be said, looking at him sternly. "Let this be a warning to you not to take vengeance into your own hands."

"Forgive me, sir," muttered James Vane. "I was deceived. A chance word I heard in that damned den set me on the wrong track."

"You had better go home, and put that pistol away, or you may get into trouble," said Dorian, turning on his heel, and going slowly down the street.

James Vane stood on the pavement in horror. He was trembling from head to foot. After a little while a black shadow that had been creeping along the dripping wall, moved out into the light and came close to him with stealthy footsteps. He felt a hand laid on his arm and looked round with a start. It was one of the women who had been drinking at the bar.

"Why didn't you kill him?" she hissed out, putting her haggard face quite close to his. "I knew you were following him when you rushed out from Daly's. You fool! You should have killed him. He has lots of money, and he's as bad as bad."

"He is not the man I am looking for," he answered, "and I want no man's money. I want a man's life. The man whose life I want must be nearly forty now. This one is little more than a boy. Thank God, I have not got his blood upon my hands."

The woman gave a bitter laugh. "Little more than a boy!" she sneered. "Why, man, it's nigh on eighteen years since Prince Charming made me what I am."

"You lie!" cried James Vane.

She raised her hand up to heaven. "Before God I am telling the truth," she cried.

"Before God?"

"Strike me dumb if it ain't so. He is the worst one that comes here. They say he has sold himself to the devil for a pretty face. It's nigh on eighteen years since I met him. He hasn't changed much since then. I have though," she added, with a sickly leer.

"You swear this?"

"I swear it," came in hoarse echo from her flat mouth. "But don't give me away to him," she whined; "I am afraid of him. Let me have some money for my night's lodging."

He broke from her with an oath, and rushed to the corner of the street, but Dorian Gray had disappeared. When he looked back, the woman had vanished also.

CHAPTER XVII

A WEEK LATER Dorian Gray was sitting in the conservatory at Selby Royal talking to the pretty Duchess of Monmouth, who with her husband, a jaded-looking man of sixty, was amongst his guests. It was tea-time, and the mellow light of the huge lace-covered lamp that stood on the table lit up the delicate china and hammered silver of the service at which the Duchess was presiding. Her white hands were moving daintily among the cups, and her full red lips were smiling at something that Dorian had whispered to her. Lord Henry was lying back in a silk-draped wicker chair looking at them. On a peach-coloured divan sat Lady Narborough pretending to listen to the Duke's description of the last Brazilian beetle that he had added to his collection. Three young men in elaborate smoking-suits were handing tea-cakes to some of the women. The house-party consisted of twelve people, and there were more expected to arrive on the next day.

"What are you two talking about?" said Lord Henry, strolling over to the table, and putting his cup down. "I hope Dorian has told you about my plan for rechristening everything, Gladys. It is a delightful idea."

"But I don't want to be rechristened, Harry," rejoined the Duchess, looking up at him with her wonderful eyes. "I am quite satisfied with my own name, and I am sure Mr. Gray should be satisfied with his."

"My dear Gladys, I would not alter either name for the world. They are both perfect. I was thinking chiefly of flowers. Yesterday I cut an orchid, for my buttonhole. It was a marvellous spotted thing, as effective as the seven deadly sins. In a thoughtless moment I asked one of the gardeners what it was called. He told me it was a fine specimen of *Robinsoniana*, or something dreadful of that kind. It is a sad truth, but we have lost the faculty of giving lovely names to things. Names are everything. I never quarrel with actions. My one quarrel is with words. This is the reason I hate vulgar realism in literature. The man who could call a spade a spade should be compelled to use one. It is the only thing he is fit for."

"Then what should we call you, Harry?" she asked.

"His name is Prince Paradox," said Dorian.

"I recognize him in a flash," exclaimed the Duchess.

"I won't hear of it," laughed Lord Henry, sinking into a chair. "From a label there is no escape! I refuse the title."

"Royalties may not abdicate," fell as a warning from pretty lips.

"You wish me to defend my throne, then?"

"Yes."

"I give the truths of to-morrow."

"I prefer the mistakes of to-day," she answered.

"You disarm me, Gladys," he cried, catching the wilfulness of her mood.

"Of your shield, Harry: not of your spear."

"I never tilt against Beauty," he said, with a wave of his hand.

"That is your error, Harry, believe me. You value beauty far too much."

"How can you say that? I admit that I think that it is better to be beautiful than to be good. But on the other hand no one is more ready than I am to acknowledge that it is better to be good than to be ugly."

"Ugliness is one of the seven deadly sins, then?" cried the Duchess. "What becomes of your simile about the orchid?"

"Ugliness is one of the seven deadly virtues, Gladys. You, as a good Tory, must not underrate them. Beer, the Bible, and the seven deadly virtues have made our England what she is."

"You don't like your country, then?" she asked.

"I live in it."

"That you may censure it the better."

"Would you have me take the verdict of Europe on it?" he enquired.

"What do they say of us?"

"That Tartuffe has emigrated to England and opened a shop."

"Is that yours, Harry?"

"I give it to you."

"I could not use it. It is too true."

"You need not be afraid. Our countrymen never recognize a description."

"They are practical."

"They are more cunning than practical. When they make up their ledger, they balance stupidity by wealth, and vice by hypocrisy."

"Still, we have done great things."

"Great things have been thrust on us, Gladys."

"We have carried their burden."

"Only as far as the Stock Exchange."

She shook her head. "I believe in the race," she cried.

"It represents the survival of the pushing."

"It has development."

"Decay fascinates me more."

"What of Art?" she asked.

"It is a malady."

"Love?"

"An illusion."

"Religion?"

"The fashionable substitute for Belief."

"You are a sceptic."

"Never! Scepticism is the beginning of Faith."

"What are you?"

"To define is to limit."

"Give me a clue."

"Threads snap. You would lose your way in the labyrinth."

"You bewilder me. Let us talk of some one else."

"Our host is a delightful topic. Years ago he was christened Prince Charming."

"Ah! don't remind me of that," cried Dorian Gray.

"Our host is rather horrid this evening," answered the Duchess, colouring. "I believe he thinks that Monmouth married me on purely scientific principles as the best specimen he could find of a modern butterfly."

"Well, I hope he won't stick pins into you, Duchess," laughed Dorian.

"Oh! my maid does that already, Mr. Gray, when she is annoyed with me."

"And what does she get annoyed with you about, Duchess?"

"For the most trivial things, Mr. Gray, I assure you. Usually because I come in at ten minutes to nine and tell her that I must be dressed by half-past eight."

"How unreasonable of her! You should give her warning."

"I daren't, Mr. Gray. Why, she invents hats for me. You remember the one I wore at Lady Hilstone's garden-party? You don't, but it is nice of you to pretend that you do. Well, she made it out of nothing. All good hats are made out of nothing."

"Like all good reputations, Gladys," interrupted Lord Henry. "Every effect that one produces gives one an enemy. To be popular one must be a mediocrity."

"Not with women," said the Duchess, shaking her head; "and women rule the world. I assure you we can't bear mediocrities. We women, as some one says, love with our ears, just as you men love with your eyes, if you ever love at all."

"It seems to me that we never do anything else," murmured Dorian.

"Ah! then, you never really love, Mr. Gray," answered the Duchess, with mock sadness.

"My dear Gladys!" cried Lord Henry. "How can you say that? Romance lives by repetition, and repetition converts an appetite into an art. Besides, each time that one loves is the only time one has ever loved. Difference of object does not alter singleness of passion. It merely intensifies it. We can have in life but one great experience at best, and the secret of life is to reproduce that experience as often as possible."

"Even when one has been wounded by it, Harry?" asked the Duchess, after a pause.

"Especially when one has been wounded by it," answered Lord Henry.

The Duchess turned and looked at Dorian Gray with a curious expression in her eyes. "What do you say to that, Mr. Gray?" she inquired.

Dorian hesitated for a moment. Then he threw his head back and laughed. "I always agree with Harry, Duchess."

"Even when he is wrong?"

"Harry is never wrong, Duchess."

"And does his philosophy make you happy?"

"I have never searched for happiness. Who wants happiness? I have searched for pleasure."

"And found it, Mr. Gray?"

"Often. Too often."

The Duchess sighed. "I am searching for peace," she said, "and if I don't go and dress, I shall have none this evening."

"Let me get you some orchids, Duchess," cried Dorian, starting to his feet, and walking down the conservatory.

"You are flirting disgracefully with him," said Lord Henry to his cousin. "You had better take care. He is very fascinating."

"If he were not, there would be no battle."

"Greek meets Greek, then?"

"I am on the side of the Trojans. They fought for a woman."

"They were defeated."

"There are worse things than capture," she answered.

"You gallop with a loose rein."

"Pace gives life," was the *riposte*.

"I shall write it in my diary to-night."

"What?"

"That a burnt child loves the fire."

"I am not even singed. My wings are untouched."

"You use them for everything, except flight."

"Courage has passed from men to women. It is a new experience for us."

"You have a rival."

"Who?"

He laughed. "Lady Narborough," he whispered. "She perfectly adores him."

"You fill me with apprehension. The appeal to Antiquity is fatal to us who are romanticists."

"Romanticists! You have all the methods of science."

"Men have educated us."

"But not explained you."

"Describe us as a sex," was her challenge.

"Sphynxes without secrets."

She looked at him, smiling. "How long Mr. Gray is!" she said. "Let us go and help him. I have not yet told him the colour of my frock."

"Ah! you must suit your frock to his flowers, Gladys."

"That would be a premature surrender."

"Romantic Art begins with its climax."

"I must keep all opportunity for retreat."

"In the Parthian manner?"

"They found safety in the desert. I could not do that."

"Women are not always allowed a choice," he answered, but hardly had he finished the sentence before from the far end of the conservatory came a stifled groan, followed by the dull sound of a heavy fall. Everybody started up. The Duchess stood motionless in horror. And with fear in his eyes Lord Henry rushed through the flapping palms, to find Dorian Gray lying face downwards on the tiled floor in a death-like swoon.

He was carried at once into the blue drawing-room, and laid upon one of the sofas. After a short time he came to himself, and looked round with a dazed expression.

"What has happened?" he asked. "Oh! I remember. Am I safe here, Harry?" He began to tremble.

"My dear Dorian," answered Lord Henry, "you merely fainted. That was all. You must have overtired yourself. You had better not come down to dinner. I will take your place."

"No, I will come down," he said, struggling to his feet. "I would rather come down. I must not be alone."

He went to his room and dressed. There was a wild recklessness of gaiety in his manner as he sat at table, but now and then a thrill of terror ran through him when he remembered that, pressed against the window of the conservatory, like a white handkerchief, he had seen the face of James Vane watching him.

CHAPTER XVIII

THE NEXT DAY he did not leave the house, and, indeed, spent most of the time in his own room, sick with a wild terror of dying, and yet indifferent to life itself. The consciousness of being hunted, snared, tracked down, had begun to dominate him. If the tapestry did but tremble in the wind, he shook. The dead leaves that were blown against the leaded panes seemed to him like his own wasted resolutions and wild regrets. When he closed his eyes, he saw again the sailor's face peering through the mist-stained glass, and horror seemed once more to lay its hand upon his heart.

But perhaps it had been only his fancy that had called vengeance out of the night, and set the hideous shapes of punishment before him. Actual life was chaos, but there was something terribly logical in the imagination. It was the imagination that set remorse to dog the feet of sin. It was the imagination that made each crime bear its misshapen brood. In the common world of fact the wicked were not punished, nor the good rewarded. Success was given to the strong, failure thrust upon the weak. That was all. Besides, had any stranger been prowling round the house he would have been seen by the servants or the keepers. Had any footmarks been found on the flowerbeds, the gardeners would have reported it. Yes: it had been merely fancy. Sibyl Vane's brother had not come back to kill him. He had sailed away in his ship to founder in some winter sea. From him, at any rate, he was safe. Why, the man did not know who he was, could not know who he was. The mask of youth had saved him.

And yet if it had been merely an illusion, how terrible it was to think that conscience could raise such fearful phantoms, and give them visible form, and make them move before one! What sort of life would his be if, day and night, shadows of his crime were to peer at him from silent corners, to mock him from secret places, to whisper in his ear as he sat at the feast, to wake him with icy fingers as he lay asleep! As the thought crept through his brain, he grew pale with terror, and the air seemed to him to have become suddenly colder. Oh! in what a wild hour of madness he had killed his friend! How ghastly the mere memory of the scene! He saw it all again. Each hideous detail came back to him with added horror. Out of the black cave of Time, terrible and swathed in scarlet, rose the image of his sin. When Lord Henry came in at six o'clock, he found him crying as one whose heart will break.

It was not till the third day that he ventured to go out. There was something in the clear, pine-scented air of that winter morning that seemed to bring him back his joyousness and his ardour for life. But it was not merely the physical conditions of environment that had caused the change. His own nature had revolted against the excess of anguish that had sought to maim and mar the perfection of its calm. With subtle and finely-wrought temperaments it is always so. Their strong passions must either bruise or bend. They either slay the man, or themselves die. Shallow sorrows and shallow loves live on. The loves and sorrows that are great are destroyed by their own plenitude. Besides, he had convinced himself that he had been the victim of a terror-stricken imagination, and looked back now on his fears with something of pity and not a little of contempt.

After breakfast he walked with the Duchess for an hour in the garden, and then drove across the park to join the shooting-party. The crisp frost lay like salt upon the grass. The sky was an inverted cup of blue metal. A thin film of ice bordered the flat reed-grown lake.

At the corner of the pine-wood he caught sight of Sir Geoffrey Clouston, the Duchess's brother, jerking two spent cartridges out of his gun. He jumped from the cart, and having told the groom to take the mare home, made his way towards his guest through the withered bracken and rough undergrowth.

"Have you had good sport, Geoffrey?" he asked.

"Not very good, Dorian. I think most of the birds have gone to the open. I dare say it will be better after lunch, when we get to new ground."

Dorian strolled along by his side. The keen aromatic air, the brown and red lights that glimmered in the wood, the hoarse cries of the beaters ringing out from time to time, and the sharp snaps of the guns that followed, fascinated him, and filled him with a sense of delightful freedom. He was dominated by the carelessness of happiness, by the high indifference of joy.

Suddenly from a lumpy tussock of old grass, some twenty yards in front of them, with black-tipped ears erect, and long hinder limbs throwing it forward, started a hare. It bolted for a thicket of alders. Sir Geoffrey put his gun to his shoulder, but there was something in the animal's grace of movement that strangely charmed Dorian Gray, and he cried out at once, "Don't shoot it, Geoffrey. Let it live."

"What nonsense, Dorian!" laughed his companion, and as the hare bounded into the thicket he fired. There were two cries heard, the cry of a hare in pain, which is dreadful, the cry of a man in agony, which is worse.

"Good heavens! I have hit a beater!" exclaimed Sir Geoffrey. "What an ass the man was to get in front of the guns! Stop shooting there!" he called out at the top of his voice. "A man is hurt."

The head-keeper came running up with a stick in his hand.

"Where, sir? Where is he?" he shouted. At the same time the firing ceased along the line.

"Here," answered Sir Geoffrey, angrily, hurrying towards the thicket. "Why on earth don't you keep your men back? Spoiled my shooting for the day."

Dorian watched them as they plunged into the alder-clump, brushing the lithe, swinging branches aside. In a few moments they emerged, dragging a body after them into the sunlight. He turned away in horror. It seemed to him that misfortune followed wherever he went. He heard Sir Geoffrey ask if the man was really dead, and the affirmative answer of the keeper. The wood seemed to him to have become suddenly alive with faces. There was the trampling of myriad feet, and the low buzz of voices. A great copper-breasted pheasant came beating through the boughs overhead.

After a few moments, that were to him, in his perturbed state, like endless hours of pain, he felt a hand laid on his shoulder. He started, and looked round.

"Dorian," said Lord Henry, "I had better tell them that the shooting is stopped for to-day. It would not look well to go on."

"I wish it were stopped for ever, Harry," he answered bitterly. "The whole thing is hideous and cruel. Is the man . . . ?"

He could not finish the sentence.

"I am afraid so," rejoined Lord Henry. "He got the whole charge of shot in his chest. He must have died almost instantaneously. Come; let us go home."

They walked side by side in the direction of the avenue for nearly fifty yards without speaking. Then Dorian looked at Lord Henry, and said, with a heavy sigh, "It is a bad omen, Harry, a very bad omen."

"What is?" asked Lord Henry. "Oh! this accident, I suppose. My dear fellow, it can't be helped. It was the man's own fault. Why did he get in front of the guns? Besides, it is nothing to us. It is rather awkward for Geoffrey, of course. It does not do to pepper beaters. It makes people think that one is a wild shot. And Geoffrey is not; he shoots very straight. But there is no use talking about the matter."

Dorian shook his head. "It is a bad omen, Harry. I feel as if something horrible were going to happen to some of us. To myself, perhaps," he added, passing his hand over his eyes, with a gesture of pain.

The elder man laughed. "The only horrible thing in the world is *ennui*, Dorian. That is the one sin for which there is no forgiveness. But we are not likely to suffer from it, unless these fellows keep chattering about this thing at dinner. I must tell them that the subject is to be tabooed. As for omens, there is no such thing as an omen. Destiny does not send us heralds. She is too wise or too cruel for that. Besides, what on earth could happen to you, Dorian? You have everything in the world that a man can want. There is no one who would not be delighted to change places with you."

"There is no one with whom I would not change places, Harry. Don't laugh like that. I am telling you the truth. The wretched peasant who has just died is better off than I am. I have no terror of Death. It is the coming of Death that terrifies me. Its monstrous wings seem to wheel in the leaden air around me. Good heavens! don't you see a man moving behind the trees there, watching me, waiting for me?"

Lord Henry looked in the direction in which the trembling gloved hand was pointing. "Yes," he said, smiling, "I see the gardener waiting for you. I suppose he wants to ask you what flowers you wish to have on the table tonight. How absurdly nervous you are, my dear fellow! You must come and see my doctor, when we get back to town."

Dorian heaved a sigh of relief as he saw the gardener approaching. The man touched his hat, glanced for a moment at Lord Henry in a hesitating manner, and then produced a letter, which he handed to his master. "Her Grace told me to wait for an answer," he murmured.

Dorian put the letter into his pocket. "Tell her Grace that I am coming in," he said, coldly. The man turned round, and went rapidly in the direction of the house.

"How fond women are of doing dangerous things!" laughed Lord Henry. "It is one of the qualities in them that I admire most. A woman will flirt with anybody in the world as long as other people are looking on."

"How fond you are of saying dangerous things, Harry! In the present instance you are quite astray. I like the Duchess very much, but I don't love her."

"And the Duchess loves you very much, but she likes you less, so you are excellently matched."

"You are talking scandal, Harry, and there is never basis for scandal."

"The basis of every scandal is an immoral certainty," said Lord Henry, lighting a cigarette.

"You would sacrifice anybody, Harry, for the sake of an epigram."

"The world goes to the altar of its own accord," was the answer.

"I wish I could love," cried Dorian Gray, with a deep note of pathos in his voice. "But I seem to have lost the passion, and forgotten the desire. I am too much concentrated on myself. My own personality has become a burden to me. I want to escape, to go away, to forget. It was silly of me to come down here at all. I think I shall send a wire to Harvey to have the yacht got ready. On a yacht one is safe."

"Safe from what, Dorian? You are in some trouble. Why not tell me what it is? You know I would help you."

"I can't tell you, Harry, " he answered, sadly. "And I dare say it is only a fancy of mine. This unfortunate accident has upset me. I have a horrible presentiment that something of the kind may happen to me."

"What nonsense!"

"I hope it is, but I can't help feeling it. Ah! here is the Duchess, looking like Artemis in a tailor-made gown. You see we have come back, Duchess."

"I have heard all about it, Mr. Gray," she answered. "Poor Geoffrey is terribly upset. And it seems that you asked him not to shoot the hare. How curious!"

"Yes, it was very curious. I don't know what made me say it. Some whim, I suppose. It looked the loveliest of little live things. But I am sorry they told you about the man. It is a hideous subject."

"It is an annoying subject," broke in Lord Henry. "It has no psychological value at all. Now if Geoffrey had done the thing on purpose, how interesting he would be! I should like to know some one who had committed a real murder."

"How horrid of you, Harry!" cried the Duchess. "Isn't it, Mr. Gray? Harry, Mr. Gray is ill again. He is going to faint."

Dorian drew himself up with an effort, and smiled. "It is nothing, Duchess," he murmured; "my nerves are dreadfully out of order. That is all. I am afraid I walked too far this morning. I didn't hear what Harry said. Was it very bad? You must tell me some other time. I think I must go and lie down. You will excuse me, won't you?"

They had reached the great flight of steps that led from the conservatory on to the terrace. As the glass door closed behind Dorian, Lord Henry turned and looked at the Duchess with his slumberous eyes. "Are you very much in love with him?" he asked.

She did not answer for some time, but stood gazing at the landscape. "I wish I knew," she said at last.

He shook his head. "Knowledge would be fatal. It is the uncertainty that charms one. A mist makes things wonderful."

"One may lose one's way."

"All ways end at the same point, my dear Gladys."

"What is that?"

"Disillusion."

"It was my début in life," she sighed.

"It came to you crowned."

"I am tired of strawberry leaves."

"They become you."

"Only in public."

"You would miss them," said Lord Henry.

"I will not part with a petal."

"Monmouth has ears."

"Old age is dull of hearing."

"Has he never been jealous?"

"I wish he had been."

He glanced about as if in search of something. "What are you looking for?" she enquired.

"The button from your foil," he answered. "You have dropped it."

She laughed. "I have still the mask."

"It makes your eyes lovelier," was his reply.

She laughed again. Her teeth showed like white seeds in a scarlet fruit.

Upstairs, in his own room, Dorian Gray was lying on a sofa, with terror in every tingling fibre of his body. Life had suddenly become too hideous a burden for him to bear. The dreadful death of the unlucky beater, shot in the thicket like a wild animal, had seemed to him to prefigure death for himself also. He had nearly swooned at what Lord Henry had said in a chance mood of cynical jesting.

At five o'clock he rang his bell for his servant and gave him orders to pack his things for the night-express to town, and to have the brougham at the door by eight-thirty. He was determined not to sleep another night at Selby Royal. It was an ill-omened place. Death walked there in the sunlight. The grass of the forest had been spotted with blood.

Then he wrote a note to Lord Henry, telling him that he was going up to town to consult his doctor, and asking him to entertain his guests in his absence. As he was putting it into the envelope, a knock came to the door, and his valet informed him that the head-keeper wished to see him. He frowned, and bit his lip. "Send him in," he muttered, after some moments' hesitation.

As soon as the man entered Dorian pulled his cheque-book out of a drawer, and spread it out before him.

"I suppose you have come about the unfortunate accident of this morning, Thornton?" he said, taking up a pen.

"Yes, sir," answered the gamekeeper.

"Was the poor fellow married? Had he any people dependent on him?" asked Dorian, looking bored. "If so, I should not like them to be left in want, and will send them any sum of money you may think necessary."

"We don't know who he is, sir. That is what I took the liberty of coming to you about."

"Don't know who he is?" said Dorian, listlessly. "What do you mean? Wasn't he one of your men?"

"No, sir. Never saw him before. Seems like a sailor, sir."

The pen dropped from Dorian Gray's hand, and he felt as if his heart had suddenly stopped beating. "A sailor?" he cried out. "Did you say a sailor?"

"Yes, sir. He looks as if he had been a sort of sailor; tattooed on both arms, and that kind of thing."

"Was there anything found on him?" said Dorian, leaning forward and looking at the man with startled eyes. "Anything that would tell his name?"

"Some money, sir—not much, and a six-shooter. There was no name of any kind. A decent-looking man, sir, but rough-like. A sort of sailor we think."

Dorian started to his feet. A terrible hope fluttered past him. He clutched at it madly. "Where is the body?" he exclaimed. "Quick! I must see it at once."

"It is in an empty stable at the Home Farm, sir. The folk don't like to have that sort of thing in their houses. They say a corpse brings bad luck."

"The Home Farm! Go there at once and meet me. Tell one of the grooms to bring my horse round. No. Never mind. I'll go to the stables myself. It will save time."

In less than a quarter of an hour Dorian Gray was galloping down the long avenue as hard as he could go. The trees seemed to sweep past him in spectral procession, and wild shadows to fling themselves across his path. Once the mare swerved at a white gate-post and nearly threw him. He lashed her across the neck with his crop. She cleft the dusky air like an arrow. The stones flew from her hoofs.

At last he reached the Home Farm. Two men were loitering in the yard. He leapt from the saddle and threw the reins to one of them. In the farthest stable a light was glimmering. Something seemed to tell him that the body was there, and he hurried to the door, and put his hand upon the latch.

There he paused for a moment, feeling that he was on the brink of a discovery that would either make or mar his life. Then he thrust the door open, and entered.

On a heap of sacking in the far corner was lying the dead body of a man dressed in a coarse shirt and a pair of blue trousers. A spotted handkerchief had been placed over the face. A coarse candle, stuck in a bottle, sputtered beside it.

Dorian Gray shuddered. He felt that his could not be the hand to take the handkerchief away, and called out to one of the farm-servants to come to him.

"Take that thing off the face. I wish to see it," he said, clutching at the door-post for support.

When the farm-servant had done so, he stepped forward. A cry of joy broke from his lips. The man who had been shot in the thicket was James Vane.

He stood there for some minutes looking at the dead body. As he rode home, his eyes were full of tears, for he knew he was safe.

CHAPTER XIX

"THERE IS NO use your telling me that you are going to be good," cried Lord Henry, dipping his white fingers into a red copper bowl filled with rose-water. "You are quite perfect. Pray, don't change."

Dorian Gray shook his head. "No, Harry, I have done too many dreadful things in my life. I am not going to do any more. I began my good actions yesterday."

"Where were you yesterday?"

"In the country, Harry. I was staying at a little inn by myself."

"My dear boy, " said Lord Henry, smiling, "anybody can be good in the country. There are no temptations there. That is the reason why people who live out of town are so absolutely uncivilized. Civilization is not by any means an easy thing to attain to. There are only two ways by which man can reach it. One is by being cultured, the other by being corrupt. Country people have no opportunity of being either, so they stagnate."

"Culture and corruption," echoed Dorian. "I have known something of both. It seems terrible to me now that they should ever be found together. For I have a new ideal, Harry. I am going to alter. I think I have altered."

"You have not yet told me what your good action was. Or did you say you had done more than one?" asked his companion, as he spilt into his plate a little crimson pyramid of seeded strawberries, and through a perforated shell-shaped spoon snowed white sugar upon them.

"I can tell you, Harry. It is not a story I could tell to any one else. I spared somebody. It sounds vain, but you understand what I mean. She was quite beautiful, and wonderfully like Sibyl Vane. I think it was that which first attracted me to her. You remember Sibyl, don't you? How long ago that seems! Well, Hetty was not one of our own class, of course. She was simply a girl in a village. But I really loved her. I am quite sure that I loved her. All during this wonderful May that we have been having, I used to run down and see her two or three times a week. Yesterday she met me in a little orchard. The apple-blossoms kept tumbling down on her hair, and she was laughing. We were to have gone away together this morning at dawn. Suddenly I determined to leave her as flower-like as I had found her."

"I should think the novelty of the emotion must have given you a thrill of real pleasure, Dorian," interrupted Lord Henry. "But I can finish your idyll for you. You gave her good advice, and broke her heart. That was the beginning of your reformation."

"Harry, you are horrible! You mustn't say these dreadful things. Hetty's heart is not broken. Of course she cried, and all that. But there is no disgrace upon her. She can live, like Perdita, in her garden of mint and marigold."

"And weep over a faithless Florizel," said Lord Henry, laughing, as he leant back in his chair. "My dear Dorian, you have the most curiously boyish moods. Do you think this girl will ever be really contented now with any one of her own rank? I suppose she will be married some day to a rough carter or a grinning ploughman. Well, the fact of having met you, and loved you, will teach her to despise her husband, and she will be wretched. From a moral point of view, I cannot say that I think much of your great renunciation. Even as a beginning, it is poor. Besides, how do you know that Hetty isn't floating at the present moment in some star-lit mill-pond, with lovely water-lilies round her, like Ophelia?"

"I can't bear this, Harry! You mock at everything, and then suggest the most serious tragedies. I am sorry I told you now. I don't care what you say to me. I know I was right in acting as I did. Poor Hetty! As I rode past the farm this morning, I saw her white face at the window, like a spray of jasmine. Don't let us talk about it any more, and don't try to persuade me that the first good action I have done for years, the first little bit of self-sacrifice I have ever known, is really a sort of sin. I want to be better. I am going to be better. Tell me something about yourself. What is going on in town? I have not been to the club for days."

"The people are still discussing poor Basil's disappearance."

"I should have thought they had got tired of that by this time," said Dorian, pouring himself out some wine, and frowning slightly.

"My dear boy, they have only been talking about it for six weeks, and the British public are really not equal to the mental strain of having more than one topic every three months. They have been very fortunate lately, however. They have had my own divorce-case, and Alan Campbell's suicide. Now they have got the mysterious disappearance of an artist. Scotland Yard still insists that the man in the grey ulster who left for Paris by the midnight train on the ninth of November was poor Basil, and the French police declare that Basil never arrived in Paris at all. I suppose in about a fortnight we shall be told that he has been seen in San Francisco. It is an odd thing, but every one who disappears is said to be seen at San Francisco. It must be a delightful city, and possess all the attractions of the next world."

"What do you think has happened to Basil?" asked Dorian, holding up his Burgundy against the light, and wondering how it was that he could discuss the matter so calmly.

"I have not the slightest idea. If Basil chooses to hide himself, it is no business of mine. If he is dead, I don't want to think about him. Death is the only thing that ever terrifies me. I hate it."

"Why?" said the younger man, wearily.

"Because," said Lord Henry, passing beneath his nostrils the gilt trellis of an open vinaigrette box, "one can survive everything nowadays except that. Death and vulgarity are the only two facts in the nineteenth century that one cannot explain away. Let us have our coffee in the music-room, Dorian. You must play Chopin to me. The man with whom my wife ran away played Chopin exquisitely. Poor Victoria! I was very fond of her. The house is rather lonely without her. Of course married life is merely a habit, a bad habit. But then one regrets the loss even of one's worst habits. Perhaps one regrets them the most. They are such an essential part of one's personality."

Dorian said nothing, but rose from the table, and, passing into the next room, sat down to the piano and let his fingers stray across the white and black ivory of the keys. After the coffee had been brought in, he stopped, and looking over at Lord Henry, said, "Harry, did it ever occur to you that Basil was murdered?"

Lord Henry yawned. "Basil was very popular, and always wore a Waterbury watch. Why should he have been murdered? He was not clever enough to have enemies. Of course he had a wonderful genius for painting. But a man can paint like Velasquez and yet be as dull as possible. Basil was really rather dull. He only interested me once, and that was when he told me, years ago, that he had a wild adoration for you, and that you were the dominant motive of his art."

"I was very fond of Basil," said Dorian, with a note of sadness in his voice. "But don't people say that he was murdered?"

"Oh, some of the papers do. It does not seem to me to be at all probable. I know there are dreadful places in Paris, but Basil was not the sort of man to have gone to them. He had no curiosity. It was his chief defect."

"What would you say, Harry, if I told you that I had murdered Basil?" said the younger man. He watched him intently after he had spoken.

"I would say, my dear fellow, that you were posing for a character that doesn't suit you. All crime is vulgar, just as all vulgarity is crime. It is not in you, Dorian, to commit a murder. I am sorry if I hurt your vanity by saying so, but I assure you it is true. Crime belongs exclusively to the lower orders. I don't blame them in the smallest degree. I should fancy that crime was to them what art is to us, simply a method of procuring extraordinary sensations."

"A method of procuring sensations? Do you think, then, that a man who has once committed a murder could possibly do the same crime again? Don't tell me that."

"Oh! anything becomes a pleasure if one does it too often," cried Lord Henry, laughing. "That is one of the most important secrets of life. I should fancy, however, that murder is always a mistake. One should never do anything that one cannot talk about after dinner. But let us pass from poor Basil. I wish I could believe that he had come to such a really romantic end as you suggest; but I can't. I dare say he fell into the Seine off an omnibus, and that the conductor hushed up the scandal. Yes: I should fancy that was his end. I see him lying now on his back under those dull-green waters with the heavy barges floating over him, and long weeds catching in his hair. Do you know, I don't think he would have done much more good work. During the last ten years his painting had gone off very much."

Dorian heaved a sigh, and Lord Henry strolled across the room and began to stroke the head of a curious Java parrot, a large grey-plumaged bird, with pink crest and tail, that was balancing itself upon a bamboo perch. As his pointed fingers touched it, it dropped the white scurf of crinkled lids over black glass-like eyes, and began to sway backwards and forwards.

"Yes," he continued, turning round, and taking his handkerchief out of his pocket; "his painting had quite gone off. It seemed to me to have lost something. It had lost an ideal. When you and he ceased to be great friends, he ceased to be a great artist. What was it separated you? I suppose he bored you. If so, he never forgave you. It's a habit bores have. By the way, what has become of that wonderful portrait he did of you? I don't think I have ever seen it since he finished it. Oh! I remember your telling me years ago that you had sent it down to Selby, and that it had got mislaid or stolen on the way. You never got it back? What a pity! It was really a masterpiece. I remember I wanted to buy it. I wish I had now. It belonged to Basil's best period. Since then, his work was that curious mixture of bad painting and good intentions that always entitles a man to be called a representative British artist. Did you advertise for it? You should."

"I forget," said Dorian. "I suppose I did. But I never really liked it. I am sorry I sat for it. The memory of the thing is hateful to me. Why do you talk of it? It used to remind me of those curious lines in some play—'Hamlet,' I think—how do they run?—

> "'Like the painting of a sorrow,
> A face without a heart.'

"Yes: that is what it was like."

Lord Henry laughed. "If a man treats life artistically, his brain is his heart," he answered, sinking into an armchair.

Dorian Gray shook his head, and struck some soft chords on the piano. "'Like the painting of a sorrow,'" he repeated, "'a face without a heart.'"

The elder man lay back and looked at him with half-closed eyes. "By the way, Dorian," he said, after a pause, "'what does it profit a man if he gain the whole world and lose'—how does the quotation run?—'his own soul'?"

The music jarred and Dorian Gray started, and stared at his friend. "Why do you ask me that, Harry?"

"My dear fellow," said Lord Henry, elevating his eyebrows in surprise, "I asked you because I thought you might be able to give me an answer. That is all.

I was going through the Park last Sunday, and close by the Marble Arch there stood a little crowd of shabby-looking people listening to some vulgar street-preacher. As I passed by, I heard the man yelling out that question to his audience. It struck me as being rather dramatic. London is very rich in curious effects of that kind. A wet Sunday, an uncouth Christian in a mackintosh, a ring of sickly white faces under a broken roof of dripping umbrellas, and a wonderful phrase flung into the air by shrill, hysterical lips—it was really very good in its way, quite a suggestion. I thought of telling the prophet that Art had a soul, but that man had not. I am afraid, however, he would not have understood me."

"Don't, Harry. The soul is a terrible reality. It can be bought, and sold, and bartered away. It can be poisoned, or made perfect. There is a soul in each one of us. I know it."

"Do you feel quite sure of that, Dorian?"

"Quite sure."

"Ah! then it must be an illusion. The things one feels absolutely certain about are never true. That is the fatality of Faith, and the lesson of Romance. How grave you are! Don't be so serious. What have you or I to do with the superstitious of our age? No: we have given up our belief in the soul. Play me something. Play me a nocturne, Dorian, and, as you play, tell me, in a low voice, how you have kept your youth. You must have some secret. I am only ten years older than you are, and I am wrinkled, and worn, and yellow. You are really wonderful, Dorian. You have never looked more charming than you do to-night. You remind me of the day I saw you first. You were rather cheeky, very shy, and absolutely extraordinary. You have changed, of course, but not in appearance. I wish you would tell me your secret. To get back my youth I would do anything in the world, except take exercise, get up early, or be respectable. Youth! There is nothing like it. It's absurd to talk of the ignorance of youth. The only people to whose opinions I listen now with any respect are people much younger than myself. They seem in front of me. Life has revealed to them her latest wonder. As for the aged, I always contradict the aged. I do it on principle. If you ask them their opinion on something that happened yesterday, they solemnly give you the opinions current in 1820, when people wore high stocks, believed in everything, and knew absolutely nothing. How lovely that thing you are playing is! I wonder did Chopin write it at Majorca, with the sea weeping round the villa, and the salt spray dashing against the panes? It is marvelously romantic. What a blessing it is that there is one art left to us that is not imitative! Don't stop. I want music to-night. It seems to me that you are the young Apollo, and that I am Marsyas listening to you. I have sorrows, Dorian, of my own, that even you know nothing of. The tragedy of old age is not that one is old, but that one is young. I am amazed sometimes at my own sincerity. Ah, Dorian, how happy you are! What an exquisite life you have led! You have drunk deeply of everything. You have crushed the grapes against your palate. Nothing has been hidden from you. And it has all been to you no more than the sound of music. It has not marred you. You are still the same."

"I am not the same, Harry."

"Yes: you are the same. I wonder what the rest of your life will be. Don't spoil it by renunciations. At present you are a perfect type. Don't make yourself incomplete. You are quite flawless now. You need not shake your head: you know you are. Besides, Dorian, don't deceive yourself. Life is not governed by will or intention. Life is a question of nerves, and fibres, and slowly built-up cells in which thought hides itself and passion has its dreams. You may fancy yourself safe, and think yourself strong. But a chance tone of colour in a room or a morning sky, a particular perfume that you had once loved and that brings subtle memories with it, a line from a forgotten poem that you had come across again, a cadence from a piece of music that you had ceased to play—I tell you, Dorian, that it is on things like these that our lives depend. Browning writes about that somewhere; but our own senses will imagine them for us. There are moments when the odour of *lilas blanc* passes suddenly across me, and I have to live the strangest month of my life over again. I wish I could change places with you, Dorian. The world has cried out against us both, but it has always worshipped you. It always will worship you. You are the type of what the age is searching for, and what it is afraid it has found. I am so glad that you have never done anything, never carved a statue, or painted a picture, or produced anything outside of yourself! Life has been your art. You have set yourself to music. Your days are your sonnets."

Dorian rose up from the piano, and passed his hand through his hair. "Yes, life has been exquisite," he murmured, "but I am not going to have the same life, Harry. And you must not say these extravagant things to me. You don't know everything about me. I think that if you did, even you would turn from me. You laugh. Don't laugh."

"Why have you stopped playing, Dorian? Go back and give me the nocturne over again. Look at that great honey-coloured moon that hangs in the dusky air. She is waiting for you to charm her, and if you play she will come closer to the earth. You won't? Let us go to the club, then. It has been a charming evening, and we must end it charmingly. There is some one at White's who wants immensely to know you—young Lord Poole, Bournemouth's eldest son. He has already copied your neckties, and has begged me to introduce him to you. He is quite delightful, and rather reminds me of you."

"I hope not," said Dorian, with a sad look in his eyes. "But I am tired to-night, Harry. I sha'n't go to the club. It is nearly eleven, and I want to go to bed early."

"Do stay. You have never played so well as to-night. There was something in your touch that was wonderful. It had more expression than I had ever heard from it before."

"It is because I am going to be good," he answered, smiling. "I am a little changed already."

"You cannot change to me, Dorian," said Lord Henry. "You and I will always be friends."

"Yet you poisoned me with a book once. I should not forgive that. Harry, promise me that you will never lend that book to any one. It does harm."

"My dear boy, you are really beginning to moralize. You will soon be going about like the converted, and the revivalist, warning people against all the sins of which you have grown tired. You are much too delightful to do that. Besides, it is no use. You and I are what we are, and will be what we will be. As for being poisoned by a book, there is no such thing as that. Art has no influence upon action. It annihilates the desire to act. It is superbly sterile. The books that the world calls immoral are books that show the world its own shame. That is all. But we won't discuss literature. Come round to-morrow. I am going to ride at eleven. We might go together, and I will take you to lunch afterwards with Lady Branksome. She is a charming woman, and wants to consult you about some tapestries she is thinking of buying. Mind you come. Or shall we lunch with our little Duchess? She says she never sees you now. Perhaps you are tired of Gladys? I thought you would be. Her clever tongue gets on one's nerves. Well, in any case, be here at eleven."

"Must I really come, Harry?"

"Certainly. The Park is quite lovely now. I don't think there have been such lilacs since the year I met you."

"Very well. I shall be here at eleven," said Dorian. "Good-night, Harry." As he reached the door he hesitated for a moment, as if he had something more to say. Then he sighed and went out.

CHAPTER XX

IT WAS A lovely night, so warm that he threw his coat over his arm, and did not even put his silk scarf round his throat. As he strolled home, smoking his cigarette, two young men in evening dress passed him. He heard one of them whisper to the other, "That is Dorian Gray." He remembered how pleased he used to be when he was pointed out, or stared at, or talked about. He was tired of hearing his own name now. Half the charm of the little village where he had been so often lately was that no one knew who he was. He had often told the girl whom he had lured to love him that he was poor, and she believed him. He had told her once that he was wicked, and she had laughed at him, and answered that wicked people were always very old and very ugly. What a laugh she had!—just like a thrush singing. And how pretty she had been in her cotton dresses and her large hats! She knew nothing, but she had everything that he had lost.

When he reached home, he found his servant waiting up for him. He sent him to bed, and threw himself down on the sofa in the library, and began to think over some of the things that Lord Henry had said to him.

Was it really true that one could never change? He felt a wild longing for the unstained purity of his boyhood—his rose-white boyhood, as Lord Henry had once called it. He knew that he had tarnished himself, filled his mind with corruption and given horror to his fancy; that he had been an evil influence to others, and had experienced a terrible joy in being so; and that of the lives that had crossed his own it had been the fairest and the most full of promise that he had brought to shame. But was it all irretrievable? Was there no hope for him?

Ah! in what a monstrous moment of pride and passion he had prayed that the portrait should bear the burden of his days, and he keep the unsullied splendour of eternal youth! All his failure had been due to that. Better for him that each sin of his life had brought its sure, swift penalty along with it. There was purification in punishment. Not "Forgive us our sins" but "Smite us for our iniquities" should be the prayer of man to a most just God.

The curiously-carved mirror that Lord Henry had given to him, so many years ago now, was standing on the table, and the white-limbed Cupids laughed round as of old. He took it up, as he had done on that night of horror, when he had first noted the change in the fatal picture, and with wild tear-dimmed eyes looked into its polished shield. Once, some one who had terribly loved him, had written to him a mad letter, ending with these idolatrous words: "The world is changed because you are made of ivory and gold. The curves of your lips rewrite history." The phrases came back to his memory, and he repeated them over and over to himself. Then he loathed his own beauty, and flinging the mirror on the floor crushed it into silver splinters beneath his heel. It was his beauty that had ruined him, his beauty and the youth that he had prayed for. But for those two things, his life might have been free from stain. His beauty had been to him but a mask, his youth but a mockery. What was youth at best? A green, an unripe time, a time of shallow moods, and sickly thoughts. Why had he worn its livery? Youth had spoiled him.

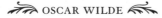

It was better not to think of the past. Nothing could alter that. It was of himself, and of his own future, that he had to think. James Vane was hidden in a nameless grave in Selby churchyard. Alan Campbell had shot himself one night in his laboratory, but had not revealed the secret that he had been forced to know. The excitement, such as it was, over Basil Hallward's disappearance would soon pass away. It was already waning. He was perfectly safe there. Nor, indeed, was it the death of Basil Hallward that weighed most upon his mind. It was the living death of his own soul that troubled him. Basil had painted the portrait that had marred his life. He could not forgive him that. It was the portrait that had done everything. Basil had said things to him that were unbearable, and that he had yet borne with patience. The murder had been simply the madness of a moment. As for Alan Campbell, his suicide had been his own act. He had chosen to do it. It was nothing to him.

A new life! That was what he wanted. That was what he was waiting for. Surely he had begun it already. He had spared one innocent thing, at any rate. He would never again tempt innocence. He would be good.

As he thought of Hetty Merton, he began to wonder if the portrait in the locked room had changed. Surely it was not still so horrible as it had been? Perhaps if his life became pure, he would be able to expel every sign of evil passion from the face. Perhaps the signs of evil had already gone away. He would go and look.

He took the lamp from the table and crept upstairs. As he unbarred the door, a smile of joy flitted across his strangely young-looking face and lingered for a moment about his lips. Yes, he would be good, and the hideous thing that he had hidden away would no longer be a terror to him. He felt as if the load had been lifted from him already.

He went in quietly, locking the door behind him, as was his custom, and dragged the purple hanging from the portrait. A cry of pain and indignation broke from him. He could see no change, save that in the eyes there was a look of cunning, and in the mouth the curved wrinkle of the hypocrite. The thing was still loathsome—more loathsome, if possible, than before—and the scarlet dew that spotted the hand seemed brighter, and more like blood newly spilt. Then he trembled. Had it been merely vanity that had made him do his one good deed? Or the desire for a new sensation, as Lord Henry had hinted, with his mocking laugh? Or that passion to act a part that sometimes makes us do things finer than we are ourselves? Or, perhaps, all these? And why was the red stain larger than it had been? It seemed to have crept like a horrible disease over the wrinkled fingers. There was blood on the painted feet, as though the thing had dripped—blood even on the hand that had not held the knife. Confess? Did it mean that he was to confess? To give himself up, and be put to death? He laughed. He felt that the idea was monstrous. Besides, even if he did confess, who would believe him? There was no trace of the murdered man anywhere. Everything belonging to him had been destroyed. He himself had burned what had been below-stairs. The world would simply say that he was mad. They would shut him up if he persisted in his story. . . . Yet it was his duty to confess, to suffer public shame, and to make public atonement. There was a God who called upon men to tell their sins to earth as well as to heaven. Nothing that he could do would cleanse him till he had told his own sin. His sin? He shrugged his shoulders. The death of Basil Hallward seemed very little to him. He was thinking of Hetty Merton. For it was an unjust mirror, this mirror of his soul that he was looking at. Vanity? Curiosity? Hypocrisy? Had there been nothing more in his renunciation than that? There had been something more. At least he thought so. But who could tell? . . . No. There had been nothing more. Through vanity he had spared her. In hypocrisy he had worn the mask of goodness. For curiosity's sake he had tried the denial of self. He recognized that now.

But this murder—was it to dog him all his life? Was he always to be burdened by his past? Was he really to confess? Never. There was only one bit of evidence left against him. The picture itself—that was evidence. He would destroy it. Why had he kept it so long? Once it had given him pleasure to watch it changing and growing old. Of late he had felt no such pleasure. It had kept him awake at night. When he had been away, he had been filled with terror lest other eyes should look upon it. It had brought melancholy across his passions. Its mere memory had marred many moments of joy. It had been like conscience to him. Yes, it had been conscience. He would destroy it.

He looked round, and saw the knife that had stabbed Basil Hallward. He had cleaned it many times, till there was no stain left upon it. It was bright, and glistened. As it had killed the painter, so it would kill the painter's work, and all that that meant. It would kill the past, and when that was dead he would be free. It would kill this monstrous soul-life, and without its hideous warnings, he would be at peace. He seized the thing, and stabbed the picture with it.

There was a cry heard, and a crash. The cry was so horrible in its agony that the frightened servants woke, and crept out of their rooms. Two gentlemen, who were passing in the Square below, stopped, and looked up at the great house. They walked on till they met a policeman, and brought him back. The man rang the bell several times, but there was no answer. Except for a light in one of the top windows, the house was all dark. After a time, he went away, and stood in an adjoining portico and watched.

"Whose house is that, constable?" asked the elder of the two gentlemen.

"Mr. Dorian Gray's, sir," answered the policeman.

They looked at each other, as they walked away, and sneered. One of them was Sir Henry Ashton's uncle.

Inside, in the servants' part of the house, the half-clad domestics were talking in low whispers to each other. Old Mrs. Leaf was crying, and wringing her hands. Francis was as pale as death.

After about a quarter of an hour, he got the coachman and one of the footmen and crept upstairs. They knocked, but there was no reply. They called out. Everything was still. Finally, after vainly trying to force the door, they got on the roof, and dropped down on to the balcony. The windows yielded easily: their bolts were old.

When they entered, they found hanging upon the wall a splendid portrait of their master as they had last seen him, in all the wonder of his exquisite youth and beauty. Lying on the floor was a dead man, in evening dress, with a knife in his heart. He was withered, wrinkled, and loathsome of visage. It was not till they had examined the rings that they recognized who it was.

George Bernard Shaw

(1856–1950)

G. Bernard Shaw (he hated the name George and did not use it) was an Irish comic dramatist known for his bombastic personality, social activism, and brilliant plays and criticism. He was born on July 26, 1856, in Dublin to George Carr Shaw and Lucinda Elizabeth Shaw. His father was an unsuccessful corn merchant with a disabling squint and a drinking problem. His mother was a gifted singer and musician.

As a young boy, Shaw was quite sensitive and thoughtful regarding the world around him, and he made ethical and moral decisions that would shape his thinking into adulthood. "My parents took no moral responsibility for me . . . I cannot remember having ever heard a single sentence uttered by my mother in the nature of moral or religious instruction. My father made an effort or two. When he caught me imitating him by pretending to smoke a pipe, he advised me very earnestly to never follow his example in any way . . . his sincerity so impressed me that to this day, I have never smoked, never shaved, or used alcoholic stimulants."

Shaw's family had little money and could only afford the barest of education for him—a governess early on, a favorite uncle's tutoring, and a few schools around Ireland. By thirteen, Shaw felt his future would not be enhanced by any further formal education. He took a post in a land agent's office but set out for London in 1876 to join his sister Lucy and his mother, who had left their father and was now living with voice teacher Vandeleur Lee.

Shaw lived in London for a few years, living off his mother and her new husband, and tried his hand at fiction. He wrote five novels, all of which were soundly rejected. He read voraciously at public libraries and the British Museum, and became involved in progressive politics. Influenced by Shelley, he became a vegetarian in 1881. He co-founded the Fabian Society, a socialist group devoted to the transformation of English society through the infiltration of the country's political and intellectual circles.

Eventually, Shaw found work as a music, theater, and book critic, finally discovering a vocation where he could stretch his creative wings. He was the theater critic for *The Saturday Review* (1895–98) and was thought of as the finest of his generation. He began to write his own plays, determined to break away from the artificial plots and predictable characters he had critiqued for the last three years.

Shaw's first play, *Widowers' House*, hit the stage in 1892. Critical of slum landlords, the play was a new form of theater in the Ibsen tradition, focusing on the social message as opposed to taking a romantic angle. This play was followed by Shaw's shocking comedy, *Mrs. Warren's Profession,* which he called "an economic exposure of the White Slave traffic as well as a melodrama." It did not sit well with the censors and was banned from performance for nine years.

Shaw called his first two plays "unpleasant" because "their dramatic power is used to force the spectator to face unpleasant facts." He wrote four subsequent works he called "the pleasant plays" in an effort to win back the audience and backers he had alienated with the first two. These four were *Arms and the Man* (1894), *Candida* (1897), *Man and Superman*, and *You Never Can Tell* (1899). *Candida* was his first moneymaker.

In 1898, a minor foot infection—that he got from lacing his shoe too tightly—worsened and Shaw was forced to resign from *The Saturday Review* to recuperate in Surrey. While on the mend, he met and married Charlotte Payne-Townshend, an Irish heiress and fellow Fabian. Their marriage, supposedly unconsummated, lasted until her death in 1943. (Shaw had intense emotional connections and correspondences with several other women, including Ellen Terry and Mrs. Patrick Campbell.)

For the next ten years Shaw—with Harley Granville-Barker (an actor-turned-producer)—took over the Court Theater, staging new and progressive drama. Ten of Shaw's plays were performed, and Shaw became a wealthy man, devoting additional time and money to social causes.

Three Plays for Puritans, issued in 1901, included *The Devil's Disciple, Caesar and Cleopatra,* and *Captain Brassbound's Conversion*. *John Bull's Other Island* (performed in 1904) was Shaw's first play to win over England's tough theater-going public. *Major Barbara* made its debut in 1905, and paired with *Androcles and the Lion* marked a journey into exploration of religious consciousness. *Pygmalion*, first performed in 1913, is considered Shaw's comic masterpiece and has certainly become his most popular play. Shaw proposed that it was a preachy story about phonetics, but the play proves to be an antic tale about love and class. (*Pygmalion* was made into a film in the United States in 1938, for which Shaw won the Academy Award for best screenplay.)

When World War I broke out, Shaw was shaken to the core. He wrote articles critical of the war, making him an outcast in his adopted country. He wrote only one play during the war, *Heartbreak House,* a drama expressing despair and bitterness about British politics and society.

After World War I, Shaw felt compelled to write drama again. He composed a group of five plays under the title *Back to Methuselah.* Then in 1923, inspired by the 1920 canonization of Joan of Arc, he wrote a chronicle play. *Saint Joan* portrays Joan not only as a martyr and a saint, but as a mystical genius. Subsequently in 1925, he won the Nobel Prize in Literature but reportedly refused the award.

Shaw lived the rest of his life as a world-renowned author, traveling and involved in local and international politics. He visited the Soviet Union at Stalin's invitation. He traveled to the U.S. to visit William Randolph Hearst at Hearst Castle in San Francisco and to lecture at the Metropolitan Opera House in New York. And he continued to write, thousands of letters and more than a dozen plays.

In 1950, Shaw tumbled off a ladder while trimming a tree in his garden; he died a few days later. He was ninety-four years old and had been working on another play, *Why She Would Not.* His estate was designated to help revamp the English alphabet. When that project failed, the money was divided among the other beneficiaries: The National Gallery of Ireland, the British Museum, and the Royal Academy of the Dramatic Art. Royalties from his plays continue to support these institutions to this day.

Mrs. Warren's Profession was written in 1894 but not performed till 1902 due to the Lord Chamberlain's censure. The subject matter—Mrs. Warren is an ex-prostitute who operates a chain of successful high-class brothels—was shocking and deemed unacceptable. Yet Shaw was not looking for a lurid subject to entice audiences, much less a taboo to violate. In his preface to the play, Shaw states: "*Mrs. Warren's Profession* was written . . . to draw attention to the truth that prostitution is caused, not by female depravity and male licentiousness, but by simply underpaying, undervaluing, and overworking women so shamefully that the poorest of them are forced to resort to prostitution to keep body and soul together."

Vivie, Mrs. Warren's daughter and the "heroine" of the play, is unaware at the start of the action that her mother is still "in the business" and that her public school and Cambridge education have been funded by her mother's morally suspect enterprise. Vivie is meant to represent what women can become if given the chance to study and think for themselves. She is smart, independent, and an actuary in an office in Chancery Row with an eye toward studying law. Yet even though she is presented as a positive alternative to her mother's example, she is lacking in humanity. She is cold, precise, as exacting as the figures she tabulates, as if somehow her "masculine" upbringing has desensitized her. The beauty of Shaw's story is that no one character is held up as ideal; every one has admirable singular qualities, but no one person in the play behaves admirably. Frank, who is after Vivie's hand and fortune, abandons her completely when he discovers they might be half-siblings and that her dowry is tainted. The Reverend, who might be Vivie's father, is living under the shadow of some love letters he wrote years ago to Mrs. Warren that she has chosen to keep. Crofts, the older gentleman also interested in Vivie, is revealed to be the bankroller of Mrs. Warren's profession. Mrs. Warren is the only character that elicits a bit of sympathy. She tells a story of an early life of poverty and then at the end of the play, begs her daughter for some small understanding and affection. Vivie cuts her mother out of her life and goes back to her tabulations.

More than a comedy, but with elements of a moral message play, *Mrs. Warren's Profession* is ironic in its attempts and almost succeeds in making prostitution seem like the last refuge of a woman with her own mind and goals. Vivie, although supposedly the audience's darling, is unappealing in her unyielding ways, letting no one love or help her. She may be young, smart, and self-sufficient, but she has no heart. Maybe Shaw was calling for a little moderation in all areas. Society should let women have more occupational choices, but allow them to retain what qualities make them "the fairer sex."

Mrs Warren's Profession

PREFACE

Mrs Warren's Profession was written in 1894 to draw attention to the truth that prostitution is caused, not by female depravity and male licentiousness, but simply by underpaying, undervaluing, and overworking women so shamefully that the poorest of them are forced to resort to prostitution to keep body and soul together. Indeed all attractive unpropertied women lose money by being infallibly virtuous or contracting marriages that are not more or less venal. If on the large social scale we get what we call vice instead of what we call virtue it is simply because we are paying more for it. No normal woman would be a professional prostitute if she could better herself by being respectable, nor marry for money if she could afford to marry for love.

Also I desired to expose the fact that prostitution is not only carried on without organization by individual enterprise in the lodgings of solitary women, each her own mistress as well as every customer's mistress, but organized and exploited as a big international commerce for the profit of capitalists like any other commerce, and very lucrative to great city estates, including Church estates, through the rents of the houses in which it is practised.

I could not have done anything more injurious to my prospects at the outset of my career. My play was immediately stigmatized by the Lord Chamberlain, who by Act of Parliament has despotic and even supermonarchical power over our theatres, as 'immoral and otherwise improper for the stage'. Its performance was prohibited, I myself being branded by implication, to my great damage, as an unscrupulous and blackguardly author. True, I have lived this defamation down, and am apparently none the worse. True too that the stage under the censorship became so licentious after the war that the ban on a comparatively prudish play like mine became ridiculous and had to be lifted. Also I admit that my career as a revolutionary critic of our most respected social institutions kept me so continually in hot water that the addition of another jugful of boiling fluid by the Lord Chamberlain troubled me too little to entitle me to personal commiseration, especially as the play greatly strengthened my repute among serious readers. Besides, in 1894 the ordinary commercial theatres would have nothing to say to me, Lord Chamberlain or no Lord Chamberlain. None the less the injury done me now admittedly indefensible, was real and considerable, and the injury to society much greater; for when the White Slave Traffic, as Mrs Warren's profession came to be called, was dealt with legislatively, all that Parliament did was to enact that prostitutes' male bullies and parasites should be flogged, leaving Mrs Warren in complete command of the situation, and its true nature more effectually masked than ever. It was the fault of the Censorship that our legislators and journalists were not better instructed.

In 1902 the Stage Society, technically a club giving private performances for the entertainment of its own members, and therefore exempt from the Lord Chamberlain's jurisdiction, resolved to perform the play. None of the public theatres dared brave his displeasure (he has absolute power to close them if they offend him) by harboring the performance; but another club which had a little stage, and which rather courted a pleasantly scandalous reputation, opened its doors for one night and one afternoon. Some idea of the resultant sensation may be gathered from the following polemic, which appeared as a preface to a special edition of the play, and was headed.

The Author's Apology

Mrs Warren's Profession has been performed at last, after a delay of only eight years; and I have once more shared with Ibsen the triumphant amusement of startling all but the strongest-headed of the London theatre critics clean out of the practice of their profession. No author who has ever known the exultation of sending the Press into an hysterical tumult of protest, of moral panic, of involuntary and frantic confession of sin, of a horror of conscience in which the power of distinguishing between the work of art on the stage and the real life of the spectator is confused and overwhelmed, will ever care for the stereotyped compliments which every successful farce or melodrama elicits from the newspapers. Give me that critic who rushed from my play to declare furiously that Sir George Crofts ought to be kicked. What a triumph for the actor, thus to reduce a jaded London journalist to the condition of the simple sailor in the Wapping gallery, who shouts execrations at Iago and warnings to Othello not to believe him! But dearer still than such simplicity is that sense of the sudden earthquake shock to the foundations of morality which sends a pallid crowd of critics into the street shrieking that the pillars of society are cracking and the ruin of the State at hand. Even the Ibsen champions of ten years ago remonstrate with me just as the veterans of those brave days remonstrated with them. Mr Grein, the hardy iconoclast who first launched my plays on the stage alongside Ghosts and The Wild Duck, exclaims that I have shattered his ideals. Actually his ideals! What would Dr Relling say? And Mr William Archer himself disowns me because I 'cannot touch pitch without wallowing in it.' Truly my play must be more needed than I knew; and yet I thought I knew how little the others know.

Do not suppose, however, that the consternation of the Press reflects any consternation among the general public. Anybody can upset the theatre critics, in a turn of the wrist, by substituting for the romantic commonplaces of the stage the moral commonplaces of the pulpit, the platform, or the library. Play Mrs Warren's Profession to an audience of clerical members of the Christian Social Union and of women well experienced in Rescue, Temperance, and Girls' Club work, and no moral panic will arise: every man and woman present will know that as long as poverty makes virtue hideous and the spare pocket-money of rich bachelordom makes vice dazzling, their daily hand-to-hand fight against prostitution with prayer and persuasion, shelters and scanty alms, will be a losing one. There was a time when they were able to urge that though 'the whitelead factory where Anne Jane was poisoned' may be a far more terrible place than Mrs Warren's house, yet hell is still more dreadful. Nowadays they no longer believe in hell; and the girls among whom they are working know that they do not believe in it, and would laugh at them if they did. So well have the rescuers learnt that Mrs Warren's defence of herself and indictment of society is the thing that most needs saying, that those who know me personally reproach me, not for writing this play, but for wasting my energies on 'pleasant plays' for the amusement of frivolous people, when I can build up such excellent stage sermons on their own work. Mrs Warren's Profession is the one play of mine which I could submit to a censorship without doubt of the result; only, it must not be the censorship of the minor theatre critic, nor of an innocent court official like the Lord Chamberlain's Examiner, much less of people who consciously profit by Mrs Warren's profession, or who personally make use of it, or who hold the widely whispered view that it is an indispensable safety-valve for the protection of domestic virtue, or, above all, who are smitten with a sentimental affection for our fallen sister, and would 'take her up tenderly, lift her with care, fashioned so slenderly, young, and so fair.' Nor am I prepared to accept the verdict of the medical gentlemen who would compulsorily examine and register Mrs Warren, whilst leaving Mrs Warren's patrons, especially her military patrons, free to destroy her health and anybody else's without fear of reprisals. But I should be quite content to have my play judged by, say, a joint committee of the Central Vigilance Society and the Salvation Army. And the sterner moralists the members of the committee were, the better.

Some of the journalists I have shocked reason so unripely that they will gather nothing from this but a confused notion that I am accusing the National Vigilance Association and the Salvation Army of complicity in my own scandalous immorality. It will seem to them that people who would stand this play would stand anything. They are quite mistaken. Such an audience as I have described would be revolted by many of our fashionable plays. They would leave the theatre convinced that the Plymouth Brother who still regards the playhouse as one of the gates of hell is perhaps the safest adviser on the subject of which he knows so little. If I do not draw the same conclusion, it is not because I am one of those who claim that art is exempt from moral obligations, and deny that the writing or performance of a play is a moral act, to be treated on exactly the same footing as theft or murder if it produces equally mischievous consequences. I am convinced that fine art is the subtlest, the most seductive, the most effective instrument of moral propaganda in the world, excepting only the example of personal conduct; and I waive even this exception in favour of the art of the stage, because it works by exhibiting examples of personal conduct made intelligible and moving to crowds of unobservant unreflecting people to whom real life means nothing. I have pointed out again and again that the influence of the theatre in England is growing so great that private conduct, religion, law, science, politics, and morals are becoming more and more theatrical, whilst the theatre itself remains impervious to common sense, religion, science, politics, and morals. That is why I fight the theatre, not with pamphlets and sermons and treatises, but with plays; and so effective do I find the dramatic method that I have no doubt I shall at last persuade even London to take its conscience and its brains with it when it goes to the theatre, instead of leaving them at home with its prayer-book as it does at present. Consequently, I am the last man to deny that if the net effect of performing Mrs Warren's Profession were an increase in the number of persons entering that profession or employing it, its performance might well be made an indictable offence.

Now let us consider how such recruiting can be encouraged by the theatre. Nothing is easier. Let the Lord Chamberlain's Examiner of Plays, backed by the Press, make an unwritten but perfectly well understood regulation that members of Mrs Warren's profession shall be tolerated on the stage only when they are beautiful, exquisitely dressed, and sumptuously lodged and fed; also that they shall, at the end of the play, die of consumption to the sympathetic tears of the whole audience, or step into the next room to commit suicide, or at least be turned out by their protectors, and passed on to be 'redeemed' by old and faithful lovers who have adored them in spite of all their levities. Naturally, the poorer girls in the gallery will believe in the beauty, in the exquisite dresses, and the luxurious living, and will see that there is no real necessity for the consumption, the suicide, or the ejectment: mere pious forms, all of them, to save the Censor's face. Even if these purely official catastrophes carried any conviction, the majority of English girls remain so poor, so dependent, so well aware that the drudgeries of such honest work as is within their reach are likely enough to lead them eventually to lung disease, premature death, and domestic desertion or brutality, that they would still see reason to prefer the primrose path to the stony way of virtue, since both, vice at worst and virtue at best, lead to the same end in poverty and overwork. It is true, that the Elementary School mistress will tell you that only girls of a certain kind will reason in this way. But alas! that certain kind turns out on inquiry to be simply the pretty, dainty kind: that is, the only kind that gets the chance of acting on such reasoning. Read the first report of the Commission on the Housing of the Working Classes (Bluebook C 4402, 1889); read the Report on Home Industries (sacred word, Home!) issued by the Women's Industrial Council (Home Industries of Women in London, 1897, IS); and ask yourself whether, if the lot in life therein described were your lot in life, you would not rather be a jewelled Vamp. If you can go deep enough into things to be able to say no, how many ignorant half-starved girls will believe you are speaking sincerely? To them the lot of the stage courtesan is heavenly in comparison with their own. Yet the Lord Chamberlain's Examiner, being an officer of the Royal Household, places the King in the position of saying to the dramatist 'Thus, and thus only, shall you present Mrs Warren's profession on the stage, or you shall starve. Witness Shaw, who told the untempting truth about it, and whom We, by the Grace of God, accordingly disallow and suppress, and do what in Us lies to silence.' Fortunately, Shaw cannot be silenced. 'The harlot's cry from street to street' is louder than the voices of all the kings. I am not dependent on the theatre, and cannot be starved into making my play a standing advertisement of the attractive side of Mrs Warren's business.

Here I must guard myself against a misunderstanding. It is not the fault of their authors that the long string of wanton's tragedies, from Antony and Cleopatra to Iris, are snares to poor girls, and are objected to on that account by many earnest men and women who consider Mrs Warren's Profession an excellent sermon. Pinero is in no way bound to suppress the fact that his Iris is a person to be envied by millions of better women. If he made his play false to life by inventing fictitious disadvantages for her, he would be acting as unscrupulously as any tract-writer. If society chooses to provide for its Irises better than for its working women, it must not expect honest playwrights to manufacture spurious evidence to save its credit. The mischief lies in the deliberate suppression of the other side of the case: the refusal to allow Mrs Warren to expose the drudgery and repulsiveness of plying for hire among coarse tedious drunkards. All that, says the Examiner in effect, is horrifying, loathsome. Precisely: what does he expect it to be? would he have us represent it as beautiful and gratifying? His answer to this question amounts, I fear, to a blunt Yes; for it seems impossible to root out of an Englishman's mind the notion that vice is delightful, and that abstention from it is privation. At all events, as long as the tempting side of it is kept towards the public, and softened by plenty of sentiment and sympathy, it is welcomed by our Censor, whereas the slightest attempt to place it in the light of the policeman's lantern or the Salvation Army shelter is checkmated at once as not merely disgusting, but, if you please, unnecessary.

Everybody will, I hope, admit that this state of things is intolerable; that the subject of Mrs Warren's profession must be either tapu altogether, or else exhibited with the warning side as freely displayed as the tempting side. But many persons will vote for a complete tapu, and an impartial clean sweep from the boards of Mrs Warren and Gretchen and the rest: in short, for banishing the sexual instincts from the stage altogether. Those who think this impossible can hardly have considered the number and importance of the subjects which are actually banished from the stage. Many plays, among them Lear, Hamlet, Macbeth, Coriolanus, Julius Ceasar, have no sex complications: the thread of their action can be followed by children who could not understand a single scene of Mrs Warren's Profession or Iris. None of our plays rouse the sympathy of the audience by an exhibition of the pains of maternity, as Chinese plays constantly do. Each nation has its particular set of tapus in addition to the common human stock; and though each of these tapus limits the scope of the dramatist, it does not make drama impossible. If the Examiner were to refuse to license plays with female characters in them, he would only be doing to the stage what our tribal customs already do to the pulpit and the bar. I have myself written a rather entertaining play with only one woman in it, and she quite heartwhole; and I could just as easily write a play without a woman in it at all. I will even go as far as to promise the Examiner my support if he will introduce this limitation for part of the year, say during Lent, so as to make a close season for that dullest of stock dramatic subjects, adultery, and force our managers and authors to find out what all great dramatists find out spontaneously: to wit, that people who sacrifice every other consideration to love are as hopelessly unheroic on the stage as lunatics or dipsomaniacs. Hector and Hamlet are the world's heroes; not Paris and Antony.

But though I do not question the possibility of a drama in which love should be as effectively ignored as cholera is at present, there is not the slightest chance of that way out of the difficulty being taken by the Examiner. If he attempted it there would be a revolt in which he would be swept away, in spite of my single-handed efforts to defend him. A complete tapu is politically impossible. A complete toleration is equally impossible to the Examiner, because his occupation would be gone if there were no tapu to enforce. He is therefor compelled to maintain the present compromise of a partial tapu, applied, to the best of his judgment, with a careful respect to persons and to public opinion. And a very sensible English solution of the difficulty, too, most readers will say. I should not dispute it if dramatic poets really were what English public opinion generally assumes them to be during their lifetime: that is, a licentiously irregular group to be kept in order in a rough and ready way by a magistrate who will stand no nonsense from them. But I cannot admit that the class represented by Eschylus, Sophocles, Aristophanes, Euripides, Shakespear, Goethe, Ibsen, and Tolstoy, not to mention our own contemporary playwrights, is as much in place in the Examiner's office as a pickpocket is in Bow Street. Further, it is not true that the Censorship, though it certainly suppresses Ibsen and Tolstoy, and would suppress Shakespear but for the absurd rule that a play once licensed is always licensed (so that Wycherly is permitted and Shelley prohibited), also suppresses unscrupulous playwrights. I challenge the Examiner to mention any extremity of sexual misconduct which any manager in his senses would risk presenting on the London stage that has not been presented under his license and that of his predecessor. The compromise, in fact, works out in practice in favor of loose plays as against earnest ones.

To carry conviction on this point, I will take the extreme course of narrating the plots of two plays witnessed within the last ten years by myself at London West End theatres, one licensed under Queen Victoria, the other under her successor. Both plots conform to the strictest rules of the period when La Dame aux Camellias was still a forbidden play, and when The Second Mrs Tanqueray would have been tolerated only on condition that she carefully explained to the audience that when she met Captain Ardale she sinned 'but in intention.'

Play number one. A prince is compelled by his parents to marry the daughter of a neighboring king, but loves another maiden. The scene represents a hall in the king's palace at night. The wedding has taken place that day; and the closed door of the nuptial chamber is in view of the audience. Inside, the princess awaits her bridegroom. A duenna is in attendance. The bridegroom enters. His sole desire is to escape from a marriage which is hateful to him. A means occurs to him. He will assault the duenna, and be ignominously expelled from the palace by his indignant father-in-law. To his horror, when he proceeds to carry out this stratagem, the duenna, far from raising an alarm is flattered, delighted, and compliant. The assaulter becomes the assaulted. He flings her angrily to the ground, where she remains placidly. He flies. The father enters; dismisses the duenna; and listens at the keyhole of his daughter's nuptial chamber, uttering various pleasantries, and declaring, with a shiver, that a sound of kissing, which he supposes to proceed from within, makes him feel young again.

Story number two. A German officer finds himself in an inn with a French lady who has wounded his national vanity. He resolves to humble her by committing a rape upon her. He announces his purpose. She remonstrates, implores, flies to the doors and finds them locked, calls for help and finds none at hand, runs screaming from side to side, and, after a harrowing scene, is overpowered and faints. Nothing further being possible on the stage without actual felony, the officer then relents and leaves her. When she recovers, she believes that he has carried out his threat; and during the rest of the play she is represented as vainly vowing vengeance upon him, whilst she is really falling in love with him under the influence of his imaginary crime against her. Finally she consents to marry him; and the curtain falls on their happiness.

This story was certified by the Examiner, acting for the Lord Chamberlain, as void in its general tendency of 'anything immoral or otherwise improper for the stage.' But let nobody conclude therefore that the Examiner is a monster, whose policy it is to deprave the theatre. As a matter of fact, both the above stories are strictly in order from the official point of view. The incidents of sex which they contain, though carried in both to the extreme point at which another step would be dealt with, not by the Examiner, but by the police, do not involve adultery, nor any allusion to Mrs Warren's profession, nor to the fact that the children of any polyandrous group will, when they grow up, inevitably be confronted, as those of Mrs Warren's group are in my play, with the insoluble problem of their own possible consanguinity. In short, by depending wholly on the coarse humors and the physical fascination of sex, they comply with all the formulable requirements of the Censorship, whereas plays in which these humors and fascinations are discarded, and the social problems created by sex seriously faced and dealt with, inevitably ignore the official formula and are suppressed. If the old rule against the exhibition of illicit sex relations on the stage were revived, and the subject absolutely barred, the only result would be that Antony and Cleopatra, Othello (because of the Bianca episode), Troilus and Cressida, Henry IV, Measure for Measure, Timon of Athens, La Dame aux Camellias, The Profligate, The Second Mrs Tanqueray, The Notorious Mrs Ebbsmith, The Gay Lord Quex, Mrs Dane's Defence, and Iris would be swept from the stage, and placed under the same ban as Tolstoy's Dominion of Darkness and Mrs Warren's Profession, whilst such plays as the two described above would have a monopoly of the theatre as far as sexual interest is concerned.

What is more, the repulsiveness of the worst of the certified plays would protect Censorship against effective exposure and criticism. Not long ago an American Review of high standing asked me for an article on the Censorship of the English Stage. I replied that such an article would involve passages too disagreeable for publication in a magazine for general family reading. The editor persisted nevertheless; but not until he had declared his readiness to face this, and had pledged himself to insert the article unaltered (the particularity of the pledge extending even to a specification of the exact number of words in the article) did I consent to the proposal. What was the result? The editor, confronted with the two stories given above, threw his pledge to the winds, and, instead of returning the article, printed it with the illustrative examples omitted, and nothing left but the argument from political principle against the Censorship. In doing this he fired my broadside after withdrawing the cannon balls; for neither the Censor nor any other Englishman, except perhaps a few veterans of the dwindling old guard of Benthamism, cares a dump about political principle. The ordinary Briton thinks that if every other Briton is not under some form of tutelage, the more childish the better, he will abuse his freedom viciously. As far as its principle is concerned, the Censorship is the most popular institution in England; and the playwright who criticizes it is slighted as a blackguard agitating for impunity. Consequently nothing can really shake the confidence of the public in the Lord Chamberlain's department except a remorseless and unbowdlerized narration of the licentious fictions which slip through its net, and are hallmarked by it with the approval of the royal household. But as such stories cannot be made public without great difficulty, owing to the obligation an editor is under not to deal unexpectedly with matters that are not virginibus puerisque, the chances are heavily in favor of the Censor escaping all remonstrance. With the exception of such comments as I was able to make in my own critical articles in The World and The Saturday Review when the pieces I have described were first produced, and a few ignorant protests by churchmen against much better plays which they confessed they had not seen nor read, nothing has been said in the press that could seriously disturb the easygoing notion that the stage would be much worse than it admittedly is but for the vigilance of the Examiner. The truth is, that no manager would dare produce on his own responsibility the pieces he can now get royal certificates for at two guineas per piece.

I hasten to add that I believe these evils to be inherent in the nature of all censorship, and not merely a consequence of the form the institution takes in London. No doubt there is a staggering absurdity in appointing an ordinary clerk to see that the leaders of European literature do not corrupt the morals of the nation, and to restrain Sir Henry Irving from presuming to impersonate Samson or David on the stage, though any other sort of artist may daub these scriptural figures on a signboard or carve them on a tombstone without hindrance. If the General Medical Council, the Royal College of Physicians, the Royal Academy of Arts, the Incorporated Law Society, and Convocation were abolished, and their functions handed over to the Examiner, the Concert of Europe would presumably certify England as mad. Yet, though neither medicine nor painting nor law nor the Church moulds the character of the nation as potently as the theatre does, nothing can come on the stage unless its dimensions admit of its first passing through the Examiner's mind! Pray do not think that I question his honesty. I am quite sure that he sincerely thinks me a blackguard, and my play a grossly improper one, because, like Tolstoy's Dominion of Darkness, it produces, as they are both meant to produce, a very strong and very painful impression of evil. I do not doubt for a moment that the rapine play which I have described, and which he licensed, was quite incapable in manuscript of producing any particular effect on his mind at all, and that when he was once satisfied that the ill-conducted hero was a German and not an English officer, he passed the play without studying its moral tendencies. Even if he had undertaken that study, there is no more reason to suppose that he is a competent moralist than there is to suppose that I am a competent mathematician. But truly it does not matter whether he is a moralist or not. Let nobody dream for a moment that what is wrong with the Censorship is the shortcoming of the gentleman who happens at any moment to be acting as Censor. Replace him tomorrow by an Academy of Letters and an Academy of Dramatic Poetry, and the new filter will still exclude original and epoch-making work, whilst passing conventional, old-fashioned, and vulgar work. The conclave which compiles the expurgatory index of the Roman Catholic Church is the most august, ancient, learned, famous, and authoritative censorship in Europe. Is it more enlightened, more liberal, more tolerant than the comparatively unqualified office of the Lord Chamberlain? On the contrary, it has reduced itself to a degree of absurdity which makes a Catholic university a contradiction in terms. All censorships exist to prevent anyone from challenging current conceptions and existing institutions. All progress is initiated by challenging current conceptions, and executed by supplanting existing institutions. Consequently the first condition of progress is the removal of censorships. There is the whole case against censorships in a nutshell.

It will be asked whether theatrical managers are to be allowed to produce what they like, without regard to the public interest. But that is not the alternative. The managers of our London music-halls are not subject to any censorship. They produce their entertainments on their own responsibility, and have no two-guinea certificates to plead if their houses are conducted viciously. They know that if they lose their character, the County Council will simply refuse to renew their license at the end of the year; and nothing in the history of popular art is more amazing than the improvement in music-halls that this simple arrangement has produced within a few years. Place the theatres on the same footing, and we shall promptly have a similar revolution: a whole class of frankly blackguardly plays, in which unscrupulous low comedians attract crowds to gaze at bevies of girls who have nothing to exhibit but their prettiness, will vanish like the obscene songs which were supposed to enliven the squalid dulness, incredible to the younger generation, of the music-halls fifteen years ago. On the other hand, plays which treat sex questions as problems for thought instead of as aphrodisiacs will be freely performed. Gentlemen of the Examiner's way of thinking will have plenty of opportunity of protesting against them in Council; but the result will be that the Examiner will find his natural level; Ibsen and Tolstoy theirs; so no harm will be done.

This question of the Censorship reminds me that I have to apologize to those who went to the recent performance of Mrs Warren's Profession expecting to find it what I have just called an aphrodisiac. That was not my fault: it was the Examiner's. After the specimens I have given of the tolerance of his department, it was natural enough for thoughtless people to infer that a play which overstepped his indulgence must be a very exciting play indeed. Accordingly, I find one critic so explicit as to the nature of his disappointment as to say candidly that 'such airy talk as there is upon the matter is utterly unworthy of acceptance as being a representation of what people with blood in them think or do on such occasions.' Thus am I crushed between the upper millstone of the Examiner, who thinks me a libertine, and the nether popular critic, who thinks me a prude. Critics of all grades and ages, middle-aged fathers of families no less than ardent young enthusiasts, are equally indignant with me. They revile me as lacking in passion, in feeling, in manhood. Some of them even sum the matter up by denying me any dramatic power: a melancholy betrayal of what dramatic power has come to mean on our stage under the Censorship! Can I be expected to refrain from laughing at the spectacle of a number of respectable gentlemen lamenting because a playwright lures them to the theatre by a promise to excite their senses in a very special and sensational manner, and then, having successfully trapped them in exceptional numbers, proceeds to ignore their senses and ruthlessly improve their minds? But I protest again that the lure was not mine. The play had been in print for four years; and I have spared no pains to make known that my plays are built to induce, not voluptuous reverie but intellectual interest, not romantic rhapsody but humane concern. Accordingly, I do not find those critics who are gifted with intellectual appetite and political conscience complaining of want of dramatic power. Rather do they protest, not altogether unjustly, against a few relapses into staginess and caricature which betray the young playwright and the old playgoer in this early work of mine. As to the voluptuaries, I can assure them that the playwright, whether he be myself or another, will always disappoint them. The drama can do little to delight the senses: all the apparent instances to the contrary are instances of the personal fascination of the performers. The drama of pure feeling is no longer in the hands of the playwright: it has been conquered by the musician, after whose enchantments all the verbal arts seem cold and tame. Romeo and Juliet with the loveliest Juliet is dry, tedious, and rhetorical in comparison with Wagner's Tristan, even though Isolde be both fourteen stone and forty, as she often is in Germany. Indeed, it needed no Wagner to convince the public of this. The voluptuous sentimentality of Gounod's Faust and Bizet's Carmen has captured the common playgoer; and there is, flatly, no future now for any drama without music except the drama of thought. The attempt to produce a genus of opera without music (and this absurdity is what our fashionable theatres have been driving at for a long time past without knowing it) is far less hopeful than my own determination to accept problem as the normal material of the drama.

That this determination will throw me into a long conflict with our theatre critics, and with the few playgoers who go to the theatre as often as the critics, I well know; but I am too well equipped for the strife to be deterred by it, or to bear malice towards the losing side. In trying to produce the sensuous effects of opera, the fashionable drama has become so flaccid in its sentimentality, and the intellect of its frequenters so atrophied by disuse, that the reintroduction of problem, with its remorseless logic and iron framework of fact, inevitably produces at first an overwhelming impression of coldness and inhuman rationalism. But this will soon pass away. When the intellectual muscle and moral nerve of the critics has been developed in the struggle with modern problem plays, the pettish luxuriousness of the clever ones, and the sulky sense of disadvantaged weakness in the sentimental ones, will clear away; and it will be seen that only in the problem play is there any real drama, because drama is no mere setting up of the camera to nature: it is the presentation in parable of the conflict between Man's will and his environment: in a word, of problem. The vapidness of such drama as the pseudo-operatic plays contain lies in the fact that in them animal passion, sentimentally diluted, is shewn in conflict, not with real circumstances, but with a set of conventions and assumptions half of which do not exist off the stage, whilst the other half can either be evaded by a pretence of compliance or defied with complete impunity by any reasonably strong-minded person. Nobody can feel that such conventions are really compulsory; and consequently nobody can believe in the stage pathos that accepts them as an inexorable fate, or in the reality of the figures who indulge in such pathos. Sitting at such plays we do not believe: we make-believe. And the habit of make-believe becomes at last so rooted, that criticism of the theatre insensibly ceases to be criticism at all, and becomes more and more a chronicle of the fashionable enterprises of the only realities left on the stage: that is, the performers in their own persons. In this phase the playwright who attempts to revive genuine drama produces the disagreeable impression of the pedant who attempts to start a serious discussion at a fashionable at-home. Later on, when he has driven the tea services out and made the people who had come to use the theatre as a drawing-room understand that it is they and not the dramatists who are the intruders, he has to face the accusation that his plays ignore human feeling, an illusion produced by that very resistance of fact and law to human feeling which creates drama. It is the *deus ex machina* who, by suspending that resistance, makes the fall of the curtain an immediate necessity, since drama ends exactly where resistance ends. Yet the introduction of this resistance produces so strong an impression of heartlessness nowadays that a distinguished critic has summed up the impression made on him by Mrs

Warren's Profession, by declaring that 'the difference between the spirit of Tolstoy and the spirit of Mr Shaw is the difference between the spirit of Christ and the spirit of Euclid.' But the epigram would be as good if Tolstoy's name were put in place of mine and D'Annunzio's in place of Tolstoy's. At the same time I accept the enormous compliment to my reasoning powers with sincere complacency; and I promise my flatterer that when he is sufficiently accustomed to and therefore undazzled by problem on the stage to be able to attend to the familiar factor of humanity in it as well as to the unfamiliar one of a real environment, he will both see and feel that Mrs Warren's Profession is no mere theorem, but a play of instincts and temperaments in conflict with each other and with a flinty social problem that never yields an inch to mere sentiment.

I go further than this. I declare that the real secret of the cynicism and inhumanity of which shallower critics accuse me is the unexpectedness with which my characters behave like human beings, instead of conforming to the romantic logic of the stage. The axioms and postulates of that dreary mimanthropometry are so well known that it is almost impossible for its slaves to write tolerable last acts to their plays, so conventionally do their conclusions follow from their premisses. Because I have thrown this logic ruthlessly overboard, I am accused of ignoring, not stage logic, but, of all things, human feeling. People with completely theatrified imaginations tell me that no girl would treat her mother as Vivie Warren does, meaning that no stage heroine would in a popular sentimental play. They say this just as they might say that no two straight lines would enclose a space. They do not see how completely inverted their vision has become even when I throw its preposterousness in their faces, as I repeatedly do in this very play. Praed, the sentimental artist (fool that I was not to make him a theatre critic instead of an architect!), burlesques them by expecting all through the piece that the feelings of the others will be logically deducible from their family relationships and from his 'conventionally unconventional' social code. The sarcasm is lost on the critics: they, saturated with the same logic, only think him the sole sensible person on the stage. Thus it comes about that the more completely the dramatist is emancipated from the illusion that men and women are primarily reasonable beings, and the more powerfully he insists on the ruthless indifference of their great dramatic antagonist, the external world, to their whims and emotions, the surer he is to be denounced as blind to the very distinction on which his whole work is built. Far from ignoring idiosyncrasy, will, passion, impulse, whim, as factors in human action, I have placed them so nakedly on the stage that the elderly citizen, accustomed to see them clothed with the veil of manufactured logic about duty, and to disguise even his own impulses from himself in this way, finds the picture as unnatural as Carlyle's suggested painting of parliament sitting without its clothes.

I now come to those critics who, intellectually baffled by the problem in Mrs Warren's Profession, have made a virtue of running away from it on the gentlemanly ground that the theatre is frequented by women as well as by men, and that such problems should not be discussed or even mentioned in the presence of women. With that sort of chivalry I cannot argue: I simply affirm that Mrs Warren's Profession is a play for women; that it was written for women; that it has been performed and produced mainly through the determination of women that it should be performed and produced; that the enthusiasm of women made its first performance excitingly successful; and that not one of these women had any inducement to support it except their belief in the timeliness and the power of the lesson the play teaches. Those who were 'surprised to see ladies present' were men; and when they proceeded to explain that the journals they represented could not possibly demoralize the public by describing such a play, their editors cruelly devoted the space saved by their delicacy to reporting at unusual length an exceptionally abominable police case.

My old Independent Theatre manager, Mr Grein, besides that reproach to me for shattering his ideals, complains that Mrs Warren is not wicked enough, and names several romancers who would have clothed her black soul with all the terrors of tragedy. I have no doubt they would; but that is just what I did not want to do. Nothing would please our sanctimonious British public more than to throw the whole guilt of Mrs Warren's profession on Mrs Warren herself. Now the whole aim of my play is to throw that guilt on the British public itself. Mr Grein may remember that when he produced my first play, Widowers' Houses, exactly the same misunderstanding arose. When the virtuous young gentleman rose up in wrath against the slum landlord, the slum landlord very effectually shewed him that slums are the product, not of individual Harpagons, but of the indifference of virtuous young gentlemen to the condition of the city they live in, provided they live at the west end of it on money earned by somebody else's labor. The notion that prostitution is created by the wickedness of Mrs Warren is as silly as the notion prevalent, nevertheless, to some extent in Temperance circles—that drunkenness is created by the wickedness of the publican. Mrs Warren is not a whit a worse woman than the reputable daughter who cannot endure her. Her indifference to the ultimate social consequence of her means of making money, and her discovery of that means by the ordinary method of taking the line of least resistance to getting it, are too common in English society to call for any special remark. Her vitality, her thrift, her energy, her outspokenness, her wise care of her daughter, and the managing capacity which has enabled her and her sister to climb from the fried fish shop down by the Mint to the establishments of which she boasts, are all high English social virtues. Her defence of herself is so overwhelming that it provokes the St James's Gazette to declare that 'the tendency of the play is wholly evil' because 'it contains one of the boldest and most specious defences of an immoral life for poor women that has ever been penned.' Happily the St James's Gazette here speaks in its haste. Mrs Warren's defence of herself is not only bold and specious, but valid and unanswerable. But it is no defence at all of the vice which she organizes. It is no defence of an immoral life to say that the alternative offered by society collectively to poor women is a miserable life, starved, overworked, fetid, ailing, ugly. Though it is quite natural and right for Mrs Warren to choose what is, according to her lights, the least immoral alternative, it is none the less infamous of society to offer such alternatives. For the alternatives offered are not morality and immorality, but two sorts of immorality. The man who cannot see that starvation, overwork, dirt, and disease are as anti-social as prostitution—that they are the vices and crimes of a nation, and not merely its misfortunes—is (to put it as politely as possible) a hopelessly Private Person.

The notion that Mrs Warren must be a fiend is only an example of the violence and passion which the slightest reference to sex rouses in undisciplined minds, and which makes it seem natural to our lawgivers to punish silly and negligible indecencies with a ferocity unknown in dealing with, for example, ruinous financial swindling. Had my play been entitled Mr Warren's Profession, and Mr Warren been a bookmaker, nobody would have expected me to make him a villain as well. Yet gambling is a vice, and bookmaking an institution, for which there is absolutely nothing to be said. The moral and economic evil done by trying to get other people's money without working for it (and this is the essence of gambling) is not only enormous but uncompensated. There are no two sides to the question of gambling, no circumstances which force us to tolerate it lest its suppression lead to worse things, no consensus of opinion among responsible classes, such as magistrates and military commanders, that it is a necessity, no Athenian records of gambling made splendid by the talents of its professors, no contention that instead of violating morals it only violates a legal institution which is in many respects oppressive and unnatural, no possible plea that the instinct on which it is founded is a vital one. Prostitution can confuse the issue with all these excuses: gambling has none of them. Consequently, if Mrs Warren must needs be a demon, a bookmaker must be a cacodemon. Well, does anybody who knows the sporting world really believe that bookmakers are worse than their neighbors? On the contrary, they have to be a good deal better; for in that world nearly everybody whose social rank does not exclude such an occupation would be a bookmaker if he could; but the strength of character required for handling large sums of money and for strict settlements and unflinching payment of losses is so rare that successful bookmakers are rare too. It may seem that at least public spirit cannot be one of a bookmaker's virtues; but I can testify from personal experience that excellent public work is done with money subscribed by bookmakers. It is true that there are abysses in bookmaking: for example, welshing. Mr Grein hints that there are abysses in Mrs Warren's profession also. So there are in every profession: the error lies in supposing that every member of them sounds these depths. I sit on a public body which prosecutes Mrs Warren zealously; and I can assure Mr Grein that she is often leniently dealt with because she has conducted her business 'respectably' and held herself above its vilest branches. The degrees in infamy are as numerous and as scrupulously observed as the degrees in the peerage: the moralist's notion that there are depths at which the moral atmosphere ceases is as delusive as the rich man's notion that there are no social jealousies or snobberies among the very poor. No: had I drawn Mrs Warren as a fiend in human form, the very people who now rebuke me for flattering her would probably be the first to deride me for deducing character logically from occupation instead of observing it accurately in society.

One critic is so enslaved by this sort of logic that he calls my portraiture of the Reverend Samuel Gardner an attack on religion. According to this view Subaltern Iago is an attack on the army, Sir John Falstaff an attack on knighthood, and King Claudius an attack on royalty. Here again the clamor for naturalness and human feeling, raised by so many critics when they are confronted by the real thing on the stage, is really a clamor for the most mechanical and superficial sort of logic. The dramatic reason for making the clergyman what Mrs Warren calls 'an old stick-in-the-mud', whose son, in spite of much capacity and charm, is a cynically worthless member of society, is to set up a mordant contrast between him and the woman of infamous profession, with her well brought-up, straightforward, hardworking daughter. The critics who have missed the contrast have doubtless observed often enough that many clergymen are in the Church through no genuine calling, but simply because, in circles which can command preferment, it is the refuge of the fool of the family; and that clergymen's sons are often conspicuous reactionists against the restraints imposed on them in childhood by their father's profession. These critics must know, too, from history if not from experience, that women as unscrupulous as Mrs Warren have distinguished themselves as administrators and rulers, both commercially and politically. But both observation and knowledge are left behind when journalists go to the theatre. Once in their stalls, they assume that it is 'natural' for clergymen to be saintly, for soldiers to be heroic, for lawyers to be hard-hearted, for sailors to be simple and generous, for doctors to perform miracles with little bottles, and for Mrs Warren to be a beast and a demon. All this is not only not natural, but not dramatic. A man's profession only enters into the drama of his life when it comes into conflict with his nature. The result of this conflict is tragic in Mrs Warren's case, and comic in the clergyman's case (at least we are savage enough to laugh at it); but in both cases it is illogical, and in both cases natural. I repeat, the critics who accuse me of sacrificing nature to logic are so sophisticated by their profession that to them logic is nature, and nature absurdity.

Many friendly critics are too little skilled in social questions and moral discussions to be able to conceive that respectable gentlemen like themselves, who would instantly call the police to remove Mrs Warren if she ventured to canvass them personally, could possibly be in any way responsible for her proceedings. They remonstrate sincerely, asking me what good such painful exposures can possibly do. They might as well ask what good Lord Shaftesbury did by devoting his life to the exposure of evils (by no means yet remedied) compared to which the worst things brought into view or even into surmise in this play are trifles. The good of mentioning them is that you make people so extremely uncomfortable about them that they finally stop blaming 'human nature' for them, and begin to support measures for their reform. Can anything be more absurd than the copy of The Echo which contains a notice of the performance of my play? It is edited by a gentleman who, having devoted his life to work of the Shaftesbury type, exposes social evils and clamors for their reform in every column except one; and that one is occupied by the declaration of the paper's kindly theatre critic, that the performance left him 'wondering what useful purpose the play was intended to serve.' The balance has to be redressed by the more fashionable papers, which usually combine capable art criticism with West-End solecism on politics and sociology. It is very noteworthy, however, on comparing the press explosion produced by Mrs Warren's Profession in 1902 with that produced by Widowers' Houses about ten years earlier, that whereas in 1892 the facts were frantically denied and the persons of the drama flouted as monsters of wickedness, in 1902 the facts are admitted, and the characters recognized, though it is suggested that this is exactly why no gentleman should mention them in public. Only one writer has ventured to imply this time that the poverty mentioned by Mrs Warren has since been quietly relieved, and need not have been dragged back to the footlights. I compliment him on his splendid mendacity, in which he is unsupported, save by a little plea in a theatrical paper which is innocent enough to think that ten guineas a year with board and lodging is an impossibly low wage for a barmaid. It goes on to cite Mr Charles Booth as having testified that there are many laborers' wives who are happy and contented on eighteen shillings a week. But I can go further than that myself. I have seen an Oxford agricultural laborer's wife looking cheerful on eight shillings a week; but that does not console me for the fact that agriculture in England is a ruined industry. If poverty does not matter as long as it is contented, then crime does not matter as long as it is unscrupulous. The truth is that it is only then that it does matter most desperately. Many persons are more comfortable when they are dirty than when they are clean; but that does not recommend dirt as a national policy.

In 1905 Arnold Daly produced Mrs Warren's Profession in New York. The press of that city instantly raised a cry that such persons as Mrs Warren are 'ordure' and should not be mentioned in the presence of decent people. This hideous repudiation of humanity and social conscience so took possession of the New York journalists that the few among them who kept their feet morally and intellectually could do nothing to check the epidemic of foul language, gross suggestion, and raving obscenity of word and thought that broke out. The writers abandoned all self-restraint under the impression that they were upholding virtue instead of outraging it. They infected each other with their hysteria until they were for all practical purposes indecently mad. They finally forced the police to arrest Daly and his company and led the magistrate to express his loathing of the duty thus forced upon him of reading an unmentionable and abominable play. Of course the convulsion soon exhausted itself. The magistrate, naturally somewhat impatient when he found that what he had to read was a strenuously ethical play forming part of a book which had been in circulation unchallenged for eight years, and had been received without protest by the whole London and New York Press, gave the journalists a piece of his mind as to their moral taste in plays. By consent, he passed the case on to a higher court, which declared that the play was not immoral; acquitted Daly; and made an end of the attempt to use the law to declare living women to be 'ordure,' and thus enforce silence as to the far-reaching fact that you cannot cheapen women in the market for industrial purposes without cheapening them for other purposes as well. I hope Mrs Warren's Profession will be played everywhere, in season and out of season, until Mrs Warren has bitten that fact into the public conscience, and shamed the newspapers which support a tariff to keep up the price of every American commodity except American manhood and womanhood.

Unfortunately, Daly had already suffered the usual fate of those who direct public attention to the profits of the sweater or the pleasures of the voluptuary. He was morally lynched side by side with me. Months elapsed before the decision of the courts vindicated him; and even then, since his vindication implied the condemnation of the Press, which was by that time sober again, and ashamed of its orgy, his triumph received a rather sulky and grudging publicity. In the meantime he had hardly been able to approach an American city, including even those cities which had heaped applause on him as the defender of hearth and home when he produced Candida, without having to face articles discussing whether mothers could allow their daughters to attend such plays as You Never Can Tell, written by the infamous author of Mrs Warren's Profession, and acted by the monster who produced it. What made this harder to bear was that though no fact is better established in theatrical business than the financial disastrousness of moral discredit, the journalists who had done all the mischief kept paying vice the homage of assuming that it is enormously popular and lucrative, and that Daly and I, being exploiters of vice, must therefore be making colossal fortunes out of the abuse heaped on us, and had in fact provoked it and welcomed it with that express object. Ignorance of real life could hardly go further.

I was deeply disgusted by this unsavory mobbing. And I have certain sensitive places in my soul: I do not like that word 'ordure'. Apply it to my work, and I can afford to smile, since the world, on the whole, will smile with me. But to apply it to the woman in the street, whose spirit is of one substance with your own and her body no less holy: to look your women folk in the face afterwards and not go out and hang yourself: that is not on the list of pardonable sins.

Shortly after these events a leading New York newspaper, which was among the most abusively clamorous for the suppression of Mrs Warren's Profession, was fined heavily for deriving part of its revenue from advertisements of Mrs Warren's houses.

Many people have been puzzled by the fact that whilst stage entertainments which are frankly meant to act on the spectators as aphrodisiacs are everywhere tolerated, plays which have an almost horrifying contrary effect are fiercely attacked by persons and papers notoriously indifferent to public morals on all other occasions. The explanation is very simple. The profits of Mrs Warren's profession are shared not only by Mrs Warren and Sir George Crofts, but by the landlords of their houses, the newspapers which advertise them, the restaurants which cater for them, and, in short, all the trades to which they are good customers, not to mention the public officials and representatives whom they silence by complicity, corruption, or blackmail. Add to these the employers who profit by cheap female labor, and the shareholders whose dividends depend on it (you find such people everywhere, even on the judicial bench and in the highest places in Church and State), and you get a large and powerful class with a strong pecuniary incentive to protect Mrs Warren's profession, and a correspondingly strong incentive to conceal, from their own consciences no less than from the world, the real sources of their gain. These are the people who declare that it is feminine vice and not poverty that drives women to the streets, as if vicious women with independent incomes ever went there. These are the people who, indulgent or indifferent to aphrodisiac plays, raise the moral hue and cry against performances of Mrs Warren's Profession, and drag actresses to the police court to be insulted, bullied, and threatened for fulfilling their engagements. For please observe that the judicial decision in New York State in favour of the play did not end the matter. In Kansas City, for instance, the municipality, finding itself restrained by the courts from preventing the performance, fell back on a local bye-law against indecency. It summoned the actress who impersonated Mrs Warren to the police court, and offered her and her colleagues the alternative of leaving the city or being prosecuted under this bye-law.

Now nothing is more possible than that the city councillors who suddenly displayed such concern for the morals of the theatre were either Mrs Warren's landlords, or employers of women at starvation wages, or restaurant keepers, or newspaper proprietors, or in some other more or less direct way sharers of the profits of her trade. No doubt it is equally possible that they were simply stupid men who thought that indecency consists, not in evil, but in mentioning it. I have, however, been myself a member of a municipal council, and have not found municipal councillors quite so simple and inexperienced as this. At all events I do not propose to give the Kansas councillors the benefit of the doubt. I therefore advise the public at large, which will finally decide the matter, to keep a vigilant eye on gentlemen who will stand anything at the theatre except a performance of Mrs Warren's Profession, and who assert in the same breath that (a) the play is too loathsome to be bearable by civilized people, and (b) that unless its performance is prohibited the whole town will throng to see it. They may be merely excited and foolish; but I am bound to warn the public that it is equally likely that they may be collected and knavish.

At all events, to prohibit the play is to protect the evil which the play exposes; and in view of that fact, I see no reason for assuming that the prohibitionists are disinterested moralists, and that the author, the managers, and the performers, who depend for their livelihood on their personal reputations and not on rents, advertisements, or dividends, are grossly inferior to them in moral sense and public responsibility.

It is true that in Mrs Warren's Profession, Society, and not any individual, is the villain of the piece; but it does not follow that the people who take offence at it are all champions of society. Their credentials cannot be too carefully examined.

PICCARD'S COTTAGE, January 1902 *(revised 1930)*

P.S. (1930) On reading the above after a lapse of 28 years, with the ban on Mrs Warren withdrawn and forgotten, I should have discarded it as an overdone fuss about nothing that now matters were it not for a recent incident. Before describing this I must explain that with the invention of the cinematograph a new censorship has come into existence, created, not this time by Act of Parliament, but by the film manufacturers to provide themselves with the certificates of propriety which have proved so useful to the theatre managers. This private censorship has acquired public power through its acceptance by the local authorities, without whose licence the films cannot be exhibited in places of public entertainment.

A lady who has devoted herself to the charitable work of relieving the homeless and penniless people who are to be found every night in London on the Thames Embankment had to deal largely with working men who had come to London from the country under the mistaken impression that there is always employment there for everybody, and with young women, also from the provinces, who had been lured to London by offers of situations which were really traps set for them by the agents of the White Slave traffic. The lady rightly concluded that much the best instrument for warning the men, and making known to the women the addresses of the organization for befriending unprotected girl travellers, is the cinema. She caused a film to be made for this purpose. The Film Censor immediately banned the part of the film which gave the addresses to the girls and shewed them the risks they ran. The lady appealed to me to help her to protest. After convincing myself by witnessing a private exhibition of the film that it was quite innocent I wrote to the Censor, begging him to examine the film personally, and remedy what seemed to be a rule-of-thumb mistake by his examiners. He not only confirmed their veto, but left uncontradicted a report in all the papers that he had given as his reason that the lady had paraded the allurements of vice, and that such parades could not be tolerated by him. The sole allurements were the smart motor car in which the heroine of the film was kidnapped, and the fashionable clothes of the two very repulsive agents who drugged her in it. In every other respect her experiences were as disagreeable as the sternest moralist could desire.

I then made a tour of the picture houses to see what the Film Censor considers allowable. Of the films duly licensed by him two were so nakedly pornographic that their exhibition could hardly have been risked without the Censor's certificate of purity. One of them presented the allurements of a supposedly French brothel so shamelessly that I rose and fled in disgust long before the end, though I am as hardened to vulgar salacity in the theatre as a surgeon is to a dissecting room.

The only logical conclusion apparent is that the White Slave traffickers are in complete control of our picture theatres, and can close them to our Rescue workers as effectively as they can reserve them for advertisements of their own trade. I spare the Film Censor that conclusion. The conclusion I press upon him and on the public is my old one of twenty-eight years ago: that all the evil effects of such corrupt control are inevitably produced gratuitously by Censors with the best intentions.

POSTSCRIPT 1933. In spite of the suppression of my play for so many years by the censorship the subject broke out into a campaign for the abolition of the White Slave Traffic which still occupies the League of Nations at Geneva. But my demonstration that the root of the evil is economic was ruthlessly ignored by the profiteering Press (that is, by the entire Press); and when at last parliament proceeded to legislate, its contribution to the question was to ordain that Mrs Warren's male competitors should be flogged instead of fined. This had the double effect of stimulating the perverted sexuality which delights in flogging, and driving the traffic into female hands, leaving Mrs Warren triumphant.

The ban on performances of the play has long since been withdrawn; and when it is performed the critics hasten to declare that the scandal of underpaid virtue and overpaid vice is a thing of the past. Yet when the war created an urgent demand for women's labor in 1914 the Government proceeded to employ women for twelve hours a day at a wage of five ha'pence an hour. It is amazing how the grossest abuses thrive on their reputation for being old unhappy far-off things in an age of imaginary progress.

ACT I

Summer afternoon in a cottage garden on the eastern slope of a hill a little south of Haslemere in Surrey. Looking up the hill, the cottage is seen in the left hand corner of the garden, with its thatched roof and porch, and a large latticed window to the left of the porch. A paling completely shuts in the garden, except for a gate on the right. The common rises uphill beyond the paling to the sky line. Some folded canvas garden chairs are leaning against the side bench in the porch. A lady's bicycle is propped against the wall, under the window. A little to the right of the porch a hammock is slung from two posts. A big canvas umbrella, stuck in the ground, keeps the sun off the hammock, in which a young lady lies reading and making notes, her head towards the cottage and her feet towards the gate. In front of the hammock, and within reach of her hand, is a common kitchen chair, with a pile of serious-looking books and a supply of writing-paper on it.

A gentleman walking on the common comes into sight from behind the cottage. He is hardly past middle age, with something of the artist about him, unconventionally but carefully dressed, and clean-shaven except for a moustache, with an eager susceptible face and very amiable and considerate manners. He has silky black hair, with waves of grey and white in it. His eyebrows are white, his moustache black. He seems not certain of his way. He looks over the paling; takes stock of the place; and sees the young lady.

THE GENTLEMAN *[taking off his hat]* I beg your pardon. Can you direct me to Hindhead View—Mrs Alison's?

THE YOUNG LADY *[glancing up from her book]* This is Mrs Alison's. *[She resumes her work]*.

THE GENTLEMAN. Indeed! Perhaps—may I ask are you Miss Vivie Warren?

THE YOUNG LADY *[sharply, as she turns on her elbow to get a good look at him]* Yes.

THE GENTLEMAN *[daunted and conciliatory]* I'm afraid I appear intrusive. My name is Praed. *[Vivie at once throws her books upon the chair, and gets out of the hammock]*. Oh, pray dont let me disturb you.

VIVIE *[striding to the gate and opening it for him]* Come in, Mr Praed. *[He comes in]*. Glad to see you. *[She proffers her hand and takes his with a resolute and hardy grip. She is an attractive specimen of the sensible, able, highly-educated young middle-class Englishwoman. Age 22. Prompt, strong, confident, self-possessed. Plain business-like dress, but not dowdy. She wears a chatelaine at her belt, with a fountain pen and a paper knife among its pendants]*.

PRAED. Very kind of you indeed, Miss Warren. *[She shuts the gate with a vigorous slam. He passes in to the middle of the garden, exercising his fingers, which are slightly numbed by her greeting]*. Has your mother arrived?

VIVIE *[quickly, evidently scenting aggression]* Is she coming?

PRAED *[surprised]* Didnt you expect us?

VIVIE. No.

PRAED. Now, goodness me, I hope Ive not mistaken the day. That would be just like me, you know. Your mother arranged that she was to come down from London and that I was to come over from Horsham to be introduced to you.

VIVIE *[not at all pleased]* Did she? Hm! My mother has rather a trick of taking me by surprise—to see how I behave myself when she's away, I suppose. I fancy I shall take my mother very much by surprise one of these days, if she makes arrangements that concern me without consulting me beforehand. She hasnt come.

PRAED *[embarrassed]* I'm really very sorry.

VIVIE *[throwing off her displeasure]* It's not your fault, Mr Praed, is it? And I'm very glad youve come. You are the only one of my mother's friends I have ever asked her to bring to see me.

PRAED *[relieved and delighted]* Oh, now this is really very good of you, Miss Warren!

VIVIE. Will you come indoors; or would you rather sit out here and talk?

PRAED. It will be nicer out here, dont you think?

VIVIE. Then I'll go and get you a chair. *[She goes to the porch for a garden chair]*.

PRAED *[following her]* Oh, pray, pray! Allow me. *[He lays hands on the chair]*.

VIVIE *[letting him take it]* Take care of your fingers: theyre rather dodgy things, those chairs. *[She goes across to the chair with the books on it; pitches them into the hammock; and brings the chair forward with one swing]*.

PRAED *[who has just unfolded his chair]* Oh, now do let me take that hard I like hard chairs.

VIVIE. So do I. Sit down, Mr Praed. *[This invitation she gives with genial peremptoriness, his anxiety to please her clearly striking her as a sign of weakness of character on his part. But he does not immediately obey]*.

PRAED. By the way, though, hadnt we better go to the station to meet your mother?

VIVIE *[coolly]* Why? She knows the way.

PRAED *[disconcerted]* Er—I suppose she does *[he sits down]*.

VIVIE. Do you know, you are just like what I expected. I hope you are disposed to be friends with me.

PRAED *[again beaming]* Thank you, my dear Miss Warren: thank you. Dear me! I'm so glad your mother hasnt spoilt you!

VIVIE. How?

PRAED. Well, in making you too conventional. You know, my dear Miss Warren, I am a born anarchist. I hate authority. It spoils the relations between parent and child: even between mother and daughter. Now I was always afraid that your mother would strain her authority to make you very conventional. It's such a relief to find that she hasnt.

VIVIE. Oh! have I been behaving unconventionally?

PRAED. Oh no: oh dear no. At least not conventionally unconventionally, you understand. *[She nods and sits down. He goes on, with a cordial outburst]*. But it was so charming of you to say that you were disposed to be friends with me! You modern young ladies are splendid: perfectly splendid!

VIVIE *[dubiously]* Eh? *[watching him with dawning disappointment as to the quality of his brains and character]*.

PRAED. When I was your age, young men and women were afraid of each other: there was no good fellowship. Nothing real. Only gallantry copied out of novels, and as vulgar and affected as it could be. Maidenly reserve! gentlemanly chivalry! always saying no when you meant yes! simple purgatory for shy and sincere souls.

VIVIE. Yes, I imagine there must have been a frightful waste of time. Especially women's time.

PRAED. Oh, waste of life, waste of everything. But things are improving. Do you know, I have been in a positive state of excitement about meeting you ever since your magnificent achievements at Cambridge: a thing unheard of in my day. It was perfectly splendid, your tieing with the third wrangler. Just the right place, you know. The first wrangler is always a dreamy, morbid fellow, in whom the thing is pushed to the length of a disease.

VIVIE. It doesnt pay. I wouldnt do it again for the same money!

PRAED *[aghast]* The same money!

VIVIE. I did it for £50.

PRAED. Fifty pounds!

VIVIE. Yes. Fifty pounds. Perhaps you dont know how it was. Mrs Latham, my tutor at Newnham, told my mother that I could distinguish myself in the mathematical tripos if I went in for it in earnest. The papers were full just then of Phillipa Summers beating the senior wrangler. You remember about it, of course.

PRAED *[shakes his head energetically]*

VIVIE. Well anyhow she did: and nothing would please my mother but that I should do the same thing. I said flatly it was not worth my while to face the grind since I was not going in for teaching; but I offered to try for fourth wrangler or thereabouts for £50. She closed with me at that, after a little grumbling; and I was better than my bargain. But I wouldnt do it again for that. £200 would have been nearer the mark.

PRAED *[much damped]* Lord bless me! Thats a very practical way of looking at it.

VIVIE. Did you expect to find me an unpractical person?

PRAED. But surely it's practical to consider not only the work these honors cost, but also the culture they bring.

VIVIE. Culture! My dear Mr Praed: do you know what the mathematical tripos means? It means grind, grind, grind for six to eight hours a day at mathematics, and nothing but mathematics. I'm supposed to know something about science; but I know nothing except the mathematics it involves. I can make calculations for engineers, electricians, insurance companies, and so on; but I know next to nothing about engineering or electricity or insurance. I dont even know arithmetic well. Outside mathematics, lawn tennis, eating, sleeping, cycling, and walking, I'm a more ignorant barbarian than any woman could possibly be who hadnt gone in for the tripos.

PRAED *[revolted]* What a monstrous, wicked, rascally system! I knew it! I felt at once that it meant destroying all that makes womanhood beautiful.

VIVIE. I dont object to it on that score in the least. I shall turn it to very good account, I assure you.

PRAED. Pooh! In what way?

VIVIE. I shall set up chambers in the City, and work at actuarial calculations and conveyancing. Under cover of that I shall do some law, with one eye on the

Stock Exchange all the time. Ive come down here by myself to read law: not for a holiday, as my mother imagines. I hate holidays.

PRAED. You make my blood run cold. Are you to have no romance, no beauty in your life?

VIVIE. I dont care for either, I assure you.

PRAED. You cant mean that.

VIVIE. Oh yes I do. I like working and getting paid for it. When I'm tired of working, I like a comfortable chair, a cigar, a little whisky, and a novel with a good detective story in it.

PRAED *[rising in a frenzy of repudiation]* I dont believe it. I am an artist; and I cant believe it: I refuse to believe it. It's only that you havnt discovered yet what a wonderful world art can open up to you.

VIVIE. Yes I have. Last May I spent six weeks in London with Honoria Fraser. Mamma thought we were doing a round of sightseeing together; but I was really at Honoria's chambers in Chancery Lane every day, working away at actuarial calculations for her, and helping her as well as a greenhorn could. In the evenings we smoked and talked, and never dreamt of going out except for exercise. And I never enjoyed myself more in my life. I cleared all my expenses, and got initiated into the business without a fee into the bargain.

YOU MAKE MY BLOOD RUN COLD. ARE YOU TO HAVE NO ROMANCE, NO BEAUTY IN YOUR LIFE?

PRAED. But bless my heart and soul, Miss Warren, do you call that discovering art?

VIVIE. Wait a bit. That wasnt the beginning. I went up to town on an invitation from some artistic people in Fitzjohn's Avenue: one of the girls was a Newnham chum. They took me to the National Gallery—

PRAED *[approving]* Ah!! *[He sits down, much relieved].*

VIVIE *[continuing]* —to the Opera—

PRAED *[still more pleased]* Good!

VIVIE. —and to a concert where the band played all the evening: Beethoven and Wagner and so on. I wouldnt go through that experience again for anything you could offer me. I held out for civility's sake until the third day; and then I said, plump out, that I couldnt stand any more of it, and went off to Chancery Lane. Now you know the sort of perfectly splendid modern young lady I am. How do you think I shall get on with my mother?

PRAED *[startled]* Well, I hope—er—

VIVIE. It's not so much what you hope as what you believe, that I want to know.

PRAED. Well, frankly, I am afraid your mother will be a little disappointed. Not from any shortcoming on your part, you know; I dont mean that. But you are so different from her ideal.

VIVIE. Her what?!

PRAED. Her ideal.

VIVIE. Do you mean her ideal of me?

PRAED. Yes.

VIVIE. What on earth is it like?

PRAED. Well, you must have observed, Miss Warren, that people who are dissatisfied with their own bringing-up generally think that the world would be all right if everybody were to be brought up quite differently. Now your mother's life has been—er—I suppose you know—

VIVIE. Dont suppose anything, Mr Praed. I hardly know my mother. Since I was a child I have lived in England, at school or college, or with people paid to take charge of me. I have been boarded out all my life. My mother has lived in Brussels or Vienna and never let me go to her. I only see her when she visits England for a few days. I dont complain: it's been very pleasant; for people have been very good to me; and there has always been plenty of money to make things smooth. But dont imagine I know anything about my mother. I know far less than you do.

PRAED *[very ill at ease]* In that case— *[He stops, quite at a loss. Then, with a forced attempt at gaiety]* But what nonsense we are talking! Of course you and your mother will get on capitally. *[He rises, and looks abroad at the view]*. What a charming little place you have here!

VIVIE *[unmoved]* Rather a violent change of subject, Mr Praed. Why wont my mother's life bear being talked about?

PRAED. Oh, you really mustnt say that. Isnt it natural that I should have a certain delicacy in talking to my old friend's daughter about her behind her back? You and she will have plenty of opportunity of talking about it when she comes.

VIVIE. No: she wont talk about it either. *[Rising]* However, I daresay you have good reasons for telling me nothing. Only, mind this, Mr Praed. I expect there will be a battle royal when my mother hears of my Chancery Lane project.

PRAED *[ruefully]* I'm afraid there will.

VIVIE. Well, I shall win, because I want nothing but my fare to London to start there to-morrow earning my own living by devilling for Honoria. Besides,

I have no mysteries to keep up; and it seems she has. I shall use that advantage over her if necessary.

PRAED *[greatly shocked]* Oh no! No, pray. Youd not do such a thing.

VIVIE. Then tell me why not.

PRAED. I really cannot. I appeal to your good feeling. *[She smiles at his sentimentality]*. Besides, you may be too bold. Your mother is not to be trifled with when she's angry.

VIVIE. You cant frighten me, Mr Praed. In that month at Chancery Lane I had opportunities of taking the measure of one or two women very like my mother. You may back me to win. But if I hit harder in my ignorance than I need, remember that it is you who refuse to enlighten me. Now, let us drop the subject. *[She takes her chair and replaces it near the hammock with the same vigorous swing as before]*.

PRAED *[taking a desperate resolution]* One word, Miss Warren. I had better tell you. It's very difficult; but—

Mrs Warren and Sir George Crofts arrive at the gate. Mrs Warren is between 40 and 50, formerly pretty, showily dressed in a brilliant hat and a gay blouse fitting tightly over her bust and flanked by fashionable sleeves. Rather spoilt and domineering, and decidedly vulgar, but, on the whole, a genial and fairly presentable old blackguard of a woman.

Crofts is a tall powerfully-built man of about 50, fashionably dressed in the style of a young man. Nasal voice, reedier than might be expected from his strong frame. Clean-shaven bulldog jaws, large flat ears, and thick neck: gentlemanly combination of the most brutal types of city man, sporting man, and man about town.

VIVIE. Here they are. *[Coming to them as they enter the garden]* How do, mater? Mr Praed's been here this half hour waiting for you.

MRS WARREN. Well, if youve been waiting, Praddy, it's your own fault: I thought youd have had the gumption to know I was coming by the 3.10 train. Vivie: put your hat on, dear—youll get sunburnt. Oh, I forgot to introduce you. Sir George Crofts: my little Vivie.

Crofts advances to Vivie with his most courtly manner. She nods, but makes no motion to shake hands.

CROFTS. May I shake hands with a young lady whom I have known by reputation very long as the daughter of one of my oldest friends?

VIVIE *[who has been looking him up and down sharply]* If you like. *[She takes his tenderly proffered hand and gives it a squeeze that makes him open his eyes; then turns away and says to her mother]* Will you come in, or shall I get a couple more chairs? *[She goes into the porch for the chairs]*.

MRS WARREN. Well, George, what do you think of her?

CROFTS *[ruefully]* She has a powerful fist. Did you shake hands with her, Praed?

PRAED. Yes: it will pass off presently.

CROFTS. I hope so. *[Vivie reappears with two more chairs. He hurries to her assistance]*. Allow me.

MRS WARREN *[patronizingly]* Let Sir George help you with the chairs, dear.

VIVIE *[pitching them into his arms]* Here you are. *[She dusts her hands and turns to Mrs Warren]*. Youd like some tea, wouldnt you?

MRS WARREN *[sitting in Praed's chair and fanning herself]* I'm dying for a drop to drink.

VIVIE. I'll see about it. *[She goes into the cottage]*.

Sir George has by this time managed to unfold a chair and plant it beside Mrs Warren, on her left. He throws the other on the grass and sits down, looking dejected and rather foolish, with the handle of his stick in his mouth. Praed, still very uneasy, fidgets about the garden on their right.

MRS WARREN *[to Praed, looking at Crofts]* Just look at him, Praddy: he looks cheerful, dont he? He's been worrying my life out these three years to have that little girl of mine shewn to him; and now that Ive done it, he's quite out of countenance. *[Briskly]* Come! sit up, George; and take your stick out of your mouth. *[Crofts sulkily obeys]*.

PRAED. I think, you know—if you dont mind my saying so—that we had better get out of the habit of thinking of her as a little girl. You see she has really distinguished herself; and I'm not sure, from what I have seen of her, that she is not older than any of us.

MRS WARREN *[greatly amused]* Only listen to him, George! Older than any of us! Well, she has been stuffing you nicely with her importance.

PRAED. But young people are particularly sensitive about being treated in that way.

MRS WARREN. Yes; and young people have to get all that nonsense taken out of them, and a good deal more besides. Dont you interfere, Praddy: I know how to treat my own child as well as you do. *[Praed, with a grave shake of his head, walks up the garden with his hands behind his back. Mrs Warren pretends to laugh, but looks after him with perceptible concern. Then she whispers to Crofts]* Whats the matter with him? What does he take it like that for?

CROFTS *[morosely]* Youre afraid of Praed.

MRS WARREN. What! Me! Afraid of dear old Praddy! Why, a fly wouldnt be afraid of him.

CROFTS. Youre afraid of him.

MRS WARREN *[angry]* I'll trouble you to mind your own business, and not try any of your sulks on me. I'm not afraid of you, anyhow. If you cant make yourself agreeable, youd better go home. *[She gets up, and, turning her back on him, finds herself face to face with Praed]*. Come, Praddy, I know it was only your tender-heartedness. Youre afraid I'll bully her.

PRAED. My dear Kitty: you think I'm offended. Dont imagine that: pray dont. But you know I often notice things that escape you; and though you never take my advice, you sometimes admit afterwards that you ought to have taken it.

MRS WARREN. Well, what do you notice now?

PRAED. Only that Vivie is a grown woman. Pray, Kitty, treat her with every respect.

MRS WARREN *[with genuine amazement]* Respect! Treat my own daughter with respect! What next, pray?

VIVIE *[appearing at the cottage door and calling to Mrs Warren]* Mother: will you come to my room before tea?

MRS WARREN. Yes, dearie. *[She laughs indulgently at Praed's gravity, and pats him on the cheek as she passes him on her way to the porch]*. Dont be cross, Praddy. *[She follows Vivie in to the cottage]*.

CROFTS *[furtively]* I say, Praed.

PRAED. Yes.

CROFTS. I want to ask you a rather particular question.

PRAED. Certainly. *[He takes Mrs Warren's chair and sits close to Crofts]*.

CROFTS. Thats right: they might hear us from the window. Look here: did Kitty ever tell you who that girl's father is?

PRAED. Never.

CROFTS. Have you any suspicion of who it might be?

PRAED. None.

CROFTS *[not believing him]* I know, of course, that you perhaps might feel bound not to tell if she had said anything to you. But it's very awkward to be uncertain about it now that we shall be meeting the girl every day. We wont exactly know how we ought to feel towards her.

PRAED. What difference can that make? We take her on her own merits. What does it matter who her father was?

CROFTS *[suspiciously]* Then you know who he was?

PRAED *[with a touch of temper]* I said no just now. Did you not hear me?

CROFTS. Look here, Praed. I ask you as a particular favor. If you do know *[movement of protest from Praed]* —I only say, if you know, you might at least set my mind at rest about her. The fact is, I feel attracted.

PRAED *[sternly]* What do you mean?

CROFTS. Oh, dont be alarmed: it's quite an innocent feeling. Thats what puzzles me about it. Why, for all I know I might be her father.

PRAED. You! Impossible!

CROFTS *[catching him up cunningly]* You know for certain that I'm not?

PRAED. I know nothing about it, I tell you, any more than you. But really, Crofts—oh no, it's out of the question. Theres not the least resemblance.

CROFTS. As to that, theres no resemblance between her and her mother that I can see. I suppose she's not your daughter, is she?

PRAED *[rising indignantly]* Really, Crofts—!

CROFTS. No offence, Praed. Quite allowable as between two men of the world.

PRAED *[recovering himself with an effort and speaking gently and gravely]* Now listen to me, my dear Crofts. *[He sits down again]*. I have nothing to do with that side of Mrs Warren's life, and never had. She has never spoken to me about it; and of course I have never spoken to her about it. Your delicacy will tell you that a handsome woman needs some friends who are not—well, not on that footing with her. The effect of her own beauty would become a torment to her if she could not escape from it occasionally. You are probably on much more confidential terms with Kitty than I am. Surely you can ask her the question yourself.

CROFTS. I have asked her, often enough. But she's so determined to keep the child all to herself that she would deny that it ever had a father if she could. *[Rising]* I'm thoroughly uncomfortable about it, Praed.

PRAED *[rising also]* Well, as you are, at all events, old enough to be her father, I dont mind agreeing that we both regard Miss Vivie in a parental way, as a young girl whom we are bound to protect and help. What do you say?

CROFTS *[aggressively]* I'm no older than you, if you come to that.

PRAED. Yes you are, my dear fellow: you were born old. I was born a boy: Ive never been able to feel the assurance of a grown-up man in my life. *[He folds his chair and carries it to the porch]*.

MRS WARREN *[calling from within the cottage]* Prad-dee! George! Tea-ea-ea-ea!

CROFTS *[hastily]* She's calling us. *[He hurries in]*.

Praed shakes his head bodingly, and is following Crofts when he is hailed by a young gentleman who has just appeared on the common, and is making for the gate. He is pleasant, pretty, smartly dressed, clever, good-for-nothing, not long turned 20, with a charming voice and agreeably disrespectful manners. He carries a light sporting magazine rifle.

THE YOUNG GENTLEMAN. Hallo! Praed!

PRAED. Why, Frank Gardner! *[Frank comes in and shakes hands cordially]*. What on earth are you doing here?

FRANK. Staying with my father.

PRAED. The Roman father?

FRANK. He's rector here. I'm living with my people this autumn for the sake of economy. Things came to a crisis in July: the Roman father had to pay my debts. He's stony broke in consequence; and so am I. What are you up to in these parts? Do you know the people here?

PRAED. Yes: I'm spending the day with a Miss Warren.

FRANK *[enthusiastically]* What! Do you know Vivie? Isnt she a jolly girl? I'm teaching her to shoot with this *[putting down the rifle]*. I'm so glad she knows you: youre just the sort of fellow she ought to know. *[He smiles, and raises the charming voice almost to a singing tone as he exclaims]* It's ever so jolly to find you here, Praed.

PRAED. I'm an old friend of her mother. Mrs Warren brought me over to make her daughter's acquaintance.

FRANK. The mother! Is she here?

PRAED. Yes: inside, at tea.

MRS WARREN *[calling from within]* Prad-dee-ee-ee-eee! The tea-cake'll be cold.

PRAED *[calling]* Yes, Mrs Warren. In a moment. Ive just met a friend here.

MRS WARREN. A what?

PRAED *[louder]* A friend.

MRS WARREN. Bring him in.

PRAED. All right. *[To Frank]* Will you accept the invitation?

FRANK *[incredulous, but immensely amused]* Is that Vivie's mother?

PRAED. Yes.

FRANK. By Jove! What a lark! Do you think she'll like me?

PRAED. Ive no doubt youll make yourself popular, as usual. Come in and try *[moving towards the house]*.

FRANK. Stop a bit. *[Seriously]* I want to take you into my confidence.

PRAED. Pray dont. It's only some fresh folly, like the barmaid at Redhill.

FRANK. It's ever so much more serious than that. You say youve only just met Vivie for the first time?

PRAED. Yes.

FRANK *[rhapsodically]* Then you can have no idea what a girl she is. Such character! Such sense! And her cleverness! Oh, my eye, Praed, but I can tell you she is clever! And—need I add?—she loves me.

CROFTS *[putting his head out of the window]* I say, Praed: what are you about? Do come along. *[He disappears]*.

FRANK. Hallo! Sort of chap that would take a prize at a dog show, aint he? Who's he?

PRAED. Sir George Crofts, an old friend of Mrs Warren's. I think we had better come in.

On their way to the porch they are interrupted by a call from the gate. Turning, they see an elderly clergyman looking over it.

THE CLERGYMAN *[calling]* Frank!

FRANK. Hallo! *[To Praed]* The Roman father. *[To the clergyman]* Yes, gov'nor: all right: presently. *[To Praed]* Look here, Praed: youd better go in to tea. I'll join you directly.

PRAED. Very good. *[He goes into the cottage]*.

The clergyman remains outside the gate, with his hands on the top of it. The Rev. Samuel Gardner, a beneficed clergyman of the Established Church, is over 50. Externally he is pretentious, booming, noisy, important. Really he is that obsolescent social phenomenon: the fool of the family dumped on the Church by his father the patron, clamorously asserting himself as father and clergyman without being able to command respect in either capacity.

REV. S. Well, sir. Who are your friends here, if I may ask?

FRANK. Oh, it's all right, gov'nor! Come in.

REV. S. No, sir; not until I know whose garden I am entering.

FRANK. It's all right. It's Miss Warren's.

REV. S. I have not seen her at church since she came.

FRANK. Of course not: she's a third wrangler. Ever so intellectual. Took a higher degree than you did; so why should she go to hear you preach?

REV. S. Dont be disrespectful, sir.

FRANK. Oh, it dont matter: nobody hears us. Come in. *[He opens the gate, unceremoniously pulling his father with it into the garden]*. I want to introduce you to her. Do you remember the advice you gave me last July, gov'nor?

REV. S. *[severely]* Yes. I advised you to conquer your idleness and flippancy, and to work your way into an honorable profession and live on it and not upon me.

FRANK. No: thats what you thought of afterwards. What you actually said was that since I had neither brains nor money, I'd better turn my good looks to account by marrying somebody with both. Well, look here, Miss Warren has brains: you cant deny that.

REV. S. Brains are not everything.

FRANK. No, of course not: theres the money—

REV. S. *[interrupting him austerely]* I was not thinking of money sir. I was speaking of higher things. Social position, for instance.

FRANK. I dont care a rap about that.

REV. S. But I do, sir.

FRANK. Well, nobody wants you to marry her. Anyhow she has what amounts to a high Cambridge degree; and she seems to have as much money as she wants.

REV. S. *[sinking into a feeble vein of humor]* I greatly doubt whether she has as much money as you will want.

FRANK. Oh, come: I havnt been so very extravagant. I live ever so quietly; I dont drink; I dont bet much; and I never go regularly on the razzle-dazzle as you did when you were my age.

REV. S. *[booming hollowly]* Silence, sir.

FRANK. Well, you told me yourself, when I was making ever such an ass of myself about the barmaid at Redhill, that you once offered a woman £50 for the letters you wrote to her when—

REV. S. *[terrified]* Sh-sh-sh, Frank, for Heaven's sake! *[He looks round apprehensively. Seeing no one within earshot he plucks up courage to boom again, but more subduedly]*. You are taking an ungentlemanly advantage of what I confided to you for your own good, to save you from an error you would have repented all your life long. Take warning by your father's follies, sir; and dont make them an excuse for your own.

FRANK. Did you ever hear the story of the Duke of Wellington and his letters?

REV. S. No, sir; and I dont want to hear it.

FRANK. The old Iron Duke didnt throw away £50: not he. He just wrote: 'Dear Jenny: publish and be damned! Yours affectionately, Wellington.' Thats what you should have done.

REV. S. *[piteously]* Frank, my boy: when I wrote those letters I put myself into that woman's power. When I told you about them I put myself, to some extent, I am sorry to say, in your power. She refused my money with these words, which I shall never forget. 'Knowledge is power,' she said; 'and I never sell power'. Thats more than twenty years ago; and she has never made use of her power or caused me a moment's uneasiness. You are behaving worse to me than she did, Frank.

FRANK. Oh yes I dare say! Did you ever preach at her the way you preach at me every day?

REV. S. *[wounded almost to tears]* I leave you, sir. You are incorrigible. *[He turns towards the gate]*.

FRANK *[utterly unmoved]* Tell them I shant be home to tea, will you, gov'nor, like a good fellow? *[He moves towards the cottage door and is met by Praed and Vivie coming out]*.

VIVIE *[to Frank]* Is that your father, Frank? I do so want to meet him.

FRANK. Certainly. *[Calling after his father]* Gov'nor. Youre wanted. *[The parson turns at the gate, fumbling nervously at his hat. Praed crosses the garden to the opposite side, beaming in anticipation of civilities]*. My father: Miss Warren.

VIVIE *[going to the clergyman and shaking his hand]* Very glad to see you here, Mr Gardner. *[Calling to the cottage]* Mother: come along: youre wanted.

Mrs Warren appears on the threshold, and is immediately transfixed recognizing the clergyman.

VIVIE *[continuing]* Let me introduce—

MRS WARREN *[swooping on the Reverend Samuel]* Why, it's Sam Gardner, gone into the Church! Well, I never! Dont you know us, Sam? This is George Crofts, as large as life and twice as natural. Dont you remember me?

REV. S. *[very red]* I really—er—

MRS WARREN. Of course you do. Why, I have a whole album of your letters still: I came across them only the other day.

REV. S. *[miserably confused]* Miss Vavasour, I believe.

MRS WARREN *[correcting him quickly in a loud whisper]* Tch! Nonsense! Mrs Warren: dont you see my daughter there?

ACT II

Inside the cottage after nightfall. Looking eastward from within instead of westward from without, the latticed window, with its curtains drawn, is now seen in the middle of the front wall of the cottage, with the porch door to the left of it. In the left-hand side wall is the door leading to the kitchen. Farther back against the same wall is a dresser with a candle and matches on it, and Frank's rifle standing beside them, with the barrel resting in the plate-rack. In the centre a table stands with a lighted lamp on it. Vivie's books and writing materials are on a table to the right of the window, against the wall. The fireplace is on the right, with a settle: there is no fire. Two of the chairs are set right and left of the table.

The cottage door opens, shewing a fine starlit night without; and Mrs Warren, her shoulders wrapped in a shawl borrowed from Vivie, enters, followed by Frank, who throws his cap on the window seat. She has had enough of walking, and gives a gasp of relief as she unpins her hat; takes it off; sticks the pin through the crown; and puts it on the table.

MRS WARREN. O Lord! I dont know which is the worst of the country, the walking or the sitting at home with nothing to do. I could do with a whisky and soda now very well, if only they had such a thing in this place.

FRANK. Perhaps Vivie's got some.

MRS WARREN. Nonsense! What would a young girl like her be doing with such things! Never mind: it dont matter. I wonder how she passes her time here! I'd a good deal rather be in Vienna.

FRANK. Let me take you there. *[He helps her to take off her shawl, gallantly giving her shoulders a very perceptible squeeze as he does so]*

MRS WARREN. Ah! would you? I'm beginning to think youre a chip of the old block.

FRANK. Like the gov'nor, eh? *[He hangs the shawl on the nearest chair and sits down]*.

MRS WARREN. Never you mind. What do you know about such things? Youre only a boy. *[She goes to the hearth, to be farther from temptation]*.

FRANK. Do come to Vienna with me? It'd be ever such larks.

MRS WARREN. No, thank you. Vienna is no place for you—at least not until youre a little older. *[She nods at him to emphasize this piece of advice. He makes a mock-piteous face, belied by his laughing eyes. She looks at him; then comes back to him]*. Now, look here, little boy *[taking his face in her hands and turning it up to her]*: I know you through and through by your likeness to your father, better than you know yourself. Dont you go taking any silly ideas into your head about me. Do you hear?

FRANK *[gallantly wooing her with his voice]* Cant help it, my dear Mrs Warren: it runs in the family.

She pretends to box his ears; then looks at the pretty laughing upturned face for a moment, tempted. At last she kisses him, and immediately turns away, out of patience with herself.

MRS WARREN. There! I shouldnt have done that. I am wicked. Never mind, my dear: it's only a motherly kiss. Go and make love to Vivie.

FRANK. So I have.

MRS WARREN *[turning on him with a sharp note of alarm in her voice]* What!

FRANK. Vivie and I are ever such chums.

MRS WARREN. What do you mean? Now see here: I wont have any young scamp tampering with my little girl. Do you hear? I wont have it.

FRANK *[quite unabashed]* My dear Mrs Warren: dont you be alarmed. My intentions are honorable: ever so honorable; and your little girl is jolly well able to take care of herself. She dont need looking after half so much as her mother. She aint so handsome, you know.

MRS WARREN *[taken aback by his assurance]* Well, you have got a nice healthy two inches thick of cheek all over you. I dont know where you got it. Not from your father, anyhow.

CROFTS *[in the garden]* The gipsies, I suppose?

REV. S. *[replying]* The broomsquires are far worse.

MRS WARREN *[to Frank]* S-sh! Remember! youve had your warning.

Crofts and the Reverend Samuel come in from the garden, the clergyman continuing his conversation as he enters.

REV. S. The perjury at the Winchester assizes is deplorable.

MRS WARREN. Well? what became of you two? And wheres Praddy and Vivie?

CROFTS *[putting his hat on the settle and his stick in the chimney corner]* They went up the hill. We went to the village. I wanted a drink. *[He sits down on the settle, putting his legs up along the seat]*.

MRS WARREN. Well, she oughtnt go off like that without telling me. *[To Frank]* Get your father a chair, Frank: where are your manners? *[Frank springs up and gracefully offers his father his chair; then takes another from the wall and sits down at the table, in the middle, with his father on his right and Mrs Warren on his left]*. George, where are you going to stay tonight? You cant stay here. And whats Praddy going to do?

CROFTS. Gardner'll put me up.

MRS WARREN. Oh, no doubt youve taken care of yourself. But what about Praddy?

CROFTS. Dont know. I suppose he can sleep at the inn.

MRS WARREN. Havnt you room for him, Sam?

REV. S. Well—er—you see, as rector here, I am not free to do as I like. Er—what is Mr Praed's social position?

MRS WARREN. Oh, he's all right: he's an architect. What an old stick-in-the-mud you are, Sam!

FRANK. Yes, it's all right, gov'nor. He built that place down in Wales for the Duke. Caernarvon Castle they call it. You must have heard of it. *[He winks with lightning smartness at Mrs Warren, and regards his father blandly]*.

REV. S. Oh, in that case, of course we shall only be too happy. I suppose he knows the Duke personally.

FRANK. Oh, ever so intimately! We can stick him in Georgina's old room.

MRS WARREN. Well, thats settled. Now if those two would only come in and let us have supper. Theyve no right to stay out after dark like this.

CROFTS *[aggressively]* What harm are they doing you?

MRS WARREN. Well, harm or not, I dont like it.

FRANK. Better not wait for them, Mrs Warren. Praed will stay out as long as possible. He has never known before what it is to stray over the heath on a summer night with my Vivie.

CROFTS *[sitting up in some consternation]* I say, you know! Come!

REV. S. *[rising, startled out of his professional manner into real force and sincerity]* Frank, once for all, it's out of the question. Mrs Warren will tell you that it's not to be thought of.

CROFTS. Of course not.

FRANK *[with enchanting placidity]* Is that so, Mrs Warren?

MRS WARREN *[reflectively]* Well, Sam, I dont know. If the girl wants to get married, no good can come of keeping her unmarried.

REV. S. *[astounded]* But married to him!—your daughter to my son! Only think: it's impossible.

CROFTS. Of course it's impossible. Dont be a fool, Kitty.

MRS WARREN *[nettled]* Why not? Isnt my daughter good enough for your son?

REV. S. But surely, my dear Mrs Warren, you know the reasons—

MRS WARREN *[defiantly]* I know no reasons. If you know any, you can tell them to the lad, or to the girl, or to your congregation, if you like.

REV. S. *[collapsing helplessly into his chair]* You know very well that I couldnt tell anyone the reasons. But my boy will believe me when I tell him there are reasons.

FRANK. Quite right, Dad: he will. But has your boy's conduct ever been influenced by your reasons?

CROFTS. You cant marry her; and thats all about it. *[He gets up and stands on the hearth, with his back to the fireplace, frowning determinedly]*.

MRS WARREN *[turning on him sharply]* What have you got to do with it, pray?

FRANK *[with his prettiest lyrical cadence]* Precisely what I was going to ask myself, in my own graceful fashion.

CROFTS *[to Mrs Warren]* I suppose you dont want to marry the girl to a man younger than herself and without either a profession or twopence to keep her on. Ask Sam, if you dont believe me. *[To the parson]* How much more money are you going to give him?

REV. S. Not another penny. He has had his patrimony and he spent the last of it in July. *[Mrs Warren's face falls]*.

CROFTS *[watching her]* There! I told you. *[He resumes his place on the settle and puts up his legs on the seat again, as if the matter were finally disposed of]*.

FRANK *[plaintively]* This is ever so mercenary. Do you suppose Miss Warren's going to marry for money? If we love one another—

MRS WARREN. Thank you. Your love's a pretty cheap commodity, my lad. If you have no means of keeping a wife, that settles it: you cant have Vivie.

FRANK *[much amused]* What do you say, gov'nor, eh?

REV. S. I agree with Mrs Warren.

FRANK. And good old Crofts has already expressed his opinion.

CROFTS *[turning angrily on his elbow]* Look here: I want none of your cheek.

FRANK *[pointedly]* I'm ever so sorry to surprise you, Crofts, but you allowed yourself the liberty of speaking to me like a father a moment ago. One father is enough, thank you.

CROFTS *[contemptuously]* Yah! *[He turns away again]*.

FRANK *[rising]* Mrs Warren: I cannot give my Vivie up, even for your sake.

MRS WARREN *[muttering]* Young scamp!

FRANK *[continuing]* And as you no doubt intend to hold out other prospects to her, I shall lose no time in placing my case before her. *[They stare at him, and he begins to declaim gracefully]*.

He either fears his fate too much,
Or his deserts are small,
That dares not put it to the touch
To gain or lose it all.

The cottage door opens whilst he is reciting; and Vivie and Praed come in. He breaks off. Praed puts his hat on the dresser. There is an immediate improvement in the company's behavior. Crofts takes down his legs from the settle and pulls himself together as Praed joins him at the fireplace. Mrs Warren loses her ease of manner and takes refuge in querulousness.

MRS WARREN. Wherever have you been, Vivie?

VIVIE *[taking off her hat and throwing it carelessly on the table]* On the hill.

MRS WARREN. Well, you shouldnt go off like that without letting me know. How could I tell what had become of you? And night coming on too!

VIVIE *[going to the door of the kitchen and opening it, ignoring her mother]* Now, about supper? *[All rise except Mrs Warren]*. We shall be rather crowded in here, I'm afraid.

MRS WARREN. Did you hear what I said, Vivie?

VIVIE *[quietly]* Yes, mother. *[Reverting to the supper difficulty]* How many are we? *[Counting]* One, two, three, four, five, six. Well, two will have to wait until the rest are done: Mrs Alison has only plates and knives for four.

PRAED. Oh, it doesnt matter about me. I—

VIVIE. You have had a long walk and are hungry, Mr Praed: you shall have your supper at once. I can wait myself. I want one person to wait with me. Frank: are you hungry?

FRANK. Not the least in the world. Completely off my peck, in fact.

MRS WARREN *[to Crofts]* Neither are you, George. You can wait.

CROFTS. Oh, hang it, Ive eaten nothing since tea-time. Cant Sam do it?

FRANK. Would you starve my poor father?

REV. S. *[testily]* Allow me to speak for myself, Sir. I am perfectly willing to wait.

VIVIE *[decisively]* Theres no need. Only two are wanted. *[She opens the door of the kitchen]*. Will you take my mother in, Mr Gardner. *[The parson takes Mrs Warren; and they pass into the kitchen. Praed and Crofts follow. All except Praed clearly disapprove of the arrangement, but do not know how to resist it. Vivie stands at the door looking in at them]*. Can you squeeze past to that corner, Mr Praed: it's rather a tight fit. Take care of your coat against the white-wash: thats right. Now, are you all comfortable?

PRAED *[within]* Quite, thank you.

MRS WARREN *[within]* Leave the door open, dearie. *[Vivie frowns; but Frank checks her with a gesture, and steals to the cottage door, which he softly sets wide open]*. Oh Lor, what a draught! Youd better shut it, dear.

Vivie shuts it with a slam, and then, noting with disgust that her mother's hat and shawl are lying about, takes them tidily to the window seat, whilst Frank noiselessly shuts the cottage door.

FRANK *[exulting]* Aha! Got rid of em. Well, Vivvums: what do you think of my governor?

VIVIE *[preoccupied and serious]* Ive hardly spoken to him. He doesnt strike me as being a particularly able person.

FRANK. Well, you know, the old man is not altogether such a fool as he looks. You see, he was shoved into the Church rather; and in trying to live up to it he makes a much bigger ass of himself than he really is. I dont dislike him as much as you might expect. He means well. How do you think youll get on with him?

IF I THOUGHT THAT I WAS LIKE THAT — THAT I WAS GOING TO BE A WASTER, SHIFTING ALONG FROM ONE MEAL TO ANOTHER WITH NO PURPOSE, AND NO CHARACTER, AND NO GRIT IN ME, I'D OPEN AN ARTERY AND BLEED TO DEATH WITHOUT ONE MOMENT'S HESITATION.

VIVIE *[rather grimly]* I dont think my future life will be much concerned with him, or with any of that old circle of my mother's, except perhaps Praed. *[She sits down on the settle]*. What do you think of my mother?

FRANK. Really and truly?

VIVIE. Yes, really and truly.

FRANK. Well, she's ever so jolly. But she's rather a caution, isnt she? And Crofts! oh, my eye, Crofts! *[He sits beside her]*.

VIVIE. What a lot, Frank!

FRANK. What a crew!

VIVIE *[with intense contempt for them]* If I thought that I was like that—that I was going to be a waster, shifting along from one meal to another with no purpose, and no character, and no grit in me, I'd open an artery and bleed to death without one moment's hesitation.

FRANK. Oh no, you wouldnt. Why should they take any grind when they can afford not to? I wish I had their luck. No: what I object to is their form. It isnt the thing: it's slovenly, ever so slovenly.

VIVIE. Do you think your form will be any better when youre as old as Crofts, if you dont work?

FRANK. Of course I do. Ever so much better. Vivvums mustnt lecture: her little boy's incorrigible. *[He attempts to take her face caressingly in his hands]*.

VIVIE *[striking his hands down sharply]* Off with you: Vivvums is not in a humor for petting her little boy this evening. *[She rises and comes forward to the other side of the room]*.

FRANK *[following her]* How unkind!

VIVIE *[stamping at him]* Be serious. I'm serious.

FRANK. Good. Let us talk learnedly. Miss Warren: do you know that all the most advanced thinkers are agreed that half the diseases of modern civilization are due to starvation of the affections in the young. Now, I—

VIVIE *[cutting him short]* You are very tiresome. *[She opens the inner door]*. Have you room for Frank there? He's complaining of starvation.

MRS WARREN *[within]* Of course there is *[clatter of knives and glasses as she moves the things on the table]*. Here! theres room now beside me. Come along, Mr Frank.

FRANK. Her little boy will be ever so even with his Vivvums for this. *[He passes into the kitchen]*.

MRS WARREN *[within]* Here, Vivie: come on you too, child. You must be famished. *[She enters, followed by Crofts, who holds the door open for Vivie with marked deference. She goes out without looking at him; and shuts the door after her]*. Why, George, you cant be done: youve eaten nothing. Is there anything wrong with you?

CROFTS. Oh, all I wanted was a drink. *[He thrusts his hands in his pockets, and begins prowling about the room, restless and sulky]*.

MRS WARREN. Well, I like enough to eat. But a little of that cold beef and cheese and lettuce goes a long way. *[With a sigh of only half-repletion she sits down lazily on the settle]*.

CROFTS. What do you go encouraging that young pup for?

MRS WARREN *[on the alert at once]* Now see here, George: what are you up to about that girl? Ive been watching your way of looking at her. Remember: I know you and what your looks mean.

CROFTS. Theres no harm in looking at her, is there?

MRS WARREN. I'd put you out and pack you back to London pretty soon if I saw any of your nonsense. My girl's little finger is more to me than your whole body and soul. *[Crofts receives this with a sneering grin. Mrs Warren, flushing a little at her failure to impose on him in the character of a theatrically devoted mother, adds in a lower key]* Make your mind easy: the young pup has no more chance than you have.

CROFTS. Maynt a man take an interest in a girl?

MRS WARREN. Not a man like you.

CROFTS. How old is she?

MRS WARREN. Never you mind how old she is.

CROFTS. Why do you make such a secret of it?

MRS WARREN. Because I choose.

CROFTS. Well, I'm not fifty yet; and my property is as good as ever it was—

MRS WARREN *[interrupting him]* Yes; because youre as stingy as youre vicious.

CROFTS *[continuing]* And a baronet isnt to be picked up every day. No other man in my position would put up with you for a mother-in-law. Why shouldnt she marry me?

MRS WARREN. You!

CROFTS. We three could live together quite comfortably: I'd die before her and leave her a bouncing widow with plenty of money. Why not? It's been growing in my mind all the time Ive been walking with that fool inside there.

MRS WARREN *[revolted]* Yes: it's the sort of thing that would grow in your mind.

He halts in his prowling; and the two look at one another, she steadfastly, with a sort of awe behind her contemptuous disgust: he stealthily, with a carnal gleam in his eye and a loose grin.

CROFTS *[suddenly becoming anxious and urgent as he sees no sign of sympathy in her]* Look here, Kitty: youre a sensible woman: you neednt put on any moral airs. I'll ask no more questions; and you need answer none. I'll settle the whole property on her; and if you want a cheque for yourself on the wedding day, you can name any figure you like—in reason.

MRS WARREN. So it's come to that with you, George, like all the other worn-out old creatures!

CROFTS *[savagely]* Damn you!

Before she can retort the door of the kitchen is opened; and the voices of the others are heard returning. Crofts, unable to recover his presence of mind, hurries out of the cottage. The clergyman appears at the kitchen door.

REV. S. *[looking round]* Where is Sir George?

MRS WARREN. Gone out to have a pipe. *[The clergyman takes his hat from the table, and joins Mrs Warren at the fireside. Meanwhile Vivie comes in, followed by Frank, who collapses into the nearest chair with an air of extreme exhaustion. Mrs Warren looks round at Vivie and says, with her affection of maternal patronage even more forced than usual]* Well, dearie: have you had a good supper?

VIVIE. You know what Mrs Alison's suppers are. *[She turns to Frank and pets him]*. Poor Frank! was all the beef gone? did it get nothing but bread and cheese and ginger beer? *[Seriously, as if she had done quite enough trifling for one evening]* Her butter is really awful. I must get some down from the stores.

FRANK. Do, in Heaven's name!

Vivie goes to the writing-table and makes a memorandum to order the butter. Praed comes in from the kitchen, putting up his handkerchief, which he has been using as a napkin.

REV. S. Frank, my boy: it is time for us to be thinking of home. Your mother does not know yet that we have visitors.

PRAED. I'm afraid we're giving trouble.

FRANK *[rising]* Not the least in the world: my mother will be delighted to see you. She's a genuinely intellectual artistic woman; and she sees nobody here from one year's end to another except the gov'nor; so you can imagine how jolly dull it pans out for her. *[To his father]* Youre not intellectual or artistic: are you, pater? So take Praed home at once; and I'll stay here and entertain Mrs Warren. Youll pick up Crofts in the garden. He'll be excellent company for the bull-pup.

PRAED *[taking his hat from the dresser, and coming close to Frank]* Come with us, Frank. Mrs Warren has not seen Miss Vivie for a long time; and we have prevented them from having a moment together yet.

FRANK *[quite softened and looking at Praed with romantic admiration]* Of course. I forgot. Ever so thanks for reminding me. Perfect gentleman, Praddy. Always were. My ideal through life. *[He rises to go, but pauses a moment between the two older men, and puts his hand on Praed's shoulder]*. Ah, if you had only been my father instead of this unworthy old man! *[He puts his other hand on his father's shoulder]*.

REV. S. *[blustering]* Silence, sir, silence: you are profane.

MRS WARREN *[laughing heartily]* You should keep him in better order, Sam. Goodnight. Here: take George his hat and stick with my compliments.

REV. S. *[taking them]* Goodnight. *[They shake hands. As he passes Vivie he shakes hands with her also and bids her goodnight. Then, in booming command, to Frank]* Come along, sir, at once. *[He goes out]*.

MRS WARREN. Byebye, Praddy.

PRAED. Byebye, Kitty.

They shake hands affectionately and go out together, she accompanying him to the garden gate.

FRANK *[to Vivie]* Kissums?

VIVIE *[fiercely]* No. I hate you. *[She takes a couple of books and some paper from the writing-table, and sits down with them at the middle table, at the end next the fireplace].*

FRANK. *[grimacing]* Sorry. *[He goes for his cap and rifle. Mrs Warren returns. He takes her hand]* Goodnight, dear Mrs Warren. *[He kisses her hand. She snatches it away, her lips tightening, and looks more than half disposed to box his ears. He laughs mischievously and runs off, clapping-to the door behind him].*

MRS WARREN *[resigning herself to an evening of boredom now that the men are gone]* Did you ever in your life hear anyone rattle on so? Isnt he a tease? *[She sits at the table]*. Now that I think of it, dearie, dont you go encouraging him. I'm sure he's a regular good-for-nothing.

VIVIE *[rising to fetch more books]* I'm afraid so. Poor Frank! I shall have to get rid of him; but I shall feel sorry for him, though he's not worth it. That man Crofts does not seem to me to be good for much either: is he? *[She throws the books on the table rather roughly].*

MRS WARREN *[galled by Vivie's indifference]* What do you know of men, child, to talk that way about them? Youll have to make up your mind to see a good deal of Sir George Crofts, as he's a friend of mine.

VIVIE *[quite unmoved]* Why? *[She sits down and opens a book]*. Do you expect that we shall be much together? You and I, I mean?

MRS WARREN *[staring at her]* Of course: until youre married. Youre not going back to college again.

VIVIE. Do you think my way of life would suit you? I doubt it.

MRS WARREN. Your way of life! What do you mean?

VIVIE *[cutting a page of her book with the paper knife on her chatelaine]* Has it really never occurred to you, mother, that I have a way of life like other people?

MRS WARREN. What nonsense is this youre trying to talk? Do you want to shew your independence, now that youre a great little person at school? Dont be a fool, child.

VIVIE *[indulgently]* Thats all you have to say on the subject, is it, mother?

MRS WARREN *[puzzled, then angry]* Dont you keep on asking me questions like that. *[Violently]* Hold your tongue. *[Vivie works on, losing no time, and saying nothing]*. You and your way of life, indeed! What next? *[She looks at Vivie again. No reply]*. Your way of life will be what I please, so it will. *[Another pause]*. Ive been noticing these airs in you ever since you got that tripos or whatever you call it. If you think I'm going to put up with them youre mistaken; and the sooner you find it out, the better. *[Muttering]* All I have to say on the subject, indeed! *[Again raising her voice angrily]* Do you know who youre speaking to, Miss?

VIVIE. *[looking across at her without raising her head from her book]* No. Who are you? What are you?

MRS WARREN *[rising breathless]* You young imp!

VIVIE. Everybody knows my reputation, my social standing, and the profession I intend to pursue. I know nothing about you. What is that way of life which you invite me to share with you and Sir George Crofts, pray?

MRS WARREN. Take care. I shall do something I'll be sorry for after, and you too.

VIVIE *[putting aside her books with cool decision]* Well, let us drop the subject until you are better able to face it. *[Looking critically at her mother]* You want some good walks and a little lawn tennis to set you up. You are shockingly out of condition: you were not able to manage twenty yards uphill today without stopping to pant; and your wrists are mere rolls of fat. Look at mine. *[She holds out her wrists]*.

MRS WARREN *[after looking at her helplessly, begins to whimper]* Vivie—

VIVIE *[springing up sharply]* Now pray dont begin to cry. Anything but that. I really cannot stand whimpering. I will go out of the room if you do.

MRS WARREN *[piteously]* Oh, my darling, how can you be so hard on me? Have I no rights over you as your mother?

VIVIE. Are you my mother?

MRS WARREN *[appalled]* Am I your mother! Oh, Vivie!

VIVIE. Then where are our relatives? my father? our family friends? You claim the rights of a mother: the right to call me fool and child; to speak to me as no woman in authority over me at college dare speak to me; to dictate my way of life; and to force on me the acquaintance of a brute whom any one can see to be the most vicious sort of London man about town. Before I give myself the trouble to resist such claims, I may as well find out whether they have any real existence.

MRS WARREN *[distracted, throwing herself on her knees]* Oh no, no. Stop, stop. I am your mother: I swear it. Oh, you cant mean to turn on me—my own child! It's not natural. You believe me, dont you? Say you believe me.

VIVIE. Who was my father?

MRS WARREN. You dont know what youre asking. I cant tell you.

VIVIE *[determinedly]* Oh yes you can, if you like. I have a right to know; and you know very well that I have that right. You can refuse to tell me, if you please; but if you do, you will see the last of me tomorrow morning.

MRS WARREN. Oh, it's too horrible to hear you talk like that. You wouldnt—you couldnt leave me.

VIVIE *[ruthlessly]* Yes, without a moment's hesitation, if you trifle with me about this. *[Shivering with disgust]* How can I feel sure that I may not have the contaminated blood of that brutal waster in my veins?

MRS WARREN. No, no. On my oath it's not he, nor any of the rest that you have ever met. I'm certain of that, at least.

Vivie's eyes fasten sternly on her mother as the significance of this flashes on her.

VIVIE *[slowly]* You are certain of that, at least. Ah! You mean that that is all you are certain of. *[Thoughtfully]* I see. *[Mrs Warren buries her face in her hands]*. Dont do that, mother: you know you dont feel it a bit. *[Mrs Warren takes down her hands and looks up deplorably at Vivie, who takes out her watch and says]* Well, that is enough for tonight. At what hour would you like breakfast? Is half-past eight too early for you?

MRS WARREN *[wildly]* My God, what sort of woman are you?

VIVIE *[coolly]* The sort the world is mostly made of, I should hope. Otherwise I dont understand how it gets its business done. Come *[taking her mother by the wrist, and pulling her up pretty resolutely]*: pull yourself together. Thats right.

MRS WARREN *[querulously]* Youre very rough with me, Vivie!

VIVIE. Nonsense. What about bed? It's past ten.

MRS WARREN *[passionately]* Whats the use of my going to bed? Do you think I could sleep?

VIVIE. Why not? I shall.

MRS WARREN. You! youve no heart. *[She suddenly breaks out vehemently in her natural tongue—the dialect of a woman of the people—with all her affectations of maternal authority and conventional manners gone, and an overwhelming inspiration of true conviction and scorn in her]* Oh, I wont bear it: I wont put up with the injustice of it. What right have you to set yourself up above me like this? You boast of what you are to me—to me, who gave you the chance of being what you are. What chance had I? Shame on you for a bad daughter and a stuck-up prude!

VIVIE *[sitting down with a shrug, no longer confident; for her replies, which have sounded sensible and strong to her so far, now begin to ring rather woodenly and even priggishly against the new tone of her mother]* Dont think for a moment I set myself above you in any way. You attacked me with the conventional authority of a mother: I defended myself with the conventional superiority of a respectable woman. Frankly, I am not going to stand any of your nonsense, and when you drop it I shall not expect you to stand any of mine. I shall always respect your right to your own opinions and your own way of life.

MRS WARREN. My own opinions and my own way of life! Listen to her talking! Do you think I was brought up like you? able to pick and choose my own way of life? Do you think I did what I did because I liked it, or thought it right, or wouldnt rather have gone to college and been a lady if I'd had the chance?

VIVIE. Everybody has some choice, mother. The poorest girl alive may not be able to choose between being Queen of England or Principal of Newnham; but she can choose between ragpicking and flowerselling, according to her taste. People are always blaming their circumstances for what they are. I dont believe in circumstances. The people who get on in this world are the people who get up and look for the circumstances they want, and, if they cant find them, make them.

MRS WARREN. Oh, it's easy to talk, very easy, isnt it? Here! would you like to know what my circumstances were?

VIVIE. Yes: you had better tell me. Wont you sit down?

MRS WARREN. Oh, I'll sit down: dont you be afraid. *[She plants her chair farther forward with brazen energy, and sits down. Vivie is impressed in spite of herself]*. D'you know what your gran'mother was?

VIVIE. No.

MRS WARREN. No, you dont. I do. She called herself a widow and had a fried-fish shop down by the Mint, and kept herself and four daughters out of it. Two of us were sisters: that was me and Liz; and we were both good-looking and well made. I suppose our father was a well-fed man: mother pretended he was a gentleman; but I dont know. The other two were only half sisters: undersized, ugly, starved looking, hard working, honest poor creatures: Liz and I would have half-murdered them if mother hadnt half-murdered us to keep our hands off them. They were the respectable ones. Well, what did they get by their respectability? I'll tell you. One of them worked in a whitelead factory twelve hours a day for nine shillings a week until she died of lead poisoning. She only expected to get her hands a little paralyzed; but she died. The other was always held up to us as a model because she married a Government laborer in the Deptford victualling yard, and kept his room and the three children neat and tidy on eighteen shillings a week—until he took to drink. That was worth being respectable for, wasnt it?

VIVIE *[now thoughtfully attentive]* Did you and your sister think so?

MRS WARREN. Liz didnt, I can tell you: she had more spirit. We both went to a church school—that was part of the ladylike airs we gave ourselves to be superior to the children that knew nothing and went nowhere—and we stayed there until Liz went out one night and never came back. I know the schoolmistress thought I'd soon follow her example; for the clergyman was always warning me that Lizzie'd end by jumping off Waterloo Bridge. Poor fool: that was all he knew about it! But I was more afraid of the whitelead factory than I was of the river; and so would you have been in my place. That clergyman got me a situation as scullery maid in a temperance restaurant where they sent out for anything you liked. Then I was waitress; and then I went to the bar at Waterloo station: fourteen hours a day serving drinks and washing glasses for four shillings a week and my board. That was considered a great promotion for me. Well, one cold, wretched night, when I was so tired I could hardly keep myself awake, who should come up for a half of Scotch but Lizzie, in a long fur cloak, elegant and comfortable, with a lot of sovereigns in her purse.

VIVIE *[grimly]* My aunt Lizzie!

MRS WARREN. Yes; and a very good aunt to have, too. She's living down at Winchester now, close to the cathedral, one of the most respectable ladies there. Chaperones girls at the county ball, if you please. No river for Liz, thank you! You remind me of Liz a little: she was a first-rate business woman—saved money from the beginning—never let herself look too like what she was—never lost her head or threw away a chance. When she saw I'd grown up good-looking she said to me across the bar 'What are you doing there, you little fool? wearing out your health and your appearance for other people's profit?' Liz was saving money then to take a house for herself in Brussels; and she thought we two could save faster than one. So she lent me some money and gave me a start; and I saved steadily and first paid her back, and then went into business with her as her partner. Why shouldnt I have done it? The house in Brussels was real high class: a much better place for a woman to be in than the factory where Anne Jane got poisoned. None of our girls were ever treated as I was treated in the scullery of that temperance place, or at the Waterloo bar, or at home. Would you have had me stay in them and become a worn out old drudge before I was forty?

VIVIE *[intensely interested by this time]* No; but why did you choose that business? Saving money and good management will succeed in any business.

MRS WARREN. Yes, saving money. But where can a woman get the money to save in any other business? Could you save out of four shillings a week and keep yourself dressed as well? Not you. Of course, if youre a plain woman and cant earn anything more; or if you have a turn for music, or the stage, or newspaper-writing: thats different. But neither Liz nor I had any turn for such things: all we had was our appearance and our turn for pleasing men. Do you think we were such fools as to let other people trade in our good looks by employing us as shopgirls, or barmaids, or waitresses, when we could trade in them ourselves and get all the profits instead of starvation wages? Not likely.

VIVIE. You were certainly quite justified—from the business point of view.

MRS WARREN. Yes; or any other point of view. What is any respectable girl brought up to do but to catch some rich man's fancy and get the benefit of his money by marrying him?—as if a marriage ceremony could make any difference in the right or wrong of the thing! Oh, the hypocrisy of the world makes me sick! Liz and I had to work and save and calculate just like other people; elseways we should be as poor as any good-for-nothing drunken waster of a woman that thinks her luck will last for ever. *[With great energy]* I despise such people: theyve no character; and if theres a thing I hate in a woman, its want of character.

VIVIE. Come now, mother: frankly! Isnt it part of what you call character in a woman that she should greatly dislike such a way of making money?

MRS WARREN. Why, of course. Everybody dislikes having to work and make money; but they have to do it all the same. I'm sure Ive often pitied a poor girl, tired out and in low spirits, having to try to please some man that she doesnt care two straws for—some half-drunken fool that thinks he's making himself agreeable when he's teasing and worrying and disgusting a woman so that hardly any money could pay her for putting up with it. But she has to bear with disagreeables and take the rough with the smooth, just like a nurse in a hospital or anyone else. It's not work that any woman would do for pleasure, goodness knows; though to hear the pious people talk you would suppose it was a bed of roses.

DO YOU THINK WE WERE SUCH FOOLS AS TO LET OTHER PEOPLE TRADE IN OUR GOOD LOOKS BY EMPLOYING US AS SHOPGIRLS, OR BARMAIDS, OR WAITRESSES, WHEN WE COULD TRADE IN THEM OURSELVES AND GET ALL THE PROFITS INSTEAD OF STARVATION WAGES? NOT LIKELY.

VIVIE. Still, you consider it worth while. It pays.

MRS WARREN. Of course it's worth while to a poor girl, if she can resist temptation and is good-looking and well conducted and sensible. It's far better than any other employment open to her. I always thought that oughtnt to be. It cant be right, Vivie, that there shouldnt be better opportunities for women. I stick to that: it's wrong. But it's so, right or wrong; and a girl must make the best of it. But of course it's not worth while for a lady. If you took to it youd be a fool; but I should have been a fool if I'd taken to anything else.

VIVIE *[more and more deeply moved]* Mother: suppose we were both as poor as you were in those wretched old days, are you quite sure that you wouldnt advise me to try the Waterloo bar, or marry a laborer, or even go into the factory?

MRS WARREN *[indignantly]* Of course not. What sort of mother do you take me for! How could you keep your self-respect in such starvation and slavery? And whats a woman worth? whats life worth? without self-respect! Why am I independent and able to give my daughter a first-rate education, when other women that had just as good opportunities are in the gutter? Because I always knew how to respect myself and control myself. Why is Liz looked up to in a cathedral town? The same reason. Where would we be now if we'd minded the clergyman's foolishness? Scrubbing floors for one and sixpence a day and nothing to look forward to but the workhouse infirmary. Dont you be led astray by people who dont know the world, my girl. The only way for a woman to provide for herself decently is for her to be good to some man that can afford to be good to her. If she's in his own station of life, let her make him marry her; but if she's far beneath him she cant expect it: why should she? it wouldnt be for her own happiness. Ask any lady in London society that has daughters; and she'll tell you the same, except that I tell you straight and she'll tell you crooked. Thats all the difference.

VIVIE *[fascinated, gazing at her]* My dear mother: you are a wonderful woman: you are stronger than all England. And are you really and truly not one wee bit doubtful—or—or—ashamed?

MRS WARREN. Well, of course, dearie, it's only good manners to be ashamed of it: it's expected from a woman. Women have to pretend to feel a great deal that they dont feel. Liz used to be angry with me for plumping out the truth about it. She used to say that when every woman could learn enough from what was going on in the world before her eyes, there was no need to talk about it to her. But then Liz was such a perfect lady! She had the true instinct of it; while I was always a bit of a vulgarian. I used to be so pleased when you sent me your photos to see that you were growing up like Liz: youve just her ladylike, determined way. But I cant stand saying one thing when everyone knows I mean another. Whats the use in such hypocrisy? If people arrange the world that way for women, theres no good pretending it's arranged the other way. No: I never was a bit ashamed really. I consider I had a right to be proud of how we managed everything so respectably, and never had a word against us, and how the girls were so well taken care of some of them did very well: one of them married an ambassador. But of course now I darent talk about such things: whatever would they think of us! *[She yawns]*. Oh dear! I do believe I'm getting sleepy after all. *[She stretches herself lazily, thoroughly relieved by her explosion, and placidly ready for her night's rest]*.

VIVIE. I believe it is I who will not be able to sleep now. *[She goes to the dresser and lights the candle. Then she extinguishes the lamp, darkening the room a good deal]*. Better let in some fresh air before locking up. *[She opens the cottage door, and finds that it is broad moonlight]*. What a beautiful night! Look! *[She draws aside the curtains of the window. The landscape is seen bathed in the radiance of the harvest moon rising over Blackdown]*.

MRS WARREN *[with a perfunctory glance at the scene]* Yes, dear; but take care you dont catch your death of cold from the night air.

VIVIE *[contemptuously]* Nonsense.

MRS WARREN *[querulously]* Oh yes: everything I say is nonsense, according to you.

VIVIE *[turning to her quickly]* No: really that is not so, mother. You have got completely the better of me tonight, though I intended it to be the other way. Let us be good friends now.

MRS WARREN *[shaking her head a little ruefully]* So it has been the other way. But I suppose I must give in to it. I always got the worst of it from Liz; and now I suppose it'll be the same with you.

VIVIE. Well, never mind. Come: goodnight, dear old mother. *[She takes her mother in her arms]*.

MRS WARREN *[fondly]* I brought you up well, didnt I, dearie?

VIVIE. You did.

MRS WARREN. And youll be good to your poor old mother for it, wont you?

VIVIE. I will, dear. *[Kissing her]* Goodnight.

MRS WARREN *[with unction]* Blessings on my own dearie darling! a mother's blessing!

She embraces her daughter protectingly, instinctively looking upward for divine sanction.

ACT III

In the Rectory garden next morning, with the sun shining from a cloudless sky. The garden wall has a five-barred wooden gate, wide enough to admit a carriage, in the middle. Beside the gate hangs a bell on a coiled spring, communicating with a pull outside. The carriage drive comes down the middle of the garden and then swerves to its left, where it ends in a little gravelled circus opposite the Rectory porch. Beyond the gate is seen the dusty high road, parallel with the wall, bounded on the farther side by a strip of turf and an unfenced pine wood. On the lawn, between the house and the drive, is a clipped yew tree, with a garden bench in its shade. On the opposite side the garden is shut in by a box hedge; and there is a sundial on the turf, with an iron chair near it. A little path leads off through the box hedge, behind the sundial.

Frank, seated on the chair near the sundial, on which he has placed the morning papers, is reading The Standard. His father comes from the house, red-eyed and shivery, and meets Frank's eye with misgiving.

FRANK *[looking at his watch]* Half-past eleven. Nice hour for a rector to come down to breakfast!

REV. S. Dont mock, Frank: dont mock. I am a little—er— *[Shivering]*.

FRANK. Off color?

REV. S. *[repudiating the expression]* No, sir: unwell this morning. Wheres your mother?

FRANK. Dont be alarmed: she's not here. Gone to town by the 11.13 with Bessie. She left several messages for you. Do you feel equal to receiving them now, or shall I wait til youve breakfasted?

REV. S. I have breakfasted, sir. I am surprised at your mother going to town when we have people staying with us. Theyll think it very strange.

FRANK. Possibly she has considered that. At all events, if Crofts is going to stay here, and you are going to sit up every night with him until four, recalling the incidents of your fiery youth, it is clearly my mother's duty, as a prudent housekeeper, to go up to the stores and order a barrel of whisky and a few hundred siphons.

REV. S. I did not observe that Sir George drank excessively.

FRANK. You were not in a condition to, gov'nor.

REV. S. Do you mean to say that I—?

FRANK *[calmly]* I never saw a beneficed clergyman less sober. The anecdotes you told about your past career were so awful that I really dont think Praed would have passed the night under your roof if it hadnt been for the way my mother and he took to one another.

REV. S. Nonsense, sir. I am Sir George Crofts' host. I must talk to him about something; and he has only one subject. Where is Mr Praed now?

FRANK. He is driving my mother and Bessie to the station.

REV. S. Is Crofts up yet?

FRANK. Oh, long ago. He hasnt turned a hair: he's in much better practice than you. He has kept it up ever since, probably. He's taken himself off somewhere to smoke.

Frank resumes his paper. The parson turns disconsolately towards the gate; then comes back irresolutely.

REV. S. Er—Frank.

FRANK. Yes.

REV. S. Do you think the Warrens will expect to be asked here after yesterday afternoon?

FRANK. Theyve been asked already.

REV. S. *[appalled]* What!!!

FRANK. Crofts informed us at breakfast that you told him to bring Mrs Warren and Vivie over here today, and to invite them to make this house their home. My mother then found she must go to town by the 11.13 train.

REV. S. *[with despairing vehemence]* I never gave any such invitation. I never thought of such a thing.

FRANK *[compassionately]* How do you know, gov'nor, what you said and thought last night?

PRAED *[coming in through the hedge]* Good morning.

REV. S. Good morning. I must apologise for not having met you at breakfast. I have a touch of—of—

FRANK. Clergyman's sore throat, Praed. Fortunately not chronic.

PRAED *[changing the subject]* Well, I must say your house is in a charming spot here. Really most charming.

REV. S. Yes: it is indeed. Frank will take you for a walk, Mr Praed, if you like. I'll ask you to excuse me: I must take the opportunity to write my sermon while Mrs Gardner is away and you are all amusing yourselves. You wont mind, will you?

PRAED. Certainly not. Dont stand on the slightest ceremony with me.

REV. S. Thank you. I'll—er—er— *[He stammers his way to the porch and vanishes into the house]*.

PRAED. Curious thing it must be writing a sermon every week.

FRANK. Ever so curious, if he did it. He buys em. He's gone for some soda water.

PRAED. My dear boy: I wish you would be more respectful to your father.

You know you can be so nice when you like.

FRANK. My dear Praddy: you forget that I have to live with the governor. When two people live together—it dont matter whether theyre father and son or husband and wife or brother and sister—they cant keep up the polite humbug thats so easy for ten minutes on an afternoon call. Now the governor, who unites to many admirable domestic qualities the irresoluteness of a sheep and the pompousness and aggressiveness of a jackass—

PRAED. No, pray, pray, my dear Frank, remember! He is your father.

FRANK. I give him due credit for that. *[Rising and flinging down his paper]* But just imagine his telling Crofts to bring the Warrens over here! He must have been ever so drunk. You know, my dear Praddy, my mother wouldnt stand Mrs Warren for a moment. Vivie mustnt come here until she's gone back to town.

PRAED. But your mother doesnt know anything about Mrs Warren, does she? *[He picks up the paper and sits down to read it]*.

FRANK. I dont know. Her journey to town looks as if she did. Not that my mother would mind in the ordinary way: she has stuck like a brick to lots of women who had got into trouble. But they were all nice women. Thats what makes the real difference. Mrs Warren, no doubt, has her merits; but she's ever so rowdy; and my mother simply wouldnt put up with her. So—hallo! *[This exclamation is provoked by the reappearance of the clergyman, who comes out of the house in haste and dismay]*.

REV. S. Frank: Mrs Warren and her daughter are coming across the heath with Crofts: I saw them from the study windows. What am I to say about your mother?

FRANK. Stick on your hat and go out and say how delighted you are to see them; and that Frank's in the garden; and that mother and Bessie have been called to the bedside of a sick relative, and were ever so sorry they couldnt stop; and that you hope Mrs Warren slept well; and—and—say any blessed thing except the truth, and leave the rest to Providence.

REV. S. But how are we to get rid of them afterwards?

FRANK. Theres no time to think of that now. Here! *[He bounds into the house]*.

REV. S. He's so impetuous. I dont know what to do with him, Mr Praed.

FRANK *[returning with a clerical felt hat, which he claps on his father's head]* Now: off with you. *[Rushing him through the gate]*. Praed and I'll wait here, to give the thing an unpremeditated air. *[The clergyman, dazed but obedient, hurries off]*.

FRANK. We must get the old girl back to town somehow, Praed. Come!

Honestly, dear Praddy, do you like seeing them together?

PRAED. Oh, why not?

FRANK *[his teeth on edge]* Dont it make your flesh creep ever so little? that wicked old devil, up to every villainy under the sun, I'll swear, and Vivie—ugh!

PRAED. Hush, pray. Theyre coming.

The clergyman and Crofts are seen coming along the road, followed by Mrs Warren and Vivie walking affectionately together.

FRANK. Look: she actually has her arm round the old woman's waist. It's her right arm: she began it. She's gone sentimental, by God! Ugh! ugh! Now do you feel the creeps? *[The clergyman opens the gate; and Mrs Warren and Vivie pass him and stand in the middle of the garden looking at the house. Frank, in an ecstasy of dissimulation, turns gaily to Mrs Warren, exclaiming]* Ever so delighted to see you, Mrs Warren. This quiet old rectory garden becomes you perfectly.

MRS WARREN. Well, I never! Did you hear that, George? He says I look well in a quiet old rectory garden.

REV. S. *[still holding the gate for Crofts, who loafs through it, heavily bored]* You look well everywhere, Mrs Warren.

FRANK. Bravo, gov'nor! Now look here: lets have a treat before lunch. First lets see the church. Everyone has to do that. It's a regular old thirteenth century church, you know; the gov'nor's ever so fond of it, because he got up a restoration fund and had it completely rebuilt six years ago. Praed will be able to shew its points.

PRAED *[rising]* Certainly, if the restoration has left any to shew.

REV. S. *[mooning hospitably at them]* I shall be pleased, I'm sure, if Sir George and Mrs Warren really care about it.

MRS WARREN. Oh, come along and get it over.

CROFTS *[turning back towards the gate]* Ive no objection.

REV. S. Not that way. We go through the fields, if you dont mind. Round here. *[He leads the way by the little path through the box hedge]*.

CROFTS. Oh, all right. *[He goes with the parson]*.

Praed follows with Mrs Warren. Vivie does not stir: she watches them until they have gone, with all the lines of purpose in her face marking it strongly.

FRANK. Aint you coming?

VIVIE. No. I want to give you a warning, Frank. You were making fun of my mother just now when you said that about the rectory garden. That is barred in future. Please treat my mother with as much respect as you treat your own.

FRANK. My dear Viv: she wouldnt appreciate it: the two cases require different treatment. But what on earth has happened to you? Last night we were perfectly agreed as to your mother and her set. This morning I find you attitudinizing sentimentally with your arm round your parent's waist.

VIVIE *[flushing]* Attitudinizing!

FRANK. That was how it struck me. First time I ever saw you do a second-rate thing.

VIVIE *[controlling herself]* Yes, Frank: there has been a change; but I dont think it a change for the worse. Yesterday I was a little prig.

FRANK. And today?

VIVIE *[wincing; then looking at him steadily]* Today I know my mother better than you do.

FRANK. Heaven forbid!

VIVIE. What do you mean?

FRANK. Viv: theres a freemasonry among thoroughly immoral people that you know nothing of. Youve too much character. Thats the bond between your mother and me: thats why I know her better than youll ever know her.

VIVIE. You are wrong: you know nothing about her. If you knew the circumstances against which my mother had to struggle—

FRANK *[adroitly finishing the sentence for her]* I should know why she is what she is, shouldnt I? What difference would that make? Circumstances or no circumstances, Viv, you wont be able to stand your mother.

VIVIE *[very angrily]* Why not?

FRANK. Because she's an old wretch, Viv. If you ever put your arm round her waist in my presence again, I'll shoot myself there and then as a protest against an exhibition which revolts me.

VIVIE. Must I choose between dropping your acquaintance and dropping my mother's?

FRANK *[gracefully]* That would put the old lady at ever such a disadvantage. No, Viv; your infatuated little boy will have to stick to you in any case. But he's all the more anxious that you shouldnt make mistakes. It's no use, Viv: your mother's impossible. She may be a good sort; but she's a bad lot, a very bad lot.

VIVIE *[hotly]* Frank—! *[He stands his ground. She turns away and sits down on the bench under the yew tree, struggling to recover her self-command. Then she says]* Is she to be deserted by all the world because she's what you call a bad lot? Has she no right to live?

FRANK. No fear of that, Viv: she wont ever be deserted. *[He sits on the bench beside her]*.

VIVIE. But I am to desert her, I suppose.

FRANK *[babyishly, lulling her and making love to her with his voice]* Musnt go live with her. Little family group of mother and daughter wouldnt be a success. Spoil our little group.

VIVIE *[falling under the spell]* What little group?

FRANK. The babes in the wood: Vivie and little Frank. *[He nestles against her like a weary child]*. Lets go and get covered up with leaves.

VIVIE *[rhythmically, rocking him like a nurse]* Fast asleep, hand in hand, under the trees.

FRANK. The wise little girl with her silly little boy.

VIVIE. The dear little boy with his dowdy little girl.

FRANK. Ever so peaceful, and relieved from the imbecility of the little boy's father and the questionableness of the little girl's—

VIVIE *[smothering the word against her breast]* Sh-sh-sh-sh! little girl wants to forget all about her mother. *[They are silent for some moments, rocking one another. Then Vivie wakes up with a shock, exclaiming]* What a pair of fools we are! Come: sit up. Gracious! your hair. *[She smooths it]*. I wonder do all grown up people play in that childish way when nobody is looking. I never did it when I was a child.

FRANK. Neither did I. You are my first playmate. *[He catches her hand to kiss it, but checks himself to look round first. Very unexpectedly, he sees Crofts emerging from the box hedge]*. Oh damn!

VIVIE. Why damn, dear?

FRANK *[whispering]* Sh! Heres this brute Crofts. *[He sits farther away from her with an unconcerned air]*.

CROFTS. Could I have a few words with you, Miss Vivie?

VIVIE. Certainly.

CROFTS *[to Frank]* Youll excuse me, Gardner. Theyre waiting for you in the church, if you dont mind.

FRANK *[rising]* Anything to oblige you, Crofts—except church. If you should happen to want me, Vivvums, ring the gate bell. *[He goes into the house with unruffled suavity]*.

CROFTS *[watching him with a crafty air as he disappears, and speaking to Vivie with an assumption of being on privileged terms with her]* Pleasant young fellow that, Miss Vivie. Pity he has no money, isnt it?

VIVIE. Do you think so?

CROFTS. Well, whats he to do? No profession. No property. Whats he good for?

VIVIE. I realize his disadvantages, Sir George.

CROFTS *[a little taken aback at being so precisely interpreted]* Oh, it's not that. But while we're in this world we're in it; and money's money. *[Vivie does not answer]*. Nice day, isnt it?

VIVIE *[with scarcely veiled contempt for this effort at conversation]* Very.

CROFTS *[with brutal good humor, as if he liked her pluck]* Well, thats not what I came to say. *[Sitting down beside her]* Now listen, Miss Vivie. I'm quite aware that I'm not a young lady's man.

VIVIE. Indeed, Sir George?

CROFTS. No; and to tell you the honest truth I dont want to be either. But when I say a thing I mean it; when I feel a sentiment I feel it in earnest; and what I value I pay hard money for. Thats the sort of man I am.

VIVIE. It does you great credit, I'm sure.

CROFTS. Oh, I dont mean to praise myself. I have my faults, Heaven knows: no man is more sensible of that than I am. I know I'm not perfect; thats one of the advantages of being a middle-aged man; for I'm not a young man, and I know it. But my code is a simple one, and, I think, a good one. Honor between man and man; fidelity between man and woman; and no cant about this religion or that religion, but an honest belief that things are making for good on the whole.

VIVIE *[with biting irony]* 'A power, not ourselves, that makes for righteousness', eh?

CROFTS *[taking her seriously]* Oh certainly. Not ourselves, of course. You understand what I mean. Well, now as to practical matters. You may have an idea that Ive flung my money about; but I havnt: I'm richer today than when I first came into the property. Ive used my knowledge of the world to invest my money in ways that other men have overlooked; and whatever else I may be, I'm a safe man from the money point of view.

VIVIE. It's very kind of you to tell me all this.

CROFTS. Oh well, come, Miss Vivie: you neednt pretend you dont see what I'm driving at. I want to settle down with a Lady Crofts. I suppose you think me very blunt, eh?

VIVIE. Not at all: I am much obliged to you for being so definite and business-like. I quite appreciate the offer: the money, the position, Lady Crofts and so on. But I think I will say no, if you dont mind. I'd rather not. *[She rises, and strolls across to the sundial to get out of his immediate neighborhood]*.

CROFTS *[not at all discouraged, and taking advantage of the additional room left him on the seat to spread himself comfortably, as if a few preliminary refusals were part of the inevitable routine of courtship]* I'm in no hurry. It was only just to let you know in case young Gardner should try to trap you. Leave the question open.

VIVIE *[sharply]* My no is final. I wont go back from it.

Crofts is not impressed. He grins; leans forward with his elbows on his knees to prod with his stick at some unfortunate insect in the grass; and looks cunningly at her. She turns away impatiently.

CROFTS. I'm a good deal older than you. Twenty-five years: quarter of a century. I shant live for ever; and I'll take care that you shall be well off when I'm gone.

VIVIE. I am proof against even that inducement, Sir George. Dont you think youd better take your answer? There is not the slightest chance of my altering it.

CROFTS *[rising, after a final slash at a daisy, and coming nearer to her]* Well, no matter. I could tell you some things that would change your mind fast enough; but I wont, because I'd rather win you by honest affection. I was a good friend to your mother: ask her whether I wasnt. She'd never have made the money that paid for your education if it hadnt been for my advice and help, not to mention the money I advanced her. There are not many men would have stood by her as I have. I put not less than £40,000 into it, from first to last.

VIVIE *[staring at him]* Do you mean to say you were my mother's business partner?

CROFTS. Yes. Now just think of all the trouble and the explanations it would save if we were to keep the whole thing in the family, so to speak. Ask your mother whether she'd like to have to explain all her affairs to a perfect stranger.

VIVIE. I see no difficulty, since I understand that the business is wound up, and the money invested.

CROFTS *[stopping short, amazed]* Wound up! I Wind up a business thats paying 35 per cent in the worst years! Not likely. Who told you that?

VIVIE *[her color quite gone]* Do you mean that it is still—? *[She stops abruptly, and puts her hand on the sundial to support herself. Then she gets quickly to the iron chair and sits down]*. What business are you talking about?

CROFTS. Well, the fact is it's not what would be considered exactly a high-class business in my set—the county set, you know—our set it will be if you think better of my offer. Not that theres any mystery about it: dont think that. Of course you know by your mother's being in it that it's perfectly straight and honest. Ive known her for many years; and I can say of her that she'd cut off her hands sooner than touch anything that was not what it ought to be. I'll tell you all about it if you like. I dont know whether youve found in travelling how hard it is to find a really comfortable private hotel.

VIVIE *[sickened, averting her face]* Yes: go on.

CROFTS. Well, thats all it is. Your mother has a genius for managing such things. Weve got two in Brussels, one in Ostend, one in Vienna, and two in Budapest. Of course there are others besides ourselves in it: but we hold most of the capital; and your mother's indispensable as managing director. Youve noticed, I daresay, that she travels a good deal. But you see you cant mention such things in society. Once let out the word hotel and everybody says you keep a public-house. You wouldnt like people to say that of your mother, would you? Thats why we're so reserved about it. By the way, youll keep it to yourself, wont you? Since its been a secret so long, it had better remain so.

VIVIE. And this is the business you invite me to join you in?

CROFTS. Oh no. My wife shant be troubled with business. Youll not be in it more than youve always been.

VIVIE. *I* always been! What do you mean?

CROFTS. Only that youve always lived on it. It paid for your education and the dress you have on your back. Dont turn up your nose at business, Miss Vivie; where would your Newnhams and Girtons be without it?

VIVIE *[rising, almost beside herself]* Take care. I know what this business is.

CROFTS *[starting, with a suppressed oath]* Who told you?

VIVIE. Your partner. My mother.

CROFTS *[black with rage]* The old—

VIVIE. Just so.

He swallows the epithet and stands for a moment swearing and raging foully to himself. But he knows that his cue is to be sympathetic. He takes refuge in generous indignation.

CROFTS. She ought to have had more consideration for you. I'd never have told you.

VIVIE. I think you would probably have told me when we were married: it would have been a convenient weapon to break me in with.

CROFTS *[quite sincerely]* I never intended that. On my word as a gentleman I didnt.

Vivie wonders at him. Her sense of the irony of his protest cools and braces her. She replies with contemptuous self-possession.

VIVIE. It does not matter. I suppose you understand that when we leave here today our acquaintance ceases.

CROFTS. Why? Is it for helping your mother?

VIVIE. My mother was a very poor woman who had no reasonable choice but to do as she did. You were a rich gentleman; and you did the same for the sake of 35 per cent. You are a pretty common sort of scoundrel, I think. That is my opinion of you.

CROFTS *[after a start; not at all displeased, and much more at his ease on these frank terms than on their former ceremonious ones]* Ha! ha! ha! ha! Go it, little missie, go it; it doesnt hurt me and it amuses you. Why the devil shouldnt I invest my money that way? I take the interest on my capital like other people: I hope you dont think I dirty my own hands with the work. Come! you wouldnt refuse the acquaintance of my mother's cousin the Duke of Belgravia because some of the rents he gets are earned in queer ways. You wouldnt cut the Archbishop of Canterbury, I suppose, because the Ecclesiastical Commissioners have a few publicans and sinners among their tenants. Do you remember your Crofts scholarship at Newnham? Well, that was founded by my brother the M.P. He gets his 22 per cent out of a factory with 600 girls in it, and not one of them getting wages enough to live on. How d'ye suppose they manage when they have no family to fall back on? Ask your mother. And do you expect me to turn my back on 35 per cent when all the rest are pocketing what they can, like sensible men? No such fool! If youre going to pick and choose your acquaintances on moral principles, youd better clear out of this country, unless you want to cut yourself out of all decent society.

VIVIE *[conscience stricken]* You might go on to point out that I myself never asked where the money I spent came from. I believe I am just as bad as you.

CROFTS *[greatly reassured]* Of course you are; and a very good thing too! What harm does it do after all? *[Rallying her jocularly]* So you dont think me such a scoundrel now you come to think it over. Eh?

VIVIE. I have shared profits with you; and I admitted you just now to the familiarity of knowing what I think of you.

CROFTS *[with serious friendliness]* To be sure you did. You wont find me a bad sort: I dont go in for being superfine intellectually: but Ive plenty of honest human feeling; and the old Crofts breed comes out in a sort of instinctive hatred of anything low, in which I'm sure youll sympathize with me. Believe me, Miss Vivie, the world isnt such a bad place as the croakers make out. As long as you dont fly openly in the face of society, society doesnt ask any inconvenient questions; and it makes precious short work of the cads who do. There are no secrets better kept than the secrets everybody guesses. In the class of people I can introduce you to, no lady or gentleman would so far forget themselves as to discuss my business affairs or your mother's. No man can offer you a safer position.

VIVIE *[studying him curiously]* I suppose you really think youre getting on famously with me.

CROFTS. Well, I hope I may flatter myself that you think better of me than you did at first.

VIVIE *[quietly]* I hardly find you worth thinking about at all now. When I think of the society that tolerates you, and the laws that protect you! when I think of how helpless nine out of ten young girls would be in the hands of you and my mother! the unmentionable woman and her capitalist bully—

CROFTS *[livid]* Damn you!

VIVIE. You need not. I feel among the damned already.

She raises the latch of the gate to open it and go out. He follows her and puts his hand heavily on the top bar to prevent its opening.

CROFTS *[panting with fury]* Do you think I'll put up with this from you, you young devil?

VIVIE *[unmoved]* Be quiet. Some one will answer the bell. *[Without flinching a step she strikes the bell with the back of her hand. It clangs harshly; and he starts back involuntarily. Almost immediately Frank appears at the porch with his rifle].*

FRANK *[with cheerful politeness]* Will you have the rifle, Viv; or shall I operate?

VIVIE. Frank: have you been listening?

FRANK *[coming down into the garden]* Only for the bell, I assure you; so that you shouldnt have to wait. I think I shewed great insight into your character, Crofts.

CROFTS. For two pins I'd take that gun from you and break it across your head.

FRANK *[stalking him cautiously]* Pray dont. I'm ever so careless in handling firearms. Sure to be a fatal accident, with a reprimand from the coroner's jury for my negligence.

VIVIE. Put the rifle away, Frank; it's quite unnecessary.

FRANK. Quite right, Viv. Much more sportsmanlike to catch him in a trap. *[Crofts, understanding the insult, makes a threatening movement].* Crofts: there are fifteen cartridges in the magazine here; and I am a dead shot at the present distance and at an object of your size.

CROFTS. Oh, you neednt be afraid. I'm not going to touch you.

FRANK. Ever so magnanimous of you under the circumstances! Thank you!

CROFTS. I'll just tell you this before I go. It may interest you, since youre so fond of one another. Allow me, Mister Frank, to introduce you to your half-sister, the eldest daughter of the Reverend Samuel Gardner. Miss Vivie: your half-brother. Good morning. *[He goes out through the gate along the road]*.

FRANK *[after a pause of stupefaction, raising the rifle]* Youll testify before the coroner that it's an accident, Viv. *[He takes aim at the retreating figure of Crofts. Vivie seizes the muzzle and pulls it round against her breast]*.

VIVIE. Fire now. You may.

FRANK *[dropping his end of the rifle hastily]* Stop! take care. *[She lets it go. It falls on the turf]*. Oh, youve given your little boy such a turn. Suppose it had gone off! ugh! *[He sinks on the garden seat overcome]*.

VIVIE. Suppose it had: do you think it would not have been a relief to have some sharp physical pain tearing through me?

FRANK *[coaxingly]* Take it ever so easy, dear Viv. Remember: even if the rifle scared that fellow into telling the truth for the first time in his life, that only makes us the babes in the wood in earnest. *[He holds out his arms to her]*. Come and be covered up with leaves again.

VIVIE *[with a cry of disgust]* Ah, not that, not that. You make all my flesh creep.

FRANK. Why, whats the matter?

VIVIE. Goodbye. *[She makes for the gate]*.

FRANK *[jumping up]* Hallo! Stop! Viv! Viv! *[She turns in the gateway]* Where are you going to? Where shall we find you?

VIVIE. At Honoria Fraser's chambers, 67 Chancery Lane, for the rest of my life. *[She goes off quickly in the opposite direction to that taken by Crofts]*.

FRANK. But I say—wait—dash it! *[He runs after her]*.

ACT IV

Honoria Fraser's chambers in Chancery Lane. An office at the top of New Stone Buildings, with a plate-glass window, distempered walls, electric light, and a patent stove. Saturday afternoon. The chimneys of Lincoln's Inn and the western sky beyond are seen through the window. There is a double writing table in the middle of the room, with a cigar box, ash pans, and a portable electric reading lamp almost snowed up in heaps of papers and books. This table has knee holes and chairs right and left and is very untidy. The clerk's desk, closed and tidy, with its high stool, is against the wall, near a door communicating with the inner rooms. In the opposite wall is the door leading to the public corridor. Its upper panel is of opaque glass, lettered in black on the outside, FRASER AND WARREN. A baize screen hides the corner between this door and the window.

Frank, in a fashionable light-colored coaching suit, with his stick, gloves, and white hat in his hands, is pacing up and down the office. Somebody tries the door with a key.

FRANK *[calling]* Come in. It's not locked.

Vivie comes in, in her hat and jacket. She stops and stares at him.

VIVIE *[sternly]* What are you doing here?

FRANK. Waiting to see you. Ive been here for hours. Is this the way you attend to your business? *[He puts his hat and stick on the table, and perches himself with a vault on the clerk's stool looking at her with every appearance of being in a specially restless, teasing, flippant mood]*.

VIVIE. Ive been away exactly twenty minutes for a cup of tea. *[She takes off her hat and jacket and hangs them up behind the screen]*. How did you get in?

FRANK. The staff had not left when I arrived. He's gone to play cricket on Primrose Hill. Why dont you employ a woman, and give your sex a chance?

VIVIE. What have you come for?

FRANK *[springing off the stool and coming close to her]* Viv: lets go and enjoy the Saturday half-holiday somewhere, like the staff. What do you say to Richmond, and then a music hall, and a jolly supper?

VIVIE. Cant afford it. I shall put in another six hours work before I go to bed.

FRANK. Cant afford it, cant we? Aha! Look here. *[He takes out a handful of sovereigns and makes them chink]*. Gold, Viv: gold!

VIVIE. Where did you get it?

FRANK. Gambling, Viv; gambling. Poker.

VIVIE. Pah! It's meaner than stealing it. No: I'm not coming. *[She sits down to work at the table, with her back to the glass door, and begins turning over the papers]*.

FRANK *[remonstrating piteously]* But, my dear Viv, I want to talk to you ever so seriously.

VIVIE. Very well: sit down in Honoria's chair and talk here. I like ten minutes chat after tea. *[He murmurs]*. No use groaning: I'm inexorable. *[He takes the opposite seat disconsolately]*. Pass that cigar box, will you?

FRANK *[pushing the cigar box across]* Nasty womanly habit. Nice men dont do it any longer.

VIVIE. Yes: they object to the smell in the office; and weve had to take to cigarets. See! *[She opens the box and takes out a cigaret, which she lights. She offers him one; but he shakes his head with a wry face. She settles herself comfortably in her chair, smoking]*. Go ahead.

FRANK. Well, I want to know what youve done—what arrangements youve made.

VIVIE. Everything was settled twenty minutes after I arrived here. Honoria has found the business too much for her this year; and she was on the point of sending for me and proposing a partnership when I walked in and told her I hadnt a farthing in the world. So I installed myself and packed her off for a fortnight's holiday. What happened at Haslemere when I left?

FRANK. Nothing at all. I said youd gone to town on particular business.

VIVIE. Well?

FRANK. Well, either they were too flabbergasted to say anything, or else Crofts had prepared your mother. Anyhow, she didnt say anything; and Crofts didnt say anything; and Praddy only stared. After tea they got up and went; and Ive not seen them since.

VIVIE *[nodding placidly with one eye on a wreath of smoke]* Thats all right.

FRANK *[looking round disparagingly]* Do you intend to stick in this confounded place?

VIVIE *[blowing the wreath decisively away, and sitting straight up]* Yes. These two days have given me back all my strength and self-possession. I will never take a holiday again as long as I live.

FRANK *[with a very wry face]* Mps! You look quite happy. And as hard as nails.

VIVIE *[grimly]* Well for me that I am!

FRANK *[rising]* Look here, Viv: we must have an explanation. We parted the other day under a complete misunderstanding. *[He sits on the table, close to her]*.

VIVIE *[putting away the cigaret]* Well: clear it up.

FRANK. You remember what Crofts said?

VIVIE. Yes.

FRANK. That revelation was supposed to bring about a complete change in the nature of our feeling for one another. It placed us on the footing of brother and sister.

VIVIE. Yes.

FRANK. Have you ever had a brother?

VIVIE. No.

FRANK. Then you dont know what being brother and sister feels like? Now I have lots of sisters; and the fraternal feeling is quite familiar to me. I assure you my feeling for you is not the least in the world like it. The girls will go their way; I will go mine; and we shant care if we never see one another again. Thats brother and sister. But as to you, I cant be easy if I have to pass a week without seeing you. Thats not brother and sister. It's exactly what I felt an hour before Crofts made his revelation. In short, dear Viv, it's love's young dream.

VIVIE *[bitingly]* The same feeling, Frank, that brought your father to my mother's feet. Is that it?

FRANK *[so revolted that he slips off the table for a moment]* I very strongly object, Viv, to have my feelings compared to any which the Reverend Samuel is capable of harboring; and I object still more to a comparison of you to your mother. *[Resuming his perch]*. Besides, I dont believe the story. I have taxed my father with it, and obtained from him what I consider tantamount to a denial.

VIVIE. What did he say?

FRANK. He said he was sure there must be some mistake.

VIVIE. Do you believe him?

FRANK. I am prepared to take his word as against Crofts.

VIVIE. Does it make any difference? I mean in your imagination or conscience; for of course it makes no real difference.

FRANK *[shaking his head]* None whatever to me.

VIVIE. Nor to me.

FRANK *[staring]* But this is ever so surprising! *[He goes back to his chair]*. I thought our whole relations were altered in your imagination and conscience, as you put it, the moment those words were out of that brute's muzzle.

VIVIE. No: it was not that. I didnt believe him. I only wish I could.

FRANK. Eh?

VIVIE. I think brother and sister would be a very suitable relation for us.

FRANK. You really mean that?

VIVIE. Yes. It's the only relation I care for, even if we could afford any other. I mean that.

FRANK *[raising his eyebrows like one on whom a new light has dawned, and rising with quite an effusion of chivalrous sentiment]* My dear Viv: why didnt you say so before? I am ever so sorry for persecuting you. I understand, of course.

VIVIE *[puzzled]* Understand what?

FRANK. Oh, I'm not a fool in the ordinary sense: only in the Scriptural sense of doing all the things the wise man declared to be folly, after trying them himself on the most extensive scale. I see I am no longer Vivvums' little boy. Dont be alarmed: I shall never call you Vivvums again—at least unless you get tired of your new little boy, however he may be.

VIVIE. My new little boy!

FRANK *[with conviction]* Must be a new little boy. Always happens that way. No other way, in fact.

VIVIE. None that you know of, fortunately for you.

Someone knocks at the door.

FRANK. My curse upon yon caller, whoe'er he be!

VIVIE. It's Praed. He's going to Italy and wants to say goodbye. I asked him to call this afternoon. Go and let him in.

FRANK. We can continue our conversation after his departure for Italy. I'll stay him out. *[He goes to the door and opens it]*. How are you, Praddy? Delighted to see you. Come in.

Praed, dressed for travelling, comes in, in high spirits.

PRAED. How do you do, Miss Warren? *[She presses his hand cordially, though a certain sentimentality in his high spirits jars on her]*. I start in an hour from Holborn Viaduct. I wish I could persuade you to try Italy.

VIVIE. What for?

PRAED. Why, to saturate yourself with beauty and romance, of course.

Vivie, with a shudder, turns her chair to the table, as if the work waiting for her there were a support to her. Praed sits opposite to her. Frank places a chair near Vivie, and drops lazily and carelessly into it, talking at her over his shoulder.

FRANK. No use, Praddy. Viv is a little Philistine. She is indifferent to my romance, and insensible to my beauty.

VIVIE. Mr Praed: once for all, there is no beauty and no romance in life for me. Life is what it is; and I am prepared to take it as it is.

PRAED *[enthusiastically]* You will not say that if you come with me to Verona and on to Venice. You will cry with delight at living in such a beautiful world.

FRANK. This is most eloquent, Praddy. Keep it up.

PRAED. Oh, I assure you *I* have cried—I shall cry again, I hope—at fifty! At your age, Miss Warren, you would not need to go so far as Verona. Your spirits would absolutely fly up at the mere sight of Ostend. You would be charmed with the gaiety, the vivacity, the happy air of Brussels.

VIVIE *[springing up with an exclamation of loathing]* Agh!

PRAED *[rising]* Whats the matter?

FRANK *[rising]* Hallo, Viv!

VIVIE *[to Praed, with deep reproach]* Can you find no better example of your beauty and romance than Brussels to talk to me about?

PRAED *[puzzled]* Of course it's very different from Verona. I dont suggest for a moment that—

VIVIE *[bitterly]* Probably the beauty and romance come to much the same in both places.

PRAED *[completely sobered and much concerned]* My dear Miss Warren: I— *[looking inquiringly at Frank]* Is anything the matter?

FRANK. She thinks your enthusiasm frivolous, Praddy. She's had ever such a serious call.

VIVIE *[sharply]* Hold your tongue, Frank. Dont be silly.

FRANK *[sitting down]* Do you call this good manners, Praed?

PRAED *[anxious and considerate]* Shall I take him away, Miss Warren? I feel sure we have disturbed you at your work.

VIVIE. Sit down: I'm not ready to go back to work yet. *[Praed sits]*. You both think I have an attack of nerves. Not a bit of it. But there are two subjects I want dropped, if you dont mind. One of them *[to Frank]* is love's young dream in any shape or form: the other *[to Praed]* is the romance and beauty of life, especially Ostend and the gaiety of Brussels. You are welcome to any illusions you may have left on these subjects: I have none. If we three are to remain friends, I must be treated as a woman of business, permanently single *[to Frank]* and permanently unromantic *[to Praed]*.

FRANK. I also shall remain permanently single until you change your mind. Praddy: change the subject. Be eloquent about something else.

PRAED *[diffidently]* I'm afraid theres nothing else in the world that I can talk about. The Gospel of Art is the only one I can preach. I know Miss Warren is a great devotee of the Gospel of Getting on; but we cant discuss that without hurting your feelings, Frank, since you are determined not to get on.

FRANK. Oh, dont mind my feelings. Give me some improving advice by all means: it does me ever so much good. Have another try to make a successful man of me, Viv. Come: lets have it all: energy, thrift, foresight, self-respect, character. Dont you hate people who have no character, Viv?

VIVIE *[wincing]* Oh, stop, stop: let us have no more of that horrible cant. Mr Praed: if there are really only those two gospels in the world, we had better all kill ourselves; for the same taint is in both, through and through.

FRANK *[looking critically at her]* There is a touch of poetry about you today, Viv, which has hitherto been lacking.

PRAED *[remonstrating]* My dear Frank: arnt you a little unsympathetic?

VIVIE *[merciless to herself]* No: it's good for me. It keeps me from being sentimental.

FRANK *[bantering her]* Checks your strong natural propensity that way, dont it?

VIVIE *[almost hysterically]* Oh yes: go on: dont spare me. I was sentimental for one moment in my life—beautifully sentimental—by moonlight; and now—

FRANK *[quickly]* I say, Viv: take care. Dont give yourself away.

VIVIE. Oh, do you think Mr Praed does not know all about my mother? *[Turning on Praed]* You had better have told me that morning, Mr Praed. You are very old fashioned in your delicacies, after all.

PRAED. Surely it is you who are a little old fashioned in your prejudices, Miss Warren. I feel bound to tell you, speaking as an artist, and believing that the most intimate human relationships are far beyond and above the scope of the law, that though I know that your mother is an unmarried woman, I do not respect her the less on that account. I respect her more.

FRANK *[airily]* Hear! Hear!

VIVIE *[staring at him]* Is that all you know?

PRAED. Certainly that is all.

VIVIE. Then you neither of you know anything. Your guesses are innocence itself compared to the truth.

PRAED *[rising, startled and indignant, and preserving his politeness with an effort]* I hope not. *[More emphatically]* I hope not, Miss Warren.

FRANK *[whistles]* Whew!

VIVIE. You are not making it easy for me to tell you, Mr Praed.

PRAED *[his chivalry drooping before their conviction]* If there is anything worse—that is, anything else—are you sure you are right to tell us, Miss Warren?

VIVIE. I am sure that if I had the courage I should spend the rest of my life in telling everybody—stamping and branding it into them until they all felt their part in its abomination as I feel mine. There is nothing I despise more than the wicked convention that protects these things by forbidding a woman to mention them. And yet I cant tell you. The two infamous words that describe what my mother is are ringing in my ears and struggling on my tongue; but I cant utter them: the shame of them is too horrible for me. *[She buries her face in her hands. The two men, astonished, stare at one another and then at her. She raises her head again desperately and snatches a sheet of paper and a pen]*. Here: let me draft you a prospectus.

FRANK. Oh, she's mad. Do you hear, Viv? mad. Come! pull yourself together.

VIVIE. You shall see. *[She writes]*. 'Paid up capital: not less than £40,000 standing in the name of Sir George Crofts, Baronet, the chief shareholder. Premises at Brussels, Ostend, Vienna and Budapest. Managing director: Mrs. Warren'; and now dont let us forget her qualifications: the two words. *[She writes the words and pushes the paper to them]*. There! Oh no: dont read it: dont! *[She snatches it back and tears it to pieces; then seizes her head in her hands and hides her face on the table]*.

Frank, who has watched the writing over her shoulder, and opened his eyes very widely at it, takes a card from his pocket; scribbles the two words on it; and silently hands it to Praed, who reads it with amazement, and hides it hastily in his pocket.

FRANK *[whispering tenderly]* Viv, dear: thats all right. I read what you wrote: so did Praddy. We understand. And we remain, as this leaves us at present, yours ever so devotedly.

PRAED. We do indeed, Miss Warren. I declare you are the most splendidly courageous woman I ever met.

This sentimental compliment braces Vivie. She throws it away from her with an impatient shake, and forces herself to stand up, though not without some support from the table.

FRANK. Dont stir, Viv, if you dont want to. Take it easy.

VIVIE. Thank you. You can always depend on me for two things: not to cry and not to faint. *[She moves a few steps towards the door of the inner room, and stops close to Praed to say]* I shall need much more courage than that when I tell my mother that we have come to the parting of the ways. Now I must go into the next room for a moment to make myself neat again, if you dont mind.

PRAED. Shall we go away?

VIVIE. No: I'll be back presently. Only for a moment. *[She goes into the other room, Praed opening the door for her]*.

PRAED. What an amazing revelation! I'm extremely disappointed in Crofts: I am indeed.

FRANK. I'm not in the least. I feel he's perfectly accounted for at last. But what a facer for me, Praddy! I cant marry her now.

PRAED *[sternly]* Frank! *[The two took at one another, Frank unruffled, Praed deeply indignant]* Let me tell you, Gardner, that if you desert her now you will behave very despicably.

FRANK. Good old Praddy! Ever chivalrous! But you mistake: it's not the moral aspect of the case: it's the money aspect. I really cant bring myself to touch the old woman's money now.

PRAED. And was that what you were going to marry on?

FRANK. What else? I havnt any money, not the smallest turn for making it. If I married Viv now she would have to support me; and I should cost her more than I am worth.

PRAED. But surely a clever bright fellow like you can make something by your own brains.

FRANK. Oh yes, a little *[He takes out his money again]*. I made all that yesterday in an hour and a half. But I made it in a highly speculative business. No, dear Praddy: even if Bessie and Georgina marry millionaires and the governor dies after cutting them off with a shilling, I shall have only four hundred a year. And he wont die until he's three score and ten: he hasnt originality enough. I shall be on short allowance for the next twenty years. No short allowance for Viv, if I can help it. I withdraw gracefully and leave the field to the gilded youth of England. So thats settled. I shant worry her about it: I'll just send her a little note after we're gone. She'll understand.

PRAED *[grasping his hand]* Good fellow, Frank! I heartily beg your pardon. But must you never see her again?

FRANK. Never see her again! Hang it all, be reasonable. I shall come along as often as possible, and be her brother. I can not understand the absurd consequences you romantic people expect from the most ordinary transactions. *[A knock at the door]*. I wonder who this is. Would you mind opening the door? If it's a client it will look more respectable than if I appeared.

PRAED. Certainly. *[He goes to the door and opens it. Frank sits down in Vivie's chair to scribble a note]*. My dear Kitty: come in: come in.

Mrs Warren comes in, looking apprehensively round for Vivie. She has done her best to make herself matronly and dignified. The brilliant hat is replaced by a sober bonnet, and the gay blouse covered by a costly black silk mantle. She is pitiably anxious and ill at ease: evidently panic-stricken.

MRS WARREN *[to Frank]* What! Youre here, are you?

FRANK *[turning in his chair from his writing, but not rising]* Here, and charmed to see you. You come like a breath of spring.

MRS WARREN. Oh, get out with your nonsense. *[In a low voice]* Wheres Vivie?

Frank points expressively to the door of the inner room, but says nothing.

MRS WARREN *[sitting down suddenly and almost beginning to cry]* Praddy: wont she see me, dont you think?

PRAED. My dear Kitty: dont distress yourself. Why should she not?

MRS WARREN. Oh, you never can see why not: youre too innocent. Mr Frank: did she say anything to you?

FRANK *[folding his note]* She must see you, if *[very expressively]* you wait til she comes in.

MRS WARREN *[frightened]* Why shouldnt I wait?

Frank looks quizzically at her; puts his note carefully on the inkbottle, so that Vivie cannot fail to find it when next she dips her pen; then rises and devotes his attention to her.

FRANK. My dear Mrs Warren: suppose you were a sparrow—ever so tiny and pretty a sparrow hopping in the roadway—and you saw a steam roller coming in your direction, would you wait for it?

MRS WARREN. Oh, dont bother me with your sparrows. What did she run away from Haslemere like that for?

FRANK. I'm afraid she'll tell you if you rashly await her return.

MRS WARREN. Do you want me to go away?

FRANK. No: I always want you to stay. But I advise you to go away.

MRS WARREN. What! And never see her again!

FRANK. Precisely.

MRS WARREN *[crying again]* Praddy: dont let him be cruel to me. *[she hastily checks her tears and wipes her eyes]*. Shell be so angry if she sees Ive been crying.

FRANK *[with a touch of real compassion in his airy tenderness]* You know that Praddy is the soul of kindness, Mrs Warren. Praddy: what do you say? Go or stay?

PRAED *[to Mrs Warren]* I really should be very sorry to cause you unnecessary pain; but I think perhaps you had better not wait. The fact is— *[Vivie is heard at the inner door]*.

FRANK. Sh! Too late. She's coming.

MRS WARREN. Dont tell her I was crying. *[Vivie comes in. She stops gravely on seeing Mrs Warren, who greets her with hysterical cheerfulness]*. Well, dearie. So here you are at last.

VIVIE. I am glad you have come: I want to speak to you. You said you were going, Frank, I think.

FRANK. Yes. Will you come with me, Mrs Warren? What do you say to a trip to Richmond, and the theatre in the evening? There is safety in Richmond. No steam roller there.

VIVIE. Nonsense, Frank. My mother will stay here.

MRS WARREN *[scared]* I dont know: perhaps I'd better go. We're disturbing you at your work.

VIVIE *[with quiet decision]* Mr Praed: please take Frank away. Sit down, mother. *[Mrs Warren obeys helplessly]*.

PRAED. Come, Frank. Goodbye, Miss Vivie.

VIVIE *[shaking hands]* Goodbye. A pleasant trip.

PRAED. Thank you: thank you. I hope so.

FRANK *[to Mrs Warren]* Goodbye: youd ever so much better have taken my advice. *[He shakes hands with her. Then airily to Vivie]* Byebye, Viv.

VIVIE. Goodbye. *[He goes out gaily without shaking hands with her]*.

PRAED *[sadly]* Goodbye, Kitty.

MRS WARREN *[snivelling]* —Goobye!

Praed goes. Vivie, composed and extremely grave, sits down in Honoria's chair, and waits for her mother to speak. Mrs Warren, dreading a pause, loses no time in beginning.

MRS WARREN. Well, Vivie, what did you go away like that for without saying a word to me? How could you do such a thing? And what have you done to poor George? I wanted him to come with me; but he shuffled out of it. I could see that he was quite afraid of you. Only fancy: he wanted me not to come. As if *[trembling]* I should be afraid of you, dearie. *[Vivie's gravity deepens]*. But of course I told him it was all settled and comfortable between us, and that we were on the best of terms. *[She breaks down]*. Vivie: whats the meaning of this? *[She produces a commercial envelope, and fumbles at the enclosure with trembling fingers]*. I got it from the bank this morning.

VIVIE. It is my month's allowance. They sent it to me as usual the other day. I simply sent it back to be placed to your credit, and asked them to send you the lodgment receipt. In future I shall support myself.

MRS WARREN *[not daring to understand]* Wasnt it enough? Why didnt you tell me? *[With a cunning gleam in her eye]* I'll double it: I was intending to double it. Only let me know how much you want.

VIVIE. You know very well that that has nothing to do with it. From this time I go my own way in my own business and among my own friends. And you will go yours. *[She rises]*. Goodbye.

MRS WARREN *[rising, appalled]* Goodbye?

VIVIE. Yes: Goodbye. Come: dont let us make a useless scene: you understand perfectly well. Sir George Crofts has told me the whole business.

MRS WARREN *[angrily]* Silly old— *[She swallows an epithet, and turns white at the narrowness of her escape from uttering it]*.

VIVIE. Just so.

MRS WARREN. He ought to have his tongue cut out. But I thought it was ended: you said you didnt mind.

VIVIE *[steadfastly]* Excuse me: I do mind.

MRS WARREN. But I explained—

VIVIE. You explained how it came about. You did not tell me that it is still going on. *[She sits]*.

Mrs Warren, silenced for a moment, looks forlornly at Vivie, who waits, secretly hoping that the combat is over. But the cunning expression comes back into Mrs Warren's face; and she bends across the table, sly and urgent, half whispering.

MRS WARREN. Vivie: do you know how rich I am?

VIVIE. I have no doubt you are very rich.

MRS WARREN. But you dont know all that that means: youre too young. It means a new dress every day; it means theatres and balls every night; it means having the pick of all the gentlemen in Europe at your feet; it means a lovely house and plenty of servants; it means the choicest of eating and drinking; it means everything you like, everything you want, everything you can think of. And what are you here? A mere drudge, toiling and moiling early and late for your bare living and two cheap dresses a year. Think over it. *[Soothingly]* Youre shocked, I know. I can enter into your feelings; and I think they do you credit; but trust me, nobody will blame you: you may take my word for that. I know what young girls are; and I know youll think better of it when youve turned it over in your mind.

VIVIE. So thats how it's done, is it? You must have said all that to many a woman, mother, to have it so pat.

MRS WARREN *[passionately]* What harm am I asking you to do? *[Vivie turns away contemptuously. Mrs Warren continues desperately]* Vivie: listen to me: you dont understand: youve been taught wrong on purpose: you dont know what the world is really like.

VIVIE *[arrested]* Taught wrong on purpose! What do you mean?

MRS WARREN. I mean that youre throwing away all your chances for nothing. You think that people are what they pretend to be: that the way you were taught at school and college to think right and proper is the way things really are. But it's not: it's all only a pretence, to keep the cowardly slavish common run of people quiet. Do you want to find that out, like other women, at forty, when youve thrown yourself away and lost your chances; or wont you take it in good time now from your own mother, that loves you and swears to you that it's truth: gospel truth? *[Urgently]* Vivie: the big people, the clever people, the managing people, all know it. They do as I do, and think what I think. I know plenty of them. I know them to speak to, to introduce you to, to make friends of for you. I dont mean anything wrong: thats what you dont understand—your head is full of ignorant ideas about me. What do the people that taught you know about life, or about people like me? When did they ever meet me, or speak to me, or let anyone tell them about me? the fools! Would they ever have done anything for you if I hadnt paid them? Havnt I told you that I want you to be respectable? Havnt I brought you up to be respectable? And how can you keep it up without my money and my influence and Lizzie's friends? Cant you see that youre cutting your own throat as well as breaking my heart in turning your back on me?

VIVIE. I recognize the Crofts philosophy of life, mother. I heard it all from him that day at the Gardners'.

MRS WARREN. You think I want to force that played-out old sot on you! I dont, Vivie: on my oath I dont.

VIVIE. It would not matter if you did: you would not succeed. *[Mrs Warren winces, deeply hurt by the implied indifference towards her affectionate intention. Vivie, neither understanding this nor concerning herself about it, goes on calmly]* Mother: you dont at all know the sort of person I am. I dont object to Crofts more than to any other coarsely built man of his class. To tell you the truth, I rather admire him for being strong-minded enough to enjoy himself in his own way and make plenty of money instead of living the usual shooting, hunting, dining-out, tailoring, loafing life of his set merely because all the rest do it. And I'm perfectly aware that if I'd been in the same circumstances as my aunt Liz, I'd have done exactly what she did. I dont think I'm more prejudiced or straitlaced than you: I think I'm less. I'm certain I'm less sentimental. I know very well that fashionable morality is all a pretence, and that if I took your money and devoted the rest of my life to spending it fashionably, I might be as worthless and vicious as the silliest woman could possibly want to be without having a word said to me about it. But I dont want to be worthless. I shouldnt enjoy trotting about the park to advertise my dressmaker and carriage builder, or being bored at the opera to shew off a shopwindowful of diamonds.

MRS WARREN *[bewildered]* But—

VIVIE. Wait a moment: Ive not done. Tell me why you continue your business now that you are independent of it. Your sister, you told me, has left all that behind her. Why dont you do the same?

MRS WARREN. Oh, it's all very easy for Liz: she likes good society, and has the air of being a lady. Imagine me in a cathedral town! Why, the very rooks in the trees would find me out even if I could stand the dulness of it. I must have work and excitement, or I should go melancholy mad. And what else is there for me to do? The life suits me: I'm fit for it and not for anything else. If I didnt do it somebody else would; so I dont do any real harm by it. And then it brings in money; and I like making money. No: it's no use: I cant give it up—not for anybody. But what need you know about it? I'll never mention it. I'll keep Crofts away. I'll not trouble you much: you see I have to be constantly running about from one place to another. Youll be quit of me altogether when I die.

VIVIE. No: I am my mother's daughter. I am like you: I must have work, and must make more money than I spend. But my work is not your work, and my way not your way. We must part. It will not make much difference to us: instead of meeting one another for perhaps a few months in twenty years, we shall never meet: thats all.

MRS WARREN *[her voice stifled in tears]* Vivie: I meant to have been more with you: I did indeed.

VIVIE. It's no use, mother: I am not to be changed by a few cheap tears and entreaties any more than you are, I daresay.

MRS WARREN *[wildly]* Oh, you call a mother's tears cheap.

VIVIE. They cost you nothing; and you ask me to give you the peace and quietness of my whole life in exchange for them. What use would my company be to you if you could get it? What have we two in common that could make either of us happy together?

WHAT DO THE PEOPLE THAT TAUGHT YOU KNOW ABOUT LIFE, OR ABOUT PEOPLE LIKE ME? WHEN DID THEY EVER MEET ME, OR SPEAK TO ME, OR LET ANYONE TELL THEM ABOUT ME? THE FOOLS! WOULD THEY EVER HAVE DONE ANYTHING FOR YOU IF I HADNT PAID THEM?

MRS WARREN *[lapsing recklessly into her dialect]* We're mother and daughter. I want my daughter. Ive a right to you. Who is to care for me when I'm old? Plenty of girls have taken to me like daughters and cried at leaving me; but I let them all go because I had you to look forward to. I kept myself lonely for you. Youve no right to turn on me now and refuse to do your duty as a daughter.

VIVIE *[jarred and antagonized by the echo of the slums in her mother's voice]* My duty as a daughter! I thought we should come to that presently. Now once for all, mother, you want a daughter and Frank wants a wife. I dont want a mother; and I dont want a husband. I have spared neither Frank nor myself in sending him about his business. Do you think I will spare you?

MRS WARREN *[violently]* Oh, I know the sort you are: no mercy for yourself or anyone else. I know. My experience has done that for me anyhow: I can tell the pious, canting, hard, selfish woman when I meet her. Well, keep yourself to yourself: I dont want you. But listen to this. Do you know what I would do with you if you were a baby again? aye, as sure as theres a Heaven above us.

VIVIE. Strangle me, perhaps.

MRS WARREN. No: I'd bring you up to be a real daughter to me, and not what you are now, with your pride and your prejudices and the college education you stole from me: yes, stole: deny it if you can: what was it but stealing? I'd bring you up in my own house, I would.

VIVIE *[quietly]* In one of your own houses.

MRS WARREN *[screaming]* Listen to her! listen to how she spits on her mother's grey hairs! Oh, may you live to have your own daughter tear and trample on you as you have trampled on me. And you will: you will. No woman ever had luck with a mother's curse on her.

VIVIE. I wish you wouldnt rant, mother. It only hardens me. Come: I suppose I am the only young woman you ever had in your power that you did good to. Dont spoil it all now.

MRS WARREN. Yes, Heaven forgive me, it's true; and you are the only one that ever turned on me. Oh, the injustice of it! the injustice! the injustice! I always wanted to be a good woman. I tried honest work; and I was slave-driven until I cursed the day I ever heard of honest work. I was a good mother; and because I made my daughter a good woman she turns me out as if I was a leper. Oh, if I only had my life to live over again! I'd talk to that lying clergyman in the school. From this time forth, so help me Heaven in my last hour, I'll do wrong and nothing but wrong. And I'll prosper on it.

VIVIE: Yes: it's better to choose your line and go through with it. If I had been you, mother, I might have done as you did: but I should not have lived one life and believed in another. You are a conventional woman at heart. That is why I am bidding you goodbye now. I am right, am I not?

MRS WARREN *[taken aback]* Right to throw away all my money?

VIVIE. No: right to get rid of you! I should be a fool not to! Isnt that so?

MRS WARREN *[sulkily]* Oh well, yes, if you come to that, I suppose you are. But Lord help the world if everybody took to doing the right thing! And now I'd better go than stay where I'm not wanted. *[She turns to the door]*.

VIVIE *[kindly]* Wont you shake hands?

MRS WARREN *[after looking at her fiercely for a moment with a savage impulse to strike her]* No, thank you. Goodbye.

VIVIE *[matter-of-factly]* Goodbye. *[Mrs Warren goes out, slamming the door behind her. The strain on Vivie's face relaxes; her grave expression breaks up into one of joyous content; her breath goes out in a half sob, half laugh of intense relief. She goes buoyantly to her place at the writing-table; pushes the electric lamp out of the way; pulls over a great sheaf of papers; and is in the act of dipping her pen in the ink when she finds Frank's note. She opens it unconcernedly and reads it quickly, giving a little laugh at some quaint turn of expression in it]*. And goodbye, Frank. *[She tears the note up and tosses the pieces into the wastepaper basket without a second thought. Then she goes at her work with a plunge, and soon becomes absorbed in its figures]*.

Saki

(Hector Hugh Munro)

(1870–1916)

The brilliant and misanthropic chronicler of Edwardian England who would become known to the world as Saki was born Hector Hugh Munro on December 18, 1870, in Akyab, Burma, where his father, Charles Augustus Munro, was Inspector General in the colonial police. When Munro's mother, Mary Frances Mercer, died two years later, Munro, along with his brother Charlie and sister Ethel, was sent back to England to live with a pair of unmarried aunts in Devonshire. It was not, by all accounts, a happy choice; the strict discipline of the household was enforced by canings and whippings and is reported to have been entirely free of affection. By the time young Munro completed his formal education—at Pencarwick School in Exmouth and Bedford grammar school—it seems that he had survived his childhood without much enjoying it.

Between Munro's seventeenth and twenty-first years, he traveled throughout Europe in the company of his father and siblings, returning in 1891 to Devon, where his father, having left the Burma police, took a job teaching school. Though Munro briefly followed in his father's footsteps, joining the Burma police in 1893, in 1896 he returned to England to take a job writing—most famously the original Reginald stories—for the *Westminster Gazette*. It was for the *Gazette* that he also wrote "The Westminster Alice," a satire of parliamentary government in the style of Lewis Carroll. Until joining the army in 1914, he focused solely on writing.

In 1900, he published his first book, a Gibbonesque history titled *The Rise of the Russian Empire*. The critics were unkind and, commencing in 1902, Munro began a six-year-long career as foreign correspondent for the *Morning Post*, working in Russia, France, and the Balkans. During this period, the world saw the first short stories published under the pseudonym "Saki" (taken from the name of a cupbearer in *The Rubaiyat of Omar Khayyam).* Though Saki produced three novels—including *When William Came,* a speculative fiction about the conquest of Britain by Germany, and *The Unbearable Bassington*—along with three plays, it is the short stories that would become the foundation for a reputation that endures to this day. Collected under the titles *Not-so Stories* (1902), *Reginald* (1904), *Reginald in Russia* (1910), *The Chronicles of Clovis* (1912), and *Beasts and Super-Beasts* (1914), they introduced such unforgettable characters as Reginald, the Baroness, and the amazing Clovis Sangrail, one of the most languidly malicious characters in all of literature.

The stories that follow—"The Reticence of Lady Anne," "The Quest," "Shock Tactics," "Hyacinth," and what is probably Saki's most frequently anthologized piece, "Tobermory"—display a cross-section of the author's most distinctive characteristics: hyperrefined malevolence, mannered speech, ironic detachment, and a touch—sometimes more like a dollop—of the macabre. The occupants of Saki's literary world are almost exclusively taken from an often witty, just as often dim-witted, but always indolent upper class. For that reason, the characters are not infrequently compared to those of P. G. Wodehouse—if not Bertie Wooster, then at least the aesthete Psmith. Nothing could be further from the truth. Wodehouse's world is sunshine incarnate compared to the mordant, seductive (and always well-bred) darkness of Saki's, whose collected stories achieve a body count that would not embarrass Edward Gorey. Whether it is the title character of "Lady Anne" driving her husband to distraction over a dinner-table argument that spills over to the drawing room, or the cat taught the power of human speech in "Tobermory," happy endings are not a reliable feature of any Saki story. Sometimes, in fact, Saki's penchant for blood (both literal and figurative) gets the better of him; in "Sredni Vashtar," a boy's pet ferret slaughters the boy's cruel cousin and guardian (a character almost certainly based on Munro's similarly cruel aunts). But more often, the tone is what Robertson Davies called "a malice without ugliness." In "The Quest," a mother exhibits "selfish absorption" regarding her missing baby, completely ignoring the worries of her houseguest—the irrepressible Clovis Sangrail—about whether hollandaise sauce is to be served with luncheon asparagus. In "Shock Tactics," Clovis returns to save his friend Bertie Heasant from his dictatorial mother (those aunts again) through a prank that is just this side of cruel. As with all of Saki's stories, they are immensely readable for their elegant style, to be sure, but also because they are hysterically funny—though with Saki, as V. S. Pritchett famously wrote, "our laughter is only a note or two short of a scream of fear."

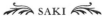

The bluff self-assurance of Edwardian England that proved such a rich source of Saki's satire perished in the trenches of World War I, and with it the satirist himself. At the outbreak of war in 1914, Munro, declining an offered commission, enlisted as a private in the 22nd Royal Fusiliers. He was posted to the Western Front in late 1915, promoted to lance-sergeant, and killed by a German sniper on August 18, 1916, during an attack on Beaumont-Hamel. His last words were reported to be, "Put that damned [*or* bloody] cigarette out!" It is, perhaps, more appropriate to close with the words of one of Saki's many fans, Christopher Morley, who wrote, "There is no greater compliment to the right kind of friend than to hand him Saki, without comment."

The Reticence of Lady Anne

Egbert came into the large, dimly lit drawing-room with the air of a man who is not certain whether he is entering a dovecote or a bomb factory, and is prepared for either eventuality. The little domestic quarrel over the luncheon-table had not been fought to a definite finish, and the question was how far Lady Anne was in a mood to renew or forgo hostilities. Her pose in the armchair by the tea-table was rather elaborately rigid; in the gloom of a December afternoon Egbert's pince-nez did not materially help him to discern the expression of her face.

By way of breaking whatever ice might be floating on the surface he made a remark about a dim religious light. He or Lady Anne were accustomed to make that remark between 4.30 and 6 on winter and late autumn evenings; it was a part of their married life. There was no recognized rejoinder to it, and Lady Anne made none.

Don Tarquinio lay astretch on the Persian rug, basking in the firelight with superb indifference to the possible ill-humour of Lady Anne. His pedigree was as flawlessly Persian as the rug, and his ruff was coming into the glory of its second winter. The page-boy, who had Renaissance tendencies, had christened him Don Tarquinio. Left to themselves, Egbert and Lady Anne would unfailingly have called him Fluff, but they were not obstinate.

Egbert poured himself out some tea. As the silence gave no sign of breaking on Lady Anne's initiative, he braced himself for another Yermak effort.

"My remark at lunch had a purely academic application," he announced; "you seem to put an unnecessarily personal significance into it."

Lady Anne maintained her defensive barrier of silence. The bullfinch lazily filled in the interval with an air from *Iphigénie en Tauride*. Egbert recognized it immediately, because it was the only air the bullfinch whistled, and he had come to them with the reputation of whistling it. Both Egbert and Lady Anne would have preferred something from *The Yeoman of the Guard*, which was their favourite opera. In matters artistic they had a similarity of taste. They leaned towards the honest and the explicit, a picture, for instance, that told its own story, with generous assistance from its title. A riderless warhorse with harness in obvious disarray, staggering into a courtyard full of pale swooning women, and marginally noted "Bad News," suggested to their minds a distinct interpretation of some military catastrophe. They could see what it was meant to convey, and explain it to friends of duller intelligence.

The silence continued. As a rule Lady Anne's displeasure became articulate and markedly voluble after four minutes of introductory muteness. Egbert seized the milk-jug and poured some of its contents in Don Tarquinio's saucer; as the saucer was already full to the brim an unsightly overflow was the result. Don Tarquinio looked on with surprised interest that evanesced into elaborate unconsciousness when he was appealed to by Egbert to come and drink up some of the spilled matter. Don Tarquinio was prepared to play many rôles in life, but a vacuum carpet-cleaner was not one of them.

"Don't you think we're being rather foolish?" Egbert said cheerfully.

If Lady Anne thought so she didn't say so.

"I daresay the fault has been partly on my side," continued Egbert, with evaporating cheerfulness. "After all, I'm only human, you know. You seem to forget that I'm only human."

He insisted on the point, as if there had been unfounded suggestions that he was built on Satyr lines, with goat continuations where the human left off.

The bullfinch recommenced its air from *Iphigénie en Tauride*. Egbert began to feel depressed. Lady Anne was not drinking her tea. Perhaps she was feeling unwell. But when Lady Anne felt unwell she was not wont to be reticent on the subject. "No one knows what I suffer from indigestion" was one of her favourite statements; but the lack of knowledge can only have been caused by defective listening; the amount of information available on the subject would have supplied material for a monograph.

Evidently Lady Anne was not feeling unwell.

Egbert began to think he was being unreasonably dealt with; naturally he began to make concessions.

"I daresay," he observed, taking as central position on the hearth-rug as Don Tarquinio could be persuaded to concede him, "I may have been to blame. I am willing, if I can thereby restore things to a happier standpoint, to undertake to lead a better life."

He wondered vaguely how it would be possible. Temptations came to him, in middle age, tentatively and without insistence, like a neglected butcher-boy who asks for a Christmas box in February for no more hopeful reason than that he didn't get one in December. He had no more idea of succumbing to them than he had of purchasing the fish-knives and fur boas that ladies are impelled to sacrifice through the medium of advertisement columns during twelve months of the year. Still, there was something impressive in the unasked-for renunciation of possibly latent enormities.

Lady Anne showed no sign of being impressed.

Egbert looked at her nervously through his glasses. To get the worst of an argument with her was no new experience. To get the worst of a monologue was a humiliating novelty.

"I shall go and dress for dinner," he announced in a voice into which he intended some shade of sternness to creep.

At the door a final access of weakness impelled him to make a final appeal.

"Aren't we being very silly?"

"A fool," was Don Tarquinio's mental comment as the door closed on Egbert's retreat. Then he lifted his velvet forepaws in the air and leapt lightly on to a bookshelf immediately under the bullfinch's cage. It was the first time he had seemed to notice the bird's existence, but he was carrying out a long-formed theory of action with the precision of mature deliberation. The bullfinch, who had fancied himself something of a despot, depressed himself of a sudden into a third of his normal displacement; then he fell to helpless wing-beating and shrill cheeping. He had cost twenty-seven shillings without the cage, but Lady Anne made no sign of interfering. She had been dead for two hours.

The Quest

An unwonted peace hung over the Villa Elsinore, broken, however, at frequent intervals, by clamorous lamentations suggestive of bewildered bereavement. The Momebys had lost their infant child; hence the peace which its absence entailed; they were looking for it in wild, undisciplined fashion, giving tongue the whole time, which accounted for the outcry which swept through house and garden whenever they returned to try the home coverts anew. Clovis, who was temporarily and unwillingly a paying guest at the villa, had been dozing in a hammock at the far end of the garden when Mrs. Momeby had broken the news to him.

"We've lost the Baby," she screamed.

"Do you mean that it's dead, or stampeded, or that you staked it at cards and lost it that way?" asked Clovis lazily.

"He was toddling about quite happily on the lawn," said Mrs. Momeby tearfully, "and Arnold had just come in, and I was asking him what sort of sauce he would like with asparagus—"

"I hope he said hollandaise," interrupted Clovis, "with a show of quickened interest, "because if there's anything I hate—"

"And all of a sudden I missed Baby," continued Mrs. Momeby in a shriller tone. "We've hunted high and low, in house and garden, and outside the gates, and he's nowhere to be seen."

"Is he anywhere to be heard?" asked Clovis; "if not, he must be at least two miles away."

"But where? And how?" asked the distracted mother.

"Perhaps an eagle or a wild beast has carried him off," suggested Clovis.

"There aren't eagles or wild beasts in Surrey," said Mrs. Momeby, but a note of horror had crept into her voice.

"They escape now and then from travelling shows. Sometimes I think they get loose for the sake of advertisement. Think what a sensational headline it would make in the local papers: 'Infant son of prominent Nonconformist devoured by spotted hyæna.' Your husband isn't a prominent Nonconformist, but his mother came of Wesleyan stock, and you must allow the newspapers some latitude."

"But we should have found his remains," sobbed Mrs. Momeby.

"If the hyæna was really hungry and not merely toying with his food there wouldn't be much in the way of remains. It would be like the small-boy-and-apple story—there ain't going to be no core."

Mrs. Momeby turned away hastily to seek comfort and counsel in some other direction. With the selfish absorption of young motherhood she entirely disregarded Clovis's obvious anxiety about the asparagus sauce. Before she had gone a yard, however, the click of the side gate caused her to pull up sharp. Miss Gilpet, from the Villa Peterhof, had come over to hear the details of the bereavement. Clovis was already rather bored with the story, but Mrs. Momeby was equipped with that merciless faculty which finds as much joy in the ninetieth time of telling as in the first.

"Arnold had just come in; he was complaining of rheumatism—"

"There are so many things to complain of in this household that it would never have occurred to me to complain of rheumatism," murmured Clovis.

"BUT IF HE'S BEING EATEN IN THE MEANTIME BY A HYÆNA AND PARTLY DIGESTED," SAID CLOVIS, WHO HUNG AFFECTIONATELY TO HIS WILD BEAST THEORY, "SURELY SOME ILL-EFFECTS WOULD BE NOTICEABLE?"

"He was complaining of rheumatism," continued Mrs. Momeby, trying to throw a chilling inflection into a voice that was already doing a good deal of sobbing and talking at high pressure as well.

She was again interrupted.

"There is no such thing as rheumatism," said Miss Gilpet. She said it with the conscious air of defiance that a waiter adopts in announcing that the cheapest-priced claret in the wine-list is no more. She did not proceed, however, to offer the alternative of some more expensive malady, but denied the existence of them all.

Mrs. Momeby's temper began to shine out through her grief.

"I suppose you'll say next that Baby hasn't really disappeared."

"He has disappeared," conceded Miss Gilpet, "but only because you haven't sufficient faith to find him. It's only lack of faith on your part that prevents him from being restored to you safe and well."

"But if he's being eaten in the meantime by a hyæna and partly digested," said Clovis, who hung affectionately to his wild beast theory, "surely some ill-effects would be noticeable?"

Miss Gilpet was rather staggered by this complication of the question.

"I feel sure that a hyæna has not eaten him," she said lamely.

"The hyæna may be equally certain that it has. You see, it may have just as much faith as you have, and more special knowledge as to the present whereabouts of the baby."

Mrs. Momeby was in tears again. "If you have faith," she sobbed, struck by a happy inspiration, "won't you find our little Erik for us? I am sure that you have powers that are denied to us.'

Rose-Marie Gilpet was thoroughly sincere in her adherence to Christian Science principles; whether she understood or correctly expounded them the learned in such manners may best decide. In the present case she was undoubtedly confronted with a great opportunity, and as she started forth on her vague search she strenuously summoned to her aid every scrap of faith that she possessed. She passed out into the bare and open high road, followed by Mrs. Momeby's warning, "It's no use going there, we've searched there a dozen times." But Rose-Marie's ears were already deaf to all things save self-congratulation; for sitting in the middle of the highway, playing contentedly with the dust and some faded buttercups, was a white-pinafored baby with a mop of tow-coloured hair tied over one temple with a pale blue ribbon. Taking first the usual feminine precaution of looking to see that no motor-car was on the distant horizon, Rose-Marie dashed at the child and bore it, despite its vigorous opposition, in through the portals of Elsinore. The child's furious screams had already announced the fact of its discovery, and the almost hysterical parents raced down the lawn to meet their restored offspring. The æsthetic value of the scene was marred in some degree by Rose-Marie's difficulty in holding the struggling infant, which was borne wrong-end foremost towards the agitated bosom of its family. "Our own little Erik come back to us," cried the Momebys in unison; as the child had rammed its fists tightly into its eye-sockets and nothing could be seen of its face but a widely gaping mouth, the recognition was in itself almost an act of faith.

"Is he glad to get back to Daddy and Mummy again?" crooned Mrs. Momeby; the preference which the child was showing for its dust and buttercup distractions was so marked that the question struck Clovis as being unnecessarily tactless.

"Give him a ride on the roly-poly," suggested the father brilliantly, as the howls continued with no sign of early abatement. In a moment the child had been placed astride the big garden roller and a preliminary tug was given to set it in motion. From the hollow depths of the cylinder came an earsplitting roar, drowning even the vocal efforts of the squalling baby, and immediately afterwards there crept forth a white-pinafored infant with a mop of tow-coloured hair tied over one temple with a pale blue ribbon. There was no mistaking either the features or the lung-power of the new arrival.

"Our own little Erik," screamed Mrs. Momeby, pouncing on him and nearly smothering him with kisses; "did he hide in the roly-poly to give us all a big fright?"

This was the obvious explanation of the child's sudden disappearance and equally abrupt discovery. There remained, however, the problem of the interloping baby, which now sat whimpering on the lawn in disfavour as chilling as its previous popularity had been unwelcome. The Momebys glared at it as though it had wormed its way into their short-lived affections by heartless and unworthy pretences. Miss Gilpet's face took on an ashen tinge as she stared helplessly at the bunched-up figure that had been such a gladsome sight to her eyes a few moments ago.

"When love is over, how little of love even the lover understands," quoted Clovis to himself.

Rose-Marie was the first to break the silence.

"If that is Erik you have in your arms, who is—that?"

"That, I think, is for you to explain," said Mrs. Momeby stiffly.

"Obviously," said Clovis, "it's a duplicate Erik that your powers of faith called into being. The question is: What are you going to do with him?"

The ashen pallor deepened in Rose-Marie's cheeks. Mrs. Momeby clutched the genuine Erik closer to her side, as though she feared her uncanny neighbour might out of sheer pique turn him into a bowl of gold-fish.

"I found him sitting in the middle of the road," said Rose-Marie weakly.

"You can't take him back and leave him there," said Clovis; "the highway is meant for traffic, not to be used as a lumber-room for disused miracles."

Rose-Marie wept. The proverb "Weep and you weep alone," broke down as badly on application as most of its kind. Both babies were wailing lugubriously, and the parent Momebys had scarcely recovered from their earlier lachrymose condition. Clovis alone maintained an unruffled cheerfulness.

"Must I keep him for always?" asked Rose-Marie dolefully.

"Not always," said Clovis consolingly; "he can go into the Navy when he's thirteen." Rose-Marie wept afresh.

"Of course," added Clovis, "there may be no end of bother about his birth certificate. You'll have to explain matters to the Admiralty, and they're dreadfully hidebound."

It was rather a relief when a breathless nursemaid from the Villa Charlotteburg over the way came running across the lawn to claim little Percy, who had slipped out of the front gate and disappeared like a twinkling from the high road.

And even then Clovis found it necessary to go in person to the kitchen to make sure about the asparagus sauce.

Shock Tactics

On a late spring afternoon Ella McCarthy sat on a green-painted chair in Kensington Gardens, staring listlessly at an uninteresting stretch of park landscape, that blossomed suddenly into tropical radiance as an expected figure appeared in the middle distance.

"Hullo, Bertie!" she exclaimed sedately, when the figure arrived at the painted chair that was the nearest neighbour to her own, and dropped into it eagerly, yet with a certain due regard for the set of its trousers; "hasn't it been a perfect spring afternoon?"

The statement was a distinct untruth as far as Ella's own feelings were concerned; until the arrival of Bertie the afternoon had been anything but perfect.

Bertie made a suitable reply, in which a questioning note seemed to hover.

"Thank you ever so much for those lovely handkerchiefs," said Ella, answering the unspoken question; "they were just what I've been wanting. There's only one thing spoilt my pleasure in your gift," she added, with a pout.

"What was that?" Bertie asked anxiously, fearful perhaps that he had chosen a size handkerchief that was not within the correct feminine limit.

"I should have liked to have written and thanked you for them as soon as I got them," said Ella, and Bertie's sky clouded at once.

"You know what mother is," he protested; "she opens all my letters, and if she found I'd been giving presents to any one there'd have been something to talk about for the next fortnight."

"Surely, at the age of twenty—" began Ella.

"I'm not twenty till September," interrupted Bertie.

"At the age of nineteen years and eight months," persisted Ella, "you might be allowed to keep your correspondence private to yourself."

"I ought to be, but things aren't always what they ought to be. Mother opens every letter that comes into the house, whoever it's for. My sisters and I have made rows about it time and again, but she goes on doing it."

"I'd find some way to stop her if I was in your place," said Ella valiantly, and Bertie felt that the glamour of his anxiously deliberated present had faded away in the disagreeable restriction that hedged round its acknowledgement.

"Is anything the matter?" asked Bertie's friend Clovis when they met that evening at the swimming-bath.

"Why do you ask?" said Bertie.

"When you wear a look of tragic gloom in a swimming-bath," said Clovis, "it's especially noticeable from the fact that you're wearing very little else. Didn't she like the handkerchiefs?"

Bertie explained the situation.

"It is rather galling, you know," he added, "when a girl has a lot of things she wants to write to you and can't send a letter except by some roundabout, unde hand way."

"One never realizes one's blessings while one enjoys them," said Clovis; "now I have to spend a considerable amount of ingenuity inventing excuses for not having written to people."

"It's not a joking matter," said Bertie resentfully: "you wouldn't find it funny if your mother opened all your letters.'

"The funny thing to me is that you should let her do it."

"I can't stop it. I've argued about it—"

"You haven't used the right kind of argument, I expect. Now, if every time one of your letters was opened you lay on your back on the dining-table during dinner and had a fit, or roused the entire family in the middle of the night to hear you recite one of Blake's 'Poems of Innocence,' you would get a far more respectful hearing for future protests. People yield more consideration to a mutilated mealtime or a broken night's rest, than ever they would to a broken heart."

"Oh, dry up," said Bertie crossly, inconsistently splashing Clovis from head to foot as he plunged into the water.

It was a day or two after the conversation in the swimming-bath that a letter addressed to Bertie Heasant slid into the letter-box at his home, and thence into the hands of his mother. Mrs. Heasant was one of those empty-minded individuals to whom other people's affairs are perpetually interesting. The more private they are intended to be the more acute is the interest they arouse. She would have opened this particular letter in any case; the fact that it was marked "private," and diffused a delicate but penetrating aroma, merely caused her to open it with headlong haste rather than matter-of-course deliberation. The harvest of sensation that rewarded her was beyond all expectations.

> "Bertie, carissimo," it began, "I wonder if you will have the nerve to do it: it will take some nerve, too. Don't forget the jewels. They

are a detail, but details interest me.

"Yours as ever,

"Clotilde.

"Your mother must not know of my existence. If questioned swear you have never heard of me."

For years Mrs. Heasant had searched Bertie's correspondence diligently for traces of possible dissipation or youthful entanglements, and at last the suspicions that had stimulated her inquisitorial zeal were justified by this one splendid haul. That any one wearing the exotic name "Clotilde" should write to Bertie under the incriminating announcement "as ever" was sufficiently electrifying, without the astounding allusion to the jewels. Mrs. Heasant could recall novels and dramas wherein jewels played an exciting and commanding rôle, and here, under her own roof, before her very eyes as it were, her own son was carrying on an intrigue in which jewels were merely an interesting detail. Bertie was not due home for another hour, but his sisters were available for the immediate unburdening of a scandal-laden mind.

"Bertie is in the toils of an adventuress," she screamed; "her name is Clotilde," she added, as if she thought they had better know the worst at once. There are occasions when more harm than good is done by shielding young girls from a knowledge of the more deplorable realities of life.

By the time Bertie arrived his mother had discussed every possible and improbable conjecture as to his guilty secret; the girls had limited themselves to the opinion that their brother had been weak rather than wicked.

"Who is Clotilde?" was the question that confronted Bertie almost before he had got into the hall. His denial of any knowledge of such a person was met with an outburst of bitter laughter.

"How well you have learned your lesson!" exclaimed Mrs. Heasant. But satire gave way to furious indignation when she realized that Bertie did not intend to throw any further light on her discovery.

"You shan't have any dinner till you've confessed everything," she stormed.

Bertie's reply took the form of hastily collecting material form an impromptu banquet from the larder and locking himself into his bedroom. His mother made frequent visits to the locked door and shouted a succession of interrogations with the persistence of one who thinks that if you ask a question often enough an answer will eventually result. Bertie did nothing to encourage the supposition.

An hour had passed in fruitless one-sided palaver when another letter addressed to Bertie and marked "private" made its appearance in the letterbox. Mrs. Heasant pounced on it with the enthusiasm of a cat that missed its mouse and to whom a second has been unexpectedly vouchsafed. If she hoped for further disclosures assuredly she was not disappointed.

> "So you have really done it!" the letter abruptly commenced; "Poor Dagmar. Now she is done for I almost pity her. You did it very well, you wicked boy, the servants think it was suicide, and there will be no fuss. Better not touch the jewels till after the inquest.
>
> "Clotilde."

Anything that Mrs. Heasant had previously done in the way of outcry was easily surpassed as she raced upstairs and beat frantically at her son's door.

"Miserable boy, what have you done to Dagmar?"

"It's Dagmar now, is it?" he snapped; "it will be Geraldine next."

"That it should come to this after all my efforts to keep you at home of an evening," sobbed Mrs. Heasant; "it's no use you trying to hide things from me; Clotilde's letter betrays everything."

"Does it betray who she is?" asked Bertie. "I've heard so much about her, I should like to know something about her home-life. Seriously, if you go on like this I shall fetch a doctor; I've often enough been preached at about nothing, but I've never had an imaginary harem dragged into the discussion."

"Are these letters imaginary?" screamed Mrs. Heasant. "What about the jewels, and Dagmar, and the theory of suicide?"

No solution of these problems was forthcoming through the bedroom door, but the last post of the evening produced another letter for Bertie, and its contents brought Mrs. Heasant the enlightenment which had already dawned on her son.

> "Dear Bertie," it ran; "I hope I haven't distracted your brain with the spoof letters I've been sending in the name of a fictitious Clotilde. You told me the other day that the servants, or somebody at your home, tampered with your letters, so I thought I would give any one that opened them something exciting to read. The shock might do them good.
>
> "Yours,
>
> "Clovis Sangrail."

Mrs. Heasant knew Clovis slightly, and was rather afraid of him. It was not difficult to read between the lines of his successful hoax. In a chastened mood she rapped once more at Bertie's door.

"A letter from Mr. Sangrail. It's all been a stupid hoax. He wrote those other letters. Why, where are you going?"

Bertie had opened the door; he had on his hat and overcoat.

"I'm going for the doctor to come and see if anything's the matter with you. Of course it was all a hoax, but no person in his right mind could have believed all that rubbish about murder and suicide and jewels. You've been making enough noise to bring the house down for the last hour or two."

"But what was I to think of those letters?" whimpered Mrs. Heasant.

"I should have known what to think of them," said Bertie; "if you choose to excite yourself over other people's correspondence it's your own fault. Anyhow, I'm going for a doctor."

It was Bertie's great opportunity, and he knew it. His mother was rather conscious of the fact that she would look rather ridiculous if the story got about. She was willing to pay the hush-money.

"I'll never open your letters again," she promised.

And Clovis has no more devoted slave than Bertie Heasant.

Hyacinth

"The new fashion of introducing the candidate's children into an election contest is a pretty one," said Mrs. Panstreppon; "it takes something away from the acerbity of party warfare, and it makes an interesting experience for the children to look back on in after years. Still, if you will listen to my advice, Matilda, you will not take Hyacinth with you down to Luffbridge on election day."

"Not take Hyacinth!" exclaimed his mother; "but why not? Jutterly is bringing his three children, and they are going to drive a pair of Nubian donkeys about the town, to emphasize the fact that their father has been appointed Colonial Secretary. We are making the demand for a strong Navy a special feature in *our* campaign, and it will be particularly appropriate to have Hyacinth dressed in his sailor suit. He'll look heavenly."

"The question is, not how he'll look, but how he'll behave. He's a delightful child, of course, but there is a strain of unbridled pugnacity in him that breaks out at times in a really alarming fashion. You may have forgotten the affair of the little Gaffin children; I haven't."

"I was in India at the time, and I've only a vague recollection of what happened; he was very naughty, I know."

"He was in his goat-carriage, and met the Gaffins in their perambulator, and he drove the goat full tilt at them and sent the perambulator spinning. Little Jacky Gaffin was pinned down under the wreckage, and while the nurse had her hands full with the goat Hyacinth was laying into Jacky's legs with his belt like a small fury."

"I'm not defending him," said Matilda, "but they must have done something to annoy him."

"Nothing intentionally, but some one had unfortunately told him that they were half French—their mother was a Duboc, you know—and he had been having a history lesson that morning, and had just heard of the final loss of Calais by the English, and was furious about it. He said he'd teach the little toads to go snatching towns from us, but we didn't know at the time he was referring to the Gaffins. I told him afterwards that all bad feeling between the two nations had died out long ago, and that anyhow the Gaffins were only half French, and he said it was only the French half of Jacky that he had been hitting; the rest had been buried under the perambulator. If the loss of Calais unloosed such a fury in him, I tremble to think what the possible loss of the election might entail."

"All that happened when he was eight; he's older know and knows better."

"Children with Hyacinth's temperament don't know better as they grow older; they merely know more."

"Nonsense. He will enjoy the fun of the election, and in any case he'll be tired out by the time the poll is declared, and the new sailor suit that I've made for him is just in the right shade of blue for our election colours, and it will exactly match the blue of his eyes. He will be a perfectly charming note of colour."

"There is such a thing as letting æsthetic sense override one's moral sense," said Mrs. Panstreppon. "I believe you would have condoned the South Sea Bubble and the persecution of the Albigenses if they had been carried out in effective colour schemes. However, if anything unfortunate should happen down at Luffbridge, don't say it wasn't foreseen by one member of the family.

The election was keenly but decorously contested. The newly appointed Colonial Secretary was personally popular, while the Government to which he adhered was distinctly unpopular, and there was some expectancy that the majority of four hundred, obtained at the last election, would be altogether wiped out. Both sides were hopeful, but neither could feel confident. The children were a great success; the little Jutterlys drove their chubby donkeys solemnly up and down the main streets, displaying posters which advocated the claims of their father, while as for Hyacinth, his conduct might have served as a model for any seraph-child that had strayed unwittingly onto the scene of an electoral contest. Of his own accord, and under the delighted eyes of half a dozen camera operators, he had gone up to the Jutterly children and presented them with a packet of butterscotch; "we needn't be enemies because we're wearing the opposite colours," he said with engaging friendliness, and the occupants of the donkey-cart accepted his offering with polite solemnity. The grown-up members of both political camps were delighted at the incident—with the exception of Mrs. Panstreppon, who shuddered.

"Never was Clytemnestra's kiss sweeter than on the night she slew me," she quoted, but made the quotation to herself.

The last hour of the poll was a period of unremitting labour for both parties; it was generally estimated that not more than a dozen votes separated the candidates, and every effort was made to bring up obstinately wavering electors. It was with a feeling of relaxation and relief that every one heard the clocks strike the hour for the close of the poll. Exclamations broke out from the tired workers, and corks flew out from bottles.

"Well, if we haven't won, we've done our level best." "It has been a clean, straight fight, with no rancour." "The children were quite a charming feature, weren't they?"

The children? It suddenly occurred to everybody that they had seen nothing of the children for the last hour. What had become of the three little Jutterlys and their donkey-cart, and, for the matter of that, what had become of Hyacinth? Hurried, anxious embassies went backwards and forwards between the respective party headquarters and the various committee-rooms, but there was blank ignorance everywhere as to the whereabouts of the children. Everyone had been too busy in the closing moments of the poll to bestow a thought on them. Then there came a telephone call at the Unionist Women's Committee-rooms, and the voice of Hyacinth was heard demanding when the poll would be declared.

"Where are you, and where are the Jutterly children?" asked his mother.

"I've just finished having high-tea at a pastry-cook's" came the answer; "and they let me telelphone. I've had a poached egg and a sausage roll and four meringues."

"You'll be ill. Are the little Jutterlys with you?"

"Rather not. They're in a pigsty."

"A pigsty? Why? What pigsty?"

"Near the Crawleigh Road. I met them driving about a back road, and told them they were to have tea with me, and put their donkeys in a yard that I knew of. Then I took them to see an old sow that had got ten little pigs. I got the sow into the outer sty by giving her bits of bread, while the Jutterlys went in to look at the litter, then I bolted the door and left them there."

"You wicked boy, do you mean to say that you've left those poor children there alone in the pigsty?"

"They're not alone, they've got ten little pigs in with them; they're jolly well crowded. They were pretty mad at being shut in, but not half as mad as the old sow is at being shut out from her young ones. If she gets in while they're their she'll bite them into mincemeat. I can get them out by letting a short ladder down through the top window, and that's what I'm going to do *if we win*. If their blighted father gets in, I'm just going to open the door for the sow, and let her do what she dashed well likes to them. That's why I want to know when the poll will be declared."

Here the narrator rang off. A wild stampede and frantic sending-off of messengers took place at other end of the telephone. Nearly all the workers on either side had disappeared to various club-rooms and public-house bars to await the declaration of the poll, but enough local information could be secured to determine the scene of Hyacinth's exploit. Mr. John Ball had a stable yard down near the Crawleigh Road, up a short lane, and his sow was known to have a litter of ten young ones. Thither went in headlong haste both the candidates, Hyacinth's mother, his aunt (Mrs. Panstreppon), and two or three hurriedly summoned friends. The two Nubian donkeys, contentedly munching at bundles of hay, met their gaze as they entered the yard. The hoarse savage grunting of an enraged animal and the shriller note of thirteen young voices, three of them human, guided them to the sty, in the outer yard of which a huge Yorkshire sow kept up a ceaseless raging patrol before a closed door. Reclining on the broad edge of an open window, from which point of vantage he could reach down and shoot the bolt of the door, was Hyacinth, his blue sailor-suit somewhat the worse for wear, and his angel smile exchanged for a look of demoniacal determination.

"If any of you come a step nearer," he shouted, "the sow will be inside in half a jiffy."

A storm of threatening, arguing, entreating expostulation broke from the baffled rescue party, but it made no more impression on Hyacinth than the squealing tempest that raged within the sty.

"If Jutterly heads the poll I'm going to let the sow in. I'll teach the blighters to win elections from us."

"He means it," said Mrs. Panstreppon; "I feared the worst when I saw that butterscotch incident."

"It's all right, my little man," said Jutterly, with the duplicity to which even a Colonial Secretary can sometimes stoop, "your father has been elected by a large majority."

"Liar!" retorted Hyacinth, with the directness of speech that is not merely excusable, but almost obligatory, in the political profession; "the votes aren't counted yet. You won't gammon me as to the result, either. A boy that I've palled with is going to fire a gun when the poll is declared; two shots if we've won, one shot if we haven't."

The situation began to look critical. "Drug the sow," whispered Hyacinth's father.

Some one went off in the motor to the nearest chemist's shop and returned presently with two large pieces of bread, liberally dosed with narcotic. The bread was thrown deftly and unostentatiously into the sty, but Hyacinth saw through this manœuvre. He set up a piercing imitation of a small pig in Purgatory, and the infuriated mother ramped round and round the sty; the pieces of bread were trampled into slush.

At any moment now the poll might be declared. Jutterly flew back to the Town Hall, where the votes were being counted. His agent met him with a smile of hope.

"You're eleven ahead at present, and only about eight more to be counted; you're just going to squeak through."

"I mustn't squeak through," exclaimed Jutterly hoarsely. "You must object to every doubtful vote on our side that can possibly be disallowed. I must *not* have the majority."

Then was seen the unprecedented sight of a party agent challenging the votes on his side with a captiousness that his opponents would have hesitated to display. One or two votes that certainly would have passed muster under ordinary circumstances were disallowed, but even so Jutterly was six a head with only thirty more to be counted.

To the watchers by the sty the moments seemed intolerable. As a last resort, some one had been sent for a gun with which to shoot the sow, though Hyacinth would probably draw the bolt the moment such a weapon was brought into the yard. Nearly all the men were away from their home, however, on election night, and the messenger had evidently gone far afield in his search. It must be a matter of minutes now to the declaration of the poll.

A sudden roar of shouting and cheering was heard from the direction of the Town Hall. Hyacinth's father clutched a pitchfork and prepared to dash into the sty in the forlorn hope of being on time.

A shot rang out in the evening air. Hyacinth stooped down from his perch and put his finger on the bolt. The sow pressed furiously against the door.

"Bang!" came another shot.

Hyacinth wriggled back and sent a short ladder down through the window of the inner sty.

"Now you can come up, you unclean little blighters," he sang out; "my daddy's got in, not yours. Hurry up, I can't keep the sow waiting much longer. And don't you jolly well come butting into any election again where I'm on the job."

In the reaction that set in after the deliverance furious recriminations were indulged in by the lately opposed candidates, their women folk, agents, and party helpers. A recount was demanded, but failed to establish the fact that the Colonial Secretary had obtained a majority. Altogether the election left a legacy of soreness behind it, apart from any that was experienced by Hyacinth in person.

"It is the last time I shall let him go to an election," exclaimed his mother.

"There I think you are going to extremes," said Mrs. Panstreppon; "if there should be a general election in Mexico I think you might safely let him go there, but I doubt whether our English politics are suited to the rough and tumble of an angel-child."

Tobermory

It was a chill, rain-washed afternoon of a late August day, that indefinite season when partridges are still in security or cold storage, and there is nothing to hunt—unless one is bounded on the north by the Bristol Channel, in which case one may lawfully gallop after fat red stags. Lady Blemley's house-party was not bounded on the north by the Bristol Channel, hence there was a full gathering of her gifts round the tea-table on this particular afternoon. And, in spite of the blankness of the season and the triteness of the occasion, there was no trace in the company of that fatigued restlessness which means a dread of the pianola and a subdued hankering for auction bridge. The undisguised open-mouthed attention of the entire party was fixed on the homely negative personality of Mr. Cornelius Appin. Of all her guests, he was the one who had come to Lady Blemley with the vaguest reputation. Some one had said that he was "clever," and he had got his invitation in the moderate expectation, on the part of his hostess, that some portion of his cleverness would be contributed to the general entertainment. Until tea-time that day she had been unable to discover in what direction, if any, his cleverness lay. He was neither a wit nor a croquet champion, a hypnotic force nor a begetter of amateur theatricals. Neither did his exterior suggest the sort of man in whom women are willing to pardon a generous measure of mental deficiency. He had subsided into mere Mr. Appin, and the Cornelius seemed a piece of transparent baptismal bluff. And now he was claiming to have launched on the world a discovery beside which the invention of gunpowder, of the printing press, and of steam locomotion were inconsiderable trifles. Science had made bewildering strides in many directions during recent decades, but this thing seemed to belong to the domain of miracle rather than scientific achievement.

"And do you really ask us to believe," Sir Wilfrid was saying, "that you have discovered a means for instructing animals in the art of human speech, and that dear old Tobermory has proved your first successful pupil?"

"It is a problem at which I have worked for the last seventeen years," said Mr. Appin, "but only during the last eight or nine months have I been rewarded with glimmerings of success. Of course I have experimented with thousands of animals, but latterly only with cats, those wonderful creatures which have assimilated themselves so marvellously with our civilization while retaining all their highly developed feral instincts. Here and there among cats one comes across an outstanding superior intellect, just as one does among the ruck of human beings, and when I made the acquaintance of Tobermory a week ago I saw at once that I was in contact with a 'Beyond-cat' of extraordinary intelligence. I had gone far along the road to success in recent experiments; with Tobermory, as you call him, I have reached the goal."

Mr. Appin concluded his remarkable statement in a voice which he strove to divest of a triumphant inflection. No one said "Rats," though Clovis's lips moved in a monosyllabic contortion which probably invoked those rodents of disbelief.

"And do you mean to say," asked Miss Resker, after a slight pause, "that you have taught Tobermory to say and understand easy sentences of one syllable?"

"My dear Miss Resker," said the wonder-worker patiently, "one teaches little children and savages and backward adults in that piecemeal fashion; when one has once solved the problem of making a beginning with an animal of highly developed intelligence one has no need for those halting methods. Tobermory can speak our language with perfect correctness."

This time Clovis very distinctly said, "Beyond-rats!" Sir Wilfrid was more polite but equally sceptical.

"Hadn't we better have the cat in and judge for ourselves?" suggested Lady Blemley.

Sir Wilfrid went in search of the animal, and the company settled themselves down to the languid expectation of witnessing some more or less adroit drawing-room ventriloquism.

In a minute Sir Wilfrid was back in the room, his face white beneath its tan and his eyes dilated with excitement.

"By Gad, it's true!"

His agitation was unmistakably genuine, and his hearers started forward in a thrill of awakened interest.

Collapsing into an armchair he continued breathlessly: "I found him dozing in the smoking-room and called out to him to come for his tea. He blinked at me in his usual way, and I said, "Come on Toby; don't keep us waiting'; and by Gad! he drawled out in a most horribly natural voice that he'd come when he dashed well pleased! I nearly jumped out of my skin!"

Appin had preached to absolutely incredulous hearers; Sir Wilfrid's statement carried instant conviction. A Babel-like chorus of startled exclamation arose, amid which the scientist sat mutely enjoying the first fruit of his stupendous discovery.

In the midst of the clamour Tobermory entered the room and made his way with velvet tread and studied unconcern across to the group seated round the tea-table.

A sudden hush of awkwardness and constraint fell on the company. Somehow there seemed an element of embarrassment in addressing on equal terms a domestic cat of acknowledged dental ability.

"Will you have some milk, Tobermory?" asked Lady Blemley in a rather strained voice.

"I don't mind if I do," was the response, couched in a tone of even indifference. A shiver of suppressed excitement went through the listeners, and Lady Blemley might be excused for pouring out the saucerful of milk rather unsteadily.

"I'm afraid I've spilt a good deal of it," she said apologetically.

"After all, it's not my Axminster," was Tobermory's rejoinder.

Another silence fell on the group, and then Miss Resker, in her best district-visitor manner, asked if the human language had been difficult to learn. Tobermory looked squarely at her for a moment and then fixed his gaze serenely on the middle distance. It was obvious that boring questions lay outside his scheme of life.

"What do you think of human intelligence?" asked Mavis Pellington lamely.

"Of whose intelligence in particular?" asked Tobermory coldly.

"Oh, well, mine for instance," said Mavis, with a feeble laugh.

"You put me in an embarrassing position," said Tobermory, whose tone and attitude certainly did not suggest a shred of embarrassment. "When your inclusion in this house-party was suggested Sir Wilfrid protested that you were the most brainless woman of his acquaintance, and that there was a wide distinction between hospitality and the care of the feeble-minded. Lady Blemley replied that your lack of brain-power was the precise quality which had earned you your invitation, as you were the only person she could think of who might be idiotic enough to buy their old car. You know, the one they call 'The Envy of Sisyphus,' because it goes quite nicely up-hill if you push it."

Lady Blemley's protestations would have had greater effect if she had not casually suggested to Mavis only that morning that the car in question would be just the thing for her down at her Devonshire home.

Major Barfield plunged in heavily to effect a diversion.

"How about your carryings-on with the tortoise-shell puss up at the stables, eh?"

The moment he had said it every one realized the blunder.

"One does not usually discuss these matters in public," said Tobermory frigidly. "From a slight observation of your ways since you've been in this house I should imagine you'd find it inconvenient if I were to shift the conversation on to your own little affairs."

The panic which ensued was not confined to the Major.

"Would you like to go and see if cook has got your dinner ready?" suggested Lady Blemley hurriedly, affecting to ignore the fact that it wanted at least two hours to Tobermory's dinner-time.

"Thanks," said Tobermory, "not quite so soon after my tea. I don't want to die of indigestion."

"Cats have nine lives, you know," said Sir Wilfrid heartily.

"Possibly," answered Tobermory; "but only one liver."

"Adelaide!" said Mrs. Cornett, "do you mean to encourage that cat to go out and gossip about us in the servants' hall?"

The panic had indeed become general. A narrow ornamental balustrade ran in front of most of the bedroom windows at the Towers, and it was recalled with dismay that this had formed a favourite promenade for Tobermory at all hours, whence he could watch the pigeons—and heaven knew what else besides. If he intended to become reminiscent in his present outspoken strain the effect would be something more than disconcerting. Mrs. Cornett, who had spent much of her time at her toilet table, and whose complexion was reputed to be of a nomadic though punctual disposition, looked as ill at ease as the Major. Miss Scrawen, who wrote fiercely sensuous poetry and led a blameless life, merely displayed irritation; if you are methodical and virtuous in private you don't necessarily want every one to know it. Bertie van Than, who was so depraved at seventeen that he had long ago given up trying to be any worse, turned a dull shade of gardenia white, but he did not commit the error of dashing out of the room like Odo Finsberry, a young gentleman who was understood to be reading for the Church and who was possibly disturbed at the thought of scandals he might hear concerning other people. Clovis had the presence of mind to maintain a composed exterior; privately he was calculating how long it would take to procure a box of fancy mice through the agency of the *Exchange and Mart* as a species of hush money.

"CATS HAVE NINE LIVES, YOU KNOW," SAID SIR WILFRID HEARTILY. "POSSIBLY," ANSWERED TOBERMORY; "BUT ONLY ONE LIVER."

Even in a delicate situation like the present, Agnes Resker could not endure to remain too long in the background.

"Why did I ever come down here?" she asked dramatically.

Tobermory immediately accepted the opening.

"Judging by what you said to Mrs. Cornett on the croquet-lawn yesterday, you were out for food. You described the Blemleys as the dullest people to stay with that you knew, but said they were clever enough to employ a first-rate cook; otherwise they'd find it difficult to get anyone to come down a second time."

"There's not a word of truth in it! I appeal to Mrs. Cornett—" exclaimed the discomfited Agnes.

"Mrs. Cornett repeated your remark afterwards to Bertie van Than," continued Tobermory, "and said, 'That woman is a regular Hunger Marcher; she'd go anywhere for four square meals a day,' and Bertie van Than said—"

At this point the chronicle mercifully ceased. Tobermory had caught a glimpse of the big yellow Tom from the Rectory working his way through the shrubbery towards the stable wing. In a flash he vanished through the open French window.

With the disappearance of his too brilliant pupil Cornelius Appin found himself beset by a hurricane of bitter upbraiding, anxious inquiry, and frightened entreaty. The responsibility for the situation lay with him, and he must prevent matters from becoming worse. Could Tobermory impart his dangerous gifts to other cats? was the first question he'd have to answer. It was possible, he replied, that he might have initiated his intimate friend the stable puss into his new accomplishment, but it was unlikely that his teaching could have taken a wider range as yet.

"Then," said Mrs. Cornett, "Tobermory may be a valuable cat and a great pet; but I'm sure you'll agree, Adelaide, that both he and the stable cat must be done away with without delay."

"You don't suppose I've enjoyed the last quarter of an hour, do you?" said Lady Blemley bitterly. "My husband and I are very fond of Tobermory—at least, we were before this horrible accomplishment was infused into him; but now, of course, the only thing is to have him destroyed as soon as possible.

"We can put some strychnine in the scraps he always gets at dinner-time," said Sir Wilfrid, "and I will go drown the stable cat myself. The coachman will be very sore at losing his pet, but I'll say a very catching form of mange has broken out in both cats and we're afraid of spreading it to the kennels."

"But my great discovery!" expostulated Mr. Appin; "after all my years of research and experiment—"

"You can go experiment on the short-horns at the farm, who are under proper control," said Mrs. Cornett, "or the elephants at the Zoological Gardens. They're said to be highly intelligent, and they have this recommendation, that they don't come creeping about our bedrooms and under chairs, and so forth."

An archangel ecstatically proclaiming the Millennium, and then finding that it clashed unpardonably with Henley and would have to be indefinitely postponed, could hardly have felt more crestfallen than Cornelius Appin at the reception of his wonderful achievement. Public opinion, however, was against him—in fact, had the general voice been consulted on the subject it is probable that a strong minority vote would have been in favour of including him in the strychnine diet.

Defective train arrangements and a nervous desire to see matters brought to a finish prevented an immediate dispersal of the party, but dinner that evening was not a social success. Sir Wilfrid had rather a trying time with the stable cat and subsequently with the coachmen. Agnes Resker ostentatiously limited her repast to a morsel of dry toast, which she bit as though it were a personal enemy; while Mavis Pellington maintained a vindictive silence throughout the meal. Lady Blemley kept up a flow of what she hoped was conversation, but her attention was fixed on the doorway. A plateful of carefully dosed fish scraps was in readiness on the sideboard, but sweets and savoury and dessert went their way, and no Tobermory appeared either in the dining-room or kitchen.

The sepulchral dinner was cheerful compared with the subsequent vigil in the smoking-room. Eating and drinking had at least supplied a distraction and cloak to the prevailing embarrassment. Bridge was out of the question in the general tension of nerves and tempers, and after Odo Finsberry had given a lugubrious rendering of "Mélisande in the Wood" to a frigid audience, music was tacitly avoided. At eleven the servants went to bed, announcing that the small window in the pantry had been left open as usual for Tobermory's private use. The guests read steadily through the current batch of magazines, and fell back gradually on the "Badminton Library" and bound volumes of *Punch*. Lady Blemley made periodic visits to the pantry, returning each time with an expression of listless depression which forestalled questioning.

At two o'clock Clovis broke the dominating silence.

"He won't turn up tonight. He's probably in the local newspaper office at the present moment, dictating the first installment of his reminiscences. Lady What's-her-name's book won't be in it. It will be the event of the day."

Having made this contribution to the general cheerfulness, Clovis went to bed. At long intervals the various members of the house-party followed his example.

The servants taking round the early tea made a uniform announcement in reply to a uniform question. Tobermory had not returned.

Breakfast was, if anything, a more unpleasant function than dinner had been, but before its conclusion the situation was relieved. Tobermory's corpse was brought in from the shrubbery, where a gardener had just discovered it. From the bites on his throat and the yellow fur which coated his claws it was evident that he had fallen in unequal combat with the big Tom from the Rectory.

By midday most of the guests had quitted the Towers, and after lunch Lady Blemley had sufficiently recovered her spirits to write an extremely nasty letter to the Rectory about the loss of her valuable pet.

Tobermory had been Appin's one successful pupil, and he was destined to have no successor. A few weeks later an elephant in the Dresden Zoological Garden, which had shown no previous sign of irritability, broke loose and killed an Englishman who had apparently been teasing it. The victim's name was variously reported in the papers as Oppin and Eppelin, but his front name was faithfully rendered Cornelius.

"If he was trying German irregular verbs on the poor beast," said Clovis, "he deserved all he got."

Flann O'Brien

(Brian O'Nolan)

(1911–1966)

Flann O'Brien was a short-story writer, novelist, and, in the guise of Myles na gCopaleen, wrote what S. J. Perelman and James Thurber rated the funniest newspaper column ever published. He was born Brian O'Nolan on October 5, 1911, in County Tyrone, Ireland. The family moved to Strabane in 1917. He and his brothers, Kevin and Ciaran, spoke only Gaelic until age ten, picking up a little English here and there despite their father's attempts to keep any such influences away from the brothers. No good Gaelic-speaking school could be found for the Nolan boys, so they were kept out of school for years. The father finally gave up and sent the boys to a Christian Brothers school where the only language was English. The family relocated to Dublin in 1923.

O'Brien spent two years at Black Rock College, then studied at University College in Dublin. While a student at university, O'Brien was charged with publishing obscene matter in the native Irish tongue in the college magazine. Fortunately neither the editor of the magazine nor the college president could read Irish. So although O'Brien was thought of as guilty, he went unpunished because of his superior scholarship. He earned a bachelor of arts degree in 1932, went on to receive a master's degree, and achieved quite a following as a member of the debating society.

When he left University College, O'Brien had not yet decided on a career. As his father had been a civil servant with good benefits and security, he thought he might give that line of work a try. There were only three civil appointments available and these were highly coveted positions, sought by hundreds of applicants. O'Brien easily passed the two exams, one in spoken Gaelic and one in general knowledge, two areas in which O'Brien excelled. He was given one of the three jobs.

After a probationary period, he was all set to relax and enjoy a life without financial worries when his father had a fatal stroke. Overnight, O'Brien became responsible for his ten siblings and mother. At the time he accepted the civil service job, he had also begun work on *At-Swim-Two-Birds.* This complex, inventive first novel was quietly published in 1939 and only upon its reissue in 1960 did it garner extensive attention and praise. It has been called "*the* major work of Irish prose after Ulysses."

O'Brien married Evelyn McDonnell on December 2, 1948. It was a quiet ceremony at the Church of Our Immaculate Lady of Refuge, with no guests but for the witnesses. He had met Evelyn, a typist, in the civil service a year earlier. She knew early on that he was Myles na gCopaleen of the *Irish Times* and thought his column was brilliant. She also had admired the direct style of his memos and reports that she had a chance to read as they passed through her section. She did not realize the extent of his drinking until after they were married but she apparently was able to cope with his condition.

O'Brien worked as a civil servant until 1953, playing the good worker in the Irish government by day and using his nights, weekends, and holidays to produce his wildly irreverent column for the *Irish Times.* His first column appeared in October 1940. As Myles na gCopaleen, he wrote his "Cruiskeen Lawn" column (cruiskeen lawn is a Gaelic phrase for "brimming jug") for twenty-six years. His column was reminiscent of H. L. Mencken, though it is said that he preferred to be viewed as an Irish Mark Twain, illustrating his ideas and inventions with colorful, dubious tales and anecdotes.

O'Brien's other books include *The Poor Mouth* (*An Beal Bocht*, written in Gaelic in 1941), *The Hard Life* (1961), *The Dalkey Archive* (1964), *The Third Policeman* (1967), and two collection of his newspaper columns titled *The Best of Myles* (1968) and *The Hair of the Dogma* (1977).

O'Brien died on April Fool's Day in 1966 in Dublin, from an assortment of alcohol-related maladies. He left behind his wife, Evelyn, and his two brothers, Kevin and Ciaran, also writers.

William Trevor once said, "Myles na gCopaleen wrote as Flann O'Brien, an identity that disguises one of Ireland's most inventive, and perceptive, novelists. But it required little perception to pinpoint the Irish passion for peopling bus stops or any other mundane setting with colourful characters, and for retelling, with innate ease, episodes of interest, wait till you've heard this." The following selection from *The Best of Myles* is a series of columns devoted to making the uninformed and ignorant appear less so through deception. "Myles" is humorously offering two services to those with money but without erudition. The first is "book-handling," to make your books seem thoroughly perused and pored over. "Popular handling—Each volume to be well and truly handled, four leaves in each to be dog-eared, and a tram-ticket, cloak-room docket . . . inserted as a forgotten bookmark." He suggests four levels of handling with a sliding price scale so "no person need appear ignorant or unlettered merely because he or she is poor. Not every vulgar person is, remember, wealthy."

The books can also be given phony inscriptions: "from your devoted friend and follower, K. Marx." Or astute comments in the margins: "I remember poor Joyce saying the very same thing to me."

The second phase in the quest for instant intelligence is the provision of a ventriloquist on excursions out for the verbally inept (presumably a veiled homage to Swift's *Gulliver's Travels,* in which servants use bellows to simulate their masters' voices). Say you are not well read but still want to be perceived as clever. The Myles na gCopaleen Escort Service is the answer, employing out-of-work ventriloquists. These trained professionals hold up both ends of the conversation, so those eavesdropping hear learned banter. "If you are dumb, you hire one of our ventriloquists to accompany you to public places, and he does absolutely all the talking." But ultimately these little set-ups do go awry, with renegade ventriloquists threatening to make people sound stupid or vulgar if they don't pay up.

O'Brien's humor was more bookish than pedestrian, more ironic than lyrical. But he did not use his education as a bludgeon. To O'Brien, a willful lack of interest in learning and reading seems to be the ultimate crime. People who wish to appear clever without the effort (and surround themselves with accoutrements of intelligence without having earned them) are his satirical targets. Also included in that group are the people who *are* well versed in art, music, and books, and feel somehow superior to the average pub-goer. To O'Brien, the phony aspirants and those they are aspiring to be are in the same barrel of bad apples.

In 1964, O'Brien wrote this dedication in the last book he saw published. It is addressed to an angel, though it could apply to any of his pub pals:

> I dedicate these pages
> To my Guardian Angel,
> Impressing upon him
> That I'm only fooling and warning him

To see to it that
There is no misunderstanding
When I go home.

Selections from the Irish Times

Buchhandlung

A VISIT THAT I paid to the house of a newly-married friend the other day set me thinking. My friend is a man of great wealth and vulgarity. When he had me set about buying bedsteads, tables, chairs, and what-not, it occurred to him to also buy a library. Whether he can read or not, I do not know, but some savage faculty for observation told him that most respectable and estimable people usually had a lot of books in their houses. So he bought several book-cases and paid some rascally middleman to stuff them with all manner of new books, some of them very costly volumes on the subject of French landscape painting.

I noticed on my visit that not one of them had ever been opened or touched, and remarked the fact.

"When I get settled down properly," said the fool, "I'll have to catch up on my reading."

This is what set me thinking. Why should a wealthy person like this be put to the trouble of pretending to read at all? Why not a professional book-handler to go in and suitably maul his library for so-much per shelf? Such a person, if properly qualified, could make a fortune.

Dog Ears Four-a-Penny

LET ME EXPLAIN exactly what I mean. The wares in a bookshop look completely unread. On the other hand, a school-boy's Latin dictionary looks read to the point of tatters. You know that dictionary has been opened and scanned perhaps a million times, and if you did not know there was such a thing as a box on the ear, you would conclude that the boy is crazy about Latin and cannot bear to be away from his dictionary. Similarly with our non-brow who wants his friends to infer from a glancing around his house that he is a high-brow. He buys an enormous book on the Russian ballet, written possibly in the language of that distant but beautiful land. Our problem is to alter that book in a reasonably short time so that anybody looking at it will conclude that its owner has practically lived, supped and slept with it for many months. You can, if you like, talk about designing a machine driven by a small but efficient petrol motor that would 'read' any book in five minutes, the equivalent of five years or ten years' 'reading' being obtained by merely turning a knob. This, however, is the cheap soulless approach of the times we live in. No machine can do the same work as the soft human fingers. The trained and experienced book-handler is the only real solution of this contemporary social problem. What does he do? How does he work? What would he charge? How many types of handling would there be?

These questions and many more I will answer the day after tomorrow.

The World of Books

YES, THIS QUESTION of book-handling. The other day I had a word to say about the necessity for the professional book-handler, a person who will maul the books of the illiterate, but wealthy, upstarts so that the books will look as if they have been read and re-read by their owners. How many uses of mauling would there be? Without giving the matter much thought, I should say four. Supposing an experienced handler is asked to quote for the handling of one shelf of books four feet in length. He would quote this under four heads:—

'Popular handling—Each volume to be well and truly handled, four leaves in each to be dog-eared, and a tram ticket, cloak-room docket or other comparable article inserted in each as a forgotten book mark. Say, £1 7s 6d. Five percent discount for civil servants.'

POPULAR HANDLING—EACH VOLUME TO BE WELL AND TRULY HANDLED, FOUR LEAVES IN EACH TO BE DOG-EARED, AND A TRAM TICKET, CLOAK-ROOM DOCKET OR OTHER COMPARABLE ARTICLE INSERTED IN EACH AS A FORGOTTEN BOOK MARK.

'Premier Handling—Each volume to be thoroughly handled, eight leaves in each to be dog-eared, a suitable passage in not less than 25 volumes to be underlined in red pencil, and a leaflet on the French works of Victor Hugo to be inserted as a forgotten book-mark in each. Say, £2 17s 6d. Five percent discount for literary university students, civil servants and lady social workers.'

A Rate to Suit all Purses

THE GREAT THING about this graduated scale is that no person need appear ignorant or unlettered merely because he or she is poor. Not every vulgar person, remember, is wealthy, although I could name . . .

But no matter. Let us get to the more expensive grades of handling. The next is well worth the extra money.

'De Luxe Handling—Each volume to be mauled savagely, the spines of the smaller volumes to be damaged in a manner that will give the impression that they have been carried around in pockets, a passage in every volume to be underlined in red pencil with an exclamation or interrogation mark inserted in the margin opposite, an old Gate Theatre programme to be inserted in each volume as a forgotten book-mark (3 percent discount if old Abbey programmes are accepted), not less than 30 volumes to be treated with old coffee, tea, porter or whiskey stains, and not less than five volumes to be inscribed with forged signatures of the authors. Five per cent discount for bank managers, county surveyors, and the heads of business houses employing not less that 35 hands. Dog-ears are extra and inserted according to instructions, twopence per half dozen per volume. Quotations for alternative old Paris theatre programmes on demand. This service is available for a limited time only, nett, £7 18s 3d.'

Order Your Copy Now

THE FOURTH CLASS is the Handling Superb, although it is not called that—*Le Traitment Superbe* being the more usual title. It is so superb that I have no space for it today. It will appear here on Monday next, and, in honour of the occasion, the *Irish Times* on that day will be printed on hand-scutched antique interwoven demidevilled superfine Dutch paper, each copy to be signed by myself and to be accompanied by an exquisite picture in tri-colour lithograph of the Old

House in College Green. The least you can do is to order your copy in advance.

And one more word. It is not sufficient just to order your copy. Order it *in advance*.

* * *

It will be remembered (how, in Heaven's name, could it be forgotten) that I was discoursing on Friday last on the subject of book-handling, my new service, which enables ignorant people who want to be suspected of reading books to have their books handled and mauled in a manner that will give the impression that their owner is very devoted to them. I described three grades of handling and promised to explain what you get under Class Four—the Superb Handling, or the Traitement Superb, as we lads who spent our honeymoon in Paris prefer to call it. It is the dearest of them all, of course, but far cheaper than dirt when you consider the amount of prestige you will gain in the eyes of your ridiculous friends. Here are the details:

'Le Traitement Superbe.' Every volume to be well and truly handled, first by a qualified handler and subsequently by a master-handler who shall have to his credit no less than 550 handling hours; suitable passages in not less than fifty percent of the books to be underlined in good-quality red ink and an appropriate phrase from the following list inserted in the margin, viz:

> Rubbish!
> Yes, indeed!
> How true, how true!
> I don't agree at all.
> Why?
> Yes, but cf. Homer, Od. iii, 151.
> Well, well, well.
> Quite, but Boussuet in his Discours sur l'histoire Universelle has already established the same point and given much more forceful explanations.
> Nonsense, nonsense!
> A point well taken!
> But *why* in heaven's name?
> I remember poor Joyce saying the very same thing to me.

Need I say that a special quotation may be obtained at any time for the supply of Special and Exclusive Phrases? The extra charge is not very much, really.

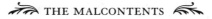

Futhermore

THAT, OF COURSE, is not all. Listen to this:

'Not less than six volumes to be inscribed with forged messages of affection and gratitude from the author of each work, e.g.,

> 'To my old friend and fellow-writer, A.B., in affectionate remembrance, from George Moore.' 'In grateful recognition of your great kindness to me, dear A.B., I send you this copy of The Crock of Gold. Your old friend, James Stephens.'
>
> 'Well, A.B., both of us are getting on. I am supposed to be a good writer now, but I am not old enough to forget the infinite patience you displayed in the old days when guiding my young feet on the path of literature. Accept this further book, poor as it may be, and please believe that I remain, as ever, your friend and admirer, G. Bernard Shaw.'
>
> 'From your devoted friend and follower, K. Marx.'
>
> Dear A.B.,—Your invaluable suggestions and assistance, not to mention your kindness, in entirely re-writing chapter 3, entitles you, surely, to this first copy of "Tess." From your old friend T. Hardy.'
>
> 'Short of the great pleasure of seeing you personally, I can only send you, dear A.B., this copy of "The Nigger." I miss your company more than I can say . . . (signature undecipherable).'

Under the last inscription, the moron who owns the book will be asked to write (and shown how if necessary) the phrase 'Poor old Conrad was not the worst.'

All of this has taken me longer to say than I thought. There is far more than this to be had for the paltry £32 7s 6d that the Superb Handling will cost you. In a day or two I hope to explain about the old letters which are inserted in some of the books by way of forgotten book-marks, every one of them an exquisite piece of forgery. Order your copy now!

Book Handling

I PROMISED TO say a little more about the fourth, or Superb, grade of book handling.

The price I quoted includes the insertion in not less than ten volumes of certain old letters, apparently used at one time as bookmarks, and forgotten. Each letter will bear the purported signature of some well-known humbug who is associated with ballet, verse-mouthing, folk-dancing, wood-cutting, or some other such activity that is sufficiently free from rules to attract the non-brows in their swarms. Each of the letters will be a flawless forgery and will thank A.B., the owner of the book, for his 'very kind interest in our work,' refer to his 'invaluable advice and guidance,' and his 'unrivalled knowledge' of the lep-as-lep-can game, his 'patient and skilful direction of the corps on Monday night,' thank him for his generous—too generous—subscription of two hundred guineas, 'which is appreciated more than I can say.' As an up-to-the-minute inducement, an extra letter will be included free of charge. It will be signed (or purport to be signed) by one or other of the noisier young non-nationals who are honouring our beautiful land with their presence. This will satisfy the half-ambition of the majority of respectable vulgarians to maintain a second establishment in that somewhat congested thoroughfare, Queer Street.

The gentlemen who are associated with me in the Dublin WAAMA League have realised that this is the off-season for harvesting the cash of simple people through the medium of the art-infected begging letter, and have turned their attention to fresh fields and impostures new. The lastest racket we have on hands is the Myles na gCopaleen Book Club. You join this and are spared the nerve-racking bother of choosing your own books. We do the choosing for you, and, when you get the book, it is *ready-rubbed*, ie, subjected free of charge to our expert handlers. You are spared the trouble of soiling and mauling it to give your friends the impression that you can read. An odd banned book will be slipped in for those who like conversation such as:—

'I say, did you read this, old man?'

'I'm not terribly certain that I did, really.'

'It's banned, you know, old boy.'

'Ow.'

There is no nonsense about completing a form, asking for a brochure, or any other such irritation. You can just send in your guinea and you immediately participate in this great cultural uprising of the Irish people.

Our New Service

THAT, HOWEVER, IS by the way. A lot of letters we receive are from well-off people *who have no books*. Nevertheless, they want to be thought educated. Can we help them, they ask?

Of course. Let nobody think that only book-owners can be smart. The Myles na gCopaleen Escort Service is the answer.

Why be a dumb dud? Do your friends shun you? Do people cross the street when they see you approaching? Do they run up the steps of strange houses, pretend they live there and force their way into the hall while you are passing by? If this is the sort of person you are, you must avail yourself today of this new service. Otherwise, you might as well be dead.

Our Service Explained

HERE IS HOW it happened. The WAAMA League has had on its hands for some time past a horde of unemployed ventriloquists who have been beseeching us to get them work. These gentleman have now been carefully trained and formed into corps to operate this new escort service.

Supposing you are a lady and so completely dumb that the dogs in the street do not think you are worth growling at. You ring up the WAAMA League and explain your trouble. You are pleased by the patient and sympathetic hearing you get. You are instructed to be in attendance at the foyer of the Gate Theatre that evening, and to look out for a tall, distinguished-looking gentleman of military bearing attired in immaculate evening dress. You go. You meet him. He advances toward you smiling, ignoring all the other handsome baggages that litter the place. In an instant his moustaches are brushing your lips.

'I trust I have not kept you waiting, Lady Charlotte,' he says pleasantly. What a delightfully low, manly voice!

'Not at all, Count,' you answer, your voice being the tinkle of silver bells. 'And what a night it is for Ibsen. One is in the mood, somehow. Yet a translation can never quite be the same. Do you remember that night . . . in Stockholm . . . long ago?'

The Secret

THE FACT OF the matter is, of course, that you have taken good care to say nothing. Your only worry throughout the evening is to shut up and keep shut up completely. The trained escort answers his own manly questions in a voice far pleasanter than your own unfeminine quack, and gives answers that will astonish the people behind for their brilliance and sparkle.

There are escorts and escorts according to the number of potatoes you are prepared to pay. Would you like to score off your escort in a literary argument during an interlude? Look out for information of this absorbing new service.

'Well, well, Godfrey, how awfully wizard being at the theatre with you!'

'Yes, it *is* fun.'

'What have you been doing with yourself?'

'Been trying to catch up with my reading, actually.'

'Ow, good show, keep in touch and all that.'

'Yes, I've been studying a lot of books on Bali. You know?'

'Ballet is terribly bewitching, isn't it? D'you like Petipa?'

'I'm not terribly sure that I do, but they seem to have developed a complete art of their own, you know. Their sense of décor and their general feeling for the plastic is quite marvellous.'

'Yes, old Dérain did some frightfully good work for them; for the Spectre, I think it was, actually. Sort of grisaille, you know.'

'But their feeling for matière is so profound and . . . almost brooding. One thinks of Courbet.'

'Yes, or Ingres.'

'Or Delacroix, don't you think?'

'Definitely. Have you read Karsavina?"

'Of course.'

'Of course, how stupid of me. I saw her, you know.'

'Ow, I hadn't realised that she herself was a Balinese.'

'Balinese? What *are* you driving at?'

'But—'

'But—'

Explanation

THIS RIDICULOUS CONVERSATION took place recently in an Irish theatre. The stuff was spoken in loud voices so that everybody could hear. It was only one of the many fine things that have been done by the Dublin WAAMA League's Escort Service. The League's horde of trained ventriloquists can now be heard carrying out their single-handed conversations all over the city and in the drawing rooms of people who are very important and equally ignorant. You know the system? If you are very dumb, you hire one of our ventriloquists to accompany you in public places, and he does absolutely all the talking. The smart replies which you appear to make will astonish yourself as much as the people around you.

The conversation I have quoted is one of the most expensive on the menu. You will note that it contains a serious misunderstanding. This makes the thing appear extraordinarily genuine. Imagine my shrewdness in making the ventriloquist misunderstand what he is saying himself! Conceive my guile, my duplicate duplicity, my play on ignorance and gullibility. Is it any wonder that I have gone into the banking business?

* * *

'Hear you were at old Lebensold's bottle do the other night. How was it, sticky and all that?'

'Pretty average grim, actually. Old Peter Piper was there.'

'Not that intoxicatingly witty painter person?'

'Sorry, one hadn't thought of him as a painter, actually. His work irritates one, you know, so derivative and all that.'

'I do quite definitely agree, but personally I trace his influences more in sorrow than in anger.'

'You do mean more in Seurat than Ingres, old thing, I s'ppowse.'

This is just a sample of the very special dialogues that our WAAMA League ventriloquist escorts have prepared for the round of Christmas parties. The extra charge is paltry.

And do not think that an escort will humiliate you by making you crack smart jokes like the one above after it has already been cracked at several other parties. Each service is exclusive. The same build-up will be retained (you can't have everything different) but the names in the last line will be changed. For instance, if the 'conversation' is on a philosophical topic the names will be Suarez and Engels. If on a literary topic , Thoreau and Béranger. And so on, until every reference book and guide to this and that has been ransacked.

Mark your envelope 'Christmas Escort' and enclose two pounds.

Serious Situation

DESPERATE IS THE only word that will do when it comes to describing the latest developments of the WAAMA League Escort Service. Several 'incidents' (using the word practically in the Japanese sense) have occurred in recent weeks, and it is now practically certain that we may expect unsavoury court sequels. Such a prospect makes me shudder, because the presence of even one small Escort in the High Court could lead to unheard of complications. Soon the nation may be faced with a vast constitutional crisis arising from pronouncements made (or, at all events, distinctly heard to have been made) by the princes of the bench and all sorts of lesser judicial dignitaries. I am afraid the astonishment of His Honour's own face will not be accepted as evidence to the contrary. Nor will a plea of gross-feasaunce be valid either.

Briefly, the ranks of my respectable and loyal Escorts have been infiltrated by cheats and disaffected elements who have, however, surpassing competence at the game of the voice-throw. Extraordinary utterances have been made in public places, but nobody knows for certain who made them. Worse, intelligent and perfectly genuine remarks made by dowdy young women have been completely ignored by the person to whom they were addressed, whose first instinct is to turn round and search the faces of inoffensive strangers to find the 'genuine' speaker.

I will have more to say on this matter in a sday or two.

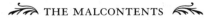

The Escort Mess

THE TROUBLE I referred to the other day began like this. A lady dumb-bell hired out what she took to be a genuine WAMMA League Escort, and went with him to the Gate Theatre. Before the play and during the first interval dozens of eavesdroppers were astounded at the brittle cut and thrust of the one-man conversation. The lady herself, who barely knew how to ask for her porridge, was pleased at the extraordinary silence that was won by her companion's conversational transports. Quite suddenly he said loudly:

'By the way, old girl, is that your old woman's dress you are wearing tonight?'

Simultaneously, the unfortunate client found a printed card shoved under her nose. It read:

'Don't look round, don't move, and don't scream for the police. Unless you sign on the dotted line promising to pay me an extra fiver for tonight, I will answer in the affirmative, and then go on to talk about your wretched tinker-woman's blouse. Play ball and nobody will be hurt. Beware! Signed, the Black Shadow.'

The poor girl, of course, had no alternative but to accept the proffered pencil and scrawl her name. Instantly she was heard to say in her merry twinkling voice:

'Really, Godfrey, it's the first time I ever wore the same gown twice, why must you be so quaint! One must make forty guineas go a bit further nowadays, you know, tightening the belt and all that.'

Worse to Come

AFTER THE SHOW there was an extraordinary scene in the foyer. The lady's husband called to fetch her home, and was immediately presented with her IOU by the 'Escort.' The demand for £5 out of the blue made his face the colour of war-time bread. He roared at his wife for an explanation. Floods of tears and mutterings were the best she could do. Then the husband rounded on the escort and denounced him as one who preyed on women, an extortionist, and a blackmailer of the deepest dye.

'And you over there with the whiskey face on you,' he added, apparently addressing a well-known and respected member of the justiciary, 'I don't like you either, and I've a damn good mind to break your red neck!'

The flabbergasted jurist (not that he was one whit less flabbergasted than the excited husband) turned the color of cigar-ash and ran out into the street in search of a Guard. In his absence the husband began to insult the wife of another bystander and to 'dar and double-dar' her companion to hit him. This favour was no sooner asked for than received. The unobtrusive 'Black Shadow' gallantly ran forward and picked up the prostrate figure, adroitly extracting in the process every item of silver and notes in his pockets. It was a chastened warrior that was delivered in due course into the arms of the rain-glistening Guard.

All this, I need hardly say, is only a beginning. Horrible slurs on our civilisation were to follow.

Those Escorts

LET ME GIVE some further details of the Escort mess I mentioned the other day. When it became generally known that a non-union man had succeeded in extracting a five-pound note from a client by menaces, hordes of unscrupulous ventriloquists descended upon the scene and made our theatre foyers a wilderness of false voices, unsaid remarks, anonymous insults, speakerless speeches and scandalous utterances which had no known utterer. Every second person wore a blank flabbergasted expression, having just offered some gratuitous insult to a stranger, or, perhaps, received one. Of course, blows were exchanged. Innocent country visitors coming to the theatre for the first time, and unaware of the situation could scarcely be expected to accept the savage jeers of some inoffensive bystander. Nor was the boot always on the same foot. The visitor's first impression of our intellectual theatres was all too frequently a haymaker in the belly, the price of some terrible remark he was heard to have made as he pushed in through the door.

PRACTISED THEATRE-GOERS HAVE TRAINED THEMSELVES TO LISTEN FOR THE ALMOST IMPERCEPTIBLE LITTLE PAUSE BETWEEN THE GENUINE ANSWER TO A QUESTION AND THE BOGUS ADDENDUM OF SOME ILL-DISPOSED VENTRILOQUIST.

Practised theatre-goers have trained themselves to listen for the almost imperceptible little pause between the genuine answer to a question and the bogus addendum of some ill-disposed ventriloquist. Thus:

'Have a cigarette?'

'No, thanks (pause), you parrot-clawed, thrush-beaked, pigeon-chested clown!'

'Do you like the play, Miss Plug? (pause) I'm only asking for politeness, because how an illiterate slut like you would presume to have an opinion on anything is more than I can understand!'

'The first act was wizard, actually. (Pause). There's egg on your tie, you pig!'

And so on, I regret to say.

Moreover

SEVERAL PEOPLE PREFER to remain inside at intervals nowadays. They are afraid of their lives of what they might blurt out if they ventured forth for a little air. This means, of course, putting up with the quieter and more deadly snake-bites of the seated malcontents, living in a phantom world of menacing mumble, ghost-whisper, and anonymous articulations of the most scandalous character, not to mention floods of threatening postcards. This sort of thing:

> 'Slip me a pound or I will see that you ask the gentleman beside you where he got the money to pay for his seat. Beware! Do not attempt to call for help! Signed, The Grey Spider.'

> 'Empty everything in your handbag into my right-hand coat pocket and make sure that nobody sees you doing it! Otherwise you will spend the evening plying strangers with salacious conundrums, even in the middle of the play. Don't think too hard of me, we all have to live. I have a wife and ten children. I do this because I have to. Signed, The Firefly.'

> 'Pay me 25s instantly or I will make a holy show of you. Be quick or you're for it. No monkey work! Signed, The Hooded Hawk.'

> 'This is a stick-up. Slip off that ring and drop it in the fold of my trousers. Otherwise you are going to heckle the players in the next act and think of what Hilton will have to say. Signed, The Mikado.'

This is merely the background of this ramp. What happened afterwards is another day's story. Just imagine Lord Longford saying: 'Has anybody here got a handball? I challenge any man here to a moonlight game above in the gardens, against the gable of the Nurses' Home!'

* * *

> 'Put five single bank notes in an envelope and stick the envelope under your seat with chewing gum before you leave the theatre for the first interval. Stay out for at least ten minutes. No monkey-work, mind. Fail me in this and I will fix your hash for you. Signed, The Green Mikado.'

The somewhat scared lady who showed me this mysterious missive at the Abbey the other night asked me what she was to do. Naturally, I counselled courage and no truck with the evil voices that were infesting the national theatre like plague-nits in a rat's back. I promised her the assistance of my genuine WAAMA League Escorts, in ever-growing volume, until the stream became a torrent. Grievous and sombre as the prospect was, I assured her, our mighty and illimitable resources would be marshalled towards the common-end. I then telephoned for my ace-escort. His wife said that he was out, but that she would send a message to him. I knew that he had no wife. He arrived just as the curtain was going up.

Dramatic Incident

MY LADY FRIEND had bravely ignored the threat and all of us sat down for the second act with some little trepidation. Just how would the dread Mikado strike? What did he mean by his threat to settle my friend's hash? I was waiting every moment to hear her make some horrible remark, of which she would be as innocent as the child unborn.

Quite suddenly the blow fell. It happened that there was a lengthy pause in the play where the story had reached a stage of crisis. A pause, but not silence. A player standing on the left of the stage electrified the audience by saying:

'Do you know, I have been wondering all night who in the name of Pete that fat cow in the fur coat is. The one second from the left in the third row!'

I turned to my own escort, thunderstruck.

'It's all right,' he whispered. 'Your lady friend is fifth from the right. The addendum was mine. I was expecting this. It is common Leipzig practice.'

Meanwhile, the unknown victim was being assisted out, the theatre was in an uproar, the curtain had been rung down and the livid husband was already on his way behind the scenes to ask the reason why.

Horrible developments have taken place in the Escort scandal. One particular theatre has become a bedlam of 'voices' and coarse badinage, notwithstanding the foolish rule of the management that 'no one who looks like a ventriloquist is to be admitted.' If you say something, no one will believe that you said it. Even a simple 'what-time-is-it?' simply evokes a knowing smile and an involuntary search of the nearest bystander's countenance; that or some extraordinary reply like 'Pie-face!' 'Who wants to know?' or 'Time we were rid of a hook like you!'

Meanwhile, decent people are taking steps to protect their interests. I was at a play the other night and could not help overhearing a scandalous monologue that was apparently being recited by my neighbor on the right, a very respectable-looking elderly man. I watched him through the corner of my eye and saw the hand go into an inside pocket. Was he searching for his card? Was he The Black Dragon about to shove some printed threat under my nose? Yes, yes, the small white card was in his claw! In a second it was held adroitly in my gaze. Imagine my astonishment when I read it:

'I give you my solemn word of honour that I am a civil servant and that the appalling language that you hear coming from me is being uttered by some other person. Signed, JUST A MINOR STAFF OFFICER.'

You see the point? He was afraid to *say* this. Because if he did, his explanation would be instantly followed up with a coarse insult to my wife, who was sitting beside me.

Each with His Own Card

I had further evidence of this later in the foyer. I was standing smoking when a small gentleman said to me: 'Excuse me for addressing a stranger, but I cannot help assuring you that it is only with the greatest difficulty that I restrain myself from letting you have a pile-driver in your grilled steak and chips, me bucko?' Instantly he produced a card and handed it to me:

'So help me, I am a crane-driver from Drogheda, and I have not opened my beak since I came in tonight. Cough twice if you believe me. Signed, NED THE DRIVER.'

I coughed and walked away. Just for fun I said to a lady who was standing near: 'Hello, hag! How's yer ould one?' Her reply was the sweet patient smile that might be exchanged between two fellow-sufferers from night starvation. What a world!

Next day I want to tell you about the lady who hired out two Escorts, thinking that each would keep the other down.

A Clash at Headquarters

THERE WAS HELL and holy bedlam at a recent meeting of the inner council of the Myles na gCopaleen WAAMA League. Our horde of literary ventriloquists sent in a demand for more pay. I agreed to hear a deputation from them, although determined to take my stand on Order 83 and to die rather than concede a blue farthing. They were barely in the room when I heard myself saying: Well, gentlem'n, I'm not surprised to see you, I may say right away that I recognise that your wages are ridiculously low and that an increase of fifty per cent is the least I would have the effrontery to offer you.

Before I had recovered from my astonishment, the spokesman said that such a response was disappointing, but that they were prepared to accept the increase under protest and without prejudice to their right to re-open the matter after consultation with their union. Then they filed out. The whole matter was over and done with before I had an opportunity of opening my beak. I mention the humiliating episode only because I see in it the idea for a new and exclusive

WAAMA League service. Why not make my ventriloquists a bulwark of the Trade Union movement? Why not use their unique gifts to bring the parasite boss class to heel? Why not arrange beforehand, beyond yea or nay, that you will get the answer you are looking for? I'm talking to Mr. O'Shannon.

Acknowledgments

This book would not have been possible without the help of a number of talented and dedicated people who made many different contributions at various stages of the book's development. Among those who deserve special thanks are Jeanine Rosen, David Rech and the staff at Scribe, Anne Hebenstreit, and Richard Miller.

Thanks are also due to several past and present members of the staff of Running Press: Nancy Armstrong, Serrin Bodmer, Marc Frey, Kathleen Greczylo, Alison Trulock, and Jennifer Worick.

Joe Queenan is the author of seven books, including *Balsamic Dreams; Confessions of a Cineplex Heckler; My Goodness: A Cynic's Short-lived Search for Sainthood;* and *Red Lobster, White Trash, and the Blue Lagoon.* He is a contributing writer at *GQ*, a contributing editor to *Movieline*, and a regular contributor to *TV Guide*. His work frequently appears in *The Wall Street Journal, The Washington Post, The New York Times, Playboy,* and *Barron's*, and he writes a monthly column for *Chief Executive* and *Barron's Online*. He lives in Tarrytown, New York, with his wife and two children.